CIVIL AI[illegible] MARKINGS 2011

REVISED 62nd EDITION

Allan S. Wright

An imprint of
Ian Allan Publishing

www.ianallanpublishing.co.uk

Contents

This 62nd edition first published 2011

ISBN 978 1 85780 348 8

Published by Midland Publishing

an imprint of Ian Allan Publishing Ltd, Hersham, Surrey KT12 4RG.
Printed in England by Ian Allan Printing Ltd, Hersham, Surrey KT12 4RG.

Visit the Ian Allan Publishing website at www.ianallanpublishing.com

Distributed in the United States of America and Canada by BookMasters Distribution Services

Cover: Boeing 787-8 Dreamliner
@ *mark wagner / aviation–images.com*

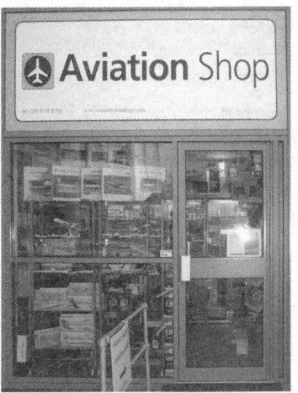

Introduction

The familiar 'G' prefixed four-letter registration system was adopted in 1919 after a short-lived spell with serial numbers commencing at K-100. Until July 1928 the UK allocations were issued in the G-Exxx range but, as a result of further international agreements, this series ended at G-EBZZ, the replacement being G-Axxx. From this point registrations were issued in a reasonably orderly manner through to G-AZZZ, the position reached in July 1972. There were, however, two exceptions. In order to prevent possible confusion with signal codes, the G-AQxx sequence was omitted, while G-AUxx was reserved for Australian use originally. In recent years however, individual requests for a mark in the latter range have been granted by the Authorities.

Although the next logical sequence was started at G-Bxxx, it was not long before the strictly applied rules relating to aircraft registration began to be relaxed. Permission was readily given for personalised marks to be issued, incorporating virtually any four-letter combination, while re-registration also became a common feature – a practice almost unheard of in the past. In this book, where this has taken place at some time, all previous UK identities carried appear in parenthesis after the operator's/owner's name. For example, during its career Twin Squirrel G-LNTY has also carried the identities G-ECOS, G-DORL and G-BPVB.

Some aircraft have also been allowed to wear military markings without displaying their civil identity. In this case the serial number actually carried is shown in parenthesis after the type's name. For example Auster 6A G-ARRX flies in military colours as VF512, its genuine previous identity. As an aid to the identification of such machines, a conversion list is provided.

Other factors caused a sudden acceleration in the number of registrations allocated by the Civil Aviation Authority in the early 1980s. The first surge followed the discovery that it was possible to register plastic bags, and other items even less likely to fly, on payment of the standard fee. This erosion of the main register was checked in early 1982 by the issue of a special sequence for such devices commencing with G-FYAA. Powered hang-gliders provided the second glut of allocations as a result of the decision that these types should be officially registered. Although a few of the early examples penetrated the current in-sequence register, in due course all new applicants were given marks in special ranges, this time G-MBxx, G-MGxx, G-MJxx, G-MMxx, G-MNxx, G-MTxx, G-MVxx, G-MWxx, G-MYxx and G-MZxx. It took some time before all microlights displayed an official mark but gradually the registration was carried, the size and position depending on the dimensions of the component to which it was applied.

There was news of a further change in mid-1998 when the CAA announced that with immediate effect microlights would be issued with registrations in the normal sequence alongside aircraft in other classes. In addition, it meant that owners could also apply for a personalised identity upon payment of the then current fee of £170 from April 1999, a low price for those wishing to display their status symbol. These various changes played their part in exhausting the current G-Bxxx range after some 26 years, with G-BZxx coming into use before the end of 1999. As this batch approached completion the next series to be used began at G-CBxx instead of the anticipated G-CAxx. The reason for this step was to avoid the re-use of marks issued in Canada during the 1920s, although a few have appeared more recently as personalised UK registrations.

Another large increase in the number of aircraft registered has resulted from the EU-inspired changes in glider registration. After many years of self-regulation by the British Gliding Association, new gliders must now comply with EASA regulations and hence receive registrations in the main G-Cxxx sequence. The phasing-in of EASA registration for the existing glider fleet has been a fairly lengthy process but has now come to an end and as at the beginning of 2011 there were over 2,250 examples on the Register.

September 2007 saw the issue of the 50,000th UK aircraft registration with G-MITC being allocated to a Robinson R44 Raven. The total number of aircraft on the Register has risen over the past 25 years from just under 10,000 at the beginning of 1985 to in excess of 21,300 by January 2009. Numbers have fallen back slightly since that time with the figure as at 1st January 2011 standing at 20,379.

Non-airworthy and preserved aircraft are shown with a star (★) after the type.

The three-letter codes used by airlines to prefix flight numbers are included for those carriers most likely to appear in or over the UK. Radio frequencies for the larger airfields/airports are also listed.

I would like to dedicate this edition to my father Alan J. Wright who sadly passed away on 15th January 2011. He was passionate about aircraft from an early age and made a significant contribution to civil aviation literature. He edited Civil Aircraft Markings every year from 1979 until 2006. He will be greatly missed by his family, friends and all who knew him.

ASW

ACKNOWLEDGEMENTS: Once again thanks are extended to the Registration Department of the Civil Aviation Authority for its assistance and allowing access to its files. Thanks are also given to all those who have contributed items for possible use and in particular to Nick Wright for his valuable assistance during the update of this edition.

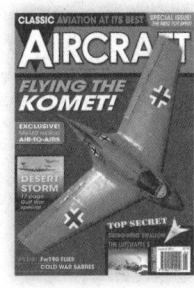

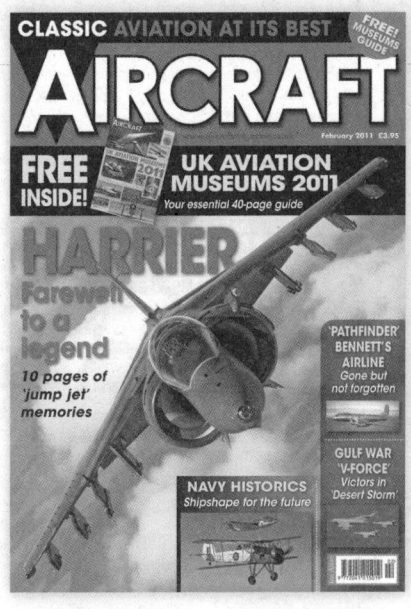

International Civil Aircraft Markings

A2-	Botswana	N-	United States of America
A3-	Tonga	OB-	Peru
A4O-	Oman	OD-	Lebanon
A5-	Bhutan	OE-	Austria
A6-	United Arab Emirates	OH-	Finland
A7-	Qatar	OK-	Czech Republic
A8-	Liberia	OM-	Slovakia
A9C-	Bahrain	OO-	Belgium
AP-	Pakistan	OY-	Denmark
B-	China/Taiwan/Hong Kong/Macao	P-	North Korea
C-	Canada	P2-	Papua New Guinea
C2-	Nauru	P4-	Aruba
C3-	Andorra	PH-	Netherlands
C5-	Gambia	PJ-	Netherlands Antilles
C6-	Bahamas	PK-	Indonesia
C9-	Mozambique	PP-	Brazil
CC-	Chile	PR-	Brazil
CN-	Morocco	PT-	Brazil
CP-	Bolivia	PU-	Brazil
CS-	Portugal	PZ-	Surinam
CU-	Cuba	RA-	Russia
CX-	Uruguay	RDPL-	Laos
D-	Germany	RP-	Philippines
D2-	Angola	S2-	Bangladesh
D4-	Cape Verde Islands	S5-	Slovenia
D6-	Comores Islands	S7-	Seychelles
DQ-	Fiji	S9-	Säo Tomé
E3-	Eritrea	SE-	Sweden
E5-	Cook Islands	SP-	Poland
EC-	Spain	ST-	Sudan
EI-	Republic of Ireland	SU-	Egypt
EK-	Armenia	SX-	Greece
EP-	Iran	T2-	Tuvalu
ER-	Moldova	T3-	Kiribati
ES-	Estonia	T7-	San Marino
ET-	Ethiopia	T8A-	Palau
EW-	Belarus	T9-	Bosnia and Herzegovina
EX-	Kyrgyzstan	TC-	Turkey
EY-	Tajikistan	TF-	Iceland
EZ-	Turkmenistan	TG-	Guatemala
F-	France, inc Colonies and Protectorates	TI-	Costa Rica
G-	United Kingdom	TJ-	Cameroon
H4-	Solomon Islands	TL-	Central African Republic
HA-	Hungary	TN-	Republic of Congo
HB-	Switzerland and Liechtenstein	TR-	Gabon
HC-	Ecuador	TS-	Tunisia
HH-	Haiti	TT-	Tchad
HI-	Dominican Republic	TU-	Ivory Coast
HK-	Colombia	TY-	Benin
HL-	South Korea	TZ-	Mali
HP-	Panama	UK-	Uzbekistan
HR-	Honduras	UN-	Kazakhstan
HS-	Thailand	UR-	Ukraine
HZ-	Saudi Arabia	V2-	Antigua
I-	Italy	V3-	Belize
J2-	Djibouti	V4	St. Kitts & Nevis
J3-	Grenada	V5-	Namibia
J5-	Guinea Bissau	V6-	Micronesia
J6-	St. Lucia	V7-	Marshall Islands
J7-	Dominica	V8-	Brunei
J8-	St. Vincent	VH-	Australia
JA-	Japan	VN-	Vietnam
JU-	Mongolia	VP-A	Anguilla
JY-	Jordan	VP-B	Bermuda
LN-	Norway	VP-C	Cayman Islands
LV-	Argentina	VP-F	Falkland Islands
LX-	Luxembourg	VP-G	Gibraltar
LY-	Lithuania	VP-L	British Virgin Islands
LZ-	Bulgaria	VP-M	Montserrat
M-	Isle of Man	VQ-B	Bermuda

VQ-H	Saint Helena/Ascension
VQ-T	Turks & Caicos Islands
VT-	India
XA-	Mexico
XB-	Mexico
XC-	Mexico
XT-	Burkina Faso
XU-	Cambodia
XW-	Laos
XY-	Myanmar
YA-	Afghanistan
YI-	Iraq
YJ-	Vanuatu
YK-	Syria
YL-	Latvia
YN-	Nicaragua
YR-	Romania
YS-	El Salvador
YU-	Serbia
YV-	Venezuela
Z-	Zimbabwe
Z3-	Macedonia
ZA-	Albania
ZK-	New Zealand
ZP-	Paraguay
ZS-	South Africa
3A-	Monaco
3B-	Mauritius
3C-	Equatorial Guinea
3D-	Swaziland
3X-	Guinea
4K-	Azerbaijan
4L-	Georgia
4O-	Montenegro
4R-	Sri Lanka
4X-	Israel
5A-	Libya
5B-	Cyprus
5H-	Tanzania
5N-	Nigeria
5R-	Malagasy Republic (Madagascar)
5T-	Mauritania
5U-	Niger
5V-	Togo
5W-	Western Samoa (Polynesia)
5X-	Uganda
5Y-	Kenya
6O-	Somalia
6V-	Senegal
6Y-	Jamaica
7O-	Yemen
7P-	Lesotho
7Q-	Malawi
7T-	Algeria
8P-	Barbados
8Q-	Maldives
8R-	Guyana
9A-	Croatia
9G-	Ghana
9H-	Malta
9J-	Zambia
9K-	Kuwait
9L-	Sierra Leone
9M-	Malaysia
9N-	Nepal
9Q-	Congo Kinshasa
9U-	Burundi
9V-	Singapore
9XR-	Rwanda
9Y-	Trinidad and Tobago

Aircraft Type Designations & Abbreviations

(for example PA-28 Piper Type 28)

A.	Beagle, Auster, Airbus
AAC	Army Air Corps
AA-	American Aviation, Grumman American
AB	Agusta-Bell
AESL	Aero Engine Services Ltd
AG	American General
An	Antonov
ANEC	Air Navigation & Engineering Co
ANG	Air National Guard
AS	Aérospatiale
A.S.	Airspeed
A.W.	Armstrong Whitworth
B.	Blackburn, Bristol, Boeing, Beagle
BA	British Airways
BAC	British Aircraft Company
BAC	British Aircraft Corporation
BAe	British Aerospace
BAPC	British Aviation Preservation Council
BAT	British Aerial Transport
B.K.	British Klemm
BN	Britten-Norman
Bo	Bolkow
Bü	Bücker
CAARP	Co-operatives des Ateliers Aéronautiques de la Région Parisienne
CAC	Commonwealth Aircraft Corporation
CAF	Canadian Air Force
CASA	Construcciones Aeronautics SA
CCF	Canadian Car & Foundry Co
CEA	Centre-Est Aviation
CH.	Chrislea
CHABA	Cambridge Hot-Air Ballooning Association
CLA.	Comper
CP.	Piel
CUAS	Cambridge University Air Squadron
Cycl	Cyclone
D.	Druine
DC-	Douglas Commercial
DH.	de Havilland
DHA.	de Havilland Australia
DHC.	de Havilland Canada
DR.	Jodel (Robin-built)
EE	English Electric
EAA	Experimental Aircraft Association
EMB	Embraer Empresa Brasileira de Aeronautica SA
EoN	Elliotts of Newbury
EP	Edgar Percival
ETPS	Empire Test Pilots School
F.	Fairchild, Fokker
F.A.A.	Fleet Air Arm
FFA	Flug und Fahrzeugwerke AG
FH	Fairchild-Hiller
FrAF	French Air Force
FRED	Flying Runabout Experimental Design
Fw	Focke-Wulf
G.	Grumman
GA	Gulfstream American
GAL.	General Aircraft
GC	Globe Aircraft
GECAS	General Electric Capital Aviation Services
GY	Gardan
H	Helio
HM.	Henri Mignet
HP.	Handley Page
HPR.	Handley Page Reading
HR.	Robin
HS.	Hawker Siddeley
ICA	Intreprinderea de Constructii Aeronau
IHM	International Helicopter Museum
I.I.I.	Iniziative Industriali Italiane
IL	Ilyushin
ILFC	International Lease Finance Corporation
IMCO	Intermountain Manufacturing Co
IWM	Imperial War Museum
KR	Rand-Robinson
L.	Lockheed
L.A.	Luton, Lake
LET	Letecky Narodny Podnik
LLP	Limited Liability Partnership
L.V.G.	Luft-Verkehrs Gesellschaft
M.	Miles, Mooney
MBA	Micro Biplane Aviation
MBB	Messerschmitt-Bölkow-Blohm
McD	McDonnell
MDH	McDonnell Douglas Helicopters
MH.	Max Holste
MHCA	Manhole Cover
MJ	Jurca
MS.	Morane-Saulnier
NA	North American
NC	Nord
NE	North East
P.	Hunting (formerly Percival), Piaggio
PA-	Piper
PC.	Pilatus
PZL	Panstwowe Zaklady Lotnicze
QAC	Quickie Aircraft Co
R.	Rockwell
RAF	Rotary Air Force
RAAF	Royal Australian Air Force
RAFGSA	Royal Air Force Gliding & Soaring Association
RCAF	Royal Canadian Air Force
RF	Fournier
R.N.	Royal Navy
S.	Short, Sikorsky
SA,SE,SO	Sud-Aviation, Aérospatiale, Scottish Aviation
SAAB	Svenska Aeroplan Aktieboleg
SC	Short
SCD	Side Cargo Door
SNCAN	Société Nationale de Constructions Aéronautiques du Nord
SOCATA	Société de Construction d'Avions de Tourisme et d'Affaires
SpA	Societa per Azioni
SPP	Strojirny Prvni Petiletky
S.R.	Saunders-Roe, Stinson
SS	Special Shape
ST	SOCATA
SW	Solar Wings
T.	Tipsy
TB	SOCATA
Tu	Tupolev
UH.	United Helicopters (Hiller)
UK	United Kingdom
USAF	United States Air Force
USAAC	United States Army Air Corps
USN	United States Navy
V.	Vickers-Armstrongs
VLM	Vlaamse Luchttransportmaatschappij
VS.	Vickers-Supermarine
WA	Wassmer
WAR	War Aircraft Replicas
WHE	W.H.Ekin
WS	Westland
Z.	Zlin

British Civil Aircraft Registrations

Reg.	Type (†False registration)	Owner or Operator	Notes
G-AAAH†	DH.60G Moth (replica) (BAPC 168) ★	Yorkshire Air Museum/Elvington	
G-AAAH	DH.60G Moth ★	Science Museum *Jason*/South Kensington	
G-AACA†	Avro 504K (BAPC 177) ★	Brooklands Museum of Aviation/Weybridge	
G-AACN	HP.39 Gugnunc ★	Science Museum/Wroughton	
G-AADR	DH.60GM Moth	E. V. Moffatt	
G-AAHI	DH.60G Moth	Nigel John Western Reid Discretionary Settlement 2008	
G-AAHY	DH.60M Moth	D. J. Elliott	
G-AAIN	Parnall Elf II	The Shuttleworth Collection/Old Warden	
G-AAJT	DH.60G Moth	M. R. Paul	
G-AALY	DH.60G Moth	K. M. Fresson	
G-AAMX	DH.60GM Moth ★	RAF Museum/Hendon	
G-AAMY	DH.60GMW Moth	Totalsure Ltd	
G-AANG	Blériot XI	The Shuttleworth Collection/Old Warden	
G-AANH	Deperdussin Monoplane	The Shuttleworth Collection/Old Warden	
G-AANI	Blackburn Monoplane	The Shuttleworth Collection/Old Warden	
G-AANJ	L.V.G. C VI (7198/18)	Aerospace Museum/Cosford	
G-AANL	DH.60M Moth	R. A. Palmer	
G-AANM	Bristol 96A F.2B (D7889) (BAPC166) ★	Aero Vintage Ltd	
G-AANO	DH.60GMW Moth	A. W. & M. E. Jenkins	
G-AANV	DH.60G Moth	R. A. Seeley	
G-AAOK	Curtiss Wright Travel Air 12Q	Shipping & Airlines Ltd	
G-AAOR	DH.60G Moth	B. R. Cox	
G-AAPZ	Desoutter I (mod.)	The Shuttleworth Collection	
G-AATC	DH.80A Puss Moth	R. A. Palmer	
G-AAUP	Klemm L.25-1A	J. I. Cooper	
G-AAWO	DH.60G Moth	I. C. Reid	
G-AAXG	DH 60M Moth	S. H. Kidston	
G-AAXK	Klemm L.25-1A ★	C. C. Russell-Vick (stored)	
G-AAYT	DH.60G Moth	P. Groves	
G-AAYX	Southern Martlet	The Shuttleworth Collection	
G-AAZG	DH.60G Moth	J. A. Pothecary & ptnrs	
G-AAZP	DH.80A Puss Moth	R. P. Williams	
G-ABAA	Avro 504K ★	Manchester Museum of Science & Industry	
G-ABAG	DH.60G Moth	A. & P. A. Wood	
G-ABBB	B.105A Bulldog IIA (K2227) ★	RAF Museum/Hendon	
G-ABDA	DH.60G Moth	R. A. Palmer	
G-ABDW	DH.80A Puss Moth (VH-UQB) ★	Museum of Flight/East Fortune	
G-ABDX	DH.60G Moth	M. D. Souch	
G-ABEV	DH.60G Moth	S. L. G. Darch	
G-ABHE	Aeronca C.2	N. S. Chittenden	
G-ABLM	Cierva C.24 ★	De Havilland Heritage Museum/London Colney	
G-ABLS	DH.80A Puss Moth	R. A. Seeley	
G-ABMR	Hart 2 (J9941) ★	RAF Museum/Hendon	
G-ABNT	Civilian C.A.C.1 Coupe	Shipping & Airlines Ltd	
G-ABNX	Redwing 2	Redwing Syndicate	
G-ABOI	Wheeler Slymph ★	Midland Air Museum/Coventry	
G-ABOX	Sopwith Pup (N5195)	C. M. D. & A. P. St. Cyrien	
G-ABSD	DHA.60G Moth	M. E. Vaisey	
G-ABUL†	DH.82A Tiger Moth ★	F.A.A. Museum/Yeovilton (G-AOXG)	
G-ABUS	Comper CLA.7 Swift	R. C. F. Bailey	
G-ABVE	Arrow Active 2	Real Aircraft Co	
G-ABWP	Spartan Arrow	R. E. Blain	
G-ABXL	Granger Archaeopteryx ★	J. R. Granger	
G-ABYA	DH.60G Gipsy Moth	M. J. Saggers	
G-ABZB	DH.60G-III Moth Major	G. M. Turner & N. Child	
G-ACBH	Blackburn B.2 ★	–/Redhill	
G-ACCB	DH.83 Fox Moth	E. A. Gautrey	
G-ACDA	DH.82A Tiger Moth	B. D. Hughes	
G-ACDC	DH.82A Tiger Moth	Tiger Club Ltd	
G-ACDI	DH.82A Tiger Moth	Doublecube Aviation LLP	
G-ACEJ	DH.83 Fox Moth	I. G. Barnett & G. R. Williams	
G-ACET	DH.84 Dragon	M. D. Souch	
G-ACGT	Avro 594 Avian IIIA ★	Yorkshire Light Aircraft Ltd/Leeds	
G-ACGZ	DH.60G-III Moth Major	N. H. Lemon	

Notes	Reg.	Type	Owner or Operator
	G-ACIT	DH.84 Dragon ★	Science Museum/Wroughton
	G-ACLL	DH.85 Leopard Moth	V. M & D. C. M. Stiles
	G-ACMA	DH.85 Leopard Moth	P. A. Vacher
	G-ACMD	DH.82A Tiger Moth	M. J. Bonnick
	G-ACMN	DH.85 Leopard Moth	M. R. & K. E. Slack
	G-ACNS	DH.60G-III Moth Major	C. T. Parry
	G-ACOJ	DH.85 Leopard Moth	Norman Aeroplane Trust
	G-ACSP	DH.88 Comet ★	T. M., M. L., D. A. & P. M. Jones
	G-ACSS	DH.88 Comet ★	The Shuttleworth Collection *Grosvenor House*/ Old Warden
	G-ACSS†	DH.88 Comet (replica) ★	G. Gayward (BAPC216)
	G-ACSS†	DH.88 Comet (replica) ★	The Galleria Hatfield (BAPC257)
	G-ACTF	Comper CLA.7 Swift ★	The Shuttleworth Collection/Old Warden
	G-ACUS	DH.85 Leopard Moth	R. A. & V. A. Gammons
	G-ACUU	Cierva C.30A (HM580) ★	G. S. Baker/Duxford
	G-ACUX	S.16 Scion (VH-UUP) ★	Ulster Folk & Transport Museum
	G-ACVA	Kay Gyroplane ★	Museum of Flight/East Fortune
	G-ACWM	Cierva C.30A (AP506) ★	IHM/Weston-super-Mare
	G-ACWP	Cierva C.30A (AP507) ★	Science Museum/South Kensington
	G-ACXB	DH.60G-III Moth Major	D. F. Hodgkinson
	G-ACXE	B.K. L-25C Swallow	J. G. Wakeford
	G-ACYK	Spartan Cruiser III ★	Museum of Flight (front fuselage)/East Fortune
	G-ACZE	DH.89A Dragon Rapide	Chewton Glen Aviation Ltd (G-AJGS)
	G-ADAH	DH.89A Dragon Rapide ★	Manchester Museum of Science & Industry *Pioneer*
	G-ADEV	Avro 504K (H5199)	The Shuttleworth Collection/Old Warden (G-ACNB)
	G-ADGP	M.2L Hawk Speed Six	R. A. Mills
	G-ADGT	DH.82A Tiger Moth (BB697)	The Tiger Club 1990 Ltd
	G-ADGV	DH.82A Tiger Moth	K. J. Whitehead (G-BACW)
	G-ADHD	DH.60G-III Moth Major	M. E. Vaisey
	G-ADIA	DH.82A Tiger Moth	S. J. Beaty
	G-ADJJ	DH.82A Tiger Moth	J. M. Preston
	G-ADKC	DH.87B Hornet Moth	A. J. Davy
	G-ADKK	DH.87B Hornet Moth	R. M. Lee
	G-ADKL	DH.87B Hornet Moth	P. R. & M. J. F. Gould
	G-ADKM	DH.87B Hornet Moth	S. G. Collyer
	G-ADLY	DH.87B Hornet Moth	Totalsure Ltd
	G-ADMT	DH.87B Hornet Moth	D. C. Reid
	G-ADMW	M.2H Hawk Major (DG590) ★	RAF Museum Storage & Restoration Centre/RAF Stafford
	G-ADND	DH.87B Hornet Moth (W9385)	D. M. & S. M. Weston
	G-ADNE	DH.87B Hornet Moth	G-ADNE Group
	G-ADNL	M.5 Sparrowhawk ★	A. P. Pearson
	G-ADNZ	DH.82A Tiger Moth (DE673)	D. C. Wall
	G-ADOT	DH.87B Hornet Moth ★	De Havilland Heritage Museum/London Colney
	G-ADPC	DH.82A Tiger Moth	D. J. Marshall
	G-ADPJ	B.A.C. Drone ★	N. H. Ponsford/Breighton
	G-ADPS	B.A. Swallow 2	J. F. Hopkins
	G-ADRA	Pietenpol Air Camper	A. J. Mason
	G-ADRG†	Mignet HM.14 (replica) ★	Lower Stondon Transport Museum (BAPC77)
	G-ADRR	Aeronca C.3	S. J. Rudkin
	G-ADRX†	Mignet HM.14 (replica) ★	S. Copeland Aviation Group (BAPC231)
	G-ADRY†	Mignet HM.14 (replica) (BAPC29)★	Brooklands Museum of Aviation/Weybridge
	G-ADVU†	Mignet HM.14 (replica) ★	North East Aircraft Museum/Usworth (BAPC211)
	G-ADWJ	DH.82A Tiger Moth	K. F. Crumplin
	G-ADWO	DH.82A Tiger Moth (BB807) ★	Solent Sky, Southampton
	G-ADWT	M.2W Hawk Trainer	R. Earl & B. Morris
	G-ADXS	Mignet HM.14 ★	Thameside Aviation Museum/Shoreham
	G-ADXT	DH.82A Tiger Moth	Conciair Ltd
	G-ADYS	Aeronca C.3	J. I. Cooper
	G-ADYV†	Mignet HM.14 (replica) ★	P. Ward (BAPC243)
	G-ADZW†	Mignet HM.14 (replica) ★	Solent Sky/Southampton (BAPC253)
	G-AEBB	Mignet HM.14 ★	The Shuttleworth Collection/Old Warden
	G-AEBJ	Blackburn B-2	BAe Systems (Operations) Ltd
	G-AEDB	B.A.C. Drone 2	R. E. Nerou & P. L. Kirk
	G-AEDU	DH.90 Dragonfly	Norman Aeroplane Trust
	G-AEEG	M.3A Falcon Skysport	P. R. Holloway
	G-AEEH	Mignet HM.14 ★	Aerospace Museum/Cosford
	G-AEFG	Mignet HM.14 (BAPC75) ★	N. H. Ponsford/Breighton

Reg.	Type	Owner or Operator	Notes
G-AEFT	Aeronca C.3	N. S. Chittenden	
G-AEGV	Mignet HM.14 ★	Midland Air Museum/Coventry	
G-AEHM	Mignet HM.14 ★	Science Museum/Wroughton	
G-AEJZ	Mignet HM.14 (BAPC120) ★	Aero Venture	
G-AEKR	Mignet HM.14 (BAPC121) ★	Doncaster Museum & Art Gallery	
G-AEKV	Kronfeld Drone ★	Brooklands Museum of Aviation/Weybridge	
G-AEKW	M.12 Mohawk ★	RAF Museum	
G-AELO	DH.87B Hornet Moth	M. J. Miller	
G-AEML	DH.89 Dragon Rapide	Fundacion Infante de Orleans/Spain	
G-AENP	Hawker Hind (K5414) (BAPC78)	The Shuttleworth Collection	
G-AEOA	DH.80A Puss Moth	P. & A. Wood/Old Warden	
G-AEOF†	Mignet HM.14 (BAPC22) ★	Aviodrome/Lelystad, Netherlands	
G-AEOF	Rearwin 8500	Shipping & Airlines Ltd	
G-AEPH	Bristol F.2B (D8096)	The Shuttleworth Collection	
G-AERV	M.11A Whitney Straight	R. A. Seeley	
G-AESB	Aeronca C.3	R. J. M. Turnbull	
G-AESE	DH.87B Hornet Moth	J. G. Green	
G-AESZ	Chilton D.W.1	R. E. Nerou	
G-AETA	Caudron G.3 (3066) ★	RAF Museum/Hendon	
G-AETG	Aeronca 100	J. Teagle and Partners	
G-AEUJ	M.11A Whitney Straight	R. E. Mitchell	
G-AEVS	Aeronca 100	R. A. Fleming	
G-AEXD	Aeronca 100	M. A. & N. Mills	
G-AEXF	P.6 Mew Gull	Real Aircraft Co/Breighton	
G-AEXT	Dart Kitten II	D. G. Scott	
G-AEXZ	Piper J-2 Cub	M. & J. R. Dowson	
G-AEZF	S.16 Scion 2 ★	Acebell Aviation/Redhill	
G-AEZJ	P.10 Vega Gull	D. P. H. Hulme	
G-AFAP†	CASA C.352L ★	Aerospace Museum/Cosford	
G-AFBS	M.14A Hawk Trainer 3 ★	G. D. Durbridge-Freeman/Duxford (G-AKKU)	
G-AFCL	B. A. Swallow 2	C. P. Bloxham	
G-AFDO	Piper J-3F-60 Cub	R. Wald	
G-AFDX	Hanriot HD.1 (HD-75) ★	RAF Museum/Hendon	
G-AFEL	Monocoupe 90A	M. Rieser	
G-AFFD	Percival Q-6 ★	B. D. Greenwood	
G-AFFH	Piper J-2 Cub	M. J. Honeychurch	
G-AFFI†	Mignet HM.14 (replica) (BAPC76) ★	Yorkshire Air Museum/Elvington	
G-AFGD	B. A. Swallow 2	A. T. Williams & ptnrs	
G-AFGE	B. A. Swallow 2	A. A. M. & C. W. N. Huke	
G-AFGH	Chilton D.W.1.	M. L. & G. L. Joseph	
G-AFGI	Chilton D.W.1.	K. A. A. McDonald	
G-AFGM	Piper J-4A Cub Coupé	P. H. Wilkinson	
G-AFGZ	DH.82A Tiger Moth	M. R. Paul (G-AMHI)	
G-AFHA	Mosscraft MA.1. ★	C. V. Butler	
G-AFIN	Chrislea LC.1 Airguard (BAPC203) ★	T. W. J. Carnall	
G-AFIR	Luton LA-4 Minor	J. Cresswell	
G-AFIU	Parker CA-4 Parasol ★	The Aeroplane Collection/Hooton Park	
G-AFJA	Watkinson Dingbat ★	A. T. Christian	
G-AFJB	Foster-Wikner G.M.1. Wicko	J. Dible	
G-AFJR	Tipsy Trainer 1	M. E. Vaisey (stored)	
G-AFJU	M.17 Monarch	Museum of Flight/East Fortune	
G-AFJV	Mosscraft MA.2 ★	C. V. Butler	
G-AFNG	DH.94 Moth Minor	The Gullwing Trust	
G-AFNI	DH.94 Moth Minor	J. Jennings	
G-AFOB	DH.94 Moth Minor	K. Cantwell/Henlow	
G-AFOJ	DH.94 Moth Minor	H. Long	
G-AFPN	DH.94 Moth Minor	A. A. A. Maitland & R. S. Jones	
G-AFRZ	M.17 Monarch	R. E. Mitchell/Sleap (G-AIDE)	
G-AFSC	Tipsy Trainer 1	D. M. Forshaw	
G-AFSV	Chilton D.W.1A	R. E. Nerou	
G-AFTA	Hawker Tomtit (K1786)	The Shuttleworth Collection	
G-AFTN	Taylorcraft Plus C2 ★	Leicestershire County Council Museums/Snibston	
G-AFUP	Luscombe 8A Silvaire	R. Dispain	
G-AFVE	DH.82A Tiger Moth (T7230)	J. Mainka	
G-AFWH	Piper J-4A Cub Coupé	C. W. Stearn & R. D. W. Norton	
G-AFWI	DH.82A Tiger Moth	P. R. Harvey	
G-AFWT	Tipsy Trainer 1	N. Parkhouse	
G-AFYD	Luscombe 8F Silvaire	J. D. Iliffe	
G-AFYO	Stinson H.W.75	M. Lodge	
G-AFZA	Piper J-4A Cub Coupe	R. A. Benson	
G-AFZK	Luscombe 8A Silvaire	M. G. Byrnes	

Notes	Reg.	Type	Owner or Operator
	G-AFZL	Porterfield CP.50	P. G. Lucas & S. H. Sharpe
	G-AFZN	Luscombe 8A Silvaire	M. Payne
	G-AGAT	Piper J-3F-50 Cub	A. S. Bathgate
	G-AGBN	GAL.42 Cygnet 2 ★	Museum of Flight/East Fortune
	G-AGEG	DH.82A Tiger Moth	Norman Aeroplane Trust
	G-AGHY	DH.82A Tiger Moth	P. Groves
	G-AGIV	Piper J-3C-65 Cub	J-3 Cub Group
	G-AGJG	DH.89A Dragon Rapide	M. J. & D. J. T. Miller
	G-AGLK	Auster 5D	C. R. Harris
	G-AGMI	Luscombe 8A Silvaire	Oscar Flying Group
	G-AGNJ	DH.82A Tiger Moth	B. P. Borsberry & ptnrs
	G-AGNV	Avro 685 York 1 (TS798) ★	Aerospace Museum/Cosford
	G-AGOS	R.S.4 Desford Trainer (VZ728) ★	Leicestershire County Council Museums
	G-AGPG	Avro 19 Srs 2 ★	The Aeroplane Collection/Hooton Park
	G-AGPK	DH.82A Tiger Moth	T. K. Butcher
	G-AGRU	V.498 Viking 1A ★	Brooklands Museum of Aviation/Weybridge
	G-AGSH	DH.89A Dragon Rapide 6	Bournemouth Aviation Museum
	G-AGTM	DH.89A Dragon Rapide 6	Air Atlantique Ltd
	G-AGTO	Auster 5 J/1 Autocrat	M. J. Barnett & D. J. T. Miller
	G-AGTT	Auster J/1 Autocrat	C. Norfolk
	G-AGVG	Auster 5 J/1 Autocrat (modified)	P. J. & S. J. Benest
	G-AGVV	Piper J-3C-65 Cub	M. Molina-Ruano/Spain
	G-AGXN	Auster J/1N Alpha	Gentleman's Aerial Touring Carriage Group
	G-AGXU	Auster J/1N Alpha	B. H. Austen
	G-AGXV	Auster J/1 Autocrat	B. S. Dowsett & I. M. Oliver
	G-AGYD	Auster J/1N Alpha	P. D. Hodson
	G-AGYH	Auster J/1N Alpha	I. M. Staves
	G-AGYK	Auster J/1 Autocrat	Autocrat Syndicate
	G-AGYT	Auster J/1N Alpha	P. J. Barrett
	G-AGYU	DH.82A Tiger Moth (DE208)	S. A. Firth
	G-AGYY	Ryan ST3KR (27)	H. de Vries/Holland
	G-AGZZ	DH.82A Tiger Moth	M. C. Jordan
	G-AHAG	DH.89A Rapide	S. G. Jones
	G-AHAL	Auster J/1N Alpha	Wickenby Aviation
	G-AHAM	Auster J/1 Autocrat	C. P. L. Jenkin
	G-AHAN	DH.82A Tiger Moth	Tiger Associates Ltd
	G-AHAP	Auster J/1 Autocrat	W. D. Hill
	G-AHAT	Auster J/1N Alpha ★	Dumfries & Galloway Aviation Museum
	G-AHAU	Auster 5 J/1 Autocrat	Andreas Auster Group
	G-AHBL	DH.87B Hornet Moth	Shipping and Airlines Ltd
	G-AHBM	DH.87B Hornet Moth	P. A. & E. P. Gliddon
	G-AHCL	Auster J/1N Alpha (modified)	D. Frankland
	G-AHCN	Auster J/1N Alpha	C. L. Towell & A. G. Boon
	G-AHCR	Gould-Taylorcraft Plus D Special	D. E. H. Balmford & D. R. Shepherd
	G-AHEC	Luscombe 8A Silvaire	C. G. Dodds
	G-AHED	DH.89A Dragon Rapide (RL962) ★	RAF Museum Storage & Restoration Centre/ RAF Stafford
	G-AHGD	DH.89A Dragon Rapide (Z7288)	S. G. Jones
	G-AHGW	Taylorcraft Plus D (LB375)	C. V. Butler
	G-AHGZ	Taylorcraft Plus D (LB367)	M. Pocock
	G-AHHH	Auster J/1 Autocrat	H. A. Jones
	G-AHHT	Auster J/1N Alpha	A. C. Barber & N. J. Hudson
	G-AHIP	Piper J-3C-65 Cub	A. D. Pearce
	G-AHIZ	DH.82A Tiger Moth	C.F.G. Flying Ltd
	G-AHKX	Avro 19 Srs 2	The Shuttleworth Collection
	G-AHKY	Miles M.18 Series 2 ★	Museum of Flight/East Fortune
	G-AHLK	Auster 3 (NJ889)	J. H. Powell-Tuck
	G-AHLT	DH.82A Tiger Moth	M. P. Waring
	G-AHNR	Taylorcraft BC-12D	Bumble Bee Group
	G-AHOO	DH.82A Tiger Moth	J. T. & A. D. Milsom
	G-AHPZ	DH.82A Tiger Moth	N. J. Wareing
	G-AHRI	DH.104 Dove 1 ★	Newark Air Museum
	G-AHSA	Avro 621 Tutor (K3241)	The Shuttleworth Collection
	G-AHSD	Taylorcraft Plus D (LB323)	A. L. Hall-Carpenter
	G-AHSP	Auster J/1 Autocrat	R. M. Weeks
	G-AHSS	Auster J/1N Alpha	A. M. Roche
	G-AHST	Auster J/1N Alpha	A. C. Frost
	G-AHTE	P.44 Proctor V	D. K. Tregilgas
	G-AHTW	A.S.40 Oxford (V3388) ★	Skyfame Collection/Duxford
	G-AHUF	DH.Tiger Moth	Dream Ventures Ltd
	G-AHUG	Taylorcraft Plus D	D. Nieman

Reg.	Type	Owner or Operator	Notes
G-AHUI	M.38 Messenger 2A ★	The Aeroplane Collection/Hooton Park	
G-AHUJ	M.14A Hawk Trainer 3 (R1914) ★	Strathallan Aircraft Collection	
G-AHUN	Globe GC-1B Swift	R. J. Hamlett	
G-AHUV	DH.82A Tiger Moth	A. D. Gordon	
G-AHVU	DH.82A Tiger Moth	J. B. Steel	
G-AHVV	DH.82A Tiger Moth	M. Arter	
G-AHWJ	Taylorcraft Plus D (LB294)	M. Pocock	
G-AHXE	Taylorcraft Plus D (LB312)	J. M. C. Pothecary	
G-AIBE	Fulmar II (N1854) ★	F.A.A. Museum/Yeovilton	
G-AIBH	Auster J/1N Alpha	M. J. Bonnick	
G-AIBM	Auster J/1 Autocrat	R. Greatrex	
G-AIBR	Auster J/1 Autocrat	P. R. Hodson	
G-AIBW	Auster J/1N Alpha	C. R. Sunter	
G-AIBX	Auster J/1 Autocrat	Wasp Flying Group	
G-AIBY	Auster J/1 Autocrat	D. Morris	
G-AICX	Luscombe 8A Silvaire	The 2177 Flying Group	
G-AIDL	DH.89A Dragon Rapide 6 (TX310)	Air Atlantique Ltd	
G-AIDN	VS.502 Spitfire Tr.VII (MT818)	P. M. Andrews	
G-AIDS	DH.82A Tiger Moth	K. D. Pogmore & T. Dann	
G-AIEK	M.38 Messenger 2A (RG333)	G. B. E. Pearce	
G-AIFZ	Auster J/1N Alpha	M. D. Ansley	
G-AIGD	Auster V J/1 Autocrat	R. B. Webber	
G-AIGF	Auster J/1N Alpha	A. R. C. Mathie	
G-AIGT	Auster J/1N Alpha	R. R. Harris	
G-AIIH	Piper J-3C-65 Cub	M. S. Pettit	
G-AIJI	Auster J/1N Alpha ★	C. J. Baker	
G-AIJM	Auster J/4	N. Huxtable	
G-AIJT	Auster J/4 Srs 100	Aberdeen Auster Flying Group	
G-AIKE	Auster 5	R. H. Cooper & T. K. Rumble	
G-AIPR	Auster J/4	M. A. & N. Mills	
G-AIPV	Auster J/1 Autocrat	W. P. Miller	
G-AIRC	Auster J/1 Autocrat	Z. J. Rockey	
G-AIRK	DH.82A Tiger Moth	J. S. & P. R. Johnson	
G-AISA	Tipsy B Srs 1	S. Slater	
G-AISC	Tipsy B Srs 1	Wagtail Flying Group	
G-AISS	Piper J-3C-65 Cub	K. W. Wood & F. Watson	
G-AIST	VS.300 Spitfire 1A (AR213/PR-D)	Sheringham Aviation UK Ltd	
G-AISX	Piper J-3C-65 Cub	Cubfly	
G-AITB	A.S.10 Oxford (MP425) ★	RAF Museum/Hendon	
G-AIUA	M.14A Hawk Trainer 3 (T9768) ★	D. S. Hunt	
G-AIUL	DH.89A Dragon Rapide 6	I. Jones	
G-AIXA	Taylorcraft Plus D (LB264)★	RAF Museum/Hendon	
G-AIXJ	DH.82A Tiger Moth	D. Green	
G-AIXN	Benes-Mraz M.1C Sokol	A. J. Wood	
G-AIYG	SNCAN Stampe SV.4B	J. E. Henny/Belgium	
G-AIYR	DH.89A Dragon Rapide (HG691)	Spectrum Leisure Ltd	
G-AIYS	DH.85 Leopard Moth	R. A. & V. A. Gammons	
G-AIZE	Fairchild F.24W Argus 2 (FS628) ★	Aerospace Museum/Cosford	
G-AIZG	VS.236 Walrus 1 (L2301) ★	F.A.A. Museum/Yeovilton	
G-AIZU	Auster J/1 Autocrat★	C. J. & J. G. B. Morley	
G-AJAD	Piper J-3C-65 Cub	C. R. Shipley	
G-AJAE	Auster J/1N Alpha	J. & B. F. Wolfe	
G-AJAJ	Auster J/1N Alpha	M. J. Whitwell	
G-AJAM	Auster J/2 Arrow	D. A. Porter	
G-AJAP	Luscombe 8A Silvaire	M. Flint	
G-AJAS	Auster J/1N Alpha	C. J. Baker	
G-AJCP	D.31 Turbulent	B. R. Pearson	
G-AJDW	Auster J/1 Autocrat	D. R. Hunt	
G-AJEB	Auster J/1N Alpha ★	The Aeroplane Collection/Hooton Park	
G-AJEE	Auster J/1 Autocrat	A. C. Whitehead	
G-AJEH	Auster J/1N Alpha	J. T. Powell-Tuck	
G-AJEI	Auster J/1N Alpha	J. Siddall	
G-AJEM	Auster J/1 Autocrat	A. L. Aish	
G-AJES	Piper J-3C-65 Cub (330485:C-44)	D. E. Jarvis	
G-AJGJ	Auster 5 (RT486)	British Classic Aircraft Restoration Flying Group	
G-AJHS	DH.82A Tiger Moth	Vliegend Museum/Netherlands	
G-AJIH	Auster J/1 Autocrat	D. G. Curran	
G-AJIS	Auster J/1N Alpha	Husthwaite Auster Group	
G-AJIT	Auster J/1 Kingsland Autocrat	G-AJIT Group	
G-AJIU	Auster J/1 Autocrat	M. D. Greenhalgh	

Notes	Reg.	Type	Owner or Operator
	G-AJIW	Auster J/1N Alpha	W. C. Walters
	G-AJJP	Fairey Jet Gyrodyne (XJ389) ★	Museum of Berkshire Aviation/Woodley
	G-AJJS	Cessna 120	Juliet Sierra Group
	G-AJJT	Cessna 120	Juliet Tango Group
	G-AJJU	Luscombe 8E Silvaire	Eenstone Luscombe Group
	G-AJKB	Luscombe 8E Silvaire	T. Carter
	G-AJOC	M.38 Messenger 2A ★	Ulster Folk & Transport Museum
	G-AJOE	M.38 Messenger 2A	P. W. Bishop
	G-AJON	Aeronca 7AC Champion	J. M. Gale
	G-AJOV†	Westland WS-51 Dragonfly ★	Aerospace Museum/Cosford
	G-AJOZ	Fairchild F.24W Argus 2 ★	Yorkshire Air Museum/Elvington
	G-AJPI	Fairchild F.24R-41a Argus 3 (314887)	R. Sijben/Netherlands
	G-AJRB	Auster J/1 Autocrat	R. W. Vince
	G-AJRE	Auster J/1 Autocrat (Lycoming)	Air Tech Spares
	G-AJRH	Auster J/1N Alpha ★	Charnwood Museum/Loughborough
	G-AJRS	M.14A Hawk Trainer 3 (P6382:C)	The Shuttleworth Collection
	G-AJTW	DH.82A Tiger Moth (N6965:FL-J)	J. A. Barker
	G-AJUE	Auster J/1 Autocrat	P. H. B. Cole
	G-AJUL	Auster J/1N Alpha	M. J. Crees
	G-AJVE	DH.82A Tiger Moth	R. A. Gammons
	G-AJWB	M.38 Messenger 2A	P. W. Bishop
	G-AJXC	Auster 5	R. D. Helliar-Symonds, K. A. & S. E. W. Williams
	G-AJXV	Auster 4 (NJ695)	B. A. Farries
	G-AJXY	Auster 4	X-Ray Yankee Group
	G-AJYB	Auster J/1N Alpha	P. J. Shotbolt
	G-AKAT	M.14A Hawk Trainer 3 (T9738)	R. A. Fleming
	G-AKAZ	Piper J-3C-65 Cub (57-G)	Frazerblades Ltd
	G-AKBO	M.38 Messenger 2A	D. O. Blackburn & P. A. Fenton
	G-AKDN	DHC.1A-1 Chipmunk	P. S. Derry/Canada
	G-AKDW	DH.89A Dragon Rapide ★	De Havilland Heritage Museum/London Colney
	G-AKEL	M.65 Gemini 1A ★	Ulster Folk & Transport Museum
	G-AKEN	M.65 Gemlni 1A	C. W. P. Turner
	G-AKEX	Percival Proctor III	M. Biddulph (G-AKIU)
	G-AKGE	M.65 Gemini 3C ★	Ulster Folk & Transport Museum
	G-AKHP	M.65 Gemini 1A	M. Hales
	G-AKHU	M.65 Gemini 1A	C. W. P. Turner
	G-AKHZ	M.65 Gemini 7 ★	The Aeroplane Collection/Hooton Park
	G-AKIB	Piper J-3C-90 Cub (480015:M-44)	M. C. Bennett
	G-AKIF	DH.89A Dragon Rapide	Airborne Taxi Services Ltd
	G-AKIN	M.38 Messenger 2A	Sywell Messenger Group
	G-AKIU	P.44 Proctor V	Air Atlantique Ltd
	G-AKKB	M.65 Gemini 1A	D. R. Gray
	G-AKKH	M.65 Gemini 1A	J. S. Allison
	G-AKKR	M.14A Magister (T9707) ★	Museum of Army Flying/Middle Wallop
	G-AKKY	M.14A Hawk Trainer 3 (L6906)★ (BAPC44)	Museum of Berkshire Aviation/Woodley
	G-AKLW	Short SA.6 Sealand 1 ★	Ulster Folk & Transport Museum
	G-AKOW	Auster 5 (TJ569) ★	Museum of Army Flying/Middle Wallop
	G-AKPF	M.14A Hawk Trainer 3 (N3788)	P. R. Holloway
	G-AKRA	Piper J-3C-65 Cub	W. R. Savin
	G-AKRP	DH.89A Dragon Rapide 4	Eaglescott Dominie Group
	G-AKSY	Auster 5 (TJ534)	A. Brier
	G-AKSZ	Auster 5C	P. W. Yates & R. G. Darbyshire
	G-AKTH	Piper J-3C-65 Cub	A. G. A. Obertelli & G. W. S. Turner
	G-AKTI	Luscombe 8A Silvaire	C. Chambers
	G-AKTO	Aeronca 7BCM Champion	R. M. Davies
	G-AKTP	PA-17 Vagabond	Golf Tango Papa Group
	G-AKTR	Aeronca 7AC Champion	R. Tarplee
	G-AKTS	Cessna 120	M. Isterling
	G-AKTT	Luscombe 8A Silvaire	S. J. Charters
	G-AKUE	DH.82A Tiger Moth	D. F. Hodgkinson
	G-AKUF	Luscombe 8E Silvaire	M. O. Loxton
	G-AKUJ	Luscombe 8E Silvaire	R. C. Green
	G-AKUK	Luscombe 8A Silvaire	O. R. Watts
	G-AKUL	Luscombe 8A Silvaire	E. A. Taylor
	G-AKUM	Luscombe 8F Silvaire	D. A. Young
	G-AKUN	Piper J-3F-65 Cub	W. R. Savin
	G-AKUO	Aeronca 11AC Chief	L. W. Richardson
	G-AKUP	Luscombe 8E Silvaire	D. A. Young
	G-AKUR	Cessna 140	J. Greenaway & C. A. Davies
	G-AKUW	Chrislea CH.3 Super Ace 2	J. & S. Rickett

Reg.	Type	Owner or Operator	Notes
G-AKVF	Chrislea CH.3 Super Ace 2	Aces High Ltd	
G-AKVM	Cessna 120	N. Wise & S. Walker	
G-AKVN	Aeronca 11AC Chief	P. A. Jackson	
G-AKVO	Taylorcraft BC-12D	A. Weir	
G-AKVP	Luscombe 8A Silvaire	J. M. Edis	
G-AKVR	Chrislea CH.3 Skyjeep 4	R. B. Webber	
G-AKVZ	M.38 Messenger 4B	Shipping & Airlines Ltd	
G-AKWS	Auster 5A-160 (RT610)	M. C. Hayes	
G-AKWT	Auster 5 ★	C. Baker	
G-AKXP	Auster 5 (NJ633)	A. D. Pearce	
G-AKXS	DH.82A Tiger Moth	J. & G. J. Eagles	
G-AKZN	P.34A Proctor 3 (Z7197) ★	RAF Museum/Hendon	
G-ALAX	DH.89A Dragon Rapide ★	Durney Aeronautical Collection/Andover	
G-ALBJ	Auster 5	P. N. Elkington	
G-ALBK	Auster 5	K. Wheatcroft	
G-ALBN	Bristol 173 (XF785) ★	RAF Museum Storage & Restoration Centre/Cardington	
G-ALCK	P.34A Proctor 3 (LZ766) ★	Skyfame Collection/Duxford	
G-ALCU	DH.104 Dove 2 ★	Midland Air Museum/Coventry	
G-ALDG	HP.81 Hermes 4 ★	Duxford Aviation Society (fuselage only)	
G-ALEH	PA-17 Vagabond	A. D. Pearce	
G-ALFA	Auster 5	A. E. Jones	
G-ALFU	DH.104 Dove 6 ★	Duxford Aviation Society	
G-ALGA	PA-15 Vagabond	S. T. Gilbert	
G-ALGT	VS.379 Spitfire F.XIVH (RM689)	Rolls-Royce PLC	
G-ALIJ	PA-17 Vagabond	Popham Flying Group	
G-ALIW	DH.82A Tiger Moth	F. R. Curry	
G-ALJF	P.34A Proctor 3	J. F. Moore	
G-ALJL	DH.82A Tiger Moth	R. I. & D. Souch	
G-ALJR	Abbott-Baynes Scud III	L. P. Woodage	
G-ALLF	Slingsby T.30A Prefect (ARK)	J. F. Hopkins & K. M. Fresson	
G-ALMA	Piper J3C-65 Cub	M. J. Butler	
G-ALNA	DH.82A Tiger Moth	R. J. Doughton	
G-ALND	DH.82A Tiger Moth (N9191)	J. T. Powell-Tuck	
G-ALOD	Cessna 140	J. R. Stainer	
G-ALSP	Bristol 171 Sycamore (WV783) ★	RAF Museum/Hendon	
G-ALSS	Bristol 171 Sycamore (WA576) ★	Dumfries & Galloway Aviation Museum	
G-ALST	Bristol 171 Sycamore (WA577) ★	North East Aircraft Museum/Usworth	
G-ALSW	Bristol 171 Sycamore (WT933) ★	Newark Air Museum	
G-ALSX	Bristol 171 Sycamore (G-48-1) ★	IHM/Weston-super-Mare	
G-ALTO	Cessna 140	T. M. Jones & ptnrs	
G-ALUC	DH.82A Tiger Moth	D. R. & M. Wood	
G-ALWB	DHC.1 Chipmunk 22A	D. M. Neville	
G-ALWF	V.701 Viscount ★	Duxford Aviation Society *RMA Sir John Franklin*	
G-ALWS	DH.82A Tiger Moth	A. P. Benyon	
G-ALWW	DH.82A Tiger Moth	D. E. Findon	
G-ALXT	DH.89A Dragon Rapide ★	Science Museum/Wroughton	
G-ALXZ	Auster 5-150	G-ALXZ Syndicate	
G-ALYB	Auster 5 (RT520) ★	South Yorkshire Aviation Museum/Doncaster	
G-ALYG	Auster 5D	A. L. Young	
G-ALYW	DH.106 Comet 1 ★	RAF Exhibition Flight (fuselage converted to 'Nimrod')	
G-ALZE	BN-1F ★	M. R. Short/Solent Sky, Southampton	
G-ALZO	A.S.57 Ambassador ★	Duxford Aviation Society	
G-AMAW	Luton LA-4 Minor	The Real Aeroplane Co.Ltd	
G-AMBB	DH.82A Tiger Moth	J. Eagles	
G-AMCK	DH.82A Tiger Moth	Liverpool Flying School Ltd	
G-AMCM	DH.82A Tiger Moth	A. K. & J. I. Cooper	
G-AMDA	Avro 652A Anson 1 (N4877:MK-V) ★	Skyfame Collection/Duxford	
G-AMEN	PA-18 Super Cub 95	The G-AMEN Flying Group	
G-AMHF	DH.82A Tiger Moth	A. J. West	
G-AMHJ	Douglas C-47A Dakota 6 (KG651) ★	Assault Glider Association/Shawbury	
G-AMIV	DH.82A Tiger Moth	K. F. Crumplin	
G-AMKU	Auster J/1B Aiglet	P. G. Lipman	
G-AMLZ	P.50 Prince 6E ★	The Jetstream Club	
G-AMMS	Auster J/5K Aiglet Trainer	R. B. Webber	
G-AMNN	DH.82A Tiger Moth	I. J. Perry	
G-AMOG	V.701 Viscount ★	Museum of Flight/East Fortune	
G-AMPG	PA-12 Super Cruiser	A. G. & S. M. Measey	
G-AMPI	SNCAN Stampe SV.4C	T. W. Harris	

Notes	Reg.	Type	Owner or Operator
	G-AMPO	Douglas C-47B (FZ626/YS-DH) ★	(gate guardian)/RAF Lyneham
	G-AMPY	Douglas C-47B (KK116)	Air Atlantique Ltd/Coventry
	G-AMPZ	Douglas C-47B ★	Air Service Berlin GmbH/Tempelhof
	G-AMRA	Douglas C-47B	Air Atlantique Ltd
	G-AMRF	Auster J/5F Aiglet Trainer	D. A. Hill
	G-AMRK	G.37 Gladiator I (K7985)	The Shuttleworth Collection
	G-AMSG	SIPA 903	S. W. Markham
	G-AMSN	Douglas C-47B ★	Aceball Aviation/Redhill
	G-AMTA	Auster J/5F Aiglet Trainer	J. D. Manson
	G-AMTF	DH.82A Tiger Moth (T7842)	H. A. D. Monro
	G-AMTK	DH.82A Tiger Moth	S. W. McKay & M. E. Vaisey
	G-AMTM	Auster J/1 Autocrat	R. J. Stobo (G-AJUJ)
	G-AMTV	DH.82A Tiger Moth	G-AMTV Flying Group
	G-AMUF	DHC.1 Chipmunk 21	Redhill Tailwheel Flying Club Ltd
	G-AMUI	Auster J/5F Aiglet Trainer	R. B. Webber
	G-AMVD	Auster 5 (TJ652)	M.Hammond
	G-AMVP	Tipsy Junior	A. R. Wershat
	G-AMVS	DH.82A Tiger Moth	J. T. Powell-Tuck
	G-AMXA	DH.106 Comet 2 (nose only) ★	(stored)
	G-AMYD	Auster J/5L Aiglet Trainer	R. D. Thomasson
	G-AMYJ	Douglas C-47B (KN353) ★	Yorkshire Air Museum/Elvington
	G-AMZI	Auster J/5F Aiglet Trainer	J. F. Moore
	G-AMZT	Auster J/5F Aiglet Trainer	D. Hyde, J. W. Saull & J. C. Hutchinson
	G-ANAF	Douglas C-47B	Air Atlantique Ltd
	G-ANAP	DH.104 Dove 6 ★	Brunel Technical College/Lulsgate
	G-ANCF	B.175 Britannia 308 ★	Bristol Aero Collection (stored)/Kemble
	G-ANCS	DH.82A Tiger Moth	C. E. Edwards & E. A. Higgins
	G-ANDE	DH.82A Tiger Moth	D. A. Nisbet
	G-ANDM	DH.82A Tiger Moth	N. J. Stagg
	G-ANEH	DH.82A Tiger Moth (N6797)	G. J. Wells
	G-ANEL	DH.82A Tiger Moth	Totalsure Ltd
	G-ANEM	DH.82A Tiger Moth	P. J. Benest
	G-ANEN	DH.82A Tiger Moth	G-ANEN Group
	G-ANEW	DH.82A Tiger Moth	K. F. Crumplin
	G-ANEZ	DH.82A Tiger Moth	C. D. J. Bland
	G-ANFH	Westland WS-55 Whirlwind ★	IHM/Weston-super-Mare
	G-ANFI	DH.82A Tiger Moth (DE623)	G. P. Graham
	G-ANFL	DH.82A Tiger Moth	Felthorpe Tiger Group Ltd
	G-ANFM	DH.82A Tiger Moth	Reading Flying Group
	G-ANFP	DH.82A Tiger Moth	G. D. Horn
	G-ANFU	Auster 5 (NJ719) ★	North East Aircraft Museum/Usworth
	G-ANFV	DH.82A Tiger Moth (DF155)	R. A. L. Falconer
	G-ANGK	Cessna 140A	M. J. Whiteman-Haywood
	G-ANHK	DH.82A Tiger Moth	J. D. Iliffe
	G-ANHR	Auster 5	H. L. Swallow
	G-ANHS	Auster 4 (MT197)	Mike Tango Group
	G-ANHU	Auster 4	J. A. & R. H. Cooper
	G-ANHX	Auster 5D	D. J. Baker
	G-ANIE	Auster 5 (TW467)	R. T. Ingram
	G-ANIJ	Auster 5D (TJ672)	G. M. Rundle
	G-ANIS	Auster 5	J. Clarke-Cockburn
	G-ANJA	DH.82A Tiger Moth	A. D. Hodgkinson
	G-ANJD	DH.82A Tiger Moth	D. O. Lewis
	G-ANKK	DH.82A Tiger Moth (T5854)	Halfpenny Green Tiger Group
	G-ANKT	DH.82A Tiger Moth (K2585)	The Shuttleworth Collection
	G-ANKV	DH.82A Tiger Moth (T7793) ★	Westmead Business Group/Croydon Airport
	G-ANKZ	DH.82A Tiger Moth (N6466)	D. W. Graham
	G-ANLD	DH.82A Tiger Moth	K. Peters
	G-ANLS	DH.82A Tiger Moth	P. A. Gliddon
	G-ANLW	Westland WS-51/2 Widgeon ★	Norfolk & Suffolk Museum/Flixton
	G-ANMO	DH.82A Tiger Moth (K4259:71)	R. J. Moore & B. S. Floodgate
	G-ANMY	DH.82A Tiger Moth (DE470)	Dog Easy Ltd
	G-ANNB	DH.82A Tiger Moth	M. C. Curtis
	G-ANNE	DH.82A Tiger Moth	C. R. Hardiman
	G-ANNG	DH.82A Tiger Moth	P. F. Walter
	G-ANNI	DH.82A Tiger Moth (T6953)	C. E. Ponsford & ptnrs
	G-ANNK	DH.82A Tiger Moth	D. R. Wilcox
	G-ANOA	Hiller UH-12A ★	Redhill Technical College
	G-ANOH	DH.82A Tiger Moth	N. Parkhouse
	G-ANOK	SAAB S.91C Safir ★	A. F. Galt & Co (stored)
	G-ANOM	DH.82A Tiger Moth	T. G. I. Dark

Reg.	Type	Owner or Operator	Notes
G-ANON	DH.82A Tiger Moth (T7909)	M. Kelly	
G-ANOO	DH.82A Tiger Moth	R. K. Packman	
G-ANOV	DH.104 Dove 6 ★	Museum of Flight/East Fortune	
G-ANPE	DH.82A Tiger Moth	I. E. S. Huddleston/Clacton (G-IESH)	
G-ANPP	P.34A Proctor 3	C. P. A. & J. Jeffrey	
G-ANRF	DH.82A Tiger Moth	C. D. Cyster	
G-ANRM	DH.82A Tiger Moth (DF112)	Spectrum Leisure Ltd	
G-ANRN	DH.82A Tiger Moth	J. J. V. Elwes	
G-ANRP	Auster 5 (TW439)	P. R. & J. S. Johnson	
G-ANRX	DH.82A Tiger Moth ★	De Havilland Heritage Museum/London Colney	
G-ANSM	DH.82A Tiger Moth	Douglas Aviation	
G-ANTE	DH.82A Tiger Moth (T6562)	G-ANTE Flyers Ltd	
G-ANTK	Avro 685 York ★	Duxford Aviation Society	
G-ANUO	DH.114 Heron 2D (G-AOXL) ★	Westmead Business Group/Croydon Airport	
G-ANUW	DH.104 Dove 6 ★	Jet Aviation Preservation Group	
G-ANWB	DHC.1 Chipmunk 21	G. Briggs	
G-ANXB	DH.114 Heron 1B ★	Newark Air Museum	
G-ANXC	Auster J/5R Alpine	Alpine Group	
G-ANXR	P.31C Proctor 4 (RM221)	N. H. T. Cottrell	
G-ANZT	Thruxton Jackaroo (T7798)	D. J. Neville & P. A. Dear	
G-ANZU	DH.82A Tiger Moth	M. I. Lodge	
G-ANZZ	DH.82A Tiger Moth	T. K. Butcher	
G-AOAA	DH.82A Tiger Moth	R. C. P. Brookhouse	
G-AOBG	Somers-Kendall SK.1	P. W. Bishop	
G-AOBH	DH.82A Tiger Moth (NL750)	P. Nutley	
G-AOBJ	DH.82A Tiger Moth	A. D. Hodgkinson	
G-AOBU	P.84 Jet Provost T.1 (XD693)	T. J. Manna	
G-AOBX	DH.82A Tiger Moth	David Ross Flying Group	
G-AOCP	Auster 5 ★	C. J. Baker (stored)	
G-AOCR	Auster 5D (NJ673)	T. Taylor	
G-AOCU	Auster 5	S. J. Ball	
G-AODA	Westland S-55 Srs 3 ★	IHM/Weston-super-Mare	
G-AODR	DH.82A Tiger Moth	G-AODR Group (G-ISIS)	
G-AODT	DH.82A Tiger Moth (R5250)	R. A. Harrowven	
G-AOEH	Aeronca 7AC Champion	A. Gregori	
G-AOEI	DH.82A Tiger Moth	C.F.G. Flying Ltd	
G-AOEL	DH.82A Tiger Moth ★	Museum of Flight/East Fortune	
G-AOES	DH.82A Tiger Moth	K. A. & A. J. Broomfield	
G-AOET	DH.82A Tiger Moth	Venom Jet Promotions Ltd	
G-AOEX	Thruxton Jackaroo	A. T. Christian	
G-AOFE	DHC.1 Chipmunk 22A (WB702)	W. J. Quinn	
G-AOFJ	Auster J/1N Alpha	L. J. Kingscott	
G-AOFS	Auster J/5L Aiglet Trainer	P. N. A. Whitehead	
G-AOGA	M.75 Aries ★	Irish Aviation Museum (stored)	
G-AOGI	DH.82A Tiger Moth	W. J. Taylor	
G-AOGR	DH.82A Tiger Moth (XL714)	R. J. S. G. Clark	
G-AOGV	Auster J/5R Alpine	R. E. Heading	
G-AOHY	DH.82A Tiger Moth (N6537)	S. W. Turley	
G-AOHZ	Auster J/5P Autocar	A. D. Hodgkinson	
G-AOIL	DH.82A Tiger Moth (XL716)	C. D. Davidson	
G-AOIM	DH.82A Tiger Moth	C. R. Hardiman	
G-AOIR	Thruxton Jackaroo	K. A. & A. J. Broomfield	
G-AOIS	DH.82A Tiger Moth (R5172)	J. K. Ellwood	
G-AOJH	DH.83C Fox Moth	Connect Properties Ltd	
G-AOJJ	DH.82A Tiger Moth (DF128)	E. & K. M. Lay	
G-AOJK	DH.82A Tiger Moth	R. J. Willies	
G-AOJR	DHC.1 Chipmunk 22	G. J-H. Caubergs & N. Marien/Belgium	
G-AOJT	DH.106 Comet 1 (F-BGNX) ★	De Havilland Heritage Museum (fuselage only)	
G-AOKH	P.40 Prentice 1	J. F. Moore/Biggin Hill	
G-AOKL	P.40 Prentice 1 (VS610)	The Shuttleworth Collection	
G-AOKO	P.40 Prentice 1 ★	Aero Venture	
G-AOKZ	P.40 Prentice 1 (VS623) ★	Midland Air Museum/Coventry	
G-AOLK	P.40 Prentice 1 ★	RAF Museum	
G-AOLU	P.40 Prentice 1 (VS356)	N. J. Butler	
G-AORB	Cessna 170B	Eaglescott Parachute Centre	
G-AORG	DH.114 Heron 2	Duchess of Brittany (Jersey) Ltd	
G-AORW	DHC.1 Chipmunk 22A	Skylark Aviation Ltd	
G-AOSF	DHC.1 Chipmunk 22 (WB571:34)	T. S. Olsen/Germany	
G-AOSK	DHC.1 Chipmunk 22 (WB726)	L. J. Irvine	
G-AOSY	DHC.1 Chipmunk 22 (WB585:M)	WFG Chipmunk Group	
G-AOTD	DHC.1 Chipmunk 22 (WB588)	S. Piech	

Notes	Reg.	Type	Owner or Operator
	G-AOTF	DHC.1 Chipmunk 23 (Lycoming)	Clevelands Gliding Club
	G-AOTI	DH.114 Heron 2D ★	De Havilland Heritage Museum/London Colney
	G-AOTK	D.53 Turbi	T. J. Adams
	G-AOTR	DHC.1 Chipmunk 22	Ace Leasing Ltd
	G-AOTY	DHC.1 Chipmunk 22A (WG472)	A. A. Hodgson
	G-AOUJ	Fairey Ultra-Light ★	IHM/Weston-super-Mare
	G-AOUO	DHC.1 Chipmunk 22 (Lycoming)	Wrekin/Cosford
	G-AOUP	DHC.1 Chipmunk 22	A. R. Harding
	G-AOUR	DH.82A Tiger Moth ★	Ulster Folk & Transport Museum
	G-AOVF	B.175 Britannia 312F ★	Aerospace Museum/Cosford
	G-AOVS	B.175 Britannia 312F ★	Airport Fire Section/Luton
	G-AOVT	B.175 Britannia 312F ★	Duxford Aviation Society
	G-AOVW	Auster 5	B. Marriott
	G-AOXN	DH.82A Tiger Moth	S. L. G. Darch
	G-AOZH	DH.82A Tiger Moth (K2572)	M. H. Blois-Brooke
	G-AOZL	Auster J/5Q Alpine	R. M. Weeks
	G-AOZP	DHC.1 Chipmunk 22	S. J. Davies
	G-APAF	Auster 5 (TW511)	J. J. J. Mostyn (G-CMAL)
	G-APAH	Auster 5	T. J. Goodwin
	G-APAJ	Thruxton Jackaroo	J. T. H. Page
	G-APAL	DH.82A Tiger Moth (N6847)	P. J. Shotbolt
	G-APAM	DH.82A Tiger Moth	R. P. Williams
	G-APAO	DH.82A Tiger Moth (R4922)	H. J. Maguire
	G-APAP	DH.82A Tiger Moth (R5136)	J. C. Wright
	G-APAS	DH.106 Comet 1XB ★	Aerospace Museum/Cosford
	G-APBE	Auster 5	R. B. Woods
	G-APBI	DH.82A Tiger Moth	C. J. Zeal
	G-APBO	D.53 Turbi	R. C. Hibberd
	G-APBW	Auster 5	C. R. W. Brown/France
	G-APCB	Auster J/5Q Alpine	A. A. Beswick
	G-APCC	DH.82A Tiger Moth	L. J. Rice/Henstridge
	G-APDB	DH.106 Comet 4 ★	Duxford Aviation Society
	G-APEP	V.953C Merchantman ★	Brooklands Museum of Aviation/Weybridge
	G-APFA	D.54 Turbi	F. J. Keitch
	G-APFJ	Boeing 707-436 ★	Museum of Flight/East Fortune
	G-APFU	DH.82A Tiger Moth	Leisure Assets Ltd
	G-APFV	PA-23-160 Apache	J. L. Thorogood (G-MOLY)
	G-APHV	Avro 19 Srs 2 (VM360) ★	Museum of Flight/East Fortune
	G-APIE	Tipsy Belfair B	D. Beale
	G-APIH	DH.82A Tiger Moth	K. Stewering
	G-APIK	Auster J/1N Alpha	J. H. Powell-Tuck
	G-APIM	V.806 Viscount ★	Brooklands Museum of Aviation/Weybridge
	G-APIT	P.40 Prentice 1 (VR192) ★	WWII Aircraft Preservation Society/Lasham
	G-APIY	P.40 Prentice 1 (VR249) ★	Newark Air Museum
	G-APIZ	D.31 Turbulent	R. G. Meredith
	G-APJB	P.40 Prentice 1 (VR259)	Air Atlantique Ltd
	G-APJJ	Fairey Ultra-light ★	Midland Aircraft Preservation Society
	G-APJZ	Auster J/1N Alpha	P. G. Lipman
	G-APLG	Auster J/5L Aiglet Trainer ★	Solway Aviation Society
	G-APLO	DHC.1 Chipmunk 22A (WD379)	Lindholme Aircraft Ltd
	G-APLU	DH.82A Tiger Moth	R. A. Bishop & M. E. Vaisey
	G-APMB	DH.106 Comet 4B ★	Gatwick Handling Ltd (ground trainer)
	G-APMH	Auster J/1U Workmaster	M. R. P. Thorogood
	G-APMX	DH.82A Tiger Moth	Foley Farm Flying Group
	G-APMY	PA-23 Apache 160 ★	Aero Venture
	G-APNJ	Cessna 310 ★	Chelsea College/Shoreham
	G-APNT	Currie Wot	B. J. Dunford
	G-APNZ	D.31 Turbulent	J. Knight
	G-APPA	DHC.1 Chipmunk 22	D. M. Squires
	G-APPL	P.40 Prentice 1	S. J. Saggers/Biggin Hill
	G-APPM	DHC.1 Chipmunk 22 (WB711)	S. D. Wilch
	G-APRL	AW.650 Argosy 101 ★	Midland Air Museum/Coventry
	G-APRO	Auster 6A	A. F. & H. Wankowski
	G-APRR	Super Aero 45	M. J. O'Donnell
	G-APRS	SA Twin Pioneer Srs 3	Aviation Heritage Ltd (G-BCWF)
	G-APRT	Taylor JT.1 Monoplane	R. A. Keech
	G-APSA	Douglas DC-6A	Air Atlantique Ltd
	G-APSR	Auster J/1U Workmaster	D. & K. Aero Services Ltd
	G-APTR	Auster J/1N Alpha	C. R. Shipley
	G-APTU	Auster 5	G-APTU Flying Group
	G-APTW	Westland WS-51/2 Widgeon ★	North East Aircraft Museum/Usworth

Reg.	Type	Owner or Operator	Notes
G-APTY	Beech G.35 Bonanza	G. E. Brennand	
G-APTZ	D.31 Turbulent	The Tiger Club (1990) Ltd	
G-APUD	Bensen B.7M (modified) ★	Manchester Museum of Science & Industry	
G-APUE	L.40 Meta Sokol	S. E. & M. J. Aherne	
G-APUP	Sopwith Pup (replica) (N5182) ★	RAF Museum/Hendon	
G-APUR	PA-22 Tri-Pacer 160	S. T. A. Hutchinson	
G-APUW	Auster J/5V-160 Autocar	E. A. J. Hibbard	
G-APUY	D.31 Turbulent	C. Jones/Barton	
G-APVF	Putzer Elster B (97+04)	A. Wiseman	
G-APVN	D.31 Turbulent	R. Sherwin	
G-APVS	Cessna 170B	N. Simpson Stormin' Norman	
G-APVU	L.40 Meta Sokol	S. E. & M. J. Aherne	
G-APVZ	D.31 Turbulent	The Tiger Club (1990) Ltd	
G-APWA	HPR.7 Herald 101 ★	Museum of Berkshire Aviation/Woodley	
G-APWJ	HPR.7 Herald 201 ★	Duxford Aviation Society	
G-APWN	Westland WS-55 Whirlwind 3 ★	Midland Air Museum/Coventry	
G-APWY	Piaggio P.166 ★	Science Museum/Wroughton	
G-APXJ	PA-24 Comanche 250	T. Wildsmith	
G-APXR	PA-22 Tri-Pacer 160	A. Troughton	
G-APXT	PA-22 Tri-Pacer 150 (modified)	A. E. Cuttler	
G-APXU	PA-22 Tri-Pacer 125 (modified)	The Scottish Aero Club Ltd	
G-APXW	EP.9 Prospector (XM819) ★	Museum of Army Flying/Middle Wallop	
G-APXX	DHA.3 Drover 2 (VH-FDT) ★	WWII Aircraft Preservation Society/Lasham	
G-APYB	Tipsy T.66 Nipper 3	B. O. Smith	
G-APYD	DH.106 Comet 4B ★	Science Museum/Wroughton	
G-APYG	DHC.1 Chipmunk 22	P. A. & J. M. Doyle	
G-APYI	PA-22 Tri-Pacer 135	Just Plane Trading Ltd	
G-APYT	Champion 7FC Tri-Traveller	B. J. Anning	
G-APZJ	PA-18 Super Cub 150	S. G. Jones	
G-APZL	PA-22 Tri-Pacer 160	B. Robins	
G-APZX	PA-22 Tri-Pacer 150	V. A. Holliday	
G-ARAD	Luton LA-5 Major ★	North East Aircraft Museum	
G-ARAI	PA-22 Tri-Pacer 160	P. McCabe	
G-ARAM	PA-18 Super Cub 150	Skymax (Aviation) Ltd	
G-ARAN	PA-18 Super Cub 150	A. P. Docherty	
G-ARAS	Champion 7FC Tri-Traveller	Alpha Sierra Flying Group	
G-ARAT	Cessna 180C	S. D. Pryke & J. Graham	
G-ARAW	Cessna 182C Skylane	Ximango UK	
G-ARAX	PA-22 Tri-Pacer 150	J. W. Iliffe	
G-ARAZ	DH.82A Tiger Moth (R4959:59)	D. A. Porter	
G-ARBE	DH.104 Dove 8	M. Whale & M. W. A. Lunn	
G-ARBG	Tipsy T.66 Nipper 2	D. Shrimpton	
G-ARBO	PA-24 Comanche 250	Tatenhill Aviation Ltd	
G-ARBS	PA-22 Tri-Pacer 160 (tailwheel)	S. D. Rowell	
G-ARBV	PA-22 Tri-Pacer 160	L. M. Williams	
G-ARBZ	D.31 Turbulent	G. Richards	
G-ARCF	PA-22 Tri-Pacer 150	M. J. Speakman	
G-ARCS	Auster D6/180	R. J. Fray	
G-ARCT	PA-18 Super Cub 95	A. H. Diver	
G-ARCV	Cessna 175A	R. Francis & C. Campbell	
G-ARCW	PA-23 Apache 160	F. W. Ellis	
G-ARCX	A.W. Meteor 14 ★	Museum of Flight/East Fortune	
G-ARDB	PA-24 Comanche 250	P. Crook	
G-ARDD	CP.301C1 Emeraude	K. N. P. Higgs	
G-ARDE	DH.104 Dove 6 ★	T. E. Evans	
G-ARDJ	Auster D.6/180	P. N. A. Whitehead	
G-ARDO	Jodel D.112	W. R. Prescott	
G-ARDS	PA-22 Caribbean 150	N. P. McGowan & C. A. Donaldson	
G-ARDV	PA-22 Tri-Pacer 160	M. D. N. Fisher	
G-ARDY	Tipsy T.66 Nipper 2	J. K. Davies	
G-ARDZ	Jodel D.140A	M. J. Wright	
G-AREA	DH.104 Dove 8 ★	De Havilland Heritage Museum/London Colney	
G-AREH	DH.82A Tiger Moth	C. D. Cyster & A. J. Hastings	
G-AREI	Auster 3 (MT438)	R. B. Webber	
G-AREL	PA-22 Caribbean 150	The Caribbean Flying Club	
G-AREO	PA-18 Super Cub 150	E. P. Parkin	
G-ARET	PA-22 Tri-Pacer 160	L. A.. Runnalls	
G-AREV	PA-22 Tri-Pacer 160	D. J. Ash/Barton	
G-AREX	Aeronca 15AC Sedan	R. J. M. Turnbull	
G-ARFB	PA-22 Caribbean 150	The Tri Pacer Group	
G-ARFD	PA-22 Tri-Pacer 160	J. R. Dunnett	

Notes	Reg.	Type	Owner or Operator
	G-ARFG	Cessna 175°	G. C. Rogers
	G-ARFI	Cessna 150A	A. R. Abrey
	G-ARFO	Cessna 150A	A. P. Amor
	G-ARFT	Jodel DR.1050	R. Shaw
	G-ARFV	Tipsy T.66 Nipper 2	J. J. Austin
	G-ARGG	DHC.1 Chipmunk 22 (WD305)	D. Curtis
	G-ARGO	PA-22 Colt 108	D. R. Smith
	G-ARGV	PA-18 Super Cub 180	Wolds Gliding Club Ltd
	G-ARGY	PA-22 Tri-Pacer 160	D. H. Tanner (G-JEST)
	G-ARGZ	D.31 Turbulent	The Tiger Club (1990) Ltd
	G-ARHB	Forney F-1A Aircoupe	K. J. Peacock & S. F. Turner
	G-ARHC	Forney F-1A Aircoupe	D. J. Hewitt
	G-ARHL	PA-23 Aztec 250	C. J. Freeman
	G-ARHM	Auster 6A	R. C. P. Brookhouse
	G-ARHN	PA-22 Caribbean 150	Popham Flying Group
	G-ARHR	PA-22 Caribbean 150	A. R. Wyatt
	G-ARHW	DH.104 Dove 8	Aviation Heritage Ltd
	G-ARHX	DH.104 Dove 8 ★	North East Aircraft Museum
	G-ARHZ	D.62 Condor	E. Shouler
	G-ARID	Cessna 172B	L. M. Edwards
	G-ARIF	Ord-Hume O-H.7 Minor Coupé ★	N. H. Ponsford (stored)
	G-ARIH	Auster 6A (TW591)	M. C. Jordan
	G-ARIK	PA-22 Caribbean 150	A. Taylor
	G-ARIL	PA-22 Caribbean 150	AJW Construction Ltd
	G-ARIM	D.31 Turbulent	J. G. McTaggart
	G-ARJB	DH.104 Dove 8	M. Whale & M. W. A. Lunn
	G-ARJE	PA-22 Colt 108	C. I. Fray
	G-ARJF	PA-22 Colt 108	M. J. Avery
	G-ARJH	PA-22 Colt 108	F. Vogels/France
	G-ARJR	PA-23 Apache 160G ★	Instructional airframe/Kidlington
	G-ARJS	PA-23 Apache 160G	Bencray Ltd/Blackpool
	G-ARJT	PA-23 Apache 160G	J. H. Ashcroft
	G-ARJU	PA-23 Apache 160G	Man Air Ltd
	G-ARKG	Auster J/5G Autocar	R. H. & J. A. Cooper
	G-ARKJ	Beech N35 Bonanza	G. D. E. Macdonald
	G-ARKK	PA-22 Colt 108	R. D. Welfare
	G-ARKM	PA-22 Colt 108	G. Cannon
	G-ARKN	PA-22 Colt 108	R. Redfern & M. Barker
	G-ARKP	PA-22 Colt 108	J. P. A. Freeman
	G-ARKS	PA-22 Colt 108	R. A. Nesbitt-Dufort
	G-ARLB	PA-24 Comanche 250	D. Heater (G-BUTL)
	G-ARLG	Auster D.4/108	Auster D4 Group
	G-ARLK	PA-24 Comanche 250	R. P. Jackson
	G-ARLP	Beagle A.61 Terrier 1	Gemini Flying Group
	G-ARLR	Beagle A.61 Terrier 2	M. Palfreman
	G-ARLU	Cessna 172B Skyhawk ★	Instructional airframe/Irish Air Corps
	G-ARLZ	D.31A Turbulent	A. D. Wilson
	G-ARMC	DHC.1 Chipmunk 22A (WB703)	John Henderson Children's Trust
	G-ARMF	DHC.1 Chipmunk 22A (WZ868:H)	D. M. Squires
	G-ARMG	DHC.1 Chipmunk 22A	M. F. Cuming
	G-ARML	Cessna 175B Skylark	D. Stephens
	G-ARMN	Cessna 175B Skylark	G-ARMN Group
	G-ARMO	Cessna 172B Skyhawk	A. J. Tobias
	G-ARMR	Cessna 172B Skyhawk	Sunsaver Ltd/Barton
	G-ARMZ	D.31 Turbulent	The Tiger Club (1990) Ltd
	G-ARNB	Auster J/5G Autocar	R. F. Tolhurst
	G-ARND	PA-22 Colt 108	J. L. & J. E. D. Rogerson
	G-ARNE	PA-22 Colt 108	The Shiny Colt Group
	G-ARNG	PA-22 Colt 108	F. B. Rothera
	G-ARNJ	PA-22 Colt 108	R. A. Keech
	G-ARNK	PA-22 Colt 108 (tailwheel)	I. P. Burnett
	G-ARNL	PA-22 Colt 108	J. A. Dodsworth/White Waltham
	G-ARNO	Beagle A.61 Terrier 1 ★ (VX113)	–/Sywell
	G-ARNP	Beagle A.109 Airedale	S. W. & M. Isbister
	G-ARNY	Jodel D.117	G-ARNY Flying Group
	G-ARNZ	D.31 Turbulent	The Tiger Club (1990) Ltd/Headcorn
	G-AROA	Cessna 172B Skyhawk	D. E. Partridge
	G-AROC	Cessna 175B	A. J. Symes (G-OTOW)
	G-AROJ	Beagle A.109 Airedale ★	D. J. Shaw (stored)
	G-ARON	PA-22 Colt 108	The G-ARON Flying Group
	G-AROO	Forney F-1A Aircoupe	W. J. McMeekan/Newtownards
	G-AROW	Jodel D.140B	A. R. Crome

Reg.	Type	Owner or Operator	Notes
G-AROY	Boeing Stearman A75N.1	I. T. Whitaker-Bethel & J. Mann	
G-ARPH	HS.121 Trident 1C ★	Museum of Flight/East Fortune	
G-ARPK	HS.121 Trident 1C ★	Manchester Airport Authority	
G-ARPO	HS.121 Trident 1C ★	CAA Fire School/Teesside	
G-ARRD	Jodel DR.1050	P. R. Watkins	
G-ARRE	Jodel DR.1050	West of Leiceter Flyers	
G-ARRI	Cessna 175B	G-ARRI Partnership	
G-ARRL	Auster J/1N Alpha	A. C. Ladd	
G-ARRM	Beagle B.206-X ★	Bristol Aero Collection (stored)	
G-ARRO	Beagle A.109 Airedale	M. & S. W. Isbister	
G-ARRS	CP.301A Emeraude	J. F. Sully	
G-ARRT	Wallis WA-116-1	K. H. Wallis	
G-ARRU	D.31 Turbulent	D. G. Huck	
G-ARRX	Auster 6A (VF512)	J. E. D. Mackie	
G-ARRY	Jodel D.140B	C. Thomas	
G-ARRZ	D.31 Turbulent	T. A. Stambach	
G-ARSG	Roe Triplane Type IV (replica)	The Shuttleworth Collection/Old Warden	
G-ARSL	Beagle A.61 Terrier 1 (VF581)	D. J. Colclough	
G-ARSU	PA-22 Colt 108	Sierra Uniform Flying Group	
G-ARTH	PA-12 Super Cruiser	R. I. Souch & B. J. Dunford	
G-ARTJ	Bensen B.8M ★	Museum of Flight/East Fortune	
G-ARTL	DH.82A Tiger Moth (T7281)	F. G. Clacherty	
G-ARTT	MS.880B Rallye Club	R. N. Scott	
G-ARTZ	McCandless M.4 gyroplane	W. R. Partridge	
G-ARUG	Auster J/5G Autocar	D. P. H. Hulme	
G-ARUH	Jodel DR.1050	A. F. Vizoso	
G-ARUI	Beagle A.61 Terrier	T. W. J. Dann	
G-ARUL	LeVier Cosmic Wind	P. G. Kynsey	
G-ARUV	CP.301A Emeraude	S. D. Glover	
G-ARUY	Auster J/1N Alpha	D. Burnham	
G-ARUZ	Cessna 175C	Cardiff Skylark Group	
G-ARVM	V.1101 VC10 ★	Brooklands Museum of Aviation/Weybridge	
G-ARVO	PA-18 Super Cub 95	Victor Oscar Group	
G-ARVT	PA-28 Cherokee 160	Red Rose Aviation Ltd	
G-ARVU	PA-28 Cherokee 160	Barton Mudwing Ltd	
G-ARVV	PA-28 Cherokee 160	G. E. Hopkins	
G-ARVZ	D.62B Condor	A. A. M. Huke	
G-ARWB	DHC.1 Chipmunk 22 (WK611)	Thruxton Chipmunk Flying Club	
G-ARWR	Cessna 172C	Devanha Flying Group	
G-ARWS	Cessna 175C	M. D. Fage	
G-ARXB	Beagle A.109 Airedale	S. W. & M. Isbister	
G-ARXD	Beagle A.109 Airedale	D. Howden	
G-ARXG	PA-24 Comanche 250	R. F. Corstin	
G-ARXH	Bell 47G	A. B. Searle	
G-ARXP	Luton LA-4 Minor	R. M. Weeks	
G-ARXT	Jodel DR.1050	CJM Flying Group	
G-ARXU	Auster 6A (VF526)	A. B. Taylor-Roberts and E. M. Le Gresley	
G-ARXW	MS.885 Super Rallye	M. J. Kirk	
G-ARYB	HS.125 Srs 1 ★	Midland Air Museum/Coventry	
G-ARYC	HS.125 Srs 1 ★	De Havilland Heritage Museum/London Colney	
G-ARYD	Auster AOP.6 (WJ358) ★	Museum of Army Flying/Middle Wallop	
G-ARYH	PA-22 Tri-Pacer 160	C. Watt	
G-ARYK	Cessna 172C	A. Winnicott	
G-ARYR	PA-28 Cherokee 180	G-ARYR Flying Group	
G-ARYS	Cessna 172C	P. A. Harvie	
G-ARYV	PA-24 Comanche 250	D. C. Hanss	
G-ARYZ	Beagle A.109 Airedale	C. W. Tomkins	
G-ARZB	Wallis WA-116 Srs 1	K. H. Wallis	
G-ARZS	Beagle A.109 Airedale	M. & S. W. Isbister	
G-ARZW	Currie Wot	B. R. Pearson	
G-ASAA	Luton LA-4 Minor	M. J. Aubrey (stored)	
G-ASAI	Beagle A.109 Airedale	K. R. Howden	
G-ASAJ	Beagle A.61 Terrier 2 (WE569)	T. Bailey	
G-ASAL	SA Bulldog Srs 120/124	Pioneer Flying Co Ltd	
G-ASAT	MS.880B Rallye Club	M. Cutovic	
G-ASAU	MS.880B Rallye Club	M. S. Lonsdale	
G-ASAX	Beagle A.61 Terrier 2	A. D. Hodgkinson	
G-ASAZ	Hiller UH-12E4 (XS165)	Hields Aviation/Sherburn	
G-ASBA	Phoenix Currie Wot	J. C. Lister	
G-ASBH	Beagle A.109 Airedale	D. T. Smollett	
G-ASCC	Beagle E3 Mk 11 (XP254)	R. Warner	
G-ASCD	Beagle A.61 Terrier 2 (TJ704) ★	Yorkshire Air Museum/Elvington	

Notes	Reg.	Type	Owner or Operator
	G-ASCH	Beagle A.61 Terrier 2	G-ASCH Group
	G-ASCM	Isaacs Fury II (K2050)	R. F. Redknap
	G-ASCZ	CP.301A Emeraude	I. Denham-Brown
	G-ASDF	Edwards Gyrocopter ★	B. King
	G-ASDK	Beagle A.61 Terrier 2	J. Swallow (G-ARLM)
	G-ASDY	Wallis WA-116/F	K. H. Wallis
	G-ASEA	Luton LA-4A Minor	D. Underwood
	G-ASEB	Luton LA-4A Minor	S. R. P. Harper
	G-ASEO	PA-24 Comanche 250	Oxbridge Investments Ltd
	G-ASEP	PA-23 Apache 235	Arrowstate Ltd
	G-ASEU	D.62A Condor	W. M. Grant
	G-ASFA	Cessna 172D	Fly BPL.com
	G-ASFD	L-200A Morava	M. Emery
	G-ASFK	Auster J/5G Autocar	B. C. C. Harrison
	G-ASFL	PA-28 Cherokee 180	G-ASFL Group
	G-ASFR	Bölkow Bö.208A1 Junior	S. T. Dauncey
	G-ASFX	D.31 Turbulent	E. F. Clapham & W. B. S. Dobie
	G-ASGC	V.1151 Super VC10 ★	Duxford Aviation Society
	G-ASHD	Brantly B.2A ★	IHM/Weston-super-Mare
	G-ASHS	SNCAN Stampe SV.4C	J. W. Beaty
	G-ASHT	D.31 Turbulent	C. W. N. Huke
	G-ASHU	PA-15 Vagabond (modified)	The Calybe Flying Group
	G-ASHX	PA-28 Cherokee 180	Powertheme Ltd
	G-ASIB	Cessna F.172D	G-ASIB Flying Group
	G-ASII	PA-28 Cherokee 180	T. R. Hart & R. W. S. Matthews
	G-ASIJ	PA-28 Cherokee 180	MK Aero Support Ltd
	G-ASIL	PA-28 Cherokee 180	R. Plant & J. Wesson
	G-ASIS	Jodel D.112	W. R. Prescott
	G-ASIT	Cessna 180	R. A. Seeley
	G-ASIY	PA-25 Pawnee 235	RAFGSA/Bicester
	G-ASJL	Beech H.35 Bonanza	R. L. Dargue
	G-ASJV	VS.361 Spitfire IX (MH434/PK-K)	Merlin Aviation Ltd/Duxford
	G-ASJZ	Jodel D.117A	M. A. Watts
	G-ASKC	DH.98 Mosquito 35 (TA719) ★	Skyfame Collection/Duxford
	G-ASKK	HPR.7 Herald 211 ★	Norwich Aviation Museum
	G-ASKL	Jodel D.150	J. M. Graty
	G-ASKP	DH.82A Tiger Moth	Tiger Club (1990) Ltd/Headcorn
	G-ASKT	PA-28 Cherokee 180	T. J. Herbert
	G-ASLH	Cessna 182F	A. L. Brown & A. L. Butcher
	G-ASLV	PA-28 Cherokee 235	Sackville Flying Group
	G-ASLX	CP.301A Emeraude	J. J. Reilly
	G-ASMA	PA-30 Twin Comanche 160 C/R	K. Cooper
	G-ASME	Bensen B.8M	R. M. Harris
	G-ASMJ	Cessna F.172E	Aeroscene Ltd
	G-ASML	Luton LA-4A Minor	R. W. Vince
	G-ASMM	D.31 Tubulent	W. J. Browning
	G-ASMS	Cessna 150A	M. & W. Long
	G-ASMT	Fairtravel Linnet 2	P. Harrison
	G-ASMV	CP.1310-C3 Super Emeraude	P. F. D. Waltham
	G-ASMW	Cessna 150D	Dukeries Aviation
	G-ASMY	PA-23 Apache 160 ★	R. D. Forster
	G-ASMZ	Beagle A.61 Terrier 2 (VF516)	B. Andrews
	G-ASNC	Beagle D.5/180 Husky	Peterborough & Spalding Gliding Club Ltd/Crowland
	G-ASNI	CP.1310-C3 Super Emeraude	D. Chapman
	G-ASNK	Cessna 205	Justgold Ltd
	G-ASNW	Cessna F.172E	G-ASNW Group
	G-ASNY	Campbell-Bensen B.8M gyroplane ★	R. Light & T. Smith
	G-ASOH	Beech 95-B55A Baron	G. Davis & C. Middlemiss
	G-ASOI	Beagle A.61 Terrier 2	G.D.B. Delmege
	G-ASOK	Cessna F.172E	D. W. Disney
	G-ASOL	Bell 47D ★	North East Aircraft Museum
	G-ASOM	Beagle A.61 Terrier 2	GASOM.org (G-JETS)
	G-ASOX	Cessna 205A	S. M. C. Harvey
	G-ASPF	Jodel D.120	T. J. Bates
	G-ASPP	Bristol Boxkite (replica)	The Shuttleworth Collection/Old Warden
	G-ASPS	Piper J-3C-90 Cub	A. J. Chalkley/Blackbushe
	G-ASPV	DH.82A Tiger Moth (T7794)	P. Zanardo
	G-ASRB	D.62B Condor	B. J. Douglas/Ireland
	G-ASRC	D.62C Condor	C. R. Isbell
	G-ASRK	Beagle A.109 Airedale	Bio Pathica Ltd/Lydd
	G-ASRO	PA-30 Twin Comanche 160	D. W. Blake

Reg.	Type	Owner or Operator	Notes
G-ASRT	Jodel 150	P. Turton	
G-ASRW	PA-28 Cherokee 180	G. N. Smith	
G-ASSF	Cessna 182G Skylane	P. S. Grellier	
G-ASSM	HS.125 Srs 1/522 ★	Science Museum/South Kensington	
G-ASSP	PA-30 Twin Comanche 160	P. H. Tavener	
G-ASSS	Cessna 172E	P. R. March & P. Turner/Filton	
G-ASST	Cessna 150D	F. R. H. Parker	
G-ASSV	Kensinger KF	C. I. Jefferson	
G-ASSW	PA-28 Cherokee 140	E. R. Curry	
G-ASSY	D.31 Turbulent	R. C. Bailey	
G-ASTI	Auster 6A	S. J. Partridge	
G-ASTL	Fairey Firefly I (Z2033) ★	F.A. A. Museum/Yeovilton	
G-ASTP	Hiller UH-12C ★	IHM/Weston-super-Mare	
G-ASUB	Mooney M.20E Super 21	S. C. Coulbeck	
G-ASUD	PA-28 Cherokee 180	G-ASUD Group	
G-ASUE	Cessna 150D	D. Huckle	
G-ASUG	Beech E18S ★	Museum of Flight/East Fortune	
G-ASUI	Beagle A.61 Terrier 2	A. L. Aish	
G-ASUP	Cessna F.172E	GASUP Air	
G-ASUR	Dornier Do 28A-1	N. J. Taafe	
G-ASUS	Jurca MJ.2B Tempete	R. Targonski	
G-ASVG	CP.301B Emeraude	K. R. H. Wingate	
G-ASVM	Cessna F.172E	R. H. Bennett	
G-ASVO	HPR.7 Herald 214 ★	Archive Visitor Centre/Shoreham (cockpit section)	
G-ASVP	PA-25 Pawnee 235	Banbury Gliding Club Ltd	
G-ASVZ	PA-28 Cherokee 140	J. S. Garvey	
G-ASWJ	Beagle 206 Srs 1 (8449M) ★	Brunel Technical College/Bristol	
G-ASWN	Bensen B.8M	D. R. Shepherd	
G-ASWX	PA-28 Cherokee 180	Gasworks Flying Group Ltd	
G-ASXC	SIPA 903	B. L. Procter (G-DWEL)	
G-ASXD	Brantly B.2B	Lousada PLC	
G-ASXI	Tipsy T.66 Nipper 3	P. G. Blenkinsopp	
G-ASXJ	Luton LA-4A Minor	C. R. Greenaway	
G-ASXS	Jodel DR.1050	R. A. Hunter	
G-ASXU	Jodel D.120A	G-ASXU Group	
G-ASXX	Avro 683 Lancaster 7 (NX611) ★	Lincolnshire Aviation Heritage Centre/East Kirkby	
G-ASXY	Jodel D.117A	Pegasus Flying Group	
G-ASXZ	Cessna 182G Skylane	Last Refuge Ltd	
G-ASYD	BAC One-Eleven 475 ★	Brooklands Museum of Aviation/Weybridge	
G-ASYG	Beagle A.61 Terrier 2 (VX927)	Terrane Auster Group	
G-ASYJ	Beech D.95A Travel Air	Crosby Aviation (Jersey) Ltd	
G-ASYP	Cessna 150E	Henlow Flying Group	
G-ASZB	Cessna 150E	R. J. Scott	
G-ASZD	Bölkow Bö.208A2 Junior	M. J. Ayers	
G-ASZE	Beagle A.61 Terrier 2	D. R. Ockleton	
G-ASZR	Fairtravel Linnet 2	R. Hodgson	
G-ASZS	Gardan GY-80 Horizon 160	ZS Group	
G-ASZU	Cessna 150E	L. J. Baker, R. Hall & C. Davies	
G-ASZV	Tipsy T.66 Nipper 2	D. H. Greenwood	
G-ASZX	Beagle A.61 Terrier 1 (WJ368)	R. B. Webber	
G-ATAF	Cessna F.172F	Summit Media Ltd	
G-ATAG	Jodel DR.1050	T. M. Dawes-Gamble	
G-ATAS	PA-28 Cherokee 180	ATAS Group	
G-ATAU	D.62B Condor	M. C. Burlock	
G-ATAV	D.62C Condor	V. A. Holliday	
G-ATBG	Nord 1002 (NJ+C11)	Ardmore Aviation Service	
G-ATBH	Aero 145	P. D. Aberbach	
G-ATBI	Beech A.23 Musketeer	Three Musketeers Flying Group	
G-ATBJ	Sikorsky S-61N	British International	
G-ATBL	DH.60G Moth	M. C. & M. R. Greenland	
G-ATBP	Fournier RF-3	D. McNicholl	
G-ATBS	D.31 Turbulent	J. A. Lear	
G-ATBU	Beagle A.61 Terrier 2	T. Jarvis	
G-ATBW	Tipsy T.66 Nipper 2	Stapleford Nipper Group	
G-ATBX	PA-20 Pacer 135	G. D. & P. M. Thomson	
G-ATBZ	Westland WS-58 Wessex 60 ★	IHM/Weston-super-Mare	
G-ATCC	Beagle A.109 Airedale	J. R. Bowden	
G-ATCD	Beagle D.5/180 Husky	T. C. O'Gorman	
G-ATCE	Cessna U.206	A. J. Hickling	
G-ATCJ	Luton LA-4A Minor	T. D. Boyle	
G-ATCL	Victa Airtourer 100	A. D. Goodall	

Notes	Reg.	Type	Owner or Operator
	G-ATCN	Luton LA-4A Minor	The Real Aeroplane Co.Ltd
	G-ATCX	Cessna 182 ★	Softnotes Ltd
	G-ATDA	PA-28 Cherokee 160	Portway Aviation Ltd/Shobdon
	G-ATDN	Beagle A.61 Terrier 2 (TW641)	S. J. SaggersBiggin Hill
	G-ATDO	Bölkow Bö.208C1 Junior	P. Thompson/Crosland Moor
	G-ATEF	Cessna 150E	Swans Aviation/Blackbushe
	G-ATEM	PA-28 Cherokee 180	G. D. Wyles
	G-ATEP	EAA Biplane ★	E. L. Martin (red)/Guernsey
	G-ATEV	Jodel DR.1050	J. C. Carter & J. L. Altrip
	G-ATEW	PA-30 Twin Comanche 160	Air Northumbria (Woolsington) Ltd
	G-ATEZ	PA-28 Cherokee 140	EFI Aviation Ltd
	G-ATFD	Jodel DR.1050	G-ATFD Group
	G-ATFF	PA-23 Aztec 250C	T. J. Wassell
	G-ATFG	Brantly B.2B ★	Museum of Flight/East Fortune
	G-ATFM	Sikorsky S-61N	British International
	G-ATFR	PA-25 Pawnee 150	Borders (Milfield) Gliding Club Ltd
	G-ATFV	Agusta-Bell 47J-2A ★	Caernarfon Air World
	G-ATFY	Cessna F.172G	J. M. Vinall
	G-ATGN	Thorn Coal Gas Balloon	British Balloon Museum/Newbury
	G-ATGP	Jodel DR.1050	Madley Flying Group
	G-ATGY	Gardan GY-80 Horizon	D. H. Mackay
	G-ATHA	PA-23 Apache 235 ★	Brunel Technical College/Bristol
	G-ATHD	DHC.1 Chipmunk 22 (WP971)	Spartan Flying Group Ltd
	G-ATHK	Aeronca 7AC Champion	The Chase Flying Group
	G-ATHM	Wallis WA-116 Srs 1	Wallis Autogyros Ltd
	G-ATHN	Nord 1101 Noralpha ★	E. L. Martin (stored)/Guernsey
	G-ATHR	PA-28 Cherokee 180	Azure Flying Club Ltd
	G-ATHT	Victa Airtourer 115	Cotswold Flying Group
	G-ATHU	Beagle A.61 Terrier 1	J. A. L. Irwin
	G-ATHV	Cessna 150F	Cessna Hotel Victor Group
	G-ATHZ	Cessna 150F	R. D. Forster
	G-ATIC	Jodel DR.1050	T. A. Major
	G-ATIG	HPR.7 Herald 214 ★	Norwich Airport towing trainer
	G-ATIN	Jodel D.117	A. Ayre
	G-ATIR	AIA Stampe SV.4C	A. Trueman
	G-ATIS	PA-28 Cherokee 160	D. E. Skertchly
	G-ATIZ	Jodel D.117	R. A. Smith
	G-ATJA	Jodel DR.1050	Bicester Flying Group
	G-ATJC	Victa Airtourer 100 (modfied)	Aviation West Ltd
	G-ATJG	PA-28 Cherokee 140	C. A. McGee
	G-ATJL	PA-24 Comanche 260	C. G. Sims t/a Juliet Lima Flying Group
	G-ATJN	Jodel D.119	J. Upex
	G-ATJT	Gardan GY-80 Horizon 160	X. Jeanjean
	G-ATJV	PA-32 Cherokee Six 260	Wingglider Ltd
	G-ATKF	Cessna 150F	P. Ashbridge
	G-ATKH	Luton LA-4A Minor	H. E. Jenner
	G-ATKI	Piper J-3C-65 Cub	B. Ryan
	G-ATKT	Cessna F.172G	KT Group
	G-ATKX	Jodel D.140C	Kilo Xray Syndicate
	G-ATLA	Cessna 182J Skylane	J. W. & J. T. Whicher
	G-ATLB	Jodel DR.1050/M1	Le Syndicate du Petit Oiseau
	G-ATLM	Cessna F.172G	Air Fotos Aviation Ltd
	G-ATLP	Bensen B.8M	R. F. G. Moyle
	G-ATLT	Cessna U.206A	Skydive UK Ltd
	G-ATLV	Jodel D.120	G. Constantine & A. Y. Leung
	G-ATMC	Cessna F.150F	G. H. Farrah & D. Cunnane
	G-ATMH	Beagle D.5/180 Husky	Dorset Gliding Club Ltd
	G-ATML	Cessna F.150F	G. I. Smith
	G-ATMM	Cessna F.150F	Cranfield Aviation Training School Ltd
	G-ATMT	PA-30 Twin Comanche 160	Montagu-Smith & Co Ltd
	G-ATNB	PA-28 Cherokee 180	Ken Macdonald and Co
	G-ATNE	Cessna F.150F	A. D. Revill
	G-ATNL	Cessna F.150F	PVI Power Services Ltd
	G-ATNV	PA-24 Comanche 260	K. Powell
	G-ATOH	D.62B Condor	Three Spires Flying Group
	G-ATOI	PA-28 Cherokee 140	R. Ronaldson
	G-ATOJ	PA-28 Cherokee 140	A Flight Aviation Ltd
	G-ATOK	PA-28 Cherokee 140	ILC Flying Group
	G-ATOM	PA-28 Cherokee 140	A. Flight Aviation Ltd
	G-ATON	PA-28 Cherokee 140	Stirling Flying Syndicate
	G-ATOO	PA-28 Cherokee 140	Caralair Aviation
	G-ATOP	PA-28 Cherokee 140	P. R. Coombs

Reg.	Type	Owner or Operator	Notes
G-ATOR	PA-28 Cherokee 140	Aligator Group	
G-ATOT	PA-28 Cherokee 180	Totair Ltd	
G-ATOU	Mooney M.20E Super 21	DbProf Doo	
G-ATOY	PA-24 Comanche 260 ★	Museum of Flight/East Fortune	
G-ATPN	PA-28 Cherokee 140	M. F. Hatt & ptnrs	
G-ATPT	Cessna 182J Skylane	C. Beer t/a Papa Tango Group	
G-ATPV	JB.01 Minicab	M. J. Cook	
G-ATRB	LET L.13 Blanik (BXW)	Bidford Gliding Ltd	
G-ATRG	PA-18 Super Cub 150	Lasham Gliding Society Ltd	
G-ATRI	Bolkow Bö. 208C1 Junior	Kingsmuir Group	
G-ATRK	Cessna F.150F	Falcon Aviation Ltd	
G-ATRL	Cessna F.150F	A. A. W. Stevens	
G-ATRM	Cessna F.150F	J. Redfearn	
G-ATRO	PA-28 Cherokee 140	G. M. Malpass	
G-ATRR	PA-28 Cherokee 140	Keen Leasing (IOM) Ltd	
G-ATRW	PA-32 Cherokee Six 260	Pringle Brandon Architects	
G-ATRX	PA-32 Cherokee Six 260	F. Chakroun	
G-ATSI	Bölkow Bö.208C1 Junior	GATSI Bolkow Ltd	
G-ATSL	Cessna F.172G	Alpha Aviation	
G-ATSR	Beech M.35 Bonanza	C. B. Linton	
G-ATSX	Bölkow Bö.208C1 Junior	Little Bear Ltd	
G-ATSY	Wassmer Wa.41 Super Baladou IV	McLean Aviation	
G-ATSZ	PA-30 Twin Comanche 160B	Sierra Zulu Aviation Ltd	
G-ATTB	Wallis WA-116-1 (XR944)	D. A. Wallis	
G-ATTD	Cessna 182J	Atlantalia Eurobusiness SL	
G-ATTI	PA-28 Cherokee 140	G-ATTI Flying Group	
G-ATTK	PA-28 Cherokee 140	G-ATTK Flying Group/Southend	
G-ATTM	Jodel DR.250-160	C. P. Tomkinson	
G-ATTN	Piccard HA Balloon ★	Science Museum/South Kensington	
G-ATTR	Bölkow Bö.208C1 Junior	S. Luck	
G-ATTV	PA-28 Cherokee 140	D. B. & M. E. Meeks	
G-ATTX	PA-28 Cherokee 180	IPAC Aviation Ltd	
G-ATUB	PA-28 Cherokee 140	J. S. Bown	
G-ATUF	Cessna F.150F	D. P. Williams	
G-ATUG	D.62B Condor	C. Gill	
G-ATUH	Tipsy T.66 Nipper 1	M. D. Barnard & C. Voelger	
G-ATUI	Bölkow Bö.208C1 Junior	M. J. Grundy	
G-ATUL	PA-28 Cherokee 180	Barry Fielding Aviation Ltd	
G-ATVF	DHC.1 Chipmunk 22 (WD327)	Four Counties Fling Club/Syerston	
G-ATVK	PA-28 Cherokee 140	R. F. Cresswell	
G-ATVO	PA-28 Cherokee 140	G. R. Bright	
G-ATVP	Vickers FB.5 Gunbus replica (2345) ★	RAF Museum/Hendon	
G-ATVS	PA-28 Cherokee 180	D. S. Olson	
G-ATVW	D.62B Condor	G. G. Roberts	
G-ATVX	Bölkow Bö.208C1 Junior	A. M. Witt	
G-ATWA	Jodel DR.1050	One Twenty Group	
G-ATWB	Jodel D.117	Andrewsfield Whisky Bravo Group	
G-ATWJ	Cessna F.172F	J. P. A. Freeman/Headcorn	
G-ATXA	PA-22 Tri-Pacer 150	S. Hildrop	
G-ATXD	PA-30 Twin Comanche 160B	C. A. Denovan	
G-ATXJ	HP.137 Jetstream 300 ★	Fire Service training airframe/Cardiff	
G-ATXN	Mitchell-Proctor Kittiwake 1	R. G. Day/Biggin Hill	
G-ATXO	SIPA 903	C. H. Morris	
G-ATXX	McCandless M.4 gyroplane ★	Ulster Folk & Transport Museum	
G-ATXZ	Bölkow Bö.208C1 Junior	G-ATXZ Group	
G-ATYM	Cessna F.150G	B. G. De Wert & M. J. Macmillan	
G-ATYN	Cessna F.150G	J. S. Grant	
G-ATYS	PA-28 Cherokee 180	D. G. Baverstock	
G-ATZK	PA-28 Cherokee 180	G-ZK Group	
G-ATZM	Piper J-3C-90 Cub	N. D. Marshall	
G-ATZS	Wassmer Wa.41 Super Baladou IV	G-ATZS Flying Group	
G-ATZY	Cessna F.150G	Aircraft Engineers Ltd	
G-AVAR	Cessna F.150G	J. A. Rees	
G-AVAW	D.62B Condor	Condor Aircraft Group	
G-AVAX	PA-28 Cherokee 180	P. J. Meakin	
G-AVBG	PA-28 Cherokee 180	M. C. Plomer-Roberts	
G-AVBH	PA-28 Cherokee 180	T. R. Smith (Agricultural Machinery) Ltd	
G-AVBS	PA-28 Cherokee 180	Bravo Sierra Flying Group	
G-AVBT	PA-28 Cherokee 180	J. F. Mitchell	
G-AVCM	PA-24 Comanche 260	R. F. Smith/Stapleford	
G-AVCN	BN-26A-8 Islander	Britten-Norman Aircraft Preservation Society	

Notes	Reg.	Type	Owner or Operator
	G-AVCV	Cessna 182J Skylane	University of Manchester, School of Earth, Atmospheric and Environmental Sciences
	G-AVDA	Cessna 182K Skylane	F. W. Ellis
	G-AVDG	Wallis WA-116 Srs 1	K. H. Wallis
	G-AVDS	Beech 65-B80 Queen Air ★	Airport Fire Service/Filton
	G-AVDT	Aeronca 7AC Champion	D. & N. Cheney
	G-AVDV	PA-22-150 Tri-Pacer	R. Burgun
	G-AVDY	Luton LA-4A Minor	J. Goodband
	G-AVEB	Morane Saulnier MS.230Et2 (157)	T. McG. Leaver
	G-AVEC	Cessna F.172 ★	S. M. Furner
	G-AVEF	Jodel 150	Heavy Install Ltd
	G-AVEH	SIAI-Marchetti S.205	EH Aviation
	G-AVEM	Cessna F.150G	M. A. Watts
	G-AVEN	Cessna F.150G	J. M. Hough
	G-AVEO	Cessna F.150G	V. Tabacek (G-DENA)
	G-AVER	Cessna F.150G	LAC Flying School
	G-AVEU	Wassmer Wa.41 Baladou IV	The Baladou Flying Group
	G-AVEX	D.62B Condor	C. A. Macleod
	G-AVEY	Currie Super Wot	C. K. Farley
	G-AVEZ	HPR.7 Herald 210 ★	Rescue trainer/Norwich
	G-AVFB	HS.121 Trident 2E ★	Duxford Aviation Society
	G-AVFE	HS.121 Trident 2E ★	Belfast Airport Authority
	G-AVFH	HS.121 Trident 2E ★	De Havilland Heritage Museum (fuselage only)/ London Colney
	G-AVFM	HS.121 Trident 2E ★	Brunel Technical College/Bristol
	G-AVFR	PA-28 Cherokee 140	R. R. Orr
	G-AVFU	PA-32 Cherokee Six 300	Trixstar Farms Ltd
	G-AVFX	PA-28 Cherokee 140	A. E. Fielding
	G-AVFZ	PA-28 Cherokee 140	G-AVFZ Flying Group
	G-AVGA	PA-24 Comanche 260	G. McD. Moir
	G-AVGC	PA-28 Cherokee 140	D. Matthews
	G-AVGE	PA-28 Cherokee 140	J. D. C. Lea
	G-AVGI	PA-28 Cherokee 140	Merseyflight Air Training School
	G-AVGU	Cessna F.150G	R. D. Luper
	G-AVGY	Cessna 182K Skylane	G. Appelback
	G-AVGZ	Jodel DR.1050	D. C. Webb
	G-AVHH	Cessna F.172	Court Farm Leisure Ltd
	G-AVHL	Jodel DR.105A	Seething Jodel Group
	G-AVHM	Cessna F.150G	D. A. & W. D. Hill
	G-AVHT	Auster AOP.9 (WZ711)	C. W. Romkins LtdSeething Jodel Group
	G-AVHY	Fournier RF.4D	I. G. K. Mitchell
	G-AVIA	Cessna F.150G	American Airplane Breakers
	G-AVIB	Cessna F.150G	Far North Aviation
	G-AVIC	Cessna F.172 ★	Leeside Flying Ltd
	G-AVIL	Alon A.2 Aircoupe (VX147)	G. D. J. Wilson
	G-AVIN	MS.880B Rallye Club	B. Bunce
	G-AVIP	Brantly B.2B	Ilkeston Contractors
	G-AVIS	Cessna F.172 ★	J. P. A. Freeman
	G-AVIT	Cessna F.150G	P. Cottrell
	G-AVIZ	Scheibe SF.25A Motorfalke	Spilsby Gliding Trust
	G-AVJF	Cessna F.172H	J. A. & D. T. A. Rees
	G-AVJJ	PA-30 Twin Comanche 160B	A. H. Manser
	G-AVJK	Jodel DR.1050/M1	Juliet Kilo Syndicate
	G-AVJO	Fokker E.III (replica) (422/15)	Flying Aces Movie Aircraft Collection
	G-AVJV	Wallis WA-117 Srs 1	K. H. Wallis (G-ATCV)
	G-AVJW	Wallis WA-118 Srs 2	K. H. Wallis (G-ATPW)
	G-AVKD	Fournier RF-4D	Lasham RF4 Group
	G-AVKE	Gadfly HDW.1 ★	IHM/Weston-super-Mare
	G-AVKG	Cessna F.172H	P. R. Brown-John
	G-AVKI	Slingsby T.66 Nipper 3	Team Nipper
	G-AVKK	Slingsby T.66 Nipper 3	C. Watson
	G-AVKP	Beagle A.109 Airedale	D. R. Williams
	G-AVKR	Bölkow Bö.208C1 Junior	L. Hawkins
	G-AVLB	PA-28 Cherokee 140	M. Wilson
	G-AVLC	PA-28 Cherokee 140	Lima Charlie Flying Group
	G-AVLE	PA-28 Cherokee 140	G. E. Wright
	G-AVLF	PA-28 Cherokee 140	Woodbine Group
	G-AVLG	PA-28 Cherokee 140	R. J. Everett
	G-AVLI	PA-28 Cherokee 140	Lima India Aviation Group
	G-AVLJ	PA-28 Cherokee 140	Cherokee Aviation Holdings Jersey Ltd
	G-AVLM	Beagle B.121 Pup 3	T. M. & D. A. Jones
	G-AVLN	Beagle B.121 Pup 2	Dogs Flying Group

Reg.	Type	Owner or Operator	Notes
G-AVLO	Bölkow Bö.208C1 Junior	G. D. Price & P. R. Teager	
G-AVLT	PA-28-140 Cherokee	Transcourt Ltd and Turweston Flying School Ltd (G-KELC)	
G-AVLW	Fournier RF-4D	J. C. A. C. da Silva	
G-AVLY	Jodel D.120A	M. E. Wills & N. V. de Candole	
G-AVMA	Gardan GY-80 Horizon 180	Z. R. Hildick	
G-AVMB	D.62B Condor	L. J. Dray	
G-AVMD	Cessna 150G	Bagby Aviation Flying Group	
G-AVMF	Cessna F. 150G	J. F. Marsh	
G-AVMJ	BAC One-Eleven 510ED ★	European Aviation Ltd (cabin trainer)	
G-AVMK	BAC One-Eleven 510ED ★	Gravesend College (fuselage only)	
G-AVMO	BAC One-Eleven 510ED ★	Museum of Flight/East Fortune	
G-AVMU	BAC One-Eleven 510ED ★	Duxford Aviation Society	
G-AVNC	Cessna F.150G	J. Turner	
G-AVNE	Westland WS-58 Wessex Mk 60 Srs 1 ★	IHM/Weston-super-Mare	
G-AVNN	PA-28 Cherokee 180	G-AVNN Flying Group	
G-AVNO	PA-28 Cherokee 180	November Oscar Flying Group	
G-AVNS	PA-28 Cherokee 180	R. J. Sharpe	
G-AVNU	PA-28 Cherokee 180	D. Durrant	
G-AVNW	PA-28 Cherokee 180	Len Smith's (Aviation) Ltd	
G-AVNY	Fournier RF-4D	J. B. Giddins (G-IVEL)	
G-AVNZ	Fournier RF-4D	C. D. Pidler	
G-AVOA	Jodel DR.1050	D. A. Willies/Cranwell	
G-AVOH	D.62B Condor	Transcourt Ltd	
G-AVOM	CEA Jodel DR.221	Avon Flying Group	
G-AVOO	PA-18 Super Cub 150	Dublin Gliding Club Ltd	
G-AVOZ	PA-28 Cherokee 180	Oscar Zulu Flying Group	
G-AVPD	Jodel D.9 Bébé ★	S. W. McKay (stored)	
G-AVPI	Cessna F.172H	Air-Tech	
G-AVPJ	DH.82A Tiger Moth	C. C. Silk	
G-AVPM	Jodel D.117	L. B. Clark & J. C. Haynes	
G-AVPN	HPR.7 Herald 213 ★	Yorkshire Air Museum/Elvington	
G-AVPO	Hindustan HAL-26 Pushpak	B. Johns	
G-AVPV	PA-18 Cherokee 180	K. A. Passmore	
G-AVPY	PA-25 Pawnee 235C	Southdown Gliding Club Ltd	
G-AVRK	PA-28 Cherokee 180	Sir W. G. Armstrong-Whitworth Flying Group	
G-AVRS	Gardan GY-80 Horizon 180	N. M. Robbins	
G-AVRU	PA-28-Cherokee 180	Lanpro	
G-AVRW	Gardan GY-20 Minicab	Kestrel Flying Group	
G-AVRZ	PA-28 Cherokee 180	Mantavia Group Ltd	
G-AVSA	PA-28 Cherokee 180	P. A. Wells	
G-AVSB	PA-28 Cherokee 180	D. L. Macdonald	
G-AVSC	PA-28 Cherokee 180	G-AVSC Syndicate	
G-AVSD	PA-28 Cherokee 180	C. B. D. Owen	
G-AVSE	PA-28 Cherokee 180	F. Glendon/Ireland	
G-AVSF	PA-28 Cherokee 180	Monday Club	
G-AVSI	PA-28 Cherokee 140	G-AVSI Flying Group	
G-AVSP	PA-28 Cherokee 180	Airways Flight Training (Exeter) Ltd	
G-AVSR	Beagle D.5/180 Husky	G. R. Greenfield & S. D. J. Holwill	
G-AVSZ	Agusta-Bell 206B JetRanger	R. H. Ryan	
G-AVTC	Slingsby Nipper T.66 RA.45 Srs 3	J. Crawford	
G-AVTP	Cessna F.172H	Tango Papa Group	
G-AVTT	Ercoupe 415D	Wright's Farm Eggs Ltd	
G-AVUG	Cessna F.150H	Skyways Flying Group	
G-AVUH	Cessna F.150H	A. G. McLaren	
G-AVUO	Luton LA4 Minor	M. E. Vaisey	
G-AVUS	PA-28 Cherokee 140	J. C. & J. Field	
G-AVUT	PA-28 Cherokee 140	Bencray Ltd	
G-AVUU	PA-28 Cherokee 140	A. Jahanfar & ptnrs	
G-AVUZ	PA-32 Cherokee Six 300	Ceesix Ltd	
G-AVVC	Cessna F.172H	Babs Flying Group	
G-AVVJ	MS.893A Rallye Commodore	M. Powell	
G-AVVO	Avro 652A Anson 19 (VL348)★	Newark Air Museum	
G-AVWA	PA-28 Cherokee 140	SFG Ltd	
G-AVWD	PA-28 Cherokee 140	M. Howells	
G-AVWI	PA-28 Cherokee 140	L. M. Veitch	
G-AVWJ	PA-28 Cherokee 140	M. R. Booker	
G-AVWL	PA-28 Cherokee 140	G-AVWL Group	
G-AVWM	PA-28 Cherokee 140	P. E. Preston & Partners	
G-AVWO	PA-28R Cherokee Arrow 180	Whiskey Oscar Group	
G-AVWR	PA-28R Cherokee Arrow 180	G-AVWR Flying Group	

Notes	Reg.	Type	Owner or Operator
	G-AVWT	PA-28R Cherokee Arrow 180	F. Brecha
	G-AVWU	PA-28R Cherokee Arrow 180	M. Ali & S. Din
	G-AVWV	PA-28R Cherokee Arrow 180	Strathtay Flying Group
	G-AVWY	Fournier RF-4D	J. P. Marriott
	G-AVXA	PA-25 Pawnee 235	S. Wales Gliding Club Ltd
	G-AVXD	Slingsby T.66 Nipper 3	J. A. Brompton
	G-AVXF	PA-28R Cherokee Arrow 180	G-AVXF Group
	G-AVXW	D.62B Condor	C. Willmott
	G-AVXY	Auster AOP.9	G. J. Siddall
	G-AVXZ	PA-28 Cherokee 140 ★	ATC Hayle (instructional airframe)
	G-AVYB	HS.121 Trident 1E-140 ★	SAS training airframe/Hereford
	G-AVYK	Beagle A.61 Terrier 3	R. Burgun
	G-AVYL	PA-28 Cherokee 180	G-AVYL Flying Group
	G-AVYM	PA-28 Cherokee 180	N. B. Le-Grys
	G-AVYR	PA-28 Cherokee 140	R. M Weeks
	G-AVYS	PA-28R Cherokee Arrow 180	C. A. Breeze
	G-AVYT	PA-28R Cherokee Arrow 180	G. N. Smith
	G-AVYV	Jodel D.120	A. J. Sephton
	G-AVZB	Aero Z-37 Cmelak ★	Science Museum/Wroughton
	G-AVZI	Bölkow Bö.208C1 Junior	C. F. Rogers
	G-AVZN	Beagle B.121 Pup 1	Shipdham Aviators Flying Group
	G-AVZP	Beagle B.121 Pup 1	T. A. White/Bagby
	G-AVZR	PA-28 Cherokee 180	Lincoln Aero Club Ltd
	G-AVZU	Cessna F.150H	R. D. Forster
	G-AVZV	Cessna F.172H	E. L. King. & D. S. Lightbown
	G-AVZW	EAA Biplane Model P	R. G. Maidment & G. R. Edmundson
	G-AWAC	Gardan GY-80 Horizon 180	P. B. Hodgson
	G-AWAJ	Beech 95-D55 Baron	B. F. Whitworth
	G-AWAT	D.62B Condor	R. E. Matthews
	G-AWAU	Vickers FB.27A Vimy (replica) (F8614) ★	RAF Museum/Hendon
	G-AWAW	Cessna F.150F ★	Science Museum/South Kensington
	G-AWAX	Cessna 150D	G-AWAX Group
	G-AWAZ	PA-28R Cherokee Arrow 180	G-AWAZ Flying Group
	G-AWBA	PA-28R Cherokee Arrow 180	March Flying Group
	G-AWBB	PA-28R Cherokee Arrow 180	P. J. Young
	G-AWBC	PA-28R Cherokee Arrow 180	Anglo Aviation (UK) Ltd
	G-AWBE	PA-28 Cherokee 140	B. E. Boyle
	G-AWBG	PA-28 Cherokee 140	M. Magrabi
	G-AWBJ	Fournier RF-4D	N. J. Arthur
	G-AWBM	D.31 Turbulent	A. D. Pratt
	G-AWBN	PA-30 Twin Comanche 160B	Stourfield Investments Ltd
	G-AWBS	PA-28 Cherokee 140	R. A. Ballard
	G-AWBT	PA-30 Twin Comanche 160B ★	Instructional airframe/Cranfield
	G-AWBU	Morane-Saulnier N (replica) (MS824)	Flying Aces Movie Aircraft Collection
	G-AWBX	Cessna F.150H	F. B. & J. W. Wolfe
	G-AWCM	Cessna F.150H	R. Garbett
	G-AWCN	Cessna FR.172E	B. & C. Stobart-Hook
	G-AWCP	Cessna F.150H (tailwheel)	C. E. Mason
	G-AWDA	Slingsby T.66 Nipper 3	J. A. Cheesebrough
	G-AWDO	D.31 Turbulent	R. N. Crosland
	G-AWDP	PA-28 Cherokee 180	B. H. & P. M. Illston
	G-AWDR	Cessna FR.172E	B. A. Wallace
	G-AWDU	Brantly B.2B	N. J. M. Freeman
	G-AWEF	SNCAN Stampe SV.4B	RAF Buchanan
	G-AWEI	D.62B Condor	P. A. Gange
	G-AWEK	Fournier RF-4D	M. P. J. Hill
	G-AWEL	Fournier RF-4D	A. B. Clymo
	G-AWEM	Fournier RF-4D	B. J. Griffin
	G-AWEP	Barritault JB-01 Minicab	R. K. Thomas
	G-AWES	Cessna 150H	D. W. Vincent
	G-AWEV	PA-28 Cherokee 140	Norflight Ltd
	G-AWEX	PA-28 Cherokee 140	Reconnaisance Ventures Ltd
	G-AWEZ	PA-28R Cherokee Arrow 180	R. G. E. Simpson
	G-AWFB	PA-28R Cherokee Arrow 180	J. C. Luke
	G-AWFC	PA-28R Cherokee Arrow 180	A. Simpson
	G-AWFD	PA-28R Cherokee Arrow 180	D. J. Hill
	G-AWFF	Cessna F.150H	R. J. Colver
	G-AWFJ	PA-28R Cherokee Arrow 180	Parplon Ltd
	G-AWFN	D.62B Condor	J. James
	G-AWFO	D.62B Condor	T. A. & R. E. Major
	G-AWFP	D.62B Condor	Blackbushe Flying Club

Reg.	Type	Owner or Operator	Notes
G-AWFT	Jodel D.9 Bébé	W. H. Cole	
G-AWFW	Jodel D.117	C. J. Rodwell	
G-AWFZ	Beech A23 Musketeer	Bob Crowe Aircraft Sales Ltd	
G-AWGA	Beagle A.109 Airedale ★	(stored)	
G-AWGD	Cessna F.172H	R. P. Vincent	
G-AWGK	Cessna F.150H	G. E. Allen	
G-AWGN	Fournier RF-4D	R. J. Grimstead	
G-AWGZ	Taylor JT.1 Monoplane	R. L. Sambell	
G-AWHB	CASA 2-111D (6J+PR) ★	Aces High Ltd/North Weald	
G-AWHE	Hispano HA.1112 M1L	Magnificent Obsessions Ltd	
G-AWHX	Rollason Beta B.2	S. G. Jones	
G-AWHY	Falconar F.11-3	Why Fly Group (G-BDPB)	
G-AWIF	Brookland Mosquito 2	C. A. Reeves	
G-AWII	VS.349 Spitfire VC (AR501)	The Shuttleworth Collection	
G-AWIR	Midget Mustang	E. C. Murgatroyd	
G-AWIT	PA-28 Cherokee 180	G-AWIT Ltd	
G-AWIV	Airmark TSR.3	P. K. Jenkins	
G-AWIW	SNCAN Stampe SV.4B	R. E. Mitchell	
G-AWJE	Slingsby T.66 Nipper 3	K G. G. Howe	
G-AWJV	DH.98 Mosquito TT Mk 35 (TA634) ★	De Havilland Heritage Museum/London Colney	
G-AWJX	Zlin Z.526 Trener Master	P. A. Colman	
G-AWKD	PA-17 Vagabond	A. T. & M. R. Dowie	
G-AWKO	Beagle B.121 Pup 1	J. Martin	
G-AWKP	Jodel DR.253	G-AWKP Group	
G-AWKX	Beech A65 Queen Air ★	(Instructional airframe)/Shoreham	
G-AWLA	Cessna F.150H	Bagby Aviation	
G-AWLF	Cessna F.172H	Gannet Aviation	
G-AWLG	SIPA 903	S. W. Markham	
G-AWLI	PA-22 Tri-Pacer 150	A. P. S. Maynard & S. Myla	
G-AWLO	Boeing Stearman E75	N. D. Pickard	
G-AWLP	Mooney M.20F	I. C. Lomax	
G-AWLR	Slingsby T.66 Nipper 3	T. D. Reid	
G-AWLS	Slingsby T.66 Nipper 3	G. A. Dunster & B. Gallagher	
G-AWLX	Auster 5 J/2 Arrow	W. J. Taylor	
G-AWLZ	Fournier RF-4D	Nympsfield RF-4 Group	
G-AWMD	Jodel D.11	J. R. Cooper	
G-AWMF	PA-18 Super Cub 150 (modified)	Booker Gliding Club Ltd	
G-AWMN	Luton LA-4A Minor	S. Penfold	
G-AWMP	Cessna F.172H	R. J. D. Blois	
G-AWMR	D.31 Turbulent	J. R. D. Bygraves	
G-AWMT	Cessna F.150H	Strategic Synergies Ltd	
G-AWNT	BN-2A Islander	Precision Terrain Surveys Ltd	
G-AWOA	MS.880B Rallye Club	G-AWOA Group	
G-AWOE	Aero Commander 680E	J. M. Houlder	
G-AWOF	PA-15 Vagabond	C. M. Hicks	
G-AWOH	PA-17 Vagabond	A. Lovejoy & K. Downes	
G-AWOT	Cessna F.150H	D. I. Flory	
G-AWOU	Cessna 170B	S. Billington	
G-AWOX	Westland WS-58 Wessex 60 (150225) ★	Paintball Adventure West/Bristol	
G-AWPH	P.56 Provost T.1	J. A. D. Bradshaw	
G-AWPJ	Cessna F.150H	W. J. Greenfield	
G-AWPN	Shield Xyla	P. A. Gasson	
G-AWPU	Cessna F.150J	LAC Flying School	
G-AWPW	PA-12 Super Cruiser	AK Leasing (Jersey) Ltd	
G-AWPZ	Andreasson BA-4B	J. M. Vening	
G-AWRP	Cierva Rotorcraft ★	IHM/Weston-super-Mare	
G-AWRS	Avro 19 Srs. 2 (TX213) ★	North East Aircraft Museum/Usworth	
G-AWRY	P.56 Provost T.1 (XF836)	A. J. House	
G-AWSA	Avro 652A Anson 19 (VL349) ★	Norfolk & Suffolk Aviation Museum/Flixton	
G-AWSH	Zlin Z.526 Trener Master	Avia Special Ltd	
G-AWSL	PA-28 Cherokee 180D	Fascia Services Ltd	
G-AWSM	PA-28 Cherokee 235	Aviation Projects Ltd	
G-AWSN	D.62B Condor	M. K. A. Blyth	
G-AWSP	D.62B Condor	R. Q. & A. S. Bond	
G-AWSS	D.62A Condor	N. J. & D. Butler	
G-AWST	D.62B Condor	J. R. Bell	
G-AWSV	Skeeter 12 (XM553)	Maj. M. Somerton-Rayner	
G-AWSW	Beagle D.5/180 Husky (XW635)	Windmill Aviation	
G-AWTL	PA-28 Cherokee 180D	G. Lloyd & M. Day	
G-AWTP	Schleicher Ka 6E	Papa Victor Syndicate	
G-AWTS	Beech A.23 Musketeer	J. G. Edwards & K. D. Maal	
G-AWTV	Beech 19A Musketeer Sport	J. Whittaker	

Notes	Reg.	Type	Owner or Operator
	G-AWTX	Cessna F.150J	R. D. Forster
	G-AWUB	Gardan GY-201 Minicab	R. A. Hand
	G-AWUE	Jodel DR.1050	K. W. Wood & F. M. Watson
	G-AWUG	Cessna F.150H	Aircraft Engineers Ltd
	G-AWUJ	Cessna F.150H	I. M. Ashpole & N. Sutton
	G-AWUL	Cessna F.150H	A. J. Baron
	G-AWUN	Cessna F.150H	G-AWUN Group
	G-AWUO	Cessna F.150H	K. A. O'Neill
	G-AWUT	Cessna F.150J	Aerospace Resources Ltd
	G-AWUU	Cessna F.150J	D. P. Ramage
	G-AWUX	Cessna F.172H	G-AWUX Group/St.Just
	G-AWUZ	Cessna F.172H	I. R. Judge
	G-AWVA	Cessna F.172H	Barton Air Ltd
	G-AWVC	Beagle B.121 Pup 1	J. J. West
	G-AWVE	Jodel DR.1050/M1	E. A. Taylor
	G-AWVG	AESL Airtourer T.2	C. J. Schofield
	G-AWVN	Aeronca 7AC Champion	Champ Flying Group
	G-AWVZ	Jodel D.112	D. C. Stokes
	G-AWWE	Beagle B.121 Pup 2	A. Bleetman
	G-AWWM	Gardan GY-201 Minicab	P. J. Brayshaw
	G-AWWN	Jodel DR.1050	The G-AWWN Group
	G-AWWP	Aerosport Woody Pusher III	M. S. Bird & R. D. Bird
	G-AWWU	Cessna FR.172F	Westward Airways (Lands End) Ltd
	G-AWXR	PA-28 Cherokee 180D	Aero Club de Portugal
	G-AWXS	PA-28 Cherokee 180D	C. R. & S. A. Hardiman
	G-AWXX	Westland Wessex 60 Srs 1	D. Brem-Wilson
	G-AWXY	MS.885 Super Rallye	K. Henderson/Hibaldstow
	G-AWXZ	SNCAN Stampe SV.4C	Bianchi Aviation Film Services Ltd
	G-AWYB	Cessna FR.172F	M.P. & S. T. Barnard & M. S. Macdonald
	G-AWYJ	Beagle B.121 Pup 2	H. C. Taylor
	G-AWYL	Jodel DR.253B	T. C. Van Lonkhuyzen
	G-AWYO	Beagle B.121 Pup 1	B. R. C. Wild
	G-AWYY	Slingsby T.57 Camel replica (B6401) ★	F.A.A. Museum/Yeovilton
	G-AWZI	HS.121 Trident 3B ★	A. Lee/FAST Museum (nose only)/Farnborough
	G-AWZJ	HS.121 Trident 3B ★	Dumfries & Galloway Museum
	G-AWZK	HS.121 Trident 3B ★	Trident Preservation Society/Manchester
	G-AWZM	HS.121 Trident 3B ★	Science Museum/Wroughton
	G-AWZP	HS.121 Trident 3B ★	Manchester Museum of Science & Industry (nose only)
	G-AWZX	HS.121 Trident 3B ★	BAA Airport Fire Services/Gatwick
	G-AXAB	PA-28 Cherokee 140	Bencray Ltd
	G-AXAN	DH.82A Tiger Moth (EM720)	D. & S. A. Firth
	G-AXAS	Wallis WA-116T	K. H. Wallis (G-AVDH)
	G-AXAT	Jodel D.117A	P. S. Wilkinson
	G-AXBF	Beagle D.5/180 Husky	M. C. R. Wills
	G-AXBJ	Cessna F.172H	BJ Flying Group
	G-AXBW	DH.82A Tiger Moth (T5879:RUC-W)	G-AXBW Ltd
	G-AXBZ	DH.82A Tiger Moth	W. J. de Jong Cleyndert
	G-AXCA	PA-28R Cherokee Arrow 200	W. H. Nelson
	G-AXCG	Jodel D.117	D. J. Millin
	G-AXCM	MS.880B Rallye Club	D. C. Manifold
	G-AXCX	Beagle B.121 Pup 2	L. A. Pink
	G-AXCY	Jodel D.117A	R. S. Marom
	G-AXDI	Cessna F.172H	M. F. & J. R. Leusby
	G-AXDK	Jodel DR.315	Delta Kilo Flying Group
	G-AXDN	BAC-Sud Concorde 01 ★	Duxford Aviation Society
	G-AXDV	Beagle B.121 Pup 1	T. A. White
	G-AXDZ	Cassutt Racer IIIM	A. Chadwick
	G-AXED	PA-25 Pawnee 235	Wolds Gliding Club Ltd
	G-AXEH	B.125 Bulldog 1 ★	Museum of Flight/East Fortune
	G-AXEI	Ward Gnome ★	Real Aeroplane Club/Breighton
	G-AXEO	Scheibe SF.25B Falke	P. F. Moffatt
	G-AXEV	Beagle B.121 Pup 2	D. S. Russell & D. G. Benson
	G-AXFG	Cessna 337D	County Garage (Cheltenham) Ltd
	G-AXFN	Jodel D.119	T. A. Appleby
	G-AXGE	MS.880B Rallye Club	R. P. Loxton
	G-AXGG	Cessna F.150J	A. J. Simpson
	G-AXGP	Piper J-3C-90 Cub	A. P. Acres
	G-AXGR	Luton LA-4A Minor	B. A. Schlussler
	G-AXGS	D.62B Condor	SAS Flying Group
	G-AXGV	D.62B Condor	R. J. Wrixon

Reg.	Type	Owner or Operator	Notes
G-AXGZ	D.62B Condor	R. M. Schweitzer	
G-AXHA	Cessna 337A	I. M. Latiff	
G-AXHC	SNCAN Stampe SV.4C	D. L. Webley	
G-AXHO	Beagle B.121 Pup 2	L. W. Grundy	
G-AXHP	Piper J-3C-65 Cub (480636:A-58)	Witham (Specialist) Vehicles Ltd	
G-AXHR	Piper J-3C-65 Cub (329601:D-44)	K. B. Raven	
G-AXHS	MS.880B Rallye Club	B. & A. Swales	
G-AXHT	MS.880B Rallye Club	P. M. Murray	
G-AXHV	Jodel D.117A	Derwent Flying Group	
G-AXIA	Beagle B.121 Pup 1	C. K. Parsons	
G-AXIE	Beagle B.121 Pup 2	J. P. Thomas	
G-AXIF	Beagle B.121 Pup 2	J. R. Faulkner	
G-AXIG	Scottish Aviation B.125 Bulldog 104	A. A. A. Hamilton	
G-AXIO	PA-28 Cherokee 140B	T. Akeroyd	
G-AXIR	PA-28 Cherokee 140B	R. W. Howard	
G-AXIW	Scheibe SF.25B Falke	M. Pedley	
G-AXIX	Glos-Airtourer 150	S. Alexander	
G-AXJB	Omega 84 balloon	Southern Balloon Group	
G-AXJH	Beagle B.121 Pup 2	The Henry Flying Group	
G-AXJI	Beagle B.121 Pup 2	J. J. Sanders & J. A. Walley	
G-AXJJ	Beagle B.121 Pup 2	M. L. Jones & ptnrs	
G-AXJO	Beagle B.121 Pup 2	J. A. D. Bradshaw	
G-AXJR	Scheibe SF.25B Falke	Falke Syndicate	
G-AXJV	PA-28 Cherokee 140B	DR Flyers	
G-AXJX	PA-28 Cherokee 140B	K. Wilson	
G-AXKH	Luton LA-4A Minor	M. E. Vaisey	
G-AXKJ	Jodel D.9	The Hinton D9 Group	
G-AXKO	Westland-Bell 47G-4A	M. Gallagher	
G-AXKS	Westland Bell 47G-4A ★	Museum of Army Flying/Middle Wallop	
G-AXKX	Westland Bell 47G-4A	R. A. Dale	
G-AXLI	Slingsby T.66 Nipper 3	D. & M. Shrimpton	
G-AXLS	Jodel DR.105A	Axle Flying Club	
G-AXLZ	PA-18 Super Cub 95	R. J. Quantrell	
G-AXMA	PA-24 Comanche 180	B. C. Faulkner	
G-AXMD	Omega O-56 balloon ★	British Balloon Museum/Newbury	
G-AXMT	Bücker Bü 133 Jungmeister	R. A. Fleming/Breighton	
G-AXMW	Beagle B.121 Pup 1	DJP Engineering (Knebworth) Ltd	
G-AXMX	Beagle B.121 Pup 2	Bob The Beagle Group	
G-AXNJ	Wassmer Jodel D.120	Clive Flying Group	
G-AXNN	Beagle B.121 Pup 2	Gabrielle Aviation Ltd	
G-AXNP	Beagle B.121 Pup 2	J. W. Ellis & R. J. Hemmings	
G-AXNR	Beagle B.121 Pup 2	The November Romeo Group	
G-AXNS	Beagle B.121 Pup 2	Derwent Aero Group	
G-AXNW	SNCAN Stampe SV.4C	C. S. Grace	
G-AXNX	Cessna 182M	T. Latky & C.Csilla	
G-AXNZ	Pitts S.1C Special	November Zulu Group	
G-AXOG	PA-E23 Aztec 250D	G. H. Nolan	
G-AXOH	MS.894 Rallye Minerva	T. A. D. Crook	
G-AXOJ	Beagle B.121 Pup 2	Pup Flying Group	
G-AXOR	PA-28 Cherokee 180D	Oscar Romeo Aviation Ltd	
G-AXOS	MS.894A Rallye Minerva	R. S. M. Fendt	
G-AXOT	MS.893 Rallye Commodore 180	P. Evans	
G-AXOZ	Beagle B.121 Pup 1	R. J. Ogborn	
G-AXPA	Beagle B.121 Pup 1	Papa-Alpha Group	
G-AXPB	Beagle B.121 Pup 1	Beagle Flying Group	
G-AXPC	Beagle B.121 Pup 2	T. A. White	
G-AXPF	Cessna F.150K	D. R. Marks	
G-AXPG	Mignet HM.293	W. H. Cole (stored)	
G-AXPM	Beagle B.121 Pup 1	S. C. Stanton	
G-AXPZ	Campbell Cricket	W. R. Partridge	
G-AXRC	Campbell Cricket	L. R. Morris	
G-AXRR	Auster AOP.9 (XR241)	R. B. Webber	
G-AXRT	Cessna FA.150K (tailwheel)	C. C. Walley	
G-AXSD	Beagle B.121 Pup 1	AURS Aviation Ltd	
G-AXSF	Nash Petrel	Nash Aircraft Ltd	
G-AXSG	PA-28 Cherokee 180	The Tago Island Co Ltd	
G-AXSI	Cessna F.172H	R. Collins (G-SNIP)	
G-AXSM	Jodel DR.1051	T. R. G. & M. S. Barnby	
G-AXSW	Cessna FA.150K	R. J. Whyham	
G-AXSZ	PA-28 Cherokee 140B	White Wings Flying Group	
G-AXTA	PA-28 Cherokee 140B	G-AXTA Aircraft Group	
G-AXTC	PA-28 Cherokee 140B	G-AXTC Group	

Notes	Reg.	Type	Owner or Operator
	G-AXTJ	PA-28 Cherokee 140B	K. Patel
	G-AXTL	PA-28 Cherokee 140B	Bristol and West Aeroplane Club Ltd
	G-AXTO	PA-24 Comanche 260	J. L. Wright
	G-AXTP	PA-28 Cherokee 180	M. Whyte/Ireland
	G-AXTX	Jodel D.112	C. Sawford
	G-AXUA	Beagle B.121 Pup 1	P. Wood
	G-AXUB	BN-2A Islander	Headcorn Parachute Club Ltd
	G-AXUC	PA-12 Super Cruiser	J. J. Bunton
	G-AXUF	Cessna FA.150K	B. T. Walsh
	G-AXUJ	Auster J/1 Autocrat	P. Gill (G-OSTA)
	G-AXUK	Jodel DR.1050	Downland Flying Group
	G-AXUM	HP.137 Jetstream 1 ★	Sodeteg Formation/France
	G-AXVB	Cessna F.172H	R. & J. Turner
	G-AXVK	Campbell Cricket	B. Jones
	G-AXVM	Campbell Cricket	D. M. Organ
	G-AXVN	McCandless M.4	W. R. Partridge
	G-AXWA	Auster AOP.9 (XN437)	C. M. Edwards
	G-AXWT	Jodel D.11	R. C. Owen
	G-AXWV	Jodel DR.253	R. Friedlander & D. C. Ray
	G-AXWZ	PA-28R Cherokee Arrow 200	Whisky Zulu Group
	G-AXXC	CP.301B Emeraude	J. C. & R. D. P. Cadle
	G-AXXV	DH.82A Tiger Moth (DE992)	C. N. Wookey
	G-AXXW	Jodel D.117	M. Breen & D. Carr
	G-AXYK	Taylor JT.1 Monoplane	O. C. Pope
	G-AXYU	Jodel D.9 Bébé	P. Turton
	G-AXZD	PA-28 Cherokee 180E	G. M. Whitmore
	G-AXZF	PA-28 Cherokee 180E	M. Arthur
	G-AXZH	Glasflugel H201B Standard Libelle	M. C. Gregorie
	G-AXZK	BN-2A-26 Islander	B-N Group Ltd
	G-AXZM	Slingsby T.66 Nipper 3	G. R. Harlow
	G-AXZO	Cessna 180	Bourne Park Flyers
	G-AXZP	PA-E23 Aztec 250D	D. M. Harbottle
	G-AXZT	Jodel D.117	P. Guest
	G-AXZU	Cessna 182N	W. Gollan
	G-AYAB	PA-28 Cherokee 180E	J. R. Green
	G-AYAC	PA-28R Cherokee Arrow 200	Fersfield Flying Group
	G-AYAJ	Cameron O-84 balloon	E. T. Hall
	G-AYAL	Omega 56 balloon ★	British Balloon Museum/Newbury
	G-AYAN	Slingsby Motor Cadet III	G. Hill & R. Moyse
	G-AYAR	PA-28 Cherokee 180E	A. Jahanfar/Southend
	G-AYAT	PA-28 Cherokee 180E	G-AYAT Flying Group
	G-AYAW	PA-28 Cherokee 180E	G-AYAW Group
	G-AYBD	Cessna F.150K	Apollo Aviation Advisory Ltd
	G-AYBG	Scheibe SF.25B Falke	Anglia Sailplanes
	G-AYBO	PA-23 Aztec 250D	A. G. Gutknecht/Austria
	G-AYBP	Jodel D.112	G. J. Langston
	G-AYBR	Jodel D.112	I. S. Parker
	G-AYCC	Campbell Cricket	D. J. M. Charity
	G-AYCE	CP.301C Emeraude	S. D. Glover
	G-AYCF	Cessna FA.150K	E. J. Atkins
	G-AYCG	SNCAN Stampe SV.4C	N. Bignall
	G-AYCJ	Cessna TP.206D	White Knuckle Airways Ltd
	G-AYCK	AIA Stampe SV.4C	The Real Flying Co Ltd (G-BUNT)
	G-AYCN	Piper J-3C-65 Cub	W. R. & B. M. Young
	G-AYCO	CEA DR.360	Charlie Oscar Club
	G-AYCP	Jodel D.112	Charlie Papa Group
	G-AYCT	Cessna F.172H	P. A. & J. Rose
	G-AYDI	DH.82A Tiger Moth	Delta India Group
	G-AYDR	SNCAN Stampe SV.4C	D. J. Ashley
	G-AYDV	Coates SA.II-1 Swalesong	D. F. Coates
	G-AYDW	Beagle A.61 Terrier 2	A. S. Topen
	G-AYDX	Beagle A.61 Terrier 2	T. S. Lee
	G-AYDY	Luton LA-4A Minor	J. Dible/Ireland
	G-AYDZ	Jodel DR.200	Zero One Group
	G-AYEB	Jodel D.112	J. Evans
	G-AYEC	CP.301A Emeraude	Redwing Flying Group
	G-AYEE	PA-28 Cherokee 180E	Demero Ltd
	G-AYEF	PA-28 Cherokee 180E	Pegasus Flying Group
	G-AYEG	Falconar F-9	A. L. Smith
	G-AYEH	Jodel DR.1050	H. L. M. Williams
	G-AYEJ	Jodel DR.1050	J. M. Newbold

Reg.	Type	Owner or Operator	Notes
G-AYEN	Piper J-3C-65 Cub	P. Warde & C. F. Morris	
G-AYET	MS.892A Rallye Commodore 150	A. T. R. Bingley	
G-AYEV	Jodel DR.1050	Conor Airpark Developments Ltd	
G-AYEW	Jodel DR.1051	J. R. Hope	
G-AYFC	D.62B Condor	A. R. Chadwick	
G-AYFD	D.62B Condor	B. G. Manning	
G-AYFE	D.62C Condor	M. Soulsby	
G-AYFF	D.62B Condor	M. A. Sims	
G-AYFG	D.62C Condor	W. A. Braim	
G-AYFJ	MS.880B Rallye Club	Rallye FJ Group	
G-AYFV	Crosby BA-4B	A. R. C. Mathie	
G-AYGA	Jodel D.117	J. W. Bowes	
G-AYGB	Cessna 310Q ★	Instructional airframe/Perth	
G-AYGC	Cessna F.150K	Alpha Aviation Group	
G-AYGD	Jodel DR.1051	J. F. M. Barlett & J. P. Liber	
G-AYGE	SNCAN Stampe SV.4C	L. J. Proudfoot & ptnrs	
G-AYGG	Jodel D.120	J. M. Dean	
G-AYGX	Cessna FR.172G	Reims Rocket Group	
G-AYHA	AA-1 Yankee	S. J. Carr	
G-AYHX	Jodel D.117A	S. Burchfield	
G-AYIA	Hughes 369HS ★	G. D. E. Bilton/Sywell	
G-AYIG	PA-28 Cherokee 140C	G. K. Clarkson	
G-AYII	PA-28R Cherokee Arrow 200	Double India Group	
G-AYIJ	SNCAN Stampe SV.4B	D. Savage	
G-AYIM	HS.748 Srs 2A	Janes Aviation Ltd	
G-AYJA	Jodel DR.1050	G. Connell	
G-AYJB	SNCAN Stampe SV.4C	F. J. M. & J. P. Esson	
G-AYJD	Alpavia-Fournier RF-3	Juliet Delta Group	
G-AYJP	PA-28 Cherokee 140C	Transcourt Ltd and Demero Ltd	
G-AYJR	PA-28 Cherokee 140C	Transcourt Ltd and Turweston Flying School	
G-AYJY	Isaacs Fury II	T. E. W. Terrell	
G-AYKD	Jodel DR.1050	G. Wright	
G-AYKJ	Jodel D.117A	R. J. Hughes	
G-AYKK	Jodel D.117	J. M. Whitham	
G-AYKS	Leopoldoff L.7 Colibri	W. B. Cooper	
G-AYKT	Jodel D.117	D. I. Walker	
G-AYKW	PA-28 Cherokee 140C	D. Wood	
G-AYKZ	SAI KZ-8	R. E. Mitchell	
G-AYLA	Glos-Airtourer 115	D. S. P. Disney	
G-AYLC	Jodel DR.1051	E. W. B. Trollope	
G-AYLF	Jodel DR.1051 (modified)	R. Twigg	
G-AYLL	Jodel DR.1050	C. Joly	
G-AYLP	AA-1 Yankee	D. Nairn	
G-AYLV	Jodel D.120	M. R. Henham	
G-AYME	Fournier RF-5	R. D. Goodger	
G-AYMK	PA-28 Cherokee 140C	W. E. Mould	
G-AYMO	PA-23 Aztec 250C	J. A. D. Richardson	
G-AYMP	Currie Wot	R. C. Hibberd	
G-AYMR	Lederlin 380L	P. J. Brayshaw	
G-AYMU	Jodel D.112	M. R. Baker	
G-AYMV	Western 20 balloon	R. G. Turnbull	
G-AYNA	Phoenix Currie Wot	D. R. Partridge	
G-AYND	Cessna 310Q	Source Group Ltd	
G-AYNF	PA-28 Cherokee 140C	BW Aviation Ltd	
G-AYNJ	PA-28 Cherokee 140C	Cherry Tree Group	
G-AYNN	Cessna 185B	Bencray Ltd	
G-AYNP	Westland WS-55 Whirlwind Srs 3 ★	IHM/Weston-super-Mare	
G-AYOW	Cessna 182N Skylane	I. F. Ellis, L. M. Hall & C. J. R. Vernon	
G-AYOY	Sikorsky S-61N Mk 2	British International	
G-AYOZ	Cessna FA.150L	P. D. Stell	
G-AYPE	MBB Bö.209 Monsun	Papa Echo Ltd	
G-AYPG	Cessna F.177RG	D. P. McDermott	
G-AYPH	Cessna F.177RG	M. L. & T. M. Jones	
G-AYPJ	PA-28 Cherokee 180	R. B. Petrie	
G-AYPM	PA-18 Super Cub 95 (115373)	R. Horner	
G-AYPO	PA-18 Super Cub 95	A. W. Knowles	
G-AYPS	PA-18 Super Cub 95	B. C. Hockley, D. G. Callow, L. G. Callow & R. J. Hamlett	
G-AYPU	PA-28R Cherokee Arrow 200	Monalto Investments Ltd	
G-AYPV	PA-28 Cherokee 140D	Ashley Gardner Flying Club Ltd	
G-AYPZ	Campbell Cricket	A. Melody	
G-AYRF	Cessna F.150L	D. T. A. Rees	

Notes	Reg.	Type	Owner or Operator
	G-AYRG	Cessna F.172K	I. G. Harrison
	G-AYRH	MS.892A Rallye Commodore 150	S. O'Ceallaigh & J. Barry
	G-AYRI	PA-28R Cherokee Arrow 200	A. E. Thompson & J. C. Houdret
	G-AYRM	PA-28 Cherokee 140D	M. J. Saggers
	G-AYRO	Cessna FA.150L Aerobat	Fat Boys Flying Club
	G-AYRS	Jodel D.120A	L. R. H. D'Eath
	G-AYRT	Cessna F.172K	P. E. Crees
	G-AYRU	BN-2A-6 Islander	Saywell International Ltd
	G-AYSB	PA-30 Twin Comanche 160C	M. J. Abbott
	G-AYSD	Slingsby T.61A Falke	P. W. Hextall
	G-AYSH	Taylor JT.1 Monoplane	C. J. Lodge
	G-AYSK	Luton LA-4A Minor	B. A. Schlussler & S. J. Rudkin
	G-AYSX	Cessna F.177RG	A. P. R. Dean
	G-AYSY	Cessna F.177RG	S. A. Tuer
	G-AYTA	SOCATA MS.880B Rallye Club ★	Manchester Museum of Science & Industry
	G-AYTR	CP.301A Emeraude	Croft Farm Flying Group
	G-AYTT	Phoenix PM-3 Duet	R. B. Webber & J. K. Houlgrave
	G-AYTV	Jurca Tempete	C. W. Kirk
	G-AYUB	CEA DR.253B	Rothwell Group
	G-AYUH	PA-28 Cherokee 180F	Broadland Flying Group Ltd
	G-AYUJ	Evans VP-1	T. N. Howard
	G-AYUM	Slingsby T.61A Falke	M. H. Simms
	G-AYUN	Slingsby T.61A Falke	G-AYUN Group
	G-AYUP	Slingsby T.61A Falke	P. R. Williams
	G-AYUR	Slingsby T.61A Falke	R. Hanningan & R. Lingard
	G-AYUS	Taylor JT.1 Monoplane	S. P. Collins
	G-AYUT	Jodel DR.1050	G. Bell
	G-AYUV	Cessna F.172H	Justgold Ltd
	G-AYVO	Wallis WA-120 Srs 1	K. H. Wallis
	G-AYVP	Woody Pusher	J. R. Wraight
	G-AYWA	Avro 19 Srs 2 ★	N. K. Geddes
	G-AYWD	Cessna 182N	Wild Dreams Group
	G-AYWH	Jodel D.117A	D. Kynaston
	G-AYWM	Glos-Airtourer Super 150	The Star Flying Group
	G-AYWT	AIA Stampe SV.4C	R. A. Palmer
	G-AYXP	Jodel D.117A	G. N. Davies
	G-AYXS	SIAI-Marchetti S205-18R	P. J. Bloore & J. M. Biles
	G-AYXT	WS-55 Whirlwind Srs 2 (XK940:911) ★	IHM/Weston-super-Mare
	G-AYXU	Champion 7KCAB Citabria	E. V. Moffatt & J. S. Peplow
	G-AYYL	Slingsby T.61A Falke	Brightman Industries Ltd
	G-AYYO	Jodel DR.1050/M1	Bustard Flying Club Ltd
	G-AYYT	Jodel DR.1050/M1	R. Johnston
	G-AYYU	Beech C23 Musketeer	G-AYYU Group
	G-AYYX	MS.880B Ralle Club	J. G. MacDonald
	G-AYZE	PA-39 Twin Comanche 160 C/R	J. E. Palmer
	G-AYZH	Taylor JT.2 Titch	T. D. Gardner
	G-AYZI	SNCAN Stampe SV.4C	D. M. & P. A. Fenton
	G-AYZJ	Westland WS-55 Whirlwind HAS.7 ★	Newark Air Museum (XM685)
	G-AYZK	Jodel DR.1050/M1	D. G. Hesketh
	G-AYZS	D.62B Condor	M. N. Thrush
	G-AYZU	Slingsby T.61A Falke	A. J. Harpley
	G-AYZW	Slingsby T.61A Falke	Y-ZW Group
	G-AZAB	PA-30 Twin Comanche 160B	Bickertons Aerodromes Ltd
	G-AZAJ	PA-28R Cherokee Arrow 200B	P. Woulfe
	G-AZAW	Gardan GY-80 Horizon 160	J. W. Foley
	G-AZAZ	Bensen B.8M ★	F.A.A. Museum/Yeovilton
	G-AZBB	MBB Bö.209 Monsun 160FV	J. A. Webb
	G-AZBE	Glos-Airtourer Super 150	R. G. Vincent
	G-AZBI	Jodel 150	F. M. Ward
	G-AZBL	Jodel D.9 Bébé	J. Hill
	G-AZBN	Noorduyn AT-16 Harvard IIB (FT391)	Swaygate Ltd
	G-AZBU	Auster AOP.9 (XR246)	Auster Nine Group
	G-AZCB	SNCAN Stampe SV.4C	M. Coward
	G-AZCK	Beagle B.121 Pup 2	I. J. Ross
	G-AZCL	Beagle B.121 Pup 2	Flew LLP & J. M. Henry
	G-AZCN	Beagle B.121 Pup 2	E. J. Spencer, D. M. Callagham & G. Wildgoose
	G-AZCP	Beagle B.121 Pup 1	T. A. White
	G-AZCT	Beagle B.121 Pup 1	J. Coleman
	G-AZCU	Beagle B.121 Pup 1	A. A. Harris
	G-AZCV	Beagle B.121 Pup 2	N. R. W. Long
	G-AZCZ	Beagle B.121 Pup 2	L. & J. M. Northover

Reg.	Type	Owner or Operator	Notes
G-AZDA	Beagle B.121 Pup 1	B. D. Deubelbeiss	
G-AZDD	MBB Bö.209 Monsun 150FF	Double Delta Flying Group	
G-AZDE	PA-28R Cherokee Arrow 200B	Metair Ltd	
G-AZDG	Beagle B.121 Pup 2	D. J. Sage & J. R. Heaps	
G-AZDJ	PA-32 Cherokee Six 300	K. J. Mansbridge & D. C. Gibbs	
G-AZDX	PA-28 Cherokee 180F	M. Cowan	
G-AZDY	DH.82A Tiger Moth	J. B. Mills	
G-AZEE	MS.880B Rallye Club	J. Shelton	
G-AZEF	Jodel D.120	P. R. Sears	
G-AZEG	PA-28 Cherokee 140D	Ashley Gardner Flying Club Ltd	
G-AZEU	Beagle B.121 Pup 2	G. M. Moir	
G-AZEV	Beagle B.121 Pup 2	G. H. Matthews	
G-AZEW	Beagle B.121 Pup 2	D. Ridley	
G-AZEY	Beagle B.121 Pup 2	M. E. Reynolds	
G-AZFA	Beagle B.121 Pup 2	J. Smith	
G-AZFC	PA-28 Cherokee 140D	WLS Flying Group	
G-AZFF	Jodel D.112	J. Bolger/Ireland	
G-AZFI	PA-28R Cherokee Arrow 200B	G-AZFI Ltd	
G-AZFM	PA-28R Cherokee Arrow 200B	P. J. Jenness	
G-AZFR	Cessna 401B	R. E. Wragg	
G-AZGA	Jodel D.120	A. R. Neal & S. A. Lowe	
G-AZGC	SNCAN Stampe SV.4C	D. J. Ashley	
G-AZGE	SNCAN Stampe SV.4C	M. R. L. Astor	
G-AZGF	Beagle B.121 Pup 2	K. Singh	
G-AZGL	MS.894A Rallye Minerva	The Cambridge Aero Club Ltd	
G-AZGY	CP.301B Emeraude	R. H. Braithwaite	
G-AZGZ	DH.82A Tiger Moth (NM181)	R. J. King	
G-AZHB	Robin HR.100/200B	J. F. Gould	
G-AZHC	Jodel D.112	Aerodel Flying Group	
G-AZHD	Slingsby T.61A Falke	R. J. Shallcrass	
G-AZHH	SA 102.5 Cavalier	D. W. Buckle	
G-AZHI	Glos-Airtourer Super 150	Flying Grasshoppers Ltd	
G-AZHK	Robin HR.100/200B	G. I. Applin (G-ILEG)	
G-AZHR	Piccard Ax6 balloon	C. Fisher	
G-AZHT	AESL Airtourer (modified)	Aviation West Ltd	
G-AZHU	Luton LA-4A Minor	W. Cawrey	
G-AZIB	ST-10 Diplomate	W. B. Bateson	
G-AZII	Jodel D.117A	J. S. Brayshaw	
G-AZIJ	Jodel DR.360	F. M. Carter	
G-AZIL	Slingsby T.61A Falke	D. W. Savage	
G-AZIP	Cameron O-65 balloon	Dante Balloon Group	
G-AZJC	Fournier RF-5	Seighford RF5 Group	
G-AZJE	Ord-Hume JB-01 Minicab	Kayee Flyers	
G-AZJN	Robin DR.300/140	J. F. Wright	
G-AZJV	Cessna F.172L	G-AZJV Flying Group	
G-AZJY	Cessna FRA.150L	J. S. Davis	
G-AZKC	MS.880B Rallye Club	L. J. Martin	
G-AZKE	MS.880B Rallye Club	D. A. Thompson & J. D. Headlam/Germany	
G-AZKO	Cessna F.337F	G. James	
G-AZKP	Jodel D.117	J. P. Dacre & I. J. F. Macdonald	
G-AZKS	AA-1A Trainer	P. Burrows, K. Harrison & P. Howlett	
G-AZKW	Cessna F.172L	D. Stewart	
G-AZKZ	Cessna F.172L	R. D. & E. Forster	
G-AZLE	Boeing N2S-5 Kaydet (1102:102)	A. E. Paulson	
G-AZLF	Jodel D.120	M. S. C. Ball	
G-AZLH	Cessna F.150L	W. Ali	
G-AZLN	PA-28 Cherokee 180F	Enstone Sales & Services Ltd and J. Logan	
G-AZLV	Cessna 172K	G-AZLV Flying Group	
G-AZLY	Cessna F.150L	S. Roberts	
G-AZMC	Slingsby T.61A Falke	P. J. R. White	
G-AZMD	Slingsby T.61C Falke	Tandem Gliding Syndicate	
G-AZMJ	AA-5 Traveler	W. R. Partridge	
G-AZMX	PA-28 Cherokee 140 ★	NE Wales Institute of Higher Education (Instructional airframe)/Flintshire	
G-AZMZ	MS.893A Rallye Commodore 150	J. Palethorpe	
G-AZNK	SNCAN Stampe SV.4A	November Kilo Group	
G-AZNL	PA-28R Cherokee Arrow 200D	B. P. Liversidge	
G-AZNO	Cessna 182P	M. S. Williams	
G-AZOA	MBB Bö.209 Monsun 150FF	M. W. Hurst	
G-AZOB	MBB Bö.209 Monsun 150FF	J. A. Webb	
G-AZOE	Glos-Airtourer 115	G-AZOE 607 Group	
G-AZOF	Glos-Airtourer Super 150	R. C. Thursby & C. Goldsmith	

Notes	Reg.	Type	Owner or Operator
	G-AZOG	PA-28R Cherokee Arrow 200D	Southend Flying Club
	G-AZOL	PA-34-200 Seneca II	Stapleford Flying Club Ltd
	G-AZOS	Jurca MJ.5-H1 Sirocco	P. J. Tanulak
	G-AZOT	PA-34-200 Seneca II	M. Soojeri
	G-AZOU	Jodel DR.1050	Horsham Flying Group
	G-AZOZ	Cessna FRA.150L	Seawing Flying Club Ltd
	G-AZPA	PA-25 Pawnee 235	Black Mountains Gliding Club Ltd
	G-AZPC	Slingsby T.61C Falke	D. Heslop & J. R. Kimberley
	G-AZPF	Fournier RF-5	R. Pye
	G-AZPH	Craft-Pitts S-1S Special ★	Science Museum/South Kensington
	G-AZRA	MBB Bö.209 Monsun 150FF	Alpha Flying Ltd
	G-AZRH	PA-28 Cherokee 140D	Trust Flying Group
	G-AZRI	Payne Free Balloon	C. A. Butter & J. J. T. Cooke
	G-AZRK	Fournier RF-5	A. B. Clymo & J. F. Rogers
	G-AZRL	PA-18 Super Cub 95	J. S. & P. R. Johnson
	G-AZRM	Fournier RF-5	Romeo Mike Group
	G-AZRN	Cameron O-84 balloon	C. J. Desmet/Belgium
	G-AZRP	Glos-Airtourer 115	B. F. Strawford
	G-AZRS	PA-22 Tri-Pacer 150	R. H. Hulls
	G-AZRZ	Cessna U.206F	Cornish Parachute Club Ltd
	G-AZSA	Stampe et Renard SV.4B	M. R. Dolman
	G-AZSC	Noorduyn AT-16 Harvard IIB (43:SC)	Goodwood Road Racing Co Ltd
	G-AZSF	PA-28R Cherokee Arrow 200D	Smart People Don't Buy Ltd
	G-AZSW	Beagle B.121 Pup 1	T. A. White
	G-AZTA	MBB Bö.209 Monsun 150FF	A. J. Court
	G-AZTF	Cessna F.177RG	R. Burgun
	G-AZTM	AESL Airtourer T2	Victa Restoration Group
	G-AZTS	Cessna F.172L	R. Murray & A. Bagley-Murray
	G-AZTV	Stolp SA.500 Starlet	G. R. Rowland
	G-AZTW	Cessna F.177RG	I. M. Richmond & G. R. Waller
	G-AZUM	Cessna F.172L	Fowlmere Flyers
	G-AZUT	MS.893A Rallye Commodore 180	J. Palethorpe
	G-AZUY	Cessna E.310L	W. B. Bateson
	G-AZUZ	Cessna FRA.150L	D. J. Parker
	G-AZVA	MBB Bö.209 Monsun 150FF	C. Elder
	G-AZVB	MBB Bö.209 Monsun 150FF	E. & P. M. L. Cliffe
	G-AZVF	MS.894A Rallye Minerva	Minerva Flying Group
	G-AZVG	AA-5 Traveler	G-AZVG Group
	G-AZVH	MS.894A Rallye Minerva	P. L. Jubb
	G-AZVI	MS.892A Rallye Commodore	G. C. Jarvis
	G-AZVL	Jodel D.119	S. P. Collins
	G-AZVP	Cessna F.177RG	C. R. Brown
	G-AZWB	PA-28 Cherokee 140	G-AZWB Flying Group
	G-AZWD	PA-28 Cherokee 140	BJ Services (Midlands) Ltd
	G-AZWF	SAN Jodel DR.1050	Cawdor Flying Group
	G-AZWS	PA-28R Cherokee Arrow 180	K. M. Turner
	G-AZWT	Westland Lysander IIIA (V9367)	The Shuttleworth Collection
	G-AZWY	PA-24 Comanche 260	Keymer Son & Co Ltd
	G-AZXB	Cameron O-65 balloon	R. J. Mitchener & P. F. Smart
	G-AZXD	Cessna F.172L	R. J. R. Williams & D. Palmer
	G-AZXG	PA-23 Aztec 250D ★	Instructional airframe/Cranfield
	G-AZYA	Gardan GY-80 Horizon 160	R. G. Whyte
	G-AZYB	Bell 47H-1 ★	IHM/Weston-super-Mare
	G-AZYD	MS.893A Rallye Commodore	Staffordshire Gliding Club Ltd
	G-AZYF	PA-28-180 Cherokee D	AZYF Group
	G-AZYS	CP.301C-1 Emeraude	C. G. Ferguson & D. Drew
	G-AZYU	PA-23 Aztec 250E	L. J. Martin
	G-AZYY	Slingsby T.61A Falke	J. A. Towers
	G-AZYZ	Wassmer Wa.51A Pacific	C. R. Buxton/France
	G-AZZO	PA-28-140 Cherokee	R. J. Hind
	G-AZZR	Cessna F.150L	N. J. Wakeling
	G-AZZV	Cessna F.172L	Zentelligence Ltd
	G-AZZZ	DH.82A Tiger Moth	S. W. McKay
	G-BAAD	Evans Super VP-1	Breighton VP-1 Group
	G-BAAF	Manning-Flanders MF1 (replica)	Aviation Film Services Ltd
	G-BAAI	MS.893A Rallye Commodore	R. D. Taylor
	G-BAAT	Cessna 182P	T. E. Earl
	G-BAAW	Jodel D.119	Alpha Whiskey Flying Group
	G-BABC	Cessna F.150L	B. B. Singh
	G-BABD	Cessna FRA.150L (modified)	Anglia Flight
	G-BABE	Taylor JT.2 Titch	M. Bonsall

Reg.	Type	Owner or Operator	Notes
G-BABG	PA-28 Cherokee 180	Mendip Flying Group	
G-BABK	PA-34-200 Seneca II	D. F. J. Flashman	
G-BACB	PA-34-200 Seneca II	Milbrooke Motors	
G-BACE	Fournier RF-5	G-BACE Fournier Group	
G-BACJ	Jodel D.120	Wearside Flying Association	
G-BACL	Jodel 150	D. F. Micklethwait	
G-BACN	Cessna FRA.150L	F. Bundy	
G-BACO	Cessna FRA.150L	T. E. C. Cushing	
G-BADC	Rollason Beta B.2A	D. H. Greenwood	
G-BADH	Slingsby T.61A Falke	I. F. Wells	
G-BADJ	PA-E23 Aztec 250E	C. Papadakis	
G-BADM	D.62B Condor	Delta Mike Condor Group	
G-BADV	Brochet MB50	W. B. Cooper	
G-BADW	Pitts S-2A Special	R. E. Mitchell	
G-BADZ	Aerotek Pitts S-2A Special	R. F. Warner	
G-BAEB	Robin DR.400/160	G. D. Jones	
G-BAEE	Jodel DR.1050/M1	R. Little	
G-BAEM	Robin DR.400/125	M. A. Webb	
G-BAEN	Robin DR.400/180	R. H. & C. R. Partington	
G-BAEO	Cessna F.172M	L. W. Scattergood	
G-BAEP	Cessna FRA.150L (modified)	A. M. Lynn	
G-BAER	Cosmic Wind	A. G. Truman	
G-BAET	Piper J-3C-65 Cub	C. J. Rees	
G-BAEU	Cessna F.150L	L. W. Scattergood	
G-BAEV	Cessna FRA.L150L	B. Doyle	
G-BAEW	Cessna F.172M ★	Westley Aircraft	
G-BAEY	Cessna F.172M	Skytrax Aviation Ltd	
G-BAEZ	Cessna FRA.150L	Donair Flying Club Ltd	
G-BAFA	AA-5 Traveler	C. F. Mackley	
G-BAFG	DH.82A Tiger Moth	Akerios International Business Co.Ltd	
G-BAFL	Cessna 182P	M. Langhammer	
G-BAFP	Robin DR.400/160	J. C. Bacon	
G-BAFT	PA-18 Super Cub 150	C. A. M. Neidt	
G-BAFU	PA-28 Cherokee 140	B. Higgins	
G-BAFV	PA-18 Super Cub 95	T. F. & S. J. Thorpe	
G-BAFW	PA-28 Cherokee 140	A. J. Peters	
G-BAFX	Robin DR.400/140	R. Foster	
G-BAGB	SIAI Marchetti SF.260	V. Balzer	
G-BAGC	Robin DR.400/140	O. C. Baars	
G-BAGF	Jodel D.92 Bébé	E. Evans	
G-BAGG	PA-32 Cherokee Six 300E	A. D. Hoy	
G-BAGN	Cessna F.177RG	R. W. J. Andrews	
G-BAGR	Robin DR.400/140	J. D. Last	
G-BAGS	Robin DR.400/180 2+2	M. Whale & M. W. A. Lunn	
G-BAGT	Helio H.295 Courier	D. C. Hanss	
G-BAGV	Cessna U.206F	Scottish Parachute Club	
G-BAGX	PA-28 Cherokee 140	I. Lwanga	
G-BAGY	Cameron O-84 balloon	P. G. Dunnington	
G-BAHD	Cessna 182P Skylane	Lambley Flying Group	
G-BAHF	PA-28 Cherokee 140	Warwickshire Aviation Ltd	
G-BAHH	Wallis WA-121	K. H. Wallis	
G-BAHI	Cessna F.150H	MJP Aviation & Sales	
G-BAHJ	PA-24 Comanche 250	K. Cooper	
G-BAHL	Robin DR.400/160	J. B. McVeighty	
G-BAHP	Volmer VJ.22 Sportsman	Seaplane Group	
G-BAHS	PA-28R Cherokee Arrow 200-II	A. R. N. Morris	
G-BAHX	Cessna 182P	M. D. J. Moore	
G-BAIG	PA-34-200-2 Seneca	Mid-Anglia School of Flying	
G-BAIH	PA-28R Cherokee Arrow 200-II	M. G. West	
G-BAIK	Cessna F.150L	M. Sollitt	
G-BAIS	Cessna F.177RG	Cardinal Syndicate	
G-BAIW	Cessna F.172M	W. J. Greenfield	
G-BAIZ	Slingsby T.61A Falke	Falke Syndicate	
G-BAJA	Cessna F.177RG	D. W. Ward	
G-BAJB	Cessna F.177RG	J. D. Loveridge	
G-BAJC	Evans VP-1	S. J. Greer	
G-BAJE	Cessna 177	Dynamic Aviation BV	
G-BAJN	AA-5 Traveler	P. J. Stead	
G-BAJO	AA-5 Traveler	Montgomery Aviation Ltd	
G-BAJR	PA-28 Cherokee 180	Spectrum Bravo Flying Group	
G-BAJZ	Robin DR.400/125	Rochester Aviation Ltd	
G-BAKD	PA-34-200 Seneca II	Andrews Professional Colour Laboratories	

Notes	Reg.	Type	Owner or Operator
	G-BAKH	PA-28 Cherokee 140	Keen Leasing (IOM) Ltd
	G-BAKJ	PA-30 Twin Comanche 160B	G. D. Colover
	G-BAKM	Robin DR.400/140	D. V. Pieri
	G-BAKN	SNCAN Stampe SV.4C	M. Holloway
	G-BAKR	Jodel D.117	R. W. Brown
	G-BAKV	PA-18 Super Cub 150	W. J. Murray
	G-BAKW	Beagle B.121 Pup 2	Cunning Stunts Flying Group
	G-BAKY	Slingsby T.61C Falke	Buckminster Gliding Club Ltd
	G-BALD	Cameron O-84 balloon	C. A. Gould
	G-BALF	Robin DR.400/140	G. & D. A. Wasey
	G-BALG	Robin DR.400/180	S. G. Jones
	G-BALH	Robin DR.400/140B	G-BALH Flying Group
	G-BALJ	Robin DR.400/180	D. A. Batt & D. de Lacey-Rowe
	G-BALN	Cessna T.310Q	O'Brien Properties Ltd
	G-BAMB	Slingsby T.61C Falke	H. J. Bradley
	G-BAMC	Cessna F.150L	K. Evans
	G-BAML	Bell 206B Jet Ranger II ★	Aero Venture
	G-BAMR	PA-16 Clipper	H. Royce
	G-BAMS	Robin DR.400/160	G-BAMS Ltd
	G-BAMT	CEA DR400/160	S. G. Jones
	G-BAMU	Robin DR.400/160	The Alternative Flying Group
	G-BAMV	Robin DR.400/180	K. Jones & E. A. Anderson
	G-BAMY	PA-28R Cherokee Arrow 200-II	C. B. Clark
	G-BANA	Robin DR.221	G. T. Pryor
	G-BANB	Robin DR.400/180	M. Ingvardsen
	G-BANC	Gardan GY-201 Minicab	C. R. Shipley
	G-BANU	Wassmer Jodel D.120	C. H. Kilner
	G-BANV	Phoenix Currie Wot	K. Knight
	G-BANW	CP.1330 Super Emeraude	P. S. Milner
	G-BANX	Cessna F.172M	Oakfleet 2000 Ltd
	G-BAOJ	MS.880B Rallye Club	R. E. Jones
	G-BAOM	MS.880B Rallye Club	P. J. D. Feehan
	G-BAOP	Cessna FRA.150L	R. D. Forster
	G-BAOU	AA-5 Traveler	R. C. Mark
	G-BAPB	DHC.1 Chipmunk 22	G. V. Bunyan
	G-BAPI	Cessna FRA.150L	Marketing Management Services Ltd
	G-BAPJ	Cessna FRA.150L	M. D. Page
	G-BAPL	PA-23 Turbo Aztec 250E	Donington Aviation Ltd
	G-BAPP	Evans VP-1 Series 2	D. H. G. Cotter
	G-BAPR	Jodel D.11	J. F. M. Bartlett
	G-BAPS	Campbell Cougar ★	IHM/Weston-super-Mare
	G-BAPV	Robin DR.400/160	J. D. & M. Millne
	G-BAPW	PA-28R Cherokee Arrow 180	A.G. Bourne & M. W. Freeman
	G-BAPX	Robin DR.400/160	G-BAPX Group
	G-BAPY	Robin HR.100/210	G-BAPY Group
	G-BARC	Cessna FR.172J	Severn Valley Aviation Group
	G-BARF	Jodel D.112 Club	V. Hughes
	G-BARG	Cessna E.310Q	IT Factor Ltd
	G-BARH	Beech C.23 Sundowner	G. Moorby & J. Hinchcliffe
	G-BARN	Taylor JT.2 Titch	R. G. W. Newton
	G-BARP	Bell 206B JetRanger 2	Western Power Distribution (South West) PLC
	G-BARS	DHC.1 Chipmunk 22 (1377)	J. Beattie
	G-BARV	Cessna 310Q	Old England Watches Ltd
	G-BARZ	Scheibe SF.28A Tandem Falke	K. Kiely
	G-BASH	AA-5 Traveler	BASH Flying Group
	G-BASJ	PA-28-180 Cherokee	Bristol Aero Club
	G-BASL	PA-28-140 Cherokee	P. N. Clynes
	G-BASM	PA-34-200 Seneca II	M. Gipps
	G-BASN	Beech C.23 Sundowner	S. R. Ford
	G-BASO	Lake LA-4 Amphibian	Uulster Seaplane Association Ltd
	G-BASP	Beagle B.121 Pup 1	B. J. Coutts
	G-BATC	MBB Bö.105D	South Georgia Heritage Trust
	G-BATJ	Jodel D.119	M. G. Davis
	G-BATN	PA-23 Aztec 250E	Marshall of Cambridge Ltd
	G-BATV	PA-28 Cherokee 180D	J. N. Rudsdale
	G-BATW	PA-28 Cherokee 140	C. D. Sainsbury
	G-BAUC	PA-25 Pawnee 235	Southdown Gliding Club Ltd
	G-BAUH	Jodel D.112	G. A. & D. Shepherd
	G-BAVB	Cessna F.172M	T. S. Sheridan-McGinnitty
	G-BAVH	DHC.1 Chipmunk 22	Portsmouth Naval Gliding Club
	G-BAVL	PA-23 Aztec 250E	S. P. & A. V. Chillott
	G-BAVO	Boeing Stearman N2S (26)	(stored)

Reg.	Type	Owner or Operator	Notes
G-BAVR	AA-5 Traveler	G. E. Murray	
G-BAWG	PA-28R Cherokee Arrow 200-II	Solent Air Ltd	
G-BAWK	PA-28 Cherokee 140	J. Stanley	
G-BAXE	Hughes 269A	Reethorpe Engineering Ltd	
G-BAXK	Thunder Ax7-77 balloon ★	A. R. Snook	
G-BAXS	Bell 47G-5	RK Helicopters	
G-BAXU	Cessna F.150L	M. W. Sheppardson	
G-BAXV	Cessna F.150L	CBM Associates Consulting Ltd	
G-BAXY	Cessna F.172M	Eaglesoar Ltd	
G-BAXZ	PA-28 Cherokee 140	G-BAXZ (87) Syndicate	
G-BAYL	SNCAN Nord 1101 Norecrin ★	(stored)/Chirk	
G-BAYO	Cessna 150L	J. A. & D. T. A. Rees	
G-BAYP	Cessna 150L	Yankee Papa Flying Group	
G-BAYR	Robin HR.100/210	P. D. Harries	
G-BAZC	Robin DR.400/160	S. G. Jones	
G-BAZM	Jodel D.11	A. F. Simpson	
G-BAZS	Cessna F.150L	L. W. Scattergood	
G-BAZT	Cessna F.172M	Aviation South West Ltd	
G-BBAW	Robin HR.100/210	F. A. Purvis	
G-BBAX	Robin DR.400/140	G. J. Bissex & P. H. Garbutt	
G-BBAY	Robin DR.400/140	J. C. Stubbs	
G-BBBB	Taylor JT.1 Monoplane	M. C. Arnold	
G-BBBC	Cessna F.150L	W. J. Greenfield	
G-BBBI	AA-5 Traveler	Go Baby Aviation Group	
G-BBBN	PA-28 Cherokee 180	Estuary Aviation Ltd	
G-BBBO	SIPA 903	G. E. Morris	
G-BBBW	FRED Srs 2	M. Palfreman	
G-BBBY	PA-28 Cherokee 140	W. R. & R. Davies	
G-BBCH	Robin DR.400/2+2	Oilburners (2006) Flying syndicate	
G-BBCI	Cessna 150H	A. M. & F. Alam	
G-BBCN	Robin HR.100/210	J. C. King	
G-BBCS	Robin DR.400/140	B. N. Stevens	
G-BBCY	Luton LA-4A Minor	A. W. McBlain	
G-BBCZ	AA-5 Traveler	Mercantile Developments Ltd	
G-BBDC	PA-28-140 Cherokee	G-BBDC Group	
G-BBDE	PA-28R Cherokee Arrow 200-II	R. L. Coleman, P. Knott & Istec Services Ltd	
G-BBDG	BAC-Aérospatiale Concorde 100 ★	Brooklands Museum	
G-BBDH	Cessna F.172M	J. D. Woodward	
G-BBDL	AA-5 Traveler	Delta Lima Flying Group	
G-BBDM	AA-5 Traveler	Jackeroo Aviation Group	
G-BBDO	PA-23 Turbo Aztec 250E	J. W. Anstee	
G-BBDP	Robin DR.400/160	Robin Lance Aviation Associates Ltd	
G-BBDS	PA-31 Turbo Navajo	Jota Aircraft Leasing Ltd (G-SKKB)	
G-BBDT	Cessna 150H	J. G. N. Wilson	
G-BBDV	SIPA S.903	Eatonair Group	
G-BBEA	Luton LA-4 Minor	D. S. Evans	
G-BBEB	PA-28R Cherokee Arrow 200-II	F. J. Stimpson & M. J. Potter	
G-BBEC	PA-28 Cherokee 180	P. & M. Corrigan	
G-BBEF	PA-28 Cherokee 140	FlyBPL.com	
G-BBEN	Bellanca 7GCBC Citabria	C. A. G. Schofield	
G-BBFD	PA-28R Cherokee Arrow 200-II	C. H. Rose & M. J. Green	
G-BBFL	Gardan GY-201 Minicab	R. Smith	
G-BBFV	PA-32 Cherokee Six 260	G-BBFV Syndicate	
G-BBGC	MS.893E Rallye 180GT	P. M. Nolan	
G-BBGI	Fuji FA.200-160	A and P West	
G-BBHF	PA-23 Aztec 250E	G. J. Williams	
G-BBHI	Cessna 177RG	T. G. W. Bunce	
G-BBHJ	Piper J-3C-65 Cub	Wellcross Flying Group	
G-BBHK	Noorduyn AT-16 Harvard IIB (FH153)	Sheringham Aviation UK Ltd	
G-BBHY	PA-28 Cherokee 180	Air Operations Ltd	
G-BBIF	PA-23 Aztec 250E	D. M. Davies	
G-BBIH	Enstrom F-28A-UK	Friebe France Aeronautique SARL	
G-BBII	Fiat G-46-3B (4-97/MM52801)	G-BBII Ltd	
G-BBIL	PA-28 Cherokee 140	Saxondale Group	
G-BBIO	Robin HR.100/210	R. P. Caley	
G-BBIX	PA-28 Cherokee 140	Sterling Aviation Ltd	
G-BBJI	Isaacs Spitfire (RN218)	S. Vince	
G-BBJU	Robin DR.400/140	J. C. Lister	
G-BBJV	Cessna F.177RG	P. R. Powell	
G-BBJX	Cessna F.150L	L. W. Scattergood	
G-BBJY	Cessna F.172M	Staverton Flying School	

Notes	Reg.	Type	Owner or Operator
	G-BBJZ	Cessna F.172M	L. P. Burrow
	G-BBKA	Cessna F.150L	W. M. Wilson
	G-BBKB	Cessna F.150L	Justgold Ltd
	G-BBKE	Cessna F.150L	G. J. Smith
	G-BBKG	Cessna FR.172J	R. Wright
	G-BBKI	Cessna F.172M	C. W. & S. A. Burman
	G-BBKL	CP.301A Emeraude	Piel G-BBKL
	G-BBKX	PA-28 Cherokee 180	DRA Flying Club Ltd
	G-BBKY	Cessna F.150L	F. W. Astbury
	G-BBKZ	Cessna 172M	KZ Flying Group
	G-BBLH	Piper J-3C-65 Cub (31145:G-26)	Shipping & Airlines Ltd
	G-BBLS	AA-5 Traveler	A. Grant
	G-BBLU	PA-34-200 Seneca II	R. H. R. Rue
	G-BBMB	Robin DR.400/180	Regent Flying Group
	G-BBMH	EAA. Sports Biplane Model P.1	G-BBMH Flying Group
	G-BBMJ	PA-23 Aztec 250E	Nationwide Caravan Rental Services Ltd
	G-BBMN	DHC.1 Chipmunk 22	R. Steiner
	G-BBMO	DHC.1 Chipmunk 22 (WK514)	Mike Oscar Group
	G-BBMR	DHC.1 Chipmunk 22 (WB763:14)	P. J. Wood
	G-BBMT	DHC.1 Chipmunk 22	MT Group
	G-BBMV	DHC.1 Chipmunk 22 (WG348)	S. P. Tilling & S. G. Howell
	G-BBMW	DHC.1 Chipmunk 22 (WK628)	G. Fielder & A. Wilson
	G-BBMZ	DHC.1 Chipmunk 22	G-BBMZ Chipmunk Syndicate
	G-BBNA	DHC.1 Chipmunk 22 (Lycoming)	Coventry Gliding Club Ltd
	G-BBNC	DHC.1 Chipmunk T.10 (WP790) ★	De Havilland Heritage Museum/London Colney
	G-BBND	DHC.1 Chipmunk 22 (WD286)	Bernoulli Syndicate
	G-BBNH	PA-34-200 Seneca II	M. G. D. Baverstock & ptnrs
	G-BBNI	PA-34-200 Seneca II	M. P. Grimshaw
	G-BBNJ	Cessna F.150L	M. C. Bellamy
	G-BBNT	PA-31-350 Navajo Chieftain	M. P. Goss
	G-BBNZ	Cessna F.172M	J. H. Sandham Aviation
	G-BBOA	Cessna F.172M	J. D & A. M. Black
	G-BBOH	Pitts S-1S Special	Venom Jet Promotions Ltd
	G-BBOL	PA-18 Super Cub 150	N. Artt
	G-BBOO	Thunder Ax6-56 balloon	K. Meehan Tigerjack
	G-BBOR	Bell 206B JetRanger 2	M. J. Easey
	G-BBPN	Enstrom F-28A-UK	D. W. C. Holmes
	G-BBPO	Enstrom F-28A-UK	Henfield Lodge Ltd
	G-BBPP	PA-28 Cherokee 180	Big Red Kite Ltd (G-WACP)
	G-BBPS	Jodel D.117	A. Appleby
	G-BBPX	PA-34-200 Seneca II	The G-BBPX Flying Group
	G-BBPY	PA-28 Cherokee 180	Sunsaver Ltd
	G-BBRA	PA-23 Aztec 250D	R. C. Lough
	G-BBRB	DH.82A Tiger Moth (DF198)	R. Barham
	G-BBRC	Fuji FA.200-180	BBRC Ltd
	G-BBRI	Bell 47G-5A	Alan Mann Helicopters Ltd
	G-BBRN	Procter Kittiwake 1 (XW784/VL)	H. M. Price
	G-BBRZ	AA-5 Traveler	B. McIntyre
	G-BBSA	AA-5 Traveler	Usworth 84 Flying Associates Ltd
	G-BBSS	DHC.1A Chipmunk 22	Coventry Gliding Club Ltd
	G-BBSW	Pietenpol Air Camper	J. K. S. Wills
	G-BBTB	Cessna FRA.150L	Solent School of Flying
	G-BBTG	Cessna F.172M	Triple X Flying Group
	G-BBTH	Cessna F.172M	Tayside Aviation Ltd
	G-BBTJ	PA-23 Aztec 250E	J. A. & R. H. Cooper
	G-BBTK	Cessna FRA.150L	Cleveland Flying School Ltd
	G-BBTY	Beech C23 Sundowner	G-BBTY Group
	G-BBUE	AA-5 Traveler	Tatenhill Aviation Ltd
	G-BBUT	Western O-65 balloon	R. G. Turnbull
	G-BBUU	Piper J-3C-65 Cub	C. Stokes
	G-BBVF	SA Twin Pioneer Srs 3 ★	Museum of Flight/East Fortune
	G-BBVO	Isaacs Fury II (S1579)	C. E. Brookes
	G-BBXB	Cessna FRA.150L	D. C. & M. Laycock
	G-BBXW	PA-28-151 Cherokee Warrior	Bristol Aero Club
	G-BBXY	Bellanca 7GCBC Citabria	R. R. L. Windus
	G-BBXZ	Evans VP-1	R. W. Burrows
	G-BBYB	PA-18 Super Cub 95	Tiger Club (1990) Ltd
	G-BBYH	Cessna 182P	Ramco (UK) Ltd
	G-BBYM	HP.137 Jetstream 200 ★	Aerospace Museum/Cosford (G-AYWR)
	G-BBYP	PA-28 Cherokee 140	E. Williams
	G-BBYS	Cessna 182P	G-BBYS Group
	G-BBYU	Cameron O-56 balloon	British Balloon Museum

Reg.	Type	Owner or Operator	Notes
G-BBZF	PA-28 Cherokee 140	East Coast Aviation	
G-BBZH	PA-28R Cherokee Arrow 200-II	G. Higgins, C. Harte and I. O'Brien	
G-BBZN	Fuji FA.200-180	D. Kynaston & ptnrs	
G-BBZV	PA-28R Cherokee Arrow 200-II	P. B. Mellor	
G-BCAH	DHC.1 Chipmunk 22 (WG316)	Century Aviation Ltd	
G-BCAP	Cameron O-56 balloon ★	Balloon Preservation Group/Lancing	
G-BCAR	Thunder Ax7-77 balloon ★	British Balloon Museum/Newbury	
G-BCAZ	PA-12 Super Cruiser	A. D. Williams	
G-BCBG	PA-23 Aztec 250E	M. J. L. Batt	
G-BCBH	Fairchild 24R-46A Argus III	Dreamticket Promotions Ltd	
G-BCBJ	PA-25 Pawnee 235	Deeside Gliding Club (Aberdeenshire) Ltd	
G-BCBL	Fairchild 24R-46A Argus III (HB751)	F. J. Cox	
G-BCBR	AJEP/Wittman W.8 Tailwind	D. P. Jones	
G-BCBX	Cessna F.150L	P. Lodge & J. G. McVey	
G-BCBZ	Cessna 337C	J. Haden	
G-BCCC	Cessna F.150L	P. J. Randell	
G-BCCE	PA-23 Aztec 250E	Golf Charlie Echo Ltd	
G-BCCF	PA-28 Cherokee 180	Charlie Foxtrot Aviation	
G-BCCK	AA-5 Traveler	Prospect Air Ltd	
G-BCCR	CP.301A Emeraude (modified)	D. C. Stokes	
G-BCCX	DHC.1 Chipmunk 22 (Lycoming)	RAFGSA	
G-BCCY	Robin HR.200/100	M. E. Hicks	
G-BCDJ	PA-28 Cherokee 140	T. J. Addison	
G-BCDK	Partenavia P.68B	Mach 014 SAS Di Albertario Michele and Co/Italy	
G-BCDL	Cameron O-42 balloon	D. P. & Mrs B. O. Turner Chums	
G-BCDN	F.27 Friendship Mk 200 ★	Instructional airframe/Norwich	
G-BCDY	Cessna FRA.150L	R. L. Nunn & T. R. Edwards	
G-BCEA	Sikorsky S-61N Mk II	British International	
G-BCEB	Sikorsky S-61N Mk II	Veritair Ltd	
G-BCEE	AA-5 Traveler	P. J. Marchant	
G-BCEF	AA-5 Traveler	G-BCEF Group	
G-BCEN	BN-2A-26 Islander	Reconnaissance Ventures Ltd	
G-BCEP	AA-5 Traveler	A. A. Kind & P. Ragan	
G-BCER	Gardan GY-201 Minicab	D. Beaumont	
G-BCEU	Cameron O-42 balloon	P. Glydon	
G-BCEX	PA-23 Aztec 250E	I. Kazi	
G-BCEY	DHC.1 Chipmunk 22 (WG465)	Gopher Flying Group	
G-BCFF	Fuji FA-200-160	S. A. Cole	
G-BCFO	PA-18 Super Cub 150	Portsmouth Naval Gliding Club	
G-BCFR	Cessna FRA.150L	Foxtrot Romeo Group	
G-BCFW	SAAB 91D Safir	D. R. Williams	
G-BCFY	Luton LA-4A Minor	M. P. Wiseman	
G-BCGB	Bensen B.8	A. Melody	
G-BCGC	DHC.1 Chipmunk 22 (WP903)	Henlow Chipmunk Group	
G-BCGH	SNCAN NC.854S	Nord Flying Group	
G-BCGI	PA-28 Cherokee 140	John West Consulting Ltd	
G-BCGJ	PA-28 Cherokee 140	Demero Ltd & Transcourt Ltd	
G-BCGM	Jodel D.120	N. J. Orchard-Armitage & I. D. Daniels	
G-BCGN	PA-28 Cherokee 140	C. F. Hessey	
G-BCGS	PA-28R Cherokee Arrow 200	Arrow Aviation Group	
G-BCGW	Jodel D.11	G. H. Chittenden	
G-BCHL	DHC.1 Chipmunk 22A (WP788)	Shropshire Soaring Ltd	
G-BCHP	CP.1310-C3 Super Emeraude	G. Hughes & A. G. Just (G-JOSI)	
G-BCHT	Schleicher ASK.16	Dunstable K16 Group	
G-BCHV	DHC.1 Chipmunk 22	K.I. Sutherland	
G-BCID	PA-34-200 Seneca II	Shenley Farms (Aviation) Ltd	
G-BCIH	DHC.1 Chipmunk 22 (WD363)	P. J. Richie	
G-BCIJ	AA-5 Traveler	Arrow Association	
G-BCIR	PA-28-151 Warrior	R. W. Harris	
G-BCJM	PA-28 Cherokee 140	APB Leasing Ltd	
G-BCJN	PA-28 Cherokee 140	Bristol and Wessex Aeroplane Club Ltd	
G-BCJO	PA-28R Cherokee Arrow 200	R. Ross	
G-BCJP	PA-28 Cherokee 140	J. Wilson	
G-BCKN	DHC.1A Chipmunk 22 (Lycoming)	RAFGSA	
G-BCKS	Fuji FA.200-180AO	G. J. Ward	
G-BCKT	Fuji FA.200-180	A. G. Dobson	
G-BCKU	Cessna FRA.150L	Mid America (UK) Ltd	
G-BCKV	Cessna FRA.150L	M. Bonsall	
G-BCLI	AA-5 Traveler	SRWN Air Services Ltd	
G-BCLL	PA-28 Cherokee 180	S. C. Hardman	
G-BCLS	Cessna 170B	N. Simpson	

Notes	Reg.	Type	Owner or Operator
	G-BCLT	MS.894A Rallye Minerva 220	K. M. Bowen
	G-BCLU	Jodel D.117	G-BCLU Group
	G-BCLW	AA-1B Trainer	C. R. White
	G-BCMD	PA-18 Super Cub 95	P. Stephenson
	G-BCMJ	Squarecraft Cavalier SA.102-5	N. F. Andrews
	G-BCMT	Isaacs Fury II	R.W. Burrows
	G-BCNC	Gardan GY-201 Minicab	J. R. Wraight
	G-BCNP	Cameron O-77 balloon	P. Spellward
	G-BCNX	Piper J-3C-65 Cub (540)	K. J. Lord
	G-BCNZ	Fuji FA.200-160	W. Dougan
	G-BCOB	Piper J-3C-65 Cub (329405:A-23)	J. W. Marjoram
	G-BCOI	DHC.1 Chipmunk 22 (WP970:12)	M. J. Diggins
	G-BCOL	Cessna F.172M	November Charlie Flying Group
	G-BCOM	Piper J-3C-65 Cub	Dougal Flying Group
	G-BCOO	DHC.1 Chipmunk 22	T. G. Fielding & M. S. Morton
	G-BCOR	SOCATA Rallye 100ST	J. A. Levey
	G-BCOU	DHC.1 Chipmunk 22 (WK522)	P. J. Loweth
	G-BCOY	DHC.1 Chipmunk 22	Coventry Gliding Club Ltd
	G-BCPD	Gardan GY-201 Minicab	P. R. Cozens
	G-BCPG	PA-28R Cherokee Arrow 200-II	Roses Flying Group
	G-BCPH	Piper J-3C-65 Cub (329934:B-72)	G. Earl
	G-BCPJ	Piper J-3C-65 Cub	Piper Cub Group
	G-BCPK	Cessna F.172M	D. C. C. Handley
	G-BCPN	AA-5 Traveler	G-BCPN Group
	G-BCPU	DHC.1 Chipmunk 22	P. Waller
	G-BCRB	Cessna F.172M	Wingstask 1995Ltd
	G-BCRE	Cameron O-77 balloon ★	Balloon Preservation Group/Lancing
	G-BCRL	PA-28-151 Warrior	BCRL Ltd
	G-BCRR	AA-5B Tiger	S. Waite
	G-BCRX	DHC.1 Chipmunk 22 (WD292)	P. J. Tuplin & M. I. Robinson
	G-BCSA	DHC.1 Chipmunk 22 (Lycoming)	RAFGSA
	G-BCSL	DHC.1 Chipmunk 22	Chipmunk Flyers Ltd
	G-BCSX	Thunder Ax7-77 balloon	C. Wolstenholm
	G-BCTF	PA-28-151 Warrior	The St. George Flight Training Ltd
	G-BCTI	Schleicher ASK 16	Tango India Syndicate
	G-BCTK	Cessna FR.172J	M. G. E. Morton
	G-BCTT	Evans VP-1	E. R. G. Ludlow
	G-BCUB	Piper J-3C-65 Cub	A. L. Brown
	G-BCUF	Cessna F.172M	Howell Plant Hire & Construction
	G-BCUH	Cessna F.150M	M. G. Montgomerie
	G-BCUJ	Cessna F.150M	j. Oleksyn & G. Astle
	G-BCUL	SOCATA Rallye 100ST	C. A. Ussher & Fountain Estates Ltd
	G-BCUO	SA Bulldog Srs 120/122	Cranfield University
	G-BCUS	SA Bulldog Srs 120/122	Falcon Group
	G-BCUV	SA Bulldog Srs 120/122 (XX704)	Flew LLP
	G-BCUW	Cessna F.177RG	S. J. Westley
	G-BCUY	Cessna FRA.150M	J. C. Carpenter
	G-BCVB	PA-17 Vagabond	A. T. Nowak
	G-BCVC	SOCATA Rallye 100ST	W. Haddow
	G-BCVE	Evans VP-2	D. Masterson & D. B. Winstanley
	G-BCVF	Practavia Pilot Sprite	D. G. Hammersley
	G-BCVG	Cessna FRA.150L	G-BCVG Flying Group
	G-BCVH	Cessna FRA.150L	M. A. James
	G-BCVJ	Cessna F.172M	Rothland Ltd
	G-BCVY	PA-34-200T Seneca II	Oxford Aviation Academy (Oxford) Ltd
	G-BCWB	Cessna 182P	M. F. Oliver & A. J. Mew
	G-BCWH	Practavia Pilot Sprite	R. Tasker
	G-BCWK	Alpavia Fournier RF-3	T. J. Hartwell
	G-BCXB	SOCATA Rallye 100ST	The Rallye Group
	G-BCXE	Robin DR.400/2+2	Weald Air Services Ltd
	G-BCXJ	Piper L-4J Cub (480752:E-39)	W. Readman
	G-BCXN	DHC.1 Chipmunk 22 (WP800)	G. M. Turner
	G-BCYH	DAW Privateer Mk. 3	G-BCYH Group
	G-BCYK	Avro CF.100 Mk 4 Canuck (18393) ★	Imperial War Museum/Duxford
	G-BCYM	DHC.1 Chipmunk 22 (WK577)	G-BCYM Group
	G-BCYR	Cessna F.172M	P. Barton, R. Ryan & P. Wayman
	G-BCZM	Cessna F.172M	Cornwall Flying Club Ltd
	G-BCZO	Cameron O-77 balloon	W. O. T. Holmes
	G-BDAD	Taylor JT.1 Monoplane	C. N. Hanson
	G-BDAG	Taylor JT.1 Monoplane	N. R. Osborne
	G-BDAH	Evans VP-1	G. H. J. Geurts

Reg.	Type	Owner or Operator	Notes
G-BDAI	Cessna FRA.150M	B. K. & W. G. Ranger	
G-BDAK	Rockwell Commander 112	M. C. Wilson	
G-BDAO	SIPA S.91	S. B. Churchill	
G-BDAP	AJEP Tailwind	J. Whiting	
G-BDAR	Evans VP-1	R. F. Powell	
G-BDAY	Thunder Ax5-42S1 balloon	T. M. Donnelly *Meconium*	
G-BDBD	Wittman W.8 Tailwind	Tailwindr Group	
G-BDBF	FRED Srs 2	G. E. & R. E. Collins	
G-BDBH	Bellanca 7GCBC Citabria	C. J. Gray	
G-BDBI	Cameron O-77 balloon	C. Jones	
G-BDBS	Short SD3-30 ★	Ulster Aviation Society	
G-BDBU	Cessna F.150M	B. Boult	
G-BDBV	Jodel D.11A	Seething Jodel Group	
G-BDBZ	Westland WS-55 Whirlwind (XJ398) ★	Aeroventure/Doncaster	
G-BDCD	Piper J-3C-85 Cub (480133:B-44)	Cubby Cub Group	
G-BDCI	CP.301A Emeraude	D. L. Sentance	
G-BDDD	DHC.1 Chipmunk 22	DRA Aero Club Ltd	
G-BDDF	Jodel D.120	J. V. Thompson	
G-BDDG	Jodel D.112	J. Pool & D. G. Palmer	
G-BDDS	PA-25 Pawnee 235	Vale of Neath Gliding Club	
G-BDDX	Whittaker MW2B Excalibur ★	Cornwall Aero Park/Helston	
G-BDDZ	CP.301A Emeraude	E. C. Mort	
G-BDEC	SOCATA Rallye 100ST	J. Fingleton	
G-BDEH	Jodel D.120A	EH Group	
G-BDEI	Jodel D.9 Bébé	The Noddy Group	
G-BDEU	DHC.1 Chipmunk 22 (WP808)	Skylark Aviation Ltd	
G-BDEX	Cessna FRA.150M	A. P. F. Tucker	
G-BDEY	Piper J-3C-65 Cub	Ducksworth Flying Club	
G-BDEZ	Piper J-3C-65 Cub	M. Housley	
G-BDFB	Currie Wot	J. Jennings	
G-BDFH	Auster AOP.9 (XR240)	R. B. Webber	
G-BDFJ	Cessna F.150M	C. J. Hopewell	
G-BDFR	Fuji FA.200-160	M. S. Bird	
G-BDFU	Dragonfly MPA Mk 1 ★	Museum of Flight/East Fortune	
G-BDFW	Rockwell Commander 112	M. E. & E. G. Reynolds	
G-BDFY	AA-5 Traveler	Grumman Group	
G-BDGB	Gardan GY-20 Minicab	S. Burchfield	
G-BDGH	Thunder Ax7-77 balloon	R. J. Mitchener & P. F. Smart	
G-BDGM	PA-28-151 Cherokee Warrior	FlyBPL.com	
G-BDHK	Piper J-3C-65 Cub (329417)	Knight Flying Group	
G-BDIE	Rockwell Commander 112	J. McAleer & R. J. Adams	
G-BDIG	Cessna 182P	Air Group 6	
G-BDIH	Jodel D.117	N. D. H. Stokes	
G-BDIX	DH.106 Comet 4C ★	Museum of Flight/East Fortune	
G-BDJD	Jodel D.112	J. E. Preston	
G-BDJG	Luton LA-4A Minor	Very Slow Flying Club	
G-BDJP	Piper J-3C-90 Cub	S. T. Gilbert	
G-BDJR	SNCAN Nord NC.858	R. F. M. Marson	
G-BDJV	BN-2A-27 Islander	Cormack (Aircraft Services) Ltd	
G-BDKC	Cessna A185F	Bridge of Tilt Co Ltd	
G-BDKD	Enstrom F-28A	P. J. Price	
G-BDKH	CP.301A Emeraude	T. A. S. Rayner	
G-BDKJ	K & S SA.102.5 Cavalier	D. A. Garner	
G-BDKM	SIPA 903	S. W. Markham	
G-BDKW	Rockwell Commander 112A	J. T. Klaschka	
G-BDLO	AA-5A Cheetah	S. & J. Dolan	
G-BDLT	Rockwell Commander 112	D. L. Churchward	
G-BDLY	K & S SA.102.5 Cavalier	P. R. Stevens	
G-BDMS	Piper J-3C-65 Cub (FR886)	A. T. H. Martin	
G-BDMW	Jodel DR.100A	Mike Whisky Group	
G-BDNC	Taylor JT.1 Monoplane	D. W. Mathie	
G-BDNG	Taylor JT.1 Monoplane	R. B. McComish	
G-BDNO	Taylor JT.1 Monoplane	R. Wilkinson	
G-BDNT	Jodel D.92 Bébé	R. J. Stobo	
G-BDNU	Cessna F.172M	J. & K. G. McVicar	
G-BDNW	AA-1B Trainer	N. A. Baxter	
G-BDNX	AA-1B Trainer	D. M. & P. A. Fenton	
G-BDOD	Cessna F.150M	OD Group	
G-BDOE	Cessna FR.172J	D. Sansome	
G-BDOG	SA Bulldog Srs 200	D. C. Bonsall	
G-BDOL	Piper J-3C-65 Cub	L. R. Balthazor	
G-BDOW	Cessna FRA.150	Joystick Aviation Ltd	

Notes	Reg.	Type	Owner or Operator
	G-BDPA	PA-28-151 Warrior	Aircraft Engineers Ltd
	G-BDPJ	PA-25 Pawnee 235B	Swift Aerobatic Display Team
	G-BDRD	Cessna FRA.150M	Aircraft Engineers Ltd
	G-BDRG	Taylor JT.2 Titch	D. R. Gray
	G-BDRJ	DHC.1 Chipmunk 22 (WP857)	WP857 Trust
	G-BDRK	Cameron O-65 balloon	R. J. Mitchener & P. F. Smart
	G-BDSB	PA-28-181 Archer II	Testair Ltd
	G-BDSF	Cameron O-56 balloon	J. H. Greensides
	G-BDSH	PA-28 Cherokee 140 (modified)	The Wright Brothers Flying Group
	G-BDSK	Cameron O-65 balloon	Southern Balloon Group *Carousel II*
	G-BDSL	Cessna F.150M	M. Howells
	G-BDSM	Slingsby T.31B Cadet III	F. C. J. Wevers/Netherlands
	G-BDTB	Evans VP-1	P. W. Boyes
	G-BDTL	Evans VP-1	T. W. Carnall
	G-BDTO	BN-2A Mk III-2 Trislander	Aurigny Air Services Ltd (G-RBSI/G-OTSB)
	G-BDTU	Omega III gas balloon	R. G. Turnbull
	G-BDTV	Mooney M.20F	S. Redfearn
	G-BDTX	Cessna F.150M	F. W. Ellis
	G-BDUI	Cameron V-56 balloon	D. C. Johnson
	G-BDUL	Evans VP-1	J. C. Lindsay
	G-BDUM	Cessna F.150M	P. B. Millington & D. Grant
	G-BDUN	PA-34-200T Seneca II	R. Paris
	G-BDUO	Cessna F.150M	D. W. Locke
	G-BDUY	Robin DR.400/140B	J. G. Anderson
	G-BDUZ	Cameron V-56 balloon	Zebedee Balloon Service
	G-BDVA	PA-17 Vagabond	I. M. Callier
	G-BDVB	PA-15 (PA-17) Vagabond	B. P. Gardner
	G-BDVC	PA-17 Vagabond	A. R. Caveen
	G-BDWE	Flaglor Scooter	P. King
	G-BDWH	SOCATA Rallye 150ST	M. A. Jones
	G-BDWJ	SE-5A (replica) (F8010:Z)	D. W. Linney
	G-BDWM	Mustang scale replica (FB226)	D. C. Bonsall
	G-BDWO	Howes Ax6 balloon	R. B. & C. Howes
	G-BDWP	PA-32R-300 Cherokee Lance	A. Belcastro & I. Bardelli/Italy
	G-BDWX	Jodel D.120A	R. P. Rochester
	G-BDWY	PA-28-140 Cherokee E	A. Boorman & D. Bishop
	G-BDWZ	Slingsby T-59J Kestrel	T. J. Wilkinson
	G-BDXX	SNCAN NC.858S	K. M. Davis
	G-BDYG	P.56 Provost T.1 (WV493) ★	Museum of Flight/East Fortune
	G-BDZA	Scheibe SF.25E Super Falke	Hereward Flying Group
	G-BDZC	Cessna F.150M	A. M. Lynn
	G-BDZD	Cessna F.172M	R. J. A. Durie
	G-BDZG	Slingsby T.59H Kestrel	R. E. Gretton
	G-BEAB	Jodel DR.1051	R. C. Hibberd
	G-BEAC	PA-28 Cherokee 140	R. Murray & A. Bagley-Murray
	G-BEAD	WG.13 Lynx ★	Instructional airframe/Middle Wallop
	G-BEAG	PA-34-200T Seneca II	Oxford Aviation Academy (Oxford) Ltd
	G-BEAH	Auster J/2 Arrow	Bedwell Hey Flying Group
	G-BEBC	Westland WS-55 Whirlwind 3 (XP355) ★	Norwich Aviation Museum
	G-BEBG	WSK-PZL SDZ-45A Ogar	The Ogar Syndicate
	G-BEBN	Cessna 177B	R. Turrell & P. Mason
	G-BEBR	GY-201 Minicab	M. J. Wood
	G-BEBS	Andreasson BA-4B	N. J. W. Reid
	G-BEBU	Rockwell Commander 112A	I. Hunt
	G-BEBZ	PA-28-151 Warrior	Airways Flight Training (Exeter) Ltd
	G-BECA	SOCATA Rallye 100ST	N. G. Ogborne
	G-BECB	SOCATA Rallye 100ST	D. H. Tonkin
	G-BECK	Cameron V-56 balloon	N. H. & A. M. Ponsford
	G-BECN	Piper J-3C-65 Cub (480480:E-44)	G. Denney
	G-BECT	CASA 1.131E Jungmann 2000 (A-57)	Alpha 57 Group
	G-BECW	CASA 1.131E Jungmann 2000 (A-10)	C. M. Rampton
	G-BECZ	CAARP CAP-10B	C. M. Thompson
	G-BEDA	CASA 1.131E Jungmann 2000	L. Atkin & M. G. Kates
	G-BEDB	Nord 1203 Norecrin ★	B. F. G. Lister (stored)/Chirk
	G-BEDD	Jodel D.117A	Dubious Group
	G-BEDF	Boeing B-17G-105-VE (124485:DF-A)	B-17 Preservation Ltd
	G-BEDG	Rockwell Commander 112	G-BEDG Group
	G-BEDJ	Piper J-3C-65 Cub (44-80594)	R. Earl
	G-BEDP	BN-2A Mk.III-2 Trislander	Blue Island Air
	G-BEDV	V.668 Varsity T.1 (WJ945) ★	Duxford Aviation Society
	G-BEEE	Thunder Ax6-56A balloon ★	British Balloon Museum/Newbury

Reg.	Type	Owner or Operator	Notes
G-BEEH	Cameron V-56 balloon	Sade Balloons Ltd	
G-BEEI	Cameron N-77 balloon	Zebedee Balloon Service Ltd	
G-BEER	Isaacs Fury II (K2075)	R. S. C. Andrews	
G-BEEU	PA-28 Cherokee 140F	E. Merkado	
G-BEFA	PA-28-151 Warrior	Verran Freight	
G-BEFF	PA-28 Cherokee 140F	E. Merkado	
G-BEGG	Scheibe SF.25E Super Falke	G-BEGG Motorfalke	
G-BEHH	PA-32R Cherokee Lance 300	K. Swallow	
G-BEHU	PA-34-200T Seneca II	Pirin Aeronautical Ltd	
G-BEHV	Cessna F.172N	Edinburgh Air Centre Ltd	
G-BEIA	Cessna FRA.150M	C. J. Hopewell	
G-BEIF	Cameron O-65 balloon	C. Vening	
G-BEIG	Cessna F.150M	R. D. Forster & M. S. B. Thorp	
G-BEII	PA-25 Pawnee 235D	Burn Gliding Club Ltd	
G-BEIL	SOCATA Rallye 150T	The Rallye Flying Group	
G-BEIP	PA-28-181 Archer II	S. Pope	
G-BEIS	Evans VP-1	P. J. Hunt	
G-BEJK	Cameron S-31 balloon	Rango Balloon and Kite Company	
G-BEJV	PA-34-200T Seneca II	Oxford Aviation Academy (Oxford) Ltd	
G-BEKL	Bede BD-4E-150	F. E.Tofield	
G-BEKM	Evans VP-1	G. J. McDill	
G-BEKO	Cessna F.182Q	G. J. & F. J. Leese	
G-BELT	Cessna F.150J	A. Kumar (G-AWUV)	
G-BEMB	Cessna F.172M	Stocklaunch Ltd	
G-BEMM	Slingsby T.31B Motor Cadet III	E. and P. McEvoy	
G-BEMU	Thunder Ax5-42 S1 balloon	M. A. Hall	
G-BEMW	PA-28-181 Archer II	Touch & Go Ltd	
G-BEMY	Cessna FRA.150M	J. R. Power	
G-BEND	Cameron V-56 balloon	Dante Balloon Group	
G-BENJ	Rockwell Commander 112B	BENJ Flying Group	
G-BENK	Cessna F.172M	Bulldog Aviation Ltd	
G-BENN	Cameron V-56 balloon	S. J. Hollingsworth & M. K. Bellamy	
G-BEOD	Cessna 180H	I. Addy	
G-BEOE	Cessna FRA.150M	W. J. Henderson	
G-BEOH	PA-28R-201T Turbo Arrow III	Gloucestershire Flying Club	
G-BEOI	PA-18 Super Cub 150	Southdown Gliding Club Ltd	
G-BEOK	Cessna F.150M	KPOW Ltd	
G-BEOL	Short SC.7 Skyvan 3 variant 100	Invicta Aviation Ltd	
G-BEOX	Lockheed 414 Hudson IV (A16-199) ★	RAF Museum/Hendon	
G-BEOY	Cessna FRA.150L	J. N. Ponsford	
G-BEOZ	A.W.650 Argosy 101 ★	Aeropark/East Midlands	
G-BEPF	SNCAN Stampe SV.4A	C. C. Rollings & F. J. Hodson	
G-BEPV	Fokker S.11-1 Instructor (174)	S. W. & M. Isbister & C. Tyers	
G-BEPY	Rockwell Commander 112B	T. L. Rippon	
G-BERA	SOCATA Rallye 150ST	A. C. Stamp	
G-BERC	SOCATA Rallye 150ST	Severn Valley Aero Group	
G-BERI	Rockwell Commander 114	K. B. Harper	
G-BERN	Saffrey S-330 balloon	B. Martin	
G-BERT	Cameron V-56 balloon	Southern Balloon Group *Bert*	
G-BERY	AA-1B Trainer	R. H. J. Levi	
G-BETD	Robin HR.200/100	C. L. Wilsher	
G-BETE	Rollason B.2A Beta	T. M. Jones	
G-BETF	Cameron 'Champion' SS balloon ★	British Balloon Museum/Newbury	
G-BETI	Pitts S-1D Special	On A Roll Aerobatics Group (G-PIII)	
G-BETL	PA-25 Pawnee 235D	Cambridge University Gliding Trust Ltd	
G-BETM	PA-25 Pawnee 235D	Yorkshire Gliding Club (Pty) Ltd	
G-BEUA	PA-18 Super Cub 150	London Gliding Club (Pty) Ltd	
G-BEUD	Robin HR.100/285R	E. A. & L. M. C. Payton	
G-BEUI	Piper J-3C-65 Cub	M. C. Jordan	
G-BEUP	Robin DR.400/180	Samuels LLP	
G-BEUU	PA-18 Super Cub 95	F. Sharples	
G-BEUX	Cessna F.172N	Multiflight Ltd	
G-BEUY	Cameron N-31 balloon	J. J. Daly	
G-BEVB	SOCATA Rallye 150ST	M. Smullen	
G-BEVC	SOCATA Rallye 150ST	Peter Bolderson (Transport and Trading) Ltd	
G-BEVG	PA-34-200T-2 Seneca	Direct Aviation Management Ltd	
G-BEVO	Sportavia-Pützer RF-5	M. Hill	
G-BEVP	Evans VP-2	G. Moscrop & R. C. Crowley	
G-BEVS	Taylor JT.1 Monoplane	D. Hunter	
G-BEVT	BN-2A Mk III-2 Trislander	Aurigny Air Services Ltd	
G-BEVW	SOCATA Rallye 150ST	S. W. Brown	
G-BEWN	DH.82A Tiger Moth	H. D. Labouchere	

Notes	Reg.	Type	Owner or Operator
	G-BEWO	Zlin Z.326 Trener Master	P. A. Colman
	G-BEWR	Cessna F.172N	C. A. Breeze & R. C. Baker
	G-BEWX	PA-28R-201 Arrow III	Three Greens Arrow Group
	G-BEWY	Bell 206B JetRanger 3	Polo Aviation Ltd (G-CULL)
	G-BEXN	AA-1C Lynx	R. J. S. Ritchie
	G-BEXW	PA-28-181 Cherokee	J. O'Keeffe
	G-BEYA	Enstrom 280C	P. George
	G-BEYB	Fairey Flycatcher (replica) (S1287) ★	F.A.A. Museum/Yeovilton
	G-BEYF	HPR.7 Herald 401 ★	Jet Heritage Museum/Bournemouth
	G-BEYL	PA-28 Cherokee 180	Yankee Lima Group
	G-BEYT	PA-28 Cherokee 140	J. N. Plange
	G-BEYV	Cessna T.210M	Castleridge Ltd
	G-BEYW	Taylor JT.1 Monoplane	R. A. Abrahams
	G-BEYZ	Jodel DR.1051/M1	M. L. Balding
	G-BEZC	AA-5 Traveler	C. M. O'Connell
	G-BEZE	Rutan Vari-Eze	S. K. Cockburn
	G-BEZF	AA-5 Traveler	The ZF Group
	G-BEZG	AA-5 Traveler	M. D. R. Harling
	G-BEZH	AA-5 Traveler	Zulu Hotel Group
	G-BEZI	AA-5 Traveler	C. J. & L. Campbell
	G-BEZK	Cessna F.172H	S. Jones
	G-BEZL	PA-31-310 Turbo Navajo C	2 Excel Aviation Ltd
	G-BEZO	Cessna F.172M	Staverton Flying School
	G-BEZP	PA-32 Cherokee Six 300D	T. P. McCormack & J. K. Zealley
	G-BEZR	Cessna F.172M	Kirmington Aviation Ltd
	G-BEZV	Cessna F.172M	Insch Flying Group
	G-BEZY	Rutan Vari-Eze	I. J. Pountney
	G-BEZZ	Jodel D.112	G-BEZZ Jodel Group
	G-BFAA	Gardan GY-80 Horizon 160	G. R. Williams
	G-BFAF	Aeronca 7BCM (7797)	D. C. W. Harper
	G-BFAH	Phoenix Currie Wot	R. W. Clarke
	G-BFAI	Rockwell Commander 114	P. Ellingford & K. Eves
	G-BFAK	GEMS MS.892A Rallye Commodore 150	J. M. Hedges
	G-BFAP	SIAI-Marchetti S.205-20R	A. O. Broin
	G-BFAS	Evans VP-1	A. I. Sutherland
	G-BFAW	DHC.1 Chipmunk 22	R. V. Bowles
	G-BFAX	DHC.1 Chipmunk 22 (WG422)	M. F. Humphries
	G-BFBA	Jodel DR.100A	A. F. Vizoso
	G-BFBB	PA-23 Aztec 250E	D. Byrne
	G-BFBE	Robin HR.200/100	A. C. Pearson
	G-BFBM	Saffery S.330 balloon	B. Martin
	G-BFBR	PA-28-161 Warrior II	Phoenix Aviation
	G-BFBU	Partenavia P.68B	Reconnaissance Ventures Ltd
	G-BFBY	Piper J-3C-65 Cub	M. Shaw
	G-BFCT	Cessna Tu.206F	D. I. Schellingerhout
	G-BFDC	DHC.1 Chipmunk 22 (WG475)	N. F. O'Neill
	G-BFDE	Sopwith Tabloid (replica) (168) ★	RAF Museum/Hendon
	G-BFDF	SOCATA Rallye 235E	M. A. Wratten
	G-BFDI	PA-28-181 Archer II	Truman Aviation Ltd
	G-BFDK	PA-28-161 Warrior II	S. T. Gilbert
	G-BFDL	Piper J-3C-65 Cub (454537:J-04)	B. A. Nicholson & P. J. Lochhead
	G-BFDO	PA-28R-201T Turbo Arrow III	J. Blackburn & J. Driver
	G-BFEB	Jodel 150	Jodel EB Group
	G-BFEF	Agusta-Bell 47G-3B1	I. F. Vaughan
	G-BFEH	Jodel D.117A	J. A. Crabb
	G-BFEK	Cessna F.152	Staverton Flying School
	G-BFEV	PA-25 Pawnee 235	Trent Valley Aerotowing Club Ltd
	G-BFFE	Cessna F.152-II	A. J. Hastings
	G-BFFJ	Sikorsky S-61N Mk II	Veritair Ltd *Tresco*
	G-BFFP	PA-18 Super Cub 150 (modified)	East Sussex Gliding Club Ltd
	G-BFFT	Cameron V-56 balloon	R. I. M. Kerr & D. C. Boxall
	G-BFFW	Cessna F.152	Aircraft Engineers Ltd
	G-BFGD	Cessna F.172N-II	J. T. Armstrong
	G-BFGG	Cessna FRA.150M	J. M. Machin
	G-BFGH	Cessna F.337G	T. Perkins
	G-BFGK	Jodel D.117	B. F. J. Hope
	G-BFGL	Cessna FA.152	E-Pane Ltd
	G-BFGS	MS.893E Rallye 180GT	Chiltern Flyers Ltd
	G-BFGX	Cessna FRA.150M	Aircraft Engineers Ltd
	G-BFGZ	Cessna FRA.150M	C. M. Barnes
	G-BFHH	DH.82A Tiger Moth	P. Harrison & M. J. Gambrell
	G-BFHI	Piper J-3C-65 Cub	N. Glass & A. J. Richardson

Reg.	Type	Owner or Operator	Notes
G-BFHP	Champion 7GCAA Citabria	Citabriation Group	
G-BFHR	Jodel DR.220/2+2	J. E. Sweetman	
G-BFHU	Cessna F.152-II	D. J. Cooke & Co Ltd	
G-BFHV	Cessna F.152-II	Falcon Flying Services	
G-BFIB	PA-31 Turbo Navajo	Richard Hannon Ltd	
G-BFID	Taylor JT.2 Titch Mk III	N. Jamieson	
G-BFIE	Cessna FRA.150M	J. P. A. Freeman	
G-BFIG	Cessna FR.172K XPII	Tenair Ltd	
G-BFIJ	AA-5A Cheetah	T. H. & M. G. Weetman	
G-BFIN	AA-5A Cheetah	Aircraft Engineers Ltd	
G-BFIP	Wallbro Monoplane 1909 (replica) ★	Norfolk & Suffolk Aviation Museum/Flixton	
G-BFIT	Thunder Ax6-56Z balloon	J. A. G. Tyson	
G-BFIU	Cessna FR.172K XP	The G-BFIU Flying Group	
G-BFIV	Cessna F.177RG	C. Fisher	
G-BFIX	Thunder Ax7-77A balloon	R. Owen	
G-BFIY	Cessna F.150M	R. J. Scott	
G-BFJJ	Evans VP-1	M. A. Watts	
G-BFJR	Cessna F.337G	Teal Aviation	
G-BFJZ	Robin DR.400/140B	Weald Air Services Ltd	
G-BFKB	Cessna F.172N	Shropshire Flying Group	
G-BFKF	Cessna FA.152	Aerolease Ltd	
G-BFKL	Cameron N-56 balloon	Merrythought Toys Ltd *Merrythought*	
G-BFLU	Cessna F.152	Swiftair Maintenance Ltd	
G-BFLX	AA-5A Cheetah	A. M. Verdon	
G-BFLZ	Beech 95-A55 Baron	R. Tang	
G-BFMF	Cassutt Racer IIIM	M. C. R. Sims	
G-BFMG	PA-28-161 Warrior II	Bills Aviation Ltd	
G-BFMH	Cessna 177B	Aerofoil Aviation Ltd	
G-BFMK	Cessna FA.152	The Leicestershire Aero Club Ltd	
G-BFMR	PA-20 Pacer 125	J. Knight	
G-BFMX	Cessna F.172N	A2Z Wholesale Fashion Jewellery Ltd	
G-BFNG	Jodel D.112	NG Group	
G-BFNI	PA-28-161 Warrior II	Lion Services	
G-BFNK	PA-28-161 Warrior II	Aviation Rentals	
G-BFNM	Globe GC-1B Swift	M. J. Butler	
G-BFOE	Cessna F.152	Redhill Air Services Ltd	
G-BFOF	Cessna F.152	Staverton Flying School	
G-BFOG	Cessna 150M	B. F. Spafford	
G-BFOJ	AA-1 Yankee	N. W. Thomas	
G-BFOP	Jodel D.120	R. J. Wesley & G. D. Western	
G-BFOU	Taylor JT.1 Monoplane	G. Bee	
G-BFOV	Cessna F.172N	D. J. Walker	
G-BFPA	Scheibe SF.25B Falke	Tay Forth Falke Syndicate	
G-BFPH	Cessna F.172K	Linc-Air Flying Group	
G-BFPO	Rockwell Commander 112B	Doerr International Ltd	
G-BFPR	PA-25 Pawnee 235D	The Windrushers Gliding Club Ltd	
G-BFPS	PA-25 Pawnee 235D	Kent Gliding Club Ltd	
G-BFPZ	Cessna F.177RG Cardinal	O. C. Baars	
G-BFRD	Bowers Fly-Baby 1A	R. A. Phillips	
G-BFRI	Sikorsky S-61N	British International	
G-BFRR	Cessna FRA.150M	Romeo Romeo Flying Group	
G-BFRS	Cessna F.172N	Aerocomm Ltd	
G-BFRV	Cessna FA.152	Cristal Air Ltd	
G-BFRY	PA-25 Pawnee 260	Yorkshire Gliding Club (Pty) Ltd	
G-BFSA	Cessna F.182Q	Ensiform Aviation Ltd	
G-BFSC	PA-25 Pawnee 235D	Essex Gliding Club Ltd	
G-BFSD	PA-25 Pawnee 235D	Deeside Gliding Club (Aberdeenshire) Ltd	
G-BFSR	Cessna F.150J	W. Ali	
G-BFSS	Cessna FR.172G	Albedale Farms Ltd	
G-BFSY	PA-28-181 Archer II	Downland Aviation	
G-BFTA	PA-28-161 Warrior II	D. A. G. Roseblade	
G-BFTC	PA-28R-201T Turbo Arrow III	Top Cat Flying Group	
G-BFTF	AA-5B Tiger	F. C. Burrow Ltd	
G-BFTG	AA-5B Tiger	D. Hepburn & G. R. Montgomery	
G-BFTH	Cessna F.172N	T. W. Oakley	
G-BFTX	Cessna F.172N	Tri Society	
G-BFUB	PA-32RT-300 Lance II	Jolida Holdings Ltd	
G-BFUD	Scheibe SF.25E Super Falke	SF25E Syndicate	
G-BFUZ	Cameron V-77 balloon	Servowarm Balloon Syndicate	
G-BFVG	PA-28-181 Archer II	P. Anderson	
G-BFVH	DH.2 (replica) (5964)	S. W. Turley	
G-BFVS	AA-5B Tiger	G-BFVS Flying Group	

Notes	Reg.	Type	Owner or Operator
	G-BFVU	Cessna 150L	Aviation South West Ltd
	G-BFWB	PA-28-161 Warrior II	Mid-Anglia School of Flying
	G-BFWD	Currie Wot (C3009)	D. Silsbury & B. Proctor
	G-BFXF	Andreasson BA.4B	P. N. Birch
	G-BFXG	D.31 Turbulent	E. J. I. Musty & M. J. Whatley
	G-BFXK	PA-28 Cherokee 140	The G-BFXK Owners Group
	G-BFXL	Albatros D.5a replica (D5397/17) ★	F.A.A. Museum/Yeovilton
	G-BFXR	Jodel D.112	R. G. Marshall
	G-BFXS	Rockwell Commander 114	Romeo Whiskey Ltd
	G-BFXW	AA-5B Tiger	Campsol Ltd
	G-BFXX	AA-5B Tiger	W. R. Gibson
	G-BFYA	MBB Bö.105DB	Sterling Helicopters Ltd
	G-BFYC	PA-32RT-300 Lance II	A. A. Barnes
	G-BFYI	Westland-Bell 47G-3B1	K. P. Mayes
	G-BFYK	Cameron V-77 balloon	L. E. Jones
	G-BFYL	Evans VP-2	W. C. Brown
	G-BFYM	PA-28-161 Warrior II	52nd Street
	G-BFYO	SPAD XIII (replica) (4513:1) ★	American Air Museum/Duxford
	G-BFYW	Slingsby T.65A Vega	S. A. Whitaker
	G-BFZB	Piper J-3C-85 Cub (480723:E5-J)	M. S. Pettit
	G-BFZD	Cessna FR.182RG	R. B. Lewis & Co
	G-BFZH	PA-28R Cherokee Arrow 200	M. Soojeri
	G-BFZM	Rockwell Commander 112TC	J. A. Hart & R. J. Lamplough
	G-BFZO	AA-5A Cheetah	J. W. Cross & A. E. Kempson
	G-BFZU	Cessna FA.152	BJ Aviation Ltd
	G-BFZV	Cessna F.172M	The Army Flying Association
	G-BGAA	Cessna 152 II	PJC Leasing Ltd
	G-BGAB	Cessna F.152 II	TG Aviation Ltd
	G-BGAE	Cessna F.152 II	Aerolease Ltd
	G-BGAF	Cessna FA.152	G-BGAF Group
	G-BGAG	Cessna F.172N	R. Clarke
	G-BGAJ	Cessna F.182Q II	B. Blumberg
	G-BGAX	PA-28 Cherokee 140	G-BGAX Group
	G-BGAZ	Cameron V-77 balloon	C. J. Madigan & D. H. McGibbon
	G-BGBA	Robin R.2100A	Cotswold Aviation Services Ltd
	G-BGBE	Jodel DR.1050	J. A. & B. Mawby
	G-BGBF	Druine D.31 Turbulent	T. A. Stambach
	G-BGBG	PA-28-181 Archer II	Harlow Printing Ltd
	G-BGBI	Cessna F.150L	T. J. Gilpin & P. M. Cobban
	G-BGBK	PA-38-112 Tomahawk	Truman Aviation Ltd
	G-BGBN	PA-38-112 Tomahawk	Bonus Aviation Ltd
	G-BGBR	Cessna F.172N	Willowair Flying Club
	G-BGBV	Slingsby T65A Vega	Vega Syndicate BGA2800
	G-BGBW	PA-38-112 Tomahawk	Truman Aviation Ltd
	G-BGBZ	Rockwell Commander 114	G. W. Dimmer
	G-BGCB	Slingsby T.65A Vega	P. W. Williams
	G-BGCM	AA-5A Cheetah	G. & S. A. Jones
	G-BGCO	PA-44-180 Seminole	BAE Systems (Operations) Ltd
	G-BGCU	Slingsby T.65A Vega	K. Challinor
	G-BGCY	Taylor JT.1 Monoplane	A. T. Lane
	G-BGEH	Monnett Sonerai II	D. & V. T. Hubbard
	G-BGEI	Baby Great Lakes	M. T. Taylor
	G-BGFC	Evans VP-2	S. W. C. Hollins
	G-BGFF	FRED Srs 2	I Pearson & P. C. Appleton
	G-BGFI	AA-5A Cheetah	T. Balstad
	G-BGFJ	Jodel D.9 Bébé	O. G. Jones
	G-BGFT	PA-34-200T Seneca II	Oxford Aviation Academy (Oxford) Ltd
	G-BGFX	Cessna F.152	Redhill Air Services Ltd
	G-BGGA	Bellanca 7GCBC Citabria	L. A. King
	G-BGGB	Bellanca 7GCBC Citabria	Citabria Syndicate
	G-BGGC	Bellanca 7GCBC Citabria	G-BGGC RPA Memorial Group
	G-BGGD	Bellanca 8GCBC Scout	Bristol & Gloucestershire Gliding Club
	G-BGGE	PA-38-112 Tomahawk	Truman Aviation Ltd
	G-BGGG	PA-38-112 Tomahawk	GGG Group
	G-BGGI	PA-38-112 Tomahawk	Truman Aviation Ltd
	G-BGGL	PA-38-112 Tomahawk	Bonus Aircraft Ltd
	G-BGGM	PA-38-112 Tomahawk	Bonus Aircraft Ltd
	G-BGGO	Cessna F.152	East Midlands Flying School Ltd
	G-BGGP	Cessna F.152	East Midlands Flying School Ltd
	G-BGGU	Wallis WA-116/RR	K. H. Wallis
	G-BGGW	Wallis WA-112	K. H. Wallis

Reg.	Type	Owner or Operator	Notes
G-BGHF	Westland WG.30 ★	IHM/Weston-super-Mare	
G-BGHI	Cessna F.152	V. R. McCready	
G-BGHJ	Cessna F.172N	Air Plane Ltd	
G-BGHM	Robin R.1180T	H. Price	
G-BGHP	Beech 76 Duchess	Magneta Ltd	
G-BGHS	Cameron N-31 balloon	G. Gray	
G-BGHT	Falconar F-12	C. R. Coates	
G-BGHU	NA T-6G Texan (115042:TA-042)	C. E. Bellhouse	
G-BGHY	Taylor JT.1 Monoplane	G. W. Hancox	
G-BGHZ	FRED Srs 2	A. J. Perry	
G-BGIB	Cessna 152 II	Redhill Air Services Ltd	
G-BGIG	PA-38-112 Tomahawk	Air Claire Ltd	
G-BGIU	Cessna F.172H	A. G. Arthur	
G-BGIX	Helio H.295 Super Courier	C. M. Lee	
G-BGIY	Cessna F.172N	Air Claire Ltd	
G-BGJU	Cameron V-65 Balloon	J. A. Folkes	
G-BGKC	SOCATA Rallye 110ST	J. H. Cranmer	
G-BGKO	Gardan GY-20 Minicab	M. N. King	
G-BGKS	PA-28-161 Warrior II	Mid America (UK) Ltd	
G-BGKT	Auster AOP.9 (XN441)	Kilo Tango Group	
G-BGKU	PA-28R-201 Arrow III	Aerolease Ltd	
G-BGKV	PA-28R-201 Arrow III	R. Haverson & A. K. Lake	
G-BGKY	PA-38-112 Tomahawk	APB Leasing Ltd	
G-BGKZ	Auster J/5F Aiglet Trainer	R. B. Webber	
G-BGLA	PA-38-112 Tomahawk	Norwich School of Flying	
G-BGLB	Bede BD-5B ★	Science Museum/Wroughton	
G-BGLF	Evans VP-1 Srs 2	B. A. Schlussler	
G-BGLG	Cessna 152	L. W. Scattergood	
G-BGLK	Monnett Sonerai 2L	J. Bradley	
G-BGLO	Cessna F.172N	J. R. Isabel	
G-BGLS	Oldfield FSuper Baby Lakes	J. F. Dowe	
G-BGLZ	Stits SA-3A Playboy	A. J. Collins	
G-BGME	SIPA 903	M. Emery (G-BCML)	
G-BGMJ	Gardan GY-201 Minicab	G-BGMJ Group	
G-BGMP	Cessna F.172G	B. M. O'Brien	
G-BGMS	Taylor JT.2 Titch	M. A. J. Spice	
G-BGMT	SOCATA Rallye 235E	C. G. Wheeler	
G-BGMV	Scheibe SF.25B Falke	I. P. Manley	
G-BGND	Cessna F.172N	A. J. M. Freeman	
G-BGNT	Cessna F.152	Aerolease Ltd	
G-BGNV	GA-7 Cougar	G. J. Bissex & D. D. Saint	
G-BGOD	Colt 77A balloon	C. Allen & M. D. Steuer	
G-BGOG	PA-28-161 Warrior II	W. D. Moore & F. J. Morris	
G-BGOL	PA-28R-201T Turbo Arrow III	R. G. Jackson	
G-BGON	GA-7 Cougar	Plane Talking Ltd	
G-BGOR	AT-6D Harvard III (14863)	P. Meyrick	
G-BGPB	CCF T-6J Texan (1747)	1959 Ltd	
G-BGPD	Piper J-3C-65 Cub (479744:M-49)	P. R. Whiteman	
G-BGPH	AA-5B Tiger	Shipping & Airlines Ltd	
G-BGPI	Plumb BGP-1	B. G. Plumb	
G-BGPJ	PA-28-161 Warrior II	W. Lancs Warrior Co Ltd	
G-BGPL	PA-28-161 Warrior II	Montash Properties Ltd	
G-BGPM	Evans VP-2	Cheap as Chips Group	
G-BGPN	PA-18 Super Cub 150	A. R. Darke	
G-BGRC	PA-28 Cherokee 140	Tecair Aviation Ltd & G. F. Haigh	
G-BGRE	Beech A200 Super King Air	Martin-Baker (Engineering) Ltd	
G-BGRG	Beech 76 Duchess	Aviation Rentals	
G-BGRI	Jodel DR.1051	R. G. Hallam	
G-BGRM	PA-38-112 Tomahawk	C. R. Salway	
G-BGRO	Cessna F.172M	Cammo Aviation	
G-BGRR	PA-38-112 Tomahawk	P. J. Montgomery	
G-BGRT	Steen Skybolt	O. Meier	
G-BGRX	PA-38-112 Tomahawk	Bonus Aviation Ltd	
G-BGSA	Morane MS.892E-150	D. C. Tonkin	
G-BGSH	PA-38-112 Tomahawk	Hatfield Ltd	
G-BGSJ	Piper J-3C-65 Cub	A. J. Higgins	
G-BGSV	Cessna F.172N	Southwell Air Services Ltd	
G-BGSW	Beech F33 Debonair	C. Wood	
G-BGSY	GA-7 Cougar	N. D. Anderson	
G-BGTC	Auster AOP.9 (XP282)	Terranne Auster Group	
G-BGTG	PA-23 Aztec 250F	ASG Leasing Ltd	
G-BGTI	Piper J-3C-65 Cub	A. P. Broad	

Notes	Reg.	Type	Owner or Operator
	G-BGTT	Cessna 310R	Capital Air Charter Ltd
	G-BGUB	PA-32 Cherokee Six 300E	A. P. Diplock
	G-BGVB	Robin DR.315	P. J. Leggo
	G-BGVE	CP.1310-C3 Super Emeraude	R. Whitwell
	G-BGVH	Beech 76 Duchess	Velco Marketing
	G-BGVK	PA-28-161 Warrior II	Aviation South West Ltd
	G-BGVN	PA-28RT-201 Arrow IV	John Wailing Ltd
	G-BGVS	Cessna F.172M	Orkney Flying Club
	G-BGVV	AA-5A Cheetah	W. A. Davidson
	G-BGVY	AA-5B Tiger	R. J. C. Neal-Smith
	G-BGVZ	PA-28-181 Archer II	M. & W. Walsh
	G-BGWC	Robin DR.400/180	M. A. Newman
	G-BGWM	PA-28-181 Archer II	Thames Valley Flying Club Ltd
	G-BGWN	PA-38-112 Tomahawk	J. R. Davison
	G-BGWO	Jodel D.112	P. Westerby-Jones
	G-BGWR	Cessna U.206A	Parachuting Aircraft Ltd (G-DISC)
	G-BGWV	Aeronca 7AC Champion	RFC Flying Group
	G-BGWZ	Eclipse Super Eagle ★	F.A.A. Museum/Yeovilton
	G-BGXA	Piper J-3C-65 Cub (329471:F-44)	P. King
	G-BGXC	SOCATA TB10 Tobago	D. H. Courtley
	G-BGXD	SOCATA TB10 Tobago	D. F. P. Finan
	G-BGXO	PA-38-112 Tomahawk	Goodwood Terrena Ltd
	G-BGXR	Robin HR.200/100	J. R. Cross
	G-BGXS	PA-28-236 Dakota	G-BGXS Group
	G-BGXT	SOCATA TB10 Tobago	J. L. Alexander
	G-BGYH	PA-28-161 Warrior II	Paper Space Ltd
	G-BGYN	PA-18 Super Cub 150	B. J. Dunford
	G-BGZF	PA-38-112 Tomahawk	APB Leasing Ltd
	G-BHAA	Cessna 152 II	Herefordshire Aero Club Ltd
	G-BHAD	Cessna A.152	Shropshire Aero Club Ltd
	G-BHAI	Cessna F.152	Scottish Aircraft Sales
	G-BHAJ	Robin DR.400/160	Rowantask Ltd
	G-BHAR	Westland-Bell 47G-3B1	T. J. Wright
	G-BHAV	Cessna F.152	T. M. & M. L. Jones
	G-BHAW	Cessna F.172N	J. Smith
	G-BHAX	Enstrom F-28C-UK-2	PVS (Barnsley) Ltd
	G-BHAY	PA-28RT-201 Arrow IV	Alpha Yankee Ltd
	G-BHBA	Campbell Cricket	S. N. McGovern
	G-BHBE	Westland-Bell 47G-3B1 (Soloy)	T. R. Smith (Agricultural Machinery) Ltd
	G-BHBG	PA-32R Cherokee Lance 300	D. E. Gee
	G-BHBT	Marquart MA.5 Charger	Charger Group
	G-BHBZ	Partenavia P.68B	Reconnaissance Ventures
	G-BHCC	Cessna 172M	D. Wood-Jenkins
	G-BHCE	Jodel D.112	D. G. Jones
	G-BHCM	Cessna F.172H	J. Dominic
	G-BHCP	Cessna F.152	Eastern Air Executive Ltd
	G-BHCZ	PA-38-112 Tomahawk	J. E. Abbott
	G-BHDD	V.668 Varsity T.1 (WL626:P) ★	Aeropark/East Midlands
	G-BHDE	SOCATA TB10 Tobago	Alpha-Alpha Ltd
	G-BHDK	Boeing B-29A-BN (461748:Y) ★	Imperial War Museum/Duxford
	G-BHDM	Cessna F.152 II	Big Red Kite Ltd
	G-BHDP	Cessna F.182Q II	Zone Travel Ltd
	G-BHDS	Cessna F.152 II	Tayside Aviation Ltd
	G-BHDV	Cameron V-77 balloon	P. Glydon
	G-BHDW	Cessna F.152 II	Aircraft Engineers Ltd
	G-BHDX	Cessna F.172N	GDX Ltd
	G-BHDZ	Cessna F.172N	Abbey Security Services Ltd
	G-BHEC	Cessna F.152 II	Stapleford Flying Club Ltd
	G-BHED	Cessna FA.152	TG Aviation Ltd
	G-BHEG	Jodel 150	D. M. Griffiths
	G-BHEK	CP.1315-C3 Super Emeraude	D. B. Winstanley
	G-BHEL	Jodel D.117	M. A. Child
	G-BHEM	Bensen B.8M	G. C. Kerr
	G-BHEN	Cessna FA.152	Leicestershire Aero Club Ltd
	G-BHEU	Thunder Ax7-65 balloon	J. A. W. Dyer
	G-BHEV	PA-28R Cherokee Arrow 200	7-Up Group
	G-BHEX	Colt 56A balloon	A. S. Dear & ptnrs
	G-BHEZ	Jodel 150	Air Yorkshire Group
	G-BHFC	Cessna F.152	P. S. Thompson
	G-BHFE	PA-44-180 Seminole	Bonus Aviation Ltd
	G-BHFG	SNCAN Stampe SV.4C	A. D. R. Northeast & S. A. Cook
	G-BHFH	PA-34-200T Seneca II	Oxford Aviation Academy (Oxford) Ltd

Reg.	Type	Owner or Operator	Notes
G-BHFI	Cessna F.152	BAe (Warton) Flying Club	
G-BHFJ	PA-28RT-201T Turbo Arrow IV	J. K. Beauchamp	
G-BHFK	PA-28-151 Warrior	Ilkeston Car Sales Ltd	
G-BHGC	PA-18 Super Cub 150	Vectis Gliding Club Ltd	
G-BHGF	Cameron V-56 balloon	P. Smallward	
G-BHGJ	Jodel D.120	Q. M. B. Oswell	
G-BHGO	PA-32 Cherokee Six 260	L. C. Myall	
G-BHGY	PA-28R Cherokee Arrow 200	Truman Aviation Ltd	
G-BHHB	Cameron V-77 balloon	R. Powell	
G-BHHE	Jodel DR.1051/M1	P. Bridges & P. C. Matthews	
G-BHHG	Cessna F.152 II	TG Aviation Ltd	
G-BHHH	Thunder Ax7-65 balloon	J. M. J. Roberts	
G-BHHK	Cameron N-77 balloon ★	British Balloon Museum	
G-BHHN	Cameron V-77 balloon	Itchen Valley Balloon Group	
G-BHHX	Jodel D.112	G-BHHX Group	
G-BHIB	Cessna F.182Q	S. N. Chater & B. Payne	
G-BHII	Cameron V-77 balloon	R. V. Brown	
G-BHIJ	Eiri PIK-20E-1 (898)	P. M. Yeoman	
G-BHIN	Cessna F.152	Target Aviation Ltd	
G-BHIR	PA-28R Cherokee Arrow 200	Factorcore Ltd	
G-BHIS	Thunder Ax7-65 balloon	Hedgehoppers Balloon Group	
G-BHIY	Cessna F.150K	G. J. Ball	
G-BHJF	SOCATA TB10 Tobago	Tyas Aviation Ltd	
G-BHJI	Mooney M.20J	Hearing Centre Aarhus/Denmark	
G-BHJK	Maule M5-235C Lunar Rocket	P. J. Kelsey	
G-BHJN	Fournier RF-4D	RF-4 Group	
G-BHJO	PA-28-161 Warrior II	Brackla Flying Group	
G-BHJS	Partenavia P.68B	Flew LLP	
G-BHJU	Robin DR.400/2+2	Ageless Aeronautics	
G-BHKJ	Cessna 421C	Totaljet Ltd	
G-BHKR	Colt 12A balloon ★	British Balloon Museum/Newbury	
G-BHKT	Jodel D.112	G. Dawes	
G-BHLE	Robin DR.400/180	A. V. Harmer	
G-BHLH	Robin DR.400/180	G-BHLH Group	
G-BHLJ	Saffery-Rigg S.200 balloon	I. A. Rigg	
G-BHLT	DH.82A Tiger Moth	Skymax (Aviation) Ltd	
G-BHLU	Fournier RF-3	G. Sabatino	
G-BHLW	Cessna 120	L. W. Scattergood	
G-BHLX	AA-5B Tiger	M. D. McPherson	
G-BHMA	SIPA 903	H. J. Taggart	
G-BHMG	Cessna FA.152	R. D. Smith	
G-BHMI	Cessna F.172N	GMI Aviation Ltd (G-WADE)	
G-BHMJ	Avenger T.200-2112 balloon	R. Light *Lord Anthony 1*	
G-BHMK	Avenger T.200-2112 balloon	P. Kinder *Lord Anthony 2*	
G-BHMT	Evans VP-1	R. T. Callow	
G-BHMY	F.27 Friendship Mk.200 ★	Norwich Aviation Museum	
G-BHNA	Cessna F.152 II	Eastern Air Executive Ltd	
G-BHNC	Cameron O-65 balloon	D. & C. Bareford	
G-BHNK	Jodel D.120A	K. R. Daly	
G-BHNL	Jodel D.112	M. D. Mold	
G-BHNO	PA-28-181 Archer II	B. J. Richardson	
G-BHNP	Eiri PIK-20E-1	D. A. Sutton	
G-BHNV	Westlan-Bell 47G-3B1	Leyline Helicopters Ltd	
G-BHNX	Jodel D.117	M. J. A. Trudgill	
G-BHOA	Robin DR.400/160	T. L. Trott	
G-BHOG	Sikorsky S-61N Mk.II	British International	
G-BHOJ	Colt 12A balloon	J. A. Folkes	
G-BHOL	Jodel DR.1050	S. J. Pearson	
G-BHOM	PA-18 Super Cub 95	Oscar Mike Flying Group	
G-BHOR	PA-28-161 Warrior II	Oscar Romeo Flying Group	
G-BHOT	Cameron V-65 balloon	Dante Balloon Group	
G-BHOZ	SOCATA TB9 Tampico	G-BHOZ Flying Group	
G-BHPK	Piper J-3C-65 Cub (238410:A-44)	L-4 Group	
G-BHPL	CASA 1.131E Jungmann 1000 (E3B-350:05-97) ★	A. Burroughes	
G-BHPS	Jodel D.120A	T. J. Price	
G-BHPY	Cessna 152 II	A. J. Gomes	
G-BHPZ	Cessna 172N	O'Brien Properties Ltd	
G-BHRC	PA-28-161 Warrior II	Sherwood Flying Club Ltd	
G-BHRH	Cessna FA.150K	Merlin Flying Club Ltd	
G-BHRO	Rockwell Commander 112	R. A. Blackwell	
G-BHRR	CP.301A Emeraude	T. W. Offen	

Notes	Reg.	Type	Owner or Operator
	G-BHRW	Jodel DR.221	Dauphin Flying Club
	G-BHSB	Cessna 172N	J. W. Cope & M. P. Wimsey
	G-BHSD	Scheibe SF.25E Super Falke	Upwood Motorglider Group
	G-BHSE	Rockwell Commander 114	604 Sqdn Flying Group Ltd
	G-BHSN	Cameron N-56 balloon	I. Bentley
	G-BHSS	Pitts S-1S Special	C. E. Oestringer
	G-BHSY	Jodel DR.1050	T. R. Allebone
	G-BHTA	PA-28-236 Dakota	Dakota Ltd
	G-BHTC	Jodel DR.1050/M1	G. Clark
	G-BHUB	Douglas C-47A (315509:W7-S) ★	Imperial War Museum/Duxford
	G-BHUE	Jodel DR.1050	M. J. Harris
	G-BHUG	Cessna 172N	G-BHUG Group
	G-BHUI	Cessna 152	South Warwickshire School of Flying Ltd
	G-BHUJ	Cessna 172N	Uniform Juliet Group
	G-BHUM	DH.82A Tiger Moth	S. G. Towers
	G-BHUU	PA-25 Pawnee 235	Booker Gliding Club Ltd
	G-BHVF	Jodel 150A	R. V. Smith
	G-BHVP	Cessna 182Q	R. J. W. Wood
	G-BHVR	Cessna 172N	Victor Romeo Group
	G-BHVV	Piper J-3C-65 Cub	C. A. Ward & C. A. Cash
	G-BHWA	Cessna F.152	Lincoln Enterprises Ltd
	G-BHWB	Cessna F.152	Lincoln Enterprises Ltd
	G-BHWH	Weedhopper JC-24A	G. A. Clephane
	G-BHWK	MS.880B Rallye Club	P. Sharpe
	G-BHWY	PA-28R Cherokee Arrow 200-II	Kilo Foxtrot Flying Group
	G-BHWZ	PA-28-181 Archer II	M. A. Abbott
	G-BHXA	SA Bulldog Srs 120/1210	Air Plan Flight Equipment Ltd
	G-BHXD	Jodel D.120	D. A. Garner
	G-BHXK	PA-28 Cherokee 140	GXK Flying Group
	G-BHXS	Jodel D.120	Plymouth Jodel Group
	G-BHXY	Piper J-3C-65 Cub (44-79609:44-S)	F. W. Rogers
	G-BHYA	Cessna R.182RG II	J-P. Jarier
	G-BHYC	Cessna 172RG II	IB Aeroplanes Ltd
	G-BHYD	Cessna R.172K XP II	Sylmar Aviation Services Ltd
	G-BHYG	PA-34-200T Seneca II	Oxford Aviation Academy (Oxford) Ltd
	G-BHYI	SNCAN Stampe SV.4A	D. Hicklin
	G-BHYP	Cessna F.172M	Avior Ltd
	G-BHYR	Cessna F.172M	G-BHYR Group
	G-BHYV	Evans VP-1	I. P. Manley
	G-BHYX	Cessna 152 II	Stapleford Flying Club Ltd
	G-BHZE	PA-28-181 Archer II	Zegruppe Ltd
	G-BHZH	Cessna F.152	Plymouth Flying School Ltd
	G-BHZK	AA-5B Tiger	ZK Group
	G-BHZO	AA-5A Cheetah	PG Air
	G-BHZR	SA Bulldog Srs 120/1210	White Knuckle Air Ltd
	G-BHZS	SA Bulldog Srs 120/1210	Air Plan Flight Equipment Ltd
	G-BHZT	SA Bulldog Srs 120/1210	D. M. Curties
	G-BHZU	Piper J-3C-65 Cub	J. K. Tomkinson
	G-BHZV	Jodel D.120A	G-BHZV Group
	G-BIAC	SOCATA Rallye 235E	G-BIAC Flying Group
	G-BIAH	Jodel D.112	P. A. Gange
	G-BIAI	WMB.2 Windtracker balloon	I. Chadwick
	G-BIAP	PA-16 Clipper	G-BIAP Flying Group
	G-BIAR	Rigg Skyliner II balloon	I. A. Rigg
	G-BIAU	Sopwith Pup (replica) (N6452) ★	F.A.A. Museum/Yeovilton
	G-BIAX	Taylor JT.2 Titch	D. M. Bland
	G-BIAY	AA-5 Traveler	P. Moderate
	G-BIBA	SOCATA TB9 Tampico	TB Aviation Ltd
	G-BIBJ	Enstrom 280C-UK-2	Startrade GmbH
	G-BIBN	Cessna FA.150K	B. V. Mayo
	G-BIBO	Cameron V-65 balloon	D. M. Hoddinott
	G-BIBS	Cameron P-20 balloon	Cameron Balloons Ltd
	G-BIBT	AA-5B Tiger	Horizon Aviation Ltd
	G-BIBW	Cessna F.172N	Shields Estates Ltd
	G-BIBX	WMB.2 Windtracker balloon	I. A. Rigg
	G-BICD	Auster 5	T. R. Parsons
	G-BICE	NA AT-6C Harvard IIA (41-33275:CE)	C. M. L. Edwards
	G-BICG	Cessna F.152 II	Falcon Flying Services
	G-BICM	Colt 56A balloon	Avon Advertiser Balloon Club
	G-BICP	Robin DR.360	B. McVeighty
	G-BICR	Jodel D.120A	Beehive Flying Group

Reg.	Type	Owner or Operator	Notes
G-BICS	Robin R.2100A	I. Young	
G-BICU	Cameron V-56 balloon	Black Pearl Balloons	
G-BICW	PA-28-161 Warrior II	Charlie Whisky Flying Group	
G-BICX	Maule M5-235C Lunar Rocket	I. S. McLeod & J. L. Yourell	
G-BIDD	Evans VP-1	J. Hodgkinson	
G-BIDF	Cessna F.172P	C. J. Chaplin & N. J. C. Howard	
G-BIDG	Jodel 150A	D. R. Gray	
G-BIDH	Cessna 152 II	Hull Aero Club Ltd (G-DONA)	
G-BIDI	PA-28R-201 Arrow III	T. A. N. Brierley & A. Lidster	
G-BIDJ	PA-18A Super Cub 150	Flight Solutions Ltd	
G-BIDK	PA-18 Super Cub 150	K. Butterfield	
G-BIDO	CP.301A Emeraude	A. R. Plumb	
G-BIDV	Colt 14A balloon ★	British Balloon Museum/Newbury	
G-BIDW	Sopwith 1½ Strutter (replica) (A8226) ★	RAF Museum/Hendon	
G-BIDX	Jodel D.112	P. Turton	
G-BIEJ	Sikorsky S-76A	Bristow Helicopters Ltd	
G-BIEN	Jodel D.120A	C. Newton/France	
G-BIEO	Jodel D.112	Clipgate Flyers	
G-BIES	Maule M5-235C Lunar Rocket	William Proctor Farms	
G-BIET	Cameron O-77 balloon	G. M. Westley	
G-BIEY	PA-28-151 Warrior	M. J. Isaac	
G-BIFA	Cessna 310R II	J. S. Lee	
G-BIFB	PA-28 Cherokee 150C	P. Coombs	
G-BIFO	Evans VP-1	D. C. Unwin	
G-BIFP	Colt 56A balloon	J. W. Adkins	
G-BIFY	Cessna F.150L	Bonus Aviation Ltd	
G-BIGJ	Cessna F.172M	Cirrus Aviation Ltd	
G-BIGK	Taylorcraft BC-12D	N. P. St. J. Ramsay	
G-BIGL	Cameron O-65 balloon	P. L. Mossman	
G-BIGR	Avenger T.200-2112 balloon	R. Light	
G-BIHD	Robin DR.400/160	G. I. J. Thomson & R. A. Hawkins	
G-BIHF	SE-5A (replica) (F943)	C. J. Zeal	
G-BIHI	Cessna 172M	E-Plane Ltd	
G-BIHO	DHC.6 Twin Otter 310	Isles of Scilly Skybus Ltd	
G-BIHT	PA-17 Vagabond	B. Carter	
G-BIHU	Saffrey S.200 balloon	B. L. King	
G-BIHX	Bensen B.8M	P. P. Willmott	
G-BIIA	Fournier RF-3	C. J. Riley	
G-BIIB	Cessna F.172M	Civil Service Flying Club (Biggin Hill) Ltd	
G-BIID	PA-18 Super Cub 95	D. A. Lacey	
G-BIIE	Cessna F.172P	Sterling Helicopters Ltd	
G-BIIK	MS.883 Rallye 115	N. J. Garbett	
G-BIIT	PA-28-161 Warrior II	Tayside Aviation Ltd	
G-BIIV	PA-28-181 Archer II	J. Thuret/France	
G-BIIZ	Great Lakes 2T-1A Sport Trainer	Circa 42 Ltd	
G-BIJB	PA-18 Super Cub 150	James Aero Ltd	
G-BIJD	Bölkow Bö.208C Junior	Sikh Sydicate	
G-BIJE	Piper J-3C-65 Cub	R. L. Hayward & A. G. Scott	
G-BIJS	Luton LA-4A Minor	I. J. Smith	
G-BIJU	CP-301A Emeraude	Eastern Taildraggers Flying Group (G-BHTX)	
G-BIJV	Cessna F.152 II	Falcon Flying Services	
G-BIJW	Cessna F.152 II	Falcon Flying Services	
G-BIJX	Cessna F.152 II	Falcon Flying Services	
G-BIKC	Boeng 757-236F	DHL Air Ltd	
G-BIKE	PA-28R Cherokee Arrow 200	R. Monette	
G-BIKF	Boeing 757-236F	DHL Air Ltd	
G-BIKG	Boeing 757-236F	DHL Air Ltd	
G-BIKI	Boeing 757-236F	DHL Air Ltd	
G-BIKJ	Boeing 757-236F	DHL Air Ltd	
G-BIKK	Boeing 757-236F	DHL Air Ltd	
G-BIKM	Boeing 757-236F	DHL Air Ltd	
G-BIKN	Boeing 757-236F	DHL Air Ltd	
G-BIKO	Boeing 757-236F	DHL Air Ltd	
G-BIKP	Boeing 757-236F	DHL Air Ltd	
G-BIKS	Boeing 757-236F	DHL Air Ltd	
G-BIKU	Boeing 757-236F	DHL Air Ltd	
G-BIKV	Boeing 757-236F	DHL Air Ltd	
G-BIKZ	Boeing 757-236F	DHL Air Ltd	
G-BILB	WMB.2 Windtracker balloon	B. L. King	
G-BILE	Scruggs BL.2B balloon	P. D. Ridout	
G-BILG	Scruggs BL.2B balloon	P. D. Ridout	
G-BILH	Slingsby T.65C Vega	M. M. Macdonald	

Notes	Reg.	Type	Owner or Operator
	G-BILI	Piper J-3C-65 Cub (454467:J-44)	G-BILI Flying Group
	G-BILL	PA-25 Pawnee 235	Pawnee Aviation
	G-BILR	Cessna 152 II	Shropshire Aero Club Ltd
	G-BILS	Cessna 152 II	Mona Flying Club
	G-BILU	Cessna 172RG	Full Sutton Flying Centre Ltd
	G-BILZ	Taylor JT.1 Monoplane	A. Petherbridge
	G-BIMK	Tiger T.200 Srs 1 balloon	M. K. Baron
	G-BIMM	PA-18 Super Cub 150	Spectrum Leisure Ltd
	G-BIMN	Steen Skybolt	R. J. Thomas
	G-BIMO	SNCAN Stampe SV.4C (394)	E. L. P. A. Dupont
	G-BIMT	Cessna FA.152	Staverton Flying Services
	G-BIMU	Sikorsky S-61N	Bristow Helicopters Ltd
	G-BIMX	Rutan Vari-Eze	D. G. Crow
	G-BIMZ	Beech 76 Duchess	R. P. Smith
	G-BINL	Scruggs BL.2B balloon	P. D. Ridout
	G-BINM	Scruggs BL.2B balloon	P. D. Ridout
	G-BINR	Unicorn UE.1A balloon	Unicorn Group
	G-BINS	Unicorn UE.2A balloon	Unicorn Group
	G-BINT	Unicorn UE.1A balloon	D. E. Bint
	G-BINX	Scruggs BL.2B balloon	P. D. Ridout
	G-BINY	Oriental balloon	J. L. Morton
	G-BIOA	Hughes 369D	AH Helicopter Services Ltd
	G-BIOB	Cessna F.172P	Network Mapping UK Ltd
	G-BIOC	Cessna F.150L	W. H. Milner
	G-BIOI	Jodel DR.1051/M	A. A. Alderdice
	G-BIOJ	Rockwell Commander 112TCA	A. T. Dalby
	G-BIOK	Cessna F.152	A. D. H. Macdonald
	G-BIOM	Cessna F.152	J. B. P. E. Fernandes
	G-BIOU	Jodel D.117A	D. C. Wellard
	G-BIOW	Slingsby T.67A	A. B. Slinger
	G-BIPA	AA-5B Tiger	Tri-Star Developments Ltd
	G-BIPH	Scruggs BL.2B balloon	C. M. Dewsnap
	G-BIPI	Everett gyroplane	C. A. Reeves
	G-BIPN	Fournier RF-3	G-BIPN Group
	G-BIPT	Jodel D.112	C. R. Davies
	G-BIPV	AA-5B Tiger	Echo Echo Ltd
	G-BIPW	Avenger T.200-2112 balloon	B. L. King
	G-BIRD	Pitts S-1D Special	N. E. Smith
	G-BIRE	Colt 56 Bottle SS balloon	D. J. Stagg
	G-BIRH	PA-18 Super Cub 135 (R-163)	Banbury Gliding Club Ltd
	G-BIRI	CASA 1.131E Jungmann 1000	D. Watt
	G-BIRL	Avenger T.200-2112 balloon	R. Light
	G-BIRP	Arena Mk 17 Skyship balloon	A. S. Viel
	G-BIRT	Robin R.1180TD	W. D'A. Hall
	G-BIRW	MS.505 Criquet (F+IS) ★	Museum of Flight/East Fortune
	G-BISG	FRED Srs 3	T. Littlefair
	G-BISH	Cameron V-65 balloon	P. J. Bish
	G-BISL	Scruggs BL.2B balloon	P. D. Ridout
	G-BISM	Scruggs BL.2B balloon	P. D. Ridout
	G-BISS	Scruggs BL.2C balloon	P. D. Ridout
	G-BIST	Scruggs BL.2C balloon	P. D. Ridout
	G-BISX	Colt 56A balloon	C. D. Steel
	G-BISZ	Sikorsky S-76A	Bristow Helicopters Ltd
	G-BITA	PA-18 Super Cub 150	Intrepid Aviation Co
	G-BITE	SOCATA TB10 Tobago	M. A. Smith
	G-BITF	Cessna F.152 II	G-BITF Owners Group
	G-BITH	Cessna F.152 II	J. R. Hyde (G-TFSA)
	G-BITK	FRED Srs 2	D. J. Wood
	G-BITM	Cessna F.172P	Dreamtrade Ltd
	G-BITO	Jodel D.112D	A. Dunbar
	G-BITY	FD.31T balloon	A. J. Bell
	G-BIUM	Cessna F.152	Eastern Air Executive Ltd
	G-BIUP	SNCAN NC.854S	J. Greenaway & T. D. Cooper
	G-BIUW	PA-28-161 Warrior II	D. R. Staley
	G-BIUY	PA-28-181 Archer II	J. S. Devlin & Z. Islam
	G-BIVA	Robin R.2112	Seahawk Flying Group
	G-BIVB	Jodel D.112	N. M. Harwood
	G-BIVC	Jodel D.112	M. J. Barmby
	G-BIVF	CP.301C-3 Emeraude	T. C. Darters
	G-BIVK	Bensen B.8M	M. J. Atyeo
	G-BIWB	Scruggs RS.5000 balloon	P. D. Ridout
	G-BIWC	Scruggs RS.5000 balloon	P. D. Ridout

Reg.	Type	Owner or Operator	Notes
G-BIWF	Warren balloon	P. D. Ridout	
G-BIWG	Zelenski Mk 2 balloon	P. D. Ridout	
G-BIWJ	Unicorn UE.1A balloon	B. L. King	
G-BIWK	Cameron V-65 balloon	I. R. Williams & R. G. Bickerdike	
G-BIWN	Jodel D.112	C. R. Coates & P. K. Morley	
G-BIWR	Mooney M.20F	M. Broady	
G-BIWU	Cameron V-65 balloon	W. Rousell & J. Tyrrell	
G-BIWW	AA-5 Traveler	Interlink Management Services Ltd	
G-BIWY	Westland WG.30 ★	Instructional airframe/Yeovil	
G-BIXA	SOCATA TB9 Tampico	W. Maxwell	
G-BIXB	SOCATA TB9 Tampico	B. G. Adams	
G-BIXH	Cessna F.152	Northumbria Flying School Ltd	
G-BIXL	P-51D Mustang (472216:HO-M)	R. Lamplough	
G-BIXN	Boeing Stearman A75N1 (FJ777)	V. S. E. Norman	
G-BIXW	Colt 56B balloon	N. A. P. Bates	
G-BIXX	Pearson Srs 2 balloon	D. Pearson	
G-BIXZ	Grob G-109	D. L. Nind & I. Allum	
G-BIYI	Cameron V-65 balloon	Sarnia Balloon Group	
G-BIYJ	PA-18 Super Cub 95	S. Russell	
G-BIYK	Isaacs Fury II	S. M. Roberts	
G-BIYP	PA-20 Pacer 125	A. W. Hoy & S. W. M. Johnson	
G-BIYR	PA-18 Super Cub 150 (R-151)	Delta Foxtrot Flying Group	
G-BIYU	Fokker S.11.1 Instructor (E-15)	Fokker Syndicate	
G-BIYW	Jodel D.112	A. Appleby	
G-BIYX	PA-28 Cherokee 140	W. B. Bateson	
G-BIYY	PA-18 Super Cub 95	A. E. & W. J. Taylor	
G-BIZE	SOCATA TB9 Tampico	Gloster Aero Group	
G-BIZF	Cessna F.172P	R. S. Bentley	
G-BIZG	Cessna F.152	M. A. Judge	
G-BIZI	Robin DR.400/120	Headcorn Flying School Ltd	
G-BIZK	Nord 3202 (78)	A. I. Milne	
G-BIZM	Nord 3202	Global Aviation Ltd	
G-BIZO	PA-28R Cherokee Arrow 200	Lemas Air	
G-BIZR	SOCATA TB9 Tampico	Fenland Flying Group (G-BSEC)	
G-BIZV	PA-18 Super Cub 95 (18-2001)	J. P. Nugent	
G-BIZW	Champion 7GCBC Citabria	G. Read & Sons	
G-BIZY	Jodel D.112	Wayland Tunley & Associates	
G-BJAD	FRED Srs 2 ★	Newark (Nottinghamshire & Lincolnshire) Air Museum	
G-BJAE	Lavadoux Starck AS.80 ★	D. J. & S. A. E. Phillips/Coventry	
G-BJAF	Piper J-3C-65 Cub	P. J. Cottle	
G-BJAG	PA-28-181 Archer II	C. R. Chubb	
G-BJAJ	AA-5B Tiger	Draycott Tiger Club	
G-BJAL	CASA 1.131E Jungmann 1000	G-BJAL Group	
G-BJAO	Bensen B.8M	A. P. Lay	
G-BJAP	DH.82A Tiger Moth (K2587)	K. Knight	
G-BJAS	Rango NA.9 balloon	A. Lindsay	
G-BJAV	Gardan GY-80 Horizon 160	W. R.Maloney	
G-BJAY	Piper J-3C-65 Cub	D. W. Finlay	
G-BJBK	PA-18 Super Cub 95	M. S. Bird	
G-BJBM	Monnett Sonerai I	I. Pearson	
G-BJBO	Jodel DR.250/160	Wiltshire Flying Group	
G-BJBW	PA-28-161 Warrior II	152 Group	
G-BJCA	PA-28-161 Warrior II	Plane Sailing (Southwest) Ltd	
G-BJCF	CP.1310-C3 Super Emeraude	K. M. Hodson & C. G. H. Gurney	
G-BJCI	PA-18 Super Cub 150 (modified)	The Borders (Milfield) Gliding Club Ltd	
G-BJCW	PA-32R-301 Saratoga SP	Golf Charlie Whisky Ltd	
G-BJDE	Cessna F.172M	J. K. P. Amor	
G-BJDF	MS.880B Rallye 100T	P. W. Johnson	
G-BJDJ	HS.125 Srs 700B	TAG Farnborough Engineering Ltd (G-RCDI)	
G-BJDK	European E.14 balloon	Aeroprint Tours	
G-BJDW	Cessna F.172M	J. Rae	
G-BJEE	BN-2T Turbine Islander	Cormack (Aircraft Services) Ltd	
G-BJEF	BN-2T Turbine Islander	Cormack (Aircraft Services) Ltd	
G-BJEI	PA-18 Super Cub 95	H. J. Cox	
G-BJEJ	BN-2T Turbine Islander	Cormack (Aircraft Services) Ltd	
G-BJEL	SNCAN NC.854	C. A. James	
G-BJEV	Aeronca 11AC Chief (897)	R. F. Willcox	
G-BJEX	Bölkow Bö.208C Junior	G. D. H. Crawford	
G-BJFC	European E.8 balloon	P. D. Ridout	
G-BJFE	PA-18 Super Cub 95	P. H. Wilmot-Allistone	

Notes	Reg.	Type	Owner or Operator
	G-BJFL	Sikorsky S-76A	Bristow Helicopters Ltd
	G-BJFM	Jodel D.120	J. V. George
	G-BJGM	Unicorn UE.1A balloon	D. Eaves & P. D. Ridout
	G-BJGX	Sikorsky S-76A	Bristow Helicopters Ltd
	G-BJGY	Cessna F.172P	K. & S. Martin
	G-BJHB	Mooney M.20J	Zitair Flying Club Ltd
	G-BJHK	EAA Acro Sport	M. R. Holden
	G-BJHV	Voisin Replica ★	Brooklands Museum of Aviation/Weybridge
	G-BJIA	Allport balloon	D. J. Allport
	G-BJIC	Dodo 1A balloon	P. D. Ridout
	G-BJID	Osprey 1B balloon	P. D. Ridout
	G-BJIG	Slingsby T.67A	A. D. Hodgkinson
	G-BJIV	PA-18 Super Cub 180	Yorkshire Gliding Club (Pty) Ltd
	G-BJKF	SOCATA TB9 Tampico	G-BJKF Group
	G-BJKW	Wills Aera II	J. K. S. Wills
	G-BJKY	Cessna F.152	Air Charter & Travel Ltd
	G-BJLC	Monnett Sonerai IIL	P. O. Yeo
	G-BJLX	Cremer balloon	P. W. May
	G-BJLY	Cremer balloon	P. Cannon
	G-BJML	Cessna 120	R. A. Smith
	G-BJMR	Cessna 310R	J. H. Sandham Aviation
	G-BJMW	Thunder Ax8-105 balloon	G. M. Westley
	G-BJMX	Jarre JR.3 balloon	P. D. Ridout
	G-BJMZ	European EA.8A balloon	P. D. Ridout
	G-BJNA	Arena Mk 117P balloon	P. D. Ridout
	G-BJND	Osprey Mk 1E balloon	A. Billington & D. Whitmore
	G-BJNG	Slingsby T.67AM	D. F. Hodgkinson
	G-BJNN	PA-38-112 Tomahawk	Carlisle Flight Training Ltd
	G-BJNY	Aeronca 11CC Super Chief	P. I. & D. M. Morgans
	G-BJNZ	PA-23 Aztec 250F	Bonus Aviation Ltd (G-FANZ)
	G-BJOB	Jodel D.140C	T. W. M. Beck & M. J. Smith
	G-BJOE	Jodel D.120A	H. Davies
	G-BJOT	Jodel D.117	R. A. Kilbride
	G-BJOV	Cessna F.150K	G-BJOV Flying Group
	G-BJPI	Bede BD-5G	M. D. McQueen
	G-BJRA	Osprey Mk 4B balloon	E. Osborn
	G-BJRG	Osprey Mk 4B balloon	A. E. de Gruchy
	G-BJRH	Rango NA.36 balloon	N. H. Ponsford
	G-BJRP	Cremer balloon	M. D. Williams
	G-BJRR	Cremer balloon	M. D. Williams
	G-BJRV	Cremer balloon	M. D. Williams
	G-BJSS	Allport balloon	D. J. Allport
	G-BJST	CCF T-6J Harvard IV (KF729)	M. F. Cuming, J. G. Fricker & N. T. Oakman
	G-BJSV	PA-28-161 Warrior II	Airways Flight Training (Exeter) Ltd
	G-BJSW	Thunder Ax7-65 balloon	J. Edwards
	G-BJSZ	Piper J-3C-65 Cub	K. Gilbert
	G-BJTB	Cessna A.150M	Cirrus Aviation Ltd
	G-BJTP	PA-18 Super Cub 95 (115302:TP)	J. T. Parkins
	G-BJTY	Osprey Mk 4B balloon	A. E. de Gruchy
	G-BJUB	BVS Special 01 balloon	P. G. Wild
	G-BJUC	Robinson R22HP	Brian Seedle Helicopters
	G-BJUD	Robin DR.400/180R	Lasham Gliding Society Ltd
	G-BJUR	PA-38-112 Tomahawk	Truman Aviation Ltd
	G-BJUS	PA-38-112 Tomahawk	J. D. Williams
	G-BJUV	Cameron V-20 balloon	P. Spellward
	G-BJVC	Evans VP-2	S. J. Greer & S. E. Clarke
	G-BJVH	Cessna F.182Q	R. J. de Courcy Cuming
	G-BJVJ	Cessna F.152	Henlow Flying Club
	G-BJVK	Grob G-109	B. Kimberley
	G-BJVM	Cessna 172N	R. D. & M. S. B. Forster
	G-BJVS	CP.1310-C3 Super Emeraude	N. F. Harris
	G-BJVT	Cessna F.152	Northumbria Flying School Ltd
	G-BJVV	Robin R.1180	J. Owens
	G-BJWH	Cessna F.152 II	J. D. Baines
	G-BJWI	Cessna F.172P	Flew LLP
	G-BJWJ	Cameron V-65 balloon	R. K. Gyselynck
	G-BJWO	BN-2A-26 Islander	Metachem Diagnostics Ltd (G-BAXC)
	G-BJWT	Wittman W.10 Tailwind	Tailwind Group
	G-BJWV	Colt 17A balloon	D. T. Meyes
	G-BJWW	Cessna F.172N	Air Charter & Travel Ltd
	G-BJWX	PA-18 Super Cub 95	G-BJWX Syndicate
	G-BJWY	S-55 Whirlwind HAR.21(WV198) ★	Solway Aviation Museum/Carlisle

Reg.	Type	Owner or Operator	Notes
G-BJWZ	PA-18 Super Cub 95	G-BJWZ Syndicate	
G-BJXB	Slingsby T.67A	X-Ray Bravo Ltd	
G-BJXK	Fournier RF-5	RF5 Syndicate	
G-BJXP	Colt 56B balloon	H. J. Anderson	
G-BJXR	Auster AOP.9	I. Churm & J. Hanson	
G-BJXX	PA-23 Aztec 250E	V. Bojovic	
G-BJXZ	Cessna 172N	T. M. Jones	
G-BJYD	Cessna F.152 II	N. J. James	
G-BJYF	Colt 56A balloon	A. J. Moore	
G-BJYK	Jodel D.120A	M. R. Baker	
G-BJYN	PA-38-112 Tomahawk	Panshanger School of Flying Ltd (G-BJTE)	
G-BJZB	Evans VP-2	R. B. McComish	
G-BJZF	DH.82A Tiger Moth	M. I. Lodge	
G-BJZN	Slingsby T.67A	P. B. Rice	
G-BJZR	Colt 42A balloon	Selfish Balloon Group	
G-BKAE	Jodel D.120	S. J. Harris	
G-BKAF	FRED Srs 2	N. Glass	
G-BKAM	Slingsby T.67M Firefly160	R. C. B. Brookhouse	
G-BKAO	Jodel D.112	H. Haigh	
G-BKAS	PA-38-112 Tomahawk	St. George Flight Training Ltd	
G-BKAY	Rockwell Commander 114	D. L. Bunning	
G-BKAZ	Cessna 152	L. W. Scattergood	
G-BKBD	Thunder Ax3 balloon	P. Donkin	
G-BKBF	MS.894A Rallye Minerva 220	K. A. Hale, L. C. Clark & P. Mickleborough	
G-BKBN	SOCATA TB10 Tobago	P. M. Clayton & D. Turner	
G-BKBP	Bellanca 7GCBC Scout	M. G. & J. R. Jefferies	
G-BKBS	Bensen B8MV	L. Harrison	
G-BKBV	SOCATA TB10 Tobago	T. C. H. Wright	
G-BKBW	SOCATA TB10 Tobago	Merlin Aviation	
G-BKCC	PA-28 Cherokee 180	DR Flying Club Ltd	
G-BKCE	Cessna F.172P II	The Leicestershire Aero Club Ltd	
G-BKCI	Brügger MB.2 Colibri	M. R. Walters	
G-BKCN	Currie Wot	N. A. A. Podmore	
G-BKCV	EAA Acro Sport II	R. J. Bower	
G-BKCW	Jodel D.120	Dundee Flying Group (G-BMYF)	
G-BKCX	Mudry/CAARP CAP-10B	G. P. Gorvett	
G-BKCZ	Jodel D.120A	I. K. Ratcliffe	
G-BKDC	Monnett Sonerai II	K. J. Towell	
G-BKDH	Robin DR.400/120	Marine & Aviation Ltd	
G-BKDJ	Robin DR.400/120	S. Pritchard & I. C. Colwell	
G-BKDK	Thunder Ax7-77Z balloon	A. J. Byrne	
G-BKDP	FRED Srs 3	M. Whittaker	
G-BKDR	Pitts S-1S Special	J. H. Milne & T. H. Bishop	
G-BKDT	SE-5A (replica) (F943) ★	Yorkshire Air Museum/Elvington	
G-BKDX	Jodel DR.1050	H. D. Colliver	
G-BKEP	Cessna F.172M	R. M. Dalley	
G-BKER	SE-5A (replica) (F5447:N)	N. K. Geddes	
G-BKET	PA-18 Super Cub 95	H. M. MacKenzie	
G-BKEV	Cessna F.172M	Derby Arrows	
G-BKEW	Bell 206B JetRanger 3	N. R. Foster	
G-BKEY	FRED Srs 3	G. S. Taylor	
G-BKFC	Cessna F.152 II	Sulby Aerial	
G-BKFI	Evans VP-1	P. L. Naylor	
G-BKFL	Aerosport Scamp	J. Sherwood	
G-BKFM	QAC Quickie 1	G. E. Meakin	
G-BKFR	CP.301C Emeraude	Devonshire Flying Group	
G-BKFW	P.56 Provost T.1 (XF597)	Sylmar Aviation & Services Ltd	
G-BKGA	MS.892E Rallye 150GT	C. J. Spradbery	
G-BKGB	Jodel D.120	B. A. Ridgway	
G-BKGC	Maule M.6-235	The Vale of the White Horse Gliding Centre Ltd	
G-BKGD	Westland WG.30 Srs.100 ★	IHM/Weston-super-Mare	
G-BKGL	Beech D.18S (1164:64)	A. T. J. Darrah	
G-BKGM	Beech D.18S (HB275)	L. S. Williams	
G-BKGR	Cameron O-65 balloon	K. Kidner & L. E. More	
G-BKGT	SOCATA Rallye 110ST	Long Marston Flying Group	
G-BKGW	Cessna F.152-II	Leicestershire Aero Club Ltd	
G-BKHG	Piper J-3C-65 Cub (479766:D-63)	H. C. Cox	
G-BKHW	Stoddard-Hamilton Glasair IIRG	P. J. Mansfield	
G-BKHY	Taylor JT.1 Monoplane	B. C. J. O'Neill	
G-BKHZ	Cessna F.172P	L. R. Leader	
G-BKIB	SOCATA TB9 Tampico	G. A. Vickers	

Notes	Reg.	Type	Owner or Operator
	G-BKIC	Cameron V-77 balloon	C. A. Butler
	G-BKIF	Fournier RF-6B	Tiger Airways
	G-BKII	Cessna F.172M	Sealand Aerial Photography Ltd
	G-BKIJ	Cessna F.172M	Cirrus Aviation Ltd
	G-BKIK	Cameron DG-19 airship ★	Balloon Preservation Group/Lancing
	G-BKIR	Jodel D.117	R. Shaw & D. M. Hardaker
	G-BKIS	SOCATA TB10 Tobago	Wessex Flyers
	G-BKIT	SOCATA TB9 Tampico	Cavendish Aviation UK Ltd
	G-BKIU	Colt 17A Cloudhopper balloon	S. R. J. Pooley
	G-BKIY	Thunder Ax3 balloon ★	Balloon Preservation Group/Lancing
	G-BKIZ	Cameron V-31 balloon	A. P. S. Cox
	G-BKJB	PA-18 Super Cub 135	W. S. Stanley
	G-BKJF	MS.880B Rallye 100T	R. Neeson
	G-BKJS	Jodel D.120A	B. F. Baldock & T. J. Nicholson
	G-BKJW	PA-23 Aztec 250E	Alan Williams Entertainments Ltd
	G-BKKN	Cessna 182R	R A. Marven
	G-BKKO	Cessna 182R	E. L. King & D. S. Lightbown
	G-BKKZ	Pitts S-1D Special	P. G. Gabriele
	G-BKLO	Cessna F.172M	Stapleford Flying Club Ltd
	G-BKMA	Mooney M.20J Srs 201	Foxtrot Whisky Aviation
	G-BKMB	Mooney M.20J Srs 201	G-BKMB Flying Group
	G-BKMG	Handley Page O/400 (replica)	The Paralyser Group
	G-BKMT	PA-32R-301 Saratoga SP	P. Ashworth
	G-BKNO	Monnett Sonerai IIL	S. Hardy
	G-BKNP	Cameron V-77 balloon	I. Lilja/Sweden
	G-BKNZ	CP.301A Emeraude	J. A. Thomas
	G-BKOA	SOCATA MS.893E Rallye 180GT	M. Jarrett
	G-BKOB	Z.326 Trener Master	A. L. Rae
	G-BKOK	BN-2B-26 Islander	Cormack (Aircraft Services) Ltd
	G-BKOT	Wassmer Wa.81 Piranha	B. N. Rolfe
	G-BKOU	P.84 Jet Provost T.3 (XN637)	G-BKOU/2 Ltd
	G-BKPA	Hoffmann H-36 Dimona	M. A. V. Gatehouse, S. J. Clark & R. Matthews
	G-BKPB	Aerosport Scamp	B. R. Thompson
	G-BKPC	Cessna A.185F	Black Knights Parachute Centre
	G-BKPD	Viking Dragonfly	E. P. Browne & G. J. Sargent
	G-BKPE	Jodel DR.250/160	Air Westward Ltd
	G-BKPS	AA-5B Tiger	A. E. T. Clarke
	G-BKPX	Jodel D.120A	D. M. Garrett & C. A. Jones
	G-BKPY	SAAB 91B/2 Safir (56321:U-AB) ★	Newark Air Museum
	G-BKPZ	Pitts S-1T Special	A. P. Mardlin
	G-BKRA	NA T-6G Texan (51-15227)	First Air Ltd
	G-BKRF	PA-18 Super Cub 95	K. M. Bishop
	G-BKRH	Brügger MB.2 Colibri	M. R. Benwell
	G-BKRK	SNCAN Stampe SV.4C	Strathgadie Stampe Group
	G-BKRL	Chichester-Miles Leopard ★	Bournemouth Aviation Museum
	G-BKRN	Beechcraft D.18S (43-35943)	A. A. Marshall & P. L. Turland
	G-BKRS	Cameron V-56 balloon	D. N. & L. J. Close
	G-BKRZ	Dragon G-77 balloon	J. R. Barber
	G-BKSC	Saro Skeeter AOP.12 (XN351) ★	R. A. L. Falconer
	G-BKSD	Colt 56A balloon	R. L. Wright
	G-BKSE	QAC Quickie Q.1	M. D. Burns
	G-BKST	Rutan Vari-Eze	R. Towle
	G-BKSX	SNCAN Stampe SV.4C	C. A. Bailey & J. A. Carr
	G-BKTA	PA-18 Super Cub 95	M. J. Dyson
	G-BKTH	CCF Hawker Sea Hurricane IB (Z7015)	The Shuttleworth Collection
	G-BKTM	PZL SZD-45A Ogar	J. T. Pajdak
	G-BKTR	Cameron V-77 balloon	C. M. Morley & C. Williamson
	G-BKTV	Cessna F.152	ACS Aviation Ltd
	G-BKTZ	Slingsby T.67M Firefly	P. R. Elvidge (G-SFTV)
	G-BKUE	SOCATA TB9 Tampico	Fife TB9ers
	G-BKUI	D.31 Turbulent	E. Shouler
	G-BKUR	CP.301A Emeraude	T. Harvey
	G-BKVA	SOCATA Rallye 180T	Buckminster Gliding Club Ltd
	G-BKVC	SOCATA TB9 Tampico	D. M. Hook
	G-BKVF	FRED Srs 3	G. E. & R. E. Collins
	G-BKVG	Scheibe SF.25E Super Falke	G-BKVG Ltd
	G-BKVK	Auster AOP.9 (WZ662)	J. K. Houlgrave
	G-BKVL	Robin DR.400/160	Tatenhill Aviation Ltd
	G-BKVM	PA-18 Super Cub 150 (115684)	D. G. Caffrey
	G-BKVO	Pietenpol Air Camper	M. C. Hayes
	G-BKVP	Pitts S-1D Special	S. W. Doyle
	G-BKVS	Campbell Cricket (modified)	K. Hughes

Reg.	Type	Owner or Operator	Notes
G-BKVT	PA-23 Aztec 250E	BKS Surveys Ltd (G-HARV)	
G-BKVW	Airtour 56 balloon	L. D. & H. Vaughan	
G-BKWD	Taylor JT.2 Titch	J. F. Sully	
G-BKWR	Cameron V-65 balloon	Window on the World Ltd	
G-BKWY	Cessna F.152	Northumbria Flying School Ltd	
G-BKXA	Robin R.2100	M. Wilson	
G-BKXD	SA.365N Dauphin 2	CHC Scotia Ltd	
G-BKXF	PA-28R Cherokee Arrow 200	P. L. Brunton/Caernarfon	
G-BKXM	Colt 17A balloon	R. G. Turnbull	
G-BKXN	ICA-Brasov IS-28M2/80HP	J. Pool	
G-BKXO	Rutan LongEz	M. G. Parsons	
G-BKXP	Auster AOP.6	B. J. Ellis	
G-BKXR	D.31A Turbulent	M. B. Hill	
G-BKZE	AS.332L Super Puma	CHC Scotia Ltd	
G-BKZF	Cameron V-56 balloon	C. F. Sanger-Davies	
G-BKZG	AS.332L Super Puma	CHC Scotia Ltd	
G-BKZI	Bell 206B JetRanger 2	Bucklefields Business Devlopments Ltd	
G-BKZT	FRED Srs 2	U. Chakravorty	
G-BKZV	Bede BD-4A	T. S. Smith	
G-BLAC	Cessna FA.152	D. C. C. Handley	
G-BLAF	Stolp SA.900 V-Star	J. D. Llewellyn	
G-BLAH	Thunder Ax7-77-1 balloon	T. M. Donnelly	
G-BLAI	Monnett Sonerai IIL	T. Simpon	
G-BLAM	Jodel DR.360	D. J. Durell	
G-BLAT	Jodel 150	G-BLAT Flying Group	
G-BLCC	Thunder Ax7-77Z balloon	W. J. Treacy & P. Murphy/Ireland	
G-BLCG	SOCATA TB10 Tobago	Contrarios Services Ltd (G-BHES)	
G-BLCH	Colt 65D balloon	S. Charlish	
G-BLCI	EAA Acro Sport	M. R. Holden	
G-BLCM	SOCATA TB9 Tampico	K. J. Steele & D. J. Hewitt	
G-BLCT	Jodel DR.220 2+2	F. N. P. Maurin	
G-BLCU	Scheibe SF.25B Falke	Charlie Uniform Syndicate	
G-BLCV	Hoffmann H-36 Dimona	R. & M. Weaver	
G-BLCW	Evans VP-1	K. Lewis	
G-BLDB	Taylor JT.1 Monoplane	J. P. J. Hefford	
G-BLDD	WAG-Aero CUBy AcroTrainer	K. Rose, N. Horseman & M. P. Comley	
G-BLDG	PA-25 Pawnee 260C	Ouse Gliding Club Ltd	
G-BLDK	Robinson R22	Flight Academy (Gyrocopters) Ltd	
G-BLDN	Rand-Robinson KR-2	P. R. Diffey	
G-BLDV	BN-2B-26 Islander	Loganair Ltd	
G-BLES	Stolp SA.750 Acroduster Too	C. J. Kingswood	
G-BLFI	PA-28-181 Archer II	Bonus Aviation Ltd	
G-BLFY	Cameron V-77 balloon	A. N. F. Pertwee	
G-BLFZ	PA-31-310 Turbo Navajo C	London Executive Aviation Ltd	
G-BLGH	Robin DR.300/180R	Booker Gliding Club Ltd	
G-BLGS	SOCATA Rallye 180T	A. Waters	
G-BLGV	Bell 206B JetRanger 3	Heliflight (UK) Ltd	
G-BLHH	Jodel DR.315	S. J. Luck	
G-BLHI	Colt 17A balloon	J. A. Folkes	
G-BLHJ	Cessna F.172P	J. H. Sandham Aviation	
G-BLHM	PA-18 Super Cub 95	A. G. Edwards	
G-BLHN	Robin HR.100/285	K. A. & L. M. C. Payton	
G-BLHR	GA-7 Cougar	W. B. Orde-Powlett	
G-BLHS	Bellanca 7ECA Citabria	Abraxas Aviation Ltd	
G-BLHW	Varga 2150A Kachina	Wilburton Flying Group	
G-BLID	DH.112 Venom FB.50 (J-1605) ★	P. G. Vallance Ltd	
G-BLIK	Wallis WA-116/F/S	K. H. Wallis	
G-BLIT	Thorp T-18 CW	A. P. Tyrwhitt-Drake	
G-BLIW	P.56 Provost T.51 (177)	A. D. M. & K. B. Edie	
G-BLIX	Saro Skeeter Mk 12 (XL809)	K. M. Scholes	
G-BLIY	MS.892A Rallye Commodore	A. J. Brasher	
G-BLJM	Beech 95-B55 Baron	A. Nitsche/Germany	
G-BLJO	Cessna F.152	J. S. Develin & Z. Islam	
G-BLKA	DH.112 Venom FB.54 (WR410:N) ★	De Havilland Heritage Museum/London Colney	
G-BLKM	Jodel DR.1051	Kilo Mike Group	
G-BLKY	Beech 95-58 Baron	R. A. Perrot	
G-BLLA	Bensen B.8M	K. T. Donaghey	
G-BLLB	Bensen B.8M	D. H. Moss	
G-BLLD	Cameron O-77 balloon	G. Birchall	
G-BLLH	Jodel DR.220A 2+2	M. D. Hughes	
G-BLLN	PA-18 Super Cub 95	P. L. Pilch & C. G. Fisher	
G-BLLO	PA-18 Super Cub 95	D. G. Margetts	

Notes	Reg.	Type	Owner or Operator
	G-BLLP	Slingsby T.67B	Air Navigation and Trading Co Ltd
	G-BLLR	Slingsby T.67B	R. L. Brinklow
	G-BLLS	Slingsby T.67B	K. Davis
	G-BLLW	Colt 56B balloon	G. Fordyce & ptnrs
	G-BLLZ	Rutan LongEz	R. S. Stoddart-Stones
	G-BLMA	Zlin 326 Trener Master	G. P. Northcott
	G-BLMC	Avro 698 Vulcan B.2A ★	Aeropark/East Midlands
	G-BLME	Robinson R22HP	Heli Air Ltd
	G-BLMG	Grob G.109B	Mike Golf Syndicate
	G-BLMN	Rutan LongEz	G. D. E. Macdonald
	G-BLMP	PA-17 Vagabond	D. & M. Shrimpton.
	G-BLMR	PA-18 Super Cub 150	M. Vickers
	G-BLMT	PA-18 Super Cub 135	I. S. Runnalls
	G-BLMW	T.66 Nipper 3	S. L. Millar
	G-BLMZ	Colt 105A balloon	M. D. Dickinson
	G-BLNO	FRED Srs 3	L. W. Smith
	G-BLOR	PA-30 Twin Comanche 160	R. L. C. Appleton
	G-BLOS	Cessna 185A (also flown with floats)	D. C. Minshaw
	G-BLOT	Colt Ax6-56B balloon	H. J. Anderson
	G-BLOV	Thunder Ax5-42 Srs 1 balloon	A. G. R. Calder
	G-BLPA	Piper J-3C-65 Cub	A. C. Frost
	G-BLPB	Turner TSW Hot Two Wot	Papa Bravo Group
	G-BLPE	PA-18 Super Cub 95	A. A. Haig-Thomas
	G-BLPF	Cessna FR.172G	S. Culpin
	G-BLPG	Auster J/1N Alpha (16693:693)	Annic Marketing (G-AZIH)
	G-BLPH	Cessna FRA.150L	J. D. Baines
	G-BLPI	Slingsby T.67B	RAF Wyton Flying Group Ltd
	G-BLPP	Cameron V-77 balloon	R. J. Gooch
	G-BLRA	BAe 146-100	BAE Systems (Operations) Ltd
	G-BLRC	PA-18 Super Cub 135	Supercub Group
	G-BLRF	Slingsby T.67C	R. C. Nicholls
	G-BLRL	CP.301C-1 Emeraude	A. M. Smith
	G-BLRM	Glaser-Dirks DG.400	J. A. & W. S. Y. Stephen
	G-BLSD	DH.112 Venom FB.54 (J-1758) ★	R. Lamplough/North Weald
	G-BLSX	Cameron O-105 balloon	B. J. Petteford
	G-BLTA	Thunder Ax7-77A	K. A. Schlussler
	G-BLTC	D.31A Turbulent	S. J. Butler
	G-BLTK	Rockwell Commander 112TC	Commander TC Group
	G-BLTM	Robin HR.200/100	Barton Robin Group
	G-BLTN	Thunder Ax7-65 balloon	A. H. Symonds
	G-BLTR	Scheibe SF.25B Falke	V. Mallon/Germany
	G-BLTS	Rutan LongEz	R. W. Cutler
	G-BLTV	Slingsby T.67B	R. L. Brinklow
	G-BLTW	Slingsby T.67B	Cheshire Air Training Services Ltd
	G-BLTY	Westland WG.30 Srs 160	D. Brem-Wilson
	G-BLUI	Thunder Ax7-65 balloon	S. Johnson
	G-BLUM	SA.365N Dauphin 2	CHC Scotia Ltd
	G-BLUV	Grob G.109B	109 Flying Group
	G-BLUX	Slingsby T.67M Firefly 200	R. L. Brinklow
	G-BLUZ	DH.82B Queen Bee (LF858)	The Bee Keepers Group
	G-BLVB	Airtour AH-56 balloon	J. J. Daly
	G-BLVI	Slingsby T.67M Firefly Mk II	Brooke Park Ltd
	G-BLVK	CAARP CAP-10B	E. K. Coventry
	G-BLVL	PA-28-161 Warrior II	TG Aviation Ltd
	G-BLVW	Cessna F.172H	R. Holloway
	G-BLWD	PA-34-200T Seneca 2	Bencray Ltd
	G-BLWF	Robin HR.100/210	M. D. Parker
	G-BLWH	Fournier RF-6B-100	I. R. March
	G-BLWM	Bristol M.1C (replica) (C4994) ★	RAF Museum/Hendon
	G-BLWP	PA-38-112 Tomahawk	APB Leasing Ltd
	G-BLWT	Evans VP-1	N. Clark
	G-BLWY	Robin R.2160D	Charlie Yankee Ltd
	G-BLXA	SOCATA TB20 Trinidad	Trinidad Flyers Ltd
	G-BLXG	Colt 21A balloon	A. Walker
	G-BLXH	Fournier RF-3	J. E. Dallison
	G-BLXI	CP.1310-C3 Super Emeraude	R. Howard
	G-BLXO	Jodel 150	P. R. Powell
	G-BLXP	PA-28R Cherokee Arrow 200	M. B. Hamlett
	G-BLXR	AS.332L Super Puma	Bristow Helicopters Ltd
	G-BLYD	SOCATA TB20 Trinidad	Yankee Delta Corporation Ltd
	G-BLYP	Robin 3000/120	Weald Air Services
	G-BLYT	Airtour AH-77 balloon	I. J. Taylor & R. C. Kincaid

Reg.	Type	Owner or Operator	Notes
G-BLZA	Scheibe SF.25B Falke	Zulu Alpha Syndicate	
G-BLZH	Cessna F.152 II	P. D'Costa	
G-BLZN	Bell 206B JetRanger	E. Miles	
G-BLZP	Cessna F.152	East Midlands Flying School Ltd	
G-BMAD	Cameron V-77 balloon	M. A. Stelling	
G-BMAO	Taylor JT.1 Monoplane	S. J. Alston	
G-BMAX	FRED Srs 2	D. A. Arkley	
G-BMAY	PA-18 Super Cub 135	R. W. Davies	
G-BMBB	Cessna F.150L	E. T. Hawkins	
G-BMBJ	Schempp-Hirth Janus CM	BJ Flying Group	
G-BMBW	Bensen B.8MR	M. E. Vahdat	
G-BMBZ	Scheibe SF.25E Super Falke	K. E. Ballington	
G-BMCC	Thunder Ax7-77 balloon	A. K. & C. M. Russell	
G-BMCD	Cameron V-65 balloon	R. Lillyman	
G-BMCG	Grob G.109B	Lagerholm Finnimport Ltd	
G-BMCI	Cessna F.172H	A. B. Davis	
G-BMCN	Cessna F.152	Cristal Air Ltd	
G-BMCS	PA-22 Tri-Pacer 135	T. A. Hodges	
G-BMCV	Cessna F.152	Leicestershire Aero Club Ltd	
G-BMCW	AS.332L Super Puma	Bristow Helicopters Ltd	
G-BMCX	AS.332L Super Puma	Bristow Southeast Asia Ltd	
G-BMDB	SE-5A (replica) (F235:B)	D. Biggs	
G-BMDE	Pietenpol AirCamper	P. B. Childs	
G-BMDJ	Price Ax7-77S balloon	R. A. Benham	
G-BMDK	PA-34-220T Seneca III	Air Medical Fleet Ltd	
G-BMDP	Partenavia P.64B Oscar 200	S. T. G. Lloyd	
G-BMDS	Jodel D.120	N. Lynch	
G-BMEA	PA-18 Super Cub 95	M. J. Butler	
G-BMEH	Jodel 150 Special Super Mascaret	R. J. & C. J. Lewis	
G-BMET	Taylor JT.1 Monoplane	M. K. A. Blyth	
G-BMEU	Isaacs Fury II	I. G. Harrison	
G-BMEX	Cessna A.150K	R. J. Grantham & D. Boatswain	
G-BMFD	PA-23 Aztec 250F	Giles Aviation Ltd (G-BGYY)	
G-BMFG	Dornier Do.27A-4	Dornier 27 Group	
G-BMFI	PZL SZD-45A Ogar	S. L. Morrey	
G-BMFP	PA-28-161 Warrior II	Bravo-Mike-Fox-Papa Group	
G-BMFU	Cameron N-90 balloon	J. J. Rudoni	
G-BMFY	Grob G.109B	P. J. Shearer	
G-BMGB	PA-28R Cherokee Arrow 200	Malmesbury Specialist Cars	
G-BMGC	Fairey Swordfish Mk II (W5856)	F.A.A. Museum/Yeovilton	
G-BMGG	Cessna 152 II	Falcon Flying Services	
G-BMGR	Grob G.109B	G-BMGR Group	
G-BMHA	Rutan LongEz	S. F. Elvins	
G-BMHC	Cessna U.206F	H. and R. Morley	
G-BMHJ	Thunder Ax7-65 balloon	M. G. Robinson	
G-BMHL	Wittman W.8 Tailwind	H. J. Bennet	
G-BMHS	Cessna F.172M	Tango X-Ray Flying Group	
G-BMHT	PA-28RT-201T Turbo Arrow	G-BMHT Flying Group	
G-BMID	Jodel D.120	G-BMID Flying Group	
G-BMIG	Cessna 172N	BMIG Group	
G-BMIM	Rutan LongEz	R. M. Smith	
G-BMIO	Stoddard-Hamilton Glasair RG	P. Bint & L. McMahon	
G-BMIP	Jodel D.112	F. J. E. Brownsill	
G-BMIR	Westland Wasp HAS.1 (XT788) ★	Park Aviation Supply/Charlwood	
G-BMIS	Monnett Sonerai II	S. R. Edwards	
G-BMIV	PA-28R-201T Turbo Arrow III	Firmbeam Ltd	
G-BMIW	PA-28-181 Archer II	Oldbus Ltd	
G-BMIX	SOCATA TB20 Trinidad	Aviation Surrey Ltd	
G-BMIY	Oldfield Baby Great Lakes	J. B. Scott (G-NOME)	
G-BMIZ	Robinson R22 Beta	Castlehill Aviation Ltd	
G-BMJA	PA-32R-301 Saratoga SP	H. Merkado	
G-BMJB	Cessna 152	Endrick Aviation LLP	
G-BMJC	Cessna 152 II	R. K. Jenkins	
G-BMJD	Cessna 152 II	Donair Flying Club Ltd	
G-BMJL	Rockwell Commander 114	D. J. & S. M. Hawkins	
G-BMJN	Cameron O-65 balloon	P. M. Traviss	
G-BMJO	PA-34-220T Seneca III	Deep Cleavage Ltd	
G-BMJR	Cessna T.337H	John Roberts Services Ltd (G-NOVA)	
G-BMJX	Wallis WA-116X	K. H. Wallis	
G-BMJY	Yakovlev C18M (07)	W. A. E. Moore	
G-BMKB	PA-18 Super Cub 135	Cubair Flight Training Ltd	

Notes	Reg.	Type	Owner or Operator
	G-BMKC	Piper J-3C-65 Cub (329854:R-44)	E. P. Parkin
	G-BMKD	Beech C90A King Air	ATC (Lasham) Ltd
	G-BMKF	Jodel DR.221	S. T. & L. A. Gilbert
	G-BMKG	PA-38-112 Tomahawk II	APB Leasing Ltd
	G-BMKI	Colt 21A balloon	A. C. Booth
	G-BMKJ	Cameron V-77 balloon	R. C. Thursby
	G-BMKK	PA-28R-200 Cherokee Arrow II	P. M. Murray
	G-BMKP	Cameron V-77 balloon	R. Bayly
	G-BMKR	PA-28-161 Warrior II	Field Flying Group (G-BGKR)
	G-BMKY	Cameron O-65 balloon	A. R. Rich
	G-BMLB	Jodel D.120A	C. A. Croucher
	G-BMLJ	Cameron N-77 balloon	C. J. Dunkley
	G-BMLK	Grob G.109B	Brams Syndicate
	G-BMLL	Grob G.109B	G-BMLL Flying Group
	G-BMLM	Beech 95-58 Baron	Atlantic Bridge Aviation Ltd
	G-BMLS	PA-28R-201 Arrow III	R. M. Shorter
	G-BMLT	Pietenpol Air Camper	W. E. R. Jenkins
	G-BMLW	Cameron O-77 balloon	M. L. & L. P. Willoughby
	G-BMLX	Cessna F.150L	J. P. A. Freeman
	G-BMMF	FRED Srs 2	R. C. Thomas
	G-BMMI	Pazmany PL.4A	P. I. Morgans
	G-BMMK	Cessna 182P	G. G. Weston
	G-BMMM	Cessna 152 II	Falcon Flying Services Ltd
	G-BMMP	Grob G.109B	G-BMMP Syndicate
	G-BMMV	ICA-Brasov IS-28M2A	C. D. King
	G-BMMW	Thunder Ax7-77 balloon	P. A. George
	G-BMNL	PA-28R Cherokee Arrow 200	C. d'Oyly
	G-BMNV	SNCAN Stampe SV.4D	Wessex Aviation & Transport Ltd
	G-BMOE	PA-28R Cherokee Arrow 200	Piper Leasing Ltd
	G-BMOF	Cessna U206G	Wild Geese Skydiving Centre
	G-BMOG	Thunder Ax7-77 balloon	R. M. Boswell
	G-BMOH	Cameron N-77 balloon	P. J. Marshall & M. A. Clarke
	G-BMOI	Partenavia P.68B	Simmette Ltd
	G-BMAD	ARV Super 2	R. E. Griffiths
	G-BMOL	PA-23 Aztec 250D	LDL Enterprises (G-BBSR)
	G-BMOT	Bensen B.8M	M. Fontolan
	G-BMPC	PA-28-181 Archer II	C. J. & R. J. Barnes
	G-BMPD	Cameron V-65 balloon	R. P. E. Phillips
	G-BMPL	Optica Industries OA.7 Optica	J. K. Edgley
	G-BMPP	Cameron N-77 balloon	The Sarnia Balloon Group
	G-BMPR	PA-28R-201 Arrow III	T. J. Brammer & D. T. Colley
	G-BMPS	Strojnik S-2A	G. J. Green
	G-BMPY	DH.82A Tiger Moth	N. M. Eisenstein
	G-BMRA	Boeing 757-236F	DHL Air Ltd
	G-BMRB	Boeing 757-236F	DHL Air Ltd
	G-BMRC	Boeing 757-236F	DHL Air Ltd
	G-BMRD	Boeing 757-236F	DHL Air Ltd
	G-BMRE	Boeing 757-236F	DHL Air Ltd
	G-BMRF	Boeing 757-236F	DHL Air Ltd
	G-BMRH	Boeing 757-236F	DHL Air Ltd
	G-BMRJ	Boeing 757-236F	DHL Air Ltd
	G-BMSB	VS.509 Spitfire IX (MJ627:9G-P)	M. S. Bayliss (G-ASOZ)
	G-BMSC	Evans VP-2	R. S. Acreman
	G-BMSD	PA-28-181 Archer II	H. Merkado
	G-BMSE	Valentin Taifun 17E	D. O'Donnell
	G-BMSF	PA-38-112 Tomahawk	B. Catlow
	G-BMSG	SAAB 32A Lansen ★	J. E. Wilkie/Cranfield
	G-BMSL	FRED Srs 3	S. Slater
	G-BMTA	Cessna 152 II	ACS Aviation Ltd
	G-BMTB	Cessna 152 II	Sky Leisure Aviation (Charters) Ltd
	G-BMTC	AS.355F1 Twin Squirrel	Cambridge & Essex Air Support Unit (G-SASU/G-BSSM/G-BKUK/G-EPOL)
	G-BMTJ	Cessna 152 II	The Pilot Centre Ltd
	G-BMTO	PA-38-112 Tomahawk	Falcon Flying Services
	G-BMTU	Pitts S-1E Special	N. A. A. Pogmore
	G-BMTX	Cameron V-77 balloon	J. A. Langley
	G-BMUD	Cessna 182P	M. E. Taylor
	G-BMUG	Rutan LongEz	A. G. Sayers
	G-BMUJ	Colt Drachenfisch balloon	Virgin Airship & Balloon Co Ltd
	G-BMUO	Cessna A.152	Sky Leisure Aviation (Charters) Ltd
	G-BMUT	PA-34-200T Seneca II	G-DAD Air Ltd
	G-BMUU	Thunder Ax7-77 balloon	A. R. Hill

Reg.	Type	Owner or Operator	Notes
G-BMUZ	PA-28-161 Warrior II	Northumbria Flying School Ltd	
G-BMVA	Scheibe SF.25B Falke	Kent Gliding Club Ltd	
G-BMVB	Cessna F.152	M. P. Barnard	
G-BMVG	QAC Quickie Q.1	P. M. Wright	
G-BMVL	PA-38-112 Tomahawk	T. Akeroyd	
G-BMVM	PA-38-112 Tomahawk	Brimpton Flying Group	
G-BMVT	Thunder Ax7-77A balloon	M. L. & L. P. Willoughby	
G-BMVU	Monnett Moni	Stacey Aviation Ltd	
G-BMWF	ARV Super 2	G. E. Collard	
G-BMWR	Rockwell Commander 112	M. & J. Edwards	
G-BMWU	Cameron N-42 balloon ★	Balloon Preservation Group/Lancing	
G-BMWV	Putzer Elster B	Magpie Group	
G-BMXA	Cessna 152 II	ACS Aviation Ltd	
G-BMXB	Cessna 152 II	C. I. J. Young	
G-BMXC	Cessna 152 II	MK Aero Support Ltd	
G-BMYC	SOCATA TB10 Tobago	E. A. Grady	
G-BMYD	Beech A36 Bonanza	Seabeam Partners Ltd	
G-BMYG	Cessna FA.152	Greer Aviation Ltd	
G-BMYI	AA-5 Traveler	W. C. & S. C. Westran	
G-BMYU	Jodel D.120	A. J. L. Gordon	
G-BMZF	WSK-Mielec LiM-2 (MiG-15*bis*) (01420) ★	F.A.A. Museum/Yeovilton	
G-BMZN	Everett gyroplane	T. A. Holmes	
G-BMZS	Everett gyroplane	L. W. Cload	
G-BMZW	Bensen B.8MR	P. D. Widdicombe	
G-BNAI	Wolf W-II Boredom Fighter (146-11083)	C. M. Bunn	
G-BNAJ	Cessna 152 II	Galair Ltd	
G-BNAN	Cameron V-65 balloon	Rango Balloon and Kite Company	
G-BNAW	Cameron V-65 balloon	A. Walker	
G-BNBW	Thunder Ax7-77 balloon	I. S. & S. W. Watthews	
G-BNBY	Beech 95-B55A Baron	J. Butler/France (G-AXXR)	
G-BNCB	Cameron V-77 balloon	C. W. Brown	
G-BNCM	Cameron N-77 balloon	C. A. Stone	
G-BNCO	PA-38-112 Tomahawk	D. K. Walker	
G-BNCR	PA-28-161 Warrior II	Airways Aero Associations Ltd	
G-BNCS	Cessna 180	C. Elwell Transport Ltd	
G-BNCU	Thunder Ax7-77 balloon	W. De Bock	
G-BNCX	Hawker Hunter T.7 (XL621) ★	Brooklands Museum of Aviation/Weybridge	
G-BNCZ	Rutan LongEz	D. G. Foreman	
G-BNDE	PA-38-112 Tomahawk	B. R. Nurthen	
G-BNDG	Wallis WA-201/R Srs1	K. H. Wallis	
G-BNDN	Cameron V-77 balloon	A. Hornshaw	
G-BNDP	Brügger MB.2 Colibri	A. C. Barber	
G-BNDR	SOCATA TB10 Tobago	I. W. Gardner	
G-BNDT	Brügger MB.2 Colibri	D. W. Rees	
G-BNDV	Cameron N-77 balloon	R. E. Jones	
G-BNDW	DH.82A Tiger Moth	C. R. Hardiman	
G-BNEE	PA-28R-201 Arrow III	Britannic Management Aviation	
G-BNEL	PA-28-161 Warrior II	S. C. Westran	
G-BNEN	PA-34-200T Seneca II	CE Ventures Ltd	
G-BNEO	Cameron V-77 balloon	J. G. O'Connell	
G-BNEV	Viking Dragonfly	N. W. Eyre	
G-BNFG	Cameron O-77 balloon	Capital Balloon Club Ltd	
G-BNFI	Cessna 150J	A. Waters	
G-BNFM	Colt 21A balloon	M. E. Dworski/France	
G-BNFN	Cameron N-105 balloon	P. Glydon	
G-BNFO	Cameron V-77 balloon	M. B. Young	
G-BNFP	Cameron O-84 balloon	M. Clarke	
G-BNFR	Cessna 152 II	A. Jahanfar	
G-BNFV	Robin DR.400/120	J. P. A. Freeman	
G-BNGE	Auster AOP.6 (TW536)	N. D. Sharpe	
G-BNGJ	Cameron N-77 balloon	S. W. K. Smeeton	
G-BNGN	Cameron N-77 balloon	N. Dykes	
G-BNGO	Thunder Ax7-77 balloon	J. S. Finlan	
G-BNGT	PA-28-181 Archer II	Edinburgh Flying Club Ltd	
G-BNGV	ARV Super 2	N. A. Onions & L. J. Russell	
G-BNGW	ARV Super 2	Southern Gas Turbines Ltd	
G-BNGY	ARV Super 2	S. C. Smith (G-BMWL)	
G-BNHB	ARV Super 2	C. J. Challener	
G-BNHG	PA-38-112 Tomahawk II	Highland Aviation Training Ltd	
G-BNHJ	Cessna 152 II	The Pilot Centre Ltd	

Notes	Reg.	Type	Owner or Operator
	G-BNHK	Cessna 152 II	Wayfarers Flying Group
	G-BNHL	Colt beer glass SS balloon	J. A. Viner
	G-BNHN	Colt Ariel Bottle SS balloon ★	British Balloon Museum
	G-BNHT	Fournier RF-3	G-BNHT Group
	G-BNID	Cessna 152 II	MK Aero Support Ltd
	G-BNII	Cameron N-90 balloon	Topless Balloon Group
	G-BNIK	Robin HR.200/120	G-BNIK Group
	G-BNIM	PA-38-112 Tomahawk	Air Claire Ltd
	G-BNIN	Cameron V-77 balloon	Cloud Nine Balloon Group
	G-BNIO	Luscombe 8A Silvaire	India Oscar Group
	G-BNIP	Luscombe 8A Silvaire	M. J. Diggins
	G-BNIU	Cameron O-77 balloon	Terre d'Envoi Blois Montgolfiere/France
	G-BNIV	Cessna 152 II	Cristal Air Ltd
	G-BNIW	Boeing Stearman PT-17	R. C. Goold
	G-BNJB	Cessna 152 II	Aerolease Ltd
	G-BNJC	Cessna 152 II	Stapleford Flying Club Ltd
	G-BNJD	Cessna 152 II	M. Howells
	G-BNJH	Cessna 152 II	ACS Aviation Ltd
	G-BNJL	Bensen B.8MR	S. Ram
	G-BNJR	PA-28RT-201T Turbo Arrow IV	D. Croker
	G-BNJT	PA-28-161 Warrior II	Hawarden Flying Group
	G-BNJX	Cameron N-90 balloon	Mars UK Ltd
	G-BNJZ	Cassutt Racer IIIM	J. Stringer
	G-BNKC	Cessna 152 II	Herefordshire Aero Club Ltd
	G-BNKD	Cessna 172N	P. J. Craig & A. D. Evans
	G-BNKE	Cessna 172N	Kilo Echo Flying Group
	G-BNKH	PA-38-112 Tomahawk	S. J. Miles
	G-BNKI	Cessna 152 II	RAF Halton Aeroplane Club Ltd
	G-BNKP	Cessna 152 II	Spectrum Leisure Ltd
	G-BNKR	Cessna 152 II	Keen Leasing (IOM) Ltd
	G-BNKS	Cessna 152 II	Shropshire Aero Club Ltd
	G-BNKT	Cameron O-77 balloon	A. A. Brown
	G-BNKV	Cessna 152 II	S. C. Westran
	G-BNLA	Boeing 747-436	British Airways
	G-BNLB	Boeing 747-436	British Airways
	G-BNLC	Boeing 747-436	British Airways
	G-BNLD	Boeing 747-436	British Airways
	G-BNLE	Boeing 747-436	British Airways
	G-BNLF	Boeing 747-436	British Airways
	G-BNLG	Boeing 747-436	British Airways
	G-BNLH	Boeing 747-436	British Airways
	G-BNLI	Boeing 747-436	British Airways
	G-BNLJ	Boeing 747-436	British Airways
	G-BNLK	Boeing 747-436	British Airways
	G-BNLL	Boeing 747-436	British Airways
	G-BNLM	Boeing 747-436	British Airways
	G-BNLN	Boeing 747-436	British Airways
	G-BNLO	Boeing 747-436	British Airways
	G-BNLP	Boeing 747-436	British Airways
	G-BNLR	Boeing 747-436	British Airways
	G-BNLS	Boeing 747-436	British Airways
	G-BNLT	Boeing 747-436	British Airways
	G-BNLU	Boeing 747-436	British Airways
	G-BNLV	Boeing 747-436	British Airways
	G-BNLW	Boeing 747-436	British Airways
	G-BNLX	Boeing 747-436	British Airways
	G-BNLY	Boeing 747-436	British Airways
	G-BNLZ	Boeing 747-436	British Airways
	G-BNMB	PA-28-151 Warrior	Azure Flying Club Ltd
	G-BNMD	Cessna 152 II	T. M. Jones/Egginton
	G-BNME	Cessna 152 II	A. R. Jury
	G-BNMF	Cessna 152 II	Redhill Air Services Ltd
	G-BNMG	Cameron O-77 balloon	J. H. Turner
	G-BNMH	Pietenpol Air Camper	N. M. Hitchman
	G-BNMI	Colt Flying Fantasy SS balloon	Air 2 Air Ltd
	G-BNML	Rand-Robinson KR-2	P. J. Brookman
	G-BNMO	Cessna TR.182RG	R. Taggart
	G-BNMX	Thunder Ax7-77 balloon	S. A. D. Beard
	G-BNNA	Stolp SA.300 Starduster Too	Banana Group
	G-BNNE	Cameron N-77 balloon	R. D. Allen, L. P. Hooper & M. J. Streat
	G-BNNO	PA-28-161 Warrior II	I. A. Anderson
	G-BNNR	Cessna 152	J. H. Sandham Aviation

Reg.	Type	Owner or Operator	Notes
G-BNNS	PA-28-161 Warrior II	S. J. French	
G-BNNT	PA-28-151 Warrior	S. T. Gilbert & D. J. Kirkwood	
G-BNNU	PA-38-112 Tomahawk	Edinburgh Flying Club Ltd	
G-BNNX	PA-28R-201T Turbo Arrow III	Bristol Flying Centre Ltd	
G-BNNY	PA-28-161 Warrior II	Falcon Flying Services	
G-BNNZ	PA-28-161 Warrior II	R. West	
G-BNOB	Wittman W.8 Tailwind	D. G. Hammersley	
G-BNOE	PA-28-161 Warrior II	Sherburn Aero Club Ltd	
G-BNOF	PA-28-161 Warrior II	Tayside Aviation Ltd	
G-BNOH	PA-28-161 Warrior II	Sherburn Aero Club Ltd	
G-BNOJ	PA-28-161 Warrior II	BAE Systems (Warton) Flying Club Ltd	
G-BNOM	PA-28-161 Warrior II	Air Navigation and Trading Co Ltd	
G-BNON	PA-28-161 Warrior II	Tayside Aviation Ltd	
G-BNOP	PA-28-161 Warrior II	BAE Systems (Warton) Flying Club Ltd	
G-BNPE	Cameron N-77 balloon	R. N. Simpkins	
G-BNPF	Slingsby T.31M	S. Luck & ptnrs	
G-BNPH	P.66 Pembroke C.1 (WV740)	A. G. & G. A. G. Dixon	
G-BNPM	PA-38-112 Tomahawk	Papa Mike Aviation	
G-BNPO	PA-28-181 Archer II	Bonus Aviation Ltd	
G-BNPV	Bowers Fly-Baby 1B	J. G. Day	
G-BNPY	Cessna 152 II	G. Tennant	
G-BNRA	SOCATA TB10 Tobago	Double D Airgroup	
G-BNRG	PA-28-161 Warrior II	Glenn Aviation Ltd	
G-BNRL	Cessna 152 II	Bulldog Aviation Ltd	
G-BNRP	PA-28-181 Archer II	Bonua Aviation Ltd	
G-BNRR	Cessna 172P	PHA Aviation Ltd	
G-BNRX	PA-34-200T Seneca II	Truman Aviation Ltd	
G-BNRY	Cessna 182Q	K. F. & S. J. Farey	
G-BNSG	PA-28R-201 Arrow III	W. R. Ronnie	
G-BNSI	Cessna 152 II	Sky Leisure Aviation (Charters) Ltd	
G-BNSL	PA-38-112 Tomahawk II	Lomac Aviators Ltd	
G-BNSM	Cessna 152 II	Cornwall Flying Club Ltd	
G-BNSN	Cessna 152 II	The Pilot Centre Ltd	
G-BNSO	Slingsby T.67M Firefly Mk II	R. M. Rennoldson	
G-BNSP	Slingsby T.67M Firefly Mk II	R. K. J. McPhee	
G-BNSR	Slingsby T.67M Firefly Mk II	Slingsby SR Group	
G-BNST	Cessna 172N	CSG Bodyshop	
G-BNSU	Cessna 152 II	Channel Aviation Ltd	
G-BNSV	Cessna 152 II	Channel Aviation Ltd	
G-BNSY	PA-28-161 Warrior II	Light Aircraft Leasing Ltd	
G-BNSZ	PA-28-161 Warrior II	Haimoss Ltd	
G-BNTC	PA-28RT-201T Turbo Arrow IV	Redhill Air Services Ltd	
G-BNTD	PA-28-161 Warrior II	P. S. Thompson	
G-BNTP	Cessna 172N	Westnet Ltd	
G-BNTZ	Cameron N-77 balloon	Balloon Team	
G-BNUL	Cessna 152 II	Big Red Kite Ltd	
G-BNUN	Beech 95-58PA Baron	SMB Aviation Ltd	
G-BNUO	Beech 76 Duchess	Pace Projects Ltd and Professional Flight Simulation Ltd	
G-BNUS	Cessna 152 II	Stapleford Flying Club Ltd	
G-BNUT	Cessna 152 Turbo	Stapleford Flying Club Ltd	
G-BNUX	Hoffmann H-36 Dimona	Buckminster Dimona Syndicate	
G-BNUY	PA-38-112 Tomahawk II	D. C. Storey	
G-BNVB	AA-5A Cheetah	Pelican Project Management Ltd	
G-BNVE	PA-28-181 Archer II	Solent Flight Ltd	
G-BNVT	PA-28R-201T Turbo Arrow III	Victor Tango Group	
G-BNWA	Boeing 767-336ER	British Airways	
G-BNWB	Boeing 767-336ER	British Airways	
G-BNWC	Boeing 767-336ER	British Airways	
G-BNWD	Boeing 767-336ER	British Airways	
G-BNWH	Boeing 767-336ER	British Airways	
G-BNWI	Boeing 767-336ER	British Airways	
G-BNWM	Boeing 767-336ER	British Airways	
G-BNWN	Boeing 767-336ER	British Airways	
G-BNWO	Boeing 767-336ER	British Airways	
G-BNWR	Boeing 767-336ER	British Airways	
G-BNWS	Boeing 767-336ER	British Airways	
G-BNWT	Boeing 767-336ER	British Airways	
G-BNWU	Boeing 767-336ER	British Airways	
G-BNWV	Boeing 767-336ER	British Airways	
G-BNWW	Boeing 767-336ER	British Airways	
G-BNWX	Boeing 767-336ER	British Airways	

Notes	Reg.	Type	Owner or Operator
	G-BNWY	Boeing 767-336ER	British Airways
	G-BNWZ	Boeing 767-336ER	British Airways
	G-BNXD	Cessna 172N	General Aero Equipment Ltd
	G-BNXE	PA-28-161 Warrior II	M. S. Brown
	G-BNXK	Nott-Cameron ULD-3 balloon	J. R. P. Nott (G-BLJN)
	G-BNXL	Glaser-Dirks DG.400	M. Lee & P. Kingwill
	G-BNXM	PA-18 Super Cub 95	C. J. Gowthorpe
	G-BNXT	PA-28-161 Warrior II	Falcon Flying Services
	G-BNXU	PA-28-161 Warrior II	Friendly Warrior Group
	G-BNXV	PA-38-112 Tomahawk	W. B. Bateson
	G-BNXX	SOCATA TB20 Trinidad	Air Touring Ltd
	G-BNXZ	Thunder Ax7-77 balloon	Hale Hot Air Balloon Group
	G-BNYD	Bell 206B JetRanger 3	Toby Blackwell Ltd
	G-BNYK	PA-38-112 Tomahawk	Lomac Aviators Ltd
	G-BNYL	Cessna 152 II	V. J. Freeman
	G-BNYM	Cessna 172N	Kestrel Syndicate
	G-BNYO	Beech 76 Duchess	Multiflight Ltd
	G-BNYP	PA-28-181 Archer II	R. D. Cooper
	G-BNYZ	SNCAN Stampe SV.4E	Bianchi Film Aviation Services Ltd
	G-BNZB	PA-28-161 Warrior II	Falcon Flying Services Ltd
	G-BNZC	DHC.1 Chipmunk 22 (18671:671)	The Shuttleworth Collection
	G-BNZK	Thunder Ax7-77 balloon	T. D. Marsden
	G-BNZL	Rotorway Scorpion 133	J. R. Wraight
	G-BNZM	Cessna T.210N	A. J. M. Freeman
	G-BNZN	Cameron N-56 balloon	Balloon Sports HB/Sweden
	G-BNZO	Rotorway Executive	J. S. David
	G-BNZV	PA-25 Pawnee 235	Aeroklub Alpski Letalski Center Lesce/Slovenia
	G-BNZZ	PA-28-161 Warrior II	Providence Aviation Ltd
	G-BOAA	BAC-Aérospatiale Concorde 102 ★	Museum Of Flight East Fortune (G-N94AA)
	G-BOAB	BAC-Aérospatiale Concorde 102 ★	Preserved at Heathrow (G-N94AB)
	G-BOAC	BAC-Aérospatiale Concorde 102 ★	Displayed in viewing area Manchester International (G-N81AC)
	G-BOAF	BAC-Aérospatiale Concorde 102 ★	Bristol Aero Collection/Filton (G-N94AF)
	G-BOAH	PA-28-161 Warrior II	Aircraft Engineers Ltd
	G-BOAI	Cessna 152 II	Aviation Spirit Ltd
	G-BOAL	Cameron V-65 balloon	N. H. & A. M. Ponsford
	G-BOAU	Cameron V-77 balloon	G. T. Barstow
	G-BOBA	PA-28R-201 Arrow III	GT Ventures Ltd
	G-BOBR	Cameron N-77 balloon	Trigger Concepts Ltd
	G-BOBT	Stolp SA.300 Starduster Too	G-BOBT Group
	G-BOBV	Cessna F.150M	Sheffield Aero Club Ltd
	G-BOBY	Monnett Sonerai II	R. G. Hallam (stored)
	G-BOCG	PA-34-200T Seneca II	Oxford Aviation Academy (Oxford) Ltd
	G-BOCI	Cessna 140A	J. B. Bonnell
	G-BOCK	Sopwith Triplane (replica) (N6290)	The Shuttleworth Collection
	G-BOCL	Slingsby T.67C	Richard Brinklow Aviation Ltd
	G-BOCM	Slingsby T.67C	Richard Brinklow Aviation Ltd
	G-BOCN	Robinson R22 Beta	Northmore Aviation Ltd
	G-BODB	PA-28-161 Warrior II	Sherburn Aero Club Ltd
	G-BODC	PA-28-161 Warrior II	Sherburn Aero Club Ltd
	G-BODD	PA-28-161 Warrior II	L. W. Scattergood
	G-BODE	PA-28-161 Warrior II	Sherburn Aero Club Ltd
	G-BODO	Cessna 152	Enstone Sales and Services Ltd
	G-BODP	PA-38-112 Tomahawk	B. Petrie
	G-BODR	PA-28-161 Warrior II	Airways Aero Associations Ltd
	G-BODS	PA-38-112 Tomahawk	Coulson Flying Services Ltd
	G-BODT	Jodel D.18	L. D. McPhillips
	G-BODU	Scheibe SF.25C Falke	Hertfordshire County Scout Council
	G-BODY	Cessna 310R	Reconnaissance Ventures Ltd
	G-BODZ	Robinson R22 Beta	Langley Aviation Ltd
	G-BOEE	PA-28-181 Archer II	J. C. & G. M. Brinkley
	G-BOEH	Jodel DR.340	Piper Flyers Group
	G-BOEK	Cameron V-77 balloon	R. I. M. Kerr & ptnrs
	G-BOEM	Pitts S-2A	M. Murphy
	G-BOEN	Cessna 172M	R. Chynoransky & M. Novansky
	G-BOER	PA-28-161 Warrior II	Just Plane Trading Ltd
	G-BOET	PA-28RT-201 Arrow IV	B. C. Chambers (G-IBEC)
	G-BOFC	Beech 76 Duchess	Magenta Ltd
	G-BOFF	Cameron N-77 balloon	R. S. McKibbin
	G-BOFL	Cessna 152 II	GEM Integrated Solutions Ltd
	G-BOFM	Cessna 152 II	GEM Integrated Solutions Ltd

Reg.	Type	Owner or Operator	Notes
G-BOFW	Cessna A.150M	D. F. Donovan	
G-BOFY	PA-28 Cherokee 140	R. A. Brown	
G-BOFZ	PA-28-161 Warrior II	R. W. Harris	
G-BOGI	Robin DR.400/180	A. L. M. Shepherd	
G-BOGK	ARV Super 2	M. K. Field	
G-BOGM	PA-28RT-201T Turbo Arrow IV	RJP Aviation	
G-BOGO	PA-32R-301T Saratoga SP	Diff Air KFT	
G-BOGY	Cameron V-77 balloon	A. Reimann & P. Spellward	
G-BOHA	PA-28-161 Warrior II	Phoenix Aviation	
G-BOHD	Colt 77A balloon	D. B. Court	
G-BOHF	Thunder Ax8-84 balloon	J. A. Harris	
G-BOHH	Cessna 172N	G-BOHH Group	
G-BOHI	Cessna 152 II	Cirrus Aviation Ltd	
G-BOHJ	Cessna 152 II	Airlaunch	
G-BOHM	PA-28 Cherokee 180	B. F. Keogh & R. A. Scott	
G-BOHO	PA-28-161 Warrior II	Egressus Flying Group	
G-BOHR	PA-28-151 Warrior	R. M. E. Garforth	
G-BOHT	PA-38-112 Tomahawk	St. George Flight Training Ltd	
G-BOHU	PA-38-112 Tomahawk	D. A. Whitmore	
G-BOHV	Wittman W.8 Tailwind	R. A. Povall	
G-BOHW	Van's RV-4	A. Mercy	
G-BOIA	Cessna 180K	R. E. Styles & ptnrs	
G-BOIB	Wittman W.10 Tailwind	C. R. Nash	
G-BOIC	PA-28R-201T Turbo Arrow III	M. J. Pearson	
G-BOID	Bellanca 7ECA Citabria	D. Mallinson	
G-BOIG	PA-28-161 Warrior II	D. Vallence-Pell	
G-BOIK	Air Command 503 Commander	F. G. Shepherd	
G-BOIL	Cessna 172N	Upperstack Ltd	
G-BOIO	Cessna 152	Sandham Aviation	
G-BOIR	Cessna 152	Shropshire Aero Club Ltd	
G-BOIT	SOCATA TB10 Tobago	G-BOIT Flying Group	
G-BOIV	Cessna 150M	India Victor Group	
G-BOIX	Cessna 172N	JR Flying Ltd	
G-BOIY	Cessna 172N	L. W. Scattergood	
G-BOIZ	PA-34-200T Seneca II	S. F. Tebby & Son	
G-BOJB	Cameron V-77 balloon	I. M. & S. D. Warner	
G-BOJI	PA-28RT-201 Arrow IV	Arrow Two Group	
G-BOJK	PA-34-220T Seneca III	Redhill Flying Club (G-BRUF)	
G-BOJM	PA-28-181 Archer II	R. P. Emms	
G-BOJR	Cessna 172P	The Exeter Flying Club 2008 Ltd	
G-BOJS	Cessna 172P	Paul's Planes Ltdl	
G-BOJU	Cameron N-77 balloon	M. A. Scholes	
G-BOJW	PA-28-161 Warrior II	B. Tearney	
G-BOJZ	PA-28-161 Warrior II	Falcon Flying Services	
G-BOKA	PA-28-201T Turbo Dakota	CBG Aviation Ltdl	
G-BOKB	PA-28-161 Warrior II	Apollo Aviation Advisory Ltd	
G-BOKH	Whittaker MW7	A. S. Watts	
G-BOKW	Bolkow Bo.208C Junior	L. S. Johnson	
G-BOKX	PA-28-161 Warrior II	Shenley Farms (Aviation) Ltd	
G-BOKY	Cessna 152 II	D. F. F. & J. E. Poore	
G-BOLB	Taylorcraft BC-12-65	C. E. Tudor	
G-BOLC	Fournier RF-6B-100	J. D. Cohen	
G-BOLD	PA-38-112 Tomahawk	G-BOLD Group	
G-BOLE	PA-38-112 Tomahawk	Double S Group	
G-BOLG	Bellanca 7KCAB Citabria	B. R. Pearson	
G-BOLI	Cessna 172P	Boli Flying Club	
G-BOLL	Lake LA-4 Skimmer	M. C. Holmes	
G-BOLN	Colt 21A balloon	G. Everett	
G-BOLO	Bell 206B JetRanger	Hargreaves Leasing Ltd	
G-BOLP	Colt 21A balloon	Spirit Balloons Ltd	
G-BOLR	Colt 21A balloon	C. J. Sanger-Davies	
G-BOLS	FRED Srs 2	I. F. Vaughan	
G-BOLT	Rockwell Commander 114	I. R. Harnett	
G-BOLU	Robin R.3000/120	M. A. Hogbin	
G-BOLV	Cessna 152 II	Synergy Aircraft Leasing Ltd	
G-BOLW	Cessna 152 II	A. Jahanfar	
G-BOLY	Cessna 172N	Simair Ltd	
G-BOMB	Cassutt Racer IIIM	D. Hart	
G-BOMN	Cessna 150F	Auburn Flying Group	
G-BOMO	PA-38-112 Tomahawk II	APB Leasing Ltd	
G-BOMP	PA-28-181 Archer II	D. Carter	
G-BOMS	Cessna 172N	Penchant Ltd	

Notes	Reg.	Type	Owner or Operator
	G-BOMU	PA-28-181 Archer II	J. Sawyer
	G-BOMY	PA-28-161 Warrior II	BOMY Group
	G-BOMZ	PA-38-112 Tomahawk	G-BOMZ Aviation
	G-BONC	PA-28RT-201 Arrow IV	G-BONC Flying Group
	G-BONG	Enstrom F-28A-UK	K. G. Ward
	G-BONP	CFM Streak Shadow	G. J. Chater
	G-BONR	Cessna 172N	D. I. Craikl
	G-BONS	Cessna 172N	BONS Group
	G-BONT	Slingsby T.67M Mk II	Etico
	G-BONU	Slingsby T.67B	R. L. Brinklow
	G-BONW	Cessna 152 II	Lincoln Aero Club Ltd
	G-BONY	Denney Kitfox Model 1	R. Dunn & P. F. Hill
	G-BONZ	Beech V35B Bonanza	P. M. Coulten
	G-BOOB	Cameron N-65 balloon	P. J. Hooper
	G-BOOC	PA-18 Super Cub 150	S. A. C. Whitcombe
	G-BOOD	Slingsby T.31M Motor Tutor	K. A. Hale
	G-BOOE	GA-7 Cougar	R. J. Moller
	G-BOOF	PA-28-181 Archer II	H. Merkado
	G-BOOG	PA-28RT-201T Turbo Arrow IV	Simair Ltd
	G-BOOH	Jodel D.112	R. M. MacCormac
	G-BOOI	Cessna 152	Stapleford Flying Club Ltd
	G-BOOL	Cessna 172N	J. R. Payne
	G-BOOW	Aerosport Scamp	D. A. Weldon/Ireland
	G-BOOX	Rutan LongEz	I. R. Wilde
	G-BOOZ	Cameron N-77 balloon	J. E. F. Kettlety
	G-BOPA	PA-28-181 Archer II	Flyco Ltd
	G-BOPC	PA-28-161 Warrior II	Aeros Ltd
	G-BOPD	Bede BD-4	S. T. Dauncey
	G-BOPH	Cessna TR.182RG	J. M. Mitchell
	G-BOPO	Brooklands OA.7 Optica	J. K. Edgley
	G-BOPR	Brooklands OA.7 Optica	Aeroelvira Ltd
	G-BOPT	Grob G.115	LAC Flying School
	G-BOPU	Grob G.115	LAC Flying School
	G-BORB	Cameron V-77 balloon	M. H. Wolff
	G-BORD	Thunder Ax7-77 balloon	D. D. Owen
	G-BORE	Colt 77A balloon	J. D. & C. J. Medcalf
	G-BORG	Campbell Cricket	R. L. Gilmore
	G-BORH	PA-34-200T Seneca II	The Construction Workers Guild Ltd
	G-BORK	PA-28-161 Warrior II	The Warrior Group (G-IIIC)
	G-BORL	PA-28-161 Warrior II	Westair Flying School Ltd
	G-BORM	HS.748 Srs 2B ★	Airport Fire Service/Exeter
	G-BORN	Cameron N-77 balloon	I. Chadwick
	G-BORS	PA-28-181 Archer II	Silverstar Aviation Ltd
	G-BORW	Cessna 172P	Briter Aviation Ltd
	G-BORY	Cessna 150L	D. H. G. Penney
	G-BOSB	Thunder Ax7-77 balloon	A. M. Holly
	G-BOSD	PA-34-200T Seneca II	Bristol Flying Centre Ltd
	G-BOSE	PA-28-181 Archer II	G-BOSE Group
	G-BOSJ	Nord 3400 (124)	A. I. Milne
	G-BOSM	Jodel DR.253B	A. G. Stevens
	G-BOSN	AS.355F1 Twin Squirrel	Helicopter Services
	G-BOSO	Cessna A.152	J. S. Develin & Z. Islam
	G-BOTD	Cameron O-105 balloon	P. J. Beglan/France
	G-BOTF	PA-28-151 Warrior	G-BOTF Group
	G-BOTG	Cessna 152 II	Donington Aviation Ltd
	G-BOTH	Cessna 182Q	P. E. Gethin
	G-BOTI	PA-28-151 Warrior	Falcon Flying Services
	G-BOTK	Cameron O-105 balloon	N. Woodham
	G-BOTN	PA-28-161 Warrior II	Apollo Aviation Advisory
	G-BOTO	Bellanca 7ECA Citabria	G-BOTO Group
	G-BOTP	Cessna 150J	R. F. Finnis & C. P. Williams
	G-BOTU	Piper J-3C-65 Cub	T. L. Giles
	G-BOTV	PA-32RT-300 Lance II	Robin Lance Aviation Association Ltd
	G-BOTW	Cameron V-77 balloon	M. R. Jeynes
	G-BOUE	Cessna 172N	P. Gray & G. N. R. Bradley
	G-BOUF	Cessna 172N	B. P. & M. I. Sneap
	G-BOUJ	Cessna 150M	UJ Flying Group
	G-BOUK	PA-34-200T Seneca II	C. J. & R. J. Barnes
	G-BOUL	PA-34-200T Seneca II	Oxford Aviation Academy (Oxford) Ltd
	G-BOUM	PA-34-200T Seneca II	Oxford Aviation Academy (Oxford) Ltd
	G-BOUN	Rand-Robinson KR-2	P. J. Brookman
	G-BOUT	Colomban MC.12 Cri-Cri	C. K. Farley

Reg.	Type	Owner or Operator	Notes
G-BOUV	Bensen B.8MR	L. R. Phillips	
G-BOUZ	Cessna 150G	Atlantic Bridge Aviation Ltd	
G-BOVB	PA-15 Vagabond	J. R. Kimberley	
G-BOVK	PA-28-161 Warrior II	Multiflight Ltd	
G-BOVT	Cessna 150M	C. J. Hopewell	
G-BOVU	Stoddard-Hamilton Glasair III	B. R. Chaplin	
G-BOVX	Hughes 269C	Arrow Aviation Services Ltd	
G-BOWB	Cameron V-77 balloon	R. A. Benham	
G-BOWE	PA-34-200T Seneca II	Oxford Aviation Academy (Oxford) Ltd	
G-BOWM	Cameron V-56 balloon	R. S. Breakwell	
G-BOWN	PA-12 Super Cruiser	T. L. Giles	
G-BOWO	Cessna R.182	D. A. H. Morris (G-BOTR)	
G-BOWP	Jodel D.120A	J. M. Pearson	
G-BOWV	Cameron V-65 balloon	R. A. Harris	
G-BOWY	PA-28RT-201T Turbo Arrow IV	J. S. Develin & Z. Islam	
G-BOWZ	Bensen B.80V	W. W. Heslop	
G-BOXA	PA-28-161 Warrior II	Channel Islands Aero Club (Jersey) Ltd	
G-BOXC	PA-28-161 Warrior II	Channel Islands Aero Club (Jersey) Ltd	
G-BOXG	Cameron O-77 balloon	R. A. Wicks	
G-BOXH	Pitts S-1S Special	G. R. Cotterell	
G-BOXJ	Piper J-3C-65 Cub	A. Bendkowski	
G-BOXR	GA-7 Cougar	Plane Talking Ltd	
G-BOXT	Hughes 269C	Goldenfly Ltd	
G-BOXU	AA-5B Tiger	Marcher Aviation Group	
G-BOXV	Pitts S-1S Special	C. Waddington	
G-BOXW	Cassutt Racer Srs IIIM	D. I. Johnson	
G-BOYB	Cessna A.152	Modi Aviation Ltd	
G-BOYC	Robinson R22 Beta	Yorkshire Helicopters	
G-BOYF	Sikorsky S-76B	Darley Stud Management Co Ltd	
G-BOYH	PA-28-151 Warrior	R. Nightingale	
G-BOYI	PA-28-161 Warrior II	G-BOYI Group	
G-BOYL	Cessna 152 II	Redhill Air Services Ltd	
G-BOYM	Cameron O-84 balloon	M. P. Ryan	
G-BOYO	Cameron V-20 balloon	J. M. Willard	
G-BOYP	Cessna 172N	I. D. & D. Brierley	
G-BOYR	Cessna F.337G	Tri-Star Farms Ltd	
G-BOYV	PA-28R-201T Turbo Arrow III	N. Halsall	
G-BOYX	Robinson R22 Beta	R. Towle	
G-BOZI	PA-28-161 Warrior II	Aerolease Ltd	
G-BOZN	Cameron N-77 balloon	Calarel Developments Ltd	
G-BOZO	AA-5B Tiger	J. Willis	
G-BOZR	Cessna 152 II	GEM Integrated Solutions Ltd	
G-BOZS	Pitts S-1C Special	S. D. Blakey	
G-BOZV	CEA DR.340 Major	C. J. Turner & S. D. Kent	
G-BOZW	Bensen B.8M	M. E. Wills	
G-BOZY	Cameron RTW-120 balloon	Magical Adventures Ltd	
G-BOZZ	AA-5B Tiger	Dolphin Property (Management) Ltd	
G-BPAA	Acro Advanced	B. O. & F. A. Smith	
G-BPAB	Cessna 150M	M. T. Farmer	
G-BPAF	PA-28-161 Warrior II	S. T. & T. W. Gilbert	
G-BPAJ	DH.82A Tiger Moth	P. A. Jackson (G-AOIX)	
G-BPAL	DHC.1 Chipmunk 22 (WG350)	K. F. & P. Tomsett (G-BCYE)	
G-BPAW	Cessna 150M	G-BPAW Group	
G-BPAY	PA-28-181 Archer II	D. A. C. Smith	
G-BPBB	Evans VP-2 (mod)	A. Bleese	
G-BPBJ	Cessna 152 II	W. Shaw & P. G. Haines	
G-BPBK	Cessna 152 II	Swiftair Maintenance Ltd	
G-BPBM	PA-28-161 Warrior II	Redhill Air Services Ltd	
G-BPBO	PA-28RT-201T Turbo Arrow IV	Tile Holdings Ltd	
G-BPBP	Brügger MB.2 Colibri	D. A. Preston	
G-BPBW	Cameron O-105 balloon	R. J. Mansfield	
G-BPCA	BN-2B-26 Islander	Loganair Ltd (G-BLNX)	
G-BPCF	Piper J-3C-65 Cub	B. M. O'Brien	
G-BPCI	Cessna R.172K	N. A. Bairstol	
G-BPCK	PA-28-161 Warrior II	Compton Abbas Airfield Ltd	
G-BPCL	SA Bulldog Srs 120/128 (HKG-6)	Isohigh Ltd	
G-BPCR	Mooney M.20K	T. & R. Harris	
G-BPCX	PA-28-236 Dakota	Blue Yonder Aviation Ltd	
G-BPDE	Colt 56A balloon	J. E. Weidema/Netherlands	
G-BPDG	Cameron V-77 balloon	F. R. Battersby	
G-BPDJ	Chris Tena Mini Coupe	J. J. Morrissey	

Notes	Reg.	Type	Owner or Operator
	G-BPDM	CASA 1.131E Jungmann 2000(781-32)	J. D. Haslam
	G-BPDT	PA-28-161 Warrior II	Channel Islands Aero Club (Jersey) Ltd
	G-BPDV	Pitts S-1S Special	J. Vize
	G-BPEM	Cessna 150K	C. G. Rice & K. McDonald
	G-BPEO	Cessna 152 II	JHP Aviation Ltd
	G-BPES	PA-38-112 Tomahawk II	Sherwood Flying Club Ltd
	G-BPEZ	Colt 77A balloon	J. W. Adkins
	G-BPFB	Colt 77A balloon	C. J. Freeman
	G-BPFC	Mooney M.20C	It's Plane Crazy Ltd
	G-BPFD	Jodel D.112	M. & S. Mills
	G-BPFH	PA-28-161 Warrior II	M. H. Kleiser
	G-BPFI	PA-28-181 Archer II	F. Teagle
	G-BPFL	Davis DA-2	B. W. Griffiths
	G-BPFM	Aeronca 7AC Champion	D. Boyce
	G-BPFZ	Cessna 152 II	Devon and Somerset Flight Training Ltd
	G-BPGC	Air Command 532 Elite	A. G. W. Davis
	G-BPGD	Cameron V-65 balloon	Gone With The Wind Ltd
	G-BPGE	Cessna U.206C	Scottish Parachute Club
	G-BPGF	Thunder Ax7-77 balloon	M. Schiavo
	G-BPGH	EAA Acro Sport II	M. F. Humphries
	G-BPGK	Aeronca 7AC Champion	D. A. Crompton & G. C. Holmes
	G-BPGT	Colt AS-80 Mk II airship	P. Porati/Italy
	G-BPGU	PA-28-181 Archer II	G. Underwood
	G-BPGZ	Cessna 150G	J. B. Scott
	G-BPHG	Robin DR.400/180	P. A. Giblett
	G-BPHH	Cameron V-77 balloon	C. D. Aindow
	G-BPHI	PA-38-112 Tomahawk	J. S. Devlin & Z. Islam
	G-BPHJ	Cameron V-77 balloon	C. W. Brown
	G-BPHK	Whittaker MW7	J. S. Shufflebottom
	G-BPHL	PA-28-161 Warrior II	J. D. Swales
	G-BPHO	Taylorcraft BC-12	B. J. Swanton
	G-BPHP	Taylorcraft BC-12-65	Bluebird Group
	G-BPHR	DH.82A Tiger Moth (A17-48)	N. Parry
	G-BPHU	Thunder Ax7-77 balloon	R. P. Waite
	G-BPHX	Cessna 140	M. J. Medland
	G-BPHZ	MS.505 Criquet (DM+BK)	Aero Vintage Ltd
	G-BPIF	Bensen-Parsons 2-place gyroplane	B. J. L. P. & W. J. A. L. de Saar
	G-BPII	Denney Kitfox	G-BPII Group
	G-BPIK	PA-38-112 Tomahawk	Carlisle Flight Training Ltd
	G-BPIP	Slingsby T.31 Motor Cadet III	V. K. Meers
	G-BPIR	Scheibe SF.25E Super Falke	A. P. Askwith
	G-BPIT	Robinson R22 Beta	NA Air Ltd
	G-BPIU	PA-28-161 Warrior II	Golf India Uniform Group
	G-BPIV	B.149 Bolingbroke Mk IVT (R3821)	Blenheim (Duxford) Ltd
	G-BPIZ	AA-5B Tiger	D. A. Horsley
	G-BPJB	Schweizer 269C	Escola de Aviacao Aerocondor SA
	G-BPJG	PA-18 Super Cub 150	M. W. Stein
	G-BPJK	Colt 77A balloon	P. Lavelle
	G-BPJP	PA-28-161 Cadet	Aviation Rentals
	G-BPJS	PA-28-161 Cadet	Plane Talking Ltd
	G-BPJU	PA-28-161 Cadet	Aviation Rentals
	G-BPJW	Cessna A.150K	G. Duck
	G-BPJZ	Cameron O-160 balloon	M. L. Gabb
	G-BPKF	Grob G.115	Swiftair Maintenance Ltd
	G-BPKK	Denney Kitfox Mk 1	C. P. Moss
	G-BPKM	PA-28-161 Warrior II	R. Cass
	G-BPKO	Cessna 140	A. Ottomaniello
	G-BPKR	PA-28-151 Warrior	Aeros Leasing Ltd
	G-BPKT	Piper J.5A Cub Cruiser	A. J. Greenslade
	G-BPLH	Jodel DR.1051	C. K. Farley
	G-BPLM	AIA Stampe SV.4C	C. J. Jessonl
	G-BPLV	Cameron V-77 balloon	V. Grenier/France
	G-BPLZ	Hughes 369HS	M. A. & R. J. Fawcett
	G-BPMB	Maule M5-235C Lunar Rocket	Maule Flying group
	G-BPME	Cessna 152 II	A. Jahanfar
	G-BPMF	PA-28-151 Warrior	Mike Foxtrot Group
	G-BPML	Cessna 172M	N. A. Bilton
	G-BPMM	Champion 7ECA Citabria	H. J. Taggart
	G-BPMU	Nord 3202B	E. C. Murgatroyd (G-BIZJ)
	G-BPMW	QAC Quickie Q.2	P. M. Wright (G-OICI/G-OGKN)
	G-BPMX	ARV Super 2	R. A. Collins
	G-BPNA	Cessna 150L	Wolds Flyers Syndicate

Reg.	Type	Owner or Operator	Notes
G-BPNI	Robinson R22 Beta	Heliflight (UK) Ltd	
G-BPNO	Zlin Z.326 Trener Master	J. A. S. Bailey & S. T. Logan	
G-BPOA	Gloster Meteor T.7 (WF877) ★	39 Restoration Group	
G-BPOB	Sopwith Camel F.1 (replica) (B2458:R)	Flying Aces Movie Aircraft Collection	
G-BPOM	PA-28-161 Warrior II	POM Flying Group	
G-BPON	PA-34-200T Seneca II	TGD Leasing Ltd	
G-BPOS	Cessna 150M	S. G. Lewis	
G-BPOT	PA-28-181 Archer II	P. S. Simpson	
G-BPOU	Luscombe 8A Silvaire	J. L. Grayer	
G-BPPA	Cameron O-65 balloon	Rix Petroleum Ltd	
G-BPPE	PA-38-112 Tomahawk	First Air Ltd	
G-BPPF	PA-38-112 Tomahawk	Bristol Strut Flying Group	
G-BPPJ	Cameron A-180 balloon	D. J. Farrar	
G-BPPK	PA-28-151 Warrior	Jazzlink Ltd	
G-BPPO	Luscombe 8A Silvaire	P. Dyer	
G-BPPP	Cameron V-77 balloon	Sarnia Balloon Group	
G-BPPS	Mudry CAARP CAP-21	L. Van Vuuren	
G-BPPY	Hughes 269B	M. D. Leeney	
G-BPPZ	Taylorcraft BC-12D	G. C. Smith	
G-BPRA	Aeronca 11AC Chief	P. L. Clements	
G-BPRC	Cameron 77 Elephant SS balloon	A. Schneider/Germany	
G-BPRD	Pitts S-1C Special	Parrot Aerobatic Group	
G-BPRI	AS.355F1 Twin Squirrel	MW Helicopters Ltd (G-TVPA)	
G-BPRJ	AS.355F1 Twin Squirrel	PLM Dollar Group Ltd	
G-BPRL	AS.355F1 Twin Squirrel	MW Helicopters Ltd	
G-BPRM	Cessna F.172L	BJ Aviation Ltd (G-AZKG)	
G-BPRN	PA-28-161 Warrior II	Air Navigation & Trading Co Ltd	
G-BPRX	Aeronca 11AC Chief	J. E. S. Turner	
G-BPRY	PA-28-161 Warrior II	White Wings Aviation Ltd	
G-BPSH	Cameron V-77 balloon	P. G. Hossack	
G-BPSJ	Thunder Ax6-56 balloon	V. Hyland	
G-BPSL	Cessna 177	K. S. Herbert	
G-BPSO	Cameron N-90 balloon	J. Oberprieler/Germany	
G-BPSR	Cameron V-77 balloon	K. J. A. Maxwell	
G-BPSS	Cameron A-120 balloon	Anglian Countryside Balloons Ltd	
G-BPTA	Stinson 108-2	M. L. Ryan	
G-BPTD	Cameron V-77 balloon	J. Lippett	
G-BPTE	PA-28-181 Archer II	J. S. Develin & Z. Islam	
G-BPTG	Rockwell Commander 112TC	B. Ogunyemi	
G-BPTI	SOCATA TB20 Trinidad	N. Davis	
G-BPTL	Cessna 172N	Tin Lizzie Group	
G-BPTS	CASA 1.131E Jungmann 1000 (E3B-153:781-75)	Aerobatic Displays Ltd	
G-BPTU	Cessna 152	A. M. Alam/Panshanger	
G-BPTV	Bensen B.8	C. Munro	
G-BPTZ	Robinson R22 Beta	Kuki Helicopter Sales Ltd and S. J. Nicholls	
G-BPUA	EAA Sport Biplane	E. J. & M. P. Hill	
G-BPUB	Cameron V-31 balloon	M. T. Evans	
G-BPUF	Thunder Ax6-56Z balloon	R. C. & M. A. Trimble (G-BHRL)	
G-BPUL	PA-18 Super Cub 150	C. D. Duthy-James	
G-BPUM	Cessna R.182RG	R. C. Chapman	
G-BPUP	Whittaker MW7	J. H. Beard	
G-BPUR	Piper J-3L-65 Cub ★	H. A. D. Monro	
G-BPUS	Rans S-9 Chaos	A. J. Sawicki	
G-BPUU	Cessna 140	D. R. Speight	
G-BPUW	Colt 90A balloon	S. Sonnenberg/Germany	
G-BPVA	Cessna 172F	S. Lancashire Flyers Group	
G-BPVE	Bleriot IX (replica) (1) ★	Bianchi Aviation Film Services Ltd/Booker	
G-BPVH	Cub Aircraft J-3C-65 Prospector	D. E. Cooper-Maguire	
G-BPVI	PA-32R-301 Saratoga SP	M. T. Coppen	
G-BPVK	Varga 2150A Kachina	D. W. Parfrey	
G-BPVM	Cameron V-77 balloon	J. Dyer	
G-BPVN	PA-32R-301T Turbo Saratoga SP	R. Weston	
G-BPVO	Cassutt Racer IIIM	K. P. Rusling	
G-BPVW	CASA 1.131E Jungmann 2000	C. & J-W. Labeij/Netherlands	
G-BPVZ	Luscombe 8E Silvaire	J. W. Macdonald, S. M. Thomas & A. P. Wilkie	
G-BPWB	Sikorsky S-61N	Bristow Helicopters Ltd/HM Coastguard	
G-BPWC	Cameron V-77 balloon	R. F. Davey	
G-BPWD	Cessna 120	Peregrine Flying Group	
G-BPWE	PA-28-161 Warrior II	RPR Associates Ltd	
G-BPWG	Cessna 150M	GB Pilots Wilsford Group	
G-BPWI	Bell 206B JetRanger 3	Warren Aviation	

Notes	Reg.	Type	Owner or Operator
	G-BPWK	Sportavia Fournier RF-5B	G-BPWK Flying Group
	G-BPWL	PA-25 Pawnee 235	Tecair Aviation Ltd
	G-BPWM	Cessna 150L	P. D. Button
	G-BPWN	Cessna 150L	A. J. & N. J. Bissex
	G-BPWP	Rutan LongEz (modified)	D. A. Field
	G-BPWR	Cessna R.172K	J. A. & D. T. A. Rees
	G-BPWS	Cessna 172P	Chartstone Ltd
	G-BPXA	PA-28-181 Archer II	Cherokee Flying Group
	G-BPXE	Enstrom 280C Shark	A. Healy
	G-BPXG	Colt 45A balloon	Zebedee Balloon Service Ltd
	G-BPXJ	PA-28RT-201T Turbo Arrow IV	J. France & M. Holubecki
	G-BPXX	PA-34-200T Seneca II	Yorkshire Aviation Ltd
	G-BPXY	Aeronca 11AC Chief	P. L. Turner
	G-BPYJ	Wittman W.8 Tailwind	J. P. & Y. Mills
	G-BPYL	Hughes 369D	Morcorp (BVI) Ltd
	G-BPYN	Piper J-3C-65 Cub	The Aquila Group
	G-BPYR	PA-31-310 Turbo Navajo	Jota Aircraft Leasing Ltd
	G-BPYS	Cameron O-77 balloon	D. J. Goldsmith
	G-BPYT	Cameron V-77 balloon	M. H. Redman
	G-BPYV	Cameron V-77 balloon	R. J. Shortall
	G-BPYY	Cameron A-180 balloon	G. D. Fitzpatrick
	G-BPYZ	Thunder Ax7-77 balloon	J. E. Astall
	G-BPZA	Luscombe 8A Silvaire	M. J. Wright
	G-BPZB	Cessna 120	Cessna 120 Group
	G-BPZC	Luscombe 8A Silvaire	C. C. & J. M. Lovell
	G-BPZD	SNCAN NC.858S	Zula Delta Syndicate
	G-BPZE	Luscombe 8E Silvaire	A. V. Harmer
	G-BPZM	PA-28RT-201 Arrow IV	Airways Flight Training (Exeter) Ltd (G-ROYW/G-CRTI)
	G-BPZP	Robin DR.400/180R	S. G. Jones
	G-BPZS	Colt 105A balloon	L. E. Giles
	G-BPZU	Scheibe SF.25C Falke	Southdown Gliding Club Ltd
	G-BPZY	Pitts S-1C Special	J. S. Mitchell
	G-BPZZ	Thunder Ax8-105 balloon	Capricorn Balloons Ltd
	G-BRAA	Pitts S-1C Special	R. J. Hodder
	G-BRAK	Cessna 172N	Falcon Flying Services Ltd
	G-BRAM	Mikoyan MiG-21PF (503) ★	FAST Museum/Farnborough
	G-BRAR	Aeronca 7AC Champion	R. B. Armitage
	G-BRBA	PA-28-161 Warrior II	B. Willis
	G-BRBB	PA-28-161 Warrior II	M. A. & A. J. Bell
	G-BRBC	NA T-6G Texan	A. P. Murphy
	G-BRBD	PA-28-151 Warrior	Compton Abbas Airfield Ltd
	G-BRBE	PA-28-161 Warrior II	Solo Services Ltd
	G-BRBG	PA-28 Cherokee 180	B. J. Millington
	G-BRBH	Cessna 150H	J. Maffia & H. Merkado
	G-BRBI	Cessna 172N	Skyhawk Flying Group
	G-BRBJ	Cessna 172M	N. Foster
	G-BRBK	Robin DR.400/180	R. Kemp
	G-BRBL	Robin DR.400/180	C. A. Merren
	G-BRBM	Robin DR.400/180	R. W. Davies
	G-BRBN	Pitts S-1S Special	D. R. Evans
	G-BRBO	Cameron V-77 balloon	M. B. Murby
	G-BRBP	Cessna 152	Just Plane Trading Ltd
	G-BRBV	Piper J-4A Cub Coupe	P. Clarke
	G-BRBW	PA-28 Cherokee 140	Air Navigation and Trading Co Ltd
	G-BRBX	PA-28-181 Archer II	Trent 199 Flying Group
	G-BRCA	Jodel D.112	R. C. Jordan
	G-BRCE	Pitts S-1C Special	M. P. & S. T. Barnard
	G-BRCF	Montgomerie-Bensen B.8MR	J. S. Walton
	G-BRCJ	Cameron H-20 balloon	P. A. Sweatman
	G-BRCM	Cessna 172L	S. G. E. Plessis & D. C. C. Handley
	G-BRCO	Cameron H-20 balloon	P. Lawman
	G-BRCT	Denney Kitfox Mk 2	M. L. Roberts
	G-BRCV	Aeronca 7AC Champion	P. I. and D. M. Morgans
	G-BRCW	Aeronca 11AC Chief	R. B. Griffin
	G-BRDD	Avions Mudry CAP-10B	T. A. Smith
	G-BRDE	Thunder Ax7-77 balloon	D. J. Keys
	G-BRDF	PA-28-161 Warrior II	White Waltham Airfield Ltd
	G-BRDG	PA-28-161 Warrior II	Falcon Flying Services
	G-BRDJ	Luscombe 8A Silvaire	P. G. Stewart
	G-BRDM	PA-28-161 Warrior II	White Waltham Airfield Ltd

Reg.	Type	Owner or Operator	Notes
G-BRDO	Cessna 177B	Cardinal Aviation	
G-BRDT	Cameron DP-70 airship	Balloon Promotion SAS	
G-BRDV	Viking Wood Products Spitfire Prototype replica (K5054) ★	Solent Sky, Southampton	
G-BRDW	PA-24 Comanche 180	I. P. Gibson	
G-BREA	Bensen B.8MR	D. J. Martin	
G-BREB	Piper J-3C-65 Cub	J. R. Wraight	
G-BREH	Cameron V-65 balloon	S. E. & V. D. Hurst	
G-BREL	Cameron O-77 balloon	R. A. Patey	
G-BREP	PA-28RT-201 Arrow IV	Jetstream Executive Travel Ltd	
G-BREU	Montgomerie-Bensen B.8MR	J. S. Firth	
G-BREX	Cameron O-84 balloon	P. Hegarty	
G-BREY	Taylorcraft BC-12D	BREY Group	
G-BREZ	Cessna 172M	Pilot Flying Group	
G-BRFB	Rutan LongEz	A. R. Oliver	
G-BRFC	Percival P.57 Sea Prince T.Mk.1 (WP321)	A. & G. A. Gainsford-Dixon	
G-BRFF	Colt 90A balloon	Amber Valley Aviation	
G-BRFI	Aeronca 7DC Champion	A. C. Lines	
G-BRFJ	Aeronca 11AC Chief	J. M. Mooney	
G-BRFL	PA-38-112 Tomahawk	D. P. Chowen	
G-BRFM	PA-28-161 Warrior II	British Disabled Flying Association	
G-BRFO	Cameron V-77 balloon	Hedge Hoppers Balloon Group	
G-BRFW	Montgomerie-Bensen B.8 2-seat	A. J. Barker	
G-BRFX	Pazmany PL.4A	D. E. Hills	
G-BRGD	Cameron O-84 balloon	R. G. Russell	
G-BRGE	Cameron N-90 balloon	Oakfield Farm Products Ltd	
G-BRGF	Luscombe 8E Silvaire	Luscombe Flying Group	
G-BRGI	PA-28 Cherokee 180	R. A. Buckfield	
G-BRGT	PA-32 Cherokee Six 260	D. A. Hitchcock	
G-BRGW	Gardan GY-201 Minicab	R. G. White	
G-BRHA	PA-32RT-300 Lance II	Lance G-BRHA Group	
G-BRHG	Colt 90A balloon	R. D. Allen	
G-BRHO	PA-34-200 Seneca	Andrews Professional Colour Laboratories Ltd	
G-BRHP	Aeronca O-58B Grasshopper (31923)	C. J. Willis/Italy	
G-BRHR	PA-38-112 Tomahawk	D. C. Hanss	
G-BRHX	Luscombe 8E Silvaire	J. Lakin	
G-BRHY	Luscombe 8E Silvaire	A. R. W. Taylor	
G-BRIE	Cameron N-77 balloon	S. F. Redman	
G-BRIH	Taylorcraft BC-12D	IH Flying Group	
G-BRIJ	Taylorcraft F-19	M. W, Olliver	
G-BRIK	T.66 Nipper 3	P. R. Bentley	
G-BRIL	Piper J-5A Cub Cruiser	D. J. Bone	
G-BRIO	Turner Super T-40A	S. Bidwell	
G-BRIR	Cameron V-56 balloon	H. G. Davies & C. Dowd	
G-BRIS	Steen Skybolt	M. R. Jones	
G-BRIV	SOCATA TB9 Tampico Club	S. J. Taft	
G-BRIY	Taylorcraft DF-65 (42-58678:IY)	S. R. Potts	
G-BRJA	Luscombe 8A Silvaire	A. D. Keen	
G-BRJC	Cessna 120	M. J. Medland	
G-BRJK	Luscombe 8A Silvaire	C. J. L. Peat & M. Richardson	
G-BRJL	PA-15 Vagabond	A. R. Williams	
G-BRJN	Pitts S-1C Special	W. Chapel	
G-BRJT	Cessna 150H	Romeo Tango Group	
G-BRJV	PA-28-161 Cadet	Northumbria Flying School Ltd	
G-BRJX	Rand-Robinson KR-2	J. R. Bell	
G-BRJY	Rand-Robinson KR-2	R. E. Taylor	
G-BRKC	Auster J/1 Autocrat	J. W. Conlon	
G-BRKH	PA-28-236 Dakota	T. A. White	
G-BRKR	Cessna 182R	A. R. D. Brooker	
G-BRKW	Cameron V-77 balloon	T. J. Parker	
G-BRKY	Viking Dragonfly Mk II	G. D. Price	
G-BRLB	Air Command 532 Elite	F. G. Shepherd	
G-BRLF	Campbell Cricket (replica)	J. L. G. McLane	
G-BRLG	PA-28RT-201T Turbo Arrow IV	P. Lodge & J. G. McVey	
G-BRLI	Piper J-5A Cub Cruiser	Little Bear Ltd	
G-BRLL	Cameron A-105 balloon	P. A. Sweatman	
G-BRLO	PA-38-112 Tomahawk	St. George Flight Training Ltd	
G-BRLP	PA-38-112 Tomahawk	P. Barton, R. Ryan & P. Wayman	
G-BRLR	Cessna 150G	Blue Skys Aviation (NE) Ltd	
G-BRLS	Thunder Ax7-77 balloon	E. C. Meek	
G-BRLV	CCF Harvard IV (93542:LTA-542)	Extraviation Ltd	

Notes	Reg.	Type	Owner or Operator
	G-BRMA	WS-51 Dragonfly HR.5 (WG719) ★	IHM/Weston-super-Mare
	G-BRMB	B.192 Belvedere HC.1	IHM/Weston-super-Mare
	G-BRME	PA-28-181 Archer II	Keen Leasing Ltd
	G-BRMT	Cameron V-31 balloon	B. Reed
	G-BRMU	Cameron V-77 balloon	K. J. & G. R. Ibbotson
	G-BRMV	Cameron O-77 balloon	P. D. Griffiths
	G-BRNC	Cessna 150M	Penny Hydraulics Ltd
	G-BRND	Cessna 152 II	T. M. & M. L. Jones
	G-BRNE	Cessna 152 II	Redhill Air Services Ltd
	G-BRNK	Cessna 152 II	D. C. & M. Bonsall
	G-BRNN	Cessna 152 II	Sheffield Aero Club Ltd
	G-BRNT	Robin DR.400/180	C. E. Ponsford & ptnrs
	G-BRNU	Robin DR.400/180	November Uniform Travel Syndicate Ltd
	G-BRNV	PA-28-181 Archer II	N. S. Lyndhurst
	G-BRNW	Cameron V-77 balloon	N. Robertson & G. Smith
	G-BRNX	PA-22 Tri-Pacer 150	S. N. Askey
	G-BROE	Cameron N-65 balloon	A. I. Attwood
	G-BROG	Cameron V-65 balloon	R. Kunert
	G-BROI	CFM Streak Shadow Srs SA	A. Collinson
	G-BROJ	Colt 31A balloon	N. J. Langley
	G-BROO	Luscombe 8E Silvaire	P. R. Bush
	G-BROR	Piper J-3C-65 Cub	White Hart Flying Group
	G-BROX	Robinson R22 Beta	J. G. Burgess
	G-BROY	Cameron V-77 balloon	C. B. McDougall
	G-BROZ	PA-18 Super Cub 150	P. G. Kynsey
	G-BRPE	Cessna 120	W. B. Bateson
	G-BRPF	Cessna 120	G. A. Robson
	G-BRPG	Cessna 120	I. C. Lomax
	G-BRPH	Cessna 120	J. A. Cook
	G-BRPK	PA-28 Cherokee 140	G-BRPK Group
	G-BRPL	PA-28-140 Cherokee	Silverstar Aviation Ltd
	G-BRPM	T.66 Nipper 3	J. H. H. Turner
	G-BRPP	Brookland Hornet (modified)	B. J. L. P. & W. J. A. L. de Saar
	G-BRPR	Aeronca O-58B Grasshopper (31952)	A. F. Kutz
	G-BRPS	Cessna 177B	E. Janssen & A. Lietaert
	G-BRPT	Rans S.10 Sakota	A. R. Hawes
	G-BRPU	Beech 76 Duchess	Plane Talking Ltd
	G-BRPV	Cessna 152	Eastern Air Executive Ltd
	G-BRPX	Taylorcraft BC-12D	G-BRPX Group
	G-BRPY	PA-15 Vagabond	J. & V. Hobday
	G-BRPZ	Luscombe 8A Silvaire	C. A. Flint
	G-BRRB	Luscombe 8E Silvaire	J. Nicholls
	G-BRRD	Scheibe SF.25B Falke	G-BRRD Group
	G-BRRF	Cameron O-77 balloon	K. P. & G. J. Storey
	G-BRRG	Glaser-Dirks DG.500M	G-BRRG Syndicate
	G-BRRK	Cessna 182Q	Werewolf Aviation Ltd
	G-BRRR	Cameron V-77 balloon	K. P. & G. J. Storey
	G-BRRU	Colt 90A balloon	Reach For The Sky Ltd
	G-BRRY	Robinson R22 Beta	Fast Helicopters Ltd
	G-BRSA	Cameron N-56 balloon	C. Wilkinson
	G-BRSD	Cameron V-77 balloon	M. E. Granger
	G-BRSE	PA-28-161 Warrior II	Falcon Flying Services Ltd
	G-BRSF	VS.361 Spitfire HF.9c (RR232)	M. B. Phillips
	G-BRSJ	PA-38-112 Tomahawk II	APB Leasing Ltd
	G-BRSL	Cameron N-56 balloon	S. Budd
	G-BRSP	Air Command 532 Elite	G. M. Hobman
	G-BRSW	Luscombe 8A Silvaire	Bloody Mary Aviation
	G-BRSX	PA-15 Vagabond	M. R. Holden
	G-BRSY	Hatz CB-1	Eaglescott Hatz Biplane Group
	G-BRTD	Cessna 152 II	152 Group
	G-BRTJ	Cessna 150F	A. G. Arthur
	G-BRTL	Hughes 369E	Road Tech Computer Systems Ltd
	G-BRTP	Cessna 152 II	R. Lee
	G-BRTT	Schweizer 269C	Fairthorpe Ltd
	G-BRTV	Cameron O-77 balloon	S. D. Wrighton
	G-BRTW	Glaser-Dirks DG.400	I. J. Carruthers
	G-BRTX	PA-28-151 Warrior	Spectrum Flying Group
	G-BRUB	PA-28-161 Warrior II	Flytrek Ltd
	G-BRUD	PA-28-181 Archer II	FlyBPL.com
	G-BRUG	Luscombe 8E Silvaire	N. W. Barratt
	G-BRUH	Colt 105A balloon	D. C. Chipping/Portugal
	G-BRUJ	Boeing Stearman A.75N1 (6136:205)	R. M. Hughes

Reg.	Type	Owner or Operator	Notes
G-BRUM	Cessna A.152	A. J. Gomes	
G-BRUN	Cessna 120	A. R. M. Eagle, J. A. Longworth & J. Peake (G-BRDH)	
G-BRUO	Taylor JT.1 Monoplane	R. Hatton	
G-BRUV	Cameron V-77 balloon	T. W. & R. F. Benbrook	
G-BRUX	PA-44-180 Seminole	C. J. Thomas	
G-BRVB	Stolp SA.300 Starduster Too	G-VB Group	
G-BRVE	Beech D.17S	Patina Ltd	
G-BRVF	Colt 77A balloon	J. Adkins	
G-BRVG	NA SNJ-7 Texan (27)	D. Gilmour/Intrepid Aviation Co	
G-BRVI	Robinson R22 Beta	York Helicopters	
G-BRVJ	Slingsby T.31 Motor Cadet III	B. Outhwaite	
G-BRVL	Pitts S-1C Special	M. F. Pocock	
G-BRVN	Thunder Ax7-77 balloon	D. L. Beckwith	
G-BRVO	AS.350B Ecureuil	Rotorhire LLP	
G-BRVY	Thunder Ax8-90 balloon	G. E. Morris	
G-BRVZ	Jodel D.117	L. Holland	
G-BRWA	Aeronca 7AC Champion	J. R. Edwards	
G-BRWB	NA T-6G Texan (526)	R. Clifford	
G-BRWD	Robinson R22 Beta	Hughes Plant Ltd	
G-BRWP	CFM Streak Shadow	R. Biffin	
G-BRWR	Aeronca 11AC Chief	A. W. Crutcher	
G-BRWT	Scheibe SF.25C Falke	Booker Gliding Club Ltd	
G-BRWU	Luton LA-4A Minor	R. B. Webber	
G-BRWV	Brügger MB.2 Colibri	M. P. Wakem	
G-BRWX	Cessna 172P	R. A. Brown & A. C. Dove	
G-BRWZ	Cameron 90 Macaw SS balloon	Forbes Global Inc	
G-BRXA	Cameron O-120 balloon	R. J. Mansfield	
G-BRXD	PA-28-181 Archer II	D. D. Stone	
G-BRXE	Taylorcraft BC-12D	B. T. Morgan & W. J. Durrad	
G-BRXF	Aeronca 11AC Chief	Aeronca Flying Group	
G-BRXG	Aeronca 7AC Champion	X-Ray Golf Flying Group	
G-BRXH	Cessna 120	BRXH Group	
G-BRXL	Aeronca 11AC Chief (42-78044)	P. L. Green	
G-BRXN	Montgomerie-Bensen B.8MR	C. M. Frerk	
G-BRXP	SNCAN Stampe SV.4C (modified)	T. Brown	
G-BRXS	Howard Special T Minus	F. A. Bakir	
G-BRXT	BAe.146-200	E1076 Trading Ltd	
G-BRXV	Robinson R22 Beta	Heliflight (UK) Ltd	
G-BRXW	PA-24 Comanche 260	Oak Group	
G-BRXY	Pietenpol Air Camper	P. S. Ganczakowski	
G-BRZA	Cameron O-77 balloon	S. Nother	
G-BRZB	Cameron A-105 balloon	Headland Services Ltd	
G-BRZD	Hapi Cygnet SF-2A	C. I. Coghill	
G-BRZG	Enstrom F-28A	P. J. Price	
G-BRZI	Cameron N-180 balloon	Eastern Balloon Rides	
G-BRZK	Stinson 108-2	Voyager G-BRZK Syndicate	
G-BRZL	Pitts S-1D Special	T. R. G. Barnby	
G-BRZS	Cessna 172P	YP Flying Group	
G-BRZW	Rans S.10 Sakota	D. L. Davies	
G-BRZX	Pitts S-1S Special	Zulu Xray Group	
G-BRZZ	CFM Streak Shadow	J. A. Weston	
G-BSAI	Stoddard-Hamilton Glasair III	K. J. & P. J. Whitehead	
G-BSAJ	CASA 1.131E Jungmann 2000	P. G. Kynsey	
G-BSAK	Colt 21A balloon	M. D. Mitchell	
G-BSAS	Cameron V-65 balloon	P. Donkin	
G-BSAV	Thunder Ax7-77 balloon	I. G. & C. A. Lloyd	
G-BSAW	PA-28-161 Warrior II	Haimoss Ltd	
G-BSAZ	Denney Kitfox Mk 2	A. J. Lloyd & ptnrs	
G-BSBA	PA-28-161 Warrior II	Falcon Flying Services Ltd	
G-BSBG	CCF Harvard IV (20310:310)	A. P. St. John	
G-BSBI	Cameron O-77 balloon	D. M. Billing	
G-BSBR	Cameron V-77 balloon	R. P. Wade	
G-BSBT	Piper J-3C-65 Cub	A. R. Elliott	
G-BSBV	Rans S.10 Sakota	S. Bain	
G-BSBW	Bell 206B JetRanger 3	Heliflight (UK) Ltd	
G-BSBZ	Cessna 150M	DTG Aviation	
G-BSCC	Colt 105A balloon	Capricorn Balloons Ltd	
G-BSCE	Robinson R22 Beta	Carpets Direct (GB) Ltd	
G-BSCG	Denney Kitfox Mk 2	A. Levitt	
G-BSCH	Denney Kitfox Mk 2	G. R. Moore	

Notes	Reg.	Type	Owner or Operator
	G-BSCI	Colt 77A balloon	J. L. & S. Wrigglesworth
	G-BSCK	Cameron H-24 balloon	J. D. Shapland
	G-BSCN	SOCATA TB20 Trinidad	B. W. Dye
	G-BSCO	Thunder Ax7-77 balloon	F. J. Whalley
	G-BSCP	Cessna 152 II	Moray Flying Club (1990) Ltd
	G-BSCS	PA-28-181 Archer II	Wingtask 1995 Ltd
	G-BSCV	PA-28-161 Warrior II	Southwood Flying Group
	G-BSCW	Taylorcraft BC-65	G. Johnson
	G-BSCX	Thunder Ax8-105 balloon	S. Charlish
	G-BSCY	PA-28-151 Warrior	Take Flight Aviation Ltd
	G-BSCZ	Cessna 152 II	The RAF Halton Aeroplane Club Ltd
	G-BSDA	Taylorcraft BC-12D	D. G. Edwards
	G-BSDD	Denney Kitfox Mk 2	D. C. Crawley
	G-BSDH	Robin DR.400/180	R. L. Brucciani
	G-BSDI	Corben Junior Ace Model E	G. N. Holland
	G-BSDJ	Piper J-4E Cub Coupe	W. J. Siertsema
	G-BSDK	Piper J-5A Cub Cruiser	J. E. Mead
	G-BSDL	SOCATA TB10 Tobago	Delta Lima Group
	G-BSDN	PA-34-200T Seneca II	Jetstream Executive Travel Ltd
	G-BSDO	Cessna 152 II	J. Vickers
	G-BSDP	Cessna 152 II	Paul's Planes Ltd
	G-BSDS	Boeing Stearman E75 (118)	L. W. Scattergood
	G-BSDW	Cessna 182P	Parker Diving Ltd
	G-BSDX	Cameron V-77 balloon	G. P. & S. J. Allen
	G-BSDZ	Enstrom 280FX	T. Ratcliffe
	G-BSED	PA-22 Tri-Pacer 160 (modified)	M. D. N. Fisher
	G-BSEE	Rans S.9	R. P. Hothersall
	G-BSEF	PA-28 Cherokee 180	I. D. Wakeling
	G-BSEG	Ken Brock KB-2 gyroplane	S. J. M. Ledingham
	G-BSEJ	Cessna 150M	C. L. Day
	G-BSEK	Robinson R22	S. J. Strange
	G-BSEL	Slingsby T.61G Super Falke	D. G. Holley
	G-BSEP	Cessna 172	EPAviation
	G-BSER	PA-28 Cherokee 160	Yorkair Ltd
	G-BSEU	PA-28-181 Archer II	K. R. Taylor
	G-BSEV	Cameron O-77 balloon	P. B. Kenington
	G-BSEX	Cameron A-180 balloon	Heart of England Balloons
	G-BSEY	Beech A36 Bonanza	P. Malam-Wilson
	G-BSFA	Aero Designs Pulsar	P. F. Lorriman
	G-BSFD	Piper J-3C-65 Cub	P. E. S. Latham
	G-BSFE	PA-38-112 Tomahawk II	ACS Aviation Ltd
	G-BSFF	Robin DR.400/180R	Lasham Gliding Society Ltd
	G-BSFP	Cessna 152T	The Pilot Centre Ltd
	G-BSFR	Cessna 152 II	Galair Ltd
	G-BSFV	Woods Woody Pusher	M. G. Parsons
	G-BSFW	PA-15 Vagabond	J. R. Kimberley
	G-BSFX	Denney Kitfox Mk 2	F. Colman
	G-BSGB	Gaertner Ax4 Skyranger balloon	B. Gaertner
	G-BSGD	PA-28 Cherokee 180	R. J. Cleverley
	G-BSGF	Robinson R22 Beta	L. B. Clark
	G-BSGG	Denney Kitfox Mk 2	C. G. Richardson
	G-BSGH	Airtour AH-56B balloon	A. R. Hardwick
	G-BSGJ	Monnett Sonerai II	J. L. Loweth
	G-BSGK	PA-34-200T Seneca II	Aeros Holdings Ltd
	G-BSGL	PA-28-161 Warrior II	Keywest Air Charter Ltd
	G-BSGP	Cameron N-65 balloon	R. Leslie
	G-BSGS	Rans S.10 Sakota	M. R. Parr
	G-BSGT	Cessna T.210N	E. A. T. Brenninkmeyer
	G-BSHA	PA-34-200T Seneca II	Justgold Ltd
	G-BSHC	Colt 69A balloon	Magical Adventures Ltd
	G-BSHD	Colt 69A balloon	F. W. Ewer
	G-BSHH	Luscombe 8E Silvaire	S. L. Lewis
	G-BSHI	Luscombe 8F Silvaire	D. Kelly
	G-BSHK	Denney Kitfox Mk 2	D. Doyle & C. Aherne
	G-BSHO	Cameron V-77 balloon	D. J. Duckworth & J. C. Stewart
	G-BSHP	PA-28-161 Warrior II	Aviation Rentals
	G-BSHR	Cessna F.172N	Deep Cleavage Ltd (G-BFGE)
	G-BSHY	EAA Acro Sport I	R. J. Hodder
	G-BSIC	Cameron V-77 balloon	T. R. Tillson
	G-BSIF	Denney Kitfox Mk 2	R. J. Humphries
	G-BSIG	Colt 21A Cloudhopper balloon	C. J. Dunkley
	G-BSIH	Rutan LongEz	W. S. Allen

Reg.	Type	Owner or Operator	Notes
G-BSII	PA-34-200T Seneca II	R. L. Burt	
G-BSIJ	Cameron V-77 balloon	G. B. Davies	
G-BSIM	PA-28-181 Archer II	Falcon Flying Services Ltd	
G-BSIO	Cameron 80 Shed SS balloon	R. E. Jones	
G-BSIU	Colt 90A balloon	S. Travaglia/Italy	
G-BSIY	Schleicher ASK.14	P. W. Andrews	
G-BSIZ	PA-28-181 Archer II	P. J. Gerrard & M. J. Cunliffe	
G-BSJU	Cessna 150M	A. C. Williamson	
G-BSJX	PA-28-161 Warrior II	MK Aero Support Ltd	
G-BSJZ	Cessna 150J	M. H. Campbell	
G-BSKA	Cessna 150M	R. J. Cushing	
G-BSKG	Maule MX-7-180	A. J. Lewis	
G-BSKW	PA-28-181 Archer II	Shropshire Aero Club Ltd	
G-BSLA	Robin DR.400/180	A. B. McCoig	
G-BSLH	CASA 1.131E Jungmann 2000	M. A. Warden	
G-BSLI	Cameron V-77 balloon	R. S. McKibbin	
G-BSLK	PA-28-161 Warrior II	R. A. Rose	
G-BSLM	PA-28 Cherokee 160	R. Fulton	
G-BSLT	PA-28-161 Warrior II	L. W. Scattergood	
G-BSLU	PA-28 Cherokee 140	W. E. Lewis	
G-BSLV	Enstrom 280FX	B. M. B Roumier	
G-BSLW	Bellanca 7ECA Citabria	Shoreham Citabria Group	
G-BSLX	WAR Focke-Wulf Fw 190 (replica) (4+)	Fw 190 Gruppe	
G-BSMD	Nord 1101 Noralpha (+14)	J. W. Hardie	
G-BSME	Bölkow Bö.208C1 Junior	D. J. Hampson	
G-BSMG	Montgomerie-Bensen B.8M	A. C. Timperley	
G-BSMK	Cameron O-84 balloon	G-BSMK Shareholders	
G-BSML	Schweizer 269C	Moorgoods Helicopters	
G-BSMM	Colt 31A balloon	D. V. Fowler	
G-BSMN	CFM Streak Shadow	P. J. Porter	
G-BSMU	Rans S.6 Coyote II	A. Wright (G-MWJE)	
G-BSMV	PA-17 Vagabond (modified)	A. Cheriton	
G-BSNE	Luscombe 8E Silvaire	C. B. Buscombe, R. Goldsworthy & G. Vitta	
G-BSNF	Piper J-3C-65 Cub	D. A. Hammant	
G-BSNG	Cessna 172N	A. J. & P. C. MacDonald	
G-BSNJ	Cameron N-90 balloon	D. P. H. Smith/France	
G-BSNP	PA-28-201T Turbo Arrow III	D. F. K. Singleton/Germany	
G-BSNR	BAe.146-300	Aviation Capital Solutions Ltd	
G-BSNT	Luscombe 8A Silvaire	Luscombe Quartet	
G-BSNU	Colt 105A balloon	Gone Ballooning	
G-BSNX	PA-28-181 Archer II	Redhill Air Services Ltd	
G-BSNZ	Cameron O-105 balloon	J. Francis	
G-BSOF	Colt 25A balloon	J. M. Bailey	
G-BSOG	Cessna 172M	R. Warner	
G-BSOJ	Thunder Ax7-77 balloon	R. J. S. Jones	
G-BSOK	PA-28-161 Warrior II	Aeros Leasing Ltd	
G-BSOM	Glaser-Dirks DG.400	G-BSOM Group	
G-BSON	Green S.25 balloon	J. J. Green	
G-BSOO	Cessna 172F	C. A. Cope	
G-BSOR	CFM Streak Shadow Srs SA	A. Parr	
G-BSOT	PA-38-112 Tomahawk II	APB Leasing Ltd	
G-BSOU	PA-38-112 Tomahawk II	D. J. Campbell	
G-BSOX	Luscombe 8AE Silvaire	P. S Lanary	
G-BSOZ	PA-28-161 Warrior II	Genavia Ltd	
G-BSPA	QAC Quickie Q.2	G. V. McKirdy & B. K. Glover	
G-BSPB	Thunder Ax8-84 balloon	A. N. F. Pertwee	
G-BSPE	Cessna F.172P	T. W. Williamson	
G-BSPG	PA-34-200T Seneca II	Andrews Professional Colour Laboratories Ltd	
G-BSPK	Cessna 195A	A. G. & D. L. Bompas	
G-BSPL	CFM Streak Shadow Srs SA	G. L. Turner	
G-BSPM	PA-28-161 Warrior II	Aviation Rentals	
G-BSPN	PA-28R-201T Turbo Arrow III	Wendex Vehicle Rental Ltd	
G-BSPT	BN-2B-26 Islander	Hebridean Air Services Ltd	
G-BSRD	Cameron N-105 balloon	A. Ockelmann	
G-BSRH	Pitts S-1C Special	C. D. Swift	
G-BSRI	Lancair 235	G. Lewis	
G-BSRK	ARV Super 2	D. M. Blair	
G-BSRL	Campbell Cricket Mk.4 gyroplane	M. Brudnicki	
G-BSRP	Rotorway Executive	R. J. Baker	
G-BSRR	Cessna 182Q	C. M. Moore	
G-BSRT	Denney Kitfox Mk 2	M. J. Freeman	
G-BSRX	CFM Streak Shadow	R. K. Dear	

Notes	Reg.	Type	Owner or Operator
	G-BSSA	Luscombe 8E Silvaire	Luscombe Flying Group
	G-BSSB	Cessna 150L	D. T. A. Rees
	G-BSSC	PA-28-161 Warrior II	Sky Blue Flight Training
	G-BSSF	Denney Kitfox Mk 2	S. R. Eskins
	G-BSSI	Rans S.6 Coyote II	J. Currell (G-MWJA)
	G-BSSK	QAC Quickie Q.2	D. G. Greatrex
	G-BSSP	Robin DR.400/180R	Soaring (Oxford) Ltd
	G-BSST	BAC-Sud Concorde 002 ★	F.A.A. Museum/Yeovilton
	G-BSSV	CFM Streak Shadow	R. W. Payne
	G-BSSW	PA-28-161 Warrior II	D. J. Skidmore & E. F. Rowland
	G-BSSY	Polikarpov Po-2	Richard Shuttleworth Trustees
	G-BSTC	Aeronca 11AC Chief	J. Armstrong & D. Lamb
	G-BSTE	AS.355F2 Twin Squirrel	Oscar Mayer Ltd
	G-BSTH	PA-25 Pawnee 235	Scottish Gliding Union Ltd
	G-BSTI	Piper J-3C-65 Cub	J. A. Scott
	G-BSTK	Thunder Ax8-90 balloon	M. Williams
	G-BSTL	Rand-Robinson KR-2	C. S. Hales & N. Brauns
	G-BSTM	Cessna 172L	G-BSTM Group
	G-BSTO	Cessna 152 II	Plymouth Flying School Ltd
	G-BSTP	Cessna 152 II	FR Aviation Ltd
	G-BSTR	AA-5 Traveler	B. D. Jones
	G-BSTT	Rans S.6 Coyote II	D. G. Palmer
	G-BSTX	Luscombe 8A Silvaire	C. Chambers
	G-BSTY	Thunder Ax8-90 balloon	R. O. Leslie
	G-BSTZ	PA-28 Cherokee 140	Air Navigation & Trading Co Ltd
	G-BSUA	Rans S.6 Coyote II	A. J. Todd
	G-BSUB	Colt 77A balloon	J. M. Foster & M. P. Hill
	G-BSUD	Luscombe 8A Silvaire	I. G. Harrison
	G-BSUF	PA-32RT-300 Lance II	S. A. Fell & J. Gibbs
	G-BSUK	Colt 77A balloon	A. J. Moore
	G-BSUO	Scheibe SF.25C Falke	Portmoak Falke Syndicate
	G-BSUU	Colt 180A balloon	British School of Ballooning
	G-BSUV	Cameron O-77 balloon	J. F. Trehern
	G-BSUW	PA-34-200T Seneca II	NPD Direct Ltd
	G-BSUX	Carlson Sparrow II	J. Cantrell
	G-BSUZ	Denney Kitfox Mk 3	C. E. Ponsford
	G-BSVB	PA-28-181 Archer II	K. A. Boost
	G-BSVE	Binder CP.301S Smaragd	Smaragd Flying Group
	G-BSVF	PA-28-161 Warrior II	Airways Aero Associations Ltd
	G-BSVG	PA-28-161 Warrior II	Airways Aero Associations Ltd
	G-BSVH	Piper J-3C-65 Cub	C. R. & K. A. Maher
	G-BSVI	PA-16 Clipper	Clipper Aviation
	G-BSVK	Denney Kitfox Mk 2	C. Cox
	G-BSVM	PA-28-161 Warrior II	EFG Flying Services
	G-BSVN	Thorp T-18	D. Prentice
	G-BSVP	PA-23-250 Aztec F	S. G. Spier
	G-BSVR	Schweizer 269C	M. K. E. Askham
	G-BSVS	Robin DR.400/100	D. McK. Chalmers
	G-BSWB	Rans S.10 Sakota	F. A. Hewitt
	G-BSWC	Boeing Stearman E75 (112)	Richard Thwaites Aviation Ltd
	G-BSWF	PA-16 Clipper	Durham Clipper Group
	G-BSWG	PA-17 Vagabond	P. E. J. Sturgeon
	G-BSWH	Cessna 152 II	Airspeed Aviation Ltd
	G-BSWI	Rans S.10 Sakota	J. M. Mooney
	G-BSWL	Slingsby T.61F Venture T.2	Bidford Gliding Ltd
	G-BSWM	Slingsby T.61F Venture T.2	Venture Gliding Group
	G-BSWR	BN-2T-26 Turbine Islander	Police Service of Northern Ireland
	G-BSWV	Cameron N-77 balloon	S. Charlish
	G-BSWX	Cameron V-90 balloon	B. J. Burrows
	G-BSWY	Cameron N-77 balloon	Nottingham Hot Air Balloon Club
	G-BSXA	PA-28-161 Warrior II	Falcon Flying Services
	G-BSXB	PA-28-161 Warrior II	Wellesbourne Flying Group
	G-BSXC	PA-28-161 Warrior II	N. Ibrahim
	G-BSXD	Soko P-2 Kraguj (30146)	S. M. Johnston
	G-BSXI	Mooney M.20E	A. N. Pain
	G-BSXM	Cameron V-77 balloon	C. A. Oxby
	G-BSXS	PA-28-181 Archer II	J. K. Milner
	G-BSXT	Piper J-5A Cub Cruiser	R. G. Trute
	G-BSYA	Jodel D.18	K. Wright
	G-BSYF	Luscombe 8A Silvaire	Atlantic Aviation
	G-BSYG	PA-12 Super Cruiser	Fat Cub Group
	G-BSYH	Luscombe 8A Silvaire	N. R. Osborne

Reg.	Type	Owner or Operator	Notes
G-BSYI	AS.355F1 Twin Squirrel	Sky Charter UK Ltd	
G-BSYJ	Cameron N-77 balloon	Chubb Fire Ltd	
G-BSYO	Piper J-3C-90 Cub	C. R. Reynolds & J. D. Fuller (G-BSMJ/G-BRHE)	
G-BSYU	Robin DR.400/180	P. D. Smoothy	
G-BSYV	Cessna 150M	E-Plane Ltd	
G-BSYW	Cessna 150M	Cada Vliegtuilgen BV/Netherlands	
G-BSYY	PA-28-161 Warrior II	British Disabled Flying Association	
G-BSYZ	PA-28-161 Warrior II	Yankee Zulu Group	
G-BSZB	Stolp SA.300 Starduster Too	D. T. Gethin	
G-BSZC	Beech C-45H (51-11701A:AF258)	Weston Ltd	
G-BSZD	Robin DR.400/180	ALG BVBA	
G-BSZF	Jodel DR.250/160	J. B. Randle	
G-BSZG	Stolp SA.100 Starduster	D. F. Chapman	
G-BSZH	Thunder Ax7-77 balloon	T. J. Wilkinson	
G-BSZI	Cessna 152 II	Eglinton Flying Club Ltd	
G-BSZJ	PA-28-181 Archer II	M. L. A. Pudney & R. D. Fuller	
G-BSZM	Montgomerie-Bensen B.8MR	A. McCredie	
G-BSZO	Cessna 152	Flight Center Ltd	
G-BSZT	PA-28-161 Warrior II	Golf Charlie Echo Ltd	
G-BSZV	Cessna 150F	C. A. Davis	
G-BSZW	Cessna 152	S. T. & T. W. Gilbert	
G-BTAG	Cameron O-77 balloon	R. A. Shapland	
G-BTAK	EAA Acrosport II	S. E. Ford	
G-BTAL	Cessna F.152 II	Hertfordshire Aero Club Ltd	
G-BTAM	PA-28-181 Archer II	Tri-Star Farms Ltd	
G-BTAS	PA-38-112 Tomahawk	Ravenair Aircraft Ltd	
G-BTAT	Denney Kitfox Mk 2	M. Lawton	
G-BTAW	PA-28-161 Warrior II	Piper Flying Group	
G-BTAZ	Evans VP-2 ★	Norwich Aviation Museum	
G-BTBA	Robinson R22 Beta	Heliflight (UK) Ltd	
G-BTBB	Thunder Ax8-105 S2 balloon	G. J. Boulden	
G-BTBC	PA-28-161 Warrior II	Synergy Aircraft Leasing Ltd	
G-BTBG	Denney Kitfox Mk 2	G. N. Lawder	
G-BTBH	Ryan ST3KR (854)	H. & S. Roberts	
G-BTBJ	Cessna 190	R. H. Reeves	
G-BTBL	Montgomerie-Bensen B.8MR	AES Radionic Surveillance Systems	
G-BTBP	Cameron N-90 balloon	M. Catalani/Italy	
G-BTBU	PA-18 Super Cub 150	G-BTBU Syndicate	
G-BTBW	Cessna 120	M. J. Willies	
G-BTBY	PA-17 Vagabond	G. W. Miller	
G-BTCB	Air Command 582 Sport	G. Scurrah	
G-BTCC	Grumman F6F-3 Hellcat (40467:19)	Patina Ltd	
G-BTCD	P-51D-25-NA Mustang (413704:87-H)	Pelham Ltd	
G-BTCE	Cessna 152	S. T. Gilbert	
G-BTCH	Luscombe 8E Silvaire	G-BTCH Flying Group	
G-BTCI	PA-17 Vagabond	T. R. Whittome	
G-BTCJ	Luscombe 8AE Silvaire	J. M. Lovell	
G-BTCM	Cameron N-90 balloon	G. Everett (G-BMPW)	
G-BTCS	Colt 90A balloon	L. A. Watts	
G-BTCZ	Cameron Chateau 84 balloon	Balleroy Developpement SAS	
G-BTDA	Slingsby T.61G Falke	Anglia Gliding Club	
G-BTDC	Denney Kitfox Mk 2	D. M. Smith	
G-BTDD	CFM Streak Shadow	S. H. Merrony	
G-BTDE	Cessna C-165 Airmaster	R. H. Screen	
G-BTDI	Robinson R22	S. Klinge	
G-BTDN	Denney Kitfox Mk 2	T. M. Williams	
G-BTDR	Aero Designs Pulsar	R. A. Blackwell	
G-BTDS	Colt 77A balloon	C. P. Witter Ltd	
G-BTDT	CASA 1.131E Jungmann 2000	T. A. Reed	
G-BTDV	PA-28-161 Warrior II	Falcon Flying Services Ltd	
G-BTDW	Cessna 152 II	J. H. Sandham Aviation	
G-BTDZ	CASA 1.131E Jungmann 2000	R. J. & M. Pickin	
G-BTEA	Cameron N-105 balloon	M. W. A. Shemilt	
G-BTEE	Cameron O-120 balloon	W. H. & J. P. Morgan	
G-BTEL	CFM Streak Shadow	J. E. Eatwell	
G-BTES	Cessna 150H	C. Burt-Brown & G. G. Saint	
G-BTET	Piper J-3C-65 Cub	K. Handley	
G-BTEU	SA.365N-2 Dauphin	CHC Scotia Ltd	
G-BTEW	Cessna 120	J. H. Milne & T. H. Bishop	
G-BTEX	PA-28 Cherokee 140	E. Latimer	
G-BTFA	Denney Kitfox Mk 2	K. R. Peek	

Notes	Reg.	Type	Owner or Operator
	G-BTFC	Cessna F.152 II	Aircraft Engineers Ltd
	G-BTFE	Bensen-Parsons 2-seat gyroplane	J. R. Goldspink
	G-BTFG	Boeing Stearman A75N1 (441)	TG Aviation Ltd
	G-BTFJ	PA-15 Vagabond	B. McCready
	G-BTFK	Taylorcraft BC-12D	A. O'Rourke
	G-BTFL	Aeronca 11AC Chief	BTFL Group
	G-BTFM	Cameron O-105 balloon	Edinburgh University Hot Air Balloon Club
	G-BTFO	PA-28-161 Warrior II	Flyfar Ltd
	G-BTFP	PA-38-112 Tomahawk	St.George Flight Training Ltd
	G-BTFT	Beech 58 Baron	Fastwing Air Charter Ltd
	G-BTFU	Cameron N-90 balloon	J. J. Rudoni & A. C. K. Rawson
	G-BTFV	Whittaker MW7	S. J. Luck
	G-BTFX	Bell 206B JetRanger 2	Amcay Ltd
	G-BTGD	Rand-Robinson KR-2 (modified)	B M. Neary
	G-BTGI	Rearwin 175 Skyranger	J. M. Fforde
	G-BTGJ	Smith DSA-1 Miniplane	G. J. Knowles
	G-BTGL	Light Aero Avid Flyer	I. Kazi
	G-BTGM	Aeronca 7AC Champion	A. J. McLuskie
	G-BTGO	PA-28 Cherokee 140	Demero Ltd & Transcourt Ltd
	G-BTGR	Cessna 152 II	A. J. Gomes
	G-BTGS	Stolp SA.300 Starduster Too	G. N. Elliott & ptnrs (G-AYMA)
	G-BTGT	CFM Streak Shadow	I. Heunis (G-MWPY)
	G-BTGV	PA-34-200T Seneca II	Oxford Aviation Academy (Oxford) Ltd
	G-BTGW	Cessna 152 II	Stapleford Flying Club Ltd
	G-BTGX	Cessna 152 II	Stapleford Flying Club Ltd
	G-BTGY	PA-28-161 Warrior II	Stapleford Flying Club Ltd
	G-BTGZ	PA-28-181 Archer II	Allzones Ltd
	G-BTHE	Cessna 150L	D. G. Williams
	G-BTHF	Cameron V-90 balloon	N. J. & S. J. Langley
	G-BTHH	Jodel DR.100A	H. R. Leefe
	G-BTHI	Robinson R22 Beta	Summerline Aviation Ltd
	G-BTHK	Thunder Ax7-77 balloon	M. S.Trend
	G-BTHM	Thunder Ax8-105 balloon	Montgolfieres Club de L'Orme/France
	G-BTHN	Murphy Renegade 912	D. Baker
	G-BTHP	Thorp T.211	M. Gardner
	G-BTHW	Beech F33C Bonanza	Robin Lance Aviation Associates Ltd
	G-BTHX	Colt 105A balloon	PSH Skypower Ltd
	G-BTHY	Bell 206B JetRanger 3	Suffolk Helicopters Ltd
	G-BTID	PA-28-161 Warrior II	Aviation South West Ltd
	G-BTIE	SOCATA TB10 Tobago	Aviation Spirit Ltd
	G-BTIF	Denney Kitfox Mk 3	K. Lally
	G-BTIG	Montgomerie-Bensen B.8MR	G. H. Leeming
	G-BTII	AA-5B Tiger	Rockside Trading Ltd
	G-BTIJ	Luscombe 8E Silvaire	S. J. Hornsby
	G-BTIL	PA-38-112 Tomahawk	B. J. Pearson
	G-BTIM	PA-28-161 Cadet	Plane Talking Ltd
	G-BTIO	SNCAN Stampe SV.4C	M. D. & C. F. Garratt
	G-BTIR	Denney Kitfox Mk 2	R. B. Wilson
	G-BTIV	PA-28-161 Warrior II	Warrior Group/Eaglescott
	G-BTJA	Luscombe 8E Silvaire	M. W. Rudkin
	G-BTJB	Luscombe 8E Silvaire	M. Loxton
	G-BTJC	Luscombe 8F Silvaire	M. Colson
	G-BTJD	Thunder Ax8-90 S2 balloon	P. Richardson
	G-BTJF	Thunder Ax10-180 balloon	Airborne Adventures Ltd
	G-BTJG	BAe.146-300	Trident Aviation Leasing Sevices (Jersey) Ltd
	G-BTJH	Cameron O-77 balloon	H. Stringer
	G-BTJK	PA-38-112 Tomahawk	Ravenair Aircraft Ltd
	G-BTJL	PA-38-112 Tomahawk	J. S. Devlin & Z. Islam
	G-BTJO	Thunder Ax9-140 balloon	G. P. Lane
	G-BTJS	Montgomerie-Bensen B.8MR	T. A. Holmes
	G-BTJU	Cameron V-90 balloon	Flambe Balloons Ltd
	G-BTJX	Rans S.10 Sakota	P. C. Avery
	G-BTKA	Piper J-5A Cub Cruiser	M. J. Walker
	G-BTKB	Renegade Spirit 912	P. J. Calvert
	G-BTKC	BAe. 146-200	Trident Aviation Leasing Services (Jersey) Ltd
	G-BTKD	Denney Kitfox Mk 4	R. A. Hills
	G-BTKG	Light Aero Avid Flyer	T. Wade/Ireland
	G-BTKL	MBB Bö.105DB-4	Gryphon Aviation Ltd
	G-BTKP	CFM Streak Shadow	C. A. Sargent & C. D. Creasey
	G-BTKT	PA-28-161 Warrior II	Biggin Hill Flying Club Ltd
	G-BTKV	PA-22 Tri-Pacer 160	R. A. Moore
	G-BTKX	PA-28-181 Archer II	D. J. Perkins

Reg.	Type	Owner or Operator	Notes
G-BTLB	Wassmer Wa.52 Europa	Popham Flying Group G-BTLB	
G-BTLG	PA-28R Cherokee Arrow 200	P. J. Moore	
G-BTLM	PA-22 Tri-Pacer 160	F & H (Aircraft)	
G-BTLP	AA-1C Lynx	Partlease Ltd	
G-BTMA	Cessna 172N	East of England Flying Group Ltd	
G-BTMK	Cessna R.172K XPII	K. E. Halford	
G-BTMO	Colt 69A balloon	Thunder & Colt	
G-BTMP	Campbell Cricket	P. W. McLaughlin	
G-BTMR	Cessna 172M	Linley Aviation Ltd	
G-BTMT	Denney Kitfox Mk 1	L. G. Horne	
G-BTMV	Everett Srs 2 gyroplane	L. Armes	
G-BTMW	Zenair CH.701 STOL	L. Lewis	
G-BTNA	Robinson R22 Beta	S. J. Adams & P. G. Eagles	
G-BTNC	AS.365N-2 Dauphin 2	CHC Scotia Ltd	
G-BTNE	PA-28-161 Warrior II	Fly Welle Ltd	
G-BTNH	PA-28-161 Warrior II	Falcon Flying Services Ltd (G-DENH)	
G-BTNO	Aeronca 7AC Champion	B. J. & B. G. Robe	
G-BTNR	Denney Kitfox Mk 3	High Notions Flying Group	
G-BTNT	PA-28-151 Warrior	Azure Flying Club Ltd	
G-BTNV	PA-28-161 Warrior II	G. M. Bauer & A. W. Davies	
G-BTNW	Rans S.6-ESA Coyote II	R. C. Holmes	
G-BTOC	Robinson R22 Beta	Summerline Aviation Ltd	
G-BTOG	DH.82A Tiger Moth	TOG Group	
G-BTOL	Denney Kitfox Mk 3	P. J. Gibbs	
G-BTON	PA-28 Cherokee 140	Group G-BTON	
G-BTOO	Pitts S-1C Special	G. H. Matthews	
G-BTOP	Cameron V-77 balloon	J. J. Winter	
G-BTOT	PA-15 Vagabond	Vagabond Flying Group	
G-BTOU	Cameron O-120 balloon	J. J. Daly	
G-BTOW	SOCATA Rallye 180GT	M. Jarrett	
G-BTOZ	Thunder Ax9-120 S2 balloon	H. G. Davies	
G-BTPA	BAe ATP	Atlantic Airlines Ltd	
G-BTPC	BAe ATP	Atlantic Airlines Ltd	
G-BTPE	BAe ATP	Atlantic Airlines Ltd	
G-BTPF	BAe ATP	Atlantic Airlines Ltd	
G-BTPG	BAe ATP	Siemans Financial Services AB	
G-BTPH	BAe ATP	Atlantic Airlines Ltd	
G-BTPJ	BAe ATP	Deutsche Leasing Sverige AB	
G-BTPL	BAe ATP	Trident Aviation Leasing Services (Jersey) Ltd	
G-BTPT	Cameron N-77 balloon	H. J. Andrews	
G-BTPV	Colt 90A balloon	Balloon Preservation Group	
G-BTPX	Thunder Ax8-90 BALLOON	B. J. Ross	
G-BTRC	Light Aero Avid Speedwing	Grangecote Ltd	
G-BTRF	Aero Designs Pulsar	P. F. Crosby & C. Smith	
G-BTRG	Aeronca 65C Super Chief	A. Welburn	
G-BTRI	Aeronca 11CC Super Chief	P. A. Wensak	
G-BTRK	PA-28-161 Warrior II	Stapleford Flying Club Ltd	
G-BTRL	Cameron N-105 balloon	J. Lippett	
G-BTRO	Thunder Ax8-90 balloon	Capital Balloon Club Ltd	
G-BTRR	Thunder Ax7-77 balloon	P. J. Wentworth	
G-BTRS	PA-28-161 Warrior II	Airwise Flying Group	
G-BTRT	PA-28R Cherokee Arrow 200-II	Romeo Tango Group	
G-BTRU	Robin DR.400/180	R. H. Mackay	
G-BTRW	Slingsby T.61F Venture T.2	The Falke Syndicate	
G-BTRY	PA-28-161 Warrior II	Oxford Aviation Academy (Oxford) Ltd	
G-BTRZ	Jodel D.18	A. P. Aspinall	
G-BTSB	Corben Baby Ace D	M. R Overall	
G-BTSJ	PA-28-161 Warrior II	Plymouth Flying School Ltd	
G-BTSN	Cessna 150G	M. L. F. Langrick	
G-BTSP	Piper J-3C-65 Cub	A. Corcoran	
G-BTSR	Aeronca 11AC Chief	J. M. Miller	
G-BTSV	Denney Kitfox Mk 3	R. J. Folwell	
G-BTSW	Colt AS-80 Mk II airship	Gefa-Flug GmbH/Germany	
G-BTSX	Thunder Ax7-77 balloon	C. Moris-Gallimore/Portugal	
G-BTSY	EE Lightning F.6 (XR724) ★	Lightning Association	
G-BTSZ	Cessna 177A	T. Akeroyd	
G-BTTB	Cameron V-90 balloon	Royal Engineers Balloon Club	
G-BTTD	Montgomerie-Bensen B.8MR	A. J. P. Herculson	
G-BTTE	Cessna 150L	C. Wilson & W. B. Murray	
G-BTTL	Cameron V-90 balloon	A. J. Baird	
G-BTTO	BAe ATP	Atlantic Airlines Ltd (G-OEDE)	
G-BTTP	BAe 146-300	Trident Aviation Leasing Services (Jersey) Ltd	

Notes	Reg.	Type	Owner or Operator
	G-BTTR	Aerotek Pitts S-2A Special	Yellowbird Adventures Ltd
	G-BTTW	Thunder Ax7-77 balloon	J. Kenny
	G-BTTY	Denney Kitfox Mk 2	G. T. Leedham
	G-BTTZ	Slingsby T.61F Venture T.2	G-BTTZ Group
	G-BTUA	Slingsby T.61F Venture T.2	Shenington Gliding Club
	G-BTUB	Yakovlev C.11	G. G. L. James
	G-BTUC	EMB-312 Tucano ★	Ulster Aviation Heritage
	G-BTUG	SOCATA Rallye 180T	Herefordshire Gliding Club Ltd
	G-BTUH	Cameron N-65 balloon	J. S. Russon
	G-BTUK	Aerotek Pitts S-2A Special	S. H. Elkington
	G-BTUL	Aerotek Pitts S-2A Special	J. M. Adams
	G-BTUM	Piper J-3C-65 Cub	G-BTUM Syndicate
	G-BTUR	PA-18 Super Cub 95 (modified)	N. T. Oakman
	G-BTUS	Whittaker MW7	C. T. Bailey
	G-BTUV	Aeronca A65TAC Defender	S. Hudson, P. McLoughlin & F. McMorrow
	G-BTUW	PA-28-151 Warrior	T. S. Kemp
	G-BTUZ	American General AG-5B Tiger	R. V. Grocott
	G-BTVA	Thunder Ax7-77 balloon	C. M. Waters
	G-BTVC	Denney Kitfox Mk 2	M. J. Downes
	G-BTVE	Hawker Demon I (K8203)	Demon Displays Ltd
	G-BTVT	BAe 146-200	Trident Aviation Leasing Services (Jersey) Ltd
	G-BTVV	Cessna FA.337G	C. Keane
	G-BTVW	Cessna 152 II	TGD Leasing Ltd
	G-BTVX	Cessna 152 II	The Flight Centre 2010 Ltd
	G-BTWB	Denney Kitfox Mk 3	J. & O. Houlihan (G-BTTM)
	G-BTWC	Slingsby T.61F Venture T.2	RAFGSA
	G-BTWD	Slingsby T.61F Venture T.2	York Gliding Centre
	G-BTWE	Slingsby T.61F Venture T.2	Aston Down G-BTWE Syndicate
	G-BTWF	DHC.1 Chipmunk 22 (WK549)	J. A. Simms
	G-BTWI	EAA Acro Sport I	S. Alexander & W. M. Coffee
	G-BTWJ	Cameron V-77 balloon	C. Gingell & M. Holden-Wadsworth
	G-BTWL	WAG-Aero Acro Sport Trainer	F. Horan
	G-BTWM	Cameron V-77 balloon	R. C. Franklin
	G-BTWV	Cameron O-90 balloon	The Cybele Flying Group
	G-BTWX	SOCATA TB9 Tampico	T. I. Murtough
	G-BTWY	Aero Designs Pulsar	R. Bishop
	G-BTWZ	Rans S.10 Sakota	J. T. Phipps
	G-BTXD	Rans S.6-ESA Coyote II	A. I. Sutherland
	G-BTXF	Cameron V-90 balloon	G. Thompson
	G-BTXG	BAe Jetstream 3102	Highland Airways Ltd
	G-BTXI	Noorduyn AT-16 Harvard IIB (FE695)	Patina Ltd
	G-BTXK	Thunder Ax7-65 balloon	A. F. Selby
	G-BTXM	Colt 21A Cloudhopper balloon	H. J. Andrews
	G-BTXN	BAe.146-300	Aviation Capital Solutions Ltd (G-JEAL)
	G-BTXS	Cameron O-120 balloon	Southern Balloon Group
	G-BTXT	Maule MXT-7-180 Star Rocket	G-BTXT Group
	G-BTXX	Bellanca 8KCAB Decathlon	Tatenhill Aviation Ltd
	G-BTXZ	Zenair CH.250	G-BTXZ Group
	G-BTYC	Cessna 150L	Polestar Aviation Ltd
	G-BTYH	Pottier P.80S	R. G. Marshall
	G-BTYI	PA-28-181 Archer II	Godiva Imaging Ltd
	G-BTYT	Cessna 152 II	Cristal Air Ltd
	G-BTYX	Cessna 140	R. F. Richards
	G-BTYY	Curtiss Robin C-2	R. R. L. Windus
	G-BTZA	Beech F33A Bonanza	G-BTZA Group
	G-BTZB	Yakovlev Yak-50 (10 yellow)	D. H. Boardman
	G-BTZD	Yakovlev Yak-1 (1342)	Historic Aircraft Collection Ltd
	G-BTZE	LET Yakovlev C.11	M. V. Rijkse
	G-BTZN	BAe.146-300	Aviation Capital Solutions Ltd
	G-BTZO	SOCATA TB20 Trinidad	A. P. Howells
	G-BTZP	SOCATA TB9 Tampico	M. W. Orr
	G-BTZS	Colt 77A balloon	P. T. R. Ollivere
	G-BTZV	Cameron V-77 balloon	D. J. & H. M. Brown
	G-BTZX	Piper J-3C-65 Cub	ZX Cub Group
	G-BTZY	Colt 56A balloon	S. J. Wardle
	G-BTZZ	CFM Streak Shadow	D. R. Stennett
	G-BUAA	Corben Baby Ace D	C. E. Brookes
	G-BUAB	Aeronca 11AC Chief	J. Reed
	G-BUAC	Slingsby T.31 Motor Cadet III	D. A. Wilson & C. R. Partington
	G-BUAF	Cameron N-77 balloon	Zebedee Balloon Service Ltd
	G-BUAG	Jodel D.18	A. L. Silcox

Reg.	Type	Owner or Operator	Notes
G-BUAI	Everett Srs 3 gyroplane	D. Stevenson	
G-BUAJ	Cameron N-90 balloon	Kent Ballooning	
G-BUAM	Cameron V-77 balloon	N. Florence	
G-BUAT	Thunder Ax9-120 balloon	J. Fenton	
G-BUAV	Cameron O-105 balloon	D. & T. Dorrell	
G-BUAX	Rans S.10 Sakota	A. W. McKee	
G-BUBL	Thunder Ax8-105 balloon ★	British Balloon Museum/Newbury	
G-BUBN	BN-2B-26 Islander	Isles of Scilly Skybus Ltd	
G-BUBS	Lindstrand LBL-77B balloon	B. J. Bower	
G-BUBT	Stoddard Hamilton Glasair IIS RG	D. Bonucchi	
G-BUBU	PA-34-220T Seneca III	Brinor (Holdings) Ltd	
G-BUBW	Robinson R22 Beta	Plane Talking Ltd	
G-BUBY	Thunder Ax8-105 S2 balloon	T. M. Donnelly	
G-BUCA	Cessna A.150K	BUCA Group	
G-BUCC	CASA 1.131E Jungmann 2000 (BU+CC)	P. L. Gaze (G-BUEM)	
G-BUCG	Schleicher ASW.20L (modified)	W. B. Andrews	
G-BUCH	Stinson V-77 Reliant	Gullwing Trading Ltd	
G-BUCI	Auster AOP.9 (XP242)	Historic Aircraft Flight Reserve Collectio	
G-BUCK	CASA 1.131E Jungmann 1000 (BU+CK)	Jungmann Flying Group	
G-BUCM	Hawker Sea Fury FB.11	Patina Ltd	
G-BUCO	Pietenpol Air Camper	A. James	
G-BUCS	Cessna 150F	London Ashford Airport Ltd	
G-BUCT	Cessna 150L	North East Flight Training Ltd	
G-BUDA	Slingsby T.61F Venture T.2	Cranwell Gliding Club	
G-BUDB	Slingsby T.61F Venture T.2	RAFGSA	
G-BUDC	Slingsby T.61F Venture T.2 (ZA652)	T.61 Group	
G-BUDE	PA-22 Tri-Pacer 135 (tailwheel)	P. Robinson	
G-BUDF	Rand-Robinson KR-2	M. Stott	
G-BUDI	Aero Designs Pulsar	R. W. L. Oliver	
G-BUDK	Thunder Ax7-77 balloon	W. Evans	
G-BUDL	Auster 3 (NX534)	K. B. Owen	
G-BUDN	Cameron 90 Shoe SS balloon	Magical Adventures Ltd	
G-BUDO	PZL-110 Koliber 150	A. S. Vine	
G-BUDR	Denney Kitfox Mk 3	N. J. P. Mayled	
G-BUDS	Rand-Robinson KR-2	D. W. Munday	
G-BUDT	Slingsby T.61F Venture T.2	G-BUDT Group	
G-BUDU	Cameron V-77 balloon	T. M. G. Amery	
G-BUDW	Brügger MB.2 Colibri	S. P. Barrett (G-GODS)	
G-BUEC	Van's RV-6	A. H. Harper	
G-BUED	Slingsby T.61F Venture T.2	617 VGS Group	
G-BUEF	Cessna 152 II	Channel Aviation	
G-BUEG	Cessna 152 II	Aviation South West Ltd	
G-BUEI	Thunder Ax8-105 balloon	K. P. Barnes	
G-BUEK	Slingsby T.61F Venture T.2	G-BUEK Group	
G-BUEN	VPM M-14 Scout	J. L. G. McLane	
G-BUEP	Maule MX-7-180	N. J. B. Bennett	
G-BUEW	Rans S-6 Coyote II	K. J. Simpson (G-MWYE)	
G-BUFG	Slingsby T.61F Venture T.2	Transcourt Ltd	
G-BUFH	PA-28-161 Warrior II	Solent School of Flying	
G-BUFN	Slingsby T.61F Venture T.2	BUFN Group	
G-BUFR	Slingsby T.61F Venture T.2	East Sussex Gliding Club Ltd	
G-BUFT	Cameron O-120 balloon	D. Bron	
G-BUFV	Light Aero Avid Speedwing Mk.4	M. & B. Gribbin	
G-BUFY	PA-28-161 Warrior II	Bickertons Aerodromes Ltd	
G-BUGE	Bellanca 7GCAA Cltabria	V. Vaughan & N. O'Brien	
G-BUGG	Cessna 150F	C. P. J. Taylor & D. M. Forshaw	
G-BUGI	Evans VP-2	J. L. Barker	
G-BUGJ	Robin DR.400/180	W. E. R. Jenkins	
G-BUGL	Slingsby T.61F Venture T.2	VMG Group	
G-BUGP	Cameron V-77 balloon	R. Churcher	
G-BUGS	Cameron V-77 balloon	S. J. Dymond	
G-BUGT	Slingsby T.61F Venture T.2	Bambi Aircraft Group	
G-BUGV	Slingsby T.61F Venture T.2	Oxfordshire Sportflying Ltd	
G-BUGW	Slingsby T.61F Venture T.2	Transcourt Ltd	
G-BUGY	Cameron V-90 balloon	Dante Balloon Group	
G-BUGZ	Slingsby T.61F Venture T.2	Dishforth Flying Group	
G-BUHA	Slingsby T.61F Venture T.2 (ZA634:C)	Buckminster Gliding Club Ltd	
G-BUHB	BAe.146-300	Trident Aviation Leasing Services Jersey) Ltd	
G-BUHM	Cameron V-77 balloon	L. A. Watts	
G-BUHO	Cessna 140	W. B. Bateson	

Notes	Reg.	Type	Owner or Operator
	G-BUHR	Slingsby T.61F Venture T.2	Connel Motor Glider Group
	G-BUHS	Stoddard-Hamilton Glasair SH TD-1	T. F. Horrocks
	G-BUHU	Cameron N-105 balloon	Unipart Balloon Club
	G-BUHZ	Cessna 120	Cessna 140 Group
	G-BUIF	PA-28-161 Warrior II	Northumbria Flying School Ltd
	G-BUIG	Campbell Cricket (replica)	J. A. English
	G-BUIH	Slingsby T.61F Venture T.2	Falcon Gliding Group
	G-BUIJ	PA-28-161 Warrior II	OPS Aero Support Services
	G-BUIK	PA-28-161 Warrior II	Falcon Flying Services
	G-BUIL	CFM Streak Shadow	J. A. McKie
	G-BUIN	Thunder Ax7-77 balloon	P. C. Johnson
	G-BUIP	Denney Kitfox Mk 2	Avcomm Developments Ltd
	G-BUIR	Light Aero Avid Speedwing Mk 4	S. J. Handley
	G-BUIU	Cameron V-90 balloon	H. Micketeit/Germany
	G-BUIZ	Cameron N-90 balloon	Balloon Preservation Flying Group
	G-BUJA	Slingsby T.61F Venture T.2	Wrekin Gliding Club
	G-BUJB	Slingsby T.61F Venture T.2	Falke Syndicate
	G-BUJE	Cessna 177B	FG93 Group
	G-BUJH	Colt 77B balloon	R. P. Cross & R. Stanley
	G-BUJI	Slingsby T.61F Venture T.2	Solent Venture Syndicate Ltd
	G-BUJJ	Avid Speedwing	R. A. Dawson
	G-BUJK	Montgomerie-Bensen B.8MR	P. C. W. Raine
	G-BUJM	Cessna 120	Cessna 120 Flying Group
	G-BUJN	Cessna 172N	Warwickshire Aviation Ltd
	G-BUJO	PA-28-161 Warrior II	Falcon Flying Services
	G-BUJP	PA-28-161 Warrior II	J. M. C. Manson
	G-BUJR	Cameron A-180 balloon	Dragon Balloon Co Ltd
	G-BUJV	Light Aero Avid Speedwing Mk 4	C. Thomas
	G-BUJW	Thunder Ax8-90 S2 balloon	G. J. Grimes
	G-BUJX	Slingsby T.61F Venture T.2	The Burn Gliding Club Ltd
	G-BUJZ	Rotorway Executive 90 (modified)	M. P. Swoboda
	G-BUKB	Rans S.10 Sakota	M. K. Blatch
	G-BUKF	Denney Kitfox Mk 4	Kilo Foxtrot Group
	G-BUKH	D.31 Turbulent	J. G. Wilkins
	G-BUKI	Thunder Ax7-77 balloon	Virgin Balloon Flights
	G-BUKK	Bücker Bü 133C Jungmeister (U-80)	E. J. F. McEntee
	G-BUKO	Cessna 120	K. Handley
	G-BUKP	Denney Kitfox Mk 2	FAA Europe Ltd
	G-BUKR	MS.880B Rallye Club 100T	G-BUKR Flying Group
	G-BUKU	Luscombe 8E Silvaire	Silvaire Flying Group
	G-BUKY	CCF Harvard IVM (52-8543)	R. A. Fleming
	G-BUKZ	Evans VP-2	P. R. Farnell
	G-BULB	Thunder Ax7-77 balloon	G. B. Davies
	G-BULC	Light Aero Avid Flyer Mk 4	C. Nice
	G-BULD	Cameron N-105 balloon	R. J. Collins
	G-BULF	Colt 77A balloon	P. Goss & T. C. Davies
	G-BULG	Van's RV-4	V. D. Long
	G-BULH	Cessna 172N Skyhawk II	FlyBPL.com
	G-BULJ	CFM Streak Shadow	C. C. Brown
	G-BULL	SA Bulldog Srs 120/128 (HKG-5)	N. V. Sills
	G-BULN	Colt 210A balloon	H. G. Davies
	G-BULO	Luscombe 8A Silvaire	B. W. Foulds
	G-BULT	Campbell Cricket	A. T. Pocklington
	G-BULY	Light Aero Avid Flyer	J. G. Stewart
	G-BULZ	Denney Kitfox Mk 2	T. G. F. Trenchard
	G-BUMP	PA-28-181 Archer II	A. J. Keen
	G-BUNB	Slingsby T.61F Venture T.2	RAFGSA
	G-BUNC	PZL-104 Wilga 35	R. F. Goodman
	G-BUND	PA-28RT-201T Turbo Arrow IV	E. Culot
	G-BUNG	Cameron N-77 balloon	A. Kaye
	G-BUNO	Lancair 320	J. Softley
	G-BUNV	Thunder Ax7-77 balloon	R. M. Garnett & R. Stone
	G-BUOA	Whittaker MW6-S Fatboy Flyer	H. N. Graham
	G-BUOB	CFM Streak Shadow	J. M. Hunter
	G-BUOD	SE-5A (replica) (B595:W)	M. D. Waldron/Belgium
	G-BUOE	Cameron V-90 balloon	A. Derbyshire
	G-BUOF	D.62B Condor	R. P. Loxton
	G-BUOI	PA-20-135 Pacer	Foley Farm Flying Group
	G-BUOK	Rans S.6-ESA Coyote II	M. Morris
	G-BUOL	Denney Kitfox Mk 3	M. Ensor & J. Howard
	G-BUON	Light Aero Avid Aerobat	I. A. J. Lappin
	G-BUOR	CASA 1.131E Jungmann 2000	M. I. M. S. Voest/Netherlands

Reg.	Type	Owner or Operator	Notes
G-BUOW	Aero Designs Pulsar XP	T. J. Hartwell	
G-BUOZ	Thunder Ax10-180 balloon	Skybus Ballooning	
G-BUPA	Rutan LongEz	N. G. Henry	
G-BUPB	Stolp SA.300 Starduster Too	J. R. Edwards & J. W. Widdows	
G-BUPC	Rollason Beta B.2	C. A. Rolph	
G-BUPF	Bensen B.8R	P. W. Hewitt-Dean	
G-BUPG	Cessna 180K	T. P. A. Norman	
G-BUPI	Cameron V-77 balloon	H. W. R. Stewart (G-BOUC)	
G-BUPM	VPM M-16 Tandem Trainer	A. Kitson	
G-BUPP	Cameron V-42 balloon	L. J. Schoeman	
G-BUPR	Jodel D.18	R. W. Burrows	
G-BUPU	Thunder Ax7-77 balloon	R. C. Barkworth & D. G. Maguire/USA	
G-BUPV	Great Lakes 2T-1A	R. J. Fray	
G-BUPW	Denney Kitfox Mk 3	S. G. Metcalfe	
G-BURD	Cessna F.172N	Tayside Aviation Ltd	
G-BURE	Jodel D.9	N. P. St.J. Ramsay	
G-BURG	Colt 77A balloon	P. A. & M. Still	
G-BURH	Cessna 150E	C. A. Davis	
G-BURI	Enstrom F-28C	D. W. C. Holmes	
G-BURJ	HS.748 Srs.2A	Clewer Aviation Ltd	
G-BURL	Colt 105A balloon	J. E. Rose	
G-BURN	Cameron O-120 balloon	I. Bentley	
G-BURP	Rotorway Executive 90	N. K. Newman	
G-BURR	Auster AOP.9	Annic Aviation	
G-BURS	Sikorsky S-76A	Premiair Aviation Services Ltd (G-OHTL)	
G-BURT	PA-28-161 Warrior II	Paul's Planes Ltd	
G-BURX	Cameron N-105 balloon	Balloon Preservation Flying Group (G-NPNP)	
G-BURZ	Hawker Nimrod II (K3661:362)	Historic Aircraft Collection Ltd	
G-BUSG	Airbus A.320-211	GA Telesis Ireland Ltd	
G-BUSH	Airbus A.320-211	British Airways	
G-BUSI	Airbus A.320-211	British Airways	
G-BUSJ	Airbus A.320-211	British Airways	
G-BUSK	Airbus A.320-211	British Airways	
G-BUSN	Rotorway Executive 90	J. A. McGinley	
G-BUSR	Aero Designs Pulsar	S. S. Bateman & R. A. Watts	
G-BUSS	Cameron 90 Bus SS balloon	Magical Adventures Ltd	
G-BUSV	Colt 105A balloon	M. N. J. Kirby	
G-BUSW	Rockwell Commander 114	J. M. J. Palmer	
G-BUTB	CFM Streak Shadow	H. O. Maclean & S. MacKechnie	
G-BUTD	Van's RV-6	N. W. Beadle	
G-BUTE	Anderson EA-1 Kingfisher	T. Crawford (G-BRCK)	
G-BUTF	Aeronca 11AC Chief	Fox Flying Group	
G-BUTG	Zenair CH.601HD	A. J. Thomas	
G-BUTH	CEA DR.220 2+2	Phoenix Flying Group	
G-BUTJ	Cameron O-77 balloon	D. Hoddinott	
G-BUTK	Murphy Rebel	R. H. Watson & M. Whyte	
G-BUTM	Rans S.6-116 Coyote II	A. B. King	
G-BUTT	Cessna FA150K	Global Engineering and Maintenance Ltd (G-AXSJ)	
G-BUTX	CASA 1.133C Jungmeister (ES.1-4)	Bucker Flying Group	
G-BUTY	Brügger MB.2 Colibri	R. M. Lawday	
G-BUTZ	PA-28 Cherokee 180C	M. H. Canning (G-DARL)	
G-BUUA	Slingsby T.67M Firefly Mk II	Babcock Defence Services	
G-BUUB	Slingsby T.67M Firefly Mk II	The Leicestershire Aero Club Ltd	
G-BUUC	Slingsby T.67M Firefly Mk II	Swiftair Maintenance Ltd	
G-BUUE	Slingsby T.67M Firefly Mk II	J. R. Bratty	
G-BUUF	Slingsby T.67M Firefly Mk II	Tiger Airways	
G-BUUI	Slingsby T.67M Firefly Mk II	Bustard Flying Club Ltd	
G-BUUJ	Slingsby T.67M Firefly Mk II	E. Hampartsoumian	
G-BUUK	Slingsby T.67M Firefly Mk II	Urop Aviation Ltd	
G-BUUM	PA-28RT-201 Arrow IV	CCHM Aviation Ltd	
G-BUUP	BAe ATP	Atlantic Airlines Ltd	
G-BUUR	BAe ATP	Atlantic Airlines Ltd	
G-BUUU	Cameron Bottle SS balloon ★	British Balloon Museum/Newbury	
G-BUUX	PA-28 Cherokee 180D	Aero Group 78	
G-BUVA	PA-22-135 Tri-Pacer	Oaksey VA Group	
G-BUVE	Colt 77B balloon	G. D. Philpot	
G-BUVL	Fisher Super Koala	A. D. Malcolm	
G-BUVM	CEA DR.250/160	G-BUVM Group	
G-BUVN	CASA 1.131E Jungmann 2000(BI-005)	W. Van Egmond/Netherlands	
G-BUVO	Cessna F.182P	Romeo Mike Flying Group (G-WTFA)	
G-BUVR	Christen A.1 Husky	A. E. Poulson	

Notes	Reg.	Type	Owner or Operator
	G-BUVT	Colt 77A balloon	N. A. Carr
	G-BUVW	Cameron N-90 balloon	P. Spellward
	G-BUVX	CFM Streak Shadow	T. J. Shaw
	G-BUVZ	Thunder Ax10-180 S2 balloon	A. Van Wyk
	G-BUWE	SE-5A (replica) (C9533:M)	Airpark Flight Centre Ltd
	G-BUWF	Cameron N-105 balloon	R. E. Jones
	G-BUWH	Parsons 2-seat gyroplane	R. V. Brunskill
	G-BUWI	Lindstrand LBL-77A balloon	Capital Balloon Club Ltd
	G-BUWJ	Pitts S-1C Special	M. A. Sims
	G-BUWK	Rans S.6-116 Coyote II	R. Warriner
	G-BUWL	Piper J-4A	M. L. Ryan
	G-BUWR	CFM Streak Shadow	T. Harvey
	G-BUWS	Denney Kitfox Mk 2	J. E. Brewis
	G-BUWT	Rand-Robinson KR-2	G. Bailey-Woods
	G-BUWU	Cameron V-77 balloon	T. R. Dews
	G-BUXA	Colt 210A balloon	Balloon School International Ltd
	G-BUXC	CFM Streak Shadow	N. R. Beale
	G-BUXD	Maule MXT-7-160	I. D. McClelland
	G-BUXI	Steen Skybolt	BUXI Group
	G-BUXK	Pietenpol Air Camper	B. M. D. Nelson
	G-BUXL	Taylor JT.1 Monoplane	P. J. Hebdon
	G-BUXN	Beech C23 Sundowner	Private Pilots Syndicate
	G-BUXS	MBB Bö.105DBS/4	Bond Air Services (G-PASA/G-BGWP)
	G-BUXW	Thunder Ax8-90 S2 balloon	Nottingham Hot Air Balloon Club
	G-BUXX	PA-17 Vagabond	R. H. Hunt
	G-BUXY	PA-25 Pawnee 235	Bath, Wilts & North Dorset Gliding Club Ltd
	G-BUYB	Aero Designs Pulsar	A. P. Fenn
	G-BUYC	Cameron 80 Concept balloon	R. P. Cross
	G-BUYD	Thunder Ax8-90 balloon	S. & P. McGuigan
	G-BUYF	Falcon XP	M. J. Hadland
	G-BUYJ	Lindstrand LBL-105A balloon	G. Fordyce
	G-BUYK	Denney Kitfox Mk 4	M. S. Shelton
	G-BUYL	RAF 2000GT gyroplane	Newtonair Gyroplanes Ltd
	G-BUYO	Colt 77A balloon	S. F. Burden/Netherlands
	G-BUYS	Robin DR.400/180	G-BUYS Flying Group
	G-BUYU	Bowers Fly-Baby 1A	R. Metcalfe
	G-BUYY	PA-28 Cherokee 180	G-BUYY Group
	G-BUZA	Denney Kitfox Mk 3	A. O'Brien/Ireland
	G-BUZB	Aero Designs Pulsar XP	S. M. Lancashire
	G-BUZC	Everett Srs 3A gyroplane	M. P. L'Hermette
	G-BUZD	AS.332L Super Puma	CHC Scotia Ltd
	G-BUZE	Light Aero Avid Speedwing	P. B. Harrison
	G-BUZG	Zenair CH.601HD	R. M. Ballard
	G-BUZH	Aero Designs Star-Lite SL-1	C. A. McDowall
	G-BUZK	Cameron V-77 balloon	J. T. Wilkinson
	G-BUZL	VPM M-6 Tandem Trainer	P. Robinson
	G-BUZM	Light Aero Avid Flyer Mk 3	R. McLuckie & O. G. Jones
	G-BUZO	Pietenpol Air Camper	D. A. Jones
	G-BUZR	Lindstrand LBL-77A balloon	Lindstrand Technologies Ltd
	G-BUZT	Kolb Twinstar Mk 3	J. A. G. Robb
	G-BUZV	Ken Brock KB-2 gyroplane	K. Hughes
	G-BUZZ	Agusta-Bell 206B JetRanger 2	Rivermead Aviation Ltd
	G-BVAB	Zenair CH.601HDS	B. N. Rides
	G-BVAC	Zenair CH.601HD	J. A. Tyndall & S. Wisedale
	G-BVAF	Piper J-3C-65 Cub	N. M. Hitchman
	G-BVAH	Denney Kitfox Mk.3	S. Allinson
	G-BVAI	PZL-110 Koliber 150	C. P. Ware and A. R. Williams
	G-BVAM	Evans VP-1	R. F. Selby
	G-BVAO	Colt 25A balloon	M. E. Dworski
	G-BVAW	Staaken Z-1 Flitzer (D-692)	L. R. Williams
	G-BVAY	Rutan Vari-Eze	D. A. Young
	G-BVAZ	Montgomerie-Bensen B.8MR	N. Steele
	G-BVBF	PA-28-151 Warrior	R. K. Spence
	G-BVBR	Light Aero Avid Speedwing	J. M. Baldwin & O. Kotova
	G-BVBS	Cameron N-77 balloon	Heart of England Balloons
	G-BVCA	Cameron N-105 balloon	Unipart Balloon Club
	G-BVCG	Van's RV-6	A. W. Shellis & I. C. Smit
	G-BVCL	Rans S.6-116 Coyote II	R. J. Powell
	G-BVCN	Colt 56A balloon	J. A. W. Dyer
	G-BVCO	FRED Srs 2	I. W. Bremner
	G-BVCP	Piper CP.1 Metisse	B. M. Diggins

Reg.	Type	Owner or Operator	Notes
G-BVCS	Aeronca 7BCM Champion	A. C. Lines	
G-BVCT	Denney Kitfox Mk 4	A. F. Reid	
G-BVCY	Cameron H-24 balloon	A. C. K. Rawson & J. J. Rudoni	
G-BVDB	Thunder Ax7-77 balloon	S. J. Hollingsworth & M. K. Bellamy (G-ORDY)	
G-BVDC	Van's RV-3	B. S. Carpenter	
G-BVDH	PA-28RT-201 Arrow IV	Dazz Aviation Ltd	
G-BVDI	Van's RV-4	J. Glen-Davis Gorman	
G-BVDJ	Campbell Cricket (replica)	S. Jennings	
G-BVDM	Cameron 60 Concept balloon	M. P. Young	
G-BVDO	Lindstrand LBL-105A balloon	K. Graham	
G-BVDP	Sequoia F.8L Falco	N. M. Turner	
G-BVDR	Cameron O-77 balloon	N. J. Logue	
G-BVDS	Lindstrand LBL-69A balloon	Lindstrand Hot-Air Balloons Ltd	
G-BVDT	CFM Streak Shadow	H. J. Bennet	
G-BVDW	Thunder Ax8-90 balloon	S. C. Vora	
G-BVDX	Cameron V-90 balloon	R. K. Scott	
G-BVDY	Cameron 60 Concept balloon	P. Baker/Ireland	
G-BVDZ	Taylorcraft BC-12D	P. N. W. England	
G-BVEA	Mosler Motors N.3 Pup	G-BVEA Group (G-MWEA)	
G-BVEH	Jodel D.112	M. L. Copland	
G-BVEL	Evans VP-1 Srs.2	M. J. & S. J. Quinn	
G-BVEN	Cameron 80 Concept balloon	R. M. Powell	
G-BVEP	Luscombe 8A Master	B. H. Austen	
G-BVER	DHC.2 Beaver 1 (XV268)	Seaflite Ltd (G-BTDM)	
G-BVEV	PA-34-200 Seneca	R. W. Harris & ptnrs	
G-BVEW	Lindstrand LBL-150A balloon	S. J. Colin	
G-BVEY	Denney Kitfox Mk 4-1200	J. H. H. Turner	
G-BVEZ	P.84 Jet Provost T.3A (XM479)	Newcastle Jet Provost Co Ltd	
G-BVFA	Rans S.10 Sakota	D. S. Wilkinson	
G-BVFB	Cameron N-31 balloon	P. Lawman	
G-BVFF	Cameron V-77 balloon	R. J. Kerr & G. P. Allen	
G-BVFM	Rans S.6-116 Coyote II	F. B. C. de Beer	
G-BVFO	Light Aero Avid Speedwing	T. G. Solomon	
G-BVFR	CFM Streak Shadow	M. A. Kelly	
G-BVFS	Slingsby T.31M	S. R. Williams	
G-BVFU	Cameron 105 Sphere SS balloon	Stichting Phoenix/Netherlands	
G-BVFZ	Maule M5-180C Lunar Rocket	R. C. Robinson	
G-BVGA	Bell 206B JetRanger3	Findon Air Services	
G-BVGB	Thunder Ax8-105 S2 balloon	E. K. Read	
G-BVGE	WS-55 Whirlwind HAR.10 (XJ729)	J. F. Kelly/Ireland	
G-BVGF	Shaw Europa	A. Graham & G. G. Beal	
G-BVGG	Lindstrand LBL-69A balloon	L. P. Hooper	
G-BVGH	Hawker Hunter T.7 (XL573)	D. J. C. Davidson	
G-BVGI	Pereira Osprey II	D. Westoby	
G-BVGJ	Cameron C-80 balloon	J. M. J. & V. F. Roberts	
G-BVGK	Lindstrand LBL Newspaper SS balloon	H. Holmqvist	
G-BVGO	Denney Kitfox Mk 4-1200	P. Madden	
G-BVGP	Bücker Bü 133 Jungmeister (U-95)	M. V. Rijkse	
G-BVGT	Auster J/1 (modified)	K. D. & C. S. Rhodes	
G-BVGW	Luscombe 8A Silvaire	J. Smith	
G-BVGX	Thunder Ax8-90 S2 balloon	G-BVGX Group/New Zealand	
G-BVGY	Luscombe 8E Silvaire	M. C. Burlock	
G-BVGZ	Fokker Dr.1 (replica) (450/17) ★	R. A. Fleming	
G-BVHC	Grob G.115D-2 Heron	Tayside Aviation Ltd	
G-BVHD	Grob G.115D-2 Heron	Tayside Aviation Ltd	
G-BVHE	Grob G.115D-2 Heron	Tayside Aviation Ltd	
G-BVHF	Grob G.115D-2 Heron	Tayside Aviation Ltd	
G-BVHG	Grob G.115D-2 Heron	Tayside Aviation Ltd	
G-BVHI	Rans S.10 Sakota	J. D. Amos	
G-BVHJ	Cameron A-180 balloon	S. J. Boxall	
G-BVHK	Cameron V-77 balloon	A. R. Rich	
G-BVHL	Nicollier HN.700 Menestrel II	W. Dobinson & D. Hawkins	
G-BVHM	PA-38-112 Tomahawk	P. J. Montgomery (G-DCAN)	
G-BVHO	Cameron V-90 balloon	N. W. B. Bews	
G-BVHR	Cameron V-90 balloon	G. P. Walton	
G-BVHS	Murphy Rebel	S. T. Raby	
G-BVHV	Cameron N-105 balloon	Wye Valley Aviation Ltd	
G-BVIA	Rand-Robinson KR-2	K. Atkinson	
G-BVIE	PA-18 Super Cub 95 (modified)	J. C. Best (G-CLIK/G-BLMB)	
G-BVIF	Montgomerie-Bensen B.8MR	R. M. & D. Mann	
G-BVIK	Maule MXT-7-180 Star Rocket	Graveley Flying Group	
G-BVIL	Maule MXT-7-180 Star Rocket	K. & S. C. Knight	

Notes	Reg.	Type	Owner or Operator
	G-BVIN	Rans S.6-ESA Coyote II	J. R. & J. M. Bartlett
	G-BVIS	Brügger MB.2 Colibri	B. H. Shaw
	G-BVIV	Light Aero Avid Speedwing	S. Styles
	G-BVIW	PA-18-Super Cub 150	I. H. Logan
	G-BVIZ	Shaw Europa	The Europa Group
	G-BVJF	Montgomerie-Bensen B.8MR	D. M. F. Harvey
	G-BVJG	Cyclone AX3/K	J. Gilroy (G-MYOP)
	G-BVJK	Glaser-Dirks DG.800A	J. S. Forster
	G-BVJN	Shaw Europa	JN Europa Group
	G-BVJT	Cessna F.406	Nor Leasing
	G-BVJU	Evans VP-1	BVJU Flying Club & Associates
	G-BVJX	Marquart MA.5 Charger	A. E. Cox
	G-BVJZ	PA-28-161 Warrior II	Aviation Management Maastricht BV/Netherlands
	G-BVKB	Boeing 737-59D	bmi Baby
	G-BVKD	Boeing 737-59D	bmi Baby
	G-BVKF	Shaw Europa	T. R. Sinclair
	G-BVKG	Colt Flying Hot Dog SS balloon	Longbreak Ltd/USA
	G-BVKH	Thunder Ax8-90 balloon	D. J. Farrar
	G-BVKK	Slingsby T.61F Venture T.2	Buckminster Gliding Club Ltd
	G-BVKL	Cameron A-180 balloon	Dragon Balloon Co Ltd
	G-BVKM	Rutan Vari-Eze	J. P. G. Lindquist/Switzerland
	G-BVKU	Slingsby T.61F Venture T.2	G-BVKU Syndicate
	G-BVLA	Lancair 320	Eaglescott Lancair Group
	G-BVLD	Campbell Cricket (replica)	C. Berry
	G-BVLF	CFM Starstreak Shadow SS-D	R. W. Chatterton
	G-BVLG	AS.355F1 Twin Squirrel	PLM Dollar Group PLC
	G-BVLH	Shaw Europa	D. Barraclough
	G-BVLJ	BAe.146-100	Inflite Engineering Services Ltd
	G-BVLL	Lindstrand LBL-210A balloon	Airborne Balloon Flights Ltd
	G-BVLN	Aero Designs Pulsar XP	D. A. Campbell
	G-BVLP	PA-38-112 Tomahawk	J. Hornby
	G-BVLR	Van's RV-4	RV4 Group
	G-BVLT	Bellanca 7GCBC Citabria	Slade Associates
	G-BVLU	D.31 Turbulent	C. D. Bancroft
	G-BVLV	Shaw Europa	Euro 39 Group
	G-BVLX	Slingsby T.61F Venture T.2	RAFGSA
	G-BVMA	Beech 200 Super King Air	Dragonfly Aviation Services LLP (G-VPLC)
	G-BVME	AS.365N2 Dauphin 2	CHC Scotia Ltd
	G-BVMH	WAG-Aero Sport Trainer (39624:D-39)	J. Mathews
	G-BVMJ	Cameron 95 Eagle SS balloon	R. D. Sargeant
	G-BVML	Lindstrand LBL-210A balloon	Ballooning Adventures Ltd
	G-BVMM	Robin HR.200/100	Gloster Aero Group
	G-BVMN	Ken Brock KB-2 gyroplane	G-BVMN Group
	G-BVMR	Cameron V-90 balloon	I. R. Comley
	G-BVMU	Yakovlev Yak-52 (09 yellow)	Ascendances SPRL/Belgium
	G-BVNG	DH.60G-III Moth Major	P. & G. Groves
	G-BVNI	Taylor JT-2 Titch	G. de Halle
	G-BVNR	Cameron N-105 balloon	John Aimo Balloons SAS/Italy
	G-BVNS	PA-28-181 Archer II	Scottish Airways Flyers (Prestwick) Ltd
	G-BVNU	FLS Aerospace Sprint Club	M. D. R. Elmes
	G-BVNY	Rans S.7 Courier	D. M. Byers-Jones
	G-BVOB	F.27 Friendship Mk 500	ACL Aircraft Trading Ltd.
	G-BVOC	Cameron V-90 balloon	H. W. R. Stewart
	G-BVOH	Campbell Cricket (replica)	A. Kitson
	G-BVOI	Rans S.6-116 Coyote II	M. J. Whiteman-Haywood
	G-BVOK	Yakovlev Yak-52 (55 grey)	Trans Holdings Ltd
	G-BVOP	Cameron N-90 balloon	October Gold Ballooning Ltd
	G-BVOR	CFM Streak Shadow	J. M. Chandler
	G-BVOS	Shaw Europa	Durham Europa Group
	G-BVOW	Shaw Europa	H. P. Brooks
	G-BVOY	Rotorway Executive 90	C. H. Drake
	G-BVOZ	Colt 56A balloon	British School of Ballooning
	G-BVPA	Thunder Ax8-105 S2 balloon	Firefly Balloon Promotions
	G-BVPD	CASA 1.131E Jungmann 2000	D. Bruton
	G-BVPM	Evans VP-2 Coupé	P. Marigold
	G-BVPN	Piper J-3C-65 Cub	C. Sarcelet (G-TAFY)
	G-BVPS	Jodel D.112	P. J. Swain
	G-BVPV	Lindstrand LBL-77B balloon	P. G. Hill
	G-BVPW	Rans S.6-116 Coyote II	T. B. Woolley
	G-BVPX	Bensen B.8 (modified) Tyro Gyro	A. W. Harvey
	G-BVPY	CFM Streak Shadow	R. J. Mitchell
	G-BVRA	Shaw Europa	N. E. Stokes

Reg.	Type	Owner or Operator	Notes
G-BVRH	Taylorcraft BL.65	M. J. Kirk	
G-BVRL	Lindstrand LBL-21A balloon	M. E. & T. J. Orchard	
G-BVRU	Lindstrand LBL-105A balloon	C & R Jemmett	
G-BVRV	Van's RV-4	A. Troughton	
G-BVRZ	PA-18 Super Cub 95	R. W. Davison	
G-BVSB	TEAM mini-MAX	D. G. Palmer	
G-BVSD	SE.3130 Alouette II (V-54)	M. J. Cuttell	
G-BVSF	Aero Designs Pulsar	R. J. & J. A. Freestone	
G-BVSN	Light Aero Avid Speedwing	R. C. Bowley	
G-BVSP	P.84 Jet Provost T.3A (XM370)	H. G. Hodges & Son Ltd	
G-BVSS	Jodel D.150	A. P. Burns	
G-BVST	Jodel D.150	A. Shipp/Breighton	
G-BVSX	TEAM mini-MAX 91	J. A. Clark	
G-BVSZ	Pitts S-1E (S) Special	H. J. Morton	
G-BVTA	Tri-R Kis	P. J. Webb	
G-BVTC	P.84 Jet Provost T.5A (XW333)	Global Aviation Ltd	
G-BVTD	CFM Streak Shadow	M. Walton	
G-BVTL	Colt 31A balloon	A. Lindsay	
G-BVTM	Cessna F.152 II	RAF Halton Aeroplane Club (G-WACS)	
G-BVTN	Cameron N-90 balloon	P. Zulehner/Austria	
G-BVTV	Rotorway Executive 90	D. W. J. Lee	
G-BVTW	Aero Designs Pulsar	R. J. Panther	
G-BVTX	DHC.1 Chipmunk 22A (WP809)	TX Flying Group	
G-BVUA	Cameron O-105 balloon	Wickers World Ltd	
G-BVUC	Colt 56A balloon	J. F. Till	
G-BVUG	Betts TB.1 (Stampe SV.4C)	H. F. Fekete (G-BEUS)	
G-BVUH	Thunder Ax6-65B balloon	K. B. Chapple	
G-BVUI	Lindstrand LBL-25A balloon	J. W. Hole	
G-BVUK	Cameron V-77 balloon	H. G. Griffiths & W. A. Steel	
G-BVUM	Rans S.6-116 Coyote II	M. A. Abbott	
G-BVUN	Van's RV-4	D. J. Harvey	
G-BVUT	Evans VP-1 Srs. 2	M. J. Barnett	
G-BVUU	Cameron C-80 balloon	T. M. C. McCoy	
G-BVUV	Shaw Europa	R. J. Mills	
G-BVUZ	Cessna 120	T. K. Duffy	
G-BVVA	Yakovlev Yak-52	S. T. G. Lloyd	
G-BVVB	Carlson Sparrow II	L. M. McCullen	
G-BVVE	Jodel D.112	M. Balls	
G-BVVG	Nanchang CJ-6A (68)	Nanchang CJ6A Group	
G-BVVH	Shaw Europa	T. G. Hoult	
G-BVVI	Hawker Audax I (K5600)	Aero Vintage Ltd	
G-BVVK	DHC.6 Twin Otter 310	Loganair Ltd/British Airways	
G-BVVL	EAA Acro Sport II	G-BVVL Syndicate	
G-BVVM	Zenair CH.601HD	D. Macdonald	
G-BVVN	Brügger MB.2 Colibri	N. F. Andrews	
G-BVVP	Shaw Europa	I. Mansfield	
G-BVVR	Stits SA-3A Playboy	R. B. Armitage	
G-BVVS	Van's RV-4	E. G. & N. S. C. English	
G-BVVU	Lindstrand LBL Four SS balloon	Magical Adventures Ltd/USA	
G-BVVW	Yakovlev Yak-52	M. Blackman	
G-BVVZ	Corby CJ-1 Starlet	P. V. Flack	
G-BVWB	Thunder Ax8-90 S2 balloon	M. A. Stelling & K. C. Tanner	
G-BVWC	EE Canberra B.6 (WK163)	Classic Aviation Projects Ltd	
G-BVWI	Cameron light bulb SS balloon	Mobberley Balloon Collection	
G-BVWM	Shaw Europa	Europa Syndicate	
G-BVWW	Lindstrand LBL-90A balloon	J. D. A. Shields	
G-BVWY	Porterfield CP.65	R. L. Earl & B. Morris	
G-BVWZ	PA-32-301 Saratoga	The Saratoga (WZ) Group	
G-BVXA	Cameron N-105 balloon	R. E. Jones	
G-BVXC	EE Canberra B.6 (WT333) ★	Classic Aviation Projects Ltd/Bruntingthorpe	
G-BVXD	Cameron O-84 balloon	Hedge Hoppers Balloon Group	
G-BVXE	Steen Skybolt	J. Buglass (G-LISA)	
G-BVXF	Cameron O-120 balloon	Zebedee Balloon Services Ltd	
G-BVXJ	CASA 1.133 Jungmeister	A. C. Mercer	
G-BVXK	Yakovlev Yak-52 (26 grey)	E. Gavazzi	
G-BVXM	AS.350B Ecureuil	The Berkeley Leisure Group Ltd	
G-BVXR	DH.104 Devon C.2 (XA880)	M. Whale & M. W. A. Lunn	
G-BVXS	Taylorcraft BC-12D	XRay Sierra Group	
G-BVYF	PA-31-350 Navajo Chieftain	J. A. Rees & D. T. Rees (G-SAVE)	
G-BVYG	CEA DR.300/180	Ulster Gliding Club Ltd	
G-BVYK	TEAM mini-MAX	A. G. Ward	
G-BVYM	CEA DR.300/180	London Gliding Club (Pty) Ltd	

Notes	Reg.	Type	Owner or Operator
	G-BVYO	Robin R.2160	D. J. S. McClean
	G-BVYP	PA-25 Pawnee 235B	Bidford Gliding Ltd
	G-BVYU	Cameron A-140 balloon	S. Charlish
	G-BVYX	Light Aero Avid Speedwing Mk 4	J. E. Lipman
	G-BVYY	Pietenpol Air Camper	Pietenpol G-BVYY Group
	G-BVYZ	Stemme S.10V	L. Gubbay
	G-BVZD	Tri-R Kis Cruiser	J. M. Angiolini & G. Melling
	G-BVZE	Boeing 737-59D	bmi Baby
	G-BVZJ	Rand-Robinson KR-2	P. D. Button
	G-BVZN	Cameron C-80 balloon	S. J. Clarke
	G-BVZO	Rans S.6-116 Coyote II	P. J. Brion
	G-BVZR	Zenair CH.601HD	R. A. Perkins
	G-BVZT	Lindstrand LBL-90A balloon	J. Edwards
	G-BVZV	Rans S.6-116 Coyote II	A. H. & F. A. Macaskill
	G-BVZX	Cameron H-34 balloon	R. H. Etherington
	G-BVZZ	DHC.1 Chipmunk 22 (WP795)	Portsmouth Naval Gliding Club
	G-BWAB	Jodel D.14	W. A. Braim
	G-BWAC	Waco YKS-7	D. N. Peters
	G-BWAD	RAF 2000GT gyroplane	A. Melody
	G-BWAF	Hawker Hunter F.6A (XG160:U) ★	Bournemouth Aviation Museum/Bournemouth
	G-BWAG	Cameron O-120 balloon	P. M. Skinner
	G-BWAH	Montgomerie-Bensen B.8MR	J. B. Allan
	G-BWAI	CFM Streak Shadow	C. M. James
	G-BWAJ	Cameron V-77 balloon	K. Graham
	G-BWAN	Cameron N-77 balloon	Balloon Preservation Flying Group
	G-BWAO	Cameron C-80 balloon	M. D. Freeston & S. Mitchell
	G-BWAP	FRED Srs 3	G. A. Shepherd
	G-BWAR	Denney Kitfox Mk 3	I. Wightman
	G-BWAT	Pietenpol Air Camper	P. W. Aitchison
	G-BWAU	Cameron V-90 balloon	K. M. & A. M. F. Hall
	G-BWAV	Schweizer 269C	Helihire
	G-BWAW	Lindstrand LBL-77A balloon	D. Bareford
	G-BWBA	Cameron V-65 balloon	Dante Balloon Group
	G-BWBB	Lindstrand LBL-14A balloon	Oxford Promotions (UK) Ltd
	G-BWBI	Taylorcraft F-22A	R. T. G. Preston
	G-BWBT	Lindstrand LBL-90A balloon	British Telecommunications PLC
	G-BWBY	Schleicher ASH.26E	J. S. Ward
	G-BWBZ	ARV-1 Super 2	P. Mitchell
	G-BWCA	CFM Streak Shadow	I. C. Pearson
	G-BWCC	Van Den Bemden Gas balloon	Piccard Balloon Group
	G-BWCG	Lindstrand LBL-42A balloon	Oxford Promotions (UK) Ltd
	G-BWCK	Everett Srs 2 gyroplane	B. F. Pearson
	G-BWCS	P.84 Jet Provost T.5 (XW293:Z)	J. H. Ashcroft
	G-BWCT	Tipsy T.66 Nipper 1	J. S. Hemmings & C. R. Steer
	G-BWCV	Shaw Europa	G. C. McKirdy
	G-BWCY	Murphy Rebel	S. Burrow
	G-BWDB	ATR-72-202	Aurigny Air Services Ltd
	G-BWDF	PZL-104 Wilga 35A	Sky Banners Ltd
	G-BWDH	Cameron N-105 balloon	Bridges Van Hire Ltd
	G-BWDM	Lindstrand LBL-120A balloon	A. N. F. Pertwee
	G-BWDP	Shaw Europa	S. Attubato
	G-BWDS	P.84 Jet Provost T.3A (XM424)	Aviation Heritage Ltd
	G-BWDT	PA-34-220T Seneca III	H. R. Chambers (G-BKHS)
	G-BWDV	Schweizer 269C	Escola de Aviacao Aerocondor SA/Portugal
	G-BWDX	Shaw Europa	J. Robson
	G-BWDZ	Sky 105-24 balloon	Blue Sky Syndicate
	G-BWEA	Lindstrand LBL-120A balloon	S. R. Seager
	G-BWEB	P.84 Jet Provost T.5A (XW422:3)	XW422 Group
	G-BWEE	Cameron V-42 balloon	A. J. Davey/Germany
	G-BWEF	SNCAN Stampe SV.4C	Acebell G-BWEF Syndicate (G-BOVL)
	G-BWEG	Shaw Europa	R. J. Marsh
	G-BWEM	VS.358 Seafire L.IIIC (RX168)	Mark One Partners LLC
	G-BWEN	Macair Merlin GT	D. A. Hill
	G-BWEU	Cessna F.152 II	Affair Aircraft Leasing LLP
	G-BWEW	Cameron N-105 balloon	Unipart Balloon Club
	G-BWEY	Bensen B.8	F. G. Shepherd
	G-BWEZ	Piper J-3C-65 Cub (436021)	J. G. McTaggart
	G-BWFG	Robin HR.200/120B	Air Atlantique Ltd
	G-BWFH	Shaw Europa	G. C. Grant
	G-BWFJ	Evans VP-1	P. A. West
	G-BWFK	Lindstrand LBL-77A balloon	Balloon Preservation Flying Group

Reg.	Type	Owner or Operator	Notes
G-BWFM	Yakovlev Yak-50	Fox Mike Group	
G-BWFN	Hapi Cygnet SF-2A	G-BWFN Group	
G-BWFO	Colomban MC.15 Cri-Cri	K. D. & C. S. Rhodes	
G-BWFP	Yakovlev Yak-52	M. C. Lee & M. L. Blaze	
G-BWFT	Hawker Hunter T.8M (XL602)	Global Aviation Services Ltd	
G-BWFX	Shaw Europa	A. D. Stewart	
G-BWFZ	Murphy Rebel	D. K. Shead (G-SAVS)	
G-BWGA	Lindstrand LBL-105A balloon	R. Thompson	
G-BWGF	P.84 Jet Provost T.5A (XW325)	Viper Jet Provost Group Ltd	
G-BWGJ	Chilton DW.1A	T. J. Harrison	
G-BWGK	Hawker Hunter GA.11 (XE689)	B. R. Pearson & GA11 Group	
G-BWGL	Hawker Hunter T.8C (XJ615)	Stichting Hawker Hunter Foundation/Netherlands	
G-BWGM	Hawker Hunter T.8C (XE665)	The Admirals Barge	
G-BWGN	Hawker Hunter T.8C (WT722)	T8C Group	
G-BWGO	Slingsby T.67M Firefly 200	R. Gray	
G-BWGS	BAC.145 Jet Provost T.5A (XW310)	M. P. Grimshaw	
G-BWGU	Cessna 150F	Goodair Leasing Ltd	
G-BWGY	HOAC Katana DV.20	Stars Fly Ltd	
G-BWHA	Hawker Hurricane IIB (Z5252)	Historic Flying Ltd	
G-BWHD	Lindstrand LBL-31A balloon	G. Lewis	
G-BWHF	PA-31-325 Navajo	Awyr Cymru Cyf	
G-BWHI	DHC.1 Chipmunk 22A (WK624)	N. E. M. Clare	
G-BWHK	Rans S.6-116 Coyote II	S. J. Wakeling	
G-BWHM	Sky 140-24 balloon	C. J. S. Limon	
G-BWHP	CASA 1.131E Jungmann (S4+A07)	J. F. Hopkins	
G-BWHR	Tipsy Nipper T.66 Srs 1	L. R. Marnef	
G-BWHS	RAF 2000 gyroplane	B. J. Payne	
G-BWHU	Westland Scout AH.1 (XR595)	N. J. F. Boston	
G-BWIA	Rans S.10 Sakota	I. D. Worthington	
G-BWIB	SA Bulldog Srs 120/122 (XX514)	B. I. Robertson/USA	
G-BWID	D.31 Turbulent	N. Huxtable	
G-BWII	Cessna 150G	J. D. G. Hicks (G-BSKB)	
G-BWIJ	Shaw Europa	R. Lloyd	
G-BWIK	DH.82A Tiger Moth (NL985)	B. J. Ellis	
G-BWIP	Cameron N-90 balloon	K. C. Tanner	
G-BWIR	Dornier 328-100	Scot Airways Ltd	
G-BWIV	Shaw Europa	T. G. Ledbury	
G-BWIW	Sky 180-24 balloon	T. M. Donnelly	
G-BWIX	Sky 120-24 balloon	J. M. Percival	
G-BWIZ	QAC Quickie Tri-Q 200	M. C. Davies	
G-BWJB	Thunder Ax8-105 balloon	Justerini & Brooks Ltd	
G-BWJG	Mooney M.20J	S. Nahum	
G-BWJH	Shaw Europa	I. R. Willis	
G-BWJI	Cameron V-90 balloon	Calarel Developments Ltd	
G-BWJM	Bristol M.1C (replica) (C4918)	The Shuttleworth Collection	
G-BWJW	Westland Scout AH.Mk.1 (XV130)	S. Dadak & G. Sobell	
G-BWJY	DHC.1 Chipmunk 22 (WG469)	K. J. Thompson	
G-BWKD	Cameron O-120 balloon	L. J. & M. Schoeman	
G-BWKE	Cameron AS-105GD airship	W. Arnold/Germany	
G-BWKF	Cameron N-105 balloon	M. Buono/Italy	
G-BWKK	Auster A.O.P.9 (XP279)	C. A. Davis & D. R. White	
G-BWKT	Stephens Akro Laser	P. D. Begley	
G-BWKU	Cameron A-250 balloon	British School of Ballooning	
G-BWKV	Cameron V-77 balloon	C. A. Bryant	
G-BWKW	Thunder Ax8-90 balloon	Gone With The Wind Ltd	
G-BWKZ	Lindstrand LBL-77A balloon	J. H. Dobson	
G-BWLD	Cameron O-120 balloon	D. Pedri & ptnrs/Italy	
G-BWLF	Cessna 404	Reconnaisance Ventures Ltd (G-BNXS)	
G-BWLJ	Taylorcraft DCO-65 (42-35870/129)	B. J. Robe	
G-BWLL	Murphy Rebel	F. W. Parker	
G-BWLM	Sky 65-24 balloon	W. J. Brogan	
G-BWLY	Rotorway Executive 90	P. W. & I. P. Bewley	
G-BWMB	Jodel D.119	C. Hughes	
G-BWMC	Cessna 182P	S. J. N. Chance & N. E. Taviner	
G-BWMF	Gloster Meteor T.7 (WA591)	Aviation Heritage Ltd	
G-BWMH	Lindstrand LBL-77B balloon	M. Gallagher	
G-BWMI	PA-28RT-201T Turbo Arrow IV	O. Cowley	
G-BWMJ	Nieuport 17/2B (replica) (N1977:8)	R. Gauld-Galliers & L. J. Day	
G-BWMK	DH.82A Tiger Moth (T8191)	APB Leasing Ltd	
G-BWMN	Rans S.7 Courier	G. J. Knee	
G-BWMO	Oldfield Baby Lakes	D. Maddocks (G-CIII)	
G-BWMS	DH.82A Tiger Moth	Foundation Early Birds/Netherlands	

Notes	Reg.	Type	Owner or Operator
	G-BWMU	Cameron 105 Monster Truck SS balloon	Magical Adventures Ltd/Canada
	G-BWMV	Colt AS-105 Mk II airship	D. Stuber/Germany
	G-BWMX	DHC.1 Chipmunk 22 (WG407:67)	407th Flying Group
	G-BWMY	Cameron Bradford & Bingley SS balloon	Magical Adventures Ltd/USA
	G-BWNB	Cessna 152 II	South Warwickshire School of Flying
	G-BWNC	Cessna 152 II	South Warwickshire School of Flying
	G-BWND	Cessna 152 II	South Warwickshire School of Flying Ltd & G. Davies
	G-BWNI	PA-24 Comanche 180	W. A. Stewart
	G-BWNJ	Hughes 269C	L. R. Fenwick
	G-BWNK	D,H,C,1 Chipmunk 22 (WD390)	WD390 Group
	G-BWNM	PA-28R Cherokee Arrow 180	M. & R. C. Ramnial
	G-BWNO	Cameron O-90 balloon	T. Knight
	G-BWNP	Cameron 90 Club SS balloon	L. P. Hooper & A. R. Hardwick
	G-BWNS	Cameron O-90 balloon	I. C. Steward
	G-BWNT	DHC.1 Chipmunk 22 (WP901)	P. G. D. Bell & A. Stafford
	G-BWNU	PA-38-112 Tomahawk	Kemble Aero Club Ltd
	G-BWNY	Aeromot AMT-200 Super Ximango	Powell-Brett Associates Ltd
	G-BWNZ	Agusta A109C	Anglo Beef Processors Ltd
	G-BWOB	Luscombe 8F Silvaire	P. J. Tanulak & H. T. Law
	G-BWOF	P.84 Jet Provost T.5	Techair London Ltd
	G-BWOH	PA-28-161 Cadet	Plane Talking Ltd
	G-BWOI	PA-28-161 Cadet	Aviation Rentals
	G-BWOJ	PA-28-161 Cadet	Aviation Rentals
	G-BWOK	Lindstrand LBL-105G balloon	Lindstrand Hot Air Balloons Ltd
	G-BWOR	PA-18 Super Cub 135	C. D. Baird
	G-BWOT	P.84 Jet Provost T.3A (XN459)	M. Soor
	G-BWOV	Enstrom F-28A	P. A. Goss
	G-BWOW	Cameron N-105 balloon	Skybus Ballooning
	G-BWOY	Sky 31-24 balloon	C. Wolstenholme
	G-BWOZ	CFM Streak Shadow SA	J. A. Lord
	G-BWPC	Cameron V-77 balloon	H. Vaughan
	G-BWPE	Murphy Renegade Spirit UK	J. Hatswell/France
	G-BWPF	Sky 120-24 balloon	J. Francis
	G-BWPH	PA-28-181 Archer II	H. Merkado
	G-BWPJ	Steen Skybolt	D. Houghton
	G-BWPP	Sky 105-24 balloon	The Sarnia Balloon Group
	G-BWPS	CFM Streak Shadow SA	P. J. Mogg
	G-BWPT	Cameron N-90 balloon	G.Everett
	G-BWPZ	Cameron N-105 balloon	D. M. Moffat
	G-BWRA	Sopwith LC-1T Triplane (replica) (N500)	S. M. Truscott & J. M. Hoblyn (G-PENY)
	G-BWRC	Light Aero Avid Speedwing	A. D. Janaway
	G-BWRM	Colt 105A balloon	N. Charbonnier/Italy
	G-BWRO	Shaw Europa	G-BWRO Group
	G-BWRR	Cessna 182Q	D. Ridley
	G-BWRS	SNCAN Stampe SV.4C	G. P. J. M. Valvekens/Belgium
	G-BWRT	Cameron 60 Concept balloon	Zebedee Balloon Service Ltd
	G-BWRZ	Lindstrand LBL-105A balloon	N. Dykes
	G-BWSB	Lindstrand LBL-105A balloon	R. Calvert-Fisher
	G-BWSC	PA-38-112 Tomahawk II	The Hawstead Flying Group
	G-BWSD	Campbell Cricket	R. F. G. Moyle
	G-BWSG	P.84 Jet Provost T.5 (XW324/K)	J. Bell
	G-BWSH	P.84 Jet Provost T.3A (XN498)	Global Aviation Ltd
	G-BWSI	K & S SA.102.5 Cavalier	B. W. Shaw
	G-BWSJ	Denney Kitfox Mk 3	J. M. Miller
	G-BWSL	Sky 77-24 balloon	D. Baggley
	G-BWSN	Denney Kitfox Mk 3	M. J. Laundy
	G-BWSU	Cameron N-105 balloon	A. M. Marten
	G-BWSV	Yakovlev Yak-52	M. W. Fitch
	G-BWTB	Lindstrand LBL-105A balloon	Servatruc Ltd
	G-BWTC	Zlin Z.242L	S. W. Turley
	G-BWTD	Zlin Z.242L	Oxford Aviation Academy (Oxford) Ltd
	G-BWTE	Cameron O-140 balloon	Cameron Flights Southern Ltd
	G-BWTG	DHC.1 Chipmunk 22 (WB671:910)	R. G. T. de Man/Netherlands
	G-BWTH	Robinson R22 Beta	Helicopter Services
	G-BWTJ	Cameron V-77 balloon	A. J. Montgomery
	G-BWTK	RAF 2000 GTX-SE gyroplane	M. Love
	G-BWTN	Lindstrand LBL-90A balloon	J. A. Lomas
	G-BWTO	DHC.1 Chipmunk 22 (WP984)	Skycraft Services Ltd
	G-BWTW	Mooney M.20C	T. J. Berry
	G-BWUA	Campbell Cricket	N. J. Orchard
	G-BWUB	PA-18S Super Cub 135	Caledonian Seaplanes Ltd

Reg.	Type	Owner or Operator	Notes
G-BWUE	Hispano HA.1112M1L	Historic Flying Ltd (G-AWHK)	
G-BWUH	PA-28-181 Archer III	A. Davis	
G-BWUJ	Rotorway Executive 162F	Southern Helicopters Ltd	
G-BWUK	Sky 160-24 balloon	Cameron Flights Southern Ltd	
G-BWUL	Noorduyn AT-16 Harvard IIB	G-BWUL Flying Group	
G-BWUN	DHC.1 Chipmunk 22 (WD310)	T. Henderson	
G-BWUP	Shaw Europa	G. W. Grant	
G-BWUS	Sky 65-24 balloon	N. A. P. Bates	
G-BWUT	DHC.1 Chipmunk 22 (WZ879)	Herbert Aviation Ltd	
G-BWUU	Cameron N-90 balloon	Bailey Balloons Ltd	
G-BWUV	DHC.1 Chipmunk 22A (WK640)	A. C. Darby	
G-BWUZ	Campbell Cricket (replica)	K. A. Touhey	
G-BWVB	Pietenpol Air Camper	E. B. Toulson	
G-BWVC	Jodel D.18	R. W. J. Cripps	
G-BWVF	Pietenpol Air Camper	N. Clark	
G-BWVI	Stern ST.80	I. Pearson	
G-BWVM	Colt AA-1050 balloon	B. B. Baxter Ltd	
G-BWVN	Whittaker MW7	C. G. Dix	
G-BWVR	Yakovlev Yak-52 (52 yellow)	I. Parkinson	
G-BWVS	Shaw Europa	D. R. Bishop	
G-BWVT	DHA.82A Tiger Moth	R. Jewitt	
G-BWVU	Cameron O-90 balloon	J. Atkinson	
G-BWVV	Jodel D.18	D. S. Howarth	
G-BWVY	DHC.1 Chipmunk 22 (WP896)	N. Gardner	
G-BWVZ	DHC.1 Chipmunk 22A (WK590)	D. Campion/Belgium	
G-BWWA	Ultravia Pelican Club GS	J. S. Aplin	
G-BWWB	Shaw Europa	P. Levi	
G-BWWC	DH.104 Dove 7 (XM223)	Air Atlantique Ltd	
G-BWWE	Lindstrand LBL-90A balloon	B. J. Newman	
G-BWWF	Cessna 185A	T. N. Bartlett & S. M. C. Harvey	
G-BWWG	SOCATA Rallye 235E	J. J. Frew	
G-BWWI	AS.332L Super Puma	Bristow Helicopters Ltd	
G-BWWJ	Hughes 269C	R. J. Scott (G-BMYZ)	
G-BWWK	Hawker Nimrod I (S1581)	Patina Ltd	
G-BWWL	Colt Flying Egg SS balloon	Magical Adventures Ltd/USA	
G-BWWN	Isaacs Fury II (K8303:D)	J. S. Marten-Hale	
G-BWWP	Rans S.6-116 Coyote II	H. R. Carey	
G-BWWT	Dornier 328-100	Scot Airways Ltd	
G-BWWU	PA-22 Tri-Pacer 150	K. M. Bowen	
G-BWWW	BAe Jetstream 3102	British Aerospace PLC	
G-BWWX	Yakovlev Yak-50	D. P. McCoy/Ireland	
G-BWWY	Lindstrand LBL-105A balloon	M. J. Smith	
G-BWXA	Slingsby T.67M Firefly 260	Babcock Defence Services	
G-BWXB	Slingsby T.67M Firefly 260	Babcock Defence Services	
G-BWXC	Slingsby T.67M Firefly 260	Babcock Defence Services	
G-BWXD	Slingsby T.67M Firefly 260	Babcock Defence Services	
G-BWXE	Slingsby T.67M Firefly 260	Babcock Defence Services	
G-BWXF	Slingsby T.67M Firefly 260	Babcock Defence Services	
G-BWXG	Slingsby T.67M Firefly 260	Babcock Defence Services	
G-BWXH	Slingsby T.67M Firefly 260	Babcock Defence Services	
G-BWXI	Slingsby T.67M Firefly 260	Babcock Defence Services	
G-BWXJ	Slingsby T.67M Firefly 260	Babcock Defence Services	
G-BWXK	Slingsby T.67M Firefly 260	Babcock Defence Services	
G-BWXL	Slingsby T.67M Firefly 260	Babcock Defence Services	
G-BWXM	Slingsby T.67M Firefly 260	Babcock Defence Services	
G-BWXN	Slingsby T.67M Firefly 260	Babcock Defence Services	
G-BWXP	Slingsby T.67M Firefly 260	D. S. McGregor	
G-BWXR	Slingsby T.67M Firefly 260	Babcock Defence Services	
G-BWXS	Slingsby T.67M Firefly 260	Babcock Defence Services	
G-BWXT	Slingsby T.67M Firefly 260	Babcock Defence Services	
G-BWXU	Slingsby T.67M Firefly 260	Babcock Defence Services	
G-BWXV	Slingsby T.67M Firefly 260	Babcock Defence Services	
G-BWXX	Slingsby T.67M Firefly 260	Babcock Defence Services	
G-BWXY	Slingsby T.67M Firefly 260	Babcock Defence Services	
G-BWXZ	Slingsby T.67M Firefly 260	Babcock Defence Services	
G-BWYB	PA-28 Cherokee 160	I. M. Latiff	
G-BWYD	Shaw Europa	F. H. Mycroft	
G-BWYE	Cessna 310R II	ACS Contracts Ltd	
G-BWYI	Denney Kitfox Mk3	D. R. Piercy	
G-BWYK	Yakovlev Yak-50	Foley Farm Flying Group	
G-BWYN	Cameron O-77 balloon	W. H. Morgan (G-ODER)	
G-BWYO	Sequoia F.8L Falco	M. C. R. Sims	

Notes	Reg.	Type	Owner or Operator
	G-BWYR	Rans S.6-116 Coyote II	K. W. Scrivens
	G-BWYU	Sky 120-24 balloon	Aerosauras Balloons Ltd
	G-BWZA	Shaw Europa	T. G. Cowlishaw
	G-BWZG	Robin R.2160	Sherburn Aero Club Ltd
	G-BWZJ	Cameron A-250 balloon	Balloon Club of Great Britain
	G-BWZU	Lindstrand LBL-90B balloon	K. D. Pierce
	G-BWZX	AS.332L Super Puma	Bristow Helicopters Ltd
	G-BWZY	Hughes 269A	Reeve Newfields Ltd (G-FSDT)
	G-BXAB	PA-28-161 Warrior II	TG Aviation Ltd (G-BTGK)
	G-BXAC	RAF 2000 GTX-SE gyroplane	J. A. Robinson
	G-BXAF	Pitts S-1D Special	N. J. Watson
	G-BXAH	CP.301A Emeraude	A. P. Goodwin
	G-BXAJ	Lindstrand LBL-14A balloon	Oscair Project AB/Sweden
	G-BXAK	Yakovlev Yak-52 (44 black)	J. Calverley
	G-BXAN	Scheibe SF-25C Falke	C. Falke Syndicate
	G-BXAO	Avtech Jabiru SK	P. J. Thompson
	G-BXAS	Avro RJ100	Trident Jet (Jersey) Ltd
	G-BXAU	Pitts S-1 Special	L. Westnage
	G-BXAV	Yakovlev Yak-52	C. J. Reeves
	G-BXAX	Cameron N-77 balloon ★	Balloon Preservation Group
	G-BXAY	Bell 206B JetRanger 3	Viewdart Ltd
	G-BXBA	Cameron A-210 balloon	Reach For The Sky Ltd
	G-BXBB	PA-20 Pacer 150	M. E. R. Coghlan
	G-BXBK	Avions Mudry CAP-10B	S. Skipworth
	G-BXBL	Lindstrand LBL-240A balloon	Firefly Balloon Promotions
	G-BXBM	Cameron O-105 balloon	Bristol University Hot Air Ballooning Society
	G-BXBU	Avions Mudry CAP-10B	J. F. Cosgrave & H. R. Pearson
	G-BXBY	Cameron A-105 balloon	D. J. Littlewood
	G-BXBZ	PZL-104 Wilga 80	J. H. Sandham Aviation
	G-BXCA	Hapi Cygnet SF-2A	J. D. C. Henslow
	G-BXCC	PA-28-201T Turbo Dakota	Greer Aviation Ltd
	G-BXCD	TEAM mini-MAX 91A	A. Maltby
	G-BXCG	Jodel DR.250/160	CG Group
	G-BXCJ	Campbell Cricket (replica)	A. G. Peel
	G-BXCL	Montgomerie-Bensen B.8MR	M. L. L. Temple
	G-BXCN	Sky 105-24 balloon	Nottingham Hot-Air Balloon Club
	G-BXCO	Colt 120A balloon	J. R. Lawson
	G-BXCP	DHC.1 Chipmunk 22 (WP859)	M. P. O'Connor
	G-BXCT	DHC.1 Chipmunk 22 (WB697)	Wickenby Aviation
	G-BXCU	Rans S.6-116 Coyote II	R. S. Gent
	G-BXCV	DHC.1 Chipmunk 22 (WP929)	Ardmore Aviation Services Ltd/Hong Kong
	G-BXCW	Denney Kitfox Mk 3	M. J. Blanchard
	G-BXDA	DHC.1 Chipmunk 22 (WP860)	D. C. Mowat
	G-BXDB	Cessna U.206F	D. A. Howard (G-BMNZ)
	G-BXDD	RAF 2000GTX-SE gyroplane	R. Harris
	G-BXDE	RAF 2000GTX-SE gyroplane	B. Jones
	G-BXDF	Beech 95-B55 Baron	Chesh-Air Ltd
	G-BXDG	DHC.1 Chipmunk 22 (WK630)	Felthorpe Flying Group
	G-BXDH	DHC.1 Chipmunk 22 (WD331)	B. K. & W. G. Ranger
	G-BXDI	DHC.1 Chipmunk 22 (WD373)	Sunrise Global Aviation Ltd
	G-BXDM	DHC.1 Chipmunk 22 (WP840)	G. Hubsch
	G-BXDN	DHC.1 Chipmunk 22 (WK609)	W. D. Lowe & L. A. Edwards
	G-BXDO	Rutan Cozy	J. Foreman
	G-BXDP	DHC.1 Chupmunk 22 (WK642)	Gipsy Captains
	G-BXDR	Lindstrand LBL-77A balloon	British Telecommunications PLC
	G-BXDS	Bell 206B JetRanger III	Toby Blackwell Ltd (G-TAMF/G-OVBJ)
	G-BXDT	Robin HR.200/120B	Multiflight Ltd
	G-BXDU	Aero Designs Pulsar	M. P. Board
	G-BXDV	Sky 105-24 balloon	N. A. Carr
	G-BXDY	Shaw Europa	D. G. & S. Watts
	G-BXDZ	Lindstrand LBL-105A balloon	D. J. & A. D. Sutcliffe
	G-BXEC	DHC.1 Chipmunk 22 (WK633)	D. S. Hunt
	G-BXEJ	VPM M-16 Tandem Trainer	AES Radionic Surveillance Systems
	G-BXEN	Cameron N-105 balloon	John Aimo Balloons SAS/Italy
	G-BXES	P.66 Pembroke C.1 (XL954)	Air Atlantique Ltd
	G-BXET	PA-38-112 Tomahawk II	Tayside Aviation Ltd
	G-BXEX	PA-28-181 Archer II	R. Mayle
	G-BXEZ	Cessna 182P	Forhawk Ltd
	G-BXFB	Pitts S-1 Special	J. F. Dowe
	G-BXFC	Jodel D.18	B. S. Godbold
	G-BXFE	Avions Mudry CAP-10B	Avion Aerobatic Ltd

Reg.	Type	Owner or Operator	Notes
G-BXFG	Shaw Europa	A. Rawicz-Szczerbo	
G-BXFI	Hawker Hunter T.7 (WV372)	Fox-One Ltd	
G-BXFK	CFM Streak Shadow	A. G. Sindrey	
G-BXFN	Colt 77A balloon	Charter Ballooning Ltd	
G-BXGA	AS.350B2 Ecureuil	PLM Dollar Group Ltd	
G-BXGD	Sky 90-24 balloon	Servo & Electronic Sales Ltd	
G-BXGG	Shaw Europa	D. J. Joyce	
G-BXGH	Diamond Katana DA20-A1	M. Dorrian	
G-BXGL	DHC.1 Chipmunk 22	Airways Aero Associations Ltd	
G-BXGM	DHC.1 Chipmunk 22 (WP928:D)	Chipmunk G-BXGM Group	
G-BXGO	DHC.1 Chipmunk 22 (WB654:U)	Trees Group	
G-BXGP	DHC.1 Chipmunk 22 (WZ882)	Eaglescott Chipmunk Group	
G-BXGS	RAF 2000 gyroplane	C. R. Gordon	
G-BXGT	I.I.I. Sky Arrow 650T	J. S. C. Goodale	
G-BXGV	Cessna 172R	Skyhawk Group	
G-BXGX	DHC.1 Chipmunk 22 (WK586:V)	Interflight (Air Charter) Ltd	
G-BXGY	Cameron V-65 balloon	Dante Balloon Group	
G-BXGZ	Stemme S.10V	D. Tucker & K. Lloyd	
G-BXHA	DHC.1 Chipmunk 22 (WP925)	H. M. & S. Roberts	
G-BXHE	Lindstrand LBL-105A balloon	L. H. Ellis	
G-BXHF	DHC.1 Chipmunk 22 (WP930:J)	Hotel Fox Syndicate	
G-BXHH	AA-5A Cheetah	Oaklands Flying	
G-BXHJ	Hapi Cygnet SF-2A	I. J. Smith	
G-BXHL	Sky 77-24 balloon	R. K. Gyselynck	
G-BXHO	Lindstrand Telewest Sphere SS balloon	Magical Adventures Ltd	
G-BXHR	Stemme S.10V	J. H. Rutherford	
G-BXHT	Bushby-Long Midget Mustang	P. P. Chapman	
G-BXHU	Campbell Cricket Mk 6	P. J. Began	
G-BXHY	Shaw Europa	Jupiter Flying Group	
G-BXIA	DHC.1 Chipmunk 22 (WB615)	Dales Aviation	
G-BXIC	Cameron A-275 balloon	Aerosaurus Balloons LLP	
G-BXIE	Colt 77B balloon	L. C. Sanders	
G-BXIF	PA-28-161 Warrior II	Piper Flight Ltd	
G-BXIG	Zenair CH.701 STOL	A. J. Perry	
G-BXIH	Sky 200-24 balloon	Kent Ballooning	
G-BXII	Shaw Europa	D. A. McFadyean	
G-BXIJ	Shaw Europa	R. James	
G-BXIM	DHC.1 Chipmunk 22 (WK512)	A. B. Ashcroft & P. R. Joshua	
G-BXIO	Jodel DR.1050M	R. S. Palmer	
G-BXIT	Zebedee V-31 balloon	Zebedee Balloon Service Ltd	
G-BXIX	VPM M-16 Tandem Trainer	D. Beevers	
G-BXIY	Blake Bluetit (BAPC37)	J. Bryant	
G-BXIZ	Lindstrand LBL-31A balloon	J. S. Russon	
G-BXJB	Yakovlev Yak-52	Bumbles Angels	
G-BXJC	Cameron A-210 balloon	British School of Ballooning	
G-BXJD	PA-28 Cherokee 180C	M. G. A. Hussein	
G-BXJG	Lindstrand LBL-105B balloon	C. E. Wood	
G-BXJH	Cameron N-42 balloon	M. J. Axtell	
G-BXJJ	PA-28-161 Cadet	Plane Talking Ltd	
G-BXJM	Cessna 152	ACS Aviation Ltd	
G-BXJO	Cameron O-90 balloon	Dragon Balloon Co Ltd	
G-BXJP	Cameron C-80 balloon	AR. Cobaleno Pasta Fresca SRL/Italy	
G-BXJS	Schempp-Hirth Janus CM	Janus Syndicate	
G-BXJT	Sky 90-24 balloon	J. G. O'Connell	
G-BXJV	Diamond Katana DA20-A1	Enniskillen Flying School Ltd	
G-BXJW	Diamond Katana DA20-A1	Enniskillen Flying School Ltd	
G-BXJY	Van's RV-6	D. J. Sharland	
G-BXJZ	Cameron C-60 balloon	J. M. Stables	
G-BXKF	Hawker Hunter T.7(XL577/V)	R. F. Harvey	
G-BXKL	Bell 206B JetRanger 3	Swattons Aviation Ltd	
G-BXKM	RAF 2000 GTX-SE gyroplane	A. H. Goddard	
G-BXKO	Sky 65-24 balloon	Ecole de Pilotage Franche-Comte Montgolfieres/France	
G-BXKU	Colt AS-120 Mk II airship	D. C. Chipping/Portugal	
G-BXKW	Slingsby T.67M Firefly 200	J-F Jansen & A. Huygens	
G-BXKX	Auster V	J. A. Clark	
G-BXLF	Lindstrand LBL-90A balloon	W. Rousell & J. Tyrrell	
G-BXLG	Cameron C-80 balloon	S. M. Anthony	
G-BXLK	Shaw Europa	R. G. Fairall	
G-BXLN	Fournier RF-4D	P. W. Cooper	
G-BXLO	P.84 Jet Provost T.4 (XR673/L)	Century Aviation Ltd	
G-BXLP	Sky 90-24 balloon	G. B. Lescott	

Notes	Reg.	Type	Owner or Operator
	G-BXLR	PZL-110 Koliber 160A	Sligo Koliber Group
	G-BXLS	PZL-110 Koliber 160A	D. C. Bayes
	G-BXLT	SOCATA TB200 Tobago XL	R. M. Shears
	G-BXLY	PA-28-151 Warrior	Multiflight Ltd (G-WATZ)
	G-BXMF	Cassutt Racer IIIM	P. R. Fabish
	G-BXMG	RAF 2000 GTX gyroplane	J. S. Wright
	G-BXMK	Lindstrand LBL-240A balloon	M. E. White
	G-BXML	Mooney M.20A	G. Kay
	G-BXMM	Cameron A-180 balloon	High Road Balloons
	G-BXMV	Scheibe SF.25C Falke 1700	K. E. Ballington
	G-BXMX	Currie Wot	M. R. Coreth
	G-BXMY	Hughes 269C	R. J. Scott
	G-BXNA	Light Aero Avid Flyer	A. P. Daines
	G-BXNC	Shaw Europa	J. K. Cantwell
	G-BXNN	DHC.1 Chipmunk 22 (WP983:B)	E. N. Skinner
	G-BXNS	Bell 206B JetRanger 3	Sterling Helicopters Ltd
	G-BXNT	Bell 206B JetRanger 3	Sterling Helicopters Ltd
	G-BXOA	Robinson R22 Beta	MG Group Ltd
	G-BXOC	Evans VP-2	H. J. & E. M. Cox
	G-BXOF	Diamond Katana DA20-A1	M. Dorrian
	G-BXOI	Cessna 172R	E. J. Watts
	G-BXOJ	PA-28-161 Warrior III	Craigard Property Trading Ltd
	G-BXOM	Isaacs Spitfire	S. Vince
	G-BXON	Auster AOP.9	C. J. & D. J. Baker
	G-BXOT	Cameron C-70 balloon	Dante Balloon Group
	G-BXOU	CEA DR.360	J. A. Lofthouse
	G-BXOW	Colt 105A balloon	M. E. White
	G-BXOX	AA-5A Cheetah	R. L. Carter & P. J. Large
	G-BXOY	QAC Quickie Q.235	C. C. Clapham
	G-BXOZ	PA-28-181 Archer II	Spritetone Ltd
	G-BXPC	Diamond Katana DA20-A1	Cubair Flight Training Ltd
	G-BXPD	Diamond Katana DA20-A1	Cubair Flight Training Ltd
	G-BXPI	Van's RV-4	S. T. G. Lloyd
	G-BXPK	Cameron A-250 balloon	Alba Ballooning Ltd
	G-BXPL	PA-28 Cherokee 140	Take Flight Aviation Ltd
	G-BXPM	Beech 58 Baron	Foyle Flyers Ltd
	G-BXPP	Sky 90-24 balloon	S. J. Farrant
	G-BXPR	Colt 110 Can SS balloon	P. O. Wagner/Germany
	G-BXPT	Ultramagic H-77 balloon	G. D. O. Bartram/Andorra
	G-BXRA	Avions Mudry CAP-10B	J. W. Scott
	G-BXRB	Avions Mudry CAP-10B	T. T. Duhig
	G-BXRC	Avions Mudry CAP-10B	Group Alpha
	G-BXRD	Enstrom 280FX	K. Payne & M. A. Stephenson
	G-BXRF	CP.1310-C3 Super Emeraude	D. T. Gethin
	G-BXRG	PA-28-181 Archer II	Alderney Flying Training Ltd
	G-BXRH	Cessna 185A	R. E. M. Holmes
	G-BXRM	Cameron A-210 balloon	Dragon Balloon Co Ltd
	G-BXRO	Cessna U.206G	M. Penny
	G-BXRP	Schweizer 269C	AH Helicopter Services Ltd
	G-BXRR	Westland Scout AH.1	M. Soor
	G-BXRS	Westland Scout AH.1 (XW613)	B-N Group Ltd
	G-BXRT	Robin DR.400-180	T. P. Usborne
	G-BXRV	Van's RV-4	Cleeve Flying Grouip
	G-BXRY	Bell 206B JetRanger	Corbett Holdings Ltd
	G-BXRZ	Rans S.6-116 Coyote II	M. P. Hallam
	G-BXSC	Cameron C-80 balloon	N. A. Apsey
	G-BXSD	Cessna 172R	R. Paston
	G-BXSE	Cessna 172R	MK Aero Support Ltd
	G-BXSG	Robinson R22 Beta II	Rivermead Aviation Ltd
	G-BXSH	Glaser-Dirks DG.800B	R. O'Conor
	G-BXSI	Avtech Jabiru SK	P. F. Gandy
	G-BXSP	Grob G.109B	Deeside Grob Group
	G-BXSR	Cessna F172N	N. C. K. G. Copeman
	G-BXST	PA-25 Pawnee 235C	The Northumbria Gliding Club Ltd
	G-BXSU	TEAM mini-MAX 91A	I. A. Coates (G-MYGL)
	G-BXSV	SNCAN Stampe SV.4C	B. A. Bower
	G-BXSX	Cameron V-77 balloon	D. R. Medcalf
	G-BXSY	Robinson R22 Beta II	N. M. G. Pearson
	G-BXTB	Cessna 152	Northumbria Flying School Ltd
	G-BXTD	Shaw Europa	P. R. Anderson
	G-BXTF	Cameron N-105 balloon	Flying Pictures Ltd
	G-BXTG	Cameron N-42 balloon	P. M. Watkins & S. M. M. Carden

Reg.	Type	Owner or Operator	Notes
G-BXTH	Westland Gazelle HT.1 (XW866)	Armstrong Aviation Ltd	
G-BXTI	Pitts S-1S Special	A. B. Treherne-Pollock	
G-BXTJ	Cameron N-77 balloon	Chubb Fire Ltd Chubb	
G-BXTO	Hindustan HAL-6 Pushpak	P. Q. Benn	
G-BXTS	Diamond Katana DA20-A1	I. M. Armitage & D. J. Short	
G-BXTT	AA-5B Tiger	M. N. Stevens	
G-BXTV	Bug Mk.4 helicopter	B. R. Cope	
G-BXTW	PA-28-181 Archer III	Davison Plant Hire	
G-BXTY	PA-28-161 Cadet	Flew LLP	
G-BXTZ	PA-28-161 Cadet	Flew LLP	
G-BXUA	Campbell Cricket Mk.5	A. W. Harvey	
G-BXUC	Robinson R22 Beta	Rivermead Aviation Ltd/Switzerland	
G-BXUF	Agusta-Bell 206B JetRanger 3	SJ Contracting Services Ltd	
G-BXUG	Lindstrand Baby Bel SS balloon	K-H. Gruenauer/Germany	
G-BXUH	Lindstrand LBL-31A balloon	Balloon Preservation Flying Groupt	
G-BXUI	Glaser-Dirks DG.800B	J. Le Coyte	
G-BXUM	Shaw Europa	D. Bosomworth	
G-BXUO	Lindstrand LBL-105A balloon	Lindstrand Technologies Ltd	
G-BXUS	Sky 65-24 balloon	PSH Skypower Ltd	
G-BXUU	Cameron V-65 balloon	M. D. Freeston & S. Mitchell	
G-BXUW	Cameron Colt 90A balloon	Zycomm Electronics Ltd	
G-BXUX	Brandli Cherry BX-2	M. F. Fountain	
G-BXUY	Cessna 310Q	G. A. Vickers	
G-BXVA	SOCATA TB200 Tobago XL	Archer Two Ltd	
G-BXVB	Cessna 152 II	PJC (Leasing) Ltd	
G-BXVD	CFM Streak Shadow SA	I. J. C. Burman	
G-BXVG	Sky 77-24 balloon	M. Wolf	
G-BXVK	Robin HR.200/120B	Modi Aviation Ltd	
G-BXVM	Van's RV-6A	J. C. Lomax	
G-BXVO	Van's RV-6A	P. J. Hynes & M. E. Holden	
G-BXVP	Sky 31-24 balloon	T. Dudman	
G-BXVR	Sky 90-24 balloon	P. Hegarty	
G-BXVS	Brügger MB.2 Colibri	G. T. Snoddon	
G-BXVT	Cameron O-77 balloon	R. P. Wade	
G-BXVU	PA-28-161 Warrior II	Jet Connections Ltd	
G-BXVV	Cameron V-90 balloon	Floating Sensations Ltd	
G-BXVX	Rutan Cozy	G. E. Murray	
G-BXVY	Cessna 152	Stapleford Flying Club Ltd	
G-BXWA	Beech 76 Duchess	Aviation South West Ltd	
G-BXWB	Robin HR.100/200B	W. A. Brunwin	
G-BXWG	Sky 120-24 balloon	M. E. White	
G-BXWH	Denney Kitfox Mk.4-1200	M. G. Porter	
G-BXWK	Rans S.6-ESA Coyote II	P. B. Davey	
G-BXWL	Sky 90-24 balloon	D. J. Baggley	
G-BXWO	PA-28-181 Archer II	J. S. Develin & Z. Islam	
G-BXWP	PA-32 Cherokee Six 300	R. J. Sharpe	
G-BXWR	CFM Streak Shadow	M. A. Hayward (G-MZMI)	
G-BXWT	Van's RV-6	R. C. Owen	
G-BXWU	FLS Aerospace Sprint 160	Aeroelvia Ltd	
G-BXWV	FLS Aerospace Sprint 160	Aeroelvia Ltd	
G-BXWX	Sky 25-16 balloon	C. O'Neill & G. Davis	
G-BXXG	Cameron N-105 balloon	R. N. Simpkins	
G-BXXH	Hatz CB-1	R. D. Shingler	
G-BXXI	Grob G.109B	M. N. Martin	
G-BXXJ	Colt Flying Yacht SS balloon	Magical Adventures Ltd/USA	
G-BXXK	Cessna FR.172N	J. A. Havers and R. A. Blackwell	
G-BXXL	Cameron N-105 balloon	Flying Pictures Ltd	
G-BXXN	Robinson R22 Beta	Helicopter Services	
G-BXXO	Lindstrand LBL-90B balloon	K. Temple	
G-BXXP	Sky 77-24 balloon	T. R. Wood	
G-BXXS	Sky 105-24 balloon	Flying Pictures Ltd	
G-BXXT	Beech 76 Duchess	Pridenote Ltd	
G-BXXU	Colt 31A balloon	Sade Balloons Ltd	
G-BXXW	Enstrom F-28F	D. A. Marks (G-SCOX)	
G-BXYD	Eurocopter EC 120B	Aero Maintenance Ltd	
G-BXYE	CP.301-C1 Emeraude	D. T. Gethin	
G-BXYF	Colt AS-105 GD airship	LN Flying Ltd	
G-BXYG	Cessna 310D	Equitus SARL/France	
G-BXYI	Cameron H-34 balloon	S. P. Harrowing	
G-BXYJ	Jodel DR.1050	G-BXYJ Group	
G-BXYK	Robinson R22 Beta	Ramsgill Aviation Ltd	
G-BXYM	PA-28 Cherokee 235	Redfly Aviation Ltd	

Notes	Reg.	Type	Owner or Operator
	G-BXYO	PA-28RT-201 Arrow IV	W. R. Tupling-Prest
	G-BXYP	PA-28RT-201 Arrow IV	G. I. Cooper
	G-BXYT	PA-28RT-201 Arrow IV	Falcon Flying Services Ltd
	G-BXYX	Van's RV-6A	A. G. Palmer
	G-BXZA	PA-38-112 Tomahawk	Aviatlantic
	G-BXZB	Nanchang CJ-6A (2632019)	Wingglider Ltd
	G-BXZF	Lindstrand LBL-90A balloon	B. T. Harris
	G-BXZI	Lindstrand LBL-90A balloon	J. A. Viner
	G-BXZK	MDH MD-900 Explorer	Dorset Police Air Support Unit
	G-BXZM	Cessna 182S	AB Integro Aviation Ltd
	G-BXZO	Pietenpol Air Camper	P. J. Cooke
	G-BXZT	MS.880B Rallye Club	Roundwood Flying Club
	G-BXZU	Micro Aviation Bantam B.22-S	M. E. Whapham & R. W. Hollamby
	G-BXZV	CFM Streak Shadow	M. D. O'Brien
	G-BXZY	CFM Streak Shadow Srs DD	Cloudbase Aviation Services Ltd
	G-BYAH	Boeing 757-204ER	Thomson Airways Ltd
	G-BYAI	Boeing 757-204ER	Thomson Airways Ltd
	G-BYAL	Boeing 757-28AER	Thomson Airways Ltd
	G-BYAO	Boeing 757-204ER	Thomson Airways Ltd
	G-BYAP	Boeing 757-204ER	Thomson Airways Ltd
	G-BYAT	Boeing 757-204ER	Thomson Airways Ltd
	G-BYAU	Boeing 757-204ER	Thomson Airways Ltd
	G-BYAV	Taylor JT.1 Monoplane	D. M. Lockley
	G-BYAW	Boeing 757-204ER	Thomson Airways Ltd
	G-BYAX	Boeing 757-204ER	Thomson Airways Ltd
	G-BYAY	Boeing 757-204ER	Thomson Airways Ltd
	G-BYAZ	CFM Streak Shadow	A. G. Wright
	G-BYBC	Agusta-Bell 206B JetRanger 2	Sky Charter UK Ltd (G-BTWW)
	G-BYBD	Cessna F.172H	D. G. Bell & J. Cartmell (G-OBHX/G-AWMU)
	G-BYBE	Jodel D.120A	J. M. Alexander
	G-BYBF	Robin R.2160i	D. J. R. Lloyd-Evans
	G-BYBH	PA-34-200T Seneca II	Goldspear (UK) Ltd
	G-BYBI	Bell 206B JetRanger 3	A. G. B. Davie-Thornhill
	G-BYBJ	Medway Hybred 44XLR	M. Gardner
	G-BYBK	Murphy Rebel	J. R. Howard
	G-BYBL	Gardan GY-80 Horizon 160D	M. J. Sutton
	G-BYBM	Avtech Jabiru SK	P. J. Hatton
	G-BYBN	Cameron N-77 balloon	M. G. Howard
	G-BYBO	Medway Hybred 44XLR Eclipser	C. Bayliss
	G-BYBP	Cessna A.185F	G. M. S. Scott
	G-BYBR	Rans S.6-116 Coyote II	S. & A. F. Williams
	G-BYBS	Sky 80-16 balloon	B. K. Rippon
	G-BYBU	Renegade Spirit UK	R. L. Williams
	G-BYBV	Mainair Rapier	M. W. Robson
	G-BYBX	Slingsby T.67M Firefly 260	Slingsby Advanced Composites Ltd
	G-BYBY	Thorp T.18C Tiger	P. G. Mair
	G-BYBZ	Jabiru SK	D. Licheri
	G-BYCA	PA-28 Cherokee 140D	R. Steptoe
	G-BYCD	Cessna 140 (modified)	G. P. James
	G-BYCE	Robinson R44	C. A. Rosenberg
	G-BYCF	Robinson R22 Beta II	Aero Maintenance Ltd
	G-BYCJ	CFM Shadow Srs DD	P. I. Hodgson
	G-BYCM	Rans S.6-ES Coyote II	E. W. McMullan
	G-BYCN	Rans S.6-ES Coyote II	T. J. Croskery
	G-BYCP	Beech B200 Super King Air	London Executive Aviation Ltd
	G-BYCS	Jodel DR.1051	C. Brown, M. N. King & P. Nelson
	G-BYCV	Meridian Maverick 430	J. K. Buckingham
	G-BYCW	Mainair Blade 912	P. C. Watson
	G-BYCX	Westland Wasp HAS.1	BN Helicopters Ltd
	G-BYCY	I.I.I. Sky Arrow 650T	K. A. Daniels
	G-BYCZ	Avtech Jabiru SK	SK Group
	G-BYDB	Grob G.115B	J. B. Baker
	G-BYDE	VS.361 Spitfire LF. IX (PT879)	P. A. Teichman
	G-BYDF	Sikorsky S-76A	Brecqhou Development Ltd
	G-BYDG	Beech C24R Sierra	Professional Flight Simulation Ltd
	G-BYDJ	Colt 120A balloon	D. K. Hempleman-Adams
	G-BYDK	SNCAN Stampe SV.4C	Bianchi Aviation Film Services Ltd
	G-BYDL	Hawker Hurricane IIB (Z5207)	P. J. Lawton
	G-BYDT	Cameron N-90 balloon	R. M. Stanley
	G-BYDU	Cameron Cart SS balloon	N. J. Langley
	G-BYDV	Van's RV-6	B. F. Hill

Reg.	Type	Owner or Operator	Notes
G-BYDY	Beech 58 Baron	Pilot Services Flying Group Ltd	
G-BYDZ	Pegasus Quantum 15-912	P. Newson	
G-BYEA	Cessna 172P	M. Gates	
G-BYEC	Glaser-Dirks DG.800B	The 23 Syndicate	
G-BYEE	Mooney M.20K	Double Echo Flying Group	
G-BYEH	CEA Jodel DR.250	Nicholson Decommissioning Ltd	
G-BYEJ	Scheibe SF-28A Tandem Falke	D. Shrimpton	
G-BYEK	Stoddard Hamilton Glastar	G. M. New	
G-BYEL	Van's RV-6	D. Millar	
G-BYEM	Cessna R.182 RG	Bickertons Aerodromes Ltd	
G-BYEO	Zenair CH.601HDS	J. R. Clarke	
G-BYER	Cameron C-80 balloon	J. M. Langley	
G-BYES	Cessna 172P	Redhill Air Services Ltd	
G-BYEW	Pegasus Quantum 15-912	D. Martin	
G-BYEY	Lindstrand LBL-21 Silver Dream balloon	Oscair Project Ltd/Sweden	
G-BYEZ	Dyn' Aero MCR-01	P. H. Milward	
G-BYFA	Cessna F.152 II	Redhill Air Services Ltd (G-WACA)	
G-BYFC	Avtech Jabiru SK	M. Flint	
G-BYFF	Pegasus Quantum 15-912	Kemble Flying Club	
G-BYFI	CFM Starstreak Shadow SA	J. A. Cook	
G-BYFJ	Cameron N-105 balloon	R. J. Mercer	
G-BYFK	Cameron Printer 105 SS balloon	Mobberley Balloon Collection	
G-BYFL	Diamond HK.36 TTS	Seahawk Gliding Club	
G-BYFM	Jodel DR.1050M-1 (replica)	A. J. Roxburgh	
G-BYFR	PA-32R-301 Saratoga II HP	Buckleton Ltd	
G-BYFT	Pietenpol Air Camper	G. Everett	
G-BYFU	Lindstrand LBL-105B balloon	ULM Decouverte/France	
G-BYFV	TEAM mini-MAX 91	W. E. Gillham	
G-BYFX	Colt 77A balloon	Wye Valley Aviation Ltd	
G-BYFY	Avions Mudry CAP-10B	R. N. Crosland	
G-BYGA	Boeing 747-436	British Airways	
G-BYGB	Boeing 747-436	British Airways	
G-BYGC	Boeing 747-436	British Airways	
G-BYGD	Boeing 747-436	British Airways	
G-BYGE	Boeing 747-436	British Airways	
G-BYGF	Boeing 747-436	British Airways	
G-BYGG	Boeing 747-436	British Airways	
G-BYHC	Cameron Z-90 balloon	S. M. Sherwin	
G-BYHE	Robinson R22 Beta	Helicopter Services Ltd	
G-BYHG	Dornier 328-100	Scot Airways Ltd	
G-BYHH	PA-28-161 Warrior III	Stapleford Flying Club Ltd	
G-BYHI	PA-28-161 Warrior II	M. G. McLarnon	
G-BYHJ	PA-28R-201 Arrow	Flew LLP	
G-BYHK	PA-28-181 Archer III	T-Air Services	
G-BYHL	DHC.1 Chipmunk 22 (WG308)	M. R. & I. D. Higgins	
G-BYHO	Mainair Blade 912	T. Porter & D. Whiteley	
G-BYHP	CEA DR.253B	HP Flying Group	
G-BYHR	Pegasus Quantum 15-912	I. D. Chantler	
G-BYHS	Mainair Blade 912	T. J. Grange, R. Beard & K. Meechan	
G-BYHT	Robin DR.400/180R	Deeside Robin Group	
G-BYHU	Cameron N-105 balloon	ABC Flights Ltd	
G-BYHV	Raj Hamsa X'Air 582	M. G. Adams	
G-BYHY	Cameron V-77 balloon	P. Spellward	
G-BYIA	Avtech Jabiru SK	E. Bentley	
G-BYIB	Rans S.6-ES Coyote II	W. Anderson	
G-BYID	Rans S.6-ES Coyote II	R. M. Watson	
G-BYIE	Robinson R22 Beta	Givens Aviation	
G-BYII	TEAM mini-MAX	G. Wilkinson	
G-BYIJ	CASA 1.131E Jungmann 2000	R. N. Crosland	
G-BYIK	Shaw Europa	P. M. Davis	
G-BYIL	Cameron N-105 balloon	Oakfield Farm Products Ltd	
G-BYIM	Avtech Jabiru UL	A. & J. McVey	
G-BYIN	RAF 2000 gyroplane	J. R. Legge	
G-BYIO	Colt 105A balloon	N. Charbonnier/Italy	
G-BYIP	Aerotek Pitts S-2A Special	D. P. Heather-Hayes	
G-BYIR	Aerotek Pitts S-1S Special	S. Kramer	
G-BYIS	Pegasus Quantum 15-912	D. J. Ramsden	
G-BYIT	Robin DR.400/500	Aero Club Basque/France	
G-BYIU	Cameron V-90 balloon	H. Micketeit/Germany	
G-BYIV	Cameron PM-80 balloon	A. Schneider/Germany	
G-BYIW	Cameron PM-80 balloon	Team Ballooning/Germany	
G-BYIX	Cameron PM-80 balloon	A. Schneider/Germany	

Notes	Reg.	Type	Owner or Operator
	G-BYIY	Lindstrand LBL-105B balloon	J. H. Dobson
	G-BYIZ	Pegasus Quantum 15-912	J. D. Gray
	G-BYJA	RAF 2000 GTX-SE	C. R. W. Lyne
	G-BYJB	Mainair Blade 912	D. C. Haslam
	G-BYJC	Cameron N-90 balloon	A. G. Merry
	G-BYJD	Avtech Jabiru UL	M. W. Knights
	G-BYJE	TEAM Mini-MAX 91	T. A. Willcox
	G-BYJF	Thorpe T.211	AD Aviation Ltd
	G-BYJG	Lindstrand LBL-77A balloon	Lindstrand Hot-Air Balloons Ltd
	G-BYJH	Grob G.109B	A. J. Buchanan
	G-BYJI	Shaw Europa	M. Gibson (G-ODTI)
	G-BYJJ	Cameron C-80 balloon	Proximm SPA/Italy
	G-BYJK	Pegasus Quantum 15-912	K. D. Smith
	G-BYJL	Aero Designs Pulsar	F. A. H. Ashmead
	G-BYJM	Cyclone AX2000	Caunton AX2000 Syndicate
	G-BYJN	Lindstrand LBL-105A balloon	B. Meeson
	G-BYJO	Rans S.6-ES Coyote II	G. Ferguson
	G-BYJP	Aerotek Pitts S-1S Special	Eaglescott Pitts Group
	G-BYJR	Lindstrand LBL-77B balloon	B. M. Reed
	G-BYJS	SOCATA TB20 Trinidad	A. P. Bedford
	G-BYJT	Zenair CH.601HD	J. D. T. Tannock
	G-BYJU	Raj Hamsa X'Air 582	G. P. Morling
	G-BYJW	Cameron Sphere 105 balloon	Balleroy Developpement SAS
	G-BYJX	Cameron C-70 balloon	B. Perona
	G-BYKA	Lindstrand LBL-69A balloon	B. Meeson
	G-BYKB	Rockwell Commander 114	A. Walton
	G-BYKC	Mainair Blade 912	G. W. Cameron & C. S. Harrison
	G-BYKD	Mainair Blade 912	D. C. Boyle
	G-BYKF	Enstrom F-28F	S. C. Severeyns & G. T. Williams
	G-BYKG	Pietenpol Air Camper	K. B. Hodge
	G-BYKI	Cameron N-105 balloon	J. A. Leahy/Ireland
	G-BYKJ	Westland Scout AH.1	Austen Associates
	G-BYKK	Robinson R44	Dragonfly Aviation
	G-BYKL	PA-28-181 Archer II	Transport Command Ltd
	G-BYKP	PA-28R-201T Turbo Arrow IV	D. W. Knox & D. L. Grimes
	G-BYKS	Leopoldoff L-6 Colibri	I. M. Callier
	G-BYKT	Pegasus Quantum 15-912	N. J. Howarth
	G-BYKU	BFC Challenger II	K. W. Seedhouse
	G-BYKW	Lindstrand LBL-77B balloon	K. Allemand/France
	G-BYKX	Cameron N-90 balloon	G. Davis
	G-BYLB	D. H. 82A Tiger Moth	P. A. Layzell
	G-BYLC	Pegasus Quantum 15-912	A. Cordes
	G-BYLD	Pietenpol Air Camper	S. Bryan
	G-BYLH	Robin HR.200/120B	Multiflight Ltd
	G-BYLI	Nova Vertex 22 hang glider	M. Hay
	G-BYLJ	Letov LK-2M Sluka	W. J. McCarroll
	G-BYLL	Sequoia F.8L Falco	N. J. Langrick
	G-BYLO	T.66 Nipper Srs 1	M. J. A. Trudgill
	G-BYLP	Rand-Robinson KR-2	C. S. Hales
	G-BYLS	Bede BD-4	G. H. Bayliss
	G-BYLT	Raj Hamsa X'Air 582	T. W. Phipps
	G-BYLV	Thunder Ax8-105 S2 balloon	kb Voli Di Chiozzi Bartolomeo EC SAS/Italy
	G-BYLW	Lindstrand LBL-77A balloon	Associazione Gran Premio Italiano
	G-BYLX	Lindstrand LBL-105A balloon	Italiana Aeronavi/Italy
	G-BYLY	Cameron V-77 balloon (1)	R. Bayly/Italy (G-ULIA)
	G-BYLZ	Rutan Cozy	W. S. Allen
	G-BYMB	Diamond Katana DA20-C1	S. Staniulis & A. Zakaras
	G-BYMC	PA-38-112 Tomahawk II	Central Aircraft Leasing Ltd
	G-BYMD	PA-38-112 Tomahawk II	M. A. Petrie
	G-BYMF	Pegasus Quantum 15-912	G. R. Stockdale
	G-BYMG	Cameron A-210 balloon	Cloud Nine Balloon Co
	G-BYMH	Cessna 152	PJC (Leasing) Ltd
	G-BYMI	Pegasus Quantum 15	N. C. Grayson
	G-BYMJ	Cessna 152	PJC (Leasing) Ltd
	G-BYMK	Dornier 328-100	Scot Airways Ltd
	G-BYMN	Rans S.6-ESA Coyote II	R. L. Barker
	G-BYMO	Campbell Cricket	P. G. Rawson
	G-BYMP	Campbell Cricket Mk 1	J. J. Fitzgerald
	G-BYMR	Raj Hamsa X'Air R100(3)	W. Drury
	G-BYMU	Rans S.6-ES Coyote II	I. R. Russell & S. Palmer
	G-BYMV	Rans S.6-ES Coyote II	T. P. R. Wright
	G-BYMW	Boland 52-12 balloon	C. Jones

Reg.	Type	Owner or Operator	Notes
G-BYMX	Cameron A-105 balloon	H. Reis/Germany	
G-BYMY	Cameron N-90 balloon	A. Cakss	
G-BYNA	Cessna F.172H	D. M. White (G-AWTH)	
G-BYND	Pegasus Quantum 15	W. J. Upton	
G-BYNE	Pilatus PC-6/B2-H4 Turbo Porter	D. M. Penny	
G-BYNF	NA-64 Yale I (3349)	R. S. Van Dijk	
G-BYNI	Rotorway Exec 90	M. Bunn	
G-BYNK	Robin HR.200/160	Penguin Flight Group	
G-BYNM	Mainair Blade 912	J. P. Hanlon & A. C. McAllister	
G-BYNN	Cameron V-90 balloon	Cloud Nine Balloon Group	
G-BYNP	Rans S.6-ES Coyote II	R. J. Lines	
G-BYNR	Avtech Jabiru UL	M. P. Maughan	
G-BYNS	Avtech Jabiru SK	D. K. Lawry	
G-BYNT	Raj Hamsa X'Air 582 (1)	A. Evans	
G-BYNU	Cameron Thunder Ax7-77 balloon	P. M. Gaines	
G-BYNV	Sky 105-24 balloon	Par Rovelli Construzioni SRL/Italy	
G-BYNW	Cameron H-34 balloon	I. M. Ashpole	
G-BYNX	Cameron RX-105 balloon	Cameron Balloons Ltd	
G-BYNY	Beech 76 Duchess	Magenta Ltd	
G-BYOB	Slingsby T.67M Firefly 260	Stapleford Flying Club Ltd	
G-BYOD	Slingsby T.67C	D. I. Stanbridge	
G-BYOG	Pegasus Quantum 15-912	M. D. Hinge	
G-BYOH	Raj Hamsa X'Air 582 (1)	D. M. Loughlin	
G-BYOI	Sky 80-16 balloon	I. S. & S. W. Watthews	
G-BYOJ	Raj Hamsa X'Air 582 (1)	C. G. Thompson	
G-BYOK	Cameron V-90 balloon	D. S. Wilson	
G-BYOM	Sikorsky S-76C (modified)	Starspeed Ltd (G-IJCB)	
G-BYON	Mainair Blade	R. Campbell-Moore	
G-BYOO	CFM Streak Shadow	G. R. Eastwood	
G-BYOR	Raj Hamsa X'Air 582(7)	P. C. Dugdale	
G-BYOT	Rans S.6-ES Coyote II	G. Shaw	
G-BYOU	Rans S.6-ES Coyote II	P. G. Bright & P. L. Parker	
G-BYOV	Pegasus Quantum 15-912	M. Howland	
G-BYOW	Mainair Blade	D. Renton	
G-BYOX	Cameron Z-90 balloon	G. A. Boyle & D. R. Rawlings	
G-BYOZ	Mainair Rapier	A. G. Lomas	
G-BYPB	Pegasus Quantum 15-912	Cleaprop Microlight School Ltd	
G-BYPD	Cameron A-105 balloon	Headland Hotel Ltd	
G-BYPE	Gardan GY-80 Horizon 160D	P. B. Hodgson	
G-BYPF	Thruster T.600N	M. A. Beadman	
G-BYPG	Thruster T.600N	G-BYPG Syndicate	
G-BYPH	Thruster T.600N	D. M. Canham	
G-BYPJ	Pegasus Quantum 15-912	M. Watson	
G-BYPL	Pegasus Quantum 15-912	IP. Lister	
G-BYPM	Shaw Europa XS	G-BYPM Group	
G-BYPN	MS.880B Rallye Club	R. Edwards and D. & S. A. Bell	
G-BYPO	Raj Hamsa X'Air 582 (1)	D. W. Willis	
G-BYPR	Zenair CH.601HD Zodiac	S. C. Ord	
G-BYPT	Rans S.6-ES Coyote II	G. P. & P. T. Willcox	
G-BYPU	PA-32R-301 Saratoga SP	AM Blatch Electrical Contractors Ltd	
G-BYPW	Raj Hamsa X'Air 583 (3)	K. J. Kimpton	
G-BYPY	Ryan ST3KR (001)	T. Curtis-Taylor	
G-BYPZ	Rans S.6-116 Super 6	R. A. Blackbourne	
G-BYRC	Westland WS-58 Wessex HC.2 (XT671)	D. Brem-Wilson	
G-BYRG	Rans S.6-ES Coyote II	S. J. Macmillan	
G-BYRH	Medway Hybred 44XLR	G. R. Puffett	
G-BYRJ	Pegasus Quantum 15-912	C. W. Docksey	
G-BYRK	Cameron V-42 balloon	R. Kunert	
G-BYRO	Mainair Blade	P. W. F. Coleman	
G-BYRR	Mainair Blade 912	G. R. Sharples	
G-BYRS	Rans S.6-ES Coyote II	A. E. Turner	
G-BYRU	Pegasus Quantum 15-912	Sarum QTM 912 Group	
G-BYRV	Raj Hamsa X'Air 582 (1)	A. D. Russell	
G-BYRX	Westland Scout AH.1 (XT634)	Edwalton Aviation Ltd	
G-BYRY	Slingsby T.67M Firefly 200	PI Air Services SPRL/Belgium	
G-BYRZ	Lindstrand LBL-77M balloon	Challenge Transatlantique/France	
G-BYSA	Shaw Europa XS	R. L. Hitchcock	
G-BYSE	Agusta-Bell 206B JetRanger 2	Alspath Properties Ltd (G-BFND)	
G-BYSF	Avtech Jabiru UL	P. F. Morgan	
G-BYSG	Robin HR.200/120B	Modi Aviation Ltd	
G-BYSI	WSK-PZL Koliber 160A	J. & D. F. Evans	
G-BYSJ	DHC.1 Chipmunk 22 (WB569:R)	C. H. Green	

Notes	Reg.	Type	Owner or Operator
	G-BYSK	Cameron A-275 balloon	Balloon School (International) Ltd
	G-BYSM	Cameron A-210 balloon	Balloon School (International) Ltd
	G-BYSN	Rans S.6-ES Coyote II	S. J. Smith
	G-BYSP	PA-28-181 Archer II	Take Flight Aviation Ltd
	G-BYSS	Medway Rebel SS	D. W. Allen
	G-BYSV	Cameron N-120 balloon	S. Simmington
	G-BYSX	Pegasus Quantum 15-912	D. W. Ormond
	G-BYSY	Raj Hamsa X'Air 582 (1)	J. M. Davidson
	G-BYTA	Kolb Twinstar Mk 3 (modified)	L. R. Morris
	G-BYTB	SOCATA TB20 Trinidad	Watchman Aircraft Ltd
	G-BYTC	Pegasus Quantum 15-912	R. J. Marriott
	G-BYTI	PA-24 Comanche 250	M. Carruthers & G. Auchterlonie
	G-BYTJ	Cameron C-80 balloon	A. J. Gregory
	G-BYTK	Avtech Jabiru UL	M. A. Potter
	G-BYTL	Mainair Blade 912	P. B. Spencer & J. T. Burrow
	G-BYTM	Dyn' Aero MCR-01	I. Lang & E. J. Clarke
	G-BYTN	DH.82A Tiger Moth (N6720:VX)	R. Merewood & J. W. Freckington
	G-BYTR	Raj Hamsa X'Air 582 (1)	B. Wyatt
	G-BYTS	Montgomerie-Bensen B.8MR gyroplane	M. G. Mee
	G-BYTU	Mainair Blade 912	J. E. Morgan
	G-BYTV	Avtech Jabiru UK	M. G. Speers
	G-BYTW	Cameron O-90 balloon	Sade Balloons Ltd
	G-BYTZ	Raj Hamsa X'Air 582 (1)	R. Armstrong
	G-BYUA	Grob G.115E Tutor	Babcock Aerospace Ltd
	G-BYUB	Grob G.115E Tutor	Babcock Aerospace Ltd
	G-BYUC	Grob G.115E Tutor	Babcock Aerospace Ltd
	G-BYUD	Grob G.115E Tutor	Babcock Aerospace Ltd
	G-BYUE	Grob G.115E Tutor	Babcock Aerospace Ltd
	G-BYUF	Grob G.115E Tutor	Babcock Aerospace Ltd
	G-BYUG	Grob G.115E Tutor	Babcock Aerospace Ltd
	G-BYUH	Grob G.115E Tutor	Babcock Aerospace Ltd
	G-BYUI	Grob G.115E Tutor	Babcock Aerospace Ltd
	G-BYUJ	Grob G.115E Tutor	Babcock Aerospace Ltd
	G-BYUK	Grob G.115E Tutor	Babcock Aerospace Ltd
	G-BYUL	Grob G.115E Tutor	Babcock Aerospace Ltd
	G-BYUM	Grob G.115E Tutor	Babcock Aerospace Ltd
	G-BYUN	Grob G.115E Tutor	Babcock Aerospace Ltd
	G-BYUO	Grob G.115E Tutor	Babcock Aerospace Ltd
	G-BYUP	Grob G.115E Tutor	Babcock Aerospace Ltd
	G-BYUR	Grob G.115E Tutor	Babcock Aerospace Ltd
	G-BYUS	Grob G.115E Tutor	Babcock Aerospace Ltd
	G-BYUU	Grob G.115E Tutor	Babcock Aerospace Ltd
	G-BYUV	Grob G.115E Tutor	Babcock Aerospace Ltd
	G-BYUW	Grob G.115E Tutor	Babcock Aerospace Ltd
	G-BYUX	Grob G.115E Tutor	Babcock Aerospace Ltd
	G-BYUY	Grob.G.115E Tutor	Babcock Aerospace Ltd
	G-BYUZ	Grob G.115E Tutor	Babcock Aerospace Ltd
	G-BYVA	Grob G.115E Tutor	Babcock Aerospace Ltd
	G-BYVB	Grob G.115E Tutor	Babcock Aerospace Ltd
	G-BYVC	Grob G.115E Tutor	Babcock Aerospace Ltd
	G-BYVD	Grob G.115E Tutor	Babcock Aerospace Ltd
	G-BYVE	Grob G.115E Tutor	Babcock Aerospace Ltd
	G-BYVF	Grob G.115E Tutor	Babcock Aerospace Ltd
	G-BYVG	Grob G.115E Tutor	Babcock Aerospace Ltd
	G-BYVH	Grob G.115E Tutor	Babcock Aerospace Ltd
	G-BYVI	Grob G.115E Tutor	Babcock Aerospace Ltd
	G-BYVJ	Grob G.115E Tutor	Babcock Aerospace Ltd
	G-BYVK	Grob G.115E Tutor	Babcock Aerospace Ltd
	G-BYVL	Grob G.115E Tutor	Babcock Aerospace Ltd
	G-BYVM	Grob G.115E Tutor	Babcock Aerospace Ltd
	G-BYVO	Grob G.115E Tutor	Babcock Aerospace Ltd
	G-BYVP	Grob G.115E Tutor	Babcock Aerospace Ltd
	G-BYVR	Grob G.115E Tutor	Babcock Aerospace Ltd
	G-BYVS	Grob G.115E Tutor	Babcock Aerospace Ltd
	G-BYVT	Grob G.115E Tutor	Babcock Aerospace Ltd
	G-BYVU	Grob G.115E Tutor	Babcock Aerospace Ltd
	G-BYVV	Grob G.115E Tutor	Babcock Aerospace Ltd
	G-BYVW	Grob G.115E Tutor	Babcock Aerospace Ltd
	G-BYVX	Grob G.115E Tutor	Babcock Aerospace Ltd
	G-BYVY	Grob G.115E Tutor	Babcock Aerospace Ltd
	G-BYVZ	Grob G.115E Tutor	Babcock Aerospace Ltd
	G-BYWA	Grob G.115E Tutor	Babcock Aerospace Ltd

Reg.	Type	Owner or Operator	Notes
G-BYWB	Grob G.115E Tutor	Babcock Aerospace Ltd	
G-BYWC	Grob G.115E Tutor	Babcock Aerospace Ltd	
G-BYWD	Grob G.115E Tutor	Babcock Aerospace Ltd	
G-BYWE	Grob G.115E Tutor	Babcock Aerospace Ltd	
G-BYWF	Grob G.115E Tutor	Babcock Aerospace Ltd	
G-BYWG	Grob G.115E Tutor	Babcock Aerospace Ltd	
G-BYWH	Grob G.115E Tutor	Babcock Aerospace Ltd	
G-BYWI	Grob G.115E Tutor	Babcock Aerospace Ltd	
G-BYWJ	Grob G.115E Tutor	Babcock Aerospace Ltd	
G-BYWK	Grob G.115E Tutor	Babcock Aerospace Ltd	
G-BYWL	Grob G.115E Tutor	Babcock Aerospace Ltd	
G-BYWM	Grob G.115E Tutor	Babcock Aerospace Ltd	
G-BYWN	Grob G.115E Tutor	Babcock Aerospace Ltd	
G-BYWO	Grob G.115E Tutor	Babcock Aerospace Ltd	
G-BYWP	Grob G.115E Tutor	Babcock Aerospace Ltd	
G-BYWR	Grob G.115E Tutor	Babcock Aerospace Ltd	
G-BYWS	Grob G.115E Tutor	Babcock Aerospace Ltd	
G-BYWT	Grob G-115E Tutor	Babcock Aerospace Ltd	
G-BYWU	Grob G.115E Tutor	Babcock Aerospace Ltd	
G-BYWV	Grob G.115E Tutor	Babcock Aerospace Ltd	
G-BYWW	Grob G.115E Tutor	Babcock Aerospace Ltd	
G-BYWX	Grob G.115E Tutor	Babcock Aerospace Ltd	
G-BYWY	Grob G.115E Tutor	Babcock Aerospace Ltd	
G-BYWZ	Grob G.115E Tutor	Babcock Aerospace Ltd	
G-BYXA	Grob G.115E Tutor	Babcock Aerospace Ltd	
G-BYXB	Grob G.115E Tutor	Babcock Aerospace Ltd	
G-BYXC	Grob G.115E Tutor	Babcock Aerospace Ltd	
G-BYXD	Grob G.115E Tutor	Babcock Aerospace Ltd	
G-BYXE	Grob G.115E Tutor	Babcock Aerospace Ltd	
G-BYXF	Grob G.115E Tutor	Babcock Aerospace Ltd	
G-BYXG	Grob G.115E Tutor	Babcock Aerospace Ltd	
G-BYXH	Grob G.115E Tutor	Babcock Aerospace Ltd	
G-BYXI	Grob G.115E Tutor	Babcock Aerospace Ltd	
G-BYXJ	Grob G.115E Tutor	Babcock Aerospace Ltd	
G-BYXK	Grob G.115E Tutor	Babcock Aerospace Ltd	
G-BYXL	Grob G.115E Tutor	Babcock Aerospace Ltd	
G-BYXM	Grob G.115E Tutor	Babcock Aerospace Ltd	
G-BYXN	Grob G.115E Tutor	Babcock Aerospace Ltd	
G-BYXO	Grob G.115E Tutor	Babcock Aerospace Ltd	
G-BYXP	Grob G.115E Tutor	Babcock Aerospace Ltd	
G-BYXS	Grob G.115E Tutor	Babcock Aerospace Ltd	
G-BYXT	Grob G.115E Tutor	Babcock Aerospace Ltd	
G-BYXW	Medway Eclipser	G. A. Hazell	
G-BYXX	Grob G.115E Tutor	Babcock Aerospace Ltd	
G-BYXY	Grob G.115E Tutor	Babcock Aerospace Ltd	
G-BYXZ	Grob G.115E Tutor	Babcock Aerospace Ltd	
G-BYYA	Grob G.115E Tutor	Babcock Aerospace Ltd	
G-BYYB	Grob G.115E Tutor	Babcock Aerospace Ltd	
G-BYYC	Hapi Cygnet SF-2A	G. H. Smith	
G-BYYE	Lindstrand LBL-77A balloon	C. Wilkinson	
G-BYYG	Slingsby T.67C	The Pathfinder Flying Club Ltd	
G-BYYL	Avtech Jabiru UL 450	M. J. Hillier & W. J. Lee	
G-BYYM	Raj Hamsa X'Air 582 (1)	S. M. S. Smith	
G-BYYN	Pegasus Quantum 15-912	V. Gledhill	
G-BYYO	PA-28R -201 Arrow III	Stapleford Flying Club Ltd	
G-BYYP	Pegasus Quantum 15	D. A. Linsey-Bloom	
G-BYYR	Raj Hamsa X'Air 582 (4)	T. D. Bawden	
G-BYYT	Avtech Jabiru UL 450	A. C. Cale and A. J. Young.	
G-BYYX	TEAM mini-MAX 91	J. Batchelor	
G-BYYY	Pegasus Quantum 15-912	Clearprop Microlight School Ltd	
G-BYYZ	Staaken Z-21A Flitzer	T. White	
G-BYZA	AS.355F2 Twin Squirrel	MMAir Ltd	
G-BYZB	Mainair Blade	A. M. Thornley	
G-BYZF	Raj Hamsa X'Air 582 (1)	R. P. Davies	
G-BYZG	Cameron A-275 balloon	Cameron Flights Southern Ltd	
G-BYZL	Cameron GP-65 balloon	P. Thibo	
G-BYZO	Rans S.6-ES Coyote II	Golf Zulu Oscar Group	
G-BYZP	Robinson R22 Beta	T. I. McGlone	
G-BYZR	I.I.I. Sky Arrow 650TC	G-BYZR Flying Group	
G-BYZS	Avtech Jabiru UL-450	N. Fielding	
G-BYZT	Nova Vertex 26	M. Hay	
G-BYZU	Pegasus Quantum 15	N. I. Clifton	

Notes	Reg.	Type	Owner or Operator
	G-BYZV	Sky 90-24 balloon	P. Farmer
	G-BYZW	Raj Hamsa X'Air 582 (2)	J. Magill
	G-BYZX	Cameron R-90 balloon	D. K. Hempleman-Adams
	G-BYZY	Pietenpol Aircamper	D. M. Hanchett
	G-BYZZ	Robinson R22 Beta II	Casdron Enterprises Ltd
	G-BZAA	Mainair Blade	B. M. Davis
	G-BZAB	Mainair Rapier	B. Myers
	G-BZAE	Cessna 152	APB Leasing Ltd
	G-BZAG	Lindstrand LBL-105A balloon	A. M. Figiel
	G-BZAI	Pegasus Quantum 15	S. I. Close
	G-BZAK	Raj Hamsa X'Air 582 (1)	C. J. Harvey
	G-BZAL	Mainair Blade 912	J. Potts
	G-BZAM	Europa	D. U. Corbett
	G-BZAO	Rans S.12XL	M. L. Robinson
	G-BZAP	Avtech Jabiru UL-450	I. J. Grindley & D. R. Griffiths
	G-BZAR	Denney Kitfox 4-1200 Speedster	N. J. France (G-LEZJ)
	G-BZAS	Isaacs Fury II (K5673)	N. C. Stone
	G-BZAT	Avro RJ100	Trident Jet (Jersey) Ltd
	G-BZAX	Avro RJ100	BAE Systems (Operations) Ltd
	G-BZAY	Avro RJ100	BAE Systems (Operations) Ltd
	G-BZAZ	Avro RJ100	BAE Systems (Operations) Ltd
	G-BZBC	Rans S.6-ES Coyote II	A. J. Baldwin
	G-BZBE	Cameron A-210 balloon	Dragon Balloon Co Ltd
	G-BZBF	Cessna 172M	L. W. Scattergood
	G-BZBH	Thunder Ax6-65 balloon	P. J. Hebdon & A. C. Fraser
	G-BZBI	Cameron V-77 balloon	C. & A. I. Gibson
	G-BZBJ	Lindstrand LBL-77A balloon	P. T. R. Ollivere
	G-BZBL	Lindstrand LBL-120A balloon	East Coast Balloons Ltd
	G-BZBO	Stoddard-Hamilton Glasair III	M. B. Hamlett/France
	G-BZBP	Raj Hamsa X'Air 582 (1)	J. L. B. Roy
	G-BZBR	Pegasus Quantum 15-912	C. P. Davies
	G-BZBS	PA-28-161 Warrior III	Aviation Rentals
	G-BZBT	Cameron H-34 Hopper balloon	British Telecommunications PLC
	G-BZBU	Robinson R22	I. C. Macdonald
	G-BZBW	Rotorway Executive 162F	Southern Helicopters Ltd
	G-BZBX	Rans S.6-ES Coyote II	N. Musgrave
	G-BZBZ	Jodel D.9	S. Morriss
	G-BZDA	PA-28-161 Warrior III	Aviation Rentals
	G-BZDB	Thruster T.600T	M. R. Jones
	G-BZDC	Mainair Blade	E. J. Wells & P. J. Smith
	G-BZDD	Mainair Blade 912	G. Devlin
	G-BZDE	Lindstrand LBL-210A balloon	Toucan Travel Ltd
	G-BZDF	CFM Streak Shadow SA	W. M. Moylan
	G-BZDH	PA-28R Cherokee Arrow 200-II	G-BZDH Ltd
	G-BZDI	Aero L-39C Albatros	C. C. Butt
	G-BZDJ	Cameron Z-105 balloon	BWS Security Systems Ltd
	G-BZDK	X'Air 582(2)	B. Park
	G-BZDM	Stoddard-Hamilton Glastar	F. G. Miskelly
	G-BZDN	Cameron N-105 balloon	I. R. Warrington & P. A. Foot
	G-BZDP	SA Bulldog Srs 120/121 (XX551:E)	R. M. Raikes
	G-BZDR	Tri-R Kis	J. M. & J. A. Jackson
	G-BZDS	Pegasus Quantum 15-912	K. C. Yeates
	G-BZDT	Maule MXT-7-180	Strongcrew Ltd
	G-BZDV	Westland Gazelle HT.2	European Plant and Machinery Sales
	G-BZEA	Cessna A.152	Sky Leisure Aviation (Charters) Ltd
	G-BZEB	Cessna 152	Sky Leisure Aviation (Charters) Ltd
	G-BZEC	Cessna 152	Sky Leisure Aviation (Charters) Ltd
	G-BZED	Pegasus Quantum 15-912	D. Crozier
	G-BZEE	Agusta-Bell 206B JetRanger 2	Atlantic Aviation 2007 Ltd
	G-BZEG	Mainair Blade	R. P. Cookson
	G-BZEH	PA-28 Cherokee 235B	R. Biddulph
	G-BZEJ	Raj Hamsa X'Air 582 (7)	H-Flight X'Air Flying Group
	G-BZEK	Cameron C-70 balloon	Ballooning 50 Degrees Nord/Luxembourg
	G-BZEL	Mainair Blade 912	T. McCormack
	G-BZEN	Avtech Jabiru UL-450	N. W. Cawley
	G-BZEP	SA Bulldog Srs 120/121 (XX561:7)	A. J. Amato
	G-BZER	Raj Hamsa X'Air R100 (1)	N. P. Lloyd & H. Lloyd-Jones
	G-BZES	Rotorway Executive 90	Southern Helicopters Ltd (G-LUFF)
	G-BZET	Robin HR.200/120B	Bulldog Aviation Ltd
	G-BZEU	Raj Hamsa X'Air 582 (2)	D. E. Foster
	G-BZEW	Rans S.6-ES Coyote II	M. J. Wooldridge

Reg.	Type	Owner or Operator	Notes
G-BZEY	Cameron N-90 balloon	Northants Auto Parts and Service Ltd	
G-BZEZ	CFM Streak Shadow	G. J. Pearce	
G-BZFA	Avro 146 RJ70	Trident Turboprop (Dublin) Ltd	
G-BZFB	Robin R.2112A	T. F. Wells	
G-BZFC	Pegasus Quantum 15-912	G. Addison	
G-BZFD	Cameron N-90 balloon	David Hataway Holdings Ltd	
G-BZFG	Sky 105 balloon	Virgin Airship & Balloon Co Ltd	
G-BZFH	Pegasus Quantum 15-912	D. W. Adams	
G-BZFI	Avtech Jabiru UL	Group Family	
G-BZFN	SA Bulldog Srs 120/121 (XX667:16)	Risk Logical Ltd	
G-BZFP	DHC.6 Twin Otter 310	Loganair Ltd/Flybe.com	
G-BZFR	Extra EA.300/L	T. C. Beadle	
G-BZFS	Mainair Blade 912	D. F. Clorley	
G-BZFT	Murphy Rebel	N. A. Evans	
G-BZFU	Lindstrand LBL HS-110 HA Airship	Lindstrand Hot Air Balloons Ltd	
G-BZFV	Zenair CH.601UL	M. E. Caton	
G-BZGA	DHC.1 Chipmunk 22 (WK585)	The Real Flying Co Ltd	
G-BZGB	DHC.1 Chipmunk 22 (WZ872:E)	Silverstar Aviation Ltd	
G-BZGF	Rans S.6-ES Coyote II	C. A. Purvis & D. F. Castle	
G-BZGH	Cessna F.172N	Golf Hotel Group	
G-BZGJ	Thunder Ax10-180 S2 balloon	Merlin Balloons	
G-BZGK	NA OV-10B Bronco (99+32)	Aircraft Restoration Co Ltd	
G-BZGL	NA OV-10B Bronco (99+26)	Aircraft Restoration Co Ltd	
G-BZGM	Mainair Blade 912	D. Avery	
G-BZGN	Raj Hamsa X'Air 582 (2)	D. I. Hall	
G-BZGO	Robinson R44	Flight Academy (Gyrocopters) Ltd	
G-BZGR	Rans S.6-ES Coyote II	J. M. Benton	
G-BZGS	Mainair Blade 912	R. J. Coppin	
G-BZGT	Avtech Jabiru UL-450	J. White	
G-BZGV	Lindstrand LBL-77A balloon	J. H. Dryden	
G-BZGW	Mainair Blade	C. S. M. Hallam	
G-BZGX	Raj Hamsa X'Air 582 (6)	A. Crowe	
G-BZGY	Dyn'Aéro CR.100	B. Appleby	
G-BZGZ	Pegasus Quantum 15-912	D. W. Beech	
G-BZHA	Boeing 767-336ER	British Airways	
G-BZHB	Boeing 767-336ER	British Airways	
G-BZHC	Boeing 767-336ER	British Airways	
G-BZHE	Cessna 152	General Aero Equipment Ltd	
G-BZHF	Cessna 152	Modi Aviation Ltd	
G-BZHG	Tecnam P92 Echo	R. W. F. Boarder	
G-BZHJ	Raj Hamsa X'Air 582 (7)	S. Hardy	
G-BZHL	Noorduyn AT-16 Harvard IIB	R. H. Cooper & S. Swallow	
G-BZHN	Pegasus Quantum 15-912	A. M. Sirant	
G-BZHO	Pegasus Quantum 15	T. H. Beales	
G-BZHR	Avtech Jabiru UL-450	G. W. Rowbotham & W. Turner	
G-BZHT	PA-18A Super Cub 150	Lakes Gliding Club	
G-BZHU	Wag-Aero Sport Trainer	Teddy Boys Flying Group	
G-BZHV	PA-28-181 Archer III	R. M. & T. A. Limb	
G-BZHX	Thunder Ax11-250 S2 balloon	Wizard Balloons Ltd	
G-BZHY	Mainair Blade 912	M. Morris	
G-BZIA	Raj Hamsa X'Air 700 (1)	J. L. Pritchett	
G-BZIC	Lindstrand LBL Sun SS balloon	Ballongaventyr 1 Sakne AB/Sweden	
G-BZID	Montgomerie-Bensen B.8MR	A. Gault	
G-BZIG	Thruster T.600N	Ultra Air Ltd	
G-BZIH	Lindstrand LBL-31A balloon	Skyart Balloons	
G-BZII	Extra EA.300/1	P. F. Brice	
G-BZIJ	Robin DR.400/500	Rob Airways Ltd	
G-BZIK	Cameron A-250 balloon	Breckland Balloons Ltd	
G-BZIL	Colt 120A balloon	Champagne Flights	
G-BZIM	Pegasus Quantum 15-912	A. & S. Cuthbertson	
G-BZIO	PA-28-161 Warrior III	Aviation Rentals	
G-BZIP	Montgomerie-Bensen B.8MR	C. D. Prebble	
G-BZIS	Raj Hamsa X'Air 582 (2)	J. O. Williams	
G-BZIT	Beech 95-B55 Baron	Propellorhead Aviation Ltd	
G-BZIV	Avtech Jabiru UL	V. R. Leggott	
G-BZIW	Pegasus Quantum 15-912	J. M. Hodgson	
G-BZIX	Cameron N-90 balloon	M. Stefanini & P. Marmugi/Italy	
G-BZIY	Raj Hamsa X'Air 582 (2)	A. L. A. Gill	
G-BZIZ	Ultramagic H-31 balloon	G. D. O. Bartram	
G-BZJA	Cameron 90 Fire SS balloon	Chubb Fire Ltd	
G-BZJC	Thruster T.600N	M. H. Moulai	
G-BZJD	Thruster T.600T	The Valentine Syndicate	

Notes	Reg.	Type	Owner or Operator
	G-BZJG	Cameron A-400 balloon	Cameron Balloons Ltd
	G-BZJH	Cameron Z-90 balloon	Balloon SpA
	G-BZJI	Nova X-Large 37 paraplane	M. Hay
	G-BZJJ	Robinson R22 Beta	E. Sorvillo/Italy
	G-BZJL	Mainair Blade 912S	D. N. Powell
	G-BZJM	VPM M-16 Tandem Trainer	D. Wood
	G-BZJN	Mainair Blade 912	L. Campbell & M. A. Haughey
	G-BZJO	Pegasus Quantum 15	W. C. Bryan
	G-BZJP	Zenair CH.701UL	B. J. Fallows
	G-BZJV	CASA 1-131E Jungmann 1000	R. A. Cumming
	G-BZJW	Cessna 150F	P. Ligertwood
	G-BZJZ	Pegasus Quantum 15	S. Baker
	G-BZKC	Raj Hamsa X'Air 582 (2)	J. E. Evans
	G-BZKD	Stolp Starduster Too	P. & C. Edmunds
	G-BZKE	Lindstrand LBL-77B balloon	D. B. Green
	G-BZKF	Rans S.6-ES Coyote II	A. W. Lowrie
	G-BZKL	PA-28R-201 Arrow III	Shoreflight Ltd
	G-BZKO	Rans S-6-ES Coyote II	G. Millar
	G-BZKU	Cameron Z-105 balloon	N. A. Fishlock
	G-BZKV	Cameron Sky 90-24 balloon	Omega Selction Services Ltd
	G-BZKW	Ultramagic M-27 balloon	T. G. Church
	G-BZLC	WSK-PZL Koliber 160A	G. F. Smith
	G-BZLE	Rans S.6-ES Coyote II	J. C. Rose
	G-BZLF	CFM Shadow Srs CD	D. W. Stacey
	G-BZLG	Robin HR.200/120B	Flew LLP
	G-BZLH	PA-28-161 Warrior II	Aviation Rentals
	G-BZLI	SOCATA TB21 Trinidad TC	K. B. Hallam
	G-BZLK	Slingsby T.31M Motor Tutor	G. Smith
	G-BZLL	Pegasus Quantum 15-912	A. J. Thomson
	G-BZLP	Robinson R44	T. A. Wells
	G-BZLS	Cameron Sky 77-24 balloon	D. W. Young
	G-BZLT	Raj Hamsa X'Air 582 (1)	J. D. McClatchey
	G-BZLU	Lindstrand LBL-90A balloon	A. E. Lusty
	G-BZLV	Avtech Jabiru UL-450	G. Dalton
	G-BZLX	Pegasus Quantum 15-912	D. McCabe & M. Harris
	G-BZLY	Grob G.109B	R. W. Hegmann
	G-BZLZ	Pegasus Quantum 15-912	A. S. Martin
	G-BZMB	PA-28R-201 Arrow III	Thurrock Arrow Group
	G-BZMC	Avtech Jabiru UL	D. Maddison
	G-BZMD	SA Bulldog Srs 120/121 (XX554)	Mad Dog Flying Group
	G-BZME	SA Bulldog Srs 120/121 (XX698:9)	S. J. Whitworth
	G-BZMF	Rutan LongEz	R. A. Gardiner
	G-BZMG	Robinson R44	Audisio Automobili Cuneo SRL
	G-BZMH	SA Bulldog Srs 120/121 (XX692:A)	M. E. J. Hingley
	G-BZMI	Pegasus Quantum 15-912	P. L. Jarvis
	G-BZMJ	Rans S-6-ES Coyote II	C. J. Arthur
	G-BZML	SA Bulldog Srs 120/121 (XX693:07)	I. D. Anderson
	G-BZMM	Robin DR.400/180R	N. A. C. Norman
	G-BZMO	Robinson R22 Beta	Time Select Ltd
	G-BZMR	Raj Hamsa X'Air 582 (2)	M. Grime
	G-BZMS	Mainair Blade	T. R. Villa
	G-BZMT	PA-28-161 Warrior III	Aviation Rentals
	G-BZMW	Pegasus Quantum 15-912	M. A. Clayton
	G-BZMY	SPP Yakovlev Yak C-11	Classic Displays Ltd
	G-BZMZ	CFM Streak Shadow	J. F. F. Fouche
	G-BZNB	Pegasus Quantum 15	M. P. & R. A. Wells
	G-BZNC	Pegasus Quantum 15-912	D. E. Wall
	G-BZND	Sopwith Pup (replica) (N5199)	M. A. Goddard
	G-BZNE	Beech B300 Super King Air	Skyhopper LLP
	G-BZNF	Colt 120A balloon	N. Charbonnier/Italy
	G-BZNH	Rans S.6-ES Coyote II	J. R. Parker
	G-BZNJ	Rans S.6-ES Coyote II	R. A. McKee
	G-BZNK	Morane Saulnier MS.315-D2	R. H. Cooper & S. Swallow
	G-BZNM	Pegasus Quantum 15	J. T. Davies
	G-BZNN	Beech 76 Duchess	Aviation Rentals
	G-BZNP	Thruster T.600N	J. D. Gibbons
	G-BZNS	Mainair Blade	A. G. Laycock
	G-BZNU	Cameron A-300 balloon	Balloon School (International) Ltd
	G-BZNV	Lindstrand LBL-31A balloon	G. R. Down
	G-BZNW	Isaacs Fury II (K2048)	S. M. Johnston
	G-BZNX	SOCATA MS.880B Rallye Club	P. C. Avery
	G-BZNY	Shaw Europa XS	W. J. Harrison

Reg.	Type	Owner or Operator	Notes
G-BZNZ	Lindstrand LBL Cake SS balloon	Oxford Promotions (UK) Ltd	
G-BZOB	Slepcev Storch (6G-ED)	B. J. Chester-Master	
G-BZOD	Pegasus Quantum 15-912	V. J. Vaughan	
G-BZOE	Pegasus Quantum 15	J. Needham	
G-BZOF	Montgomerie-Bensen B.8MR gyroplane	S. J. M. Ledingham	
G-BZOG	Dornier 328-100	Scot Airways Ltd	
G-BZOI	Nicollier HN.700 Menestrel II	S. J. McCollum	
G-BZOL	Robin R.3000/140	S. D. Baker	
G-BZOM	Rotorway Executive 162F	R. L. Cole	
G-BZON	SA Bulldog Srs 120/121 (XX528:D)	D. J. Critchley	
G-BZOO	Pegasus Quantum 15-912	A. J. Maxfield	
G-BZOP	Robinson R44	CN Joinery and Building Services Ltd	
G-BZOR	TEAM mini-MAX 91	J. F. Govan	
G-BZOU	Pegasus Quantum 15-912	D. T. Moeller	
G-BZOV	Pegasus Quantum 15-912	D. Turner	
G-BZOW	Whittaker MW7	G. W. Peacock	
G-BZOX	Cameron Colt 90B balloon	D. J. Head	
G-BZOY	Beech 76 Duchess	Aviation Rentals	
G-BZOZ	Van's RV-6	M. & S. Sheppard	
G-BZPA	Mainair Blade 912S	J. McGoldrick	
G-BZPB	Hawker Hunter GA.11 (XF300)	B. R. Pearson	
G-BZPC	Hawker Hunter GA.11 (WV256)	B. R. Pearson	
G-BZPD	Cameron V-65 balloon	P. Spellward	
G-BZPE	Lindstrand LBL-310 balloon	Aerosaurus Balloons Ltd	
G-BZPG	Beech C24R Sierra 200	Wycombe Air Centre Ltd	
G-BZPH	Van's RV-4	G-BZPH RV-4 Group	
G-BZPI	SOCATA TB20 Trinidad	K. M. Brennan	
G-BZPJ	Beech 76 Duchess	Aviation Rentals	
G-BZPK	Cameron C-80 balloon	D. L. Homer	
G-BZPN	Mainair Blade 912S	G. R. Barker	
G-BZPP	Westland Wasp HAS.1 (XT793:456)	C. J. Marsden	
G-BZPR	Ultramagic N-210 balloon	European Balloon Display Co Ltd	
G-BZPS	SA Bulldog Srs 120/121 (XX658:07)	A. J. Robinson & M. J. Miller	
G-BZPT	Ultramagic N-210 balloon	European Balloon Display Co Ltd	
G-BZPV	Lindstrand LBL-90B balloon	D. P. Hopkins	
G-BZPW	Cameron V-77 balloon	J. Vonka	
G-BZPX	Ultramagic S-105 balloon	Scotair Balloons	
G-BZPY	Ultramagic H-31 balloon	Scotair Balloons	
G-BZPZ	Mainair Blade	J. W. Edwards	
G-BZRA	Rans S.6-ES Coyote II	M. Allen	
G-BZRB	Mainair Blade	J-B. Weber	
G-BZRJ	Pegasus Quantum 15-912	G-BZRJ Group	
G-BZRO	PA-30 Twin Comanche C	Gloucester Comanche Group	
G-BZRP	Pegasus Quantum 15-912	T. P. Williams	
G-BZRR	Pegasus Quantum 15-912	S. E. Garner	
G-BZRS	Eurocopter EC 135T2	Bond Air Services Ltd	
G-BZRT	Beech 76 Duchess	Aviation Rentals	
G-BZRU	Cameron V-90 balloon	Aerostatica Monte/Italy	
G-BZRV	Van's RV-6	N. M. Hitchman	
G-BZRW	Mainair Blade 912S	G. J. E. Alcorn	
G-BZRY	Rans S.6-ES Coyote II	A. G. Smith	
G-BZRZ	Thunder Ax11-250 S2 balloon	A. C. K. Rawson & J. J. Rudoni	
G-BZSB	Pitts S-1S Special	A. D. Ingold	
G-BZSC	Sopwith Camel F.1 (replica)	The Shuttleworth Collection	
G-BZSE	Hawker Hunter T.8B (WV322:Y)	Towerdrive 2000 Ltd	
G-BZSG	Pegasus Quantum 15-912	S. Andrews	
G-BZSH	Ultramagic H-77 balloon	P. M. G. Vale	
G-BZSI	Pegasus Quantum 15	M. O. O'Brien	
G-BZSM	Pegasus Quantum 15	C. A. Brock	
G-BZSO	Ultramagic M-77C balloon	C. C. Duppa-Miller	
G-BZSP	Stemme S.10	A. Flewelling & L. Bleaken	
G-BZSS	Pegasus Quantum 15-912	T. R. Marsh	
G-BZST	Jabiru SPL-450	D. J and L. Rhys	
G-BZSU	Cameron A-315 balloon	Ballooning Network Ltd	
G-BZSX	Pegasus Quantum 15-912	G. L. Hall	
G-BZSY	SNCAN Stampe SV.4A	G. J. N. Valvekens/Belgium	
G-BZSZ	Avtech Jabiru UL-450	M. P. Gurr & D. R. Burridge	
G-BZTA	Robinson R44	Jarretts Motors Ltd	
G-BZTC	TEAM mini-MAX 91	G. G. Clayton	
G-BZTD	Thruster T.600T 450 JAB	B. O. McCartan	
G-BZTF	Yakovlev Yak-52	KY Flying Group	
G-BZTH	Shaw Europa	T. J. Houlihan	

Notes	Reg.	Type	Owner or Operator
	G-BZTI	Shaw Europa XS	D. E. Puttock
	G-BZTJ	CASA Bü 133C Jungmeister	R. A. Seeley
	G-BZTK	Cameron V-90 balloon	E. Appollodorus
	G-BZTM	Mainair Blade	A. J. Hubbard
	G-BZTN	Shaw Europa XS	M. K. McGreavey & W. R. Montgomery
	G-BZTR	Mainair Blade	D. J. Puxley
	G-BZTS	Cameron 90 Bertie Bassett SS balloon	Trebor Bassett Ltd
	G-BZTT	Cameron A-275 balloon	Cameron Flights Southern Ltd
	G-BZTU	Mainair Blade 912	C. T. Halliday
	G-BZTV	Mainair Blade 912S	R. D. McManus
	G-BZTW	Hunt Wing Avon 582 (1)	T. S. Walker
	G-BZTX	Mainair Blade 912	K. A. Ingham
	G-BZTY	Avtech Jabiru UL	R. P. Lewis
	G-BZUB	Mainair Blade	J. Campbell
	G-BZUC	Pegasus Quantum 15-912	G. Breen/Portugal
	G-BZUD	Lindstrand LBL-105A balloon	A. Nimmo
	G-BZUE	Pagasus Quantum 15-912	P. O'Rourke
	G-BZUF	Mainair Rapier	B. Craig
	G-BZUG	RL.7A XP Sherwood Ranger	J. G. Boxall
	G-BZUH	Rans S.6-ES Coyote II	J. D. Sinclair-Day
	G-BZUI	Pegasus Quantum 15-912	A. P. Slade
	G-BZUK	Lindstrand LBL-31A balloon	G. R. J. Luckett/USA
	G-BZUL	Avtech Jabiru UL	A. M. Hemmings
	G-BZUO	Cameron A-340HL balloon	Anglian Countryside Balloons Ltd
	G-BZUP	Raj Hamsa X'Air Jabiru(3)	P. O'Hagan
	G-BZUU	Cameron C-90 balloon	D. C. Ball
	G-BZUV	Cameron H-24 balloon	J. N. Race
	G-BZUX	Pegasus Quantum 15	C. Gorvett
	G-BZUY	Van's RV-6	Uniform Yankee Group
	G-BZUZ	Hunt Avon-Blade R.100 (1)	C. F. Janes
	G-BZVA	Zenair CH.701UL	M. W. Taylor
	G-BZVB	Cessna FR.172H	Victor Bravo Group (G-BLMX)
	G-BZVE	Cameron N-133 balloon	A. Bellini
	G-BZVI	Nova Vertex 24 hang glider	M. Hay
	G-BZVJ	Pegasus Quantum 15	R. Blackhall
	G-BZVK	Raj Hamsa X'Air 582 (2)	P. F. Berry
	G-BZVM	Rans S.6-ES Coyote II	D. P. Sudworth
	G-BZVN	Van's RV-6	Syndicate RV6 G-BZVN
	G-BZVR	Raj Hamsa X'Air 582 (4)	Hummingbird Club
	G-BZVT	I.I.I. Sky Arrow 650T	D. J. Goldsmith
	G-BZVU	Cameron Z-105 balloon	The Mall Balloon Team Ltd
	G-BZVV	Pegasus Quantum 15-912	S. Runcie
	G-BZVW	Ilyushin IL-2 Stormovik	S. Swallow & R. H. Cooper
	G-BZVX	Ilyushin IL-2 Stormovik	S. Swallow & R. H. Cooper
	G-BZWB	Mainair Blade 912	L. Parker
	G-BZWC	Raj Hamsa X'Air Falcon 912 (1)	T. A. Dobbins
	G-BZWG	PA-28 Cherokee 140	H. Merkado
	G-BZWH	Cessna 152	J. & H. Aviation Services Ltd
	G-BZWJ	CFM Streak Shadow	T. A. Morgan
	G-BZWK	Avtech Jabiru SK	G. M. Bolger
	G-BZWM	Pegasus XL-Q	D. T. Evans
	G-BZWN	Van's RV-8	A. J. Symms & R. D. Harper
	G-BZWR	Mainair Rapier	M. A. Steele
	G-BZWS	Pegasus Quantum 15-912	G-BZWS Syndicate
	G-BZWT	Technam P.92-EM Echo	R. F. Cooper
	G-BZWU	Pegasus Quantum 15-912	C. A. Reynolds
	G-BZWV	Steen Skybolt	D. E. Blaxland
	G-BZWX	Whittaker MW5D Sorcerer	P. A. Gardner
	G-BZWZ	Van's RV-6	A. P. Mardlin
	G-BZXA	Raj Hamsa X'Air V2 (1)	A. R. Walker
	G-BZXB	Van's RV-6	B. J. King-Smith & D. J. Akerman
	G-BZXC	SA Bulldog Srs 120/121 (XX612:A, 03)★	Carnegie College
	G-BZXI	Nova Philou 26 hang glider	M. Hay
	G-BZXJ	Schweizer 269-1	D. M. McGarrity
	G-BZXK	Robin HR.200/120B	Aviation Rentals
	G-BZXM	Mainair Blade 912	M. Liptrot & A. D. Taylor
	G-BZXN	Avtech Jabiru UL-450	V. G. J. Davies & D. A. Hall
	G-BZXO	Cameron Z-105 balloon	D. K. Jones & K. D. Thomas
	G-BZXP	Kiss 400-582 (1)	A. Fairbrother
	G-BZXR	Cameron N-90 balloon	H. J. Andrews
	G-BZXS	SA Bulldog Srs 120/121 (XX631:W)	K. J. Thompson
	G-BZXT	Mainair Blade 912	Barton 912 Flyers

Reg.	Type	Owner or Operator	Notes
G-BZXV	Pegasus Quantum 15-912	P. I. Oliver	
G-BZXW	VPM M-16 Tandem Trainer	P. J. Troy-Davies (G-NANA)	
G-BZXX	Pegasus Quantum 15-912	B. Hall	
G-BZXY	Robinson R44	Helicopter Services Ltd	
G-BZXZ	SA Bulldog Srs 120/121 (XX629:V)	D. Haworth	
G-BZYA	Rans S.6-ES Coyote II	M. R. Osbourn	
G-BZYD	Westland Gazelle AH.1 (XZ239)	Aerocars Ltd	
G-BZYG	Glaser-Dirks DG.500MB	R. C. Bromwich	
G-BZYI	Nova Phocus 123 hang glider	M. Hay	
G-BZYK	Avtech Jabiru UL	Cloudbase Aviation G-BZYK	
G-BZYM	Raj Hamsa X'Air 700 (1A)	R. R. Celentano	
G-BZYN	Pegasus Quantum 15-912	J. Cannon	
G-BZYR	Cameron N-31 balloon	C. J. Sanger-Davies	
G-BZYS	Micro Aviation Bantam B.22-S	D. L. Howell	
G-BZYT	Interavia 80TA	J. King	
G-BZYU	Whittaker MW6 Merlin	K. J. Cole	
G-BZYV	Snowbird Mk.V 582 (1)	M. A. Oakley	
G-BZYW	Cameron N-90 balloon	M. Catalani	
G-BZYX	Raj Hamsa X'Air 700 (1A)	A. M. Sutton	
G-BZYY	Cameron N-90 balloon	M. E. Mason	
G-BZZD	Cessna F.172M	R. H. M. Richardson-Bunbury (G-BDPF)	
G-CAHA	PA-34-200T Seneca II	TGD Leasing Ltd	
G-CALL	PA-23 Aztec 250F	J. D. Moon	
G-CAMM	Hawker Cygnet (replica)	Richard Shuttleworth Trustees	
G-CAMP	Cameron N-105 balloon	Hong Kong Balloon & Airship Club	
G-CAMR	BFC Challenger II	P. R. A. Walker	
G-CAPI	Mudry/CAARP CAP-10B	PI Group (G-BEXR)	
G-CAPX	Avions Mudry CAP-10B	H. J. Pessall	
G-CARS†	Pitts S-2A Special (replica)★	Toyota Ltd	
G-CBAB	SA Bulldog Srs 120/121 (XX543:F)	J. N. R. Davidson, L. C. T. George & P. J. R. Hill	
G-CBAD	Mainair Blade 912	J. Stocking	
G-CBAF	Lancair 320	L. H. & M. van Cleeff	
G-CBAH	Raj Hamsa X'Air 133 (1)	J. C. Macmillan	
G-CBAI	Flight Design CT2K	Newtownards Microlight Group	
G-CBAK	Robinson R44	CEL Electrical Logistics Ltd	
G-CBAL	PA-28-161 Warrior II	Azure Flying Club Ltd	
G-CBAN	SA Bulldog Srs 120/121 (XX668:1)	C. Hilliker	
G-CBAP	Zenair CH.601UL	A. G. Marsh	
G-CBAR	Stoddard-Hamilton Glastar	C. M. Barnes	
G-CBAS	Rans S.6-ES Coyote II	S. Stockill	
G-CBAT	Cameron Z-90 balloon	British Telecommunications PLC	
G-CBAU	Rand-Robinson KR-2	C. B. Copsey	
G-CBAV	Raj Hamsa X'Air V.2 (1)	D. W. Stamp & G. J. Lampitt	
G-CBAW	Cameron A-300 balloon	D. K. Hempleman-Adams	
G-CBAX	Tecnam P92-EA Echo	L. Collier	
G-CBAZ	Rans S.6-ES Coyote II	E. S. Wills	
G-CBBA	Robin DR.400/180	Whitby Seafoods Ltd	
G-CBBB	Pegasus Quantum 15-912	F. A. Dimmock	
G-CBBC	SA Bulldog Srs 120/121 (XX515:4)	Bulldog Support Ltd	
G-CBBF	Beech 76 Duchess	Flew LLP	
G-CBBG	Mainair Blade	S. L. Cogger	
G-CBBH	Raj Hamsa X'Air 582 (11)	S. P. Macdonald	
G-CBBK	Robinson R22	R. J. Everett	
G-CBBL	SA Bulldog Srs 120/121 (XX550:Z)	A. Cunningham	
G-CBBM	Savannah VG Jabiru (1)	C. E. Passmore	
G-CBBN	Pegasus Quantum 15-912	G-CBBN Flying Group	
G-CBBO	Whittaker MW5D Sorcerer	P. J. Gripton	
G-CBBP	Pegasus Quantum 15-912	C. E. Thompson	
G-CBBS	SA Bulldog Srs 120/121 (XX694:E)	Newcastle Aerobatic Academy Ltd	
G-CBBT	SA Bulldog Srs 120/121 (XX695:3)	Newcastle Bulldog Group Ltd	
G-CBBW	SA Bulldog Srs 120/121 (XX619:T)	S. E. Robottom-Scott	
G-CBCB	SA Bulldog Srs 120/121 (XX537:C)	M. W. Minary The General Aviation Trading Co Ltd	
G-CBCD	Pegasus Quantum 15	I. A. Lumley	
G-CBCF	Pegasus Quantum 15-912	P. A. Bromley	
G-CBCH	Zenair CH.701UL	L. G. Millen	
G-CBCI	Raj Hamsa X'Air 582 (2)	C. P. Lincoln	
G-CBCK	Tipsy T.66 Nipper Srs 3	N. M. Bloom (G-TEDZ)	
G-CBCL	Stoddard-Hamilton Glastar	M. I. Weaver	
G-CBCM	Raj Hamsa X'Air 700 (1A)	M. Ellis	

Notes	Reg.	Type	Owner or Operator
	G-CBCN	Schweizer 269C-1	D. M. McGarrity
	G-CBCP	Van's RV-6A	G-CBCP Group
	G-CBCR	SA Bulldog Srs 120/121 (XX702:P)	D. Wells
	G-CBCV	SA Bulldog Srs 120/121 (XX699:F)	C. A. Patter
	G-CBCX	Pegasus Quantum 15	T. J. Heaton
	G-CBCY	Beech C24R Sierra Super	Wycombe Air Centre Ltd
	G-CBCZ	CFM Streak Shadow SLA	J. O'Malley-Kane
	G-CBDC	Thruster T.600N 450-JAB	E. Maguire
	G-CBDD	Mainair Blade	G. Hird
	G-CBDG	Zenair CH.601HD	R. E. Lasnier
	G-CBDH	Flight Design CT2K	K. Tuck
	G-CBDI	Denney Kitfox Mk.2	J. G. D. Barbour
	G-CBDJ	Flight Design CT2K	P. J. Walker
	G-CBDK	SA Bulldog Srs 120/121 (XX611:7)	J. N. Randle
	G-CBDL	Mainair Blade	M. D. Howe
	G-CBDM	Tecnam P92-EM Echo	J. J. Cozens
	G-CBDN	Mainair Blade	T. Peckham
	G-CBDO	Raj Hamsa X'Air 582(1)	A. Campbell
	G-CBDP	Mainair Blade 912	D. S. Parker
	G-CBDS	SA Bulldog Srs 120/121 (XX707:4)	J. R. Parry
	G-CBDT	Zenair CH.601HD	D. G. Watt
	G-CBDU	Quad City Challenger II	E. J. Brooks
	G-CBDV	Raj Hamsa X'Air 582	E. J. Girling
	G-CBDX	Pegasus Quantum 15	P. Sinkler
	G-CBDZ	Pegasus Quantum 15-912	J. J. Brutnell
	G-CBEB	Kiss 400-582 (1)	M. Harris
	G-CBEC	Cameron Z-105 balloon	A. L. Ballarino/Italy
	G-CBED	Cameron Z-90 balloon	John Aimo Balloons SAS/Italy
	G-CBEE	PA-28R Cherokee Arrow 200	IHC Ltd
	G-CBEF	SA Bulldog Srs 120/121 (XX621:H)	A. M. Farmer & J. A. Ingram
	G-CBEH	SA Bulldog Srs 120/121 (XX521:H)	J. E. Lewis
	G-CBEI	PA-22 Colt 108	D. Sharp
	G-CBEJ	Colt 120A balloon	J. A. Gray
	G-CBEK	SA Bulldog Srs 120/121 (XX700:17)	B. P. Robinson
	G-CBEM	Mainair Blade	S. Beardsell
	G-CBEN	Pegasus Quantum 15-912	S. Clarke
	G-CBES	Shaw Europa XS	M. R. Hexley
	G-CBEU	Pegasus Quantum 15-912	S. D. Cox
	G-CBEV	Pegasus Quantum 15-912	A. S. R. Czajka
	G-CBEW	Flight Design CT2K	Shy Talk Group
	G-CBEX	Flight Design CT2K	A. G. Quinn
	G-CBEY	Cameron C-80 balloon	D. V. Fowler
	G-CBEZ	Robin DR.400/180	K. V. Field
	G-CBFA	Diamond DA40 Star	Lyrastar Ltd
	G-CBFE	Raj Hamsa X'Air V.2 (1)	T. D. Wolstenholme
	G-CBFF	Cameron O-120 balloon	T. M. C. McCoy
	G-CBFH	Thunder Ax8-105 S2 balloon	D. V. Fowler & A. N. F. Pertwee
	G-CBFJ	Robinson R44	HJS Helicopters Ltd
	G-CBFK	Murphy Rebel	P. J. Gibbs
	G-CBFM	SOCATA TB21 Trinidad	Exec Flight Ltd
	G-CBFN	Robin DR.100/200B	Foxtrot November Group
	G-CBFO	Cessna 172S	P. Gray
	G-CBFP	SA Bulldog Srs 120/121 (XX636:Y)	R. Nisbet & A. R. Dix
	G-CBFU	SA Bulldog Srs 120/121 (XX628:9)	J. R. & S. J. Huggins
	G-CBFV	Ikarus C.42	A. W. Leadley
	G-CBFW	Bensen B.8	A. J. Thomas
	G-CBFX	Rans S.6-ES Coyote II	A. E. Ciantar
	G-CBFY	Cameron Z-250 balloon	M. L. Gabb
	G-CBGB	Zenair CH.601UL	J. F. Woodham
	G-CBGC	SOCATA TB10 Tobago	Tobago Aviation Ltd
	G-CBGD	Zenair CH.701UL	I. S. Walsh
	G-CBGE	Tecnam P92-EM Echo	J. P. Spiteri
	G-CBGG	Pegasus Quantum 15	T. E. Davies
	G-CBGH	Teverson Bisport	R. C. Teverson
	G-CBGJ	Aeroprakt A.22 Foxbat	M. McCall
	G-CBGL	MH.1521M Broussard	MAXB Group
	G-CBGO	Murphy Maverick 430	C. R. Ellis & E. A. Wrathall
	G-CBGP	Ikarus C.42 FB UK	C. F. Welby
	G-CBGR	Avtech Jabiru UL-450	R. G. Kirkland
	G-CBGS	Cyclone AX2000	JAT Group
	G-CBGU	Thruster T.600N 450-JAB	B. R. Cardosi
	G-CBGV	Thruster T.600N 450	J. R. Nutter

Reg.	Type	Owner or Operator	Notes
G-CBGW	Thruster T.600N 450-JAB	M. C. Arnold & A. R. Pluck	
G-CBGX	SA Bulldog Srs 120/121 (XX622:B)	Henfield Lodge Ltd	
G-CBGZ	Westland Gazelle HT.2 (ZB646:59/CU)	D. Weatherhead Ltd	
G-CBHA	SOCATA TB10 Tobago	Oscar Romeo Aviation Ltd	
G-CBHB	Raj Hamsa X'Air 582 (5)	F. G. Shepherd	
G-CBHC	RAF 2000 GTX-SE gyroplane	A. J. Thomas	
G-CBHD	Cameron Z-160 balloon	Ballooning 50 Degrees Nord/Luxembourg	
G-CBHG	Mainair Blade 912S	B. S. Hope	
G-CBHI	Shaw Europa XS	Active Aviation Ltd	
G-CBHJ	Mainair Blade 912	B. C. Jones	
G-CBHK	Pegasus Quantum 15 (HKS)	B. Dossett	
G-CBHM	Mainair Blade 912	F. J. Thorne	
G-CBHN	Pegasus Quantum 15-912	G. G. Cook	
G-CBHO	Gloster Gladiator II (N5719)	Retro Track & Air (UK) Ltd	
G-CBHP	Corby CJ-1 Starlet	R. F. Cresswell	
G-CBHR	Lazer Z200	The Space Creative Partnership Ltd	
G-CBHT	Dassault Falcon 900EX	TAG Aviation (UK) Ltd (G-GPWH)	
G-CBHU	RL.5A Sherwood Ranger	G-CBHU Group	
G-CBHW	Cameron Z-105 balloon	Bristol Chamber of Commerce, Industry & Shipping	
G-CBHX	Cameron V-77 balloon	N. A. Apsey	
G-CBHY	Pegasus Quantum 15-912	A. Hope	
G-CBHZ	RAF 2000 GTX-SE gyroplane	M. P. Donnelly	
G-CBIB	Flight Design CT2K	T. R. Villa	
G-CBIC	Raj Hamsa X'Air V2 (2)	J. T. Blackburn & D. R. Sutton	
G-CBID	SA Bulldog Srs 120/121(XX549:6)	Red Dog Group/Bulldog Group	
G-CBIE	Flight Design CT2K	B. M. Jones & S. R. McKiernan	
G-CBIF	Avtech Jabiru SPL-450	S. N. J. Huxtable	
G-CBIH	Cameron Z-31 balloon	Gone With The Wind Ltd	
G-CBIJ	Ikarus C.42 FB UK Cyclone	J. A. Smith	
G-CBIL	Cessna 182K	E. Bannister & J. R. C. Spooner(G-BFZZ)	
G-CBIM	Lindstrand LBL-90A balloon	R. K. Parsons	
G-CBIN	TEAM mini-MAX 91	A. R. Mikolaczyk	
G-CBIO	Thruster T.600N 450-JAB	Sandown Microlights	
G-CBIP	Thruster T.600N 450-JAB	K. D. Mitchell	
G-CBIR	Thruster T.600N 450-JAB	E. G. White	
G-CBIS	Raj Hamsa X'Air 582 (2)	P. T. W. T. Derges	
G-CBIT	RAF 2000 GTX-SE gyroplane	Terrafirma Services Ltd	
G-CBIU	Cameron 95 Flame SS balloon	PSH Skypower Ltd	
G-CBIV	Skyranger 912 (1)	R. K. W. Moss	
G-CBIW	Lindstrand LBL-310A balloon	C. E. Wood	
G-CBIX	Zenair CH.601UL	R. A. & B. M. Roberts	
G-CBIY	Aerotechnik EV-97 Eurostar	R. Soltysik	
G-CBIZ	Pegasus Quantum 15-912	M. Morris	
G-CBJD	Stoddard-Hamilton Glastar	K. F. Farey	
G-CBJE	RAF 2000 GTX-SE gyroplane	V. G. Freke	
G-CBJG	DHC.1 Chipmunk 20 (1373)	C. J. Rees	
G-CBJH	Aeroprakt A.22 Foxbat	H. Smith	
G-CBJJ	SA Bulldog Srs 120/121 (XX525)	G. V. Crowe, T. Marnix & H. V. Snick	
G-CBJL	Kiss 400-582 (1)	R. E. Morris	
G-CBJM	Avtech Jabiru SP-470	G. R. T. Elliott	
G-CBJN	RAF 2000 GTX-SE gyroplane	R. Hall	
G-CBJO	Pegasus Quantum 15-912	M. Johnson	
G-CBJP	Zenair CH.601UL	R. E. Peirse	
G-CBJR	Aerotechnik EV-97A Eurostar	Madley Flying Group	
G-CBJS	Cameron C-60 balloon	N. Ivison	
G-CBJT	Mainair Blade	J. McGrath	
G-CBJV	Rotorway Executive 162F	R. J. Green	
G-CBJW	Ikarus C.42 Cyclone FB UK	J. A. Robinson	
G-CBJX	Raj Hamsa X'Air Falcon J22	N. & E. Hart	
G-CBJZ	Westland Gazelle HT.3	K. G. Theurer/Germany	
G-CBKA	Westland Gazelle HT.3 (XZ937:Y)	J. Windmill	
G-CBKB	Bücker Bü 181C Bestmann	W. R. & G. D. Snadden	
G-CBKD	Westland Gazelle HT.2	Flying Scout Ltd	
G-CBKE	Kiss 400-582 (1)	P. Blackbourn	
G-CBKF	Easy Raider J2.2 (1)	R. R. Armstrong	
G-CBKG	Thruster T.600N 450 JAB	Silver Shadow Group	
G-CBKI	Cameron Z-90 balloon	Wheatfields Park Ltd	
G-CBKJ	Cameron Z-90 balloon	Invista (UK) Holdings Ltd	
G-CBKK	Ultramagic S-130 balloon	Airbourne Adventures Ltd	
G-CBKL	Raj Hamsa X'Air 582 (1)	Caithness X-Air Group	
G-CBKM	Mainair Blade 912	N. Purdy	

Notes	Reg.	Type	Owner or Operator
	G-CBKN	Mainair Blade 912	D. S. Clews
	G-CBKR	PA-28-161 Warrior III	Yeovil Auto Tuning
	G-CBKS	Kiss 400-582 (1)	S. Kilpin
	G-CBKU	Ikarus C.42 Cyclone FB UK	C. Blackburn
	G-CBKV	Cameron Z-77 balloon	Blue Albatross SRL/Italy
	G-CBKW	Pegasus Quantum 15-912	W. G. Coulter
	G-CBKY	Avtech Jabiru SP-470	P. R. Sistern
	G-CBLA	Aero Designs Pulsar XP	J. P. Kynaston
	G-CBLB	Technam P.92-EM Echo	R. Lewis-Evans
	G-CBLD	Mainair Blade 912S	N. E. King
	G-CBLE	Robin R.2120U	Flew LLP
	G-CBLF	Raj Hamsa X'Air 582 (11)	B. J. Harper & P. J. Soukup
	G-CBLJ	Aerostar Yakovlev Yak-52	P. Joly
	G-CBLK	Hawker Hind	Aero Vintage Ltd
	G-CBLL	Pegasus Quantum 15-912	G. J. McNally
	G-CBLM	Mainair Blade 912	A. S. Saunders
	G-CBLN	Cameron Z-31 balloon	P. M. Oggioni
	G-CBLO	Lindstrand LBL-42A balloon	R. J. Clements
	G-CBLP	Raj Hamsa X'Air Falcon	A. C. Parsons
	G-CBLS	Fiat CR.42	Fighter Collection Ltd
	G-CBLT	Mainair Blade 912	B. J. Bader
	G-CBLU	Cameron C-90 balloon	A. G. Martin
	G-CBLW	Raj Hamsa X'Air Falcon 582(3)	R. G. Halliwell
	G-CBLX	Kiss 400-582 (1)	I. G. Parker
	G-CBLY	Grob G.109B	G-CBLY Syndicate
	G-CBLZ	Rutan LongEz	S. K. Cockburn
	G-CBMA	Raj Hamsa X'Air 582 (10)	K. G. Winter
	G-CBMB	Cyclone Ax2000	York Microlight Centre Ltd
	G-CBMC	Cameron Z-105 balloon	B. R. Whatley
	G-CBMD	IDA Bacau Yakovlev Yak-52 (10 yellow)	R. J. Hunter
	G-CBME	Cessna F.172M	Skytrax Aviation Ltd
	G-CBMI	Yakovlev Yak-52	I. A. Harding
	G-CBMK	Cameron Z-120 balloon	G. Davies
	G-CBML	DHC.6 Twin Otter 310	Isles of Scilly Skybus Ltd
	G-CBMM	Mainair Blade 912	W. L. Millar
	G-CBMO	PA-28 Cherokee 180	C. Woodliffe
	G-CBMP	Cessna R.182	Orman (Carrolls Farm) Ltd
	G-CBMR	Medway Eclipser	D. S. Blofeld
	G-CBMT	Robin DR.400/180	A. C. Williamson
	G-CBMU	Whittaker MW6-S Fat Boy Flyer	F. J. Brown
	G-CBMV	Pegasus Quantum 15	G. Poulett
	G-CBMW	Zenair CH.701 UL	I. Park
	G-CBMX	Kiss 400-582 (1)	D. L. Turner
	G-CBMZ	Aerotechnik EV-97 Eurostar	J. C. O'Donnell
	G-CBNA	Flight Design CT2K	D. M. Wood
	G-CBNB	Eurocopter EC 120B	Arenberg Consultadoria E Servicos LDA/Madeira
	G-CBNC	Mainair Blade 912	A. C. Rowlands
	G-CBNF	Rans S.7 Courier	M. Henderson
	G-CBNG	Robin R.2112	R. K. Galbally & E. W. Russell
	G-CBNI	Lindstrand LBL-180A balloon	Cancer Research UK
	G-CBNJ	Raj Hamsa X'Air 912 (1)	P. S. Chapman
	G-CBNL	Dyn'Aéro MCR-01 Club	D. H. Wilson
	G-CBNO	CFM Streak Shadow	D. J. Goldsmith
	G-CBNT	Pegasus Quantum 15-912	B. H. Goldsmith
	G-CBNV	Rans S.6-ES Coyote II	F. H. Cook
	G-CBNW	Cameron N-105 balloon	Bailey Balloons
	G-CBNX	Mongomerie-Bensen B.8MR	A. C. S. M. Hart
	G-CBNY	Kiss 400-582 (1)	R. Redman
	G-CBNZ	TEAM hi-MAX 1700R	A. P. S. John
	G-CBOA	Auster B.8 Agricola Srs 1	C. J. Baker
	G-CBOC	Raj Hamsa X'Air 582 (5)	A. J. McAleer
	G-CBOE	Hawker Hurricane IIB	P. J. Tuplin & P. W. Portelli
	G-CBOF	Shaw Europa XS	I. W. Ligertwood
	G-CBOG	Mainair Blade 912S	W. Birchall & J. S. Little
	G-CBOK	Rans S.6-ES Coyote II	I. Johnson
	G-CBOM	Mainair Blade 912	G. Suckling
	G-CBOP	Avtech Jabiru UL-450	D. W. Batchelor
	G-CBOR	Cessna F.172N	P. Seville
	G-CBOS	Rans S.6-ES Coyote II	J. T. Athulathmudali
	G-CBOT	Robinson R44	G. Fairburn
	G-CBOU	Bensen-Parsons 2-place gyroplane	R. Collin & M.S.Sparkes
	G-CBOW	Cameron Z-120 balloon	Associated Technologies Ltd

Reg.	Type	Owner or Operator	Notes
G-CBOY	Pegasus Quantum 15-912	Charlie Boy Syndicate	
G-CBOZ	IDA Bacau Yakovlev Yak-52	T. M. Boxall	
G-CBPC	Sportavia-Putzer RF-5B Sperber	Lee RF-5B Group	
G-CBPD	Ikarus C.42 Cyclone FB UK	Waxwing Group	
G-CBPE	SOCATA TB10 Tobago	A. F. Welch	
G-CBPH	Lindstrand LBL-105A balloon	I. Vastano/Italy	
G-CBPI	PA-28R-201 Arrow III	M. J. Richardson	
G-CBPL	TEAM mini-MAX 93	K. M. Moores	
G-CBPM	Yakovlev Yak-50 (50 black)	P. W. Ansell	
G-CBPP	Avtech Jabiru UL-450	D. G. Bennett	
G-CBPR	Avtech Jabiru UL-450	F. B. Hall	
G-CBPU	Raj Hamsa X'Air R100(3)	O. Sanda	
G-CBPV	Zenair CH.601UL	R. D. Barnard	
G-CBPW	Lindstrand LBL-105A balloon	A. C. Elson	
G-CBRB	Ultramagic S-105 balloon	I. S. Bridge	
G-CBRC	Jodel D.18	B. W. Shaw	
G-CBRD	Jodel D.18	J. D. Haslam	
G-CBRE	Mainair Blade 912	J. Jones	
G-CBRF	Ikarus C.42 FB100 VLA	T. W. Gale	
G-CBRG	Cessna 560XL Citation Excel	Queensway Aviation Ltd	
G-CBRJ	Mainair Blade 912S	R. W. Janion	
G-CBRK	Ultramagic M-77 balloon	R. T. Revel	
G-CBRM	Mainair Blade	M. H. Levy	
G-CBRO	Robinson R44	R. D. Jordan	
G-CBRR	Aerotechnik EV-97 Eurostar	T. O. Powley	
G-CBRT	Murphy Elite	T. W. Baylie	
G-CBRU	IDA Bacau Yakovlev Yak-52 (42 white)	R. Rawicz-Szczerbo	
G-CBRV	Cameron C-90 balloon	C. J. Teall	
G-CBRW	Aerostar Yakovlev Yak-52 (50 grey)	Max-Alpha Aviation GmbH/Germany	
G-CBRX	Zenair CH.601UL Zodiac	C. J. Meadows	
G-CBRZ	Kiss 400-582(1)	J. J. Ryan/Ireland	
G-CBSF	Westland Gazelle HT.2	Falcon Aviation Ltd	
G-CBSH	Westland Gazelle HT.3 (XX406:P)	Alltask Ltd	
G-CBSI	Westland Gazelle HT.3 (XZ934:U)	P. S. Unwin	
G-CBSK	Westland Gazelle HT.3 (ZB627:A)	Falcon Flying Group	
G-CBSL	IDA Bacau Yakovlev Yak-52 (67 red)	N. & A. D. Barton	
G-CBSO	PA-28-181 Archer II	Archer One Ltd	
G-CBSP	Pegasus Quantum 15-912	D. S. Carstairs	
G-CBSR	Yakovlev Yak-52	Grovinvest Srl	
G-CBSS	IDA Bacau Yakovlev Yak-52	E. J. F. Verhellen/Belgium	
G-CBSU	Avtech Jabiru UL	K. R. Crawley	
G-CBSV	Montgomerie-Bensen B.8MR	J. A. McGill	
G-CBSZ	Mainair Blade 912S	S. L. Lightbody	
G-CBTB	I.I.I. Sky Arrow 650TS	J. S. Hudson	
G-CBTD	Pegasus Quantum 15-912	D. Baillie	
G-CBTE	Mainair Blade 912|S	K. J. Miles	
G-CBTG	Ikarus C42 FB UK Cyclone	R. McLaughlin	
G-CBTK	Raj Hamsa X'Air 582 (5)	A. R. Cook	
G-CBTL	Monnett Moni	G. Dawes	
G-CBTM	Mainair Blade	D. A. A. Hewitt	
G-CBTN	PA-31 Navajo C	Durban Aviation Services Ltd	
G-CBTO	Rans S.6-ES Coyote II	C. G. Deeley	
G-CBTR	Lindstrand LBL-120A balloon	R. H. Etherington	
G-CBTS	Gloster Gamecock (replica)	Retro Track & Air (UK) Ltd	
G-CBTT	PA-28-181 Archer II	Citicourt Aviation Ltd (G-BFMM)	
G-CBTW	Mainair Blade 912	D. Hyatt	
G-CBTX	Denney Kitfox Mk.2	G. I. Doake	
G-CBTZ	Pegasus Quantum 15-912	M. Carter	
G-CBUA	Extra EA.230	S. Pedersen	
G-CBUC	Raj Hamsa X'Air 582 (5)	M. N. Watson	
G-CBUD	Pegasus Quantum 15-912	G. N. S. Farrant	
G-CBUE	Ultramagic N-250 balloon	Elinore French Ltd	
G-CBUF	Flight Design CT2K	J. T. James	
G-CBUG	Technam P.92-EM Echo	J. J. Bodnarec	
G-CBUI	Westland Wasp HAS.1 (XT420:606)	The Helicopter Squadron Ltd	
G-CBUJ	Raj Hamsa X'Air 582 (10)	G-CBUJ Flying Group	
G-CBUK	Van's RV-6A	P. G. Greenslade	
G-CBUN	Barker Charade	D. R. Wilkinson & T. Coldwell	
G-CBUO	Cameron O-90 balloon	W. J. Treacy & P. M. Smith	
G-CBUP	VPM M-16 Tandem Trainer	J. S. Firth	
G-CBUR	Zenair CH.601UL	N. A. Jack	
G-CBUS	Pegasus Quantum 15	J. Liddiard	

Notes	Reg.	Type	Owner or Operator
	G-CBUU	Pegasus Quantum 15-912	Hadair
	G-CBUW	Cameron Z-133 balloon	Balloon School (International) Ltd
	G-CBUX	Cyclone AX2000	R. Thompson
	G-CBUY	Rans S.6-ES Coyote II	I. L. Johnson
	G-CBUZ	Pegasus Quantum 15	D. G. Seymour
	G-CBVA	Thruster T.600N 450	D. J. Clingan
	G-CBVB	Robin R.2120U	Flew LLP
	G-CBVC	Raj Hamsa X'Air 582 (5)	M. A. Curtis
	G-CBVD	Cameron C-60 balloon	Phoenix Balloons Ltd
	G-CBVF	Murphy Maverick	H. A. Leek
	G-CBVG	Mainair Blade 912S	A. M. Buchanan
	G-CBVH	Lindstrand LBL-120A balloon	Line Packaging & Display Ltd
	G-CBVK	Schroeder Fire Balloons G balloon	S. Travaglia
	G-CBVL	Robinson R22 Beta II	Spiral Wing Ltd
	G-CBVM	Aerotechnik EV-97 Eurostar	M. Sharpe
	G-CBVN	Pegasus Quik	C. Kearney
	G-CBVO	Raj Hamsa X'Air 582 (5)	D. E. Rubery
	G-CBVR	Skyranger 912 (2)	S. H. Lunney
	G-CBVS	Skyranger 912 (2)	S. C. Cornock
	G-CBVU	PA-28R Cherokee Arrow 200-II	S. Crowley
	G-CBVV	Cameron N-120 balloon	John Aimo Balloons SAS/Italy
	G-CBVX	Cessna 182P	P. & A. de Weerdt
	G-CBVY	Ikarus C.42 Cyclone FB UK	M. J. Hendra & Gossage
	G-CBVZ	Flight Design CT2K	A. N. D. Arthur
	G-CBWA	Flight Design CT2K	G-CBWA Group
	G-CBWB	PA-34-200T Seneca II	Fairoaks Airport Ltd
	G-CBWD	PA-28-161 Warrior III	Plane Talking Ltd
	G-CBWE	Aerotechnik EV-97 Eurostar	J. & C. W. Hood
	G-CBWG	Aerotechnik EV-97A Eurostar	Southside Flyers
	G-CBWI	Thruster T. 600N 450	P. L. Jarvis
	G-CBWJ	Thruster T. 600N 450	Voliamo Group
	G-CBWK	Ultramagic H-77 balloon	H. C. Peel
	G-CBWN	Campbell Cricket Mk.6	P. G. Rawson
	G-CBWO	Rotorway Executive 162F	Handyvalue Ltd
	G-CBWP	Shaw Europa	T. W. Greaves
	G-CBWS	Whittaker MW6 Merlin	D. W. McCormack
	G-CBWU	Rotorway Executive 162F	Usk Valley Trout Farm
	G-CBWV	Falconar F-12A Cruiser	A. Ackland
	G-CBWW	Skyranger 912 (2)	N. S. Wellsl
	G-CBWY	Raj Hamsa X'Air 582 (6)	J. C. Rose
	G-CBWZ	Robinson R22 Beta	Plane Talking Ltd
	G-CBXA	Raj Hamsa X'Air 582 (5)	K. & K. P. Kormi
	G-CBXB	Lindstrand LBL-150A balloon	M. A. Webb
	G-CBXC	Ikarus C.42 Cyclone FB UK	J. A. Robinson
	G-CBXE	Easy Raider J2.2 (2)	D. A. Lord
	G-CBXF	Easy Raider J2.2 (2)	M. R. Grunwell
	G-CBXG	Thruster T.600N 450	Newtownards Microlight Group
	G-CBXJ	Cessna 172S	Steptoe and Sons Properties Ltd
	G-CBXK	Robinson R22 Mariner	Tiger Helicopters Ltd
	G-CBXM	Mainair Blade	B. A. Coombe
	G-CBXN	Robinson R22 Beta II	N. M. G. Pearson
	G-CBXR	Raj Hamsa X-Air Falcon 582 (1)	A. R. Rhodes
	G-CBXS	Skyranger J2.2 (1)	C. J. Erith
	G-CBXU	TEAM mini-MAX 91A	C. D. Hatcher
	G-CBXV	Mainair Blade	S. E. Harper
	G-CBXW	Shaw Europa XS	R. G. Fairall
	G-CBXZ	Rans S.6-ES Coyote II	D. Tole
	G-CBYB	Rotorway Executive 162F	Clark Contracting
	G-CBYC	Cameron Z-275 balloon	P. Baker
	G-CBYD	Rans S.6-ES Coyote II	R. Burland
	G-CBYE	Pegasus Quik	C. E. Morris
	G-CBYF	Mainair Blade	J. Ayre
	G-CBYH	Aeroprakt A.22 Foxbat	G. C. Moore
	G-CBYI	Pegasus Quantum 15-503	The G-BCYI Group
	G-CBYJ	Steen Skybolt	The Skybolt Group
	G-CBYM	Mainair Blade	P. E. Hudson
	G-CBYN	Shaw Europa XS	G. M. Tagg
	G-CBYO	Pegasus Quik	C. J. Roper & P. F. Mayo
	G-CBYP	Whittaker MW6-S Fat Boy Flyer	R. J. Grainger
	G-CBYS	Lindstrand LBL-21 balloon France	B. M. Reed/France
	G-CBYT	Thruster T.600N 450	P. Bartle & J. Paterson
	G-CBYU	PA-28-161 Warrior II	Stapleford Flying Club Ltd

Reg.	Type	Owner or Operator	Notes
G-CBYV	Pegasus Quantum 15-912	A. R. Wright	
G-CBYW	Hatz CB-1	T. A. Hinton	
G-CBYX	Bell 206B JetRanger 3	Sky Charter UK Ltd	
G-CBYY	Robinson R44	AMS Aviation Ltd	
G-CBYZ	Tecnam P92-EM Echo-Super	B. Weaver	
G-CBZA	Mainair Blade	D. Wilkinson	
G-CBZB	Mainair Blade	A. Bennion	
G-CBZD	Mainair Blade	G. F. Jones	
G-CBZE	Robinson R44	Alps (Scotland) Ltd	
G-CBZF	Robinson R22 Beta	Fly Executive Ltd	
G-CBZG	Rans S.6-ES Coyote II	W. Chang	
G-CBZH	Pegasus Quik	B. D. Searle	
G-CBZI	Rotorway Executive 162F	T. D. Stock	
G-CBZJ	Lindstrand LBL-25A balloon	Pegasus Ballooning	
G-CBZK	Robin DR.400/180	R. A. Fleming	
G-CBZL	Westland Gazelle HT.3	Armstrong Aviation Ltd	
G-CBZM	Avtech Jabiru SPL-450	M. E. Ledward	
G-CBZN	Rans S.6-ES Coyote II	R. G. Morris	
G-CBZP	Hawker Fury 1 (K5674)	Historic Aircraft Collection	
G-CBZR	PA-28R-201 Arrow III	Plane Talking Ltd/Elstree	
G-CBZS	Aurora	J. Lynden	
G-CBZT	Pegasus Quik	A. P. Portsmouth	
G-CBZU	Lindstrand LBL-180A balloon	European Balloon Co.Ltd	
G-CBZV	Ultramagic S-130 balloon	P. Goldschmidt	
G-CBZW	Zenair CH.701UL	T. M. Siles	
G-CBZX	Dyn' Aero MCR-01 ULC	A. C. N. Freeman & M. P. Wilson	
G-CBZZ	Cameron Z-275 balloon	A. C. K. Rawson & J. J. Rudoni	
G-CCAB	Mainair Blade	A. J. Morris	
G-CCAC	Aerotech EV-97 Eurostar	D. C. Lugg	
G-CCAD	Mainair Pegasus Quik	L. A. Hosegood & M. J. Mawle	
G-CCAE	Avtech Jabiru UL-450	G-CCAE Group	
G-CCAF	Skyranger 912 (1)	D. W. & M. L. Squire	
G-CCAG	Mainair Blade 912	W. Cope	
G-CCAK	Zenair CN.601HD	A. Kimmond	
G-CCAL	Technam P.92-EA Echo	M. Rudd	
G-CCAM	Mainair Blade	M. Richardson	
G-CCAP	Robinson R22 Beta II	Development Charter Ltd	
G-CCAR	Cameron N-77 balloon	D. P. Turner	
G-CCAS	Pegasus Quik	Caunton Alpha Syndicate	
G-CCAT	AA-55A Cheetah	A. Ohringer (G-OAJH/G-KILT/G-BJFA)	
G-CCAU	Eurocopter EC 135T1	Eurocopter UK Ltd	
G-CCAV	PA-28-181 Archer II	Archer II Ltd	
G-CCAW	Mainair Blade 912	A. D. Carr	
G-CCAY	Cameron Z-42 balloon	P. Stern	
G-CCAZ	Mainair Pegasus Quik	J. P. Floyd	
G-CCBA	Skyranger R.100	Fourstrokes Group	
G-CCBB	Cameron N-90 balloon	S. C. A. & L. D. Craze	
G-CCBC	Thruster T.600N 450	E. J. Girling & J. A. E. Bowen	
G-CCBF	Maule M.5-235C	C. G. Sims (G-NHVH)	
G-CCBG	Skyranger V.2 + (1)	P. R. Mailer	
G-CCBH	PA-28 Cherokee 236	J. R. Hunt, M. Kenny & S. M. Packer	
G-CCBI	X'Air R100 (2)	B.McStravog	
G-CCBJ	Skyranger 912 (2)	M. A. Russell	
G-CCBK	Aerotechnik EV-97 Eurostar	B. S. Waycott	
G-CCBL	Agusta-Bell 206B JetRanger 3	Formula Karting Ltd	
G-CCBM	Aerotechnik EV-97 Eurostar	W. Graves	
G-CCBN	Scale Replica SE-5a (80105/19)	V. C. Lockwood	
G-CCBP	Lindstrand LBL-60X balloon	D. Strasmann	
G-CCBR	Jodel D.120	A. Dunne & M. Munnelly	
G-CCBT	Cameron Z-90 balloon	I. J. Sharpe	
G-CCBV	Cameron Z-225 balloon	New Spirit Baloons ASBL, Luxembourg	
G-CCBW	Sherwood Ranger	A. L. Virgoe	
G-CCBX	Raj Hamsa X'Air 133 (2)	R. G. Cheshire	
G-CCBY	Avtech Jabiru UL-450	D. M. Goodman	
G-CCCA	VS.509 Spifire Tr.IX	Historic Flying Ltd (G-BHRH/G-TRIX)	
G-CCCB	Thruster T.600N 450	J. Williams	
G-CCCD	Mainair Pegasus Quantum 15	R. N. Gamble	
G-CCCE	Aeroprakt A.22 Foxbat	P. Sykes	
G-CCCF	Thruster T.600N 450	G. A. Fowler	
G-CCCG	Mainair Pegasus Quik	S. I. Laurence	
G-CCCH	Thruster T600N 450	P. J. Scullion	

Notes	Reg.	Type	Owner or Operator
	G-CCCI	Medway Eclipse R	V. Grayson
	G-CCCJ	Nicollier HN.700 Menestrel II	G. A. Rodmell
	G-CCCK	Skyranger 912 (2)	P. L. Braniff
	G-CCCM	Skyranger 912 (2)	I. A Forrest & C. K. Richardson
	G-CCCN	Robin R.3000/160	DR Flyers 2
	G-CCCO	Aerotechnik EV-97 Eurostar	D. R. G. Whitelaw
	G-CCCP	IDA Yakovlev Yak-52	A. H. Soper
	G-CCCR	Best Off Sky Ranger 912(2)	E. Foster & J. H. Peet
	G-CCCU	Thruster T.600N 450	A. F. Cashin
	G-CCCV	Raj Hamsa X'Air Falcon 133 (1)	G. J. Boyer
	G-CCCW	Pereira Osprey 2	D. J. Southward
	G-CCCY	Skyranger 912 (2)	A. Watson
	G-CCDB	Mainair Pegasus Quik	M. Dodd
	G-CCDC	Rans S.6-ES Coyote II	A. S. Luketa
	G-CCDD	Mainair Pegasus Quik	M. P. Hadden & M. H. Rollins
	G-CCDF	Mainair Pegasus Quik	R. P. McGann
	G-CCDG	Skyranger 912 (1)	Freebird Group
	G-CCDH	Skyranger 912 (2)	P. K. Goff
	G-CCDJ	Raj Hamsa X'Air Falcon 582 (2)	P. White
	G-CCDK	Pegasus Quantum 15-912	S. Brock
	G-CCDL	Raj Hamsa X'Air Falcon 582 (2)	G. M. Brown
	G-CCDM	Mainair Blade	P. R. G. Morley
	G-CCDO	Mainair Pegasus Quik	S. T. Welsh
	G-CCDP	Raj Hamsa X'Air R.100 (3)	F. J. McGuigan
	G-CCDR	Raj Hamsa X'Air Falcon Jabiru	P. D. Sibbons
	G-CCDS	Nicollier HN.700 Menestrel II	B. W. Gowland
	G-CCDU	Tecnam P92-EM Echo	B. N. Thresher
	G-CCDV	Thruster T.600N 450	G. C. Hobson
	G-CCDW	Skyranger 582 (1)	Debts R Us Family Group
	G-CCDX	Aerotechnik EV-97 Eurostar	J. M. Swash
	G-CCDY	Skyranger 912 (2)	N. H. Copperthwaite
	G-CCDZ	Pegasus Quantum 15-912	K. D. Baldwin
	G-CCEA	Mainair Pegasus Quik	G. D. Ritchie
	G-CCEB	Thruster T.600N 450	Thruster Air Services Ltd
	G-CCED	Zenair CH.601UL	R. P. Reynolds
	G-CCEE	PA-15 Vagabond	I. M. Callier (G-VAGA)
	G-CCEF	Shaw Europa	C. P. Garner
	G-CCEG	Rans S.6-ES Coyote II	W. Goldsmith
	G-CCEH	Skyranger 912 (2)	ZC Owners
	G-CCEJ	Aerotechnik EV-97 Eurostar	N. A. Quintin
	G-CCEK	Kiss 400-582 (1)	G. S. Sage
	G-CCEL	Avtech Jabiru UL	S. K. Armstrong
	G-CCEM	Aerotechnik EV-97 Eurostar	Oxenhope Flying Group
	G-CCEN	Cameron Z-120 balloon	R. Hunt
	G-CCEO	Thunder Ax10-180 S2 balloon	P. Heitzeneder/Austria
	G-CCEP	Raj Hamsa X'Air Falcon Jabiru	K. Angel
	G-CCES	Raj Hamsa X'Air 3203(1)	G. V. McCloskey
	G-CCET	Nova Vertex 28 hang glider	M. Hay
	G-CCEU	RAF 2000 GTX-SE gyroplane	N. G. Dovaston
	G-CCEW	Mainair Pegasus Quik	N. F. Mackenzie
	G-CCEY	Raj Hamsa X'582 (11)	P. F. F. Spedding
	G-CCEZ	Easy Raider J2.2	P. J Clegg
	G-CCFA	Kiss 400-582 (1)	A. E. Barron
	G-CCFB	Mainair Pegasus Quik	P. Bailey
	G-CCFC	Robinson R44 II	The Winning Zone Ltd
	G-CCFD	BFC Challenger II	W. Oswald
	G-CCFE	Tipsy Nipper T.66 Srs 2	G-CCFE Group
	G-CCFG	Dyn'Aéro MCR-01 Club	A. Jones
	G-CCFI	PA-32 Cherokee Six 260	McManus Truck & Trailer Spares Ltd
	G-CCFJ	Kolb Twinstar Mk.3	D. Travers
	G-CCFK	Shaw Europa	C. R. Knapton
	G-CCFL	Mainair Pegasus Quik	P. G. Mallon
	G-CCFO	Pitts S-1S Special	R. J. Anderson
	G-CCFS	Diamond DA40D Star	R. H. Butterfield
	G-CCFT	Mainair Pegasus Quantum 15-912	P. Simpson
	G-CCFU	Diamond DA40D Star	Jetstream Aviation Academy/Greece
	G-CCFV	Lindstrand LBL-77A balloon	Alton Aviation Ltd
	G-CCFW	WAR Focke-Wulf Fw.190	D. B. Conway
	G-CCFX	EAA Acrosport 2	C. D. Ward
	G-CCFY	Rotorway Executive 162F	Southern Helicopters Ltd
	G-CCFZ	Ikarus C.42 FB UK	B. W. Drake
	G-CCGB	TEAM mini-MAX	A. D, Pentland

Reg.	Type	Owner or Operator	Notes
G-CCGC	Mainair Pegasus Quik	R. W. Street	
G-CCGE	Robinson R22 Beta	Patriot Aviation Ltd	
G-CCGF	Robinson R22 Beta	Multiflight Ltd	
G-CCGG	Jabiru Aircraft Jabiru J400	G. E. Hall	
G-CCGH	Supermarine Aircraft Spitfire Mk.26 (AB196)	Cokebusters Ltd	
G-CCGI	Mainair Pegasus Quik	M. C. Kerr	
G-CCGK	Mainair Blade	C. M. Babiy & M. Hurn	
G-CCGM	Kiss 450-582 (1)	A. I. Lea	
G-CCGP	Bristol Type 200	R. L. Holman	
G-CCGR	Raj Hamsa X'Air 133 (1)	C. J. Roberts	
G-CCGS	Dornier 328-100	Scot Airways Ltd	
G-CCGT	Cameron Z-425 balloon	A. A. Brown	
G-CCGU	Van's RV-9A	B. J. Main & ptnrs	
G-CCGW	Shaw Europa	D. Buckley	
G-CCGY	Cameron Z-105 balloon	Cameron Balloons Ltd	
G-CCGZ	Cameron Z-250 balloon	Cameron Flights Southern Ltd	
G-CCHA	Diamond DA40D Star	Diamond Hire UK Ltd	
G-CCHD	Diamond DA40D Star	Flying Time Ltd	
G-CCHH	Pegasus Quik	C. A. Green	
G-CCHI	Mainair Pegasus Quik	M. R. Starling	
G-CCHJ	Kiss 400-582 (1)	H. C. Jones	
G-CCHL	PA-28-181 Archer iii	Archer Three Ltd	
G-CCHM	Kiss 450	M. J. Jessup	
G-CCHN	Corby CJ.1 Starlet	D. C. Mayle	
G-CCHO	Mainair Pegasus Quik	M. Allan	
G-CCHP	Cameron Z-31 balloon	M. H. Redman	
G-CCHR	Easy Raider 583 (1)	M. P. Wiseman	
G-CCHS	Raj Hamsa X'Air 582	N. H. Gokul	
G-CCHT	Cessna 152	J. S. Devlin & Z. Islam	
G-CCHV	Mainair Rapier	K. A. Wright	
G-CCHW	Cameron Z-77 balloon	A. Murphy	
G-CCHX	Scheibe SF.25C Falke	Lasham Gliding Society Ltd	
G-CCHY	Bücker Bü 131 Jungmann (A+12)	M. V. Rijkse	
G-CCID	Jabiru Aircraft Jabiru J400	J. Bailey	
G-CCIF	Mainair Blade	S. P. Moores	
G-CCIG	Aero Designs Pulsar	P. Maguire	
G-CCIH	Mainair Pegasus Quantum 15	T. Smith	
G-CCII	ICP Savannah Jabiru (3)	D. Chaloner	
G-CCIJ	PA-28R Cherokee Arrow 180	S. A. Hughes	
G-CCIK	Skyranger 912 (2)	M. D. Kirby	
G-CCIO	Skyranger 912 (2)	B. Berry	
G-CCIR	Van's RV-8	N. W. Charles	
G-CCIS	Scheibe SF.28A Tandem Falke	The Tandem-Falke Syndicate	
G-CCIT	Zenair CH.701UL	J. A. R. Hughes	
G-CCIU	Cameron N-105 balloon	W. W. Leitlein	
G-CCIV	Mainair Pegasus Quik	F. Omaraie-Hamdanie	
G-CCIW	Raj Hamsa X'Air 582 (2)	N. Watts	
G-CCIY	Skyranger 912 (2)	L. F. Tanner	
G-CCIZ	PZL-110 Koliber 160A	J. P. Nugent	
G-CCJA	Skyranger 912 (2)	C. Day	
G-CCJB	Zenair CH.701 STOL	E. G. Brown	
G-CCJD	Mainair Pegasus Quantum 15	P. Clark	
G-CCJF	Cameron C-90 balloon	Balloon School International Ltd	
G-CCJH	Lindstrand LBL-90A balloon	J. R. Hoare	
G-CCJI	Van's RV-6	N. A. Thomas	
G-CCJJ	Medway Pirana	P. K. Bennett	
G-CCJK	Aerostar Yakovlev Yak-52	G-CCJK Group	
G-CCJL	Super Marine Aircraft Spitfire XXVI	M. W. Hanley & P. M. Whitaker	
G-CCJM	Mainair Pegasus Quik	P. Crosby	
G-CCJN	Rans S.6ES Coyote II	M. G. A. Wood	
G-CCJO	ICP-740 Savannah Jabiru 4	R. & I. Fletcher	
G-CCJT	Skyranger 912 (2)	Juliet Tango Group	
G-CCJU	ICP MXP-740 Savannah Jabiru (4)	A. R. & M. A. Baxter	
G-CCJV	Aeroprakt A.22 Foxbat	Foxbat UK015 Syndicate	
G-CCJW	Skyranger 912 (2)	J. R. Walter	
G-CCJX	Shaw Europa XS	J. S. Baranski	
G-CCJY	Cameron Z-42 balloon	D. J. Griffin	
G-CCKF	Skyranger 912 (2)	D. McCabe & M. Harris	
G-CCKG	Skyranger 912 (2)	J. Young	
G-CCKH	Diamond DA40D Star	Flying Time Ltd	
G-CCKI	Diamond DA40D Star	S. C. Horwood	

Notes	Reg.	Type	Owner or Operator
	G-CCKJ	Raj Hamsa X'Air 133 (3)	D. Robertson
	G-CCKL	Aerotechnik EV-97A Eurostar	G-CCKL Group
	G-CCKM	Mainair Pegasus Quik	W. T. Milburn & P. A. Kershaw
	G-CCKN	Nicollier HN.700 Menestrel II	C. R. Partington
	G-CCKO	Mainair Pegasus Quik	A. Voyce
	G-CCKP	Robin DR.400/120	Duxford Flying Group
	G-CCKR	Pietenpol Air Camper	C. R. Thompson
	G-CCKT	Hapi Cygnet SF-2	P. W. Abraham
	G-CCKV	Isaacs Fury II	S. T. G. Ingram
	G-CCKW	PA-18 Super Cub 135	P. A. Layzell (G-GDAM)
	G-CCKX	Lindstrand LBL-210A balloon	Alba Ballooning Ltd
	G-CCKY	Lindstrand LBL-240A balloon	Cameron Flights Southern Ltd
	G-CCLF	Best Off Skyranger 912 (2)	J. Bannister & N. J. Sutherland
	G-CCLG	Lindstrand LBL-105A balloon	M. A. Derbyshire
	G-CCLH	Rans S.6-ES Coyote II	K. R. Browne
	G-CCLM	Mainair Pegasus Quik	D. J. Shippen & C. C. Colclough
	G-CCLO	Ultramagic H-77 balloon-	J. P. Moore
	G-CCLP	ICP MXP-740 Savannah	C. J. Powell & P. R. Whitmore
	G-CCLR	Schleicher Ash 26E	M. T. Burton & A. Darby
	G-CCLS	Comco Ikarus C.42 FB UK	B. D. Wykes
	G-CCLU	Best Off Skyranger 912	C. M. Babiy
	G-CCLV	Diamond DA40D Star	D. J. Watson
	G-CCLW	Diamond DA40D Star	Shacklewell Diamond Group
	G-CCLX	Mainair Pegasus Quik	R. Maude
	G-CCMC	Jabiru Aircraft Jabiru UL 450	J. Johnston
	G-CCMD	Mainair Pegasus Quik	J. T. McCormack
	G-CCME	Mainair Pegasus Quik	Caunton Graphites Syndicate
	G-CCMH	M.2H Hawk Major	J. A. Pothecary
	G-CCMI	SA Bulldog Srs 120/121 (XX513:10)	H. R. M. Tyrrell (G-KKKK)
	G-CCMJ	Easy Raider J2.2 (1)	G. F. Clews
	G-CCMK	Raj Hamsa X'Air Falcon	G. J. Digby
	G-CCML	Mainair Pegasus Quik	G. G. Wood
	G-CCMM	Dyn'Aéro MCR-01 ULC Banbi	J. D. Harris
	G-CCMN	Cameron C-90 balloon	A.E. Austin
	G-CCMO	Aerotechnik EV-97A Eurostar	E. M and P. M Woods
	G-CCMP	Aerotechnik EV-97A Eurostar	E. K. McAlinden
	G-CCMR	Robinson R22 Beta	G. F. Smith
	G-CCMS	Mainair Pegasus Quik	Barton Charlie Charlie Group
	G-CCMT	Thruster T.600N 450	S. P. McCaffrey
	G-CCMU	Rotorway Executive 162F	D. J. Fravigar & J. Smith
	G-CCMW	CFM Shadow Srs.DD	M. Wilkinson
	G-CCMX	Skyranger 912 (2)	K. J. Cole
	G-CCMZ	Best Off Skyranger 912 (2)	D. D. Appleford
	G-CCNA	Jodel DR.100A (Replica)	R. Everitt
	G-CCNB	Rans S.6ES Coyote II	M. S. Lawrence
	G-CCNC	Cameron Z-275 balloon	Ladybird Balloons Ltd
	G-CCND	Van's RV-9A	K. S. Woodard
	G-CCNE	Mainair Pegasus Quantum 15	G. D. Barker
	G-CCNF	Raj Hamsa X'Air 582 Falcon 133	R. E. Williams
	G-CCNG	Flight Design CT2K	D. Ewing
	G-CCNH	Rans S.6ES Coyote II	J. E. Howard
	G-CCNJ	Skyranger 912 (2)	J. D. Buchanan
	G-CCNM	Mainair Pegasus Quik	N. M. & H. M. M. Corr
	G.CCNN	Cameron Z-90 balloon	J. H. Turner
	G-CCNP	Flight Design CT2K	M. J. Hawkins
	G-CCNR	Skyranger 912 (2)	K. Washbourne
	G-CCNS	Skyranger 912 (2)	G. G. Rowley
	G-CCNT	Ikarus C.42 FB80	G-CCNT Group
	G-CCNU	Skyranger J2.2 (2)	P. D. Priestley
	G-CCNV	Cameron Z-210 balloon	J. A. Cooper
	G-CCNW	Mainair Pegasus Quantum Lite	J. Childs
	G-CCNX	CAB CAP-10B	Arc Input Ltd
	G-CCNY	Robinson R44	J. & S. J. Strange
	G-CCNZ	Raj Hamsa X'Air 133 (1)	A. Tucker
	G-CCOB	Aero C.104 Jungmann	C. W. Tomkins
	G-CCOC	Mainair Pegasus Quantum 15	S. I. P. Hardman
	G-CCOF	Rans S.6-ESA Coyote II	A. J. Wright & M. Govan
	G-CCOG	Mainair Pegasus Quik	A. O. Sutherland
	G-CCOK	Mainair Pegasus Quik	R. Cotterrell
	G-CCOM	Westland Lysander IIIA (V9312)	Propshop Ltd
	G-CCOP	Ultramagic M-105 balloon	M. E. J. Whitewood
	G-CCOR	Sequoia F.8L Falco	D. J. Thoma

Reg.	Type	Owner or Operator	Notes
G-CCOS	Cameron Z-350 balloon	Wickers World Ltd	
G-CCOT	Cameron Z-105 balloon	Airborne Adventures Ltd	
G-CCOU	Mainair Pegasus Quik	D. E. J. McVicker	
G-CCOV	Shaw Europa XS	B. C. Barton	
G-CCOW	Mainair Pegasus Quik	R. F. Dye & G. S. B. Airth	
G-CCOY	NA AT-6D Harvard II	Classic Flying Machine Collection Ltd	
G-CCOZ	Monnett Sonerai II	W. H. Cole	
G-CCPA	Kiss 400-582(1)	C.P. Astridge	
G-CCPC	Mainair Pegasus Quik	P. M. Coppola	
G-CCPD	Campbell Cricket Mk.4	T. H. Geake	
G-CCPE	Steen Skybolt	C. Moore	
G-CCPF	Skyranger 912 (2)	A. R. Tomlinson	
G-CCPG	Mainair Pegasus Quik	A.W. Lowrie	
G-CCPH	EV-97 TeamEurostar UK	A. H. Woolley	
G-CCPJ	EV-97 TeamEurostar UK	J. S. Webb	
G-CCPK	Murphy Rebel	B. A. W. Bridgewater	
G-CCPL	Skyranger 912 (2)	G-CCPL Group	
G-CCPM	Mainair Blade 912	T.D. Thompson	
G-CCPN	Dyn'Aéro MCR-01 Club	M. Sibson	
G-CCPO	Cameron N-77 balloon	A. C. Booth & M. J. Woodcock (G-MITS)	
G-CCPP	Cameron 70 Concept balloon	Sarnia Balloon Group	
G-CCPS	Ikarus C.42 FB100 VLA	H. Cullens	
G-CCPT	Cameron Z-90 balloon	Charter Ballooning Ltd	
G-CCPV	Jabiru J400	J. R. Lawrence & M. J. Worrall	
G-CCPW	BAe Jetstream 3102	Linksair Ltd	
G-CCPX	Diamond DA400 Star	R. T. Dickinson	
G-CCPY	Hughes 369D	Alpha Properties (London) Ltd	
G-CCPZ	Cameron Z-225 balloon	Cameron Flights Southern Ltd	
G-CCRA	Glaser-Dirks DG-800B	R. Fischer	
G-CCRB	Kolb Twinstar Mk.3 (modified)	R. W. Burge	
G-CCRC	Cessna Tu.206G	D. M. Penny	
G-CCRF	Mainair Pegasus Quantum 15	D. W. Pearce	
G-CCRG	Ultramagic M-77 balloon	Wickers World Ltd	
G-CCRH	Cameron Z-315 balloon	B. J. Palfreyman	
G-CCRI	Raj Hamsa X'Air 582 (5)	B. M. Tibenham	
G-CCRJ	Shaw Europa	J. F. Cliff	
G-CCRK	Luscombe 8A Silvaire	J. R. Kimberley	
G-CCRN	Thruster T.600N 450	R. A. Wright	
G-CCRP	Thruster T.600N 450	M. M. Lane (G-ULLY)	
G-CCRR	Skyranger 912 (1)	M. Cheetham	
G-CCRS	Lindstrand LBL-210A balloon	Aerosaurus Ballooning Ltd	
G-CCRT	Mainair Pegasus Quantum 15	C. R. Whitton	
G-CCRV	Skyranger 912 (2)	A. C. Thomson	
G-CCRW	Mainair Pegasus Quik	S. O. Hutchinson	
G-CCRX	Jabiru UL-450	M. Everest	
G-CCSA	Cameron Z-350 balloon	Ballooning Network Ltd	
G-CCSD	Mainair Pegasus Quik	S. J. M. Morling	
G-CCSF	Mainair Pegasus Quik	D. G. Barnes & A. Sorah	
G-CCSG	Cameron Z-275 balloon	Wickers World Ltd	
G-CCSH	Mainair Pegasus Quik	D. G. Ardley	
G-CCSI	Cameron Z-42 balloon	IKEA Ltd	
G-CCSJ	Cameron A-275 balloon	Dragon Balloon Co Ltd	
G-CCSL	Mainair Pegasus Quik	A. J. Harper	
G-CCSN	Cessna U.206G	K. Brady	
G-CCSO	Raj Hamsa X'Air Falcon	D. G. McHugh	
G-CCSP	Cameron N-77 balloon	Ballongforeningen Oscair I Goteberg/Sweden	
G-CCSR	Aerotechnik EV-97A Eurostar	Sierra Romeo Flying Group	
G-CCSS	Lindstrand LBL-90A balloon	British Telecom	
G-CCST	PA-32R-301 Saratoga	G. R. Balls	
G-CCSU	IDA Bacau Yakovlev Yak-52	S. Ullrich/Germany	
G-CCSV	ICP MXP-740 Savannah Jabiru	R. D. Wood	
G-CCSW	Nott PA balloon	J. R. P.Nott	
G-CCSX	Skyranger 912	T. Jackson	
G-CCSY	Mainair Pegasus Quik	I. K. Macleod	
G-CCTA	Zenair CH.601UL Zodiac	G. E. Reynolds	
G-CCTB	BAe. RJ100	Trident Jet Leasing (Ireland) Ltd	
G-CCTC	Mainair Pegasus Quik	D. R. Purslow	
G-CCTD	Mainair Pegasus Quik	R. N. S. Taylor	
G-CCTE	Dyn'Aéro MCR-01 Banbi	B. F. Walker	
G-CCTF	Aerotek Pitts S-2A Special	M. S. Hill	
G-CCTG	Van's RV-3B	A. Donald	
G-CCTH	Aerotechnik EV-97 TeamEurostar UK	M. W. Fitch	

Notes	Reg.	Type	Owner or Operator
	G-CCTI	Aerotechnik EV-97 Teameurostar	Flylight Airsports Ltd
	G-CCTL	Robinson R44 II	L. Davis
	G-CCTM	Mainair Blade	J. N. Hanso
	G-CCTN	Ultramagic T-180 balloon	A. Derbyshire
	G-CCTO	Aerotechnik EV-97 Eurostar	A. J. Bolton
	G-CCTP	Aerotechnik EV-97 Eurostar	P. E. Rose
	G-CCTR	Skyranger 912	A. H. Trapp
	G-CCTS	Cameron Z-120 balloon	F. R. Hart
	G-CCTT	Cessna 172S	Aerodynamic Research Innovations Ltd
	G-CCTU	Mainair Pegasus Quik	R. S. Swift
	G-CCTV	Rans S.6ESA Coyote II	G. & S. Simons
	G-CCTW	Cessna 152	R. J. Dempsey
	G-CCTX	Rans S.8ES Coyote II	G-CCTX Group
	G-CCTZ	Mainair Pegasus Quik 912S	S. Baker
	G-CCUA	Mainair Pegasus Quik	C. Gane
	G-CCUB	Piper J-3C-65 Cub	G. Cormack
	G-CCUD	Skyranger J.2	A. D. Haughey
	G-CCUE	Ultramagic T-180 balloon	Cameron Flights Southern Ltd
	G-CCUF	Skyranger 912(2)	R. E. Parker
	G-CCUH	RAF 2000 GTX-SE gyroplane	J. H. Haverhals
	G-CCUI	Dyn'Aéro MCR-01 Banbi	J. T. Morgan
	G-CCUK	Agusta A109-II	Simon Wright Homes Ltd
	G-CCUL	Shaw Europa XS	Europa 6
	G-CCUO	Hughes 369D	Claremont Air Services
	G-CCUP	Wessex 60 Mk.2 (XR502:Z)	D. Brem-Wilson & J. Buswell
	G-CCUR	Mainair Pegasus Quantum 15-912	D. W. Power & D. James
	G-CCUT	Aerotechnik EV-97 Eurostar	Doctor and the Medics
	G-CCUY	Shaw Europa	N. Evans
	G-CCUZ	Thruster T.600N 450	Fly 365 Ltd
	G-CCVA	Aerotechnik EV-97 Eurostar	K. J. Scott
	G-CCVD	Cameron Z-105 balloon	F. Morselli/Italy
	G-CCVF	Lindstrand LBL-105 balloon	Alan Patterson Design
	G-CCVH	Curtiss H-75A-1 (82:8)	The Fighter Collection
	G-CCVI	Zenair CH.701 SP	The 701 Group
	G-CCVJ	Raj Hamsa X'Air Falcon 133	I. S. Doig
	G-CCVK	Aerotechnik EV-97 TeamEurostar UK	J. Holditch
	G-CCVL	Zenair CH.601XL Zodiac	A. Y-T. Leungr & G. Constantine
	G-CCVM	Van's RV-7A	J. G. Small
	G-CCVN	Jabiru SP-470	Teesside Aviators Group
	G-CCVP	Beech 58	Richard Nash Cars Ltd
	G-CCVR	Skyranger 912(2)	M. J. Batchelor
	G-CCVS	Van's RV-6A	J. Edgeworth (G-CCVC)
	G-CCVT	Zenair CH.601UL Zodiac	P. Millar
	G-CCVU	Robinson R22 Beta II	Fly Excecutive Ltd
	G-CCVW	Nicollier HN.700 Menestrel II	B. F. Enock
	G-CCVX	Mainair Tri Flyer 330	J. A. Shufflebotham
	G-CCVZ	Cameron O-120 balloon	T. M. C. McCoy
	G-CCWC	Skyranger 912	W. Goldsmith
	G-CCWE	Lindstrand LBL-330A balloon	Adventure Balloons Ltd
	G-CCWF	Raj Hamsa X'Air 133	F. Loughran
	G-CCWH	Dyn'Aéro MCR-01 Bambi	B. J. Mills & N. J. Mines
	G-CCWJ	Robinson R44 II	Saxon Logistics Ltd
	G-CCWL	Mainair Blade	M. E. Rushworth
	G-CCWM	Robin DR.400/180	M. R. Clark
	G-CCWO	Mainair Pegasus Quantum 15-912	R. Fitzgerald
	G-CCWP	Aerotechnik EV-97 TeamEurostar UK	Sky Blue Flight Training
	G-CCWR	Mainair Pegasus Quik	C. J. Meadows
	G-CCWU	Skyranger 912	W. J. Byrd
	G-CCWV	Mainair Pegasus Quik	W. J. Dawson
	G-CCWW	Mainair Pegasus Quantum 15-912	I. W. Barlow
	G-CCWZ	Raj Hamsa X'Air Falcon 133	M. A. Evans
	G-CCXA	Boeing Stearman A75N-1 Kaydet (669)	Skymax (Aviation) Ltd
	G-CCXB	Boeing Stearman B75N1	C. D. Walker
	G-CCXC	Avion Mudry CAP-10B	Skymax (Aviation) Ltd
	G-CCXD	Lindstrand LBL-105B balloon	Silver Ghost Balloon Club
	G-CCXE	Cameron Z-120 balloon	M. R. Andreas
	G-CCXF	Cameron Z-90 balloon	R. G. March & T. J. Maycock
	G-CCXG	SE-5A (replica) (C5430)	C. Morris
	G-CCXH	Skyranger J2.2	M. J. O'Connor
	G-CCXK	Pitts S-1S Special	P. G. Bond
	G-CCXM	Skyranger 912(1)	C. J. Finnigan
	G-CCXN	Skyranger 912(1)	P. D. Brisco & G. P. Martin

Reg.	Type	Owner or Operator	Notes
G-CCXO	Corgy CJ-1 Starlet	S. C. Ord	
G-CCXP	ICP Savannah Jabiru	B. J. Harper	
G-CCXR	Mainair Pegasus Blade	J. McErlain	
G-CCXS	Montgomerie-Bensen B.8MR	A. Morgan	
G-CCXT	Mainair Pegasus Quik	C. Turner	
G-CCXU	Diamond DA40D Star	R. J. & L. Hole	
G-CCXV	Thruster T.600N 450	Caunton Thruster Group	
G-CCXW	Thruster T.600N 450	G-CCXW Syndicate	
G-CCXX	AG-5B Tiger	P. D. Lock	
G-CCXZ	Mainair Pegasus Quik	K. J. Sene	
G-CCYB	Escapade 912(1)	B. E. & S. M. Renehan	
G-CCYC	Robinson R44 II	Derg Developments Ltd/Ireland	
G-CCYE	Mainair Pegasus Quik	J. Lane	
G-CCYG	Robinson R44	Moorland Windows	
G-CCYI	Cameron O-105 balloon	Media Balloons Ltd	
G-CCYJ	Mainair Pegasus Quik	YJ Syndicate	
G-CCYL	MainairPegasus Quantum 15	A. M. Goulden	
G-CCYM	Skyranger 912	I. Pilton	
G-CCYO	Christen Eagle II	P. C. Woolley	
G-CCYP	Colt 56A balloon	Magical Adventures Ltd	
G-CCYR	Ikarus C.42 FB80	Airbourne Aviation Ltd	
G-CCYS	Cessna F.182Q	S. Dyson	
G-CCYU	Ultramagic S-90 balloon	A. R. Craze	
G-CCYX	Bell 412	RCR Aviation Ltd	
G-CCYY	PA-28-161 Warrior II	Flightcontrol Ltd	
G-CCYZ	Dornier EKW C3605	CW Tomkins Ltd	
G-CCZA	SOCATA MS.894A Rallye Minerva 220	R. N. Aylett	
G-CCZB	Mainair Pegasus Quantum 15	A. Johnson	
G-CCZD	Van's RV-7	D. Powell	
G-CCZI	Cameron A-275 balloon	Balloon School (International) Ltd	
G-CCZJ	Raj Hamsa X' Air Falcon 582	P. A. Lindford	
G-CCZK	Zenair CH.601 UL Zodiac	R. J. Hopkins	
G-CCZM	Skyranger 912S	D. Woodward	
G-CCZN	Rans S.6-ES Coyote II	R. D. Proctor	
G-CCZO	Mainair Pegasus Quik	J. V. Cleaver	
G-CCZP	Super Marine Aircraft Spitfire 26 (JF343:JW-P)	J. W. E. Pearson	
G-CCZR	Medway Raven Eclipse R	K. A. Sutton	
G-CCZS	Raj Hamsa X'Air Falcon 582	A. T. Kilpatrick	
G-CCZT	Van's RV-9A	Zulu Tango Flying Group	
G-CCZU	Diamond DA40D Star	Diamond Finance Services GmbH	
G-CCZV	PA-28-151 Warrior	P. D. P. Deal	
G-CCZW	Mainair Pegasus Blade	P. J. Webster	
G-CCZX	Robin DR.400/180	M. Conrad	
G-CCZY	Van's RV-9A	Mona RV-9 Group	
G-CCZZ	Aerotechnik EV-97 Eurostar	B. M Starck & J. P. Aitken	
G-CDAA	Mainair Pegasus Quantum 15-912	I. A. Macadam	
G-CDAB	Glasair Super IISRG	W. L. Hitchins	
G-GDAC	Aerotechnik EV-97 TeamEurostar	Nene Valley Microlights Ltd	
G-CDAD	Lindstrand LBL-25A balloon	G. J. Madelin	
G-CDAE	Van's RV-6A	K. J. Fleming	
G-CDAG	Mainair Blade	K. I. Making	
G-CDAI	Robin DR.400/140B	D. Hardy & J. Sambrook	
G-CDAK	Zenair CH.601 UK Zodiac	W. K. Evans	
G-CDAL	Zenair CH.601UL Zodiac	R. J. Howell	
G-CDAO	Mainair Pegasus Quantum 15 -912	J. C. Duncan	
G-CDAP	Aerotechnik EV-97 TeamEurostar UK	R. W. Caress	
G-CDAR	Mainair Pegasus Quik	A. R. Pitcher	
G-CDAT	ICP MXP-740 Savannah Jabiru	R. Simpson	
G-CDAW	Robinson R22 Beta	Airtask Group PLC	
G-CDAX	Mainair Pegasus Quik	L. Hurman	
G-CDAY	Skyranger 912	D. A. Perkins t/a G-CDAY Group	
G-CDAZ	Aerotechnik EV-97 Eurostar	M. C. J. Ludlow	
G-CDBA	Skyranger 912(S)	P. J. Brennan	
G-CDBB	Mainair Pegasus Quik	D. W. Watson	
G-CDBC	Aviation Enterprises Magnum	Aviation Enterprises Ltd	
G-CDBD	Jabiru J400	I. D. Rutherford	
G-CDBE	Montgomerie-Bensen B.8M	P. Harwood	
G-CDBG	Robinson R22 Beta	Jepar Rotorcraft	
G-CDBJ	Yakovlev Yak-3	C. E. Bellhouse	
G-CDBK	Rotorway Executive 162F	Car Builder Solutions Ltd	
G-CDBM	Robin DR.400/180	C. M. Simmonds	

Notes	Reg.	Type	Owner or Operator
	G-CDBO	Skyranger 912	A. C. Turnbull
	G-CDBR	Stolp SA.300 Starduster Too	R. J. Warren
	G-CDBS	MBB Bö.105DBS-4	Bond Air Services Ltd
	G-CDBU	Ikarus C.42 FB100	S. E. Meehan
	G-CDBV	Skyranger 912S	K. Hall
	G-CDBX	Shaw Europa XS	R. Marston
	G-CDBY	Dyn'Aero MCR-01 ULC	A. Thornton
	G-CDBZ	Thruster T.600N 450	J. A. Lynch
	G-CDCB	Robinson R44 II	Microwave Sales and Services Ltd
	G-CDCC	Aerotechnik EV-97A Eurostar	R. E. & & N. G. Nicholson
	G-CDCD	Van's RVF-9A	RV9ers
	G-CDCE	Avions Mudry CAP-10B	The Tiger Club (1990) Ltd
	G-CDCF	Mainair Pegasus Quik	T. J. Gayton-Polley
	G-CDCG	Ikarus C.42 FB UK	N. E. Ashton & R. H. J. Jenkins
	G-CDCH	Skyranger 912(2)	G. C. Long
	G-CDCI	Pegasus Quik	S. G. Murray
	G-CDCK	Mainair Pegasus Quik	R. Solomons
	G-CDCM	Ikarus C.42 FB UK	S. T. Allen
	G-CDCO	Ikarus C.42 FB UK	Churchill Trading Ltd
	G-CDCP	Avtech Jabiru J400	M. W. T. Wilson
	G-CDCR	Savannah Jabiru(1)	T. Davidson
	G-CDCS	PA-12 Super Cruiser	D. Todorovic
	G-CDCT	Aerotechnik EV-97 TeamEurostar UK	G. R. Nicholson
	G-CDCU	Mainair Pegasus Blade	W. S. Clare
	G-CDCV	Robinson R44 II	C. A. W. Godfrey
	G-CDCW	Escapade 912 (1)	P. Nicholls
	G-CDCX	Citation 750	Pendley Farm Ltd
	G-CDDA	SOCATA TB20 Trinidad	Oxford Aviation Academy (Oxford) Ltd
	G-CDDB	Grob/Schemmp-Hirth CS-11	K. D. Barber/France
	G-CDDC	Cameron A-275 balloon	Airborne Balloon Flights Ltd
	G-CDDF	Mainair Pegasus Quantum 15-912	B. C. Blackburn & J. L. Dalgetty
	G-CDDG	PA-26-161 Warrior II	A. Oxenham
	G-CDDH	Raj Hamsa X'Air Falcon	B. & L. Stanbridge
	G-CDDI	Thruster T.600N 450	R. Nayak
	G-CDDK	Cessna 172M	M. H. & P. R. Kavern
	G-CDDL	Cameron Z-350 balloon	Balloon School (International) Ltd
	G-CDDM	Lindstrand LBL 90A balloon	A. M. Holly
	G-CDDN	Lindstrand LBL 90A balloon	Flying Enterprises
	G-CDDO	Raj Hamsa X'Air 133(2)	S. Bain
	G-CDDP	Lazer Z.230	A. Smith
	G-CDDR	Skyranger 582(1)	R. L. Nyman
	G-CDDS	Zenair CH.601HD	S. Foreman
	G-CDDT	SOCATA TB20 Trinidad	Oxford Aviation Academy (Oxford) Ltd
	G-CDDU	Skyranger 912(2)	J. S. G. Down, A. Rastall & R. Newton
	G-CDDV	Cameron Z-250 balloon	Alba Ballooning Ltd
	G-CDDW	Aeroprakt A.22 Foxbat	M. Raflewski
	G-CDDX	Thruster T.600N 450	P. A. G. Harper
	G-CDDY	Van's RV-8	The AV8ors
	G-CDEA	SAAB 2000	Air Kilroe Ltd
	G-CDEB	SAAB 2000	Eastern Airways
	G-CDED	Robinson R22 Beta	Flight Solutions Ltd
	G-CDEF	PA-28-161 Cadet	Western Air (Thruxton) Ltd
	G-CDEH	ICP MXP-740 Savannah	P. E. Terrell
	G-CDEM	Raj Hamsa X' Air 133	R. J. Froud
	G-CDEN	Mainair Pegasus Quantum 15 912	J. D. J. Spragg
	G-CDEO	PA-28 Cherokee 180	VVB Engineering Services Ltd
	G-CDEP	Aerotechnik EV-97 TeamEurostar	Echo Papa Group
	G-CDER	PA-28-161 Warrior II	Archer Five Ltd
	G-CDET	Culver LCA Cadet	J. Gregson
	G-CDEV	Escapade 912 (1)	M. B. Devenport
	G-CDEW	Pegasus Quik	K. M. Sullivan
	G-CDEX	Shaw Europa	J. M. Carter
	G-CDEZ	Robinson R44 II	Heli Air Ltd
	G-CDFA	Kolb Twinstar Mk3 Extra	S. Soar & W. A. Douthwaite
	G-CDFC	Ultramagic S-160 balloon	Over The Rainbow Balloon Flights Ltd
	G-CDFD	Scheibe SF.25C Falke	T. M. Holloway
	G-CDFE	IAV Bacau Yakolev YAK-52	D. P. Curtis
	G-CDFG	Mainair Pegasus Quik	D. Gabbott
	G-CDFI	Colt 31A balloon	A. M. Holly
	G-CDFJ	Skyranger 912	L. A. Hosegood
	G-CDFK	Jabiru SPL-450	H. J. Bradley
	G-CDFL	Zenair CH.601UL	Caunton Zodiac Group

Reg.	Type	Owner or Operator	Notes
G-CDFM	Raj Hamsa X'Air 582 (5)	W. A. Keel-Stocker	
G-CDFN	Thunder Ax7-77 balloon	E. Rullo/Italy	
G-CDFO	Pegasus Quik	G-CDFO Syndicate	
G-CDFP	Skyranger 912 (2)	J. M. Gammidge	
G-CDFR	Mainair Pegasus Quantum 15	A. Jopp	
G-CDFU	Rans S.6-ES	P. W. Taylor	
G-CDFY	Beech B.200 Super King Air	BAE Systems Marine Ltd	
G-CDGA	Taylor JT.1 Monoplane	R. M. Larimore	
G-CDGB	Rans S.6-116 Coyote	S. Penoyre	
G-CDGC	Pegasus Quik	A. T. K. Crozier	
G-CDGD	Pegasus Quik	I. D. & V. A. Milne	
G-CDGE	Edge XT912-IIIB	M. R. Leyshon	
G-CDGF	Ultramagic S-105 balloon	D. & K. Bareford	
G-CDGG	Dyn'Aéro MCR-01 Club	N. Rollins	
G-CDGH	Rans S.6-ES Coyote	G-CDGH Group	
G-CDGI	Thruster T600N 450	R. North	
G-CDGN	Cameron C-90 balloon	M. C. Gibbons	
G-CDGO	Pegasus Quik	J. C. Townsend	
G-CDGP	Zenair CH 601XL	T. J. Bax	
G-CDGR	Zenair CH 701UL	I. A. R. Sim	
G-CDGS	AG-5B Tiger	S. M. R. Hickman & M. R. O. Thompson	
G-CDGT	Montgomerie-Parsons Two Place g/p	J. B. Allan	
G-CDGU	VS.300 Spitfire I (X4276)	Peter Monk Ltd	
G-CDGW	PA-28-181 Archer III	Rutland Flying Group	
G-CDGX	Pegasus Quantum 15-912	S. R. Green	
G-CDGY	VS.349 Spitfire Mk VC	Aero Vintage Ltd	
G-CDHA	Skyranger 912S(1)	A. T. Cameron	
G-CDHC	Slingsby T67C	N. J. Morgan	
G-CDHD	Balóny Kubíček BB-22 balloon	R. C. Franklin	
G-CDHE	Skyranger 912(2)	Barton Syndicate	
G-CDHF	PA-30 Twin Comanche B	Reid International (Guernsey) Ltd	
G-CDHG	Mainair Pegasus Quik	T. W. Pelan	
G-CDHH	Robinson R44 II	Abwood Homes/Ireland	
G-CDHJ	Lindstrand LBL-90B balloon	Lindstrand Hot Air Balloons Ltd	
G-CDHL	Lindstrand LBL-330A balloon	Richard Nash Cars Ltd	
G-CDHM	Pegasus Quantum 15	S. T. Hayes	
G-CDHN	Lindstrand LBL-317A balloon	Aerosaurus Balloons Ltd	
G-CDHO	Raj Hamsa X'Air 133 (1)	G. P. Masters	
G-CDHP	Lindstrand LBL-150A balloon	Floating Sensations Ltd (G-OHRH)	
G-CDHR	Ikarus C.42 FB80	Airbourne Aviation Ltd/Popham	
G-CDHS	Cameron N-90 balloon	C. Moulin	
G-CDHU	Skyranger 912 (2)	A. R. Parker & N. H. Tomkins	
G-CDHX	Aeroprakt A.22 Foxbat	N. E. Stokes	
G-CDHY	Cameron Z-90 balloon	D. M. Roberts	
G-CDHZ	Nicollier HN.700 Menestrel II	G. E. Whittaker	
G-CDIA	Thruster T.600N 450	T. Davidson	
G-CDIB	Cameron Z-350Z balloon	Ballooning Network Ltd	
G-CDIF	Mudry CAP-10B	J. D. Gordon	
G-CDIG	Aerotechnik EV-97 Eurostar	M. Sanders	
G-CDIH	Cameron Z-275 balloon	Bailey Balloons Ltd	
G-CDIJ	Skyranger 912 (2)	E. B. Toulson	
G-CDIK	Cameron Z-120 balloon	Cameron Balloons Ltd	
G-CDIL	Pegasus Quantum 15-912	S. J. Wooltorton	
G-CDIO	Cameron Z-90 balloon	Slowfly Montgolfiere SNC/Italy	
G-CDIP	Skyranger 912S(1)	J. Parke	
G-CDIR	Mainair Pegasus Quantum 15-912	M. Smith & A. S. Turner	
G-CDIS	Cessna 150F	S. P. Fox	
G-CDIT	Cameron Z-105 balloon	Bailey Balloons Ltd	
G-CDIU	Skyranger 912S(1)	C. P. Dawes & J. English	
G-CDIV	Lindstrand LBL-90A balloon	The Packhouse Ltd	
G-CDIX	Ikarus C.42 FB.100	T. G. Greenhill & J. G. Spinks	
G-CDIY	Aerotechnik EV-97A Eurostar	R. E. Woolsey	
G-CDIZ	Escapade 912(1)	E. G. Bishop & E. N. Dunn	
G-CDJB	Van's RV-4	W. D. Garlick & R. J. Napp	
G-CDJC	Skyranger 912 (2)	J. L. A. Campell	
G-CDJD	ICP MXP-740 Savannah Jabiru (4)	D. W. Mullin	
G-CDJE	Thruster T.600N 450	K. R. Ford	
G-CDJF	Flight Design CT2K	P. A. James	
G-CDJG	Zenair 601UL Zodiac	D. Garcia	
G-CDJI	Ultramagic M-120 balloon	The Ballooning Business Ltd	
G-CDJJ	IAV Yakovlev Yak-52	J. J. Miles	
G-CDJK	Ikarus C.42 FB 80	Cornish Aviation Ltd	

Notes	Reg.	Type	Owner or Operator
	G-CDJL	Avtech Jabiru J400	J. Gardiner and R. Holden-White
	G-CDJM	Zenair CH.601XL	S. A. Rennison
	G-CDJN	RAF 2000 GTX-SE gyroplane	D. J. North
	G-CDJO	DH.82A Tiger Moth	D. Dal Bon
	G-CDJP	Skyranger 912(2)	J. S. Potts
	G-CDJR	Aerotechnik EV-97 TeamEurostar	K. C. Lye & M. D. White
	G-CDJT	Aérospatiale SA.341G Gazelle 1	Simlot Ltd
	G-CDJU	CASA 1.131E Jungmann Srs.1000	P. Gaskell
	G-CDJV	Beech A.36 Bonanza	Atlantic Bridge Aviation Ltd/Lydd
	G-CDJW	Van's RV-7	J. B. Shaw
	G-CDJX	Cameron N-56 balloon	Cameron Balloons Ltd
	G-CDJY	Cameron C-80 balloon	British Airways PLC
	G-CDKA	SAAB 2000	Eastern Airways
	G-CDKB	SAAB 2000	Eastern Airways
	G-CDKE	Rans S6-ES Coyote II	J. E. Holloway
	G-CDKF	Escapade 912 (1)	Kilo Fox Flying Group
	G-CDKH	Skyranger 912S (1)	C. Lenaghan
	G-CDKI	Skyranger 912S (1)	J. M. Hucker
	G-CDKJ	Silence Twister	A. H. R. Stansfield
	G-CDKK	Mainair Pegasus Quik	P. M. Knight
	G-CDKL	Escapade 912 (2)	M. A. Hodgson & D. Maidment
	G-CDKM	Pegasus Quik	P. Lister
	G-CDKN	ICP MXP-740 Savannah Jabiru (4)	J. Bate
	G-CDKO	ICP MXP-740 Savannah Jabiru (4)	C. Jones & B. Hunter
	G-CDKP	Avtech Jabiru UL-D Calypso	Rochester Microlights Ltd
	G-CDKX	Skyranger J.2 .2 (1)	E. Lewis
	G-CDKY	Robinson R44	Bernard Hunter Ltd
	G-CDKZ	Thunder Ax10-160 S2 balloon	Cameron Flights Southern Ltd
	G-CDLA	Mainair Pegasus Quik	C. R. Stevens
	G-CDLB	Cameron Z-120 balloon	J. A. Hibberd and Tchemma Products
	G-CDLC	CASA 1.131E Jungmann 2000	R. D. Loder
	G-CDLD	Mainair Pegasus Quik 912S	W. Williams
	G-CDLG	Skyranger 912 (2)	D. J. Saunders
	G-CDLI	Airco DH.9 (E8894)	Aero Vintage Ltd
	G-CDLJ	Mainair Pegasus Quik	J. S. James & R. S. Keyser
	G-CDLK	Skyranger 912S	L. E. Cowling
	G-CDLL	Dyn'Aéro MCR-01 ULC	D. Cassidy
	G-CDLR	ICP MXP / 740 Savannah Jabiru (4)	A. J. Burton & P. Read
	G-CDLS	Jabiru Aircrraft Jabiru J400	E. Bentley
	G-CDLT	Raytheon Hawker 800XP	Gama Aviation Ltd
	G-CDLV	Lindstrand LBL-105A balloon	Smartfusion SV Ltd
	G-CDLW	Zenair ZH.601UL Zodiac	W. A. Stphen
	G-CDLY	Cirrus SR20	Partside Aviation Ltd
	G-CDLZ	Mainair Pegasus Quantum 15-912	C. M. Jeffrey & J. L. Dalgetty
	G-CDMA	PA-28-151 Warrior	A. Cabre
	G-CDMC	Cameron Z-105 balloon	First Flight
	G-CDMD	Robin DR.400/500	P. R. Liddle
	G-CDME	Van's RV-7	M. W. Elliott
	G-CDMF	Van's RV-9A	S. R. Neale & T. R. Donovan
	G-CDMG	Robinson R22 Beta	Heli Aitch Be Ltd
	G-CDMH	Cessna P.210N	J. G. Hinley
	G-CDMJ	Mainair Pegasus Quik	M. J. R. Dean
	G-CDMK	Montgomerie-Bensen B8MR	P. Rentell
	G-CDML	Mainair Pegasus Quik	Ducky Group
	G-CDMM	Cessna 172P Skyhawk	Cristal Air Ltd
	G-CDMN	Van's RV-9	G. J. Smith
	G-CDMO	Cameron S Can-100 balloon	A. Schneider/Germany
	G-CDMP	Best Off Skyranger 912(1)	J. A. Charlton
	G-CDMS	Ikarus C,42 FB 80	Airbourne Aviation Ltd
	G-CDMT	Zenair CH.601XL Zodiac	B. A. Ritchie
	G-CDMU	Mainair Pegasus Quik	T. M. Bolton & S. D. Jones
	G-CDMV	Best Off Skyranger 912S(1)	D. O'Keeffe & K. E. Rutter
	G-CDMX	PA-28-161 Warrior II	S. Collins
	G-CDMY	PA-28-161 Warrior II	J. S. Develin & Z. Islam
	G-CDMZ	Mainair Pegasus Quik	R. Solomons
	G-CDNA	Grob G.109A	Army Gliding Association
	G-CDND	GA-7 Cougar	C. J. Chaplin
	G-CDNE	Best Off Skyranger 912S(1)	G-CDNE Syndicate
	G-CDNF	Aero Design Pulsar 3	D. Ringer
	G-CDNG	Aerotechnik EV-97 TeamEurostar UK	H. Wilson
	G-CDNH	Mainair Pegasus Quik	C. D. Andrews
	G-CDNI	Aerotechnik EV-97 TeamEurostar UK	G-CDNI Group

Reg.	Type	Owner or Operator	Notes
G-CDNJ	Colomban MC-15 Cri Cri	Cri Cri Group	
G-CDNK	Learjet 45	Balholm Leasing BV	
G-CDNM	Aerotechnik EV-97 TeamEurostar UK	H. C. Lowther	
G-CDNO	Westland Gazelle AH.1 (XX432)	Falcon Aviation Ltd	
G-CDNP	Aerotechnik EV-97 TeamEurostar UK	Eaglescott Eurostar Group	
G-CDNR	Ikarus C.42 FB1000	M. T. Sheelan	
G-CDNS	Westland Gazelle AH.1 (XZ321)	Falcon Aviation Ltd	
G-CDNT	Zenair CH.601XL Zodiac	W. McCormack	
G-CDNW	Ikarus C.42 FB UK	W. Gabbott	
G-CDNY	Jabiru SP-470	G. Lucey	
G-CDNZ	Ultramagic M-120 balloon	R. H. Etherington/Italy	
G-CDOA	EV-97 TeamEurostar UK	Mainair Microlight School Ltd	
G-CDOB	Cameron C-90 balloon	G. D. & S. M. Philpot	
G-CDOC	Mainair Quik GT450	D. M. Broom	
G-CDOE	Avro 146 RJ70	Trident Turboprop (Dublin) Ltd	
G-CDOF	Avro 146 RJ70	Trident Turboprop (Dublin) Ltd	
G-CDOG	Lindstrand LBL-Dog SS balloon	ABC Flights Ltd	
G-CDOJ	Schweizer 269C-1	Sterling Helicopters Ltd	
G-CDOK	Ikarus C.42 FB 100	M Aviation Ltd	
G-CDOM	Mainair Pegasus Quik	G-CDOM Flying Group	
G-CDON	PA-28-161 Warrior II	G-CDON Group	
G-CDOO	Mainair Pegasus Quantum 15-912	O. C. Harding	
G-CDOP	Mainair Pegasus Quik	H. A. Duthie & R. C. Tadman	
G-CDOR	Mainair Blade	J. D. Otter	
G-CDOT	Ikarus C.42 FB 100	A. C. Anderson	
G-CDOV	Skyranger 912(2)	B. Richardson	
G-CDOY	Robin DR.400/180R	Lasham Gliding Society Ltd	
G-CDOZ	EV-97 TeamEurostar UK	J. P. McCall	
G-CDPA	Alpi Pioneer 300	N. D. White & N. G. Dowding	
G-CDPB	Skyranger 982(1)	N. S. Bishop	
G-CDPC	Cameron C-90 balloon	Cameron Balloons Ltd	
G-CDPD	Mainair Pegasus Quik	M. D. Vearncombe	
G-CDPE	Skyranger 912(2)	D. Workman	
G-CDPG	Crofton Auster J1-A	P. & T. Groves	
G-CDPH	Tiger Cub RL5A LW Sherwood Ranger ST	K. F. Crumplin	
G-CDPI	Zenair CH.601UL Zodiac	R. M. Cornwell & A. D. Janaway	
G-CDPJ	Van's RV-8	P. Johnson	
G-CDPL	EV-97 TeamEurostar UK	C. I. D. H Garrison	
G-CDPM	Jurca Spitfire	J. E. D. Rogerson	
G-CDPN	Ultramagic S-105	D. J. MacInnes	
G-CDPP	Ikarus C42 FB UK	H. M. Owen	
G-CDPR	PA-18 Super Cub 95	J. P. Hibble	
G-CDPS	Raj Hamsa X'Air 133	N. Brown	
G-CDPV	PA-34-200T Seneca II	Partside Aviation Ltd	
G-CDPW	Mainair Pegasus Quantum 15-912	T. P. R. Wright	
G-CDPY	Shaw Europa	A. Burrill	
G-CDPZ	Flight Design CT2K	M. E. Henwick	
G-CDRC	Cessna 182Q Skylane	R. S. Hill and Sons	
G-CDRD	AirBorne XT912-B Edge/Streak III-B	Fly NI Ltd	
G-CDRF	Cameron Z-90 balloon	Chalmers Ballong Corps	
G-CDRG	Mainair Pegasus Quik	R. J. Gabriel	
G-CDRH	Thruster T.600N	Carlisle Thruster Group	
G-CDRI	Cameron O-105 balloon	Snapdragon Balloon Group	
G-CDRJ	Tanarg/Ixess 15 912S(1)	J. H. Hayday	
G-CDRM	Van's RV-7A	R. Keppelmueller	
G-CDRN	Cameron Z-225 balloon	Balloon School (International) Ltd	
G-CDRO	Ikarus C42 F880	Airbourne Aviation Ltd	
G-CDRP	Ikarus C42 FB80	D. S. Parker	
G-CDRR	Mainair Pegasus Quantum 15-912	G. J. Crago	
G-CDRS	Rotorway Executive 162F	R. C. Swann	
G-CDRT	Mainair Pegasus Quik	R. Tetlow	
G-CDRU	CASA 1.131E Jungmann 2000	P. Cunniff	
G-CDRV	Van's RV-9A	R. J. Woodford	
G-CDRW	Mainair Pegasus Quik	G. L. Fearon	
G-CDRX	Cameron Z-225 balloon	Balloon School (International) Ltd	
G-CDRY	Ikarus C42 FB100 VLA	R. J. Mitchell	
G-CDRZ	Balóny Kubíček BB22 balloon	Club Amatori Del Volo In Montgolfiera	
G-CDSA	Mainair Pegasus Quik	D. J. Cornelius	
G-CDSB	Alpi Pioneer 200	T. A. & P. M. Pugh	
G-CDSC	Scheibe SF.25C Rotax-Falke	Devon & Somerset Motorglider Group	
G-CDSD	Alpi Pioneer 200	J. A. R. Blick	

Notes	Reg.	Type	Owner or Operator
	G-CDSF	Diamond DA40D Star	Flying Time Ltd
	G-CDSH	ICP MXP-740 Savannah Jabiru(5)	J. P. Bell
	G-CDSK	Reality Escapade Jabiru(3)	R. H. Sear
	G-CDSM	P & M Aviation Quik GT450	A. Munro
	G-CDSN	Raj Hamsa X'Air Jabiru(3)	S. P. Heard
	G-CDSO	Thruster T.600N	The Red Barons
	G-CDSS	Mainair Pegasus Quik	P. A. Bass
	G-CDST	Ultramagic N-250 balloon	A. Derbyshire
	G-CDSU	Robinson R22	Sloane Helicopters Ltd
	G-CDSW	Ikarus C.42 FB UK	P. W. Lupton
	G-CDSX	EE Canberra T.Mk.4 (VN799)	Aviation Heritage Ltd
	G-CDSY	Robinson R44	E. Meegan
	G-CDTA	EV-97 TeamEurostar UK	R. D. Stein
	G-CDTB	Mainair Pegasus Quantum 15-912	D. W. Corbett
	G-CDTD	Eurocopter AS350B2 Ecureuil	TEC Aircraft Leasing GmbH & Co KG
	G-CDTE	Tecnam P2002-JF	Tecnam General Aviation Ltd
	G-CDTG	Diamond DA42 Twin Star	Twinstar Ltd
	G-CDTH	Schempp-Hirth Nimbus 4DM	M. A. V. Gatehouse
	G-CDTI	Messerschmitt Bf.109E (4034)	Rare Aero Ltd
	G-CDTJ	Just/Reality Escapade Jabiru	P. Anning
	G-CDTL	Avtech Jabiru J-400	M. I. Sistern
	G-CDTO	P & M Quik GT450	J. R. Houston
	G-CDTP	Skyranger 912S (1)	P. M. Whitaker
	G-CDTR	P & M Quik GT450	M. G. Freeman
	G-CDTT	Savannah Jabiru(4)	M. J. Day
	G-CDTU	EV-97 TeamEurostar UK	G-CDTU Group
	G-CDTV	Tecnam P2002 EA Sierra	S. A. Noble
	G-CDTX	Cessna F.152	J. S. Develin & Z. Islam
	G-CDTY	Savannah Jabiru (5)	D. McCormack
	G-CDTZ	Aeroprakt A.22 Foxbat	P. C. Piggott & M. E. Hughes
	G-CDUE	Robinson R44	Scotia Helicopters Ltd
	G-CDUH	P & M Quik GT450	R. W. Thornborough
	G-CDUJ	Lindstrand LBL 31A balloon	J. M. Frazer
	G-CDUK	Ikarus C.42 FB UK	D. M. Lane
	G-CDUL	Skyranger 912S (2)	T. W. Thiele & C. D. Hogbourne
	G-CDUS	Skyranger 912S (1)	C. S. Robinson
	G-CDUT	Jabiru J400	T. W. & A. Pullin.
	G-CDUU	P & M Quik GT450	Caunton Charlie Delta Group
	G-CDUV	Savannah Jabiru(5)	D. M. Blackman
	G-CDUW	Aeronca C3	N. K. Geddes
	G-CDUX	PA-32 Cherokee Six 300	D. J. Mason
	G-CDUY	Thunder & Colt 77A balloon	G. Birchall
	G-CDVA	Skyranger 912 (2)	D. C. Mole
	G-CDVD	Aerotechnik EV-97 Eurostar	P. Ritchie
	G-CDVF	Rans S.6-ES Coyote II	S. G. Beeson
	G-CDVG	Pegasus Quik	C. M. Lewis
	G-CDVH	Pegasus Quantum 15	M. J. Hyde
	G-CDVI	Ikarus C42 FB80	Airbourne Aviation Ltd
	G-CDVJ	Montgomerie-Bensen B8MR	D. J. Martin
	G-CDVK	Savannah Jabiru (5)	M. Peters
	G-CDVL	Alpi Pioneer 300	J. D. Clabon
	G-CDVN	P & M Quik GT450	P. Warrener
	G-CDVO	P & M Quik	D. Sykes
	G-CDVR	P & M Quik GT450	N. H. McCorquodale
	G-CDVS	Europa XS	J. F. Lawn
	G-CDVT	Van's RV-6	P. J. Wood
	G-CDVU	Aerotechnik EV-97 TeamEurostar	W. D. Kyle & T. J. Dowling
	G-CDVV	SA Bulldog Srs. 120/121 (XX626:02, W)	W. H. M. Mott
	G-CDVX	Republic TP-47G-10-GU Thunderbolt	Patina Ltd
	G-CDVZ	P & M Quik GT450	S. M. Green & M. D. Peacock
	G-CDWB	Skyranger 912(2)	V. J. Morris
	G-CDWD	Cameron Z-105 balloon	Bristol University Ballooning Society
	G-CDWE	Nord NC.856 Norvigie	R. H. & J. A. Cooper
	G-CDWG	Dyn'Aéro MCR-01 Club	S. E. Gribble
	G-CDWH	Curtiss P-40B	The Fighter Collection
	G-CDWI	Ikarus C42 FB80	The Scottish Flying Club
	G-CDWJ	Flight Design CTSW	B. W. T. Rood
	G-CDWK	Robinson R44	Speedyparts Direct
	G-CDWL	Raj Hamsa X'Air 582 (5)	The CDWL Flying Group
	G-CDWM	Skyranger 912S (1)	R. W. Marshall
	G-CDWN	Ultramagic N-210 balloon	S. R. Seager
	G-CDWO	P & M Quik GT450	G. W. Carwardine

Reg.	Type	Owner or Operator	Notes
G-CDWP	P & M Quik GT450	J. R. North	
G-CDWR	P & M Quik GT450	D. P. Creedy	
G-CDWS	P & M Quik GT450	H. N. Barrott	
G-CDWT	Flight Design CTSW	R. Scammell	
G-CDWU	Zenair CH.601UL Zodiac	A. D. Worrall	
G-CDWV	Lindstrand LBL House SS balloon	LSB Public Relations Ltd	
G-CDWW	P & M Quik GT450	J. H. Bradbury	
G-CDWX	Lindstrand LBL 77A balloon	LSB Public Relations Ltd	
G-CDWY	Agusta A109S Grand	Sportsdirect.com Retail Ltd	
G-CDWZ	P & M Quik GT450	B. J. Holloway	
G-CDXA	Robinson R44 Raven	Northumbria Helicopters Ltd	
G-CDXD	Medway SLA100 Executive	A. J. Baker	
G-CDXF	Lindstrand LBL 31A balloon	R. S. Mohr	
G-CDXG	P & M Pegasus Quantum 15-912	A. P. Hutchinson	
G-CDXH	Avro RJ100	Trident Jet Leasing (Ireland) Ltd	
G-CDXI	Cessna 182P	B. G. McBeath	
G-CDXJ	Jabiru J400	J. C. Collingwood	
G-CDXK	Diamond DA42 Twin Star	A. M. Healy	
G-CDXL	Flight Design CTSW	A. K. Paterson	
G-CDXM	Pegasus Quik	Mainair Microlight Centre Ltd	
G-CDXN	P & M Quik GT450	Microflight Aviation Ltd	
G-CDXO	Zenair CH.601UL Zodiac	T. W. Lorimer	
G-CDXP	Aerotechnik EV-97 Eurostar	R. J. Crockett	
G-CDXR	Replica Fokker DR.1	J. G. Day	
G-CDXS	Aerotechnik EV-97 Eurostar	R. T. P. Harris	
G-CDXT	Van's RV-9	T. M. Storey	
G-CDXU	Chilton DW.1A	M. Gibbs	
G-CDXV	Campbell Cricket Mk.6A	W. G. Spencer	
G-CDXW	Cameron Orange 120 SS balloon	You've Been Tangoed	
G-CDXX	Robinson R44 Raven II	Emsway Developments Ltd	
G-CDXY	Skystar Kitfox Mk.7	D. E. Steade	
G-CDYA	Gippsland GA-8 Airvan	P. Marsden	
G-CDYB	Rans S.6-ES Coyote II	J. M. Fearn	
G-CDYC	PA-28RT-201 Arrow IV	Arrowflight Ltd	
G-CDYD	Ikarus C42 FB80	C42 Group	
G-CDYG	Cameron Z-105 balloon	A. Service Di Tartaglini Emanuela	
G-CDYI	BAe Jetstream 4100	Eastern Airways	
G-CDYL	Lindstrand LBL-77A balloon	J. H. Dobson	
G-CDYM	Murphy Maverick 430	M. R. Cann	
G-CDYO	Ikarus C42 FB80	B. Goodridge	
G-CDYP	Aerotechnik EV-97 TeamEurostar UK	R. V. Buxton & R. Cranborne	
G-CDYR	Bell 206L-3 LongRanger III	Yorkshire Helicopters	
G-CDYT	Ikarus C42 FB80	J. W. D. Blythe	
G-CDYU	Zenair CH.701UL	A. Gannon	
G-CDYX	Lindstrand LBL-77B balloon	H. M. Savage	
G-CDYY	Alpi Pioneer 300	B. Williams	
G-CDYZ	Van's RV-7	Holden Group Ltd	
G-CDZA	Alpi Pioneer 300	J. F. Dowe	
G-CDZB	Zenair CH.601UL Zodiac	L. J. Dutch	
G-CDZD	Van's RV-9A	R. D. Masters	
G-CDZG	Ikarus C42-FB80	Mainair Microlight School Ltd	
G-CDZH	Boeing 737-804	Thomsonfly	
G-CDZI	Boeing 737-804	Thomsonfly	
G-CDZK	Tecnam P92-JS	Tecnam General Aviation Ltd	
G-CDZL	Boeing 737-804	Thomsonfly (G-BYNC)	
G-CDZM	Boeing 737-804	Thomsonfly (G-BYNB)	
G-CDZO	Lindstrand LBL-60X balloon	R. D. Parry	
G-CDZR	Nicollier HN.700 Menestrel II	P. Berkin	
G-CDZS	Kolb Twinstar Mk.3 Extra	P. W. Heywood	
G-CDZT	Beech B200 Super King Air	BAE Systems Ltd	
G-CDZU	ICP MXP-740 Savannah Jabiru (5)	P. J. Cheney	
G-CDZW	Cameron N-105 balloon	Backetorp Byggconsult AB	
G-CDZY	Medway SLA 80 Executive	Medway Microlights	
G-CDZZ	Rotorsport UK MT-03	S. J. Boxall	
G-CEAE	Boeing 737-229	European Skybus Ltd	
G-CEAF	Boeing 737-229	European Skybus Ltd	
G-CEAH	Boeing 737-229	European Aviation Ltd	
G-CEAK	Ikarus C42 FB80	Barton Heritage Flying Group	
G-CEAM	Aerotechnik EV-97 TeamEurostar UK	Flylight Airsports Ltd	
G-CEAN	Ikarus C42 FB80	Airbourne Aviation Ltd	
G-CEAO	Jurca MJ.5 Sirocco	P. S. Watts	

Notes	Reg.	Type	Owner or Operator
	G-CEAR	Alpi Pioneer 300	A. Parker
	G-CEAT	Zenair CH.601HDS Zodiac	T. B. Smith
	G-CEAU	Robinson R44	Mullahead Property Co Ltd
	G-CEAV	Ultramagic M-105 balloon	G. Everett
	G-CEAX	Ultramagic S-130 balloon	Anglian Countryside Balloons Ltd
	G-CEAY	Ultramagic H-42 balloon	J. D. A. Shields
	G-CEBA	Zenair CH.601XL Zodiac	P. G. Morris
	G-CEBC	ICP MXP-740 Savannah Jabiru (5)	E. W. Chapman
	G-CEBE	Schweizer 269C-1	Milburn World Travel Services Ltd
	G-CEBF	Aerotechnik EV-97A Eurostar	M. Lang
	G-CEBG	Balóny Kubíček BB26 balloon	P. M. Smith
	G-CEBH	Tanarg/Ixess 15 912S (1)	D. A. Chamberlain
	G-CEBI	Kolb Twinstar Mk.3	R. W. Livingstone
	G-CEBK	PA-31-350 Navajo Chieftain	De Jong Management BV
	G-CEBL	Balóny Kubíček BB20GP balloon	Associazione Sportiva Aerostatica Lombada/Italy
	G-CEBM	P & M Quik GT450	G. Oliver
	G-CEBN	Avro RJ100	Trident Jet Leasing (Ireland) Ltd
	G-CEBO	Ultramagic M-65C balloon	M. J. Woodcock
	G-CEBP	EV-97 TeamEurostar UK	T. R. Southall
	G-CEBT	P & M Quik GT450	A. J. Riddell
	G-CEBW	P-51D Mustang	Dental Insurance Solutions Ltd
	G-CEBZ	Zenair CH.601UL Zodiac	I. M. Ross & A Watt
	G-CECA	P & M Quik GT450	A. Weatherall
	G-CECC	Ikarus C42 FB80	G-CECC Group
	G-CECD	Cameron C-90 balloon	S. P. Harrowing
	G-CECE	Jabiru UL-D	ST Aviation Ltd
	G-CECF	Just/Reality Escapade Jabiru (3)	M. M. Bayle
	G-CECG	Jabiru UL-D	R. K. Watson
	G-CECH	Jodel D.150	W. R. Prescott
	G-CECI	Pilatus PC-6/B2-H4 Turbo Porter	D. M. Penny
	G-CECJ	Aeromot AMT-200S Super Ximango	C. J. & S. C. Partridge
	G-CECK	ICP MXP-740 Savannah Jabiru (5)	K. W. Eskins
	G-CECL	Ikarus C42 FB80	C. Lee
	G-CECO	Hughes 269C	P. A. Leverton
	G-CECP	Best Off Skyranger 912(2)	A. Asslanian
	G-CECS	Lindstrand LBL-105A balloon	Beam Global Distribution (UK) Ltd
	G-CECU	Boeing 767-222	UK International Airlines Ltd
	G-CECV	Van's RV-7	D. M. Stevens
	G-CECW	Robinson R44 II	A. Bauer
	G-CECX	Robinson R44	Dolphin Property (Management) Ltd
	G-CECY	EV-97 Eurostar	M. R. M. Welch
	G-CECZ	Zenair CH.601XL Zodiac	P. A. Foulds & J. A. Kentzer
	G-CEDA	Cameron Z-105 balloon	Charbonnier di Charbonnier E CSNC/Italy
	G-CEDB	Just/Reality Escapade Jabiru (3)	P. Travis
	G-CEDC	Ikarus C42 FB100	P. D. Ashley
	G-CEDD	PA-28RT-201 Arrow IV	A. Zoechling
	G-CEDE	Flight Design CTSW	F. Williams & J. A. R. Hartley
	G-CEDF	Cameron N-105 balloon	Bailey Balloons Ltd
	G-CEDG	Robinson R44	P. J. Barnes
	G-CEDI	Best Off Skyranger 912(2)	L. Call & G. Finney
	G-CEDJ	Aero Designs Pulsar XP	P. F. Lorriman
	G-CEDK	Cessna 750 Citation X	The Duke of Westminster
	G-CEDL	TEAM Minimax 91	K. N. Cobb
	G-CEDM	Flight Design CTSW	A. P. Sellars
	G-CEDN	Pegasus Quik	R. G. Beecham
	G-CEDO	Raj Hamsa X'Air Falcon 133(2)	J. Lane & A. P. Lambert
	G-CEDR	Ikarus C42 FB80	R. S. O'Carroll
	G-CEDT	Tanarg/Ixess 15 912S(1)	N. S. Brayn
	G-CEDV	Evektor EV-97 TeamEurostar UK	Airbourne Aviation Ltd
	G-CEDW	TEAM Minimax 91	A. J. Sharratt
	G-CEDX	Evektor EV-97 TeamEurostar UK	C. P. Davis
	G-CEDZ	Best Off Skyranger 912(2)	J. E. Walendowski & I. Bell
	G-CEEB	Cameron C-80 balloon	Cameron Balloons Ltd
	G-CEEC	Raj Hamsa X'Air Hawk	B. G. King
	G-CEED	ICP MXP-740 Savannah Jabiru(5)	J. Rademaker
	G-CEEE	Robinson R44	C. R. Caswell
	G-CEEF	ELA 07R	G. Millward
	G-CEEG	Alpi Pioneer 300	D. McCormack
	G-CEEI	P & M Quik GT450	R. A. Hill
	G-CEEJ	Rans S-7S Courier	J. M. Lister
	G-CEEK	Cameron Z-105 balloon	PSH Skypower Ltd
	G-CEEL	Ultramagic S-90 balloon	San Paolo Company SRL

Reg.	Type	Owner or Operator	Notes
G-CEEM	P & M Quik GT450	D. P. Sayer	
G-CEEN	PA-28-161 Cadet	Plane Talking Ltd	
G-CEEO	Flight Design CTSW	E. McCallum	
G-CEEP	Van's RV-9A	J. M. Ghosh & M. P. Wiseman	
G-CEER	ELA 07R	F. G. Shepherd	
G-CEES	Cameron C-90 balloon	P. C. May	
G-CEEU	PA-28-161 Cadet	Plane Talking Ltd	
G-CEEV	PA-28-161 Warrior III	Plane Talking Ltd	
G-CEEW	Ikarus C42 FB100	D. McCartan	
G-CEEX	ICP MXP-740 Savannah Jabiru(5)	G. M. Teasdale	
G-CEEY	PA-28-161 Warrior III	Plane Talking Ltd	
G-CEEZ	PA-28-161 Warrior III	Plane Talking Ltd	
G-CEFA	Ikarus C42 FB UK	J. Morrisroe	
G-CEFB	Ultramagic H-31 balloon	P. Dickinson	
G-CEFC	Super Marine Spitfire 26	D. R. Bishop	
G-CEFJ	Sonex	M. H. Moulai	
G-CEFK	Evektor EV-97 TeamEurostar UK	P. Morgan	
G-CEFM	Cessna 152	Cristal Air Ltd	
G-CEFP	Jabiru J430	G. Hammond	
G-CEFS	Cameron C-100 balloon	Gone With The Wind Ltd	
G-CEFT	Whittaker MW5-D Sorcerer	W. Bruce	
G-CEFV	Cessna 182T Skylane	G. H. Smith and Son	
G-CEFY	ICP MXP-740 Savannah Jabiru(4)	B. Hartley	
G-CEFZ	Evektor EV-97 TeamEurostar UK	Robo Flying Group	
G-CEGE	Fairchild SA.226TC Metro II	Blue City Aviation Ltd	
G-CEGG	Lindstrand LBL-25A Cloudhopper balloon	C. G. Dobson	
G-CEGH	Van's RV-9A	M. E. Creasey	
G-CEGI	Van's RV-8	C. W. N. & A. A. M. Huke	
G-CEGJ	P & M Quik GT450	Flylight Airsports Ltd	
G-CEGK	ICP MXP-740 Savannah VG Jabiru(1)	Sandtoft Ultralights Partnership	
G-CEGL	Ikarus C42 FB100	FES Autogas Ltd	
G-CEGO	Evektor EV-97A Eurostar	N. J. Keeling, R. F. McLachlan & J. A. Charlton	
G-CEGP	Beech 200 Super King Air	Cega Air Ambulance UK Ltd (G-BXMA)	
G-CEGR	Beech 200 Super King Air	Henfield Lodge Ltd	
G-CEGS	PA-28-161 Warrior II	Aviation Rentals	
G-CEGT	P & M Quik GT450	J. Plenderleith	
G-CEGU	PA-28-151 Warrior	Aviation Rentals	
G-CEGV	P & M Quik GT450	G. Shaw	
G-CEGW	P & M Quik GT450	P. Barrow	
G-CEGY	ELA 07R	A. Buchanan	
G-CEGZ	Ikarus C42 FB80	A. D. Tomlins	
G-CEHC	P & M Quik GT450	G. H. Sharwood-Smith	
G-CEHD	Best Off Skyranger 912(2)	A. A. Howland	
G-CEHE	Medway SLA 100 Executive	R. P. Stoner	
G-CEHG	Ikarus C42 FB100	G. E. Cole	
G-CEHI	P & M Quik GT450	A. Costello	
G-CEHL	EV-97 TeamEurostar UK	B. P. Connally	
G-CEHM	Rotorsport UK MT-03	R. C. Slight	
G-CEHN	Rotorsport UK MT-03	P. A. Harwood	
G-CEHR	Auster AOP.9	J. Cooke & R. B. Webber	
G-CEHS	CAP.10B	G. Hutchinson	
G-CEHT	Rand KR-2	P. P. Geoghegan	
G-CEHV	Ikarus C42 FB80	Mainair Microlight School Ltd	
G-CEHW	P & M Quik GT450	G-CEHW Group	
G-CEHX	Lindstrand LBL-9A balloon	P. Baker	
G-CEHZ	Edge XT912-B/Streak III-B	J. Horan	
G-CEIA	Rotorsport UK MT-03	M. P Chetwynd-Talbot	
G-CEIB	Yakovlev Yak-18A	G. M. Bauer	
G-CEID	Van's RV-7	A. Moyce	
G-CEIE	Flight Design CTSW	D. K. Ross	
G-CEIG	Van's RV-7	W. K. Wilkie	
G-CEIH	Avro RJ100	Trident Jet Leasing (Ireland) Ltd	
G-CEII	Medway SLA80 Executive	F. J. Clarehugh	
G-CEIK	Ultramagic M-90 ballon	Imagination Balloon Flights	
G-CEIL	Bassett Escapade 912(2)	D. E. Bassett	
G-CEIS	Jodel DR.1050	M. Hales	
G-CEIT	Van's RV-7	S. S. Gould	
G-CEIV	Tanarg/Ixess 15 912S(2)	W. R. Cross	
G-CEIW	Europa	R. Scanlan	
G-CEIX	Alpi Pioneer 300	R. F. Bond	
G-CEIY	Ultramagic M-120 balloon	Societa Cooperativa Sociale Il Paraticchio/Italy	
G-CEIZ	PA-28-161 Warrior II	India Zulu Flying Group	

Notes	Reg.	Type	Owner or Operator
	G-CEJA	Cameron V-77 balloon	G. Gray (G-BTOF)
	G-CEJC	Cameron N-77 balloon	D. J. Stagg
	G-CEJD	PA-28-161 Warrior III	Western Air (Thruxton) Ltd
	G-CEJE	Wittman W.10 Tailwind	R. A. Povall
	G-CEJF	PA-28-161 Cadet	Aviation Rentals
	G-CEJG	Ultramagic M-56 balloon	Dragon Balloon Co.Ltd
	G-CEJI	Lindstrand LBL-105A balloon	Richard Nash Cars Ltd
	G-CEJJ	P & M Quik GT450	Juliet Juliet Group
	G-CEJK	Lindstrand LBL-260A balloon	Cameron Flights Southen Ltd
	G-CEJL	Ultramagic H-31 balloon	Robert Wiseman Dairies PLC
	G-CEJN	Mooney M.20F	G. R. Wakeley
	G-CEJR	Cameron Z-90 balloon	KB Voli Di Chiozzi Bartolomeo EC SAS/Italy
	G-CEJT	Cameron Z-31 balloon	Cameron Balloons Ltd
	G-CEJV	PA-28-161 Cadet	Aviation Rentals
	G-CEJW	Ikarus C42 FB80	M. I. Deeley
	G-CEJX	P & M Quik GT450	P. Stewart & A. J. Huntly
	G-CEJY	Aerospool Dynamic WT9 UK	R. G. Bennett
	G-CEJZ	Cameron C-90 balloon	A. M. Holly
	G-CEKA	Robinson R-44 II	P. L. Lunnon
	G-CEKB	Taylor JT.1 Monoplane	C. J. Bush
	G-CEKC	Medway SLA100 Executive	B. W. Webb
	G-CEKD	Flight Design CTSW	M. K. Arora
	G-CEKE	Robin DR400/180	M. F. Cuming
	G-CEKG	P & M Quik GT450	G-CEKG Flying Group
	G-CEKI	Cessna 172P	N. Houghton
	G-CEKJ	Evektor EV-97A Eurostar	C. W. J. Vershoyle-Greene
	G-CEKK	Best Off Sky Ranger Swift 912S(1)	J. A. Hunt
	G-CEKO	Robin DR400/100	R. J. Hopkins
	G-CEKS	Cameron Z-105 balloon	Phoenix Balloons Ltd
	G-CEKT	Flight Design CTSW	Charlie Tango Group
	G-CEKV	Europa	K. Atkinson
	G-CEKW	Jabiru J430	J430 Syndicate
	G-CELA	Boeing 737-377	Jet 2
	G-CELB	Boeing 737-377	Jet 2
	G-CELC	Boeing 737-377	Jet 2 (G-OBMA)
	G-CELD	Boeing 737-377	Jet 2 (G-OBMB)
	G-CELE	Boeing 737-377	Jet 2 (G-MONN)
	G-CELF	Boeing 737-377	Jet 2
	G-CELG	Boeing 737-377	Jet 2
	G-CELH	Boeing 737-330	Jet 2
	G-CELI	Boeing 737-330	Jet 2
	G-CELJ	Boeing 737-330	Jet 2
	G-CELK	Boeing 737-330	Jet 2
	G-CELM	Cameron C-80 balloon	L. Greaves
	G-CELO	Boeing 737-33AQC	Jet 2
	G-CELP	Boeing 737-330QC	Jet 2
	G-CELR	Boeing 737-330QC	Jet 2
	G-CELS	Boeing 737-377	Jet 2
	G-CELU	Boeing 737-377	Jet 2
	G-CELV	Boeing 737-377	Jet 2
	G-CELW	Boeing 737-377	Jet 2
	G-CELX	Boeing 737-377	Jet 2
	G-CELY	Boeing 737-377	Jet 2
	G-CELZ	Boeing 737-377	Jet 2
	G-CEMA	Alpi Pioneer 200	D. M. Bracken
	G-CEMB	P & M Quik GT450	RAF Microlight Flying Association
	G-CEMC	Robinson R44 Raven II	Helicentre Holdings Ltd
	G-CEMD	PA-28-161 Warrior II	Steptoe and Son Properties Ltd
	G-CEME	Evektor EV-97 Eurostar	F. W. McCann
	G-CEMF	Cameron C-80 balloon	Linear Communications Consultants Ltd
	G-CEMG	Ultramagic M-105 balloon	Comunicazione In Volo SRL/Italy
	G-CEMI	Europa XS	B. D. A. Morris
	G-CEMK	Boeing 767-222	UK International Airlines Ltd
	G-CEML	P & M Pegasus Quik	C. J. Kew
	G-CEMM	P & M Quik GT450	M. A. Rhodes
	G-CEMN	Ultramagic S-130 balloon	F. Morselli/Italy
	G-CEMO	P & M Quik GT450	L. E. Craig
	G-CEMP	BB UK Tria 503(1)	P. Robshaw
	G-CEMR	Mainair Blade 912	A. D. Cameron
	G-CEMS	MDH MD900 Explorer	Yorkshire Air Ambulance Ltd.
	G-CEMT	P & M Quik GT450	A. Dixon
	G-CEMU	Cameron C-80 balloon	J. G. O'Connell

Reg.	Type	Owner or Operator	Notes
G-CEMV	Lindstrand LBL-105A balloon	R. G. Turnbull	
G-CEMW	Lindstrand LBL Bananas balloon	Top Banana Balloon Team (G-OCAW)	
G-CEMX	P & M Pegasus Quik	S. J. Meehan	
G-CEMY	Alpi Pioneer 300	J. C. A. Garland & P. F. Salter	
G-CEMZ	Pegasus Quik	D. Jessop	
G-CENA	Dyn'Aero MCR-01 ULC Banbi	I. N. Drury, R. Germany & D. Goodman	
G-CENB	Evektor EV-97 TeamEurostar UK	K. J. Gay	
G-CENC	Christen Eagle II	J. R. Pearce	
G-CEND	Evektor EV-97 TeamEurostar UK	Flylight Airsports Ltd	
G-CENE	Flight Design CTSW	The CT Flying Group	
G-CENG	SkyRanger 912(2)	R. A. Knight	
G-CENH	Tecnam P2002-EA Sierra	M. W. Taylor	
G-CENI	Supermarine Spitfire Mk.26	D. B. Smith	
G-CENJ	Medway SLA 951	M. Ingleton	
G-CENK	Schempp-Hirth Nimbus 4DT	R. A. Christie	
G-CENL	P & M Quik GT450	P. Von Sydow & S. Baker	
G-CENM	Evektor EV-97 Eurostar	N. D. Meer	
G-CENN	Cameron C-60 balloon	Stonebee Ltd	
G-CENO	Aerospool Dynamic WT9 UK	R. O. Lewthwaite	
G-CENP	Ace Magic Laser	C. S. Robinson	
G-CENR	ELA 07S	M. S. Gough	
G-CENS	SkyRanger Swift 912S(1)	M. & N. D. Stannard	
G-CENU	Savannah Jabiru(5)	N. Farrell	
G-CENV	P & M Quik GT450	RAF Microlight Flying Association	
G-CENW	Evektor EV-97A Eurostar	W. S. Long	
G-CENX	Lindstrand LBL-360A	Richard Nash Cars Ltd	
G-CENZ	Aeros Discus/Alize	J. D. Buchanan	
G-CEOB	Pitts S-1 Special	I. Gallagher & P. A. Moslin	
G-CEOC	Tecnam P2002-EA Sierra	M. A. Lomas	
G-CEOE	Champion 8KCAB	R. Boucher	
G-CEOF	PA-28R-201 Arrow	J. H. Sandham Aviation	
G-CEOG	PA-28R-201 Arrow	A. J. Gardiner	
G-CEOH	Raj Hamsa X'Air Falcon ULP(1)	Miles Blackburn Ltd	
G-CEOI	Cameron C-60 balloon	M. E. White	
G-CEOJ	Eurocopter EC 155B	Starspeed Ltd	
G-CEOK	Cessna 150M	G. Johnson	
G-CEOL	Flylight Lightfly-Discus	A. Bill	
G-CEOM	Jabiru UL-450	J. R. Caylow	
G-CEON	Raj Hamsa X'Air Hawk	K. S. Campbell	
G-CEOO	P & M Quik GT450	S. Moran	
G-CEOP	Aeroprakt A22-L Foxbat	P. M. Ford	
G-CEOS	Cameron C-90 balloon	British School of Ballooning	
G-CEOT	Dudek ReAction Sport/Bailey Quattro 175	J. Kelly	
G-CEOU	Lindstrand LBL-31A balloon	Lindstrand Hot Air Balloons Ltd	
G-CEOV	Lindstrand LBL-120A balloon	Lindstrand Hot Air Balloons Ltd	
G-CEOW	Europa XS	R. W. Wood	
G-CEOX	Rotorsport UK MT-03	L. C. Griffiths	
G-CEOZ	Paramania Action GT26/PAP Chariot Z	A. M. Shepherd	
G-CEPC	MDD DC-9-82	P. L. Aviation Ltd	
G-CEPE	MDD DC-9-82	P. L. Aviation Ltd	
G-CEPL	Super Marine Spitfire Mk.26	S. R. Marsh	
G-CEPM	Jabiru J430	T. R. Sinclair	
G-CEPN	Kolb Firefly	I. Brewster	
G-CEPP	P & M Quik GT450	W. M. Studley	
G-CEPR	Cameron Z-90 balloon	Sport Promotion SRL/Italy	
G-CEPS	TL2000UK Sting Carbon	C. E. & R. P. Reeves	
G-CEPU	Cameron Z-77 balloon	Liquigas SPA	
G-CEPV	Cameron Z-77 balloon	Liquigas SPA	
G-CEPW	Alpi Pioneer 300	N. K. Spedding	
G-CEPX	Cessna 152	Cristal Air Ltd	
G-CEPY	Ikarus C42 FB80	L. Lay	
G-CEPZ	DR.107 One Design	CEPZ Flying Group	
G-CERB	SkyRanger Swift 912S(1)	J. J. Littler	
G-CERC	Cameron Z-350 balloon	Ballooning Network Ltd	
G-CERD	D.H.C.1 Chipmunk 22	A. C. Darby	
G-CERE	Evektor EV-97 TeamEurostar UK	Airbourne Aviation Ltd	
G-CERF	Rotorsport UK MT-03	P. J. Robinson	
G-CERH	Cameron C-90 balloon	A. Walker	
G-CERI	Shaw Europa XS	S. J. M. Shepherd	
G-CERK	Van's RV-9A	P. E. Brown	
G-CERL	Ultramagic M-77 balloon	A. M. Holly	
G-CERM	Kubicek BB22Z balloon	A. M. Holly	

Notes	Reg.	Type	Owner or Operator
	G-CERN	P & M Quik GT450	P. M. Jackson
	G-CERO	Agusta A109C	Castle Air Charters Ltd (G-OBEK/G-CDDJ)
	G-CERP	P & M Quik GT450	G. R. Cassie, A. J. L. Coulson, D. A. Howe & S. O. Kennedy
	G-CERT	Mooney M.20K	J. A. Nisbet
	G-CERV	P & M Quik GT450	East Fortune Flyers
	G-CERW	P & M Pegasus Quik	J. I. Smith
	G-CERX	Hawker 850XP	Hangar 8 Management Ltd
	G-CERY	SAAB 2000	Eastern Airways
	G-CERZ	SAAB 2000	Eastern Airways
	G-CESA	Replica Jodel DR.1050	P. D. Thomas & T. J. Bates
	G-CESC	Cameron Z-105 balloon	M. Miller
	G-CESD	SkyRanger Swift 912S(1)	S. E. Dancaster
	G-CESF	EV-97 TeamEurostar UK	W. F. Whitfield
	G-CESG	P & M Quik GT450	L. Greco
	G-CESH	Cameron Z-90 balloon	First Flight
	G-CESI	Aeroprakt A22-L Foxbat	D. J. Ashley
	G-CESJ	Raj Hamsa X'Air Hawk	J. Bolton & R. Shewan
	G-CESM	TL2000UK Sting Carbon	E. Stephenson
	G-CESR	P & M Quik GT450	G. Kerr
	G-CESS	Cessna F.172G	V. Bojovic (G-ATGO)
	G-CEST	Robinson R44	P. Sturdy
	G-CESU	Robinson R22 Beta	Northwestern Helicopters AB
	G-CESV	EV-97 TeamEurostar UK	N. Jones
	G-CESW	Flight Design CTSW	A. Costello & J. Cunliffe
	G-CESX	Cameron Z-31 balloon	Wye Valley Aviation Ltd
	G-CESY	Cameron Z-31 balloon	Wye Valley Aviation Ltd
	G-CESZ	CZAW Sportcruiser	A. F. Hayes & M. G. Titmus
	G-CETB	Robin DR.400/180	QR Flying Club
	G-CETD	PA-28-161 Warrior III	Plane Talking Ltd
	G-CETE	PA-28-161 Warrior III	Plane Talking Ltd
	G-CETF	Flight Design CTSW	P and M Aviation Ltd
	G-CETG	Alpha R2160I	D. J. Lawrence
	G-CETK	Cameron Z-145 balloon	R. H. Etherington
	G-CETL	P & M Quik GT450	J. I. Greenshields
	G-CETM	P & M Quik GT450	I. Burnside
	G-CETN	Hummel Bird	A. A. Haseldine
	G-CETO	Best Off Sky Ranger Swift 912S(1)	J. & B. Hudson
	G-CETP	Van's RV-9A	D. Boxall & S. Hill
	G-CETR	Ikarus C42 FB100	A. E. Lacy-Hulbert
	G-CETS	Van's RV-7	TS Group
	G-CETT	Evektor EV-97 TeamEurostar UK	Tango Tango Group
	G-CETU	Best Off Sky Ranger Swift 912S(1)	A. Raithby & N. McCusker
	G-CETV	Best Off Sky Ranger Swift 912S(1)	C. J. Johnson
	G-CETX	Alpi Pioneer 300	J. M. P. Ree
	G-CETY	Rans S-6-ES Coyote II	J. North
	G-CETZ	Ikarus C42 FB100	Airways Airsports Ltd
	G-CEUE	BN-2B-20 Islander	Britten-Norman Aircraft Ltd
	G-CEUF	P & M Quik GT450	G. T. Snoddon
	G-CEUH	P & M Quik GT450	North West Turf Ltd
	G-CEUJ	SkyRanger Swift 912S(1)	J. P. Batty & J. R. C. Brightman
	G-CEUL	Ultramagic M-105 balloon	R. A. Vale
	G-CEUM	Ultramagic M-120 balloon	Bridges Van Hire Ltd
	G-CEUN	Orlican Discus CS	RAF Gliding and Soaring Association
	G-CEUO	Cessna F550 Citation 1	Air Charter Scotland Ltd
	G-CEUR	Schempp-Hirth Ventus 2cT	G. Coppin
	G-CEUT	Hoffman H-36 Dimona II	P. Pozerskis
	G-CEUU	Robinson R44 II	A. Stafford-Jones
	G-CEUV	Cameron C-90 balloon	A. M. Holly
	G-CEUW	Zenair CH.601XL Zodiac	J. S. Griffiths
	G-CEUZ	P & M Quik GT450	B. S. Smy
	G-CEVA	Ikarus C42 FB80	The Scottish Flying Group
	G-CEVB	P & M Quik GT450	N. Hartley & J. L. Guy.
	G-CEVC	Van's RV-4	P. A. Brook
	G-CEVD	Rolladen-Schneider LS3	Victor Delta Syndicate
	G-CEVE	Centrair 101A	J. W. North & T. Newham
	G-CEVF	BAe.146-200	BAE Systems (Operations) Ltd
	G-CEVG	P & M Pegasus Quik	Bartn Quik Group
	G-CEVH	Cameron V-65 balloon	J. A. Atkinson
	G-CEVJ	Alpi Pioneer 200	B. W. Bartlett
	G-CEVK	Schleicher Ka 6CR	K6 Syndicate
	G-CEVL	Fairchild M-62A-4 Cornell	UK Cornell Group

Reg.	Type	Owner or Operator	Notes
G-CEVM	Tecnam P2002-EA Sierra	R. C. Mincik	
G-CEVN	Rolladen-Schneider LS7	N. Gaunt & B. C. Toon	
G-CEVO	Grob G.109B	T.J. Wilkinson	
G-CEVP	P & M Quik GT450	S. G. Ward	
G-CEVS	EV-97 TeamEurostar UK	Eurostar Group	
G-CEVT	Dudek Reaction 27/Bailey Quattro 175	J. Kelly	
G-CEVU	Savannah VG Jabiru(1)	B. L. Cook	
G-CEVV	Rolladen-Schneider LS3	LS3 307 Syndicate	
G-CEVW	P & M Quik GT450	R. W. Sutherland	
G-CEVX	Aeriane Swift Light PAS	J. S. Firth	
G-CEVY	Rotorsport UK MT-03	P. Robinson	
G-CEVZ	Centrair ASW-20FL	J. R. Rainer & J. R. Matthews	
G-CEWC	Schleicher ASK-21	London Gliding Club Proprietary Ltd	
G-CEWD	P & M Quik GT450	J. Murphy	
G-CEWE	Schempp-Hirth Nimbus 2	T. Clark	
G-CEWF	Jacobs V35 Airchair balloon	D. J. Farrar	
G-CEWG	Aerola Alatus-M	Flylight Airsports Ltd	
G-CEWH	P & M Quik GT450	B. W. Hunter	
G-CEWI	Schleicher ASW-19B	K. Steele & S. R. Edwards	
G-CEWK	Cessna 172S	Skytrek Aviation Services	
G-CEWL	Alpi Pioneer 200	M. A. Hogg	
G-CEWM	DHC.6 Twin Otter 300	Isles of Scilly Skybus Ltd	
G-CEWN	Diamond DA-42 Twin Star	Airedale Mechanical and Electrical Ltd	
G-CEWO	Schleicher Ka 6CR	DQS Group	
G-CEWP	Grob G.102 Astir CS	R. D. Slater	
G-CEWR	Aeroprakt A22-L Foxbat	C. S. Bourne & G. P. Wiley	
G-CEWS	Zenair CH.701SP	G. E. MacCuish	
G-CEWT	Flight Design CTSW	A and R. W. Osborne	
G-CEWU	Ultramagic H-77 balloon	P. C. Waterhouse	
G-CEWW	Grob G.102 Astir CS	M. R. Woodiwiss	
G-CEWX	Cameron Z-350 balloon	Original Bristol FM Ltd	
G-CEWY	Quicksilver GT500	R. J. Scott	
G-CEWZ	Schempp-Hirth Discus bT	J. F. Goudie	
G-CEXL	Ikarus C42 FB80	Syndicate C42-1	
G-CEXM	Best Off Sky Ranger Swift 912S(1)	A. F. Batchelor	
G-CEXN	Cameron A-120 balloon	Dragon Balloon Company Ltd	
G-CEXO	PA-28-161 Warrior III	Durham Tees Flight Training Ltd	
G-CEXP	HPR.7 Herald 209 ★	Towing and rescue trainer/Gatwick	
G-CEXR	PA-28-161 Warrior III	Plane Talking Ltd	
G-CEXX	Rotorsport UK MT-03	D. B. Roberts	
G-CEYC	DG Flugzeugbau DG-505 Elan Orion	Scottish Gliding Union Ltd	
G-CEYD	Cameron N-31 balloon	Black Pearl Balloons (G-LLYD)	
G-CEYE	PA-32R-300 Cherokee Lance	D. L. Claydon	
G-CEYF	Eurocopter EC135 T1	Starspeed Ltd (G-HARP)	
G-CEYG	Cessna 152	S. J. & T. Powell and A. H. Haynes	
G-CEYH	Cessna 152	Cornwall Flying Club Ltd	
G-CEYI	Cessna 152	Blackburn Aeroplane Co.Ltd	
G-CEYK	Europa XS	A. B. Milne	
G-CEYL	Bombardier BD-700-1A10 Global Express	Aravco Ltd	
G-CEYM	Van's RV-6	R. B. Skinner	
G-CEYN	Grob G.109B	Lasham Gliding Society Ltd	
G-CEYO	Aerospatiale AS.350B2 Ecureuil	FBS Ltd	
G-CEYP	North Wing Design Stratus/ATF	J. S. James	
G-CEYR	Rotorsport UK MT-03	N. Wright	
G-CEYU	SA.365N1 Dauphin 2	Multiflight Ltd	
G-CEYX	Rotorsport UK MT-03	N. Creveul	
G-CEYY	EV-97 TeamEurostar UK	N. J. James	
G-CEYZ	Sikorsky S-76C	Bristow Helicoipters Ltd	
G-CEZA	Ikarus C42 FB80	P. Harper & P. J. Morton	
G-CEZB	Savannah VG Jabiru(1)	D. D. J. Rossdale	
G-CEZD	EV-97 TeamEurostar	G. P. Jones	
G-CEZE	Best Off Sky Ranger Swift 912S	G-CEZE Group	
G-CEZF	EV-97 TeamEurostar UK	D. J. Dick	
G-CEZG	Diamond DA.42 Twin Star	Diamond Aircraft UK Ltd	
G-CEZH	Aerochute Dual	G. Stokes	
G-CEZI	PA-28-161 Cadet	Chalrey Ltd	
G-CEZK	Stolp S.750 Acroduster Too	R. I. M. Hague	
G-CEZL	PA-28-161 Cadet	Chalrey Ltd	
G-CEZM	Cessna 152	Cristal Air Ltd	
G-CEZN	Pacific Airwave Pulse 2/Skycycle	G. W. Cameron	
G-CEZO	PA-28-161 Cadet	Chalrey Ltd	
G-CEZP	Diamond DA.40D Star	Dusky Aviation Ltd	

Notes	Reg.	Type	Owner or Operator
	G-CEZR	Diamond DA.40D Star	Flying Time Ltd
	G-CEZS	Zenair CH.601HDS Zodiac	R. Wyness
	G-CEZT	P & M Aviation Quik GT450	B. C. Blackburn
	G-CEZU	CFM Streak Shadow SA	M. R. Foreman
	G-CEZV	Zenair CH.601HDS Zodiac	G. Waters
	G-CEZW	Jodel D.150 Mascaret	N. J. Kilford
	G-CEZX	P & M Aviation Quik GT450	N. J. Braund
	G-CEZZ	Flight Design CTSW	S. Emery
	G-CFAG	Rotorsport UK MT-03	M. D. Cole
	G-CFAJ	DG-300 Elan	S. Marriott
	G-CFAK	Rotorsport UK MT-03	R. M. Savage
	G-CFAM	Schempp-Hirth Nimbus 3/24.5	Nimbus III Syndicate J15
	G-CFAO	Rolladen-Schneider LS4	V. R. Roberts
	G-CFAP	Interplane ZJ-Viera	Flylight Airsports Ltd
	G-CFAR	Rotorsport UK MT-03	P. M. Twose
	G-CFAS	Escapade Jabiru(3)	C. G. N. Boyd
	G-CFAT	P & M Aviation Quik GT450	T. G. Jackson
	G-CFAU	Cameron Z-105 balloon	High On Adventure Balloons Ltd
	G-CFAV	Ikarus C42 FB80	G. Shaw
	G-CFAW	Lindstrand LBL-35A Cloudhopper balloon	A. Walker
	G-CFAX	Ikarus C42 FB80	R. E. Parker & B. Cook
	G-CFAY	Sky 120-24 balloon	G. B. Lescott
	G-CFBA	Schleicher ASW-20BL	T. J. Hatton & C. R. Little
	G-CFBB	Schempp-Hirth Standard Cirrus	B. F. R. Smyth & R. Andrewartha
	G-CFBC	Schleicher ASW-15B	CFBC Group
	G-CFBE	Ikarus C42 FB80	GS Aviation (Europe) Ltd
	G-CFBF	Lindstrand LBL 203T gas balloon	S and D Leisure (Europe) Ltd
	G-CFBH	Glaser-Dirks DG-100G Elan	IBM Gliding Club
	G-CFBJ	Rotorsport UK MT-03	C-More Flying Ltd
	G-CFBK	BAC 167 Strikemaster Mk.80A (1125)	Trans Holdings Ltd
	G-CFBL	Best Off Sky Ranger Swift 912S(1)	D. Hemmings
	G-CFBM	P & M Quantum 15-912	F. W. & N. A. Milne
	G-CFBN	Glasflugel Mosquito B	S. R. & J. Nash
	G-CFBO	Reality Escapade Jabiru(3)	J. F. Thornton
	G-CFBP	BAe 125 Srs.700A	Hawker 700 Ltd
	G-CFBS	Best Off Sky Ranger Swift 912S(1)	A. J. Tyler
	G-CFBT	Schempp-Hirth Ventus bT	488 (Gransden) Group
	G-CFBV	Schleicher ASK-21	London Gliding Club Proprietary Ltd
	G-CFBW	DG-100G Elan	G-CFBW Syndicate
	G-CFBX	Beech C90GTI King Air	J. M. Lynch
	G-CFBY	Best Off Sky Ranger Swift 912S(1)	J. A. Armin
	G-CFBZ	Schleicher Ka 6CR	R. H. W. Martyn
	G-CFCA	Schempp-Hirth Discus b	M. R. Hayden
	G-CFCB	Centrair 101	G. N. Fraser & G. A. Marshall
	G-CFCC	Cameron Z-275 balloon	Ballooning Network Ltd
	G-CFCD	SkyRanger Swift 912S(1)	D. & L. Payn
	G-CFCE	Raj Hamsa X'Air Hawk	T. Collins
	G-CFCF	Aerochute Dual	C. J. Kendal & S. G. Smith
	G-CFCH	Campbell Cricket Mk.4	E. J. Barton
	G-CFCI	Cessna F.172N	J. Blacklock
	G-CFCJ	Grob G.102 Astir CS	A. J. C. Beaumont & P. Hardwick
	G-CFCK	Best Off Sky Ranger 912S(1)	C. M. Sperring
	G-CFCL	Rotorsport UK MT-03	M. D. Reece
	G-CFCM	Robinson R44	A. J. Brough
	G-CFCN	Schempp-Hirth Standard Cirrus	S. M. Robinson
	G-CFCO	Ultramagic M-130 balloon	I. Vastano
	G-CFCP	Rolladen-Schneider LS6-a	R. E. Robertson
	G-CFCR	Schleicher Ka-6E	R. F. Whittaker
	G-CFCS	Schempp-Hirth Nimbus 2C	J. Luck & P. Dolling
	G-CFCT	EV-97 TeamEurostar UK	Sutton Eurostar Group
	G-CFCU	Lindstrand LBL-203T gas balloon	Lindstrand Aeroplatforms Ltd
	G-CFCV	Schleicher ASW-20	M. J. Davis
	G-CFCW	Rotorsport UK MT-03	C. M. Jones
	G-CFCX	Rans S-6-ES Coyote II	D. & S. Morrison
	G-CFCY	Best Off Sky Ranger Swift 912S(1)	M. E. & T. E. Simpson
	G-CFCZ	P & M Quik GT450	P. K. Dale
	G-CFDA	Schleicher ASW-15	7 Delta Group
	G-CFDC	P & M Aviation Quik GT450	P. R. Davies
	G-CFDE	Schempp-Hirth Ventus bT	P. Clay
	G-CFDF	Ultramagic S-90 balloon	Edinburgh University Hot Air Balloon Club
	G-CFDG	Schleicher Ka 6CR	Delta-Golf Group

Reg.	Type	Owner or Operator	Notes
G-CFDI	Van's RV-6	M. D. Challoner	
G-CFDJ	EV-97 TeamEurostar UK	J. D. J. Spragg & M. Jones	
G-CFDK	Rans S-6-ES Coyote II	Conair Sports Ltd	
G-CFDL	P & M QuikR	P and M Aviation Ltd	
G-CFDM	Schempp-Hirth Discus b	J. L. & T. G. M. Whiting	
G-CFDN	Best Off Sky Ranger Swift 912S(1)	D. A. Perkins	
G-CFDO	Flight Design CTSW	D. I. Waller	
G-CFDP	Flight Design CTSW	N. Fielding	
G-CFDR	Schleicher Ka 6CR	Dartmoor Gliding Society Ltd	
G-CFDS	TL2000UK Sting Carbon	TL Sting G-CFDS Group	
G-CFDT	Aerola Alatus-M	B. T. Green	
G-CFDU	BB03 Trya/BB103	J. M. Macleod	
G-CFDV	Sikorsky S-76C	Bristow Helicopters Ltd	
G-CFDX	PZL-Bielsko SZD-48-1 Jantar Standard 2	The Jantar Syndicate	
G-CFDY	P &M Quik GT450	C. N. Thornton	
G-CFDZ	Flight Design Exxtacy/Alize	N. C. O. Watney	
G-CFEA	Cameron C-90 balloon	A. M. Holly	
G-CFEB	Cameron C-80 balloon	A. M. Holly	
G-CFED	Van's RV-9	E. Taylor & P. Robinson	
G-CFEE	Evektor EV-97 Eurostar	G.CFEE Flying Group	
G-CFEF	Grob G.102 Astir CS	Oxford University Gliding Club	
G-CFEG	Schempp-Hirth Ventus b/16.6	K. F. Moorhouse & R. W. Partridge	
G-CFEH	Centrair 101 Pegase	Booker Gliding Club Ltd	
G-CFEJ	Schempp-Hirth Discus b	L. Coles	
G-CFEK	Cameron Z-105 balloon	R. M. Penny (Plant Hire and Demolition) Ltd	
G-CFEL	EV-97 Eurostar	S. R. Green	
G-CFEI	RAF 2000 GTX-SE	A. M. Wells	
G-CFEM	P & M Aviation Quik GT450	H. Cooke	
G-CFEN	PZL-Bielsko SZD-50-3 Puchacz	The Northumbria Gliding Club Ltd	
G-CFEO	EV-97 Eurostar	J. B. Binks	
G-CFER	Schempp-Hirth Discus b	S. R. Westlake	
G-CFES	Schempp-Hirth Discus b	P. W. Berridge	
G-CFET	Van's RV-7	J. Astor	
G-CFEV	P & M Pegasus Quik	W. T. Davis	
G-CFEW	Lindstrand LBL-240A balloon	M. E. White	
G-CFEX	P & M Quik GT450	H. Wilson	
G-CFEY	Aerola Alatus-M	P. D. Harvey	
G-CFEZ	CZAW Sportcruiser	J. F. Barber & J. R. Large	
G-CFFA	Ultramagic M-90 balloon	Proxim SPA/Italy	
G-CFFB	Grob G.102 Astir CS	M. H. Simms	
G-CFFC	Centrair 101A	B. Douglas	
G-CFFE	EV-97 TeamEurostar UK	J. A. Warters	
G-CFFF	Pitts S-1S Special	N. N. Bentley	
G-CFFG	Aerochute Dual	R. J. Watkin & W. A. Kimberlin	
G-CFFH	Aeros Discus 15T Dragonfly	D. Wilson	
G-CFFJ	Flight Design CTSW	R. Germany	
G-CFFK	Schempp-Hirth Nimbus 3/24.5	I. Ashdown	
G-CFFL	Lindstrand LBL-317A balloon	Aerosarus Balloons Ltd	
G-CFFN	P & M Quik GT450	Kent County Scout Council	
G-CFFO	P & M Quik GT450	D. E. McGauley	
G-CFFP	Eurocopter EC.120B Colibri	Eurocopter UK Ltd	
G-CFFS	Centrair 101A	W. Murray	
G-CFFT	Schempp-Hirth Discus b	R. Maskell	
G-CFFU	Glaser-Dirks DG-101G Elan	FFU Group	
G-CFFV	PZL-Bielsko SZD-51-1 Junior	Herefordshire Gliding Club Ltd	
G-CFFW	Eurocopter AS.365N Dauphin 2	Eurocopter UK Ltd	
G-CFFX	Schempp-Hirth Discus b	P. J. Richards	
G-CFFY	PZL-Bielsko SZD-51-1 Junior	Scottish Gliding Union Ltd	
G-CFGA	VS Spitfire VIII	The Pembrokeshire Spitfire Aeroplane Company Ltd	
G-CFGB	Cessna 680 Citation Sovereign	Keepflying LLP	
G-CFGC	Demoiselle	R. B. Hewing	
G-CFGD	P & M Quik GT450	D. J. Revell	
G-CFGE	Stinson 108-1 Voyager	M. J. Medland	
G-CFGF	Schempp-Hirth Nimbus 3T	R. E. Cross	
G-CFGG	Rotorsport UK MT-03	C. M. Jones	
G-CFGH	Jabiru J160	D. F. Sargant & D. J. Royce	
G-CFGI	VS.358 Seafire Mk.II (MB293)	Mark One Partners LLC	
G-CFGJ	VS.300 Spitfire I (N3200)	Mark One Partners LLC	
G-CFGK	Grob G.102 Astir CS	P. Allingham	
G-CFGM	Ikarus C42	R. S. O'Carroll	
G-CFGN	VS.300 Spitfire IA	Mark One Partners LLC	

Notes	Reg.	Type	Owner or Operator
	G-CFGO	Best Off Sky Ranger Swift 912S	C. Lamb
	G-CFGP	Schleicher ASW-19	A. E. Prime
	G-CFGR	Schleicher ASK-13	Portsmouth Naval Gliding Centre
	G-CFGT	P & M Aviation Quik GT450	G. I. Taylor
	G-CFGU	Schempp-Hirth Standard Cirrus	D. Higginbottom
	G-CFGV	P & M Quik GT450	R. Bennett
	G-CFGX	EV-97 TeamEurostar UK	Golf XRay Group
	G-CFGY	Rotorsport UK MT-03	G. J. Slater & N. D. Leak
	G-CFGW	Centrair 101A	L. P. Smith
	G-CFGZ	Flight Design CTSW	B. Gorvett
	G-CFHB	Micro Aviation B.22J Bantam	Micro Aviation (UK and Ireland)
	G-CFHC	Micro Aviation B.22J Bantam	B. J. Syson
	G-CFHD	Schleicher ASW-20 BL	196 Syndicate
	G-CFHF	PZL-Bielsko SZD-51-1	Black Mountains Gliding Club
	G-CFHG	Schempp-Hirth Mini Nimbus C	R. W. & M. P. Weaver
	G-CFHI	Van's RV-9	J. R. Dawe
	G-CFHJ	Centrair 101A Pegase	Booker Gliding Club Ltd
	G-CFHK	Aeroprakt A22-L Foxbat	R. Bellew
	G-CFHL	Rolladen-Schneider LS4	I. P. Hicks & R. Puritz
	G-CFHM	Schleicher ASK-13	Lasham Gliding Society Ltd
	G-CFHN	Schleicher K 8B	The Nene Valley Gliding Club Ltd
	G-CFHO	Grob G.103 Twin Astir II	The Surrey Hills Gliding Club Ltd
	G-CFHP	Ikarus C42 FB80	Airbourne Aviation Ltd
	G-CFHR	Schempp-Hirth Discus b	M. Fursedon, J. Jervis & T. Turner
	G-CFHS	Tchemma T01/77 balloon	D. J. Farrar
	G-CFHU	Robinson R22 Beta	Cameron and Brown Partnership
	G-CFHW	Grob G.102 Astir CS	P. Haliday
	G-CFHX	Schroeder Fire Balloons G22/24 balloon	T. J. Ellenrieder
	G-CFHY	Fokker Dr.1 Triplane replica	P. G. Bond
	G-CFHZ	Schleicher Ka 6CR	G. D. Leatherland
	G-CFIA	Best Off Sky Ranger Swift 912S(1)	D. I. Hall
	G-CFIC	Jodel DR.1050/M1	J. H. & P. I. Kempton
	G-CFID	Tanarg/Ixess 15 912S	D. Smith
	G-CFIE	Rotorsport UK MT-03	A. McCredie
	G-CFIF	Christen Eagle II	A. Corcoran
	G-CFIG	P & M Aviation Quik GT450	J. Whitfield
	G-CFIH	Piel CP.1320	I. W. L. Aikman
	G-CFII	DH.82A Tiger Moth	Motair LLP
	G-CFIJ	Christen Eagle II	U. Wendt
	G-CFIK	Lindstrand LBL-60X balloon	A. M. Holly
	G-CFIL	P & M Aviation Quik GT450	S. N. Catchpole
	G-CFIM	P & M Aviation Quik GT450	A. Szczepanek
	G-CFIO	Cessna 172S	Skytrek Air Services
	G-CFIP	Raj Hamsa X'Air Falcon 700(1)	M. Skinner
	G-CFIS	Jabiru UL-D	O. Matthews
	G-CFIT	Ikarus C42 FB100	N. Hammerton
	G-CFIU	CZAW Sportcruiser	G. Everett & D. Smith
	G-CFIW	Balony Kubicek BB20XR balloon	H. C. J. Williams
	G-CFIY	Ikarus C42 FB100	Hadair
	G-CFIZ	Best Off Sky Ranger 912(2)	J. A. Hartshorne
	G-CFJA	Embraer EMB-135BJ Legacy	TAG Aviation (UK) Ltd
	G-CFJB	Rotorsport UK MT-03	N. J. Hargreaves
	G-CFJC	Sikorsky S-76C	Bristow Helicopters Ltd
	G-CFJD	Campbell Cricket Mk.6A	C. Seaman
	G-CFJF	Schempp-Hirth SHK-1	J. F. Mills
	G-CFJG	Best Off Sky Ranger Swift 912S(1)	C. M. Gray
	G-CFJH	Grob G.102 Astir CS77	P. Hardman
	G-CFJI	Ultramagic M-105 balloon	Comunicazione In Volo Srl/Italy
	G-CFJJ	Best Off Sky Ranger Swift 912S(1)	J. J. Ewing
	G-CFJK	Centrair 101A	T. J. Parker
	G-CFJL	Raj Hamsa X'Air Hawk	G. L. Craig
	G-CFJM	Rolladen-Schneider LS4-a	K. Woods & S. Hill
	G-CFJN	Diamond DA.40D Star	Atlantic Flight Training Ltd
	G-CFJO	Diamond DA.40D Star	Atlantic Flight Training Ltd
	G-CFJP	Cameron N-56 balloon	K-H Gruenauer/Germany
	G-CFJR	Glaser-Dirks DG-300 Club Elan	W. Palmer & H. Smith
	G-CFJS	Glaser-Dirks DG-300 Club Elan	K. L. Goldsmith
	G-CFJU	Raj Hamsa X'Air Hawk	R. J. Minns & H. M. Wooldridge
	G-CFJV	Schleicher ASW-15	R. Abercrombie
	G-CFJW	Schleicher K7	K7 Group
	G-CFJX	DG-300 Elan	Crown Service Gliding Club
	G-CFJZ	Schempp-Hirth SHK-1	B. C. Irwin & R. H. Hanna

Reg.	Type	Owner or Operator	Notes
G-CFKA	Rotorsport UK MT-03	R. J. Haggas	
G-CFKB	CZAW Sportcruiser	B. S. Williams	
G-CFKD	Raj Hamsa X'Air Falcon Jabiru(4)	A. M. Fawthrop	
G-CFKE	Raj Hamsa X'Air Hawk	S. Rance	
G-CFKF	Cameron Z-210 balloon	First Flight	
G-CFKG	Rolladen-Schneider LS4-a	FKG Group	
G-CFKH	Zenair CH.601XL Zodiac	M. A. Baker	
G-CFKI	Cameron Z-120 balloon	KB Voli Di Chiozzi Bartolomeo EC SAS/Italy	
G-CFKJ	P & M Aviation Quik GT450	B. Geary	
G-CFKK	Flylight Dragonfly	P. B. J. Eveleigh	
G-CFKL	Schleicher ASW-20 BL	J. Ley	
G-CFKM	Schempp-Hirth Discus b	Lasham Gliding Society Ltd	
G-CFKN	Lindstrand GA22 Mk.II airship	Lindstrand Technologies Ltd	
G-CFKO	P & M Aviation Quik GT450	P. Millership	
G-CFKP	Performance Designs Barnstormer/ Voyager	B. J. V. Gardiner	
G-CFKR	P & M Aviation Pegasus Quik	R. D. Ballard	
G-CFKS	Flight Design CTSW	D. J. M. Williams	
G-CFKT	Schleicher K 8B	FKT Group	
G-CFKU	P & M Aviation Quik GT450	C. A. Hasell	
G-CFKV	Savannah VG Jabiru(1)	D. Thorpe & K. N. Rigley	
G-CFKW	Alpi Pioneer 200	P. Rayson	
G-CFKX	Cameron Z-160 balloon	Tiger Aspect Productions Ltd	
G-CFKY	Schleicher Ka 6CR	J. A. Timmis	
G-CFKZ	Europa XS	N. P. Davis	
G-CFLA	P & M Aviation Quik GT450	D. Blake	
G-CFLB	Paratoys 28/Lowboy 313	P. R. Nation	
G-CFLC	Glaser-Dirks DG-300 Club Elan	J. L.Hey	
G-CFLD	Ikarus C42 FB80	L. McWilliams	
G-CFLE	Schempp-Hirth Discus b	Booker Gliding Club Ltd	
G-CFLF	Rolladen-Schneider LS4-a	D. Lamb	
G-CFLG	CZAW Sportcruiser	D. A. Buttress	
G-CFLH	Schleicher K8B	The South Wales Gliding Club Ltd	
G-CFLI	Europa Aviation Europa	A. & E. Bennett	
G-CFLK	Cameron C-90 balloon	A. M. Holly	
G-CFLL	EV-97 Eurostar	D. R. Lewis	
G-CFLM	P & M Pegasus Quik	JAG Flyers	
G-CFLN	Best Off Sky Ranger Swift 912S(1)	D. Bletcher	
G-CFLO	Rotorsport UK MT-03	R. G. Mulford	
G-CFLP	D.31 Turbulent	Eaglescott Turbulent Group	
G-CFLR	P & M Aviation Quik GT450	G. Shaw	
G-CFLS	Schleicher Ka 6CR	University College London Union	
G-CFLU	SAAB 2000	Eastern Airways	
G-CFLV	SAAB 2000	Eastern Airways	
G-CFLW	Schempp-Hirth Standard Cirrus 75	J. Pack	
G-CFLX	DG-300 Club Elan	R. Emms	
G-CFLZ	Scheibe SF-27A Zugvogel V	SF Group	
G-CFMA	BB03 Trya/BB103	D. Sykes	
G-CFMB	P & M Aviation Quik GT450	Countermine PLC	
G-CFMC	Van's RV-9A	G-CFMC Flying Group	
G-CFMD	P & M Aviation Quik GT450	Wilson G. Jamieson Ltd	
G-CFME	SOCATA TB10 Tobago	Charles Funke Associates Ltd	
G-CFMF	Lindstrand LBL-203T gas balloon	Hiflyer Polska SP.zoo/Poland	
G-CFMH	Schleicher ASK-13	Lasham Gliding Society Ltd	
G-CFMI	Best Off Sky Ranger 912(1)	P. Shelton	
G-CFMK	Centrair 101 Pegase	S. R. Phelps	
G-CFMM	Cessna 172S	Cristal Air Ltd	
G-CFMN	Schempp-Hirth Ventus cT	FMN Glider Syndicate	
G-CFMO	Schempp-Hirth Discus b	P. D. Bagnall	
G-CFMP	Europa XS	M. P. Gamble	
G-CFMR	Ultramagic V-14 balloon	M. W. A. Shemilt	
G-CFMS	Schleicher ASW-15	C. Bessent	
G-CFMT	Schempp-Hirth Standard Cirrus	J. M. Brooke	
G-CFMU	Schempp-Hirth Standard Cirrus	A. Harrison & J. Gammage	
G-CFMV	Aerola Alatus-M	M. G. Lynes	
G-CFMW	Scheibe SF-25C	The Windrushers Gliding Club Ltd	
G-CFMX	PA-28-161 Warrior II	Stapleford Flying Club Ltd	
G-CFMY	Rolladen-Schneider LS7	G-CFMY Group	
G-CFNB	Cameron TR-70 balloon	Balslooning Team BVBA/Belgium	
G-CFNC	Flylight Dragonfly	W. G. Minns	
G-CFND	Schleicher Ka 6E	C. Scutt & P. Bryant	
G-CFNE	PZL-Bielsko SZD-38A Jantar 1	T. Robson, J. Murray & I. Gordon	

Notes	Reg.	Type	Owner or Operator
	G-CFNF	Robinson R44 II	Sloane Helicopters Ltd
	G-CFNG	Schleicher ASW-24	P. H. Pickett
	G-CFNH	Schleicher ASW-19	S. N. & P. E. S. Longland
	G-CFNI	Airborne Edge XT912-B/Streak III-B	Fly NI Ltd
	G-CFNK	Slingsby T.65A Vega	I. P. Goldstraw & V. Luscombe-Mahoney
	G-CFNL	Schempp-Hirth Discus b	A. S. Ramsay & P. P. Musto
	G-CFNM	Centrair 101B Pegase	D. T. Hartley
	G-CFNO	Best Off Sky Ranger Swift 912S(1)	J. W. Taylor
	G-CFNP	Schleicher Ka 6CR	P. Pollard-Wilkins
	G-CFNR	Schempp-Hirth Discus b	R. A. Amor
	G-CFNS	Glaser-Dirks DG-300 Club Elan	P. E. Williams, K. F. Byrne & J. M. Price
	G-CFNT	Glaser-Dirks DG-600	G-CFNT Group
	G-CFNU	Rolladen Schneider LS4-a	R. J. Simpson
	G-CFNV	CZAW Sportcruiser	N. D. McAllister & D. J. Turner
	G-CFNW	EV-97 TeamEurostar UK	The Scottish Aero Club Ltd
	G-CFNX	Tanarg/Ixess 13 912S(1)	Flylight Airsports Ltd
	G-CFNY	Flylight Dragonfly	J. K. Evans
	G-CFNZ	Airborne Edge XT912-B/Streak III-B	R. G. Mason
	G-CFOB	Schleicher ASW-15B	A. Maitland
	G-CFOC	Glaser-Dirks DG200/17	R. & C. Nunn
	G-CFOE	Cameron Z-210 balloon	Charbonnier di Nello Charbonnier E C SNC
	G-CFOF	Scheibe SF-27A Zugvogel V	S. Maddex
	G-CFOG	Ikarus C42 FB UK	P. D. Coppin
	G-CFOH	GA Gulfstream IV	Gama Aviation Ltd
	G-CFOI	Cessna 172N	P. Fearon
	G-CFOJ	Eurocopter EC.155 B1	Starspeed Ltd
	G-CFOK	Grob G.103C Twin III Acro	York Gliding Centre Ltd
	G-CFOL	Ultramagic M-90 balloon	M. G. Howard
	G-CFOM	Scheibe SF27A	K. A. Ford & R. D. Noon
	G-CFON	Wittman W8 Tailwind	C. F. O'Neill
	G-CFOO	P & M Aviation Quik R	Microavionics
	G-CFOR	Schleicher K 8B	Dorset Gliding Club Ltd
	G-CFOS	Flylight Dragonfly	P. S. Bendall
	G-CFOT	PZL-Bielsko SZD-48-3 Jantar Standard 3	T. Greenwood
	G-CFOU	Schleicher Ka-7	Channel Gliding Club Ltd
	G-CFOV	CZAW Sportcruiser	J. G. Murphy
	G-CFOW	Best Off Sky Ranger Swift 912S(1)	A. Chappell
	G-CFOX	Marganski MDM-1	Fox Glider Syndicate
	G-CFOY	Schempp-Hirth Discus b	B. W. Mills, J. W. Slater & R. F. Dowty
	G-CFOZ	Rolladen-Schneider LS1-f	L51 Group
	G-CFPA	CZAW Sportcruiser	P. Gazinski
	G-CFPB	Schleicher ASW-15B	G-CFPB Syndicate
	G-CFPC	AA-5B Tiger	Airtime Aviation France Ltd (G-JENN)
	G-CFPD	Rolladen-Schneider LS7	S. Wilson & M. White
	G-CFPE	Schempp-Hirth Ventus cT	R. Palmer
	G-CFPF	Scheibe L-Spatz 55	N. C. Stone
	G-CFPG	AMS-Flight Carat A	A. Collinson
	G-CFPH	Centrair ASW-20F	GB2 Syndicate
	G-CFPI	P & M Aviation Quik GT450	G-CFPI Group
	G-CFPJ	CZAW Sportcruiser	S. R. Winter
	G-CFPL	Schempp-Hirth Ventus c	R. V. Barrett
	G-CFPM	PZL-Bielsko SZD-51-1 Junior	Kent Gliding Club Ltd
	G-CFPN	Schleicher ASW-20	M. Rayner
	G-CFPP	Schempp-Hirth Nimbus 2B	R. Jones & R. Murfitt
	G-CFPR	P & M Aviation Quik R	S. Pearson
	G-CFPS	Sky 25-16 balloon	G. B. Lescott
	G-CFPT	Schleicher ASW-20	L. Hornsey and L. Weeks Syndicate
	G-CFPW	Glaser-Dirks DG-600	P. B. Gray
	G-CFPZ	Sikorsky S-76C	Bristow Helicopters (International) Ltd
	G-CFRC	Schempp-Hirth Nimbus 2B	Tim and Martin Nimbus 2B Group
	G-CFRE	Schleicher Ka 6E	K6-FRE Syndicate
	G-CFRF	Lindstrand LBL-31A	RAF Halton Hot Air Balloon Club
	G-CFRH	Schleicher ASW-20CL	J. N. Wilton
	G-CFRI	Ultramagic N-355 balloon	Kent Ballooning
	G-CFRJ	Schempp-Hirth Standard Cirrus	J. Francis, P. Gould & C. J. Lawrence
	G-CFRK	Schleicher ASW-15B	ASW 15B Syndicate
	G-CFRL	Grob G.102 Astir CS	The South Wales Gliding Club Ltd
	G-CFRM	SkyRanger Swift 912S(1)	R. K. & T. A. Willcox
	G-CFRN	Rotorsport UK MTO Sport	G. Shaw
	G-CFRP	Centrair 101A Pegase	C. Bessent
	G-CFRR	Centrair 101A	P. A. Lewis
	G-CFRS	Scheibe Zugvogel IIIB	R. C. Theobald & S. W. Vallei

Reg.	Type	Owner or Operator	Notes
G-CFRT	EV-97 TeamEurostar UK	G. J. Slater & N. D. Leak	
G-CFRV	Centrair 101A	P. J. Britten	
G-CFRW	Schleicher ASW-20L	R. M. Green	
G-CFRX	Centrair 101A	S. Woolrich	
G-CFRY	Zenair CH 601UL	C. K. Fry	
G-CFRZ	Schempp-Hirth Standard Cirrus	S. G. Lapworth & N. E. Smith	
G-CFSB	Tecnam P2002-RG Sierra	W. J. Gale and Son	
G-CFSD	Schleicher ASK-13	Portsmouth Naval Gliding Centre	
G-CFSE	Cameron H-340HL balloon	Balloon School (International) Ltd	
G-CFSF	P & M Aviation QuikR	A. M. Dalgetty	
G-CFSG	Van's RV-9	R. A. L. Hubbard	
G-CFSH	Grob G.102 Astir CS Jeans	Buckminster Gliding Club Ltd	
G-CFSI	Aerola Alatus-M	T. J. Birkbeck	
G-CFSJ	Jabiru J160	D. P. Bird	
G-CFSK	Dyn'Aero MCR-01 VLA Sportster	S. Collins	
G-CFSL	Kubicek BB-26Z balloon	M. R. Jeynes	
G-CFSM	Cessna 172Q	Zentelligence Ltd	
G-CFSN	Aerola Alatus-M	A. G. Phillips	
G-CFSO	Flylight Dragonfly	C. J. Haste	
G-CFSR	DG-300 Elan	A. P. Montague	
G-CFSS	Schleicher Ka 6E	FSS Syndicate	
G-CFST	Schleicher ASH-25E	D. Tucker & K. H. Lloyd	
G-CFSU	Scheibe Zugvogel IIIA	F. F. Dobbs	
G-CFSW	Skyranger Swift 912S(1)	S. B. & L. S. Williams	
G-CFSX	Savannah VG Jabiru(1)	J. P. Swadling	
G-CFTA	Ace Magic Laser	P and M Aviation Ltd	
G-CFTB	Schleicher Ka 6CR	L. V. Blair	
G-CFTC	PZL-Bielsko SZD-51-1 Junior	Seahawk Gliding Club	
G-CFTD	Schleicher ASW-15B	E. Stephenson	
G-CFTE	P & M Aviation Quik R	M. E. Fowler	
G-CFTF	Roe 1 Triplane Replica	E. A. Verdon-Roe	
G-CFTG	P & M Aviation Quik R	A. V. Cosser	
G-CFTH	PZL-Bielsko SZD-50-3 Puchacz	Buckminster Gliding Club Ltd	
G-CFTI	Evektor EV-97A Eurostar	G. R. Pritchard	
G-CFTJ	Aerotechnik EV-97A Eurostar	C. B. Flood	
G-CFTK	Grob G.102 Astir CS Jeans	Ulster Gliding Club Ltd	
G-CFTL	Schleicher ASW-20CL	J. S. & S. V. Shaw	
G-CFTM	Cameron C-80 balloon	P. A. Meecham	
G-CFTN	Schleicher K 8B	Mendip Gliding Club Ltd	
G-CFTO	Ikarus C42 FB80	Fly Hire Ltd	
G-CFTP	Schleicher ASW-20CL	D. J. Pengilley & M. S. Hawkins	
G-CFTR	Grob G.102 Astir CS77	Lakes Gliding Club	
G-CFTS	Glaser-Dirks DG-300 Club Elan	FTS Syndicate	
G-CFTT	Van's RV-7	R. I. & D. J. Blain	
C-CFTU	Flylight Dragonfly	R. J. Cook	
G-CFTV	Rolladen-Schneider LS7-WL	D. Hilton	
G-CFTW	Schempp-Hirth Discus b	P. A. Startup	
G-CFTX	Jabiru J160	R. K. Creasey	
G-CFTY	Rolladen-Schneider LS7-WL	J. A. Thomson & A. Burgess	
G-CFTZ	Evektor EV-97 Eurostar	G. G. Bevis	
G-CFUA	Van's RV-9A	P. J. Roy & N. A. Onions	
G-CFUB	Schleicher Ka 6CR	D. E. Hooper	
G-CFUD	Skyranger Swift 912S(1)	G-CFUD Group	
G-CFUE	Alpi Pioneer 300 Hawk	A. Dayani	
G-CFUF	Ultramagic N-300 balloon	Merlin Balloons	
G-CFUG	Grob G.109B	Portsmouth Naval Gliding Centre	
G-CFUH	Schempp-Hirth Ventus c	C. G. T. Huck	
G-CFUI	Hunt Wing/Avon 503(4)	R. F. G. Moyle	
G-CFUJ	Glaser-Dirks DG-300 Elan	Foxtrot Uniform Juliet Group	
G-CFUL	Schempp-Hirth Discus b	Discus 803 Syndicate	
G-CFUN	Schleicher ASW-20CL	D. C. W. Sanders	
G-CFUP	Schempp-Hirth Discus b	Lasham Gliding Society Ltd	
G-CFUR	Schempp-Hirth Ventus cT	K. Martin & D. Towson	
G-CFUS	PZL-Bielsko SZD-51-1 Junior	Scottish Gliding Union Ltd	
G-CFUT	Glaser-Dirks DG-300 Club Elan	M. J. Barnett & A. C. Eltis	
G-CFUU	DG-300 Club Elan	G-CFUU Syndicate	
G-CFUV	Rolladen-Schneider LS7-WL	E. Alston	
G-CFUW	Rotorsport UK MTO Sport	D. A. Robertson	
G-CFUX	Cameron C-80 balloon	A. M. Holly	
G-CFUY	PZL-Bielsko SZD-50-3 Puchacz	The Bath, Wilts and North Dorset Gliding Club	
G-CFUZ	CZAW Sportcruiser	M. W. Bush	
G-CFVA	P & M Quik GT450	Countermine PLC	

Notes	Reg.	Type	Owner or Operator
	G-CFVB	Agusta A.109E Power	Qinetiq Ltd
	G-CFVC	Schleicher ASK-13	Mendip Gliding Club Ltd
	G-CFVE	Schempp-Hirth Nimbus 2	L. Mitchell
	G-CFVF	Kiss 400-582(1)	J. D. Pinkney
	G-CFVG	Rotorsport UK MTO Sport	K. J. Whitehead
	G-CFVH	Rolladen-Schneider LS7	C. C. & J. C. Marshall
	G-CFVI	Evektor EV-97 TeamEurostar	Nene Valley Microlights Ltd
	G-CFVJ	Cvjetkovic CA-65 Skyfly	D. Hunter
	G-CFVK	Skyranger HKS(1)	B. Barrass
	G-CFVL	Scheibe Zugvogel IIIB	T. G. Homan & M. Balogh
	G-CFVM	Centrair 101A Pegase	S. H. North
	G-CFVN	Centrair 101A Pegase	S. W. Bradford
	G-CFVO	Beech B.200 Super King Air	Unity Aviation Ltd
	G-CFVP	Centrair 101A Pegase	Foxtrot Victor Papa Group
	G-CFVR	Europa XS	M. T. Fuller
	G-CFVT	Schempp-Hirth Nimbus 2	I. Dunkley
	G-CFVU	Schleicher ASK-13	The Vale of the White Horse Gliding Centre Ltd
	G-CFVV	Centrair 101A Pegase	Cambridge Gliding Club Ltd
	G-CFVW	Schempp-Hirth Ventus bT	I. C. Champness & R. F. Barber
	G-CFVX	Cameron C-80 balloon	A. M. Holly
	G-CFVY	Cameron A-120 balloon	Rocket M edia (UK) Ltd
	G-CFWA	Schleicher Ka 6CR	C. C. Walley
	G-CFWB	Schleicher ASK-13	Cotswold Gliding Club
	G-CFWC	Grob G.103C Twin III Acro	The South Wales Gliding Club Ltd
	G-CFWD	Rotorsport UK MTO Sport	Gower Gyronautics
	G-CFWE	PZL-Bielsko SZD-50-3 Puchacz	Deeside Gliding Club (Aberdeenshire) Ltd
	G-CFWF	Rolladen-Schneider LS7	G. B. Hibberd
	G-CFWH	Scheibe SF27A	M. D. Smith
	G-CFWI	Kubicek BB-22Z balloon	N. Charbonnier
	G-CFWJ	P & M Quik GT450	D. Little
	G-CFWK	Schempp-Hirth Nimbus-3DT	29 Syndicate
	G-CFWL	Schleicher K8B	A. S. Burton
	G-CFWM	Glaser-Dirks DG-300 Club Elan	FWM Group
	G-CFWN	P & M Quik GT450	G-CFWN Group
	G-CFWO	Murphy Maverick 430	S. P. Rice
	G-CFWP	Schleicher ASW-19B	B. Spriggs
	G-CFWR	Skyranger 912 (2)	A. M. Wood & J. Mills
	G-CFWS	Schleicher ASW-20C	662 Syndicate
	G-CFWT	PZL-Bielsko SZD-50-3 Puchacz	Coventry Gliding Club Ltd
	G-CFWU	Rolladen-Schneider LS7-WL	Whiskey Uniform Group
	G-CFWV	Van's RV-7	S. J. Carr & D. K. Sington
	G-CFWW	Schleicher ASH-25E	ASH25E FWW Syndicate
	G-CFWY	Centrair 101A Pegase	S. Foster
	G-CFWZ	Schleicher ASW-19B	G-CFWZ Flying Group
	G-CFXA	Grob G.104 Speed Astir IIB	A. V. Jupp & D. C. White
	G-CFXB	Schleicher K 8B	R. Sansom
	G-CFXC	Schleicher Ka 6E	A. K. Bailey & G. Pook
	G-CFXD	Centrair 101A Pegase	D. G. England & R. Banks
	G-CFXF	Magni M-16C Tandem Trainer	M. W. King
	G-CFXG	Flylight Dragonfly	N. L. Stammers
	G-CFXH	Schleicher K 7	Vale of Neath Gliding Club
	G-CFXI	Lindstrand LBL Box balloon	A. M. Holly
	G-CFXJ	Schleicher ASW-24	G. S. J. Bambrook & A. Purcell
	G-CFXK	Flylight Dragonfly	P. J. Clegg
	G-CFXL	Lindstrand LBL-90A balloon	A. M. Holly
	G-CFXM	Schempp-Hirth Discus bT	G. R. E. Bottomley
	G-CFXN	CZAW Sportcruiser	R. Underwood & J. D. Boyce
	G-CFXO	PZL-Bielsko SZD-50-3 Puchacz	Coventry Gliding Club Ltd
	G-CFXP	Lindstrand LBL-105A balloon	Shaun Bradley Project Services Ltd
	G-CFXR	Lindstrand LBL-105A balloon	Lindstrand Hot Air Balloons Ltd
	G-CFXS	Schleicher Ka 6E	B. C. F. Wade & R. B. Woodhouse
	G-CFXT	Naval Aircraft Factory N3N-3	R. H. & J. A. Cooper
	G-CFXU	Schleicher Ka-6E	FXU Syndicate
	G-CFXW	Schleicher K8B	The South Wales Gliding Club Ltd
	G-CFXX	P & M Quik R	M. C. Shortman
	G-CFXY	Schleicher ASW-15B	E. L. Armstrong
	G-CFXZ	P & M Quik R	Skymasts Antennas Ltd
	G-CFYA	PZL-Bielsko SZD-50-3 Puchacz	Cairngorm Gliding Club
	G-CFYB	Rolladen-Schneider LS7	A. T. Macdonald & V. P. Haley
	G-CFYC	Schempp-Hirth Ventus b	G. Smith
	G-CFYD	Aeroprakt A22-L Foxbat	A. P. Fenn
	G-CFYE	Scheibe Zugvogel IIIB	R. Staines

Reg.	Type	Owner or Operator	Notes
G-CFYF	Schleicher ASK-21	London Gliding Club Proprietary Ltd	
G-CFYG	Glasflugel Club Libelle 205	FYG Syndicate	
G-CFYH	Rolladen-Schneider LS4-a	G. W. & C. A. Craig	
G-CFYI	Grob G.102 Astir CS	Astir 216 Syndicate	
G-CFYJ	Schempp-Hirth Standard Cirrus	FYJ Syndicate	
G-CFYK	Rolladen-Schneider LS7-WL	R. R. Ward	
G-CFYL	PZL-Bielsko SZD-50-3 Puchacz	Deeside Gliding Club (Aberdeenshire) Ltd	
G-CFYM	Schempp-Hirth Discus bT	B. F. Laverick-Smith	
G-CFYN	Schempp-Hirth Discus b	N. White & P. R. Foulger	
G-CFYO	P & M Quik R	M. H. Bond	
G-CFYP	FBM & W Silex M/Flyke/Monster	A. J. R. Carver	
G-CFYR	LET L-23 Super Blanik	G-CFYR Group	
G-CFYS	Dynamic WT9 UK	E. M. Middleton	
G-CFYT	Beech 58 Baron	Conciair Ltd	
G-CFYU	Glaser-Dirks DG-100 Elan	I. M. & C. Shepherd	
G-CFYV	Schleicher ASK-21	The Bristol Gliding Club Proprietary Ltd	
G-CFYW	Rolladen-Schneider LS7	C. Bessant	
G-CFYX	Schempp-Hirth Discus b	Discus FYX Group	
G-CFYY	Schleicher ASK-13	Lasham Gliding Society Ltd	
G-CFYZ	Schleicher ASH-25	A. J. Nurse	
G-CFZA	PZL-Bielsko SZD-51-1	Booker Gliding Club Ltd	
G-CFZB	Glasflugel H201B Standard Libelle	J. C. Meyer	
G-CFZD	Jabiru J430	C. J. Judd & A. Macknish	
G-CFZF	PZL-Bielsko SZD-51-1 Junior	Devon and Somerset Gliding Club Ltd	
G-CFZG	Colt 77A balloon	K. A. O'Kines	
G-CFZH	Schempp-Hirth Ventus c	FZH Group	
G-CFZI	Savannah Jabiru (5)	J. T., A. L. & O. D. Lewis	
G-CFZJ	VS.388 Seafire F.46	C. T. Charleston	
G-CFZK	Schempp-Hirth Standard Cirrus	S. Lucas & R. Burgoyne	
G-CFZL	Schleicher ASW-20 CL	A. L. & R. M. Housden	
G-CFZM	Avro RJ85	BAE Systems (Operations) Ltd	
G-CFZO	Schempp-Hirth Nimbus 3	D. Tanner	
G-CFZP	PZL-Bielsko SZD-51-1 Junior	Portsmouth Naval Gliding Centre	
G-CFZR	Schleicher Ka 6CR	I. McHardy	
G-CFZS	Cameron A-140 balloon	Eastern Safaris Europe Ltd	
G-CFZT	Ace Magic Laser	P and M Aviation Ltd	
G-CFZV	Rolladen-Schneider LS7	R. N. Boddy	
G-CFZW	Glaser-Dirks DG-300 Club Elan	D. O'Flanagan, G. Rogers & G. Stilgoe	
G-CFZX	Rotorsport UK MTO Sport	Gyro-I Ltd	
G-CFZZ	LET L-33 Solo	D. A. R. Wiseman	
G-CGAA	Flylight Dragonfly	G. Adkins	
G-CGAB	AB Sportine LAK-12 Lietuva	W. T. Emery	
G-CGAC	P & M Quik GT450	A. Gillett	
G-CGAD	Rolladen-Schneider LS3	P. B. Turner	
G-CGAF	Schleicher ASK-21	Lasham Gliding Society Ltd	
G-CGAG	Scleicher ASK-21	Stratford on Avon Gliding Club Ltd	
G-CGAH	Schempp-Hirth Standard Cirrus	J. W. Williams	
G-CGAI	Raj Hamsa X'Air Hawk	P. J. Kilshaw	
G-CGAJ	Alpi Pioneer 400	C. Rusalen	
G-CGAK	Acrosport II	P. D. Sibbons	
G-CGAL	P & M Quik R	R. A. Keene	
G-CGAM	Schleicher ASK-21	Oxford University Gliding Club	
G-CGAN	Glasflugel H301 Libelle	S. & C. A. Noujaim	
G-CGAO	DHC.1 Chipmunk 22	P. Jeffery	
G-CGAP	Schempp-Hirth Ventus bT	J. R. Greenwell	
G-CGAR	Rolladen-Schneider LS6-c	A. Warbrick	
G-CGAS	Schempp-Hirth Ventus cT	G. M. J. Monaghan	
G-CGAT	Grob G.102 Astir CS	N. J. Hooper & C. Smales	
G-CGAU	Glasflugel H201B Standard Libelle	G-CGAU Group	
G-CGAV	Scheibe SF-27A Zugvogel V	GAV Syndicate	
G-CGAW	Beech 200 Super King Air	Fort Alice Aviation Ltd	
G-CGAX	PZL-Bielsko SZD-55-1 Promyk	I. D. Macro & P. Gold	
G-CGAZ	P & M Aviation Quik R	E. J. Douglas	
G-CGBA	Schleicher ASK-13	The Burn Gliding Club Ltd	
G-CGBB	Schleicher ASK-21	Edinburgh University Gliding Club	
G-CGBC	Balony Kubicek BB26Z balloon	N. Charbonnier	
G-CGBD	PZL-Bielsko SZD-50-3	The Northumbria Gliding Club Ltd	
G-CGBF	Schleicher ASK-21	BBC (London) Club	
G-CGBG	Rolladen-Schneider LS6-18w	C. Villa	
G-CGBH	Raj Hamsa X'Air Hawk	S. E. McEwen	
G-CGBI	VS.349 Spitfire LF.VB	R. W. H. Cole	

Notes	Reg.	Type	Owner or Operator
	G-CGBJ	Grob G.102 Astir CS	Banbury Gliding Club Ltd
	G-CGBK	Grob G.102 Astir CS	B. J. Griffiths
	G-CGBL	Rolladen-Schneider LS7-WL	P. A. Roche
	G-CGBM	Flight Design CTSW	Mainair Microlight School Ltd
	G-CGBN	Schleicher ASK-21	Essex and Suffolk Gliding Club Ltd
	G-CGBO	Rolladen-Schneider LS6	J. R. W. Luxton
	G-CGBR	Rolladen-Schneider LS6-c	V. L. Brown
	G-CGBS	Glaser-Dirks DG-300 Club Elan	A. Gillanders & M. C. Chalmers
	G-CGBU	Centrair 101A Pegase	S. I. Ross, A. D. Wood & P. S. Tickner
	G-CGBV	Schleicher ASK-21	Wolds Gliding Club Ltd
	G-CGBX	Schleicher ASW-22	D. A. Ashby
	G-CGBY	Rolladen-Schneider LS7	W. J. & S. E. Morecraft
	G-CGBZ	Glaser-Dirks DG-500 Elan Trainer	Needwood Forest Gliding Club Ltd
	G-CGCA	Schleicher ASW-19B	Deeside Gliding Club (Aberdeenshire) Ltd
	G-CGCC	PZL-Bielsko SZD-51-1 Junior	Coventry Gliding Club Ltd
	G-CGCD	Schempp-Hirth Standard Cirrus	Cirrus Syndicate
	G-CGCE	Magni M16C Tandem Trainer	D. C. Fairbrass
	G-CGCF	Schleicher ASK-23	Needwood Forest Gliding Club Ltd
	G-CGCH	CZAW Sportcruiser	C. Harrison
	G-CGCK	PZL-Bielsko SZD-50-3 Puchacz	Kent Gliding Club Ltd (G-BTJV)
	G-CGCL	Grob G.102 Astir CS	J. A. Williams
	G-CGCM	Rolladen-Schneider LS6-c	G. R. Glazebrook
	G-CGCN	MCR-01 Club	D. J. Smith
	G-CGCO	Schempp-Hirth Cirrus VTC	T. W. Slater
	G-CGCP	Schleicher Ka-6CR	D. & B. Clarke
	G-CGCR	Schleicher ASW-15B	R. C. Page
	G-CGCS	Glasflugel Club Libelle 205	D. G. Coats
	G-CGCT	Schempp-Hirth Discus b	D. A. White
	G-CGCU	PZL-Bielsko SZD-50-3 Puchacz	Buckminster Gliding Club Ltd
	G-CGCV	Raj Hamsa X'Air Hawk	W. J. Whyte
	G-CGCW	Skyranger Swift 912(1)	C. M. Wilkes
	G-CGCX	Schleicher ASW-15	C. D. Bingham
	G-BGCY	Centrair 101A Pegase	M. S. W. Meagher
	G-CGDA	Rolladen-Schneider LS3-17	A. R. Fish
	G-CGDB	Schleicher K 8B	The Welland Gliding Club Ltd
	G-CGDC	Rotorsport UK MTO Sport	R. E. Derham & T. R. Kingsley
	G-CGDD	Bolkow Phoebus C	G. C. Kench
	G-CGDE	Schleicher Ka 6CR	K6 Syndicate
	G-CGDF	Schleicher Ka 6BR	T. D. Lynch & H. Marshall
	G-CGDG	Cameron C-80 balloon	A. M. Holly
	G-CGDI	EV-97A Eurostar	D. Street
	G-CGDJ	PA-28-161 Warrior II	C. G. D. Jones (G-ETDA)
	G-CGDK	Schleicher K 8B	Vale of Neath Gliding Club
	G-CGDL	P & M Quik R	S. J. Bunce
	G-CGDM	Sonex Sonex	D. Scott
	G-CGDN	Rolladen-Schneider LS3-17	S. J. Pepler
	G-CGDO	Grob G.102 Astir CS	P. Lowe & R. Bostock
	G-CGDP	Thunder Ax10-160 S2 balloon	The Ballooning Business Ltd
	G-CGDR	Schempp-Hirth Discus CS	J. H. C. Friend
	G-CGDS	Schleicher ASW-15B	B. Birk & P. A. Crouch
	G-CGDT	Schleicher ASW-24	Tango 54 Syndicate
	G-CGDU	Schleicher ASK-24	G. J. Moore
	G-CGDV	CSA Sportcruiser	D. R. Stevens
	G-CGDW	CSA Sportcruiser	Onega Ltd
	G-CGDX	Orlican Discus CS	Coventry Gliding Club Ltd
	G-CGDY	Schleicher ASW-15B	Cloud Nine Syndicate
	G-CGDZ	Schleicher ASW-24	J. M. Norman
	G-CGEA	Schleicher Ka 6CR	S. D. Hawkin
	G-CGEB	Grob G.102 Astir CS77	T. R. Dews
	G-CGEC	Flight Design CTLS	S. Munday
	G-CGEE	Glasflugel H201B Standard Libelle	C. Metcalfe & J. Kelsey
	G-CGEF	La Mouette Hytrike Srs A	A. Lucchesi & G. Thevenot
	G-CGEG	Schleicher K 8B	Darlton Gliding Club Ltd
	G-CGEH	Schleicher ASW-15B	P. Nayeri
	G-CGEI	Cessna 550 Citation Bravo	S. W. Bond
	G-CGEJ	Alpi Pioneer 200-M	P. S. & N. Bewley
	G-CGEK	Ace Magic Laser	P. L. Wilkinson
	G-CGEL	PZL-Bielsko SZD-50-3	The Northumbria Gliding Club Ltd
	G-CGEM	Schleicher Ka 6CR	GEM Syndicate
	G-CGEN	RAF 2000	D. E. Worley
	G-CGEO	CSA Sportcruiser	The Jester Flying Group
	G-CGEP	Schempp-Hirth Standard Cirrus	D. J. Bundock

Reg.	Type	Owner or Operator	Notes
G-CGER	Cameron Z-105 balloon	CV Fly Communication SRL/Italy	
G-CGET	Boeing 737-33A	Jet 2 (G-TOYE)	
G-CGEU	Flylight Dragonfly	D. Newbrook	
G-CGEV	Heliopolis Gomhouria Mk.6	A. Brier	
G-CGEW	Rotorsport UK MTO Sport	G-CGEW Group	
G-CGEX	P & M Quik GT450	D. L. Clark	
G-CGEY	Julian CD Dingbat	G. Carr	
G-CGEZ	Raj Hamsa X'Air Hawk	M. Howes & B. J. Ellis	
G-CGFB	BB03 Trya/BB103	B. J. Fallows	
G-CGFG	Cessna 152	Cristal Air Ltd	
G-CGFH	Cessna T182T Turbo Skylane	P. P. D. Howard-Johnston	
G-CGFI	MS.885 Super Rallye	AC Civil Engineering Ltd	
G-CGFJ	Cessna 172M	T. I. Murtough	
G-CGFK	Ace Magic Laser	C. J. Boseley	
G-CGFN	Cameron C-60 balloon	R. S. Mohr	
G-CGFO	Ultramagic H-42 balloon	J. Dyer	
G-CGFP	Pietenpol Aircamper	D. Hetherington	
G-CGFR	Lindstrand LBL HS-120 Airship	Lindstrand Hot Air Balloons Ltd	
G-CGFS	Nanchang CJ-6A	L. C. Myall	
G-CGFU	Schempp-Hirth Mini-Nimbus C	Mini Nimbus Syndicate	
G-CGFY	Lindstrand LBL-105A balloon	J. A. Lawton	
G-CGFZ	Thruster T.600N 450	K. J. Crompton	
G-CGGA	P & M Quik R	Stichting Mat Aeroteam	
G-CGGB	P & M Quik R	Stichting Mat Aeroteam	
G-CGGC	P & M Quik R	Stichting Mat Aeroteam	
G-CGGE	Cameron Z-275 balloon	Wickers World Ltd	
G-CGGF	Robinson R44 II	Sky Helicopteros SL	
G-CGGG	Robinson R44	Fly Executive Ltd (G-SJDI)	
G-CGGH	Sky 220-24 balloon	Zebedee Balloon Service Ltd	
G-CGGI	Schweizer 269C-1	Patriot Aviation Ltd	
G-CGGJ	Schweizer 269C-1	Patriot Aviation Ltd	
G-CGGK	Westland Wasp HAS Mk.1	The Real Aeroplane Co.Ltd	
G-CGGL	Rotorsport UK MTOSport	A. D. Lysser	
G-CGGM	EV-97 TeamEurostar UK	GM Group	
G-CGGN	Dassault Falcon 7X	TAG Aviation (UK) Ltd	
G-CGGO	Robin DR.400-180 Regent	AWE Holdings Ltd	
G-CGGP	Autogyro MTOSport	N. Cowley	
G-CGGS	Robinson R44 II	Oakfield Investments Ltd	
G-CGGT	P & M Quik GT450	M. Earp	
G-CGGU	Bombardier CL.600-2B16 Challenger	Jet Aviation Business Jets Deutschland GmbH/Germany	
G-CGGV	Rotorsport UK MTO Sport	R. W. Bottom	
G-CGGW	Rotorsport UK MTO Sport	P. Adams	
G-CGGX	TEAM Minimax 91A	P. D. Parry	
G-CGGY	UltraMagic N-425 balloon	Anglian Countryside Balloons Ltd	
G-CGGZ	UltraMagic S-90 balloon	P. Lawman	
G-CGHA	P & M Quik R	K. M. Hughes	
G-CGHB	NAMC CJ-6A	M. J. Harvey	
G-CGHC	Pioneer 300 Hawk	M. Bettaglio	
G-CGHD	Cessna 172S	Patriot Aviation Ltd	
G-CGHE	Flight Design CTSW	P & M Aviation Ltd	
G-CGHG	P & M Quik GT450	Bruch and Co.Ltd	
G-CGHH	P & M Quik R	D. J. Tiplady	
G-CGHI	Dassault Falcon 2000	Warton Ltd	
G-CGHJ	Staaken Z-21A Flitzer	D. J. Ashley	
G-CGHK	Alpi Pioneer 300 Hawk	D. J. Ashley	
G-CGHL	Rotorsport UK MTOSport	C. S. Mackenzie	
G-CGHM	PA-28 Cherokee 140	R. Steptoe	
G-CGHN	Aeros Discus/Alize	R. Simpson & N. Sutton	
G-CGHO	P & M Quik R	N. Creveau	
G-CGHR	Magic Laser	N. P. Power	
G-CGHS	DG Flugzeugbau DG-808C	M. A. V. Gatehouse	
G-CGHT	Dyn'Aero MCR-01 Banbi	A. Battiato (G-POOP)	
G-CGHU	Hawker Hunter T.Mk.8C	Hawker Hunter Aviation Ltd	
G-CGHW	Czech Sport Aircraft Sportcruiser	Sport Cruiser 290 Group	
G-CGHX	Beagle B.121 Pup	N. F. Foden	
G-CGHY	Raytheon Hawker 800XP	Xclusive Jet Charter Ltd	
G-CGHZ	P & M Quik R	P. J. Shergold	
G-CGIA	Paramania Action/Bailey Quattro 175	A. E. C. Phillips	
G-CGIB	Magic Cyclone	P and M Aviation Ltd	
G-CGIC	Rotorsport MTO Sport	J. Harmon & K. Snell	
G-CGID	PA-31-350 Navajo Chieftain	T. Michaels	

Notes	Reg.	Type	Owner or Operator
	G-CGIE	Flylight Dragonfly	Flylight Airsports Ltd
	G-CGIF	Flylight Dragonfly	G. Nicholas
	G-CGIG	Lindstrand LBL-90A balloon	Fly Me Home Ltd
	G-CGIH	Cameron C-90 balloon	W. Bracken
	G-CGIJ	Agusta Westland AW139	HM Coastguard
	G-CGIK	Isaacs Spitfire	A. J. Harpley
	G-CGIL	CZAW Sportcruiser	G-CGIL Group
	G-CGIM	Ace Aviation Magic Laser	C. Royle
	G-CGIN	Paramania Action GT/Bailey Quattro 175	A. E. C. Phillips
	G-CGIO	Medway SLA100 Executive	C. J. Draper
	G-CGIP	CZAW Sportcruiser	R. Vincent
	G-CGIR	Remos GX	L. R. Marks & J. A. Pereira
	G-CGIS	Cameron Parachutist 110 SS balloon	K. Gruenauer (G-RIPS)
	G-CGIU	AX1 balloon	M. W. A. Shemilt
	G-CGIV	Kolb Firefly	W. A. Emmerson
	G-CGIW	Sikorsky S-76C-2	Bristow Helicopters (International) Ltd
	G-CGIX	Rotorsport UK MTO Sport	J. K. Houldcroft
	G-CGIY	Piper J3C-65	R. C. Cummings
	G-CGIZ	Flight Design CTSW	J. Hilton
	G-CGJA	Bombardier CL600-2B16 Challenger	TAG Aviation (UK) Ltd
	G-CGJB	Schempp-Hirth Duo Discus T	G. J. Basey
	G-CGJC	Rotorsport UK MTO Sport	J. C. Collingwood
	G-CGJD	Rotorsport UK Calidus	C. Collins
	G-CGJE	VS.361 Spitfire IX	Historic Flight Ltd
	G-CGJF	Fokker E.111 Replica	I. Brewster
	G-CGJH	P & M Quik GT450	B. Montila
	G-CGJI	Best Off Skyranger 912S(1)	Flylight Airsports Ltd
	G-CGJJ	P & M Quik R	S. E. Bettley
	G-CGJL	CZAW Sportcruiser	G-CGJL Flying Group
	G-CGJM	Skyranger Swift 912S(1)	J. P. Metcalfe
	G-CGJN	Van's RV-7	J. R. & M. G. Jefferies
	G-CGJO	P & M Quik R	C. W. J. Davis
	G-CGJP	Van's RV-10	F. G. Morris
	G-CGJS	CZAW Sportcruiser	J. M. Tiley
	G-CGJT	CZAW Sportcruiser	D. F. Toller
	G-CGJV	Lindstrand LBL Motorbike SS balloon	Lindstrand Hot Air Balloons Ltd
	G-CGJW	RAF 2000 GTX-SE	J. J. Wollen
	G-CGJX	SA.341B Gazelle AH Mk.1	B. W. Stuart
	G-CGJY	SA.341D Gazelle HT Mk.3	P. J. Whitaker
	G-CGJZ	SA.341D Gazelle HT Mk.3	A. W. J. Stuart
	G-CGKA	Grob G115E Tutor	Babcock Aerospace Ltd
	G-CGKB	Grob G115E Tutor	Babcock Aerospace Ltd
	G-CGKC	Grob G115E Tutor	Babcock Aerospace Ltd
	G-CGKD	Grob G115E Tutor	Babcock Aerospace Ltd
	G-CGKE	Grob G115E Tutor	Babcock Aerospace Ltd
	G-CGKF	Grob G115E Tutor	Babcock Aerospace Ltd
	G-CGKG	Grob G115E Tutor	Babcock Aerospace Ltd
	G-CGKH	Grob G115E Tutor	Babcock Aerospace Ltd
	G-CGKI	Grob G115E Tutor	Babcock Aerospace Ltd
	G-CGKJ	Grob G115E Tutor	Babcock Aerospace Ltd
	G-CGKK	Grob G115E Tutor	Babcock Aerospace Ltd
	G-CGKL	Grob G115E Tutor	Babcock Aerospace Ltd
	G-CGKM	Grob G115E Tutor	Babcock Aerospace Ltd
	G-CGKN	Grob G115E Tutor	Babcock Aerospace Ltd
	G-CGKO	Grob G115E Tutor	Babcock Aerospace Ltd
	G-CGKP	Grob G115E Tutor	Babcock Aerospace Ltd
	G-CGKR	Grob G115E Tutor	Babcock Aerospace Ltd
	G-CGKS	Grob G115E Tutor	Babcock Aerospace Ltd
	G-CGKT	Grob G115E Tutor	Babcock Aerospace Ltd
	G-CGKU	Grob G115E Tutor	Babcock Aerospace Ltd
	G-CGKV	Grob G115E Tutor	Babcock Aerospace Ltd
	G-CGKW	Grob G115E Tutor	Babcock Aerospace Ltd
	G-CGKX	Grob G115E Tutor	Babcock Aerospace Ltd
	G-CGKY	Cessna 182T	T. A. E. Dobell
	G-CGKZ	Best Off Sky Ranger 912S(1)	A. Worthington
	G-CGLA	Cameron Z-105 balloon	Novartis Animal Health UK Ltd
	G-CGLB	Airdrome Dream Classic	S. J. Ball
	G-CGLC	Czech Sport Aircraft Sportcruiser	P. Taylor
	G-CGLE	Flylight Dragonfly	B. Skelding
	G-CGLF	Magni M-16C Tandem Trainer	J. S. Walton
	G-CGLG	P & M Quik GT450	P & M Aviation Ltd
	G-CGLH	Rotorsport UK Calidus	A. J. Turner

Reg.	Type	Owner or Operator	Notes
G-CGLI	Alpi Pioneer 200	B. A. Lyford	
G-CGLJ	TL 2000UK Sting Carbon	L. A. James	
G-CGLK	Magni M-16C Tandem Trainer	K. Kerr	
G-CGLL	Rotorsport UK MTO Sport	P. J. Troy-Davies	
G-CGLM	Rotorsport UK MTO Sport	J. Owen	
G-CGLN	Jabiru J430	J. R. Frohnsdorff & C. H. K. Hood	
G-CGLO	P & M Quik R	A. P. Watkins	
G-CGLP	CZAW Sportcruiser	P. A. Cruttenden & P. J. Reilly	
G-CGLR	Czech Sport Aircraft Sportcruiser	G-CGLR Group	
G-CGLT	Czech Sport Aircraft Sportcruiser	D. J. Fawcett	
G-CGLV	Beech 58 Baron	Conciair Ltd (G-DAFY)	
G-CGLW	P & M Pegasus Quik	C. D. Waldron	
G-CGLX	Rotorsport UK MTO Sport	The Gyrocopter Co.Ltd	
G-CGLY	Rotorsport UK Calidus	A. G. A. Edwards	
G-CGLZ	TL 2000UK Sting Carbon	D. Nieman	
G-CGMA	Ace Magic Laser	J. N. Hanson	
G-CGMB	Embraer EMB-135ER	Eastern Airways	
G-CGMC	Embraer EMB-135ER	Eastern Airways	
G-CGMD	Rotorsport UK Calidus	D.W. Leeming	
G-CGME	Ellipse Fuji/Pulma 2000	I. M. Vass	
G-CGMF	Cessna 560XL Citation XLS	Multiflight Charter Services LLP	
G-CGMG	Van's RV-9	D. J. Bone	
G-CGMH	Jodel D150A Mascaret	M. Hales	
G-CGMI	P & M Quik GT450	W. G. Reynolds	
G-CGMJ	P & M Quik R	J. Rodgers	
G-CGMK	Best Off Sky Ranger 582(1)	F. Omaraie-Hamdanie	
G-CGML	TL 2000UK Sting Carbon	G. T. Leedham	
G-CGMM	CZAW Sportcruiser	TAF and Co	
G-CGMN	Best Off Sky Ranger Swift 912S	T. C. Butterworth	
G-CGMO	Ace Magic Laser	G. J. Latham	
G-CGMP	CZAW Sportcruiser	M. Payne	
G-CGMR	Colt Bibendum-110 balloon	Mobberley Balloon Collection (G-GRIP)	
G-CGMS	Sutton/Aquilair KID 1	K. A. Sutton	
G-CGMU	Sikorsky S-92A	HM Coastguard	
G-CGMV	Roko Aero NG 4HD	Eshott NG4 Group	
G-CGMW	Alpi Pioneer 200M	M. S. McCrudden	
G-CGMX	Cameron TR-70 balloon	Cameron Balloons Ltd	
G-CGMY	PA-28-181 Archer III	GEFA Gesellschaft FUR Absatzfinanzierung GmbH/Germany	
G-CGMZ	P & M Quik R	M. W. Houghton	
G-CGNA	Cameron Super FMG-100 balloon	Cameron Balloons Ltd	
G-CGNB	SOCATA Rallye 100ST	RM Goodman Ltd	
G-CGNC	Rotorsport UK MTO Sport	Comedy South West Ltd	
G-CGND	Robinson R44 II	Ajax Machinery	
G-CGNE	Robinson R44 II	Heli Air Ltd	
G-CGNG	CZAW Sportcruiser	T. Dounias	
G-CGNH	Escapade Jabiru(1)	A. H. Paul	
G-CGNI	Ikarus C42 FB80	G. J. Slater	
G-CGNJ	Cameron Z-105 balloon	Loughborough Students Union Hot Air Balloon Club	
G-CGNK	P & M Quik GT450	G. W. Hillidge	
G-CGNL	Cameron Z-90 balloon	A. M. Holly	
G-CGNM	Magni M-16C Tandem Trainer	Evolo Ltd	
G-CGNN	Montgomerie-Bensen B.8MR	P. M. Ryder	
G-CGNO	P & M Quik GT450	Airways Airsports Ltd	
G-CGNP	Embraer EMB-500 Phenom 100	London Executive Aviation Ltd	
G-CGNR	Van's RV-6	N. Rawlinson	
G-CGNS	Sky 65-24 balloon	R. L. Bovell	
G-CGNT	Avro RJ100	BAE Systems (Operations) Ltd	
G-CGNU	Avro RJ100	BAE Systems (Operations) Ltd	
G-CGNV	Reality Escapade	M. J. Whatley	
G-CGNW	Scheibe SF-25C Falke	The Royal Air Force Gliding and Soaring Association	
G-CGNX	Rotorsport UK MTO Sport	L. McCallum	
G-CGNY	Cessna 340A	P. W. J. Sharpe-Brash	
G-CGNZ	Europa XS	J. L. Almney	
G-CGOA	Cessna 550 Citation II	Xclusive Jet Charter Ltd (G-JMDW)	
G-CGOB	P & M Quik R	P & M Aviation Ltd	
G-CGOC	Sikorsky S-92A	HM Coastguard	
G-CGOD	Cameron N-77 balloon	G. P. Lane	
G-CGOE	Magni M-16C Tandem Trainer	Gyromania Ltd	
G-CGOG	Evektor EV-97A Eurostar	J. S. Holden	

Notes	Reg.	Type	Owner or Operator
	G-CGOH	Cameron C-80 balloon	Spirit Balloons Ltd
	G-CGOI	Stewart S-51 Mustang (413926 E2-S)	K. E. Armstrong
	G-CGOJ	Jodel D.11	J. A. Macleod
	G-CGOK	Ace Magic Cyclone	C. M. Theakstone
	G-CGOL	Jabiru J430	J. V. Sanders
	G-CGOM	Flight Design MC	P and M Aviation Ltd
	G-CGOO	Sorrell SNS-8 Hyperlight	W. F. Hayward
	G-CGOP	Sikorsky S-76C	Bristow Helicopters Ltd
	G-CGOR	Jodel D.18	R. D. Cook
	G-CGOS	PA-28-161 Warrior III	S. H. B. Smith
	G-CGOT	Rotorsport UK Calidus	P. Slater
	G-CGOU	Sikorsky S-76C	Bristow Helicopters Ltd
	G-CGOV	Raj Hamsa X'Air Falcon 582(2)	A. Hipkin
	G-CGOW	Cameron Z-77 balloon	J. F. Till
	G-CGOX	Raj Hamsa X'Air Hawk	Oscar Xray Group
	G-CGOZ	Cameron GB-1000 free gas balloon	Cameron Balloons Ltd
	G-CGPA	Ace Magic Cyclone	M. A. Sweet
	G-CGPB	Magni M-24C	Magni Gyro Ltd
	G-CGPC	P & M Pegasus Quik	A. C. Barnes
	G-CGPD	Ultramagic S-90 balloon	S. J. Farrant
	G-CGPE	P & M Quik GT450	E. H. Gatehouse
	G-CGPF	Flylight Dragonfly	Flylight Airsports Ltd
	G-CGPG	Rotosport UK MTO Sport	K. O. Maurer
	G-CGPH	Ultramagic S-50 balloon	The Packhouse Ltd
	G-CGPI	Eurocopter EC135 T2+	Bond Air Services Ltd (G-TAGG)
	G-CGPJ	Robin DR.400-140	W. H. Cole & P. Dass
	G-CGPK	Rotorsport UK MT-03	Ellis Flying Group (G-RIFS)
	G-CGPL	Sonex Sonex	P. C. Askew
	G-CGPO	TL2000UK Sting Carbon	G. A. Squires
	G-CGPR	Czech Sport Aircraft Pipersport	A. Daltry-Cooke
	G-CGPS	EV-97 Eurostar SL	P. R. Jenson & R. A. Morris
	G-CGPT	Dassault Falcon 900EX	TAG Aviation (UK) Ltd
	G-CGPV	Cameron C-80 balloon	D. G. Such & M. Tomlin
	G-CGPW	Raj Hamsa X'Air Hawk	K. Worthington
	G-CGPX	Zenair CH.601XL Zodiac	A. James
	G-CGPY	Boeing E75 N1 Stearman	M. P. Dentith
	G-CGPZ	Rans S-4 Coyote	C. Saunders
	G-CGRA	Flight Design MC	P & M Aviation Ltd
	G-CGRB	Flight Design CTLS	P & M Aviation Ltd
	G-CGRC	P & M Quik R	R. J. Cook
	G-CGRD	Cirrus SR22	Craigard Property Trading Ltd
	G-CGRE	Cessna F.172H	Parachuting Aircraft Ltd
	G-CGRF	Lindstrand LBL-140A balloon	Lindstrand Hot Air Balloons Ltd
	G-CGRG	Agusta AW139	CHC Scotia Ltd
	G-CGRH	Agusta AW139	CHC Scotia Ltd
	G-CGRJ	Carnet Paramotor	M. Carnet
	G-CGRK	Sikorsky S-76C	Bristow Helicopters Ltd
	G-CGRL	Robinson R44	A. Williamson
	G-CGRM	VS.329 Spitfire Mk.IIA	J. C. Radford
	G-CGRN	Pazmany PL-4A	G. Hudson
	G-CGRO	Robin DR.400/140B	Exeter Aviation Ltd
	G-CGRP	Pitts P12	R. F. Warner
	G-CGRR	P & M Quik	A. W. Buchan
	G-CGRS	P & M Quik	R. Stalker
	G-CGRT	Magni M-24C	A. Parker
	G-CGRU	Sikorsky S-76C	Bristow Helicopters Ltd
	G-CGRW	P & M Quik	W. B. Russell
	G-CGRX	Cessna F.172N	Iscavia Ltd
	G-CGRY	Magni M-24C	K. Herbert
	G-CGRZ	Magni M-24C	J. M. Foster
	G-CGSA	Flylight Dragonfly	W. Lofts
	G-CGSB	Cessna 525A Citationjet CJ2	Sol Aviation Companhia de Aviaco Lda/Portugal
	G-CGSC	Quad City Challenger II	L. Gregory
	G-CGSD	Magni M-16C	The Gyrocopter Company UK Ltf
	G-CGSE	Embraer EMB-135BJ Legacy 650	GE Capital Corporation (Leasing) Ltd
	G-CGSH	Evektor EV-97 TeamEurostar UK	S. Hoyle
	G-CGSI	Zenair CH.601HDS Zodiac	E. McHugh
	G-CGSJ	Bombardier BD700-1A10 Global Express	TAG Aviation (UK) Ltd
	G-CGSM	Avro RJ-85	Trident Aviation Leasing Services (Jersey) Ltd
	G-CGSN	Agusta AW139	Bristow Helicopters Ltd
	G-CGSO	P & M Quik GT450	Light Vending Ltd
	G-CGST	Boeing 737-33A	Aergo Leasing 112 Ltd

Reg.	Type	Owner or Operator	Notes
G-CGSU	Cassutt Racer IIIM	D. J. Howell	
G-CGSV	Lindstrand LBL-400C balloon	Lindstrand Hot Air Balloons Ltd	
G-CGSW	Flylight Motorfloater	Flylight Airsports Ltd	
G-CGSX	Aeroprakt A22-L Foxbat	P. J. Trimble	
G-CGTA	Taylorcraft BC-12-65	D. P. Busby	
G-CGTB	Taylorcraft BC-12D	D. P. & D. S. Busby	
G-CGTC	BN-2T-4S Islander	Britten-Norman Aircraft Ltd	
G-CGTE	Cherry BX-2	D.Roberts	
G-CGTG	Skyranger 912S(1)	C. Trollope	
G-CGTH	Pacific Wings Must 12.5/Trike	B. Plunkett	
G-CGTI	Magni M-24C	S. G. Bradley	
G-CGTS	Cameron A-140 balloon	A. A. Brown	
G-CGTT	EV-97 Eurostar SL	D. L. Walker	
G-CGTZ	Reality Escapade Kid	E. O. Otun	
G-CGUG	P & M Quik R	J. D. Lawrance	
G-CGUL	Gulfstream V-SP	Gama Aviation Ltd	
G-CGUN	Alpha R2160	Quo Vadis UK Ltd	
G-CGVA	Aeroprakt A-22-L Foxbat	T. R. C. Griffin	
G-CGVG	Flight Design CTSW	J. T. James	
G-CGVV	Cameron Z-90 Balloon	Cameron Balloons Ltd	
G-CGWB	Agusta AW139	CHC Scotia Ltd/HM Coastguard	
G-CGWD	Robinson R-44	J. M. Henderson	
G-CGWW	Cameron A-120 balloon	Bristol Airways Ltd (G-VIKY)	
G-CHAB	Schleicher Ka 6CR	W. J. Hunter	
G-CHAC	PZL-Bielsko SZD-50-3 Puchacz	Peterborough and Spalding Gliding Club Ltd	
G-CHAD	Aeroprakt A.22 Foxbat	DJB Foxbat	
G-CHAE	Glasflugel H205 Club Libelle	K. G. Guest	
G-CHAF	PZL-Bielsko SZD-50-3 Puchacz	Seahawk Gliding Club	
G-CHAH	Shaw Europa	T. Higgins	
G-CHAI	Bombardier CL.601-3R	Hangar 8 Management Ltd (G-FBFI)	
G-CHAM	Cameron 90 Pot SS balloon	Pendle Balloon Company	
G-CHAN	Robinson R22 Beta	Artall Air LLP	
G-CHAO	Rolladen-Schneider LS6-b	A. R. J. Hughes	
G-CHAP	Robinson R44	Brierley Lifting Tackle Co Ltd	
G-CHAR	Grob G.109B	RAFGSA	
G-CHAS	PA-28-181 Archer II	G-CHAS Flying Group	
G-CHAX	Schempp-Hirth Standard Cirrus	C. Keating & R. Jarvis	
G-CHAY	Rolladen-Schneider LS7	N. J. Leaton	
G-CHBA	Rolladen-Schneider LS7	LS7 729 Group	
G-CHBB	Schleicher ASW-24	London Gliding Club Propietary Ltd	
G-CHBC	Rolladen-Schneider LS6-c	A. Crowden	
G-CHBD	Glaser-Dirks DG-200	D. A. Clempson	
G-CHBE	Glaser-Dirks DG-300 Club Elan	DG 356 Group	
G-CHBF	Schempp-Hirth Nimbus 2C	K. Richards & J. Clark	
G-CHBG	Schleicher ASW-24	Imperial College of Science, Technology and Medicine	
G-CHBH	Grob G.103C Twin III Acro	Imperial College of Science, Technology and Medicine	
G-CHBK	Grob G.103 Twin Astir II	S. Naylor	
G-CHBL	Grob G.102 Astir CS77	Bidford Gliding Ltd	
G-CHBM	Grob G.102 Astir CS77	P. W. Brown & J. D. M. Sharp	
G-CHBO	Schleicher Ka 6CR	M. I. Perrier & H. Southworth	
G-CHBP	Glaser-Dirks DG-500	A. Taverna	
G-CHBS	PZL-Bielsko SZD-41A Jantar Standard 1	P. J. Chaisty & D. Hendry	
G-CHBT	Grob G.102 Astir CS Jeans	Astir Syndicate	
G-CHBU	Centrair ASW-20F	M. Staljan, S. Brogger & C. Behrendt	
G-CHBV	Schempp-Hirth Nimbus 2B	G. J. Evison, J. Lynas & R. Strarup	
G-CHCF	AS.332L-2 Super Puma	CHC Scotia Ltd	
G-CHCG	AS.332L-2 Super Puma	CHC Scotia Ltd	
G-CHCH	AS.332L-2 Super Puma	CHC Scotia Ltd	
G-CHCI	AS.332L-2 Super Puma	CHC Scotia Ltd	
G-CHCJ	EC.225LP Super Puma	CHC Scotia Ltd	
G-CHCK	Sikorsky S-92A	CHC Scotia Ltd	
G-CHCL	EC.225LP Super Puma	CHC Scotia Ltd	
G-CHCM	EC.225LP Super Puma	CHC Scotia Ltd	
G-CHCN	EC.225LP Super Puma	CHC Scotia Ltd	
G-CHCO	AS.365N2 Dauphin 2	CHC Scotia Ltd	
G-CHCP	Agusta AB.139	CHC Scotia Ltd	
G-CHCR	AS.365N2 Dauphin 2	CHC Scotia Ltd	
G-CHCS	Sikorsky S-92A	CHC Scotia Ltd	
G-CHCT	Agusta AB.139	CHC Scotia Ltd	

Notes	Reg.	Type	Owner or Operator
	G-CHCV	Agusta AW.139	CHC Scotia Ltd
	G-CHCW	Agusta AW.139	CHC Scotia Ltd
	G-CHDA	Pilatus B4-PC11AF	F. P. & C. M. E. Bois
	G-CHDB	PZL-Bielsko SZD-51-1 Junior	Stratford on Avon Gliding Club Ltd
	G-CHDC	Schleicher ASK-13	Derbyshire and Lancashire Gliding Club Ltd
	G-CHDD	Centrair 101B Pegase 90	591 Glider Syndicate
	G-CHDE	Pilatus B4-PC11AF	A. A. Jenkins
	G-CHDJ	Schleicher ASW-20CL	G. E. G. Lambert & L. M. M. Sebreights
	G-CHDL	Schleicher ASW-20	137 Syndicate
	G-CHDN	Schleicher K 8B	Upward Bound Trust
	G-CHDP	PZL-Bielsko SZD-50-3 Puchacz	Heron Gliding Club
	G-CHDR	DG-300 Elan	R. Robins
	G-CHDU	PZL-Bielsko SZD-51-1 Junior	Cambridge Gliding Club Ltd
	G-CHDV	Schleicher ASW-19B	ASW Aviation
	G-CHDX	Rolladen-Schneider LS7-WL	D. Holborn & R. T. Halliburton
	G-CHDY	Schleicher K 8B	V. Mallon
	G-CHEB	Shaw Europa	I. C. Smit & P. Whittingham
	G-CHEC	PZL-Bielsko SZD-55-1	D. Pye
	G-CHEE	Schempp-Hirth Discus b	A. Henderson
	G-CHEF	Glaser-Dirks DG-500 Elan Trainer	Yorkshire Gliding Club (Proprietary) Ltd
	G-CHEG	AB Sportine Aviacija LAK-12	Z. Kmita, R. Hannigan & S. Grant
	G-CHEH	Rolladen-Schneider LS7-WL	P. Candler
	G-CHEJ	Schleicher ASW-15B	A. F. F. Webb
	G-CHEK	PZL-Bielsko SZD-51-1	Cambridge Gliding Club Ltd
	G-CHEL	Colt 77B balloon	Chelsea Financial Services PLC
	G-CHEM	PA-34-200T Seneca II	London Executive Aviation Ltd
	G-CHEN	Schempp-Hirth Discus b	G-CHEN Group
	G-CHEO	Schleicher ASW-20	The Eleven Group
	G-CHEP	PZL-Bielsko SZD-50-3 Puchacz	Peterborough and Spalding Gliding Club Ltd
	G-CHER	PA-38-112 Tomahawk II	Carlisle Flight Training Ltd
	G-CHEW	Rolladen-Schneider LS6-c18	486 Group
	G-CHEY	PA-31T2 Cheyenne IIXL	Provident Partners Ltd
	G-CHEZ	BN-2B-20 Islander	Cheshire Police Authority (G-BSAG)
	G-CHFA	Schempp-Hirth Ventus b/16.6	A. K. Lincoln
	G-CHFB	Schleicher Ka-6CR	P. J. Galloway
	G-CHFF	Schempp-Hirth Standard Cirrus	Foxtrot 2 Group
	G-CHFH	PZL-Bielsko SZD-50-3	Trent Valley Aerotowing Club Ltd
	G-CHFV	Schempp-Hirth Ventus B/16.6	A. Cliffe & B. Pearson
	G-CHFW	Schleicher K 8B	Oxford Gliding Co.Ltd
	G-CHFX	Schempp-Hirth Nimbus 4T	S. G. Jones
	G-CHFY	Schempp-Hirth Ventus cT	D. J. Ellis & M. Day
	G-CHGB	Grob G.102 Astir CS	A. A. M. Wahlberg, P. Hollamby & G. Clark
	G-CHGF	Schleicher ASW-15B	HGF Flying Group
	G-CHGG	Schempp-Hirth Standard Cirrus	S. Shah
	G-CHGH	Schleicher ASW-19B	F. R. Marks
	G-CHGK	Schempp-Hirth Discus bT	HGK Syndicate
	G-CHGL	Bell 206B JetRanger II	Vantage Aviation Ltd (G-BPNG/G-ORTC)
	G-CHGO	AB Sportine Aviacija LAK-12	P. Raymond & J-M Peuffier
	G-CHGP	Rolladen-Schneider LS6-c	D. R. Elrington
	G-CHGR	AB Sportline Aviacija LAK-12	M. R. Garwood
	G-CHGS	Schempp-Hirth Discus b	G-CHGS Syndicate
	G-CHGT	FFA Diamant 16.5	T. E. Lynch
	G-CHGV	Glaser-Dirks DG500/22 Elan	Hotel Golf Victor Syndicate
	G-CHGW	Centrair ASW-20F	S. C. Moss
	G-CHGX	AB Sportine LAK-12 Lietuva	M. Jenks
	G-CHGZ	Schempp-Hirth Discus bT	G-CHGZ Syndicate
	G-CHHH	Rolladen-Schneider LS6-c	P. H. Rackham
	G-CHHK	Schleicher ASW-19B	M. Walker
	G-CHHM	AB Sportline LAK-12 Lietuva	D. Martin
	G-CHHN	Schempp-Hirth Ventus b/16.6	N. A. C. Norman & R. K. Forrest
	G-CHHO	Schempp-Hirth Discus bT	97Z Syndicate
	G-CHHP	Schempp-Hirth Discus b	F. R. Knowles
	G-CHHR	PZL-Bielsko SZD-55-1 Promyk	R. T. & G. Starling
	G-CHHS	Schleicher ASW-20	P.J. Rocks & D. Britt
	G-CHHT	Rolladen-Schneider LS6-c	F. Roles
	G-CHHU	Rolladen-Schneider LS6-c	J. M. Hall & P. Shuttleworth
	G-CHHW	AB Sportine LAK-12	A. J. Dibdin
	G-CHHX	Wassmer WA.26P Squale	M. H. Gagg
	G-CHIK	Cessna F.152	Stapleford Flying Club Ltd (G-BHAZ)
	G-CHIP	PA-28-181 Archer II	J. A. Divis
	G-CHIS	Robinson R22 Beta	Staffordshire Helicopters Ltd
	G-CHIX	Robin DR.400/500	P. A. & R. Stephens

Reg.	Type	Owner or Operator	Notes
G-CHJA	VFW-Fokker FK-3	M. A. Johnson	
G-CHJC	Rolladen-Schneider LS6-c	F. J. Davies	
G-CHJD	Schleicher Ka 6E	Shenington Gliding Club	
G-CHJE	Schleicher K 8B	J. J. Sconce	
G-CHJF	Rolladen-Schneider LS6-c	J. L. Bridge	
G-CHJH	Schempp-Hirth Discus bT	Hotel Juliet Hotel Group	
G-CHJL	Schempp-Hirth Discus bT	Discus JL Group	
G-CHJN	Schempp-Hirth Standard Cirrus	J. F. Bowles	
G-CHJP	Schleicher Ka-6CR	D. M. Cornelius	
G-CHJR	Glasflugel H201B Standard Libelle	B. O. Marcham & B. Magnani	
G-CHJT	Centrair ASW-20F	R. J. Pirie & M. S. R. Broadway	
G-CHJV	Grob G.102 Astir CS	Cotswold Gliding Club	
G-CHJX	Rolladen-Schneider LS6-c	M. R. Haynes & P. Robinson	
G-CHJY	Schempp-Hirth Standard Cirrus	Cirrus Group	
G-CHKA	Orlican Discus CS	R. W. & M. P. Weaver	
G-CHKB	Grob G.102 Astir CS77	G-CHKB Group	
G-CHKC	Schempp-Hirth Standard Cirrus	S. Foster	
G-CHKD	Schempp-Hirth Standard Cirrus	R. Jeffcoate	
G-CHKK	Schleicher K8B	R. E. Johnston	
G-CHKL	Cameron 120 Kookaburra SS balloon	Eagle Ltd/Australia	
G-CHKM	Grob G.102 Astir CS Jeans	Essex and Suffolk Gliding Club Ltd	
G-CHKN	Kiss 400-582(1)	P. J. Higgins	
G-CHKR	Jastreb Standard Cirrus G/81	N. A. White	
G-CHKS	Jastreb Standard Cirrus G/81	G. G. Butler	
G-CHKU	Schempp-Hirth Standard Cirrus	T. J. Wheeler & T. M. O'Sullivan	
G-CHKV	Scheibe Zugvogel IIIA	Dartmoor Gliding Society Ltd	
G-CHKX	Rolladen-Schneider LS4-B	HKX Group	
G-CHKY	Schempp-Hirth Discus b	C. V. Hill & O. J. Anderson	
G-CHKZ	CARMAM JP 15-36AR Aiglon	T. A. & A. J. Hollings	
G-CHLB	Rolladen-Schneider LS4-b	E. G. Leach & K. F. Rogers	
G-CHLC	Pilatus B4-PC11AF	E. Lockhart	
G-CHLH	Schleicher K 8B	Shenington Gliding Club	
G-CHLK	Glasflugel H.301 Libelle	G. L. J. Barrett & H. Fletcher	
G-CHLL	Lindstrand LBL-90A balloon	P. J. Hollingsworth	
G-CHLM	Schleicher ASW-19B	R. A. Colbeck	
G-CHLN	Schempp-Hirth Discus CS	Portsmouth Naval Gliding Centre	
G-CHLO	Grob G.109B	F. Waller	
G-CHLP	Schleicher ASK-21	Southdown Gliding Club Ltd	
G-CHLS	Schempp-Hirth Discus b	R. A. Lennard	
G-CHLV	Schleicher ASW-19B	P. J. Belcher & R. I. Brickwood	
G-CHLX	Schleicher ASH-25	F. Huselstein	
G-CHLY	Schempp-Hirth Discus CS	S. J. Pearce	
G-CHMA	PZL-Bielsko SZD-51-1 Junior	The Welland Gliding Club Ltd	
G-CHMB	Glaser-Dirks DG-300 Elan	A. D. & P. Langlands	
G-CHMG	ICA IS-28B2	A. Sutton, R. Wood & A. J. Palfreyman	
G-CHMH	Schleicher K8B	Shenington Gliding Club	
G-CHMK	Rolladen-Schneider LS6-18W	A. S. Decloux	
G-CHML	Schempp-Hirth Discus CS	I. D. Bateman	
G-CHMM	Glasflugel 304B	Delta 19 Group	
G-CHMO	Orlican Discus CS	S. Barter	
G-CHMP	Bellanca 7ACA Champ	I. J. Langley	
G-CHMS	Glaser-Dirks DG-100	D. A. Fall	
G-CHMT	Glasflugel Mosquito B	J. Taberham	
G-CHMU	CARMAM JP-15/36AR Aiglon	HMU Group	
G-CHMV	Schleicher ASK-13	The Windrushers Gliding Club Ltd	
G-CHMX	Rolladen-Schneider LS4-a	K. P. Nakhla & L Couval	
G-CHMY	Schempp-Hirth Standard Cirrus	HMY Syndicate	
G-CHMZ	Fedorov ME7 Mechta	R. Andrews	
G-CHNA	Glaser-Dirks DG-500/20 Elan	G-CHNA Group	
G-CHNC	Schleicher ASK-19B	T. J. Highton	
G-CHNE	Schempp-Hirth Nimbus 2B	P. J. Uden	
G-CHNF	Schempp-Hirth Duo Discus	Booker Gliding Club Ltd	
G-CHNG	Schleicher K 8B	Bidford Gliding Ltd	
G-CHNH	Schempp-Hirth Nimbus 2C	C. J. Pollard	
G-CHNK	PZL-Bielsko SZD-51-1 Junior	Booker Gliding Club Ltd	
G-CHNM	Standard Cirrus G/81	The 55 Syndicate	
G-CHNN	Schempp-Hirth Duo Discus	R. Fremerey, N. Lauer & J. Meurs	
G-CHNT	Schleicher ASW-15	S. J. Lintott & I. Dawkins	
G-CHNU	Schempp-Hirth Nimbus 4DT	D. E. Findon	
G-CHNV	Rolladen-Schneider LS4-b	S. K. Armstrong & P. H. Dixon	
G-CHNW	Schempp-Hirth Duo Discus	G-CHNW Group	
G-CHNY	Centrair 101A Pegase	M. O. Breen	

Notes	Reg.	Type	Owner or Operator
	G-CHNZ	Centrair 101A Pegase	R. H. Partington
	G-CHOD	Schleicher ASW-20	S. E. Archer-Jones
	G-CHOF	CARMAM M100S	M. A. Farrelly
	G-CHOG	AB Sportine LAK-12	J. M. Pursey
	G-CHON	Schempp-Hirth Nimbus 2B	A. J. Nurse
	G-CHOP	Westland-Bell 47G-3B1	Leamington Hobby Centre Ltd
	G-CHOR	Schempp-Hirth Discus b	The Windrushers Gliding Club Ltd
	G-CHOS	Grob G.103 Twin Astir	Essex and Suffolk Gliding Club Ltd
	G-CHOV	PZL-Bielsko SZD-51-1 Junior	Coventry Gliding Club Ltd
	G-CHOW	Schempp-Hirth Discus b	M. H. Hardwick
	G-CHOX	Shaw Europa XS	Chocs Away Ltd
	G-CHOY	Schempp-Hirth Mini Nimbus C	A. H. Sparrow
	G-CHOZ	Rolladen-Schneider LS6-18W	R. E. Scott
	G-CHPA	Robinson R22 Beta	Rivermead Aviation Ltd/Switzerland
	G-CHPC	Schleicher ASW-20 CL	B. L. Liddard & P. J. Williams
	G-CHPD	Rolladen-Schneider LS6-c18	C. J. & K. A. Teagle
	G-CHPE	Schleicher ASK-13	Dumfries and District Gliding Club
	G-CHPH	Schempp-Hirth Discus CS	S. G. Jones
	G-CHPI	DHC.1 Chipmunk Mk.22	K. F. Tomsett
	G-CHPK	Van's RV-8	Viscount A. C. Andover (G-JILS)
	G-CHPL	Rolladen-Schneider LS4-b	Southdown Gliding Club Ltd
	G-CHPO	Schleicher Ka-6CR	N. Robinson
	G-CHPR	Robinson R22 Beta	C. Gozzi
	G-CHPT	Federov ME7 Mechta	A. E. Griffiths
	G-CHPV	Schleicher ASK-21	Scottish Gliding Union Ltd
	G-CHPW	Schleicher ASK-21	Scottish Gliding Union Ltd
	G-CHPX	Schempp-Hirth Discus CS	G-CHPX Group
	G-CHPY	DHC.1 Chipmunk 22 (WB652:V)	Devonair Executive Business Travel Ltd
	G-CHRC	Glaser-Dirks DG500/20 Elan	DG500-390 Syndicate
	G-CHRG	PZL-Bielsko SZD-51-1 Junior	Scottish Gliding Union Ltd
	G-CHRH	Schempp-Hirth Discus 2cT	C. Hyett
	G-CHRJ	Schleicher K 8B	Shenington Gliding Club
	G-CHRK	Centrair 101 Pegase	P. T. Bushill & M. Morris
	G-CHRL	Schempp-Hirth Standard Cirrus	A. Smurthwaite & M. Harbour
	G-CHRN	Schleicher ASK-18	Stratford on Avon Gliding Club Ltd
	G-CHRS	Orlican Discus CS	M. Santopinto
	G-CHRW	Schempp-Hirth Duo Discus	802 Syndicate
	G-CHRX	Schempp-Hirth Discus a	N. Worrell & G. S. Bird
	G-CHSA	Rolladen-Schneider LS6-18W	D. A. Benton
	G-CHSB	Glaser-Dirks DG-303 Elan	C. M. Hawkes
	G-CHSD	Schempp-Hirth Discus b	G-CHSD Group
	G-CHSE	Grob G.102 Astir CS77	K. J. Sleigh
	G-CHSG	Scheibe SF27A	HSG Syndicate
	G-CHSK	Schleicher ASW-20CL	A. J. Watson & C. C. Ramshorn
	G-CHSM	Schleicher ASK-13	Stratford on Avon Gliding Club Ltd
	G-CHSN	Schleicher Ka-6CR	Needwood Forest Gliding Club Ltd
	G-CHSO	Schempp-Hirth Discus b	Midland Gliding Club Ltd
	G-CHSU	Eurocopter EC 135T1	Eurocopter UK Ltd
	G-CHSX	Scheibe SF-27A	Essex & Suffolk Gliding Club Ltd
	G-CHSZ	Rolladen-Schneider LS8-a	I. G. Garden
	G-CHTA	AA-5A Cheetah	T. Hale (G-BFRC)
	G-CHTB	Schempp-Hirth Janus	Janus G-CHTB Syndicate
	G-CHTC	Schleicher ASW-15B	HTC Syndicate
	G-CHTD	Grob G.102 Astir CS	S. Waldie
	G-CHTE	Grob G.102 Astir CS77	HTE Group
	G-CHTF	AB Sportline LAK-12	M. Tolson
	G-CHTJ	Schleicher ASK-13	Queen's University Gliding Club
	G-CHTM	Rolladen-Schneider LS8-18	M. J. Chapman
	G-CHTR	Grob G.102 Astir CS	I. P. & D. M. Wright
	G-CHTS	Rolladen-Schneider LS8-18	P. T. Cunnison & P. Rowden
	G-CHTN	Schleicher ASW-22	R. C. Hodge
	G-CHTU	Schempp-Hirth Cirrus	Open Cirrus Group
	G-CHTV	Schleicher ASK-21	Cambridge Gliding Club Ltd
	G-CHTY	LET L-13 Blanik	Vectis Gliding Club Ltd
	G-CHUA	Schleicher ASW-19B	G. D. Vaughan
	G-CHUD	Schleicher ASK-13	London Gliding Club Propietary Ltd
	G-CHUE	Schleicher ASW-27	M. J. Smith
	G-CHUF	Schleicher ASK-13	The Welland Gliding Club Ltd
	G-CHUG	Shaw Europa	C. M. Washington
	G-CHUH	Schempp-Hirth Janus	Janus D31 Syndicate
	G-CHUJ	Centrair ASW-20F	P. D. Ruskin
	G-CHUK	Cameron O-77 balloon	R. P. E. Phillips

Reg.	Type	Owner or Operator	Notes
G-CHUL	Schempp-Hirth Cirrus	I. Ashton	
G-CHUN	Grob G.102 Astir CS Jeans	Staffordshire Gliding Club Ltd	
G-CHUO	Federov ME7 Mechta	J. D. A. Cooper & W. H. Ollis	
G-CHUR	Schempp-Hirth Cirrus	M. Rossiter & A. G. Thomas	
G-CHUS	Scheibe SF27A Zugvogel V	SF27 HUS Syndicate	
G-CHUT	Centrair ASW-20F	G. Macfadyen	
G-CHUU	Schleicher ASK-13	Upward Bound Trust	
G-CHUY	Schempp-Hirth Ventus cT	M. A. & M. N. Challans	
G-CHUZ	Schempp-Hirth Discus bT	P. A. Gelsthorpe	
G-CHVF	Rolladen-Schneider LS8-18	J. Haigh & R. B. Coote	
G-CHVG	Schleicher ASK-21	Rattlesden Gliding Club Ltd	
G-CHVH	Pilatus B4-PC11	London Gliding Club Proprietary Ltd	
G-CHVK	Grob G.102 Astir CS	P. G. Goulding	
G-CHVL	Rolladen-Schneider LS8-18	Cumulus Gliding Syndicate	
G-CHVM	Glaser-Dirks DG-300	Glider Syndicate 303	
G-CHVO	Schleicher ASK-13	R. Brown	
G-CHVP	Schleicher ASW-20	P. J. Williams	
G-CHVR	Schempp-Hirth Discus b	Yorkshire Gliding Club (Proprietary) Ltd	
G-CHVT	Schempp-Hirth Ventus 2b	Victor Tango Group	
G-CHVU	Rolladen-Schneider LS8-a	European Soaring Club	
G-CHVV	Rolladen-Schneider LS4-b	A. J. Bardgett	
G-CHUW	Rolladen-Schneider LS8-18	S8 Group	
G-CHVX	Centrair ASW-20F	Banbury Gliding Club Ltd	
G-CHVW	Scleicher ASK-13	Rattlesden Gliding Club Ltd	
G-CHVZ	Schempp-Hirth Standard Cirrus	ABC Soaring	
G-CHWA	Schempp-Hirth Ventus 2c	C. Garton	
G-CHWB	Schempp-Hirth Duo Discus	Lasham Gliding Society Ltd	
G-CHWC	Glasflugel Standard Libelle 201B	Whiskey Charlie Group	
G-CHWF	Jastreb Standard Cirrus G/81	M. D. Langford & M. C. Mann	
G-CHWG	Glasflugel Standard Libelle 201B	M. Kalweit	
G-CHWH	Schempp-Hirth Ventus cT	H. R. Browning	
G-CHWL	Rolladen-Schneider LS8-a	W. M. Coffee	
G-CHWP	Glaser-Dirks DG-100G Elan	D. Procter	
G-CHWS	Rolladen-Schneider LS8-18	G. E. & H. B. Chalmers	
G-CHWT	Schleicher K 8B	Shenington Gliding Club	
G-CHWW	Grob G.103A Twin II Acro	Crown Service Gliding Club	
G-CHWY	Schempp-Hirth Standard Cirrus	D. D. Copeland	
G-CHXA	Scheibe Zugvogel IIIB	G-CHXA Group	
G-CHXB	Grob G.102 Astir CS77	T. S. Miller	
G-CHXD	Schleicher ASW-27	J. Quartermaine & M. Jerman	
G-CHXE	Schleicher ASW-19B	M. J. Hargreaves	
G-CHXH	Schempp-Hirth Discus b	Deeside Gliding Club (Aberdeenshire) Ltd	
G-CHXJ	Schleicher ASK-13	Cotswold Gliding Club	
G-CHXM	Grob G.102 Astir CS	Bristol University Gliding Club	
G-CHXO	Schleicher ASH-25	The Eleven Group	
G-CHXP	Schleicher ASK-13	The Vale of the White Horse Gliding Centre Ltd	
G-CHXR	Schempp-Hirth Ventus cT	560 Group	
G-CHXT	Rolladen-Schneider LS-4a	H. Hingley	
G-CHXU	Schleicher ASW-19B	D. P. Binney	
G-CHXV	Schleicher ASK-13	Aquila Gliding Club Ltd	
G-CHXW	Rolladen-Schneider LS8-18	W. Aspland	
G-CHXX	Schempp-Hirth Standard Cirrus	A. Coatsworth & R. M. Wootten	
G-CHXZ	Rolladen-Schneider LS4	E. J. Foggin	
G-CHYA	Rolladen-Schneider LS6c-18	Y. Melou	
G-CHYD	Schleicher ASW-24	E. S. Adlard	
G-CHYE	DG-505 Elan Orion	The Bristol Gliding Club Proprietary Ltd	
G-CHYF	Rolladen-Schneider LS8-18	R. E. Francis	
G-CHYH	Rolladen-Schneider LS3-17	B. Silke	
G-CHYJ	Schleicher ASK-21	Highland Gliding Club Ltd	
G-CHYK	Centrair ASW-20FL	Yankee Kilo Group	
G-CHYP	PZL-Bielsko SZD-50-3 Puchacz	Rattlesden Gliding Club Ltd	
G-CHYR	Schleicher ASW-27	A. J. Manwaring & A. R. Hutchings	
G-CHYS	Schleicher ASK-21	Army Gliding Association	
G-CHYT	Schleicher ASK-21	Army Gliding Association	
G-CHYU	Schempp-Hirth Discus CS	Army Gliding Association	
G-CHYW	Schleicher K 8B	Lincolnshire Gliding Club Ltd	
G-CHYX	Schleicher K 8B	Oxford University Gliding Club	
G-CHYY	Schempp-Hirth Nimbus 3DT	G-CHYY Syndicate	
G-CHZA	Schempp-Hirth Nimbus 3/24.5	374 Syndicate	
G-CHZB	PZL-Swidnik PW-5 Smyk	The Burn Gliding Club Ltd	
G-CHZD	Schleicher ASW-15B	C. P. Ellison & W. C. Davis	
G-CHZE	Schempp-Hirth Discus CS	HZE Glider Syndicate	

Notes	Reg.	Type	Owner or Operator
	G-CHZG	Rolladen-Schneider LS8-18	M. J. & T. J. Webb
	G-CHZH	Schleicher Ka 6CR	M. E. de Torre
	G-CHZJ	Schempp-Hirth Standard Cirrus	P. Fletcher & R. H. D. Adams
	G-CHZM	Rolladen-Schneider LS4-a	B. Toulson & J. M. Bevan
	G-CHZN	Robinson R22 Beta	Hi-Range Ltd (G-GHZM/G-FENI)
	G-CHZO	Schleicher ASW-27	A. A. Gilmore
	G-CHZR	Schleicher ASK-21	K21 HZR Group
	G-CHZU	Schempp-Hirth Standard Cirrus	N. S. Murning
	G-CHZV	Schempp-Hirth Standard Cirrus	S. M. Sheard
	G-CHZX	Schleicher K 8B	S. M. Chapman & S. Potter
	G-CHZY	Rolladen-Schneider LS4-a	N. P. Wedi
	G-CHZZ	Schleicher ASW-20L	LD Syndicate
	G-CIAO	I.I.I. Sky Arrow 1450-L	G. Arscott
	G-CIAS	BN-2B-21 Islander	Channel Island Air Search Ltd (G-BKJM)
	G-CIBO	Cessna 180K	CIBO Ops Ltd
	G-CIDD	Bellanca 7ECA Citabria	M. J. Medland
	G-CIEL	Cessna 560XL Citation Excel	Enerway Ltd
	G-CIGY	Westland-Bell 47G-3B1	Heli-Highland Ltd (G-BGXP)
	G-CIRI	Cirrus SR20	Cirrus Flyers Group
	G-CIRS	Cirrus SR20	J. McCloskey
	G-CITJ	Cessna 525 CitationJet	Centreline Air Charter Ltd/Bristol
	G-CITY	PA-31-350 Navajo Chieftain	Woodgate Aviation (IOM) Ltd
	G-CIVA	Boeing 747-436	British Airways
	G-CIVB	Boeing 747-436	British Airways
	G-CIVC	Boeing 747-436	British Airways
	G-CIVD	Boeing 747-436	British Airways
	G-CIVE	Boeing 747-436	British Airways
	G-CIVF	Boeing 747-436	British Airways
	G-CIVG	Boeing 747-436	British Airways
	G-CIVH	Boeing 747-436	British Airways
	G-CIVI	Boeing 747-436	British Airways
	G-CIVJ	Boeing 747-436	British Airways
	G-CIVK	Boeing 747-436	British Airways
	G-CIVL	Boeing 747-436	British Airways
	G-CIVM	Boeing 747-436	British Airways
	G-CIVN	Boeing 747-436	British Airways
	G-CIVO	Boeing 747-436	British Airways
	G-CIVP	Boeing 747-436	British Airways
	G-CIVR	Boeing 747-436	British Airways
	G-CIVS	Boeing 747-436	British Airways
	G-CIVT	Boeing 747-436	British Airways
	G-CIVU	Boeing 747-436	British Airways
	G-CIVV	Boeing 747-436	British Airways
	G-CIVW	Boeing 747-436	British Airways
	G-CIVX	Boeing 747-436	British Airways
	G-CIVY	Boeing 747-436	British Airways
	G-CIVZ	Boeing 747-436	British Airways
	G-CIXB	Grob G.109B	G-CIXB Syndicate
	G-CIZZ	Beech 58 Baron	Bonanza Flying Club Ltd
	G-CJAB	Dornier 328-300 JET	Corporate Jet Realisations Ltd
	G-CJAD	Cessna 525 CitationJet	Carisle Bay Ltd
	G-CJAI	P & M Quik GT450	J. C. Kitchen
	G-CJAL	Schleicher Ka 6E	JAL Syndicate
	G-CJAO	Schempp-Hirth Discus b	A. Lyth & J. Weddell
	G-CJAP	Ikarus C42 FB80	J. A. Paley
	G-CJAR	Schempp-Hirth Discus bT	D. G. Maddicks & S. P. Withey
	G-CJAS	Glasflugel Standard Libelle 201B	M. J. Collett
	G-CJAT	Schleicher K8B	Wolds Gliding Club Ltd
	G-CJAV	Schleicher ASK-21	Wolds Gliding Club Ltd
	G-CJAW	Glaser-Dirks DG-200/17	D. J. Blackman
	G-CJAX	Schleicher ASK-21	Wolds Gliding Club Ltd
	G-CJAY	Mainair Pegasus Quik GT450	J. C. Kitchen
	G-CJAZ	Grob G.102 Astir CS Jeans	The Bath, Wilts and North Dorset Gliding Club
	G-CJBB	Rolladen-Schneider LS8-a	C. Bruce
	G-CJBC	PA-28 Cherokee 180	J. B. Cave
	G-CJBH	Eiriavion PIK-20D	537 Syndicate
	G-CJBJ	Schempp-Hirth Standard Cirrus	S. T. Dutton
	G-CJBK	Schleicher ASW-19B	D. Caielli & P. Sharpe
	G-CJBM	Schleicher ASK-21	Midland Gliding Club Ltd
	G-CJBO	Rolladen-Schneider LS8-18	L7 Syndicate
	G-CJBR	Schempp-Hirth Discus b	G-CJBR Group

Reg.	Type	Owner or Operator	Notes
G-CJBS	AB Sportine LAK-12	Bravo Sierra Bigwigs Flying Group	
G-CJBT	Schleicher ASW-19B	G. Dennis	
G-CJBW	Schempp-Hirth Discus bT	G-CJBW Syndicate	
G-CJBX	Rolladen-Schneider LS4-a	P. W. Lee & P. A. Ivens	
G-CJBY	AB Sportine LAK-12	P. G. Steggles & N. Clarke	
G-CJCA	Schleicher ASW-15B	S. Briggs	
G-CJCC	Cessna 680 Citation Sovereign	Viking Airways Ltd	
G-CJCD	Schleicher ASW-24	M. D. Evershed	
G-CJCF	Grob G.102 Astir CS77	The Northumbria Gliding Club Ltd	
G-CJCG	PZL-Swidnik PW-5 Smyk	M. Evans & T. J Wallace	
G-CJCJ	Schempp-Hirth Standard Cirrus	R. Johnson & R. Carter	
G-CJCK	Schempp-Hirth Discus bT	P. J. Tiller & T. Wright	
G-CJCM	Schleicher ASW-27	J. R. Klunder & K. E. Singer	
G-CJCN	Schempp-Hirth Standard Cirrus 75	S. C. J. Barker	
G-CJCT	Schempp-Hirth Nimbus 4T	D. S. Innes	
G-CJCU	Schempp-Hirth Standard Cirrus B	R. A. Davenport	
G-CJCW	Grob G.102 Astir CS77	N. G. Smith	
G-CJCX	Schempp-Hirth Discus bT	C. W. M. Claxton	
G-CJCY	Rolladen-Schneider LS8-18	R. Zaccour	
G-CJCZ	Schleicher Ka 6CR	N. Barnes	
G-CJDB	Cessna 525 Citationjet	Breed Aircraft Ltd	
G-CJDC	Schleicher ASW-27	J. J. Marshall	
G-CJDD	Glaser-Dirks DG-200/17	Juliet Delta Delta Group	
G-CJDE	Rolladen-Schneider LS8-18	B. Kerby & M. Davies	
G-CJDF	Schleicher ASH-25E	522 Syndicate	
G-CJDG	Rolladen-Schneider LS6-b	R. H. & A. Moss	
G-CJDJ	Rolladen-Schneider LS3	J. C. Burdett	
G-CJDK	Rolladen-Schneider LS8-18	B. Bredenbeck	
G-CJDM	Schleicher ASW-15B	C. J. H. Donnelly	
G-CJDN	Cameron C-90 balloon	N. Ivison	
G-CJDP	Glaser-Dirks DG-200/17	The Owners of JDP	
G-CJDR	Schleicher ASW-15	M. J. Waters	
G-CJDS	Schempp-Hirth Standard Cirrus 75	P. Nicholls	
G-CJDT	Rolladen-Schneider LS8-a	H. A. Rebbeck	
G-CJDU	LET L-13 Blanik	Herefordshire Gliding Club Ltd	
G-CJDV	DG Flugzeugbau DG-300 Elan Acro	J. M. Gilbey & B. D. Michael	
G-CJDX	Wassmer WA-28	R. Hutchinson	
G-CJDY	Rolladen-Schneider LS8-18	P. O. R. Paterson	
G-CJDZ	Schempp-Hirth Nimbus 4T	P. J. Harvey	
G-CJEA	Rolladen-Schneider LS8-18	D. J. Westwood & R. I. Davidson	
G-CJEB	Schleicher ASW-24	P. C. Scholz	
G-CJEC	PZL-Bielsko SZD-50-3 Puchasz	Cambridge Gliding Club Ltd	
G-CJED	Schempp-Hirth Nimbus 3/24.5	J. Edyvean	
G-CJEE	Schleicher ASW-20L	B. Pridgeon	
G-CJEH	Glasflugel Mosquito B	M. J. Vickery	
G-CJEL	Schleicher ASW-24	N. K. Shepherd & S. J. Lintott	
G-CJEM	Schempp-Hirth Duo Discus	Duo Discus 572 Flying Group	
G-CJEP	Rolladen-Schneider LS4-b	C. F. Carter & N. Backes	
G-CJER	Schempp-Hirth Standard Cirrus 75	Cirrus Group	
G-CJEU	Glasflugel Standard Libelle	D. B. Johns	
G-CJEV	Schempp-Hirth Standard Cirrus	E. Perrin & G. F. C. King	
G-CJEW	Schleicher Ka 6CR	CJEW Syndicate	
G-CJEX	Schempp-Hirth Ventus 2a	D. S. Watt	
G-CJEZ	Glaser-Dirks DG-100	R. Kehr	
G-CJFA	Schempp-Hirth Standard Cirrus	P. M. Sheahan	
G-CJFC	Schempp-Hirth Discus CS	RAF Gliding and Soaring Association	
G-CJFE	Schempp-Hirth Janus CE	RAF Gliding and Soaring Association	
G-CJFH	Schempp-Hirth Duo Discus	RAF Gliding and Soaring Association	
G-CJFJ	Schleicher ASW-20CL	R. J. Stirk	
G-CJFK	Schleicher ASW-20L	D. Holt	
G-CJFM	Schleicher ASK-13	Darlton Gliding Club Ltd	
G-CJFR	Schempp-Hirth Ventus cT	L. Rayment, D. Ryall & D. W. Smith	
G-CJFT	Schleicher K-8B	The Surrey Hills Gliding Club Ltd	
G-CJFU	Schleicher ASW-19B	M. T. Stanley	
G-CJFX	Rolladen-Schneider LS8-a	P. E. Baker	
G-CJFZ	Fedorov ME7 Mechta	R. J. Colbourne	
G-CJGB	Schleicher K 8B	Richard Walker and Partners	
G-CJGD	Scleicher K 8B	R. E. Pettifer & C. A. McLay	
G-CJGE	Schleicher ASK-21	M. R. Wall	
G-CJGF	Schempp-Hirth Ventus c	J.G. Fisher	
G-CJGG	P & M Quik GT450	J. M. Pearce	
G-CJGH	Schempp-Hirth Nimbus 2C	G-CJGH Syndicate	

Notes	Reg.	Type	Owner or Operator
	G-CJGJ	Schleicher ASK-21	Midland Gliding Club Ltd
	G-CJGK	Eiri PIL-200	The Four Aces
	G-CJGL	Schempp-Hirth Discus CS	RAF Gliding and Soaring Association
	G-CJGM	Schempp-Hirth Discus CS	RAF Gliding and Soaring Association
	G-CJGN	Schempp-Hirth Standard Cirrus	P. A. Shuttleworth
	G-CJGR	Schempp-Hirth Discus bT	S. P. Wareham & D. A. Smith
	G-CJGS	Rolladen-Schneider LS8-18	T. Stupnik
	G-CJGU	Schempp-Hirth Mini-Nimbus B	N. D. Ashton
	G-CJGW	Schleicher ASK-13	Darlton Gliding Club Ltd
	G-CJGX	Schleicher K 8B	Andreas K8 Group
	G-CJGY	Schempp-Hirth Standard Cirrus	P. J. Shout
	G-CJGZ	Glasflugel Standard Libelle 201B	C. J. Davison
	G-CJHD	Schleicher Ka 6E	W. Kilroy & C. Sinclair
	G-CJHE	Astir CS77	Aero Club de Portugal
	G-CJHG	Grob G.102 Astir CS	P. L. E. Zelazowski
	G-CJHJ	Glasflugel Standard Libelle 201B	G-CJHJ Group
	G-CJHK	Schleicher K8B	Stratford on Avon Gliding Club Ltd
	G-CJHL	Schleicher Ka 6E	M. R. Doran & J. R. Gilbert
	G-CJHM	Schempp-Hirth Discus b	J. C. Thwaites
	G-CJHN	Grob G.102 Astir CS Jeans	A. M. Percival & J. C. Hurne
	G-CJHO	Schleicher ASK-18	RAF Gliding and Soaring Association
	G-CJHP	Flight Design CTSW	S. J. Reader
	G-CJHR	Centrair SNC34C Alliance	The Borders (Milfield) Gliding Club Ltd
	G-CJHS	Schleicher ASW-19B	JHS Syndicate
	G-CJHU	Rolladen-Schneider LS8-18	S. P. Ball
	G-CJHW	Glaser-Dirks DG-200	A. W. Thornhill & S. Webster
	G-CJHX	Bolkow Phoebus C	J. Hewitt
	G-CJHY	Rolladen-Schneider LS8-18	L. E. N. Tanner & N. Wall
	G-CJHZ	Schleicher ASW-20	T. J. Stanley
	G-CJJB	Rolladen-Schneider LS4	M. Tomlinson
	G-CJJD	Schempp-Hirth Discus bT	C. E. Turner & D. Wilson
	G-CJJE	Schempp-Hirth Discus a	A. Soffici
	G-CJJF	Schleicher ASW-27	G. F. Read
	G-CJJH	DG Flugzeugbau DG-800S	J. S. Weston
	G-CJJJ	Schempp-Hirth Standard Cirrus	R. McLuckie
	G-CJJK	Rolladen-Schneider LS8-18	A. D. Roch
	G-CJJL	Schleicher ASW-19B	G-CJJL Group
	G-CJJP	Schempp-Hirth Duo Discus	N. Clements
	G-CJJT	Schleicher ASW-27	Portsmouth Naval Gliding Centre
	G-CJJU	Rolladen-Schneider LS8-a	A. J. French
	G-CJJX	Schleicher ASW-15B	STJ Syndicate
	G-CJJZ	Schempp-Hirth Discus bT	S. J. C. Parker
	G-CJKA	Schleicher ASK-21	East Sussex Gliding Club Ltd
	G-CJKB	PZL-Swidnik PW-5 Smyk	J. C. Gibson
	G-CJKD	Rolladen-Schneider LS8-18	D. Abbey & G. Glover
	G-CJKE	PZL-Swidnik PW-5 Smyk	The Burn Gliding Club Ltd
	G-CJKF	Glaser-Dirks DG-200	D. O. Sandells & R. K. Stafford
	G-CJKG	Schleicher ASK-18	RAF Gliding and Soaring Association
	G-CJKJ	Schleicher ASK-21	RAF Gliding and Soaring Association
	G-CJKK	Schleicher ASK-21	Army Gliding Association
	G-CJKM	Glaser-Dirks DG200/17	E. W. Russell
	G-CJKN	Rolladen-Schneider LS8-18	D. A. Booth
	G-CJKO	Schleicher ASK-21	RAF Gliding and Soaring Association
	G-CJKP	Rolladen-Schneider LS4-b	D. M. Hope
	G-CJKS	Schleicher ASW-19B	R. J. P. Lancaster & P. D. F. Adshead
	G-CJKT	Schleicher ASK-13	RAF Gliding and Soaring Association
	G-CJKU	Schleicher ASK-18	RAF Gliding and Soaring Association
	G-CJKV	Grob G.103A Twin II Acro	The Welland Gliding Club Ltd
	G-CJKW	Grob G.102 Astir CS77	The Bath, Wilts and North Dorset Gliding Club Ltd
	G-CJKX	Schempp-Hirth Discus B	A. R. Armstrong
	G-CJKY	Schempp-Hirth Ventus cT	G. V. Matthews & M. P. Osborn
	G-CJKZ	Schleicher ASK-21	RAF Gliding and Soaring Association
	G-CJLA	Schempp-Hirth Ventus 2cT	E. C. & P. M. Neighbour
	G-CJLC	Schempp-Hirth Discus CS	RAF Gliding and Soaring Association
	G-CJLF	Schleicher ASK-13	Army Gliding Association
	G-CJLG	PZL-Bielsko SZD-51-1 Junior	Army Gliding Association
	G-CJLH	Rolladen-Schneider LS4	JLH Syndicate
	G-CJLJ	Rolladen-Schneider LS4-b	Army Gliding Association
	G-CJLK	Rolladen-Schneider LS7	D. N. Munro & S. G. Hamilton
	G-CJLL	Robinson R44 II	AT and P Rentals Ltd
	G-CJLN	Rolladen-Schneider LS8-18	RAF Gliding and Soaring Association
	G-CJLO	Schleicher ASK-13	Bowland Forest Gliding Club Ltd

Reg.	Type	Owner or Operator	Notes
G-CJLP	Schempp-Hirth Discus CS	RAF Gliding and Soaring Association	
G-CJLR	Grob G.102 Astir CS	RAF Gliding and Soaring Association	
G-CJLS	Schleicher K-8B	RAF Gliding and Soaring Association	
G-CJLV	Schleicher Ka 6E	J. M. & J. C. Cooper	
G-CJLW	Schempp-Hirth Discus CS	RAF Gliding and Soaring Association	
G-CJLY	Schleicher ASW-27	L. M. Astle & P. C. Piggott	
G-CJLZ	Grob G.103A Twin II Acro	21 Syndicate	
G-CJMA	Schleicher ASK-18	RAF Gliding and Soaring Association	
G-CJMD	Embraer RJ135BJ	Corporate Jet Management Ltd	
G-CJMG	PZL-Bielsko SZD-51-1 Junior	Kent Gliding Club Ltd	
G-CJMH	Schempp-Hirth Standard Cirrus	J. Van Der Hoek & J. G Walker	
G-CJMJ	Schleicher ASK-13	RAF Gliding and Soaring Association	
G-CJMK	Schleicher ASK-18	RAF Gliding and Soaring Association	
G-CJML	Grob G.102 Astir CS77	RAF Gliding and Soaring Association	
G-CJMN	Schempp-Hirth Nimbus 2	R. A. Holroyd	
G-CJMO	Rolladen-Schneider LS8-18	D. J. Langrick	
G-CJMP	Schleicher ASK-13	East Sussex Gliding Club Ltd	
G-CJMR	Rolladen-Schneider LS8-18	J. N. Rebbeck	
G-CJMS	Schleicher ASK-21	RAF Gliding and Soaring Association	
G-CJMT	Rolladen-Schneider LS8-18	D. P. & K. M. Draper	
G-CJMU	Rolladen-Schneider LS8-18	G-CJMU Group	
G-CJMV	Schempp-Hirth Nimbus-2C	G. Tucker & K. R. Walton	
G-CJMW	Schleicher ASK-13	RAF Gliding and Soaring Association	
G-CJMX	Schleicher ASK-13	Shalbourne Soaring Society Ltd	
G-CJMY	PZL-Bielsko SZD-51-1 Junior	Highland Gliding Club Ltd	
G-CJMZ	Schleicher ASK-13	RAF Gliding and Soaring Association	
G-CJNA	Grob G.102 Astir CS Jeans	Shenington Gliding Club	
G-CJNB	Rolladen-Schneider LS8-18	Tatenhill Aviation Ltd	
G-CJNE	Schempp-Hirth Discus 2a	R. Priest	
G-CJNF	Schempp-Hirth Discus 2a	H. Hay	
G-CJNG	Glasflugel Standard Libelle 201B	C. A. Willson	
G-CJNJ	Rolladen-Schneider LS8-18	A. B. Laws	
G-CJNK	Rolladen-Schneider LS8-18	Army Gliding Association	
G-CJNM	Rolladen-Schneider LS8-18	M. H. Patel & P. Onn	
G-CJNN	Schleicher K 8B	Buckminster Gliding Club Ltd	
G-CJNO	Glaser-Dirks DG-300 Elan	Yankee Kilo Group	
G-CJNP	Rolladen-Schneider LS6-b	P. S. Fink	
G-CJNR	Glasflugel Mosquito B	S. L. Barnes & C. R. North	
G-CJNT	Schleicher ASW-19B	M. D. Borrowdale	
G-CJNX	LET L-13 Blanik	Vectis Gliding Club Ltd	
G-CJNZ	Glaser-Dirks DG-100	T. Tordoff & R. Jones	
G-CJOA	Schempp-Hirth Discus b	RAF Gliding and Soaring Association	
G-CJOB	Schleicher K 8B	JQB Syndicate	
G-CJOC	Schempp-Hirth Discus bT	287 Syndicate	
G-CJOD	Rolladen-Schneider LS8-18	RAF Gliding and Soaring Association	
G-CJOE	Schempp-Hirth Standard Cirrus	P. T. Johnson	
G-CJOG	Grob G.103A Twin II Acro	Acro Syundicate	
G-CJOH	AB Sportine LAK-12 Lietuva	J. M. Sherman	
G-CJOJ	Schleicher K 8B	P. W. Burgess	
G-CJON	Grob G.102 Astir CS77	RAF Gliding and Soaring Association	
G-CJOO	Schempp-Hirth Duo Discus	185 Syndicate	
G-CJOP	Centrair 101A Pegase	P. A. Woodcock	
G-CJOR	Schempp-Hirth Ventus 2cT	A. M. George & N. A. Maclean	
G-CJOS	Schempp-Hirth Standard Cirrus	G-CJOS Group	
G-CJOU	AB Sportline Aviacija LAK-17A	B. Dorozko	
G-CJOV	Schleicher ASW-27	J. W. White	
G-CJOW	Schempp-Hirth Cirrus VTC	North Wales Gliding Club Ltd	
G-CJOX	Schleicher ASK-21	Southdown Gliding Club Ltd	
G-CJOZ	Schleicher K 8B	Derbyshire and Lancashire Gliding Club Ltd	
G-CJPA	Schempp-Hirth Duo Discus	Coventry Gliding Club Ltd	
G-CJPC	Schleicher ASK-13	Shalbourne Soaring Society Ltd	
G-CJPH	Rolladen-Schneider LS8-18	R. E. D. Bailey	
G-CJPJ	Grob G.104 Speed Astir IIB	R. J. L. Maisonpierre	
G-CJPL	Rolladen-Schneider LS8-18	I. A. Reekie	
G-CJPM	Grob G.102 Astir CS Jeans	G-CJPM Syndicate	
G-CJPO	Schleicher ASK-18	RAF Gliding and Soaring Association	
G-CJPP	Schempp-Hirth Discus b	Scottish Gliding Union Ltd	
G-CJPR	Rolladen-Schneider LS8-18	D. M. Byass & J. A. McCoshim	
G-CJPT	Schleicher ASW-27	R. C. Willis-Fleming	
G-CJPV	Schleicher ASK-13	RAF Gliding and Soaring Association	
G-CJPW	Glaser-Dirks DG-200	J. R. Parr	
G-CJPX	Schleicher ASW-15	R. Hayden & P. Daly	

Notes	Reg.	Type	Owner or Operator
	G-CJPY	Schleicher ASK-13	RAF Gliding and Soaring Association
	G-CJPZ	Schleicher ASK-18	RAF Gliding and Soaring Association
	G-CJRA	Rolladen-Schneider LS8-18	J. Williams
	G-CJRB	Schleicher ASW-19B	S33 Syndicate
	G-CJRC	Glaser-Dirks DG-300 Elan	P. J. Sillett
	G-CJRD	Grob G.102 Astir CS	A. J. Hadwin & S. J. Kape
	G-CJRE	Scleicher ASW-15	R. A. Starling
	G-CJRF	PZL-Bielsko SZD-50-3 Puchacz	Wolds Gliding Club Ltd
	G-CJRG	Schempp-Hirth Standard Cirrus	N. J. Laux
	G-CJRH	Schleicher ASW-27	C. Jackson & P. C. Jarvis
	G-CJRJ	PZL-Bielsko SZD-50-3 Puchacz	Derbyshire & Lancashire Gliding Club Ltd
	G-CJRL	Glaser-Dirks DG-100G Elan	P. Lazenby
	G-CJRM	Grob G.102 Astir CS	M. Spittal
	G-CJRN	Glaser-Dirks DG-200/17	T. G. Roberts
	G-CJRR	Schempp-Hirth Discus bT	N. A. Hays
	G-CJRT	Schempp-Hirth Standard Cirrus	JRT Syndicate
	G-CJRU	Schleicher ASW-24	S. A. Kerby
	G-CJRV	Schleicher ASW-19B	M. Roome
	G-CJRX	Schleicher ASK-13	RAF Gliding and Soaring Association
	G-CJSA	Nanchang NAMC CJ-6A	Bogaerts Aviation BVBA
	G-CJSC	Schempp-Hirth Nimbus-3DT	S. G. Jones
	G-CJSD	Grob G.102 Astir CS	RAF Gliding and Soaring Association
	G-CJSE	Schempp-Hirth Discus b	Imperial College of Science, Technology and Medicine
	G-CJSG	Schleicher Ka 6E	A. J. Emck
	G-CJSH	Grob G.102 Club Astir IIIB	Lasham Gliding Society Ltd
	G-CJSJ	Rolladen-Schneider LS7-WL	S. P. Woolcock
	G-CJSK	Grob G.102 Astir CS	Sierra Kilo Group
	G-CJSL	Schempp-Hirth Ventus cT	D. Latimer
	G-CJSN	Schleicher K 8B	Cotswold Gliding Club
	G-CJSS	Schleicher ASW-27	G. K. & S. R. Drury
	G-CJST	Rolladen-Schneider LS1-c	W. A. Bowness & E. Richar
	G-CJSU	Rolladen-Schneider LS8-18	J. G. Bell
	G-CJSV	Schleicher ASK-13	RAF Gliding and Soaring Association
	G-CJSW	Rolladen-Schneider LS4-a	C. Benoit
	G-CJSX	AMS-Flight DG-500	Oxford Gliding Company Ltd
	G-CJSZ	Schleicher ASK-18	C. Weston
	G-CJTB	Schleicher ASW-24	V17 Syndicate
	G-CJTF	Schleicher ASW-27	T. J. Scott
	G-CJTH	Schleicher ASW-24	R. J. & J. E. Lodge
	G-CJTJ	Schempp-Hirth Mini-Nimbus B	A. Richards
	G-CJTK	DG Flugzeugbau DG-300 Elan Acro	A. Jorgensen
	G-CJTL	Rolladen-Schneider LS8-18	L. S., J. M. & R. S. Hood
	G-CJTM	Rolladen-Schneider LS8-18	A. D. Holmes
	G-CJTN	Glaser-Dirks DG-300 Elan	A. D. Noble & P. W. Schartau
	G-CJTO	Glasflugel H303A Mosquito	Tango Oscar Group
	G-CJTP	Schleicher ASW-20L	C. A. Sheldon
	G-CJTR	Rolladen-Schneider LS7-WL	D53 Syndicate
	G-CJTS	Schempp-Hirth Cirrus VTC	G-CJTS Cirrus Group
	G-CJTU	Schempp-Hirth Duo Discus T	G-CJTU Syndicate
	G-CJTW	Glasflugel Mosquito B	S. Urry
	G-CJTY	Rolladen-Schneider LS8-a	BBC (London) Club
	G-CJUB	Schempp-Hirth Discus CS	Coventry Gliding Club Ltd
	G-CJUD	Denney Kitfox Mk 3	P. J. And B-J Chandler
	G-CJUF	Schempp-Hirth Ventus 2cT	M. H. B. Pope
	G-CJUG	Issoire E78B Silene	J. M. Sanders
	G-CJUH	Schleicher ASW-27	R. A. Johnson
	G-CJUJ	Schleicher ASW-27	P. A. Ivens
	G-CJUK	Grob G.102 Astir CS	P. Freer & S. J. Calvert
	G-CJUM	Schempp-Hirth Duo Discus T	2 UP Group
	G-CJUN	Schleicher ASW-19B	M. P. S. Roberts
	G-CJUP	Schempp-Hirth Discus 2b	The Discuss 2 Uniform papa group
	G-CJUR	Valentin Mistral C	Essex Gliding Trust Ltd
	G-CJUS	Grob G.102 Astir CS	East Sussex Gliding Club Ltd
	G-CJUU	Schempp-Hirth Standard Cirrus	H. R. Fraser
	G-CJUV	Schempp-Hirth Discus b	Lasham Gliding Society Ltd
	G-CJUX	Aviastroitel AC-4C	R. J. Walton
	G-CJUZ	Schleicher ASW-19B	K. W. Clarke
	G-CJVA	Schempp-Hirth Ventus 2cT	M. S. Armstrong
	G-CJVB	Schempp-Hirth Discus bT	C. J. Edwards
	G-CJVC	PZL-Bielsko SZD-51-1 Junior	York Gliding Centre Ltd
	G-CJVE	Eiriavion PIK-20D	S. R. Wilkinson

Reg.	Type	Owner or Operator	Notes
G-CJVF	Schempp-Hirth Discus CS	J. Hodgson	
G-CJVG	Schempp-Hirth Discus bT	S. J. Bryan & P. J. Bramley	
G-CJVJ	AB Sportine LAK-17A	J. A. Sutton	
G-CJVL	DG-300 Elan	A. T. Vidion & A. Griffiths	
G-CJVM	Schleicher ASW-27	G. K. Payne	
G-CJVP	Glaser-Dirks DG-200	M. S. Howey & S. Leadbeater	
G-CJVS	Schleicher ASW-28	Zulu Glasstek Ltd	
G-CJVU	Standard Cirrus CS-11-75L	Cirrus 75 Syndicate	
G-CJVV	Schempp-Hirth Janus C	G. Jenkins & G. Smith	
G-CJVW	Schleicher ASW-15	C. F.McGinn & E. Hawke	
G-CJVX	Schempp-Hirth Discus CS	G-CJVX Syndicate	
G-CJVZ	Schleicher ASK-21	Yorkshire Gliding Club (Proprietary) Ltd	
G-CJWA	Schleicher ASW-28	P. R. Porter & M. J. Taylor	
G-CJWB	Schleicher ASK-13	East Sussex Gliding Club Ltd	
G-CJWD	Schleicher ASK-21	London Gliding Club Proprietary Ltd	
G-CJWF	Schleicher ASW-27	B. A. Fairston & A. Stotter	
G-CJWG	Schempp-Hirth Nimbus 3	880 Group	
G-CJWJ	Schleicher ASK-13	RAF Gliding and Soaring Association	
G-CJWK	Schempp-Hirth Discus bT	722 Syndicate	
G-CJWM	Grob G.103 Twin Astir II	Norfolk Gliding Club Ltd	
G-CJWP	Bolkow Phoebus B1	A. Fidler	
G-CJWR	Grob G.102 Astir CS	Cairngorn Gliding Club	
G-CJWT	Glaser-Dirks DG-200	K. R. Nash	
G-CJWU	Schempp-Hirth Ventus bT	G. Tabbner	
G-CJWX	Schempp-Hirth Ventus 2cT	S. G. Olender	
G-CJXA	Schempp-Hirth Nimbus 3	Y44 Syndicate	
G-CJXB	Centrair 201B Marianne	Marianne Syndicate	
G-CJXC	Wassmer WA28	A. P. Montague	
G-CJXG	Eiriavion PIK-20D	D. Ingledew, N. Clark & S. Ingason	
G-CJXL	Schempp-Hirth Discus CS	J. Hall & M. J. Hasluck	
G-CJXM	Schleicher ASK-13	The Windrushers Gliding Club	
G-CJXN	Centrair 201B	R. D. Trussell	
G-CJXP	Glaser-Dirks DG-100	T. M. Bell	
G-CJXR	Schempp-Hirth Discus b	Cambridge Gliding Club Ltd	
G-CJXT	Schleicher ASW-24B	P. McAuley	
G-CJXW	Schempp-Hirth Duo Discus T	R. A. Beatty	
G-CJXX	Pilatus B4-PC11AF	N. H. Buckenham	
G-CJXY	Neukom Elfe S4A	J. Hunt	
G-CJYC	Grob G.102 Astir CS	R. A. Christie	
G-CJYD	Schleicher ASW-27	J. E. Gatfield	
G-CJYE	Schleicher ASK-13	North Wales Gliding Club Ltd	
G-CJYF	Schempp Hirth Discus CS	W. J. Winthrop	
G-CJYL	AB Sportine Aviacija LAK-12	A. Camerotto	
G-CJYO	Glaser-Dirks DG-100G Elan	A. M. Booth	
G-CJYP	Grob G.102 Club Astir II	Astir Syndicate BGA4891	
G-CJYR	Schempp-Hirth Duo Discus T	G-CJYR Group	
G-CJYS	Schempp-Hirth Mini Nimbus C	A. Jenkins	
G-CJYU	Schempp-Hirth Ventus 2cT	RAF Gliding and Soaring Association	
G-CJYX	Rolladen-Schneider LS3-17	D. Meyer-Beeck & V. G. Diaz	
G-CJZB	DG-500 Elan Orion	Bicester JZB Syndicate	
G-CJZE	Schleicher ASK-13	Needwood Forest Gliding Club Ltd	
G-CJZG	Schempp-Hirth Discus bT	R. H. C. Acreman	
G-CJZH	Schleicher ASW-20 CL	C. P. Gibson & C. A. Hunt	
G-CJZK	DG-505 Elan Orion	Devon and Somerset Gliding Club Ltd	
G-CJZL	Schempp-Hirth Mini Nimbus B	S. J. Aldridge	
G-CJZM	Schempp-Hirth Ventus 2a	S. Crabb	
G-CJZN	Schleicher ASW-28	P. J. Coward	
G-CJZY	Grob G.102 Standard Astir III	Lasham Gliding Society Ltd	
G-CJZZ	Rolladen-Schneider LS7	J. H. Tucker	
G-CKAC	Glaser-Dirks DG-200	C. Morton-Fincham	
G-CKAE	Centrair 101A Pegase	Rattlesden Gliding Club Ltd	
G-CKAK	Schleicher ASW-28	S. J. Kelman	
G-CKAL	Schleicher ASW-28	D. A. Smith & P. A. Ivens	
G-CKAM	Glasflugel Club Libelle 205	P. A. Cronk & R. C. Tallowin	
G-CKAN	PZL-Bielsko SZD-50-3 Puchacz	The Bath Wilts and North Dorset Gliding Club Ltd	
G-CKAP	Schempp-Hirth Discus CS	KAP Syndicate	
G-CKAR	Schempp-Hirth Duo Discus T	977 Syndicate	
G-CKAS	Schempp-Hirth Ventus 2cT	KAS Club	
G-CKAU	DG Flugzeugbau DG-303 Elan Acro	G. Earle	
G-CKAV	Rolladen-Schneider LS4-a	A. J. Cockerell	
G-CKAW	AMS-Flight DG-505 Elan	Midland Gliding Club Ltd	

Notes	Reg.	Type	Owner or Operator
	G-CKAX	AMS-Flight DG-500 Elan Orion	York Gliding Centre Ltd
	G-CKAY	Grob G.102 Astir CS	D. Ryder & P. Carrington
	G-CKBA	Centrair 101A Pegase	KBA Pegase 101A Syndicate
	G-CKBC	Rolladen-Schneider LS6-c	M. Schlotter
	G-CKBD	Grob G.102 Astir CS	R. A. Morriss
	G-CKBF	AMS-Flight DG-303 Elan	A. L. Garfield
	G-CKBG	Schempp-Hirth Ventus 2cT	71 Syndicate
	G-CKBH	Rolladen-Schneider LS6	F. C. Ballard & P. Walker
	G-CKBK	Schempp-Hirth Ventus 2cT	D. Rhys-Jones
	G-CKBL	Grob G.102 Astir CS	Norfolk Gliding Club Ltd
	G-CKBM	Schleicher ASW-28	C. S. & M. E. Newland-Smith
	G-CKBN	PZL-Bielsko SZD-55-1 Promyk	N. D. Pearson
	G-CKBS	Glaser-Dirks DG-600	C. R. R. Audissou
	G-CKBT	Schempp-Hirth Standard Cirrus	P. R. Johnson
	G-CKBU	Schleicher ASW-28	G. C. Metcalfe
	G-CKBV	Schleicher ASW-28	P. Whipp
	G-CKBX	Schleicher ASW-27	M. Wright & T. J. Davies
	G-CKCB	Rolladen-Schneider LS4-a	The Bristol Gliding Club Proprietary Ltd
	G-CKCD	Schempp-Hirth Ventus 2cT	R. S. Jobar & S. G. Jones
	G-CKCE	Schempp-Hirth Ventus 2cT	M. W. Cater & J. P. Walker
	G-CKCH	Schempp-Hirth Ventus 2cT	J. J. Pridal & L. R. Marks
	G-CKCJ	Schleicher ASW-28	S. L. Withall
	G-CKCK	Enstrom 280FX	Rhoburt Ltd
	G-CKCM	Glasflugel Standard Libelle 201B	G. A. Cox
	G-CKCN	Schleicher ASW-27	W. J. Head
	G-CKCP	Grob G.102 Astir CS	Norfolk Gliding Club Ltd
	G-CKCR	AB Sportine Aviacija LAK-17A	L. Bertoncini/Italy
	G-CKCT	Schleicher ASK-21	Kent Gliding Club Aircraft Ltd
	G-CKCV	Schempp-Hirth Duo Discus T	WE4 Group
	G-CKCW	Glaser-Dirks DG200/17	R. W. Adamson & K. A. B. Morgan
	G-CKCY	Schleicher ASW-20	A. J. Wilson & S. R. Tromans
	G-CKCZ	Schleicher ASK-21	Booker Gliding Club Ltd
	G-CKDA	Schempp-Hirth Ventus 2B	D. J. Eade
	G-CKDB	Schleicher Ka 6CR	Banbury Gliding Club Ltd
	G-CKDC	Centrair ASW-20F	M. Staljan, S. Brogger & C. Behrendt
	G-CKDF	Schleicher ASK-21	Portsmouth Naval Gliding Centre
	G-CKDH	Schleicher K-8B	Midland Gliding Club Ltd
	G-CKDK	Rolladen-Schneider LS4-a	M. C. & P. A. Ridger
	G-CKDN	Schleicher ASW-27B	J. S. McCullagh
	G-CKDO	Schempp-Hirth Ventus 2cT	M. W. Edwards
	G-CKDP	Schleicher ASK-21	Kent Gliding Club Aircraft Ltd
	G-CKDR	PZL-Bielsko SZD-48-3 Jantar Standard 3	G. Hyrkowski
	G-CKDS	Schleicher ASW-27	A. W. Gillett & G. D. Morris
	G-CKDU	Glaser-Dirks DG-200/17	P. G. Noonan
	G-CKDV	Schempp-Hirth Ventus B/16.6	M. A. Codd
	G-CKDW	Schleicher ASW-27	C. Colton
	G-CKDX	Glaser-Dirks DG-200	Delta X Ray Group
	G-CKDY	Glaser-Dirks DG-100	503 Group
	G-CKDZ	Schempp-Hirth Standard Cirrus 75	Charlie 75
	G-CKEA	Schempp-Hirth Cirrus 18	C. M. Reed
	G-CKEB	Schempp-Hirth Standard Cirrus	A. J. Mugleston
	G-CKED	Schleicher ASW-27B	M. H. Bull
	G-CKEE	Grob G.102 Astir CS	Essex and Suffolk Gliding Club Ltd
	G-CKEJ	Schleicher ASK-21	London Gliding Club Proprietary Ltd
	G-CKEK	Schleicher ASK-21	Devon and Somerset Gliding Club Ltd
	G-CKEM	Robinson R44	True Course Helicopter Ltd
	G-CKEP	Rolladen-Schneider LS6-b	T. W. M. Beck
	G-CKER	Schleicher ASW-19B	G-CKER Syndicate
	G-CKES	Schempp-Hirth Cirrus 18	D. Judd & N. Hawley
	G-CKET	Rolladen-Schneider LS8-8	M. B. Jefferyes & J. C. Taylor
	G-CKEV	Schempp-Hirth Duo Discus	RAF Gliding and Soaring Association
	G-CKEY	PA-28-161 Warrior II	Warwickshire Aviation Ltd
	G-CKEZ	DG Flugzeugbau LS8	D. A. Jesty
	G-CKFA	Schempp-Hirth Standard Cirrus 75	C. F. Jordan
	G-CKFB	Schempp-Hirth Discus-2T	P. L. & P. A. G. Holland
	G-CKFC	Schempp-Hirth Ventus 2cT	P. Lecci
	G-CKFD	Schleicher ASW-27B	W. T. Craig
	G-CKFE	Eiriavion PIK-20D	M. J. McSorley
	G-CKFG	Grob G.103A Twin II Acro	The Surrey Hills Gliding Club Ltd
	G-CKFH	Schempp-Hirth Mini Nimbus	G-CKFH Flying Group
	G-CKFJ	Schleicher ASK-13	York Gliding Centre Ltd
	G-CKFK	Schempp-Hirth Standard Cirrus 75	P. R. Wilkinson

Reg.	Type	Owner or Operator	Notes
G-CKFL	Rolladen-Schneider LS4	D. O'Brien & D. R. Taylor	
G-CKFM	Rolladen-Schneider LS8-18	A. J. H. Smith	
G-CKFN	DG Flugzeugbau DG1000	Yorkshire Gliding Club (Proprietary) Ltd	
G-CKFP	Schempp-Hirth Ventus 2cxT	C. R. Sutton	
G-CKFR	Schleicher ASK-13	Club Acrupacion de Pilotos del Sureste/Spain	
G-CKFT	Schempp-Hirth Duo Discus T	Duo Discus Syndicate	
G-CKFV	DG Flugzeugbau LS8-t	G. A. Rowden & K. I. Arkley	
G-CKFY	Schleicher ASK.21	Cambridge Gliding Club	
G-CKGA	Schempp-Hirth Ventus 2cxT	D. R. Campbell	
G-CKGB	Schempp-Hirth Ventus 2cxT	D. R. Irving	
G-CKGC	Schempp-Hirth Ventus 2cxT	C. P. A. Jeffery	
G-CKGD	Schempp-Hirth Ventus 2cxT	C. Morris	
G-CKGF	Schempp-Hirth Duo Discus T	Duo 233 Group	
G-CKGH	Grob G.102 Club Astir II	I. M. Gavan	
G-CKGK	Schleicher ASK-21	RAF Gliding & Soaring Association	
G-CKGL	Schempp-Hirth Ventus 2cT	Kilo Golf Lima Syndicate	
G-CKGM	Centrair 101A Pegase	S. France	
G-CKGU	Schleicher ASW-19B	ASW 19 KGU Group	
G-CKGV	Schleicher ASW-20	A. H. Reynolds	
G-CKGX	Schleicher ASK-21	Coventry Gliding Club Ltd	
G-CKGY	Scheibe Bergfalke IV	B. R. Pearson	
G-CKHA	PZL SZD-51-1 Junior	Devon & Somerset Gliding Club Ltd	
G-CKHB	Rolladen-Schneider LS3	R. Lemin	
G-CKHC	DG Flugzeugbau DG.505	G-CKHC Group	
G-CKHD	Schleicher ASW-27B	N. D Tillett	
G-CKHE	AB Sportine Aviacija LAK-17AT	N. J. Gough & A. J. Garrity	
G-CKHG	Schleicher ASW-27B	R. A. F. King	
G-CKHH	Schleicher ASK-13	Lincolnshire Gliding Club Ltd	
G-CKHK	Schempp-Hirth Duo Discus T	Duo Discus Syndicate	
G-CKHM	Centrair 101A Pegase 90	A. J. Rowlands	
G-CKHN	PZL SZD-51-1 Junior	The Nene Valley Gliding Club Ltd	
G-CKHP	Rolladen-Schneider LS8-18	A. D. May	
G-CKHR	PZL-Bielsko SZD-51-1 Junior	Wolds Gliding Club Ltd	
G-CKHS	Rolladen-Schneider LS7-WL	M. Lawson & D. Wallis	
G-CKHV	Glaser-Dirks DG-100	M. J. Brown & M. E. Laxaback	
G-CKHW	PZL SZD-50-3 Puchacz	Derbyshire and Lancashire Gliding Club Ltd	
G-CKJB	Schempp-Hirth Ventus bT	J. D. Sorrell	
G-CKJC	Schempp-Hirth Nimbus 3T	A. C. Wright	
G-CKJD	Schempp-Hirth Cirrus 75-VTC	P. J. P. Vanden Boer	
G-CKJE	DG Flugzeugbau LS8-18	M. D. Wells	
G-CKJF	Schempp-Hirth Standard Cirrus	G-CKJF Group	
G-CKJG	Schempp-Hirth Cirrus VTC	S. J. Wright	
G-CKJH	Glaser-Dirks DG.300 Elan	Yorkshire Gliding Club	
G-CKJJ	DG Flugzeugbau DG-500 Elan Orion	Ulster Gliding Club Ltd	
G-CKJL	Scleicher ASK-13	Lincolnshire Gliding Club Ltd	
G-CKJM	Schempp-Hirth Ventus cT	G-CKJM Group	
G-CKJN	Schleicher ASW-20	R. Logan	
G-CKJP	Schleicher ASK-21	T. M. Holloway	
G-CKJS	Schleicher ASW-28-18E	G-CKJS Syndicate	
G-CKJV	Schleicher ASW-28-18E	A. C. Price	
G-CKJZ	Schempp-Hirth Discus bT	G-CKJZ Group	
G-CKKB	Centrair 101A Pegase	D. M. Rushton	
G-CKKC	DG Flugzeugbau DG-300 Elan Acro	Charlie Kilo Kilo Charlie Syndicate	
G-CKKE	Schempp-Hirth Duo Discus T	The Foxtrot Group	
G-CKKF	Schempp-Hirth Ventus 2cT	A. R. MacGregor	
G-CKKH	Schleicher ASW-27	P. L. Hurd	
G-CKKK	AB Sportine Aviacija LAK-17A	C. J. Nicolas	
G-CKKP	Schleicher ASK-21	Bowland Forest Gliding Club Ltd	
G-CKKR	Schleicher ASK-13	Banbury Gliding Club Ltd	
G-CKKV	DG Flugzeugbau DG-1000S	Lasham Gliding Society Ltd	
G-CKKX	Rolladen-Schneider LS4-A	B. W. Svenson	
G-CKKY	Schempp-Hirth Duo Discus T	P. D. Duffin	
G-CKLA	Schleicher ASK-13	Booker Gliding Club Ltd	
G-CKLC	Glasflugel H206 Hornet	L. P. Woodage	
G-CKLD	Schempp-Hirth Discus 2cT	J. P. Galloway	
G-CKLF	Schempp-Hirth Janus	T. J. Highton & C. J. Lawrence	
G-CKLG	Rolladen-Schneider LS4	P. M. Scheiwiller, P. S. Graham & J. P. Heath	
G-CKLN	Rolladen-Schneider LS4-A	Army Gliding Association	
G-CKLP	Scleicher ASW-28-18	J. T. Birch	
G-CKLR	Pezetel SZD-55-1	Zulu Five Gliding Group (G-CKLM)	
G-CKLS	Rolladen-Schneider LS4	Wolds Gliding Club Ltd	
G-CKLT	Schempp-Hirth Nimbus 3/24.5	G. N. Thomas	

Notes	Reg.	Type	Owner or Operator
	G-CKLV	Schempp-Hirth Discus 2cT	J. Iglehart
	G-CKLW	Schleicher ASK-21	Yorkshire Gliding Club
	G-CKLY	DG Flugzeugbau DG-1000T	G-CKLY Group
	G-CKMA	DG Flugzeugbau LS8-T	W. J. Morecraft
	G-CKMB	AB Sportline Aviacija LAK-19T	D. J. McKenzie
	G-CKMD	Schempp-Hirth Standard Cirrus	S. A. Crabb
	G-CKME	DG Flugzeugbau LS8-T	S. M. Smith
	G-CKMF	Centrair 101A Pegase	D. L. M. Jamin
	G-CKMG	Glaser-Dirks DG-101G Elan	G. G. Dale
	G-CKMI	Schleicher K8C	V. Mallon
	G-CKMJ	Schleicher Ka 6CR	V. Mallon
	G-CKML	Schempp-Hirth Duo Discus T	KML Group
	G-CKMM	Schleicher ASW-28-18E	R. G. Munro
	G-CKMO	Rolladen-Schneider LS7-WL	G. E. M. Turpin
	G-CKMP	AB Sportine Aviacija LAK-17A	J. L. McIver
	G-CKMT	Grob G103C	The Borders (Milfield) Gliding Club Ltd
	G-CKMV	Rolladen-Schneider LS3-17	S. Procter & M. P. Woolmer
	G-CKMW	Schleicher ASK-21	RAF Gliding & Soaring Association
	G-CKMZ	Schleicher ASW-28-18	J. R. Martindale
	G-CKNB	Schempp-Hirth Standard Cirrus	A. Booker
	G-CKNC	Caproni Calif A21S	J. J. & M. E. Pritchard
	G-CKND	DG Flugzeugbau DG-1000T	KND Group
	G-CKNE	Schempp-Hirth Standard Cirrus 75-VTC	G. D. E. Macdonald
	G-CKNF	DG Flugzeugbau DG-1000T	Six November Fox
	G-CKNG	Schleicher ASW-28-18E	M. P. Brockinhton
	G-CKNK	Glaser-Dirks DG.500	Cotswold Gliding Club
	G-CKNL	Schleicher ASK-21	Buckminster Gliding Club Ltd
	G-CKNM	Scleicher ASK-18	I. L. Pattingale
	G-CKNO	Schempp-Hirth Ventus 2cxT	C. McEwen
	G-CKNR	Schempp-Hirth Ventus 2cxT	R. J. Nicholls
	G-CKNS	Rolladen-Schneider LS4-A	I. R. Willows
	G-CKNU	Schleicher ASW-27-18E	R. A. Cheetham
	G-CKNV	Schleicher ASW-28-18E	D. G. Brain
	G-CKOD	Schempp-Hirth Discus BT	A. L. Harris & M. W. Talbot
	G-CKOE	Schleicher ASW-27-18	R. C. Bromwich
	G-CKOH	DG Flugzeugbau DG-1000T	Lasham Gliding Society Ltd
	G-CKOI	AB Sportine Aviacija LAK-17AT	C. G. Corbett
	G-CKOK	Schempp-Hirth Discus 2cT	B. D. Scougall
	G-CKOL	Schempp-Hirth Duo Discus T	Oscar Lima Syndicate
	G-CKOM	Schleicher ASW-27-18	L. M. P. Wells
	G-CKON	Schleicher ASW-27-18E	J. P. Gorringe
	G-CKOO	Schleicher ASW-27-18E	A. Darlington, J. P. Lewis & C. T. P. Williams
	G-CKOR	Glaser-Dirks DG-300 Elan	J. A. Sparrow
	G-CKOT	Schleicher ASK-21	Ulster Gliding Club Ltd
	G-CKOU	AB Sportine Aviacija LAK-19T	A. Challenor D. Le Roux & R. Walker
	G-CKOW	DG-505 Elan Orion	Southdown Gliding Club Ltd
	G-CKOX	AMS-Flight DG-505 Elan Orion	Seahawk Gliding Club
	G-CKOY	Schleicher ASW-27-18E	G-CKOY Group
	G-CKOZ	Schleicher ASW-27-18E	E. W. Johnston
	G-CKPA	AB Sportline Aviacija LAK-19T	O. R. Momege
	G-CKPE	Schempp-Hirth Duo Discus	Portsmouth Naval Gliding Centre
	G-CKPG	Schempp-Hirth Discus 2cT	G. Knight & P. Rowden
	G-CKPJ	Neukom S-4D Elfe	S. Szladowski
	G-CKPK	Schempp-Hirth Ventus 2cxT	I. C. Lees
	G-CKPM	DG Flugzeugbau LS8-T	8T Soaring
	G-CKPN	PZL-Bielsko SZD-51-1 Junior	Rattlesden Gliding Club Ltd
	G-CKPO	Schempp-Hirth Duo Discus xT	KPO Syndicate
	G-CKPP	Schleicher ASK-21	The Gliding Centre
	G-CKPU	Schleicher ASW-27-18E	A. J. Kellerman
	G-CKPV	Schempp-Hirth HS.7 Mini-Nimbus B	C. J. Pollard
	G-CKPX	ZS Jezow PW-6U	KPX Syndicate
	G-CKPY	Schempp-Hirth Duo Discus xT	Duo-Discus Syndicate
	G-CKPZ	Schleicher ASW-20	T. Davies
	G-CKRB	Schleicher ASK-13	Derbyshire and Lancashire Gliding Club Ltd
	G-CKRC	Schleicher ASW-28-18E	M. Woodcock
	G-CKRD	Schleicher ASW-27-18E	R. F. Thirkell
	G-CKRF	DG-300 Elan	G. A. King
	G-CKRH	Grob G.103 Twin Astir II	Staffordshire Gliding Club Ltd
	G-CKRI	Schleicher ASK-21	Kent Gliding Club Aircraft Ltd
	G-CKRJ	Schleicher ASW-27-18E	J. C. Thompson
	G-CKRN	Grob G.102 Astir CS	Yorkshire Gliding Club (Proprietary) Ltd
	G-CKRO	Schempp-Hirth Duo Discus T	Duo Discus Syndicate KRO

Reg.	Type	Owner or Operator	Notes
G-CKRR	Schleicher ASW-15B	S. A. Day	
G-CKRS	FFA Diamant 16.5	G-CKRS Syndicate	
G-CKRT	Schleicher ASW-27-18E	J. D. Spencer	
G-CKRU	ZS Jezow PW-6U	Cotswold Gliding Club	
G-CKRV	Schleicher ASW-27-18E	J. Cruttenden & J. Taylor	
G-CKRW	Schleicher ASK-21	RAF Gliding and Soaring Association	
G-CKRX	Jezow PW-6U	Cotswold Gliding Club	
G-CKSC	Czech Sport Aircraft Sportcruiser	Czechmate Syndicate	
G-CKSD	Rolladen-Schneider LS8-a	C. Emson	
G-CKSH	PZL-Bielsko SZD-30 Pirat	J. K. Hoffmann	
G-CKSK	Pilatus B4-PC11	R. Mauthner	
G-CKSL	Schleicher ASW-15B	Sierra Lima Group	
G-CKSM	Schempp-Hirth Duo Discus T	J. H. May & S. P. Ball	
G-CKSX	Schleicher ASW-27-18E	M. C. Foreman	
G-CKSY	Rolladen-Schneider LS-7-WL	C. M. Lewis	
G-CKTB	Schempp-Hirth Ventus 2cT	M. H. Player	
G-CKTC	Schleicher Ka 6CR	Tango Charlie Group	
G-CKZT	PA-28-235 Cherokee Pathfinder	U. Chakravorty	
G-CLAC	PA-28-161 Warrior II	G-CLAC Group	
G-CLAR	EC.225LP Super Puma	CHC Scotia Ltd	
G-CLAV	Shaw Europa	G. Laverty	
G-CLAX	Jurca MJ.5 Sirocco F2/39	G. D. Claxton (G-AWKB)	
G-CLAY	Bell 206B JetRanger 3	Claygate Distribution Ltd (G-DENN)	
G-CLDS	Rotorsport UK Calidus	Rotorsport UK Ltd	
G-CLEA	PA-28-161 Warrior II	G-CLEA Group	
G-CLEE	Rans S.6-ES Coyote II	J. Bell	
G-CLEG	Flight Design CTSW	C. A. S. Powell	
G-CLEM	Bölkow Bö.208A2 Junior	G-CLEM Group (G-ASWE)	
G-CLEO	Zenair CH.601HD	K. M. Bowen	
G-CLES	Scheicher ASW-27-18E	A. P. Brown & N. D. Tillett	
G-CLEU	Glaser-Dirks DG-200	S. F. Tape	
G-CLFB	Rolladen-Schneider LS4-A	B. Harker	
G-CLFC	Mainair Blade	G. N. Cliffe & G. Marshall	
G-CLFH	Schleicher ASW-20C	T. Fordwich-Gorefly & P. Armstrong	
G-CLFX	Schempp-Hirth Duo Discus T	A. L. Baillie	
G-CLFZ	Schleicher ASW-18E	C. F. Cownden & J. P. Davies	
G-CLGC	Schempp-Hirth Duo Discus	London Gliding Club Proprietary Ltd	
G-CLGL	Schempp-Hirth Ventus 2c	M. J. Collett and S. & A. Roberts	
G-CLIC	Cameron A-105 balloon	R. S. Mohr	
G-CLIF	Ikarus C42 FB UK	C. Sims	
G-CLIN	Ikarus C42 FB100	G. C. Linley	
G-CLOE	Sky 90-24 balloon	J. Skinner	
G-CLOS	PA-34-200 Seneca II	R. A. Doherty	
G-CLOT	Robinson R44	Tracey Plant Ltd	
G-CLOW	Beech 200 Super King Air	Clowes (Estates) Ltd	
G-CLRK	Sky 77-24 balloon	William Clark & Son (Parkgate) Ltd	
G-CLUB	Cessna FRA.150N	D. A. N. Pergue	
G-CLUE	PA-34-200T Seneca II	P. Pigg	
G-CLUX	Cessna F.172N	J. & K. Aviation	
G-CLWN	Cameron Clown SS balloon	Magical Adventures Ltd (G-UBBE)	
G-CMAF	Embraer RJ135BJ Legacy	TAG Aviation (UK) Ltd	
G-CMBR	Cessna 172S	C. M. B. Reid	
G-CMBS	MDH MD-900 Explorer	Cambridgeshire Constabulary	
G-CMCC	Robinson R44 II	C. McCann	
G-CMED	SOCATA TB9 Tampico	D. Primorac	
G-CMGC	PA-25 Pawnee 235	Midland Gliding Club Ltd (G-BFEX)	
G-CMJK	Eurocopter EC.225LP	CHC Scotia Ltd	
G-CMLS	Cirrus SR20	Cumulus Aircraft Rentals Ltd	
G-CMOR	Skyranger 912(2)	N. R. Henry	
G-CMOS	Cessna T.303 Crusader	C. J. Moss	
G-CMSN	Robinson R22 Beta	Kuki Helicopter Sales Ltd (G-MGEE//G-RUMP)	
G-CMWK	Grob G.102 Astir CS	S. J. Saunders	
G-CMXX	Robinson R44 II	Northern Excavators Ltd	
G-CNAB	Avtech Jabiru UL	W. A. Brighouse	
G-CNCN	Rockwell Commander 112CA	G. R. Frost	
G-CNHB	Van's RV-7	M. E. Wood	
G-CNUK	Dassault Falcon 7X	TAG Aviation (UK) Ltd	
G-COAI	Cranfield A.1	Cranfield University (G-BCIT)	
G-COBH	Beech 200 Super King Air	Cobham Flight Inspection Ltd (G-FPLA)	

Notes	Reg.	Type	Owner or Operator
	G-COBI	Beech 300 Super King Air	Cobham Flight Inspection Ltd
	G-COBM	Beech 300 Super King Air	Cobham Flight Inspection Ltd
	G-COBO	ATR-72-212A	Aurigny Air Services Ltd
	G-COCO	Cessna F.172M	P. C. Sheard & R. C. Larder
	G-CODY	Kolb Twinstar Mk.3 Extra	J. W. Codd
	G-COIN	Bell 206B JetRanger 2	J. P. Niehorster
	G-COLA	Beech F33C Bonanza	J. R. C. Spooner (G-BUAZ)
	G-COLH	PA-28 Cherokee 140	Full Sutton Flying Centre Ltd (G-AVRT)
	G-COLI	Rotorsport UK MT-03	C. Gilholm
	G-COLR	Colt 69A balloon ★	British School of Ballooning/Lancing
	G-COLS	Van's RV-7A	C. Terry
	G-COMB	PA-30 Twin Comanche 160B	M. R. Booker (G-AVBL)
	G-COML	Eurocopter EC120B	Combilift
	G-COMP	Cameron N-90 balloon	Computacenter Ltd
	G-COMU	Flight Design CT2K	K. Brown
	G-CONA	Flight Design CTLS	S. Connah (G-CGED)
	G-CONB	Robin DR.400/180	M. D. Souster (G-BUPX)
	G-CONC	Cameron N-90 balloon	A. A. Brown
	G-CONL	SOCATA TB10 Tobago	J. M. Huntington
	G-CONR	Champion 7GCBC Scout	N. O'Brien
	G-CONV	Convair CV-440-54 ★	Reynard Nursery/Carluke
	G-COOK	Cameron N-77 balloon	IAZ (International) Ltd
	G-COOT	Taylor Coot A	P. M. Napp
	G-COPS	Piper J-3C-65 Cub	R. W. Sproat
	G-CORA	Shaw Europa XS	A. P. Gardner (G-ILUM)
	G-CORB	SOCATA TB20 Trinidad	G. D. Corbin
	G-CORD	Slingsby T.66 Nipper 3	A. V. Lamprell (G-AVTB)
	G-CORL	AS.350B3 Ecureuil	Abbeyflight Ltd
	G-COSF	PA-28-161 Warrior II	PA-28 Warrior Ltd
	G-COSY	Lindstrand LBL-56A balloon	M. H. Read & J. E. Wetters
	G-COTH	MD-900 Explorer	Police Aviation Services Ltd
	G-COTT	Cameron 60 Cottage SS balloon	Dragon Balloon Co Ltd
	G-COUP	Ercoupe 415C	R. C. van Haarlem
	G-COUZ	X'Air 582(2)	D. J. Couzens
	G-COVA	PA-26-161 Warrior III	Coventry (Civil) Aviation Ltd (G-CDCL)
	G-COVB	PA-28-161 Warror III	Coventry (Civil) Aviation Ltd
	G-COVE	Avtech Jabiru UL	A. A. Rowson
	G-COVZ	Cessna F.150M	R. A. Doherty (G-BCRT)
	G-COXS	Aeroprakt A.22 Foxbat	S. Cox
	G-COXY	Kiss 400-582 (1)	J. R. Pearce
	G-COZI	Rutan Cozy III	R. Machin
	G-CPAO	Eurocopter EC.135P2+	Cheshire Police Authority
	G-CPAS	Eurocopter EC.135P2+	Eurocopter UK Ltd
	G-CPCD	CEA DR.221	P. J. Taylor
	G-CPDA	DH.106 Comet 4C (XS235) ★	C. Walton Ltd/Bruntingthorpe
	G-CPDW	Avions Mudry CAP.10B	Hilfa Ltd
	G-CPEM	Boeing 757-236	British Airways
	G-CPEN	Boeing 757-236	British Airways
	G-CPEO	Boeing 757-236	British Airways
	G-CPEP	Boeing 757-2Y0	Thomson Airways Ltd
	G-CPER	Boeing 757-236	British Airways
	G-CPES	Boeing 757-236	British Airways
	G-CPET	Boeing 757-236	British Airways
	G-CPEU	Boeing 757-236	Thomson Airways Ltd
	G-CPEV	Boeing 757-236	Thomson Airways Ltd
	G-CPFC	Cessna F.152 II	Falcon Flying Services Ltd
	G-CPHA	Robinson R44 II	Heli Air Ltd
	G-CPMK	DHC.1 Chipmunk 22 (WZ847)	P. A. Walley
	G-CPMS	SOCATA TB20 Trinidad	Charlotte Park Management Services Ltd
	G-CPOL	AS.355F1 Twin Squirrel	MW Helicopters Ltd
	G-CPPM	North American Harvard II	S. D. Wilch
	G-CPRI	Learjet 45	Capri UK Investments Ltd
	G-CPRR	Cessna 680 Citation Sovereign	Eurojet Aviation Ltd
	G-CPSH	Eurocopter EC 135T1	Thames Valley Police Authority
	G-CPSS	Cessna 208B Grand Caravan	Aerodynamics Ltd
	G-CPTM	PA-28-151 Warrior	T. J. & C. Mackay (G-BTOE)
	G-CPTS	Agusta-Bell 206B JetRanger 2	A. R. B. Aspinall
	G-CPXC	Avions Mudry CAP-10C	Cunning Plan Development Ltd
	G-CRAB	Skyranger 912 (1)	R. A. Weller
	G-CRAR	CZAW Sportcruiser	J. S. Kinsey

Reg.	Type	Owner or Operator	Notes
G-CRBV	Balóny Kubíček BB26 balloon	Charter Ballooning Ltd	
G-CRDY	Agusta-Bell 206A JetRanger	Loughbeigh Properties Ltd (G-WHAZ)	
G-CRES	Denney Kitfox Mk 3	J. McGoldrick	
G-CREY	SeaRey Amphibian	A. F. Reid & P. J. Gallagher	
G-CRIC	Colomban MC.15 Cri-Cri	R. S. Stoddart-Stones	
G-CRIK	Colomban MC.15 Cri-Cri	A.R. Robinson	
G-CRIL	Rockwell Commander 112B	Rockwell Aviation Group	
G-CRIS	Taylor JT.1 Monoplane	C. R. Steer	
G-CRJW	Schleicher ASW-27-18	R. J. Welford	
G-CRLA	Cirrus SR20	Aero Club Heidelberg EV/Germany	
G-CROB	Shaw Europa XS T-G	R. G. Hallam	
G-CROL	Maule MXT-7-180	W. E. Willets	
G-CROO	Cessna 525A Citationjet CJ2	Rooney Air Ltd	
G-CROP	Cameron Z-105 balloon	PSH Skypower Ltd	
G-CROW	Robinson R44	Longmoore Ltd	
G-CROY	Shaw Europa	M. T. Austin	
G-CRPH	Airbus A.320-231	Thomas Cook Airlines Ltd	
G-CRUI	CZAW Sportcruiser	J. Massey	
G-CRUM	Westland Scout AH.1 (XV137)	G-CRUM Group	
G-CRUZ	Cessna T.303	Bank Farm Ltd	
G-CRWZ	CZAW Sportcruiser	P. B. Lowry	
G-CRZA	CZAW Sportcruiser	A. J. Radford	
G-CSAM	Van's RV-9A	B. G. Murray	
G-CSAV	Thruster T.600N 450	D. J. N. Brown	
G-CSAW	CZAW Sportcruiser	B. C. Fitzgerald-O'Connor	
G-CSBD	PA-28-236 Dakota	S. B. & S-J. Dunnett (G-CSBO)	
G-CSBM	Cessna F.150M	Transcourt Ltd	
G-CSCS	Cessna F.172N	C.Sullivan	
G-CSDJ	Avtech Jabiru UL	G-CSDJ Group	
G-CSDR	Corvus CA22	J. B. Mills	
G-CSFC	Cessna 150L	Foxtrot Charlie Flying Group	
G-CSFD	Ultramagic M-90 balloon	L. A. Watts	
G-CSFT	PA-23 Aztec 250D ★	Aces High Ltd (G-AYKU)	
G-CSGT	PA-28-161 Warrior II	M. J. Wade (G-BPHB)	
G-CSIX	PA-32 Cherokee Six 300	A. J. Hodge	
G-CSMK	Aerotechnik EV-97 Eurostar	R. Frey	
G-CSPR	Van's RV-6A	P. J. Pengilly	
G-CSUE	ICP MXP-740 Savannah Jabiru (5)	J. R. Stratton	
G-CSZM	Zenair CH.601XL Zodiac	C. Budd	
G-CTAA	Schempp-Hirth Janus	AA group	
G-CTAG	Rolladen-Schneider LS8-18	C. D. R. Tagg	
G-CTAM	Cirrus SR22	M. R. Munn	
G-CTAV	Aerotechnik EV-97 Eurostar	P. Simpson	
G-CTCD	Diamond DA42 Twin Star	CTC Aviation Group PLC	
G-CTCE	Diamond DA42 Twin Star	CTC Aviation Group PLC	
G-CTCF	Diamond DA42 Twin Star	CTC Aviation Group PLC	
G-CTCG	Diamond DA42 Twin Star	Royce Marshall and Co.	
G-CTCH	Diamond DA42 Twin Star	CTC Aviation Group PLC	
G-CTCL	SOCATA TB10 Tobago	Gift Aviation Ltd (G-BSIV)	
G-CTDH	Flight Design CT2K	A. D. Thelwall	
G-CTDW	Flight Design CTSW	S. L. Morris	
G-CTED	Van's RV-7A	E. W. Lyon	
G-CTEL	Cameron N-90 balloon	M. R. Noyce	
G-CTEN	Cessna 750 Citation X	Pendley Aviation LLP	
G-CTIO	SOCATA TB20 Trinidad	I. R. Hunt	
G-CTIX	VS.509 Spitfire T.IX (PT462)	A. A. Hodgson	
G-CTKL	Noorduyn AT-16 Harvard IIB (54137)	M. R. Simpson	
G-CTLS	Flight Design CTLS	D. J. Haygreen	
G-CTNG	Cirrus SR20	K. D. Brown	
G-CTOY	Denney Kitfox Mk 3	B. McNeilly	
G-CTPW	Bell 206B JetRanger 3	Aviation Rentals	
G-CTRL	Robinson R22 Beta	Central Helicopters Ltd	
G-CTSW	Flight Design CTSW	K. Dickson	
G-CTUG	PA-25 Pawnee 235	The Borders (Milfield) Gliding Club Ltd	
G-CTWO	Schempp-Hirth Standard Cirrus	R. J. Griffin	
G-CTWW	PA-34-200T Seneca II	Fly (CI) Ltd (G-ROYZ/G-GALE)	
G-CTZO	SOCATA TB20 Trinidad GT	D. T. White	
G-CUBB	PA-18 Super Cub 180	Bidford Gliding Ltd	
G-CUBE	Skyranger 912 (2)	A. I. Medler	

Notes	Reg.	Type	Owner or Operator
	G-CUBI	PA-18 Super Cub 125	G. T. Fisher
	G-CUBJ	PA-18 Super Cub 150 (18-5395:CDG)	A. L. Grisay
	G-CUBN	PA-18 Super Cub 150	N. J. R. Minchin
	G-CUBP	PA-18 Super Cub 150	D. W. Berger
	G-CUBS	Piper J-3C-65 Cub	S. M. Rolfe (G-BHPT)
	G-CUBW	WAG-Aero Acro Trainer	B. G. Plumb & ptnrs
	G-CUBY	Piper J-3C-65 Cub	C. A. Bloom (G-BTZW)
	G-CUCU	Colt 180A balloon	S. R. Seage
	G-CUDY	Enstrom 480B	D'Arcy Holdings Ltd (G-REAN)
	G-CUGC	Schleicher ASW-19B	Cambridge University Gliding Club (G-CKEX)
	G-CUIK	QAC Quickie Q.200	C. S. Rayner
	G-CUMU	Schempp-Hirth Discus b	C. E. Fernando
	G-CUPP	Pitts S-2A	Avmarine Ltd
	G-CURV	Avid Speedwing	K. S. Kelso
	G-CUTE	Dyn'Aéro MCR-01	E. G. Shimmin
	G-CUTH	P & M Quik R	A. R. & S. Cuthbertson
	G-CVAL	Ikarus C42 FB100	G. W. F. Morton
	G-CVBF	Cameron A-210 balloon	Virgin Balloon Flights Ltd
	G-CVII	Dan Rihn DR.107 One Design	One Design Group
	G-CVIX	DH.110 Sea Vixen D.3 (XP924)	Drilling Systems Ltd
	G-CVMI	PA-18 Super Cub 150	D. Heslop & T. P. Spurge
	G-CVPM	VPM M-16 Tandem Trainer	P. L. Newman
	G-CVST	Jodel D.140E	D. Runnalls & R. Sheridan
	G-CVXN	Cessna F.406 Caravan	Caledonian Airborne Systems Ltd (G-SFPA)
	G-CVZT	Schempp-Hirth Ventus 2cT	C. D. Sterritt & M. W. Conboy
	G-CWAG	Sequoia F. 8L Falco	D. R. Austin
	G-CWAL	Raj Hamsa X'Air 133	L. R. Morris
	G-CWAY	Ikarus C42 FB100	M. Conway
	G-CWBM	Phoenix Currie Wot	M. J. Bond (G-BTVP)
	G-CWEB	P & M Quik GT450	M & K. A. Forsyth
	G-CWFA	PA-38-112 Tomahawk	F. P. Hermann (G-BTGC)
	G-CWFC	PA-38-112 Tomahawk ★	Cardiff-Wales Flying Club Ltd (G-BRTA)
	G-CWIC	Mainair Pegasus Quik	G-CWIC Group
	G-CWIK	Mainair Pegasus Quik	C. D. Jackson
	G-CWIS	Diamond DA.20 Star	R. A. Eve
	G-CWLC	Schleicher ASH-25	C. L. Withall
	G-CWMC	P & M Quik GT450	A. R. Hughes
	G-CWMT	Dyn'Aéro MCR-01 Bambi	J. Jones
	G-CWOT	Currie Wot	D. Doyle & H. Duggan
	G-CWTD	Aeroprakt A.22 Foxbat	J. V. Harris
	G-CWVY	Mainair Pegasus Quik	G-CWVY Group
	G-CXCX	Cameron N-90 balloon	Cathay Pacific Airways (London) Ltd
	G-CXDZ	Cassutt Speed Two	J. A. H. Chadwick
	G-CXIP	Thruster T.600N	India Papa Syndicate
	G-CXLS	Cessna 560 XL Citation XLS	Aviation Beauport Ltd (G-PKRG)
	G-CXSM	Cessna 172R	S. Eustathiou (G-BXSM)
	G-CYGI	HAPI Cygnet SF-2A	B. Brown
	G-CYLL	Sequoia F.8L Falco	N. J. Langrick & A. J. Newall
	G-CYLS	Cessna T.303	Oasis 303 Ltd (G-BKXI
	G-CYMA	GA-7 Cougar	Cyma Petroleum (UK) Ltd (G-BKOM)
	G-CYPM	Cirrus SR22	R. M. Steeves
	G-CYRA	Kolb Twinstar Mk. 3 (Modified)	S. J. Fox (G-MYRA)
	G-CYRS	Bell 206L Long Ranger	HJS Helicopters Ltd
	G-CZAC	Zenair CH.601XL	D. Pitt
	G-CZAG	Sky 90-24 balloon	S. Paszkowicz
	G-CZAW	CZAW Sportcruiser	Sprite Aviation Services Ltd
	G-CZCZ	Avions Mudry CAP-10B	M. Farmer
	G-CZMI	Skyranger 912 (2)	L. M. Bassett
	G-CZNE	BN-2B-20 Islander	Skyhopper LLP (G-BWZF)
	G-CZOS	Cirrus SR20	Caseright Ltd
	G-CZSC	CZAW Sportcruiser	A. K. Lynn
	G-DAAH	PA-28RT-201T Turbo Arrow IV	D. A. H. Morris
	G-DAAM	Robinson R22 Beta	Helispin SRL/Italy
	G-DAAT	Eurocopter EC 135T2	Bond Air Services Ltd
	G-DAAZ	PA-28RT-201T Turbo Arrow IV	Calais Ltd
	G-DABS	Robinson R22 Beta II	B16 Ltd

Reg.	Type	Owner or Operator	Notes
G-DACA	P.57 Sea Prince T.1 (WF118) ★	P. G. Vallance Ltd/Charlwood	
G-DACF	Cessna 152 II	T. M. & M. L. Jones (G-BURY)	
G-DADA	Rotorsport UK MT-03	P. J. Troy-Davies	
G-DADG	PA-18-150 Super Cub	F. J. Cox	
G-DADJ	Glaser-Dirks DG-200	T. Forsey	
G-DADZ	CZAW Sportcruiser	Meon Flying Group	
G-DAGF	EAA Acrosport II	D. A. G. Fraser	
G-DAGJ	Zenair CH.601HD Zodiac	D. A. G. Johnson	
G-DAIR	Luscombe 8A Silvaire	D. F. Soul (G-BURK)	
G-DAIV	Ultramagic H-77 balloon	D. Harrison-Morris	
G-DAJB	Boeing 757-2T7	Monarch Airlines Ltd	
G-DAJC	Boeing 757-31K	Thomas Cook Airlines Ltd	
G-DAKI	Pilatus PC-12/47	Aquarelle Investments Ltd	
G-DAKK	Douglas C-47A	General Technics Ltd	
G-DAKM	Diamond DA40D Star	K. MacDonald	
G-DAKO	PA-28-236 Dakota	Methods Consulting Ltd	
G-DAME	Vans RV-7	A. D. Heath	
G-DAMY	Shaw Europa	U. A. Schliessler & R. J. Kelly	
G-DANA	Jodel DR.200 (replica)	Cheshire Eagles (G-DAST)	
G-DAND	SOCATA TB10 Tobago	Portway Aviation Ltd	
G-DANT	Rockwell Commander 114	J Terreaux	
G-DANY	Avtech Jabiru UL	D. A. Crosbie	
G-DANZ	AS.355N Twin Squirrel	Melesey Ltd	
G-DAPH	Cessna 180K	T. W. Harris	
G-DASH	Rockwell Commander 112	D. & M. Nelson (G-BDAJ)	
G-DASS	Ikarus C.42 FB100	R. I. Hackett	
G-DASY	Hughes 369E	Puddleduck Plane Partnership	
G-DATG	Cessna F.182P	Oxford Aeroplane Co Ltd	
G-DAVB	Aerosport Scamp	D. R. Burns	
G-DAVD	Cessna FR.172K	D. M. Driver & S. Copeland	
G-DAVE	Jodel D.112	D. Evans	
G-DAVG	Robinson R44 II	AG Aviation Ltd (G-WOWW)	
G-DAVM	Akrotech Europe CAP.10B	D. Moorman	
G-DAVS	AB Sportine Aviacija LAK-17AT	G-DAVS Syndicate	
G-DAVV	Robinson R44 Raven II	D. A. Gold	
G-DAVZ	Cessna 182T Skylane	Heli-4 Charter Ltd	
G-DAWG	SA Bulldog Srs 120/121 (XX522:06)	R. H. Goldstone	
G-DAWZ	Glasflugel 304 CZ	D. A. Whitley	
G-DAYS	Shaw Europa	D. A. Gittins	
G-DAYZ	Pietenpol Air Camper	N. S. Lomax	
G-DAZY	PA-34-200T Seneca	Fly (CI) Ltd	
G-DAZZ	Van's RV-8	Wishanger RV8	
G-DBAT	Lindstrand LBL-56A balloon	G. R. J. Luckett	
G-DBCA	Airbus A.319-131	bmi british midland	
G-DBCB	Airbus A.319-131	bmi british midland	
G-DBCC	Airbus A.319-131	bmi british midland	
G-DBCD	Airbus A.319-131	bmi british midland	
G-DBCE	Airbus A.319-131	bmi british midland	
G-DBCF	Airbus A.319-131	bmi british midland	
G-DBCG	Airbus A.319-131	bmi british midland	
G-DBCH	Airbus A.319-131	bmi british midland	
G-DBCI	Airbus A.319-131	bmi british midland	
G-DBCJ	Airbus A.319-131	bmi british midland	
G-DBCK	Airbus A.319-131	bmi british midland	
G-DBDB	VPM M-16 Tandem Trainer	D. R. Bolsover (G-IROW)	
G-DBIN	Medway SLA 80 Executive	D. Binnington	
G-DBJD	PZL-Bielsko SZD-9BIS Bocian 1D	Bertie the Bocian Glider Syndicate	
G-DBKL	VS.379 Spitfire F.Mk.XIV	P. M. Andrews	
G-DBLA	Boeing 767-35EER	Thomson Airways Ltd	
G-DBLX	Aviat A-18 Husky	Aviat Aircraft (UK) Ltd	
G-DBMK	Ikarus C42 FB100 VLA	GDBMK Ltd (G-MROY)	
G-DBND	Schleicher Ka 6CR	A. H. Hall	
G-DBNH	Schleicher Ka 6CR	The Bath, Wilts and North Dorset Gliding Club Ltd	
G-DBOD	Cessna 172S	Goodwood Road Racing Co.Ltd	
G-DBOL	Schleicher Ka 6CR	A. C. Thorne	
G-DBRT	Slingsby T.51 Dart	C. W. Logue	
G-DBRU	Slingsby T.51 Dart	L. J. Stephenson	
G-DBRY	Slingsby T.51 Dart	D. J. Knights	
G-DBSA	Slingsby T.51 Dart	G. Burton	
G-DBSL	Slingsby T.51 Dart	G-DBSL Group	
G-DBSR	Kubicek BB26Z balloon	G. J. Bell	

Notes	Reg.	Type	Owner or Operator
	G-DBTF	Schleicher Ka 6CR	T. Fletcher
	G-DBTJ	Schleicher Ka 6CR	I. G. Robinson
	G-DBUF	Slingsby T.51 Dart 17R	K. W. Clarke & N. G. Harrison
	G-DBUZ	Schleicher Ka 6CR	J. J. Leacroft
	G-DBVB	Schleicher K7	Dartmoor Gliding Society Ltd
	G-DBVH	Slingsby T.51 Dart 17R	P. G. Addy
	G-DBVR	Schleicher Ka 6CR	C. S. Warren
	G-DBVX	Schleicher Ka 6CR	R. Lynch
	G-DBVY	LET L-13 Blanik	Victor Yankee Group
	G-DBVZ	Schleicher Ka 6CR	G-DBVZ Group
	G-DBWC	Schleicher Ka 6CR	K6CR BWC Syndicate
	G-DBWJ	Slingsby T.51 Dart 17R	M. F. Defendi
	G-DBWM	Slingsby T.51 Dart 17R	P. L. Poole
	G-DBWO	Slingsby T.51 Dart	G. Winch
	G-DBWP	Slingsby T-51 Dart 17R	R. Johnson
	G-DBWS	Slingsby T.51 Dart 17R	R. D. Broome
	G-DBXE	Slingsby T.51 Dart	Group G-DBXE
	G-DBXG	Slingsby T.51 Dart 17R	J. M. Whelan
	G-DBXH	Slingsby T.51 Dart 17R	S. Foster
	G-DBXT	Schleicher Ka 6CR	C. I. Knowles
	G-DBYC	Slingsby T.51 Dart 17R	N. A. Jaffray
	G-DBYG	Slingsby T.51 Dart 17R	W. T. Emery
	G-DBYL	Schleicher Ka 6CR	Channel Gliding Club Ltd
	G-DBYM	Schleicher Ka 6CR	K. S. Smith
	G-DBYU	Schleicher Ka-6CR	G. B. Sutton
	G-DBYX	Schleicher Ka-6E	J. R. Dent
	G-DBZF	Slingsby T.51 Dart 17R	S. Rhenius & D. Charles
	G-DBZX	Schleicher Ka 6CR	Leeds University Union Gliding Society
	G-DBZZ	SZD-24-4A Foka 4	A. P. Benbow
	G-DCAE	Schleicher Ka 6E	N. Rolfe
	G-DCAG	Schleicher Ka 6E	715 Syndicate
	G-DCAM	Eurocopter AS.355NP Ecureuil 2	Cameron Charters LLP
	G-DCAO	Schempp-Hirth SHK-1	M. G. Entwisle & A. K. Bartlett
	G-DCAS	Schleicher Ka 6E	R. F. Tindall
	G-DCAZ	Slingsby T-51 Dart 17R	D. A. Bullock & Man L. C.
	G-DCBA	Slingsby T.51 Dart 17R	M. Parsons
	G-DCBI	Schweizer 269C-1	Helicentre Holdings Ltd
	G-DCBM	Schleicher Ka 6CR	R. J. Shepherd
	G-DCBW	Schleicher ASK-13	Stratford on Avon Gliding Club Ltd
	G-DCBY	Schleicher Ka 6CR	Talgarth 475
	G-DCCA	Schleicher Ka 6E	R. K. Forrest
	G-DCCB	Schempp-Hirth SHK-1	CCB Syndicate
	G-DCCD	Schleicher Ka 6E	Charlie Charlie Delta Group
	G-DCCE	Schleicher ASK-13	Oxford Gliding Co.Ltd
	G-DCCF	Schleicher ASK-13	Norfolk Gliding Club Ltd
	G-DCCG	Schleicher Ka 6E	R. J. Playle
	G-DCCJ	Schleicher Ka 6CR	S. Badby
	G-DCCL	Schleicher Ka 6E	G-DCCL Group
	G-DCCM	Schleicher ASK-13	The Burn Gliding Club Ltd
	G-DCCP	Schleicher ASK-13	Lima 99 Syndicate
	G-DCCR	Schleicher Ka 6E	A. Shaw
	G-DCCT	Schleicher ASK-13	Stratford on Avon Gliding Club Ltd
	G-DCCU	Schleicher Ka 6E	J. L. Hasker
	G-DCCV	Schleicher Ka 6E	C. H. Page & J. A. Wade
	G-DCCW	Schleicher ASK-13	Needwood Forest Gliding Club Ltd
	G-DCCX	Schleicher ASK-13	Trent Valley Gliding Club Ltd
	G-DCCY	Schleicher ASK-13	Devon and Somerset Gliding Club Ltd
	G-DCCZ	Schleicher ASK-13	The Windrushers Gliding Club Ltd
	G-DCDA	Schleicher Ka 6E	D. Close, A. Smith & J. Tonkin
	G-DCDC	Lange E1 Antares	J. D. Williams
	G-DCDF	Schleicher Ka 6E	CDF Syndicate
	G-DCDG	FFA Diamant 18	J. Cashin & D. McCarty
	G-DCDH	Schempp-Hirth Cirrus	DCDH Syndicate
	G-DCDO	Ikarus C42 FB80	C42 Dodo Syndicate
	G-DCDW	Diamant 18	D. R. Chapman
	G-DCDZ	Schleicher Ka 6E	J. R. J. Minns
	G-DCEB	PZL-Bielsko SZD-9BIS Bocian 1E	The Bath, Wilts and North Dorset Gliding Club Ltd
	G-DCEC	Schempp-Hirth Cirrus	Cirrus 18 Group
	G-DCEL	Schleicher Ka 6E	Essex and Suffolk Gliding Club Ltd
	G-DCEM	Schleicher Ka 6E	E. W. Black
	G-DCEN	PZL-Bielsko SZD-30 Pirat	D. P. Aherne

Reg.	Type	Owner or Operator	Notes
G-DCEO	Schleicher Ka 6E	C. L. Lagden & J. C. Green	
G-DCEW	Schleicher Ka 6E	J. W. Richardson and Partners Group	
G-DCEX	Schleicher ASK-13	R. B. Walker	
G-DCEY	Schleicher Ka 6E	R. Saunders	
G-DCFA	Schleicher ASK-13	Booker Gliding Club Ltd	
G-DCFE	Schleicher ASK-13	Loughborough Students Union Gliding Club	
G-DCFF	Schleicher K 8B	Derbyshire and Lancashire Gliding Club Ltd	
G-DCFG	Schleicher ASK-13	The Nene Valley Gliding Club Ltd	
G-DCFK	Schempp-Hirth Cirrus	M. P. Webb	
G-DCFL	Schleicher Ka 6E	L. M. Causer	
G-DCFS	Glasflugel Standard Libelle 201B	P. J. Flack	
G-DCFW	Glasflugel Standard Libelle 201B	D. J. Edwardes & T. J. Price	
G-DCFX	Glasflugel Standard Libelle 201B	K. D. Fishenden	
G-DCFY	Glasflugel Standard Libelle 201B	C. W. Stevens	
G-DCGB	Schleicher Ka 6E	P. M. Turner & S. C. Male	
G-DCGD	Schleicher Ka 6E	Charlie Golf Delta Group	
G-DCGE	Schleicher Ka 6E	C. V. Hill & P. C. Hazlehurst	
G-DCGH	Schleicher K 8B	K7 (1971) Syndicate	
G-DCGM	FFA Diamant 18	J. G. Batch	
G-DCGO	Schleicher ASK-13	Oxford Gliding Company Ltd	
G-DCGY	Schempp-Hirth Cirrus	R. A. J. Jones & G. Nevisky	
G-DCHB	Schleicher Ka 6E	D. L. Jones	
G-DCHC	Bolkow Phoebus C	D. A. Gardner & D. C. Ephraim	
G-DCHJ	Bolkow Phoebus C	D. C. Austin	
G-DCHL	PZL-Bielsko SZD-30	A. P. P. Scorer & A. Stocks	
G-DCHO	Aquila AT01	D. R and C. A Ho	
G-DCHT	Schleicher ASW-15	P. G. Roberts & J. M. Verrill	
G-DCHU	Schleicher K 8B	Highland Gliding Club K8 Syndicate	
G-DCHW	Schleicher ASK-13	Dorset Gliding Club Ltd	
G-DCHZ	Schleicher Ka 6E	V. Harrington	
G-DCJB	Bolkow Phoebus C	D. Clarke & R. Idle	
G-DCJJ	Bolkow Phoebus C	P. N. Maddocks	
G-DCJK	Schempp-Hirth SHK-1	R. H. Short	
G-DCJM	Schleicher K-8B	Midland Gliding Club Ltd	
G-DCJN	Schempp-Hirth SHK-1	R. J. Makin	
G-DCJR	Schempp-Hirth Cirrus	CJR Syndicate	
G-DCJY	Schleicher Ka 6CR	CJY Syndicate	
G-DCKD	PZL-Bielsko SZD-30	The Borders (Milfield) Gliding Club Ltd	
G-DCKK	Cessna F.172N	KK Group	
G-DCKL	Schleicher Ka 6E	BGA1603 Owners Syndicate	
G-DCKN	PZL-Bielsko SZD-9bis Bocian 1E	DCKN Bocian Syndicate	
G-DCKP	Schleicher ASW-15	ASW 15-BGA1606 Partnership	
G-DCKR	Schleicher ASK-13	Bidford Gliding Ltd	
G-DCKV	Schleicher ASK-13	Black Mountains Gliding Club	
G-DCKY	Glasflugel Standard Libelle 201B	G. Herbert	
G-DCKZ	Schempp-Hirth Standard Cirrus	G. I. Bustin	
G-DCLA	Schempp-Hirth Standard Cirrus	C. J. Hughes & D. J. Dye	
G-DCLM	Glasflugel Standard Libelle 201B	C. J. Heide & J. H. Newberry	
G-DCLO	Schempp-Hirth Cirrus	Bravo Delta Group	
G-DCLP	Glasflugel Standard Libelle 201B	D. Heaton	
G-DCLT	Schleicher K7	A. H. Watkins	
G-DCLV	Glasflugel Standard Libelle 201B	P. Ottomaniello	
G-DCLZ	Schleicher Ka 6E	T. D. Fielder & R. M. King	
G-DCMF	PZL-Bielsko SZD-32A Foka 5	K. Szent-Wanyi	
G-DCMG	Schleicher K7	J. P. Bakker	
G-DCMH	Glasflugel H201B Standard Libelle	D. Williams	
G-DCMI	Mainair Pegasus Quik	S. J. E. Smith	
G-DCMK	Schleicher ASK-13	The South Wales Gliding Club Ltd	
G-DCMN	Schleicher K 8B	The Bristol Gliding Club Proprietary Ltd	
G-DCMO	Glasflugel Standard Libelle 201B	L. C. Wood & E. V. Todd	
G-DCMR	Glasflugel Standard Libelle 201B	S. F. Scougall	
G-DCMS	Glasflugel Standard Libelle 201B	Libelle 602 Syndicate	
G-DCMV	Glasflugel Standard Libelle 201B	L. B. Roberts	
G-DCMW	Glasflugel Standard Libelle 201B	T. Rose	
G-DCNC	Schempp-Hirth Standard Cirrus	Cirrus 273 Syndicate	
G-DCND	PZL-Bielsko SZD-9bis Bocian 1E	Angus Gliding Club Ltd	
G-DCNE	Glasflugel Standard Libelle 201B	25 Syndicate	
G-DCNG	Glasflugel Standard Libelle 201B	J. Mitcheson	
G-DCNJ	Glasflugel Standard Libelle 201B	R. Thornley	
G-DCNM	PZL-Bielsko SZD-9bis Bocian 1E	Bocian Syndicate	
G-DCNP	Glasflugel Standard Libelle 201B	I. G. Carrick & I. R.Thompson	
G-DCNS	Slingsby T.59A Kestrel	J. R. Greenwell	

Notes	Reg.	Type	Owner or Operator
	G-DCNW	Slingsby T.59F Kestrel	S. R. Watson
	G-DCNX	Slingsby T.59F Kestrel	M. Boxall
	G-DCNY	Glasflugel Standard Libelle 201B	Libelle 151 Syndicate
	G-DCOJ	Slingsby T.59A Kestrel	T. W. Treadaway
	G-DCON	Robinson R44	D. Connolly/Ireland
	G-DCOR	Schempp-Hirth Standard Cirrus	J. D. Drury
	G-DCOY	Schempp-Hirth Standard Cirrus	A. D. Walsh & M. R. Latham
	G-DCPA	MBB BK.117C-1C	Veritair Aviation Ltd (G-LFBA)
	G-DCPB	Eurocopter MBB-BK 117C-2	Devon & Cornwall Constabulary
	G-DCPD	Schleicher ASW-17	A. J. Hewitt
	G-DCPG	Schleicher K7	A. L. Maitland & D. N. Mackay
	G-DCPJ	Schleicher KA6E	E. Lown
	G-DCPM	Glasflugel Standard Libelle 201B	K. Marsden & P. E. Jessop
	G-DCPU	Schempp-Hirth Standard Cirrus	P. J. Ketelaar
	G-DCPV	PZL-Bielsko SZD-30 Pirat	CPV Group
	G-DCRB	Glasflugel Standard Libelle 201B	A. I. Mawer
	G-DCRH	Schempp-Hirth Standard Cirrus	P. E. Thelwall
	G-DCRN	Schempp-Hirth Standard Cirrus	S. McLaughlin & J. Craig
	G-DCRO	Glasflugel Standard Libelle 201B	G-DCRO Group
	G-DCRS	Glasflugel standard Libelle 201B	J. R. Hiley
	G-DCRT	Schleicher ASK-13	Bowland Forest Gliding Club Ltd
	G-DCRV	Glasflugel Standard Libelle 201B	I. Ashdown
	G-DCRW	Glasflugel Standard Libelle 201B	417 Syndicate
	G-DCSB	Slingsby T.59F Kestrel	W. Fischer
	G-DCSD	Slingsby T.59D Kestrel	P. G. Fairness
	G-DCSE	Robinson R44	Heli Air Ltd
	G-DCSF	Slingsby T.59F Kestrel 19	R. Birch
	G-DCSG	Robinson R44	Voute Sales Ltd (G-TRYG)
	G-DCSJ	Glasflugel Standard Libelle 201B	P. J. Gill
	G-DCSK	Slingsby T.59D Kestrel	Kestrel CSK Group
	G-DCSN	Pilatus B4-PC11AF	J. S. Firth
	G-DCSP	Pilatus B4-PC11	G-DCSP Group
	G-DCSR	Glasflugel Standard Libelle 201B	Glasgow and West
	G-DCTB	Schempp-Hirth Standard Cirrus	I. M. Young & S. McCurdy
	G-DCTE	Schleicher ASW-17	C. A. & S. C. Noujaim
	G-DCTJ	Slingsby T.59D Kestrel	H. B. Walrond
	G-DCTL	Slingsby T.59D Kestrel	E. S. E. Hibbard
	G-DCTM	Slingsby T.59D Kestrel	C. Roney
	G-DCTO	Slingsby T.59D Kestrel	K. A. Moules
	G-DCTP	Slingsby T.59D Kestrel	D. C. Austin
	G-DCTR	Slingsby T.59D Kestrel	M. W. Hands
	G-DCTT	Schempp-Hirth Standard Cirrus	E. Sparrow
	G-DCTU	Glasflugel Standard Libelle 201B	F. K. Hutchinson & P. M. Davies
	G-DCTV	PZL-Bielsko SZD-30	Black Mountains Gliding Club
	G-DCTX	PZL-Bielsko SZD-30	Dave King, John Cooper, Ben Fantham Group
	G-DCUB	Pilatus B4-PC11	Staffordshire Gliding Club Ltd
	G-DCUC	Pilatus B4-PC11	G. M. Cumner
	G-DCUD	Yorkshire Sailplanes YS53 Sovereign	T. J. Wilkinson
	G-DCUJ	Glasflugel Standard Libelle 201B	T. G. B. Hobbis
	G-DCUO	Pilatus B4-PC11	Cotswold Gliding Club
	G-DCUS	Schempp-Hirth Cirrus VTC	G. Wearing and Partners
	G-DCUT	Pilatus B4 PC11AF	A. L. Walker
	G-DCVA	LET L-13 Blanik	Andreas Gliding Club Ltd
	G-DCVB	LET L-13 Blanik	Blanik Syndicate
	G-DCVE	Schempp-Hirth Cirrus VTC	H. Whybrow
	G-DCVG	Pilatus B4-PC11AF	J. Paepke
	G-DCVK	Pilatus B4-PC11AF	J. P. Marriott
	G-DCVL	Glasflugel Standard Libelle 201B	J. Williams
	G-DCVM	Pilatus B4-PC11AF	R. P. F. Aguiar & C. J. D. Gorjao
	G-DCVR	PZL-Bielsko SZD-30 Pirat	M. H. Sims
	G-DCVS	PZL-Bielsko SZD-36A	CVS Group
	G-DCVV	Pilatus B4-PC11AF	Syndicate CVV
	G-DCVW	Slingsby T.59D Kestrel	J. J. Green
	G-DCVY	Slingsby T.59D Kestrel	N. Dickenson
	G-DCWA	Slingsby T.59D Kestrel	D. J. Jeffries
	G-DCWB	Slingsby T.59D Kestrel	Kestrel 677 Syndicate
	G-DCWD	Slingsby T.59D Kestrel	Deeside Kestrel Group
	G-DCWE	Glasflugel Standard Libelle 201B	T. W. J. Stoker
	G-DCWF	Slingsby T.59D Kestrel	P. F. Nicholson
	G-DCWG	Glasflugel Standard Libelle 201B	Libelle 322 Group
	G-DCWH	Schleicher ASK-13	York Gliding Centre Ltd
	G-DCWJ	Schleicher K7	Angus Gliding Club K7 Syndicate

Reg.	Type	Owner or Operator	Notes
G-DCWR	Schempp-Hirth Cirrus VTC	CWR Group	
G-DCWS	Schempp-Hirth Cirrus VTC	K. Ruxton, R. Cassels, D. Fairbank & B. A. Hutchins	
G-DCWT	Glasflugel Standard Libelle 201B	B. J. Darton	
G-DCWX	Glasflugel Standard Libelle	C. A. Weyman	
G-DCWY	Glasflugel Standard Libelle 201B	S. J. Taylor	
G-DCWZ	Glasflugel Standard Libelle 201B	F. C. F. Van der Linden	
G-DCXK	Glasflugel Standard Libelle 201B	C. A. Turner	
G-DCXL	Jodel D.140C	A. C. D. Norris/France	
G-DCXM	Slingsby T.59D Kestrel	R. P. Beck & T. Potter	
G-DCXV	Yorkshire Sailplanes YS-53 Sovereign	T53 Syndicate	
G-DCYA	Pilatus B4 PC-11	B4-072 Group	
G-DCYD	PZL-Bielsko SZD-30 Pirat	J. P. Thompson & E. Vyorlova	
G-DCYG	Glasflugel H201B Standard Libelle	R. Barsby & A. C. S. Lintott	
G-DCYM	Schempp-Hirth Standard Cirrus	K. M. Fisher	
G-DCYO	Schempp-Hirth Standard Cirrus	M. D. Wright	
G-DCYP	Schempp-Hirth Standard Cirrus	A. F. Scott	
G-DCYT	Schempp-Hirth Standard Cirrus	R. Robertson	
G-DCYZ	Schleicher K 8B	Oxford Gliding Co.Ltd	
G-DCZD	Pilatus B4 PC-11	S. E. Marples	
G-DCZE	PZL-Bielsko SZD-30	L. A. Bean	
G-DCZG	PZL-Bielsko SZD-30	J. T. Pajdak	
G-DCZJ	PZL-Bielsko SZD-30	B. L. C. Gordon	
G-DCZN	Schleicher ASW-15B	G-DCZN Group	
G-DCZO	Slingsby T.59D Kestrel	P. W. Schartau	
G-DCZR	Slingsby T.59D Kestrel	R. P. Brisbourne	
G-DCZU	Slingsby T.59D Kestrel	M. P. Edwards	
G-DCZZ	Slingsby T.59D Kestrel	C. J. Lowrie	
G-DDAC	PZL-Bielsko SZD-36A	R. J. A. Colenso	
G-DDAJ	Shempp-Hirth Nimbus 2	J. D. Jones	
G-DDAK	Schleicher K-7	Vale of Neath Gliding Club	
G-DDAN	PZL-Bielsko SZD-30	J. M. A. Shannon	
G-DDAP	SZL-Bielsko SZD-30	Delta Alpha Papa Group	
G-DDAS	Schempp-Hirth Standard Cirrus	G. Goodenough	
G-DDAU	PZL-Bielsko SZD-30	Buckminster Gliding Club Ltd	
G-DDAV	Robinson R44 II	Heli Air Ltd	
G-DDAW	Schleicher Ka 6CR	P. S. Holmes & R. G. Charlesson	
G-DDAY	PA-28R-201T Turbo Arrow III	G-DDAY Group (G-BPDO)	
G-DDBB	Slingsby T.51 Dart 17R	M. D. J. Ladley	
G-DDBC	Pilatus B4-PC11	J. H. France & G. R. Harris	
G-DDBD	Shaw Europa XS	B. Davies	
G-DDBG	ICA IS-29D	P. S. Whitehead	
G-DDBK	Slingsby T.59D Kestrel	523 Syndicate	
G-DDBN	Slingsby T.59D Kestrel	I. B. Kennedy	
G-DDBP	Glasflugel Club Libelle 205	J. P. Beach	
G-DDBS	Slingsby T.59D Kestrel	M. Bond	
G-DDBV	PZL-Bielsko SZD-30	L. Clarke	
G-DDCA	PZL-Bielsko SZD-36A Cobra 15	J. Young & J. R. Aylesbury	
G-DDCC	Glasflugel Standard Libelle 201B	G-DDCC Syndicate	
G-DDCW	Schleicher Ka 6CR	B. W. Rendall	
G-DDDA	Schempp-Hirth Standard Cirrus	A. J. Davis & C. G. Wrigley	
G-DDDB	Schleicher ASK-13	Shenington Gliding Club	
G-DDDD	Evektor EV-97 TeamEurostar UK	S. Sebastian	
G-DDDE	PZL-Bielsko SZD-38A Jantar 1	Jantar One Syndicate	
G-DDDL	Schleicher K8B	York Gliding Centre Ltd	
G-DDDM	Schempp-Hirth Cirrus	DDM Syndicate	
G-DDDR	Schempp-Hirth Standard Cirrus	J. D. Ewence	
G-DDDW	PZL-Bielsko SZD-30	R. M. Golding, D. Gear & S. B. Butcher	
G-DDDY	P & M Quik GT450	J. W. Dodson	
G-DDEA	Slingsby T.59D Kestrel	A. Pickles	
G-DDEB	Slingsby T.59D Kestrel	J. L. Smoker	
G-DDEG	ICA IS-28B2	P. S. Whitehead	
G-DDEO	Glasflugel H205 Club Libelle	N. J. Mitchell	
G-DDEP	Schleicher Ka-6CR	M. D. Brooks	
G-DDEV	Schleicher Ka-6CR	A. N. & L. M. Morley	
G-DDEW	ICA-Brasov IS-29D	G. V. Prater	
G-DDEX	LET-13 Blanik	Blanik DEX Group	
G-DDFC	Schempp-Hirth Standard Cirrus	C. E. & I. Helme	
G-DDFE	Molino PIK-20B	M. A. Roff-Jarrett	
G-DDFK	Molino PIK-20B	B. H. & M. J. Fairclough	

Notes	Reg.	Type	Owner or Operator
	G-DDFL	PZL-Bielsko SZD-38A Jantar 1	P. Bellham
	G-DDFN	Glaser-Dirks DG-100	D. J. Clarke & J. Melling
	G-DDFR	Grob G.102 Astir CS	The Windrushers Gliding Club Ltd
	G-DDFV	PZL-Bielsko SZD-38A Jantar 1	G. S. J. Bambrook & A. Purcell
	G-DDFW	PZL-Bielsko SZD-30	Cloud Nine Syndicate
	G-DDFX	PZL-Bielsko SZD-41A Jantar Standard 1	T. D. Lynch
	G-DDGA	Schleicher K-8B	The Welland Gliding Club Ltd
	G-DDGE	Schempp-Hirth Standard Cirrus	A. S. Cobbett
	G-DDGG	Schleicher Ka 6E	N. F. Holmes & F. D. Platt
	G-DDGH	PZL-Bielsko SZD-30 Pirat	M. Ling
	G-DDGJ	Champion 8KCAB	Western Air (Thruxton) Ltd
	G-DDGK	Schleicher Ka 6CR	R. G. Olsen
	G-DDGV	Breguet 905S Fauvette	J. N. Lee
	G-DDGX	Schempp-Hirth Standard Cirrus 75	USKGC Group
	G-DDGY	Schempp-Hirth Nimbus 2B	Nimbus 195 Group
	G-DDHA	Schleicher K 8B	Shalborne Soaring Society Ltd
	G-DDHC	PZL-Bielsko SZD-41A	P. J. Kelly
	G-DDHE	Slingsby T.53B	Aviation Preservation Society of Scotland
	G-DDHG	Schleicher Ka 6CR	Angus Gliding Club Ltd
	G-DDHH	Eiriavion PIK-20B	D. M. Steed
	G-DDHJ	Glaser-Dirks DG-100	G. E. McLaughlin
	G-DDHK	Glaser-Dirks DG-100	B. J. Griffin
	G-DDHL	Glaser-Dirks DG-100	DHL Syndicate
	G-DDHM	Schleicher Ka 6E	J. G. Heard
	G-DDHN	Eiriavion PIK-20B	G. Bass and Partners
	G-DDHT	Schleicher Ka 6E	M. A. Jones
	G-DDHW	Schempp-Hirth Nimbus 2	M. J. Carruthers & D. Thompson
	G-DDHX	Schempp-Hirth Standard Cirrus B	J. Franke
	G-DDHZ	PZL-Bielsko SZD-30	Peterborough and Spalding Gliding Club
	G-DDIG	Rockwell Commander 114	Daedalus Flying Group (G-CCDT)
	G-DDJB	Schleicher K-8B	Portsmouth Naval Gliding Centre
	G-DDJD	Grob G.102 Astir CS	P. E. Gascoigne
	G-DDJE	Schleicher Ka-6CR	The Friday Syndicate
	G-DDJF	Schempp-Hirth Duo Discus T	R. J. H. Fack
	G-DDJK	Schleicher ASK-18	Booker Gliding Club Ltd
	G-DDJM	PZL-Bielsko SZD-41A Jantar Standard 1	G. Dennis, T. Davies & P. Moorehead
	G-DDJN	Eiriavion PIK-20B	M. Ireland & S. Lambourne
	G-DDJR	Schleicher Ka 6CR	Syndicate K6
	G-DDJX	Grob G.102 Astir CS	P. Barnwell & R. Duke
	G-DDKC	Schleicher K 8B	Yorkshire Gliding Club (Proprietary) Ltd
	G-DDKD	Glasflugel Hornet	Hornet Syndicate
	G-DDKE	Schleicher ASK-13	The South Wales Gliding Club Ltd
	G-DDKG	Schleicher Ka 6CR	Kilo Golf Group
	G-DDKL	Schempp-Hirth Nimbus 2	G. J. Croll
	G-DDKM	Glasflugel Hornet	R. S. Lee
	G-DDKN	Schleicher Ka 6CR	A. Ciccone
	G-DDKR	Grob G.102 Astir CS	Oxford Gliding Co.Ltd
	G-DDKS	Grob G.102 Astir CS	Oxford Gliding Co.Ltd
	G-DDKT	Eiriavion PIK-20B	F. P. Wilson
	G-DDKU	Grob G.102 Astir CS	Delta Kilo Uniform Syndicate
	G-DDKV	Grob G.102 Astir CS	T. J. Ireson
	G-DDKW	Grob G.102 Astir CS	Southdown Gliding Club Ltd
	G-DDKX	Grob G.102 Astir CS	L. R. Bennett
	G-DDLA	Pilatus B4 PC-11	P. R. Seddon
	G-DDLB	Schleicher ASK-18	The Vale of the White Horse Gliding Centre Ltd
	G-DDLC	Schleicher ASK-13	Lasham Gliding Society Ltd
	G-DDLE	Schleicher Ka 6E	P. J. Abbott & J. Banks
	G-DDLG	Schempp-Hirth Standard Cirrus 75	S. Naylor
	G-DDLH	Grob G.102 Astir CS77	M. D. & M. E. Saunders
	G-DDLJ	Eiriavion PIK-20B	M. S. Parkes
	G-DDLM	Grob G.102 Astir CS	K. Dyer & D. Hilton
	G-DDLP	Schleicher Ka 6CR	J. R. Crosse
	G-DDLS	Schleicher K 8B	North Devon Gliding Club
	G-DDLT	ICA IS-28B2	M. P. Wiseman
	G-DDLY	Eiriavion PIK-20D	M. Conrad
	G-DDMB	Schleicher K 8B	Crown Service Gliding Club
	G-DDMD	Glaser-Dirks DG-100	N. M. Hill
	G-DDMG	Schleicher K 8B	Dorset Gliding Club Ltd
	G-DDMH	Grob G.102 Astir CS	C. K. Lewis
	G-DDMK	Schempp-Hirth SHK-1	D. Breeze
	G-DDML	Schleicher K-7	Dumfries and District Gliding Club
	G-DDMM	Schempp-Hirth Nimbus 2	T. Linee

Reg.	Type	Owner or Operator	Notes
G-DDMN	Glasflugel Mosquito	DMN Group	
G-DDMO	Schleicher Ka 6E	Trent Valley Gliding Club Ltd	
G-DDMP	Grob G.102 Astir CS	Kingswood Syndicate	
G-DDMR	Grob G.102 Astir CS	Mendip Gliding Club Ltd	
G-DDMS	Glasflugel Standard Libelle 201B	G-DDMS Group	
G-DDMU	Eiriavion PIK-20D	J. Mjels	
G-DDMV	NA T-6G Texan (493209)	C. Dabin	
G-DDMX	Schleicher ASK-13	Dartmoor Gliding Society Ltd	
G-DDNC	Grob G.102 Astir CS	K. S. Wells & R. A. Lovegrove	
G-DDND	Pilatus B4-PC11AF	DND Group	
G-DDNE	Grob G.102 Astir CS77	621 Astir Syndicate	
G-DDNF	PZL-Bielsko SZD-9bis Bocian 1D	Portmoak Bocian (DNF) Syndicate	
G-DDNG	Schempp-Hirth Nimbus 2	Nimbus 265 Syndicate	
G-DDNJ	Schleicher ASK-18	Derbyshire and Lancashire Gliding Club Ltd	
G-DDNK	Grob G.102 Astir CS	G-DDNK Group	
G-DDNT	PZL-Bielsko SZD-30	R. K. Lashly	
G-DDNU	PZL-Bielsko SZD-42-1 Jantar 2	C. D. Rowland & D. Chalmers-Brown	
G-DDNV	Schleicher ASK-13	Channel Gliding Club Ltd	
G-DDNW	Schleicher Ks 6CR	K. Marchant & P. Carey	
G-DDNX	Schleicher Ka 6CR	Black Mountains Gliding Club	
G-DDNZ	Schleicher K 8B	Southampton University Gliding Club	
G-DDOA	Schleicher ASK-13	Essex and Suffolk Gliding Club Ltd	
G-DDOB	Grob G.102 Astir CS77	C. E. Hutson	
G-DDOC	Schleicher Ka 6CR	W. St. G. V. Stoney	
G-DDOE	Grob G.102 Astir CS77	Heron Gliding Club	
G-DDOF	Schleicher Ka 6CR	A. J. Watson	
G-DDOG	SA Bulldog Srs 120/121 (XX524:04)	Deltaero Ltd	
G-DDOK	Schleicher Ka 6E	R. S. Hawley & S. Y. Duxbury	
G-DDOR	Grob G.102 Astir CS77	V. A. Watt	
G-DDOU	Eiriavion PIK-20D	DQU Syndicate	
G-DDOX	Schleicher K-7	The Nene Valley Gliding Club Ltd	
G-DDOY	Schleicher K-8B	Mendip Gliding Club Ltd	
G-DDPA	Schleicher ASK-18	J. P. Kirby	
G-DDPH	Schempp-Hirth Mini-Nimbus B	J. W. Murdoch	
G-DDPK	Glasflugel H303A Mosquito	G. Lawley	
G-DDPL	Eiriavion PIK-20D	437 Syndicate	
G-DDPO	Grob G.102 Astrir CS77	Dorset Gliding Club Ltd	
G-DDPY	Grob G.102 Astir CS77	D. S. Burton	
G-DDRA	Schleicher Ka 6CR	K6CR Group Shobdon	
G-DDRB	Glaser-Dirks DG-100	DRB Syndicate	
G-DDRD	Schleicher Ka 6CR	Essex and Suffolk Gliding Club Ltd	
G-DDRE	Schleicher Ka 6CR	J. H. Jowett & I. D. King	
G-DDRJ	Schleicher ASK-13	Lasham Gliding Society Ltd	
G-DDRL	Scheibe SF26A	T. A. Lipinski	
G-DDRM	Schleicher K 7	K7 DRM Syndicate	
G-DDRN	Glasflugel H303A Mosquito	A. & V. R. Roberts	
G-DDRO	Grob G.103 Twin Astir	Astir 258 Syndicate	
G-DDRP	Pilatus B4-PC11	DRP Syndicate	
G-DDRT	Eiriavion PIK-20D	PIK 688 Syndicate	
G-DDRU	Grob G.102 Astir CS77	I. P. Stork	
G-DDRV	Schleicher K 8B	DRV Syndicate	
G-DDRW	Grob G.102 Astir CS	I. W. & J. R. King	
G-DDRY	Schleicher Ka 6CR	M. K. Bradford	
G-DDRZ	Schleicher K-8B	East Sussex Gliding Club Ltd	
G-DDSB	Schleicher Ka-6E	G. B. Griffiths	
G-DDSF	Schleicher K-8B	Edinburgh University Gliding Club	
G-DDSG	Schleicher Ka 6CR	S. Montandon	
G-DDSH	Grob G.102 Astir CS77	Astir 648 Syndicate	
G-DDSJ	Grob G.103 Twin Astir II	Herefordshire Gliding Club Ltd	
G-DDSL	Grob G.103 Twin Astir	DSL Group	
G-DDSP	Schempp-Hirth Mini Nimbus B	270 Syndicate	
G-DDST	Schleicher ASW-20L	D. J. Miller	
G-DDSU	Grob G.102 Astir CS77	Bowland Forest Gliding Club Ltd	
G-DDSV	Pilatus B4-PC11AF	G. M. Drinkell & S. J. Brenton	
G-DDSX	Schleicher ASW-19B	B. Ashbourn & G. Kamp	
G-DDSY	Schleicher Ka-6CR	W. G. Johnson & P. J. Shuff	
G-DDTA	Glaser-Dirks DG-200	M. D. Bowman	
G-DDTC	Schempp-Hirth Janus B	Darlton Gliding Club Ltd	
G-DDTE	Schleicher ASW-19B	G. R. & A. Purcell	
G-DDTG	Schempp-Hirth SHK-1	D. B. Smith	
G-DDTK	Glasflugel Mosquito B	P. France	
G-DDTM	Glaser-Dirks DG-200	R. S. Skinner	

Notes	Reg.	Type	Owner or Operator
	G-DDTN	Schleicher K 8B	C. G. & G. N. Thomas
	G-DDTP	Schleicher ASW-20	T. S. & S. M. Hills
	G-DDTS	CARMAM M-100S	I. A. Macadam
	G-DDTU	Schempp-Hirth Nimbus 2B	Nimbus Syndicate
	G-DDTV	Glasflugel Mosquito B	S. R. Evans
	G-DDTW	PZL-Bielsko SZD-30 Pirat	NDGC Pirat Syndicate
	G-DDTX	Glasflugel Mosquito B	P. T. S. Nash
	G-DDTY	Glasflugel H303 Mosquito B	W. H. L. Bullimore
	G-DDUB	Glasflugel H303 Mosquito B	Mosquito Group
	G-DDUE	Schleicher ASK-13	Army Gliding Association
	G-DDUF	Schleicher K 8B	M. Staljan
	G-DDUH	Scheibe L-Spatz 55	R. J. Aylesbury & J. Young
	G-DDUK	Schleicher K-8B	The Bristol Gliding Club Propietary Ltd
	G-DDUL	Grob G.102 Astir CS77	G. R. Davey
	G-DDUR	Schleicher Ka 6CR	B. N. Bromley & M. Witthread
	G-DDUS	Schleicher Ka 6E	R. A. Bartlett
	G-DDUT	Schleicher ASW-20	M. E. Doig & E. T. J. Murphy
	G-DDUY	Glaser-Dirks DG-100	R. L. & K. P. McLean
	G-DDVB	Schleicher ASK-13	Essex and Suffolk Gliding Club Ltd
	G-DDVC	Schleicher ASK-13	Staffordshire Gliding Club Ltd
	G-DDVD	LET L-13 Blanik	Vectis Gliding Club Ltd
	G-DDVG	Schleicher Ka-6CR	G-DDVG Banana Group
	G-DDVH	Schleicher Ka 6E	M. A. K. Cropper
	G-DDVK	PZL-Bielsko SZD-48 Jantar Standard 2	G. P. Nuttall
	G-DDVL	Schleicher ASW-19	A. C. M. Phillips
	G-DDVM	Glasflugel H205 Club Libelle	M. A. Field
	G-DDVN	Eiriavion PIL-20D-78	T. P. Bassett & A. D. Butler
	G-DDVP	Schleicher ASW-19B	VP Syndicate
	G-DDVS	Schempp-Hirth Standard Cirrus	J. C. & T. J. Milner
	G-DDVV	Schleicher ASW-20L	A. M. Hooper
	G-DDVX	Schleicher ASK-13	Shenington Gliding Club
	G-DDVY	Schempp-Hirth Cirrus	M. G. Ashton & G. Martin
	G-DDVZ	Glasflugel H303 Mosquito B	B. H. Shaw & R. Spreckley
	G-DDWB	Glasflugel H303 Mosquito B	D. T. Edwards
	G-DDWC	Schleicher Ka 6E	D. E. Jones
	G-DDWG	Schleicher K-8B	Dartmoor Gliding Society Ltd
	G-DDWJ	Glaser-Dirks DG-200	A. P. Kamp & P. R. Desmond
	G-DDWL	Glasflugel Mosquito B	H. A. Stanford
	G-DDWN	Schleicher K7 Rhonadler	L. R. & J. E. Merritt
	G-DDWP	Glasflugel Mosquito B	I. H. Murdoch
	G-DDWR	Glasflugel Mosquito B	C. D. Lovell
	G-DDWS	Eiriavion PIK-20D	D. G. Slocombe
	G-DDWT	Slingsby T.65C Vega	A. P. Grimley
	G-DDWU	Grob G.102 Astir CS	G-DDWU Syndicate
	G-DDWW	Slingsby T.65A Vega	G-DDWW Flying Group
	G-DDWZ	Schleicher ASW-19B	P. Woodcock
	G-DDXA	Glasflugel H303 Mosquito B	G-DDXA Group
	G-DDXB	Schleicher ASW-20	81 Syndicate
	G-DDXD	Slingsby T.65A Vega	G-DDXD Flying Group
	G-DDXE	Slingsby T.65A Vega	H. K. Rattray
	G-DDXF	Slingsby T.65A Vega	B. A. Walker
	G-DDXG	Slingsby T.65A Vega	DXG Group
	G-DDXH	Schleicher Ka 6E	D. E. Findon
	G-DDXJ	Grob G.102 Astir CS77	M. T. Stickland
	G-DDXK	Centrair ASW-20F	E. & A. Townsend
	G-DDXL	Schempp-Hirth Standard Cirrus	C. J. Button
	G-DDXN	Glaser-Dirks DG-200	J. A. Johnston
	G-DDXT	Schempp-Hirth Mini-Nimbus C	G-DDXT Mini-Nimbus
	G-DDXW	Glasflugel Mosquito B	I. W. Myles & J. E. Shaw
	G-DDXX	Schleicher ASW-19B	B. C. P. Crook
	G-DDYC	Schleicher Ka 6CR	F. J. Bradley
	G-DDYE	Schleicher ASW-20L	828 Syndicate
	G-DDYF	Grob G.102 Astir CS77	York Gliding Centre Ltd
	G-DDYH	Glaser-Dirks DG-200	P. Johnson
	G-DDYJ	Schleicher Ka 6CR	Upward Bound Trust
	G-DDYL	CARMAM JP 15-36AR	P. A. Pickering
	G-DDYR	Schleicher K7	University of the West of England Gliding Club
	G-DDYU	Schempp-Hirth Nimbus -2C	K. Richards
	G-DDYX	Schleicher ASW-20	J. L. Bugbee
	G-DDZA	Slingsby T.65A Vega	K-H. Kuntze
	G-DDZB	Slingsby T.65A Vega	A. A. Black
	G-DDZF	Schempp-Hirth Standard Cirrus	L. S., J. M. & R. S. Hood

Reg.	Type	Owner or Operator	Notes
G-DDZG	Schleicher ASW-19B	M. P. Theo	
G-DDZJ	Grob G.102 Astir CS Jeans	Mendip Astir Syndicate	
G-DDZM	Slingsby T.65A Vega	Vega Syndicate	
G-DDZN	Slingsby T.65A Vega	D. A. White	
G-DDZP	Slingsby T.65A Vega	M. T. Crews	
G-DDZR	IS-28B2	The Furness Gliding Club Proprietary Ltd	
G-DDZT	Eiriavion PIK-20D	PIK-20D 106 Group	
G-DDZU	Grob G.102 Astir CS	P. Clarke	
G-DDZV	Scheibe SF-27A	N. Newham	
G-DDZW	Schleicher Ka 6CR	S. W. Naylor	
G-DDZY	Schleicher ASW-19B	M. C. Fairman	
G-DEAE	Schleicher ASW-20L	R. Burghall	
G-DEAF	Grob G.102 Astir CS77	The Borders (Milfield) Gliding Club Ltd	
G-DEAG	Slingsby T.65A Vega	D. L. King	
G-DEAH	Schleicher Ka 6E	M. Lodge	
G-DEAJ	Schempp-Hirth Nimbus 2	R. M. Crockett	
G-DEAK	Glasflugel H303 Mosquito B	T. A. L. Barnes	
G-DEAM	Schempp-Hirth Nimbus 2B	Alpha Mike Syndicate	
G-DEAN	Solar Wings Pegasus XL-Q	Y. G. Richardson (G-MVJV)	
G-DEAR	Eiriavion PIK-20D	G-DEAR Group	
G-DEAT	Eiriavion PIK-20D	A. Spencer & D. Bieniasz	
G-DEAU	Schleicher K7	The Welland Gliding Club Ltd	
G-DEAV	Schempp-Hirth Mini-Nimbus C	G. D. H. Crawford	
G-DEAW	Grob G.102 Astir CS77	EAW Group	
G-DEBR	Shaw Europa	P. Curley	
G-DEBT	Pioneer 300	N. J. T. Tonks	
G-DEBX	Schleicher ASW-20	R. J. L. Clark	
G-DECC	Schleicher Ka 6CR	Redwing	
G-DECF	Schleicher Ka 6CR	ECF Group	
G-DECG	Schempp-Hirth SHK-1	J. L. Williams & M. F. Hardy	
G-DECH	Glasflugel H303 Mosquito B	A. & R. Walker	
G-DECJ	Slingsby T.65A Vega	J. Hart	
G-DECK	Cessna T.210N	C. E. Wright	
G-DECL	Slingsby T.65A Vega	J. E. Strzebrakowski	
G-DECM	Slingsby T.65A Vega	F. Wilson	
G-DECO	Dyn'Aéro MCR-01 Club	G-DECO Flying Group	
G-DECP	Rolladen-Schneider LS3-17	M. H. Ewer & K. Fear	
G-DECR	P & M Quik R	D. V. Lawrence	
G-DECS	Glasflugel H303 Mosquito B	A. C. Cummins & K. L. Fixter	
G-DECW	Schleicher ASK-21	Norfolk Gliding Club Ltd	
G-DECZ	Schleicher ASK-21	Booker Gliding Club Ltd	
G-DEDB	CARMAM JP-15-36AR Aiglon	CARMAM EDB Group	
G-DEDG	Schleicher Ka 6CR	S. J. Wood	
G-DEDH	Glasflugel H303 Mosquito B	B. L. Liddiard	
G-DEDJ	Glasflugel H303 Mosquito B	D. Martin & R. Bollow	
G-DEDK	Schleicher K7 Rhonadler	North Wales Gliding Club Ltd	
G-DEDM	Glaser-Dirks DG-200	A. H. G. St.Pierre	
G-DEDN	Glaser-Dirks DG-100G	DG 280 Syndicate	
G-DEDU	Schleicher ASK-13	Channel Gliding Club Ltd	
G-DEDX	Slingsby T.65D Vega	G. Kirkham	
G-DEDY	Slingsby T.65D Vega	T. McKinley	
G-DEDZ	Slingsby T.65C Vega	Echo Delta Zulu Group	
G-DEEA	Slingsby T.65C Vega	Borders Sport Vega Syndicate	
G-DEEC	Schleicher ASW-20L	D. Beams	
G-DEED	Schleicher K-8B	The Windrushers Gliding Club Ltd	
G-DEEF	Rolladen-Schneider LS3-17	Echo Echo Foxtrot Group	
G-DEEG	Slingsby T.65C Vega	Vega Syndicate	
G-DEEH	Schleicher ASW-19	K. Kiely	
G-DEEJ	Schleicher ASW-20L	G-DEEJ Group	
G-DEEK	Schempp-Hirth Nimbus 2C	R. Cassidy & W. P. Stephen	
G-DEEM	Schleicher K-8	The South Wales Gliding Club Ltd	
G-DEEN	Schempp-Hirth Standard Cirrus 75	G-DEEN Flying Group	
G-DEEO	Grob G.102 Club Astir II	G-DEEO Group	
G-DEEP	Wassmer WA.26P Squale	B. J. Key	
G-DEES	Rolladen-Schneider LS3-17	J. B. Illidge	
G-DEEW	Schleicher Ka 6CR	S. M. Dodds	
G-DEEX	Rolladen-Schneider LS3-17	M. A. M. Pirie	
G-DEEZ	Denney Kitfox Mk.3	J. D. & D. Cheesman	
G-DEFA	Schleicher ASW-20L	Eight Eighties Syndicate	
G-DEFB	Schempp-Hirth Nimbus 2C	N. Revell	
G-DEFE	Centrair ASW-20F	W. A. Horne & D. A. Mackenzie	

Notes	Reg.	Type	Owner or Operator
	G-DEFF	Schempp-Hirth Nimbus 2C	J. W. L. Clarke and P. J. D. Smith
	G-DEFN	Scheibe L-Spatz 55	P. L. E. Duguay
	G-DEFS	Rolladen-Schneider LS3	P. R. Thomas
	G-DEFT	Flight Design CTSW	D. Arnold
	G-DEFV	Schleicher ASW-20	A. R. McKillen
	G-DEFW	Slingsby T.65C Sport Vega	Darlton Gliding Club Ltd
	G-DEFY	Robinson R22 Beta	P. M. M. P. Silveira/Portugal
	G-DEFZ	Rolladen-Schneider LS3-a	EFZ Syndicate
	G-DEGD	Schleicher ASW-17	H. Wucherer
	G-DEGE	Rolladen-Schneider LS3-a	EGE Glider Syndicate
	G-DEGF	Slingsby T.65D Vega	Shalbourne Soaring Society Ltd
	G-DEGH	Slingsby T.65C Vega	K. Dykes, M. J. Davies & R. A. Starling
	G-DEGJ	Slingsby T.65C Vega	Cotswold Vega Syndicate
	G-DEGK	Schempp-Hirth Standard Cirrus	P. H. Robinson
	G-DEGN	Grob G.103 Twin Astir II	Staffordshire Gliding Club Ltd
	G-DEGP	Schleicher ASW-20L	S. Pozerskis
	G-DEGR	Breguet 905 Fauvette	P. Parker
	G-DEGS	Schempp-Hirth Nimbus 2CS	R. C. Nichols
	G-DEGT	Slingsby T.65D Vega	Vega Syndicate EGT
	G-DEGW	Schempp-Hirth Mini-Nimbus C	I. F. Barnes and Partners
	G-DEGX	Slingsby T.65C Vega	Haddenham Vega Syndicate
	G-DEGZ	Schleicher ASK-21	Black Mountains Gliding Club
	G-DEHG	Slingsby T.65C Vega	Vega Syndicate
	G-DEHH	Schempp-Hirth Ventus a	J. A. White
	G-DEHK	Rolladen-Schneider LS4	S. Eyles & D. Puttock
	G-DEHM	Schleicher Ka 6E	J. B. Symonds
	G-DEHO	Schleicher ASK-21	Lasham Gliding Society Ltd
	G-DEHP	Schempp-Hirth Nimbus 2C	D. J. King
	G-DEHT	Schempp-Hirth Nimbus 2C	Nimbus 2C Syndicate
	G-DEHU	Glasflugel 304	F. Townsend
	G-DEHV	Schleicher ASW-20L	M. A. & B. A. Roberts
	G-DEHW	ICA IS-28B2	Y6 Group/Netherlands
	G-DEHY	Slingsby T.65D Vega	Vega Syndicate
	G-DEHZ	Schleicher ASW-20L	D. Crimmins
	G-DEJA	ICA IS-28B2	M. H. Simms
	G-DEJB	Slingsby T.65C Vega	D. Tait & I. G. Walker
	G-DEJC	Slingsby T-65C Vega	I. Powis
	G-DEJD	Slingsby T.65D Vega	R. L. & K. P. McLean
	G-DEJE	Slingsby T-65C Vega	Crown Service Gliding Club
	G-DEJF	Schleicher K 8B	Cotswold Gliding Club
	G-DEJH	Eichelsdorfer SB-5E	S. E. Richardson & B. J. Dawson
	G-DEJR	Schleicher ASW-19B	193 Syndicate
	G-DEJY	PZL-Bielsko SZD-9bis Bocian 1D	G-DEJY Group
	G-DEJZ	Scheibe SF26A	J. M. Collin
	G-DEKA	Cameron Z-90 balloon	P. G. Bogliaccino
	G-DEKC	Schleicher Ka 6E	S. L. Benn
	G-DEKD	Schleicher ASK-13	Midland Gliding Club Ltd
	G-DEKF	Grob G.102 Club Astir III	The Bristol Gliding Club Proprietary Ltd
	G-DEKG	Schleicher ASK-21	Army Gliding Association
	G-DEKJ	Schempp-Hirth Ventus b	I. J. Metcalfe
	G-DEKS	Scheibe SF27A Zugvogel V	J. C. Johnson
	G-DEKT	Wassmer WA.30	D. C. Reynolds
	G-DEKU	Schleicher ASW-20L	A. J. Gillson
	G-DEKV	Rolladen-Schneider LS4	S. L. Helstrip
	G-DEKW	Schempp-Hirth Nimbus 2B	V. Luscombe-Mahoney
	G-DELA	Schleicher ASW-19B	ELA Syndicate
	G-DELB	Robinson R-22 Beta ★	Aero Venture
	G-DELD	Slingsby T65C Vega	ELD Syndicate
	G-DELF	Aero L-29A Delfin	B. R. Green
	G-DELG	Schempp-Hirth Ventus b/16.6	A. G. Machin
	G-DELN	Grob G.102 Astir CS Jeans	Bowland Forest Gliding Club Ltd
	G-DELO	Slingsby T.65D Vega	I. Sim
	G-DELR	Schempp-Hirth Ventus b	I. D. Smith
	G-DELX	Schleicher K-7	The Nene Valley Gliding Club Ltd
	G-DELZ	Schleicher ASW-20L	D. A. Fogden
	G-DEMB	Rolladen-Schneider LS4	R. A. Hine
	G-DEME	Glaser-Dirks DG-200/17	E. D. Casagrande
	G-DEMF	Rolladen-Schneider LS4	R. N. Johnston & M. C. Oggelsby
	G-DEMG	Rolladen-Schneider LS4	R. C. Bowsfield
	G-DEMH	Cessna F.172M (modified)	M. Hammond (G-BFLO)
	G-DEMJ	Slingsby T65C Sport Vega	D. J. Miles
	G-DEMM	AS.350B2 Ecureuil	Three Counties Helicopter Co.Ltd

Reg.	Type	Owner or Operator	Notes
G-DEMN	Slingsby T.65D Vega	C. D. Sword	
G-DEMP	Slingsby T.65C Vega	The Surrey Hills Gliding Club Ltd	
G-DEMR	Slingsby T.65C Vega	D. A. Woodforth	
G-DEMT	Rolladen-Schneider LS4	M. R. Fox	
G-DEMU	Glaser-Dirks DG-202/17	A. Butterfield & N. Swinton	
G-DEMZ	Slingsby T65A Vega	Vega Syndicate (G-BGCA)	
G-DENB	Cessna F.150G	C. R. Haden (G-ATZZ)	
G-DENC	Cessna F.150G	G-DENC Cessna Group (G-AVAP)	
G-DEND	Cessna F.150M	R. N. Tate (G-WAFC/G-BDFI)	
G-DENE	PA-28 Cherokee 140	D. V. Magee (G-ATOS)	
G-DENI	PA-32 Cherokee Six 300	A. Bendkowski (G-BAIA)	
G-DENJ	Schempp-Hirth Ventus b/16.6	S. Boyden	
G-DENO	Glasflugel Standard Libelle 201B	D. M. Bland	
G-DENS	Binder CP.301S Smaragd	Garston Smaragd Group	
G-DENT	Cameron N-145 balloon	P. D. Claridge	
G-DENU	Glaser-Dirks DG-100G	435 Syndicate	
G-DENV	Schleicher ASW-20L	R. D. Hone	
G-DENX	PZL-Bielsko SZD-48 Jantar Standard 2	J. M. Hire	
G-DEOA	Rolladen-Schneider LS4	A. A. Jenkins & R. L. Smith	
G-DEOB	PZL-Bielsko SZD-30	R. A. Firmin	
G-DEOD	Grob G.102 Astir CS77	D. S. Fenton	
G-DEOE	Schleicher ASK-13	Essex Gliding Club Ltd	
G-DEOF	Schleicher ASK-13	Essex Gliding Club Ltd	
G-DEOJ	Centrair ASW-20FL	R. Grey & J. Sanders	
G-DEOK	Centrair 101A Pegase	The Pegase Group	
G-DEOM	Carman M100S	S. W. Hutchinson	
G-DEON	Schempp-Hirth Nimbus 3	N3 Group	
G-DEOT	Grob G.103A Twin II Acro	R. Tyrrell	
G-DEOU	Pilatus B4-PC11	G-DEOU Group	
G-DEOV	Schempp-Hirth Janus C	Burn Gliding Club Ltd	
G-DEOW	Schempp-Hirth Janus C	383 Syndicate	
G-DEOX	Carmam M-200 Foehn	B. S. Goodspeed	
G-DEOZ	Schleicher K 8B	Cotswold Gliding Club	
G-DEPD	Schleicher ASK-21	EPD Glider Syndicate	
G-DEPE	Schleicher ASW-19B	P. A. Goulding	
G-DEPF	Centrair ASW-20FL	323 Syndicate	
G-DEPM	Scheibe SF-34	M. H. Sims	
G-DEPP	Schleicher ASK-13	Mendip Gliding Club Ltd	
G-DEPS	Schleicher ASW-20L	C. Beveridge	
G-DEPT	Schleicher K-8B	C. S. Warren	
G-DEPU	Glaser-Dirks DG-101G Elan	J. F. Rogers	
G-DEPX	Schempp-Hirth Ventus b/16.6	M. E. S. Thomas	
G-DERA	Centrair ASW-20FL	R. J. Lockett	
G-DERB	Robinson R22 Beta	Heli Air Ltd (G-BPYH)	
G-DERH	Schleicher ASK-21	The Burn Gliding Club Ltd	
G-DERJ	Schleicher ASK-21	RAF Gliding and Soaring Association	
G-DERR	Schleicher ASW-19B	D. Clarke	
G-DERS	Schleicher ASW-19B	G-DERS Flying Group	
G-DERV	Cameron Truck SS balloon	J. M. Percival	
G-DERX	Centrair 101A Pegase	A. Delaney & J. Innes	
G-DESB	Schleicher ASK-21	The Old Boys	
G-DESC	Rolladen-Schneider LS4	J. Crawford & J. M. Staley	
G-DESH	Centrair 101A	J. E. Moore	
G-DESJ	Schleicher K8B	Bowland Forest Gliding Club Ltd	
G-DESO	Glaser-Dirks DG-300 Elan	G. R. P. Brown	
G-DESU	Schleicher ASK-21	Banbury Gliding Club Ltd	
G-DETA	Schleicher ASK-21	P. Hawkins	
G-DETD	Schleicher K8B	Cotswold Gliding Club	
G-DETG	Rolladen-Schneider LS4	K. J. Woods	
G-DETJ	Centrair 101A	S. C. Phillips	
G-DETK	PZL-Bielsko SZD-48 Jantar Standard 2	I. W. Paterson	
G-DETM	Centrair 101A	D. Bowden	
G-DETS	Schleicher ASK-13	Upward Bound Trust	
G-DETV	Rolladen-Schneider LS4	P. Fabian	
G-DETY	Rolladen-Schneider LS4	D. T. Staff	
G-DETZ	Schleicher ASW-20CL	The 20 Syndicate	
G-DEUC	Schleicher ASK-13	The Bristol Gliding Club Proprietary Ltd	
G-DEUD	Schleicher ASW-20C	R. Tietema	
G-DEUF	PZL-Bielsko SZD-50-3	Puchacz Group	
G-DEUH	Rolladen-Schneider LS4	A. R. Turner & F. J. Parkinson	
G-DEUJ	Schempp-Hirth Ventus b/16.6	S. C. Renfrew	
G-DEUK	Centrair ASW-20FL	P. A. Clark	

Notes	Reg.	Type	Owner or Operator
	G-DEUS	Schempp-Hirth Ventus b/16.6	R. J. Whitaker
	G-DEUV	PZL-Bielsko SZD-42-2 Jantar 2B	G. V. McKirdy
	G-DEUX	AS.355F Ecureuil 2	Elmridge Ltd
	G-DEUY	Schleicher ASW-20BL	ASW20BL-G-DUEY Group
	G-DEVF	Schempp-Hirth Nimbus 3T	A. G. Leach
	G-DEVH	Schleicher Ka 10	C. W. & K. T. Matten
	G-DEVJ	Schleicher ASK-13	Lasham Gliding Society Ltd
	G-DEVK	Grob G.102 Astir CS	Peterborough and Spalding Gliding Club Ltd
	G-DEVL	Eurocopter EC 120B	Saxon Logistics Ltd
	G-DEVM	Centrair 101A	Seahawk Gliding Club
	G-DEVO	Centrair 101A	P. G. Scott
	G-DEVP	Schleicher ASK-13	Lasham Gliding Society Ltd
	G-DEVS	PA-28 Cherokee 180	180 Group/Blackbushe (G-BGVJ)
	G-DEVV	Schleicher ASK-23	Midland Gliding Club Ltd
	G-DEVW	Schleicher ASK-23	London Gliding Club Proprietary Ltd
	G-DEVX	Schleicher ASK-23	London Gliding Club Proprietary Ltd
	G-DEVY	Schleicher ASK-23	London Gliding Club Proprietary Ltd
	G-DEWE	P & M Flight Design CTSW	Comunica Industries International Ltd
	G-DEWG	Grob G.103A Twin II Acro	J. P. Ryan
	G-DEWI	Rotorsport UK MTO Sport	D. V. Nockels
	G-DEWP	Grob G.103A Twin II Acro	Cambridge Gliding Club Ltd
	G-DEWR	Grob G.103A Twin II Acro	The Bristol Gliding Club Proprietary Ltd
	G-DEWZ	Grob G.103A Twin II Acro	T. R. Dews
	G-DEXA	Grob G.103A Twin II Acro	Trent Valley Aerotowing Club Ltd
	G-DEXP	ARV Super 2	M. Davies
	G-DEXT	Robinson R44 II	Berkley Properties Ltd
	G-DFAF	Schleicher ASW-20L	A. S. Miller
	G-DFAR	Glasflugel H205 Club Libelle	Alpha Romeo Syndicate
	G-DFAT	Schleicher ASK-13	Dorset Gliding Club Ltd
	G-DFAV	ICA IS-32A	Ibis 32 Syndicate
	G-DFAW	Schempp-Hirth Ventus b/16.6	P. R. Stafford-Allen
	G-DFBD	Schleicher ASW-15B	D. A. Wilson
	G-DFBE	Rolladen-Schneider LS6	J. B. Van Woerden
	G-DFBJ	Schleicher K 8B	Bidford Gliding Ltd
	G-DFBM	Schempp-Hirth Nimbus 3/24.5	D. Gardiner
	G-DFBO	Schleicher ASW-20BL	454 Syndicate
	G-DFBR	Grob G.102 Astir CS77	773 Syndicate
	G-DFBY	Schempp-Hirth Discus b	D. Latimer
	G-DFCD	Centrair 101A	G. J. Bass
	G-DFCK	Schempp-Hirth Ventus b	Bidford Gliding Ltd
	G-DFCL	Schleicher K 8B	Bidford Gliding Ltd
	G-DFCM	Glaser-Dirks DG-300	A. Davis & I. D. Roberts
	G-DFCW	Schleicher ASK-13	Lasham Gliding Society Ltd
	G-DFCY	Schleicher ASW-15	M. R. Shaw
	G-DFDF	Grob G.102 Astir CS	The Bristol Gliding Club Proprietary Ltd
	G-DFDP	ICA IS-30	J. Hewitt
	G-DFDW	Glaser-Dirks DG-300	C. M. Hadley
	G-DFEA	Grob G.103 Twin Astir	FEA Twin Astir Syndicate
	G-DFEB	Grob G.102 Club Astir III	Lasham Gliding Society Ltd
	G-DFEO	Schleicher ASK-13	Lasham Gliding Society Ltd
	G-DFEX	Grob G.102 Astir CS77	J. Taylor
	G-DFFP	Schleicher ASW-19B	J. M. Hutchinson
	G-DFGJ	Schleicher Ka 6CR	K6 Syndicate
	G-DFGT	Glaser-Dirks DG-300 Elan	T. J. Gray
	G-DFHS	Schempp-Hirth Ventus cT	154 Group
	G-DFHY	Scheibe SF-27A	J. M. Pursey
	G-DFJJ	Schempp-Hirth Ventus cT	S. G. Jones
	G-DFJO	Schempp-Hirth Ventus cT	B. W. T. Rood
	G-DFKH	Schleicher Ka 6CR	I. A. Megarry
	G-DFKI	Westland Gazelle HT.2	A. P. Foreman (G-BZOT)
	G-DFKX	Schleicher Ka 6CR	J. E. Herring
	G-DFLL	PZL-Bielsko SZD-9bis Bocian 10	The Bath, Wilts and North Dorset Gliding Club Ltd
	G-DFLY	PA-38-112 Tomahawk	Ravenair Aircraft Ltd/Liverpool
	G-DFMG	Schempp-Hirth Discus b	M. T. Davis
	G-DFOG	Rolladen-Schneider LS7	D. W. Smith
	G-DFOX	AS.355F1 Twin Squirrel	Potter Aviation Ltd (G-NAAS/G-BPRG/G-NWPA)
	G-DFRA	Rolladen-Schneider LS6-b	79 Syndicate
	G-DFSA	Grob G.102 Astir CS	Astir 498 Syndicate
	G-DFTJ	PZL-Bielsko SZD-48-1 Jantar Standard 2	P. Nock
	G-DFUN	Van's RV-6	G-DFUN Flying Group

Reg.	Type	Owner or Operator	Notes
G-DFWJ	Rolladen-Schneider LS7-WL	G-DFWJ Group	
G-DGAW	Schleicher Ka 6CR	H. C. Yorke & D. Searle	
G-DGCL	Glaser-Dirks DG.800B	C. J. Lowrie	
G-DGDJ	Rolladen-Schneider LS4-a	450 Syndicate	
G-DGFD	Robinson R44 II	FD Aviarion Ltd (G-CGNF)	
G-DGHI	Dyn'Aéro MCR-01 Club	D. G. Hall	
G-DGIK	DG Flugzeugbau DG.1000S	R. P. Davis	
G-DGIO	Glaser-Dirks DG-100G Elan	EDP Group	
G-DGIV	Glaser-Dirks DG.800B	S. M. Tilling & J. Vella-Grech	
G-DGOD	Robinson R22 Beta	Casdron Enterprises Ltd	
G-DGRA	DG Flugzeugbau DG-808C	R. Arkle	
G-DGSC	CZAW Sportcruiser	D. J. Gunn	
G-DGSM	Glaser-Dirks DG-400-17	T. E. Snoddy & L. J. McKelvie	
G-DHAA	Glasflugel H201B Standard Libelle	D. J. Jones & R. N. Turner	
G-DHAD	Glasflugel H201B Standard Libelle	R. Hines	
G-DHAH	Aeronca 7BCM Champion	G. D. Horn (G-JTYE)	
G-DHAL	Schleicher ASK-13	The Windrushers Gliding Club Ltd	
G-DHAP	Schleicher Ka 6E	M.Fursedon & T. Turner	
G-DHAT	Glaser-Dirks DG-200/17	G-DHAT Group	
G-DHCA	Grob G.103 Twin Astir	A. Jordan & P. Burton	
G-DHCC	DHC.1 Chipmunk 22 (WG321:G)	Eureka Aviation BVBA/Belgium	
G-DHCE	Schleicher ASW-19B	G-DHCE Syndicate	
G-DHCF	PZL-Bielsko SZD-50-3	Shalbourne Soaring Society Ltd	
G-DHCH	Centrair ASW-20F	A. C. Turk	
G-DHCJ	Grob G.103A Twin II Acro	Peterborough and Spalding Gliding Club Ltd	
G-DHCL	Schempp-Hirth Discus b	C. E. Broom & L. Chicot	
G-DHCO	Glasflugel Standard Libelle 201B	M. J. Birch	
G-DHCR	PZL-Bielsko SZD-51-1	East Sussex Gliding Club Ltd	
G-DHCU	DG-300 Club Elan	J. C. A. Garland & M. S. Smith	
G-DHCV	Schleicher ASW-19B	Birkett Air Services Ltd	
G-DHCW	PZL-Bielsko SZD-51-1	Deeside Gliding Club (Aberdeenshire) Ltd	
G-DHCX	Schleicher ASK-21	Devon and Somerset Gliding Club Ltd	
G-DHCZ	DHC.2 Beaver 1	Propshop Ltd (G-BUCJ)	
G-DHDH	Glaser-Dirks DG-200	J. T. Newbery	
G-DHDV	DH.104 Dove 8 (VP981)	Air Atlantique Ltd	
G-DHEB	Schleicher Ka 6CR	J. Burrow	
G-DHEM	Schempp-Hirth Discus CS	473 Syndicate	
G-DHER	Schleicher ASW-19B	B. Meech	
G-DHES	Centrair 101A	C. J. Cole & D. R. Bennett	
G-DHET	Rolladen-Schneider LS6-c18	M. P. Brooks	
G-DHEV	Schempp-Hirth Cirrus	HEV Group	
G-DHEZ	Rolladen-Schneider LS6-c	J. Herman & S. C. Williams	
G-DHGL	Schempp-Hirth Discus b	R. G. Corbin & S. E. Buckley	
G-DHGS	Robinson R22 Beta	RSW Aviation Ltd	
G-DHJH	Airbus A.321-211	Thomas Cook Airlines Ltd	
G-DHJZ	Airbus A.320-214	Thomas Cook Airlines Ltd	
G-DHKL	Schempp-Hirth Discus bT	M. A. Thorne	
G-DHLE	Boeing 767-3JHF	DHL Air Ltd	
G-DHLF	Boeing 767-3JHF	DHL Air Ltd	
G-DHLG	Boeing 767-3JHF	DHL Air Ltd	
G-DHMP	Schempp-Hirth Discus b	HMP Discus Syndicate	
G-DHNX	Rolladen-Schneider LS4-b	C. S. Crocker & K. J. Screen	
G-DHOC	Scheibe Bergfalke II-55	D. M. Hook	
G-DHOK	Schleicher ASW-20CL	S. D. Minson	
G-DHOP	Van's RV-9A	A. S. Orme	
G-DHOX	Schleicher ASW-15B	P. Ridgill & R. Sibley	
G-DHPA	Issoire E-78 Silene	P. Woodcock	
G-DHPM	OGMA DHC.1 Chipmunk 20 (1365)	P. Meyrick	
G-DHPR	Schempp-Hirth Discus b	G. J. Bowser	
G-DHRG	Airbus A.320-214	Thomas Cook Airlines Ltd	
G-DHRR	Schleicher ASK-21	Lakes Gliding Club	
G-DHSJ	Schempp-Hirth Discus b	A. A. Jenkins	
G-DHSL	Schempp-Hirth Ventus 2c	H. G. Woodsend	
G-DHSR	AB Sportine LAK-12 Lietuva	G. Forster	
G-DHSS	DH.112 Venom FB.50 (WR360:K)	Aviation and Computer Consultancy Ltd	
G-DHTG	Grob G.102 Astir CS	Trent Valley Gliding Club Ltd	
G-DHTM	DH.82A Tiger Moth (replica)	C. R. Hardiman	
G-DHTT	DH.112 Venom FB.50 (WR421)	Aviation and Computer Consultancy Ltd (G-BMOC)	
G-DHUB	PZL-Bielsko SZD-48-3	C. J. M. Chatburn	

Notes	Reg.	Type	Owner or Operator
	G-DHUK	Schleicher Ka 6CR	Essex Gliding Club Ltd
	G-DHUU	DH.112 Venom FB.50 (WR410)	Aviation and Computer Consultancy Ltd (G-BMOD)
	G-DHVM	DH.112 Venom FB.50 (WR470)	Air Atlantique Ltd/Coventry (G-GONE)
	G-DHYL	Schempp-Hirth Ventus 2a	M. J. Cook
	G-DHZF	DH.82A Tiger Moth (N9192)	C. A.Parker & M. R. Johnson/Sywell (G-BSTJ)
	G-DIAM	Diamond DA40D Star	Airshare LLP
	G-DIAT	PA-28 Cherokee 140	D. J. Skidmore (G-BCGK)
	G-DICK	Thunder Ax6-56Z balloon	R. D. Sargeant
	G-DIDG	Van's RV-7	E. T. & D. K. Steele
	G-DIDY	Thruster T600T 450	D. R. Sims
	G-DIGG	Robinson R44 II	Thames Materials Ltd
	G-DIGI	PA-32 Cherokee Six 300	D. Stokes
	G-DIGN	Robin DR.400/180 Regent	D. M. Green
	G-DIKY	Murphy Rebel	R. J. P. Herivel
	G-DIME	Rockwell Commander 114	H. B. Richardson
	G-DINA	AA-5B Tiger	Portway Aviation Ltd
	G-DING	Colt 77A balloon	G. J. Bell
	G-DINO	Pegasus Quantum 15	P. W. Day (G-MGMT)
	G-DIPI	Cameron 80 Tub SS balloon	C. G. Dobson
	G-DIPM	PA-46-350P Malibu Mirage	MAS Mix Ltd
	G-DIRK	Glaser-Dirks DG.400	G-DIRK Syndicate
	G-DISA	SA Bulldog Srs 120/125	British Disabled Flying Association
	G-DISK	PA-24 Comanche 250	A. M. & Harrhy (G-APZG)
	G-DISO	Jodel 150	P. F. Craven
	G-DIWY	PA-32 Cherokee Six 300	IFS Chemicals Ltd
	G-DIXY	PA-28-181 Archer III	Modern Air (UK) Ltd
	G-DIZI	Escapade	J. A. & J. M. Iszard
	G-DIZO	Jodel D.120A	D. Aldersea (G-EMKM)
	G-DIZY	PA-28R-201T Turbo Arrow III	Calverton Flying Club Ltd
	G-DIZZ	Hughes 369HE	Hopkinsons Fairdeals Remarking LLP
	G-DJAA	Schempp-Hirth Janus B	S. G. Jones
	G-DJAB	Glaser-Dirks DG-300 Elan	I. G. Johnston
	G-DJAC	Schempp-Hirth Duo Discus	G-DJAC Group
	G-DJAD	Schleicher ASK-21	The Borders (Milfield) Gliding Club Ltd
	G-DJAE	Cessna 500 Citation	Kenmare Bay Homes Ltd (G-JEAN)
	G-DJAH	Schempp-Hirth Discus b	K. Neave & C. F. M. Smith
	G-DJAN	Schempp-Hirth Discus b	N. F. Perren
	G-DJAY	Avtech Jabiru UL-450	G. S. Stokes
	G-DJBC	Ikarus C42 FB100	D. Meegan
	G-DJCR	Varga 2150A Kachina	D. J. C. Robertson (G-BLWG)
	G-DJED	Schleicher ASW-15B	Grupo JED/Portugal
	G-DJET	Diamond DA42 Twin Star	Papa Bravo Aviation Ltd
	G-DJGG	Schleicher ASW-15B	A. A. Cole
	G-DJHP	Valentin Mistral C	P. B. Higgs
	G-DJJA	PA-28-181 Archer II	Interactive Aviation Ltd
	G-DJLL	Schleicher ASK-13	Portsmouth Naval Gliding Centre
	G-DJMC	Schleicher ASK-21	RAF Gliding and Soaring Association
	G-DJMD	Schempp-Hirth Discus b	Papa 23 Group
	G-DJMM	Cessna 172S	J. Browne & M. Manston
	G-DJNC	ICA-Brasov IS-28B2	Delta Juliet November Group
	G-DJNH	Denney Kitfox Mk 3	S. M. Morgan & M. J. Turner
	G-DJST	Ixess 912(1)	D. J. Stimpson
	G-DJWS	Schleicher ASW-15B	B. Pridgeon
	G-DKBA	DKBA AT 0301-0 balloon	I. Chadwick
	G-DKDP	Grob G.109	Grob 4
	G-DKEM	Bell 407	True Course Helicopter Ltd
	G-DKEN	Rolladen-Schneider LS4-a	K. L. Sangster and B. Lytollis
	G-DKEY	PA-28-161 Warrior II	PA-28 Warrior Ltd
	G-DKFU	Schempp-Hirth Ventus 2cxT	W. F. Payton (G-CKFU)
	G-DKGF	Viking Dragonfly ★	(stored)/Enstone
	G-DKNY	Robinson R44 II	Williamair Ltd
	G-DKTA	PA-28-236 Dakota	G. Beattie & C. J. T. Kitchen
	G-DLAA	Cessna 208 Caravan 1	Aerodynamics Ltd
	G-DLAC	Cessna 208B Grand Caravan	Aerodynamics Ltd
	G-DLAL	Beech E90 King Air	Aerodynamics Ltd
	G-DLCB	Shaw Europa	K. Richards
	G-DLDL	Robinson R22 Beta	Airtask Group PLC

Reg.	Type	Owner or Operator	Notes
G-DLEE	SOCATA TB9 Tampico Club	D. A. Lee (G-BPGX)	
G-DLOM	SOCATA TB20 Trinidad	J. N. A. Adderley	
G-DLTR	PA-28 Cherokee 180E	Light Aircraft Leasing Ltd (G-AYAV)	
G-DMAC	Avtech Jabiru SP-430	C. J. Pratt	
G-DMAH	SOCATA TB20 Trinidad	William Cook Aviation Ltd	
G-DMBO	Van's RV-7	C. J. Goodwin	
G-DMCA	Douglas DC-10-30 ★	Forward fuselage/Manchester Airport Viewing Park	
G-DMCI	Ikarus C42 FB100	D. McCartan	
G-DMCS	PA-28R Cherokee Arrow 200-II	Arrow Associates (G-CPAC)	
G-DMCT	Flight Design CT2K	A. M. Sirant	
G-DMND	Diamond DA42 Twin Star	MC Air Ltd	
G-DMRA	Robinson R44 II	D. M. Richards	
G-DMRS	Robinson R44 II	Nottinghamshire Helicopters (2004) Ltd	
G-DMSS	Westland Gazelle HT.3 (XW858:C)	G. Wood	
G-DMWW	CFM Shadow Srs DD	Microlight Sport Aviation Ltd	
G-DNBH	Raj Hamsa X'Air Hawk	D. N. B. Hearn	
G-DNGA	Balóny Kubíček BB.20	G. J. Bell	
G-DNGR	Colt 31A balloon	G. J. Bell	
G-DKNY	Ikarus C42 FB80	D. N. K. & M. A. Symon	
G-DNOP	PA-46-350P Malibu Mirage	Campbell Aviation Ltd	
G-DOCA	Boeing 737-436	British Airways	
G-DOCB	Boeing 737-436	British Airways	
G-DOCE	Boeing 737-436	British Airways	
G-DOCF	Boeing 737-436	British Airways	
G-DOCG	Boeing 737-436	British Airways	
G-DOCH	Boeing 737-436	British Airways	
G-DOCL	Boeing 737-436	British Airways	
G-DOCN	Boeing 737-436	British Airways	
G-DOCO	Boeing 737-436	British Airways	
G-DOCS	Boeing 737-436	British Airways	
G-DOCT	Boeing 737-436	British Airways	
G-DOCU	Boeing 737-436	British Airways	
G-DOCV	Boeing 737-436	British Airways	
G-DOCW	Boeing 737-436	British Airways	
G-DOCX	Boeing 737-436	British Airways	
G-DOCY	Boeing 737-436	British Airways (G-BVBY)	
G-DOCZ	Boeing 737-436	British Airways (G-BVBZ)	
G-DODB	Robinson R22 Beta	Heliyorks Ltd	
G-DODD	Cessna F.172P-II	K. Watts	
G-DODG	Aerotechnik EV-97A Eurostar	K. G. Vaughan	
G-DOEA	AA-5A Cheetah	Fairway Flying Services (G-RJMI)	
G-DOFY	Bell 206B JetRanger 3	Carnigill Aviation Ltd	
G-DOGE	SA Bulldog Srs 100/101	W. P. Cooper (G-AZHX)	
G-DOGG	SA Bulldog Srs 120/121 (XX638)	P. Sengupta	
G-DOGI	Robinson R22 Beta	Northumbria Helicopters Ltd (G-BVGS)	
G-DOGZ	Horizon 1	M. J. Nolan	
G-DOIG	CZAW Sportcruiser	J. H. Doyle	
G-DOIN	Skyranger 912(S)1	A. G. Borer	
G-DOIT	AS.350B1 Ecureuil	FBS Ltd	
G-DOLF	AS.365N3 Dauphin II	Profred Partners LLP	
G-DOLI	Cirrus SR20	Furness Asset Management Ltd	
G-DOLY	Cessna T.303	KW Aviation Ltd (G-BJZK)	
G-DOME	PA-28-161 Warrior III	Target Aviation Ltd	
G-DOMS	Aerotechnik EV-97A Eurostar	R. K. & C. A. Stewart	
G-DONI	AA-5B Tiger	W. P. Moritz (G-BLLT)	
G-DONS	PA-28RT-201T Turbo Arrow IV	C. E. Griffiths	
G-DONT	Xenair CH.601XL Zodiac	A. C. J. Butcher	
G-DOOM	Cameron Z-105 balloon	Test Flight	
G-DORM	Robinson R44 II	M. McGlone	
G-DORN	EKW C-3605	R. G. Gray	
G-DORS	Eurocopter EC 135T2+	Premier Fund Leasing	
G-DORY	Cameron Z-315 balloon	P. Baker	
G-DOSA	Diamond DA42 Twin Star	DO Systems Ltd	
G-DOSB	Diamond DA42 Twin Star	DO Systems Ltd	
G-DOSC	Diamond DA42 Twin Star	DO Systems Ltd	
G-DOTT	CFM Streak Shadow	R. J. Bell	
G-DOTW	Savannah VG Jabiru(1)	I. S. Wright	
G-DOTY	Van's RV-7	H. A. Daines	

Notes	Reg.	Type	Owner or Operator
	G-DOVE	Cessna 182Q	Patriot Aviation Ltd
	G-DOVE†	D. H. 104 Devon C.2 ★	E. Surrey College/Gatton Point, Redhill (G-KOOL)
	G-DOVS	Robinson R44 II	D. B. Hamilton
	G-DOWN	Colt 31A balloon	M. Williams
	G-DOZI	Ikarus C.42 FB100	D. A. Izod
	G-DOZZ	Best Off Sky Ranger Swift 912S(1)	J. P. Doswell
	G-DPEP	Aero AT-3 R100	Cunning Plan Development Ltd
	G-DPHN	SA.365N1 Dauphin 2	Atlantic Air Ltd
	G-DPJR	Sikorsky S-76B	Blackbird Logistics Ltd (G-JCBA)
	G-DPPF	Augusta A.109E Power	Dyfed-Powys Police Authority
	G-DPYE	Robin DR400/500	C. R. J. Walker
	G-DRAM	Cessna FR.172F (floatplane)	Clyde River Rats
	G-DRAT	Slingsby T.51 Dart 17R	W. R. Longstaff
	G-DRAW	Colt 77A balloon	A. G. Odell
	G-DRBG	Cessna 172M	Henlow Flying Club Ltd (G-MUIL)
	G-DRBN	Embraer EMB-500 Phenom 100	Flairjet Ltd
	G-DRCS	Schleicher ASH-25E	C. R. Smithers
	G-DREG	Superchaser	N. R. Beale
	G-DREX	Cameron Saturn-110 balloon	M. A. Trimble
	G-DRFC	ATR-42-300	Air Atlantique
	G-DRGS	Cessna 182S	Walter Scott & Partners Ltd
	G-DRIV	Robinson R44 II	C. P. Vaudin
	G-DRLH	Eurocopter EC 120B Colibri	R. L. Hartshorn
	G-DRMM	Shaw Europa	T. J. Harrison
	G-DROL	Robinson R44 II	M. R. Lord (G-OPDG)
	G-DROP	Cessna U.206C	K. Brady (G-UKNO/G-BAMN)
	G-DRPK	Reality Escapade	P. A. Kirkham
	G-DRSV	CEA DR.315 (modified)	R. S. Voice
	G-DRYI	Cameron N-77 balloon	C. A. Butter
	G-DRYS	Cameron N-90 balloon	C. A. Butter
	G-DRZF	CEA DR.360	P. K. Kaufeler
	G-DSFT	PA-28R Cherokee Arrow 200-II	J. Jones (G-LFSE/G-BAXT)
	G-DSGC	PA-25 Pawnee 235C	Devon & Somerset Gliding Club Ltd
	G-DSID	PA-34-220T Seneca III	I. S. Gillbe
	G-DSKI	Aerotechnik EV-97 Eurostar	G-DSKI Group
	G-DSKY	Diamond DA.42 Twin Star	Papa Bravo Aviation Ltd (G-CDSZ)
	G-DSLL	Pegasus Quantum 15-912	R. G. Jeffery
	G-DSMA	P & M Aviation Quik R	Forestair Dragoons Ltd
	G-DSPI	Robinson R44	Central Helicopters Ltd (G-DPSI)
	G-DSPK	Cameron Z-140	Bailey Balloons Ltd
	G-DSPL	Diamond DA40 Star	Dynamic Signal Processing Ltd (G-GBOS)
	G-DSPZ	Robinson R44 II	Focal Point Communications Ltd
	G-DSVN	Rolladen-Schneider LS8-18	A. R. Paul
	G-DTAR	P & M Aviation Quik GT450	D. Tarvit
	G-DTCP	PA-32R-300 Cherokee Lance	R. S. Cook (G-TEEM)
	G-DTFF	Cessna T.182T Turbo Skylane	Rajair Ltd
	G-DTFL	PA-46-500TP Malibu Meridian	Tyrone Fabrication Ltd
	G-DTOY	Ikarus C.42.FB100	C. W. Laske
	G-DTSM	EV-97 TeamEurostar UK	J. R. Stothart
	G-DTUG	Wag-Aero Super Sport	D. A. Bullock
	G-DTWO	Schempp-Hirth Discus 2A	O. Walters
	G-DUBI	Lindstrans LBL-120A balloon	A. Nimmo
	G-DUDE	Van's RV-8	W. M. Hodgkins
	G-DUDI	Rotorsport UK MTO Sport	D. Watson
	G-DUDZ	Robin DR.400/180	D. H. Pattison (G-BXNK)
	G-DUFF	Rand Robinson KR-2	J. I. B. Duff
	G-DUGE	Ikarus C42 FB UK	D. Stevenson
	G-DUGI	Lindstrand LBL-90A balloon	J. A. Folkes
	G-DUKY	Robinson R44	English Braids Ltd
	G-DUMP	Customcraft A-25 balloon	P. C. Bailey
	G-DUNK	Cessna F172M Skyhawk	Devon and Somerset Flight Training Ltd
	G-DUNS	Lindstrand LBL-90A balloon	A. Murphy
	G-DUOT	Schempp-Hirth Duo Discus T	G-DUOT Group
	G-DURO	Shaw Europa	W. R. C. Williams-Wynne
	G-DURX	Thunder 77A balloon	R. C. and M. A. Trimble
	G-DUSK	DH.115 Vampire T.11 (XE856) ★	Bournemouth Aviation Museum

Reg.	Type	Owner or Operator	Notes
G-DUST	Stolp SA.300 Starduster Too	N. M. Robinson	
G-DUTY	Hughes 369E	Toure International Ltd	
G-DUVL	Cessna F.172N	G-DUVL Flying Group	
G-DVAA	Eurocopter EC135 T2+	Devon Air Ambulance Trading Co.Ltd	
G-DVBF	Lindstrand LBL-210A balloon	Virgin Balloon Flights	
G-DVON	DH.104 Devon C.2 (VP955)	C. L. Thatcher	
G-DWAL	Ahusta A.109A II	Surrey Heli Charters Ltd (G-JODI/G-BVCJ/ G-CLRL/G-EJCB)	
G-DWCE	Robinson R44 II	Jim Davies Civil Engineering Ltd	
G-DWDW	Rotorsport UK MTO Sport	D. J. Watson	
G-DWEM	Eurocopter EC135 T2	Bond Air Services Ltd (G-SSXX/G-SSSX)	
G-DWIA	Chilton D.W.1A	D. Elliott	
G-DWIB	Chilton D.W.1B (replica)	J. Jennings	
G-DWJM	Cessna 550 Citation II	TL Aviation Instrad LLP (G-BJIR)	
G-DWMS	Avtech Jabiru UL-450	B. J. Weighell	
G-DWPH	Ultramagic M-77 balloon	Ultramagic SA/Spain	
G-DXCC	Ultramagic M-77 balloon	A. Murphy	
G-DYCE	Robinson R44 II	Moorland Windows	
G-DYKE	Dyke JD.2 Delta	M. S. Bird	
G-DYMC	Aerospool Dynamic WT9 UK	S. Hoyle	
G-DYNA	Dynamic WT9 UK	Yeoman Light Aircraft Co.Ltd	
G-DYNM	Aerospool Dynamic WT9 UK	D. M. Pearson	
G-DZDZ	Rolladen-Schneider LS4	I. MacArthur	
G-DZZY	Champion 8KCAB	Paul's Planes Ltd	
G-EAGA	Sopwith Dove (replica)	A. Wood	
G-EAOU†	Vickers Vimy (replica)(NX71MY)	Greenco (UK) Ltd	
G-EASD	Avro 504L	G. M. New	
G-EASQ†	Bristol Babe (replica) (BAPC87) ★	Bristol Aero Collection (stored)/Kemble	
G-EAVX	Sopwith Pup (B1807)	K. A. M. Baker	
G-EBED†	Vickers 60 Viking (replica) (BAPC114)★	Brooklands Museum of Aviation/Weybridge	
G-EBHX	DH.53 Humming Bird	The Shuttleworth Collection	
G-EBIA	RAF SE-5A (F904)	The Shuttleworth Collection	
G-EBIB	RAF SE-5A ★	Science Museum/South Kensington	
G-EBIC	RAF SE-5A (F938) ★	RAF Museum/Hendon	
G-EBIR	DH.51	The Shuttleworth Collection	
G-EBJE	Avro 504K (E449) ★	RAF Museum/Hendon	
G-EBJG	Parnall Pixie IIIH	Midland Aircraft Preservation Society	
G-EBJI	Hawker Cygnet (replica)	C. J. Essex	
G-EBJO	ANEC IIH	The Shuttleworth Collection	
G-EBKY	Sopwith Pup (9917)	The Shuttleworth Collection	
G-EBLV	DH.60 Cirrus Moth	British Aerospace PLC	
G-EBMB	Hawker Cygnet I ★	RAF Museum/Cosford	
G-EBNV	English Electric Wren	The Shuttleworth Collection	
G-EBQP	DH.53 Humming Bird (J7326) ★	P. L. Kirk & T. G. Pankhurst	
G-EBWD	DH.60X Hermes Moth	The Shuttleworth Collection	
G-EBZM	Avro 594 Avian IIIA ★	Manchester Museum of Science & Industry	
G-EBZN	DH.60X Moth	J. Hodgkinson (G-UAAP)	
G-ECAC	Alpha R21620U	Bulldog Aviation Ltd	
G-ECAD	Cessna FA.152	Bulldog Aviation Ltd (G-JEET/G-BHMF)	
G-ECAE	Royal Aircraft Factory SE.5A	H. A. D. Monro	
G-ECAN	DH.84 Dragon	Norman Aircraft Trust	
G-ECBH	Cessna F.150K	ECBH Flying Group	
G-ECBI	Schweizer 269C-1	Iris Aviation Ltd	
G-ECBO	Eurocopter EC-130 B4	Hawkrise Aviation LLP	
G-ECDB	Schleicher Ka 6E	C. W. R. Neve	
G-ECDS	DH.82A Tiger Moth	N. C. Wilson	
G-ECDX	DH.71 Tiger Moth (replica)	M. D. Souch	
G-ECEA	Schempp-Hirth Cirrus	CEA Group	
G-ECGC	Cessna F.172N	S. Din	
G-ECGO	Bölkow Bö.208C1 Junior	A Flight Aviation Ltd	
G-ECJI	Dassault Falcon 10	Fleet International Avn. and Maritime Finance Ltd	
G-ECJM	PA-28R-201T Turbo Arrow III	Regishire Ltd (G-FESL/G-BNRN)	
G-ECKB	Escapade 912(2)	C. M. & C. P. Bradford	
G-ECLW	Glasflugel Standard Libelle 201B	R. G. Parker	

Notes	Reg.	Type	Owner or Operator
	G-ECMC	Robinson R22 Beta	Bulldog Aviation Ltd (G-LSWL)
	G-ECMK	PA-18-150 Super Cub	111 Supercub Group
	G-ECOA	DHC.8-402 Dash Eight	Flybe.com
	G-ECOB	DHC.8-402 Dash Eight	Flybe.com
	G-ECOC	DHC.8-402 Dash Eight	Flybe.com
	G-ECOD	DHC.8-402 Dash Eight	Flybe.com
	G-ECOE	DHC.8-402 Dash Eight	Flybe.com
	G-ECOF	DHC.8-402 Dash Eight	Flybe.com
	G-ECOG	DHC.8-402 Dash Eight	Flybe.com
	G-ECOH	DHC.8-402 Dash Eight	Flybe.com
	G-ECOI	DHC.8-402 Dash Eight	Flybe.com
	G-ECOJ	DHC.8-402 Dash Eight	Flybe.com
	G-ECOK	DHC.8-402 Dash Eight	Flybe.com
	G-ECOL	Schempp-Hirth Nimbus 2B	A. D. F. Flintoft & L. I. Rigby
	G-ECOM	DHC.8-402 Dash Eight	Flybe.com
	G-ECON	Cessna 172M	Aviation Rentals (G-JONE)
	G-ECOO	DHC.8-402 Dash Eight	Flybe.com
	G-ECOP	DHC.8-402 Dash Eight	Flybe.com
	G-ECOR	DHC.8-402 Dash Eight	Flybe.com
	G-ECOT	DHC.8-402 Dash Eight	Flybe.com
	G-ECOU	AS.355F2 Twin Squirrel	Rulegate Ltd
	G-ECOV	DHC.8-402 Dash Eight	Flybe.com
	G-ECOW	DHC.8-402 Dash Eight	Bombardier Services (UK) Ltd
	G-ECOX	Grega GN.1 Air Camper	H. C. Cox
	G-ECOY	DHC.8-402 Dash Eight	Bombardier Services (UK) Ltd
	G-ECOZ	DHC.8-402 Dash Eight	Flybe.com
	G-ECPA	Glasflugel H201B Standard Libelle	M. J. Witton
	G-ECSW	Pilatus B4-PC11AF	I. H. Keyser
	G-ECTF	Comper CLA.7 Swift Replica	P. R. Cozens
	G-ECUB	PA-18 Super Cub 150	J. K. Padden (G-CBFI)
	G-ECVB	Pietenpol Air Camper	G. Edwards
	G-ECXL	PZL-Bielsko SZD-30 Pirat	Charlie X-Ray Lima Group
	G-ECZA	BN-21-21 Islander	B-N Group Ltd (G-BDPN)
	G-EDAV	SA Bulldog Srs 120/121 (XX534:B)	Edwalton Aviation Ltd
	G-EDAY	BAe Jetstream 3101	Skylease Sweden AB
	G-EDCJ	Cessna 525 CitationJet	Jetphase Ltd
	G-EDCL	Cessna 525 CitationJet	Air Charter Scotland (Holdings) Ltd
	G-EDCM	Cessna 525 CitationJet	Air Charter Scotland (Holdings) Ltd
	G-EDCS	Raytheon 400A	Mountain Aviation Ltd
	G-EDDD	Schempp-Hirth Nimbus 2	C. A. Mansfield (G-BKPM)
	G-EDDS	CZAW Sportcruiser	E. H. Bishop
	G-EDDV	PZL-Bielsko SZD-38A Jantar 1	S. R. Bruce
	G-EDEE	Comco Ikarus C.42 FB100	Microavionics
	G-EDEL	PA-32-300 Cherokee Six D	I. Blamire
	G-EDEN	SOCATA TB10 Tobago	Group Eden
	G-EDEO	Beech B.24R Sierra 200	G-EDEO Group
	G-EDGA	PA-28-161 Warrior II	The RAF Halton Aeroplane Club Ltd
	G-EDGE	Jodel 150	A. D. Edge
	G-EDGI	PA-28-161 Warrior II	Cunning Plan Development Ltd
	G-EDGJ	Zivko Edge 360	D. G. Jenkins
	G-EDGY	Flight Test Edge 540	C. R. A. Scrope
	G-EDHO	Cirrus SR20	Singers Corporate Asset Finance Ltd
	G-EDHY	Dassault Falcon 2000EX	Victoria Aviation Ltd
	G-EDLY	Airborne Edge 912/Streak IIIB	M. & P. L. Eardley
	G-EDMV	Eiriavion PIK-20D	BNA MV
	G-EDNA	PA-38-112 Tomahawk	P. J. Montgomery
	G-EDRE	Lindstrand LBL 90A balloon	Edren Homes Ltd
	G-EDRV	Van's RV-6A	G-EDRV Flying Group
	G-EDTO	Cessna FR.172F	N. G. Hopkinson
	G-EDVL	PA-28R Cherokee Arrow 200-II	J. S. Devlin & Z. Islam (G-BXIN)
	G-EDYO	PA-32-260 Cherokee Six	R. Bursey & A. D. Paton
	G-EEAD	Slingsby T.65A Vega	D. S. Smith
	G-EEBA	Slingsby T.65A Vega	J. A. Cowie & K. Robertson
	G-EEBB	Sikorsky S-76C	Haughey Air Ltd
	G-EEBD	Scheibe Bergfalke IV	F. A. P. M. Otten
	G-EEBE	Issoire E-78B Silene	Silene Group
	G-EEBF	Schempp-Hirth Mini Nimbus C	M. Pingel
	G-EEBK	Schempp-Hirth Mini Nimbus C	G. S. Bell
	G-EEBL	Schleicher ASK-13	Derbyshire and Lancashire Gliding Club Ltd
	G-EEBM	Grob G.102 Astir CS77	Yorkshire Gliding Club (Proprietary) Ltd

Reg.	Type	Owner or Operator	Notes
G-EEBN	Centrair ASW-20FL	S. MacArthur & R. Carlisle	
G-EEBR	Glaser-Dirks DG200/17	N. J. L. Busvine	
G-EEBS	Scheibe Zugvogel IIIA	J. A. Stockford	
G-EEBZ	Schleicher ASK-13	Booker Gliding Club Ltd	
G-EECC	Aerospool Dynamic WT9 UK	C. V. Ellingworth	
G-EECK	Slingsby T65A Vega	The ECK Syndicate	
G-EECO	Lindstrand LBL-25A balloon	A. Jay	
G-EEDE	Centrair ASW-20F	G. M. Cumner	
G-EEEK	Extra EA.300/200	A. R. Willis	
G-EEER	Schempp-Hirth Mini Nimbus C	D. J. Uren	
G-EEEZ	Champion 8KCAB	Les Wallen Manufacturing Ltd	
G-EEFA	Cameron Z-90 balloon	A. Murphy	
G-EEFK	Centrair ASW-20FL	A. P. Balkwill & G. B. Monslow	
G-EEFT	Schempp-Hirth Nimbus 2B	S. A. Adlard	
G-EEGL	Christen Eagle II	M. P. Swoboda & S. L. Nicholson	
G-EEGU	PA-28-161 Warrior II	Premier Flight Training Ltd	
G-EEJE	PA-31 Navajo B	Geeje Ltd	
G-EEKA	Glaser-Dirks DG-202/17	M. J. R. Lindsay & P. Hayward	
G-EEKY	PA-28 Cherokee 140B	Gauntlet Holdings	
G-EELS	Cessna 208B Caravan 1	Glass Eels Ltd	
G-EELT	Rolladen-Schneider LS4	ELT Syndicate	
G-EELY	Schleicher Ka 6CR	K6 ELY Syndicate	
G-EENA	PA-32R-301 Saratoga SP	Gamit Ltd	
G-EENE	Rolladen-Schneider LS4	R. A. Hine	
G-EENI	Shaw Europa	M. P. Grimshaw	
G-EENK	Schleicher ASK-21	Essex Gliding Club Ltd	
G-EENN	Schempp-Hirth Nimbus 3	M. W. Dickson	
G-EENT	Glasflugel 304	M. Hastings & P. D. Morrison	
G-EENW	Schleicher ASW-20L	G-EENW Group	
G-EENY	GA-7 Cougar	Jade Air PLC	
G-EENZ	Schleicher ASW-19B	O. L. Pugh	
G-EERH	Ruschmeyer R.90-230RG	D. Sadler	
G-EERV	Van's RV-6	M. Crunden & C. B. Stirling	
G-EERY	Robinson R22	EGB (Helicopters) Ltd	
G-EESA	Shaw Europa	C. Deith (G-HIIL)	
G-EESY	Rolladen-Schneider LS4	G. S. Morley	
G-EETG	Cessna 172Q Cutlass	Tango Golf Flying Group	
G-EEUP	SNCAN Stampe SV.4C	A. M. Wajih	
G-EEVL	Grob G.102 Astir CS77	G. D. E. Macdonald	
G-EEWS	Cessna T.210N	A. N. Macdonald & S. M. Jack	
G-EEWZ	Mainair Pegasus Quik	A. J. Roche	
G-EEYE	Mainair Blade 912	B. J. Egerton	
G-EEZA	Robinson R44 II	Teleology Ltd	
G-EEZO	DG Flugzeugbau DG-808C	G-ZO Syndicate	
G-EEZR	Robinson R44	AC Helicopters Ltd	
G-EEZS	Cessna 182P	D. A. G. Johnson	
G-EEZZ	Zenair CH.601XL Zodiac	K. W. Allan	
G-EFAM	Cessna 182S Skylane	G-EFAM Flying Group	
G-EFBP	Cessna FR.172K	A. Webster	
G-EFCM	PA-28-180 Cherokee D	ATC Trading Ltd	
G-EFFI	Rotorway Executive 162F	P. D. Annison	
G-EFGH	Robinson R22 Beta	Ryvoan Aviation Ltd	
G-EFIR	PA-28-181 Archer II	Leicestershire Aero Club Ltd	
G-EFJD	MBB Bo.209 Monsun	E. J. Smith	
G-EFLT	Glasflugel Standard Libelle 201B	P. A. Pearson	
G-EFLY	Centrair ASW-20FL	I. D. & J. H. Atherton	
G-EFOF	Robinson R22 Beta	NT Burton Aviation	
G-EFOX	Eurofox 912(2)	R. M. Cornwell	
G-EFSM	Slingsby T.67M Firefly 260	A. G. Bell (G-BPLK)	
G-EFTE	Bölkow Bö.207	B. Morris & R. L. Earl	
G-EFTF	AS.350B Ecureuil	T. J. French (G-CWIZ/G-DJEM/G-ZBAC/ G-SEBI/G-BMCU)	
G-EFUN	E-Plane	A. W. Bishop & G. Castelli	
G-EFVS	Wassmer WA.52 Europa	D. F. Hurn	
G-EGAG	SOCATA TB20 Trinidad	D. & E. Booth	
G-EGAL	Christen Eagle II	Eagle Partners	
G-EGBS	Van's RV-9A	Shobdon RV-9A Group	
G-EGEE	Cessna 310Q	R. C. Devine	
G-EGEG	Cessna 172R	C. D. Lever	
G-EGEL	Christen Eagle II	G-EGEL Flying Group	

Notes	Reg.	Type	Owner or Operator
	G-EGGI	Ikarus C.42FB UK	A. G. & G. J. Higgins
	G-EGGS	Robin DR.400/180	G-EGGS Syndicate
	G-EGGZ	Best Off Sky Ranger Swift 912S(1)	J. C. Sheardown
	G-EGHH	Hawker Hunter F.58 (J-4083)	Heritage Aviation Developments Ltd
	G-EGIA	UltraMagic M-65C balloon	Balloon Promotion SAS/Italy
	G-EGIL	Christen Eagle II	Smoke On Go Ltd
	G-EGJA	SOCATA TB20 Trinidad	D. A. Williamson
	G-EGKE	SOCATA Rallye 180TS	Suffolk Soaring Tug Group
	G-EGLE	Christen Eagle II	D. Thorpe t/a Eagle Group
	G-EGLG	PA-31 Turbo Navajo C	H. Merkado (G-OATC/G-OJPW/G-BGCC)
	G-EGLL	PA-28-161 Warrior II	Airways Aero Associations Ltd (G-BLEJ)
	G-EGLS	PA-28-181 Archer III	O. Sylvester
	G-EGLT	Cessna 310R	Reconnaissance Ventures Ltd (G-BHTV)
	G-EGNS	Gulfstream 550	Pobedy Corporation
	G-EGPG	PA-18-135 Super Cub	G. Cormack (G-BWUC)
	G-EGSJ	Jabiru J400	Seething Jabiru Group (G-MGRK)
	G-EGTB	PA-28-161 Warrior II	Airways Aero Association Ltd (G-BPWA)
	G-EGTC	Robinson R44	MFH Helicopters Ltd (G-CCNK)
	G-EGTR	PA-28-161 Cadet	Aviation Rentals (G-BRSI)
	G-EGUR	Jodel D.140B	S. H. Williams
	G-EGVO	Dassault Falcon 900EX	TAG Aviation (UK) Ltd
	G-EGWN	American Champion 7ECA	The Royal Air Force Halton Aeroplane Club Ltd
	G-EHAA	MDH MD.900 Explorer	Police Aviation Services Ltd (G-GNAA)
	G-EHAV	Glasflugel Standard Libelle 201B	A. Liran & M. Truelove
	G-EHBJ	CASA 1.131E Jungmann 2000	E. P. Howard
	G-EHCB	Schempp-Hirth Nimbus 3DT	G-EHCB Group
	G-EHCC	PZL-Bielsko SZD-50-3 Puchacz	Heron Gliding Club
	G-EHCZ	Schleicher K8B	The Surrey Hills Gliding Club Ltd
	G-EHDS	CASA 1.131E Jungmann 2000	C. W. N. & A. A. M. Huke (G-DUDS)
	G-EHGF	PA-28-181 Archer II	G. P. Robinson
	G-EHIC	Jodel D.140B	India Charlie Consortium
	G-EHLX	PA-28-181 Archer II	ASG Leasing Ltd
	G-EHMF	Isaacs Fury II	M. A. Farrelly
	G-EHMJ	Beech S35 Bonanza	A. J. Daley
	G-EHMM	Robin DR.400/180R	Booker Gliding Club Ltd
	G-EHMS	MD Helicopters MD-900	Virgin HEMS (London) Ltd
	G-EHTT	Schleicher ASW-20CL	HTT Syndicate
	G-EHUP	Aérospatiale SA.341G Gazelle 1	MW Helicopters Ltd
	G-EHXP	Rockwell Commander 112A	A. L. Stewart
	G-EIBM	Robinson R22 Beta	HJS Helicopters Ltd (G-BUCL)
	G-EICK	Cessna 172S	Centenary Flying Group
	G-EIER	Marganski Swift S-1	D. Poll & C Cain
	G-EIGG	BAe Jetstream 3102	Bravo Aviation Ltd
	G-EIKY	Shaw Europa	J. D. Milbank
	G-EIRE	Cessna T.182T	J. Byrne
	G-EISG	Beech A36 Bonanza	R. J. & B. Howard
	G-EISO	SOCATA MS.892A Rallye Commodore 150	EISO Group
	G-EITE	Luscombe 8F Silvaire	S. R. H. Martin
	G-EIWT	Cessna FR.182RG	J. R. Pybus
	G-EIZO	Eurocopter EC 120B	R. M. Bailey
	G-EJAE	GlaserDirks DG-200	D. I. P. H. Waller
	G-EJAR	Airbus A.319-111	EasyJet Airline Co Ltd
	G-EJBI	Bolkow Bo.207	J. O'Donnell & J. L. Bone
	G-EJEL	Cessna 550 Citation II	Futura Trading SAS
	G-EJGO	Z.226HE Trener	S. K. T. & C. M. Neofytou
	G-EJIM	Schempp-Hirth Discus 2cT	J. Lynchehaun
	G-EJJB	Airbus A.319-111	EasyJet Airline Co Ltd
	G-EJOC	AS.350B Ecureuil	Air and Ground Aviation Ltd (G-GEDS/G-HMAN/G-SKIM/G-BIVP)
	G-EJRC	Robinson R44 II	Perry Farming Co.
	G-EJRS	PA-28-161 Cadet	Carlisle Flight Traing Ltd
	G-EJTC	Robinson R44	N. Parkhouse
	G-EJWI	Flight Design CTLS	E. Wright
	G-EKEY	Schleicher ASW-20 CL	K. W. Payne
	G-EKIM	Alpi Pioneer 300	M. Langmead
	G-EKIR	PA-28-262 Cadet	Aeros Leasing Ltd
	G-EKKL	PA-28-161 Warrior II	Apollo Aviation Advisory Ltd/Shoreham

Reg.	Type	Owner or Operator	Notes
G-EKMN	Zlin Z.242L	TGD Leasing Ltd	
G-EKOS	Cessna FR.182 RG	S. Charlton	
G-ELAM	PA-30 Twin Comanche160B	Hangar 39 Ltd (G-BAWU/G-BAWV)	
G-ELDR	PA-32 Cherokee Six 260	Demero Ltd	
G-ELEE	Cameron Z-105 balloon	D. Eliot	
G-ELEN	Robin DR.400/180	N. R. & E. Foster	
G-ELIS	PA-34-200T Seneca II	Bristol Flying Centre Ltd (G-BOPV)	
G-ELIZ	Denney Kitfox Mk 2	A. J. Ellis	
G-ELKA	Christen Eagle II	J. T. Matthews	
G-ELKS	Avid Speedwing Mk 4	H. S. Elkins	
G-ELLA	PA-32R-301 Saratoga IIHP	C. C. W. Hart	
G-ELLE	Cameron N-90 balloon	D. J. Stagg	
G-ELLI	Bell 206B JetRanger 3	Italian Clothes Ltd	
G-ELMH	NA AT-6D Harvard III (42-84555:EP-H)	M. Hammond	
G-ELMO	Robinson R44 II	Locumlink Associates Ltd/Ireland	
G-ELOA	Cessna 560XL Citation Excel	Krypton Aviation Ltd	
G-ELSE	Diamond DA42 Twin Star	R. Swann	
G-ELSI	Tanarg/Ixess 15 912S(1)	D. Daniel	
G-ELTE	Agusta A109A II	Henfield Lodge Ltd (G-BWZI)	
G-ELUE	PA-28-161 Warrior II	Freedom Aviation Ltd	
G-ELUN	Robin DR.400/180R	Cotswold DR.400 Syndicate	
G-ELUT	PA-28R Cherokee Arrow 200-II	Green Arrow Europe Ltd	
G-ELZN	PA-28-161 Warrior II	ZN Flying Group	
G-ELZY	PA-28-161 Warrior II	Goodwood Road Racing School Ltd	
G-EMAA	Eurocopter EC 135T2	Bond Air Services Ltd	
G-EMAX	PA-31-350 Navajo Chieftain	Atlantic Bridge Aviation Ltd	
G-EMBC	Embraer RJ145EP	Port One Ltd	
G-EMBI	Embraer RJ145EP	bmi regional	
G-EMBJ	Embraer RJ145EP	bmi regional	
G-EMBN	Embraer RJ145EP	bmi regional	
G-EMBO	Embraer RJ145EP	Aircraft Solutions ERJ-145LLC	
G-EMBP	Embraer RJ145EU	Aircraft Solutions ERJ-145 LLC	
G-EMBW	Embraer RJ145EU	Aircraft Solutions ERJ-145 LLC	
G-EMBX	Embraer RJ145EU	Aircraft Solutions ERJ-145 LLC	
G-EMBY	Embraer RJ145EU	Aircraft Solutions ERJ-145 LLC	
G-EMCA	Commander Aircraft 114B	S. Roberts	
G-EMDM	Diamond DA40-P9 Star	D. J. Munson	
G-EMHC	Agusta A109E Power	East Midlands Helicopters	
G-EMHK	MBB Bö.209 Monsun 150FV	T. A. Crone (G-BLRD)	
G-EMID	Eurocopter EC 135P2	East Midlands Air Support Unit	
G-EMIN	Shaw Europa	S. A. Lamb	
G-EMJA	CASA 1.131E Jungmann 2000	N. J. Radford	
G-EMLE	Aerotechnik EV-97 Eurostar	A. R. White	
G-EMLS	Cessna T210L Turbo Centurion	I. K. F. Simcock	
G-EMLY	Pegasus Quantum 15	S. J. Reid	
G-EMMM	Diamond DA40 Star	A. J. Leigh	
G-EMMS	PA-38-112 Tomahawk	Ravenair Aircraft Ltd/Liverpool	
G-EMMY	Rutan Vari-Eze	M. J. Tooze	
G-EMSA	Czech Sport Aircraft Sportcruiser	A. C. & M. A. Naylor	
G-EMSB	PA-22-160 Tri-Pacer	M. S. Bird (G-ARHU)	
G-EMSI	Shaw Europa	P. W. L. Thomas	
G-EMSL	PA-28-161 Warrior II	Falcon Flying Services Ltd	
G-EMSY	DH.82A Tiger Moth	G-EMSY Group (G-ASPZ)	
G-ENBD	Lindstrand LBL-120A balloon	A. Nimmo	
G-ENBW	Robin DR.400-180R	Bicester Robin Crew	
G-ENCE	Partenavia P.68B	Bicton Aviation (G-OROY/G-BFSU)	
G-ENEA	Cessna 182P	Air Ads Ltd	
G-ENEE	CFM Streak Shadow SA	S. D. J. Harvey	
G-ENES	Bell 206B JetRanger III	Celtic Energy Ltd	
G-ENGO	Steen Skybolt	R. G. Fulton	
G-ENGR	Head AX8-105 balloon	Royal Engineers Balloon Club	
G-ENHP	Enstrom 480B	H. J. Pelham	
G-ENIA	Staaken Z-21 Flitzer	A. F. Wankowski	
G-ENIE	Tipsy T.66 Nipper 3	R. J. Ripley	
G-ENII	Cessna F.172M	J. Howley	
G-ENIO	Pitts S-2C Special	Advanced Flying (London) Ltd	
G-ENNA	PA-28-161 Warrior II	Falcon Flying Serices Ltd (G-ESFT)	
G-ENNI	Robin R.3000/180	I. F. Doubtfire	
G-ENNK	Cessna 172S	Pooler-LMT Ltd	

Notes	Reg.	Type	Owner or Operator
	G-ENNY	Cameron V-77 balloon	J. H. Dobson
	G-ENOA	Cessna F.172F	M. K. Acors (G-ASZW)
	G-ENRE	Avtech Jabiru UL	P. R. Turton
	G-ENRI	Lindstrand LBL-105A balloon	P. G. Hall
	G-ENST	CZAW Sportcruiser	L. M. Radcliffe, C. Slater & D. G. Price
	G-ENTS	Van's RV-9A	L. G. Johnson
	G-ENTT	Cessna F.152 II	C. & A. R. Hyett (G-BHHI)
	G-ENTW	Cessna F.152 II	Firecrest Aviation Ltd, C. Oates & C. Castledine (G-BFLK)
	G-ENVO	MBB Bo.105CBS-4	F. C. Owen
	G-ENVY	Mainair Blade 912	P. J. Lomax & J. A. Robinson
	G-ENXA	Falcon 900EX	Enex Aviation Ltd
	G-ENZO	Cameron Z-105 balloon	Garelli VI SPA
	G-EOFS	Shaw Europa	A. Fletcher & G. Plenderleith
	G-EOFW	Pegasus Quantum 15-912	G-EOFW Microlight Group
	G-EOHL	Cessna 182L	G. B. Dale & M. C. Terris
	G-EOID	Aeroprakt A22-L Foxbat	M. D. Northwood
	G-EOIN	Zenair CH.701UL	D. G. Palmer
	G-EOJB	Robinson R44 II	G. J. Braithwaite (G-EDES)
	G-EOLD	PA-28-161 Warrior II	M. A . Ward
	G-EOLX	Cessna 172N	Westward Airways (Lands End) Ltd
	G-EOMA	Airbus A.330-243	Monarch Airlines Ltd
	G-EOMK	Robin DR400/180	F. Warin
	G-EOPH	Cameron C-90 balloon	A. J. Cherrett
	G-EORG	PA-38-112 Tomahawk	Control Developments (UK) Ltd
	G-EORJ	Shaw Europa	P. E. George
	G-EPAR	Robinson R22 Beta II	Jepar Rotorcraft
	G-EPDI	Cameron N-77 balloon	R. Moss
	G-EPIC	Jabiru UL-450	T. Chadwick
	G-EPOC	Jabiru UL-450	S. Cope
	G-EPOX	Aero Designs Pulsar XP	D. R. Stansfield
	G-EPSN	Ultramagic M-105 balloon	G. Everett
	G-EPTR	PA-28R Cherokee Arrow 200-II	ACS Aviation Ltd
	G-ERCO	Ercoupe 415D	A. R. & M. V. Tapp
	G-ERDA	Staaken Z-21A Flitzer	J. Cresswell
	G-ERDS	DH.82A Tiger Moth	W. A. Gerdes
	G-ERFS	PA-28-161 Warrior II	Cunning Plan Development Ltd
	G-ERIC	Rockwell Commander 112TC	J. A. L. Irwin
	G-ERIK	Cameron N-77 balloon	T. M. Donnelly
	G-ERIS	Hughes 369D	R. J. Howard (G-PJMD/G-BMJV)
	G-ERIW	Staaken Z-21 Flitzer	R. I. Wasey
	G-ERJA	Embraer RJ145EP	Falak Fin Nine Ltd
	G-ERJC	Embraer RJ145EP	Falak Fin Ten Ltd
	G-ERMO	ARV Super 2	S. Vince (G-BMWK)
	G-ERNI	PA-28-181 Archer II	J. Gardener & N. F. P. Hopwood (G-OSSY)
	G-EROB	Europa XS	R. J. Bull (G-RBJW)
	G-EROL	Westland SA.341G Gazelle 1	MW Helicopters Ltd (G-NONA/G-FDAV/G-RIFA/G-ORGE/G-BBHU)
	G-EROM	Robinson R22 Beta	EBG (Helicopters) Ltd
	G-EROS	Cameron H-34 balloon	Evening Standard Co Ltd
	G-ERRY	AA-5B Tiger	Haniel Aviation Ltd (G-BFMJ)
	G-ERTE	Skyranger 912S (1)	A. P. Trumper
	G-ERTI	Staaken Z-21A Flitzer	B. S. Carpenter
	G-ERYR	P & M Aviation Quik GT450	R. D. Ellis
	G-ESCA	Escapade Jabiru (1)	G. W. E. & R. H. May
	G-ESCC	Escapade 912	G. & S. Simons
	G-ESCP	Escapade 912(1)	R. G. Hughes
	G-ESEX	Eurocopter EC 135T2	Essex Police Authority
	G-ESGA	Reality Escapade	I. Bamford
	G-ESKA	Escapade 912	J. H. Beard
	G-ESME	Cessna R.182 II (15211)	G. C. Cherrington (G-BNOX)
	G-ESSL	Cessna 182R Skylane II	Euro Seaplane Services Ltd
	G-ESSY	Robinson R44	EW Guess (Holdings) Ltd
	G-ESTA	Cessna 550 Citation II	Executive Aviation Services Ltd (G-GAUL)
	G-ESTR	Van's RV-6	R. M. Johnson
	G-ESUS	Rotorway Executive 162F	J. Tickner
	G-ETAT	Cessna 172S Skyhawk	ADR Aviation

Reg.	Type	Owner or Operator	Notes
G-ETBY	PA-32 Cherokee Six 260	G-ETBY Group (G-AWCY)	
G-ETCW	Stoddard-Hamilton Glastar	P. G. Hayward	
G-ETDC	Cessna 172P	The Moray Flying Club	
G-ETFF	Robinson R44	Rajair Ltd (G-HSLJ)	
G-ETHY	Cessna 208	N. A. Moore	
G-ETIM	Eurocopter EC 120B	Agricultural Machinery Ltdl	
G-ETIN	Robinson R22 Beta	J. M. Lynch	
G-ETIV	Robin DR.400/180	L. A. Seers	
G-ETME	Nord 1002 Pingouin (KG+EM)	108 Flying Group	
G-ETNT	Robinson R44	Irwin Plant Hire	
G-ETOU	Agusta A.109S Grand	P. J. Ogden	
G-ETPS	Hawker Hunter FGA.9 (XE601)	FGA 9 Ltd	
G-ETUS	Bell 206B-2 JetRanger II	D & G Cars Ltd (G-JBHH/G-SCOO/G-CORC/ G-CJHI/G-BBFB)	
G-ETVS	Alpi Pioneer 300 Hawk	T. W. Skinner	
G-EUAB	Europa XS	A. D. Stephens	
G-EUAN	Jabiru UL-D	M. Wade & M. Lusted	
G-EUFO	Rolladen-Schneider LS7-WL	J. R. Bane & R. Hardy	
G-EUJG	Avro 594 Avian IIIA	R. I. & D. E. Souch	
G-EUKS	Westland Widgeon III	R. I. Souch	
G-EUNA	Airbus A.318-112	British Airways	
G-EUNB	Airbus A.318-112	British Airways	
G-EUNI	Beech B200 Super King Air	Universita Telematica E-Campus (G-TAGH)	
G-EUOA	Airbus A.319-131	British Airways	
G-EUOB	Airbus A.319-131	British Airways	
G-EUOC	Airbus A.319-131	British Airways	
G-EUOD	Airbus A.319-131	British Airways	
G-EUOE	Airbus A.319-131	British Airways	
G-EUOF	Airbus A.319-131	British Airways	
G-EUOG	Airbus A.319-131	British Airways	
G-EUOH	Airbus A.319-131	British Airways	
G-EUOI	Airbus A.319-131	British Airways	
G-EUOJ	Airbus A.319-131	British Airways	
G-EUOK	Airbus A.319-131	British Airways	
G-EUOL	Airbus A.319-131	British Airways	
G-EUPA	Airbus A.319-131	British Airways	
G-EUPB	Airbus A.319-131	British Airways	
G-EUPC	Airbus A.319-131	British Airways	
G-EUPD	Airbus A.319-131	British Airways	
G-EUPE	Airbus A.319-131	British Airways	
G-EUPF	Airbus A.319-131	British Airways	
G-EUPG	Airbus A.319-131	British Airways	
G-EUPH	Airbus A.319-131	British Airways	
G-EUPJ	Airbus A.319-131	British Airways	
G-EUPK	Airbus A.319-131	British Airways	
G-EUPL	Airbus A.319-131	British Airways	
G-EUPM	Airbus A.319-131	British Airways	
G-EUPN	Airbus A.319-131	British Airways	
G-EUPO	Airbus A.319-131	British Airways	
G-EUPP	Airbus A.319-131	British Airways	
G-EUPR	Airbus A.319-131	British Airways	
G-EUPS	Airbus A.319-131	British Airways	
G-EUPT	Airbus A.319-131	British Airways	
G-EUPU	Airbus A.319-131	British Airways	
G-EUPV	Airbus A.319-131	British Airways	
G-EUPW	Airbus A.319-131	British Airways	
G-EUPX	Airbus A.319-131	British Airways	
G-EUPY	Airbus A.319-131	British Airways	
G-EUPZ	Airbus A.319-131	British Airways	
G-EURT	Eurocopter EC155 B1	William Ewart Properties Ltd (G-EWAT)	
G-EUSO	Robin DR.400/140 Major	Weald Air Services Ltd	
G-EUUA	Airbus A.320-232	British Airways	
G-EUUB	Airbus A.320-232	British Airways	
G-EUUC	Airbus A.320-232	British Airways	
G-EUUD	Airbus A.320-232	British Airways	
G-EUUE	Airbus A.320-232	British Airways	
G-EUUF	Airbus A.320-232	British Airways	
G-EUUG	Airbus A.320-232	British Airways	
G-EUUH	Airbus A.320-232	British Airways	
G-EUUI	Airbus A.320-232	British Airways	
G-EUUJ	Airbus A.320-232	British Airways	

Notes	Reg.	Type	Owner or Operator
	G-EUUK	Airbus A.320-232	British Airways
	G-EUUL	Airbus A.320-232	British Airways
	G-EUUM	Airbus A.320-232	British Airways
	G-EUUN	Airbus A.320-232	British Airways
	G-EUUO	Airbus A.320-232	British Airways
	G-EUUP	Airbus A.320-232	British Airways
	G-EUUR	Airbus A.320-232	British Airways
	G-EUUS	Airbus A.320-232	British Airways
	G-EUUT	Airbus A.320-232	British Airways
	G-EUUU	Airbus A.320-232	British Airways
	G-EUUV	Airbus A.320-232	British Airways
	G-EUUW	Airbus A.320-232	British Airways
	G-EUUX	Airbus A.320-232	British Airways
	G-EUUY	Airbus A.320-232	British Airways
	G-EUUZ	Airbus A.320-232	British Airways
	G-EUXC	Airbus A.321-231	British Airways
	G-EUXD	Airbus A.321-231	British Airways
	G-EUXE	Airbus A.321-231	British Airways
	G-EUXF	Airbus A.321-231	British Airways
	G-EUXG	Airbus A.321-231	British Airways
	G-EUXH	Airbus A.321-231	British Airways
	G-EUXI	Airbus A.321-231	British Airways
	G-EUXJ	Airbus A.321-231	British Airways
	G-EUXK	Airbus A.321-231	British Airways
	G-EUXL	Airbus A.321-231	British Airways
	G-EUXM	Airbus A.321-231	British Airways
	G-EUYA	Airbus A.320-232	British Airways
	G-EUYB	Airbus A.320-232	British Airways
	G-EUYC	Airbus A.320-232	British Airways
	G-EUYD	Airbus A.320-232	British Airways
	G-EUYE	Airbus A.320-232	British Airways
	G-EUYF	Airbus A.320-232	British Airways
	G-EUYG	Airbus A.320-232	British Airways
	G-EUYH	Airbus A.320-232	British Airways
	G-EUYI	Airbus A.320-232	British Airways
	G-EUYJ	Airbus A.320-232	British Airways
	G-EUYK	Airbus A.320-232	British Airways
	G-EVAJ	Best Off Skyranger 912S(1)	A. B. Gridley
	G-EVBF	Cameron Z-350 balloon	Virgin Balloon Flights
	G-EVET	Cameron 80 Concept balloon	L. O. & H. Vaughan
	G-EVEV	Robinson R44 II	M. P. Wilkinson
	G-EVEY	Thruster T.600N 450-JAB	The G-EVEY Flying Group
	G-EVIE	PA-28-181 Warrior II	Tayside Aviation Ltd (G-ZULU)
	G-EVIG	Evektor EV-97 TeamEurostar UK	A. S. Mitchell
	G-EVII	Schempp-Hirth Ventus 2cT	Active Aviation Ltd
	G-EVLE	Rearwin 8125 Cloudster	M. C. Hiscock (G-BVLK)
	G-EVLN	Gulfstream 4	Metropix Ltd
	G-EVPH	Aerotechnik EV-97 Eurostar	A. H. Woolley
	G-EVPI	Evans VP-1 Srs 2	C. P. Martyr
	G-EVRD	Beech 390 Premier 1	Commercial Aviation Charters Ltd
	G-EVRO	Aerotechnik EV-97 Eurostar	J. G. McMinn
	G-EVSL	Aerotechnik EV-97 Eurostar SL	C. M. Theakstone
	G-EVTO	PA-28-161 Warrior II	Redhill Air Services Ltd
	G-EWAD	Robinson R44 II	Excel Law Ltd
	G-EWAN	Prostar PT-2C	C. G. Shaw
	G-EWAW	Bell 206B-3 JetRanger 3	J. Tobias (G-DORB)
	G-EWBC	Avtec Jabiru SK	E. W. B. Comber
	G-EWES	Pioneer 300	D. A. Ions
	G-EWEW	AB Sportine Aviacija LAK-19T	G. Paul
	G-EWHT	Robinson R-2112	Cotswold Aviation Services
	G-EWIZ	Pitts S-2E Special	Pelham Ltd
	G-EWME	PA-28 Cherokee 235	C. J. Mewis & E. S. Ewen
	G-EWZZ	CZAW Sportcruiser	G. Fraser
	G-EXAM	PA-28RT-201T Turbo Arrow IV	RR. S. Urquhart & A. Cameron
	G-EXEC	PA-34-200 Seneca	Sky Air Travel Ltd
	G-EXES	Shaw Europa XS	D. Barraclough
	G-EXEX	Cessna 404	Reconnaissance Ventures Ltd
	G-EXGC	Extra EA.300/200	P. J. Bull
	G-EXHL	Cameron C-70 balloon	R. K. Gyselynck

Reg.	Type	Owner or Operator	Notes
G-EXII	Extra EA.300	A. D. Hoy	
G-EXIL	Extra EA.300/S	C. W. Burkett & S. French	
G-EXIT	MS.893E Rallye 180GT	G-EXIT Group	
G-EXLL	Zenair CH.601	J. P. Ashford	
G-EXPD	Stemme S.10-VT	Global Gliding Expeditions	
G-EXPL	Champion 7GCBC Citabria	M. W. Meynell	
G-EXRS	Bombardier BD-700-1A10 Global Express	Ocean Sky Aircraft Management Ltd	
G-EXTR	Extra EA.260	S. J. Carver	
G-EYAK	Yakovlev Yak-50 (50 yellow)	P. N. A. Whitehead	
G-EYAS	Denney Kitfox Mk 2	R. E. Hughes	
G-EYCO	Robin DR.400/180	S. J. York	
G-EYNL	MBB Bö.105DBS/5	Sterling Helicopters Ltd	
G-EYOR	Van's RV-6	S. I. Fraser	
G-EYRE	Bell 206L-1 LongRanger	European Aviation and Technical Services Ltd	
G-EZAA	Airbus A.319-111	easyJet Airline Co Ltd	
G-EZAB	Airbus A.319-111	easyJet Airline Co Ltd	
G-EZAC	Airbus A.319-111	easyJet Airline Co Ltd	
G-EZAD	Airbus A.319-111	easyJet Airline Co Ltd	
G-EZAF	Airbus A.319-111	easyJet Airline Co Ltd	
G-EZAG	Airbus A.319-111	easyJet Airline Co Ltd	
G-EZAI	Airbus A.319-111	easyJet Airline Co Ltd	
G-EZAJ	Airbus A.319-111	easyJet Airline Co Ltd	
G-EZAK	Airbus A.319-111	easyJet Airline Co Ltd	
G-EZAL	Airbus A.319-111	easyJet Airline Co Ltd	
G-EZAM	Airbus A.319-111	easyJet Airline Co Ltd (G-CCKA)	
G-EZAN	Airbus A.319-111	easyJet Airline Co Ltd	
G-EZAO	Airbus A.319-111	easyJet Airline Co Ltd	
G-EZAP	Airbus A.319-111	easyJet Airline Co Ltd	
G-EZAR	Pegasus Quik	B. Robertson	
G-EZAS	Airbus A.319-111	easyJet Airline Co Ltd	
G-EZAT	Airbus A.319-111	easyJet Airline Co Ltd	
G-EZAU	Airbus A.319-111	easyJet Airline Co Ltd	
G-EZAV	Airbus A.319-111	easyJet Airline Co Ltd	
G-EZAW	Airbus A.319-111	easyJet Airline Co Ltd	
G-EZAX	Airbus A.319-111	easyJet Airline Co Ltd	
G-EZAY	Airbus A.319-111	easyJet Airline Co Ltd	
G-EZAZ	Airbus A.319-111	easyJet Airline Co Ltd	
G-EZBA	Airbus A.319-111	easyJet Airline Co Ltd	
G-EZBB	Airbus A.319-111	easyJet Airline Co Ltd	
G-EZBC	Airbus A.319-111	easyJet Airline Co Ltd	
G-EZBD	Airbus A.319-111	easyJet Airline Co Ltd	
G-EZBE	Airbus A.319-111	easyJet Airline Co Ltd	
G-EZBF	Airbus A.319-111	easyJet Airline Co Ltd	
G-EZBG	Airbus A.319-111	easyJet Airline Co Ltd	
G-EZBH	Airbus A.319-111	easyJet Airline Co Ltd	
G-EZBI	Airbus A.319-111	easyJet Airline Co Ltd	
G-EZBJ	Airbus A.319-111	easyJet Airline Co Ltd	
G-EZBK	Airbus A.319-111	easyJet Airline Co Ltd	
G-EZBL	Airbus A.319-111	easyJet Airline Co Ltd	
G-EZBM	Airbus A.319-111	easyJet Airline Co Ltd	
G-EZBN	Airbus A.319-111	easyJet Airline Co Ltd	
G-EZBO	Airbus A.319-111	easyJet Airline Co Ltd	
G-EZBR	Airbus A.319-111	easyJet Airline Co Ltd	
G-EZBT	Airbus A.319-111	easyJet Airline Co Ltd	
G-EZBU	Airbus A.319-111	easyJet Airline Co.Ltd	
G-EZBV	Airbus A.319-111	easyJet Airline Co.Ltd	
G-EZBW	Airbus A.319-111	easyJet Airline.Co.Ltd	
G-EZBX	Airbus A.319-111	easyJet Airline Co.Ltd	
G-EZBY	Airbus A.319-111	easyJet Airline Co.Ltd	
G-EZBZ	Airbus A.319-111	easyJet Airline Co.Ltd	
G-EZDA	Airbus A.319-111	easyJet Airline Co.Ltd	
G-EZDB	Airbus A.319-111	easyJet Airline Co.Ltd	
G-EZDC	Airbus A.319-111	easyJet Airline Co Ltd (G-CCKB)	
G-EZDD	Airbus A.319-111	easyJet Airline Co.Ltd	
G-EZDE	Airbus A.319-111	easyJet Airline Co.Ltd	
G-EZDF	Airbus A.319-111	easyJet Airline Co.Ltd	
G-EZDG	Rutan Vari-Eze	D. M. Gale (G-EZOS)	
G-EZDH	Airbus A.319-111	easyJet Airline Co.Ltd	
G-EZDI	Airbus A.319-111	easyJet Airline Co.Ltd	

Notes	Reg.	Type	Owner or Operator
	G-EZDJ	Airbus A.319-111	easyJet Airline Co.Ltd
	G-EZDK	Airbus A.319-111	easyJet Airline Co.Ltd
	G-EZDL	Airbus A.319-111	easyJet Airline Co.Ltd
	G-EZDM	Airbus A.319-111	easyJet Airline Co.Ltd
	G-EZDN	Airbus A.319-111	easyJet Airline Co.Ltd
	G-EZDO	Airbus A.319-111	easyJet Airline Co.Ltd
	G-EZDP	Airbus A.319-111	easyJet Airline Co.Ltd
	G-EZDR	Airbus A.319-111	easyJet Airline Co.Ltd
	G-EZDS	Airbus A.319-111	easyJet Airline Co.Ltd
	G-EZDT	Airbus A.319-111	easyJet Airline Co.Ltd
	G-EZDU	Airbus A.319-111	easyJet Airline Co.Ltd
	G-EZDV	Airbus A.319-111	easyJet Airline Co.Ltd
	G-EZDW	Airbus A.319-111	easyJet Airline Co.Ltd
	G-EZDX	Airbus A.319-111	easyJet Airline Co.Ltd
	G-EZDY	Airbus A.319-111	easyJet Airline Co.Ltd
	G-EZDZ	Airbus A.319-111	easyJet Airline Co.Ltd
	G-EZEA	Airbus A.319-111	easyJet Airline Co Ltd
	G-EZEB	Airbus A.319-111	easyJet Airline Co Ltd
	G-EZEC	Airbus A.319-111	easyJet Airline Co Ltd
	G-EZED	Airbus A.319-111	easyJet Airline Co Ltd
	G-EZEF	Airbus A.319-111	easyJet Airline Co Ltd
	G-EZEG	Airbus A.319-111	easyJet Airline Co Ltd
	G-EZEJ	Airbus A.319-111	easyJet Airline Co Ltd
	G-EZEK	Airbus A.319-111	easyJet Airline Co Ltd
	G-EZEL	Westland SA.341G Gazelle 1	W. R. Pitcher (G-BAZL)
	G-EZEO	Airbus A.319-111	easyJet Airline Co Ltd
	G-EZEP	Airbus A.319-111	easyJet Airline Co Ltd
	G-EZES	Airbus A.319-111	easyJet Airline Co Ltd
	G-EZET	Airbus A.319-111	easyJet Airline Co Ltd
	G-EZEU	Airbus A.319-111	easyJet Airline Co Ltd
	G-EZEV	Airbus A.319-111	easyJet Airline Co Ltd
	G-EZEW	Airbus A.319-111	easyJet Airline Co Ltd
	G-EZEZ	Airbus A.319-111	easyJet Airline Co Ltd
	G-EZFA	Airbus A.319-111	easyJet Airline Co.Ltd
	G-EZFB	Airbus A.319-111	easyJet Airline Co.Ltd
	G-EZFC	Airbus A.319-111	easyJet Airline Co.Ltd
	G-EZFD	Airbus A.319-111	easyJet Airline Co.Ltd
	G-EZFE	Airbus A.319-111	easyJet Airline Co.Ltd
	G-EZFF	Airbus A.319-111	easyJet Airline Co.Ltd
	G-EZFG	Airbus A.319-111	easyJet Airline Co.Ltd
	G-EZFH	Airbus A.319-111	easyJet Airline Co.Ltd
	G-EZFI	Airbus A.319-111	easyJet Airline Co.Ltd
	G-EZFJ	Airbus A.319-111	easyJet Airline Co.Ltd
	G-EZFK	Airbus A.319-111	easyJet Airline Co.Ltd
	G-EZFL	Airbus A.319-111	easyJet Airline Co.Ltd
	G-EZFM	Airbus A.319-111	easyJet Airline Co.Ltd
	G-EZFN	Airbus A.319-111	easyJet Airline Co.Ltd
	G-EZFO	Airbus A.319-111	easyJet Airline Co.Ltd
	G-EZFP	Airbus A.319-111	easyJet Airline Co.Ltd
	G-EZFR	Airbus A.319-111	easyJet Airline Co.Ltd
	G-EZFS	Airbus A.319-111	easyJet Airline Co.Ltd
	G-EZFT	Airbus A.319-111	easyJet Airline Co.Ltd
	G-EZFU	Airbus A.319-111	easyJet Airline Co.Ltd
	G-EZFV	Airbus A.319-111	easyJet Airline Co.Ltd
	G-EZFW	Airbus A.319-111	easyJet Airline Co.Ltd
	G-EZFX	Airbus A.319-111	easyJet Airline Co.Ltd
	G-EZFY	Airbus A.319-111	easyJet Airline Co.Ltd
	G-EZFZ	Airbus A.319-111	easyJet Airline Co.Ltd
	G-EZGA	Airbus A.319-111	easyJet Airline Co.Ltd
	G-EZGB	Airbus A.319-111	easyJet Airline Co.Ltd
	G-EZGC	Airbus A.319-111	easyJet Airline Co.Ltd
	G-EZGD	Airbus A.319-111	easyJet Airline Co.Ltd
	G-EZGE	Airbus A.319-111	easyJet Airline Co.Ltd
	G-EZGF	Airbus A.319-111	easyJet Airline Co.Ltd
	G-EZGG	Airbus A.319-111	easyJet Airline Co.Ltd
	G-EZGH	Airbus A.319-111	easyJet Airline Co.Ltd
	G-EZGI	Airbus A.319-111	easyJet Airline Co.Ltd
	G-EZIC	Airbus A.319-111	easyJet Airline Co Ltd
	G-EZID	Airbus A.319-111	easyJet Airline Co Ltd
	G-EZIE	Airbus A.319-111	easyJet Airline Co Ltd
	G-EZIG	Airbus A.319-111	easyJet Airline Co Ltd
	G-EZIH	Airbus A.319-111	easyJet Airline Co Ltd

Reg.	Type	Owner or Operator	Notes
G-EZII	Airbus A.319-111	easyJet Airline Co Ltd	
G-EZIJ	Airbus A.319-111	easyJet Airline Co Ltd	
G-EZIK	Airbus A.319-111	easyJet Airline Co Ltd	
G-EZIL	Airbus A.319-111	easyJet Airline Co Ltd	
G-EZIM	Airbus A.319-111	easyJet Airline Co Ltd	
G-EZIN	Airbus A.319-111	easyJet Airline Co Ltd	
G-EZIO	Airbus A.319-111	easyJet Airline Co Ltd	
G-EZIP	Airbus A.319-111	easyJet Airline Co Ltd	
G-EZIR	Airbus A.319-111	easyJet Airline Co Ltd	
G-EZIS	Airbus A.319-111	easyJet Airline Co Ltd	
G-EZIT	Airbus A.319-111	easyJet Airline Co Ltd	
G-EZIU	Airbus A.319-111	easyJet Airline Co Ltd	
G-EZIV	Airbus A.319-111	easyJet Airline Co Ltd	
G-EZIW	Airbus A.319-111	easyJet Airline Co Ltd	
G-EZIX	Airbus A.319-111	easyJet Airline Co Ltd	
G-EZIY	Airbus A.319-111	easyJet Airline Co Ltd	
G-EZIZ	Airbus A.319-111	easyJet Airline Co Ltd	
G-EZJZ	Boeing 737-73V	easyJet Airline Co Ltd	
G-EZKA	Boeing 737-73V	easyJet Airline Co Ltd	
G-EZKB	Boeing 737-73V	easyJet Airline Co Ltd	
G-EZKC	Boeing 737-73V	easyJet Airline Co Ltd	
G-EZKD	Boeing 737-73V	easyJet Airline Co Ltd	
G-EZKE	Boeing 737-73V	easyJet Airline Co Ltd	
G-EZKF	Boeing 737-73V	easyJet Airline Co Ltd	
G-EZKG	Boeing 737-73V	easyJet Airline Co Ltd	
G-EZMH	Airbus A.319-111	easyJet Airline Co Ltd (G-CCKD)	
G-EZMS	Airbus A.319-111	easyJet Airline Co Ltd	
G-EZNC	Airbus A.319-111	easyJet Airline Co Ltd (G-CCKC)	
G-EZPG	Airbus A.319-111	easyJet Airline Co Ltd	
G-EZSM	Airbus A.319-111	easyJet Airline Co Ltd (G-CCKE)	
G-EZTA	Airbus A.320-214	easyJet Airline Co.Ltd	
G-EZTB	Airbus A.320-214	easyJet Airline Co.Ltd	
G-EZTC	Airbus A.320-214	easyJet Airline Co.Ltd	
G-EZTD	Airbus A.320-214	easyJet Airline Co.Ltd	
G-EZTE	Airbus A.320-214	easyJet Airline Co.Ltd	
G-EZTF	Airbus A.320-214	easyJet Airline Co.Ltd	
G-EZTG	Airbus A.320-214	easyJet Airline Co.Ltd	
G-EZTH	Airbus A.320-214	easyJet Airline Co.Ltd	
G-EZTI	Airbus A.320-214	easyJet Airline Co.Ltd	
G-EZTJ	Airbus A.320-214	easyJet Airline Co.Ltd	
G-EZTK	Airbus A.320-214	easyJet Airline Co.Ltd	
G-EZTL	Airbus A.320-214	easyJet Airline Co.Ltd	
G-EZTM	Airbus A.320-214	easyJet Airline Co.Ltd	
G-EZTN	Airbus A.320-214	easyJet Airline Co.Ltd	
G-EZTP	Airbus A.320-214	easyJet Airline Co.Ltd	
G-EZTR	Airbus A.320-214	easyJet Airline Co.Ltd	
G-EZTS	Airbus A.320-214	easyJet Airline Co.Ltd	
G-EZTT	Airbus A.320-214	easyJet Airline Co.Ltd	
G-EZTU	Airbus A.320-214	easyJet Airline Co.Ltd	
G-EZTV	Airbus A.320-214	easyJet Airline Co.Ltd	
G-EZTW	Airbus A.320-214	easyJet Airline Co.Ltd	
G-EZTX	Airbus A.320-214	easyJet Airline Co.Ltd	
G-EZTY	Airbus A.320-214	easyJet Airline Co.Ltd	
G-EZTZ	Airbus A.320-214	easyJet Airline Co.Ltd	
G-EZUA	Airbus A.320-214	easyJet Airline Co.Ltd	
G-EZUB	Zenair CH.601HD Zodiac	R. A. C. Stephens	
G-EZVS	Colt 77B balloon	A. J. Lovell	
G-EZXO	Colt 56A balloon	A. J. Lovell	
G-EZZA	Shaw Europa XS	J. C. R. Davey	
G-EZZE	CZAW Sportcruiser	G. Verity	
G-EZZL	Westland Gazelle HT.3	Regal Group UK (G-CBKC)	
G-EZZY	Evektor EV-97 Eurostar	G. & P. M. G. Verity	
G-FABB	Cameron V-77 balloon	T. J. Wilkinson	
G-FACE	Cessna 172S	Oxford Aviation Services Ltd	
G-FAIR	SOCATA TB10 Tobago	Fairwings Ltd	
G-FAJC	Alpi Pioneer 300 Hawk	F. A. Cavaciuti	
G-FAJM	Robinson R44 II	Ryvoan Aviation Ltd	
G-FALC	Aeromere F.8L Falco	D. M. Burbridge (G-AROT)	
G-FAME	Starstreak Shadow SA-II	S. R. Whitehead	
G-FAMH	Zenair CH.701	F. Omaraie-Hamdanie	
G-FAMT	Bombardier BD700-1A10 Global Express	Gama Aviation Ltd	

Notes	Reg.	Type	Owner or Operator
	G-FANC	Fairchild 24R-46 Argus III	A. T. Fines
	G-FANL	Cessna FR.172K XP-II	J. A. Rees
	G-FARA	BAe Jetstream 3102	Spitfire Investments Ltd
	G-FARE	Robinson R44 II	Toriamos Ltd/Ireland
	G-FARL	Pitts S-1E Special	T. I. Williams
	G-FARO	Aero Designs Star-Lite SL.1	M. K. Faro
	G-FARR	Jodel 150	G. H. Farr
	G-FARY	QAC Quickie Tri-Q	A. Bloomfield and A. Underwood
	G-FATB	Rockwell Commander 114B	James D. Pearce & Co
	G-FATE	Falco F8L	G-FATE Flying Group
	G-FAVC	DH.80A Puss Moth	Liddell Aircraft Ltd
	G-FAVS	PA-32-300 Cherokee Six	Favourites Racing Ltd (G-BKEK)
	G-FAZA	Cameron Z-180 balloon	M. G. Howard
	G-FBAT	Aeroprakt A.22 Foxbat	J. Jordan
	G-FBEA	Embraer ERJ190-200LR	Flybe.com
	G-FBEB	Embraer ERJ190-200LR	Flybe.com
	G-FBEC	Embraer ERJ190-200LR	Flybe.com
	G-FBED	Embraer ERJ190-200LR	Flybe.com
	G-FBEE	Embraer ERJ190-200LR	Flybe.com
	G-FBEF	Embraer ERJ190-200LR	Flybe.com
	G-FBEG	Embraer ERJ190-200LR	Flybe.com
	G-FBEH	Embraer ERJ190-200LR	Flybe.com
	G-FBEI	Embraer ERJ190-200LR	Flybe.com
	G-FBEJ	Embraer ERJ190-200LR	Flybe.com
	G-FBEK	Embraer ERJ190-200LR	Flybe.com
	G-FBEL	Embraer ERJ190-200LR	Flybe.com
	G-FBEM	Embraer ERJ190-200LR	Flybe.com
	G-FBEN	Embraer ERJ190-200LR	Flybe.com
	G-FBHA	Agusta AW.139	FB Heliservices Ltd
	G-FBII	Ikarus C.42 FB100	F. Beeson
	G-FBKA	Cessna 510 Citation Mustang	Blink Ltd
	G-FBKB	Cessna 510 Citation Mustang	Blink Ltd
	G-FBKC	Cessna 510 Citation Mustang	Blink Ltd
	G-FBKD	Cessna 510 Citation Mustang	Blink Ltd
	G-FBLI	Cessna 510 Citation Mustang	Blink Ltd
	G-FBLK	Cessna 510 Citation Mustang	Blink Ltd
	G-FBNK	Cessna 510 Citation Mustang	Blink Ltd
	G-FBOY	Skystar Kitfox Mk 7	A. Bray
	G-FBPL	PA-34-200 Seneca	FlyBlackpool Ltd (G-BBXK)
	G-FBRN	PA-28-181 Archer II	Herefordshire Aero Club Ltd
	G-FBTT	Aeroprakt A22-L Foxbat	T. D. Reid
	G-FBWH	PA-28R Cherokee Arrow 180	F. A. Short
	G-FCAB	Diamond DA42 Twin Star	Diamond Finance Services GmbH
	G-FCAV	Schleicher ASK-13	M. F. Cuming
	G-FCBI	Schweizer 269C-1	CSL Industrial Ltd
	G-FCCC	Schleicher ASK-13	Shenington Gliding Club
	G-FCDB	Cessna 550 Citation Bravo	Eurojet Aviation Ltd
	G-FCED	PA-31T2 Cheyenne IIXL	Provident Partners Ltd
	G-FCFC	Bombardier BD700-1A10 Global Express	Ocean Sky (UK) Ltd
	G-FCKD	Eurocopter EC 120B	Pacific Helicopters Ltd
	G-FCLA	Boeing 757-28A	Thomas Cook Airlines Ltd
	G-FCLB	Boeing 757-28A	Thomas Cook Airlines Ltd
	G-FCLC	Boeing 757-38A	Thomas Cook Airlines Ltd
	G-FCLD	Boeing 757-25F	Thomas Cook Airlines Ltd
	G-FCLE	Boeing 757-28A	Thomas Cook Airlines Ltd
	G-FCLF	Boeing 757-28A	Thomas Cook Airlines Ltd
	G-FCLH	Boeing 757-28A	Thomas Cook Airlines Ltd
	G-FCLI	Boeing 757-28A	Thomas Cook Airlines Ltd
	G-FCLJ	Boeing 757-2Y0	Thomas Cook Airlines Ltd
	G-FCLK	Boeing 757-2Y0	Thomas Cook Airlines Ltd
	G-FCOM	Slingsby T.59F Kestrel	P. A. C. Wheatcroft & A. G. Truman
	G-FCON	Schempp-Hirth Standard Cirrus	M. G. Sankey & I. Keen
	G-FCSL	PA-32-350 Navajo Chieftain	Culross Aerospace Ltd (G-CLAN)
	G-FCSP	Robin DR.400/180	S. Eustace
	G-FCUK	Pitts S-1C Special	D. Stephens
	G-FCUM	Robinson R44 II	The Grange Country Club Ltd
	G-FDDY	Schleicher Ka 6CR	DDY Group
	G-FDPS	Aviat Pitts S-2C Special	Flights and Dreams Ltd

Reg.	Type	Owner or Operator	Notes
G-FDZA	Boeing 737-8K5	Thomsonfly Ltd	
G-FDZB	Boeing 737-8K5	Thomsonfly Ltd	
G-FDZD	Boeing 737-8K5	Thomsonfly Ltd	
G-FDZE	Boeing 737-8K5	Thomsonfly Ltd	
G-FDZF	Boeing 737-8K5	Thomsonfly Ltd	
G-FDZG	Boeing 737-8K5	Thomsonfly Ltd	
G-FDZR	Boeing 737-8K5	Thomsonfly Ltd	
G-FDZS	Boeing 737-8K5	Thomsonfly Ltd	
G-FDZT	Boeing 737-8K5	Thomsonfly Ltd	
G-FEAB	PA-28-181 Archer III	Feabrex Ltd	
G-FEBB	Grob G.104 Speed Astir IIB	The Astir Group	
G-FEBJ	Schleicher ASW-19B	A. P. Hatton	
G-FECO	Grob G.102 Astir CS77	C. Peterson	
G-FEDA	Eurocopter EC 120B	J. Henshall	
G-FEET	Mainair Pegasus Quik	M. P. Duckett	
G-FELD	Rotorsport UK MTO Sport	S. Pearce	
G-FELL	Shaw Europa	M. C. Costin & J. A. Inglis	
G-FELT	Cameron N-77 balloon	Allan Industries Ltd	
G-FELX	CZAW Sportcruiser	T. F. Smith	
G-FERN	Mainair Blade 912	M. H. Moulai	
G-FERV	Rolladen-Schneider LS4	R. J. J. Bennett	
G-FESS	Pegasus Quantum 15-912	P. M. Fessi (G-CBBZ)	
G-FEVS	PZL-Bielsko SZD-50-3 Puchacz	Deeside Gliding Club (Aberdeenshire) Ltd	
G-FEWG	Fuji FA.200-160	Caseright Ltd (G-BBNV)	
G-FEZZ	Bell 206B JetRanger II	R. J. Myram	
G-FFAB	Cameron N-105 balloon	B. J. Hammond	
G-FFAF	Cessna F.150L	R. Henderson	
G-FFEN	Cessna F.150M	B. Emerson & J. Tuckwell	
G-FFFG	Dassault Falcon 900EX	TAG Aviation (UK) Ltd	
G-FFFT	Lindstrand LBL-31A balloon	W. Rousell & J. Tyrrell	
G-FFIT	Pegasus Quik	G. Turner	
G-FFOX	Hawker Hunter T.7B (WV318:D)	WV318 Group	
G-FFRA	Dassault Falcon 20DC	FR Aviation Ltd	
G-FFRI	AS.355F1 Twin Squirrel	Sterling Helicopters Ltd (G-GLOW/G-PAPA/ G-CNET/G-MCAH)	
G-FFTI	SOCATA TB20 Trinidad	R. Lenk	
G-FFUN	Pegasus Quantum 15	J. R. F. Hollingshead	
G-FFWD	Cessna 310R	T. S. Courtman (G-TVKE/G-EURO)	
G-FGAZ	Schleicher Ka 6E	C. M. Billings, B. A. & M. A. Roberts	
G-FGID	Vought FG-1D Corsair (KD345:130-A)	Patina Ltd	
G-FGSI	Montgomerie-Bensen B8MR	F. G. Shepherd	
G-FGSK	Cameron 120 Beer Crate SS balloon	Ballon-Sport und Luftwerbung Dresden GmbH/ Germany	
G-FHAS	Scheibe SF.25E Super Falke	D. C. Mason	
G-FIAT	PA-28 Cherokee 140	Demero Ltd & Transcourt Ltd (G-BBYW)	
G-FIBS	AS.350BA Ecureuil	Elitop SRL/Italy	
G-FICS	Flight Design CTSW	J. R. Phillips	
G-FIFA	Cessna 404 Titan	Fly (CI) Ltd (G-TVIP/G-KIWI/G-BHNI)	
G-FIFE	Cessna FA.152	Tayside Aviation Ltd (G-BFYN)	
G-FIFI	SOCATA TB20 Trinidad	F. A. Saker (G-BMWS)	
G-FIFO	Cessna 152	A. Kitts & C. Salway (G-OAFT/G-BNKM)	
G-FIFT	Ikarus C.42 FB 100	A. R. Jones	
G-FIGA	Cessna 152	Merseyflight Ltd	
G-FIGB	Cessna 152	A. J. Gomes	
G-FIGP	Boeing 737-2E7	European Skybus Ltd (G-BMDF)	
G-FIII	Extra EA.300/L	J. S. Allison (G-RGEE)	
G-FIJJ	Cessna F.177RG	D. R. Vale (G-AZFP)	
G-FIJV	Lockheed L.188CF Electra	Atlantic Airlines Ltd	
G-FIKI	Cirrus SR22	Caseright Ltd	
G-FILE	PA-34-200T Seneca	Bristol Flying Centre Ltd	
G-FILL	PA-31-310 Navajo	P. V. Naylor-Leyland	
G-FINA	Cessna F.150L	A. G. Freeman (G-BIFT)	
G-FIND	Cessna F.406	Reconnaissance Ventures Ltd	
G-FINT	Piper L-4B Grasshopper	G. & H. M. Picarella	
G-FINZ	I.I.I Sky Arrow 650T	A. G. Counsell	
G-FIRM	Cessna 550 Citation Bravo	The Cambridge Aero Club Ltd	
G-FIRS	Robinson R22 Beta II	Helitrain Ltd	

Notes	Reg.	Type	Owner or Operator
	G-FIRZ	Murphy Renegade Spirit UK	S. Koutsoukos
	G-FISH	Cessna 310R-II	ACS Contracts Ltd
	G-FITY	Europa XS	D. C. A. Moore & M. Fielder
	G-FIXX	Van's RV-7	Hambilton Engineering Ltd
	G-FIZU	Lockheed L.188CF Electra	Atlantic Airlines Ltd
	G-FIZY	Shaw Europa XS	R. Eyles & R. C. Winter (G-DDSC)
	G-FIZZ	PA-28-161 Warrior II	G-FIZZ Group
	G-FJET	Cessna 550 Citation II	London Executive Aviation Ltd (G-DCFR/ G-WYLX/G-JETD)
	G-FJMS	Partenavia P.68B	J. B. Randle (G-SVHA)
	G-FJTH	Aeroprakt A.22 Foxbat	F. J. T. Hancock
	G-FKNH	PA-15 Vagabond	M. J. Mothershaw
	G-FKOS	PA-28-181 Archer II	M. K. Johnson
	G-FLAG	Colt 77A balloon	B. A. Williams
	G-FLAV	PA-28-161 Warrior II	The Crew Flying Group
	G-FLBA	DHC.8-402 Dash Eight	Flybe.com
	G-FLBB	DHC.8-402 Dash Eight	Flybe.com
	G-FLBC	DHC.8-402 Dash Eight	Flybe.com
	G-FLBD	DHC.8-402 Dash Eight	Flybe.com
	G-FLBE	DHC.8-402 Dash Eight	Flybe.com
	G-FLBI	Robinson R44 II	Hopkinsons Fairdeals Remarketing
	G-FLBK	Cessna 510 Citation Mustang	Blink Ltd
	G-FLCA	Fleet Model 80 Canuck	E. C. Taylor
	G-FLCT	Hallam Fleche	R. G. Hallam
	G-FLDG	Skyranger 912	A. J. Gay
	G-FLEA	SOCATA TB10 Tobago	TB Group
	G-FLEE	ZJ-Viera	P. C. Piggott
	G-FLEW	Lindstrand LBL-90A balloon	A. Nimmo
	G-FLEX	Mainair Pegasus Quik	L. A. Read
	G-FLGT	Lindstrand LBL-105A balloon	Ballongaventyr I. Skane AB/Sweden
	G-FLIK	Pitts S-1S Special	R. P. Millinship
	G-FLIP	Cessna FA.152	Cristal Air Ltd (G-BOES)
	G-FLIS	Magni M.16C	M. L. L. Temple
	G-FLIT	Rotorway Executive 162F	R. S. Snell
	G-FLIZ	Staaken Z-21 Flitzer	M. J. Clark
	G-FLKE	Scheibe SF.25C Falke	RAF Gliding & Soaring Association
	G-FLKS	Scheibe SF.25C Falke	London Gliding Club Propietary Ltd
	G-FLKY	Cessna 172S	M. E. Falkingham
	G-FLOA	Cameron O-120 balloon	Floating Sensations Ltd
	G-FLOR	Shaw Europa	A. F. C. van Eldik
	G-FLOW	Cessna 172N	P. H. Archard
	G-FLOX	Shaw Europa	DPT Group
	G-FLPI	Rockwell Commander 112	H. J. Freeman
	G-FLSH	Yak-52	M. A. Wright
	G-FLTA	BAe 146-200	Westall Ltd
	G-FLTC	BAe 146-300	E3205 Trading Ltd (G-JEBH/G-BVTO/G-NJID)
	G-FLTF	BAe 146-300	Rangefield Holdings Ltd (G-DEBE)
	G-FLTG	Cameron A-140 balloon	Floating Sensations Ltd
	G-FLTZ	Beech 58 Baron	Calder Group Ltd (G-PSVS)
	G-FLUZ	Rolladen-Schneider LS8-18	D. M. King
	G-FLYA	Mooney M.20J	B. Willis
	G-FLYB	Ikarus C.42 FB100	G-FLYB Group
	G-FLYC	Ikarus C.42 FB100	Solent Flight Ltd
	G-FLYF	Mainair Blade 912	Cool Water Direct Ltd
	G-FLYG	Slingsby T.67C	G. Laden
	G-FLYH	Robinson R22 Beta	J. R. Huggins (G-BXMR)
	G-FLYI	PA-34-200 Seneca II	Falcon Flying Services Ltd (G-BHVO)
	G-FLYM	Ikarus C42 FB100	R. A. McKee
	G-FLYP	Beagle B.206 Srs 2	Key Publishing Ltd (G-AVHO)
	G-FLYT	Shaw Europa	K. F. & R. Richardson
	G-FLYX	Robinson R44 II	Sitecrest Aviation LLP
	G-FLYY	BAC.167 Strikemaster 80A	B. T. Barber
	G-FLZA	Staaken Z-21A Flitzer	G. R. Pybus
	G-FMAM	PA-28-151 Warrior (modified)	Lima Tango Flying Group (G-BBXV)
	G-FMGG	Maule M5-235C Lunar Rocket	S. Bierbaum (G-RAGG)
	G-FMKA	Diamond HK.36TC Super Dimona	G. P. Davis
	G-FMSG	Cessna FA.150K	G. Owen/Gamston (G-POTS/G-AYUY)

Reg.	Type	Owner or Operator	Notes
G-FNES	Dassault Falcon 900EX	Matrix Aviation Ltd	
G-FNEY	Cessna F.177RG	F. Ney	
G-FNLD	Cessna 172N	Papa Hotel Flying Group	
G-FNPT	PA-28-161 Warrior III	Plane Talking Ltd	
G-FOFO	Robinson R44 II	Kuki Helicopter Sales Ltd	
G-FOGG	Cameron N-90 balloon	J. P. E. Money-Kyrle	
G-FOGI	Shaw Europa XS	B. Fogg	
G-FOGY	Robinson R22 Beta	Helicentre Holdings Ltd	
G-FOKK	Fokker DR1 (replica)	P. D. & S. E. Ford	
G-FOKR	Fokker E.III Replica	D. Stephens	
G-FOLD	Light Aero Avid Speedwing	B. W. & G. Evans	
G-FOLI	Robinson R22 Beta II	G. M. Duckworth	
G-FOLY	Aerotek Pitts S-2A Modified	C. T. Charleston	
G-FOPP	Lancair 320	Airsport (UK) Ltd	
G-FORA	Schempp-Hirth Ventus cT	G. Bailey & J. D. Sorrell	
G-FORC	SNCAN Stampe SV.4C	C. C. Rollings & F. J. Hodson	
G-FORD	SNCAN Stampe SV.4C	P. H. Meeson	
G-FORM	Learjet 45	Broomco 3598 Ltd	
G-FORZ	Pitts S-1S Special	N. W. Parkinson	
G-FOSY	MS.880B Rallye Club	A. G. Foster (G-AXAK)	
G-FOWL	Colt 90A balloon	The Packhouse Ltd	
G-FOWS	Cameron N-105 balloon	Ezmerelda Balloon Syndicate	
G-FOXA	PA-28-161 Cadet	Leicestershire Aero Club Ltd	
G-FOXB	Aeroprakt A.22 Foxbat	G. D. McCullough	
G-FOXC	Denney Kitfox Mk 3	G. Hawkins	
G-FOXD	Denney Kitfox Mk 2	P. P. Trangmar	
G-FOXE	Denney Kitfox Mk 2	K. M. Pinkar	
G-FOXF	Denney Kitfox Mk 4	M. S. Goodwin	
G-FOXG	Denney Kitfox Mk 2	J. U. McKercher	
G-FOXI	Denney Kitfox	I. M. Walton	
G-FOXL	Zenair CH.601XL Zodiac	R. W. Taylor	
G-FOXM	Bell 206B JetRanger 2	Tyringham Charter & Group Services (G-STAK/ G-BNIS)	
G-FOXS	Denney Kitfox Mk 2	S. P. Watkins & C. C. Rea	
G-FOXX	Denney Kitfox	A. W. Hodder	
G-FOXZ	Denney Kitfox	S. C. Goozee	
G-FOZY	Van's RV-7	M. G. Forrest (G-COPZ)	
G-FOZZ	Beech A36 Bonanza	Go To Air Ltd	
G-FPIG	PA-28-151 Warrior	G. F. Strain (G-BSSR)	
G-FPLB	Beech 200 Super King Air	Cobham Flight Inspection Ltd	
G-FPLD	Beech 200 Super King Air	Cobham Flight Inspection Ltd	
G-FPLE	Beech 200 Super King Air	Cobham Flight Inspection Ltd	
G-FPSA	PA-28-161 Warrior II	Deep Cleavage Ltd (G-RSFT/G-WARI)	
G-FRAD	Dassault Falcon 20E	Cobham Leasing Ltd (G-BCYF)	
G-FRAF	Dassault Falcon 20E	FR Aviation Ltd	
G-FRAG	PA-32 Cherokee Six 300E	T. A. Houghton	
G-FRAH	Dassault Falcon 20DC	FR Aviation Ltd	
G-FRAI	Dassault Falcon 20E	FR Aviation Ltd	
G-FRAJ	Dassault Falcon 20E	FR Aviation Ltd	
G-FRAK	Dassault Falcon 20DC	FR Aviation Ltd	
G-FRAL	Dassault Falcon 20DC	FR Aviation Ltd	
G-FRAN	Piper J-3C-90 Cub(480321:H-44)	Essex L-4 Group (G-BIXY)	
G-FRAO	Dassault Falcon 20DC	FR Aviation Ltd	
G-FRAP	Dassault Falcon 20DC	FR Aviation Ltd	
G-FRAR	Dassault Falcon 20DC	FR Aviation Ltd	
G-FRAS	Dassault Falcon 20C	FR Aviation Ltd	
G-FRAT	Dassault Falcon 20C	FR Aviation Ltd	
G-FRAU	Dassault Falcon 20C	FR Aviation Ltd	
G-FRAW	Dassault Falcon 20ECM	FR Aviation Ltd	
G-FRAY	Cassutt IIIM (modified)	C. I. Fray	
G-FRBA	Dassault Falcon 20C	FR Aviation Ltd	
G-FRCE	Folland Gnat T.Mk.1	Red Gnat Ltd	
G-FRDY	Dynamic WT9 UK	Peter Dodd Consultants	
G-FRGN	PA-28-236 Dakota	P. J. Vacher	
G-FRGT	P & M Quik GT450	G-FRGT Group	
G-FRIL	Lindstrand LBL-105A balloon	S. Travaglia	
G-FRJB	Britten Sheriff SA-1 ★	Aeropark	
G-FRNK	Skyranger 912(2)	D. L. Foxley & G. Lace	
G-FROM	Ikarus C.42 FB100	G-FROM Group	

Notes	Reg.	Type	Owner or Operator
	G-FRSX	VS.388 Seafire F.46 (LA564)	Seafire Displays Ltd
	G-FRYI	Beech 200 Super King Air	London Executive Aviation Ltd (G-OAVX/ G-IBCA/G-BMCA)
	G-FRYL	Beech 390 Premier 1	Hawk Air Ltd/Farnborough
	G-FRZN	Agusta A109S Grand	Iceland Foods Ltd
	G-FSEU	Beech 200 Super King Air	Air Mercia Ltd
	G-FSHA	Denney Kitfox Mk 2	P. P. Trangmar
	G-FSZY	TB-10 Tobago	Fuzzy Flying Group
	G-FTAX	Cessna 421C	Gold Air International Ltd (G-BFFM)
	G-FTDF	Airbus A.320-231	Thomas Cook Airlines Ltd (G-EPFR/G-BVJV)
	G-FTIL	Robin DR.400/180R	RAF Wyton Flying Club Ltd
	G-FTIN	Robin DR.400/100	YP Flying Group
	G-FTSE	BN-2A Mk.III-2 Trislander	Aurigny Air Services Ltd (G-BEPI)
	G-FTSL	Canadair CL.600-2B16 604	Farglobe transport Services Ltd
	G-FUEL	Robin DR.400/180	R. Darch
	G-FUFU	Agusta A.109 Grand	Air Harrods Ltd
	G-FUKM	Westland Gazelle AH.1 (ZA730)	Falcon Aviation Ltd
	G-FULL	PA-28R Cherokee Arrow 200-II	Stapleford Flying Club Ltd (G-HWAY/G-JULI)
	G-FULM	Sikorsky S-76C	Air Harrods Ltd
	G-FUND	Thunder Ax7-65Z balloon	G. Everett
	G-FUNK	Yakovlev Yak-50	Redstar Aero Services Ltd
	G-FUNN	Plumb BGP-1	P. E. Barker
	G-FURI	Isaacs Fury II	S. M. Johnston
	G-FUSE	Cameron N-105 balloon	S. A. Lacey
	G-FUZZ	PA-18 Super Cub 95 (51-15319)	G. W. Cline
	G-FVEL	Cameron Z-90 balloon	Fort Vale Engineering Ltd
	G-FWAY	Lindstrand LBL-90A balloon	Fairway Furniture Ltd
	G-FWKS	Tanarg/Ixess 15 912S(1)	M. A. Coffin (G-SYUT)
	G-FWPW	PA-28-236 Dakota	P. A. & F. C. Winters
	G-FXBT	Aeroprakt A.22 Foxbat	R. H. Jago
	G-FXII	VS.366 Spitfire F.XII (EN224)	P. R. Arnold
	G-FYAN	Williams Westwind MLB	M. D. Williams
	G-FYAO	Williams Westwind MLB	M. D. Williams
	G-FYAU	Williams Westwind Mk 2 MLB	M. D. Williams
	G-FYAV	Osprey Mk 4E2 MLB	C. D. Egan & C. Stiles
	G-FYBX	Portswood Mk XVI MLB	I. Chadwick
	G-FYCL	Osprey Mk 4G MLB	P. J. Rogers
	G-FYCV	Osprey Mk 4D MLB	M. Thomson
	G-FYCZ	Osprey Mk 4D2 MLB	P. Middleton
	G-FYDF	Osprey Mk 4DV	K. A. Jones
	G-FYDI	Williams Westwind Two MLB	M. D. Williams
	G-FYDN	European 8C MLB	P. D. Ridout
	G-FYDO	Osprey Mk 4D MLB	N. L. Scallan
	G-FYDP	Williams Westwind Three MLB	M. D. Williams
	G-FYDS	Osprey Mk 4D MLB	N. L. Scallan
	G-FYEK	Unicorn UE.1C MLB	D. & D. Eaves
	G-FYEO	Eagle Mk 1 MLB	M. E. Scallan
	G-FYEV	Osprey Mk 1C MLB	M. E. Scallan
	G-FYEZ	Firefly Mk 1 MLB	M. E. & N. L. Scallan
	G-FYFI	European E.84DS MLB	M. Stelling
	G-FYFJ	Williams Westland 2 MLB	M. D. Williams
	G-FYFN	Osprey Saturn 2 MLB	J. & M. Woods
	G-FYFW	Rango NA-55 MLB	Rango Balloon and Kite Company
	G-FYFY	Rango NA-55RC MLB	Rango Balloon and Kite Company
	G-FYGC	Rango NA-42B MLB	L. J. Wardle
	G-FYGJ	Airspeed 300 MLB	N. Wells
	G-FYGM	Saffrey/Smith Princess MLB	A. Smith
	G-FZZA	General Avia F22-A	APB Leasing Ltd
	G-FZZI	Cameron H-34 balloon	Magical Adventures Ltd
	G-GABI	Lindstrand LBL-35A Cloudhopper balloon	R. D. Sargeant
	G-GABS	Cameron TR-70 balloon	N. M. Gabriel
	G-GABY	Bombardier BD-700-1A10 Global Express	Ocean Sky (UK) Ltd
	G-GACA	P.57 Sea Prince T.1 (WP308:572CU) ★	P. G. Vallance Ltd/Charlwood

Reg.	Type	Owner or Operator	Notes
G-GACB	Robinson R44 II	A. C. Barker	
G-GAEA	Aquila AT01	Stamp Aviation Ltd	
G-GAEB	Aquila AT01	Stamp Aviation Ltd	
G-GAFA	PA-34-200T Seneca II	Oxford Aviation Academy (Oxford) Ltd	
G-GAFT	PA-44-180 Seminole	GT Ventures Ltd	
G-GAII	Hawker Hunter GA.11 (XE685)	GA11 Ltd	
G-GAJB	AA-5B Tiger	G-GAJB Group (G-BHZN)	
G-GALA	PA-28 Cherokee 180E	FlyBPL.com	
G-GALB	PA-28-161 Warrior II	LB Aviation Ltd	
G-GALL	PA-38-112 Tomahawk	M. Lowe & K. Hazelwood (G-BTEV)	
G-GALX	Dassault Falcon 900 EX	Charter Air Ltd	
G-GAME	Cessna T.303	J. & R. K. Hyatt	
G-GAND	Agusta-Bell 206B Jet Ranger	The Henderson Group (G-AWMK)	
G-GANE	Sequoia F.8L Falco	S. J. Gane	
G-GANG	Bell 206L-4 Long Ranger IV	The Henderson Group	
G-GAOH	Robin DR.400 / 2 +2.	S. D. Baker & M. Stott	
G-GAOM	Robin DR.400 / 2+2	P. M. & P. A. Chapman	
G-GASP	PA-28-181 Archer II	G-GASP Flying Group	
G-GASS	Thunder Ax7-77 balloon	Servowarm Balloon Syndicate	
G-GAST	Van's RV-8	G. M. R. Abrey	
G-GATE	Robinson R44 II	J. W. Gate	
G-GATT	Robinson R44 II	B. W. Faulkner	
G-GAVH	P & M Quik	G. Hardman	
G-GAWA	Cessna 140	C140 Group (G-BRSM)	
G-GAZA	Aérospatiale SA.341G Gazelle 1	The Auster Aircraft Co Ltd (G-RALE/G-SFTG)	
G-GAZN	P & M Quik GT450	P. C. Bishop	
G-GAZO	Ace Magic Cyclone	G. J. Pearce	
G-GAZZ	Aérospatiale SA.341G Gazelle 1	Cheqair Ltd	
G-GBAO	Robin R1180TD	J. Toulorge	
G-GBBB	Schleicher ASH-25	ASH25 BB Glider Syndicate	
G-GBBT	Ultramagic M-90 balloon	British Telecommunications PLC	
G-GBCC	Ikarus C42 FB100	I. R. Westrope	
G-GBEE	Mainair Pegasus Quik	M. G. Evans	
G-GBFF	Cessna F.172N	Aviation Rentals	
G-GBFR	Cessna F.177RG	Airspeed Aviation Ltd	
G-GBGA	Scheibe SF.25C Falke	Bidford Gliding Ltd	
G-GBGB	Ultramagic M.105 balloon	Universal Car Services Ltd	
G-GBGF	Cameron Dragon SS balloon	Magical Adventures Ltd (G-BUVH)	
G-GBHI	SOCATA TB10 Tobago	Robert Purvis Plant Hire Ltd	
G-GBJP	Mainair Pegasus Quantum 15	M. P. Chew	
G-GBJS	Robin HR200/100S Club	R. Bowen	
G-GBLP	Cessna F.172M	Aviate Scotland Ltd (G-GWEN)	
G-GBMR	Beech B200 Super King Air	M and R Aviation LLP	
G-GBOB	Alpi Pioneer 300 Hawk	R. E. Burgess	
G-GBPP	Rolladen-Schneider LS6-c18	G. J. Lyons & R. Sinden	
G-GBRB	PA-28 Cherokee 180C	M. S. Marsland	
G-GBRU	Bell 206B JetRanger 3	R. A. Fleming Ltd (G-CDGV)	
G-GBRV	Van's RV-9A	G. Carter & K. L. Chorley (G-THMB)	
G-GBSL	Beech 76 Duchess	M. H. Cundsy (G-BGVG)	
G-GBTA	Boeing 737-436	British Airways (G-BVHA)	
G-GBTB	Boeing 737-436	British Airways (G-BVHB)	
G-GBTL	Cessna 172S	Bohana Technology Ltd	
G-GBUE	Robin DR.400/120A	J. A. Kane (G-BPXD)	
G-GBUN	Cessna 182T	G. M. Bunn	
G-GBVX	Robin DR400/120A	The Leuchars Flying Co.Ltd	
G-GBXF	Robin HR200/120	B. A. Mills	
G-GBXS	Shaw Europa XS	D. J. Newton & M. Shea	
G-GCAC	Shaw Europa XS T-G	J. L. Gunn	
G-GCAT	PA-28 Cherokee 140B	Group Cat (G-BFRH)	
G-GCCL	Beech 76 Duchess	Aerolease Ltd	
G-GCDA	Cirrus SR20	Aircraft Grouping Ltd	
G-GCDB	Cirrus SR20	Aircraft Grouping Ltd	
G-GCDC	Cirrus SR20	Stamp Aviation Ltd	
G-GCDD	Cirrus SR20	Stamp Aviation Ltd	
G-GCEA	Pegasus Quik	J. D. Ash	
G-GCFM	Diamond DA.40D Star	B. Viforel	
G-GCIY	Robin DR.400-140B	Exavia Ltd	
G-GCJA	Rolladen-Schneider LS8-18	N. T. Mallender	
G-GCKI	Mooney M.20K	B. Barr	
G-GCMM	Agusta A109E	Meade Air LLP	
G-GCMW	Grob G.102 Astir CS	E. F. Weaver	

Notes	Reg.	Type	Owner or Operator
	G-GCUF	Robin DR400/160	S. T. Bates
	G-GCYC	Cessna F.182Q	A. G. Dodd
	G-GDAV	Robinson R44 II	G. H. Weston
	G-GDEF	Robin DR.400/120	J. M. Shackleton
	G-GDER	Robin R.1180TD	Berkshire Aviation Services Ltd
	G-GDFA	Beoing 737-3G7	Jet 2
	G-GDFB	Boeing 737-33A	Jet 2
	G-GDFC	Boeing 737-8K2	Jet 2
	G-GDJF	Robinson R44 II	Berkley Properties Ltd (G-DEXT)
	G-GDKR	Robin DR400/140B	L. J. Milbank
	G-GDMW	Beech 76 Duchess	Flew LLP
	G-GDOG	PA-28R Cherokee Arrow 200-II	The Mutley Crew Group (G-BDXW)
	G-GDOV	Robinson R44	E. K. Richardson
	G-GDSG	Agusta A109E Power	Pendley Aviation LLP
	G-GDRV	Van's RV-6	J. R. S. Heaton & R. Feather
	G-GDTL	Airbus A.320-231	MyTravel Airways
	G-GDTU	Avions Mudry CAP-10B	D. C. Cooper & A. L. Farr
	G-GEEP	Robin R.1180TD	The Aiglon Flying Group
	G-GEHL	Cessna 172S	Ebryl Ltd
	G-GEHP	PA-28RT-201 Arrow IV	Aeros Leasing Ltd
	G-GEIR	Embraer EMB-505 Phenom 300	F-Partners Ltd
	G-GEMM	Cirrus SR20	Schmolke Grosskuechensysteme GmbH
	G-GEMX	P&M Quik GT450	A. R. Oliver
	G-GEOF	Pereira Osprey 2	G. Crossley
	G-GEOS	Diamond HK.36 TTC-ECO Super Dimona	University Court (School of Geosciences) of the University of Edinburgh
	G-GERS	Robinson R44 II	M. Virdee
	G-GERT	Van's RV-7	Barnstormers
	G-GERY	Stoddard-Hamilton Glastar	S. G. Brown
	G-GEZZ	Bell 206B JetRanger II	Rivermead Aviation Ltd
	G-GFAA	Slingsbt T.67A	Aircraft Grouping Ltd (G-BJXA)
	G-GFCA	PA-28-161 Cadet	Aeros Leasing Ltd
	G-GFCB	PA-28-161 Cadet	A. J. Warren
	G-GFCD	PA-34-220T Seneca III	Stonehurst Aviation Ltd (G-KIDS)
	G-GFDA	Diamond DA.42 Twin Star	Saltaire Motor Co.Ltd (G-CEFX)
	G-GFEA	Cessna 172S	Allan Jefferies (G-CEDY)
	G-GFEY	PA-34-200T Seneca II	G-GFEY Owners Club
	G-GFFD	Boeing 737-59D	Charleston Partners Ltd (G-OBMY)
	G-GFFE	Boeing 737-528	Pineapple Ltd
	G-GFIA	Cessna 152	Aircraft Grouping Ltd
	G-GFIB	Cessna F.152	Aircraft Grouping Ltd (G-BPIO)
	G-GFIC	Cessna 152	Aircraft Grouping Ltd (G-BORI)
	G-GFID	Cessna 152 II	Silverstar Maintenance Services Ltd (G-BORJ)
	G-GFIE	Cessna 152	S. J. Taylor (G-CEUS)
	G-GFIF	Cessna FA.152	J. Viner (G-JONI/G-BFTU)
	G-GFIG	Cessna 152	J. Viner (G-BNOZ)
	G-GFKY	Zenair CH.250	R. G. Kelsall
	G-GFLY	Cessna F.150L	Leagate Ltd
	G-GFNO	Robin ATL	D. J. Watson
	G-GFOX	Aeroprakt A.22 Foxbat	I. A. Love & G. F. Elvis
	G-GFRA	PA-28RT-201T Turbo Arrow IV	S. Viner (G-LROY/G-BNTS)
	G-GFRD	Robin ATL L	H. Joosten & S. Kumpen
	G-GFRO	Robin ATL	B. F. Walker
	G-GFSA	Cessna 172R Skyhawk	Aircraft Grouping Ltd
	G-GFTA	PA-28-161 Warrior III	One Zero Three Ltd
	G-GFTB	PA-28-161 Warrior III	One Zero Three Ltd
	G-GGDV	Schleicher Ka 6E	A. R. Barton
	G-GGGG	Thunder Ax7-77A balloon	T. A. Gilmour
	G-GGHZ	Robin ATL	Modesto's Bakeries Ltd
	G-GGJK	Robin DR.400/140B	Headcorn Jodelers
	G-GGLE	PA-22 Colt 108 (tailwheel)	K. de Dobbelaere/Belgium
	G-GGNG	Robinson R44	Patriot Aviation Ltd
	G-GGOW	Colt 77A balloon	R. Foster
	G-GGRR	SA Bulldog Srs 120/121 (XX614:V)	M. Litherland (G-CBAM)
	G-GGTT	Agusta-Bell 47G-4A	P. R. Smith
	G-GHEE	Aerotechnik EV-97 Eurostar	C. J. Ball
	G-GHIA	Cameron N-120 balloon	J. A. Marshall
	G-GHKX	PA-28-161 Warrior II	Aviation Rentals

Reg.	Type	Owner or Operator	Notes
G-GHOW	Cessna F.182Q	J. F. Busby	
G-GHPG	Cesna 550 Citation 2	Concolor Ltd	
G-GHRW	PA-28RT-201 Arrow IV	Bonus Aircraft Ltd (G-ONAB/G-BHAK)	
G-GHZJ	SOCATA TB9 Tampico	P. K. Hayward	
G-GIBB	Robinson R44 II	Tingdene Aviation Ltd	
G-GIBP	Moravan Zlin Z.526 Trener Master	D. G. Cowden	
G-GIDY	Shaw Europa XS	Gidy Group	
G-GIGI	MS.893A Rallye Commodore	D. J. Moore (G-AYVX)	
G-GIGZ	Van's RV-8	C. D. Mitchell	
G-GILI	Robinson R44	Twylight Management Ltd	
G-GIRY	AG-5B Tiger	Romeo Yankee Flying Group	
G-GIST	Luscombe 8E Silvaire	J. B. Brown (G-AKUH)	
G-GIVE	Cameron A-300 balloon	Cameron Flights Southern Ltd	
G-GIWT	Shaw Europa XS	A. Twigg	
G-GJCD	Robinson R22 Beta	J. C. Lane	
G-GJMB	Bombardier CL-600-2B19 Challenger 850	Corporate Jet Management Ltd (G-CJMB)	
G-GKAT	Enstrom 280C	D. G. Allsop & A. J. Clark	
G-GKEV	Alpi Pioneer 300	K. D. Taylor	
G-GKFC	RL-5A LW Sherwood Ranger	P. A. Durrans (G-MYZI)	
G-GKKI	Avions Mudry CAP 231EX	Acro Laser Company Ltd	
G-GKRC	Cessna 180K	S. J. Beaty	
G-GKUE	SOCATA TB-9 Tampico Club	I. Parkinson	
G-GLAD	Gloster G.37 Gladiator II (N5903:H)	Patina Ltd	
G-GLAK	AB Sportine LAK-12	L. M. Middleton	
G-GLAW	Cameron N-90 balloon	R. A. Vale	
G-GLED	Cessna 150M	Firecrest Aviation Ltd and H. Vara	
G-GLHI	Skyranger 912	S. F. Winter	
G-GLIB	Robinson R44	G. P. Glibbery	
G-GLID	Schleicher ASW-28-18E	S. Bovin and Compagnie Belge d'Assurances Aviation	
G-GLII	Great Lakes 2T-1A-2	T. J. Richardson	
G-GLKE	Robin DR400/180	Karrek Financial Management Ltd	
G-GLOC	Extra EA.300/200	The Cambridge Aero Club Ltd	
G-GLST	Great Lakes Sport Trainer	D. A. Graham	
G-GLTT	PA-31-350 Navajo Chieftain	Redhill Aviation Ltd	
G-GLUC	Van's RV-6	Speedfreak Ltd	
G-GLUE	Cameron N-65 balloon	L. J. M. Muir & G. D. Hallett	
G-GMAA	Learjet 45	Gama Aviation Ltd	
G-GMAB	BAe 125 Srs 1000A	Gama Aviation Ltd (G-BUWX)	
G-GMAC	Gulfstream G-IVSP	Gama Aviation Ltd	
G-GMAX	SNCAN Stampe SV.4C	Glidegold Ltd (G-BXNW)	
G-GMCM	AS.350B3 Ecureuil	T. J. Morris Ltd	
G-GMED	PA-42-720 Cheyenne IIA	Air Medical Fleet Ltd	
G-GMIB	Robin DR400/500	St. David's Farm & Equine Practice	
G-GMKD	Robin HR200/120B	J. Owens	
G-GMKE	Robin HR200/120B	Pilot Flying Group	
G-GMPB	BN-2T-4S Defender 4000	Greater Manchester Police Authority (G-BWPU)	
G-GMPX	MDH MD-900 Explorer	Greater Manchester Police Authority	
G-GMSI	SOCATA TB9 Tampico	M. L. Rhodes	
G-GNJW	Ikarus C.42	N. C. Pearse	
G-GNRV	Van's RV-9A	N. K. Beavins	
G-GNTB	SAAB SF.340A	Loganair Ltd	
G-GNTF	SAAB SF.340A	Loganair Ltd	
G-GOAC	PA-34-200T Seneca II	Oxford Aviation Academy (Oxford) Ltd	
G-GOBD	PA-32R-301 Saratoga IIHP	F. & M. Garventa (G-OARW)	
G-GOBT	Colt 77A balloon	British Telecom PLC	
G-GOCX	Cameron N-90 balloon	R. D. Parry/Hong Kong	
G-GOES	Robinson R44-II	JG Commercials	
G-GOGB	Lindstrand LBL ,90A	J. Dyer (G-CDFX)	
G-GOGW	Cameron N-90 balloon	S. E. Carroll	
G-GOLF	SOCATA TB10 Tobago	B. Lee	
G-GOOF	Flylight Dragonfly	P. C. Bailey	
G-GORE	CFM Streak Shadow	M. S. Clinton	
G-GORV	Van's RV-8	G-GORV Group	
G-GOSL	Robin DR.400/180	R. M. Gosling (G-BSDG)	

Notes	Reg.	Type	Owner or Operator
	G-GOSS	Jodel DR.221	Avon Flying Group
	G-GOTC	GA-7 Cougar	Western Air (Thruxton) Ltd and Bucklefield Business Developments Ltd
	G-GOTH	PA-28-161 Warrior III	A. Jerreries
	G-GOUP	Robinson R22 Beta	M. A. Bennett (G-DIRE)
	G-GOWF	Eurocopter EC.135 T2+	Bond Air Services Ltd
	G-GPAG	Van's RV-6	P. A. Green
	G-GPAS	Avtech Jabiru UL-450	G. D. Allen
	G-GPAT	Beech 76 Duchess	Folada Aero & Technical Services Ltd
	G-GPEG	Sky 90-24 balloon	N. T. Parry
	G-GPFI	Boeing 737-229	European Skybus Ltd
	G-GPMW	PA-28RT-201T Turbo Arrow IV	Calverton Flying Group Ltd
	G-GPPN	Cameron TR-70 balloon	Backetorp Byggconsult AB
	G-GPSF	Jabiru J430	P. S. Furlow
	G-GREY	PA-46-350P Malibu Mirage	S. T. Day & S. C. Askham
	G-GRIN	Van's RV-6	A. Phillips
	G-GRIZ	PA-18-135 Super Cub	P. N. Elkington (G-BSHV)
	G-GRMN	Aerospool Dynamic WT9 UK	R. M. North
	G-GRND	Agusta A109S	Galegrove 2 LBG
	G-GROE	Grob G.115A	H. Merkado
	G-GROL	Maule MXT-7-180	D. C. Croll & ptnrs
	G-GROW	Cameron N-77 balloon	Derbyshire Building Society
	G-GRPA	Ikarus C.42 FB100	R. Wood
	G-GGRH	Robinson R44	Heli Air Ltd
	G-GRRR	SA Bulldog Srs 120/122	Horizons Europe Ltd (G-BXGU)
	G-GRSR	Schempp-Hirth Discus bT	SR Group
	G-GRVE	Van's RV-6	R. D. Carswell
	G-GRVY	Van's RV-8	A. P. Lawton & A. Page
	G-GRWL	Lilliput Type 4 balloon	A. E. & D. E. Thomas
	G-GRWW	Robinson R44 II	G. R. Williams (G-HEEL)
	G-GRYN	Rotorsport UK Calidus	K. Hedger
	G-GRYZ	Beech F33A Bonanza	J. Kawadri & M. Kaveh
	G-GRZZ	Robinson R44 II	Graegill Aviation Ltd
	G-GSAL	Fokker E.III Reolica	Grass Strip Aviation Ltd
	G-GSCV	Ikarus C42 FB UK	Jabeque Ltd
	G-GSGZ	Mudry CAP.232	J. Paulson
	G-GSJH	Bell 206B JetRanger 3	T. J. Morris Ltd (G-PENT/G-IIRB)
	G-GSMT	Rotorsport UK MTOSport	Rotorsport UK Ltd
	G-GSPG	Hughes 369HS	S. Giddings Aviation
	G-GSPY	Robinson R44 II	Percy Wood Leisure Ltd
	G-GSRV	Robin DR.400/500	R. G. Fairall
	G-GSSA	Boeing 747-47UF	Global Supply Systems Ltd
	G-GSSB	Boeing 747-47UF	Global Supply Systems Ltd
	G-GSSC	Boeing 747-47UF	Global Supply Systems Ltd
	G-GSSO	Gulfstream GV-SP	TAG Aviation (UK) Ltd
	G-GSST	Grob G.102 Astir CS77	770 Group
	G-GSYJ	Diamond DA42 Twin Star	Crosby Aviation (Jersey) Ltd
	G-GSYS	PA-34-220T Seneca V	SYS (Scaffolding Contractors) Ltd
	G-GTAX	PA-31-350 Navajo Chieftain	Hadagain Investments Ltd (G-OIAS)
	G-GTDL	Airbus A.320-231	Thomas Cook Airlines Ltd
	G-GTEE	P & M Quik GT450	Fly Hire Ltd
	G-GTFC	P & M Quik	A. J. Fell
	G-GTGT	P & M Quik GT.450	G. C. Weighell
	G-GTHM	PA-38-112 Tomahawk	A. B. King & T. P. Powley
	G-GTJD	P & M Quik GT450	F. E. Hall
	G-GTJM	Eurocopter EC 120B Colibri	T. J. Morris Ltd
	G-GTOM	Alpi Pioneer 300	T. F. Freake
	G-GTSO	P & M Quik GT450	C. Bayliss
	G-GTTP	P & M Quik GT450	J. A. Lockert
	G-GTVM	Beech 58 Baron	Baron Flying Club Ltd
	G-GTWO	Schleicher ASW-15	J. M. G. Carlton & R. Jackson
	G-GUCK	Beech C23 Sundowner 180	J. T. Francis (G-BPYG)
	G-GUFO	Cameron 80 Saucer SS balloon	Magical Adventures Ltd (G-BOUB)
	G-GULP	I.I.I. Sky Arrow 650T	S. Marriott
	G-GULZ	Christen Eagle II	T. N. Jinks
	G-GUMS	Cessna 182P	L. W. Scattergood (G-CBMN)
	G-GUNS	Cameron V-77 balloon	V. Grenier

Reg.	Type	Owner or Operator	Notes
G-GUNZ	Van's RV-8	R. Ellingworth & A. G. Thomas	
G-GURN	PA-31 Navajo C	Batair Ltd (G-BHGA)	
G-GURU	PA-28-161 Warrior II	Fly Guru LLP	
G-GUSS	PA-28-151 Warrior	M. J. Cleaver & J. M. Newman (G-BJRY)	
G-GUST	Agusta-Bell 206B JetRanger 2	DNH Helicopters Ltd (G-CBHH/G-AYBE)	
G-GUYS	PA-34-200T Seneca	G. B. Faulkner (G-BMWT)	
G-GVPI	Evans VP-1 srs.2	G. Martin	
G-GWIZ	Colt Clown SS balloon	Magical Adventures Ltd	
G-GWYN	Cessna F.172M	Magic Carpet Flying Co	
G-GXAL	Remos GX	A. B. Atkinson	
G-GYAK	Yakovlev Yak-50	M. W. Levy & M. V. Rijske	
G-GYAT	Gardan GY-80 Horizon 180	Rochester GYAT Flying Group Club	
G-GYAV	Cessna 172N	Southport & Merseyside Aero Club (1979) Ltd	
G-GYBO	Gardan GY-80 Horizon 160	A. L. Fogg	
G-GYMM	PA-28R Cherokee Arrow 200	MRR Aviation Ltd (G-AYWW)	
G-GYRO	Campbell Cricket	J. W. Pavitt	
G-GYTO	PA-28-161 Warrior III	Smart People Don't Buy Ltd	
G-GZDO	Cessna 172N	Cambridge Hall Aviation	
G-GZIP	Rolladen-Schneider LS8-18	D. S. S. Haughton	
G-GZRP	PA-42-720 Cheyenne IIIA	Air Medical Fleet Ltd	
G-HAAH	Schempp-Hirth Ventus 2cT	The V66 Syndicate	
G-HAAT	MDH MD.900 Explorer	Police Aviation Services Ltd (G-GMPS)	
G-HABI	Best Off SkyRanger 912S(1)	J. Habicht	
G-HABT	Supermarine Aircraft Spitfire Mk.26	M. R. Overall	
G-HACE	Van's RV-6A	D. C. McElroy	
G-HACK	PA-18 Super Cub 150	Intrepid Aviation Co	
G-HADD	P & M Quik R	T. J. Barker	
G-HAEC	CAC-18 Mustang 23 (472218:WZ-I)	R. W. Davies	
G-HAEF	EV-97 TeamEurostar UK	RAF Microlight Flying Association	
G-HAFG	Cessna 340A	Pavilion Aviation Ltd	
G-HAFT	Diamond DA42 Twin Star	Atlantic Flight Training Ltd	
G-HAGL	Robinson R44 II	Devon Helicopters Ltd	
G-HAIB	Aviat A-1B Husky	H. Brockmueller	
G-HAIG	Rutan LongEz	C. Docherty	
G-HAIR	Robin DR.400/180	S. P. Copson	
G-HAJJ	Glaser-Dirks DG.400	W. G. Upton & J. G. Kosak	
G-HALC	PA-28R Cherokee Arrow 200	Halcyon Aviation Ltd	
G-HALJ	Cessna 140	Hangar 1 Ltd	
G-HALL	PA-22 Tri-Pacer 160	F. P. Hall (G-ARAH)	
G-HALP	SOCATA TB10 Tobago	D. H. Halpern	
G-HALT	Mainair Pegasus Quik	S. Dixon	
G-HAMI	Fuji FA.200-180	K. G. Cameron & M. P. Antoniak & P. Fairlie (G-OISF/G-BAPT)	
G-HAMM	Yakovlev Yak-50	Propeller Studios Ltd	
G-HAMP	Bellanca 7ACA Champ	R. J. Grimstead	
G-HAMR	PA-28-161 Warrior II	Electric Scribe 2000 Ltd	
G-HAMS	Pegasus Quik	D. R. Morton	
G-HANA	Westland WS-58 Wessex HC.2	R. A. Fidler	
G-HANG	Diamond DA42 Twin Star	Atlantic Flight Training Ltd	
G-HANS	Robin DR.400 2+2	J. S. Russell	
G-HANY	Agusta-Bell 206B JetRanger 3	Beech Holdings Ltd (G-ESAL/G-BHXW/G-JEKP)	
G-HAPE	Pietenpol Aircamper	J. P. Chape	
G-HAPI	Lindstrand LBL-105A balloon	Adventure Balloons Ltd	
G-HAPY	DHC.1 Chipmunk 22A (WP803)	Astrojet Ltd	
G-HARD	Dyn'Aéro MCR-01 ULC	N. A. Burnet	
G-HARE	Cameron N-77 balloon	D. H. Sheryn & C. A. Buck	
G-HARI	Raj Hamsa X'Air V2 (2)	J. Blackburn	
G-HARK	Canadair CL.600-2B16	Corbridge Ltd	
G-HARN	PA-28-181 Archer II	K. Saxton (G-DENK/G-BXRJ)	
G-HARR	Robinson R22 Beta	Unique Helicopters Ltd	
G-HART	Cessna 152 (tailwheel)	Air Atlantique Ltd (G-BPBF)	
G-HARY	Alon A-2 Aircoupe	M. B. Willis (G-ATWP)	
G-HATF	Thorp T-18CW	A. T. Fraser	
G-HATZ	Hatz CB-1	S. P. Rollason	
G-HAUL	Westland WG.30 Srs 300 ★	IHM/Weston-super-Mare	
G-HAUS	Hughes 369HM	The Uniform Group (G-KBOT/G-RAMM)	

Notes	Reg.	Type	Owner or Operator
	G-HAUT	Schempp-Hirth Mini Nimbus C	530 Syndicate
	G-HAVI	Eurocopter EC.130B4	J. & J. Havakin
	G-HAYY	Czech Sport Aircraft Sportcruiser	B. R. W. Hay
	G-HAZE	Thunder Ax8-90 balloon	T. G. Church
	G-HBBC	DH.104 Dove 8	Roger Gawn 2007 Family Trust (G-ALFM)
	G-HBBH	Ikarus C42 FB100	Golf Bravo Hotel Group
	G-HBEK	Agusta A109C	HPM Investments Ltd (G-RNLD/G-DATE)
	G-HBJT	Eurocopter EC.155B1	Starspeed Ltd
	G-HBMW	Robinson R22	Durham Flying Syndicate (G-BOFA)
	G-HBOB	Eurocopter EC135 T2+	Bond Air Services Ltd/Thames Valley Air Ambulance
	G-HBOS	Scheibe SF-25C Rotax-Falke	Coventry Gliding Club Ltd
	G-HBRO	Eurocopter AS.355NP Ecureuil 2	Henry Brothers (Magherafelt) Ltd
	G-HBUG	Cameron N-90 balloon	Black Horse Ballooning Club (G-BRCN)
	G-HCAC	Schleicher Ka 6E	M. Burridge
	G-HCFC	Agusta A.109E Power	Castle Air Charters Ltd
	G-HCGD	Learjet 45	TAG Aviation (UK) Ltd
	G-HCSA	Cessna 525A CJ2	Bookajet Aircraft Management Ltd
	G-HCSL	PA-34-220T Seneca III	Fly (CI) Ltd
	G-HDAE	DHC.1 Chipmunk 22	Airborne Classics Ltd
	G-HDEF	Robinson R44 II	Arena Aviation Ltd (G-LOCO/G-TEMM)
	G-HDEW	PA-32R-301 Saratoga SP	A. H. Biddulph & P. R. Ellis
	G-HDTV	Agusta A109A-II	Castle Air Charters Ltd (G-BXWD)
	G-HDIX	Enstrom 280FX	Clovetree Ltd
	G-HEAD	Colt Flying Head SS balloon	Ikeair
	G-HEAN	AS.355NP Ecureuil 2	Brookview Developments Ltd
	G-HEBB	Schleicher ASW-27-18E	E. Y. Heinonen
	G-HEBJ	Cessna 525 Citationjet	Air Charter Scotland Ltd
	G-HEBR	BN-2B-21 Islander	Hebridean Air Services Ltd (G-BJOP)
	G-HEBS	BN-2B-26 Islander	Hebridean Air Services Ltd (G-BUBJ)
	G-HEBZ	BN-2A-26 Islander	Cormack (Aircraft Services) Ltd (G-BELF)
	G-HECB	Fuji FA.200-160	H. E. W. E. Bailey (G-BBZO)
	G-HEHE	Eurocopter EC.120B Colibri	HE Group Ltd
	G-HEJB	Cirrus SR22 GTS	G. A. J. Bowles
	G-HEKK	RAF 2000 GTX-SE gyroplane	C. J. Watkinson (G-BXEB)
	G-HEKL	Percival Mew Gull Replica	Innomech Ltd
	G-HELA	SOCATA TB10 Tobago	S. E. Bond
	G-HELE	Bell 206B JetRanger 3	B. E. E. Smith (G-OJFR)
	G-HELM	AS.350B2 Ecureuil	FS Aviation LLP
	G-HELN	Piper PA-28-95	Helen Group
	G-HELV	DH.115 Vampire T.55 (XJ771)	Aviation Heritage Ltd
	G-HEMS	SA.365N Dauphin 2	PLM Dollar Group Ltd
	G-HEMZ	Agusta A109S Grand	Sloane Helicopters Ltd
	G-HENT	SOCATA Rallye 110ST	F. Monds
	G-HENY	Cameron V-77 balloon	R. S. D'Alton
	G-HEOI	Eurocopter EC135 P2+	Staffordshire & West Mercia Police Authorities
	G-HERB	PA-28R-201 Arrow III	Icarus Flyers Ltd
	G-HERC	Cessna 172S	Cambridge Aero Club Ltd
	G-HERD	Lindstrand LBL-77B balloon	S. W. Herd
	G-HERT	BAE Herti	BAe Systems (Operations) Ltd
	G-HEVN	SOCATA TB200 Tobago XL	Valley Flying Co.Ltd
	G-HEWI	Piper J-3C-90 Cub	Denham Grasshopper Group (G-BLEN)
	G-HEWS	Hughes 369D ★	Spares' use
	G-HEXE	Colr 17A balloon	A. Dunnington
	G-HEYY	Cameron 72 Bear SS balloon	Magical Adventures Ltd
	G-HFAA	Raytheon 390 Premier 1	SARL Av'Rent
	G-HFBM	Curtiss Robin C-2	D. M. Forshaw
	G-HFCA	Cessna A.150L	T. H. Scott
	G-HFCB	Cessna F.150L	P. R. Mortimer
	G-HFCL	Cessna F.152	MK Aero Support Ltd (G-BGLR)
	G-HFCT	Cessna F.152	Stapleford Flying Club Ltd
	G-HFLY	Robinson R44 II	Helifly (UK) Ltd
	G-HFRH	DHC-1 Chipmunk 22	Sunrise Global Aviation Ltd
	G-HGAS	Cameron N-77 balloon	N. J. Tovey
	G-HGPI	SOCATA TB20 Trinidad	M. J. Jackson
	G-HGRB	Robinson R44	Ramsgill Aviation Ltd (G-BZIN)

Reg.	Type	Owner or Operator	Notes
G-HHAA	HS. Buccaneer S.2B (XX885)	Hawker Hunter Aviation Ltd	
G-HHAC	Hawker Hunter F.58 (J-4021)	Hawker Hunter Aviation Ltd (G-BWIU)	
G-HHDR	Cessna 182T	D. R. & H. Howell	
G-HHII	Hawker Hurricane 2B (BE505: XP-L)	Hangar 11 Collection (G-HRLO)	
G-HHOG	Robinson R44 II	Fast Helicopters Ltd	
G-HIBM	Cameron N-145 balloon	Alba Ballooning Ltd	
G-HIEL	Robinson R22 Beta	M. C. Mitchell	
G-HIJK	Cessna 421C	G. R. Case (G-OSAL)	
G-HIJN	Ikarus C.42 FB100	J. R. North	
G-HILI	Van's RV-3B	A. G. & E. A. Hill	
G-HILO	Rockwell Commander 114	J. G. Gleeson & J. J. Toomey	
G-HILS	Cessna F.172H	G-HILS Aviation Group (G-AWCH)	
G-HILT	SOCATA TB10 Tobago	S. Harrison	
G-HILY	Zenair CH.600 Zodiac	K. V. Hill & D. Woolliscroft (G-BRII)	
G-HILZ	Van's RV-8	A. G. & E. A. Hill	
G-HIMM	Cameron Z-105 balloon	C. M. D. Haynes	
G-HIND	Maule MT-7-235	M. A. Ashmole	
G-HINZ	Avtec Jabiru SK	E. Faupel	
G-HIPE	Sorrell SNS-7 Hiperbipe	B. G. Ell	
G-HIPO	Robinson R22 Beta	SI Plan Electronics (Research) Ltd (G-BTGB)	
G-HIRE	GA-7 Cougar	London Aerial Tours Ltd (G-BGSZ)	
G-HITM	Raj Hamsa X'Air 582 (1)	A. Davis	
G-HITT	Hawker Hurricane 1	Hawker Hurricane Ltd	
G-HIUP	Cameron A-250 balloon	Ladybird Balloons Ltd	
G-HIVA	Cessna 337A	G. J. Banfield (G-BAES)	
G-HIVE	Cessna F.150M	M. P. Lynn (G-BCXT)	
G-HIYA	Best Off Skyranger 912(2)	R. D. & C. M. Parkinson	
G-HIZZ	Robinson R22 II	Flyfare (G-CNDY/G-BXEW)	
G-HJSM	Schempp-Hirth Nimbus 4DM	60 Syndicate (G-ROAM)	
G-HJSS	AIA Stampe SV.4C (modified)	H. J. Smith (G-AZNF)	
G-HKAA	Schempp-Hirth Duo Discus T	A. Aveling	
G-HKCF	Enstrom 280C-UK	HKC Helicopter Services (G-MHCF/G-GSML/ G-BNNV)	
G-HKHM	Hughes 369B	Heli Air Ltd	
G-HKSD	Diamond HK-36 TC Super Dimona	D. King & N. Everett	
G-HLCF	Starstreak Shadow SA-II	F. E. Tofield	
G-HLEE	Best Off Sky Ranger J2.2(1)	P. G. Hill	
G-HLMB	Schempp-Hirth Ventus 2b	U. Hofinghoff	
G-HLOB	Cessna 172S	Goodwood Road Racing Co.Ltd	
G-HMBJ	Rockwell Commander 114B	D. W. R. Best	
G-HMCA	EV-97 TeamEurostar UK	RAF Microlight Flying Association	
G-HMCB	Skyranger Swift 912S(1)	R. W. Goddin	
G-HMED	PA-28-161 Warrior III	Eglinton Flying Club Ltd	
G-HMEI	Dassault Falcon 900	Executive Jet Group Ltd	
G-HMEV	Dassault Falcon 900	Maughold Ltd	
G-HMHM	Rotorsport UK MTO Sport	S. D. Evans	
G-HMPS	CZAW Sportcruiser	H. & P. Shedden	
G-HMPT	Agusta-Bell 206B JetRanger 2	Yorkshire Helicopters	
G-HNGE	Ikarus C42 FB100	Compton Abbas Airfield Ltd	
G-HNLY	Bell 206L LongRanger III	Henley Aviation Ltd	
G-HNTR	Hawker Hunter T.7 (XL571:V) ★	Yorkshire Air Museum/Elvington	
G-HOBO	Denney Kitfox Mk 4	J. P. Donovan	
G-HOCA	Robinson R44 II	Howcan Air Services Ltd	
G-HOCK	PA-28 Cherokee 180	G-HOCK Flying Club (G-AVSH)	
G-HOFF	P & M Aviation Quik GT450	P. J. Oakey	
G-HOFM	Cameron N-56 balloon	Magical Adventures Ltd	
G-HOGS	Cameron 90 Pig SS balloon	Magical Adventures Ltd	
G-HOGZ	Yakovlev Yak-52	G. P. Williams	
G-HOJO	Schempp-Hirth Discus 2a	S. G. Jones	
G-HOLA	PA-28-201T Turbo Dakota	J. Prescott (G-BNYB)	
G-HOLE	P & M Quik GT450	P. Boardman (G-CEBD)	
G-HOLI	Ultramagic M-77 balloon	G. Everett	
G-HOLM	Eurocopter EC.120B Colibri	Oxford Air Services Ltd	
G-HOLY	ST.10 Diplomate	M. K. Barsham	
G-HONG	Slingsby T.67M Firefly 200	Jewel Aviation and Technology Ltd	

Notes	Reg.	Type	Owner or Operator
	G-HONI	Robinson R22 Beta	Patriot Aviation Ltd (G-SEGO)
	G-HONK	Cameron O-105 balloon	M. A. Green
	G-HONY	Lilliput Type 1 Srs A balloon	A. E. & D. E. Thomas
	G-HOOD	SOCATA TB20 Trinidad GT	M. J. Hoodless
	G-HOPA	Lindstrand LBL-35A balloon	S. F. Burden/Netherlands
	G-HOPE	Beech F33A Bonanza	Hope Aviation
	G-HOPR	Lindstrand LBL-25A balloon	K. C. Tanner
	G-HOPY	Van's RV-6A	R. C. Hopkinson
	G-HORK	Pioneer 300 Hawk	R. Y. Kendal
	G-HOSS	Beech F33A	T. D. Broadhurst
	G-HOTA	EV-97 TeamEurostar UK	A. C. Aiken
	G-HOTB	Eurocopter EC155 B1	Noirmont (EC155) Ltd (G-CEXZ)
	G-HOTM	Cameron C-80 balloon	J. K. Macleod
	G-HOTZ	Colt 77B balloon	C. J. & S. M. Davies
	G-HOUS	Colt 31A balloon ★	The British Balloon Museum and Library
	G-HOWE	Thunder Ax7-77 balloon	C. Suggitt
	G-HOWI	Cessna F.182Q	H. Poulson
	G-HOWL	RAF 2000 GTX-SE gyroplane	C. J. Watkinson
	G-HOXN	Van's RV-9	XRay November Flying Club
	G-HPAD	Bell 206B JetRanger 2	Helipad Ltd (G-CITZ/G-BRTB)
	G-HPEN	Ultramagic M-120 balloon	G. Holtam
	G-HPOL	MDH MD-902 Explorer	Humberside Police Authority
	G-HPPY	Learjet 40	European Skyjets Ltd
	G-HPSF	Rockwell Commander 114B	R. W. Scandrett
	G-HPSL	Rockwell Commander 114B	M. B. Endean
	G-HPUX	Hawker Hunter T.7 (XL587)	Hawker Hunter Aviation Ltd
	G-HPWA	Van's RV-8	M. de Ferranti
	G-HRBS	Robinson R22 Beta	Fly Executive Ltd
	G-HRCC	Robin HR200/100	P. R and J. S. Johnson
	G-HRDS	Gulfstream GV-SP(550)	Fayair (Jersey) Ltd
	G-HRHE	Robinson R22 Beta	Irwin Plant Sales (G-BTWP)
	G-HRIO	Robin HR.100/120	R. Mullender
	G-HRLI	Hawker Hurricane 1 (V7497)	Hawker Restorations Ltd
	G-HRLK	SAAB 91D/2 Safir	Sylmar Aviation & Services Ltd (G-BRZY)
	G-HRLM	Brügger MB.2 Colibri	M. W. Bodger & M. H. Hoffmann
	G-HRND	Cessna 182T	Dingle Star Ltd
	G-HRNT	Cessna 182S	C. R. Thompson
	G-HROI	Rockwell Commander RC.112	Intereuropean Aviation Ltd
	G-HRPN	Robinson R44 II	M. Lazzari
	G-HRVD	CCF Harvard IV	Anglia Flight (G-BSBC)
	G-HRVS	Van's RV-8	D. J. Harvey & M. S. Pettit
	G-HRYZ	PA-28-180 Cherokee Archer	Lees Avionics Ltd (G-WACR/G-BCZF)
	G-HSAR	Agusta A.109E	Caste Air Charters Ltd
	G-HSBC	Lindstrand LBL-69X balloon	A. Nimmo
	G-HSKE	Aviat A-18 Husky	R. B. Armitage & S. L. Davis
	G-HSKI	Aviat A-1B	C. J. R. Flint
	G-HSOO	Hughes 369HE	Kuki Helicopter Sales Ltd & S. J. Nicholls (G-BFYJ)
	G-HSTH	Lindstrand LBL. HS-110 balloon	Lindstrand Hot Air Balloons Ltd
	G-HSXP	Raytheon Hawker 850XP	Fowey Services Ltd
	G-HTAX	PA-31-350 Navajo Chieftain	Hadagain Investments Ltd
	G-HTBT	Rotorsport UK Calidus	H. T. Beattie
	G-HTEL	Robinson R44	A. G. & R. S. Higgins
	G-HTML	P & M Aviation Quik R	P. Leigh
	G-HTRL	PA-34-220T Seneca III	Air Medical Fleet Ltd (G-BXXY)
	G-HTWE	Rans S6-116	H. C. C. Coleridge
	G-HUBB	Partenavia P.68B	Ravenair Aircraft Ltd
	G-HUBY	Embraer EMB-135BJ Legacy	London Executive Aviation Ltd
	G-HUCH	Cameron 80 Carrots SS balloon	Magical Adventures Ltd (G-BYPS)
	G-HUES	Hughes 369HS	A. C. Richardson (G-GASC/G-WELD/G-FROG)
	G-HUEW	Shaw Europa XS	C, R. Wright
	G-HUEY	Bell UH-1H	G-HUEY Partnership
	G-HUFF	Cessna 182P	Highfine Ltd
	G-HUGS	Robinson R22 Beta	Unique Helicopters (NI) Ltd (G-BYHD)
	G-HUKA	MDH Hughes 369E	B. P. Stein (G-OSOO)
	G-HULK	Skyranger 912(2)	L. C. Stockman
	G-HULL	Cessna F.150M	Hull Aero Club Ltd

Reg.	Type	Owner or Operator	Notes
G-HUMH	Van's RV-9A	H. A. Daines	
G-HUND	Aviat A-1B Husky	U Ladurner	
G-HUNI	Bellanca 7GCBC Scout	The Pilot Centre Ltd	
G-HUPW	Hawker Hurricane 1 (R4118:UP-W)	Minmere Farm Partnership	
G-HURI	CCF Hawker Hurricane XIIA (Z5140/HA-C)	Historic Aircraft Collection Ltd	
G-HURN	Robinson R22 Beta	Sloane Helicopters Ltd	
G-HUSK	Aviat A-1B	G. D. Ettlmayr	
G-HUTE	Aerochute Dual	R. J. Watkin & W. A. Kimberlin	
G-HUTT	Denney Kitfox Mk.2	H. D. Colliver	
G-HUTY	Van's RV-7	S. A. Hutt	
G-HVAN	RL-5A LW Sherwood Ranger ST	P. S. Taylor	
G-HVBF	Lindstrand LBL-210A balloon	Virgin Balloon Flights	
G-HVER	Robinson R44 II	Equation Associates Ltd	
G-HVRD	PA-31-350 Navajo Chieftain	N. Singh (G-BEZU)	
G-HVRZ	Eurocopter EC 120B	EDM Helicopters Ltd	
G-HWAA	Eurocopter EC 135T2	Bond Air Services Ltd	
G-HXTD	Robin DR.400/180	Richmond Aviation Ltd	
G-HYLT	PA-32R-301 Saratoga SP	T. G. Gordon	
G-HYST	Enstrom 280FX	S. Patten	
G-IACA	Sikorsky S-92A	Bristow Helicopters Ltd	
G-IACB	Sikorsky S-92A	Bristow Helicopters Ltd	
G-IACC	Sikorsky S-92A	Bristow Helicopters Ltd	
G-IACD	Sikorsky S-92A	Bristow Helicopters Ltd	
G-IACE	Sikorsky S-92A	Bristow Helicopters Ltd	
G-IACF	Sikorsky S-92A	Bristow Helicopters Ltd	
G-IAJJ	Robinson R44 II	O'Connor Utilities Ltd	
G-IAJS	Ikarus C.42 FB UK	A. J. Slater	
G-IANB	Glaser-Dirks DG-800B	I. S. Bullous	
G-IANC	SOCATA TB10 Tobago	I. Corbin & P. D. Seed (G-BIAK)	
G-IANH	SOCATA TB10 Tobago	R. J. Wright	
G-IANI	Shaw Europa XS T-G	I. F. Rickard & I. A. Watson	
G-IANJ	Cessna F.150K	J. A. & D. T. A. Rees (G-AXVW)	
G-IANN	Kolb Twinstar Mk 3	I. Newman	
G-IANV	Diamond DA42 Twin Star	Plane Talking Ltd	
G-IANW	AS.350B3 Ecureuil	Milford Aviation Services Ltd	
G-IARC	Stoddard-Hamilton Glastar	A. A. Craig	
G-IASM	Beech 200 Super King Air	European Air Services Ltd (G-OEAS)	
G-IBAZ	Ikarus C.42 FB100	B. R. Underwood	
G-IBBC	Cameron 105 Sphere SS balloon	Balloon Preservation Group	
G-IBBS	Shaw Europa	R. H. Gibbs	
G-IBED	Robinson R22A	Brian Seedle Helicopters Blackpool (G-BMHN)	
G-IBFC	BFC Challenger II	K. V. Hill	
G-IBFP	VPM .M.16 Tandem Trainer	B. F. Pearson	
G-IBFW	PA-28R-201 Arrow III	Archer Four Ltd	
G-IBHH	Hughes 269C	Alpha Properties (London) Ltd (G-BSCD)	
G-IBIG	Bell 206B JetRanger 3	Big Heli-Charter Ltd (G-BORV)	
G-IBII	Pitts S-2A Special	Aerobatic Displays Ltd (G-XATS)	
G-IBLP	P & M Quik GT450	B. L. Prime	
G-IBMS	Robinson R44	Beoley Mill Software Ltd	
G-IBUZ	CZAW Sportcruiser	G. L. Fearon	
G-IBZS	Cessna 182S	D. C. Shepherd	
G-ICAS	Pitts S-2B Special	J. C. Smith	
G-ICBM	Stoddard-Hamilton Glasair III Turbine	G. V. Walters & D. N. Brown	
G-ICDM	Jabiru UL-450	C. D. Meek (G-CEKM)	
G-ICES	Thunder Ax6-56 balloon ★	British Balloon Museum & Library Ltd	
G-ICKY	Lindstrand LBL-77A balloon	R. J. Percival & J. Tyrrell	
G-ICMT	Evektor EV-97 Eurostar	R. Haslam	
G-ICOI	Lindstrand LBL-105A balloon	F. Schroeder/Germany	
G-ICOM	Cessna F.172M	C. G. Elesmore (G-BFXI)	
G-ICON	Rutan LongEz	S. J. & M. A. Carradice	
G-ICRS	Ikarus C.42 FB UK Cyclone	Ikarus Flying Group Ltd	
G-ICSG	AS.355F1 Twin Squirrel	Sky Charter UK Ltd (G-PAMI/G-BUSA)	
G-ICWT	Pegasus Quantum 15-912	D. H. Evans	

Notes	Reg.	Type	Owner or Operator
	G-IDAB	Cessna 550 Citation Bravo	Mail Handling International Ltd
	G-IDAY	Skyfox CA-25N Gazelle	G. G. Johnstone
	G-IDEB	AS.355F1 Ecureuil 2	MW Helicopters Ltd (G-ORMA/G-SITE/G-BPHC)
	G-IDER	Orlican Discus CS	A. J. Preston & D. B. Keith
	G-IDII	Dan Rihn DR.107 One Design	C. Darlow
	G-IDOL	Evektor EV-97 Eurostar	K. L. Manning
	G-IDSL	Flight Design CT2K	W. D. Dewey
	G-IDUP	Enstrom 280C Shark	Antique Buildings Ltd (G-BRZF)
	G-IDWR	Hughes 369HS	Copley Electrical Contractors (G-AXEJ)
	G-IEIO	PA-34-200T Seneca II	Sky Zone Servicos Aereos Lda
	G-IEJH	Jodel 150A	A. Turner & D. Worth (G-BPAM)
	G-IEYE	Robin DR.400/180	G. Wood
	G-IFAB	Cessna F.182Q	Manda Construction Ltd
	G-IFBP	AS.350B2 Ecureuil	Frank Bird Aviation
	G-IFDM	Robinson R44	MFH Helicopters Ltd
	G-IFFR	PA-32 Cherokee Six 300	Brendair (G-BWVO)
	G-IFFY	Flylight Dragonfly	R. D. Leigh
	G-IFIF	Cameron TR-60 balloon	M. G. Howard
	G-IFIT	PA-31-350 Navajo Chieftain	Dart Group PLC (G-NABI/G-MARG)
	G-IFLE	Aerotechnik EV-97 TeamEurostar UK	M. R. Smith
	G-IFLI	AA-5A Cheetah	I-Fly Group Ltd
	G-IFLP	PA-34-200T Seneca II	ACS Aviation Ltd
	G-IFRH	Agusta A109C	Helicopter Services Ltd
	G-IFTE	HS.125 Srs 700B	Albion Aviation Management Ltd (G-BFVI)
	G-IFTF	BAe 125 Srs 800B	Albion Aviation Management Ltd (G-RCEJ/ G-GEIL)
	G-IFWD	Schempp-Hirth Ventus cT	J. C. Ferguson & C. J. Hamilton
	G-IGEL	Cameron N-90 balloon	Computacenter Ltd
	G-IGGL	SOCATA TB10 Tobago	G-IGGL Flying Group (G-BYDC)
	G-IGHH	Enstrom 480	Raw Sports Ltd
	G-IGHT	Van's RV-8	E. A. Yates
	G-IGIA	AS.350B3 Ecureuil	Faloria Ltd
	G-IGIE	SIAI Marchetti SF.260	Flew LLP
	G-IGII	Shaw Europa	C. D. Peacock
	G-IGLE	Cameron V-90 balloon	G-IGLE Group
	G-IGLI	Schempp-Hirth Duo Discus T	C. Fox
	G-IGLY	P & M Aviation Quik GT450	VFR Ltd
	G-IGLZ	Champion 8KCAB	Woodgate Aviation (IOM) Ltd
	G-IGPW	Eurocopter EC 120B	Helihopper Ltd (G-CBRI)
	G-IGTE	SIAI Marchetti F.260	D. Fletcher & J. J. Watts
	G-IGWT	Bombardier CL600-2B19	Ocean Sky Aircraft Management Ltd
	G-IGZZ	Robinson R44 II	Rivermead Aviation Ltd
	G-IHOP	Cameron Z-31 balloon	N. W. Roberts
	G-IHOT	Aerotechnik EV-97 Eurostar UK	Exodos Airsports Ltd
	G-IIAC	Aeronca 11AC Chief	F. & M. R. Overall (G-BTPY)
	G-IIAI	Mudry CAP.232	C. Butler
	G-IIAN	Aero Designs Pulsar	I. G. Harrison
	G-IICI	Aviat Pitts S-2C Special	D. G. Cowden
	G-IICT	Schempp-Hirth Ventus 2Ct	P. McLean
	G-IICX	Schempp-Hirth Ventus 2cxT	S. G. Jones
	G-IIDI	Extra EA.300/L	Power Aerobatics Ltd (G-XTRS)
	G-IIDY	Aerotek Pitts S-2B Special	The S-2B Group (G-BPVP
	G-IIEX	Extra EA.300/L	S. G. Jones
	G-IIFM	Edge 360	F. L. McGee
	G-IIFR	Robinson R22 Beta II	OK Aero SRO/Czech Republic
	G-IIGI	Van's RV-4	IIGI Flying Club
	G-IIHI	Extra 300/SC	YAK UK Ltd
	G-IIID	Dan Rihn DR.107 One Design	D. A. Kean
	G-IIIE	Aerotek Pitts S-2B Special	D. S. A. Gomes da Silva
	G-IIIG	Boeing Stearman A75N1	O. Josse & S. Bolyn /Belgium (G-BSDR)
	G-IIII	Aerotek Pitts S-2B Special	R. J. Allan, N. Jones & A. J. Maxwell
	G-IIIK	Extra EA.300/SC	Extra 300SC LLP
	G-IIIL	Pitts S-1T Special	Empyreal Airways Ltd
	G-IIIM	Stolp SA.100 Starduster	H. Mackintosh
	G-IIIO	Schempp-Hirth Ventus 2CM	S. J. Clark
	G-IIIP	Pitts S-1D Special	R. S. Grace (G-BLAG)
	G-IIIR	Pitts S-1S Special	R. O. Rogers

Reg.	Type	Owner or Operator	Notes
G-IIIS	Sukhoi Su-26M2	Airtime Aerobatics Ltd	
G-IIIT	Aerotek Pitts S-2A Special	Aerobatic Displays Ltd	
G-IIIV	Pitts Super Stinker 11-260	S. D. Barnard	
G-IIIX	Pitts S-1S Special	D. S. T. Eggleton (G-LBAT/G-UCCI/G-BIYN)	
G-IIIZ	Sukhoi Su-26M	P. M. M. Bonhommy	
G-IIJC	Midget Mustang	Longacre Aviation Ltd (G-CEKU)	
G-IIMI	Extra EA.300/L	Firebird Aerobatics Ltd	
G-IIMT	Midget Mustang	P. J. Hebdon	
G-IINI	Van's RV-9A	R. D. Masters	
G-IIOO	Schleicher ASW-27-18E	M. Clarke	
G-IIPB	DR.107 One Design	P. D. Baisden	
G-IIPT	Robinson R22 Beta	Highmark Aviation Ltd (G-FUSI)	
G-IIPZ	Mudry CAP.232	S. P. R. Madle & J. Murfitt	
G-IIRG	Stoddard-Hamilton Glasair IIS RG	A. C. Lang	
G-IIRP	Mudry CAP.232	R. J. Pickin	
G-IIRW	Van's RV-8	R. Winward	
G-IITC	Mudry CAP.232	T. W. Cassells	
G-IIVI	CAP-232	Skylane Aviation Ltd	
G-IIXF	Van's RV-7	C. A. & S. Noujaim	
G-IIXI	Extra EA.300/L	B. H. D. H. Frere	
G-IIXX	Parsons 2-seat gyroplane	J. M. Montgomerie	
G-IIYK	Yakovlev Yak-50	D. A. Hammant	
G-IIZI	Extra EA.300	Power Aerobatics Ltd	
G-IJAC	Light Aero Avid Speedwing Mk 4	I. J. A. Charlton	
G-IJAG	Cessna 182T Skylane	AG Group	
G-IJBB	Enstrom 480	R. P. Bateman (G-LIVA/G-PBTT)	
G-IJMI	Extra EA.300/L	DEP Promotions Ltd	
G-IJNK	Robinson R44	Hi-Range Ltd (G-KTOL/G-DCOM)	
G-IJOE	PA-28RT-201T Turbo Arrow IV	J. H. Bailey	
G-IJYS	BAe Jetstream 3102	Avient Ltd (G-BTZT)	
G-IKAH	Slingsby T.51 Dart 17R	K. A. Hale	
G-IKAP	Cessna T.303	T. M. Beresford	
G-IKBP	PA-28-161 Warrior II	F. J. Page	
G-IKEA	Cameron 120 Ikea SS balloon	IKEA Ltd	
G-IKES	Stoddard-Hamilton GlaStar	M. Stow	
G-IKEV	Jabiru UL-450	D. I. Taylor	
G-IKON	Van's RV-4	S. Sampson	
G-IKOS	Cessna 550 Citation Bravo	Medox Enterprises Ltd	
G-IKRK	Shaw Europa	K. R. Kesterton	
G-IKRS	Ikarus C.42 FK UK Cyclone	K. J. Warburton	
G-IKUS	Ikarus C.42 FB UK Cyclone	C. I. Law	
G-ILBO	Rolladen-Schneider LS3-A	J. P. Gilbert	
G-ILDA	VS.361 Spitfire HF.IX (SM520 : KJ-1)	Spitfire Display Ltd (G-BXHZ)	
G-ILEE	Colt 56A balloon	G. I. Lindsay	
G-ILES	Cameron O-90 balloon	G. N. Lantos	
G-ILET	Robinson R44 II	Carisson Properties Ltd	
G-ILIB	PZL-Bielsko SZD-36A	D. Poll	
G-ILLE	Boeing Stearman A75L3 (379)	M. Minkler	
G-ILLG	Robinson R44 II	C. B. Ellis	
G-ILLY	PA-28-181 Archer II	R. A. & G. M. Spiers	
G-ILPY	Cessna 172S	D. R. Turner	
G-ILRS	Ikarus C.42 FB UK Cyclone	Knitsley Mill Leisure Ltd	
G-ILSE	Corby CJ-1 Starlet	S. Stride	
G-ILTS	PA-32 Cherokee Six 300	P. G. Teasdale & Foremans Aviation Ltd (G-CVOK)	
G-ILUA	Alpha R2160I	A. R. Haynes	
G-IMAB	Europa XS	T. J. Price	
G-IMAC	Canadair CL-600-2A12 Challenger	Gama Aviation Ltd	
G-IMAD	Cessna 172P	Leus Aviation Ltd	
G-IMAG	Colt 77A balloon ★	Balloon Preservation Group	
G-IMBI	QAC Quickie 1	J. D. King (G-BWIT)	
G-IMBL	Bell 407	Northern Flights Ltd	
G-IMBY	Pietenpol AirCamper	C. Brockis	
G-IMCD	Van's RV-7	I. G. McDowell	
G-IMEA	Beech 200 Super King Air	MIAW LLP (G-OWAX)	
G-IMEC	PA-31 Navajo C	Planeco Ltd (G-BFOM)	
G-IMEL	Rotary Air Force RAF 2000 GTX-SE	P. F. Murphy	
G-IMHK	P & M Quik R	J. Waite	

Notes	Reg.	Type	Owner or Operator
	G-IMIC	IDA Bacau Yakovlev Yak-52	J. S. & H. A. Jewell
	G-IMME	Zenair CH.701 STOL	M. Spearman
	G-IMMI	Escapade Kid	J. Pearce
	G-IMMY	Robinson R44	Tony Cain Leisure Services
	G-IMNY	Escapade 912	D. S. Bremner
	G-IMOK	Hoffmann HK-36R Super Dimona	A. L. Garfield
	G-IMPS	Skyranger Nynja 912S	S. J. Brooks & B. J. Killick
	G-IMPX	Rockwell Commander 112B	Impatex Computer Systems Ltd
	G-IMPY	Light Aero Avid Flyer C	T. R. C. Griffin
	G-IMUP	Tanarg/Ixess 15 912S (1)	P. D. Hill
	G-INCA	Glaser-Dirks DG.400	K. D. Hook
	G-INCE	Skyranger 912(2)	N.P. Sleigh
	G-INDC	Cessna T.303	J-Ross Developments Ltd
	G-INDI	Pitts S-2C Special	L. Coesens
	G-INDX	Robinson R44	Kinetic Computers Ltd
	G-INDY	Robinson R44	Lincoln Aviation
	G-INGA	Thunder Ax8-84 balloon	M. L. J. Ritchie
	G-INGE	Thruster T.600N	Thruster 1 Group
	G-INGS	American Champion 8KCAB	Scotflight Ltd
	G-INII	Pitts S-1 Special	C. Davidson (G-BTEF)
	G-INJA	Ikarus C42 FB UK	C. E. Walls
	G-INNI	Jodel D.112	S. Barry
	G-INNY	SE-5A (replica) (F5459:Y)	M. J. Speakman
	G-INOW	Monnett Moni	G. C. Bridges
	G-INSR	Cameron N-90 balloon	P. J. Waller and The Smith and Pinching Group Ltd
	G-INTS	Van's RV-4	N. J. F. Campbell
	G-INTV	AS.355F2 Ecureuil 2	Arena Aviation Ltd (G-JETU)
	G-IOCO	Beech 58 Baron	Anchor Shipping Agents SpA/Italy
	G-IOFR	Lindstrand LBL-105A balloon	RAF Halton Hot Air Balloon Club
	G-IOIA	I.I.I. Sky Arrow 650T	P.J. Lynch, P.G. Ward, N.J.C. Ray
	G-IOMI	Cameron Z-105 balloon	Elgas SRL/Italy
	G-IOOI	Robin DR.400/160	N. B. Mason
	G-IOOP	Christen Eagle II	A. P. S. Maynard
	G-IOOZ	Agusta A109S Grand	Hundred Percent Aviation Ltd
	G-IOPT	Cessna 182P	Indy Oscar Group
	G-IORG	Robinson R22 Beta	Highmark Aviation Ltd
	G-IORV	Van's RV-10	A. F. S. & B. L. Caldecourt
	G-IOSI	Jodel DR.1051	D. C. & M. Brooks
	G-IOSL	Van's RV-9	S. Leach (G-CFIX)
	G-IOSO	Jodel DR.1050	A. E. Jackson
	G-IOWE	Shaw Europa XS	P. A. Lowe
	G-IPAT	Jabiru SP	H. Adams
	G-IPAX	Cessna 560XL Citation Excel	Pacific Aviation Ltd
	G-IPEP	Beech 95-B55 Baron	P. E. T. Price (G-FABM)
	G-IPKA	Alpi Pioneer 300	M. E. Hughes
	G-IPOD	Europa XS	Ultraflight Ltd (G-CEBV)
	G-IPSI	Grob G.109B	D. G. Margetts (G-BMLO)
	G-IPUP	Beagle B.121 Pup 2	Swift Flying Group
	G-IRAF	RAF 2000 GTX-SE gyroplane	P. Robichaud
	G-IRAL	Thruster T600N 450	J. Giraldez
	G-IRAP	Bombardier BD-700-1A10 Global Express	TAG Aviation (UK) Ltd (G-CJME)
	G-IRAR	Van's RV-9	J. Maplethorpe
	G-IREN	SOCATA TB-20 Trinidad GT	Chios Aeroclub
	G-IRGJ	Champion 7ECA Citabria Aurora	T. A. Mann
	G-IRIS	AA-5B Tiger	C. Nichol (G-BIXU)
	G-IRJX	Avro RJX-100 ★	Manchester Heritage Museum
	G-IRKB	PA-28R-201 Arrow III	M. Ruter
	G-IRLE	Schempp-Hirth Ventus cT	D. J. Scholey
	G-IRLY	Colt 90A balloon	C. E. R. Smart
	G-IRLZ	Lindstrand LBL-60X balloon	A. M. Holly
	G-IROE	Flight Design CTSW	S. Roe
	G-IRON	Shaw Europa XS	T. M. Clark
	G-IROS	Rotorsport UK Calidus	JB Aviation Ltd
	G-IRPC	Cessna 182Q	A. T. Jeans (G-BSKM)
	G-IRPW	Europa XS	R. P. Wheelwright
	G-IRSH	Embraer EMB-135RJ	Legemb Ltd

Reg.	Type	Owner or Operator	Notes
G-IRYC	Schweizer 269-1	CSL Industrial Ltd	
G-ISAX	PA-28-181 Archer III	M. S. Kontowtt	
G-ISAY	BAe Jetstream 4102	Enar Lindstrom AB (G-MAJN)/Sweden	
G-ISCA	PA-28RT-201 Arrow IV	D. J. & P. Pay	
G-ISCD	Czech Sport Aircraft Sportcruiser	P. W. Shepherd	
G-ISDB	PA-28-161 Warrior II	Action Air Services Ltd (G-BWET)	
G-ISDN	Boeing Stearman A75N1	D. R. L. Jones	
G-ISEH	Cessna 182R	S. J. Nash (G-BIWS)	
G-ISEL	Best Off Skyranger 912 (2)	P. A. Robertson	
G-ISEW	P & M Quik GT450	J. D. Doran	
G-ISFC	PA-31-310 Turbo Navajo B	T. M. Latiff (G-BNEF)	
G-ISHA	PA-28-161 Warrior III	LAC Flying School	
G-ISHK	Cessna 172S	Matchpage Ltd	
G-ISLB	BAe Jetstream 3201	Blue Island Air	
G-ISLC	BAe Jetstream 3202	Blue Island Air	
G-ISLD	BAe Jetstream 3202	Blue Island Air	
G-ISMA	Van's RV-7A	S. Marriott (G-STAF)	
G-ISMO	Robinson R22 Beta	Moy Motorsport Ltd	
G-ISPH	Bell 206B JetRanger 2	Blades Aviation (UK) LLP (G-OPJM)	
G-ISST	Eurocopter EC 155B1	Bristow Helicopters Ltd	
G-ISSU	Eurocopter EC 155B1	Bristow Helicopters Ltd	
G-ISSV	Eurocopter EC 155B1	Bristow Helicopters Ltd	
G-ISSW	Eurocopter EC 155B1	Bristow Helicopters Ltd	
G-ISSY	Eurocopter EC 120B	D. R. Williams (G-CBCG)	
G-ISZA	Aerotek Pitts S-2A Special	F. L. McGee (G-HISS/G-BLVU)	
G-ITAF	SIAI-Marchetti SF.260AM	N. A. Whatling	
G-ITBT	Alpi Pioneer 300 Hawk	F. Paolini	
G-ITFL	Diamond DA42 Twin Star	AAAS AF 8 November 2009 A/S Under Konkurs	
G-ITII	Aerotech Pitts S-2A Special	P. J. Kirkpatrick	
G-ITOI	Cameron N-90 balloon	Flying Pictures Ltd	
G-ITPH	Robinson R44 II	Helicopter Services Europe Ltd	
G-ITUG	PA-28 Cherokee 180	S. I. Tugwell (G-AVNR)	
G-ITVM	Lindstrand LBL-105A balloon	Elmer Balloon Team	
G-ITWB	DHC.1 Chipmunk 22	I. T. Whitaker-Bethe	
G-IUAN	Cessna 525 CitationJet	R. F. Celada SPA/Italy	
G-IUII	Aerostar Yakovlev Yak-52	D. J. C. Davidson	
G-IUMB	Schleicher ASW-20L	M. S. Szymkowicz	
G-IVAC	Airtour AH-77B balloon	T. D. Gibbs	
G-IVAL	CAB CAP-10B	I. Valentine	
G-IVAN	Shaw TwinEze	A. M. Aldridge	
G-IVAR	Yakovlev Yak-50	A. H. Soper	
G-IVDM	Schempp Hirth Nimbus 4DM	G. W. Lynch	
G-IVEN	Robinson R44 II	OKR Group/Ireland	
G-IVER	Shaw Europa XS	I. Phillips	
G-IVET	Shaw Europa	K. J. Fraser	
G-IVII	Vqn's RV-7	M. A. N. Newall	
G-IVIV	Robinson R44	D. Brown	
G-IVJM	Agusta A109E Power	Air Harrods Ltd (G-MOMO)	
G-IVOR	Aeronca 11AC Chief	South Western Aeronca Group	
G-IVYS	Parsons 2-seat gyroplane	R. M. Harris	
G-IWIN	Raj Hamsa X'Air Hawk	H. R. Bethune	
G-IWIZ	Flylight Dragonfly	S. Wilson	
G-IWON	Cameron V-90 balloon	D. P. P. Jenkinson (G-BTCV)	
G-IWRB	Agusta A109A-II	Maison Air Ltd (G-VIPT)	
G-IXII	Christen Eagle II	Eagle Flying Group (G-BPZI)	
G-IXXI	Schleicher ASW-27-18E	G. P. Stingemore	
G-IYCO	Robin DR.400/500	Timgee Holdings Ltd	
G-IZAP	Learjet 45	Premiair Business Aviation Ltd (G-OLDK)	
G-IZII	Marganski Swift S-1	G. C. Westgate	
G-IZIP	Learjet 45	Premiair Business Aviation Ltd (G-OLDW)	
G-IZIT	Rans S.6-116 Coyote II	D. J. Flower & M. C. Watson	
G-IZZI	Cessna T.182T	D. J. & E-S Lucey	
G-IZZS	Cessna 172S	Air Claire Ltd	
G-IZZY	Cesna 172R	P. A. Adams & T. S. Davies (G-BXSF)	
G-IZZZ	Champion 8KCAB	A.M. Read	

Notes	Reg.	Type	Owner or Operator
	G-JAAB	Avtech Jabiru UL	R. Holt
	G-JABA	Jabiru SK	G. L. Turner
	G-JABB	Avtech Jabiru UL	R. J. Sutherland
	G-JABE	Jabiru Aircraft Jabiru UL-D	H. M. Manning and P. M. Jones
	G-JABI	Jabiru Aircraft Jabiru J400	Anvilles Flying Group
	G-JABJ	Jabiru Aircraft Jabiru J400	L. B. W. & F. H. Hancock
	G-JABS	Avtech Jabiru UL-450	Jabiru Flying Group
	G-JABU	Jabiru J430	S. D. Miller
	G-JABY	Avtech Jabiru UL	P. R. Smith
	G-JACA	PA-28-161 Warrior II	Channel Islands Aero Club (Jersey) Ltd
	G-JACB	PA-28-181 Archer III	Channel Islands Aero Club (Jersey) Ltd (G-PNNI)
	G-JACH	PA-28-181 Archer III	Goldcrest 2001 Ltd (G-IDPH)
	G-JACK	Cessna 421C	JCT 600 Ltd
	G-JACO	Avtech Jabiru UL	C. D. Matthews/Ireland
	G-JACS	PA-28-181 Archer III	Modern Air (UK) Ltd
	G-JADJ	PA-28-181 Archer III	ACS Aviation Ltd
	G-JADW	Ikarus C42 FB80	J. W. & D. A. Wilding
	G-JAEE	Van's RV-6A	J. A. E. Edser
	G-JAES	Bell 206B JetRanger 3	Audisio Automobili Cuneo SRL/Italy (G-STOX/ G-BNIR)
	G-JAGS	Cessna FRA.150L	RAF Marham Flying Club (G-BAUY)
	G-JAIR	Mainair Blade	W. R. Astbury
	G-JAJA	Robinson R44 II	J. D. Richardson
	G-JAJB	AA-5A Cheetah	Active Aviation Ltd
	G-JAJK	PA-31-350 Navajo Chieftain	Keen Leasing (IOM) Ltd (G-OLDB/G-DIXI)
	G-JAJP	Avtech Jabiru UL	J. W. E. Pearson & J. Anderson
	G-JAKF	Robinson R44 Raven II	J. G. Froggatt
	G-JAKI	Mooney M.20R	J. M. Moss & D. M. Abrahamson
	G-JAKS	PA-28 Cherokee 160	K. Harper (G-ARVS)
	G-JAMA	Schweizer 269C-1	R. J. Scott
	G-JAME	Zenair CH 601UL	A. Batters (G-CDFZ)
	G-JAMP	PA-28-151 Warrior	Lapwing Flying Group Ltd (G-BRJU)
	G-JAMY	Shaw Europa XS	J. P. Sharp
	G-JANA	PA-28-181 Archer II	S. Hoo-Hing
	G-JANB	Colt Flying Bottle SS balloon	Justerini & Brooks Ltd
	G-JANI	Robinson R44	JT Helicopters Ltd
	G-JANN	PA-34-220T Seneca III	D. J. Whitcombe
	G-JANS	Cessna FR.172J	C. M. Aizlewood
	G-JANT	PA-28-181 Archer II	Janair Aviation Ltd
	G-JAOC	Best Off Sky Ranger Swift 912S(1)	A. C. Bell
	G-JAPK	Grob G.130A Twin II Acro	Cairngorm Gliding Club
	G-JARM	Robinson R44	J. Armstrong
	G-JASE	PA-28-161 Warrior II	Mid-Anglia School of Flying
	G-JASS	Beech B200 Super King Air	Platinum Executive Aviation LLP
	G-JAST	Mooney M.20J -201	M. J. Willis
	G-JAVO	PA-28-161 Warrior II	Victor Oscar Ltd (G-BSXW)
	G-JAWC	Pegasus Quantum 15-912	S. Suckling
	G-JAWZ	Pitts S-1S Special	A. R. Harding
	G-JAXS	Avtech Jabiru UL	J. P. Pullin
	G-JAYI	Auster J/1 Autocrat	Aviation Heritage Ltd
	G-JAYS	Skyranger 912S(1)	R. A. Green
	G-JAYZ	CZAW Sportcruiser	J. Williams
	G-JBAS	Neico Lancair 200	A. Slater
	G-JBBZ	AS.350B3 Ecureuil	BZ Air Ltd
	G-JBDB	Agusta-Bell 206B JetRanger	Dicksons Van World Ltd (G-OOPS/G-BNRD)
	G-JBDH	Robin DR.400/180	W. A. Clark
	G-JBEN	Mainair Blade 912	G. J. Bentley
	G-JBII	Robinson R22 Beta	Fast Helicopters Ltd (G-BXLA)
	G-JBIS	Cessna 550 Citation II	247 Jet Ltd
	G-JBIZ	Cessna 550 Citation II	247 Jet Ltd
	G-JBKA	Robinson R44	J. G. Harrison
	G-JBLZ	Cessna 550 Citation Bravo	247 Jet Ltd
	G-JBMW	Bell 407	Magell Ltd
	G-JBRE	Rotorsport UK MT-03	J. B. R. Elliot & D. F. Sargant
	G-JBRG	Agusta A109A II	Interceptor Aviation Ltd (G-TMUR/G-CEPO)
	G-JBRN	Cessna 182S	SB Aviation Ltd (G-RITZ)
	G-JBRS	Van's RV-8	C. Jobling
	G-JBSP	Avtech Jabiru SP-470	C. R. James
	G-JBTR	Van's RV-8	R. A. Ellis
	G-JBUZ	Robin DR400/180R Remorqueur	D. A. Saywell

Reg.	Type	Owner or Operator	Notes
G-JCAP	Robinson R22 Beta	R. D. Masters	
G-JCAR	PA-46-350P Malibu Mirage	Aquarelle Investments Ltd	
G-JCAS	PA-28-181 Archer II	Charlie Alpha Ltd	
G-JCBB	Gulfstream V-SP	J. C. Bamford Excavators Ltd	
G-JCBJ	Sikorsky S-76C	J. C. Bamford Excavators Ltd	
G-JCBX	Dassault Falcon 900EX	J. C. Bamford Excavators Ltd	
G-JCJC	Colt Flying Jeans SS balloon	Magical Adventures Ltd	
G-JCKT	Stemme S.10VT	J. C. Taylor	
G-JCOP	Eurocopter AS.350B3 Ecureuil	Optimum Ltd	
G-JCUB	PA-18 Super Cub 135	Vintage Aircraft Flying Group	
G-JCWM	Robinson R44 II	M. L. J. Goff	
G-JDBC	PA-34-200T Seneca II	Bowdon Aviation Ltd (G-BDEF)	
G-JDEE	SOCATA TB20 Trinidad	JDEE Group	
G-JDEL	Jodel 150	K. F. & R. Richardson (G-JDLI)	
G-JDIX	Mooney M.20B	P. Sedlacek (G-ARTB)	
G-JDJM	PA-28 Cherokee 140	Hare Flying Group (G-HSJM/G-AYIF)	
G-JDPB	PA-28R-201T Turbo Arrow III	BC Arrow Ltd (G-DNCS)	
G-JDRD	Alpi Pioneer 300	R. J. Doughton	
G-JEAF	Fokker F.27 Friendship Mk.500	Executive Jet Support Ltd	
G-JEAJ	BAe 146-200	Trident Aviation Leasing Services (Jersey) Ltd (G-OLCA)	
G-JEAX	BAe 146-200	BAE Systems (Operations) Ltd	
G-JEAY	BAe-146-200	BAE Systems (Operations) Ltd	
G-JEBV	Avro RJ100	Trident Jet Leasing (Ireland) Ltd (G-CDCN)	
G-JECE	DHC.8-402 Dash Eight	Flybe.com	
G-JECF	DHC.8-402 Dash Eight	Flybe.com	
G-JECG	DHC.8-402 Dash Eight	Flybe.com	
G-JECH	DHC.8-402 Dash Eight	Flybe.com	
G-JECI	DHC.8-402 Dash Eight	Flybe.com	
G-JECJ	DHC.8-402 Dash Eight	Flybe.com	
G-JECK	DHC.8-402 Dash Eight	Flybe.com	
G-JECL	DHC.8-402 Dash Eight	Flybe.com	
G-JECM	DHC.8-402 Dash Eight	Flybe.com	
G-JECN	DHC.8-402 Dash Eight	Flybe.com	
G-JECO	DHC.8-402 Dash Eight	Flybe.com	
G-JECP	DHC.8-402 Dash Eight	Flybe.com	
G-JECR	DHC.8-402 Dash Eight	Flybe.com	
G-JECS	DHC.8-402 Dash Eight	Flybe.com	
G-JECT	DHC.8-402 Dash Eight	Flybe.com	
G-JECU	DHC.8-402 Dash Eight	Flybe.com	
G-JECX	DHC.8-402 Dash Eight	Flybe.com	
G-JECY	DHC.8-402 Dash Eight	Flybe.com	
G-JECZ	DHC.8-402 Dash Eight	Flybe.com	
G-JEDH	Robin DR.400/180	J. B. Hoolahan	
G-JEDI	DHC.8-402 Dash Eight	Flybe.com	
G-JEDJ	DHC.8-402 Dash Eight	Flybe.com	
G-JEDK	DHC.8-402 Dash Eight	Flybe.com	
G-JEDL	DHC.8-402 Dash Eight	Flybe.com	
G-JEDM	DHC.8-402 Dash Eight	Flybe.com	
G-JEDN	DHC.8-402 Dash Eight	Flybe.com	
G-JEDO	DHC.8-402 Dash Eight	Flybe.com	
G-JEDP	DHC.8-402 Dash Eight	Flybe com	
G-JEDR	DHC.8-402 Dash Eight	Flybe com	
G-JEDS	Andreasson BA-4B	S. B. Jedburgh (G-BEBT)	
G-JEDT	DHC.8-402 Dash Eight	Flybe com	
G-JEDU	DHC.8-402 Dash Eight	Flybe com	
G-JEDV	DHC.8-402 Dash Eight	Flybe.com	
G-JEDW	DHC.8-402 Dash Eight	Flybe.com	
G-JEEP	Evektor EV-97 Eurostar	G-JEEP Group (G-CBNK)	
G-JEFA	Robinson R44	Simlot Ltd	
G-JEJE	RAF 2000 GTX-SE gyroplane	J. W. Erswell	
G-JEJH	Jodel DR.1050 Ambassadeur	Bredon Hill Flying Group	
G-JELI	Schweizer 269C-1	Jelico Ltd (G-CCVG)	
G-JEMA	BAe ATP	PTB (Emerald) Pty Ltd	
G-JEMC	BAe ATP	PTB (Emerald) Pty Ltd	
G-JEMI	Lindstrand LBL-90A balloon	J. A. Lawton	
G-JENA	Mooney M.20K	Jena Air Force	
G-JENI	Cessna R.182	R. A. Bentley	
G-JENK	Ikarus C42 FB80	R. K. Jenkins	
G-JERO	Shaw Europa XS	P. Jenkinson and N. Robshaw	

Notes	Reg.	Type	Owner or Operator
	G-JERS	Robinson R22 Beta	Scotia Helicopters Ltd
	G-JESA	Southdown Raven X (modified)	A. E. James (G-MNLB)
	G-JESE	AS.355F2 Ecureuil 2	Arena Aviation Ltd (G-EMHH/G-BYKH)
	G-JESI	AS.350B Ecureuil	Staske Construction Ltd (G-JOSS/G-WILX/ G-RAHM/G-UNIC/G-COLN/G-BHIV)
	G-JESS	PA-28R-201T Turbo Arrow III	R. E. Trawicki (G-REIS)
	G-JETA	Cessna 550 Citation II	Icon Two Ltd (G-RDBS)
	G-JETC	Cessna 550 Citation II	Interceptor Aviation Ltd (G-JCFR)
	G-JETH	Hawker Sea Hawk FGA.6 (XE489) ★	P. G. Vallance Ltd/Charlwood
	G-JETJ	Cessna 550 Citation II	G-JETJ Ltd (G-EJET/G-DJBE)
	G-JETM	Gloster Meteor T.7 (VZ638) ★	P. G. Vallance Ltd/Charlwood
	G-JETO	Cessna 550 Citation II	Air Charter Scotland Ltd (G-RVHT)
	G-JETX	Bell 206B JetRanger 3	L. B. Oldham
	G-JETZ	Hughes 369E	GJP Helicopters Ltd
	G-JEZA	Agusta AW.139	CHC Scotia Ltd
	G-JEZZ	Skyranger 582	A. S. Ashton
	G-JFAN	P & M Quik R	J. F. A. Nicol
	G-JFDI	Dynamic WT9 UK	M. S. Gregory
	G-JFER	Rockwell Commander 114B	J. C. & J. A. Ferguson (G-HPSE)
	G-JFLO	Aerospool Dynamic WT9 UK	J. Flood
	G-JFLY	Schleicher ASW-24	Cambridge Gliding Club Ltd
	G-JFMK	Zenair CH.701SP	J. D. Pearson
	G-JFRV	Van's RV-7A	J. H. Fisher
	G-JFWI	Cessna F.172N	Staryear Ltd
	G-JGBI	Bell 206L-4 LongRanger	Dorbcrest Homes Ltd
	G-JGCA	VS.361 Spitfire LF.IXe (TE517)	P. M. Andrews (G-CCIX/G-BIXP)
	G-JGMN	CASA 1.131E Jungmann 2000	P. D. Scandrett
	G-JGSI	Pegasus Quantum 15-912	A. Fern
	G-JHAC	Cessna FRA.150L	J. H. A. Clarke (G-BACM)
	G-JHDD	Czech Sport Aircraft Sportcruiser	D. Draper & J. W. Hagley
	G-JHEW	Robinson R22 Beta	Heli Air Ltd
	G-JHKP	Shaw Europa XS	J. D. Heykoop
	G-JHNY	Cameron A.210 balloon	Floarting Sensations Ltd
	G-JHPC	Cessna 182T	JHP Aviation Ltd
	G-JHYS	Shaw Europa	B. C. Moorhouse
	G-JIBO	BAe Jetstream 3102	Links Asset Management Ltd (G-OJSA/G-BTYG)
	G-JIFI	Schempp-Hirth Duo Discus T	D. K. McCarthy
	G-JIII	Stolp SA.300 Starduster Too	VTIO Co
	G-JIIL	Pitts S-2A Special	A. G. Griffiths
	G-JILY	Robinson R44	R. R. Orr
	G-JIMB	Beagle B.121 Pup 1	K. D. H. Gray & P. G. Fowler (G-AWWF)
	G-JIMH	Cessna F.152 II	Emmalin (G-SHAH)
	G-JIMM	Shaw Europa XS	J. Riley
	G-JIMZ	Van's RV-4	J.W.Hale
	G-JINI	Cameron V-77 balloon	I. R. Warrington
	G-JIVE	MDH Hughes 369E	Sleekform Ltd (G-DRAR)
	G-JJAB	Jabiru J400	K. Ingebrigsten
	G-JJAN	PA-28-181 Archer II	J. S. Develin & Z. Islam
	G-JJEN	PA-28-181 Archer III	K. M. R. Jenkins
	G-JJFB	Eurocopter EC.120B Colibri	J. G. Rhoden
	G-JJIL	Extra EA.300/L	Link Goals SP ZOO
	G-JJJL	Agusta A.109E Power	Brookes Air Charter LLP (G-CEJS)
	G-JJSI	BAe 125 Srs 800B	Gama Leasing Ltd (G-OMGG)
	G-JJWL	Robinson R44	Willbeth Ltd
	G-JKAY	Robinson R44	Jamiroquai Ltd
	G-JKKK	Cessna 172S	P. Eaton
	G-JKMH	Diamond DA42 Twin Star	ADR Aviation
	G-JKMJ	Diamond DA42 Twin Star	Medox Enterprises Ltd
	G-JLAT	Aerotechnik EV-97 Eurostar	J. Latimer
	G-JLCA	PA-34-200T Seneca II	Tayside Aviation Ltd (G-BOKE)
	G-JLEE	Agusta-Bell 206B JetRanger 3	J. S. Lee (G-JOKE/G-CSKY/G-TALY)
	G-JLHS	Beech A36 Bonanza	I. G. Meredith
	G-JLIN	PA-28-161 Cadet	JH Sandham Aviation
	G-JLLT	Aerotechnik EV-97 Eurostar	J. Latimer
	G-JLRW	Beech 76 Duchess	Airways Flight Training

Reg.	Type	Owner or Operator	Notes
G-JMAA	Boeing 757-3CQ	Thomas Cook Airlines Ltd	
G-JMAB	Boeing 757-3CQ	Thomas Cook Airlines Ltd	
G-JMAC	BAe Jetstream 4100 ★	Jetstream Club, Liverpool Marriott Hotel South, Speke (G-JAMD/G-JXLI)	
G-JMAL	Jabiru UL-D	A. D. Sutton	
G-JMAX	Hawker 800XP	J-Max Air Services	
G-JMCD	Boeing 757-25F	Thomas Cook Airlines Ltd	
G-JMCE	Boeing 757-25F	Thomas Cook Airlines Ltd	
G-JMCG	Boeing 757-2G5	Thomas Cook Airlines Ltd	
G-JMCL	Boeing 737-322	Atlantic Airlines Ltd	
G-JMDI	Schweizer 269C	D. A. Sempers (G-FLAT)	
G-JMED	Learjet 35A	Air Medical Fleet Ltd	
G-JMJR	Cameron Z-90	J. M. Reck/France	
G-JMKE	Cessna 172S	115CR (146) Ltd	
G-JMMX	Dassault Falcon 900EX	Jaymax Jersey Ltd	
G-JMON	Agusta A109A-II	C. J. Thomas (G-RFDS/G-BOLA)	
G-JMOS	PA-34-220T Seneca V	Moss Aviation LLP	
G-JMRV	Van's RV-7	J. W. Marshall	
G-JMTS	Robin DR.400/180	G-JMTS Group	
G-JMXA	Agusta A109E Power	J-Max Air Services	
G-JNAS	AA-5A Cheetah	C. J. Williams	
G-JNET	Robinson R22 Beta	R. L. Hartshorn	
G-JNMA	VS.379 Spitfire FR.Mk.XIVe	P. M. Andrews	
G-JNNB	Colt 90A balloon	N. A. P. Godfrey	
G-JNSC	Schempp-Hirth Janus CT	D. S. Bramwell	
G-JNUS	Schempp-Hirth Janus C	N. A. Peatfield	
G-JOAL	Beech B200 Super King Air	South Coast Air Charter LLP	
G-JOBA	P & M Quik GT450	T. H. Parr	
G-JOBS	Cessna T182T	Tech Travel Ltd (G-BZVF)	
G-JODL	Jodel D.1050/M	D. Silsbury	
G-JOEL	Bensen B.8MR	C. Quinn	
G-JOEY	BN-2A Mk III-2 Trislander	Aurigny Air Services (G-BDGG)	
G-JOHA	Cirrus SR20	N. Harris	
G-JOJO	Cameron A-210 balloon	A. C. Rawson & J. J. Rudoni	
G-JOKR	Extra EA.300/L	R. Hockey & C. Vogelgesang	
G-JOLY	Cessna 120	B. V. Meade	
G-JONB	Robinson R22 Beta	J. Bignall	
G-JONG	Rotorway Executive 162F	J. V. George	
G-JONH	Robinson R22 Beta	Polar Helicopters Ltd	
G-JONL	CZAW Sportcruiser	J. R. Linford	
G-JONM	PA-28-181 Archer III	J. H. Massey	
G-JONO	Colt 77A balloon★	British Balloon Museum and Library	
G-JONT	Cirrus SR22	J. A. Green	
G-JONX	Aeropro Eurofox 912(1)	J. M. Walsh	
G-JONY	Cyclone AX2000 HKS	K. R. Matheson	
G-JONZ	Cessna 172P	Truman Aviation Ltd	
G-JONT	Cirrus SR22	J. A. Green	
G-JOOL	Mainair Blade 912	P. C. Collins	
G-JOON	Cessna 182D	Go Adventure Ireland Ltd	
G-JOPT	Cessna 560 Citation V	Air Charter Scotland Ltd	
G-JORD	Robinson R44 II	Overby Ltd	
G-JOST	Shaw Europa	M. W. Olliver	
G-JOYT	PA-28-181 Archer II	John K. Cathcart Ltd (G-BOVO)	
G-JOYZ	PA-28-181 Archer III	S. W. & J. E. Taylor	
G-JPAL	AS.355N Twin Squirrel	JPM Ltd	
G-JPAT	Robin HR.200/100	L. Girardier & A. J. McCulloch	
G-JPEG	BN-2A-20 Islander	Apem Ltd (G-BEDW)	
G-JPIP	Schempp-Hirth Discus bT	I. W. Paterson	
G-JPJR	Robinson R44 II	Longstop Investments Ltd	
G-JPMA	Avtech Jabiru UL	G. J. Stafford	
G-JPOT	PA-32R-301 Saratoga SP	P.J.Wolstencroft (G-BIYM)	
G-JPRO	P.84 Jet Provost T.5A (XW433)	Air Atlantique Ltd	
G-JPSZ	Dassault Falcon 900EX Easy	Sorven Aviation Ltd	
G-JPTT	Enstrom 480	P. G. Lawrence (G-PPAH)	
G-JPTV	P.84 Jet Provost T.5A (XW354)	Century Aviation Ltd	
G-JPVA	P.84 Jet Provost T.5A (XW289)	H. Cooke (G-BVXT)	
G-JPWM	Skyranger 912 (2)	R. S. Waters & M. Pittock	
G-JRED	Robinson R44	J. Reddington Ltd	

Notes	Reg.	Type	Owner or Operator
	G-JREE	Maule MX-7-180	C. R. P. Briand
	G-JRKD	Jodel D.18	R. K. Davies
	G-JRME	Jodel D.140E	J. E. & L. L. Rex
	G-JRSL	Agusta A109E Power	Perment Ltd
	G-JSAK	Robinson R22 Beta II	Tukair Aircraft Charter
	G-JSAT	BN-2T Turbine Islander	Rhine Army Parachute Association/Germany (G-BVFK)
	G-JSEY	Bollonbau Worner NL-STU/1000	M. Leblanc
	G-JSON	Cameron N-105 balloon	Up and Away Ballooning Ltd
	G-JSPL	Avtech Jabiru SPL-450	A. E. Stowe
	G-JSRV	Van's RV-6	J. Stringer
	G-JSSD	HP.137 Jetstream 3001 ★	Museum of Flight/East Fortune
	G-JTEM	Van's RV-7	J. C. Bacon
	G-JTNC	Cessna 500 Citation	Eurojet Aviation Ltd (G-OEJA/G-BWFL)
	G-JTPC	Aeromot AMT-200 Super Ximango	G. J. & J. T. Potter
	G-JTSA	Robinson R44 II	JTS Aviation Ltd
	G-JTWO	Piper J-2 Cub	O. D. Usherwood
	G-JUDD	Avtech Jabiru UL-450H	G. S. Elder
	G-JUDE	Robin DR.400/180	Bravo India Flying Group Ltd
	G-JUDY	AA-5A Cheetah	Gray Hooper Holt LLP
	G-JUGE	Aerotechnik EV-97 TeamEurostar UK	L. J. Appleby
	G-JUGS	Autogyro MTOSport	S. J. M. Hornsby
	G-JUIN	Cessna T.303 Crusader	F. Kratky
	G-JULE	P & M Quik GT450	A. J. A. Fowler
	G-JULL	Stemme S.10VT	J. P. C. Fuchs
	G-JULU	Cameron V-90 balloon	J. M. Searle
	G-JULZ	Shaw Europa	J. S. Firth
	G-JUNG	CASA 1.131E Jungmann 1000 (E3B-143)	K. H. Wilson
	G-JUPP	PA-32RT-300 Lance II	Jupp Air Ltd (G-BNJF)
	G-JURA	BAe Jetstream 3102	Highland Airways Ltd
	G-JURG	Rockwell Commander 114A	Wright Aviation Dunchurch Ltd
	G-JUST	Beech F33A Bonanza	P. Thompson
	G-JVBF	Lindstrand LBL-210A balloon	Virgin Balloon Flights
	G-JVBP	Aerotechnik EV-97 Team Eurostar UK	B. J. Partridge & J. A. Valentine
	G-JVJK	Alpi Pioneer 300 Hawk	D. R. Vale
	G-JWBI	Agusta-Bell 206B JetRanger 2	J. W. Bonser (G-RODS/G-NOEL/G-BCWN)
	G-JWCM	SA Bulldog Srs 120/1210	Goon Aviation Ltd
	G-JWDB	Ikarus C.42 FB80	A. R. Hughes
	G-JWDS	Cessna F.150G	G. Sayer (G-AVNB)
	G-JWEB	Robinson R44	P. T. Birdsall
	G-JWIV	Jodel DR.1051	C. M. Fitton
	G-JWJW	CASA 1-131E Jungmann Srs.2000	J. W. & J. T. Whicher
	G-JWNW	Magni M-16C Tandem Trainer	W. N. Garton-Jones
	G-JWXS	Shaw Europa XS T-G	J. Wishart
	G-JXTA	BAe Jetstream 3103	Jetstream Executive Travel Ltd
	G-JXTC	BAe Jetstream 3108	Jetstream Executive Travel Ltd (G-LOGT/ G-BSFH)
	G-JYAK	Yakovlev Yak-50 (93 white outline)	J. W. Stow
	G-JYRO	Rotorsport UK MT-03	A. Richards
	G-KAAT	MDH MD-902 Explorer	Police Aviation Services Ltd (G-PASS)
	G-KAFT	Diamond DA40D Star	Atlantic Flight Training Ltd
	G-KAIR	PA-28-181 Archer II	Keen Leasing (IOM) Ltd
	G-KALS	Bombardier BD-100-1A10	Concolor Ltd
	G-KAMP	PA-18 Super Cub 135	J. R. G. Furnell
	G-KANE	Aerospatiale SA.341G Gazelle 1	MW Helicopters Ltd (G-GAZI)
	G-KANL	Bombardier BD-700-1A10 Global Express	Ocean Sky (UK) Ltd
	G-KANZ	Westland Wasp HAS.1	T. J. Manna
	G-KAOM	Scheibe SF.25C Falke	Falke G-KAOM Syndicate
	G-KAOS	Van's RV-7	A. E. N. Nicholas, D. F. McGarvey
	G-KAPW	P.56 Provost T.1 (XF603)	The Shuttleworth Collection
	G-KARA	Brügger MB.2 Colibri	C. L. Hill (G-BMUI)
	G-KARI	Fuji FA.200-160	C. P. Rowley
	G-KARK	Dyn'Aéro MCR-01 Club	R. Bailes-Brown

Reg.	Type	Owner or Operator	Notes
G-KART	PA-28-161 Warrior II	N. Clark	
G-KASW	Rotorsport UK Calidus	K. C. Wigley	
G-KASX	VS.384 Seafire Mk.XVII (SX336)	T. J. Manna (G-BRMG)	
G-KATE	Westland WG.30 Srs 100 ★	(stored)/Yeovil	
G-KATG	Bell 206L-1 LongRanger	Lothian Helicopters Ltd	
G-KATI	Rans S.7 Courier	T. S. D. Lyle	
G-KATS	PA-28 Cherokee 140	G-KATS Group (G-BIRC)	
G-KATT	Cessna 152 II	Redhill Air Services Ltd (G-BMTK)	
G-KATZ	Flight Design CT2K	A. N. D. Arthur	
G-KAWA	Denney Kitfox Mk 2	L. E. Donaldson	
G-KAXF	Hawker Hunter F.6A (N-294)	Stichting Dutch Hawker Hunter Foundation/Netherlands	
G-KAXT	Westland Wasp HAS.1 (XT787)	Kennet Aviation	
G-KAYH	Extra EA.300/L	R. C. Howe/Netherlands	
G-KAYI	Cameron Z-90 balloon	Snow Business International Ltd	
G-KAZA	Sikorsky S-76C	Bristow Helicopters Ltd	
G-KAZB	Sikorsky S-76C	Bristow Helicopters Ltd	
G-KAZI	Mainair Pegasus Quantum 15-912	Edren Homes Ltd	
G-KBOJ	Autogyro MTOSport	K. M. G. Barnett	
G-KBOX	Flight Design CTSW	C. R. Mason	
G-KBPI	PA-28-161 Warrior II	Goodwood Aerodrome & Motor Circuit Ltd (G-BFSZ)	
G-KCHG	Schempp-Hirth Ventus Ct	Ventus KJW Syndicate	
G-KCIG	Sportavia RF-5B	Deeside Fournier Group	
G-KCIN	PA-28-161 Cadet	Jetstream Executive Travel Ltd (G-CDOX)	
G-KCWJ	Schempp-Hirth Duo Discus T	8F Group	
G-KDCC	Shaw Europa XS	K. A. C. Dodd	
G-KDCD	Thruster T600N	J. T. Fisher & R. D. Pyne (G-MZNW)	
G-KDEY	Scheibe SF.25E Super Falke	Falke Syndicate	
G-KDIX	Jodel D.9 Bébé	P. M. Bowden	
G-KDMA	Cessna 560 Citation V	Gamston Aviation Ltd	
G-KDOG	SA Bulldog Srs 120/121 (XX624:E)	Gamit Ltd	
G-KEAM	Schleicher ASH 26E	D. T. Reilly	
G-KEDK	Discus BT	G. N. Fraser	
G-KEEF	Commander Aircraft 112A	K. D. Pearse	
G-KEEN	Stolp SA.300 Starduster Too	Sharp Aerobatics Ltd/Netherlands	
G-KEES	PA-28 Cherokee 180	C. N. Ellerbrook	
G-KEJY	Aerotechnik EV-97 TeamEurostar UK	Kemble Eurostar 1	
G-KELI	Robinson R44 Raven II	KN Network Services Ltd	
G-KELL	Van's RV-6	R. G. Stephens/Ireland	
G-KELS	Van's RV-7	J. Verroen	
G-KELV	Diamond DA42 Twin Star	K. K. Freeman (G-CTCH)	
G-KELX	Van's RV-6	J. D. Kelsall (G-HAMY)	
G-KELY	AS.350B Ecureuil	Kelly Sales and Services Donegal Ltd (G-WKRD/G-BUJG/G-HEAR)	
G-KELZ	Van's RV-8	M. O'Leary (G-DJRV)	
G-KEMC	Grob G.109	Norfolk Gliding Club Ltd	
G-KEMI	PA-28-181 Archer III	Modern Air (UK) Ltd	
G-KEMY	Cessna 182T	Allen Aircraft Rental Ltd	
G-KENB	Air Command 503 Commander	K. Brogden	
G-KENG	Rotorsport UK MT-03	K. A. Graham	
G-KENI	Rotorway Executive	P. A. Taylor	
G-KENM	Luscombe 8EF Silvaire	M. G. Waters	
G-KENW	Robin DR400/500	K. J. White	
G-KENZ	Rutan Vari-Eze	K. M. McConnel l (G-BNUI)	
G-KEPE	Schempp-Hirth Nimbus 3DT	Nimbus Syndicate	
G-KEPP	Rans S.6-ES Coyote II	R. G. Johnston	
G-KERK	Piper J-3C-65 Cub	C. C. Kirk (G-OINK/G-BILD)	
G-KESS	Glaser-Dirks DG-400	N. H. T. Cottrell & T. Flude	
G-KEST	Steen Skybolt	G-KEST Syndicate	
G-KESY	Slingsby T.59D Kestrel	A. J. Whiteman	
G-KETH	Agusta-Bell 206B JetRanger 2	DAC Leasing Ltd	
G-KEVB	PA-28-181 Archer III	Palmair Ltd	
G-KEVG	Rotorsport UK MT-03	K. J. Robinson & R. N. Bodley	
G-KEVI	Jabiru J400	P. Horth & P. G. Macintosh	
G-KEVK	Flight Design CTSW	K. Kirby	
G-KEVL	Rotorway Executive 162F	K. D. Longhurst (G-CBIK)	
G-KEVS	P & M Quik GT450	K. Mallin	

Notes	Reg.	Type	Owner or Operator
	G-KEWT	Ultramagic M.90 balloon	R. F. Penney
	G-KEYS	PA-23 Aztec 250F	Giles Aviation Ltd
	G-KEYY	Cameron N-77 balloon	B. N. Trowbridge (G-BORZ)
	G-KFAN	Scheibe SF.25B Falke	R. G. & J. A. Boyes
	G-KFLY	Flight Design CTSW	G-KFLY Group (G-LFLY)
	G-KFOX	Denney Kitfox	I. R. Lawrence & R. Hampshire
	G-KFZI	KFZ-1 Tigerfalck	L. R. Williams
	G-KGAO	Scheibe SF.25C Falke 1700	Falke 2000 Group
	G-KHCC	Schempp-Hirth Ventus Bt	J. L. G. McLane
	G-KHCG	AS.355F2 Ecureuil II	London Helicopter Centres Ltd (G-SDAY/ G-SYPA/G-BPRE)
	G-KHEH	Grob G.109B	N. A. Tziros
	G-KHOM	Aeromot AMT-200 Super Ximango	Bowland Ximango Group
	G-KHOP	Zenair CH.601HDS Zodiac	K. Hopkins
	G-KHRE	MS.893E Rallye 150SV	D. M. Gale & K. F. Crumplin
	G-KICK	Pegasus Quantum 15-912	G. van der Gaag
	G-KIDD	Jabiru J430	R. L. Lidd (G-CEBB)
	G-KIEV	DKBA AT 0300-0 balloon	The Volga Balloon Team
	G-KIGR	Schleicher ASH-25E	G-KIGR ASH Syndicate
	G-KIII	Extra EA.300/L	Extra 200 Ltd
	G-KIKX	Cessna T.206H Turbo Stationair	Airkix Aircraft Ltd
	G-KIMA	Zenair CH.601XL Zodiac	K. Martindale
	G-KIMB	Robin DR.340/140	R. M. Kimbell
	G-KIMH	Rotorsport UK MTO Sport	P. B. Harrison
	G-KIMK	Partenavia P.68B	M. Konstantinovic (G-BCPO)
	G-KIMM	Shaw Europa XS	P. A. D. Clarke
	G-KIMY	Robin DR.400/140B	S. G. Jones
	G-KIPP	Thruster T.600 450	Compton Abbas Airfield Ltd
	G-KIRB	Europa XS	D. E. Steade (G-OIZI)
	G-KIRC	Pietenpol Air Camper	M. Kirk (G-BSVZ)
	G-KIRK	Piper J-3C-65 Cub	M. Kirk
	G-KISS	Rand-Robinson KR-2	E. A. Rooney
	G-KITF	Denney Kitfox	T. Wright
	G-KITH	Alpi Pioneer 300	K. G. Atkinson
	G-KITI	Pitts S-2E Special	B. R. Cornes
	G-KITS	Shaw Europa	J. R. Evernden
	G-KITT	Curtiss P-40M Kittyhawk (49)	P.A. Teichman
	G-KITY	Denney Kitfox Mk 2	Kitfox KFM Group
	G-KIZZ	Kiss 450-582	J. C. A. Page
	G-KJBS	CSA Sportcruiser	S. M. Lowe
	G-KKAM	Schleicher ASW-22BLE	D. P. Taylor
	G-KKAZ	Airbus A.320-214	Thomas Cook Airlines Ltd
	G-KKCW	Flight Design CT2K	M. A. D. Bowden
	G-KKER	Avtech Jabiru UL-450	E. A. Pearson
	G-KKEV	DHC.8-402 Dash Eight	Flybe.com
	G-KLAS	Robinson R44	Coates Aviation Ltd
	G-KLAW	Christen Eagle II	R. S. Goodwin & B. Lovering
	G-KLNB	Beech 300 Super King Air	Saxonair Charter Ltd
	G-KLNK	Eurocopter EC135 P2+	Saxonair Charter Ltd (G-VGMB)
	G-KLNP	Eurocopter EC120B Colibri	Saxonair Charter Ltd
	G-KLNR	Hawker 400A	Saxonair Charter Ltd
	G-KLNW	Cessna 510 Citation Mustang	Saxonair Charter Ltd
	G-KLYE	Best Off Sky Ranger Swift 912S(1)	J. F. Murphy
	G-KMRV	Van-s RV-9A	G. K. Mutch
	G-KNCG	PA-32-301FT 6X	MJC Aviation Ltd
	G-KNEE	Ultramagic M-77C balloon	M. A.Green
	G-KNEK	Grob G.109B	Syndicate 109
	G-KNIB	Robinson R22 Beta II	C. G. Knibb
	G-KNIX	Cameron Z-315 balloon	Cameron Flights Southern Ltd
	G-KNOW	PA-32 Cherokee Six 300	A. S. Bansal
	G-KNYT	Robinson R44	Aircol
	G-KOBH	Schempp-Hirth Discus bT	C. F. M. Smith & K. Neave

Reg.	Type	Owner or Operator	Notes
G-KOCO	Cirrus SR22	R. Fitzgerald	
G-KODA	Cameron O-77 balloon	K. Stamurs	
G-KOFM	Glaser-Dirks DG.600/18M	A. Mossman	
G-KOHF	Schleicher ASK.14	J. Houlihan	
G-KOKL	Hoffmann H-36 Dimona	Dimona Syndicate	
G-KOLB	Kolb Twinstar Mk 3A	M. P. Wiseman	
G-KOLI	WSK PZL-110 Koliber 150	J. R. Powell	
G-KONG	Slingsby T.67M Firefly 200	R. C. Morton	
G-KOOL	DH.104 Devon C.2	D. S. Hunt (G-DOVE)	
G-KOTA	PA-28-236 Dakota	H. C. L. & P. Greatrex	
G-KOYY	Schempp-Hirth Nimbus 4T	R. Kalin	
G-KPAO	Robinson R44	Avonair Ltd (G-SSSS)	
G-KPEI	Cessna 560XL Citation	Queensway Aviation Ltd	
G-KPLG	Schempp-Hirth Ventus 2cM	M. F. Lassan	
G-KPTN	Dassault Falcon 50	TAG Aviation (UK) Ltd	
G-KPTT	SOCATA TB20 Trinidad	Pelican Air Ltd	
G-KRES	Stoddard-Hamilton Glasair IIS RG	A. D. Murray	
G-KRIB	Robinson R44 II	Cribarth Helicopters	
G-KRII	Rand-Robinson KR-2	M. R. Cleveley	
G-KRMA	Cessna 425 Corsair	Speedstar Holdings Ltd	
G-KRNW	Eurocopter EC 135T2	Bond Air Services Ltd	
G-KRUZ	CZAW Sportcruiser	A. W. Shellis & P. Whittingham	
G-KSFR	Bombardier BD-100-1A10 Challenger	The Lily Partnership LLP	
G-KSHI	Beech A36 Bonanza	Hangar 11 Collection	
G-KSIR	Stoddard-Hamilton Glasair IIS RG	K. M. Bowen	
G-KSIX	Schleicher Ka 6E	C. D. Sterritt	
G-KSKS	Cameron N-105 balloon	Kiss the Sky Ballooning	
G-KSKY	Sky 77-24 balloon	J. W. Dale	
G-KSSH	MDH MD-900 Explorer	Police Aviation Services Ltd (G-WMID)	
G-KSVB	PA-24 Comanche 260	Knockin Flying Club Ltd	
G-KSWI	Hughes 369E	K. S. Williams (G-OOCS/G-ODTB/G-BXUR)	
G-KTEE	Cameron V-77 balloon	D. C. & N. P. Bull	
G-KTIA	Hawker 900XP	TAG Aviation (UK) Ltd	
G-KTKT	Sky 260-24 balloon	Adventure Balloons Ltd	
G-KTSG	Robinson R22 Beta	Sienna Gold Ltd	
G-KTTY	Denney Kitfox Model 3	S. D. Morris (G-LESJ)	
G-KTWO	Cessna 182T	S. J. G. Mole	
G-KUIK	Mainair Pegasus Quik	P. Nugent	
G-KUIP	CZAW Sportcruiser	A. J. Kuipers	
G-KUKI	Robinson R22 Beta	HJS Helicopters Ltd	
G-KULA	Best Off Skyranger 912ULS	G. S. Cridland	
G-KUPP	Flight Design CTSW	S. J. Peet	
G-KURK	Piper J3C-65 Cub	G. V. E. Kirk (G-BJTO)	
G-KUTI	Flight Design CTSW	D. F. & S. M. Kenny	
G-KUTU	Quickie Q.2	R. Nash & J. Parkinson	
G-KUUI	J-3C-65 Cub	V. S. E. Norman	
G-KVBF	Cameron A-340HL balloon	Virgin Balloon Flights	
G-KVIP	Beech 200 Super King Air	Capital Air Charter Ltd	
G-KWAK	Scheibe SF.25C	Mendip Gliding Club Ltd	
G-KWIC	Mainair Pegasus Quik	B. F. Levey	
G-KWIN	Dassault Falcon 2000EX	Quinn Aviation Ltd	
G-KWKI	QAC Quickie Q.200	R. Greatrex	
G-KWKR	P and M Aviation QuikR	L. G. White	
G-KWLI	Cessna 421C	Langley Aviation Ltd (G-DARR/G-BNEZ)	
G-KXXI	Schleicher ASK-21	R. C. & C. G. Bell	
G-KYLE	Thruster T600N 450	MKS Syndicate	
G-KYTE	Piper PA-28-161 Warrior II	G. Whitlow (G-BRRN)	
G-LABS	Shaw Europa	C. T. H. Pattinson	
G-LACA	PA-28-161 Warrior II	LAC Flying School	
G-LACB	PA-28-161 Warrior II	LAC Flying School	
G-LACC	Cameron C-90 balloon	Directorate Army Aviation	
G-LACD	PA-28-181 Archer III	Target Aviation Ltd (G-BYBG)	

Notes	Reg.	Type	Owner or Operator
	G-LACI	Cessna 172S Skyhawk	L. Endresz
	G-LACR	Denney Kitfox	C. M. Rose
	G-LADD	Enstrom 480	R. C. G. Davidson
	G-LADS	Rockwell Commander 114	D. F. Soul
	G-LADZ	Enstrom 480	Falcon Helicopters Ltd
	G-LAFF	Cameron TR-84 Srs.2 balloon	Balloonists Supporting Barretstown
	G-LAFT	Diamond DA40D Star	Atlantic Flight Training Ltd
	G-LAGR	Cameron N-90 balloon	J. R. Clifton
	G-LAID	Robinson R44 II	SARL Tolla Ciel
	G-LAIN	Robinson R22 Beta	Patriot Aviation Ltd
	G-LAIR	Stoddard-Hamilton Glasair IIS FT	A. I.O'Broin & S. T. Raby
	G-LAKE	Lake LA-250 Renegade	Lake Aviation Ltd
	G-LAKI	Jodel DR.1050	G. Cameron (G-JWBB)
	G-LALE	Embraer EMB-135BJ Legacy	London Executive Avition Ltd
	G-LAMM	Shaw Europa	S. A. Lamb
	G-LAMP	Cameron 110 Lampbulb SS balloon	S. A. Lacey
	G-LAMS	Cessna F.152 II	APB Leasing Ltd
	G-LANC	Avro 683 Lancaster X (KB889) ★	Imperial War Museum/Duxford
	G-LAND	Robinson R22 Beta	Heli Air Ltd
	G-LANE	Cessna F.172N	A. Holmes
	G-LANS	Cessna 182T	AK Enterprises Ltd
	G-LAOL	PA-28RT-201 Arrow IV	Goodwood Road Racing Co Ltd
	G-LAPS	Lindstrand LBL 203T gas balloon	Lindstrand Aeroplatforms Ltd
	G-LARA	Robin DR.400/180	K. D. & C. A. Brackwell
	G-LARE	PA-39 Twin Comanche 160 C/R	Glareways (Neasden) Ltd
	G-LARK	Helton Lark 95	J. Fox
	G-LARR	AS.350B3 Squirrel	Larsen Manufacturing Ltd
	G-LARY	Robinson R44 II	Air 86 SARL/France (G-CCRZ)
	G-LASN	Skyranger J2.2	L. C. F. Lasne
	G-LASR	Stoddard-Hamilton Glasair II	G. Lewis
	G-LASS	Rutan Vari-Eze	J. Mellor
	G-LASU	Eurocopter EC 135T2	Lancashire Constabulary Air Support Unit
	G-LATE	Falcon 2000EX	Hangar 8 Management Ltd
	G-LAVE	Cessna 172R	M. L. Roland (G-BYEV)
	G-LAWX	Sikorsky S-92A	Air Harrods Ltd
	G-LAXY	Everett Gyroplane Srs.3	E. J. Barton
	G-LAZA	Lazer Z.200	D. G. Jenkins
	G-LAZL	PA-28-161 Warrior II	Highland Aviation Training Ltd
	G-LAZZ	Stoddard-Hamilton Glastar	A. N. Evans
	G-LBAI	Eurocopter EC.155B1	Polaris Aviation Ltd
	G-LBDC	Bell 206B JetRanger III	Fresh Direct Travel Ltd
	G-LBMM	PA-28-161 Warrior II	M. A. Jones
	G-LBRC	PA-28RT-201 Arrow IV	D. J. V. Morgan
	G-LBUK	Lindstrand LBL-77A balloon	Morrison Design Ltd
	G-LBUZ	Aerotechnick EV-97A Eurostar	D. P. Tassart
	G-LCGL	Comper CLA.7 Swift (replica)	M. C. & M. R. Greenland
	G-LCKY	Flight Design CTSW	G. D. Honey
	G-LCMW	TL 2000UK Sting Carbon	M. J. White & L. Chadwick
	G-LCOC	BN-2A Mk III Trislander	Blue Island Air
	G-LCOK	Colt 69A balloon	Hot-Air Balloon Co Ltd (G-BLWI)
	G-LCPL	AS.365N-2 Dauphin 2	Charterstyle Ltd
	G-LCUB	PA-18 Super Cub 95	The Tiger Club 1990 Ltd (G-AYPR)
	G-LCYA	Dassault 900EX	Airport Management and Investment Ltd
	G-LCYD	Embraer ERJ170-100STD	BA Cityflyer Ltd
	G-LCYE	Embraer ERJ170-100STD	BA Cityflyer Ltd
	G-LCYF	Embraer ERJ170-100STD	BA Cityflyer Ltd
	G-LCYG	Embraer ERJ170-100STD	BA Cityflyer Ltd
	G-LCYH	Embraer ERJ170-100STD	BA Cityflyer Ltd
	G-LCYI	Embraer ERJ170-100STD	BA Cityflyer Ltd
	G-LCYJ	Embraer ERJ190-100SR	BA Cityflyer Ltd
	G-LCYK	Embraer ERJ190-100SR	BA Cityflyer Ltd
	G-LCYL	Embraer ERJ190-100SR	BA Cityflyer Ltd
	G-LCYM	Embraer ERJ190-100SR	BA Cityflyer Ltd
	G-LCYN	Embraer ERJ190-100SR	BA Cityflyer Ltd
	G-LDAH	Skyranger 912 (2)	P. D. Brookes & L. Dickinson
	G-LDER	Schleicher ASW-22	P. Shrosbree & D. Starer
	G-LDFM	Cessna 560XL Citation Excel	Granard Ltd
	G-LDVO	Europa Aviation Europa XS	D. J. Park
	G-LDWS	Jodel D.150	D. H. Wilson Spratt (G-BKSS)

Reg.	Type	Owner or Operator	Notes
G-LDYS	Colt 56A balloon	M. J. Myddelton	
G-LEAA	Cessna 510 Citation Mustang	London Executive Aviation Ltd	
G-LEAB	Cessna 510 Citation Mustang	London Executive Aviation Ltd	
G-LEAC	Cessna 510 Citation Mustang	London Executive Aviation Ltd	
G-LEAF	Cessna F.406	Reconnaisance Ventures Ltd	
G-LEAH	Alpi Pioneer 300	A. Bortolan	
G-LEAI	Cessna 510	London Executive Aviation Ltd	
G-LEAM	PA-28-236 Dakota	G-LEAM Group (G-BHLS)	
G-LEAP	BN-2T Turbine Islander	Skydive Swansea Ltd	
G-LEAR	Learjet 35A	Agrevia Holdings Ltd (G-ZEST)	
G-LEAS	Sky 90-24 balloon	C. I. Humphrey	
G-LEAU	Cameron N-31 balloon	P. L. Mossman	
G-LEAX	Cessna 560XL Citation XLS	London Executive Aviation Ltd	
G-LEBE	Shaw Europa	P. Atkinson	
G-LECA	AS.355F1 Twin Squirrel	Western Power Distribution (South West) PLC (G-BNBK)	
G-LEDE	Zenair CH.601UL Zodiac	A. R. Cattell	
G-LEDR	Westland Gazelle HT.2	R. D. Leader (G-CBSB)	
G-LEED	Denney Kitfox Mk 2	S. J. Walker	
G-LEEE	Avtech Jabiru UL-450	J. P. Mimnagh& L. E. G. Fekete	
G-LEEH	Ultramagic M-90 balloon	Sport Promotion SRL/Italy	
G-LEEJ	Hughes 369HS	L. Jones	
G-LEEK	Reality Escapade	Phoenix Group	
G-LEEN	Aero Designs Pulsar XP	R. B. Hemsworth (G-BZMP/G-DESI)	
G-LEES	Glaser-Dirks DG.400 (800)	Active Aviation Ltd	
G-LEEZ	Bell 206L-1 LongRanger 2	Pennine Helicopters Ltd (G-BPCT)	
G-LEGG	Cessna F.182Q	W. A. L. Mitchell (G-GOOS)	
G-LEGO	Cameron O-77 balloon	P. M. Traviss	
G-LEGY	Flight Design CTLS	P. J. Clegg	
G-LEIC	Cessna FA.152	Leicestershire Aero Club Ltd	
G-LELE	Lindstrand LBL-31A balloon	D. S. Wilson	
G-LEMM	Ultramagic Z-90 balloon	M. Maranoni/Italy	
G-LENF	Mainair Blade 912S	G. D. Fuller	
G-LENI	AS.355F1 Twin Squirrel	Grid Defence Systems Ltd (G-ZFDB/G-BLEV)	
G-LENN	Cameron V-56 balloon	D. J. Groombridge	
G-LENS	Thunder Ax7-77Z balloon	R. S. Breakwell	
G-LENX	Cessna 172N	November XRay Ltd	
G-LEOD	Pietenpol Aircamper	I. D. McCleod	
G-LEOS	Robin DR.400/120	R. J. O. Walker	
G-LESH	BB Microlight BB03 Trya/Alien	L. R. Hodgson	
G-LESZ	Denney Kitfox Mk 5	J. C. Holland	
G-LETS	Vans RV-7	M. O'Hearne	
G-LEVI	Aeronca 7AC Champion	G-LEVI Group	
G-LEVO	Robinson R44 II	Leavesley Aviation Ltd	
G-LEXX	Van's RV-8	S. Emery	
G-LEXY	Van's RV-8	A. A. Wordsworth	
G-LEZE	Rutan LongEz	Bill Allen's Autos Ltd	
G-LFIX	VS.509 Spitfire T.IX (ML407)	C. S. Grace	
G-LFOR	Piper J3C-65 Cub	A. Hoskins & J. C. Gowdy	
G-LFPT	Cessna 510 Citation Mustang	Ambeo PLC	
G-LFSA	PA-38-112 Tomahawk	Liverpool Flying School Ltd (G-BSFC)	
G-LFSB	PA-38-112 Tomahawk	J. D. Burford	
G-LFSC	PA-28 Cherokee 140	R. C. Boyall (G-BGTR)	
G-LFSG	PA-28 Cherokee 180E	Liverpool Flying School Ltd (G-AYAA)	
G-LFSH	PA-38-112 Tomahawk	Liverpool Flying School Ltd (G-BOZM)	
G-LFSI	PA-28 Cherokee 140	Flying Group G-LFSI (G-AYKV)	
G-LFSJ	PA-28-161 Warrior II	FlyBPL.com	
G-LFSM	PA-38-112 Tomahawk	Liverpool Flying School Ltd (G-BWNR)	
G-LFSN	PA-38-112 Tomahawk	Liverpool Flying School Ltd (G-BNYV)	
G-LFSR	PA-28RT-201 Arrow IV	Liverpool Flying School Ltd (G-JANO)	
G-LFVB	VS.349 Spitfire LF.Vb (EP120)	Patina Ltd	
G-LGAR	Learjet 60	TAG Aviation (UK) Ltd	
G-LGCA	Robin DR.400/180R	London Gliding Club Proprietary Ltd	
G-LGCB	Robin DR.400/180R	London Gliding Club Proprietary Ltd	
G-LGCC	Robin DR 400/180R	London Gliding Club Proprietary Ltd (G-BNXI)	
G-LGEZ	Rutan Long-EZ	P. C. Elliott	
G-LGKD	Gulfstream 550	TAG Aviation (UK) Ltd	
G-LGLG	Cameron Z-210 balloon	Flying Circus SRL/Spain	
G-LGNA	SAAB SF.340B	Loganair Ltd/Flybe.com	

Notes	Reg.	Type	Owner or Operator
	G-LGNB	SAAB SF.340B	Loganair Ltd/Flybe.com
	G-LGNC	SAAB SF.340B	Loganair Ltd/Flybe.com
	G-LGND	SAAB SF.340B	Loganair Ltd/Flybe.com (G-GNTH)
	G-LGNE	SAAB SF.340B	Loganair Ltd/Flybe.com (G-GNTI)
	G-LGNF	SAAB SF.340B	Loganair Ltd/Flybe.com (G-GNTJ)
	G-LGNG	SAAB SF.340B	Loganair Ltd/Flybe.com
	G-LGNH	SAAB SF.340B	Loganair Ltd/Flybe.com
	G-LGNI	SAAB SF.340B	Loganair Ltd/Flybe.com
	G-LGNJ	SAAB SF.340B	Loganair Ltd/Flybe.com
	G-LGNK	SAAB SF.340B	Loganair Ltd/Flybe.com
	G-LGNL	SAAB SF.340B	Loganair Ltd/Flybe.com
	G-LGNM	SAAB SF.340B	Loganair Ltd/Flybe.com
	G-LGNN	SAAB SF.340B	Loganair Ltd/Flybe.com
	G-LGOC	Aero AT-3 R100	London Transport Flying Club Ltd
	G-LHCA	Robinson R22 Beta	London Helicopter Centres Ltd
	G-LHCB	Robinson R22 Beta	London Helicopter Centres Ltd (G-SIVX)
	G-LHCI	Bell 47G-5	Heli-Highland Ltd (G-SOLH/G-AZMB)
	G-LHEL	AS.355F2 Twin Squirrel	Beechview Aviation Ltd
	G-LHER	Czech Sport Aircraft Piper Sport	M. P. Lhermette
	G-LHMS	Eurocopter EC 120B Colibri	Hadley Helicopters Ltd
	G-LHXL	Robinson R44	Lloyd Helicopters Europe Ltd
	G-LIBB	Cameron V-77 balloon	R. J. Mercer
	G-LIBI	Glasflugel Standard Libelle 201B	G. Spreckley
	G-LIBL	Glasflugel Standard Libelle 201B	P. A. Pearson
	G-LIBS	Hughes 369HS	R. J. H. Strong
	G-LIBY	Glasflugel Standard Libelle 201B	R. P. Hardcastle
	G-LICK	Cessna 172N II	Sky Back Ltd (G-BNTR)
	G-LIDA	Hoffmann H36 Dimona	Bidford Airfield Ltd
	G-LIDE	PA-31-350 Navajo Chieftain	Keen Leasing (IOM) Ltd
	G-LIDY	Schleicher ASW-27B	T. Stuart
	G-LILA	Bell 206L-1 LongRanger 2	Lothian Helicopters Ltd (G-NEUF/G-BVVV)
	G-LILP	Shaw Europa XS	G. L. Jennings
	G-LILY	Bell 206B JetRanger 3	T. S. Brown (G-NTBI)
	G-LIMO	Bell 206L-1 LongRanger	Heliplayer Ltd
	G-LIMP	Cameron C-80 balloon	T. & B. Chamberlain
	G-LINC	Hughes 369HS	Wavendon Social Housing Ltd
	G-LINE	AS.355N Twin Squirrel	National Grid Electricity Transmission PLC
	G-LINN	Shaw Europa XS	T. Pond
	G-LINS	Robinson R22 Beta	Heli Air Ltd (G-DMCD/G-OOLI)
	G-LIOA	Lockheed 10A ElectraH (NC5171N) ★	Science Museum/South Kensington
	G-LION	PA-18 Super Cub 135 (R-167)	JG Jones Haulage Ltd
	G-LIOT	Cameron O-77 balloon	N. D. Eliot
	G-LIPE	Robinson R22 Beta	Spiral Wing Ltd (G-BTXJ)
	G-LIPS	Cameron 90 Lips SS balloon	Reach For The Sky Ltd (G-BZBV)
	G-LITE	Rockwell Commander 112A	B. G. Rhodes
	G-LITS	P & M Quik R	A. Dixon
	G-LITZ	Pitts S-1E Special	H. J. Morton
	G-LIVH	Piper J-3C-65 Cub (330238:A-24)	U. E. Allman
	G-LIVS	Schleicher ASH-26E	P. O. Sturley
	G-LIZA	Cessna 340A II	Air Charter Scotland Ltd
	G-LIZI	PA-28 Cherokee 160	G-LIZI Group (G-ARRP)
	G-LIZY	Westland Lysander III (V9673) ★	G. A. Warner/Duxford
	G-LIZZ	PA-E23 Aztec 250E	I. Kazi & T. J. Nathan (G-BBWM)
	G-LJCC	Murphy Rebel	P. H. Hyde
	G-LKTB	PA-28-181 Archer III	Top Cat Aviation Ltd
	G-LLAN	Grob G.109B	J. D. Scott
	G-LLCH	Cessna 172S	N. A. Smith (G-PLBI)
	G-LLEW	Aeromot AMT-200S Super Ximango	Echo Whiskey Ximango Syndicate
	G-LLIZ	Robinson R44 II	W. R. Harford
	G-LLLL	Rolladen-Schneider LS8-18	P. C. Fritche
	G-LLMW	Diamond DA42 Twin Star	Ming W. L.
	G-LLOY	Alpi Pioneer 300	A. R. Lloyd
	G-LMBO	Robinson R44	Jewel Aviation and Technology Ltd
	G-LMLV	Dyn'Aéro MCR-01	G-LMLV Flying Group
	G-LNAA	MDH MD-900 Explorer	Police Aviation Services Ltd
	G-LNCT	MDH MD-900 Explorer	Police Aviation Services Ltd

Reg.	Type	Owner or Operator	Notes
G-LNDS	Robinson R44	MC Air Ltd	
G-LNIG	Flylight Dragonfly	N. R. Henry	
G-LNNE	Van's RV-7	G-LNNE Group	
G-LNTY	AS.355F1 Twin Squirrel	Sky Select Ltd (G-ECOS/G-DORL/G-BPVB)	
G-LOAD	Dan Rihn DR.107 One Design	M. J. Clark	
G-LOAN	Cameron N-77 balloon	P. Lawman	
G-LOBO	Cameron O-120 balloon	Solo Aerostatics	
G-LOCH	Piper J-3C-90 Cub	M. C. & M. R. Greenland	
G-LOFB	Lockheed L.188CF Electra	Atlantic Airlines Ltd	
G-LOFC	Lockheed L.188CF Electra	Atlantic Airlines Ltd	
G-LOFE	Lockheed L.188CF Electra	Atlantic Airlines Ltd	
G-LOFM	Maule MX-7-180A	Air Atlantique Ltd	
G-LOFT	Cessna 500 Citation I	Fox Tango (Jersey) Ltd	
G-LOIS	Avtech Jabiru UL	D. W. Newman	
G-LOKI	Ultramagic M-77C balloon	L. J. M. Muir & G. D. Hallett	
G-LOLA	Beech A36 Bonanza	K. Payne	
G-LONE	Bell 206L-1 LongRanger	Central Helicopters Ltd	
G-LOOC	Cessna 172S	Goodwood Road Racing Co.Ltd	
G-LOON	Cameron C-60 balloon	C. Wolstenholme	
G-LOOP	Pitts S-1C Special	D. Shutter	
G-LORC	PA-28-161 Cadet	Sherburn Aero Club Ltd	
G-LORD	PA-34-200T Seneca II	M. A. Rooney	
G-LORN	Avions Mudry CAP-10B	J. D. Gailey	
G-LORR	PA-28-181 Archer III	S. J. Sylvester	
G-LORT	Light Aero Avid Speedwing 4	L. M. Thomas	
G-LORY	Thunder Ax4-31Z balloon	A. J. Moore	
G-LOSI	Cameron Z-105 balloon	Aeropubblicita Vicenza SRL/Italy	
G-LOSM	Gloster Meteor NF.11 (WM167)	Aviation Heritage Ltd	
G-LOST	Denney Kitfox Mk 3	J. H. S. Booth	
G-LOSY	Aerotechnik EV-97 Eurostar	C. D. Reeves	
G-LOTA	Robinson R44	Rahtol Ltd	
G-LOTI	Bleriot XI (replica) ★	Brooklands Museum Trust Ltd	
G-LOVB	BAe Jetstream 3102	Sky Aeronautical Ltd (G-BLCB)	
G-LOWS	Sky 77-24 balloon	A. J. Byrne & D. J. Bellinger	
G-LOYA	Cessna FR.172J	K. A. D. Mitchell (G-BLVT)	
G-LOYD	Aérospatiale SA.341G Gazelle 1	I. G. Lloyd (G-SFTC)	
G-LOYN	Robinson R44 II	C. J. Siva-Jothy	
G-LPAD	Lindstrand LBL-105A balloon	Line Packaging & Display Ltd	
G-LPIN	P & M Aviation Quik R	Arnold Gilpin Associates Ltd	
G-LREE	Grob G.109B	G-LREE Group	
G-LRGE	Lindstrand LBL-330A balloon	Adventure Balloons Ltd	
G-LRSN	Robinson R44	Kidmane Developments Ltd	
G-LSAA	Boeing 757-236	Jet 2 (G-BNSF)	
G-LSAB	Boeing 757-27B	Jet 2 (G-OAHF)	
G-LSAC	Boeing 757-23A	Jet 2	
G-LSAD	Boeing 757-236	Jet 2 (G-OOOS/G-BRJD)	
G-LSAE	Boeing 757-27B	Jet 2	
G-LSAG	Boeing 757-21B	Jet 2	
G-LSAH	Boeing 757-21B	Jet 2	
G-LSAI	Boeing 757-21B	Jet 2	
G-LSAJ	Boeing 757-236	Jet 2 (G-CDUP/G-OOOT/G-BRJJ)	
G-LSAK	Boeing 757-23N	Jet 2	
G-LSCM	Cessna 172S	G. A. Luscombe	
G-LSCP	Rolladen-Schneider LS6-18W	L. G. Blows & M. F. Collins	
G-LSED	Rolladen-Schneider LS6-c	McKnight/Baker Syndicate	
G-LSFB	Rolladen-Schneider LS7-WL	P. Thomson	
G-LSFI	AA-5A Cheetah	J. Ibbotson (G-BGSK)	
G-LSFR	Rolladen-Schneider LS4	A. Mulder	
G-LSFT	PA-28-161 Warrior II	Biggin Hill Flying Club Ltd (G-BXTX)	
G-LSGB	Rolladen-Schneider LS6-b	T. J. Brenton	
G-LSGM	Rolladen-Schneider LS3-17	M. R. W. Crook	
G-LSHI	Colt 77A balloon	J. H. Dobson	
G-LSIF	Rolladen-Schneider LS1-f	R. C. Godden	
G-LSIV	Rolladen-Schneider LS4	264 Syndicate	
G-LSIX	Rolladen-Schneider LS6-18W	D. P. Masson & A. V. W. Nunn	
G-LSJE	Escapade Jabiru(1)	L. S. J. Webb	
G-LSKV	Rolladen-Schneider LS8-18	D. Pitman	

Notes	Reg.	Type	Owner or Operator
	G-LSKY	Mainair Pegasus Quik	G. R. Hall & P. R. Brooker
	G-LSLS	Rolladen-Schneider LS4	288 Syndicate
	G-LSMB	Dassault Falcon 2000EX	Aviation Beauport Ltd
	G-LSPH	Van's RV-8	R. S. Partridge-Hicks
	G-LSTR	Stoddard-Hamilton Glastar	A. Vaughan
	G-LSVI	Rolladen-Schneider LS6-c18	J. Saakwa-Mante
	G-LTFB	PA-28 Cherokee 140	Fly (CI) Ltd (G-AVLU)
	G-LTFC	PA-28 Cherokee 140B	N. M. G. Pearson (G-AXTI)
	G-LTRF	Sportavia Fournier RF-7	E. & N. Hart (G-EHAP)
	G-LTSB	Cameron LTSB-90 balloon	ABC Flights Ltd
	G-LTWA	Robinson R44	L. T. W. Alderman
	G-LUBE	Cameron N-77 balloon	A. C. K. Rawson
	G-LUBY	Jabiru J430	K. Luby
	G-LUCI	Robinson R44 II	ABO Services Ltd (G-CULF)
	G-LUCK	Cessna F.150M	MK Consulting Engineers Ltd
	G-LUCL	Colomban MC-30 Luciole	R. C. Teverson
	G-LUDM	Van's RV-8	D. F. Sargant
	G-LUED	Aero Designs Pulsar	J. C. Anderson
	G-LUEK	Cessna 182T	B. F. Lueken
	G-LUEY	Rans S-7S Courier	S. Garfield
	G-LUKE	Rutan LongEz	R. A. Pearson
	G-LUKY	Robinson R44	Hack Aviation and Executive Aviation Services Ltd
	G-LULA	Cameron C-90 balloon	S. D. Davis
	G-LULI	Robinson R44 II	Luxtronic Ltd
	G-LULU	Grob G.109	A. P. Bowden
	G-LULV	Diamond DA-42 Twin Star	Deltabond Ltd
	G-LUND	Cessna 340 II	Prospect Developments (Northern) Ltd (G-LAST/G-UNDY/G-BBNR)
	G-LUNE	Mainair Pegasus Quik	D. Muir
	G-LUNG	Rotorsport UK MT-03	P. Krysiak & R. H. Sawyer
	G-LUNY	Pitts S-1S Special	G-LUNY Group
	G-LUON	Schleicher ASW-27-18E	P. C. Naegeli
	G-LUPY	Marganski Swift S-1	P. R. J. Conran
	G-LUSC	Luscombe 8E Silvaire	M. Fowler
	G-LUSH	PA-28-151 Warrior	S. Papi
	G-LUSI	Luscombe 8F Silvaire	D. M. Robinson
	G-LUSK	Luscombe 8A Silvaire	M. A. Lamprell & P. J. Laycock (G-BRGG)
	G-LUST	Luscombe 8E Silvaire	C. J. Watson
	G-LUXE	BAe 146-301	BAE Systems (Operations) Ltd (G-SSSH)
	G-LUXY	Cessna 551	Hitachi Capital (UK) plc
	G-LVBF	Lindstrand LBL-330A balloon	Virgin Balloon Flights
	G-LVDC	Bell 206L Long Ranger III	Freshair UK Ltd (G-OFST/G-BXIB)
	G-LVES	Cessna 182S	R. W. & A. M. Glaves (G-ELIE)
	G-LVLV	Canadair CL.604 Challenger	Gama Aviation Ltd
	G-LVPL	Edge XT912 B/Streak III/B	C. D. Connor
	G-LWAY	Robinson R44	MFH Helicopters Ltd
	G-LWDC	Canadair CL600-2A12 Challenger	ISM Aviation Services Ltd
	G-LWNG	Aero Designs Pulsar	C. Moffat (G-OMKF)
	G-LXRS	Bombardier BD-700 Global Express	Profed Partners LLP
	G-LXUS	Alpi Pioneer 300	W. C. Walters
	G-LYAK	IDA Bacau Yakovlev Yak-52	Lee52 Ltd
	G-LYDA	Hoffmann H-36 Dimona	G-LYDA Flying Group
	G-LYDC	PA-31-350 Navajo Chieftain	Atlantic Bridge Aviation Ltd
	G-LYDF	PA-31-350 Navajo Chieftain	Atlantic Bridge Aviation Ltd
	G-LYDS	Schempp-Hirth Nimbus 3T	D. H. Smith
	G-LYFA	IDABacau Yakovlev Yak-52	Fox Alpha Group
	G-LYNC	Robinson R22 Beta II	Airborne Adventures Ltd
	G-LYND	PA-25 Pawnee 235	York Gliding Centre Ltd (G-ASFX/G-BSFZ)
	G-LYNI	Aerotechnik EV-97 Eurostar	G. Evans
	G-LYNK	CFM Shadow Srs DD	B. A. Richards
	G-LYNX	Westland WG.13 Lynx (ZB500)	IHM/Weston-super-Mare
	G-LYPG	Avtech Jabiru UL	A. J. Geary
	G-LYSA	Schleicher ASW-20L	L. A. Humphries
	G-LYTE	Thunder Ax7-77 balloon	G. M. Bulme
	G-LZED	AutoGyro MTO Sport	L. Zivanovic

Reg.	Type	Owner or Operator	Notes
G-LZII	Laser Z200	K. G. Begley	
G-LZZY	PA-28RT-201T Turbo Arrow IV	A. C. Gradidge (G-BMHZ)	
G-MAAN	Shaw Europa XS	P. S. Mann	
G-MAAX	Bell 206L-1 LongRanger 2	Lothian Helicopters Ltd (G-EYLE/G-OCRP/G-BWCU)	
G-MABE	Cessna F.150L	I. D. McClelland (G-BLJP)	
G-MACA	Robinson R22 Beta	Jepar Rotorcraft	
G-MACE	Hughes 369E	West Country Helicopters Ltd	
G-MACH	SIAI-Marchetti SF.260	Cheyne Motors Ltd	
G-MACK	PA-28R Cherokee Arrow 200-II	M. D. Hinge	
G-MACN	Cirrus SR22	J. D. M. Tickell	
G-MACP	Bombardier CL600-2B16 Challenger	Ocean Sky Aircraft Management Ltd (G-CGFF/G-OCSF)	
G-MADV	P & M Quik GT450	D. A. Valentine	
G-MAFA	Cessna F.406	Directflight Ltd (G-DFLT)	
G-MAFB	Cessna F.406	Directflight Ltd	
G-MAFE	Dornier 228-202K	FR Aviation Ltd (G-OALF/G-MLDO)	
G-MAFF	BN-2T Turbine Islander	FR Aviation Ltd (G-BJEO)	
G-MAFI	Dornier 228-202K	FR Aviation Ltd	
G-MAFT	Diamond DA.40 Star	Atlantic Flight Training Ltd	
G-MAGC	Cameron Grand Illusion SS balloon	Magical Adventures Ltd	
G-MAGG	Pitts S-1SE Special	O. T. Elmer	
G-MAGK	Schleicher ASW-20L	A. G. K. Mackenzie	
G-MAGL	Sky 77-24 balloon	RCM SRL/Luxembourg	
G-MAGZ	Robin DR.400/500	T. J. Thomas	
G-MAIE	PA-32RT-301T Turbo Saratoga II TC	Sub Marine Services Ltd	
G-MAIK	PA-34-220T Seneca V	Air Prive SA	
G-MAIN	Mainair Blade 912	D. P. Pryke	
G-MAIR	PA-34-200T Seneca II	Bristol Flying Centre Ltd	
G-MAJA	BAe Jetstream 4102	Eastern Airways	
G-MAJB	BAe Jetstream 4102	Eastern Airways (G-BVKT)	
G-MAJC	BAe Jetstream 4102	Eastern Airways (G-LOGJ)	
G-MAJD	BAe Jetstream 4102	Eastern Airways (G-WAWR)	
G-MAJE	BAe Jetstream 4102	Eastern Airways (G-LOGK)	
G-MAJF	BAe Jetstream 4102	Eastern Airways (G-WAWL)	
G-MAJG	BAe Jetstream 4102	Eastern Airways (G-LOGL)	
G-MAJH	BAe Jetstream 4102	Eastern Airways (G-WAYR)	
G-MAJI	BAe Jetstream 4102	Eastern Airways (G-WAND)	
G-MAJJ	BAe Jetstream 4102	Eastern Airways (G-WAFT)	
G-MAJL	BAe Jetstream 4102	Eastern Airways	
G-MAJP	BAe Jetstream 4100	Eastern Airways	
G-MAJR	DHC.1 Chipmunk 22 (WP805)	Chipmunk Shareholders	
G-MAJS	Airbus A.300B4-605R	Monarch Airlines Ltd	
G-MAJU	BAe Jetstream 4100	Eastern Airways	
G-MAJV	BAe Jetstream 4100	Eastern Airways	
G-MAJW	BAe Jetstream 4100	Eastern Airways	
G-MAJX	BAe Jetstream 4100	Eastern Airways	
G-MAJY	BAe Jetstream 4100	Eastern Airways	
G-MAJZ	BAe Jetstream 4100	Eastern Airways	
G-MAKE	Rotorsport UK Calidus	S. Pearce	
G-MAKI	Robinson R44	Hoe Leasing Ltd	
G-MAKK	Aeroprakt A22-L Foxbat	M. A. McKillop	
G-MAKS	Cirrus SR22	J. E. Morris	
G-MALA	PA-28-181 Archer II	M. & D. Aviation (G-BIIU)	
G-MALC	AA-5 Traveler	B. P. Hogan (G-BCPM)	
G-MALS	Mooney M.20K-231	P. Mouterde	
G-MALT	Colt Flying Hop SS balloon	P. J. Stapley	
G-MALU	Czech Sport Aircraft Sportcruiser	B. Borghi, N. Mastrorillo & P. Spano/Italy	
G-MAMD	Beech B.200 Super King Air	Forest Aviation Ltd	
G-MAML	Robinson R44 II	Barley Mo Ltd	
G-MANC	BAe ATP	Trident Aviation Leasing Services (Jersey) Ltd (G-LOGF)	
G-MANH	BAe ATP	Atlantic Airlines Ltd (G-LOGC/G-OLCC)	
G-MANN	Aérospatiale SA.341G Gazelle 1	MW Helicopters Ltd	
G-MANW	Tri-R Kis	M. T. Manwaring	
G-MANX	FRED Srs 2	S. Styles	
G-MANZ	Robinson R44 II	Meadow Helicopters Ltd	
G-MAPL	Robinson R44	Sky Service SRL/Italy	
G-MAPP	Cessna 402B	Reconnaisance Ventures Ltd	
G-MAPR	Beech A36 Bonanza	M. J. B. Cozens	
G-MARA	Airbus A.321-231	Monarch Airlines Ltd	

Notes	Reg.	Type	Owner or Operator
	G-MARE	Schweizer 269C	The Earl of Caledon
	G-MARO	Skyranger J2.2 (2)	J. F. Northey
	G-MARX	Van's RV-4	The Marx Brothers Flying Group
	G-MARZ	Thruster T.600N 450	S. W. Plume
	G-MASC	Jodel 150A	K. F. & R. Richardson
	G-MASF	PA-28-181 Archer II	Mid-Anglia School of Flying
	G-MASH	Westland-Bell 47G-4A	Kinetic Avionics Ltd (G-AXKU)
	G-MASI	P & M Quik GT450	D. M. Merritt-Holman
	G-MASS	Cessna 152 II	MK Aero Support Ltd (G-BSHN)
	G-MATE	Moravan Zlin Z.50LX	S. A. W. Becker
	G-MATF	Gulfstream G-IV	Westgate Ltd
	G-MATS	Colt GA-42 airship	P. A. Lindstrand
	G-MATT	Robin R.2160	Flew LLP (G-BKRC)
	G-MATX	Pilatus PC-12/45	Air Matrix Ltd
	G-MATY	Robinson R22 Beta	MT Aviation
	G-MATZ	PA-28 Cherokee 140	Midland Air Training School (G-BASI)
	G-MAUK	Colt 77A balloon	B. Meeson
	G-MAUS	Shaw Europa XS	A. P. Ringrose
	G-MAVI	Robinson R22 Beta	Northumbria Helicopters Ltd
	G-MAVV	Aero AT-3 R100	Cunning Plan Development Ltd
	G-MAXG	Pitts S-1S Special	MAXG Group
	G-MAXI	PA-34-200T Seneca II	Draycott Seneca Syndicate Ltd
	G-MAXS	Mainair Pegasus Quik 912S	W. J. Walker
	G-MAXV	Van's RV-4	R. S. Partridge-Hicks
	G-MAYB	Robinson R44	Highmark Aviation Ltd
	G-MAYE	Bell 407	M. Maye
	G-MAZA	Rotorsport UK MT-03	N. Crownshaw & M. Manson
	G-MAZY†	DH.82A Tiger Moth ★	Newark Air Museum
	G-MBAA	Hiway Skytrike Mk 2	M. J. Aubrey
	G-MBAB	Hovey Whing-Ding II	M. J. Aubrey
	G-MBAD	Weedhopper JC-24A	M. Stott
	G-MBAF	R. J. Swift 3	C. G. Wrzesien
	G-MBAW	Pterodactyl Ptraveller	J. C. K. Scardifield
	G-MBBB	Skycraft Scout 2	A. J. & B. Chalkley
	G-MBBJ	Hiway Demon	M. J. Aubrey
	G-MBBM	Eipper Quicksilver MX	J. Brown
	G-MBCJ	Mainair Sports Tri-Flyer	R. A. Smith
	G-MBCK	Eipper Quicksilver MX	P. Rowbotham
	G-MBCL	Sky-Trike/Typhoon	P. J. Callis
	G-MBCX	Airwave Nimrod 165	M. Maylor
	G-MBDG	Eurowing Goldwing	A. J. Glynn
	G-MBDL	AES Lone Ranger ★	North East Aircraft Museum
	G-MBDM	Southdown Sigma Trike	A. R. Prentice
	G-MBET	MEA Mistral Trainer	B. H. Stephens
	G-MBGF	Twamley Trike	T. B. Woolley
	G-MBHE	American Aerolights Eagle	R. J. Osborne
	G-MBHK	Flexiform Skytrike	K. T. Vinning
	G-MBHZ	Pterodactyl Ptraveller	J. C. K. Scardifield
	G-MBIA	Flexiform Sealander Skytrike	I. P. Cook
	G-MBIT	Hiway Demon Skytrike	K. S. Hodgson
	G-MBIZ	Mainair Tri-Flyer	D. M. A. Templeman/E. F. C. Clapham/ S. P. Slade/W. B. S. Dobie
	G-MBJF	Hiway Skytrike Mk II	C. H. Bestwick
	G-MBJK	American Aerolights Eagle	B. W. Olley
	G-MBJL	Airwave Nimrod	A. G. Lowe
	G-MBJM	Striplin Lone Ranger	C. K. Brown
	G-MBKY	American Aerolight Eagle	M. J. Aubrey
	G-MBKZ	Hiway Skytrike	S. I. Harding
	G-MBLU	Southdown Lightning L.195	C. R. Franklin
	G-MBMG	Rotec Rally 2B	J. R. Pyper
	G-MBOF	Pakes Jackdaw	L. G. Pakes
	G-MBOH	Microlight Engineering Mistral	N. A. Bell
	G-MBPB	Pterodactyl Ptraveller	N. A. Bell
	G-MBPJ	Moto-Delta	J. B. Jackson
	G-MBPX	Eurowing Goldwing	A. R. Channon
	G-MBRB	Electraflyer Eagle 1	R. C. Bott
	G-MBRD	American Aerolights Eagle	R. J. Osborne
	G-MBRH	Ultraflight Mirage Mk II	R. W. F. Boarder
	G-MBSX	Ultraflight Mirage II	C. J. Draper
	G-MBTH	Whittaker MW4	M. W. J. Whittaker
	G-MBTJ	Solar Wings Microlight	H. A. Comber

Reg.	Type	Owner or Operator	Notes
G-MBTW	Raven Vector 600	W. A. Fuller	
G-MBUZ	Wheeler Scout Mk II	A. C. Thorne	
G-MBYI	Ultraflight Lazair	C. M. Mackinnon	
G-MBYL	Huntair Pathfinder	S. Porter	
G-MBYM	Eipper Quicksilver MX	M. P. Harper & L. L. Perry	
G-MBZO	Tri-Pacer 330	A. N. Burrows	
G-MBZV	American Aerolights Eagle	M. J. Aubrey	
G-MCAB	Gardan GY-201 Minicab	P. G. Hooper	
G-MCAI	Robinson R44 II	M. C. Allen	
G-MCAN	Agusta A109S Grand	Cannon Air LLP	
G-MCAP	Cameron C-80 balloon	L. D. Thurgar	
G-MCCF	Thruster T.600N	C. C. F. Fuller	
G-MCCY	IDA Bacau Yakolev Yak-52	D. P. McCoy/Ireland	
G-MCDB	VS.361 Spitfire LF.IX	M. Collenette	
G-MCEL	Pegasus Quantum 15-912	F. Hodgson	
G-MCJL	Pegasus Quantum 15-912	Lincoln Enterprises Ltd	
G-MCLY	Cessna 172P	McAully Flying Group Ltd	
G-MCMC	SOCATA TBM-700	SogestaoAdministraca Gerencia SA	
G-MCMS	Aero Designs Pulsar	R. J. Bost	
G-MCOW	Lindstrand LBL-77A balloon	S. & S. Villiers	
G-MCOX	Fuji FA.200-180AO	W. Surrey Engineering (Shepperton) Ltd	
G-MCOY	Flight Design CT2K	C. & P. Moore	
G-MCPI	Bell 206B JetRanger 3	Castle Air Charters Ltd (G-ONTB)	
G-MCRO	Dyn'Aero MCR-01	M. K. Faro	
G-MCUB	Escapade	W. H. Bliss	
G-MCXV	Colomban MC.15 Cri-Cri	P. C. Appleton	
G-MDAC	PA-28-181 Archer II	S. A. Nicklen	
G-MDAY	Cessna 170B	M. Day	
G-MDBA	Dassault Falcon 2000	TAG Aviation (UK) Ltd	
G-MDBC	Pegasus Quantum 15-912	J. H. Bradbury	
G-MDBD	Airbus A.330-243	Thomas Cook Airlines Ltd	
G-MDDT	Robinson R44 II	M. D. Tracey	
G-MDGE	Robinson R22 Beta	C. J. Siva-Jothy (G-OGOG/G-TILL)	
G-MDJE	Cessna 208 Caravan 1 (amphibian)	Loch Lomond Seaplanes Ltd	
G-MDJN	Beech 95-B55 Baron	WAFO Schnecken und Zylinder GmbH (G-SUZI/G-BAXR)	
G-MDKD	Robinson R22 Beta	Euro Systems Projects Ltd	
G-MDPI	Agusta A109A-II	Langfast Ltd (G-PERI/G-EXEK/G-SLNE/ G-EEVS/G-OTSL)	
G-MEDF	Airbus A.321-231	bmi British Midland	
G-MEDG	Airbus A.321-231	bmi British Midland	
G-MEDH	Airbus A.320-232	bmi British Midland	
G-MEDJ	Airbus A.321-232	bmi British Midland	
G-MEDK	Airbus A.320-232	bmi British Midland	
G-MEDL	Airbus A.321-231	bmi British Midland	
G-MEDM	Airbus A.321-231	bmi British Midland	
G-MEDN	Airbus A.321-231	bmi British Midland	
G-MEDU	Airbus A.321-231	bmi British Midland	
G-MEDX	Agusta A109E Power	Sloane Helicopters Ltd	
G-MEEE	Schleicher ASW-20L	T. E. Macfadyen	
G-MEET	Learjet 40	TAG Aviation (UK) Ltd	
G-MEGA	PA-28R-201T Turbo Arrow III	H. de Vries	
G-MEGG	Shaw Europa XS	M. E. Mavers	
G-MEGN	Beech B200 Super King Air	Dragonfly Aviation Services LLP	
G-MEGP	Bombardier BD-100-1A10 Challenger 300	Marcus Evans (Aviation) Ltd	
G-MEGS	Cessna 172S	The Cambridge Aero Club Ltd	
G-MELL	CZAW Sportcruiser	G. A. & J. A. Mellins	
G-MELS	PA-28-181 Archer III	P. J. Sowood	
G-MELT	Cessna F.172H	Falcon Aviation Ltd (G-AWTI)	
G-MEME	PA-28R-201 Arrow III	Henry J. Clare Ltd	
G-MENU	Robinson R44 II	Eagles in Flight Ltd	
G-MEOW	CFM Streak Shadow	G. J. Moor	
G-MEPU	Rotorsport UK MT-03	M. C. Elliott	
G-MERC	Colt 56A balloon	A. F. & C. D. Selby	
G-MERE	Lindstrand LBL-77A balloon	R. D. Baker	
G-MERF	Grob G.115A	G-MERF Group	
G-MERL	PA-28RT-201 Arrow IV	W. T. Jenkins	
G-MESH	CZAW Sportcruiser	M. E. S. Heaton	

Notes	Reg.	Type	Owner or Operator
	G-METH	Cameron C-90 balloon	A. & D. Methley
	G-MEUP	Cameron A-120 balloon	I. Bentley
	G-MFAC	Cessna F.172H	Cezzy Flying Group (G-AVGZ)
	G-MFEF	Cessna FR.172J	M. & E. N. Ford
	G-MFHI	Shaw Europa	Hi Fliers
	G-MFLA	Robin HR200/120B	Multiflight Ltd (G-HHUK)
	G-MFLB	Robin HR200/120B	Multiflight Ltd (G-BXOR)
	G-MFLC	Robin HR200/120B	Multiflight Ltd (G-BXGW)
	G-MFLI	Cameron V-90 balloon	J. M. Percival
	G-MFLJ	P & M Quik GT450	M. F. Jakeman
	G-MFLM	Cessna F.152 II	Multiflight Ltd (G-BFFC)
	G-MFLY	Mainair Rapier	J. J. Tierney
	G-MFMF	Bell 206B JetRanger 3	Western Power Distribution (South West) PLC (G-BJNJ)
	G-MFMM	Scheibe SF.25C Falke	J. E. Selman
	G-MGAN	Robinson R44	A. Taylor
	G-MGCA	Jabiru Aircraft Jabiru UL	K. D. Pearce
	G-MGCB	Pegasus XL-Q	M. G. Gomez
	G-MGCK	Whittaker MW6-S FT	G-MGCK Group
	G-MGDL	Pegasus Quantum 15	M. J. Buchanan
	G-MGEC	Rans S.6-ESD-XL Coyote II	Mike and Andy Group
	G-MGEF	Pegasus Quantum 15	G. D. Castell
	G-MGFK	Pegasus Quantum 15	F. A. A. Kay
	G-MGGG	Pegasus Quantum 15	R. A. Beauchamp
	G-MGGT	CFM Streak Shadow SAM	D. R. Stansfield
	G-MGGV	Pegasus Quantum 15-912	K. Loder
	G-MGMC	Pegasus Quantum 15	G. J. Slater
	G-MGMM	PA-18 Super Cub 150	Alice's Flying Group
	G-MGND	Rans S.6-ESD Coyote IIXL	Moorside Aviation Ltd
	G-MGNE	Embraer EMB-505 Phenom 300	Flairjet Ltd
	G-MGOD	Medway Raven	A. Wherrett/N. R. Andrew/D. J. Millward
	G-MGOO	Renegade Spirit UK Ltd	P. J. Dale
	G-MGPA	Ikarus C42 FB100	S. Ashley
	G-MGPD	Pegasus XL-R	H. T. Mounfield
	G-MGPH	CFM Streak Shadow	V. C. Readhead (G-RSPH)
	G-MGPX	Kolb Twinstar Mk.3 Extra	S. P. Garton
	G-MGRH	Quad City Challenger II	A. C. T. Hardy
	G-MGTG	Pegasus Quantum 15	R. B. Milton (G-MZIO)
	G-MGTR	Hunt Wing	A. C. Ryall
	G-MGTV	Thruster T.600N 450	R. Bingham
	G-MGTW	CFM Shadow Srs DD	G. T. Webster
	G-MGUN	Cyclone AX2000	D. A. Perkins
	G-MGUY	CFM Shadow Srs BD	Shadow Flight Centre Ltd
	G-MGWH	Thruster T300	J. J. Hill
	G-MGWI	Robinson R44	Ed Murray and Sons Ltd (G-BZEF)
	G-MHAR	PA-42-720 Cheyenne IIIA	BAE Systems (Operations) Ltd
	G-MHCB	Enstrom 280C	Springbank Aviation Ltd
	G-MHCE	Enstrom F-28A	Wyke CommercialServices (G-BBHD)
	G-MHCJ	Enstrom F-28C-UK	Paradise Helicopters (G-CTRN)
	G-MHCK	Enstrom 280FX	D. Shakespeare (G-BXXB)
	G-MHCM	Enstrom 280FX	Kingswood Bank LLP (G-IBWF/G-ZZWW/G-BSIE)
	G-MHGS	Stoddard-Hamilton Glastar	M. Henderson
	G-MHJK	Diamond DA42 Twin Star	Plane Talking Ltd
	G-MHMH	Agusta-Bell 206B JetRanger II	Helicopter Hire LLP (G-HOLZ/G-CDBT)
	G-MHMR	Pegasus Quantum 15-912	L. Zivanovic
	G-MHRV	Van's RV-6A	M. R. Harris
	G-MICE	Cessna 510 Citation Mustang	Fteron Ltd
	G-MICH	Robinson R22 Beta	Tiger Helicopters Ltd (G-BNKY)
	G-MICI	Cessna 182S	Steve Parrish Racing (G-WARF)
	G-MICK	Cessna F.172N	Branscombe Airfield Ltd
	G-MICY	Everett Srs 1 gyroplane	D. M. Hughes
	G-MIDD	PA-28 Cherokee 140	Midland Air Training School (G-BBDD)
	G-MIDG	Midget Mustang	C. E. Bellhouse
	G-MIDO	Airbus A.320-232	bmi british midland
	G-MIDS	Airbus A.320-232	bmi british midland
	G-MIDT	Airbus A.320-232	bmi british midland
	G-MIDX	Airbus A.320-232	bmi british midland
	G-MIDY	Airbus A.320-232	bmi british midland

Reg.	Type	Owner or Operator	Notes
G-MIFF	Robin DR.400/180	G. E. Snushall	
G-MIGG	WSK-Mielec LiM-5 (1211) ★	D. Miles (G-BWUF)	
G-MIII	Extra EA.300/L	Angels High Ltd	
G-MIKE	Brookland Hornet	M. H. J. Goldring	
G-MIKI	Rans S.6-ESA Coyote II	S. P. Slade	
G-MIKS	Robinson R44 II	M. Glastyonbury	
G-MILA	Cessna F.172N	P. J. Miller	
G-MILD	Scheibe SF.25C Falke	The Borders (Milfield) Gliding Club Ltd	
G-MILE	Cameron N-77 balloon	Miles Air Ltd	
G-MILF	Harmon Rocket II	E. Stinton	
G-MILI	Bell 206B JetRanger 3	Wsetflor AG) Ltd	
G-MILN	Cessna 182Q	Meon Hill Farms (Stockbridge) Ltd	
G-MILO	Cessna T.303	Fortisair Ltd	
G-MIME	Shaw Europa	P. Lewis & N. G. Ley	
G-MIND	Cessna 404	Reconnaissance Ventures Ltd	
G-MINN	Lindstrand LBL-90A balloon	S. M. & D. Johnson (G-SKKC/G-OHUB)	
G-MINS	Nicollier HN.700 Menestrel II	R. Fenion	
G-MINT	Pitts S-1S Special	T. G. Sanderson	
G-MIOO	M.100 Student ★	Museum of Berkshire Aviation/Woodley (G-APLK)	
G-MIRA	Jabiru SP-340	C. P. L. Helson/Belgium (G-LUMA)	
G-MIRM	Stinson HW-75 Voyager	M. Howells (G-BMSA/G-BCUM)	
G-MIRN	Remos GX	M. Kurkic	
G-MISH	Cessna 182R	Graham Churchill Plant Ltd (G-RFAB/G-BIXT)	
G-MISJ	CZAW Sportcruiser	M. T. Dawson	
G-MISS	Taylor JT.2 Titch	D. Beale	
G-MITE	Raj Hamsa X'Air Falcon	R. Hooper & T. G. V. Oyston & R. Hooper	
G-MITZ	Cameron N-77 balloon	Colt Car Co Ltd	
G-MJAD	Eipper Quicksilver MX	J. McCullough	
G-MJAE	American Aerolights Eagle	T. B. Woolley	
G-MJAJ	Eurowing Goldwing	M. J. Aubrey	
G-MJAM	Eipper Quicksilver MX	J. C. Larkin	
G-MJAN	Hiway Skytrike	G. M. Sutcliffe	
G-MJBK	Swallow B	M. A. Newbould	
G-MJBL	American Aerolights Eagle	B. W. Olley	
G-MJBS	Ultralight Stormbuggy	G. I. Sargeant	
G-MJCU	Tarjani	J. K. Ewing	
G-MJDE	Huntair Pathfinder	P. Rayson	
G-MJDJ	Hiway Skytrike Demon	A. J. Cowan	
G-MJDP	Eurowing Goldwing	B. L. R. J. Keeping	
G-MJEO	American Aerolights Eagle	A. M. Shaw	
G-MJER	Flexiform Striker	D. S. Simpson	
G-MJFM	Huntair Pathfinder	R. Gillespie & S. P. Girr	
G-MJFX	Skyhook TR-1	M. R. Dean	
G-MJFZ	Hiway Demon/Tri-flyer	A. W. Lowrie	
G-MJHC	Ultrasports Tripacer 330	E. J. Allen	
G-MJHR	Southdown Lightning	B. R. Barnes	
G-MJHV	Hiway Demon 250	A. G. Griffiths	
G-MJIA	Flexiform Striker	D. G. Ellis	
G-MJIC	Ultrasports Puma 330	T. J. Gayton-Polley	
G-MJIR	Eipper Quicksilver MX	H. Feeney	
G-MJJA	Huntair Pathfinder	J. M. Watkins & R. D. Bateman	
G-MJJK	Eipper Quicksilver MXII	J. McCullough	
G-MJKB	Striplin Skyranger	A. P. Booth	
G-MJKO	Goldmarque 250 Skytrike	M. J. Barry	
G-MJKP	Super Scorpion/Sky-Trike ★	Aero Venture	
G-MJKX	Ultralight Skyrider Phantom	L. R. Graham	
G-MJMN	Flexiform Striker/Tri-flyer 330	A. Bishop	
G-MJMR	Solar Wings Typhoon	J. C. S. Jones	
G-MJMS	Hiway Skytrike	D. E. Peace	
G-MJOC	Huntair Pathfinder	A. J. Glynn	
G-MJOE	Eurowing Goldwing	R. J. Osborne	
G-MJPE	Hiway Demon Skytrike	T. G. Elmhirst	
G-MJPV	Eipper Quicksilver MX	F. W. Ellis	
G-MJRL	Eurowing Goldwing	M. Daniels	
G-MJRO	Eurowing Goldwing	T. B. Smith	
G-MJRU	MBA Tiger Cub 440	S. R. Davis	
G-MJSF	Skyrider Airsports Phantom	B. J. Towers	
G-MJSL	Dragon 200	M. J. Aubrey	
G-MJSO	Hiway Skytrike	D. C. Read	
G-MJSP	Romain Tiger Cub 440	A. R. Sunley	
G-MJST	Pterodactyl Ptraveller	B. W. Olley	

Notes	Reg.	Type	Owner or Operator
	G-MJSY	Eurowing Goldwing	A. J. Rex
	G-MJSZ	DH Wasp	J. J. Hill
	G-MJTM	Aerostructure Pipistrelle 2B	A. M. Sirant
	G-MJTX	Skyrider Airsports Phantom	P. D. Coppin
	G-MJTZ	Skyrider Airsports Phantom	B. J. Towers
	G-MJUR	Skyrider Aviation Phantom	M. J. Whiteman-Haywood
	G-MJUW	MBA Tiger Cub 440	D. G. Palmer
	G-MJUX	Skyrider Airsports Phantom	N. Flint
	G-MJVF	CFM Shadow	J. A. Cook
	G-MJVN	Ultrasports Puma 440	R. McGookin
	G-MJVP	Eipper Quicksilver MX II	G. J. Ward
	G-MJVU	Eipper Quicksilver MX II	F. J. Griffith
	G-MJVX	Skyrider Phantom	J. R. Harris
	G-MJVY	Dragon Srs 150	J. C. Craddock
	G-MJWB	Eurowing Goldwing	D. G. Palmer
	G-MJWF	Tiger Cub 440	R. A. & T. Maycock
	G-MJWK	Huntair Pathfinder	D. Young
	G-MJYV	Mainair Triflyer 2 Seat	H. L. Phillips
	G-MJYW	Wasp Gryphon III	P. D. Lawrence
	G-MJZK	Southdown Puma Sprint 440	R. J. Osborne
	G-MKAA	Boeing 747-2S4F	MK Airlines Ltd
	G-MKAK	Colt 77A balloon	A. C. Ritchie
	G-MKAS	PA-28 Cherokee 140	MK Aero Support Ltd (G-BKVR)
	G-MKBA	Boeing 747-2B5F	MK Airlines Ltd
	G-MKCA	Boeing 747-2B5B	MK Airlines Ltd
	G-MKDA	Boeing 747-2B5F	MK Airlines Ltd
	G-MKEA	Boeing 747-249F	MK Airlines Ltd
	G-MKEV	EV-96 Eurostar	K. Laud
	G-MKGA	Boeing 747-2R7F	MK Airlines Ltd
	G-MKHA	Boeing 747-2J6B	MK Airlines Ltd
	G-MKIA	VS.300 Spitfire 1 (P9374)	Mark One Partners LLC
	G-MKKA	Boeing 747-219B	MK Airlines Ltd
	G-MKVB	VS.349 Spitfire LF.VB (BM597)	Historic Aircraft Collection
	G-MKXI	VS.365 Spitfire PR.XI (PL624:R)	P. A. Teichman
	G-MLAL	Jabiru J400	J. M. Pipping
	G-MLAS	Cessna 182E ★	Parachute jump trainer/St. Merryn
	G-MLAW	P & M Quik GT450	S. M. Redding
	G-MLHI	Maule MX-7-180 Star Rocket	Maulehigh (G-BTMJ)
	G-MLJL	Airbus A.330-243	Thomas Cook Airlines Ltd
	G-MLKE	P & M Aviation Quik R	M. A. Scholes
	G-MLLE	CEA DR.200A-B	A. D. Evans
	G-MLWI	Thunder Ax7-77 balloon	M. L. & L. P. Willoughby
	G-MLZZ	Best Off Sky Ranger Swift 912S(1)	D. M. Robbins
	G-MMAC	Dragon Srs.200	J. F. Ashton & J. P. Kirwan
	G-MMAG	MBA Tiger Cub 440	M. J. Aubrey
	G-MMBE	MBA Tiger Cub 440	A. Gannon
	G-MMBL	Southdown Puma	B. J. Farrell
	G-MMBU	Eipper Quicksilver MX II	D. A. Norwood
	G-MMCI	Southdown Puma Sprint	L. A. Davies
	G-MMCV	Solar Wings Typhoon III	G. Addison
	G-MMDF	Southdown Lightning II	J. C. Haigh
	G-MMDN	Flexiform Striker	M. G. Griffiths
	G-MMEK	Medway Hybred 44XL	M. G. J. Bridges
	G-MMFE	Flexiform Striker	W. Camm
	G-MMFV	Flexiform Striker	R. A. Walton
	G-MMGF	MBA Tiger Cub 440	J. G. Boxall
	G-MMGL	MBA Tiger Cub 440	H. E. Dunning
	G-MMGS	Solar Wings Panther XL	R. J. Hood
	G-MMGT	Solar Wings Typhoon	H. Cook
	G-MMGU	Flexiform Sealander	A. D. Cranfield
	G-MMGV	Whittaker MW5 Sorcerer	M. W. J. Whittaker & G. N. Haffey
	G-MMHE	Gemini Sprint	N. L. Zaman
	G-MMHL	Hiway Super Scorpion	E. J. Blyth
	G-MMHN	MBA Tiger Cub 440	M. J. Aubrey
	G-MMHS	SMD Viper	C. J. Meadows
	G-MMIE	MBA Tiger Cub 440	B. M. Olliver
	G-MMIZ	Lightning MkII	D. Coging
	G-MMJD	Southdown Puma Sprint	M. P. Robertshaw
	G-MMJF	Ultrasports Panther Dual 440	J. Benn

Reg.	Type	Owner or Operator	Notes
G-MMJV	MBA Tiger Cub 440	D. G. Palmer	
G-MMKA	Ultrasports Panther Dual	R. S. Wood	
G-MMKM	Flexiform Dual Striker	S. W. Hutchinson	
G-MMKP	MBA Tiger Cub 440	J. W. Beaty	
G-MMKR	Southdown Lightning DS	C. R. Madden	
G-MMKX	Skyrider Phantom 330	G. J. Lampitt	
G-MMLE	Eurowing Goldwing SP	M. J. Aubrey	
G-MMMG	Eipper Quicksilver MXL	J. G. Campbell	
G-MMMH	Hadland Willow	M. J. Hadland	
G-MMML	Dragon 150	M. J. Aubrey	
G-MMMN	Ultrasports Panther Dual 440	C. Downton	
G-MMNB	Eipper Quicksilver MX	M. J. Lindop	
G-MMNC	Eipper Quicksilver MX	W. S. Toulmin	
G-MMNH	Dragon 150	T. J. Barlow	
G-MMNN	Buzzard	E. W. Sherry	
G-MMOB	Southdown Sprint	D. Woolcock	
G-MMOK	Solar Wings Panther XL	R. F. & A. J. Foster	
G-MMOW	Mainair Gemini/Flash	D. P. Quaintrell	
G-MMPH	Southdown Puma Sprint	J. Siddle	
G-MMPL	Flexiform Dual Striker	P. D. Lawrence	
G-MMPO	Mainair Gemini/Flash	M.A Feber	
G-MMPZ	Teman Mono-Fly	H. Smith	
G-MMRH	Highway Skytrike	A. M. Sirant	
G-MMRL	Solar Wings Panther XL	R. J. Hood	
G-MMRN	Southdown Puma Sprint	D. C. Read	
G-MMRP	Mainair Gemini	J. C. S. Jones	
G-MMRW	Flexiform Dual Striker	M. D. Hinge	
G-MMSA	Ultrasports Panther XL	T. W. Thiele & G. Savage	
G-MMSG	Solar Wings Panther XL-S	R. W. McKee	
G-MMSH	Solar Wings Panther XL	I. J. Drake	
G-MMSO	Mainair Tri-Flyer 440	K. A. Maughan	
G-MMSP	Mainair Gemini/Flash	J. Whiteford	
G-MMTD	Mainair Tri-Flyer 330	W. E. Teare	
G-MMTL	Mainair Gemini	K. Birkett	
G-MMTR	Ultrasports Panther	P. M. Kelsey	
G-MMTY	Fisher FP.202U	M. A. Welch	
G-MMUA	Southdown Puma Sprint	M. R. Crowhurst	
G-MMUM	MBA Tiger Cub 440	Coulson Flying Services Ltd	
G-MMUO	Mainair Gemini/Flash	D. R. Howells & B. D. Bastin	
G-MMUV	Southdown Puma Sprint	D. C. Read	
G-MMUW	Mainair Gemini/Flash	J. C. K. Scardifield	
G-MMUX	Gemini Sprint	A. S. Gillespie	
G-MMVA	Southdown Puma Sprint	C. E. Tomkins	
G-MMVH	Southdown Raven	G. W. & K. M. Carwardine	
G-MMVI	Southdown Puma Sprint	G. R. Williams	
G-MMVS	Skyhook Pixie	B. W. Olley	
G-MMWG	Greenslade Mono-Trike	G-MMWG Group	
G-MMWS	Mainair Tri-Flyer	P. H. Risdale	
G-MMWX	Southdown Puma Sprint	G. A. Webb	
G-MMXL	Mainair Gemini Flash	G. W. Warner	
G-MMXO	Southdown Puma Sprint	D. J. Tasker	
G-MMXU	Mainair Gemini/Flash	T. J. Franklin	
G-MMXV	Mainair Gemini/Flash	M. A. Boffin	
G-MMXW	Mainair Gemini/Sprint	A. Hodgson	
G-MMYA	Solar Wings Pegasus XL	R. G. Mason	
G-MMYL	Cyclone 70	A. W. Nancarrow	
G-MMYO	Southdown Puma Sprint	P. R. Whitehouse	
G-MMZA	Mainair Gemini/Flash	G. T. Johnston	
G-MMZD	Mainair Gemini/Flash	P. L. Dowd	
G-MMZG	Ultrasports Panther XL-S	P. W. Maddocks	
G-MMZK	Mainair Gemini/Flash	G. Jones & B. Lee	
G-MMZV	Mainair Gemini/Flash	D. Sauntson	
G-MMZW	Southdown Puma Sprint	M. G. Ashbee	
G-MNAE	Mainair Gemini/Flash	G. C. luddington	
G-MNAI	Ultrasports Panther XL-S	R. G. Cameron	
G-MNAW	Solar Wings Pegasus XL-R	C. T. H. Tenison	
G-MNAZ	Solar Wings Pegasus XL-R	R. W. houldsworth	
G-MNBA	Solar Wings Pegasus XL-R	J. G. H. Featherstone	
G-MNBB	Solar Wings Pegasus XL-R	D. A. Blackston	
G-MNBC	Solar Wings Pegasus XL-R	N. Kelly	
G-MNBF	Mainair Gemini/Flash	P. Mokryk & S. King	

Notes	Reg.	Type	Owner or Operator
	G-MNBG	Mainair Gemini/Flash	T. Barnett
	G-MNBI	Solar Wings Panther XL-S	M. O'Connell
	G-MNBJ	Skyhook Pixie	G. Sykes
	G-MNBM	Southdown Puma Sprint	C. Hall-Gardiner
	G-MNBN	Mainair Gemini/Flash	I. Bond
	G-MNBP	Mainair Gemini/Flash	G. A. Harper
	G-MNBS	Mainair Gemini/Flash	P. A. Comins
	G-MNBT	Mainair Gemini/Flash	R. R. A. Dean
	G-MNCA	Hiway Demon 175	M. A. Sirant
	G-MNCF	Mainair Gemini/Flash	C. F. Janes
	G-MNCG	Mainair Gemini/Flash	J. E. F. Fletcher
	G-MNCM	CFM Shadow Srs B	K. G. D. Macrae
	G-MNCO	Eipper Quicksilver MXII	S. Lawton
	G-MNCP	Southdown Puma Sprint	D. A. Payne
	G-MNCS	Skyrider Airsports Phantom	K. J. Underwood
	G-MNCU	Medway Hybred 44XL	J. E. Evans
	G-MNCV	Medway Hybred 44XL	P. F. Brightmore
	G-MNDC	Mainair Gemini/Flash	M. Medlock
	G-MNDD	Mainair Scorcher Solo	L. Hurman
	G-MNDE	Medway Half Pint	Delta Echo Half Pint Group
	G-MNDM	Mainair Gemini/Flash	J. C. Birkbeck
	G-MNDU	Midland Sirocco 377GB	M. A. Collins
	G-MNDY	Southdown Puma Sprint	A. M. Coupland
	G-MNEG	Mainair Gemini/Flash	A. Sexton/Ireland
	G-MNEH	Mainair Gemini/Flash	I. Rawson
	G-MNER	CFM Shadow Srs B	F. C. Claydon
	G-MNET	Mainair Gemini/Flash	I. P. Stubbins
	G-MNEV	Mainair Gemini/Flash	M. Gardiner
	G-MNEY	Mainair Gemini/Flash	D. A. Spiers
	G-MNFB	Southdown Puma Sprint	C. Lawrence
	G-MNFF	Mainair Gemini/Flash	C. H. Spencer & R. P. Cook
	G-MNFG	Southdown Puma Sprint	M. Ingleton
	G-MNFL	AMF Chevvron	S. S. M. Turner
	G-MNFM	Mainair Gemini/Flash	P. M. Fidell
	G-MNFN	Mainair Gemini/Flash	J. R. Martin
	G-MNFP	Mainair Gemini/Flash	S. E. Walsh
	G-MNGG	Solar Wings Pegasus XL-R	I. D. Mallinson
	G-MNGK	Mainair Gemini/Flash	R. G. Wyatt
	G-MNGM	Mainair Gemini/Flash	R. J. Webb
	G-MNGT	Mainair Gemini/Flash	J. W. Biegus
	G-MNGW	Mainair Gemini/Flash	F. R. Stephens
	G-MNHD	Solar Wings Pegasus XL-R	P. D. Stiles
	G-MNHE	Solar Wings Pegasus XL-R	D.Stevens
	G-MNHF	Solar Wings Pegasus XL-R	J. E. Cox
	G-MNHH	Solar Wings Panther XL-S	F. J. Williams
	G-MNHI	Solar Wings Pegasus XL-R	R. W. Matthews
	G-MNHJ	Solar Wings Pegasus XL-R	C. Council
	G-MNHK	Solar Wings Pegasus XL-R	K. Buckley
	G-MNHL	Solar Wings Pegasus XL-R	The Microlight School (Lichfield) Ltd
	G-MNHM	Solar Wings Pegasus XL-R	P. A. Howell
	G-MNHN	Solar Wings Pegasus XL-R	M. Devlin
	G-MNHR	Solar Wings Pegasus XL-R	B. D. Jackson
	G-MNHT	Solar Wings Pegasus XL-R	J. W. Coventry
	G-MNHZ	Mainair Gemini/Flash	I. O. S. Ross
	G-MNIA	Mainair Gemini/Flash	A. E. Dix
	G-MNID	Mainair Gemini/Flash	M. I. Potts
	G-MNIG	Mainair Gemini/Flash	A. B. Woods
	G-MNIH	Mainair Gemini/Flash	N. H. S. Insall
	G-MNII	Mainair Gemini/Flash	R. F. Finnis
	G-MNIK	Pegasus Photon	M. Belemet
	G-MNIM	Maxair Hummer	K. Wood
	G-MNIW	Airwave Nimrod/Tri-Flyer	G. S. Highley
	G-MNIZ	Mainair Gemini/Flash	A. G. Power
	G-MNJB	Southdown Raven	W. Flood
	G-MNJD	Southdown Puma Sprint	S. D. Smith
	G-MNJG	Gemini Sprint MS	S. Earl
	G-MNJJ	Solar Wings Pegasus Flash	P. A. Shelley
	G-MNJL	Solar Wings Pegasus Flash	S. D. Thomas
	G-MNJN	Solar Wings Pegasus Flash	G. J. Crago
	G-MNJR	Solar Wings Pegasus Flash	M. G. Ashbee
	G-MNJS	Southdown Puma Sprint	E. A. Frost
	G-MNJX	Medway Hybred 44XL	H. A. Stewart

Reg.	Type	Owner or Operator	Notes
G-MNKB	Solar Wings Pegasus Photon	M. E. Gilbert	
G-MNKC	Solar Wings Pegasus Photon	K. B. Woods	
G-MNKD	Solar Wings Pegasus Photon	A. M. Sirant	
G-MNKE	Solar Wings Pegasus Photon	G. Forster	
G-MNKG	Solar Wings Pegasus Photon	S. N. Robson	
G-MNKK	Solar Wings Pegasus Photon	M. E. Gilbert	
G-MNKM	MBA Tiger Cub 440	A. R. Sunley	
G-MNKN	Skycraft Scout Mk.3-3R	M. A. Aubrey	
G-MNKO	Solar Wings Pegasus Flash	T. A. Goundry	
G-MNKP	Solar Wings Pegasus Flash	I. N. Miller	
G-MNKU	Southdown Puma Sprint	S. P. O'Hannrachain	
G-MNKW	Solar Wings Pegasus Flash	S. P. Halford	
G-MNKX	Solar Wings Pegasus Flash	T. A. Newton	
G-MNKZ	Southdown Raven	G. B. Gratton	
G-MNLI	Mainair Gemini/Flash	P. M. Fessi	
G-MNLT	Southdown Raven	J. L. Stachini	
G-MNLY	Mainair Gemini/Flash	P. D. Parry	
G-MNMC	Mainair Gemini Sprint	G. A. Davidson	
G-MNMD	Southdown Raven	P. G. Overall	
G-MNMG	Mainair Gemini/Flash	N. A. M. Beyer-Kay	
G-MNMK	Solar Wings Pegasus XL-R	A. F. Smallacombe	
G-MNMM	Aerotech MW5 Sorcerer	S. F. N. Warnell	
G-MNMU	Southdown Raven	M. J. Curley	
G-MNMV	Mainair Gemini/Flash	S. Staig	
G-MNMW	Aerotech MW6 Merlin	E. F. Clapham	
G-MNMY	Cyclone 70	N. R. Beale	
G-MNNA	Southdown Raven	D. & G. D. Palfrey	
G-MNNF	Mainair Gemini/Flash	W. J. Gunn	
G-MNNG	Solar Wings Photon	K. B. Woods	
G-MNNL	Mainair Gemini/Flash II	C. L. Rumney	
G-MNNM	Mainair Scorcher Solo	L. L. Perry & S. R. Leeper	
G-MNNO	Southdown Raven	M. J. Robbins	
G-MNNS	Eurowing Goldwing	J. S. R. Moodie	
G-MNNV	Mainair Gemini/Flash II	F. Whitfield	
G-MNNY	Solar Wings Pegasus Flash	C. W. Payne	
G-MNPC	Mainair Gemini/Flash	M. S. McGimpsey	
G-MNPZ	Mainair Scorcher Solo	S. Stevens	
G-MNRD	Ultraflight Lazair IIIE	Sywell Lazair Group	
G-MNRE	Mainair Scorcher Solo	A. P. Pearce	
G-MNRI	Hornet Dual Trainer	R. H. Goll	
G-MNRM	Hornet Dual Trainer	I. C. Cannan	
G-MNRS	Southdown Raven	M. C. Newman	
G-MNRT	Midland Ultralights Sirocco	R. F. Hinton	
G-MNRX	Mainair Gemini/Flash II	R. Downham	
G-MNRZ	Mainair Scorcher Solo	R. Pattrick & K. Medd	
G-MNSJ	Mainair Gemini/Flash	P. Cooney	
G-MNSL	Southdown Raven X	P. B. Robinson	
G-MNSY	Southdown Raven X	L. A. Hosegood	
G-MNTC	Southdown Raven X	D. S. Bancarlari	
G-MNTD	Aerial Arts Chaser 110SX	B. Richardson	
G-MNTE	Southdown Raven X	E. Foster	
G-MNTK	CFM Shadow Srs B	M. J. Bromley	
G-MNTP	CFM Shadow Srs B	E. G. White	
G-MNTV	Mainair Gemini/Flash II	A.M. Sirant	
G-MNUF	Mainair Gemini/Flash II	K. Jones	
G-MNUI	Skyhook Cutlass Dual	M. Holling	
G-MNUR	Mainair Gemini/Flash II	J. S. Hawkins	
G-MNUU	Southdown Raven X	P. N. Jackson	
G-MNVB	Solar Wings Pegasus XL-R	L. R. Ingram	
G-MNVE	Solar Wings Pegasus XL-R	M. P. Aris	
G-MNVG	Solar Wings Pegasus Flash II	D. J. Ward	
G-MNVH	Solar Wings Pegasus Flash II	J. A. Clarke & C. Hall	
G-MNVI	CFM Shadow Srs B	D. R. C. Pugh	
G-MNVJ	CFM Shadow Srs CD	G. Mudd	
G-MNVK	CFM Shadow Srs B	A. K. Atwell	
G-MNVL	Aerial Arts 130SX/Half Pint	P. J. Hopkins	
G-MNVO	Hovey Whing-Ding II	C. Wilson	
G-MNVT	Mainair Gemini/Flash II	ACB Hydraulics	
G-MNVV	Mainair Gemini/Flash II	T. Wilbor	
G-MNVW	Mainair Gemini/Flash II	J. C. Munro-Hunt	
G-MNVZ	Solar Wings Pegasus Photon	J. J. Russ	
G-MNWG	Southdown Raven X	D. Murray	

Notes	Reg.	Type	Owner or Operator
	G-MNWI	Mainair Gemini/Flash II	I. E. Chapman
	G-MNWL	Aerial Arts 130SX	E. H. Snook
	G-MNXE	Southdown Raven X	A. E. Silvey
	G-MNXF	Southdown Raven X	D. E. Gwenin
	G-MNXG	Southdown Raven X	E. M. & M. A. Williams
	G-MNXO	Medway Hybred 44XLR	R. P. Taylor
	G-MNXS	Mainair Gemini/Flash II	J. M. Macdonald
	G-MNXU	Mainair Gemini/Flash II	J. M. Hucker
	G-MNXX	CFM Shadow Srs BD	M. Nazm
	G-MNXZ	Whittaker MW5 Sorcerer	A. J. Glynn
	G-MNYA	Solar Wings Pegasus Flash II	C. Trollope
	G-MNYC	Solar Wings Pegasus XL-R	J. S. Hawkins
	G-MNYD	Aerial Arts 110SX Chaser	B. Richardson
	G-MNYE	Aerial Arts 110SX Chaser	R. J. Ripley
	G-MNYF	Aerial Arts 110SX Chaser	R. W. Twamley
	G-MNYM	Southdown Raven X	R. L. Davis
	G-MNYP	Southdown Raven X	A. G. Davies
	G-MNYU	Pegasus XL-R	G. L. Turner
	G-MNYW	Solar Wings Pegasus XL-R	M. P. Waldock
	G-MNYX	Solar Wings Pegasus XL-R	P. F. Mayes
	G-MNZB	Mainair Gemini/Flash II	P. A. Ryder
	G-MNZC	Mainair Gemini/Flash II	C. J. Whittaker
	G-MNZD	Mainair Gemini/Flash II	N. D. Carter
	G-MNZF	Mainair Gemini/Flash II	M. Lally
	G-MNZJ	CFM Shadow Srs BD	E. W. Laidlaw
	G-MNZK	Solar Wings Pegasus XL-R	P. J. Appleby
	G-MNZP	CFM Shadow Srs B	J. G. Wakeford
	G-MNZR	CFM Shadown Srs BD	G. Taylor
	G-MNZS	Aerial Arts 130SX	N. R. Beale
	G-MNZU	Eurowing Goldwing	P. D. Coppin & P. R. Millen
	G-MNZW	Southdown Raven X	T. A. Willcox
	G-MNZZ	CFM Shadow Srs B	Shadow Aviation Ltd
	G-MOAC	Beech F33A Bonanza	R. M. Camrass
	G-MOAN	Aeromot AMT-200S Super Ximango	A. E. Mayhew
	G-MODE	Eurocopter EC 120B	Cardy Construction Ltd
	G-MOFB	Cameron O-120 balloon	D. M. Moffat
	G-MOFZ	Cameron O-90 balloon	D. M. Moffat
	G-MOGI	AA-5A Cheetah	J. G. Stewart (G-BFMU)
	G-MOGS	CZAW Sportcruiser	J. M. Oliver
	G-MOGY	Robinson R22 Beta	Northumbria Helicopters Ltd
	G-MOKE	Cameron V-77 balloon	G-MOKE ASBC/Luxembourg
	G-MOLE	Taylor JT.2 Titch	R. Calverley
	G-MOLO	Pilatus PC-12/47E	Breckenridge Ltd
	G-MOLL	PA-32-301T Turbo Saratoga	M. S. Bennett
	G-MOMA	Thruster T.600N 450	S. W. Turley (G-CCIB)
	G-MONI	Monnett Moni	R. M. Edworthy
	G-MONJ	Boeing 757-2T7	Monarch Airlines Ltd
	G-MONK	Boeing 757-2T7	Monarch Airlines Ltd
	G-MONR	Airbus A.300-605R	Monarch Airlines Ltd
	G-MONS	Airbus A.300-605R	Monarch Airlines Ltd
	G-MONX	Airbus A.320-212	Monarch Airlines Ltd
	G-MOOR	SOCATA TB10 Tobago	P. D. Kirkham (G-MILK)
	G-MOOS	P.56 Provost T.1 (XF690)	H. Cooke (G-BGKA)
	G-MOOV	CZAW Sportcruiser	G-MOOV Syndicate
	G-MOPS	Best Off Sky Ranger Swift 912S	P. Stretton
	G-MOSA	Morane Saulnier MS317	A. C. Whitehead
	G-MOSS	Beech D55 Baron	D. J. da Costa Marques (G-AWAD)
	G-MOSY	Cameron O-84 balloon	P. L. Mossman
	G-MOTA	Bell 206B JetRanger 3	J. W. Sandle
	G-MOTH	DH.82A Tiger Moth (K2567)	P. T. Szluha
	G-MOTI	Robin DR.400/500	Tango India Flying Group
	G-MOTO	PA-24 Comanche 180	J. J. Woodhouse (G-EDHE/G-ASFH)
	G-MOTR	Enstrom 280C Shark	Vehicle Provider Ltd (G-BGWS)
	G-MOUL	Maule M6-235	M. Klinge
	G-MOUR	HS. Gnat T.1 (XR991)	Heritage Aircraft Ltd
	G-MOUT	Cessna 182T	C. Mountain
	G-MOVE	PA-60-601P Aerostar	Airtime Aviation France Ltd
	G-MOVI	PA-32R-301 Saratoga SP	G-BOON Ltd (G-MARI)
	G-MOWG	Aeroprakt A22-L Foxbat	J. Smith
	G-MOZI	Glasflugel Mosquito	J. Christensen & P. Smith
	G-MOZZ	Avions Mudry CAP-10B	N. Skipworth

Reg.	Type	Owner or Operator	Notes
G-MPAA	PA-28-181 Archer III	MPFC Ltd	
G-MPAC	Ultravia Pelican PL	J. H. Leigh t/a The Clipgate Flying Grp	
G-MPAT	EV-97 TeamEurostar UK	Exodus Airsports Ltd	
G-MPBH	Cessna FA.152	The Moray Flying Club (1996) Ltd (G-FLIC/ G-BILV)	
G-MPBI	Cessna 310R	B. Davies	
G-MPCD	Airbus A.320-212	Monarch Airlines Ltd	
G-MPMP	Bombardier CL600-2B16 Challenger	Patronus Aviation Ltd (G-JMMP)	
G-MPRL	Cessna 210M	Myriad Public Relations Ltd	
G-MPSA	Eurocopter MBB BK-117C-2	Metropolitan Police Authority	
G-MPSB	Eurocopter MBB BK-117C-2	Metropolitan Police Authority	
G-MPSC	Eurocopter MBB BK-117C-2	Metropolitan Police Authority	
G-MPSP	Bombardier CL600-2B16 Challenger	Patronus Aviation Ltd (G-MPCW/G-JMMD)	
G-MPTP	Bombardier CL600-2B16 Challenger	Patronus Aviation Ltd (G-MPJM/G-JMCW)	
G-MPWI	Robin HR.100/210	P. G. Clarkson & S. King	
G-MRAJ	Hughes 369E	A. Jardine	
G-MRAM	Mignet HM.1000 Balerit	R. A. Marven	
G-MRDC	Robinson R44 II	E. M. Montefusco	
G-MRDS	CZAW Sportcruiser	D. I. Scott	
G-MRED	Christavia Mk 1	The Barton Group	
G-MRJJ	Mainair Pegasus Quik	J.H. Sparks	
G-MRJK	Airbus A.320-214	Monarch Airlines Ltd	
G-MRJP	Silence Twister	M. D. Carruthers	
G-MRKS	Robinson R44	TJD Trade Ltd (G-RAYC)	
G-MRKT	Lindstrand LBL-90A balloon	Marketplace Public Relations (London) Ltd	
G-MRLL	NA P-51D Mustang (413521:5Q-B)	M. Hammond	
G-MRLN	Sky 240-24 balloon	Merlin Balloons	
G-MRMJ	Eurocopter AS.365N3 Dauphin 2	Whirligig Ltd	
G-MROC	Pegasus Quantum 15-912	M. A. Metzler	
G-MROD	Van's RV-7A	K. R. Emery	
G-MROO	Cessna 525A Citationjet CJ2	Rooney Air Ltd (G-EEBJ)	
G-MRPH	Murphy Rebel	P. & B. S. Metson	
G-MRRR	Hughes 369E	J. Paxton	
G-MRRY	Robinson R44 II	F. V. Neefs	
G-MRSN	Robinson R22 Beta	Yorkshire Helicopters Ltd	
G-MRST	PA-28 RT-201 Arrow IV	Calverton Flying Group Ltd	
G-MRTN	SOCATA TB10 Tobago	P. A Gange & M. S. Colebrook (G-BHET)	
G-MRTY	Cameron N-77 balloon	R. A. Vale & ptnrs	
G-MRVK	Czech Sport Aircraft Pipersport	M. Farrugia	
G-MRVL	Van's RV-7	L. W. Taylor	
G-MSAL	MS.733 Alcyon (143)	M. Isbister t/a Alcyon Flying Group	
G-MSCM	Denney Kitfox Mk 2	D. J. Thomas (G-BSCM)	
G-MSFC	PA-38-112 Tomahawk	Sherwood Flying Club Ltd	
G-MSFT	PA-28-161 Warrior II	Western Air (Thruxton) Ltd (G-MUMS)	
G-MSIX	Glaser-Dirks DG.800B	G-MSIX Group	
G-MSKY	Ikarus C.42 FB100 VLA	P. M. Yeoman & J. S. Mason	
G-MSON	Cameron Z-90 balloon	K. D. Peirce	
G-MSOO	Revolution Mini 500 helicopter	R. H. Ryan	
G-MSPT	Eurocopter EC 135T2	M Sport Ltd	
G-MSPY	Pegasus Quantum 15-912	B. E. Wagenhauser	
G-MSTG	NA P-51D Mustang (414419:LH-F)	M. Hammond	
G-MSTR	Cameron 110 Monster SS Baloon	ABC Flights Ltd (G-OJOB)	
G-MTAB	Mainair Gemini/Flash II	L. Clarkson	
G-MTAC	Mainair Gemini/Flash II	R. Massey	
G-MTAF	Mainair Gemini/Flash II	A. G. Lister	
G-MTAG	Mainair Gemini/Flash II	M. J. Cowie & J. P. Hardy	
G-MTAH	Mainair Gemini/Flash II	G. F. Atkinson	
G-MTAI	Solar Wings Pegasus XL-R	S. T. Elkington	
G-MTAJ	Solar Wings Pegasus XL-R	S. Lyman	
G-MTAL	Solar Wings Photon	J. W. Coventry	
G-MTAP	Southdown Raven X	M. C. Newman	
G-MTAS	Whittaker MW5 Sorcerer	R. J. Scott	
G-MTAV	Solar Wings Pegasus XL-R	C. L. Harris & S. Fairweather	
G-MTAW	Solar Wings Pegasus XL-R	M. G. Ralph	
G-MTAX	Solar Wings Pegasus XL-R	J. Pool	
G-MTAY	Solar Wings Pegasus XL-R	S. A. McLatchie	
G-MTAZ	Solar Wings Pegasus XL-R	M. O'Connell	
G-MTBB	Southdown Raven X	A. Miller	
G-MTBD	Mainair Gemini/Flash II	I. E. Regan	

Notes	Reg.	Type	Owner or Operator
	G-MTBE	CFM Shadow Srs BD	S. K. Brown
	G-MTBH	Mainair Gemini/Flash II	P. & T. Sludds
	G-MTBJ	Mainair Gemini/Flash II	P. J. & R. M. Perry
	G-MTBL	Solar Wings Pegasus XL-R	R. N. Whiting
	G-MTBN	Southdown Raven X	A. J. & S. E. Crosby-Jones
	G-MTBO	Southdown Raven X	J. Liversuch
	G-MTBP	Aerotech MW5 Sorcerer	L. J. Greenhough
	G-MTBR	Aerotech MW5 Sorcerer	R. Poulter
	G-MTBS	Aerotech MW5 Sorcerer	T. B. Fowler
	G-MTCH	Solar Wings Pegasus XL-R	M. Doyle
	G-MTCK	SW Pegasus Flash	R. H. de C. Ribeiro
	G-MTCM	Southdown Raven X	J. C. Rose
	G-MTCP	Aerial Arts Chaser 110SX	B. Richardson
	G-MTCU	Mainair Gemini/Flash II	T. J. Philip
	G-MTDD	Aerial Arts Chaser 110SX	B. Richardson
	G-MTDE	American Aerolights 110SX	J. T. Meager
	G-MTDF	Mainair Gemini/Flash II	P. G. Barnes
	G-MTDO	Eipper Quicksilver MXII	D. L. Ham
	G-MTDR	Mainair Gemini/Flash II	D. J. Morriss
	G-MTDU	CFM Shadow Srs BD	A. Harris
	G-MTDW	Mainair Gemini/Flash II	S. R. Leeper
	G-MTDY	Mainair Gemini/Flash II	S. Penoyre
	G-MTEC	Solar Wings Pegasus XL-R	R. W. Glover
	G-MTEE	Solar Wings Pegasus XL-R	The Microlight School (Lichfield) Ltd
	G-MTEK	Mainair Gemini/Flash II	G. M. Wrigley & M. O'Hearne
	G-MTER	Solar Wings Pegasus XL-R	M. Lowe
	G-MTES	Solar Wings Pegasus XL-R	N. P. Read
	G-MTET	Solar Wings Pegasus XL-R	K. Gilsenan
	G-MTEU	Solar Wings Pegasus XL-R	T. E. Thomas
	G-MTEW	Solar Wings Pegasus XL-R	S. P. Halford
	G-MTEY	Mainair Gemini/Flash II	A. Wells
	G-MTFA	Pegasus XL-R	S. Hindle
	G-MTFB	Solar Wings Pegasus XL-R	H. Tuvey
	G-MTFC	Medway Hybred 44XLR	J. K. Masters
	G-MTFG	AMF Chevvron 232	J. Batchelor
	G-MTFM	Solar Wings Pegasus XL-R	P. R. G. Morley
	G-MTFN	Aerotech MW5 Sorcerer	S. M. King
	G-MTFT	Solar Wings Pegasus XL-R	S. J. Ward
	G-MTFU	CFM Shadow Srs CD	G. J. Jones & D. C. Lees
	G-MTGA	Mainair Gemini/Flash	I. White
	G-MTGB	Thruster TST Mk 1	M. J. Aubrey
	G-MTGC	Thruster TST Mk 1	H. Tuvey
	G-MTGD	Thruster TST Mk 1	J. Edwards
	G-MTGF	Thruster TST Mk 1	B. Swindon
	G-MTGH	Mainair Gemini/Flash II	M. Nazm
	G-MTGL	Solar Wings Pegasus XL-R	R. & P. J. Openshaw
	G-MTGM	Solar Wings Pegasus XL-R	I. J. Steele
	G-MTGO	Mainair Gemini/Flash	J. Ouru
	G-MTGR	Thruster TST Mk 1	M. R. Grunwell
	G-MTGS	Thruster TST Mk 1	R. J. Nelson
	G-MTGV	CFM Shadow Srs BD	V. R. Riley
	G-MTGW	CFM Shadow Srs BD	A. D. Grix
	G-MTHH	Solar Wings Pegasus XL-R	J. Palmer
	G-MTHJ	Solar Wings Pegasus XL-R	M. R. Harrison
	G-MTHN	Solar Wings Pegasus XL-R	M. T. Seal
	G-MTHT	CFM Shadow Srs BD	A. P. Jones
	G-MTHV	CFM Shadow Srs BD	K. R. Bircher
	G-MTIA	Mainair Gemini/Flash IIA	G. W. Jennings
	G-MTIB	Mainair Gemini/Flash IIA	M. D. Maclagan
	G-MTIE	Solar Wings Pegasus XL-R	P. Wibberley
	G-MTIJ	Solar Wings Pegasus XL-R	M. J. F. Gilbody
	G-MTIK	Southdown Raven X	G. A. Oldershaw
	G-MTIL	Mainair Gemini/Flash IIA	M. Ward
	G-MTIM	Mainair Gemini/Flash IIA	T. M. Swan
	G-MTIO	Solar Wings Pegasus XL-R	A. R. Wade
	G-MTIR	Solar Wings Pegasus XL-R	P. Jolley
	G-MTIS	Solar Wings Pegasus XL-R	Upottery Aerotow Club
	G-MTIW	Solar Wings Pegasus XL-R	G. S. Francis
	G-MTIX	Solar Wings Pegasus XL-R	S. Pickering
	G-MTIZ	Solar Wings Pegasus XL-R	S. L. Blount
	G-MTJA	Mainair Gemini/Flash IIA	W. O. Flannery
	G-MTJB	Mainair Gemini/Flash IIA	B. Skidmore

Reg.	Type	Owner or Operator	Notes
G-MTJC	Mainair Gemini/Flash IIA	T. A. Dockrell	
G-MTJE	Mainair Gemini/Flash IIA	M. P. Tilzey	
G-MTJG	Medway Hybred 44XLR	M. A. Trodden	
G-MTJH	SW Pegasus Flash	C. G. Ludgate	
G-MTJL	Mainair Gemini/Flash IIA	J. Hunter	
G-MTJS	Solar Wings Pegasus XL-Q	R. J. H. Hayward	
G-MTJT	Mainair Gemini/Flash IIA	D. F. Greatbanks	
G-MTJV	Mainair Gemini/Flash IIA	R. W. Hocking	
G-MTJX	Hornet Dual Trainer/Raven	J. P. Kirwan	
G-MTKA	Thruster TST Mk 1	Poet Pilot (UK) Ltd	
G-MTKB	Thruster TST Mk 1	M. Hanna	
G-MTKD	Thruster TST Mk 1	E. Spain/Ireland	
G-MTKG	Solar Wings Pegasus XL-R	D. J. Wilkinson & D. H. May	
G-MTKH	Solar Wings Pegasus XL-R	K. Brooker	
G-MTKI	Solar Wings Pegasus XL-R	M. Wady	
G-MTKR	CFM Shadow Srs BD	D. P. Eichhorn	
G-MTKW	Mainair Gemini/Flash IIA	J. H. McIvor	
G-MTKZ	Mainair Gemini/Flash IIA	I. S. McNeill	
G-MTLB	Mainair Gemini/Flash IIA	M. J. Jones	
G-MTLC	Mainair Gemini/Flash IIA	R. J. Alston	
G-MTLG	Solar Wings Pegasus XL-R	G. J. Simoni	
G-MTLL	Mainair Gemini/Flash IIA	M. S. Lawrence	
G-MTLM	Thruster TST Mk 1	R.J. Nelson	
G-MTLN	Thruster TST Mk 1	P. W. Taylor	
G-MTLT	Solar Wings Pegasus XL-R	K. M. Mayling	
G-MTLV	Solar Wings Pegasus XL-R	P. Cave	
G-MTLX	Medway Hybred 44XLR	D. A. Coupland	
G-MTLY	Solar Wings Pegasus XL-R	I. Johnston	
G-MTLZ	Whittaker MW5 Sorceror	J. O'Keeffe	
G-MTMA	Mainair Gemini/Flash IIA	R. Stafford	
G-MTMC	Mainair Gemini/Flash IIA	Rovogate Ltd	
G-MTME	Solar Wings Pegasus XL-R	R. J. Turner	
G-MTMF	Solar Wings Pegasus XL-R	H. T. M. Smith	
G-MTMG	Solar Wings Pegasus XL-R	C. W. & P. E. F. Suckling	
G-MTJV	Mainair Gemini/Flash IIA	J. F. Ashton	
G-MTMO	Raven X	H. Tuvey	
G-MTMP	Hornet Dual Trainer/Raven	P. G. Owen	
G-MTMR	Hornet Dual Trainer/Raven	D. J. Smith	
G-MTMT	Mainair Gemini/Flash IIA	C. Pickvance	
G-MTMV	Mainair Gemini/Flash IIA	G. J. Small	
G-MTMW	Mainair Gemini/Flash IIA	F. Lees	
G-MTMX	CFM Shadow Srs BD	D. R. White	
G-MTNC	Mainair Gemini/Flash IIA	M. G. Titmus & M. E. Cook	
G-MTND	Medway Hybred 44XLR	Butty Boys Flying Group	
G-MTNE	Medway Hybred 44XLR	A. G. Rodenburg	
G-MTNF	Medway Hybred 44XLR	P. A. Bedford	
G-MTNG	Mainair Gemini/Flash IIA	A. N. Bellis	
G-MTNI	Mainair Gemini/Flash IIA	F. J. Clarehugh	
G-MTNJ	Mainair Gemini/Flash IIA	S. M. Cook	
G-MTNL	Mainair Gemini/Flash IIA	R. A. Matthews	
G-MTNM	Mainair Gemini/Flash IIA	P. M. Cary	
G-MTNO	Solar Wings Pegasus XL-Q	A. F. Batchelor	
G-MTNP	Solar Wings Pegasus XL-Q	R. J. Kelly	
G-MTNR	Thruster TST Mk 1	A. M. Sirant	
G-MTNT	Thruster TST Mk 1	M. McKenzie	
G-MTNU	Thruster TST Mk 1	T. H. Brearley	
G-MTNV	Thruster TST Mk 1	J. B. Russell	
G-MTOA	Solar Wings Pegasus XL-R	R. A. Bird	
G-MTOB	Solar Wings Pegasus XL-R	P. S. Lemm	
G-MTOE	Solar Wings Pegasus XL-R	G. W. F. J. Dear	
G-MTOF	Solar Wings Pegasus XL-R	J. C. Ettridge	
G-MTOH	Solar Wings Pegasus XL-R	H. Cook	
G-MTON	Solar Wings Pegasus XL-R	D. J. Willett	
G-MTOT	Solar Wings Pegasus XL-R	A. J. Lloyd	
G-MTOY	Solar Wings Pegasus XL-R	G-MTOY Group	
G-MTOZ	Solar Wings Pegasus XL-R	C. P. Davies	
G-MTPB	Mainair Gemini/Flash IIA	D. J. Houlding & R. Swan	
G-MTPC	Raven X	G. W. Carwardine	
G-MTPE	Solar Wings Pegasus XL-R	J. Bassett	
G-MTPF	Solar Wings Pegasus XL-R	P. M. Watts & A. S. Mitchel	
G-MTPH	Solar Wings Pegasus XL-R	G. Barker & L. Blight	
G-MTPI	Solar Wings Pegasus XL-R	R. J. Bullock	

Notes	Reg.	Type	Owner or Operator
	G-MTPJ	Solar Wings Pegasus XL-R	D. Lockwood
	G-MTPK	Solar Wings Pegasus XL-R	S. H. James
	G-MTPL	Solar Wings Pegasus XL-R	C. J. Jones
	G-MTPM	Solar Wings Pegasus XL-R	D. K. Seal
	G-MTPR	Solar Wings Pegasus XL-R	T. Kenny
	G-MTPT	Thruster TST Mk 1	Chilbolton Thruster Group
	G-MTPU	Thruster TST Mk 1	N. Hay
	G-MTPW	Thruster TST Mk 1	K. Hawthorne
	G-MTPX	Thruster TST Mk 1	T. Snook
	G-MTPY	Thruster TST Mk 1	H. N. Baumgartner
	G-MTRA	Mainair Gemini/Flash IIA	E. N. Alms
	G-MTRC	Midlands Ultralights Sirocco 377G	D. Thorpe
	G-MTRM	Solar Wings Pegasus XL-R	M. Morris
	G-MTRO	Solar Wings Pegasus XL-R	D. Rowland
	G-MTRS	Solar Wings Pegasus XL-R	J. J. R. Tickle
	G-MTRV	Solar Wings Pegasus XL-Q	E. R. Termini
	G-MTRX	Whittaker MW5 Sorceror	W. Turner
	G-MTRZ	Mainair Gemini/Flash IIA	D. F. G. Barlow
	G-MTSC	Mainair Gemini/Flash IIA	K. Wilson
	G-MTSH	Thruster TST Mk 1	R. R. Orr
	G-MTSJ	Thruster TST Mk 1	C. M. Gall
	G-MTSK	Thruster TST Mk 1	J. S. Pyke
	G-MTSM	Thruster TST Mk 1	R. J. Webb
	G-MTSS	Solar Wings Pegasus XL-R	P. Ayres
	G-MTSY	Solar Wings Pegasus XL-R	N. F. Waldron
	G-MTSZ	Solar Wings Pegasus XL-R	D. L. Pickover
	G-MTTA	Solar Wings Pegasus XL-R	J. J. McMennum
	G-MTTE	Solar Wings Pegasus XL-R	M. C. Mawson
	G-MTTF	Aerotech MW6 Merlin	P. Cotton
	G-MTTI	Mainair Gemini/Flash IIA	P. Geddes
	G-MTTM	Mainair Gemini/Flash IIA	M. Anderson
	G-MTTN	Ultralight Flight Phantom	T. M. Weaver
	G-MTTP	Mainair Gemini/Flash IIA	A. Ormson
	G-MTTU	Solar Wings Pegasus XL-R	A. Friend
	G-MTTW	Mainair Gemini/Flash IIA	L. A. Howell
	G-MTTY	Solar Wings Pegasus XL-Q	P. M. Scrivener
	G-MTTZ	Solar Wings Pegasus XL-Q	J. Haskett
	G-MTUA	Solar Wings Pegasus XL-R	Fly Hire Ltd
	G-MTUC	Thruster TST Mk 1	E. J. Girling
	G-MTUD	Thruster TST Mk 1	S. Cooper & J. Parker
	G-MTUK	Solar Wings Pegasus XL-R	G. McLaughlin
	G-MTUN	Solar Wings Pegasus XL-Q	M. J. O'Connor
	G-MTUP	Solar Wings Pegasus XL-Q	G. Davies
	G-MTUR	Solar Wings Pegasus XL-Q	G. Ball
	G-MTUS	Solar Wings Pegasus XL-Q	G. Nicol
	G-MTUT	Solar Wings Pegasus XL-Q	R. E. Bull
	G-MTUU	Mainair Gemini/Flash IIA	M. Harris
	G-MTUV	Mainair Gemini/Flash IIA	D. Baker & S. Taylor
	G-MTUY	Solar Wings Pegasus XL-Q	H. C. Lowther
	G-MTVH	Mainair Gemini/Flash IIA	P. H. Statham
	G-MTVI	Mainair Gemini/Flash IIA	R. A. McDowell
	G-MTVJ	Mainair Gemini/Flash IIA	D. W. Buck
	G-MTVO	Solar Wings Pegasus XL-R	D. A. Payne
	G-MTVP	Thruster TST Mk 1	J. M. Evans
	G-MTVR	Thruster TST Mk 1	D. R. Lucas
	G-MTVT	Thruster TST Mk.1	W. H. J. Knowles
	G-MTVV	Thruster TST Mk 1	J. H. Askew
	G-MTVX	Solar Wings Pegasus XL-Q	D. A. Foster
	G-MTWG	Mainair Gemini/Flash IIA	N. Mackenzie & P. S. Bunting
	G-MTWH	CFM Shadow Srs BD	I. W. Hogg
	G-MTWK	CFM Shadow Srs BD	J. P. Batty & J. R. C. Brightman
	G-MTWR	Mainair Gemini/Flash IIA	J. B. Hodson
	G-MTWS	Mainair Gemini/Flash IIA	M. Sanderson
	G-MTWX	Mainair Gemini/Flash IIA	J. Donley
	G-MTWY	Thruster TST Mk 1	J. F. Gardner
	G-MTWZ	Thruster TST Mk 1	T. A. Colman
	G-MTXA	Thruster TST Mk 1	B. Dennis
	G-MTXB	Thruster TST Mk 1	J. J. Hill
	G-MTXC	Thruster TST Mk.1	W. Macleod
	G-MTXD	Thruster TST Mk 1	D. J. Flower
	G-MTXI	Solar Wings Pegasus XL-Q	S. A. Mallett
	G-MTXJ	Solar Wings Pegasus XL-Q	E. W. Laidlaw

Reg.	Type	Owner or Operator	Notes
G-MTXL	Noble Hardman Snowbird Mk IV	P. J. Collins	
G-MTXM	Mainair Gemini/Flash IIA	C. Blount, J. D. Penman & R. Tomlinson	
G-MTXO	Whittaker MW6	M. W. Shepherd	
G-MTXR	CFM Shadow Srs BD	S. A. O'Neill	
G-MTXU	Snowbird Mk.IV	M. A. Oakley	
G-MTXZ	Mainair Gemini/Flash IIA	J. S. Hawkins	
G-MTYA	Solar Wings Pegasus XL-Q	R. Howieson	
G-MTYC	Solar Wings Pegasus XL-Q	C. I. D. H. Garrison	
G-MTYD	Solar Wings Pegasus XL-Q	R. S. Colebrook	
G-MTYE	Solar Wings Pegasus XL-Q	D. P. Graham	
G-MTYF	Solar Wings Pegasus XL-Q	M. Quarterman	
G-MTYH	Solar Wings Pegasus XL-Q	I. B. Currer	
G-MTYI	Solar Wings Pegasus XL-Q	D. Ewing	
G-MTYL	Solar Wings Pegasus XL-Q	E. T. H. Cox	
G-MTYR	Solar Wings Pegasus XL-Q	D. T. Evans	
G-MTYS	Solar Wings Pegasus XL-Q	R. G. Wall	
G-MTYV	Southdown Raven X	S. R. Jones	
G-MTYW	Raven X	R. Solomons	
G-MTYY	Solar Wings Pegasus XL-R	L. A. Hosegood	
G-MTZA	Thruster TST Mk 1	J. F. Gallagher	
G-MTZB	Thruster TST Mk 1	J. E. Davies	
G-MTZC	Thruster TST Mk 1	R. W. Marshall	
G-MTZE	Thruster TST Mk 1	B. S. P. Finch	
G-MTZF	Thruster TST Mk 1	D. C. Marsh	
G-MTZG	Mainair Gemini/Flash IIA	A. P. Fenn	
G-MTZH	Mainair Gemini/Flash IIA	D. C. Hughes	
G-MTZJ	Solar Wings Pegasus XL-R	W. G. Harling	
G-MTZK	Solar Wings Pegasus XL-R	G. F. Jones	
G-MTZL	Mainair Gemini/Flash IIA	N. S. Brayn	
G-MTZM	Mainair Gemini/Flash IIA	K. L. Smith	
G-MTZO	Mainair Gemini/Flash IIA	R. C. Hinds	
G-MTZR	Solar Wings Pegasus XL-Q	P. J. Hatchett	
G-MTZS	Solar Wings Pegasus XL-Q	P. A. Darling	
G-MTZV	Mainair Gemini/Flash IIA	G. H. Williams	
G-MTZW	Mainair Gemini/Flash IIA	J. E. Rourke	
G-MTZX	Mainair Gemini/Flash IIA	R. G. Cuckow	
G-MTZY	Mainair Gemini/Flash IIA	K. M. Gough & R. Dunn	
G-MTZZ	Mainair Gemini/Flash IIA	G. J. Cadden	
G-MUCK	Lindstrand LBL 77A	C. J. Wootton	
G-MUDD	Hughes 369E	Derwen Plant Co.Ltd	
G-MUDY	PA-18-150 Super Cub	C. S. Grace (G-OTUG)	
G-MUIR	Cameron V-65 balloon	L. C. M. Muir	
G-MULT	Beech 76 Duchess	Folada Aero & Technical Services Ltd	
G-MUMM	Colt 180A balloon	D. K. Hempleman-Davis	
G-MUMY	Vans RV-4	S. D. Howes	
G-MUNI	Mooney M.20J	P. R. Williams	
G-MURG	Van's RV-6	Cadmium Lake Ltd	
G-MUSH	Robinson R44 II	Heli Air Ltd/Wellesbourne	
G-MUSO	Rutan LongEz	C. J. Tadjeran/Sweden	
G-MUTT	CZAW Sportcruiser	W. Gillam	
G-MUTZ	Avtech Jabiru J430	N. C. Dean	
G-MUVG	Cessna 421C	Centurion Airlines Ltd	
G-MUZY	Titan T-51 Mustang	D. Stephens	
G-MVAC	CFM Shadow Srs BD	R. G. Place	
G-MVAD	Mainair Gemini/Flash IIA	N. D. Fox & C. J. Hemmingway	
G-MVAG	Thruster TST Mk 1	P. Higgins/Ireland	
G-MVAH	Thruster TST Mk 1	M. W. H. Henton	
G-MVAJ	Thruster TST Mk 1	D. Watson	
G-MVAM	CFM Shadow Srs BD	C. P. Barber	
G-MVAN	CFM Shadow Srs BD	R. W. Frost	
G-MVAO	Mainair Gemini/Flash IIA	S. W. Grainger	
G-MVAP	Mainair Gemini/Flash IIA	R. J. Miller	
G-MVAR	Solar Wings Pegasus XL-R	A. J. Thomas	
G-MVAV	Solar Wings Pegasus XL-R	D. J. Utting	
G-MVAW	Solar Wings Pegasus XL-Q	G. Sharman	
G-MVAX	Solar Wings Pegasus XL-Q	N. M. Cuthbertson	
G-MVAY	Solar Wings Pegasus XL-Q	V. O. Morris	
G-MVBC	Aerial Arts Tri-Flyer 130SX	D. Beer	
G-MVBE	Mainair Scorcher	M. Laycock	
G-MVBF	Mainair Gemini/Flash IIA	E. McCallum	

Notes	Reg.	Type	Owner or Operator
	G-MVBG	Mainair Gemini/Flash IIA	D. W. Curtis
	G-MVBI	Mainair Gemini/Flash IIA	S. Irwin
	G-MVBJ	Solar Wings Pegasus XL-R	R. J. O. Page
	G-MVBK	Mainair Gemini/Flash IIA	B. R. McLoughlin
	G-MVBL	Mainair Gemini/Flash IIA	S. T. Cain
	G-MVBM	Mainair Gemini/Flash IIA	G. Hall
	G-MVBN	Mainair Gemini/Flash IIA	N. C. Stone
	G-MVBO	Mainair Gemini/Flash IIA	J. A. Brown
	G-MVBP	Thruster TST Mk 1	G-MVBP Group
	G-MVBT	Thruster TST Mk 1	TST Group Flying
	G-MVBZ	Solar Wings Pegasus XL-R	A. G. Butler
	G-MVCA	Solar Wings Pegasus XL-R	R. Walker
	G-MVCB	Solar Wings Pegasus XL-R	L. Briscoe
	G-MVCC	CFM Shadow Srs BD	P. B. Davey
	G-MVCD	Medway Hybred 44XLR	V. W. Beynon
	G-MVCE	Mainair Gemini/Flash IIA	N. Ford
	G-MVCF	Mainair Gemini/Flash IIA	M. W. Luke
	G-MVCL	Solar Wings Pegasus XL-Q	T. E. Robinson
	G-MVCM	Solar Wings Pegasus XL-Q	P. J. Croney
	G-MVCN	Solar Wings Pegasus XL-Q	C. J. Lamb
	G-MVCR	Solar Wings Pegasus XL-Q	P. Hoeft
	G-MVCS	Solar Wings Pegasus XL-Q	J. J. Sparrow
	G-MVCT	Solar Wings Pegasus XL-Q	G. S. Lampitt
	G-MVCV	Solar Wings Pegasus XL-Q	G. Stewart
	G-MVCW	CFM Shadow Srs BD	D. A. Coupland
	G-MVCY	Mainair Gemini/Flash IIA	A. M. Smith
	G-MVCZ	Mainair Gemini/Flash IIA	P. J. Devine
	G-MVDA	Mainair Gemini/Flash IIA	C. Tweedley
	G-MVDE	Thruster TST Mk 1	K. N. Cobb
	G-MVDF	Thruster TST Mk 1	G-MVDF Syndicate
	G-MVDG	Thruster TST Mk 1	B. M. Grant
	G-MVDH	Thruster TST Mk 1	E. H. Snook
	G-MVDJ	Medway Hybred 44XLR	W. D. Hutchins
	G-MVDK	Aerial Arts Chaser S	S. Adams
	G-MVDL	Aerial Arts Chaser S	N. P. Lloyd
	G-MVDP	Aerial Arts Chaser S	R. G. Mason
	G-MVDT	Mainair Gemini/Flash IIA	D. C. Stephens
	G-MVDV	Solar Wings Pegasus XL-R	K. Taggerty
	G-MVDY	Solar Wings Pegasus XL-R	C. G. Murphy
	G-MVDZ	Solar Wings Pegasus XL-R	A. K. Pickering
	G-MVEC	Solar Wings Pegasus XL-R	J. A. Jarvis
	G-MVEG	Solar Wings Pegasus XL-R	A. M. Shaw
	G-MVEH	Mainair Gemini/Flash IIA	E. J. Elliott
	G-MVEI	CFM Shadow Srs BD	I. G. Ferguson
	G-MVEL	Mainair Gemini/Flash IIA	M. R. Starling
	G-MVEN	CFM Shadow Srs BD	C. Langley
	G-MVER	Mainair Gemini/Flash IIA	J. R. Davis
	G-MVES	Mainair Gemini/Flash IIA	J. Helm
	G-MVET	Mainair Gemini/Flash IIA	C. Buttery
	G-MVEZ	Solar Wings Pegasus XL-Q	P. W. Millar
	G-MVFA	Solar Wings Pegasus XL-Q	D. J. Bromley
	G-MVFB	Solar Wings Pegasus XL-Q	M. O. Bloy
	G-MVFC	Solar Wings Pegasus XL-Q	D. R. Joint
	G-MVFD	Solar Wings Pegasus XL-Q	C. D. Humphries
	G-MVFE	Solar Wings Pegasus XL-Q	S. J. Weeks
	G-MVFF	Solar Wings Pegasus XL-Q	A. Makepiece
	G-MVFH	CFM Shadow Srs BD	M. D. Goad
	G-MVFJ	Thruster TST Mk 1	B. E. Reneham
	G-MVFL	Thruster TST Mk 1	E. J. Wallington
	G-MVFM	Thruster TST Mk 1	G. J. Boyer
	G-MVFO	Thruster TST Mk 1	S. R. James Humberstone & A. L. Higgins
	G-MVFT	Solar Wings Pegasus XL-R	J. Bohea
	G-MVFX	Thruster TST Mk 1	A. M. Dalgetty
	G-MVFZ	Solar Wings Pegasus XL-R	R. K. Johnson
	G-MVGA	Aerial Arts Chaser S	N. R. Beale
	G-MVGC	AMF Chevvron 2-32	W. Fletcher
	G-MVGD	AMF Chevvron 2-32	T. R. James
	G-MVGF	Aerial Arts Chaser S	P. J. Higgins
	G-MVGG	Aerial Arts Chaser S	P. D. Curtis
	G-MVGH	Aerial Arts Chaser S	J. A. Horn
	G-MVGK	Aerial Arts Chaser S	D. J. Smith
	G-MVGM	Mainair Gemini/Flash IIA	P. A. C. R. Stephens

Reg.	Type	Owner or Operator	Notes
G-MVGN	Solar Wings Pegasus XL-R	M. J. Smith	
G-MVGO	Solar Wings Pegasus XL-R	J. B. Peacock	
G-MVGP	Solar Wings Pegasus XL-R	J. P. Cox	
G-MVGU	Solar Wings Pegasus XL-Q	I. A. Macadam	
G-MVGY	Medway Hybred 44XL	M. Vines	
G-MVGZ	Ultraflight Lazair IIIE	D. M. Broom	
G-MVHD	CFM Shadow Srs BD	D. Raybould	
G-MVHE	Mainair Gemini/Flash IIA	B. J. Thomas	
G-MVHG	Mainair Gemini/Flash II	C. A. J. Elder	
G-MVHH	Mainair Gemini/Flash IIA	A. M. Lynch	
G-MVHI	Thruster TST Mk 1	L. Hurman	
G-MVHJ	Thruster TST Mk 1	F. Omaraie-Hamdanie	
G-MVHK	Thruster TST Mk 1	D. J. Gordon	
G-MVHL	Thruster TST Mk 1	G. Jones	
G-MVHN	Aerial Arts Chaser S	N. D. Townend	
G-MVHP	Solar Wings Pegasus XL-Q	J. B. Gasson	
G-MVHR	Solar Wings Pegasus XL-Q	J. M. Hucker	
G-MVHS	Solar Wings Pegasus XL-Q	A. P. Clarke	
G-MVHW	Solar Wings Pegasus XL-Q	Ultralight Training Ltd	
G-MVIB	Mainair Gemini/Flash IIA	LSA Systems	
G-MVIE	Aerial Arts Chaser S	T. M. Stiles	
G-MVIF	Medway Raven X	A. C. Hing	
G-MVIG	CFM Shadow Srs BD	M. J. Green	
G-MVIH	Mainair Gemini/Flash IIA	T. M. Gilesnan	
G-MVIL	Noble Hardman Snowbird Mk IV	Marine Power (Scotland) Ltd	
G-MVIN	Noble Hardman Snowbird Mk.IV	C. P. Dawes	
G-MVIO	Noble Hardman Snowbird Mk.IV	C. R. Taylor	
G-MVIP	AMF Chevvron 232	P. C. Avery	
G-MVIR	Thruster TST Mk 1	T. D. B. Gardner	
G-MVIT	Thruster TST Mk 1	A. C. Bell	
G-MVIU	Thruster TST Mk 1	Anglesey Thrusters Syndicate	
G-MVIV	Thruster TST Mk 1	G. Rainey	
G-MVIX	Mainair Gemini/Flash IIA	D. Ostle & D. J. Johnston	
G-MVIZ	Mainair Gemini/Flash IIA	D. Reston	
G-MVJC	Mainair Gemini/Flash IIA	B. Temple	
G-MVJD	Solar Wings Pegasus XL-R	D. L. Price	
G-MVJE	Mainair Gemini/Flash IIA	G. Zuchowski	
G-MVJF	Aerial Arts Chaser S	V. S. Rudham	
G-MVJG	Aerial Arts Chaser S	T. H. Scott	
G-MVJK	Aerial Arts Chaser S	S. P. Maher	
G-MVJM	Microflight Spectrum	S. E. Whitehouse	
G-MVJN	Solar Wings Pegasus XL-Q	A. L. Brown	
G-MVJP	Solar Wings Pegasus XL-Q	S. H. Bakowski	
G-MVJR	Solar Wings Pegasus XL-Q	Group JR	
G-MVJS	Solar Wings Pegasus XL-Q	D. Pecheur	
G-MVJU	Solar Wings Pegasus XL-Q	J. C. Longmore	
G-MVKB	Medway Hybred 44XLR	J. Newby	
G-MVKC	Mainair Gemini/Flash IIA	M. Faulkner	
G-MVKH	Solar Wings Pegasus XL-R	K. M. Elson	
G-MVKJ	Solar Wings Pegasus XL-R	G. V. Warner	
G-MVKK	Solar Wings Pegasus XL-R	G. P. Burns	
G-MVKL	Solar Wings Pegasus XL-R	J. Powell-Tuck	
G-MVKM	Solar Wings Pegasus XL-R	A. J. Clarke	
G-MVKN	Solar Wings Pegasus XL-Q	A. S. Mason	
G-MVKO	Solar Wings Pegasus XL-Q	A. R. Hughes	
G-MVKP	Solar Wings Pegasus XL-Q	J. Williams	
G-MVKS	Solar Wings Pegasus XL-Q	K. S. Wright	
G-MVKT	Solar Wings Pegasus XL-Q	P. W. Ruffle	
G-MVKU	Solar Wings Pegasus XL-Q	I. K. Priestley	
G-MVKV	Solar Wings Pegasus XL-Q	D. R. Stansfield	
G-MVKW	Solar Wings Pegasus XL-Q	A. T. Scott	
G-MVLA	Aerial Arts Chaser S	K. R. Emery	
G-MVLB	Aerial Arts Chaser S	R. P. Wilkinson	
G-MVLC	Aerial Arts Chaser S	B. R. Barnes	
G-MVLD	Aerial Arts Chaser S	J. D. Doran	
G-MVLE	Aerial Arts Chaser S	R. G. hooker	
G-MVLJ	CFM Shadow Srs B	R. S. Cochrane	
G-MVLL	Mainair Gemini/Flash IIA	S. Coldicott	
G-MVLR	Mainair Gemini/Flash IIA	P. A. Louis	
G-MVLS	Aerial Arts Chaser S	C. Murphy	
G-MVLT	Aerial Arts Chaser S	T. J. Gayton-Polley	
G-MVLX	Solar Wings Pegasus XL-Q	J. F. Smith	

Notes	Reg.	Type	Owner or Operator
	G-MVLY	Solar Wings Pegasus XL-Q	I. B. Osborn
	G-MVMA	Solar Wings Pegasus XL-Q	G. C. Winter-Goodwin
	G-MVMC	Solar Wings Pegasus XL-Q	P. Smith & I. W. Barlow
	G-MVMG	Thruster TST Mk 1	A. D. McCaldin
	G-MVMI	Thruster TST Mk 1	L. M. Hamblyn
	G-MVMK	Medway Hybred 44XLR	D. J. Lewis
	G-MVML	Aerial Arts Chaser S	G. C. Luddington
	G-MVMM	Aerial Arts Chaser S	D. Margereson
	G-MVMR	Mainair Gemini/Flash IIA	P. W. Ramage
	G-MVMT	Mainair Gemini/Flash IIA	R. F. Sanders
	G-MVMU	Mainair Gemini/Flash IIA	P. A. Brunt
	G-MVMV	Aerotech MW5 (K) Sorcerer	J. M. Macdonald
	G-MVMW	Mainair Gemini/Flash IIA	G. Jones
	G-MVMX	Mainair Gemini/Flash IIA	D. J. Rooney
	G-MVNA	Powerchute Raider	J. McGoldrick
	G-MVNB	Powerchute Raider	A. L. Inwood
	G-MVNC	Powerchute Raider	R. S. McFadyen
	G-MVNE	Powerchute Raider	A. E. Askew
	G-MVNL	Powerchute Raider	M/ A/ Stevenson
	G-MVNM	Gemini/Flash IIA	C. D. Phillips
	G-MVNP	Aerotech MW5 (K) Sorcerer	A. M. Edwards
	G-MVNR	Aerotech MW5 (K) Sorcerer	E. I. Rowlands-Jones
	G-MVNS	Aerotech MW5 (K) Sorcerer	A. M. Sirant
	G-MVNT	Whittaker MW5 (K) Sorcerer	P. E. Blyth
	G-MVNW	Mainair Gemini/Flash IIA	D. J. Gregory
	G-MVNX	Mainair Gemini/Flash IIA	J. P. Neilan
	G-MVNY	Mainair Gemini/Flash IIA	M. K. Buckland
	G-MVNZ	Mainair Gemini/Flash IIA	J. Howarth
	G-MVOB	Mainair Gemini/Flash IIA	G. L. Logan
	G-MVOD	Aerial Arts Chaser 110SX	N. R. Beale
	G-MVOF	Mainair Gemini/Flash IIA	P. J. Nolan
	G-MVOH	CFM Shadow Srs B	D. I. Farmer
	G-MVOJ	Noble Hardman Snowbird Mk IV	C. D. Beetham
	G-MVOL	Noble Hardman Snowbird Mk IV	Swansea Snowbird Flyers
	G-MVOO	AMF Chevvron 2-32	M. K. Field
	G-MVOP	Aerial Arts Chaser S	D. Thorpe
	G-MVOR	Mainair Gemini/Flash IIA	P. T. & R. M. Jenkins
	G-MVOT	Thruster TST Mk 1	C. S. Ashley-Cooper
	G-MVOU	Thruster TST Mk.1	D. W. Tewson
	G-MVOV	Thruster TST Mk 1	G-MVOV Group
	G-MVOX	Thruster TST Mk 1	J. E. Davies
	G-MVPA	Mainair Gemini/Flash IIA	J. E. Milburn
	G-MVPB	Mainair Gemini/Flash IIA	G. A. Harper
	G-MVPC	Mainair Gemini/Flash IIA	W. O. Flannery
	G-MVPD	Mainair Gemini/Flash IIA	P. Thelwel
	G-MVPE	Mainair Gemini/Flash IIA	M. D. Jealous & M. Goodrick
	G-MVPF	Medway Hybred 44XLR	G. H. Crick
	G-MVPH	Whittaker MW6 Merlin	A. K. Mascord
	G-MVPI	Mainair Gemini/Flash IIA	A. Shand
	G-MVPK	CFM Shadow Srs B	P. Sarfas
	G-MVPM	Whittaker MW6 Merlin	K. W. Curry
	G-MVPN	Whittaker MW6 Merlin	A. M. Field
	G-MVPR	Solar Wings Pegasus XL-Q	R. A. Smith
	G-MVPS	Solar Wings Pegasus XL-Q	R. J. Hood
	G-MVPX	Solar Wings Pegasus XL-Q	N. Ionita
	G-MVPY	Solar Wings Pegasus XL-Q	G. H. Dawson
	G-MVRA	Mainair Gemini/Flash IIA	F. Flood
	G-MVRB	Mainair Gemini/Flash	G. Callaghan/Northern Ireland
	G-MVRD	Mainair Gemini/Flash IIA	A. R. Helm
	G-MVRG	Aerial Arts Chaser S	J. P. Kynaston
	G-MVRH	Solar Wings Pegasus XL-Q	K. Farr
	G-MVRI	Solar Wings Pegasus XL-Q	P. Martin
	G-MVRM	Mainair Gemini/Flash IIA	J. S. Stevenson
	G-MVRO	CFM Shadow Srs CD	K. H. Creed
	G-MVRP	CFM Shadow Srs BD	M. A. Kelly
	G-MVRR	CFM Shadow Srs BD	S. P. Christian
	G-MVRS	CFM Shadow Srs BD ★	Aero Venture
	G-MVRT	CFM Shadow Srs BD	L. A. Hosegood & M. J. Mawle
	G-MVRW	Solar Wings Pegasus XL-Q	D. L. Hadley
	G-MVRX	Solar Wings Pegasus XL-Q	M. Everest
	G-MVRZ	Medway Hybred 44XLR	I. Oswald
	G-MVSE	Solar Wings Pegasus XL-Q	L. B. Richardson

Reg.	Type	Owner or Operator	Notes
G-MVSG	Aerial Arts Chaser S	M. Roberts	
G-MVSI	Medway Hybred 44XLR	C. T. H. Tenison	
G-MVSJ	Aviasud Mistral 532	D. W. Curtis	
G-MVSM	Midland Ultralights Sirocco	C. G. Benham	
G-MVSN	Mainair Gemini/Flash IIA	G. B. Wade	
G-MVSO	Mainair Gemini/Flash IIA	W. R. Furness	
G-MVSP	Mainair Gemini/Flash IIA	D. R. Buchanan	
G-MVST	Mainair Gemini/Flash IIA	M. D. Harper	
G-MVSV	Mainair Gemini/Flash IIA	P. Shelton	
G-MVSW	Solar Wings Pegasus XL-Q	K. Perratt	
G-MVSX	Solar Wings Pegasus XL-Q	A. R. Law	
G-MVSZ	Solar Wings Pegasus XL-Q	M. Jones	
G-MVTA	Solar Wings Pegasus XL-Q	P. Hanby	
G-MVTD	Whittaker MW6 Merlin	G. J. Green	
G-MVTF	Aerial Arts Chaser S 447	S. R. McKiernan	
G-MVTI	Solar Wings Pegasus XL-Q	P. J. Taylor	
G-MVTJ	Solar Wings Pegasus XL-Q	M. P. & R. A. Wells	
G-MVTK	Solar Wings Pegasus XL-Q	A. J. Owen	
G-MVTL	Aerial Arts Chaser S	N. D. Meer	
G-MVTM	Aerial Arts Chaser S	G. L. Davies	
G-MVUA	Mainair Gemini/Flash IIA	E. W. Hughes	
G-MVUB	Thruster T.300	A. K. Grayson	
G-MVUC	Medway Hybred 44XLR	B. Pounder	
G-MVUF	Solar Wings Pegasus XL-Q	G. P. Blakemore	
G-MVUG	Solar Wings Pegasus XL-Q	I. J. Morgan	
G-MVUI	Solar Wings Pegasus XL-Q	J. K. Edgecombe & P. E. Hadley	
G-MVUJ	Solar Wings Pegasus XL-Q	J. H. Cooper	
G-MVUM	Solar Wings Pegasus XL-Q	S. Clay	
G-MVUO	AMF Chevvron 2-32	W. D. M. Turtle	
G-MVUR	Hornet RS-ZA	G. R. Puffett	
G-MVUS	Aerial Arts Chaser S	H. Poyzer	
G-MVUU	Hornet ZA	K. W. Warn	
G-MVVI	Medway Hybred 44XLR	J. L. Ford	
G-MVVK	Solar Wings Pegasus XL-R	A. J. Weir	
G-MVVN	Solar Wings Pegasus XL-Q	J. R. Butler	
G-MVVO	Solar Wings Pegasus XL-Q	A. L. Scarlett	
G-MVVP	Solar Wings Pegasus XL-Q	I. Pite	
G-MVVR	Medway Hybred 44XLR	H. J. Long	
G-MVVT	CFM Shadow Srs BD	W. F. Hayward	
G-MVVV	AMF Chevvron 2-32	J. S. Firth	
G-MVVZ	Powerchute Raider	A. E. Askew	
G-MVWJ	Powerchute Raider	N. J. Doubek	
G-MVWN	Thruster T.300	Whisky November Group	
G-MVWR	Thruster T.300	G. Rainey	
G-MVWS	Thruster T.300	R. J. Hunphries	
G-MVWV	Medway Hybred 44XLR	H. Tuvey	
G-MVWW	Aviasud Mistral	Golf Whisky Whisky Group	
G-MVWZ	Aviasud Mistral	K. Green	
G-MVXA	Brewster I MW6	I. Brewster	
G-MVXB	Mainair Gemini/Flash IIA	M. E. Clennell	
G-MVXC	Mainair Gemini/Flash IIA	A. Worthington	
G-MVXJ	Medway Hybred 44XLR	P. J. Wilks	
G-MVXN	Aviasud Mistral	P. W. Cade	
G-MVXR	Mainair Gemini/Flash IIA	D. M. Bayne	
G-MVXV	Aviasud Mistral	M. F. E. Chalk	
G-MVXX	AMF Chevvron 232	C. K. Brown	
G-MVYC	Solar Wings Pegasus XL-Q	P. E. L. Street	
G-MVYD	Solar Wings Pegasus XL-Q	B. Birtle	
G-MVYE	Thruster TST Mk 1	M. J. Aubrey	
G-MVYK	Hornet R-ZA	P. Asbridge	
G-MVYN	Hornet RS-ZA	C. F. Janes	
G-MVYR	Medway Hybred 44XLR	K. J. Clarke	
G-MVYS	Mainair Gemini/Flash IIA	P. D. Finch	
G-MVYT	Noble Hardman Snowbird Mk IV	M. A. Oakley	
G-MVYV	Noble Hardman Snowbird Mk IV	D. W. Hayden	
G-MVYW	Noble Hardman Snowbird Mk IV	T. J. Harrison	
G-MVYX	Noble Hardman Snowbird Mk IV	R. McBlain	
G-MVYY	Aerial Arts Chaser S508	C. J. Gordon & R. H. Bird	
G-MVYZ	CFM Shadow Srs BD	T. G. Solomon	
G-MVZA	Thruster T.300	C. C. Belcher	
G-MVZC	Thruster T.300	S. Dougan	
G-MVZD	Thruster T.300	G-MVZD Syndicate	

Notes	Reg.	Type	Owner or Operator
	G-MVZI	Thruster T.300	R. R. R. Whittern
	G-MVZJ	Solar Wings Pegasus XL-Q	G. P. Burns
	G-MVZK	Quad City Challenger II	G. Carr
	G-MVZL	Solar Wings Pegasus XL-Q	P. R. Dobson
	G-MVZM	Aerial Arts Chaser S	J. L. Parker
	G-MVZO	Medway Hybred 44XLR	S. J. Taft
	G-MVZP	Murphy Renegade Spirit UK	The North American Syndicate
	G-MVZS	Mainair Gemini/Flash IIA	R. L. Beese
	G-MVZT	Solar Wings Pegasus XL-Q	C. J. Meadows
	G-MVZU	Solar Wings Pegasus XL-Q	M. G. McMurray
	G-MVZV	Solar Wings Pegasus XL-Q	K. D. Masters
	G-MVZX	Renegade Spirit UK	G. Holmes
	G-MVZZ	AMF Chevvron 232	W. A. L. Mitchell
	G-MWAB	Mainair Gemini/Flash IIA	J. E. Buckley
	G-MWAC	Solar Wings Pegasus XL-Q	H. Lloyd-Hughes
	G-MWAD	Solar Wings Pegasus XL-Q	J. K.Evans
	G-MWAE	CFM Shadow Srs BD	M. D. Brown
	G-MWAF	Solar Wings Pegasus XL-R	J. P. Bonner
	G-MWAN	Thruster T.300	E. J. Girling
	G-MWAP	Thruster T.300	A. G. Spurway & S. F. Chave
	G-MWAT	Solar Wings Pegasus XL-Q	D. G. Seymour
	G-MWAV	Solar Wings Pegasus XL-R	T. Woodward
	G-MWAW	Whittaker MW6 Merlin	G. J. Chater
	G-MWBI	Medway Hybred 44XLR	G. E. Coates
	G-MWBJ	Medway Sprint	C. C. Strong
	G-MWBK	Solar Wings Pegasus XL-Q	A. W. Jarvis
	G-MWBS	Hornet RS-ZA	P. D. Jaques
	G-MWBW	Hornet RS-ZA	C. G. Bentley
	G-MWBY	Hornet RS-ZA	Forestair Dragoons Ltd
	G-MWCB	Solar Wings Pegasus XL-Q	J. C. Whiting
	G-MWCC	Solar Wings Pegasus XL-R	I. K. Priestley
	G-MWCE	Mainair Gemini/Flash IIA	B. A. Tooze
	G-MWCF	Solar Wings Pegasus XL-R	R. McKie
	G-MWCG	Microflight Spectrum	C. Ricketts
	G-MWCH	Rans S.6 Coyote	G-MWCH Group
	G-MWCK	Powerchute Kestrel	A. E. Askew
	G-MWCM	Powerchute Kestrel	G. E. Lockyer
	G-MWCN	Powerchute Kestrel	J. D. McKibben
	G-MWCO	Powerchute Kestrel	J. R. E. Gladstone
	G-MWCR	Southdown Puma Sprint	S. R. Hall
	G-MWCS	Powerchute Kestrel	R. S. McFadyen
	G-MWCY	Medway Hybred 44XLR	J. K. Masters
	G-MWDB	CFM Shadow Srs BD	M. D. Meade
	G-MWDC	Solar Wings Pegasus XL-R	R. Littler
	G-MWDD	Solar Wings Pegasus XL-Q	M. Wachowiak
	G-MWDE	Hornet RS-ZA	H. G. Reid
	G-MWDI	Hornet RS-ZA	R. J. Perrin
	G-MWDK	Solar Wings Pegasus XL-R	T. Wicks
	G-MWDL	Solar Wings Pegasus XL-R	D. J. Windsor
	G-MWDN	CFM Shadow Srs BD	A. A. Duffas
	G-MWDS	Thruster T.300	S. Hazelden
	G-MWDZ	Eipper Quicksilver MXL II	R. G. Cook
	G-MWEG	Solar Wings Pegasus XL-Q	S. P. Michlig
	G-MWEH	Solar Wings Pegasus XL-Q	K. A. Davidson
	G-MWEK	Whittaker MW5 Sorcerer	D. W. & M. L. Squire
	G-MWEL	Mainair Gemini/Flash IIA	E. St John-Foti
	G-MWEN	CFM Shadow Srs BD	C. Dawn
	G-MWEO	Whittaker MW5 Sorcerer	J. Morton
	G-MWEP	Rans S.4 Coyote	E. J. Wallington
	G-MWER	Solar Wings Pegasus XL-Q	J. A. O'Neill
	G-MWES	Rans S.4 Coyote	M. A. McLoughlin
	G-MWEY	Hornet RS-ZA	J. Kidd
	G-MWEZ	CFM Shadow Srs CD	G-MWEZ Group
	G-MWFB	CFM Shadow Srs CD	J. S. Morgan
	G-MWFC	TEAM mini-MAX (G-BTXC)	P. C. C. H. Crossley
	G-MWFD	TEAM mini-MAX	J. T. Blackburn
	G-MWFF	Rans S.4 Coyote	P. J. Greenrod
	G-MWFG	Powerchute Kestrel	R. I. Simpson
	G-MWFI	Powerchute Kestrel	R. R. O'Neill
	G-MWFL	Powerchute Kestrel	M. A. Stevenson
	G-MWFT	MBA Tiger Cub 440	J. R. Ravenhill
	G-MWFU	Quad City Challenger II UK	I. C. Lewis

Reg.	Type	Owner or Operator	Notes
G-MWFV	Quad City Challenger II UK	M. Liptrot	
G-MWFW	Rans S.4 Coyote	M. P. Hallam	
G-MWFX	Quad City Challenger II UK	I. M. Walton	
G-MWFY	Quad City Challenger II UK	C. C. B. Soden	
G-MWFZ	Quad City Challenger II UK	A. Slade	
G-MWGA	Rans S.5 Coyote	A. W. Lowrie	
G-MWGG	Mainair Gemini/Flash IIA	D. Lopez	
G-MWGI	Whittaker MW5 (K) Sorcerer	G. E. Norton	
G-MWGJ	Whittaker MW5 (K) Sorcerer	I. Pearson	
G-MWGK	Whittaker MW5 (K) Sorcerer	R. J. Cook	
G-MWGL	Solar Wings Pegasus XL-Q	F. McGlynn	
G-MWGN	Rans S.4 Coyote II	V. Hallam	
G-MWGR	Solar Wings Pegasus XL-Q	N. Ionita	
G-MWGU	Powerchute Kestrel	M. Pandolfino	
G-MWGZ	Powerchute Kestrel	J. L. Lynch	
G-MWHC	Solar Wings Pegasus XL-Q	P. J. Lowery	
G-MWHF	Solar Wings Pegasus XL-Q	N. J. Troke	
G-MWHG	Solar Wings Pegasus XL-Q	I. A. Lumley	
G-MWHH	TEAM mini-MAX	I. D. Worthington	
G-MWHI	Mainair Gemini/Flash	P. Harwood	
G-MWHL	Solar Wings Pegasus XL-Q	S. J. Reader	
G-MWHO	Mainair Gemini/Flash IIA	B. Epps	
G-MWHP	Rans S.6-ESD Coyote	J. F. Bickerstaffe	
G-MWHR	Mainair Gemini/Flash IIA	B. Brazier	
G-MWHT	Solar Wings Pegasus Quasar	C. G. Jarvis	
G-MWHX	Solar Wings Pegasus XL-Q	N. P. Kelly	
G-MWIA	Mainair Gemini/Flash IIA	G. R. Reynolds	
G-MWIB	Aviasud Mistral	J. Broome	
G-MWIC	Whittaker MW5 Sorcerer	A. M. Witt	
G-MWIE	Solar Wings Pegasus XL-Q	X. S. Norman	
G-MWIF	Rans S.6-ESD Coyote II	K. Kelly	
G-MWIG	Mainair Gemini/Flash IIA	A. P. Purbrick	
G-MWIL	Medway Hybred 44XLR	P. J. Bosworth	
G-MWIM	Solar Wings Pegasus Quasar	G. C. James	
G-MWIO	Rans S.4 Coyote	K. T. Short	
G-MWIP	Whittaker MW6 Merlin	B. J. Merret & D. Beer	
G-MWIS	Solar Wings Pegasus XL-Q	P. G. Strangward	
G-MWIU	Pegasus Quasar TC	W. Hepburn	
G-MWIW	Solar Wings Pegasus Quasar	P. A. Patterson	
G-MWIX	Solar Wings Pegasus Quasar	G. Hawes	
G-MWIY	Solar Wings Pegasus Quasar	G. Bullock & A. Turner	
G-MWIZ	CFM Shadow Srs BD	T. P. Ryan	
G-MWJF	CFM Shadow Srs BD	S. N. White	
G-MWJH	Solar Wings Pegasus Quasar	S. W. Walker	
G-MWJI	Solar Wings Pegasus Quasar	L. Luscombe	
G-MWJJ	Solar Wings Pegasus Quasar	S. H. Hailstone	
G-MWJK	Solar Wings Pegasus Quasar	M. Richardson	
G-MWJN	Solar Wings Pegasus XL-Q	J. C. Corrall	
G-MWJP	Medway Hybred 44XLR	C. D. Simmons	
G-MWJR	Medway Hybred 44XLR	T. G. Almond	
G-MWJT	Solar Wings Pegasus Quasar	D. L. Mitchell	
G-MWJX	Medway Puma Sprint	C. D. Hignell	
G-MWKE	Hornet R-ZA	D. R. Stapleton	
G-MWKO	Solar Wings Pegasus XL-Q	P. M. Golden	
G-MWKX	Microflight Spectrum	C. R. Ions	
G-MWKY	Solar Wings Pegasus XL-Q	I. D. Edwards	
G-MWKZ	Solar Wings Pegasus XL-Q	T. G. Burston & I. A. Fox-Mills	
G-MWLA	Rans S.4 Coyote	J. A. R. Hughes	
G-MWLB	Medway Hybred 44XLR	G. P. D. Coan	
G-MWLD	CFM Shadow Srs BD	J. J. Hansen	
G-MWLE	Solar Wings Pegasus XL-R	D. Stevenson	
G-MWLG	Solar Wings Pegasus XL-R	C. Cohen	
G-MWLJ	Solar Wings Pegasus Quasar	P 7 M Aviation Ltd	
G-MWLK	Solar Wings Pegasus Quasar	D. J. Shippen	
G-MWLL	Solar Wings Pegasus XL-Q	A. J. Bacon	
G-MWLM	Solar Wings Pegasus XL-Q	A. McWilliam	
G-MWLN	Whittaker MW6-S Fatboy Flyer	S. J. Field	
G-MWLO	Whittaker MW6 Merlin	G-MWLO Flying Group	
G-MWLP	Mainair Gemini/Flash IIA	C. E. J. Moultrie	
G-MWLS	Medway Hybred 44XLR	M. A. Oliver	
G-MWLU	Solar Wings Pegasus XL-R	T. P. G. Ward	
G-MWLW	TEAM mini-MAX	E. J. Oteng	

Notes	Reg.	Type	Owner or Operator
	G-MWLX	Mainair Gemini/Flash IIA	J. K. Kerr, B. O. Lyell & C. Usher
	G-MWLZ	Rans S.4 Coyote	B. O. McCartan
	G-MWMB	Powerchute Kestrel	D.W. & K. P. Larder
	G-MWMC	Powerchute Kestrel	Talgarreg Flying Club
	G-MWMD	Powerchute Kestrel	D. J. Jackson
	G-MWMF	Powerchute Kestrel	P. J. Blundell
	G-MWMG	Powerchute Kestrel	M. D. Walton
	G-MWMH	Powerchute Kestrel	E. W. Potts
	G-MWMI	SolarWings Pegasus Quasar	N. J. Hopkins
	G-MWMK	SolarWings Pegasus Quasar TC	T. M. Frost
	G-MWML	SolarWings Pegasus Quasar	S. C. Key
	G-MWMM	Mainair Gemini/Flash IIA	R. H. Church
	G-MWMN	Solar Wings Pegasus XL-Q	P. A. Arnold & N. A. Rathbone
	G-MWMO	Solar Wings Pegasus XL-Q	D. S. F. McNair
	G-MWMP	Solar Wings Pegasus XL-Q	L. W. Caudwell
	G-MWMS	Mainair Gemini/Flash	J. Swindail
	G-MWMV	Solar Wings Pegasus XL-R	M. Nutting
	G-MWMW	Renegade Spirit UK	A. L. & S. Roberts
	G-MWMX	Mainair Gemini/Flash IIA	P. G. Hughes/Ireland
	G-MWMY	Mainair Gemini/Flash IIA	O. C. Rash
	G-MWMZ	Solar Wings Pegasus XL-Q	P. M. Scrivener
	G-MWNB	Solar Wings Pegasus XL-Q	P. F. J. Rogers
	G-MWND	Tiger Cub Developments RL.5A	D. A. Pike
	G-MWNE	Mainair Gemini/Flash IIA	D. Matthews
	G-MWNF	Renegade Spirit UK	D. J. White
	G-MWNG	Solar Wings Pegasus XL-Q	H. C. TRhomson
	G-MWNK	Solar Wings Pegasus Quasar	G. S. Lynn
	G-MWNL	Solar Wings Pegasus Quasar	B. J. Lyford
	G-MWNO	AMF Chevvron 232	I. K. Hogg
	G-MWNP	AMF Chevvron 232	M. K. Field
	G-MWNR	Renegade Spirit UK	RJR Flying Group
	G-MWNS	Mainair Gemini/Flash IIA	J. G. Hilliard
	G-MWNT	Mainair Gemini/Flash IIA	November Tango Group
	G-MWNU	Mainair Gemini/Flash IIA	C. C. Muir
	G-MWNX	Powerchute Kestrel	J. H. Greenroyd
	G-MWOC	Powerchute Kestrel	D. M. F. Harvey
	G-MWOD	Powerchute Kestrel	T. Morgan
	G-MWOE	Powerchute Raider	R. K. Sorrentino
	G-MWOH	Solar Wings Pegasus XL-R	J. D. Buchanan
	G-MWOI	Solar Wings Pegasus XL-R	B. T. Geoghegan
	G-MWOJ	Mainair Gemini/Flash IIA	C. J. Pryce
	G-MWOM	Pegasus Quasar TC	M. S. Ahmadu
	G-MWOO	Renegade Spirit UK	R. C. Wood
	G-MWOR	Solar Wings Pegasus XL-Q	S. E. Smith
	G-MWOV	Whittaker MW6 Merlin	S. Jeffs
	G-MWOY	Solar Wings Pegasus XL-Q	S. P. Griffin
	G-MWPB	Mainair Gemini/Flash IIA	J. Fenton
	G-MWPC	Mainair Gemini/Flash IIA	S. J. Ware
	G-MWPD	Mainair Gemini/Flash IIA	M. R. Picksley
	G-MWPE	Solar Wings Pegasus XL-Q	E. C. R. Hudson
	G-MWPF	Mainair Gemini/Flash IIA	G. P. Taggart
	G-MWPG	Microflight Spectrum	D. Brunton
	G-MWPH	Microflight Spectrum	A. Whittaker
	G-MWPN	CFM Shadow Srs CD	W. R. H. Thomas
	G-MWPP	CFM Streak Shadow	A. J. Price
	G-MWPR	Whittaker MW6 Merlin	S. F. N. Warnell
	G-MWPS	Renegade Spirit UK	M. D. Stewart
	G-MWPW	AMF Chevvron 2-32C	M. S. Westman
	G-MWPX	Solar Wings Pegasus XL-R	R. J. Wheeler
	G-MWPZ	Renegade Spirit UK	J. Ievers
	G-MWRC	Mainair Gemini/Flash IIA	D. R. Talbot
	G-MWRD	Mainair Gemini/Flash IIA	D. Morton
	G-MWRE	Mainair Gemini/Flash IIA	A. Williams
	G-MWRF	Mainair Gemini/Flash IIA	N. Hay
	G-MWRH	Mainair Gemini/Flash IIA	E. G. Astin
	G-MWRI	Mainair Gemini/Flash IIA	J. F. Booth
	G-MWRJ	Mainair Gemini/Flash IIA	J. M. Breaks
	G-MWRL	CFM Shadow Srs.CD	M. R. Jones
	G-MWRM	Medway Hybred 44XLR	I. R. M. Scott
	G-MWRN	Solar Wings Pegasus XL-R	D. T. Mackenzie
	G-MWRR	Mainair Gemini/Flash IIA	J. Clark t/a G-MWRR Group
	G-MWRS	Ultravia Super Pelican	T. B. Woolley

Reg.	Type	Owner or Operator	Notes
G-MWRT	Solar Wings Pegasus XL-R	G. L. Gunnell	
G-MWRU	Solar Wings Pegasus XL-R	A. Harding	
G-MWRY	CFM Shadow Srs CD	A. T. Armstrong	
G-MWSA	TEAM mini-MAX	G. J. Jones	
G-MWSB	Mainair Gemini/Flash IIA	P. J. Bosworth	
G-MWSC	Rans S.6-ESD Coyote II	I. Fernihough	
G-MWSD	Solar Wings Pegasus XL-Q	A. M. Harley	
G-MWSF	Solar Wings Pegasus XL-R	J. J. Freeman	
G-MWSI	Solar Wings Pegasus Quasar TC	J. J. C. Parrish	
G-MWSJ	Solar Wings Pegasus XL-Q	R. J. Collison	
G-MWSK	Solar Wings Pegasus XL-Q	J. Doogan	
G-MWSL	Mainair Gemini/Flash IIA	C. W. Frost	
G-MWSM	Mainair Gemini/Flash IIA	R. M. Wall	
G-MWSO	Solar Wings Pegasus XL-R	M. A. Clayton	
G-MWSP	Solar Wings Pegasus XL-R	S. I. Hatherall	
G-MWSR	Solar Wings Pegasus XL-R	G. P. J. Davies	
G-MWSS	Medway Hybred 44XLR	C. D. Hannam & J. W. Taylor	
G-MWST	Medway Hybred 44XLR	A. Ferguson	
G-MWSU	Medway Hybred 44XLR	T. De Landro	
G-MWSW	Whittaker MW6 Merlin	S. F. N. Warnell	
G-MWSX	Whittaker MW5 Sorcerer	P. J. Hellyer	
G-MWSY	Whittaker MW5 Sorcerer	J. E. Holloway	
G-MWSZ	CFM Shadow Srs CD	M. W. W. Clotworthy	
G-MWTC	Solar Wings Pegasus XL-Q	M. M. Chittenden	
G-MWTI	Solar Wings Pegasus XL-Q	O. G. Johns	
G-MWTJ	CFM Shadow Srs CD	T. D. Wolstenholme	
G-MWTL	Solar Wings Pegasus XL-R	B. Lindsay	
G-MWTN	CFM Shadow Srs CD	M. J. Broom	
G-MWTO	Mainair Gemini/Flash IIA	E. Beckett	
G-MWTP	CFM Shadow Srs CD	R. E. M. Gibson-Bevan	
G-MWTR	Mainair Gemini/Flash IIA	C. Montlake	
G-MWTT	Rans S.6-ESD Coyote II	L. E. Duffin	
G-MWTZ	Mainair Gemini/Flash IIA	C. W. R. Felce	
G-MWUA	CFM Shadow Srs CD	Cloudbase Aviation	
G-MWUB	Solar Wings Pegasus XL-R	T. R. L. Bayley	
G-MWUD	Solar Wings Pegasus XL-R	A. J. Weir	
G-MWUI	AMF Chevvron 2-32C	N. D. A. Graham	
G-MWUK	Rans S.6-ESD Coyote II	G. K. Hoult & S. J. C. Pollock	
G-MWUL	Rans S.6-ESD Coyote II	D. M. Bayne	
G-MWUN	Rans S.6-ESD Coyote II	J. Parke	
G-MWUO	Solar Wings Pegasus XL-Q	A. P. Slade	
G-MWUR	Solar Wings Pegasus XL-R	Nottingham Aerotow Club	
G-MWUS	Solar Wings Pegasus XL-R	H. R. Loxton	
G-MWUU	Solar Wings Pegasus XL-R	B. R. Underwood	
G-MWUV	Solar Wings Pegasus XL-R	C. D. Baines	
G-MWUW	Solar Wings Pegasus XL-R	Ultraflight Microlights Ltd	
G-MWUX	Solar Wings Pegasus XL-Q	B. D. Attwell	
G-MWUY	Solar Wings Pegasus XL-Q	M. J. Sharp	
G-MWUZ	Solar Wings Pegasus XL-Q	S. R. Nanson	
G-MWVA	Solar Wings Pegasus XL-Q	G. Charles-Jones	
G-MWVE	Solar Wings Pegasus XL-R	W. A. Keel-Stocker	
G-MWVF	Solar Wings Pegasus XL-R	J. B. Wright	
G-MWVG	CFM Shadow Srs CD	Shadow Aviation Ltd	
G-MWVH	CFM Shadow Srs CD	M. McKenzie	
G-MWVL	Rans S.6-ESD Coyote II	A. J. T., O. D. & A. Lewis	
G-MWVM	Solar Wings Pegasus Quasar II	A. A. Edmonds	
G-MWVN	Mainair Gemini/Flash IIA	J. McCafferty	
G-MWVO	Mainair Gemini/Flash IIA	P. Webb	
G-MWVP	Renegade Spirit UK	P. D. Mickleburgh	
G-MWVR	Mainair Gemini/Flash IIA	J. Brook	
G-MWVT	Mainair Gemini/Flash IIA	R. M. Wigman	
G-MWVY	Mainair Gemini/Flash IIA	A. Mundy	
G-MWVZ	Mainair Gemini/Flash IIA	S. N. Pryor	
G-MWWB	Mainair Gemini/Flash IIA	W. P. Seward	
G-MWWC	Mainair Gemini/Flash IIA	D. & A. Margereson	
G-MWWD	Renegade Spirit	J. & A. Oswald	
G-MWWH	Solar Wings Pegasus XL-Q	A. J. Alexander	
G-MWWI	Mainair Gemini/Flash IIA	M. A. S. Nesbitt	
G-MWWK	Mainair Gemini/Flash IIA	S. D. Puddle	
G-MWWN	Mainair Gemini/Flash IIA	R. Whitby	
G-MWWR	Microflight Spectrum	T. H. Evans	
G-MWWS	Thruster T.300	D. P. Wring	

Notes	Reg.	Type	Owner or Operator
	G-MWWV	Solar Wings Pegasus XL-Q	R. W. Livingstone
	G-MWWZ	Cyclone Chaser S	P. K. Dale
	G-MWXA	Mainair Gemini/Flash IIA	M. Briongos
	G-MWXC	Mainair Gemini/Flash IIA	N. J. Lindsay
	G-MWXF	Mainair Mercury	D. F. Hampson
	G-MWXG	Solar Wings Pegasus Quasar IITC	J. E. Moseley
	G-MWXH	Solar Wings Pegasus Quasar IITC	R. P. Wilkinson
	G-MWXJ	Mainair Mercury	P. J. Taylor
	G-MWXK	Mainair Mercury	M. P. Wilkinson
	G-MWXP	Solar Wings Pegasus XL-Q	A. P. Attfield
	G-MWXU	Mainair Gemini/Flash IIA	C. M. Mackinnon
	G-MWXV	Mainair Gemini/Flash IIA	G. G. Wilson & R. Winstanley
	G-MWXW	Cyclone Chaser S	K. C. Dodd
	G-MWXX	Cyclone Chaser S 447	P. I. Frost
	G-MWXY	Cyclone Chaser S 447	D. Curtis
	G-MWXZ	Cyclone Chaser S 508	D. L. Hadley
	G-MWYA	Mainair Gemini/Flash IIA	R. F. Hunt
	G-MWYC	Solar Wings Pegasus XL-Q	M. A. Collins
	G-MWYD	CFM Shadow Srs C	F. E. Greenfield
	G-MWYE	Rans S.6-ESD Coyote II	G. A. M. Moffat
	G-MWYG	Mainair Gemini/Flash IIA	R. D. Saulters
	G-MWYH	Mainair Gemini/Flash IIA	R. Haslam
	G-MWYI	Solar Wings Pegasus Quasar II	T. S. Chadfield
	G-MWYJ	Solar Wings Pegasus Quasar II	A. Clarke & L. B. Hughes
	G-MWYL	Mainair Gemini/Flash IIA	A. J. Hinks
	G-MWYM	Cyclone Chaser S 1000	C. J. Meadows
	G-MWYS	CGS Hawk 1 Arrow	Civilair
	G-MWYT	Mainair Gemini/Flash IIA	J. R. Kendall
	G-MWYU	Solar Wings Pegasus XL-Q	L. A. Dotchin
	G-MWYV	Mainair Gemini/Flash IIA	R. Bricknell
	G-MWYY	Mainair Gemini/Flash IIA	R. D. Allard
	G-MWYZ	Solar Wings Pegasus XL-Q	D. P. Graham
	G-MWZA	Mainair Mercury	A. J. Malham
	G-MWZB	AMF Microlight Chevvron 2-32C	E. Ratcliffe
	G-MWZD	Solar Wings Pegasus Quasar IITC	A. R. Walker
	G-MWZF	Solar Wings Pegasus Quasar IITC	R. G. T. Corney
	G-MWZI	Solar Wings Pegasus XL-R	K. J. Slater
	G-MWZJ	Solar Wings Pegasus XL-R	P. Kitchen
	G-MWZL	Mainair Gemini/Flash IIA	D. Renton
	G-MWZM	TEAM mini-MAX 91	I. D. Worthington
	G-MWZO	Solar Wings Pegasus Quasar IITC	A. Robinson
	G-MWZP	Solar Wings Pegasus Quasar IITC	C. Garton
	G-MWZR	Solar Wings Pegasus Quasar IITC	R. Veart
	G-MWZS	Solar Wings Pegasus Quasar IITC	G. Bennett
	G-MWZU	Solar Wings Pegasus XL-R	A. D. Winebloom
	G-MWZV	Solar Wings Pegasus XL-R	D. J. Newby
	G-MWZY	Solar Wings Pegasus XL-R	S. J. Barkworth
	G-MWZZ	Solar Wings Pegasus XL-R	The Microlight School (Lichfield) Ltd
	G-MXMX	PA-46R-350T Malibu Matrix	Feabrex Ltd
	G-MXPH	BAC.167 Strikemaster Mk 84 (311)	R. S. Partridge-Hicks (G-SARK)
	G-MXVI	VS.361 Spitfire LF.XVIe (TE184:D)	P. M. Andrews
	G-MYAB	Solar Wings Pegasus XL-R	A. N. F. Stewart
	G-MYAE	Solar Wings Pegasus XL-Q	C. R. Bunce
	G-MYAF	Solar Wings Pegasus XL-Q	M. Rees
	G-MYAG	Quad City Challenger II	I. Murray
	G-MYAH	Whittaker MW5 Sorcerer	J. Bolton
	G-MYAI	Mainair Mercury	J. Ellerton
	G-MYAJ	Rans S.6-ESD Coyote II	R. M. Moulton
	G-MYAN	Whittaker MW5 (K) Sorcerer	A. F. Reid
	G-MYAO	Mainair Gemini/Flash IIA	R. A. Chapman
	G-MYAR	Thruster T.300	G. Hawkins
	G-MYAS	Mainair Gemini/Flash IIA	J. R. Davis
	G-MYAT	TEAM mini-MAX	M. W. Hands
	G-MYAZ	Renegade Spirit UK	R. Smith
	G-MYBA	Rans S.6-ESD Coyote II	A. M. Hughes
	G-MYBB	Maxair Drifter	M. Ingleton
	G-MYBC	CFM Shadow Srs CD	M. E. Gilbert
	G-MYBF	Solar Wings Pegasus XL-Q	K. H. Pead
	G-MYBI	Rans S.6-ESD Coyote II	N. C. Tambiah
	G-MYBJ	Mainair Gemini/Flash IIA	G. C. Bowers

Reg.	Type	Owner or Operator	Notes
G-MYBL	CFM Shadow Srs C	R. G. Hicks	
G-MYBM	TEAM mini-MAX	B. Hunter	
G-MYBN	Hiway Demon 175	B. R. Lamming	
G-MYBO	Solar Wings Pegasus XL-R	D. Gledhill	
G-MYBR	Solar Wings Pegasus XL-Q	M. J. Larbey & G. T. Hunt	
G-MYBT	Solar Wings Pegasus Quasar IITC	G. A. Rainbow-Ockwell	
G-MYBU	Cyclone Chaser S 447	R. L. Arscott	
G-MYBV	Solar Wings Pegasus XL-Q	P. M. Langdon	
G-MYBW	Solar Wings Pegasus XL-Q	J. S. Chapman	
G-MYCA	Whittaker MW6 Merlin	R. A. L-V. Harris	
G-MYCB	Cyclone Chaser S 447	P. Sykes	
G-MYCE	Solar Wings Pegasus Quasar IITC	S. W. Barker	
G-MYCJ	Mainair Mercury	A. Gannon	
G-MYCK	Mainair Gemini/Flash IIA	J. E. Orbell	
G-MYCL	Mainair Mercury	P. B. Cole	
G-MYCM	CFM Shadow Srs CD	T. Jones	
G-MYCN	Mainair Mercury	P. Lowham	
G-MYCO	Renegade Spirit UK	S. Desormes	
G-MYCP	Whittaker MW6 Merlin	A. C. Jones	
G-MYCR	Mainair Gemini/Flash IIA	A. P. King	
G-MYCS	Mainair Gemini/Flash IIA	Husthwaite Alpha Group	
G-MYCX	Powerchute Kestrel	S. J. Pugh-Jones	
G-MYCZ	Powerchute Kestrel	R. R. O'Neill	
G-MYDA	Powerchute Kestrel	K. J. Greatrix	
G-MYDC	Mainair Mercury	M. Howard & K. Littlefair	
G-MYDD	CFM Shadow Srs CD	C. H. Gem/Spain	
G-MYDE	CFM Shadow Srs CD	D. N. L. Howell	
G-MYDF	TEAM mini-MAX	J. G. Bright	
G-MYDJ	Solar Wings Pegasus XL-R	Cambridgeshire Aerotow Club	
G-MYDK	Rans S.6-ESD Coyote II	J. W. Caush & W. Doyle	
G-MYDM	Whittaker MW6-S Fatboy Flyer	K. Gregan	
G-MYDN	Quad City Challenger II	T. C. Hooks	
G-MYDP	Kolb Twinstar Mk 3	Norberts Flying Group	
G-MYDR	Thruster Tn.300	H. G. Soper	
G-MYDT	Thruster T.300	J. B. Grotrian	
G-MYDU	Thruster T.300	S. Collins	
G-MYDV	Mainair Gemini /Flash IIA	S. J. Mazilis	
G-MYDX	Rans S.6-ESD Coyote II	V. Donskovas	
G-MYDZ	Mignet HM.1000 Balerit	D. S. Simpson	
G-MYEA	Solar Wings Pegasus XL-Q	A. M. Taylor	
G-MYED	Solar Wings Pegasus XL-R	V. Adamson	
G-MYEH	Solar Wings Pegasus XL-R	J. Spuffard	
G-MYEI	Cyclone Chaser S447	D. J. Hyatt	
G-MYEJ	Cyclone Chaser S447	S. C. Reeve	
G-MYEK	Solar Wings Pegasus Quasar IITC	M. N. Dando	
G-MYEM	Solar Wings Pegasus Quasar IITC	D. J. Moore	
G-MYEN	Solar Wings Pegasus Quasar IITC	T. J. Feeney	
G-MYEO	Solar Wings Pegasus Quasar IITC	A. G. Curtis	
G-MYER	Cyclone AX3/503	T. F. Horrocks	
G-MYES	Rans S.6-ESD Coyote II	S. J. Mathison	
G-MYET	Whittaker MW6 Merlin	G. Campbell	
G-MYEX	Powerchute Kestrel	R. J. Watkin	
G-MYFA	Powerchute Kestrel	M. Phillips	
G-MYFH	Quad City Challenger II	W. I. McMillan	
G-MYFI	Cyclone AX3/503	R. Dilkes	
G-MYFK	Solar Wings Pegasus Quasar IITC	M. A. Azeem	
G-MYFL	Solar Wings Pegasus Quasar IITC	S. B. Wilkes	
G-MYFM	Renegade Spirit UK	P. J. Houtman	
G-MYFO	Cyclone Airsports Chaser S	O. J. Neece	
G-MYFP	Mainair Gemini/Flash IIA	R. C. Reynolds	
G-MYFR	Mainair Gemini/Flash IIA	S. B. Brady	
G-MYFT	Mainair Scorcher	T. Williams	
G-MYFU	Mainair Gemini/Flash IIA	J. Payne	
G-MYFV	Cyclone AX3/503	J. K. Sargent	
G-MYFW	Cyclone AX3/503	Microlight School (Lichfield) Ltd	
G-MYFX	Solar Wings Pegasus XL-Q	J. Urrutia	
G-MYGD	Cyclone AX3/503	K. B. Vickers	
G-MYGF	TEAM mini-MAX	R. D. Barnard	
G-MYGH	Rans S.6ESD Coyote II	N. Blair & D. G. Higgins	
G-MYGK	Cyclone Chaser S 508	P. C. Collins	
G-MYGM	Quad City Challenger II	G. J. Williams & J. White	
G-MYGN	AMF Chevvron 2-32C	P. J. Huston	

Notes	Reg.	Type	Owner or Operator
	G-MYGO	CFM ShadowSrs CD	D. A. Crosbie
	G-MYGP	Rans S.6-ESD Coyote II	D. J. Millin
	G-MYGR	Rans S.6-ESD Coyote II	D. J. Warren
	G-MYGT	Solar Wings Pegasus XL-R	Condors Aerotow Syndicate
	G-MYGU	Solar Wings Pegasus XL-R	J. A. Sims
	G-MYGV	Solar Wings Pegasus XL-R	J. A. Crofts & G. M. Birkett
	G-MYGZ	Mainair Gemini/Flash IIA	C. Roadnight
	G-MYHG	Cyclone AX/503	N. P. Thomson & C. Alsop
	G-MYHH	Cyclone AX/503	D. J. Harber
	G-MYHI	Rans S.6-ESD Coyote II	G. F. Clews
	G-MYHK	Rans S.6-ESD Coyote II	M. R. Williamson
	G-MYHL	Mainair Gemini/Flash IIA	B. J. Riley
	G-MYHM	Cyclone AX3/503	G-MYHM Group
	G-MYHN	Mainair Gemini/Flash IIA	H. J. Timms
	G-MYHP	Rans S.6-ESD Coyote II	K. E. Gair & J. G. E. Lane
	G-MYHR	Cyclone AX3/503	C. W. Williams
	G-MYHS	Powerchute Kestrel	R. R. O'Neill
	G-MYIA	Quad City Challenger II	I. Pearson
	G-MYIF	CFM Shadow Srs CD	P. J. Edwards
	G-MYIH	Mainair Gemini/Flash IIA	A. N. Huddart
	G-MYII	TEAM mini-MAX	G. H. Crick
	G-MYIJ	Cyclone AX3/503	Ultralight Training Ltd
	G-MYIK	Kolb Twinstar Mk 3	B. A. Janaway
	G-MYIL	Cyclone Chaser S 508	R. A. Rawes
	G-MYIN	Solar Wings Pegasus Quasar IITC	W. P. Hughes
	G-MYIO	Solar Wings Pegasus Quasar IITC	E. Foster & J. H. Peet
	G-MYIP	CFM Shadow Srs CD	T. Bailey
	G-MYIR	Rans S.6-ESD Coyote II	P. D. Smalley
	G-MYIS	Rans S.6-ESD Coyote II	I. S. Everett & M. Stott
	G-MYIT	Cyclone Chaser S 508	R. Barringer
	G-MYIV	Mainair Gemini/Flash IIA	P. S. Nicholls
	G-MYIX	Quad City Challenger II	J. R. Appleton
	G-MYIY	Mainair Gemini/Flash IIA	D. Jackson
	G-MYIZ	TEAM mini-MAX 2	J. C. Longmore
	G-MYJC	Mainair Gemini/Flash IIA	M. N. Irven
	G-MYJD	Rans S.6-ESD Coyote II	A. A. Ross
	G-MYJF	Thruster T.300	P. F. McConville
	G-MYJG	Thruster T.300	J. W. Rice
	G-MYJJ	Solar Wings Pegasus Quasar IITC	D. Murray
	G-MYJK	Solar Wings Pegasus Quasar IITC	The Microlight School (Lichfield) Ltd
	G-MYJM	Mainair Gemini/Flash IIA	F. Tumelty
	G-MYJO	Cyclone Chaser S 508	A. W. Rawlings
	G-MYJS	Solar Wings Pegasus Quasar IITC	J. P. Rooms
	G-MYJT	Solar Wings Pegasus Quasar IITC	S. Ferguson
	G-MYJU	Solar Wings Pegasus Quasar IITC	P. G. Penhaligan
	G-MYJZ	Whittaker MW5D Sorcerer	D. L. Brown
	G-MYKA	Cyclone AX3/503	T. Whittall
	G-MYKB	Kolb Twinstar Mk 3	T. Antell
	G-MYKD	Cyclone Chaser S 508	H. Tuvey
	G-MYKE	CFM Shadow Srs BD	MKH Engineering
	G-MYKF	Cyclone AX3/503	M. A. Collins
	G-MYKG	Mainair Gemini/Flash IIA	B. D. Walker
	G-MYKH	Mainair Gemini/Flash IIA	A. W. Leadley
	G-MYKJ	TEAM mini-MAX	T. de Breffe Gardner
	G-MYKO	Whittaker MW6-S Fat Boy Flyer	J. A. Weston
	G-MYKR	Solar Wings Pegasus Quasar IITC	C. Stallard
	G-MYKS	Solar Wings Pegasus Quasar IITC	D. J. Oskis
	G-MYKT	Cyclone AX3/503	J. D. Sanger & J. E. Seager
	G-MYKV	Mainair Gemini/Flash IIA	P. J. Gulliver
	G-MYKX	Mainair Mercury	D. T. McAfee & A. F. Allan
	G-MYKW	Mainair Mercury	J. D. Hylton
	G-MYKZ	TEAM mini-MAX	R. Targonski
	G-MYLB	TEAM mini-MAX	J. G. Burns
	G-MYLC	Solar Wings Pegasus Quantum 15	C. McKay
	G-MYLD	Rans S.6-ESD Coyote II	B. Cartwright
	G-MYLE	Solar Wings Pegasus Quantum 15	S. E. Powell
	G-MYLF	Rans S.6-ESD Coyote II	A. J. Spencer
	G-MYLG	Mainair Gemini/Flash IIA	N. J. Axworthy
	G-MYLH	Solar Wings Pegasus Quantum 15	G. Carr
	G-MYLI	Solar Wings Pegasus Quantum 15	A. M. Keyte
	G-MYLK	Solar Wings Pegasus Quantum 15	G-MYLK Group
	G-MYLL	Solar Wings Pegasus Quantum 15	I. A. Macadam

Reg.	Type	Owner or Operator	Notes
G-MYLM	Solar Wings Pegasus Quasar IITC	P. Osborne & S. B. Walters	
G-MYLN	Kolb Twinstar Mk 3	J. F. Joyes	
G-MYLO	Rans S.6-ESD Coyote II	P. Bowers	
G-MYLP	Kolb Twinstar Mk 3	R. Thompson (G-BVCR)	
G-MYLR	Mainair Gemini/Flash IIA	I. J. Cleland & M. D. Calder	
G-MYLS	Mainair Mercury	W. K. C. Davies	
G-MYLT	Mainair Blade	T. D. Hall	
G-MYLV	CFM Shadow Srs CD	Aviation for Paraplegics and Tetraplegics Trust	
G-MYLW	Rans S.6-ESD Coyote II	A. D. Dias	
G-MYLX	Medway Raven	T. M. Knight	
G-MYLZ	Solar Wings Pegasus Quantum 15	W. G. McPherson	
G-MYMB	Solar Wings Pegasus Quantum 15	D. B. Jones	
G-MYMC	Solar Wings Pegasus Quantum 15	P. B. Smith	
G-MYME	Cyclone AX3/503	G-MYME Group	
G-MYMH	Rans S.6-ESD Coyote II	A. R. Cattell	
G-MYMI	Kolb Twinstar Mk.3	F. J. Brown	
G-MYMJ	Medway Raven	N. Brigginshaw	
G-MYMK	Mainair Gemini/Flash IIA	A. Britton	
G-MYML	Mainair Mercury	D. J. Dalley	
G-MYMM	Ultraflight Fun 18S	N. P. Power	
G-MYMN	Whittaker MW6 Merlin	K. J. Cole	
G-MYMP	Rans S.6-ESD Coyote II	R. L. Flowerday (G-CHAZ)	
G-MYMR	Rans S.6-ESD Coyote II	J. Minogue	
G-MYMS	Rans S.6-ESD Coyote II	P. G. Briscoe	
G-MYMV	Mainair Gemini/Flash IIA	A. J. Evans	
G-MYMW	Cyclone AX3/503	L. J. Perring	
G-MYMX	Solar Wings Pegasus Quantum 15	A. R. Watt	
G-MYMZ	Cyclone AX3/503	Microlight School (Lichfield) Ltd	
G-MYNB	Solar Wings Pegasus Quantum 15	J. A. Gregorig	
G-MYND	Mainair Gemini/Flash IIA	S. Wild	
G-MYNE	Rans S.6-ESD Coyote II	J. L. Smoker	
G-MYNF	Mainair Mercury	C. I. Hemingway	
G-MYNH	Rans S.6-ESD Coyote II	E. F. & V. M. Clapham	
G-MYNI	TEAM mini-MAX	I. Pearson	
G-MYNK	Solar Wings Pegasus Quantum 15	J. Britton	
G-MYNL	Solar Wings Pegasus Quantum 15	S. J. Whalley	
G-MYNN	Solar Wings Pegasus Quantum 15	V. Loy	
G-MYNO	Solar Wings Pegasus Quantum 15	P. A. C. R. Stephens	
G-MYNP	Solar Wings Pegasus Quantum 15	K. A. Davidson	
G-MYNR	Solar Wings Pegasus Quantum 15	C. A. Reynolds	
G-MYNS	Solar Wings Pegasus Quantum 15	F. J. McVey	
G-MYNT	Solar Wings Pegasus Quantum 15	C. D. Arnold	
G-MYNV	Solar Wings Pegasus Quantum 15	J. Goldsmith-Ryan	
G-MYNX	CFM Streak Shadow SA	S. P. Fletcher	
G-MYNY	Kolb Twinstar Mk 3	I. F. Hill	
G-MYNZ	Solar Wings Pegasus Quantum 15	P. W. Rogers	
G-MYOA	Rans S6-ESD Coyote II	N. S. M. Day	
G-MYOG	Kolb Twinstar Mk 3	T. A. Womersley	
G-MYOH	CFM Shadow Srs CD	D. R. Sutton	
G-MYOI	Rans S.6-ESD Coyote II	A. W. Paterson	
G-MYOL	Air Creation Fun 18S GTBIS	S. N. Bond	
G-MYOM	Mainair Gemini/Flash IIA	M. A. Haughey	
G-MYON	CFM Shadow Srs CD	D. W. & S. E. Suttill	
G-MYOO	Kolb Twinstar Mk 3	P. D. Coppin	
G-MYOR	Kolb Twinstar Mk 3	R. W. Hocking	
G-MYOS	CFM Shadow Srs CD	C. A. & E. J. Bowles	
G-MYOT	Rans S.6-ESD Coyote II	D. E. Wilson	
G-MYOU	Solar Wings Pegasus Quantum 15	D. J. Tasker	
G-MYOV	Mainair Mercury	P. Newton	
G-MYOX	Mainair Mercury	K. Driver	
G-MYOZ	Quad City Challenger II UK	A. R. Thomson	
G-MYPA	Rans S.6-ESD Coyote II	N. C. Marciano	
G-MYPC	Kolb Twinstar Mk 3	S. J. Ball	
G-MYPE	Mainair Gemini/Flash IIA	R. Cant & J. Davies	
G-MYPG	Solar Wings Pegasus XL-Q	R. D. Howie	
G-MYPH	Solar Wings Pegasus Quantum 15	P. M. J. White	
G-MYPI	Solar Wings Pegasus Quantum 15	P. L. Jarvis	
G-MYPJ	Rans S.6-ESD Coyote II	K. A. Eden	
G-MYPL	CFM Shadow Srs CD	G. I. Madden	
G-MYPN	Solar Wings Pegasus Quantum 15	P. J. S. Albon	
G-MYPP	Whittaker MW6-S Fat Boy Flyer	G. Everett & D. Smith	
G-MYPR	Cyclone AX3/503	K. D. Parnell	

Notes	Reg.	Type	Owner or Operator
	G-MYPS	Whittaker MW6 Merlin	I. S. Bishop
	G-MYPT	CFM Shadow Srs CD	R. Gray
	G-MYPV	Mainair Mercury	B. Donnan
	G-MYPW	Mainair Gemini/Flash IIA	T. C. Edwards
	G-MYPX	Solar Wings Pegasus Quantum 15	C. Cleveland & M. M. P. Evans
	G-MYPY	Solar Wings Pegasus Quantum 15	C. Cheasman
	G-MYPZ	Quad City Challenger II	E. G. Astin
	G-MYRC	Mainair Blade	J. Owen
	G-MYRD	Mainair Blade	D. R. Slater
	G-MYRE	Cyclone Chaser S	S. W. Barker
	G-MYRF	Solar Wings Pegasus Quantum 15	P. D. Gregory
	G-MYRG	TEAM mini-MAX	I. Macleod
	G-MYRH	Quad City Challenger II	G. Cousins
	G-MYRJ	BFC Challenger II	C. G. Trow
	G-MYRK	Renegade Spirit UK	D. J. Newton
	G-MYRL	TEAM mini-MAX	J. N. Hanson
	G-MYRM	Solar Wings Pegasus Quantum 15	B. R. & B. Dale
	G-MYRN	Solar Wings Pegasus Quantum 15	J. Houston & I. Waghorn
	G-MYRO	Cyclone AX3/503	R. S. Mole
	G-MYRP	Letov LK-2M Sluka	R. M. C. Hunter
	G-MYRS	Solar Wings Pegasus Quantum 15	M. Howland
	G-MYRT	Solar Wings Pegasus Quantum 15	A. M. Taylor
	G-MYRU	Cyclone AX3/503	W. A. Emmerson
	G-MYRV	Cyclone AX3/503	M. Gardiner
	G-MYRW	Mainair Mercury	G. C. Hobson
	G-MYRY	Solar Wings Pegasus Quantum 15	N. J. Lindsay
	G-MYRZ	Solar Wings Pegasus Quantum 15	R. E. Forbes
	G-MYSA	Cyclone Chaser S 508	S. D. J. Harvey
	G-MYSB	Solar Wings Pegasus Quantum 15	P. H. Woodward
	G-MYSC	Solar Wings Pegasus Quantum 15	K. R. White
	G-MYSD	BFC Challlenger II	C. W. Udale
	G-MYSG	Mainair Mercury	P. T. Flanagan
	G-MYSI	HM14/93	A. R. D. Seaman
	G-MYSJ	Mainair Gemini/Flash IIA	A. Warnock
	G-MYSL	Aviasud Mistral	J. E. Midder
	G-MYSM	CFM Shadow Srs CD	L. W. Stevens
	G-MYSO	Cyclone AX3/50	R. Bowden
	G-MYSP	Rans S.6-ESD Coyote II	A. J. Alexander, B. Knight & K. G. Diamond
	G-MYSR	Solar Wings Pegasus Quatum 15	W. G. Craig
	G-MYSU	Rans S.6-ESD Coyote II	C. N. Nairn
	G-MYSV	Aerial Arts Chaser	S. H. Hailstone
	G-MYSW	Solar Wings Pegasus Quantum 1	C. T. D. Whipps
	G-MYSX	Solar Wings Pegasus Quantum 1	J. L. Treves
	G-MYSY	Solar Wings Pegasus Quantum 15	B. D. S. Vere
	G-MYSZ	Mainair Mercury	W. Fletcher & S. D. J. Harvey
	G-MYTB	Mainair Mercur	P. J. Higgins
	G-MYTD	Mainair Blade	B. E. Warburton & D. B. Meades
	G-MYTE	Rans S.6-ESD Coyote II	M. Botten
	G-MYTG	Mainair Blade	O. P. Farrell
	G-MYTH	CFM Shadow Srs CD	S. G. Smith
	G-MYTI	Solar Wings Pegasus Quantum 15	K. M. Gaffney
	G-MYTJ	Solar Wings Pegasus Quantum 15	L. Blight
	G-MYTK	Mainair Mercury	D. A. Holroyd
	G-MYTL	Mainair Blade	I. T. Callagham & J. W. Coventry
	G-MYTN	Solar Wings Pegasus Quantum 15	R. Nicholson
	G-MYTO	Quad City Challenger II	A. Studley
	G-MYTP	Arrowflight Hawk II	R. J. Turner
	G-MYTT	Quad City Challenger II	D. M. Lockley
	G-MYTU	Mainair Blade	C. J. Barker
	G-MYTV	Hunt Avon Skytrike	M. Carson
	G-MYTY	CFM Streak Shadow Srs M	D. M. Broom
	G-MYUA	Air Creation Fun 18S GTBIS	J. Leden
	G-MYUC	Mainair Blade	A. D. Clayton
	G-MYUD	Mainair Mercury	P. W. Margetson
	G-MYUE	Mainair Mercury	T. H. R. Jamin
	G-MYUF	Renegade Spirit	F. Overall
	G-MYUH	Solar Wings Pegasus XL-Q	K. S. Daniels
	G-MYUI	Cyclone AX3/503	R. & M. Bailey
	G-MYUL	Quad City Challenger II UK	N. V. & B. M. R. Van Cleve
	G-MYUN	Mainair Blade	G. A. Barratt
	G-MYUO	Solar Wings Pegasus Quantum 15	E. J. Hughes
	G-MYUP	Letov LK-2M Sluka	J. C. Dawson

Reg.	Type	Owner or Operator	Notes
G-MYUR	Hunt Wing	T. C. Saltmarsh	
G-MYUS	CFM Shadow Srs CD	Aviation for Paraplegics and Tetraplegics Trust	
G-MYUU	Pegasus Quantum 15	J. A. Slocombe	
G-MYUV	Pegasus Quantum 15	D. W. Wilson	
G-MYUW	Mainair Mercury	G. C. Hobson	
G-MYUZ	Rans S.6-ESD Coyote II	A. R. Trace	
G-MYVA	Kolb Twinstar Mk 3	E. Bayliss	
G-MYVB	Mainair Blade	P. Mountain	
G-MYVC	Pegasus Quantum 15	D. P. Clarke	
G-MYVE	Mainair Blade	S. Cooke	
G-MYVG	Letov LK-2M Sluka	C. I. Chegwen	
G-MYVH	Mainair Mercury	S. E. Wilks	
G-MYVI	Air Creation Fun 18S GTBIS	Flylight Airsports Ltd	
G-MYVJ	Pegasus Quantum 15	A. I. McPherson & P. W. Davidson	
G-MYVK	Pegasus Quantum 15	N. C. Milnes	
G-MYVL	Mainair Mercury	P. J. Judge	
G-MYVM	Pegasus Quantum 15	G. J. Gibson	
G-MYVO	Mainair Blade	S. S. Raines	
G-MYVP	Rans S.6-ESD Coyote II	K. J. Legg & G. Cross	
G-MYVR	Pegasus Quantum 15	J. M. Webster	
G-MYVS	Mainair Mercury	P. S. Flynn	
G-MYVV	Medway Hybred 44XLR	S. Perity	
G-MYVY	Mainair Blade	G. Heeks	
G-MYVZ	Mainair Blade	R. Llewellyn	
G-MYWC	Hunt Wing	M. A. Coffin	
G-MYWE	Thruster T.600	W. A. Stephenson	
G-MYWG	Pegasus Quantum 15	S. L. Greene	
G-MYWH	Hunt Wing/Experience	G. N. Hatchett	
G-MYWI	Pegasus Quantum 15	J. R. Fulcher	
G-MYWJ	Pegasus Quantum 15	L. M. Sams & I. Clarkson	
G-MYWK	Pegasus Quantum 15	G. McGrane	
G-MYWL	Pegasus Quantum 15	S. J. Prouse	
G-MYWM	CFM Shadow Srs CD	N. J. McKinley	
G-MYWN	Cyclone Chaser S 508	R. A. Rawes	
G-MYWO	Pegasus Quantum 15	S. Gill & D. Hume	
G-MYWP	Kolb Twinstar Mk 3	P. R. Day	
G-MYWR	Pegasus Quantum 15	R. Horton	
G-MYWS	Cyclone Chaser S 447	M. H. Broadbent	
G-MYWT	Pegasus Quantum 1	A. G. Ransom	
G-MYWU	Pegasus Quantum 15	J. R. Buttle	
G-MYWV	Rans S.4C Coyote	P. G. Anthony & D. A. Crouchman	
G-MYWW	Pegasus Quantum 15	C. W. Bailie	
G-MYWY	Pegasus Quantum 15	A. S. R. Czajka	
G-MYXA	TEAM mini-MAX 91	P. J. Fahie	
G-MYXB	Rans S.6-ESD Coyote II	K. Gerrard	
G-MYXC	Quad City Challenger II	K. N. Dickinson	
G-MYXD	Pegasus Quasar IITC	A. Cochrane	
G-MYXE	Pegasus Quantum 15	J. F. Bolton	
G-MYXF	Air Creation Fun GT503	D. J. N. Brown	
G-MYXH	Cyclone AX3/503	S. Bond	
G-MYXI	Aries 1	H. Cook	
G-MYXJ	Mainair Blade	S. N. Robson	
G-MYXK	Quad City Challenger II	P. J. Collins	
G-MYXL	Mignet HM.1000 Baleri	R. W. Hollamby	
G-MYXM	Mainair Blade	S. C. Hodgson	
G-MYXN	Mainair Blade	M. R. Sands	
G-MYXO	Letov LK-2M Sluka	G. W. Allport	
G-MYXP	Rans S.6-ESD Coyote II	R. S. Amor	
G-MYXS	Kolb Twinstar Mk 3	B. B. Boniface	
G-MYXT	Pegasus Quantum 15	L. Harland	
G-MYXU	Thruster T.300	D. W. Wilson	
G-MYXV	Quad City Challenger II	T. S. Savage	
G-MYXW	Pegasus Quantum 15	P. J. Oakey	
G-MYXX	Pegasus Quantum 15	G. Fish	
G-MYXY	CFM Shadow Srs CD	A. P. Watkins & C. W. J. Davis	
G-MYXZ	Pegasus Quantum 15	A. K. Hole	
G-MYYA	Mainair Blade	K. J. Watt	
G-MYYB	Pegasus Quantum 15	A. L. Johnson	
G-MYYC	Pegasus Quantum 15	A. J. Rowe	
G-MYYD	Cyclone Chaser S 447	E. Kelly	
G-MYYF	Quad City Challenger II	J. G. & J. A. Smith	
G-MYYG	Mainair Blade	S. D. Pryke	

Notes	Reg.	Type	Owner or Operator
	G-MYYH	Mainair Blade	C. Nicholson
	G-MYYI	Pegasus Quantum 15	C. M. Day
	G-MYYJ	Hunt Wing	R. M. Jarvis
	G-MYYK	Pegasus Quantum 15	J. D. & N. G. Philp
	G-MYYL	Cyclone AX3/503	C. A. Fletcher
	G-MYYP	AMF Chevvron 2-45CS	J. Cook
	G-MYYR	TEAM mini-MAX 91	L. S. Bailey
	G-MYYS	TEAM mini-MAX	J. Pulford
	G-MYYV	Rans S.6-ESD Coyote IIXL	J. Rochead
	G-MYYW	Mainair Blade	M. D. Kirby
	G-MYYX	Pegasus Quantum 15	B. J. Chapman
	G-MYYY	Mainair Blade	E. D. Lockie
	G-MYYZ	Medway Raven X	J. W. Leaper
	G-MYZB	Pegasus Quantum 15	M. A. Lovatt
	G-MYZC	Cyclone AX3/503	P. E. Owen
	G-MYZE	TEAM mini-MAX	A. D. Bales
	G-MYZF	Cyclone AX3/503	Microflight (Ireland) Ltd
	G-MYZG	Cyclone AX3/503	D. S. Thomas
	G-MYZH	Chargus Titan 38	T. J. Gayton-Polley
	G-MYZJ	Pegasus Quantum 15	N. P. Gallon & G. R. L. Shrimp
	G-MYZK	Pegasus Quantum 15	D. Logan
	G-MYZL	Pegasus Quantum 15	S. Jelley
	G-MYZM	Pegasus Quantum 15	D. Hope
	G-MYZP	CFM Shadow Srs DD	R. M. Davies & P. I. Hodgson
	G-MYZR	Rans S.6-ESD Coyote II	Rans Clan
	G-MYZV	Rans S.6-ESD Coyote II	B. W. Savory
	G-MYZY	Pegasus Quantum 15	N. C. O. Watney
	G-MZAA	Mainair Blade	A. G. Butler
	G-MZAC	Quad City Challenger II	M. N. Calhaem
	G-MZAE	Mainair Blade	D. J. Guild
	G-MZAF	Mainair Blade	N. R. Stockton
	G-MZAG	Mainair Blade	D. R. G. Cornwell
	G-MZAH	Rans S.6-ESD Coyote II	C. J. Collett
	G-MZAJ	Mainair Blade	M. P. Daley
	G-MZAK	Mainair Mercury	I. Rawson
	G-MZAM	Mainair Blade	B. M. Marsh & P. David
	G-MZAN	Pegasus Quantum 15	P. M. Leahy
	G-MZAP	Mainair Blade	K. D. Adams
	G-MZAR	Mainair Blade	P. Bowden
	G-MZAS	Mainair Blade	T. Carter
	G-MZAT	Mainair Blade	M. J. Moulton
	G-MZAU	Mainair Blade	A. F. Glover
	G-MZAV	Mainair Blade	G. Taylor
	G-MZAW	Pegasus Quantum 15	C. A. Mackenzie
	G-MZAX	Pegasus Quantum 15	M. J. J. Clutterbuck
	G-MZAY	Mainair Blade	P. J. Harrison
	G-MZAZ	Mainair Blade	T. Porter & D. Whiteley
	G-MZBA	Mainair Blade 912	M. Leyden & S. Cronin
	G-MZBB	Pegasus Quantum 15	T. Campbell
	G-MZBC	Pegasus Quantum 15	B. M. Quinn
	G-MZBF	Letov LK-2M Sluka	V. Simpson
	G-MZBG	Hodder MW6-A	E. I. Rowlands-Jons & M. W. Kilvert
	G-MZBH	Rans S.6-ESD Coyote II	D. Sutherland
	G-MZBK	Letov LK-2M Sluka	A. W. Hodder
	G-MZBL	Mainair Blade	C. J. Rubery
	G-MZBN	CFM Shadow Srs B	W. J. Buskell
	G-MZBO	Pegasus Quantum 15	K. C. Beattie
	G-MZBR	Southdown Raven	D. M. Lane
	G-MZBS	CFM Shadow Srs D	S. K. Ryan
	G-MZBT	Pegasus Quantum 15	A. P. Whitmarsh
	G-MZBU	Rans S.6-ESD Coyote II	R. S. Marriott
	G-MZBV	Rans S.6-ESD Coyote II	C. L. Barham & R. I. Cannan
	G-MZBW	Quad City Challenger II UK	R. M. C. Hunter
	G-MZBY	Pegasus Quantum 15	I. J. Rawlingson
	G-MZBZ	Quad City Challenger II UK	T. R. Gregory
	G-MZCA	Rans S.6-ESD Coyote II	W. Scott
	G-MZCB	Cyclone Chaser S 447	R. W. Keene
	G-MZCC	Mainair Blade 912	K. S. Rissmann
	G-MZCD	Mainair Blade	T. Drury & S. P. Maxwell
	G-MZCE	Mainair Blade	I. C. Hindle
	G-MZCF	Mainair Blade	C. Hannanby

Reg.	Type	Owner or Operator	Notes
G-MZCG	Mainair Blade	J. C. Sutton	
G-MZCH	Whittaker MW6-S Fatboy Flyer	J. T. Moore	
G-MZCI	Pegasus Quantum 15	P. H. Risdale	
G-MZCJ	Pegasus Quantum 15	C. R. Madden	
G-MZCK	AMF Chevvron 2-32C	M. Daly	
G-MZCM	Pegasus Quantum 15	J. E. Bullock	
G-MZCN	Mainair Blade	P. Mulvey	
G-MZCR	Pegasus Quantum 15	J. E. P. Stubberfield	
G-MZCS	TEAM mini-MAX	R. F. Morton	
G-MZCT	CFM Shadow Srs CD	W. G. Gill	
G-MZCU	Mainair Blade	C. E. Pearce	
G-MZCV	Pegasus Quantum 15	I. Davidson	
G-MZCW	Pegasus Quantum 15	K. L. Baldwin	
G-MZDA	Rans S.6-ESD Coyote IIXL	S. Day & R. Plummer	
G-MZDB	Pegasus Quantum 15	Scottish Aerotow Club	
G-MZDC	Pegasus Quantum 15	M. T. Jones	
G-MZDD	Pegasus Quantum 15	A. J. Todd	
G-MZDE	Pegasus Quantum 15	R. G. Hedley	
G-MZDG	Rans S.6-ESD Coyote IIXL	J. M. Coffin	
G-MZDH	Pegasus Quantum 15	R. C. Reynolds	
G-MZDJ	Medway Raven X	R. Bryan & S. Digby	
G-MZDK	Mainair Blade	B. L. Cook	
G-MZDL	Whittaker MW6-S Fatboy Flyer	N. Hogarth	
G-MZDM	Rans S.6-ESD Coyote II	M. E. Nicholas	
G-MZDN	Pegasus Quantum 15	P. G. Ford	
G-MZDP	AMF Chevvron 2-32	J. Pool	
G-MZDS	Cyclone AX3/503	S. F. N. Warnell	
G-MZDT	Mainair Blade	G. A. Davidson & I. Lee	
G-MZDU	Pegasus Quantum 15	G. Breen/Portugal	
G-MZDV	Pegasus Quantum 15	S. A. Mallett	
G-MZDX	Letov LK-2M Sluka	J. L. Barker	
G-MZDY	Pegasus Quantum 15	R. Bailey	
G-MZDZ	Hunt Wing	E. W. Laidlaw	
G-MZEA	BFC Challenger II	G. S. Cridland	
G-MZEB	Mainair Blade	G. Todd & A. R. Campbell	
G-MZEC	Pegasus Quantum 15	A. B. Godber	
G-MZED	Mainair Blade	C. W. Potts	
G-MZEE	Pegasus Quantum 15	J. L. Brogan	
G-MZEG	Mainair Blade	R. Jacques	
G-MZEH	Pegasus Quantum 15	P. S. Hall	
G-MZEJ	Mainair Blade	P. G. Thomas	
G-MZEK	Mainair Mercury	G. Crane	
G-MZEL	Cyclone Airsports AX3/503	R. I. Simpson	
G-MZEM	Pegasus Quantum 15	L. H. Black	
G-MZEN	Rans S.6-ESD Coyote II	P. R. Hutty	
G-MZEO	Rans S.6-ESD Coyote IIXL	R. W. Lenthall	
G-MZEP	Mainair Rapier	A. G. Bird	
G-MZER	Cyclone AX2000	J. H. Keep	
G-MZES	Letov LK-2N Sluka	J. L. Self	
G-MZEU	Rans S.6-ESD Coyote IIXL	N. Grugan	
G-MZEV	Mainair Rapier	W. T. Gardner	
G-MZEW	Mainair Blade	T. D. Holder	
G-MZEX	Pegasus Quantum 15	J. P. Quinlan	
G-MZEY	Micro Bantam B.22	P. J. Glover	
G-MZEZ	Pegasus Quantum 15	M. J. Ing	
G-MZFA	Cyclone AX2000	G. S. Highley	
G-MZFB	Mainair Blade	A. J. Plant	
G-MZFC	Letov LK-2M Sluka	F. Overall	
G-MZFD	Mainair Rapier	R. J. Allerton	
G-MZFE	Hunt Wing	G. J. Latham	
G-MZFF	Hunt Wing	B. J. Adamson	
G-MZFG	Pegasus Quantum 15	A. M. Prentice	
G-MZFH	AMF Chevvron 2-32C	A. Greenwell	
G-MZFL	Rans S.6-ESD Coyote IIXL	H. Adams	
G-MZFM	Pegasus Quantum 15	M. McLaughlin	
G-MZFN	Rans S.6.ESD Coyote IIXL	C. J. & W. R. Wallbank	
G-MZFO	Thruster T.600N	S. J. P. Stevenson	
G-MZFS	Mainair Blade	S. L. Rowlands	
G-MZFT	Pegasus Quantum 15	C. Childs	
G-MZFU	Thruster T.600N	P. G. Hullett	
G-MZFX	Cyclone AX2000	Avon Aerotow Group	
G-MZFY	Rans S.6-ESD Coyote IIXL	L. G. Tserkezos	

Notes	Reg.	Type	Owner or Operator
	G-MZFZ	Mainair Blade	D. J. Bateman
	G-MZGA	Cyclone AX2000	R. G. Crampton
	G-MZGB	Cyclone AX2000	P. Hegarty
	G-MZGC	Cyclone AX2000	C. E. Walls
	G-MZGD	Rans S.5 Coyote II	P. J. Greenrod
	G-MZGF	Letov LK-2M Sluka	G. Lombardi & R. C. Hinkins
	G-MZGG	Pegasus Quantum 15	N. I. Garland
	G-MZGH	Hunt Wing/Avon 462	J. H. Cole
	G-MZGI	Mainair Blade 912	H. M. Roberts
	G-MZGJ	Kolb Twinstar Mk 1	C. D. Gates
	G-MZGK	Pegasus Quantum 15	C. D. Cross & S. H. Moss
	G-MZGL	Mainair Rapier	D. Thrower
	G-MZGM	Cyclone AX2000	A. F. Smallacombe
	G-MZGN	Pegasus Quantum 15	B. J. Youngs
	G-MZGO	Pegasus Quantum 15	S. F. G. Allen
	G-MZGP	Cyclone AX2000	Buchan Light Aeroplane Club
	G-MZGR	TEAM mini-MAX	K. G. Seeley
	G-MZGS	CFM Shadow Srs BD	P. Bayliss
	G-MZGT	RH78 Tiger Light	C. L. G. Innocent
	G-MZGU	Arrowflight Hawk II (UK)	J. N. Holden
	G-MZGV	Pegasus Quantum 15	H. Millington
	G-MZGW	Mainair Blade	R. Almond
	G-MZGY	Thruster T.600N 450	P. E. Young
	G-MZHA	Thruster T.600N	P. Stark
	G-MZHB	Mainair Blade	M. R. Hilton
	G-MZHD	Thruster T.600N	B. E. Foster
	G-MZHF	Thruster T.600N	R. Benner & K. Harmston
	G-MZHI	Pegasus Quantum 15	F. R. Macdonald
	G-MZHJ	Mainair Rapier	G. Standish & R. Jones
	G-MZHK	Pegasus Quantum 15	R. Hussain
	G-MZHM	Team Himax 1700R	M. H. McKeown
	G-MZHN	Pegasus Quantum 15	F. W. Ferichs
	G-MZHO	Quad City Challenger II	J. Pavelin
	G-MZHP	Pegasus Quantum 15	P. C. J. Coidan
	G-MZHR	Cyclone AX2000	T. N. Farley
	G-MZHS	Thruster T.600T	J. R. Davis
	G-MZHT	Whittaker MW6 Merlin	G. J. Chadwick
	G-MZHU	Thruster T.600T	D. R. Baker
	G-MZHV	Thruster T.600T	H. G. Denton
	G-MZHW	Thruster T.600N	H. & G. Willingham
	G-MZHY	Thruster T.600N	J. P. & R. E. Jones
	G-MZIB	Pegasus Quantum 15	S. Murphy
	G-MZID	Whittaker MW6 Merlin	C. P. F. Sheppard
	G-MZIE	Pegasus Quantum 15	Flylight Airsports Ltd
	G-MZIF	Pegasus Quantum 15	D. Parsons
	G-MZIH	Mainair Blade	N. J. Waller
	G-MZIJ	Pegasus Quantum 15	D. L. Wright
	G-MZIK	Pegasus Quantum 15	C. M. Wilkinson
	G-MZIL	Mainair Rapier	A. J. Owen & J. C. Price
	G-MZIM	Mainair Rapier	M. J. McKegney
	G-MZIR	Mainair Blade	S. Connor
	G-MZIS	Mainair Blade	M. K. Richings
	G-MZIT	Mainair Blade 912	P. M. Horn
	G-MZIU	Pegasus Quantum 15	A. P. Douglas-Dixon
	G-MZIV	Cyclone AX2000	C. J. Tomlin
	G-MZIW	Mainair Blade	S. R. Pickering
	G-MZIX	Mignet HM.1000 Balerit	P. E. H. Scott
	G-MZIY	Rans S.6-ESD Coyote II	G. Munro
	G-MZIZ	Renegade Spirit UK (G-MWGP)	B. L. R. J. Keeping
	G-MZJA	Mainair Blade	R. C. McArthur
	G-MZJD	Mainair Blade	D. A. Meek
	G-MZJE	Mainair Rapier	E. Woods
	G-MZJF	Cyclone AX2000	D. J. Lewis & V. E. Booth
	G-MZJG	Pegasus Quantum 15	K. M. C. Compton
	G-MZJH	Pegasus Quantum 15	P. Copping
	G-MZJI	Rans S.6-ESD Coyote II	M. A. Newbould & C. Topp
	G-MZJJ	Maverick	S. J. Spavins
	G-MZJK	Mainair Blade	P. G. Angus
	G-MZJL	Cyclone AX2000	M. H. Owen
	G-MZJM	Rans S.6-ESD Coyote IIXL	K. A. Hastie
	G-MZJO	Pegasus Quantum 15	D. J. Cook
	G-MZJP	Whittaker MW6-S Fatboy Flyer	R. C. Funnell & D. J. Burton

Reg.	Type	Owner or Operator	Notes
G-MZJR	Cyclone AX2000	N. A. Martin	
G-MZJS	Meridian Maverick	M. F. Farrer	
G-MZJT	Pegasus Quantum 15	N. Hammerton	
G-MZJV	Mainair Blade 912	M. A. Roberts	
G-MZJX	Mainair Blade	A. D. Taylor	
G-MZJY	Pegasus Quantum 15	M. F. Turff	
G-MZJZ	Mainair Blade	A. Openshaw	
G-MZKA	Pegasus Quantum 15	S. P. Tkaczyk	
G-MZKC	Cyclone AX2000	G-MZKC Group	
G-MZKD	Pegasus Quantum 15	T. M. Frost	
G-MZKE	Rans S.6-ESD Coyote IIXL	P. A. Flaherty	
G-MZKF	Pegasus Quantum 15	R. G. Hearsey	
G-MZKG	Mainair Blade	N. S. Rigby	
G-MZKH	CFM Shadow Srs DD	S. P. H. Calvert	
G-MZKI	Mainair Rapier	D. L. Aspinall	
G-MZKJ	Mainair Blade	The G-MZKJ Group	
G-MZKK	Mainair Blade 912	I. M. Ferdinand	
G-MZKL	Pegasus Quantum 15	G. Williams	
G-MZKN	Mainair Rapier	J. McAloney	
G-MZKR	Thruster T.600N	R. J. Arnett	
G-MZKS	Thruster T.600N	P. J. Hepburn	
G-MZKT	Thruster T.600N	Great Thornes Flying Group	
G-MZKU	Thruster T.600N	A. S. Day	
G-MZKV	Mainair Blade 912	J. D. Harriman	
G-MZKW	Quad City Challenger II	K. W. Warn	
G-MZKY	Pegasus Quantum 15	P. S. Constable	
G-MZKZ	Mainair Blade	R. P. Wolstenholme	
G-MZLA	Pegasus Quantum 15	A. J. Harris	
G-MZLC	Mainair Blade 912	R. A. L. Harris	
G-MZLD	Pegasus Quantum 15	D. Hamilton	
G-MZLE	Maverick (G-BXSZ)	J. S. Hill	
G-MZLF	Pegasus Quantum 15	S. Seymour	
G-MZLG	Rans S.6-ESD Coyote IIXL	F. Y. Allery	
G-MZLI	Mignet HM.1000 Balerit	A. G. Barr	
G-MZLJ	Pegasus Quantum 15	R. M. Williams	
G-MZLK	Solar Wings Typhoon/Tri-Pacer	A. Leak	
G-MZLL	Rans S.6-ESD Coyote II	J. A. Willats & G. W. Champion	
G-MZLM	Cyclone AX2000	P. E. Hadley	
G-MZLN	Pegasus Quantum 15	P. A. Greening	
G-MZLP	CFM Shadow Srs D	D. J. Gordon	
G-MZLR	Solar Wings Pegasus XL-Q	B. Lorraine	
G-MZLS	Cyclone AX2000	A. C. A. Hayes	
G-MZLT	Pegasus Quantum 15	V. T. Betts	
G-MZLU	Cyclone AX2000	E. Pashley & A. W. Lees	
G-MZLV	Pegasus Quantum 15	A. Armsby	
G-MZLW	Pegasus Quantum 15	R. W. R. Crevel & R. J. Nixon	
G-MZLX	Micro Aviation B.22S Bantam	V. J. Vaughan	
G-MZLY	Letov LK-2M Sluka	W. McCarthy	
G-MZLZ	Mainair Blade	D. Allan	
G-MZMA	Solar Wings Pegasus Quasar IITC	M. L. Pardoe	
G-MZMC	Pegasus Quantum 15	J. J. Baker	
G-MZMD	Mainair Blade 912	S. George	
G-MZME	Medway Eclipser	P. A. Wenham	
G-MZMF	Pegasus Quantum 15	A. J. Tranter	
G-MZMG	Pegasus Quantum 15	A. G. Kemp	
G-MZMH	Pegasus Quantum 15	M. Hurtubise	
G-MZMJ	Mainair Blade	D. Wilson	
G-MZMK	Chevvron 2-32C	P. J. Tyler	
G-MZML	Mainair Blade 912	S. C. Stoodley	
G-MZMM	Mainair Blade 912	J. Lynch	
G-MZMN	Pegasus Quantum 912	R. H. Cheesley	
G-MZMO	TEAM mini-MAX 91	R. E. Main	
G-MZMP	Mainair Blade	A. M. Beale	
G-MZMS	Rans S.6-ESD Coyote II	J. Morris	
G-MZMT	Pegasus Quantum 15	Z. Cantel	
G-MZMU	Rans S.6-ESD Coyote II	J. W. Willcox	
G-MZMV	Mainair Blade	M. D. Harris	
G-MZMW	Mignet HM.1000 Balerit	M. E. Whapham	
G-MZMX	Cyclone AX2000	L. A. Lacy	
G-MZMY	Mainair Blade	C. J. Millership	
G-MZMZ	Mainair Blade	W. A. Stacey	
G-MZNA	Quad City Challenger II UK	S. Hennessy	

Notes	Reg.	Type	Owner or Operator
	G-MZNB	Pegasus Quantum 15	F. Gorse
	G-MZNC	Mainair Blade 912	A. J. Harrison
	G-MZND	Mainair Rapier	D. W. Stamp
	G-MZNG	Pegasus Quantum 15	The Scottish Flying Club
	G-MZNH	CFM Shadow Srs DD	Cloudbase Aviation
	G-MZNJ	Mainair Blade	S. J. Taft
	G-MZNL	Mainair Blade 912	M. A. Williams
	G-MZNM	TEAM mini-MAX	P. J. Fahie
	G-MZNN	TEAM mini-MAX	P. J. Bishop
	G-MZNO	Mainair Blade	F. Poirot
	G-MZNR	Pegasus Quantum 15	E. S. Wills
	G-MZNS	Pegasus Quantum 15	M. J. Robbins
	G-MZNT	Pegasus Quantum 15-912	M. B. Sears
	G-MZNU	Mainair Rapier	B. Johnson
	G-MZNV	Rans S.6-ESD Coyote II	A. P. Thomas
	G-MZNX	Thruster T.600N	B. Rogan
	G-MZNY	Thruster T.600N	G. Price
	G-MZNZ	Letov LK-2M Sluka	B. F. Crick
	G-MZOC	Mainair Blade	T. D. Clarry
	G-MZOD	Pegasus Quantum 15	M. C. Robinson
	G-MZOE	Cyclone AX2000	M. F. Hadley
	G-MZOF	Mainair Blade	R. M. Ellis
	G-MZOG	Pegasus Quantum 15-912	D. Smith
	G-MZOH	Whittaker MW5D Sorcerer	I. Pearson
	G-MZOI	Letov LK-2M Sluka	B. S. P. Finch
	G-MZOJ	Pegasus Quantum 15	M. K. Ashmore
	G-MZOK	Whittaker MW6 Merlin	G-MZOK Syndicate
	G-MZOM	CFM Shadow Srs DD	G-MZOM Shadow Flyers
	G-MZOP	Mainair Blade 912	K. M. Thorogood
	G-MZOS	Pegasus Quantum 15-912	R. J. Field
	G-MZOV	Pegasus Quantum 15	Pegasus XL Group
	G-MZOW	Pegasus Quantum 15-912	G. P. Burns
	G-MZOX	Letov LK-2M Sluka	D. L. Hadley
	G-MZOY	TEAM Mini-MAX 91	P. R. & S. E. Whitehouse
	G-MZOZ	Rans S.6-ESD Coyote IIXL	S. G. & D. C. Emmons
	G-MZPH	Mainair Blade	J. D. Hoyland
	G-MZPJ	TEAM mini-MAX	P. R. Jenson
	G-MZPW	Pegasus Quasar IITC	N. S. Payne
	G-MZRC	Pegasus Quantum 15	M. Hopkins
	G-MZRM	Pegasus Quantum 15	A. Robinson
	G-MZRS	CFM Shadow Srs CD	M. Booth
	G-MZSC	Pegasus Quantum 15-912	J. Urrutia
	G-MZSM	Mainair Blade	R. R. Anderson
	G-MZTS	Aerial Arts Chaser S	D. G. Ellis (G-MVDM)
	G-MZUB	Rans S.6-ESD Coyote IIXL	B. O. Dowsett
	G-MZZT	Kolb Twinstar Mk 3	D. E. Martin
	G-MZZY	Mainair Blade 912	A. Mucznik
	G-NAAA	MBB Bö.105DBS/4	Bond Air Services Ltd (G-BUTN/G-AZTI)
	G-NAAB	MBB Bo.105DBS/4	Bond Air Services Ltd
	G-NAAL	Bombardier CL600-2B16 Challenger	Ocean Sky Aircraft Management Ltd
	G-NACA	Norman NAC-2 Freelance 180	A. R. Norman
	G-NACI	Norman NAC-1 Srs 100	L. J. Martin & D. G. French (G-AXFB)
	G-NACL	Norman NAC-6 Fieldmaster	EPA Aircraft Co Ltd (G-BNEG)
	G-NACO	Norman NAC-6 Fieldmaster	EPA Aircraft Co Ltd
	G-NACP	Norman NAC-6 Fieldmaster	EPA Aircraft Co Ltd
	G-NADO	Titan Tornado SS	Euro Aviation LLP
	G-NADS	TEAM mini-MAX 91	R. L. Williams
	G-NADZ	Van's RV-4	J. K. Cook (G-BROP)
	G-NAGG	Rotorsport UK MT-03	C. A. Clements
	G-NANI	Robinson R44 II	MOS Gmbh
	G-NANO	Avid Speed Wing	T. M. C. Handley
	G-NAPP	Van's RV-7	E. Fogarty
	G-NARG	Tanarg/Ixess 15 912S (1)	K. Kirby
	G-NARO	Cassutt Racer	C. Ball & R. Supply (G-BTXR)
	G-NARR	Stolp SA300 Starduster Too	G. J. D. Thomson
	G-NATT	Rockwell Commander 114A	Northgleam Ltd
	G-NATX	Cameron O-65 balloon	A. G. E. Faulkner
	G-NATY	HS. Gnat T.1 (XR537) ★	Drilling Systems Ltd
	G-NBDD	Robin DR.400/180	B. & S. E. Chambers
	G-NBEL	AS.355F1 Ecureuil 2	Latitude Aviation Ltd (G-SKYW/G-TBIS/G-TALI)

Reg.	Type	Owner or Operator	Notes
G-NBSI	Cameron N-77 balloon	Nottingham Hot-Air Balloon Club	
G-NCCC	Bombardier CL600-2B16	TAG Aviation (UK) Ltd	
G-NCFC	PA-38-112 Tomahawk II	A. M. Heynen	
G-NCUB	Piper J-3C-65 Cub	R. J. Willies (G-BGXV)	
G-NDAA	MBB Bö.105DBS-4	Bond Air Services Ltd (G-WMAA/G-PASB/G-BDMC)	
G-NDOL	Shaw Europa	S. Longstaff	
G-NDOT	Thruster T.600N	P. C. Bailey	
G-NDPA	Ikarus C42 FB UK	P. A. Pilkington	
G-NEAL	PA-32-260 Cherokee Six	I. Parkinson (G-BFPY)	
G-NEAT	Shaw Europa	M. Burton	
G-NEAU	Eurocopter EC 135T2	Northumbria Police Authority	
G-NEEL	Rotorway Executive 90	I. C. Bedford	
G-NELI	PA-28R Cherokee Arrow 180	R. Drysdale	
G-NEMO	Raj Hamsa X'Air Jabiru (4)	G. F. Allen	
G-NEON	PA-32 Cherokee Six 300B	S. C. A. Lever	
G-NEPB	Cameron N-77 balloon	The Post Office	
G-NESA	Shaw Europa XS	A. M. Kay	
G-NESE	Tecnam P2002-JF	N. & S. Easton	
G-NESH	Robinson R44 II	M. Tancock	
G-NEST	Christen Eagle II	A. F. R. Pruniaux	
G-NESV	Eurocopter EC 135T1	Cleveland Police Authority	
G-NESW	PA-34-220T Seneca III	G. C. U. Guida	
G-NESY	PA-18 Super Cub 95	V. Featherstone	
G-NETB	Cirrus SR22	N. Caminada	
G-NETR	AS.355F1 Twin Squirrel	PLM Dollar Group Ltd (G-JARV/G-OGHL)	
G-NETT	Cessna 172S	Air-Unlimited Sweden AB	
G-NETY	PA-18 Super Cub 150	N. B. Mason	
G-NEWS	Bell 206B-3 JetRanger III	Apple International Inc.Ltd & JAC Heli	
G-NEWT	Beech 35 Bonanza	J. S. Allison (G-APVW)	
G-NEWZ	Bell 206B JetRanger 3	Guay Tulliemet Aviation Ltd	
G-NFLA	BAe Jetstream 3102	Cranfield University (G-BRGN/G-BLHC)	
G-NFLC	HP.137 Jetstream 1H (G-AXUI) ★	Instructional airframe/Perth	
G-NFLY	Tecnam P2002-EA Sierra	C. N. Hodgson	
G-NFNF	Robin DR.400/180	M. Child, W. Cobb & J. Archer	
G-NFON	Van's RV-8	N. F. O'Neill	
G-NGLS	Aerospool Dynamic WT9 UK	The Nigels Ltd	
G-NHAA	AS.365N-2 Dauphin 2	The Great North Air Ambulance Service (G-MLTY)	
G-NHAB	AS.365N-2 Dauphin 2	The Great North Air Ambulance Service (G-DAUF)	
G-NHRH	PA-28 Cherokee 140	C. J. Milsom	
G-NHRJ	Shaw Europa XS	D. A. Lowe	
G-NICC	Aerotechnik EV-97 Team Eurostar UK	Pickup and Son Ltd	
G-NICI	Robinson R44	David Fishwick Vehicles Sales Ltd	
G-NICK	PA-18 Super Cub	M. W. Zipfell	
G-NICS	Best Off Sky Ranger Swift 912S(1)	N. G. Heywood	
G-NIDG	Aerotechnik EV-97 Eurostar	Skydrive Ltd	
G-NIEN	Van's RV-9A	G. R. Pybus	
G-NIFE	SNCAN Stampe SV.4A (156)	Tiger Airways	
G-NIGC	Avtech Jabiru UL-450	W. D. Brereton	
G-NIGE	Luscombe 8E Silvaire	Garden Party Ltd (G-BSHG)	
G-NIGL	Shaw Europa	N. M. Graham	
G-NIGS	Thunder Ax7-65 balloon	S. D. Annett	
G-NIJM	PA-28R Cherokee Arrow 180	G-NIJM Syndicate	
G-NIKE	PA-28-181 Archer II	Key Properties Ltd	
G-NIKK	Diamond Katana DA20-C1	Cubair Flight Training Ltd	
G-NIKO	Airbus A.321-211	Thomas Cook Airlines Ltd	
G-NIKX	Robinson R-44 II	P. R. Holloway	
G-NIMA	Balóny Kubíček BB30Z balloon	C. Williamson	
G-NIMB	Schempp-Hirth Nimbus 2C	M. J. Slade	
G-NINA	PA-28-161 Warrior II	A. P. Gorrod (G-BEUC)	
G-NINB	PA-28-180 Cherokee	P. A. Layzell	
G-NINC	PA-28-180 Cherokee	P. A. Layzell	
G-NIND	PA-28-180 Cherokee	P. A. Layzell	
G-NINE	Murphy Renegade 912	R. C. McCarthy	
G-NIOG	Robinson R44 II	Alu-Fix Contracts Ltd	
G-NIOS	PA-32R-301 Saratoga SP	Plant Aviation	

Notes	Reg.	Type	Owner or Operator
	G-NIPA	Slingsby T.66 Nipper 3	R. J. O. Walker (G-AWDD)
	G-NIPP	Slingsby T.66 Nipper 3	R. J. Porter (G-AVKJ)
	G-NIPR	Slingsby T.66 Nipper 3	P. A. Gibbs (G-AVXC)
	G-NIPS	Tipsy T.66 Nipper 2	B. W. Faulkner
	G-NIPY	Hughes 369HS	Jet Aviation (Northwest) Ltd
	G-NISA	Robinson R44 II	G. P. Jones (G-HTMT)
	G-NISH	Van's RV-8	N. H. F. Hampton & S. R. Whitling
	G-NITA	PA-28 Cherokee 180	T. Clifford (G-AVVG)
	G-NIVA	Eurocopter EC 155B1	Lanthwaite Aviation Ltd
	G-NIVT	Schempp-Hirth Nimbus 4T	G-NIVT Gliding Group
	G-NJBA	Rotorway Executive 162F	British Waterproofing Ltd
	G-NJET	Schempp-Hirth Ventus cT	V. S. Bettle
	G-NJIM	PA-32R-301T Turbo Saratoga	J. L. Rivers
	G-NJPW	P & M Quik GT450	N. J. P. West
	G-NJSH	Robinson R22 Beta	A. J. Hawes
	G-NJSP	Jabiru J430	N. J. S. Pitman
	G-NJTC	Aeroprakt A22-L Foxbat	B. Jackson & T. F. Casey
	G-NLCH	Lindstrand LBL-35A balloon	S. A. Lacey
	G-NLEE	Cessna 182Q	C. G. D. Jones (G-TLTD)
	G-NLMB	Zenair CH.601UL Zodiac	N. Lamb
	G-NLPA	Hawker 750	Hangar 8 Management Ltd
	G-NLYB	Cameron N-105 balloon	P. H. E. Van Overwalle/Belgium
	G-NMAK	Airbus A.319-115	Twinjet Aircraft Sales Ltd
	G-NMBG	Jabiru J400	P. R. Hendry-Smith & H. I. Smith
	G-NMID	Eurocopter EC 135T2	Derbyshire Constabulary
	G-NMOS	Cameron C-80 balloon	C. J. Thomas & M. C. East
	G-NMRV	Van's RV-6	W. H. Greenwood
	G-NNAC	PA-18 Super Cub 135	PAW Flying Services Ltd
	G-NNCY	Eurocopter EC.225LP Super Puma	CHC Scotia Ltd
	G-NNON	Mainair Blade	D. R. Kennedy
	G-NOAH	Airbus A.319-115CJ	Acropolis Aviation Ltd
	G-NOCK	Cessna FR.182RG II	R. D. Masters (G-BGTK)
	G-NODE	AA-5B Tiger	Strategic Telecom Networks Ltd
	G-NOIR	Bell 222	Heron Helicopters Ltd (G-OJLC/G-OSEB/ G-BNDA)
	G-NOIZ	Yakovlev Yak-55M	S. C. Cattlin
	G-NOMO	Cameron O-31 balloon	Balloon Promotion SAS/Italy
	G-NOMZ	Balony Kubicek BB-S Gnome SS balloon	A. M. Holly
	G-NONE	Dyn'Aéro MCR-01 ULC	T. W. Lorimer
	G-NONI	AA-5 Traveler	November India Group (G-BBDA)
	G-NOOK	Mainair Blade 912S	D. J. S. Sevin
	G-NOOR	Commander 114B	As-Al Ltd
	G-NORA	Ikarus C.42 FB UK	N. A. Rathbone
	G-NORB	Saturne S110K hang glider	R. N. Pearce
	G-NORD	SNCAN NC.854	A. D. Pearce
	G-NOSE	Cessna 402B	Reconnaissance Ventures Ltd (G-MPCU)
	G-NOSS	BAe Jetstream 3102	Spitfire Investments Ltd
	G-NOTE	PA-28-181 Archer III	J. Beach
	G-NOTS	Skyranger 912S(1)	E. A. J. Chalk
	G-NOTT	Nott ULD-2 balloon	J. R. P. Nott
	G-NOTY	Westland Scout AH.1	R. P. Coplestone
	G-NOUS	Cessna 172S	Flyglass Ltd
	G-NOWW	Mainair Blade 912	C. Bodill
	G-NOXY	Robinson R44	T. A. Knox Shopfitters Ltd (G-VALV)
	G-NPKJ	Van's RV-6	M. R. Turner
	G-NPPL	Comco Ikarus C.42 FB.100	Papa Lima Group
	G-NRIA	Beech 23 Musketeer	Respondmatte Flugeliclub
	G-NROY	PA-32RT-300 Lance II	B. Nedjati-Gilani (G-LYNN/G-BGNY)
	G-NRRA	SIAI-Marchetti SF.260 ★	G. Boot
	G-NSBB	Ikarus C.42 FB-100 VLA	B. Bayes & N. E. Sams
	G-NSEW	Robinson R44	G-NSEW Ltd
	G-NSJS	Cessna 680 Citation Sovereign	Ferncroft Ltd
	G-NSKB	Aeroprakt A22-L Foxbat	N. F. Smith
	G-NSOF	Robin HR.200/120B	Modi Aviation Ltd

Reg.	Type	Owner or Operator	Notes
G-NSTG	Cessna F.150F	Westair Flying Services Ltd (G-ATNI)	
G-NSUK	PA-34-220T Seneca V	Langsteiner Flugbetrieb KEG	
G-NTWK	AS.355F2 Twin Squirrel	PLM Dollar Group (G-FTWO/G-OJOR/G-BMUS)	
G-NUDE	Robinson R44	The Last Great Journey Ltd (G-NSYT)	
G-NUFC	Best Off Skyranger 912S(1)	C. R. Rosby	
G-NUGC	Grob G.103A Twin II Acro	University of Nottingham Gliding Club	
G-NUKA	PA-28-181 Archer II	N. Ibrahim	
G-NULA	Flight Design CT2K	L. I. Bailey	
G-NUNI	Lindstrand LBL-77A balloon	J. A. Folkes	
G-NUTA	Christen Eagle II	Blue Eagle Group	
G-NUTT	Mainair Pegasus Quik	NUTT Syndicate	
G-NUTY	AS.350B Ecureuil	Eli Airbust SRL (G-BXKT)	
G-NVBF	Lindstrand LBL-210A balloon	Virgin Balloon Flights	
G-NWAA	Eurocopter EC 135T2	Bond Air Services Ltd	
G-NWDC	Robinson R22 Beta	J. Porter (G-SBAR)	
G-NWFA	Cessna 150M	North Weald Flying Group Ltd (G-CFBD)	
G-NWFC	Cessna 172P	North Weald Flying Group Ltd	
G-NWFG	Cessna 172P	North Weald Flying Group Ltd	
G-NWOI	Eurocopter EC135 P2+	North Wales Police Authority	
G-NWPR	Cameron N-77 balloon	D. B. Court	
G-NWPS	Eurocopter EC 135T1	North-West Police Authority	
G-NXOE	Cessna 172S	Goodwood Road Racing Co.Ltd	
G-NXUS	Nexus Mustang	G. W. Miller	
G-NYMB	Schempp-Hirth Nimbus 3	Nimbus Syndicate	
G-NYMF	PA-25 Pawnee 235D	Bristol Gliding Club Pty Ltd	
G-NYNA	Van's RV-9A	B. Greathead & S. Hiscox	
G-NYNE	Schleicher ASW-27-18E	R. C. W. Ellis	
G-NZGL	Cameron O-105 balloon	R. A. Vale & ptnrs	
G-NZSS	Boeing Stearman N2S-5 (343251:27)	P. R. Bennett & M. J. Nice	
G-OAAA	PA-28-161 Warrior II	Red Hill Air Services Ltd	
G-OAAF	BAe ATP	Atlantic Airlines Ltd (G-JEMB)	
G-OABB	Jodel D.150	K. Manley	
G-OABC	Colt 69A balloon	P. A. C. Stuart-Kregor	
G-OABO	Enstrom F-28A	C. R. Taylor (G-BAIB)	
G-OABR	AG-5B Tiger	A. J. Neale	
G-OACA	PA-44-180 Seminole	Lenham Motorsport (G-GSFT)	
G-OACE	Valentin Taifun 17E	I. F. Wells	
G-OACF	Robin DR.400/180	A. C. Fletcher	
G-OACI	MS.893E Rallye 180GT	Full Sutton Flying Centre Ltd	
G-OACP	OGMA DHC.1 Chipmunk 20	Aeroclub de Portugal	
G-OADY	Beech 76 Duchess	Multiflight Ltd	
G-OAER	Lindstrand LBL-105A balloon	M. P. Rowley	
G-OAFF	Cessna 208 Caravan 1	Army Parachute Association	
G-OAFR	Cameron Z-105 balloon	PSH Skypower Ltd	
G-OAGI	FLS Aerospace Sprint 160	Black Art Composites Ltd (G-FLSI)	
G-OAGL	Bell 206B JetRanger 3	AGL Helicopters (G-CORN/G-BHTR)	
G-OAHC	Beech F33C Bonanza	Cirrus Aviation Ltd (G-BTTF)	
G-OAJB	Cyclone AX2000	H. Tovey (G-MZFJ)	
G-OAJC	Robinson R44	Adare International Transport Ltd	
G-OAJL	Ikarus C.42 FB100	G. D. M. McCullogh	
G-OAJS	PA-39 Twin Comanche 160 C/R	S. Vansteenkiste (G-BCIO)	
G-OAKI	BAe Jetstream 3102	Jetstream Executive Travel Ltd	
G-OAKR	Cessna 172S	A. K. Robson)	
G-OALD	SOCATA TB20 Trinidad	Gold Aviation	
G-OALH	Tecnam P92-EM Echo	T. J. Adams-Lewis	
G-OAMB	Cessna 510 Citation Mustang	Ambeo PLC	
G-OAMF	Pegasus Quantum 15-912	C. Parkinson	
G-OAMG	Bell 206B JetRanger 3	Toby Blackwell Ltd	
G-OAMI	Bell 206B JetRanger 2	Leamington Hobby Centre Ltd (G-BAUN)	
G-OAML	Cameron AML-105 balloon	Stratton Motor Co (Norfolk) Ltd	
G-OAMP	Cessna F.177RG	J-F. Pitot (G-AYPF)	
G-OANI	PA-28-161 Warrior II	J. F. Mitchell	
G-OANN	Zenair CH.601HD	Zodiac Group Mona	
G-OAPE	Cessna T.303	C. Twiston-Davies & P. L. Drew	

Notes	Reg.	Type	Owner or Operator
	G-OAPR	Brantly B.2B	Helicopter International Magazine
	G-OAPW	Glaser-Dirks DG.400	P. L. Poole
	G-OARA	PA-28R-201 Arrow III	Obmit Ltd
	G-OARC	PA-28RT-201 Arrow IV	Plane Talking Ltd (G-BMVE)
	G-OARI	PA-28R-201 Arrow III	Plane Talking Ltd
	G-OARO	PA-28R-201 Arrow III	Plane Talking Ltd
	G-OARS	Cessna 172S	AK Enterprises Ltd
	G-OART	PA-23 Aztec 250D	A. N. J. & S. L. Palmer (G-AXKD)
	G-OARU	PA-28R-201 Arrow III	Plane Talking Ltd
	G-OARV	ARV Super 2	I. F. Davidson
	G-OASH	Robinson R22 Beta	J. C. Lane
	G-OASJ	Thruster T.600N 450	R. C. Reynolds
	G-OASP	AS.355F2 Twin Squirrel	Helicopter Services Ltd
	G-OASW	Schleicher ASW-27	M. P. W. Mee
	G-OATE	Mainair Pegasus Quantum 15-912	S. J. Goate
	G-OATV	Cameron V-77 balloon	A. W. & E. P. Braund-Smith
	G-OAVA	Robinson R22 Beta	J. Sargent
	G-OAWS	Colt 77A balloon	P. Lawman
	G-OBAB	Lindstrand LBL-35A Cloudhopper balloon	B. A. Bower
	G-OBAK	PA-28R-201T Turbo Arrow III	G-OBAK Group Aviation
	G-OBAL	Mooney M.20J	G-OBAL Group
	G-OBAN	Jodel D.140B	S. R. Cameron (G-ATSU)
	G-OBAX	Thruster T.600N 450-JAB	J. Northage & M. E. Hutchinson
	G-OBAZ	Best Off Skyranger 912(2)	B. J. Marsh
	G-OBBO	Cessna 182S	A. E. Kedros
	G-OBBY	Robinson R44	Holdsmart Ltd
	G-OBCC	Cessna 560	Patronus Aviation Ltd
	G-OBDA	Diamond Katana DA20-A1	Oscar Papa Ltd
	G-OBDN	PA-28-161 Warrior II	R. M. Bennett
	G-OBEE	Boeing Stearman A75N-1 (3397:174)	P. G. Smith
	G-OBEI	SOCATA TB200 Tobago XL	Rapido Aviation Ltd/Ireland
	G-OBEN	Cessna 152 II	Globibussola Lda (G-NALI/G-BHVM)
	G-OBET	Sky 77-24 balloon	P. M. Watkins & S. M. Carden
	G-OBEV	Shaw Europa	M. B. & N. I. Hill
	G-OBFE	Sky 120-24 balloon	J. Sonnabend
	G-OBFS	PA-28-161 Warrior III	Plane Talking Ltd
	G-OBHD	Short SD3-60 Variant 100	BAC Leasing Ltd (G-BNDK)
	G-OBIB	Colt 120A balloon	M. W. A. Shemilt
	G-OBIL	Robinson R22 Beta	Fly Executive Ltd
	G-OBIO	Robinson R22 Beta	Heli Air Ltd
	G-OBJB	Lindstrand LBL-90A balloon	B. J. Bower
	G-OBJH	Colt 77A balloon	Hayrick Ltd
	G-OBJM	Taylor JT.1 Monoplane	B. J. Main
	G-OBJP	Pegasus Quantum 15-912	S. J. Baker
	G-OBJT	Shaw Europa	B. J. Tarmar (G-MUZO)
	G-OBLC	Beech 76 Duchess	Pridenote Ltd
	G-OBLU	Cameron H-34 balloon	John Aimo Balloons SAS/Italy
	G-OBMI	Mainair Blade	S. R. Kirkham & D. F. Reeves
	G-OBMP	Boeing 737-3Q8	bmi Baby
	G-OBMS	Cessna F.172N	A. J. Ransome, D. Beverley and K. Brown
	G-OBMW	AA-5 Traveler	Fretcourt Ltd (G-BDFV)
	G-OBNA	PA-34-220T Seneca V	Palmair Ltd
	G-OBNC	BN-2B-20 Islander	Britten-Norman Aircraft Ltd
	G-OBOF	Remos GX	D. Hawkins
	G-OBPP	Schleicher ASG-29E	M. H. Patel
	G-OBRA	Cameron Z-315 balloon	Cameron Flights Southern Ltd
	G-OBRY	Cameron N-180 balloon	A. C. K. Rawson & J. J. Rudoni
	G-OBSM	Robinson R44 Raven	Flight Solutions Ltd (G-CDSE)
	G-OBTS	Cameron C-80 balloon	C. F. Cushion
	G-OBUP	DG Flugzeugbau DG-808C	R. A. Roberts
	G-OBUU	Replica Comper CLA Swift	J. A. Pothecary & R. H. Hunt
	G-OBUY	Colt 69A balloon	Balloon Preservation Flying Group
	G-OBUZ	Van's RV-6	A. F. Hall
	G-OBWP	BAe ATP	Trident Aviation Leasing Services (Jersey) Ltd (G-BTPO)
	G-OBYD	Boeing 767-304ER	Thomsonfly Ltd
	G-OBYE	Boeing 767-304ER	Thomsonfly Ltd
	G-OBYF	Boeing 767-304ER	Thomsonfly Ltd
	G-OBYG	Boeing 767-3Q8ER	Thomsonfly Ltd
	G-OBYH	Boeing 767-304ER	Thomsonfly Ltd
	G-OBYJ	Boeing 767-304ER	Thomsonfly Ltd

Reg.	Type	Owner or Operator	Notes
G-OBYT	Agusta-Bell 206A JetRanger	R. J. Everett (G-BNRC)	
G-OCAD	Sequoia F.8L Falco	Falco Flying Group	
G-OCAM	AA-5A Cheetah	R. E. Dagless (G-BLHO)	
G-OCBI	Schweizer 269C-1	Alpha Properties (London) Ltd	
G-OCBT	IDA Bacau Yakovlev Yak-52	Cambridge Business Travel	
G-OCCD	Diamond DA40D Star	Flying Pictures Ltd	
G-OCCE	Diamond DA40D Star	Plane Talking Ltd	
G-OCCF	Diamond DA40D Star	Plane Talking Ltd	
G-OCCG	Diamond DA40D Star	Plane Talking Ltd	
G-OCCH	Diamond DA40D Star	Venturi Capital Ltd	
G-OCCK	Diamond DA40D Star	Venturi Capital Ltd	
G-OCCL	Diamond DA40D Star	Venturi Capital Ltd	
G-OCCM	Diamond DA40D Star	Plane Talking Ltd	
G-OCCN	Diamond DA40D Star	Venturi Capital Ltd	
G-OCCO	Diamond DA40D Star	Plane Talking Ltd	
G-OCCP	Diamond DA40D Star	Plane Talking Ltd	
G-OCCR	Diamond DA40D Star	P. Plaisted	
G-OCCS	Diamond DA40D Star	Plane Talking Ltd	
G-OCCT	Diamond DA40D Star	Plane Talking Ltd	
G-OCCU	Diamond DA40D Star	Chalrey Ltd	
G-OCCV	Diamond DA42 Twin Star	Plane Talking Ltd	
G-OCCW	Diamond DA42 Twin Star	Plane Talking Ltd	
G-OCCX	Diamond DA42 Twin Star	Plane Talking Ltd	
G-OCCY	Diamond DA42 Twin Star	Venturi Capital Ltd	
G-OCCZ	Diamond DA42 Twin Star	Venturi Capital Ltd	
G-OCDP	Flight Design CTSW	M. A. Beadman	
G-OCDW	Jabiru UL	H. Burroughs	
G-OCEG	Beech B.200 Super King Air	Cega Aviation Ambulance UK Ltd.	
G-OCFC	Robin R.2160	Cornwall Flying Club Ltd	
G-OCFD	Bell 206B JetRanger 3	Rushmere Helicopters LLP (G-WGAL/G-OICS)	
G-OCFM	PA-34-200 Seneca II	Stapleford Flying Club Ltd (G-ELBC/G-BANS)	
G-OCGC	Robin DR.400-180R	Cambridge Gliding Club Ltd	
G-OCHM	Robinson R44	Westleigh Developments Ltd	
G-OCJK	Schweizer 269C	P. Crawley	
G-OCJZ	Cessna 525A Citationjet CJ2	Go West Ltd	
G-OCLC	Aviat A-1B Husky	Caledonian Seaplanes Ltd	
G-OCMM	Agusta A109A II	Castle Air Charters Ltd (G-BXCB/G-ISEB/ G-IADT/G-HBCA)	
G-OCMS	EV-97 TeamEurostar UK	C. M. Saysell	
G-OCMT	EV-97 TeamEurostar UK	P. Crowhurst	
G-OCOK	American Champion 8KCAB Super Decathlon	J. D. May	
G-OCON	Robinson R44	Da Vinci Helicopters Ltd	
G-OCOV	Robinson R22 Beta	Heli Air Ltd	
G-OCPC	Cessna FA.152	F. H. Hancock & M. S. Hillier	
G-OCRI	Colomban MC.15 Cri-Cri	M. J. J. Dunning	
G-OCRZ	CZAW Sportcruiser	P. Marsden	
G-OCST	Agusta-Bell 206B JetRanger 3	Lift West Ltd (G-BMKM)	
G-OCTI	PA-32 Cherokee Six 260	D. G. Williams (G-BGZX)	
G-OCTU	PA-28-161 Cadet	Plane Talking Ltd	
G-OCUB	Piper J-3C-90 Cub	Zebedee Flying Group	
G-OCZA	CZAW Sportcruiser	S. M. Dawson	
G-ODAC	Cessna F.152 II	T. M. Jones (G-BITG)	
G-ODAD	Colt 77A balloon	J. H. Dobson	
G-ODAF	Lindstrand LBL-105A balloon	T. J. Horne	
G-ODAG	Cessna 525A Citationjet CJ2	Air Charter Scotland Ltd	
G-ODAK	PA-28-236 Dakota	Airways Aero Associations Ltd	
G-ODAY	Cameron N-56 balloon	British Balloon Museum & Library	
G-ODAZ	Robinson R44 II	D. Robson	
G-ODBN	Lindstrand LBL Flowers SS balloon	Magical Adventures Ltd	
G-ODCC	Bell 206L-3 Long Ranger III	DCC Aviation	
G-ODCH	Schleicher ASW-20L	D. C. Heath	
G-ODCR	Robinson R44 II	D. Lynn	
G-ODCS	Robinson R22 Beta II	C. Carola	
G-ODDS	Aerotek Pitts S-2A	A. C. Cassidy	
G-ODDY	Lindstrand LBL-105A balloon	P. & T. Huckle	
G-ODDZ	Schempp-Hirth Duo Discus T	D. B. Smith	
G-ODEB	Cameron A-250 balloon	A. Derbyshire	
G-ODEE	Van's RV-6	D. Cook	
G-ODEL	Falconar F-11-3	G. F. Brummell	

Notes	Reg.	Type	Owner or Operator
	G-ODEX	Cessna 182T	C. G. Bauer-Schlichtegroli
	G-ODGS	Avtech Jabiru UL-450	S. R. Eskins
	G-ODHB	Robinson R44	A. J. Mossop
	G-ODHL	Cameron N-77 balloon	DHL International (UK) Ltd
	G-ODIN	Avions Mudry CAP-10B	CAP Ten
	G-ODJD	Raj Hamsa X'Air 582 (7)	M. Bastin
	G-ODJF	Lindstrand LBL-90B balloon	Helena Dos Santos SA/Portugal
	G-ODJG	Shaw Europa	K. R. Challis & C. S. Andersson
	G-ODJH	Mooney M.20C	R. M. Schweitzer/Netherlands (G-BMLH)
	G-ODOC	Robinson R44	Gas & Air Ltd
	G-ODOG	PA-28R Cherokee Arrow 200-II	Advanced Investments Ltd (G-BAAR)
	G-ODPJ	VPM M-16 Tandem Trainer	K. J. Robinson & S. Palmer (G-BVWX)
	G-ODRD	PA-32R-301T Saratoga II	Interceptor Properties Ltd
	G-ODSK	Boeing 737-37Q	bmi Baby
	G-ODTW	Shaw Europa	D. T. Walters
	G-ODUD	PA-28-181 Archer II	G-ODUD Aviation Ltd (G-IBBO)
	G-ODUO	Schempp-Hirth Duo Discus	3D Syndicate
	G-ODUR	Raytheon Hawker 900XP	Hangar 8 Ltd
	G-ODVB	CFM Shadow Srs DD	L. J. E. Moss
	G-ODXB	Lindstrand LBL-120A balloon	A. Nimmo
	G-OEAC	Mooney M.20J	S. Lovatt
	G-OEAT	Robinson R22 Beta	C. Y. O. Seeds Ltd (G-RACH)
	G-OEBC	Ultramagic N-300 balloon	European Balloon Display Co.Ltd
	G-OECM	Commander 114B	ECM (Vehicle Delivery Service) Ltd
	G-OECO	Flylight Dragonfly	P. A. & M. W. Aston
	G-OEDB	PA-38-112 Tomahawk	M. A. Petrie (G-BGGJ)
	G-OEDP	Cameron N-77 balloon	M. J. Betts
	G-OEGG	Cameron Egg-65 SS balloon	Calorie Watch Balloon Team
	G-OEGL	Christen Eagle II	The Eagle Flight Syndicate
	G-OEKS	Ikarus C42 FB80	J. D. Smith
	G-OELD	Pegasus Quantum 15-912	R. P. Butler
	G-OELZ	Wassmer WA.52 Europa	G-OELZ Group
	G-OEMT	MBB BK-117 C-1	Sterling Helicopters Ltd
	G-OERR	Lindstrand LBL-60A balloon	P. C. Gooch
	G-OERS	Cessna 172N	E. R. Stevens (G-SSRS)
	G-OESY	Easy Raider J2.2 (1)	J. Gray
	G-OETI	Bell 206B JetRanger 3	T. A. Wells (G-RMIE/G-BPIE)
	G-OETV	PA-31-350 Navajo Chieftain	Hinde Holdings Ltd
	G-OEVA	PA-32-260 Cherokee Six	M. G. Cookson (G-FLJA/G-AVTJ)
	G-OEWD	Raytheon 390 Premier 1	Bookajet Aircraft Management Ltd
	G-OEZI	Easy Raider J2.2(2)	C. D. Pidler
	G-OEZY	Shaw Europa	A. W. Wakefield
	G-OFAA	Cameron Z-105 balloon	R. A. Schwab
	G-OFAL	Ozone Roadster/Bailey Quattro	Malcolm Roberts Heating, Plumbing and Electrical Ltd
	G-OFAS	Robinson R22 Beta	Fast Helicopters Ltd
	G-OFBJ	Thunder Ax7-77 balloon	J. C. Harris
	G-OFBU	Ikarus C.42 FB UK	Old Sarum C42 Group
	G-OFCM	Cessna F.172L	Sirius Aviation Ltd (G-AZUN)
	G-OFDT	Mainair Pegasus Quik	D. Bardsley
	G-OFER	PA-18 Super Cub 150	M. S. W. Meagher
	G-OFFA	Pietenpol Air Camper	OFFA Group
	G-OFFO	Extra EA.300/L	2 Excel Aviation Ltd
	G-OFIT	SOCATA TB10 Tobago	GFI Aviation Group (G-BRIU)
	G-OFIX	Grob G.109B	T. R. Dews
	G-OFLI	Colt 105A balloon	Virgin Airship & Balloon Co Ltd
	G-OFLT	EMB-110P1 Bandeirante ★	Rescue trainer/Aveley, Essex (G-MOBL/G-BGCS)
	G-OFLY	Cessna 210M	A. P. Mothew
	G-OFMC	Avro RJ100	Ford Motor Co.Ltd (G-CDUI)
	G-OFOA	BAe 146-100	Formula One Administration Ltd (G-BKMN/G-ODAN)
	G-OFOM	BAe 146-100	Formula One Management Ltd (G-BSLP/G-BRLM)
	G-OFOX	Denney Kitfox	P. R. Skeels
	G-OFRB	Everett gyroplane	T. N. Holcroft-Smith
	G-OFRY	Cessna 152	Devon and Somerset Flight Training Ltd
	G-OFSP	CZAW Sportcruiser	F. S. Pullman
	G-OFTI	PA-28 Cherokee 140	G-OFTI Group
	G-OGAN	Shaw Europa	J. R. Malpass
	G-OGAR	PZL SZD-45A Ogar	P. Rasmussen t/a Perranporth Ogar Flying Group

vReg.	Type	Owner or Operator	Notes
G-OGAS	Westland WG.30 Srs 100 ★	(stored)/Yeovil (G-BKNW)	
G-OGAY	Baloney Kubicek BB-26 balloon	J. W. Soukup	
G-OGAZ	Aérospatiale SA.341G Gazelle 1	Killochries Fold (G-OCJR/G-BRGS)	
G-OGBD	Boeing 737-3L9	bmi Baby	
G-OGBR	Mudry CAP.232	G. C. J. Cooper & E. Vazeille	
G-OGCA	PA-28-161 Warrior II	Cardiff-Wales Aviation Services Ltd	
G-OGEM	PA-28-181 Archer II	GEM Integrated Solutions Ltd	
G-OGEO	Aérospatiale SA.341G Gazelle 1	George Steel Contract Services (G-BXJK)	
G-OGET	PA-39 Twin Comanche	D. Saxton (G-AYXY)	
G-OGFS	BAe.125 Srs 800B	Aircraft Holdings Ltd (G-GRGA/G-DCTA/G-OSPG/G-ETOM/G-BVFC/G-TPHK/G-FDSL)	
G-OGGB	Grob G.102 Astir CS	M. Ogbe	
G-OGGS	Thunder Ax8-84 balloon	G. Gamble & Sons (Quorn) Ltd	
G-OGGY	Aviat A.1B	C. A. I. Hickling	
G-OGIL	Short SD3-30 Variant 100 ★	North East Aircraft Museum/Usworth (G-BITV)	
G-OGJC	Robinson R44 II	G. Corbett	
G-OGJM	Cameron C-80 balloon	G. F. Madelin	
G-OGJP	Commander 114B	MJ Church Plant Ltd	
G-OGJS	Puffer Cozy	G. J. Stamper	
G-OGKB	Sequoia Falco F8L	G. K. Brothwood	
G-OGLY	Cameron Z-105 balloon	H. M. Ogston	
G-OGOD	P & M Quik GT450	J. R. Elcocks	
G-OGOS	Everett gyroplane	N. A. Seymour	
G-OGSA	Avtech Jabiru SPL-450	R. G. J. Tait	
G-OGSK	Embraer EMB-135BJ Legacy	TAG Aviation (UK) Ltd	
G-OGTS	Air Command 532 Elite	GTS Engineering (Coventry) Ltd	
G-OHAC	Cessna F.182Q	The RAF Halton Aeroplane Club	
G-OHAL	Pietenpol Air Camper	J. F. Morris	
G-OHAM	Robinson R44 II	Hamsters Wheel Productions Ltd (G-GBEN/G-CDJZ)	
G-OHAV	ATG Ltd HAV-3	Hybrid Air Vehicles Ltd	
G-OHCP	AS.355F1 Twin Squirrel	Staske Construction Ltd (G-BTVS/G-STVE/G-TOFF/G-BKJX)	
G-OHDC	Colt Film Cassette SS balloon ★	Balloon Preservation Group	
G-OHGA	Hughes O-6A	MSS Holdings (UK) Ltd	
G-OHGC	Scheibe SF.25C Falke	Heron Gliding Club	
G-OHHI	Bell 206L-1 LongRanger	Sky Charter UK Ltd (G-BWYJ)	
G-OHIG	EMB-110P1 Bandeirante ★	Air Salvage International/Alton (G-OPPP)	
G-OHIY	Van's RV-10	M. A. Hutton	
G-OHJE	Alpi Pioneer 300 Hawk	H. J. Edwards	
G-OHJV	Robinson R44	HJV Ltd	
G-OHKS	Pegasus Quantum 15-912	S. J. Farr	
G-OHLI	Robinson R44 II	NCS Partnership	
G-OHMS	AS.355F1 Twin Squirrel	Western Power Distribution (South West) PLC	
G-OHNO	Yakovlev Yak-55	R. Graham E. Mason & s. Whatmough	
G-OHOV	Rotorway Executive 162F	M. G. Bird	
G-OHPC	Cessna 208 Caravan 1	S. Ulrich	
G-OHVR	Robinson R44 II	Transparent Film Products Ltd	
G-OHWV	Raj Hamsa X'Air 582(4)	C. W. Bridge	
G-OHYE	Thruster T.600N 450	G-OHYE Group (G-CCRO)	
G-OIBM	Rockwell Commander 114	H. A. Barrs (G-BLVZ)	
G-OIBO	PA-28 Cherokee 180	Azure Flying Club Ltd (G-AVAZ)	
G-OICO	Lindstrand LBL-42A balloon	B. Esposito	
G-OIFM	Cameron 90 Dude SS balloon	Magical Adventures Ltd	
G-OIHC	PA-32R-301 Saratoga IIHP	N. J. Lipczynski (G-PUSK)	
G-OIIO	Robinson R22 Beta	Whizzard Helicopters (G-ULAB)	
G-OIMC	Cessna 152 II	East Midlands Flying School Ltd	
G-OINN	UltraMagic H-31 balloon	G. Everett	
G-OIOB	Mudry CAP.10B	A. L. Hall-Carpenter	
G-OIOZ	Thunder Ax9-120 S2 balloon	R. H. Etherington	
G-OISO	Cessna FRA.150L	L. A. Mills & B. A. Mills (G-BBJW)	
G-OITV	Enstrom 280C-UK-2	C. W. Brierley Jones (G-HRVY/G-DUGY/G-BEEL)	
G-OIVN	Liberty XL-2	I. Shaw	
G-OJAB	Avtech Jabiru SK	Flying Spanners Group	
G-OJAC	Mooney M.20J	Hornet Engineering Ltd	
G-OJAE	Hughes 269C	R. W. Cutler	
G-OJAG	Cessna 172S	Chalrey Ltd	
G-OJAJ	Dassault Falcon 2000EX	tag Aviation (UK) Ltd	
G-OJAN	Robinson R22 Beta	J. C. Lane (G-SANS/G-BUHX)	

Notes	Reg.	Type	Owner or Operator
	G-OJAS	Auster J/1U Workmaster	D. S. Hunt
	G-OJAZ	Robinson R44	P. C. Twigg
	G-OJBB	Enstrom 280FX	Pendragon (Design & Build) Ltd
	G-OJBM	Cameron N-90 balloon	P. Spinlove
	G-OJBS	Cameron N-105A balloon	Up & Away Ballooning Ltd
	G-OJBW	Lindstrand LBL J & B Bottle SS balloon	N. A. P. Godfrey
	G-OJCW	PA-32RT-300 Lance II	P. G. Dobson
	G-OJDA	EAA Acrosport II	D. B. Almey
	G-OJDC	Thunder Ax7-77 balloon	A. Heginbottom
	G-OJDS	Ikarus C.42 FB 80	L. C. Wellington-Graham
	G-OJEG	Airbus A.321-231	Monarch Airlines Ltd
	G-OJEH	PA-28-181 Archer II	P. C. & M. A. Greenaway
	G-OJEN	Cameron V-77 balloon	C. Westwood
	G-OJGC	Van's RV-4	J. G. Claridge
	G-OJGT	Maule M.5-235C	Newnham Joint Flying Syndicate
	G-OJHC	Cessna 182P	Stapleford Flying Club Ltd
	G-OJHL	Shaw Europa	M. D. Burns & G. Rainey
	G-OJIB	Boeing 757-23A	Astraeus Ltd (G-OOOG)
	G-OJIL	PA-31-350 Navajo Chieftain	Redhill Aviation Ltd
	G-OJIM	PA-28R-201T Turbo Arrow III	G-OJIM Flyers Ltd
	G-OJJV	P & M Pegasus Quik	J. J. Valentine
	G-OJKM	Rans S.7 Courier	G. Lewis & J. Mellor
	G-OJLD	Van's RV-7	J. L. Dixon
	G-OJLH	TEAM mini-MAX 91	A. J. Weir (G-MYAW)
	G-OJMB	Airbus A.330-243	Thomas Cook Airlines Ltd
	G-OJMC	Airbus A.330-243	Thomas Cook Airlines Ltd
	G-OJMF	Enstrom 280FX	Manchester Helicopter Centre Ltd (G-DDOD)
	G-OJMR	Airbus A.300B4-605R	Monarch Airlines Ltd
	G-OJMS	Cameron Z-90 balloon	Joinerysoft Ltd
	G-OJNB	Linsdstrand LBL-21A balloon	N. A. P. Godfrey
	G-OJNE	Schempp-Hirth Nimbus 3T	J. N. Ellis
	G-OJOD	Jodel D.18	D. Hawkes & C. Poundes
	G-OJON	Taylor JT.2 Titch	N. M. Robbins
	G-OJPS	Bell 206B JetRanger 2	Milford Aviation (G-UEST/G-ROYB/G-BLWU)
	G-OJRH	Robinson R44	Holgate Construction Ltd
	G-OJRM	Cessna T.182T	Colne Airways Ltd
	G-OJSA	BAe Jetstream 3102	Diamond Air Charter Ltd
	G-OJSF	PA-23 Aztec 250F	Comed Aviation Ltd (G-SFHR/G-BHSO)
	G-OJSH	Thruster T.600N 450 JAB	G-OJSH Group
	G-OJVA	Van's RV-6	J. A. Village
	G-OJVH	Cessna F.150H	A. W. Cairns (G-AWJZ)
	G-OJVL	Van's RV-6	S. E. Tomlinson
	G-OJWB	Hawker 800XP	Langford Lane Ltd
	G-OJWS	PA-28-161 Warrior II	P. J. Ward
	G-OKAG	PA-28R Cherokee Arrow 180	Alpha-Golf Flying Group
	G-OKAY	Pitts S-1E Special	S. R. S. Evans
	G-OKBT	Colt 25A Mk II balloon	British Telecommunications PLC
	G-OKCC	Cameron N-90 balloon	D. J. Head
	G-OKCP	Lindstrand LBL Battery SS balloon	A. M. Holly (G-MAXX)
	G-OKED	Cessna 150L	L. J. Pluck
	G-OKEM	Mainair Pegasus Quik	W. J. Hardy
	G-OKEN	PA-28R-201T Turbo Arrow III	K. Woodcock
	G-OKER	Van's RV-7	R. M. Johnson
	G-OKEV	Shaw Europa	K. A. Kedward
	G-OKEY	Robinson R22 Beta	Fast Helicopters Ltd
	G-OKID	Reality Escapade Kid	P. M. Francis
	G-OKIM	Best Off Sykyranger 912 (2)	K. P. Taylor
	G-OKIS	Tri-R Kis	M. R. Cleveley
	G-OKMA	Tri-R Kis	K. Miller
	G-OKPW	Tri-R Kis	K. P. Wordsworth
	G-OKTI	Aquila AT01	P. H. Ferdinand
	G-OKYA	Cameron V-77 balloon	R. J. Pearce
	G-OKYM	PA-28 Cherokee 140	North Wales Air Academy Ltd (G-AVLS)
	G-OLAA	Alpi Pioneer 300 Hawk	G. G. Hammond
	G-OLAU	Robinson R22 Beta	MPW Aviation Ltd
	G-OLAW	Lindstrand LBL-25A balloon	George Law Plant
	G-OLCP	AS.355N Twin Squirrel	Charterstyle Ltd (G-CLIP)
	G-OLDG	Cessna T.182T	Gold Aviation Ltd (G-CBTJ)
	G-OLDH	Aérospatiale SA.341G Gazelle 1	Gold Aviation Ltd (G-UTZY/G-BKLV)
	G-OLDM	Pegasus Quantum 15-912	P. R. Biggs

Reg.	Type	Owner or Operator	Notes
G-OLDN	Bell 206L LongRanger	Sky Charter UK Ltd (G-TBCA/G-BFAL)	
G-OLDO	Eurocopter EC.120B Colibri	Gold Aviation Ltd (G-HIGI)	
G-OLDP	Mainair Pegasus Quik	A. G. Woodward	
G-OLDT	Learjet 45	Shed Three Ltd	
G-OLDX	Cessna 182T	Gold Air International Ltd (G-IBZT)	
G-OLEE	Cessna F.152	Redhill Air Services Ltd	
G-OLEM	Jodel D.18	G. E. Roe (G-BSBP)	
G-OLEO	Thunder Ax10-210 S2 balloon	Charter Ballooning Ltd	
G-OLEW	Vans RV-7A	A. Burani	
G-OLEZ	Piper J-3C-65 Cub	L. Powell (G-BSAX)	
G-OLFA	AS.350B3 Ecureuil	Heliaviation Ltd	
G-OLFB	Pegasus Quantum 15-912	J. G. & P. Callan	
G-OLFF	Cameron Z-120 balloon	A. Nimmo	
G-OLFO	Robinson R44	Crinstown Aviation Ltd	
G-OLFT	Rockwell Commander 114	D. A. Tubby (G-WJMN)	
G-OLFZ	P & M Quik GT450	A. J. Boyd	
G-OLGA	CFM Starstreak Shadow SA-II	N. F. Smith	
G-OLLI	Cameron O-31 SS balloon	The British Balloon Museum & Library Ltd	
G-OLLS	Cessna U.206H Floatplane	Loch Lomond Seaplanes Ltd	
G-OLMA	Partenavia P.68B	C. M. Evans (G-BGBT)	
G-OLNT	SA.365N1 Dauphin 2	LNT Aviation Ltd (G-POAV/G-BOPI)	
G-OLOW	Robinson R44	C. O. Semik	
G-OLRT	Robinson R22 Beta	The Henderson Group	
G-OLSF	PA-28-161 Cadet	Flew LLP (G-OTYJ)	
G-OLUG	Cameron Z-120 balloon	K. H. Gruenauer	
G-OMAF	Dornier 228-200	FR Aviation Ltd	
G-OMAG	Cessna 182B	Bodmin Light Aeroplane Services Ltd	
G-OMAL	Thruster T.600N 450	M. Howland	
G-OMAO	SOCATA TB-20 Trinidad	Alpha Oscar Group (G-GDGR)	
G-OMAS	Cessna A.150M	M. A. Segar (G-BTFS)	
G-OMAT	PA-28 Cherokee 140	Midland Air Training School (G-JIMY/G-AYUG)	
G-OMAX	Brantly B.2B	A. Murzyn (G-AVJN)	
G-OMBI	Cessna 525B Citationjet CJ3	Ravenheat Manufacturing Ltd	
G-OMCC	AS.350B Ecureuil	Michael Car Centres Ltd (G-JTCM/G-HLEN/ G-LOLY)	
G-OMDB	Van's V-6A	D. A. Roseblade	
G-OMDD	Thunder Ax8-90 S2 balloon	M. D. Dickinson	
G-OMDH	Hughes 369E	Stilgate Ltd	
G-OMDR	Agusta-Bell 206B JetRanger 3	Castle Air Charters Ltd (G-HRAY/G-VANG/ G-BIZA)	
G-OMEA	Cessna 560XL Citation XLS	Marshall Executive Aviation	
G-OMEL	Robinson R44	Helitrain Ltd (G-BVPB)	
G-OMEN	Cameron Z-90 balloon	M. G. Howard	
G-OMEX	Zenair CH.701 UL	S. J. Perry	
G-OMEZ	Zenair CH.601HDS	T. D. Dawson	
G-OMGH	Robinson R44 II	Universal Energy Ltd	
G-OMGR	Cameron Z-105 balloon	Omega Resource Group PLC	
G-OMHC	PA-28RT-201 Arrow IV	Halfpenny Green Flight Centre Ltd	
G-OMHD	EE Canberra PR.Mk.9 (XH134)	Midair SA	
G-OMHI	Mills MH-1	J. P. Mills	
G-OMHP	Avtech Jabiru UL	J. Livingstone	
G-OMIA	MS.893A Rallye Commodore 180	L. Portelli	
G-OMIK	Shaw Europa	M. J. Clews	
G-OMIW	Pegasus Quik	M. I. Woodward	
G-OMJA	PA-28-181 Archer II	R. D. Masters & S. Walker	
G-OMJC	Beech 390 Premier 1	Manhattan Jet Charter	
G-OMJT	Rutan LongEz	M. J. Timmons	
G-OMKA	Robinson R44 II	S. Shepherd	
G-OMLC	EAA Acrosport 2	M. A. C. Chapman	
G-OMLS	Bell 206B JetRanger 2	M. L. Scott	
G-OMMA	Robinson R44 II	L. de Lange (G-CFRU)	
G-OMMG	Robinson R22 Beta	CDS Aviation Ltd (G-BPYX)	
G-OMMM	Colt 90A balloon	A. & M. Frayling	
G-OMNI	PA-28R Cherokee Arrow 200D	Cotswold Aviation Services Ltd (G-BAWA)	
G-OMOO	Ultramagic T-150 balloon	Robert Wiseman Dairies PLC	
G-OMPW	Mainair Pegasus Quik	M. P. Wimsey	
G-OMRB	Cameron V-77 balloon	I. J. Jevons	
G-OMRH	Cessna 550 Citation Bravo	McAir Services LLP	
G-OMRP	Flight Design CTSW	M. E. Parker	
G-OMSA	Flight Design CTSW	Microlight Sport Aviation Ltd	
G-OMST	PA-28-161 Warrior III	Mid-Sussex Timber Co Ltd (G-BZUA)	

Notes	Reg.	Type	Owner or Operator
	G-OMSV	Beech B.200GT King Air	JPM Ltd
	G-OMUM	Rockwell Commander 114	C. E. Campbell
	G-OMYA	Airbus A.320-214	Thomas Cook Airlines Ltd (G-BXKB)
	G-OMYJ	Airbus A.321-211	Thomas Cook Airlines Ltd (G-OOAF/G-UNID/ G-UKLO)
	G-OMYT	Airbus A.330-243	Thomas Cook Airlines Ltd (G-MOJO)
	G-ONAF	Naval Aircraft Factory N3N-3 (4406:12)	N3N-3 Group
	G-ONAL	Beech 200 Super King Air	Unity Aviation Ltd (G-HAMA)
	G-ONAT	Grob G.102 Astir CS77	N. A. Toogood
	G-ONAV	PA-31-310 Turbo Navajo C	Panther Aviation Ltd (G-IGAR)
	G-ONCB	Lindstrand LBL-31A balloon	M. R. Noyce & R. P. E. Phillips
	G-ONCL	Colt 77A balloon	T. J. Gouder
	G-ONCS	Slingsby T.66 Nipper 3	Ardleigh Flying Group (G-AZBA)
	G-ONEP	Robinson R44 II	Neptune Property Developments Ltd
	G-ONER	Van's RV-8	J. N. Grunwell & G. Lawrence
	G-ONES	Slingsby T.67M Firefly 200	Aquaman Aviation Ltd
	G-ONET	PA-28 Cherokee 180E	Hatfield Flying Club Ltd (G-AYAU)
	G-ONEZ	Glaser-Dirks DG-200/17	One Zulu Group
	G-ONFL	Murphy Maverick 430	G. J. Johnson (G-MYUJ)
	G-ONGA	Robinson R44 II	Chopper Holding BV
	G-ONGC	Robin DR.400/180R	Norfolk Gliding Club Ltd
	G-ONHH	Forney F-1A Aircoupe	R. D. I. Tarry (G-ARHA)
	G-ONIG	Murphy Elite	N. S. Smith
	G-ONIX	Cameron C-80 balloon	D. J. Griffin
	G-ONKA	Aeronca K	N. J. R. Minchin
	G-ONMT	Robinson R22 Beta II	Polar Helicopters Ltd
	G-ONON	RAF 2000 GTX-SE gyroplane	M. P. Lhermette
	G-ONPA	PA-31-350 Navajo Chieftain	Synergy Aircraft Leasing Ltd
	G-ONSO	Pitts S-1C Special	A. P. S. Maynard (G-BRRS)
	G-ONTV	Agusta-Bell 206B JetRanger 3	Castle Air Charters Ltd
	G-ONUN	Van's RV-6A	K. R. H. Wingate
	G-OOAN	Boeing 767-39HER	Thomson Airways Ltd (G-UKLH)
	G-OOAR	Airbus A.320-214	Thomson Airways Ltd
	G-OOBA	Boeing 757-26N	Thomson Airways Ltd
	G-OOBB	Boeing 757-28A	Thomson Airways Ltd
	G-OOBC	Boeing 757-28A	Thomson Airways Ltd
	G-OOBD	Boeing 757-28A	Thomson Airways Ltd
	G-OOBE	Boeing 757-28A	Thomson Airways Ltd
	G-OOBF	Boeing 757-28A	Thomson Airways Ltd
	G-OOBG	Boeing 757-236	Thomson Airways Ltd
	G-OOBH	Boeing 757-236	Thomson Airways Ltd
	G-OOBI	Boeing 757-2B7	Thomson Airways Ltd
	G-OOBJ	Boeing 757-2B7	Thomson Airways Ltd
	G-OOBK	Boeing 767-324ER	Thomsonf AirwaysLtd
	G-OOBL	Boeing 767-324ER	Thomson Airways Ltd
	G-OOBM	Boeing 767-324ER	Thomson Airways Ltd
	G-OOBN	Boeing 757-2G5	Thomson Airways Ltd
	G-OOBP	Boeing 757-2G5	Thomson Airways Ltd
	G-OOCH	Ultramagic H-42 balloon	P. C. Gooch
	G-OODE	SNCAN Stampe SV.4C (modified)	G-OODE Flying Group (G-AZNN)
	G-OODI	Pitts S-1D Special	C. Hutson & R. S. Wood (G-BBBU)
	G-OODM	Cessna 525A Citation CJ2	Air Charter Scotland Ltd
	G-OODW	PA-28-181 Archer II	Goodwood Terrena Ltd
	G-OOER	Lindstrand LBL-25A balloon	Airborne Adventures Ltd
	G-OOEX	Cirrus SR22T	Data Interchange PLC
	G-OOEY	Balony Kubicek BB-222 balloon	A. W. Holly
	G-OOFE	Thruster T.600N 450	R. P. Tribe
	G-OOFT	PA-28-161 Warrior III	Plane Talking Ltd
	G-OOGA	GA-7 Cougar	B. Robinson
	G-OOGI	GA-7 Cougar	Plane Talking Ltd (G-PLAS/G-BGHL)
	G-OOGO	GA-7 Cougar	M. M. Naviede
	G-OOGS	GA-7 Cougar	P. Pigg (G-BGJW)
	G-OOGY	P & M Quik R	Cambridge Road Professional Services Ltd
	G-OOIO	AS.350B3 Ecureuil	Hovering Ltd
	G-OOJC	Bensen B.8MR	S. Henley
	G-OOJP	Commander 114B	R. J. Rother
	G-OOLE	Cessna 172M	P. S. Eccersley (G-BOSI)
	G-OOLL	Tanarg/Ixess 15 912S(1)	M. A. Furber
	G-OOMF	PA-18-150 Super Cub	C. G. Bell
	G-OONA	Robinson R44 II	Honeybee Aviation Ltd

Reg.	Type	Owner or Operator	Notes
G-OONE	Mooney M.20J	Go One Aviation Ltd	
G-OONK	Cirrus SR22	Heathfield Rentals Ltd	
G-OONY	PA-28-161 Warrior II	D. A. Field	
G-OONZ	P & M Quik	A. Barrett	
G-OOON	PA-34-220T Seneca III	P. Webb	
G-OOOX	Boeing 757-2Y0	Thomson Airways Ltd	
G-OOOZ	Boeing 757-236	Thomson Airways Ltd (G-BUDZ)	
G-OOPE	Airbus A.321-211	Thomson Airways Ltd (G-OOAE/ G-UNIF)	
G-OOPH	Airbus A.321-211	Thomson Airways Ltd (G-OOAH/G-UNIE)	
G-OOPP	Airbus A.320-214	Thomson Airways Ltd (G-OOAS)	
G-OOPT	Airbus A.320-214	Thomson Airways Ltd (G-OOAT)	
G-OOPU	Airbus A.320-214	Thomson Airways Ltd (G-OOAU)	
G-OOPX	Airbus A.320-214	Thomson Airways Ltd (G-OOAX)	
G-OORV	Van's RV-6	T. I. Williams	
G-OOSE	Rutan Vari-Eze	B. O. Smith & J. A. Towers	
G-OOSH	Zenair CH.601UL Zodiac	P. C. Bishop	
G-OOSI	Cessna 404	Aerodata International Surveys BVBA/Belgium	
G-OOSY	DH.82A Tiger Moth	Flying Tigers	
G-OOTC	PA-28R-201T Turbo Arrow III	D. G. & C. M. King (G-CLIV)	
G-OOTT	Eurocopter AS.350B3 Ecureuil	R. J. Green	
G-OOTW	Cameron Z-275 balloon	Airborne Balloon Flights Ltd	
G-OOUK	Cirrus SR22	R. S. Tomlinson	
G-OOWS	Eurocopter AS.350B3 Ecureuil	Millburn World Travel Services Ltd	
G-OOXP	Aero Designs Pulsar XP	C. Cartwright & B. Vincent	
G-OPAG	PA-34-200 Seneca II	A. H. Lavender (G-BNGB)	
G-OPAM	Cessna F.152 II (tailwheel)	PJC Leasing Ltd (G-BFZS)	
G-OPAT	Beech 76 Duchess	R. D. J. Axford (G-BHAO)	
G-OPAZ	Pazmany PL.2	P. M. Harrison	
G-OPCG	Cessna 182T	P. L. Nolan	
G-OPEJ	TEAM Minimax 91A	P. E. Jackson	
G-OPEN	Bell 206B	Gazelle Aviation LLP	
G-OPEP	PA-28RT-201T Turbo Arrow IV	SAM Ltd	
G-OPET	PA-28-181 Archer II	Cambrian Flying Group Ltd	
G-OPFA	Pioneer 300	S. Eddison & R. Minett	
G-OPFT	Cessna 172R Skyhawk	AJW Construction Ltd	
G-OPHA	Robinson R44	H. W. Euridge	
G-OPHT	Schleicher ASH-26E	P. Turner	
G-OPIC	Cessna FRA.150L	A. V. Harmer (G-BGNZ)	
G-OPIK	Eiri PIK-20E	G-OPIK Syndicate	
G-OPIT	CFM Streak Shadow Srs SA	I. J. Guy	
G-OPJD	PA-28RT-201T Turbo Arrow IV	J. M. McMillan	
G-OPJK	Shaw Europa	P. J. Kember	
G-OPJS	Pietenpol Air Camper	P. J. Shenton	
G-OPKF	Cameron 90 Bowler SS balloon	D. K. Fish	
G-OPLC	DH.104 Dove 8	W. G. T. Pritchard (G-BLRB)	
G-OPME	PA-23 Aztec 250D	J. F. Gosling (G-ODIR/G-AZGB)	
G-OPMP	Robinson R44 II	Phillips Commercials Ltd (G-HHHH)	
G-OPMT	Lindstrand LBL-105A balloon	K. R. Karlstrom	
G-OPNH	Stoddard-Hamilton Glasair IIRG	A. J. E. & A. E. Smith (G-CINY)	
G-OPRC	Shaw Europa XS	M. J. Ashby-Arnold	
G-OPSF	PA-38-112 Tomahawk	P. I. Higham (G-BGZI)	
G-OPSL	PA-32R-301 Saratoga SP	P. R. Tomkins (G-IMPW)	
G-OPSS	Cirrus SR20	Dunster House Ltd	
G-OPST	Cessna 182R	M. J. G. Wellings & Welmacs Ltd	
G-OPTF	Robinson R44 II	Heli Air Ltd	
G-OPTI	PA-28-161 Warrior II	A. K. Hulme	
G-OPUB	Slingsby T.67M Firefly 160	P. M. Barker (G-DLTA/G-SFTX)	
G-OPUK	PA-28-161 Warrior III	Dennis and Robinson Ltd	
G-OPUP	Beagle B.121 Pup 2	F. A. Zubiel (G-AXEU)	
G-OPUS	Avtech Jabiru SK	K. W. Whistance	
G-OPVM	Van's RV-9A	P. Mather	
G-OPWK	AA-5A Cheetah	J. H. Sandham Aviation (G-OAEL)	
G-OPWS	Mooney M.20K	A. R. Mills	
G-OPYE	Cessna 172S	Far North Aviation	
G-OPYO	Alpi Pioneer 300 Hawk	T. J. Franklin & D. S. Simpson	
G-ORAC	Cameron 110 Van SS balloon	A. G. Kennedy	
G-ORAE	Van's RV-7	R. W. Eaton	
G-ORAF	CFM Streak Shadow	A. P. Hunn	
G-ORAM	Thruster T600N 450	A. Brown	
G-ORAR	PA-28-181 Archer III	P. N. & S. M. Thornton	

Notes	Reg.	Type	Owner or Operator
	G-ORAS	Clutton FRED Srs 2	A. I. Sutherland
	G-ORAU	Evektor EV-97A Eurostar	W. R. C. Williams-Wynne
	G-ORAY	Cessna F.182Q II	Unicorn Consultants Ltd (G-BHDN)
	G-ORBK	Robinson R44 II	GTC (UK) Ltd (G-CCNO)
	G-ORBS	Mainair Blade	J. W. Dodson
	G-ORCA	Van's RV-4	J. J. & B. P. Waites
	G-ORCW	Schempp-Hirth Ventus 2cT	R. C. Wilson
	G-ORDB	Cessna 550 Citation Bravo	Equipe Air Ltd
	G-ORDH	AS.355N Twin Squirrel	Harpin Ltd
	G-ORDS	Thruster T.600N 450	G. J. Pill
	G-ORED	BN-2T Turbine Islander	B-N Group Ltd (G-BJYW)
	G-ORGY	Cameron Z-210 balloon	Cameron Flights Southern Ltd
	G-ORHE	Cessna 500 Citation	Eassda Ireland Ltd (G-BOGA/G-OBEL)
	G-ORIG	Glaser-Dirks DG.800A	I. Godfrey
	G-ORIX	ARV K1 Super 2	T. M. Lyons (G-BUXH/G-BNVK)
	G-ORJA	Beech B.200 Super King Air	Airwest Ltd
	G-ORJW	Laverda F.8L Falco Srs 4	Viking BV/Netherlands
	G-ORKY	AS.350B2 Ecureuil	MCJ Helicopters
	G-ORLA	P & M Pegasus Quik	J. Summers
	G-ORLE	Agusta A109A	Sofitro SA (G-USTB)
	G-ORMB	Robinson R22 Beta	Scotia Helicopters Ltd
	G-ORMG	Cessna 172R II	J. R. T. Royle
	G-ORMW	Ikarus C.42 FB100	B. J. Jenkins
	G-OROD	PA-18 Super Cub 150	B. W. Faulkner
	G-OROO	Cessna 560XL Citation XLS	Rooney Air Ltd
	G-OROS	Ikarus C.42 FB80	R. I. Simpson
	G-ORPC	Shaw Europa XS	P. W. Churms
	G-ORPR	Cameron O-77 balloon	S. R. Vining
	G-ORRG	Robin DR.400-180 Regent	Radley Robin Group
	G-ORTH	Beech E90 King Air	Gorthair Ltd
	G-ORUG	Thruster T.600N 450	D. J. N. Brown
	G-ORVE	Van's RV-6	R. J. F. Swain & F. M. Sperryn
	G-ORVG	Van's RV-6	RV Group
	G-ORVI	Van's RV-6	J. D. N. Cooke
	G-ORVR	Partenavia P.68B	Ravenair Aircraft Ltd (G-BFBD)
	G-ORVS	Van's RV-9	C. J. Marsh
	G-ORXI	Beech RB390 Premier 1A	Oryx Jet Ltd (G-RIZA)
	G-ORYX	Hawker 900XP	Oryx Jet Ltd
	G-ORZA	Diamond DA42 Twin Star	M. J. Hill (G-FCAC)
	G-OSAT	Cameron Z-105 balloon	Lotus Balloons Ltd
	G-OSAW	QAC Quickie Q.2	S. A. Wilson (G-BVYT)
	G-OSCC	PA-32 Cherokee Six 300	BG & G Airlines Ltd (G-BGFD)
	G-OSCO	TEAM mini-MAX 91	M. A. Perry
	G-OSDF	Schempp-Hirth Ventus a	S. D. Foster
	G-OSDI	Beech 95-58 Baron	A. W. Eldridge & J. A. Heard (G-BHFY)
	G-OSEA	BN-2B-26 Islander	W. T. Johnson & Sons (Huddersfield) Ltd (G-BKOL)
	G-OSEP	Mainair Blade 912	J. D. Smith
	G-OSFB	Diamond HK.36TTC Super Dimona	Oxfordshire Sportflying Ltd
	G-OSFS	Cessan F.177RG	Staverton Flying School
	G-OSHK	Schempp-Hirth SHK-1	P. B. Hibbard
	G-OSHL	Robinson R22 Beta	Sloane Helicopters Ltd
	G-OSIC	Pitts S-1C Special	J. A. Dodd (G-BUAW)
	G-OSII	Cessna 172N	India India Flying Group (G-BIVY)
	G-OSIS	Pitts S-1S Special	C. Butler
	G-OSIT	Pitts S-1T Special	C. J. J. Robertson
	G-OSJF	PA-23-250 Aztec F	Equity Air Charter Ltd (G-SFHR/G-BHSO)
	G-OSJL	Robinson R44 II	Darlo Air Ltd
	G-OSJN	Shaw Europa XS	N. Landell-Mills & R. J. Tobin
	G-OSKP	Enstrom 480	C. C. Butt
	G-OSKR	Skyranger 912 (2)	K. Clark
	G-OSKY	Cessna 172M	Skyhawk Leasing Ltd
	G-OSLD	Shaw Europa XS	S. Percy & C. Davies
	G-OSLO	Schweizer 269C	A. H. Helicopter Services Ltd
	G-OSMD	Bell 206B JetRanger 2	Overby Ltd (G-LTEK/G-BMIB)
	G-OSND	Cessna FRA.150M	Group G-OSND (G-BDOU)
	G-OSOE	HS.748 Srs 2A	PTB (Emerald) Pty Ltd (G-AYYG)
	G-OSOH	Cessna 525 Citationjet	Hangar 8 Management Ltd
	G-OSPD	Aerotechnik EV-97 TeamEurostar UK	I. Nicholls
	G-OSPK	Cessna 172S	R. W. Denny
	G-OSPS	PA-18 Super Cub 95	J. P. Orrissey

Reg.	Type	Owner or Operator	Notes
G-OSPY	Cirrus SR20	Cambridge Guarantee Ltd	
G-OSRL	Learjet 45	S. R. Lloyd	
G-OSSA	Cessna Tu.206B	Skydive St.Andrews Ltd	
G-OSST	Colt 77A balloon	A. A. Brown	
G-OSTC	AA-5A Cheetah	5th Generation Designs Ltd	
G-OSTL	Ikarus C.42 FB 100	G-OSTL Syndicate	
G-OSTU	AA-5A Cheetah	M. Lynch (G-BGCL)	
G-OSTY	Cessna F.150G	R. F. Newman (G-AVCU)	
G-OSUP	Lindstrand LBL-90A balloon	M. E. Orchard	
G-OSUS	Mooney M.20K	J. B. King	
G-OSUT	Scheibe SF-25C Rotax-Falke	Yorkshire Gliding Club (Pty.) Ltd	
G-OSZA	Aerotek Pitts S-2A	Septieme Ciel	
G-OSZB	Christen Pitts S-2B Special	P. M. Ambrose (G-OGEE)	
G-OSZS	Pitts S-2S Special	Airtime Aerobatics Ltd	
G-OTAG	Bombardier CL600-2B16 Challenger	TAG Aviation (UK) Ltd	
G-OTAL	ARV Super 2	N. R. Beale (G-BNGZ)	
G-OTAM	Cessna 172M	G. V. White	
G-OTAN	PA-18 Super Cub 135 (54-2445)	S. D. Turner & C. G. Dodds	
G-OTAZ	Hawker 900XP	Hangar 8 Management Ltd	
G-OTCH	CFM Streak Shadow	D. Goodman & I. N. Drury	
G-OTCV	Skyranger 912S (1)	T. C. Viner	
G-OTCZ	Schempp-Hirth Ventus 2cT	D. H. Conway t/a CZ Group	
G-OTDI	Diamond DA40D Star	Atrium Ltd	
G-OTEC	Tecnam P2002-EA Sierra	C. W. Thirtle	
G-OTEL	Thunder Ax8-90 balloon	J. Edwards	
G-OTFL	Eurocopter EC 120B	Tyrone Fabrication Ltd (G-IBRI)	
G-OTFT	PA-38-112 Tomahawk	P. Tribble (G-BNKW)	
G-OTGA	PA-28R-201 Arrow III	TG Aviation Ltd	
G-OTHE	Enstrom 280C-UK Shark	G. E. Heritage (G-OPJT/G-BKCO)	
G-OTIB	Robin DR.400/180R	The Windrushers Gliding Club Ltd	
G-OTIG	AA-5B Tiger	L. Burke (G-PENN)	
G-OTIM	Bensen B.8MV	T. J. Deane	
G-OTIV	Aerospool Dynamic WT9 UK	D. N. E. d'Ath	
G-OTJH	Pegasus Quantum 15-912	L. R. Gartside	
G-OTJS	Robinson R44 II	TJS Self Drive	
G-OTLC	Grumman AA-5 Traveller	Total Logistics Concepts Ltd (G-BBUF)	
G-OTNA	Robinson R44 Raven II	Abel Developments Ltd	
G-OTOE	Aeronca 7AC Champion	J. M. Gale (G-BRWW)	
G-OTOO	Stolp SA.300 Starduster Too	I. M. Castle	
G-OTOP	P & M Quik R	S. D. Pain	
G-OTRV	Van's RV-6	W. R. C. Williams-Wynne	
G-OTRY	Schleicher ASW-24	A. R. Harrison & G. Pursey	
G-OTSP	AS.355F1 Twin Squirrel	MW Helicopters Ltd (G-XPOL/G-BPRF)	
G-OTTY	Rotorsport UK Calidus	C. A. Ho	
G-OTUI	SOCATA TB20 Trinidad	D. J. Taylor & J. T. Flint (G-KKDL/G-BSHU)	
G-OTUN	Aerotechnik EV-97 Eurostar	S. P. Slater	
G-OTUP	Lindstrand LBL-180A balloon	A. N. Sharp	
G-OTVI	Robinson R44 II	Hields Aviation	
G-OTVR	PA-34-220T Seneca V	Bladerunner Aviation Ltd	
G-OTWO	Rutan Defiant	B. Wronski	
G-OTYE	Aerotechnik EV-97 Eurostar	A. B. Godber & J. Tye	
G-OTYP	PA-28 Cherokee 180	T. C. Lewis	
G-OUCH	Cameron N-105 balloon	A. C. Elson	
G-OUDA	Aeroprakt A22-L Foxbat	A. R. Cattell	
G-OUGH	Yakovlev Yak-52	I. M. Gough (G-LAOK)	
G-OUHI	Shaw Europa XS	Airplan Flight Equipment Ltd	
G-OUIK	Mainair Pegasus Quik	D. G. Baker	
G-OUMC	Lindstrand LBL-105A balloon	Executive Ballooning	
G-OUNI	Cirrus SR20	Unique Helicopters (NI) Ltd (G-TABI)	
G-OURO	Shaw Europa	I. M. Mackay	
G-OUVI	Cameron O-105 balloon	Bristol University Hot Air Ballooning Society	
G-OVAG	Tipsy Nipper T.66 Srs 1	L. D. Johnston	
G-OVAL	Ikarus C.42 FB100	N. G. Tomes	
G-OVBF	Cameron A-250 balloon	Virgin Balloon Flights	
G-OVBL	Lindstrand LBL-150A balloon	R. J. Henderson	
G-OVET	Cameron O-56 balloon	A. R. Hardwick & E. Fearon	
G-OVFM	Cessna 120	T. B. Parmenter	
G-OVFR	Cessna F.172N	Marine and Aviation Ltd	
G-OVIA	Lindstrand LBL-105A balloon	N. C. Lindsey	

Notes	Reg.	Type	Owner or Operator
	G-OVID	Light Aero Avid Flyer	W. J. Lister
	G-OVII	Van's RV-7	T. J. Richardson
	G-OVIN	Rockwell Commander 112TC	G. Vekaria
	G-OVLA	Ikarus C.42 FB	Webb Plant Sales
	G-OVMC	Cessna F.152 II	Swiftair Maintenance Ltd
	G-OVNE	Cessna 401A H	Norwich Aviation Museum
	G-OVNR	Robinson R22 Beta	Glenntrade Ltd
	G-OVOL	Skyranger 912S(1)	A. S. Docherty
	G-OVON	PA-18-95 Super Cub	V. F. A. Stanley
	G-OWAI	Schleicher ASK-21	Scottish Gliding Union
	G-OWAL	PA-34-220T Seneca III	R. G. & W. Allison
	G-OWAN	Cessna 210D Centurion	G. Owen
	G-OWAP	PA-28-161 Cherokee Warrior II	Airways Aero Association Ltd (G-BXNH)
	G-OWAR	PA-28-161 Warrior II	Bickertons Aerodromes Ltd
	G-OWAZ	Pitts S-1C Special	P. E. S. Latham (G-BRPI)
	G-OWEL	Colt 105A balloon	S. R. Seager
	G-OWEN	K & S Jungster	R. C. Owen
	G-OWET	Thurston TSC-1A2 Teal	J. Reddington
	G-OWFS	Cessna A.152	Westair Flying Services Ltd (G-DESY/G-BNJE)
	G-OWGC	Slingsby T.61F Venture T.2	Wolds Gliding Club Ltd
	G-OWIL	Cessna 120	R. Flanagan (G-BTYW)
	G-OWLC	PA-31 Turbo Navajo	Channel Airways Ltd (G-AYFZ)
	G-OWMC	Thruster T.600N	Wilts Microlight Centre
	G-OWND	Robinson R44 Astro	R. E. Todd
	G-OWOW	Cessna 152 II	Plane Talking Ltd (G-BMSZ)
	G-OWRC	Cessna F.152 II	Unimat SA/France
	G-OWRD	Agusta A109C	MW Helicopters Ltd (G-USTC/G-LAXO)
	G-OWRT	Cessna 182G	L. Townsend (G-ASUL)
	G-OWWW	Shaw Europa	R. F. W. Holder
	G-OWYE	Lindstrand LBL-240A balloon	Wye Valley Aviation Ltd
	G-OWYN	Aviamilano F.14 Nibbio	R. Nash
	G-OXBA	Cameron Z-160 balloon	J. E. Rose
	G-OXBC	Cameron A-140 balloon	J. E. Rose
	G-OXBY	Cameron N-90 balloon	C. A. Oxby
	G-OXII	Van's RV-12	J. A. King
	G-OXKB	Cameron 110 Sports Car SS balloon	D. M. Moffat
	G-OXLS	Cessna 560XL Citation XLS	Go XLS Ltd
	G-OXOM	PA-28-161 Cadet	Aviation Rentals (G-BRSG)
	G-OXPS	Falcon XPS	J. C. Greenslade (G-BUXP)
	G-OXRS	Bombardier BD700 1A10 Global Express	Profred Partners LLP
	G-OXVI	VS.361 Spitfire LF.XVIe (TD248:CR-S)	Spitfire Ltd
	G-OYAK	Yakovlev C-11 (9 white)	A. H. Soper
	G-OYES	Mainair Blade 912	B. McAdam & A. Hatton
	G-OYIO	Robin DR.400/120	Bustard Flying Club Ltd
	G-OYST	Agusta-Bell 206B JetRanger 2	Adroit Services Corporation (G-JIMW/G-UNIK/G-TPPH/G-BCYP)
	G-OYTE	Rans S.6ES Coyote II	N. D. Major
	G-OZAC	Bell 407	Helilux
	G-OZAR	Enstrom 480	Benham Helicopters Ltd (G-BWFF)
	G-OZAT	Hawker 900XP	Hangar 8 Management Ltd
	G-OZBB	Airbus A.320-212	Monarch Airlines Ltd
	G-OZBE	Airbus A.321-231	Monarch Airlines Ltd
	G-OZBF	Airbus A.321-231	Monarch Airlines Ltd
	G-OZBG	Airbus A.321-231	Monarch Airlines Ltd
	G-OZBH	Airbus A.321-231	Monarch Airlines Ltd
	G-OZBI	Airbus A.321-231	Monarch Airlines Ltd
	G-OZBK	Airbus A.320-214	Monarch Airlines Ltd
	G-OZBL	Airbus A.321-231	Monarch Airlines Ltd (G-MIDE)
	G-OZBM	Airbus A.321-231	Monarch Airlines Ltd (G-MIDJ)
	G-OZBN	Airbus A.321-231	Monarch Airlines Ltd (G-MIDK)
	G-OZBO	Airbus A.321-231	Monarch Airlines Ltd (G-MIDM)
	G-OZBP	Airbus A.321-231	Monarch Airlines Ltd (G-TTIB)
	G-OZBR	Airbus A.321-231	Monarch Airlines Ltd
	G-OZBS	Airbus A.321-231	Monarch Airlines Ltd (G-TTIA)
	G-OZBT	Airbus A.321-231	Monarch Airlines Ltd (G-TTIH)
	G-OZBU	Airbus A.321-231	Monarch Airlines Ltd (G-TTII)
	G-OZEE	Light Aero Avid Speedwing Mk 4	G. D. Bailey
	G-OZEF	Shaw Europa XS	Z. M. Ahmad

Reg.	Type	Owner or Operator	Notes
G-OZIE	Jabiru J400	S. A. Bowkett	
G-OZIO	Aquila AT01	Caseright Ltd	
G-OZOI	Cessna R.182	J. R. G. & F. L. G. Fleming (G-ROBK)	
G-OZOO	Cessna 172N	R. A. Brown (G-BWEI)	
G-OZOZ	Schempp-Hirth Nimbus 3DT	OZ Syndicate	
G-OZRH	BAe 146-200	Calder Ltd	
G-OZZI	Jabiru SK	A. H. Godfrey	
G-OZZO	Avions Mudry CAP.231	R. M. Buchan	
G-PACE	Robin R.1180T	M. T. Fitzpatrick & T. C. Wise	
G-PACL	Robinson R22 Beta	Whizzard Helicopters	
G-PACO	Sikorsky S-76C	Cardinal Helicopter Services	
G-PACT	PA-28-181 Archer III	A. Parsons	
G-PADD	AA-5A Cheetah	Caseright Ltd (G-ESTE/G-GHNC)	
G-PADE	Escapade Jabiru(3)	C. L. G. Innocent	
G-PADI	Cameron V-77 balloon	R. M. Trotter	
G-PAFC	Cameron C-70 balloon	Cameron Balloons Ltd	
G-PAFR	Glaser-Dirks DG-300 Elan	P. Morgan	
G-PAIZ	PA-12 Super Cruiser	B. R. Pearson	
G-PALI	Czech Sport Aircraft Piper Sport	P. A. Langley	
G-PAMY	Robinson R44 II	Batchelor Aviation Ltd	
G-PARG	Pitts S-1C Special	M. Kotsageridis	
G-PARI	Cessna 172RG Cutlass	V. A. Holliday	
G-PASH	AS.355F1 Twin Squirrel	Diamond Aviation Ltd	
G-PASN	Enstrom F-28F	Passion 4 Health International Ltd (G-BSHZ)	
G-PATF	Shaw Europa	E. P. Farrell	
G-PATG	Cameron O-90 balloon	P. Mackley	
G-PATI	Cessna F.172M	Nigel Kenny Aviation Ltd (G-WACZ/G-BCUK)	
G-PATM	AS.350B2 Ecureuil	Mealey Construction Ltd	
G-PATN	SOCATA TB10 Tobago	G-PATN Owners Group (G-LUAR)	
G-PATO	Zenair CH.601UL Zodiac	N. D. Townend	
G-PATP	Lindstrand LBL-77A balloon	P. Pruchnickyj	
G-PATS	Shaw Europa	G-PATS Flying Group	
G-PATX	Lindstrand LBL-90A balloon	P. C. Gooch	
G-PATZ	Shaw Europa	H. P. H. Griffin	
G-PAVL	Robin R.3000/120	Autogas Worldwide Ltd	
G-PAWL	PA-28 Cherokee 140	G-PAWL Group (G-AWEU)	
G-PAWN	PA-25 Pawnee 260C	A. P. Meredith (G-BEHS)	
G-PAWS	AA-5A Cheetah	M. J. Patrick	
G-PAWZ	Best Off Sky Ranger Swift 912S(1)	S. D. McMurran	
G-PAXX	PA-20 Pacer 135 (modified)	D. W. Grace	
G-PAYD	Robin DR.400/180	A. Head	
G-PAZY	Pazmany PL.4A	M. Richardson (G-BLAJ)	
G-PBAT	Czech Sport Aircraft Sportcruiser	P. M. W. Bath	
G-PBEC	Van's RV-7	P. G. Reid	
G-PBEE	Robinson R44	Echo Echo Syndicate	
G-PBEK	Agusta A109A	Castle Air Charters Ltd (G-BXIV)	
G-PBEL	CFM Shadow Srs DD	S. Fairweather	
G-PBIX	VS.361 Spitfire LF XVI E	Pemberton-Billing LLP (G-XVIA)	
G-PBRL	Robinson R22	Cardy Construction Ltd	
G-PBUS	Avtech Jabiru SK	R. D. Bennett	
G-PBYA	Consolidated PBY-5A Catalina (433915)	Catalina Aircraft Ltd	
G-PBYY	Enstrom 280FX	B. Morgan (G-BXKV)	
G-PBZN	AS.350B Ecureuil	Quarry and Mining Equipment Ltd (G-MURP)	
G-PCAF	Pietenpol Air Camper	C. C. & F. M. Barley	
G-PCAT	SOCATA TB10 Tobago	S. D. Johnson (G-BHER)	
G-PCCC	Alpi Pioneer 300	R. Pidcock	
G-PCDP	Zlin Z.526F Trener Master	J. Mann	
G-PCMC	P & M Quik R	M. J. & P. J. Canty	
G-PCOP	Beech B200 Super King Air	Albert Batlett and Sons (Airdrie) Ltd	
G-PDGE	Eurocopter EC 120B	A. J. Wicklow	
G-PDGF	AS.350B2 Ecureuil	PLM Dollar Group Ltd (G-FROH)	
G-PDGG	Aeromere F.8L Falco Srs 3	P. D. G. Grist	
G-PDGN	SA.365N Dauphin 2	PLM Dollar Group Ltd (G-TRAF/G-BLDR)	
G-PDGR	AS.350B2 Ecureuil	PLM Dollar Group Ltd (G-RICC/G-BTXA)	
G-PDGT	AS.355F2 Ecureuil 2	PLM Dollar Group Ltd (G-BOOV)	
G-PDHJ	Cessna T.182R	P. G. Vallance Ltd	
G-PDOC	PA-44-180 Seminole	Medicare (G-PVAF)	

Notes	Reg.	Type	Owner or Operator
	G-PDOG	Cessna O-1E Bird Dog (24550)	J. D. Needham
	G-PDSI	Cessna 172N	DA Flying Group
	G-PEAR	P &M Pegasus Quik	C. D. Hayle
	G-PECK	PA-32-300 Cherokee Six D	S. Empson (G-ETAV/G-MCAR/G-LADA/G-AYWK)
	G-PEGA	Pegasus Quantum 15-912	E. Schoonbrood
	G-PEGE	Skyranger 912	A. N. Hughes
	G-PEGI	PA-34-200T Seneca II	ACS Aviation Ltd
	G-PEGY	Shaw Europa	M. Powell
	G-PEGZ	Centrair 101A Pegase	G-PEGZ Group
	G-PEJM	PA-28-181 Archer III	S. J. Clark
	G-PEKT	SOCATA TB20 Trinidad	A. J. Dales
	G-PENH	Ultramagic M-90 balloon	G. Holtam
	G-PEPA	Cessna 206H	R. D. Lygo (G-MGMG)
	G-PEPE	Cessna 560XL Citation XLS	Fram Partners LLP
	G-PEPS	Robinson R44	PEP Aviation (G-LFBW/G-ODES)
	G-PERC	Cameron N-90 balloon	P. A. Foot & I. R. Warrington
	G-PERE	Robinson R22 Beta	R. F. McLachlan
	G-PERR	Cameron 60 Bottle SS balloon ★	British Balloon Museum/Newbury
	G-PEST	Hawker Tempest II (MW401)	Tempest Two Ltd
	G-PETH	PA-24-260C Comanche	J. V. Hutchinson
	G-PETR	PA-28-140 Cherokee	A. A. Gardner (G-BCJL)
	G-PETS	Diamond DA42NG Twin Star	Airways Aircraft Leasing Ltd
	G-PEYO	Gefa-Flug AS 105 GD airship	International Merchandising Promotion and Services SA
	G-PFAA	EAA Biplane Model P	T. A. Fulcher
	G-PFAF	FRED Srs 2	M. S. Perkins
	G-PFAH	Evans VP-1	J. A. Scott
	G-PFAP	Currie Wot/SE-5A (C1904:Z)	J. H. Seed
	G-PFAR	Isaacs Fury II (K2059)	M. A. Watts
	G-PFAT	Monnett Sonerai II	H. B. Carter
	G-PFAW	Evans VP-1	R. F. Shingler
	G-PFCI	PA-34-220T Seneca IV	Magnum Holdings Ltd
	G-PFCL	Cessna 172S	J. Crego
	G-PFCT	Learjet 45	The Fighter Collection Ltd (G-GOMO/G-OLDF/G-JRJR)
	G-PFFN	Beech 200 Super King Air	The Puffin Club Ltd
	G-PFSL	Cessna F.152	P. A. Simon
	G-PGAC	MCR-01	G. A. Coatesworth
	G-PGBR	Vulcanair P-68	Caseright Ltd
	G-PGFG	Tecnam P92-EM Echo	P. G. Fitzgerald
	G-PGGY	Robinson R44	Linic Consultants Ltd
	G-PGHM	Air Creation Kiss 450	P. G. H. Millbank
	G-PGRP	Embraer EMB-135BJ Legacy	Gama Aviation Ltd
	G-PGSA	Thruster T.600N	T. Davis
	G-PGSI	Pierre Robin R2160	M. A. Spencer
	G-PHAA	Cessna F.150M	PHA Aviation (G-BCPE)
	G-PHAB	Cirrus SR22	G3 Aviation Ltd (G-MACL)
	G-PHAT	Cirrus SR20	Synergy Aircraft Leasing Ltd
	G-PHLY	Cessna FRA150L	M. Bonsall
	G-PHMG	Van's RV-8	A. C. Fletcher
	G-PHNM	Embraer EMB-500 Phenom 100	Errigal Aviation Ltd
	G-PHNX	Schempp-Hirth Duo Discus Xt	J. L. Birch & R. Maskell
	G-PHOR	Cessna FRA.150L Aerobat	M. Bonsall (G-BACC)
	G-PHOX	Aeroprakt A22-L Foxbat	J. D. Webb
	G-PHSI	Colt 90A balloon	P. H. Strickland
	G-PHTG	SOCATA TB10 Tobago	A. J. Baggarley
	G-PHUN	Cessna FRA.150L Aerobat	M. Bonsall (G-BAIN)
	G-PHVM	Van's RV-8	G. Howes & V. Millard
	G-PHXS	Shaw Europa XS	P. Handford
	G-PHYL	Denney Kitfox Mk 4	L. A. James
	G-PHYS	Jabiru SP-470	G-PHYS Group
	G-PHYZ	Jabiru J430	P. C. Knight
	G-PIAF	Thunder Ax7-65 balloon	L. Battersley
	G-PICX	P & M Aviation QuikR	M. D. Thomas
	G-PIDG	Robinson R44	K. J. O. Goodyear
	G-PIEL	CP.301A Emeraude	P. R. Thorne (G-BARY)
	G-PIES	Thunder Ax7-77Z balloon	S. J. Hollingsworth & M. K. Bellamy
	G-PIET	Pietenpol Air Camper	A. R. Wyatt

Reg.	Type	Owner or Operator	Notes
G-PIGG	Lindstrand LBL Pig SS balloon	I. Heidenreich/Germany	
G-PIGI	Aerotechnik EV-97 Eurostar	Pigs Might Fly Group	
G-PIGS	SOCATA Rallye 150ST	Boonhill Flying Group (G-BDWB)	
G-PIGY	Short SC.7 Skyvan Srs 3A Variant 100	Invicta Aviation Ltd	
G-PIIT	Pitts S-2 Special	R. Reid	
G-PIIX	Cessna P.210N	D. L. Harrisberg & R. Dennis (G-KATH)	
G-PIKD	Eiriavion PIK-20D-78	M. C. Hayes	
G-PIKE	Robinson R22 Mariner	Sloane Helicopters Ltd	
G-PIKK	PA-28 Cherokee 140	Coventry Aviators Flying Group (G-AVLA)	
G-PILE	Rotorway Executive 90	J. B. Russell	
G-PILL	Light Aero Avid Flyer Mk 4	D. R. Meston	
G-PILY	Pilatus B4 PC-11	N. Frost	
G-PIMM	Ultramagic M-77 balloon	G. Everett	
G-PIMP	Robinson R44	Maxim Gestioni SRL	
G-PINC	Cameron Z-90 balloon	M. Cowling	
G-PING	AA-5A Cheetah	J. A. Newbold	
G-PINT	Cameron 65 Barrel SS balloon	D. K. Fish	
G-PINX	Lindstrand Pink Panther SS balloon	Magical Adventures Ltd/USA	
G-PIOM	Robinson R44	Karl Hayes Plant Hire (G-BXUK)	
G-PION	Alpi Pioneer 300	P. F. J. Burton	
G-PIPI	Mainair Pegasus Quik	N. R. Williams	
G-PIPP	PA-32R-301T Saratoga II TC	Poores Travel Consultants Ltd	
G-PIPR	PA-18 Super Cub 95	R. Forfitt & A. J. J. Sproule (G-BCDC)	
G-PIPS	Van's RV-4	F. W. Hardiman	
G-PIPY	Cameron 105 Pipe SS balloon	D. M. Moffat	
G-PITS	Pitts S-2AE Special	P. N. A. & S. N. Whithead	
G-PITT	Pitts S-2 Special	Mansfield Property Consultancy Ltd	
G-PITZ	Pitts S-2A Special	J. A. Coutts	
G-PIXE	Colt 31A balloon	N. D. Eliot	
G-PIXI	Pegasus Quantum 15-912	K. J. Rexter	
G-PIXL	Robinson R44 II	Flying TV Ltd	
G-PIXX	Robinson R44 II	Flying TV Ltd	
G-PIXY	Supermarine Aircraft Spitfire Mk.26	R. Collenette	
G-PJLO	Boeing 767-35EER	Thomson Airways Ltd	
G-PJMT	Lancair 320	V. Hatton & P. Gilroy	
G-PJNZ	Commander 114B	C. R. Barr	
G-PJPJ	Boeing 737-5H6	Astraeus Ltd (G-GFFJ)	
G-PJSY	Van's RV-6	P. J. York	
G-PJTM	Cessna FR.172K II	R. & J. R. Emery (G-BFIF)	
G-PKPK	Schweizer 269C	C. H. Dobson	
G-PLAD	Kolb Twinstar Mk 3 Extra	P. J. Ladd	
G-PLAJ	BAe Jetstream 3102	Amber Airways Ltd	
G-PLAL	Eurocopter EC 135T2	Saville Air Services	
G-PLAN	Cessna F.150L	G-PLAN Flying Group	
G-PLAR	Vans RV-9A	P. M. & L. Riglar	
G-PLAY	Robin R.2112	A. M. and G. F. Granger t/a Alpha Flying Group	
G-PLAZ	Rockwell Commander 112	I. Hunt (G-RDCI/G-BFWG)	
G-PLEE	Cessna 182Q	Peterlee Parachute Centre	
G-PLLT	Lindstrand Box SS balloon	Lindstrand Hot Air Balloons Ltd	
G-PLMB	AS.350B Ecureuil	Aeromecanic (G-BMMB)	
G-PLMH	AS.350B2 Ecureuil	PLM Dollar Group Ltd	
G-PLMI	SA.365C-1 Dauphin	PLM Dollar Group Ltd	
G-PLOW	Hughes 269B	Sulby Aerial Surveys (G-AVUM)	
G-PLPC	Schweizer Hughes 269C	A. R. Baker	
G-PLPL	Agusta A109E Power	Iceland Foods Ltd (G-TMWC)	
G-PLPM	Shaw Europa XS	P. L. P. Mansfield	
G-PLSA	Aero Designs Pulsar XP	Air Ads Ltd (G-NEVS)	
G-PMAM	Cameron V-65 balloon	P. A. Meecham	
G-PMGG	Agusta-Bell 206A JetRanger	P. M. Gallagher & M. J. Lee (G-EEGO/G-PELS/ G-DNCN)	
G-PMHT	SOCATA TBM850	Ewan Air	
G-PMNF	VS.361 Spitfire HF.IX (TA805:FX-M)	P. R. Monk	
G-PNEU	Colt 110 Bibendum SS balloon	A. M. Holly	
G-PNGC	Schleicher ASK-21	Portsmouth Naval Gliding Centre	
G-PNIX	Cessna FRA.150L	Dukeries Aviation (G-BBEO)	
G-POCO	Cessna 152	K. M. Watts	

Notes	Reg.	Type	Owner or Operator
	G-POET	Robinson R44 II	C. L. Farrell
	G-POGO	Flight Design CT2K	L. I. Bailey
	G-POLA	Eurocopter EC 135 P2+	West Midlands Police Authority
	G-POLI	Robinson R44 II	Luxtronic Ltd
	G-POLL	Skyranger 912 (1)	D. L. Pollitt
	G-POLY	Cameron N-77 balloon	S. Church & S. Jenkins
	G-POND	Oldfield Baby Lakes	U. Reichert/Germany
	G-POOH	Piper J-3C-65 Cub	P. Robinson
	G-POOL	ARV Super 2	P. A. Dawson (G-BNHA)
	G-POPA	Beech A36 Bonanza	C. J. O'Sullivan
	G-POPE	Eiri PIK-20E-1	G-POPE Syndicate
	G-POPI	SOCATA TB10 Tobago	I. S. Hacon & C. J. Earle (G-BKEN)
	G-POPW	Cessna 182S	D. L. Price
	G-POPY	Best Off Sky Ranger Swift 912S(1)	C. D. & L. J. Church
	G-PORK	AA-5B Tiger	R. A. Lambert (G-BFHS)
	G-POSH	Colt 56A balloon	B. K. Rippon (G-BMPT)
	G-POUX	Pou du Ciel-Bifly	G. D. Priest
	G-POWB	Beech B300 Super King Air	Titan Airways Ltd
	G-POWC	Boeing 737-33A	Titan Airways Ltd
	G-POWD	Boeing 767-36N	Titan Airways Ltd
	G-POWF	Avro RJ100	Titan Airways Ltd
	G-POWL	Cessna 182R	B. W. Powell
	G-POZA	Escapade Jabiru ULP (1)	M. R. Jones
	G-PPIO	Cameron C-90 balloon	A. Murphy
	G-PPLC	Cessna 560 Citation V	Sterling Aviation
	G-PPLG	Rotorsport UK MT-03	J. E. Butler
	G-PPLL	Van's RV-7A	P. G. Leonard
	G-PPLO	Fournier RF-4D	J. B. Giddins & J. Marriott
	G-PPOD	Europa Aviation Europa XS	S. Easom
	G-PPPP	Denney Kitfox Mk 3	R. Powers
	G-PPTS	Robinson R44	J. & L. Prowse
	G-PRAG	Brügger MB.2 Colibri	Colibri Flying Group
	G-PRAH	Flight Design CT2K	G. N. S. Farrant
	G-PRDH	AS.355F2 Ecureuil 2	EZ-Int Ltd
	G-PREI	Raytheon 390 Premier 1	Craft Air SA/Luxembourg
	G-PRET	Robinson R44	J. A. Wilson
	G-PREY	Pereira Osprey II	N. S. Dalrymple (G-BEPB)
	G-PREZ	Robin DR.400/500	Regent Group
	G-PRII	Hawker Hunter PR.11 (XG164/A)	Deep Cleavage Ltd
	G-PRIM	PA-38-112 Tomahawk	Braddock Ltd
	G-PRIV	VS.353 Spitfire PR.IV	P. R. Arnold
	G-PRKR	Canadair CL600-2B16 Challenger 604	TAG Aviation (UK) Ltd
	G-PRLY	Avtech Jabiru SK	N. C. Cowell (G-BYKY)
	G-PROJ	Robinson R44 II	Project Racing Team Ltd
	G-PROM	AS.350B Ecureuil	General Cabins & Engineering Ltd (G-MAGY/ G-BIYC)
	G-PROO	Hawker 4000 Horizon	Hangar 8 Management Ltd
	G-PROS	Van's RV-7A	S. A. Jarrett
	G-PROV	P.84 Jet Provost T.52A (T.4)	Provost Group
	G-PROW	Aerotechnik EV-97A Eurostar	R. A. Smith
	G-PRSI	Pegasus Quantum 15-912	A. P. Shoobert
	G-PRTT	Cameron N-31 balloon	A. Kaye
	G-PRXI	VS.365 Spitfire PR.XI (PL983)	Propshop Ltd
	G-PSAX	Lindstrand LBL-77B balloon	M. V. Farrant
	G-PSFG	Robin R.21601	Mardenair Ltd (G-COVD/G-BYOF)
	G-PSGC	PA-25 Pawnee 260C (modified)	Peterborough & Spalding Gliding Club Ltd (G-BDDT)
	G-PSHK	Schempp-Hirth SHK-1	P. Gentil
	G-PSIR	Jurca MJ.77 Gnatsum (474008 'VF-R')	P. W. Carlton & T. R. Grief
	G-PSKY	Skyranger 912S(1)	P. W. Curnock & J. W. Wilcox
	G-PSNI	Eurocopter EC 135T2	Police Service of Northern Ireland
	G-PSNO	Eurocopter MBB BK-117C-2	Police Service of Northern Ireland
	G-PSON	Colt Cylinder One SS balloon	Balloon Preservation Flying Group
	G-PSRT	PA-28-151 Warrior	P. A. S. Dyke (G-BSGN)
	G-PSST	Hunter F.58A	Heritage Aviation Developments Ltd
	G-PSTR	Beech B.200 Super King Air	Red Air LLP
	G-PSUE	CFM Shadow Srs CD	D. A. Crosbie (G-MYAA)
	G-PSUK	Thruster T.600N 450	Thruster Syndicate

Reg.	Type	Owner or Operator	Notes
G-PTAG	Shaw Europa	R. C. Harrison	
G-PTAR	Best Off Skyranger 912S(1)	P. Vergette	
G-PTDP	Bücker Bü133C Jungmeister	T. J. Reeve (G-AEZX)	
G-PTEA	PA-46-350P Malibu Mirage	P. J. Caiger	
G-PTOO	Bell 206L-4 LongRanger 4	P2 Air Ltd	
G-PTRE	SOCATA TB20 Trinidad	Trantshore Ltd (G-BNKU)	
G-PTRI	Cessna 182T	G-PTRI LLP	
G-PTTS	Aerotek Pitts S-2A	P. & J. Voce	
G-PTWO	Pilatus P2-05 (U-110)	R. G. Meredith	
G-PUDL	PA-18 Super Cub 150	C. M. Edwards	
G-PUDS	Shaw Europa	M. J. Riley	
G-PUFF	Thunder Ax7-77A balloon	Intervarsity Balloon Club	
G-PUGS	Cessna 182H	N. C. & M. F. Shaw	
G-PUKA	Jabiru Aircraft Jabiru J400	D. P. Harris	
G-PULR	Pitts S-2AE	A. Ayre	
G-PUMA	AS.332L Super Puma	CHC Scotia Ltd	
G-PUME	AS.332L Super Puma	CHC Scotia Ltd	
G-PUMN	AS.332L Super Puma	CHC Scotia Ltd	
G-PUMO	AS.332L-2 Super Puma	CHC Scotia Ltd	
G-PUMS	AS.332L-2 Super Puma	CHC Scotia Ltd	
G-PUNK	Thunder Ax8-105 balloon	S. C. Kinsey	
G-PUNT	Robinson R44 II	R. D. Cameron	
G-PUPP	Beagle B.121 Pup 2	B. R. Hunter & A. D. Wood (G-BASD)	
G-PUPS	Cameron Z-210 balloon	High On Adventure Balloons Ltd	
G-PUPY	Shaw Europa XS	V. L. Flett	
G-PURE	Cameron can 70 SS balloon	Mobberley Balloon Collection	
G-PURL	PA-32R-301 Saratoga II	A. P.H. & E. Hay	
G-PURR	AA-5A Cheetah	D. H. Green (G-BJDN)	
G-PURS	Rotorway Executive	J. E. Houseman	
G-PUSA	Gefa-Flug AS105GD Hot Air Airship	Skyking Aviation Ltd	
G-PUSI	Cessna T.303	Crusader Craft	
G-PUSS	Cameron N-77 balloon	L. D. Thurgar	
G-PVBF	Lindstrand LBL-260S balloon	Virgin Balloon Flights	
G-PVCV	Robin DR400/140	P. N. Bevan & L. M. Poor	
G-PVEL	Bombardier BD700-1A11 Global 5000	Ocean Sky (UK) Ltd	
G-PVET	DHC.1 Chipmunk 22 (WB565)	Connect Properties Ltd	
G-PVHT	Dassault Falcon 7X	TAG Aviation (UK) Ltd	
G-PVML	Robin DR400/140B	Weald Air Services Ltd	
G-PVSS	P & M Quik GT450	K. & L. Ramsay	
G-PVST	Thruster T.600N 450	R. J. Davey	
G-PWBE	DH.82A Tiger Moth	M. F. Newman	
G-PWIT	Bell 206L-1 LongRanger	Formal Holdings Ltd (G-DWMI)	
G-PWNS	Cessna 525 Citationjet	Langford Lane Ltd	
G-PWUL	Van's RV-6	S. King	
G-PYNE	Thruster T.600N 450	R. Dereham	
G-PYPE	Van's RV-7	R. & L. Pyper	
G-PYPA	Robinson R44 II	E. P. Arditti	
G-PYRO	Cameron N-65 balloon	A. C. Booth	
G-PZAS	Schleicher ASW-27-18	A. P. C. Sampson	
G-PZAZ	PA-31-350 Navajo Chieftain	Air Medical Fleet Ltd (G-VTAX/G-UTAX)	
G-RAAF	VS.359 Spitfire VIII	Composite Mast Engineering and Technology Ltd	
G-RAAL	Embraer EMB-500 Phenom 100	Flairjet Ltd	
G-RABA	Cessna FR.172H	Air Ads Ltd	
G-RABS	Alpi Pioneer 300	J. Mullen	
G-RACA	P.57 Sea Prince T.1 (571/CU) ★	(stored)/Long Marston	
G-RACI	Beech C90 King Air (modified)	E Flight SRL/Italy (G-SHAM)	
G-RACO	PA-28R Cherokee Arrow 200-II	Graco Group Ltd	
G-RACR	Ultramagic M-65C balloon	R. A. Vale	
G-RACY	Cessna 182S	N. J. Fuller	
G-RADI	PA-28-181 Archer II	I. Davidson	
G-RADR	Douglas AD-4NA Skyraider (126922:402)	T. J. Manna (G-RAID)	
G-RAEF	Schempp-Hirth SHK-1	R. A. Earnshaw-Fretwell	
G-RAEM	Rutan LongEz	G. F. H. Singleton	
G-RAES	Boeing 777-236	British Airways	
G-RAFA	Grob G.115	RAF College Flying Club Ltd	

Notes	Reg.	Type	Owner or Operator
	G-RAFB	Grob G.115	RAF College Flying Club Ltd
	G-RAFC	Robin R.2112	RAF Charlie Group
	G-RAFE	Thunder Ax7-77 balloon	Giraffe Balloon Syndicate
	G-RAFG	Slingsby T.67C Firefly	A. Brinkley
	G-RAFH	Thruster T.600N 450	RAF Microlight Flying Association (FH)
	G-RAFR	Skyranger J2.2(1)	M. D. Gregory
	G-RAFS	Thruster T.600N 450	RAF Microlight Flying Association (FS)
	G-RAFT	Rutan LongEz	W. S. Allen
	G-RAFV	Avid Speedwing	Fox Victor Group (G-MOTT)
	G-RAFW	Mooney M.20E	Vinola (Knitwear) Manufacturing Co Ltd (G-ATHW)
	G-RAFY	Best Off Sky Ranger Swift 912S(1)	M. A. Evans & C. R. Cawley
	G-RAFZ	RAF 2000 GTX-SE	John Pavitt (Engineers) Ltd
	G-RAGE	Wilson Cassutt IIIM	R. S. Grace (G-BEUN)
	G-RAGS	Pietenpol Air Camper	S. H. Leonard
	G-RAGT	PA-32-301FT Cherokee Six	Oxhill Aviation
	G-RAIG	SA Bulldog Srs 100/101	Power Aerobatics Ltd (G-AZMR)
	G-RAIR	Schleicher ASH-25	P. T. Reading & Viscount Cobham
	G-RAIX	CCF AT-16 Harvard 4 (KF584)	M. R. Paul (G-BIWX)
	G-RAJA	Raj Hamsa X'Air 582 (2)	P. Smith
	G-RAJJ	BAe 146-200	Cello Aviation Ltd (G-CFDH)
	G-RALA	Robinson R44 Clipper II	Rala Aviation Ltd
	G-RALD	Robinson R22HP	Interceptor Aviation Ltd (G-CHIL)
	G-RAMA	Cameron C-70 balloon	Poppies (UK) Ltd
	G-RAMI	Bell 206B JetRanger 3	Yorkshire Helicopters
	G-RAMP	Piper J-3C-65 Cub	J. A. Holman & T. A. Hinton
	G-RAMS	PA-32R-301 Saratoga SP	Mike Sierra LLP
	G-RAMY	Bell 206B JetRanger 2	Lincair Ltd
	G-RAPD	Hughes 369E	FS Aviation LLP
	G-RAPH	Cameron O-77 balloon	P. A. Sweatman
	G-RAPI	Lindstrand LBL-105A balloon	P. A. Foot
	G-RAPT	Robinson R44 II	Heli Air Ltd
	G-RARB	Cessna 172N	Prior Group Holdings Ltd
	G-RARE	Thunder Ax5-42 SS balloon ★	Balloon Preservation Group
	G-RASA	Diamond DA42 Twin Star	C. D. Hill
	G-RASC	Evans VP-2	R. F. Powell
	G-RASH	Grob G.109E	G-RASH Syndicate
	G-RATC	Van's RV-4	A. F. Ratcliffe
	G-RATD	Van's RV-8	J. R. Pike
	G-RATE	AA-5A Cheetah	G-RATE Flying Group (G-BIFF)
	G-RATH	Rotorway Executive 162F	M. S. Cole
	G-RATI	Cessna F.172M	D. Daniel (G-PATI/G-WACZ/G-BCUK)
	G-RATV	PA-28RT-201T Turbo Arrow IV	Tango Victor Ltd (G-WILS)
	G-RATZ	Shaw Europa	W. Goldsmith
	G-RAVE	Southdown Raven X	M. J. Robbins (G-MNZV)
	G-RAVN	Robinson R44	Brambledown Aircraft Hire
	G-RAWB	P & M Quik GT450	R. Blatchford
	G-RAWS	Rotorway Executive 162F	R. P. Robinson
	G-RAYA	Denney Kitfox Mk 4	G. M. Park
	G-RAYB	P & M Quik GT450	R. Blatchford
	G-RAYH	Zenair CH.701UL	R. Horner
	G-RAYO	Lindstrand LBL-90A balloon	R. Owen
	G-RAYS	Zenair CH.250	A. D. Lowe
	G-RAYY	Cirrus SR22	Alquiler de Veleros SL/Spain
	G-RAYZ	Tecnam P2002-EA Sierra	R. Wells
	G-RAZY	PA-28-181 Archer II	T. H. Pemberton (G-REXS)
	G-RAZZ	Maule MX-7-180	C. S. Baird
	G-RBBB	Shaw Europa	T. J. Hartwell
	G-RBCI	BN-2A Mk.III-2 Trislander	Aurigny Air Services Ltd (G-BDWV)
	G-RBCT	Schempp-Hirth Ventus 2Ct	M. J. Weston & J. D. Huband
	G-RBMS	Cirrus 22	D. J. Bowie
	G-RBMV	Cameron O-31 balloon	P. D. Griffiths
	G-RBNB	Embraer ERJ190-100ECJ	Hangar 8 Management Ltd
	G-RBNS	Embraer EMB-135BJ Legacy 650	Portrack Global Ltd
	G-RBOS	Colt AS-105 airship ★	Science Museum/Wroughton
	G-RBOW	Thunder Ax-7-65 balloon	R. S. McDonald
	G-RBSN	Ikarus C.42 FB80	P. B. & M. Robinson
	G-RCED	Rockwell Commander 114	D. J. and D. Pitman
	G-RCHY	Aerotechnik EV-97 Eurostar	N. McKenzie
	G-RCKT	Harmon Rocket II	K. E. Armstrong

Reg.	Type	Owner or Operator	Notes
G-RCMC	Murphy Renegade 912	J. Matcham	
G-RCMF	Cameron V-77 balloon	J. M. Percival	
G-RCML	Sky 77-24 balloon	R. C. M. Sarl/Luxembourg	
G-RCNB	Eurocopter EC 120B	Furbs Pension Fund	
G-RCOM	Bell 206L-3 LongRanger 3	3GRComm Ltd	
G-RCRC	P & M Quik	R. M. Brown	
G-RCST	Jabiru J430	G. R. Cotterell	
G-RCWK	Cessna 182T Skylane	R. C. W. King	
G-RDCO	Avtech Jabiru J430	RDCO (International) LLP	
G-RDDT	Schempp-Hirth Duo Discus T	R. Witter	
G-RDEL	Robinson R44	Isaonas SL/Spain	
G-RDFX	Aero AT-3	B. Wilson	
G-RDHS	Shaw Europa XS	R. D. H. Spencer	
G-RDNS	Rans S.6-S Super Coyote	P. G. Cowling & J. S. Crofts	
G-RDPH	P & M Quik R	R. S. Partidge-Hicks	
G-READ	Colt 77A balloon	Intervarsity Balloon Club	
G-REAF	Jabiru J400	R. E. Afia	
G-REAH	PA-32R-301 Saratoga SP	M. Q. Tolbod & S. J. Rogers (G-CELL)	
G-REAP	Pitts S-1S Special	R. Dixon	
G-REAR	Lindstrand LBL-69X balloon	A. M. Holly	
G-REAS	Van's RV-6A	T. J. Smith	
G-REBB	Murphy Rebel	M. Stow	
G-RECK	PA-28 Cherokee 140B	D. Barron & S. G. Brown (G-AXJW)	
G-RECO	Jurca MJ-5L Sirocco	J. D. Tseliki	
G-REDC	Pegasus Quantum 15-912	S. Houghton	
G-REDD	Cessna 310R II	G. Wightman (G-BMGT)	
G-REDE	Eurocopter AS.365N3 Dauphin 2	Bond European Aviation Leasing Ltd	
G-REDF	Eurocopter AS.365N3 Dauphin 2	Bond European Aviation Leasing Ltd	
G-REDG	Eurocopter AS.365N3 Dauphin 2	Bond Offshore Helicopters Ltd	
G-REDH	Eurocopter AS.365N3 Dauphin 2	Bond Offshore Helicopters Ltd	
G-REDJ	Eurocopter AS.332L-2 Super Puma	International Aviation Leasing Ltd	
G-REDK	Eurocopter AS.332L-2 Super Puma	International Aviation Leasing Ltd	
G-REDL	Eurocopter AS.332L-2 Super Puma	International Aviation Leasing Ltd	
G-REDM	Eurocopter AS.332L-2 Super Puma	International Aviation Leasing Ltd	
G-REDN	Eurocopter AS.332L-2 Super Puma	International Aviation Leasing Ltd	
G-REDO	Eurocopter AS.332L-2 Super Puma	International Aviation Leasing Ltd	
G-REDP	Eurocopter AS.332L-2 Super Puma	International Aviation Leasing Ltd	
G-REDR	Eurocopter AS.225LP Super Puma	International Aviation Leasing Ltd	
G-REDS	Cessna 560XL Citation Excel	Air Charter Scotland (Holdings) Ltd	
G-REDT	Eurocopter EC.225LP Super Puma	International Aviation Leasing LLP	
G-REDV	Eurocopter EC.225LP Super Puma	Bond Offshore Helicopters Ltd	
G-REDW	Eurocopter EC.225LP Super Puma	Bond Offshore Helicopters Ltd	
G-REDX	Experimental Aviation Berkut	G. V. Waters	
G-REDY	Robinson R22 Beta	P. de Santis	
G-REDZ	Thruster T.600N 450	N. S. Dell	
G-REEC	Sequoia F.8L Falco	J. D. Tseliki	
G-REED	Mainair Blade 912S	I. C. Macbeth	
G-REEF	Mainair Blade 912S	G. Mowll	
G-REEM	AS.355F1 Twin Squirrel	Heliking Ltd (G-EMAN/G-WEKR/G-CHLA)	
G-REER	Centrair 101A Pegase	R. L. Howorth & G. C. Stinchcombe	
G-REES	Jodel D.140C	G-REES Flying Group	
G-REGC	Zenair CH.601XL Zodiac	G. P. Coutie	
G-REGE	Robinson R44	Rotorvation Helicopters	
G-REGI	Cyclone Chaser S508	G. S. Stokes (G-MYZW)	
G-REGS	Thunder Ax7-77 balloon	D. R. Rawlings	
G-REJP	Europa XS	A. Milner	
G-REKO	Pegasus Quasar IITC	M. Sims (G-MWWA)	
G-RELL	D.62B Condor	P. S. Grellier (G-OPJH/G-AVDW)	
G-REMH	Bell 206B-3 JetRanger III	Nottinghamshire Helicopters (2008) Ltd	
G-RENO	SOCATA TB10 Tobago	V. W. Ood	
G-RESC	MBB BK.117C-1	Sterling Helicopters Ltd	
G-RESG	Dyn'Aéro MCR-01 Club	R. E. S. Greenwood	
G-REST	Beech P35 Bonanza	C. R. Taylor (G-ASFJ)	
G-RETA	CASA 1.131 Jungmann 2000	Richard Shuttleworth Trustees (G-BGZC)	
G-REVE	Van's RV-6	R. C. Dyer	
G-REVO	Skyranger 912(2)	H. Murray	
G-REYS	Canadair CL600-2B16 Challenger 604	TAG Aviation	
G-RFIO	Aeromot AMT-200 Super Ximango	M. D. Evans	
G-RFLY	Extra EA.300/L	Firefly Aero Services Ltd	

Notes	Reg.	Type	Owner or Operator
	G-RFOX	Denney Kitfox Mk 3	L. G. G. Faulkner
	G-RFSB	Sportavia RF-5B	G-RFSB Group
	G-RFUN	Robinson R44	Brooklands Developments Ltd
	G-RGAP	Cessna 172S	Certrain Ltd
	G-RGNT	Robinson R44 II	Regent Aviation (G-DMCG)
	G-RGSG	Raytheon Hawker 900XP	Hangar 8 Management Ltd
	G-RGTS	Schempp-Hirth Discus b	G. R. Green
	G-RGUS	Fairchild 24A-46A Argus III (44-83184)	T. R. Coulton & J. L. Bryan
	G-RGZT	Cirrus SR20	D. Whalley
	G-RHAM	Skyranger 582(1)	I. Smart & T. Driffield
	G-RHCB	Schweizer 269C-1	Aviation Rentals
	G-RHHT	PA-32RT-300 Lance II	M. R. Boutel
	G-RHMS	Embraer EMB-135BJ Legacy	Astra Fire Ltd
	G-RHOS	ICP MXP-740 Savannah VG Jabiru(1)	J. C. Munro-Hunt
	G-RHYM	PA-31-310 Turbo Navajo B	2 Excel Aviation Ltd (G-BJLO)
	G-RHYS	Rotorway Executive 90	A. K. Voase
	G-RIAM	SOCATA TB10 Tobago	H. Varia
	G-RIBA	P & M Quik GT450	R. J. Murphy
	G-RICK	Beech 95-B55 Baron	J. Jack (G-BAAG)
	G-RICO	AG-5B Tiger	I. J. Ward
	G-RICS	Shaw Europa	The Flying Property Doctor
	G-RIDA	Eurocopter AS.355NP Ecureuil 2	National Grid Electricity Transmission PLC
	G-RIDE	Stephens Akro	R. Mitchell
	G-RIDG	Van's RV-7	B. A. Ridgway
	G-RIEF	DG Flugzeugbau DG-1000T	EF Gliding Group
	G-RIET	Hoffmann H.36 Dimona	Dimona Gliding Group
	G-RIEV	Rolladen-Schneider LS8-18	R. D. Grieve
	G-RIFB	Hughes 269C	Puddleduck Plane Partnership
	G-RIFN	Avion Mudry CAP-10B	D. E. Starkey & R. A. J. Spurrell
	G-RIFO	Schempp-Hirth Standard Cirrus 75-VTC	L. de Marchi (G-CKGT)
	G-RIFY	Christen Eagle II	C. J. Gow
	G-RIGB	Thunder Ax7-77 balloon	N. J. Bettin
	G-RIGH	PA-32R-301 Saratoga IIHP	G. M. R. Graham
	G-RIGS	PA-60 Aerostar 601P	G. G. Caravatti & P. G. Penati/Italy
	G-RIHN	Dan Rihn DR.107 One Design	P. J. Burgess
	G-RIII	Vans RV-3B	R. S. Grace & D. H. Burge
	G-RIIV	Van's RV-4	C. Baldwin
	G-RIKI	Mainair Blade 912	J. W. Strachan
	G-RIKS	Shaw Europa XS	R. Morris
	G-RIKY	Mainair Pegasus Quik	P. J. Bent
	G-RILA	Flight Design CTSW	P. Mahony
	G-RILY	Monnett Sonnerai 2L	P. C. Avery
	G-RIMB	Lindstrand LBL-105A balloon	D. Grimshaw
	G-RIME	Lindstrand LBL-25A balloon	N. Ivison
	G-RIMM	Westland Wasp HAS.1 (XT435:430)	G. P. Hinkley
	G-RINN	Mainair Blade	P. Hind
	G-RINO	Thunder Ax7-77 balloon	D. J. Head
	G-RINS	Rans S.6-ESD Coyote II	D. Watt
	G-RINT	CFM Streak Shadow	D. Grint
	G-RINZ	Van's RV-7	P. Chaplin (G-UZZL)
	G-RIPA	Partenavia P68 Observer 2	Apem Ltd
	G-RIPH	VS.384 Seafire F.XVII	Seafire Displays Ltd (G-CDTM)
	G-RISE	Cameron V-77 balloon	D. L. Smith
	G-RISH	Rotorway Exeecutive 162F	C. S. Rische
	G-RISK	Hughes 369E	Wavendon Social Housing Ltd
	G-RISY	Van's RV-7	A. J. A. Weal
	G-RITT	Pegasus Quik	I. A. Macadam
	G-RIVE	Jodel D.153	P. Fines
	G-RIVR	Thruster T.600N	Thruster Air Services Ltd
	G-RIVT	Van's RV-6	N. Reddish
	G-RIXA	J-3C-65 Cub	J. J. Rix
	G-RIXS	Shaw Europa XS	R. Iddon
	G-RIXY	Cameron Z-77 balloon	Rix Petroleum Ltd
	G-RIZE	Cameron O-90 balloon	S. F. Burden/Netherlands
	G-RIZI	Cameron N-90 balloon	R. Wiles
	G-RIZZ	PA-28-161 Warrior II	Modi Aviation Ltd
	G-RJAH	Boeing Stearman A75N1	R. J. Horne
	G-RJAM	Sequoia F.8L Falco	A. Marks

Reg.	Type	Owner or Operator	Notes
G-RJCC	Cessna 172S	R. J. Chapman	
G-RJCP	Rockwell Commander 114B	Heltor Ltd	
G-RJCS	Hughes 369E	C. Springthorpe	
G-RJMS	PA-28R-201 Arrow III	M. G. Hill	
G-RJRJ	Evektor EV-97A Eurostar	G-RJRJ Flying Group	
G-RJWW	Maule M5-235C Lunar Rocket	D. E. Priest (G-BRWG)	
G-RJWX	Shaw Europa XS	J. R. Jones	
G-RJXA	Embraer RJ145EP	bmi regional	
G-RJXB	Embraer RJ145EP	bmi regional	
G-RJXC	Embraer RJ145EP	bmi regional	
G-RJXD	Embraer RJ145EP	bmi regional	
G-RJXE	Embraer RJ145EP	bmi regional	
G-RJXF	Embraer RJ145EP	bmi regional	
G-RJXG	Embraer RJ145EP	bmi regional	
G-RJXH	Embraer RJ145EP	bmi regional	
G-RJXI	Embraer RJ145EP	bmi regional	
G-RJXJ	Embraer RJ135LR	bmi regional	
G-RJXK	Embraer RJ135LR	bmi regional	
G-RJXL	Embraer RJ135LR	bmi regional	
G-RJXM	Embraer RJ145MP	bmi regional	
G-RJXO	Embraer RJ145MP	ECC Leasing Co.Ltd	
G-RJXP	Embraer RJ135ER	bmi regional (G-CDFS)	
G-RJXR	Embraer RJ145EP	bmi regional (G-CCYH)	
G-RKEL	Agusta-Bell 206B JetRanger 3	Nunkeeling Ltd	
G-RKKT	Cessna FR.172G	K. L. Irvine (G-AYJW)	
G-RLEF	Hawker Hurricane XII	P. J. Lawton	
G-RLMW	Tecnam P2002-EA Sierra	R. O'Malley-White	
G-RLON	BN-2A Mk III-2 Trislander	Aurigny Air Services Ltd (G-ITEX/G-OCTA/ G-BCXW)	
G-RLWG	Ryan ST3KR	R. A. Fleming	
G-RMAC	Shaw Europa	P. J. Lawless	
G-RMAN	Aero Designs Pulsar	M. B. Redman	
G-RMAX	Cameron C-80 balloon	RE/MAX Ireland Ltd	
G-RMCM	EV-97 TeamEurostar UK	Nene Valley Microlights Ltd	
G-RMCS	Cessna 182R	R. W. C. Sears	
G-RMHE	Aerospool Dynamic WT9 UK	R. M. Hughes-Ellis	
G-RMIT	Van's RV-4	J. P. Kloos	
G-RMMA	Dassault Falcon 900EX	Execujet (UK) Ltd	
G-RMMT	Europa XS	N. Schmitt	
G-RMPI	Whittaker MW5D Sorcerer	N. R. Beale	
G-RMPS	Van's RV-12	K. D. Boardman	
G-RMPY	Aerotechnik EV-97 Eurostar	N. R. Beale	
G-RMRV	Van's RV-7A	R. Morris	
G-RMSM	American Champion 8KCAB	S. Anstalt	
G-RMSY	Cameron TR-70 balloon	A. M. Holly	
G-RMTO	Rotorsport UK MTO Sport	J. R. S. Heaton	
G-RNAC	IDA Bacau Yakovlev Yak-52	RNAEC Group	
G-RNAS	DH.104 Sea Devon C.20 (XK896) ★	Airport Fire Service/Filton	
G-RNBW	Bell 206B JetRanger 2	Rainbow Helicopters Ltd	
G-RNCH	PA-28-181 Archer II	Carlisle Flight Training Ltd	
G-RNDD	Robin DR.400/500	Witham (Specialist Vehicles) Ltd	
G-RNGO	Robinson R22 Beta II	M. Flandina	
G-RNHF	Hawker Sea Fury T.Mk.20 (VX281)	Naval Aviation Ltd (G-BCOW)	
G-RNIE	Cameron 70 Ball SS balloon	N. J. Bland	
G-RNLI	VS.236 Walrus I (W2718) ★	Walrus Aviation Ltd	
G-RNRM	Cessna A.185F	Skydive St. Andrews Ltd	
G-RNRS	SA Bulldog Srs.100/101	Power Aerobatics Ltd (G-AZIT)	
G-ROAD	Robinson R44 II	IntecPC Ltd	
G-ROBD	Shaw Europa	M. P. Wiseman	
G-ROBG	P & M Quik GT450	Exodus Airsports Ltd	
G-ROBJ	Robin DR.500/200i	D. R. L. Jones	
G-ROBN	Pierre Robin R1180T	N. D. Anderson	
G-ROBT	Hawker Hurricane I (P2902:DX-X)	R. A. Roberts	
G-ROBY	Colt 17A balloon	Virgin Airship & Balloon Co Ltd	
G-ROBZ	Grob G109B	Bravo Zulu Group	
G-ROCH	Cessna T.303	R. S. Bentley	
G-ROCK	Thunder Ax7-77 balloon	M. A. Green	

Notes	Reg.	Type	Owner or Operator
	G-ROCO	ACLA Sirocco	The Light Aircraft Co.Ltd
	G-ROCR	Schweizer 269C	Hayles Aviation
	G-ROCT	Robinson R44 II	A. von Liechtenstein
	G-RODC	Steen Skybolt	J. S. Firth & A. P. Ransome
	G-RODD	Cessna 310R II	R. J. Herbert Engineering Ltd (G-TEDD/G-MADI)
	G-RODG	Avtech Jabiru UL	G-RODG Group
	G-RODI	Isaacs Fury (K3731)	P. K. Morley
	G-RODJ	Ikarus C42 FB80	Swansea Sport Flying
	G-RODZ	Van's RV-3A	P. Davis
	G-ROEI	Avro Roe 1 Replica	Brooklands Museum Trust Ltd
	G-ROGE	Robinson R44 II	Hacheston Properties Ltd
	G-ROGY	Cameron 60 Concept balloon	S. A. Laing
	G-ROKO	Roko-Aero NG-4HD	M. Coaten & D. S. Watson
	G-ROKT	Cessna FR.172E	G-ROKT Flying Club Ltd
	G-ROLF	PA-32R-301 Saratoga SP	P. F. Larkins
	G-ROLL	Pitts S-2A Special	Aerobatic Displays Ltd
	G-ROLY	Cessna F.172N	M. Bonsall (G-BHIH)
	G-ROME	I.I.I. Sky Arrow 650TC	Sky Arrow (Kits) UK Ltd
	G-ROMP	Extra 230H	G. G. Ferriman
	G-ROMW	Cyclone AX2000	K. V. Falvey
	G-RONA	Shaw Europa	C. M. Noakes
	G-RONG	PA-28R Cherokee Arrow 200-II	D. Griffiths & S. P. Rooney
	G-RONI	Cameron V-77 balloon	R. E. Simpson
	G-RONS	Robin DR.400/180	R. & K. Baker
	G-RONW	FRED Srs 2	F. J. Keitch
	G-ROOB	Embraer EMB-500 Phenom 100	Flairjet Ltd
	G-ROOK	Cessna F.172P	Rolim Ltd
	G-ROOV	Shaw Europa XS	P. W. Hawkins & K. Siggery
	G-RORB	Spitfire Mk.26	Golf Romeo Bravo Club
	G-RORI	Folland Gnat T.1 (01)	Heritage Aircraft Ltd
	G-RORY	Piaggio FWP.149D	M. Edwards (G-TOWN)
	G-ROSI	Thunder Ax7-77 balloon	J. E. Rose
	G-ROTG	Robinson R44 II	Aldwick Court Farm
	G-ROTS	CFM Streak Shadow Srs SA	A. G. Vallis & C. J. Kendal
	G-ROUP	Cessna F.172M	Perranporth Flying School Ltd (G-BDPH)
	G-ROUS	PA-34-200T Seneca II	Oxford Aviation Training Ltd
	G-ROVE	PA-18 Super Cub 135	S. J. Gaveston
	G-ROVY	Robinson R22 Beta	Fly Executive Ltd
	G-ROWA	Aquila AT01	Chicory Crops Ltd
	G-ROWE	Cessna F.182P	D. Rowe
	G-ROWI	Shaw Europa XS	R. M. Carson
	G-ROWL	AA-5B Tiger	T. A. Timms
	G-ROWR	Robinson R44	R. A. Oldworth
	G-ROWS	PA-28-151 Warrior	S. Goodchild
	G-ROXI	Cameron C-90 balloon	A. Murphy
	G-ROYC	Avtech Jabiru UL450	M. Daleki
	G-ROYM	Robinson R44 II	Business Agility Ltd
	G-ROZI	Robinson R44	Rotormotive Ltd
	G-ROZZ	Ikarus C.42 FB 80	A. J. Blackwell
	G-RPAF	Europa XS	R. P. Frost
	G-RPBM	Cameron Z-210 balloon	First Flight
	G-RPCC	Europa XS	R. P. Churchill-Coleman
	G-RPEZ	Rutan LongEz	M. P. Dunlop
	G-RPPO	Groppo Trail	G. N. Smith
	G-RPRV	Van's RV-9A	C. B. Amery
	G-RRAK	Enstrom 480B	B. Satherley (G-RIBZ)
	G-RRAT	CZAW Sportcruiser	G. Sipson
	G-RRCU	CEA DR.221B Dauphin	Merlin Flying Club Ltd
	G-RRED	PA-28-181 Archer II	J. P. Reddington
	G-RRFC	SOCATA TB20 Trinidad GT	C. A. Hawkins
	G-RRFF	VS.329 Spitfire Mk.IIB	P. Maksimczyk
	G-RRGN	VS.390 Spitfire PR.XIX (PS853)	Rolls-Royce PLC (G-MXIX)
	G-RROB	Robinson R44 II	Something Different Charters LLP
	G-RROD	PA-30 Twin Comanche 160B	R. McFadyen (G-SHAW)
	G-RRRT	Beech F.33A Bonanza	R. S. Earl
	G-RRSR	Piper J-3C-65 Cub (480173:57-H)	R. W. Roberts
	G-RRVX	Van's RV-10	R. E. Garforth
	G-RSAF	BAC.167 Strikemaster 80A	Viper Classics Ltd
	G-RSCU	Agusta A.109E	Sloane Helicopters Ltd

Reg.	Type	Owner or Operator	Notes
G-RSHI	PA-34-220T Seneca V	R. S. Hill and Sons	
G-RSKR	PA-28-161 Warrior II	ACS Engineering Ltd (G-BOJY)	
G-RSKY	Skyranger 912(2)	C. G. Benham & C. H. Tregonning	
G-RSMC	Medway SLA 100 Executive	W. S. C. Toulmin	
G-RSMT	Rotorsport UK MT-03	A. G. Jones	
G-RSSF	Denney Kitfox Mk 2	R. W. Somerville	
G-RSWO	Cessna 172R	AC Management Associates Ltd	
G-RSWW	Robinson R22 Beta	Tiger Helicopters Ltd	
G-RSXL	Cessna 560 Citation XLS	Aircraft Leasing Overseas Ltd	
G-RTBI	Thunder Ax6-56 balloon	P. J. Waller	
G-RTFM	Jabiru J400	I. A. Macphee	
G-RTHS	Rans S-6-ES Coyote II	T. Harrison-Smith	
G-RTIN	Rotorsport UK MT-03	P. McCrory	
G-RTMS	Rans S.6 ES Coyote II	C. J. Arthur	
G-RTMY	Ikarus C.42 FB 100	Mike Yankee Group	
G-RTRT	PZL-104MA Wilga 2000	E. A. M. Austin	
G-RUBB	AA-5B Tiger	D. E. Gee	
G-RUBE	Embraer EMB-135BJ Legacy	Autumn Breeze International Ltd	
G-RUBO	Embraer EMB-500 Phenom 100	Flairjet Ltd	
G-RUBY	PA-28RT-201T Turbo Arrow IV	Arrow Aircraft Group (G-BROU)	
G-RUCK	Bell 206B-3 JetRanger III	J. A. Ruck	
G-RUES	Robin HR.100/210	R. H. R. Rue	
G-RUFF	Mainair Blade 912	C. W. THompson	
G-RUFS	Avtech Jabiru UL	S. Richens	
G-RUGS	Campbell Cricket Mk 4 gyroplane	J. L. G. McLane	
G-RUIA	Cessna F.172N	P/G. Morris	
G-RULE	Robinson R44 Raven II	Huckair	
G-RUMI	Noble Harman Snowbird Mk.IV	G. Crossley (G-MVOI)	
G-RUMM	Grumman F8F-2P Bearcat (121714:201B)	Patina Ltd	
G-RUMN	AA-1A Trainer	M. T. Manwaring	
G-RUMW	Grumman FM-2 Wildcat (JV579:F)	Patina Ltd	
G-RUNT	Cassutt Racer IIIM	D. P. Lightfoot	
G-RUSL	Van's RV-6A	G. R. Russell	
G-RUSO	Robinson R22 Beta	R. M. Barnes-Gorell	
G-RUSS	Cessna 172N ★	Leisure Lease (stored)/Southend	
G-RUVE	Van's RV-8	J. P. Brady & D. J. Taylor	
G-RUVI	Zenair CH.601UL	P. G. Depper	
G-RUVY	Van's RV-9A	R. D. Taylor	
G-RUZZ	Robinson R44 II	Russell Harrison PLC	
G-RVAB	Van's RV-7	I. M. Belmore & A. T. Banks	
G-RVAC	Van's RV-7	A. F. S. & B. Caldecourt	
G-RVAL	Van's RV-8	R. N. York	
G-RVAN	Van's RV-6	D. Broom	
G-RVAT	Van's RV-8	T. R. Grief	
G-RVAW	Van's RV-6	C. Rawlings & R. J. Tomlinson	
G-RVBA	Van's RV-8A	D. P. Richard	
G-RVBC	Van's RV-6A	B. J. Clifford	
G-RVBF	Cameron A-340 balloon	Virgin Balloon Flights	
G-RVBI	Van's RV-8	M. A. N. Newall	
G-RVCE	Van's RV-6A	M. D. Barnard & C. Voelger	
G-RVCH	Van's RV-8A	C. R. Harrison	
G-RVCL	Van's RV-6	M. A. Wyer	
G-RVDG	Van's RV-9	D. M. Gill	
G-RVDJ	Van's RV-6	J. D. Jewitt	
G-RVDP	Van's RV-4	O. Florin	
G-RVDR	Van's RV-6A	P. R. Redfern	
G-RVDX	Van's RV-4	M. R. Tingle (G-FTUO)	
G-RVEE	Van's RV-6	J. C. A. Wheeler	
G-RVEI	Van's RV-8	D. Stephens	
G-RVET	Van's RV-6	D. R. Coleman	
G-RVGA	Van's RV-6A	D. C. Arnold	
G-RVGC	Van's RV-6A	G. C. Calder (G-RVCG)	
G-RVIA	Van's RV-6A	K. R. W. Scull & J. Watkins	
G-RVIB	Van's RV-6	K. Martin & P. Gorman	
G-RVIC	Van's RV-6A	I. T. Corse	
G-RVII	Van's RV-7	P. H. C. Hall	
G-RVIN	Van's RV-6	R. G. Jines	
G-RVIO	Van's RV-10	R. C. Hopkinson	

Notes	Reg.	Type	Owner or Operator
	G-RVIS	Van's RV-8	I. V. Sharman
	G-RVIT	Van's RV-6	P. J. Shotbolt
	G-RVIV	Van's RV-4	S. B. Robson
	G-RVIW	Van's RV-9	G. S. Scott
	G-RVIX	Van's RV-9A	J. R. Holt & C. S. Simmons
	G-RVIZ	Van's RV-12	J. E. Singleton
	G-RVJM	Van's RV-6	M. D. Challoner
	G-RVJO	Van's RV-9A	J. C. Simpson
	G-RVJP	Van's RV-9A	R. M. Palmer
	G-RVJW	Van's RV-4	J. M. Williams
	G-RVLC	Van's RV-9A	L. J. Clark
	G-RVMB	Van's RV-9A	M. James & R. W. Littledale
	G-RVMC	Van's RV-7	M. R. McNeil
	G-RVMT	Van's RV-6	M. J. Aldridge
	G-RVMZ	Van's RV-8	A. E. Kay
	G-RVNH	Van's RV-9A	N. R. Haines
	G-RVNI	Van's RV-6A	G-RVNI Group
	G-RVNS	Van's RV-4	N. P. D. Smith (G-CBGN)
	G-RVPH	Van's RV-8	J. C. P. Herbert
	G-RVPL	Van's RV-8	B. J. Summers
	G-RVPM	Van's RV-4	P. J. McMahon (G-RVDS)
	G-RVPW	Van's RV-6A	P. Waldron
	G-RVRA	PA-28 Cherokee 140	Par Contractors Ltd (G-OWVA)
	G-RVRB	PA-34-200T Seneca II	Ravenair Aircraft Ltd (G-BTAJ)
	G-RVRC	PA-23 Aztec 250E	West-Tec Ltd (G-BNPD)
	G-RVRD	PA-23 Aztec 250E	Ravenair Aircraft Ltd (G-BRAV/G-BBCM)
	G-RVRE	Partenavia P.68B	Ravenair Aircraft Ltd
	G-RVRF	PA-38-112 Tomahawk	Ravenair Aircraft Ltd (G-BGEL)
	G-RVRI	Cessna 172H Skyhawk	Truro Aerodrome Ltd (G-CCCC)
	G-RVRJ	PA-E23 Aztec 250E	Ravenair Aircraft Ltd (G-BBGB)
	G-RVRK	PA-38-112 Tomahawk	Ravenair Aircraft Ltd (G-BGZW)
	G-RVRL	PA-38-112 Tomahawk	Ravenair Aircraft Ltd (G-BGZW/G-BGBY)
	G-RVRM	PA-38-112 Tomahawk	Ravenair Aircraft Ltd (G-BGEK)
	G-RVRN	PA-28-161 Warrior II	Ravenair Aircraft Ltd (G-BPID)
	G-RVRO	PA-38-112 Tomahawk II	Ravenair Aircraft Ltd (G-BOUD)
	G-RVRP	Van's RV-7	R. C. Parris
	G-RVRR	PA-38-112 Tomahawk	Ravenair Aircraft Ltd (G-BRHT)
	G-RVRT	PA-28-140 Cherokee C	Ravenair Aircraft Ltd (G-AYKX)
	G-RVRU	PA-38-112 Tomahawk	Ravenair Aircraft Ltd (G-NCFE/G-BKMK)
	G-RVRV	Van's RV-4	P. Jenkins
	G-RVRW	PA-23 Aztec 250E	Ravenair Aircraft Ltd (G-BAVZ)
	G-RVRX	Partenavia P.68B	Ravenair Aircraft Ltd (G-PART)
	G-RVRY	PA-38-112 Tomahawk	Ravenair Aircraft Ltd (G-BTND)
	G-RVRZ	PA-23-250 Aztec E	Ravenair Aircraft Ltd (G-NRSC/G-BSFL)
	G-RVSA	Van's RV-6A	W. H. Knott
	G-RVSD	Van's RV-9A	S. W. Damarell
	G-RVSG	Van's RV-9A	S. Gerrish
	G-RVSH	Van's RV-6A	S. J. D. Hall
	G-RVSR	Van's RV-8	R. K. & S. W. Elders
	G-RVSX	Van's RV-6	R. L. & V. A. West
	G-RVTE	Van's RV-6	E. McShane & T. Feeny
	G-RVTN	Van's RV-10	C. I. Law
	G-RVTT	Van's RV-7	A. Phillips
	G-RVUK	Van's RV-7	R. J. Fray
	G-RVVI	Van's RV-6	John Reynolds Racing Ltd
	G-RVVY	Van's RV-10	P. R. Marskell
	G-RWAY	Rotorway Executive 162F	A. G. Rackstraw (G-URCH)
	G-RWEW	Robinson R44	Northern Heli Charters
	G-RWGS	Robinson R44 II	R. W. G. Simpson
	G-RWGW	Learjet 45	Woodlands Air LLP (G-MUTD)
	G-RWIA	Robinson R22 Beta	R. W. I'Anson (G-BOEZ)
	G-RWIN	Rearwin 175	A. B. Bourne & N. D. Battye
	G-RWLA	Eurocopter EC135 T2	Oxford Air Services Ltd
	G-RWLY	Shaw Europa XS	C. R. Arcle
	G-RWMW	Zenair CH.601XL Zodiac	R. W. H. Watson & M. Whyte (G-DROO)
	G-RWPL	Eurocopter EC.155 B1	Pure Leisure Air Ltd
	G-RWSS	Denney Kitfox Mk 2	R. W. Somerville
	G-RWWW	WS-55 Whirlwind HCC.12 (XR486)★	IHM/Weston-super-Mare
	G-RXUK	Lindstrand LBL-105A balloon	R. K. Scott & E. C. Fouracre
	G-RYAL	Avtech Jabiru UL	N. Palmer & D. J. Piper

Reg.	Type	Owner or Operator	Notes
G-RYDR	Rotorsport UK MT-03	A. D. McCutcheon	
G-RYNS	PA-32-301FT Cherokee Six	D. A. Earle	
G-RYPE	DG Flugzeugbau DG-1000T	DG-1000T Partners	
G-RYPH	Mainair Blade 912	I. A. Cunningham	
G-RYZZ	Robinson R44 II	Rivermead Aviation Ltd	
G-RZEE	Schleicher ASW-19B	R. Johnson	
G-RZLY	Flight Design CTSW	J. D. Macnamara	
G-SAAA	Flight Design CTSW	P. J. Watson & A. J. Kolleng	
G-SAAB	Rockwell Commander 112TC	Zytech Ltd (G-BEFS)	
G-SABA	PA-28R-201T Turbo Arrow III	C. A. Burton (G-BFEN)	
G-SABB	Eurocopter EC 135T1	Bond Air Services Ltd	
G-SABI	Dassault Falcon 900EX	TAG Aviation (UK) Ltd	
G-SABR	NA F-86A Sabre (8178:FU-178)	Golden Apple Operations Ltd	
G-SACB	Cessna F.152 II	P. Wilson (G-BFRB)	
G-SACH	Stoddard-Hamilton Glastar	R. S. Holt	
G-SACI	PA-28-161 Warrior II	PJC (Leasing) Ltd	
G-SACK	Robin R.2160	Sherburn Aero Club Ltd	
G-SACM	TL2000UK Sting Carbon	M. Clare	
G-SACO	PA-28-161 Warrior II	Stapleford Flying Club Ltd	
G-SACR	PA-28-161 Cadet	Sherburn Aero Club Ltd	
G-SACS	PA-28-161 Cadet	Sherburn Aero Club Ltd	
G-SACT	PA-28-161 Cadet	Sherburn Aero Club Ltd	
G-SACX	Aero AT-3 R100	Sherburn Aero Club Ltd	
G-SACY	Aero AT-3 R100	Sherburn Aero Club Ltd	
G-SADC	Gulfstream G450	Ocean Sky (UK) Ltd	
G-SAFE	Cameron N-77 balloon	P. J. Waller	
G-SAFI	CP.1320 Super Emeraude	C. S. Carleton-Smith	
G-SAFR	SAAB 91D Safir	Sylmar Aviation & Services Ltd	
G-SAGA	Grob G.109B	G-GROB Ltd/Booker	
G-SAGE	Luscombe 8A Silvaire	C. Howell (G-AKTL)	
G-SAHI	Trago Mills SAH-1	Hotel India Group	
G-SAIG	Robinson R44 II	Torfield Aviation Ltd	
G-SAIR	Cessna 421C	Air Support Aviation Services Ltd (G-OBCA)	
G-SAJA	Schempp-Hirth Discus 2	J. G. Arnold	
G-SALA	PA-32 Cherokee Six 300E	Stonebold Ltd	
G-SALE	Cameron Z-90 balloon	R. D. Baker	
G-SAMG	Grob G.109B	RAFGSA	
G-SAMJ	Partenavia P.68B	Ravenair Aircraft Ltd	
G-SAMM	Cessna 340A	D. M. Harbottle	
G-SAMP	Agusta A109E Power	Deans Foods Ltd	
G-SAMY	Shaw Europa	K. R. Tallent	
G-SAMZ	Cessna 150D	F. A. Bakir (G-ASSO)	
G-SANL	Bombardier BD700-1A10 Global Express	Sanctuary Aviation LLP	
G-SAOC	Schempp-Hirth Discus 2cT	RAF Gliding and Soaring Association	
G-SAPM	SOCATA TB20 Trinidad	G-SAPM Ltd (G-EWFN)	
G-SARA	PA-28-181 Archer II	Apollo Aviation Advisory Ltd	
G-SARB	Sikorsky S-92A	CHC Scotia Ltd (HM Coastguard)	
G-SARC	Sikorsky S-92A	CHC Scotia Ltd (HM Coastguard)	
G-SARD	Agusta Westland AW139	CHC Scotia Ltd (HM Coastguard)	
G-SARH	PA-28-161 Warrior II	Solo Services Ltd and Tempora Ltd	
G-SARJ	P & M Quik GT450	A. R. Jones	
G-SARM	Ikarus C.42 FB100	G-SARM Group	
G-SARV	Van's RV-4	Hinton Flying Group	
G-SASA	Eurocopter EC 135T1	Bond Air Services Ltd	
G-SASB	Eurocopter EC 135T2+	Bond Air Services Ltd	
G-SASC	Beech B200C Super King Air	Gama Aviation Ltd	
G-SASD	Beech B200C Super King Air	Gama Aviation Ltd	
G-SASG	Schleicher ASW-27-18E	F. B. Jeynes	
G-SASH	MDH MD.900 Explorer	Yorkshire Air Ambulance Ltd	
G-SASI	CZAW Sportcruiser	A. S. Arundell	
G-SASK	PA-31P Pressurised Navajo	Middle East Business Club Ltd (G-BFAM)	
G-SASM	Westland Scout AH.Mk.1	C. J. Marsden	
G-SASY	Eurocopter EC.130 B4	R. J. H. Smith	
G-SATN	PA-25-260 Pawnee C	RAF Gliding and Soaring Association	
G-SAUO	Cessna A.185F	T. G. Lloyd	
G-SAUK	Rans S6-ES	M. D. Tulloch	
G-SAVY	Savannah VG Jabiru(1)	C. S. Hollingworth & S. P. Yardley	
G-SAWI	PA-32RT-300T Turbo Lance II	Regularity Ltd	
G-SAXT	Schempp-Hirth Duo Discus Xt	RAF Gliding and Soaring Association	

Notes	Reg.	Type	Owner or Operator
	G-SAYS	RAF 2000 GTX-SE gyroplane	D. Beevers
	G-SAZY	Avtech Jabiru J400	S.M. Pink
	G-SAZZ	CP.328 Super Emeraude	D. J. Long
	G-SBAE	Cessna F.172P	Warton Flying Club
	G-SBDB	Remos GX	G-SBDB Group
	G-SBHH	Schweizer 269C	Ag-Raum GmbH/Germany (G-XALP)
	G-SBIZ	Cameron Z-90 balloon	Snow Business International Ltd
	G-SBKR	SOCATA TB10 Tobago	S. C. M. Bagley
	G-SBKS	Cessna 206H Stationair	Alard Properties Ltd
	G-SBLT	Steen Skybolt	Skybolt Group
	G-SBMM	PA-28R Cherokee Arrow 180	K. S. Kalsi (G-BBEL)
	G-SBOL	Steen Skybolt	M. P. Barley
	G-SBRK	Aero AT-3 R100	Sywell Aerodrome Ltd
	G-SBUS	BN-2A-26 Islander	Isles of Scilly Skybus Ltd (G-BMMH)
	G-SCAN	Vinten-Wallis WA-116/100	K. H. Wallis
	G-SCBI	SOCATA TB20 Trinidad	Ace Services
	G-SCCZ	CZAW Sportcruiser	J. W. Ellis
	G-SCHI	AS.350B2 Ecureuil	Patriot Aviation Ltd
	G-SCHO	Robinson R22 Beta	Blades Aviation (UK) LLP
	G-SCII	Agusta A109C	C and M Coldstores (G-JONA)
	G-SCIP	SOCATA TB20 Trinidad GT	The Studio People Ltd
	G-SCLX	FLS Aerospace Sprint 160	E. J. F. McEntee (G-PLYM)
	G-SCNN	Schempp-Hirth Standard Cirrus	G. C. Short
	G-SCOL	Gippsland GA-8 Airvan	Sunderland Parachute Centre Ltd
	G-SCPD	Escapade 912 (1)	R. W. L. Breckell
	G-SCPI	CZAW Sportcruiser	I. M. Speight & P. R. W. Goslin
	G-SCPL	PA-28 Cherokee 140	Aeros Leasing Ltd (G-BPVL)
	G-SCRZ	CZAW Sportcruiser	P. H. Grant
	G-SCSC	CZAW Sportcruiser	G-SCSC Group
	G-SCTA	Westland Scout AH.1	G. R. Harrison
	G-SCUB	PA-18 Super Cub 135 (542447)	M. E. Needham
	G-SCUL	Rutan Cozy	K. R. W. Scull
	G-SCVF	Czech Sprt Aircraft Sportcruiser	V. Flintham
	G-SCZR	CZAW Sportcruiser	Kestrel Group
	G-SDAT	Flight Design CTSW	A. R. Wade
	G-SDCI	Bell 206B JetRanger 2	S. D. Coomes (G-GHCL/G-SHVV)
	G-SDEC	American Champion 8KCAB	D. Boag
	G-SDEV	DH. 104 Sea Devon C.20 (XK895)	Aviation Heritage Ltd
	G-SDFM	Aerotechnik EV-97 Eurostar	G-SDFM Group
	G-SDNI	VS.361 Spitfire LF.IX E	P. M. Andrews
	G-SDOB	Tecnam P2002-EA Sierra	S. P. S. Dornan
	G-SDOI	Aeroprakt A.22 Foxbat	S. A. Owen
	G-SDOZ	Tecnam P92-EA Echo Super	Cumbernauld Flyers G-SDOZ
	G-SEAI	Cessna U.206G (amphibian)	K. O'Conner
	G-SEAJ	Cessna 525 Citationjet	CJ 525 Ltd
	G-SEAT	Colt 42A balloon	R. M. Horn
	G-SEBA	Ultramagic M-130 balloon	Prestige Milano Group SRL/Italy
	G-SEBN	Skyranger 912S(1)	C. M. James
	G-SEDO	Cameron N-105 balloon	Wye Valley Aviation Ltd
	G-SEED	Piper J-3C-65 Cub	J. H. Seed
	G-SEEE	Pegasus Quik GT450	R. Meredith-Hardy
	G-SEEK	Cessna T.210N	A. Hopper
	G-SEFI	Robinson R44 II	Kermann Avionics Sales Ltd
	G-SEIL	BN-2B-27 Islander	Highland Airways Ltd (G-BIIP)
	G-SEJW	PA-28-161 Warrior II	Keen Leasing Ltd
	G-SELA	Cessna 152	L. W. Scattergood (G-FLOP)
	G-SELB	PA-28-161 Warrior II	L. W. Scattergood (G-LFSK)
	G-SELC	Diamond DA42 Twin Star	Stapleford Flying Club Ltd
	G-SELF	Shaw Europa	N. D. Crisp & ptnrs
	G-SELL	Robin DR.400/180	c. r. Beard Farmers Ltd
	G-SELY	Agusta-Bell 206B JetRanger 3	DSC North Ltd
	G-SEMR	Cessna T206H Turbo Stationair	Semer LLP
	G-SENA	Rutan LongEz	G. Bennett
	G-SEND	Colt 90A balloon	Air du Vent/France
	G-SENE	PA-34-200T Seneca II	M. O'Hara
	G-SENS	Eurocopter EC.135T2+	Eurocopter UK Ltd
	G-SENX	PA-34-200T Seneca II	First Air Ltd (G-DARE/G-WOTS/G-SEVL)
	G-SEPT	Cameron N-105 balloon	P. Gooch
	G-SERE	Diamond DA42 Twin Star	Sere Ltd

Reg.	Type	Owner or Operator	Notes
G-SERL	SOCATA TB10 Tobago	R. J. Searle (G-LANA)	
G-SERV	Cameron N-105 balloon	PSH Skypower Ltd	
G-SESA	RAF SE.5A 75 replica	D. J. Calvert	
G-SETI	Cameron Sky 80-16 balloon	R. P. Allan	
G-SEUK	Cameron TV-80 ss balloon	Mobberley Balloon Collection	
G-SEVA	SE-5A (replica) (F141:G)	I. D. Gregory	
G-SEVE	Cessna 172N	MK Aero Support Ltd	
G-SEVN	Van's RV-7	N. Reddish	
G-SEWP	AS.355F2 Ecureuil II	Gryphon Aviation LLP (G-OFIN/G-DANS/ G-BTNM)	
G-SEXE	Scheibe SF.25C Falke	Repulor Ltd	
G-SEXX	PA-28-161 Warrior II	Weald Air Services Ltd	
G-SEXY	AA-1 Yankee ★	Jetstream Club, Liverpool Marriott Hotel South, Speke (G-AYLM)	
G-SFAR	Ikarus C42 FB100	D. S. Luke	
G-SFCJ	Cessna 525 CitationJet	Sureflight Aviation Ltd	
G-SFLA	Ikarus C42 FB80	Solent Flight Ltd	
G-SFLB	Ikarus C42 FB80	Solent Flight Ltd	
G-SFLY	Diamond DA40 Star	L. & N. P. L. Turner	
G-SFPB	Cessna F.406	Reims Aviation Industries SA/France	
G-SFRY	Thunder Ax7-77 balloon	M. Rowlands	
G-SFSL	Cameron Z-105 balloon	A. J. Gregory	
G-SFTZ	Slingsby T.67M Firefly 160	Western Air (Thruxton) Ltd	
G-SGEN	Ikarus C.42 FB 80	G. A. Arturi	
G-SGSE	PA-28-181 Archer II	U. Patel (G-BOJX)	
G-SHAA	Enstrom 280-UK	C. J. Vincent	
G-SHAF	Robinson R44 II	Tresillian Leisure Ltd	
G-SHAK	Cameron Cabin SS balloon	Magical Adventures Ltd (G-ODIS)	
G-SHAL	Bombardier CL-600-2B19	TAG Aviation (UK) Ltd	
G-SHAN	Robinson R44 II	F. Katzenstein	
G-SHAR	Cessna 182T Skylane	J. E. R. Gardner	
G-SHAY	PA-28R-201T Turbo Arrow III	Alpha Yankee Flying Group (G-BFDG/G-JEFS)	
G-SHED	PA-28-181 Archer II	G-SHED Flying Group (G-BRAU)	
G-SHEE	P & M Quik GT450	L. Cottle	
G-SHEF	Bombardier BD700-1A10 Global Express	TAG Aviation (UK) Ltd	
G-SHEZ	Mainair Pegasus Quik	R. Wells	
G-SHHH	Glaser-Dirks DG-100G	P. J. Masson	
G-SHIM	CFM Streak Shadow	K. R. Anderson	
G-SHIP	PA-23 Aztec 250F ★	Midland Air Museum/Coventry	
G-SHMI	Evektor EV-97 Team EuroStar UK	Poet Pilot (UK) Ltd	
G-SHOG	Colomban MC.15 Cri-Cri	K. D. & C. S. Rhodes (G-PFAB)	
G-SHOW	MS.733 Alycon	Vintage Aircraft Team	
G-SHRK	Enstrom 280C-UK	Flighthire Ltd/Belgium (G-BGMX)	
G-SHRN	Schweizer 269C-1	CSL Industrial Ltd	
G-SHRT	Robinson R44 II	Air and Ground Aviation Ltd	
G-SHSH	Shaw Europa	S. G. Hayman & J. Price	
G-SHSI	Embraer EMB-135BJ Legacy	TAG Aviation (UK) Ltd	
G-SHSP	Cessna 172S	Shropshire Aero Club Ltd	
G-SHUC	Rans S-6-ESD Coyote II	T. A. England (G-MYKN)	
G-SHUF	Mainair Blade	R. G. Bradley & S. Webb	
G-SHUG	PA-28R-201T Turbo Arrow III	G-SHUG Ltd	
G-SHUU	Enstrom 280C-UK-2	D. Ellis (G-OMCP/G-KENY/G-BJFG)	
G-SHUV	Aerosport Woody Pusher	J. R. Wraigh	
G-SHWK	Cessna 172S	Cambridge Aero Club Ltd	
G-SIAI	SIAI-Marchetti SF.260W	Air Training Services	
G-SICA	BN-2B-20 Islander	Shetland Leasing and Property Development Ltd (G-SLAP)	
G-SICB	BN-2B-20 Islander	Shetlands Islands Council (G-NESU/G-BTVN)	
G-SIGN	PA-39 Twin Comanche 160 C/R	D. Buttle	
G-SIIE	Christen Pitts S-2B Special	J. & T. J. Bennett (G-SKYD)	
G-SIII	Extra EA.300	Fun Flight Ltd	
G-SIIS	Pitts S-1S Special	I. H. Searson (G-RIPE)	
G-SIJJ	North American P-51D-NA Mustang (472035)	P. A. Teichman	
G-SIJW	SA Bulldog Srs 120/121 (XX630:5)	M. Miles	
G-SILS	Pietenpol Skyscout	D. Silsbury	
G-SILY	Pegasus Quantum 15	N. J. Brownlow	

Notes	Reg.	Type	Owner or Operator
	G-SIMI	Cameron A-315 balloon	Balloon Safaris
	G-SIMM	Ikarus C.42 FB 100 VLA	D. Simmons
	G-SIMP	Avtech Jabiru SP	P. J. V. Dibble
	G-SIMS	Robinson R22 Beta	CDS Aviation Ltd
	G-SIMY	PA-32-300 Cherokee Six	I. Simpson (G-OCPF/G-BOCH)
	G-SINK	Schleicher ASH-25	G-SINK Group
	G-SIPA	SIPA 903	A. C. Leak & J. H. Dilland (G-BGBM)
	G-SIPP	Lindstrand lbl-35a Cloudhopper balloon	N. Bourke
	G-SIRA	Embraer EMB-135BJ Legacy	ECC Leasing Company Ltd
	G-SIRD	Robinson R44 II	Peglington Productions Ltd
	G-SIRE	Best Off Sky Ranger Swift 912S(1)	P. Rigby
	G-SIRJ	Cessna 680 Citation Sovereign	Bookajet Ltd
	G-SIRO	Dassault Falcon 900EX	Condor Aviation LLP
	G-SIRS	Cessna 560XL Citation Excel	London Executive Aviation Ltd
	G-SISI	Schempp-Hirth Duo Discus	Glider Sierra India
	G-SISU	P & M Quik GT450	Executive and Business Aviation Support Ltd
	G-SITA	Pegasus Quantum 15-912	A. F. S. McDougall
	G-SIVJ	Westland Gazelle HT.2	Skytrace (UK) Ltd (G-CBSG)
	G-SIVK	MBB Bolkow Bo.105DBS-4	C. J. Siva-Jothy (G-PASX)
	G-SIVR	MDH MD.900 Explorer	C. J. Siva-Jothy
	G-SIVW	Lake LA-250 Renegade	C. J. Siva-Jothy
	G-SIXC	Douglas DC-6A	Air Atlantique Ltd
	G-SIXD	PA-32 Cherokee Six 300D	M. B. Paine & I. Gordon
	G-SIXT	PA-28-161 Warrior II	Airways Aero Associations Ltd (G-BSSX)
	G-SIXX	Colt 77A balloon	P. & M. Still
	G-SIXY	Van's RV-6	C. J. Hall & C. R. P. Hamlett
	G-SIZZ	Jabiru J400	K. J. Betteley
	G-SJBI	Pitts S-2C Special	S. L. Walton
	G-SJCH	BN-2T-4S Defender 4000	Hampshire Police Authority (G-BWPK)
	G-SJES	Evektor EV-97 TeamEurostar UK	Purple Aviation Ltd
	G-SJKR	Lindstrand LBL-90A balloon	S. J. Roake
	G-SJMH	Robin DR.400-140B	C. S. & J. A. Bailey
	G-SJPI	Dynamic WT9 UK	S. J. Phillips
	G-SJSS	Bombardier CL600-2B16	TAG Aviation (UK) Ltd
	G-SKAN	Cessna F.172M	M. Richardson & J. Williams (G-BFKT)
	G-SKAZ	Aero AT-3 r100	G-SKAZ Flying Group
	G-SKCI	Rutan Vari-Eze	C. Hannan
	G-SKEN	Cessna 182T	Kenward Orthopaedic Ltd
	G-SKEW	Mudry CAP-232	J. H. Askew
	G-SKIE	Steen Skybolt	K. G. G. Howe and M. J. Coles
	G-SKII	Augusta-Bell 206B JetRanger 3	K. P. Toner (Developments)
	G-SKKY	Cessna 172S Skyhawk	Skyquest Ltd
	G-SKNT	Pitts S-2A	First Light Aviation Ltd (G-PEAL)
	G-SKOT	Cameron V-42 balloon	S. A. Laing
	G-SKPG	Best Off Skyranger 912 (2)	P. Gibbs
	G-SKPH	Yakovlev Yak-50	R. S. Partridge-Hicks & I. C. Austin (G-BWWH)
	G-SKPP	Eurocopter EC.120B Colbri	Bournemouth Helicopters Ltd (G-MKII)
	G-SKRA	Best Off Skyranger 912S (1)	P. A. Banks
	G-SKRG	Best Off Skyranger 912 (2)	I. D. Town
	G-SKSW	Best Off Sky Ranger Swift 912S	M. D. & S. M. North
	G-SKUA	Stoddard-Hamilton Glastar	F. P. Smiddy (G-LEZZ/G-BYCR)
	G-SKYC	Slingsby T.67M Firefly	T. W. Cassells (G-BLDP)
	G-SKYE	Cessna TU.206G	RAF Sport Parachute Association
	G-SKYF	SOCATA TB10 Tobago	W. L. McNeil
	G-SKYJ	Cameron Z-315 balloon	Cameron Flights Southern Ltd
	G-SKYK	Cameron A-275 balloon	Cameron Flights Southern Ltd
	G-SKYL	Cessna 182S	Skylane Aviation Ltd
	G-SKYN	AS.355F1 Twin Squirrel	Arena Aviation Ltd (G-OGRK/G-BWZC/G-MODZ)
	G-SKYO	Slingsby T.67M-200	R. H. Evelyn
	G-SKYR	Cameron A-180 balloon	Cameron Flights Southern Ltd
	G-SKYT	I.I.I. Sky Arrow 650TC	W. M. Bell & S. J. Brooks
	G-SKYU	Cameron A-210 balloon	Cameron Flights Southern Ltd
	G-SKYV	PA-28RT-201T Turbo Arrow IV	North Yorks Properties Ltd (G-BNZG)
	G-SKYW	AS355F1	Skywalker Aviation Ltd (G-BTIS/G-TALI)
	G-SKYX	Cameron A-210 balloon	Cameron Flights Southern Ltd
	G-SKYY	Cameron A-275 balloon	Cameron Flights Southern Ltd
	G-SLAC	Cameron N-77 balloon	B. L. Alderson
	G-SLAK	Thruster T.600N 450	M. P. Williams (G-CBXH)
	G-SLCE	Cameron C-80 balloon	A. M. Holly

Reg.	Type	Owner or Operator	Notes
G-SLCT	Diamond DA42 Twin Star	Stapleford Flying Club Ltd	
G-SLEA	Mudry/CAARP CAP-10B	M. J. M. Jenkins & N. R. Thorburn	
G-SLII	Cameron O-90 balloon	C. W. Clarke	
G-SLIP	Easy Raider	D. R. Squires	
G-SLMG	Diamond HK.36 TTC Super Dimona	G-SLMG Syndicate	
G-SLNM	EV-97 TeamEurostar UK	N. W. Mayes	
G-SLNT	Flight Design CTSW	K. Kirby	
G-SLNW	Robinson R22 Beta	Heli-4 Charter LLP (G-LNIC)	
G-SLOK	Robinson R44 II	Heli-4-Charter LLP	
G-SLTN	SOCATA TB20 Trinidad	Paikea Aviation Ltd	
G-SLYN	PA-28-161 Warrior II	Flew LLP	
G-SMAN	Airbus A.330-243	Monarch Airlines Ltd	
G-SMAS	BAC.167 Strikemaster 80A (1104)	M. A. Petrie	
G-SMBM	Pegasus Quantum 15-912	N. Charles & P. A. Henretty	
G-SMDH	Shaw Europa XS	S. W. Pitt	
G-SMDJ	AS.350B2 Ecureuil	Denis Ferranti Hoverknights Ltd	
G-SMIG	Cameron O-65 balloon	R. D. Parry	
G-SMMA	Cessna F.406 Caravan II	Secretary of State for Scotland per Environmental and Rural Affairs Department	
G-SMMB	Cessna F.406 Caravan II	Secretary of State for Scotland per Environmental and Rural Affairs Department	
G-SMRS	Cessna 172F	M. R. Sarling	
G-SMRT	Lindstrand LBL-260A balloon	Cameron Flights Southern Ltd	
G-SMTH	PA-28 Cherokee 140	R. W. Harris & A. Jahanfar (G-AYJS)	
G-SMYK	PZL-Swidnik PW-5 Smyk	PW-5 Syndicate	
G-SNAK	Lindstrand LBL-105A balloon	Ballooning Adventures Ltd	
G-SNAL	Cessna 182T	N. S. Lyndhurst	
G-SNAP	Cameron V-77 balloon	M. B. Young	
G-SNEV	CFM Streak Shadow SA	J. D. Reed	
G-SNIF	Cameron A-300 balloon	A. C. K. Rowson & Sudoni	
G-SNOG	Kiss 400-582 (1)	B. H. Ashman	
G-SNOP	Shaw Europa	Bob Crowe Aircraft Sales Ltd (G-DESL/ G-WWWG)	
G-SNOW	Cameron V-77 balloon	G. G. Cannon & P. Haworth	
G-SNOZ	Shaw Europa	P. O. Bayliss (G-DONZ)	
G-SNSA	Agusta AW139	CHC Scotia Ltd	
G-SNUZ	PA-28-161 Warrior II	Freedom Aviation Ltd	
G-SNZY	Learjet 45	European Skyjets Ltd	
G-SOAF	BAC.167 Strikemaster Mk. 82A (425)	Strikemaster Flying Club	
G-SOAR	Eiri PIK-20E	R. I. Huttlestone	
G-SOAY	Cessna T.303	Wrekin Construction Co Ltd	
G-SOBI	PA-28-181 Archer II	E. F. Mangion	
G-SOCK	Mainair Pegasus Quik	K. R. McCartney	
G-SOCT	Yakovlev Yak-50 (AR-B)	C. R. Turton	
G-SOHO	Diamond DA40D Star	Soho Aviation Ltd	
G-SOKO	Soko P-2 Kraguj (30149)	P. C. Avery (G-BRXK)	
G-SOLA	Aero Designs Star-Lite SL.1	G. P. Thomas	
G-SONA	SOCATA TB10 Tobago	J. Freeman (G-BIBI)	
G-SONE	Cessna 525A Citationjet	CJ 525 Ltd	
G-SONX	Sonex	M. Chambers	
G-SOOA	Cessna172S	Goodwood Road Racing Co.Ltd	
G-SOOC	Hughes 369HS	R.J.H. Strong (G-BRRX)	
G-SOOS	Colt 21A balloon	P. J. Stapley	
G-SOOT	PA-28 Cherokee 180	J. A. Bridger (G-AVNM)	
G-SOOZ	Rans S.6-ES Coyote II	S. N. Lawrence	
G-SOPH	Skyranger 912(2)	S. Marathe	
G-SOPP	Enstrom 280FX	F. J. Sopp (G-OSAB)	
G-SORA	Glaser-Dirks DG.500/22	C. A. Boyle, C. P. Arthur, B. Douglas & R. Jackson	
G-SORT	Cameron N-90 balloon	A. Brown	
G-SOUL	Cessna 310R	Reconnaissance Ventures Ltd	
G-SOVA	Cessna 550 Citation II	Mitre Aviation Ltd	
G-SOVB	Learjet 45	Murray Air Ltd (G-OLDJ)	
G-SPAM	Avid Aerobat (modified)	M. Durcan	
G-SPAO	Eurocopter EC135	Bond Air Services Ltd	
G-SPAT	Aero AT-3 R100	S2T Aero Ltd	
G-SPCZ	CZAW Sportcruiser	R. J. Robinson	
G-SPDR	DH.115 Sea Vampire T.22 (N6-766)	M. J. Cobb	

Notes	Reg.	Type	Owner or Operator
	G-SPDY	Raj Hamsa X'Air Hawk	G. H. Gilmour-White
	G-SPED	Alpi Pioneer 300	M. Taylor
	G-SPEE	Robinson R22 Beta	Heliclub de laValle du Loing (G-BPJC)
	G-SPEL	Sky 220-24 balloon	Cameron Flights Southern Ltd
	G-SPEY	Agusta-Bell 206B JetRanger 3	Castle Air Charters Ltd (G-BIGO)
	G-SPFX	Rutan Cozy	B. D. Tutty
	G-SPHU	Eurocopter EC 135T2+	Bond Air Services Ltd
	G-SPIN	Pitts S-2A Special	P. Avery
	G-SPIT	VS.379 Spitfire FR.XIV (MV268)	Patina Ltd (G-BGHB)
	G-SPJE	Robinson R44 II	Abel Alarm Co.Ltd
	G-SPMM	Best Off Sky Ranger Swift 912S(1)	L. Chesworth & M. L. Sumner
	G-SPOG	Jodel DR.1050	P. D. Thomas & T. J. Bates (G-AXVS)
	G-SPTR	Robinson R44 II	Heli Air Ltd
	G-SPUR	Cessna 550 Citation II	London Executive Aviation Ltd
	G-SPVK	AS.350B3 Ecureuil	GBL Aviation LLP (G-CERU)
	G-SPYS	Robinson R44 II	SKB Partners LLP
	G-SRAH	Schempp-Hirth Mini-Nimbus C	P. Hawkins
	G-SRAW	Alpi Pioneer 300	M. Clare & A. R. Lloyd
	G-SRBN	Embraer EMB-500 Phenom 100	Flaijet Ltd
	G-SRDG	Dassault Falcon 7X	Triair (Bermuda) Ltd
	G-SRII	Easy Raider 503	K. Myles
	G-SROE	Westland Scout AH.1 (XP907)	Bolenda Engineering Ltd
	G-SRPH	Robinson R44	Rooney Helicopter Hire
	G-SRRA	Tecnam P2002-EA Sierra	J. Dunn
	G-SRUM	Aero AT-3 R100	Cunning Plan Development Ltd
	G-SRVA	Cirrus SR20	Harineras del Mediterraneo SL
	G-SRVO	Cameron N-90 balloon	Servo & Electronic Sales Ltd
	G-SRWN	PA-28-161 Warrior II	S. Smith (G-MAND/G-BRKT)
	G-SRYY	Shaw Europa XS	I. O'Brien
	G-SRZZ	Cirrus SR22	M. P. Bowcock
	G-SSCL	MDH Hughes 369E	Shaun Stevens Contractors Ltd
	G-SSDR	Scooter	J. Attard
	G-SSEX	Rotorway Executive 162F	M. Middleby
	G-SSIX	Rans S.6-116 Coyote II	R. I. Kelly
	G-SSKY	BN-2B-26 Islander	Isles of Scilly Skybus Ltd (G-BSWT)
	G-SSSC	Sikorsky S-76C	CHC Scotia Ltd
	G-SSSD	Sikorsky S-76C	CHC Scotia Ltd
	G-SSSE	Sikorsky S-76C	CHC Scotia Ltd
	G-SSTI	Cameron N-105 balloon	A. A. Brown
	G-SSWV	Sportavia Fournier RF-5B	Fournier Flying Group
	G-STAA	Robinson R44	Elicotteri Molise SRL (G-HALE)
	G-STAV	Cameron O-84 balloon	Blenheim Scout Group
	G-STAY	Cessna FR.172K	J. M. Wilkins
	G-STBA	Boeing 777-336ER	British Airways
	G-STBB	Boeing 777-36NER	British Airways
	G-STBC	Boeing 777-36NER	British Airways
	G-STCH	Fiesler Fi 156A-1 Storch (GM+AI)	P. R. Holloway
	G-STDL	Phillips ST.2 Speedtwin	Speedtwin Developments Ltd (G-DPST)
	G-STEA	PA-28R Cherokee Arrow 200	D. W. Breden
	G-STEM	Stemme S.10V	G-STEM Group
	G-STEN	Stemme S.10 (4)	G-STEN Syndicate
	G-STEP	Schweizer 269C	M. Johnson
	G-STER	Bell 206B JetRanger 3	Maintopic Ltd
	G-STEU	Rolladen-Schneider LS6-18W	F. K. Russell
	G-STEV	Jodel DR.221	S. W. Talbot
	G-STGR	Agusta 109S Grand	WA Developments International Ltd
	G-STHA	PA-31-350 Navajo Chieftain	Jota Aircraft Leasing Ltd (G-GLUG/G-BLOE/ G-NITE)
	G-STIN	TL 2000UK Sting Carbon	N. A. Smith
	G-STIX	Van's RV-7	R. D. S. Jackson
	G-STME	Stemme S 10-VT	R. A. Roberts
	G-STMP	SNCAN Stampe SV.4A	A. C. Thorne
	G-STNG	TL2000 Sting Carbon	Geesting 3 Syndicate
	G-STNR	IDA Bacau Yakovlev Yak-52	S. M. Norman (G-BWOD)
	G-STNS	Agusta A109A-II	Heliflight (UK) Ltd
	G-STOD	ICP MXP-740 Savannah VG Jabiru(1)	S. B. Todd
	G-STOK	Colt 77B balloon	A. C. Booth
	G-STON	AS355N Ecureuil II	Gryphon Aviation LLP
	G-STOO	Stolp Starduster Too	K. F. Crumplin

Reg.	Type	Owner or Operator	Notes
G-STOP	Robinson R44 Raven II	HLQ Services Ltd/Ireland	
G-STOW	Cameron 90 Wine Box SS balloon	Flying Enterprises	
G-STPI	Cameron A-210 balloon	The Ballooning Business Ltd	
G-STRF	Boeing 737-76N	Astraeus Ltd	
G-STRG	Cyclone AX2000	Pegasus Flight Training (Cotswolds)	
G-STRI	Boeing 737-33A	Astraeus Ltd	
G-STRJ	Boeing 737-33A	Astraeus Ltd	
G-STRK	CFM Streak Shadow SA	E. J. Hadley	
G-STRL	AS.355N Twin Squirrel	Harrier Enterprises Ltd	
G-STRM	Cameron N-90 balloon	A. Brown	
G-STRN	Boeing 737-7L9	Astraeus Ltd	
G-STRP	Airbus A.320-211	Astraeus Ltd	
G-STRW	Boeing 757-28A	Astraeus Ltd	
G-STRX	Boeing 757-28A	Astraeus Ltd	
G-STRY	Boeing 757-28A	Astraeus Ltd	
G-STRZ	Boeing 757-258	Astraeus Ltd	
G-STSN	Stinson 108-3 Voyager	M. S. Colebrook (G-BHMR)	
G-STUA	Aerotek Pitts S-2A Special (modified)	G-STUA Group	
G-STUB	Christen Pitts S-2B Special	A. F. D. Kingdon	
G-STUF	Learjet 40	Concierge Aviation Ltd	
G-STUI	Pitts S-2AE	S. L. Goldspink	
G-STUN	TL2000 Sting Carbon	D. Russell (G-KEVT)	
G-STUY	Robinson R44 II	HP Rentals Ltd	
G-STVT	CZAW Sportcruiser	S. Taylor	
G-STWO	ARV Super 2	P. M. Paul	
G-STYL	Pitts S-1S Special	T. G. Lloyd	
G-STZZ	TL2000UK Sting Carbon	W. R. Field	
G-SUCH	Cameron V-77 balloon	D. G. Such (G-BIGD)	
G-SUCK	Cameron Z-105 balloon	R. P. Wade	
G-SUCT	Robinson R22	Irwin Plant Sales	
G-SUEB	PA-28-181 Archer III	ACS Aviation Ltd	
G-SUED	Thunder Ax8-90 balloon	E. C. Lubbock & S. A. Kidd (G-PINE)	
G-SUEI	Diamond DA.42 Twin Star	Sue Air	
G-SUEL	P & M Quik GT450	J. M. Ingram	
G-SUEW	Airbus A.320-214	Thomas Cook Airlines Ltd	
G-SUEX	Agusta-Bell 206B JetRanger 2	Aerospeed Ltd (G-AYBC/G-BTWW)	
G-SUEY	Bell 206L-1 Long Ranger	Aerospeed Ltd	
G-SUEZ	Agusta-Bell 206B JetRanger 2	Aerospeed Ltd	
G-SUFF	Eurocopter EC 135T1	Eurocopter UK Ltd	
G-SUFK	Eurocopter EC 135P2+	Suffolk Police Authority	
G-SUGA	Embraer EMB-135BJ Legacy 650	Amsair Aircraft Ltd	
G-SUKI	PA-38-112 Tomahawk	Ravenair Aircraft Ltd (G-BPNV)	
G-SUKY	P & M Quik R	S. J. Reid	
G-SUMX	Robinson R22 Beta	J. A. Bickerstaffe	
G-SUMZ	Robinson R44 II	Frankham Bros Ltd	
G-SUNN	Robinson R44	R. Purchase	
G-SUPA	PA-18 Super Cub 150	Supa Group	
G-SURG	PA-30 Twin Comanche 160B	A. R. Taylor (G-VIST/G-AVHG)	
G-SURY	Eurocopter EC 135T2	Surrey Police Authority	
G-SUSE	Shaw Europa XS	P. R. Tunney	
G-SUSI	Cameron V-77 balloon	J. H. Dryden	
G-SUSX	MDH MD-902 Explorer	Sussex Police Authority	
G-SUTD	Jabiru UL-D	E. Bentley	
G-SUTN	I.I.I. Sky Arrow 650TC	D. J. Goldsmith	
G-SUZN	PA-28-161 Warrior II	St. George Flight Training Ltd	
G-SVAS	PA-18-150 Super Cub	Richard Shuttleworth Trustees	
G-SVDG	Jabiru SK	R. Tellegen	
G-SVEA	PA-28-161 Warrior II	G-SVEA Group	
G-SVEN	Centrair 101A Pegase	G7 Group	
G-SVET	Yakovlev Yak-50	Yak-50 Group	
G-SVEY	Vulcanair P-68 Observer 2	C Aviation Ltd	
G-SVIP	Cessna 421B Golden Eagle II	R. P. Bateman	
G-SVIV	SNCAN Stampe SV.4C	J. E. Keighley	
G-SVNC	Rolladen-Schneider LS4	M. C. Jenkins	
G-SVPN	PA-32R-301T Turbo Saratoga	LAC Marine Ltd	
G-SVSB	Cessna 680 Citation Sovereign	Ferron Trading Ltd	
G-SWAY	PA-18-150 Super Cub	R. Lillywhite	
G-SWCT	Flight Design CTSW	J. A. Shufflebotham	
G-SWEE	Beech 95-B55 Baron	Orman (Carrolls Farm) Ltd (G-AZDK)	

Notes	Reg.	Type	Owner or Operator
	G-SWEL	Hughes 369HS	M. A. Crook & A. E. Wright (G-RBUT)
	G-SWIF	VS.541 Swift F.7 (XF114) ★	Solent Sky, Southampton
	G-SWIG	Robinson R44	S. Goddard & S. Walsh
	G-SWIP	Silence Twister	Zulu Glasstek Ltd (G-RIOT)
	G-SWLL	Aero AT-3 R100	Sywell Aerodrome Ltd
	G-SWON	Pitts S-1S Special	S. L. Goldspink
	G-SWOT	Currie Wot (C3011:S)	D. A. Porter
	G-SWPR	Cameron N-56 balloon	A. Brown
	G-SWSW	Schempp-Hirth Ventus bT	W. H. Greenwood
	G-SWWM	Westland Gazelle HT.Mk.2 (XW853)	M. S. Beaton
	G-SWYM	CZAW Sportcruiser	R. W. Beal
	G-SXIX	Rans S.19	J. L. Almey
	G-SXTY	Learjet 60	TAG Aviation (UK) Ltd
	G-SYCO	Europa	P. J. Tiller
	G-SYEL	Aero AT-3 R100	Sywell Aerodrome Ltd
	G-SYFW	Focke-Wulf Fw.190 replica (2+1)	J. E. Cull
	G-SYGA	Beech B200 Super King Air	Synergy Aircraft Leasing Ltd (G-BPPM)
	G-SYGC	Cessna 525A Citationjet CJ2	Synergy Aviation Ltd (G-HGRC)
	G-SYLJ	Embraer RJ135BJ	TAG Aviation (UK) Ltd
	G-SYPS	MDH MD.900 Explorer	South Yorkshire Police Authority
	G-SYWL	Aero AT-3 R100	Sywell Aerodrome Ltd
	G-TAAB	Cirrus SR22	TAA UK Ltd
	G-TAAC	Cirrus SR20	TAA UK Ltd
	G-TABS	EMB-110P1 Bandeirante	Skydrift Ltd (G-PBAC)
	G-TABY	Cirrus SR20	N. Carter
	G-TACK	Grob G.109B	A. P. Mayne
	G-TAFC	Maule M7-2358 Super Rocket	The Amphibious Flying Club Ltd
	G-TAFF	CASA 1.131E Jungmann 1000	A. J. E. Smith (G-BFNE)
	G-TAFI	Bücker Bü 133C Jungmeister	R. P. Lamplough
	G-TAGR	Europa	C. G. Sutton
	G-TAIR	PA-34-200T Seneca II	AWA Aeronautical Web Academy lda
	G-TAJF	Lindstrand LBL-77A balloon	T. A. J. Fowles
	G-TAKE	AS.355F1 Ecureuil II	Arena Aviation Ltd (G-OITN)
	G-TALA	Cessna 152 II	Tatenhill Aviation Ltd (G-BNPZ)
	G-TALB	Cessna 152 II	Tatenhill Aviation Ltd (G-BORO)
	G-TALC	Cessna 152	Tatenhill Aviation Ltd (G-BPBG)
	G-TALD	Cessna F.152	Tatenhill Aviation Ltd (G-BHRM)
	G-TALE	PA-28-181 Archer II	Tatenhill Aviation Ltd (G-BJOA)
	G-TALF	PA-24-250 Comanche	Tatenhill Aviation Ltd (G-APUZ)
	G-TALG	PA-28-151 Warrior	Tatenhill Aviation Ltd (G-BELP)
	G-TALH	PA-28-181 Archer II	Tatenhill Aviation Ltd (G-CIFR)
	G-TALN	Rotorway A600 Talon	Southern Helicopters Ltd
	G-TAMB	Schweizer 269D	Total Air Management Services Ltd
	G-TAMC	Schweizer 269D	Total Air Management Services Ltd
	G-TAMD	Schweizer 269D	Total Air Management Services Ltd
	G-TAME	Schweizer 269D	Total Air Management Services Ltd
	G-TAMR	Cessna 172S	Caledonian Air Surveys Ltd
	G-TAMS	Beech A23-24 Musketeer Super	Aerograde Ltd
	G-TANA	Tanarg 912S(2)/Ixess 15	A. P. Marks
	G-TANG	Tanarg 912S(2)/Ixess 15	N. L. Stammers
	G-TANJ	Raj Hamsa X'Air 582(5)	M. M. & P. M. Stoney
	G-TANK	Cameron N-90 balloon	D. J., A. H. & A. M. Mercer
	G-TANS	SOCATA TB20 Trinidad	B. J. Ryan
	G-TANY	EAA Acrosport 2	P. J. Tanulak
	G-TAPE	PA-23 Aztec 250D	M. Spittle
	G-TAPS	PA-28RT-201T Turbo Arrow IV	P. G. Doble
	G-TARN	Pietenpol Air Camper	P. J. Heilbron
	G-TARR	P & M Quik	A. Edwards
	G-TART	PA-28-236 Dakota	N. K. G. Prescot
	G-TASH	Cessna 172N (modified)	Just Plane Trading Ltd
	G-TASK	Cessna 404	Reconnaissance Ventures Ltd
	G-TATO	Robinson R22	Skyrunner Aviation Ltd
	G-TATR	Replica Travelair R Type	R. A. Seeley
	G-TATS	AS.350BA Ecureuil	T. J. Hoare
	G-TATT	Gardan GY-20 Minicab	Tatt's Group
	G-TAXI	PA-23 Aztec 250E	M. Roberts
	G-TAYC	Gulfstream G450	TAG Aviation (UK) Ltd
	G-TAYI	Grob G.115	K. P. Widdowson & K. Hackshall (G-DODO)
	G-TAYS	Cessna F.152 II	Tayside Aviation Ltd (G-LFCA)

Reg.	Type	Owner or Operator	Notes
G-TAZZ	Dan Rihn DR.107 One Design	C. J. Gow	
G-TBAE	BAe 146-200	BAE Systems (Corporate Travel Ltd) (G-HWPB/G-BSRU/G-OSKI/G-JEAR)	
G-TBAG	Murphy Renegade II	M. R. Tetley	
G-TBBC	Pegasus Quantum 15-912	J. Horn	
G-TBEA	Cessna 525A Citation CJ2	Xclusive Jet Charter Ltd	
G-TBGL	Agusta A109A-II	Bulford Holdings Ltd (G-VJCB/G-BOUA)	
G-TBGT	SOCATA TB10 Tobago GT	P. G. Sherry & A. J. Simmonds	
G-TBHH	AS355F2 Twin Squirrel	Alpha Properties (London) Ltd (G-HOOT/G-SCOW/G-POON/G-MCAL)	
G-TBIC	BAe 146-200	Nex Aviation Aircrafts Ltd	
G-TBIO	SOCATA TB10 Tobago	R. G. L. Solomon and J. S. Ritchie	
G-TBJP	Mainair Pegasus Quik	R. J. Price	
G-TBLB	P & M Quik GT450	B. L. Benson	
G-TBLY	Eurocopter EC 120B	AD Bly Aircraft Leasing Ltd	
G-TBMR	P & M Aviation Quik GT450	B. Robertson	
G-TBMW	Murphy Renegade Spirit	S. J. & M. J. Spavins (G-MYIG)	
G-TBOK	SOCATA TB10 Tobago	TB10 Ltd	
G-TBSV	SOCATA TB20 Trinidad GT	Condron Concrete Ltd	
G-TBTB	Robinson R44	ARB Helicopters (G-CDUN)	
G-TBTN	SOCATA TB10 Tobago	Airways International Ltd (G-BKIA)	
G-TBXX	SOCATA TB20 Trinidad	Aeroplane Ltd	
G-TBZO	SOCATA TB20 Trinidad	R. P. Lewis & D. L. Clarke	
G-TCAC	Airbus A.320-232	Thomas Cook Airlines Ltd (G-ERAA)	
G-TCAD	Airbus A.320-214	Thomas Cook Airlines Ltd	
G-TCAL	Robinson R44 II	C. M. Gough-Cooper	
G-TCAN	Colt 69A balloon	H. C. J. Williams	
G-TCAS	Cameron Z-275 balloon	The Ballooning Business Ltd	
G-TCBA	Boeing 757-28A	Thomas Cook Airlines Ltd (G-OOOY)	
G-TCCA	Boeing 767-31K	Thomas Cook Airlines Ltd (G-SJMC)	
G-TCCB	Boeing 767-31KER	Thomas Cook Airlines Ltd (G-DIMB)	
G-TCDA	Airbus A.321-211	Thomas Cook Airlines Ltd (G-JOEE)	
G-TCEE	Hughes 369HS	Aviation Styling Ltd (G-AZVM)	
G-TCHI	VS.509 Spitfire Tr.9	M. B. Phillips	
G-TCHO	VS Spitfire Mk.IX	B. Phillips	
G-TCMM	Agusta-Bell 206B-3 Jet Ranger 3	R and M Crane Hire Ltd (G-JMVB/G-OIML)	
G-TCNM	Tecnam P92-EA Echo	F. G. Walker	
G-TCNY	Mainair Pegasus Quik	L. A. Maynard	
G-TCSM	Bell 206B-3 JetRanger III	Aerial Helicopters Ltd (G-CDYS/G-BOTM)	
G-TCTC	PA-28RT-200 Arrow IV	Marie-Dominique Lopez	
G-TCUB	Piper J-3C-65 Cub	C. Kirk	
G-TCXA	Airbus A.330-243	Thomas Cook Airlines Ltd	
G-TDKI	CZAW Sportcruiser	D. R. Kendall	
G-TDOG	SA Bulldog Srs 120/121 (XX538:O)	G. S. Taylor	
G-TDRA	Cessna 172S Skyhawk	TDR Aviation Ltd	
G-TDSA	Cessna F.406 Caravan II	Nor Leasing	
G-TDVB	Dyn' Aero MCR-01ULC	D. V. Brunt	
G-TDYN	Aerospool Dynamic WT9 UK	A. A. & L. J. Rice	
G-TEAS	Tanarg/Ixess 15 912S(1)	G. T. Lewis	
G-TEBZ	PA-28R-201 Arrow III	Bowen-Air Ltd	
G-TECC	Aeronca 7AC Champion	N. J. Orchard-Armitage	
G-TECH	Rockwell Commander 114	M. A. Rooney (G-BEDH)	
G-TECI	Tecnam P2002-JF	Polarb Air Ltd	
G-TECK	Cameron V-77 balloon	M. W. A. Shemilt	
G-TECM	Tecnam P92-EM Echo	N. G. H. Staunton	
G-TECO	Tecnam P92-EM Echo	A. N. Buchan	
G-TECS	Tecnam P2002-EA Sierra	D. A. Lawrence	
G-TEDB	Cessna F.150L	E. L. Bamford (G-AZLZ)	
G-TEDF	Cameron N-90 balloon	Fort Vale Engineering Ltd	
G-TEDI	Best Off Skyranger J2.2(1)	J. E. McGee	
G-TEDW	Kiss 450-582 (2)	K. Buckley	
G-TEDY	Evans VP-1	N. K. Marston (G-BHGN)	
G-TEEE	P & M Quik GT450	S. E. Bettley	
G-TEFC	PA-28 Cherokee 140	Foxtrot Charlie Flyers	
G-TEGS	Bell 206B JetRanger III	E. Drinkwater	
G-TEHL	CFM Streak Shadow Srs M	J. Anderson (G-MYJE)	
G-TELC	Rotorsport UK MT-03	C. M. Jones	
G-TELY	Agusta A109A-II	Castle Air Charters Ltd	

Notes	Reg.	Type	Owner or Operator
	G-TEMB	Tecnam P2000-EA Sierra	M. B. Hill
	G-TEMP	PA-28 Cherokee 180	F. Busch International Ltd (G-AYBK)
	G-TEMT	Hawker Tempest II (MW763)	Tempest Two Ltd
	G-TENG	Extra EA.300/L	D. McGinn
	G-TENT	Auster J/1N Alpha	R. Callaway-Lewis (G-AKJU)
	G-TERN	Shaw Europa	J. Smith
	G-TERR	Mainair Pegasus Quik	T. R. Thomas
	G-TERY	PA-28-181 Archer II	J. R. Bratherton (G-BOXZ)
	G-TESI	Tecnam P2002 EA Sierra	C. C. Burgess
	G-TESR	Tecnam P2002-RG Sierra	Tecnam UK Ltd
	G-TEST	PA-34-200 Seneca	Stapleford Flying Club Ltd (G-BLCD)
	G-TEWS	PA-28 Cherokee 140	P. M. Ireland (G-KEAN/G-AWTM)
	G-TEXA	BAe Jetstream 4100	Bravo Aviation Ltd
	G-TEXN	North American T-6G Texan (3072:72)	Thunderprop Ltd (G-BHTH)
	G-TEZZ	CZAW Sportcruiser	T. D. Baker
	G-TFIX	Mainair Pegasus Quantum 15-912	T. G. Jones
	G-TFLX	P & M Quik GT450	L. A. Wood
	G-TFLY	Air Creation Kiss 450-582 (1)	A. J. Ladell
	G-TFOG	Best Off Skyranger 912(2)	T. J. Fogg
	G-TFOX	Denney Kitfox Mk.2	R. Janek
	G-TFRB	Air Command 532 Elite	F. R. Blennerhassett
	G-TFUN	Valentin Taifun 17E	North West Taifun Group
	G-TFYN	PA-32RT-300 Lance II	R. C. Poolman
	G-TGDL	Robinsn R44 II	Enable International Ltd
	G-TGER	AA-5B Tiger	D. T. Pangbourne (G-BFZP)
	G-TGGR	Eurocopter EC 120B	Messiah Corporation Ltd
	G-TGRA	Agusta A109A	Tiger Helicopters Ltd
	G-TGRD	Robinson R22 Beta II	Tiger Helicopters Ltd (G-OPTS)
	G-TGRE	Robinson R22A	Tiger Helicopters Ltd (G-SOLD)
	G-TGRS	Robinson R22 Beta	Tiger Helicopters Ltd (G-DELL)
	G-TGRZ	Bell 206B JetRanger 3	Tiger Helicopters Ltd (G-BXZX)
	G-TGTT	Robinson R44 II	London Helicopter Centres Ltd (G-STUS)
	G-TGUN	Aero AT-3 R100	Cunning Plan Development Ltd
	G-THAT	Raj Hamsa X'Air Falcon 912 (1)	A. N. Green
	G-THEO	TEAM mini-MAX 91	D. W. Melville
	G-THFC	Embraer RJ135BJ Legacy	Raz Air Ltd (G-RRAZ/G-RUBN)
	G-THIN	Cessna FR.172E	I. C. A. Ussher (G-BXYY)
	G-THLA	Robinson R22 Beta	Thurston Helicopters Ltd and Tukair Aircraft Charter
	G-THNX	Cessna 525 Citationjet	Synery Aviation Ltd (G-BVCM)
	G-THOL	Boeing 737-36N	Thomsonfly Ltd (G-IGOK)
	G-THOM	Thunder Ax-6-56 balloon	T. H. Wilson
	G-THON	Boeing 737-36N	Thomsonfly Ltd (G-IGOL)
	G-THOO	Boeing 737-33V	Thomsonfly Ltd (G-EZYK)
	G-THOP	Boeing 737-3U3	Thomsonfly Ltd
	G-THOT	Avtech Jabiru SK	S. G. Holton
	G-THRE	Cessna 182S	J. P. Monjalet
	G-THRM	Schleicher ASW-27	C. G. Starkey (G-CJWC)
	G-THSL	PA-28R-201 Arrow III	D. M. Markscheffe
	G-TICH	Taylor JT.2 Titch	R. Davitt
	G-TIDS	Jodel 150	M. R. Parker
	G-TIFG	Ikarus C42 FB80	The Ikarus Flying Group
	G-TIGA	DH.82A Tiger Moth	D. E. Leatherland (G-AOEG)
	G-TIGC	AS.332L Super Puma	Bristow Helicopters Ltd (G-BJYH)
	G-TIGE	AS.332L Super Puma	Bristow Helicopters Ltd (G-BJYJ)
	G-TIGF	AS.332L Super Puma	Bristow Helicopters Ltd
	G-TIGG	AS.332L Super Puma	Bristow Helicopters Ltd
	G-TIGJ	AS.332L Super Puma	Bristow Helicopters Ltd
	G-TIGS	AS.332L Super Puma	Bristow Helicopters Ltd
	G-TIGV	AS.332L Super Puma	Bristow Helicopters Ltd
	G-TIII	Aerotek Pitts S-2A Special	Treble India Group
	G-TILE	Robinson R22 Beta	Fenland Helicopters Ltd
	G-TIMB	Rutan Vari-Eze	P. G. Kavanagh (G-BKXJ)
	G-TIMC	Robinson R44	T. Clark Aviation LLP (G-CDUR)
	G-TIMH	Robinson R22	Central Helicopters Ltd
	G-TIMK	PA-28-181 Archer II	Minimal Risk Consultancy Ltd
	G-TIML	Cessna 172S Skyhawk	Air Unlimited Sweden AB/Sweden
	G-TIMM	Folland Gnat T.1 (XM693)	Heritage Aircraft Ltd

Reg.	Type	Owner or Operator	Notes
G-TIMP	Aeronca 7BCM Champion	R. B. Valler	
G-TIMS	Falconar F-12A	T. Sheridan	
G-TIMX	Head AX8-88B balloon	T. S. Crowdy	
G-TIMY	Gardan GY-80 Horizon 160	R. G. Whyte	
G-TIMZ	Robinson R44	D. E. Burt	
G-TINA	SOCATA TB10 Tobago	A. Lister	
G-TING	Cameron O-120 balloon	Floating Sensations Ltd	
G-TINK	Robinson R22 Beta	Heli Air Ltd	
G-TINS	Cameron N-90 balloon	J. R. Clifton	
G-TINT	Aerotechnik EV-97 Team Eurostar UK	I. A. Cunningham	
G-TINY	Z.526F Trener Master	D. Evans	
G-TIVS	Rans S.6-ES Coyote II	A. P. Michell	
G-TIVV	Aerotechnik EV-97 Team Eurostar UK	I. Shulver	
G-TIZZ	Westland SA.341C Gazelle HT.2	R. H. Kirke (G-CBSD)	
G-TJAG	PA-34-220T Seneca V	Morgan Airbourne LLP	
G-TJAL	Jabiru SPL-430	D. W. Cross	
G-TJAV	Mainair Pegasus Quik	T. Scott	
G-TJAY	PA-22 Tri-Pacer 135	D. Pegley	
G-TJDM	Van's RV-6A	J. D. Michie	
G-TKAY	Shaw Europa	A. M. Kay	
G-TKEV	P & M Quik R	O. P. Gall	
G-TKIS	Tri-R Kis	T. J. Bone	
G-TKPZ	Cessna 310R	Aircraft Engineers Ltd (G-BRAH)	
G-TLAC	Sherwood Ranger ST	The Light Aircraft Co.Ltd	
G-TLDL	Medway SLA 100 Executive	D. T. Lucas	
G-TLEL	American Blimp Corp A.60+ airship	Lightship Europe Ltd	
G-TLET	PA-28-161 Cadet	ADR Aviation (G-GFCF/G-RHBH)	
G-TLFK	Cessna 680 Citation Sovereign	International Jetclub Ltd	
G-TLST	TL 2000 Sting Carbon	B. McFadden	
G-TLTL	Schempp-Hirth Discus CS	E. K. Armitage	
G-TMAN	Roadster/Adventure Funflyer Quattro	P. A. Mahony	
G-TMAX	Evektor EV-97 Sportstar Max	Cosmik Aviation Ltd	
G-TMCB	Best Off Skyranger 912 (2)	P. R. Hanman	
G-TMCC	Cameron N-90 balloon	M. S. Jennings	
G-TMKI	P.56 Provost T.1 (WW453)	B. L. Robinson	
G-TMOL	SOCATA TB20 Trinidad	Blackbrooks LLP	
G-TMRB	Short SD3-60 Variant 100	HD Air Ltd (G-SSWB/G-BMLE)	
G-TNGO	Van's RV-6	R. Marsden	
G-TNJB	P & M Quik R	C. J. Shorter	
G-TNRG	Tanarg/Ixess 15 912S(2)	J. W. Mann	
G-TNTN	Thunder Ax6-56 balloon	H. M. Savage & J. F. Trehern	
G-TOAD	Jodel D.140B	J. H. Stevens	
G-TOAK	SOCATA TB20 Trinidad	J. E. Howe	
G-TOBA	SOCATA TB10 Tobago	E. Downing	
G-TOBI	Cessna F.172K	TOBI Group (G-AYVB)	
G-TODD	ICA IS-28M2A	C. I. Roberts & C. D. King	
G-TODG	Flight Design CTSW	S. J. Sykes	
G-TOFT	Colt 90A balloon	C. S. Perceval	
G-TOGO	Van's RV-6	I. R. Thomas	
G-TOHS	Cameron V-31 balloon	J. P. Moore	
G-TOLI	Robinson R44 II	Coleman Cantle Partnership	
G-TOLL	PA-28R-201 Arrow III	Arrow Aircraft Ltd	
G-TOLY	Robinson R22 Beta	Helicopter Services Ltd (G-NSHR)	
G-TOMC	NA AT-6D Harvard III	A. A. Marshall	
G-TOMJ	Flight Design CT2K	J. Fleming	
G-TOMM	Robinson R22 Beta	EBG (Helicopters) Ltd	
G-TOMS	PA-38-112 Tomahawk	G-TOMS Group	
G-TOMX	MCR-01 VLA Sportster	P. T. Knight	
G-TOMZ	Denney Kitfox Mk.2	S. J. Spavins	
G-TONE	Pazmany PL-4	A. D. Worrall	
G-TONN	Mainair Pegasus Quik	J. C. Boyd	
G-TONS	Slingsby T.67M-200	D. I. Stanbridge	
G-TOOB	Schempp-Hirth Discus 2b	M. F. Evans & P. Davis	
G-TOOL	Thunder Ax8-105 balloon	D. V. Howard	
G-TOPC	AS.355F1 Twin Squirrel	Kinetic Avionics Ltd	
G-TOPK	Shaw Europa XS	P. J. Kember	

Notes	Reg.	Type	Owner or Operator
	G-TOPO	PA-23-250 Turbo Aztec	Keen Leasing (IOM) Ltd (G-BGWW)
	G-TOPS	AS.355F1 Twin Squirrel	Sterling Helicopters (G-BPRH)
	G-TOPZ	Aérospatiale SA.342J Gazelle	Top Yachts Ltd
	G-TORC	PA-28R Cherokee Arrow 200	Haimoss Ltd
	G-TORE	P.84 Jet Provost T.3A ★	Instructional airframe/City University, Islington
	G-TORI	Zenair CH.701SP	M. J. Maddock (G-CCSK)
	G-TORK	Cameron Z-105 balloon	M. E. Dunstan-Sewell
	G-TORN	Flight Design CTSW	J. A. Moss
	G-TOSH	Robinson R22 Beta	JT Helicopters Ltd
	G-TOTN	Cessna 210M	Quay Financial Strategies Ltd (G-BVZM)
	G-TOTO	Cessna F.177RG	TOTO Flying Group (G-OADE/G-AZKH)
	G-TOUR	Robin R.2112	A. Carnegie
	G-TOWS	PA-25 Pawnee 260	Lasham Gliding Society Ltd
	G-TOYD	Boeing 737-33V	bmi Baby (G-EZYT)
	G-TOYF	Boeing 737-36N	bmi Baby (G-IGOO/G-SMDB)
	G-TOYG	Boeing 737-36N	bmi Baby (G-IGOJ)
	G-TOYH	Boeing 737-36N	bmi Baby (G-IGOY)
	G-TOYI	Boeing 737-3Q8	bmi Baby
	G-TOYJ	Boeing 737-36M	bmi Baby
	G-TOYK	Boeing 737-33R	bmi Baby
	G-TOYM	Boeing 737-36Q	bmi Baby (G-OHAJ)
	G-TOYZ	Bell 206B JetRanger 3	Potter Aviation Ltd (G-RGER)
	G-TPAL	P & M Aviation Quik GT450	R. Robertson
	G-TPSL	Cessna 182S	A. N. Purslow
	G-TPWL	P & M Quik GT450	The G-TPWL Group
	G-TRAC	Robinson R44	C. J. Sharples
	G-TRAM	Pegasus Quantum 15-912	G-TRAM Group
	G-TRAN	Beech 76 Duchess	Multiflight Ltd (G-NIFR)
	G-TRAT	Pilatus PC-12/45	Sky Elite Ltd
	G-TRAX	Cessna F.172M	Skytrax Aviation Ltd
	G-TRBO	Schleicher ASW-28-18E	A. Cluskey
	G-TRCY	Robinson R44	Sugarfree Air Ltd
	G-TREC	Cessna 421C	Sovereign Business Integration PLC (G-TLOL)
	G-TREE	Bell 206B JetRanger 3	Bush Woodlands
	G-TREK	Jodel D.18	R. H. Mole
	G-TREX	Alpi Pioneer 300	S. R. Winter
	G-TRIB	Lindstrand LBL HS-110 airship	S. L. Bell
	G-TRIC	DHC.1 Chipmunk 22 (18013:013)	A. A. Fernandez (G-AOSZ)
	G-TRIG	Cameron Z-90 balloon	Hedge Hoppers Balloon Group
	G-TRIM	Monnett Moni	E. A. Brotherton-Ratcliffe
	G-TRIN	SOCATA TB20 Trinidad	M. Hardy & M. J. Porter
	G-TROY	NA T-28A Fennec (51-7692)	S. G. Howell & S. Tilling
	G-TRTM	DG Flugzeugbau DG-808C	ATSI Ltd
	G-TRUD	Enstrom 480	Sussex Aviation Ltd
	G-TRUE	MDH Hughes 369E	N. E. Bailey
	G-TRUK	Stoddard-Hamilton Glasair RG	M. P. Jackson
	G-TRUX	Colt 77A balloon	Servowarm Baloon Syndicate
	G-TRYK	Kiss 400-582 (1)	M. A. Pantling
	G-TRYX	Enstrom 480B	Atryx Aviation LLP
	G-TSAC	Tecnam P2002-EA Sierra	A. G. Cozens
	G-TSDS	PA-32R-301 Saratoga SP	I. R. Jones (G-TRIP/G-HOSK)
	G-TSGA	PA-28R-201 Arrow III	TSG Aviation Ltd (G-ONSF/G-EMAK)
	G-TSGE	Cirrus SR20	Renneta Ltd
	G-TSGJ	PA-28-181 Archer II	Golf Juliet Flying Club
	G-TSIM	Titan T-51 Mustang	B. J. Chester-Master
	G-TSIX	AT-6C Harvard IIA (111836:JZ-6)	Century Aviation Ltd
	G-TSJF	Cessna 525B CitationJet CJ3	Lunar Jet Ltd
	G-TSKD	Raj Hamsa X'Air Jabiru J.2.2.	T. Sexton & K. B. Dupuy
	G-TSKS	EV-97 TeamEurostar UK	Purple Aviation Ltd
	G-TSKY	Beagle B.121 Pup 2	R. G. Hayes (G-AWDY)
	G-TSLC	Schweizer 269C-1	Bournemouth Helicopters Ltd
	G-TSLS	Bombardier BD-700-1A11 Global 5000	TAG Aviation (UK) Ltd
	G-TSOB	Rans S.6-ES Coyote II	S. Luck
	G-TSOL	EAA Acrosport 1	J. A. Wojda (G-BPKI)
	G-TSUE	Shaw Europa	H. J. C. Maclean
	G-TSWI	Lindstrand LBL-90A balloon	Dylan Harvey Group Ltd
	G-TTAT	ICP MXP-740 Savannah VG Jabiru(1)	A. N. Green
	G-TTDD	Zenair CH.701 STOL	D. B. Dainton & V. D. Asque

Reg.	Type	Owner or Operator	Notes
G-TTFG	Colt 77B balloon	T. J. & M. J. Turner (G-BUZF)	
G-TTID	Airbus A.321-231	easyJet Airline Co.Ltd	
G-TTIE	Airbus A.321-231	easyJet Airline Co.Ltd	
G-TTMB	Bell 206B JetRanger 3	Sky Charter UK Ltd (G-RNME/G-CBDF)	
G-TTOB	Airbus A.320-232	British Airways PLC	
G-TTOE	Airbus A.320-232	British Airways PLC	
G-TTOY	CFM Streak Shadow SA	J. Softley	
G-TTRL	Van's RV-9A	J. E. Gattrell	
G-TUBB	Avtech Jabiru UL	A. H. Bower	
G-TUCK	Van's RV-8	N. G. R. Moffat	
G-TUGG	PA-18 Super Cub 150	Ulster Gliding Club Ltd	
G-TUGI	CZAW Sportcruiser	T. J. Wilson	
G-TUGS	PA-25-235 Pawnee D	J. A. Stephen (G-BFEW)	
G-TUGY	Robin DR.400/180	TUGY Group	
G-TULP	Lindstrand LBL Tulips SS balloon	Oxford Promotions (UK) Ltd	
G-TUNE	Robinson R22 Beta	Tune Aviation (G-OJVI)	
G-TURF	Cessna F.406	Reconnaissance Ventures Ltd	
G-TUTU	Cameron O-105 balloon	A. C. K. Rawson & J. J. Rudoni	
G-TVAM	MBB Bo105DBS-4	Bond Air Services Ltd (G-SPOL)	
G-TVBF	Lindstrand LBL-310A balloon	Virgin Balloons Flights	
G-TVCO	Gippsland GA-8 Airvan	Zyox Ltd	
G-TVEE	Hughes 369HS	Eastern Atlantic Helicopters Ltd	
G-TVHB	Eurocopter EC 135 P2+	Thames Valley Police Authority	
G-TVHD	AS.355F2 Ecureuil 2	Arena Aviation Ltd	
G-TVII	Hawker Hunter T.7 (XX467:86)	G-TVII Group/Exeter	
G-TVIJ	CCF Harvard IV (T-6J) (28521:TA-521)	R. W. Davies (G-BSBE)	
G-TVSI	Campbell Cricket Replica	C. Smith	
G-TWAZ	Rolladen-Schneider LS7-WL	S. Derwin and M. Boulton	
G-TWEL	PA-28-181 Archer II	International Aerospace Engineering Ltd	
G-TWEY	Colt 69A balloon	N. Bland	
G-TWIN	PA-44-180 Seminole	Bonus Aircraft Ltd	
G-TWIS	Silence Twister	C. S. & K. D. Rhodes	
G-TWIZ	Rockwell Commander 114	B. C. & P. M. Cox	
G-TWLV	Van's RV-12	J. N. Parr	
G-TWNN	Beech 76 Duchess	Folada Aero and Technical Services Ltd	
G-TWOA	Schempp-Hirth Discus 2a	A. J. McNamara	
G-TWOC	Schempp-Hirth Ventus 2cT	D. Heslop	
G-TWOO	Extra EA.300/200	Extra 200 Aviation Ltd (G-MRKI)	
G-TWOT	Schempp-Hirth Discus 2T	C. Gulich	
G-TWRL	Pitts S-1S Special	C. Dennis	
G-TWSR	Silence Twister	J. A. Hallam	
G-TWSS	Silence Twister	A. P. Hatton	
G-TWTR	Robinson R44 II	Heli Aviation Ltd	
G-TWTW	Denney Kitfox Mk.2	T. Willford	
G-TXAN	AT-6D Harvard III (FX301)	P. Squires (G-JUDI)	
G-TYAK	IDA Bacau Yakovlev Yak-52	S. J. Ducker	
G-TYCN	Agusta A109E Power	A. J. Walter (Aviation) Ltd (G-VMCO)	
G-TYER	Robin DR.400/500	Robin Group	
G-TYGA	AA-5B Tiger	D. H. & R. J. Carman (G-BHNZ)	
G-TYGR	Best Off Skyranger 912S (1)	M. J. Poole	
G-TYKE	Avtech Jabiru UL-450	K. W. Allan	
G-TYMO	DH.82A Tiger Moth	N. Rose	
G-TYMS	Cessna 172P	Sorel Flying Group	
G-TYNA	PA-28-181 Archer II	Winged Bull Aviation	
G-TYNE	SOCATA TB20 Trinidad	N. V. Price	
G-TYRE	Cessna F.172M	J. S. C. English	
G-TZEE	SOCATA TB10 Tobago	Zytech Ltd	
G-TZII	Thorp T.211B	M. J. Newton	
G-UACA	Skyranger R.100	R. G. Openshaw	
G-UAKE	NA P-51D-5-NA Mustang	P. S. Warner	
G-UANO	DHC.1 Chipmunk 22	Advanced Flight Training Ltd (G-BYYW)	
G-UANT	PA-28 Cherokee 140	Air Navigation & Trading Co Ltd	
G-UAPA	Robin DR.400/140B	Carlos Saraive Lda/Portugal	
G-UAPO	Ruschmeyer R.90-230RG	P. Randall	
G-UAVA	PA-30 Twin Comanche	Small World Aviation Ltd	

Notes	Reg.	Type	Owner or Operator
	G-UCAM	PA-31-350 Navajo Chieftain	University of Cambridge Department of Geography (G-NERC/G-BBXX)
	G-UCCC	Cameron 90 Sign SS balloon	Unipart Group of Companies Ltd
	G-UCLU	Schleicher ASK-21	University College London Union
	G-UDET	Replica Fokker E.111	M. J. Clark
	G-UDGE	Thruster T.600N	G-UDGE Syndicate (G-BYPI)
	G-UDMS	PA-46R-350T Malibu Matrix	J. C. M. Critchley & S. S. Harding
	G-UDOG	SA Bulldog Srs 120/121 (XX518:S)	Gamit Ltd
	G-UFAW	Raj Hamsa X'Air 582 (5)	P. Batchelor
	G-UFCB	Cessna 172S	The Cambridge Aero Club Ltd
	G-UFCC	Cessna 172S	Oxford Aviation Services Ltd
	G-UFCF	Cessna 172S	Global Traffic Network UK Ltd
	G-UFCG	Cessna 172S	Ulster Flying Club (1961) Ltd
	G-UFCH	Cessna 172S	Global Traffic Network UK Ltd
	G-UFCI	Cessna 172S	Ulster Flying Club (1961) Ltd
	G-UFCJ	Cessna 172S	Ulster Flying Club (1961) Ltd (G-RMIN)
	G-UFLY	Cessna F.150H	Westair Flying Services Ltd (G-AVVY)
	G-UHIH	Bell UH-1H Iroquois (21509)	MSS Holdings Ltd
	G-UHOP	UltraMagic H-31 balloon	S. J. Roake
	G-UIKR	P & M Quik R	A. M. Sirant
	G-UILA	Aquila AT01	Aquila Sport Aeroplanes LLP
	G-UILD	Grob G.109B	K. Butterfield
	G-UILE	Lancair 320	R. J. Martin
	G-UILT	Cessna T.303	Rock Seat Ltd (G-EDRY)
	G-UINN	Stolp SA.300 Starduster Too	J. D. H. Gordon
	G-UIST	BAe Jetstream 3102	Highland Airways Ltd
	G-UJAB	Avtech Jabiru UL	C. A. Thomas
	G-UJGK	Avtech Jabiru UL	W. G. Upton & J. G. Kosak
	G-UKAG	BAe.146-300	Trident Aviation Leasing Services (Jersey) Ltd
	G-UKAW	Agusta A.109E	Westland Helicopters Ltd
	G-UKHP	BAe.146-300	Trident Aviation Leasing Services (Jersey) Ltd
	G-UKOZ	Avtech Jabiru SK	D. J. Burnett
	G-UKPS	Cessna 208 Caravan 1	UK Parachute Services Ltd
	G-UKRB	Colt 105A balloon	Virgin Airship & Balloon Co Ltd
	G-UKRC	BAe.146-300	Aviation Capital Solutions Ltd (G-BSMR)
	G-UKSC	BAe.146-300	Trident Aviation Leasing Services (Jersey) Ltd
	G-UKUK	Head Ax8-105 balloon	P. A. George
	G-ULAS	DHC.1 Chipmunk 22 (WK517)	ULAS Flying Club Ltd/Denham
	G-ULES	AS.355F2 Twin Squirrel	Select Plant Hire Company Ltd (G-OBHL/-HARO/G-DAFT/G-BNNN)
	G-ULHI	SA Bulldog Srs.100/101	Power Aerobatics Ltd (G-OPOD/G-AZMS)
	G-ULIA	Cameron V-77 balloon	J. T. Wilkinson
	G-ULPS	Everett Srs 1 gyroplane	C. J. Watkinson (G-BMNY)
	G-ULSY	Ikarus C.42 FB 80	Ikarus 1 Flying Group
	G-ULTA	Ultramagic M-65C	G. A. Board
	G-ULTR	Cameron A-105 balloon	P. Glydon
	G-UMAS	Rotorsport UK MT-03	BAE Systems (Operations) Ltd
	G-UMBO	Thunder Ax7-77A balloon	Virgin Airship & Balloon Co Ltd
	G-UMMI	PA-31-310 Turbo Navajo	J. A. & D. T. A. Rees (G-BGSO)
	G-UMMS	EV-97 TeamEurostar UK	A. C. Lees (G-ODRY)
	G-UMMY	Best Off Skyranger J2.2(2)	A. R. Williams
	G-UNDD	PA-23 Aztec 250E	G. J. & D. P. Deadman (G-BATX)
	G-UNER	Lindstrand LBL-90A balloon	St. Dunstans
	G-UNES	Van's RV-6	R. C. Dyer
	G-UNGE	Lindstrand LBL-90A balloon	Silver Ghost Balloon Club (G-BVPJ)
	G-UNGO	Pietenpol Air Camper	A. R. Wyatt
	G-UNIN	Schempp-Hirth Ventus b	U9 Syndicate
	G-UNIV	Montgomerie-Parsons 2-seat gyroplane	University of Glasgow (G-BWTP)
	G-UNIX	VPM M16 Tandem Trainer	A. P. Wilkinson
	G-UNNA	Jabiru UL-450WW	N. D. A. Graham
	G-UNRL	Lindstrand LBL-RR21 balloon	Alton Aviation Ltd
	G-UORO	Shaw Europa	D. Dufton

Reg.	Type	Owner or Operator	Notes
G-UPFS	Waco UPS-7	D. N. Peters & N. R. Finlayson	
G-UPHI	Best Off Skyranger Swift 912S(1)	Flylight Airsports Ltd	
G-UPID	Bowers Fly Baby 1A	R. D. Taylor	
G-UPOI	Cameron TR-84 S1 balloon	Beatwax Ltd	
G-UPPI	BAC 167 Strikemaster Mk.80A	G. P. Williams (G-CBPB)	
G-UPTA	Skyranger 912S (1)	D. Minnock	
G-UPUP	Cameron V-77 balloon	S. F. Burden/Netherlands	
G-UPUZ	Lindstrand LBL-120A balloon	C.J. Sanger-Davies	
G-UROP	Beech 95-B55 Baron	T. B. Jenkins	
G-URRR	Air Command 582 Sport	L. Armes	
G-URRU	Bombardier CL600-2B16 Challenger	Executive Jet Charter Ltd	
G-URSA	Sikorsky S-76C	Premiair Aviation Services Ltd (G-URSS)	
G-URUH	Robinson R44	Heli Air Ltd	
G-URUS	Maule MX7-180B Super Rocket	Broomco Ltd	
G-USAA	Cessna F.150G	A. Naish (G-OIDW)	
G-USAR	Cessna 441 Conquest	I. Annenskiy	
G-USIL	Thunder Ax7-77 balloon	Window On The World Ltd	
G-USKY	Aviat A-1B Husky	B. Walker and Co (Dursley) Ltd	
G-USMC	Cameron Chestie 90 SS balloon	J. W. Soukup	
G-USRV	Van's RV-6	C. Cartwright & B. Vincent	
G-USSY	PA-28-181 Archer II	Western Air (Thruxton) Ltd	
G-USTH	Agusta A109A-II	Stratton Motor Co.(Norfolk) Ltd	
G-USTS	Agusta A109A-II	MB Air Ltd (G-MKSF)	
G-USTY	FRED Srs 2	Gusty Group	
G-UTSI	Rand-Robinson KR-2	K. B. Gutridge	
G-UTSY	PA-28R-201 Arrow III	Arrow Aviation Ltd	
G-UTTS	Robinson R44	HS (Holdings) Ltd (G-ROAP)	
G-UTZI	Robinson R44 II	S. K. Miles/Spain	
G-UURO	Aerotechnik EV-97 Eurostar	Romeo Oscar Syndicate	
G-UVBF	Lindstrand LBL-400A balloon	Virgin Balloon Flights	
G-UVIP	Cessna 421C	MM Air Ltd (G-BSKH)	
G-UVNR	BAC.167 Strikemaster Mk 87	G. P. Williams (G-BXFS)	
G-UYAD	Bombardier CL600-2B16	Coldstream SARL/Luxembourg	
G-UZEL	Aérospatiale SA.341G Gazelle 1	Fairalls of Godstone Ltd (G-BRNH)	
G-UZLE	Colt 77A balloon	G. B. Davies	
G-UZUP	Aerotechnik EV-97A Eurostar	G-UZUP EV-97 Flying Group	
G-VAAC	PA-28-181 Archer III	A. J. Catzelfis (G-CCDN)	
G-VAIR	Airbus A.340-313	Virgin Atlantic Airways Ltd *Maiden Tokyo*	
G-VALS	Pietenpol Air Camper	J. R. D. Bygraves	
G-VALY	SOCATA TB21 Trinidad GT Turbo	R. J. Thwaites and Westflight Aviation Ltd	
G-VALZ	Cameron N-120 balloon	Ladybird Balloons Ltd	
G-VANA	Gippsland GA-8 Airvan	P. Marsden	
G-VAND	Gippsland GA-8 Airvan	Go Adventure Ireland Ltd	
G-VANN	Van's RV-7A	D. N. & J. A. Carnegie	
G-VANS	Van's RV-4	R. J. Marshall and M. J. Wells	
G-VANX	Gippsland GA-8 Airvan	Airkix Aircraft Ltd	
G-VANZ	Van's RV-6A	S. J. Baxter	
G-VARG	Varga 2150A Kachina	J. Denton	
G-VART	Rotorway Executive 90	I. R. Brown & K. E. Parker (G-BSUR)	
G-VAST	Boeing 747-41R	Virgin Atlantic Airways Ltd *Ladybird*	
G-VATL	Airbus A.340-642	Virgin Atlantic Airways Ltd *Miss Kitty*	
G-VBCA	Cirrus SR22	C. A. S. Atha	
G-VBFA	Ultramagic N-250 balloon	Virgin Balloon Flights	
G-VBFB	Ultramagic N-355 balloon	Virgin Balloon Flights	
G-VBFC	Ultramagic N-250 balloon	Virgin Balloon Flights	
G-VBFD	Ultramagic N-250 balloon	Virgin Balloon Flights	
G-VBFE	Ultramagic N-255 balloon	Virgin Balloon Flights	
G-VBFF	Lindstrand LBL-360A balloon	Virgin Balloon Flights	
G-VBFG	Cameron Z-350 balloon	Virgin Balloon Flights	
G-VBFH	Cameron Z-350 balloon	Virgin Balloon Flights	
G-VBFI	Cameron Z-350 balloon	Virgin Balloon Flights	
G-VBFJ	Cameron Z-350 balloon	Virgin Balloon Flights	
G-VBFK	Cameron Z-350 balloon	Virgin Balloon Flights	

Notes	Reg.	Type	Owner or Operator
	G-VBFL	Cameron Z-400 balloon	Virgin Balloon Flights
	G-VBFM	Cameron Z-375 balloon	Virgin Balloon Flights
	G-VBFN	Cameron Z-375 balloon	Virgin Balloon Flights
	G-VBFO	Cameron Z-375 balloon	Virgin Balloon Flights
	G-VBFP	Ultramagic N-425 balloon	Virgin Balloon Flights
	G-VBFR	Cameron Z-375 balloon	Virgin Balloon Flights
	G-VBFS	Cameron Z-375 balloon	Virgin Balloon Flights
	G-VBFT	Cameron Z-375 balloon	Virgin Balloon Flights
	G-VBFV	Cameron Z-400 balloon	Virgin Balloon Flights
	G-VBFW	Cameron Z-77 balloon	Virgin Balloon Flights
	G-VBFX	Cameron Z-400 balloon	Virgin Balloon Flights
	G-VBFY	Cameron Z-400 balloon	Virgin Balloon Flights
	G-VBIG	Boeing 747-4Q8	Virgin Atlantic Airways Ltd *Tinker Belle*
	G-VBLU	Airbus A.340-642	Virgin Atlantic Airways Ltd *Soul Sister*
	G-VBPM	Cirrus SR22	Pestrin Ltd
	G-VBUG	Airbus A.340-642	Virgin Atlantic Airways Ltd
	G-VCIO	EAA Acro Sport II	C. M. Knight
	G-VCJH	Robinson R22 Beta	Hughes Plant Ltd
	G-VCML	Beech 58 Baron	St. Angelo Aviation Ltd
	G-VCXT	Schempp-Hirth Ventus 2cT	R. F. Aldous/Germany
	G-VDIR	Cessna T.310R	J. Driver
	G-VDOG	Cessna 305C Bird Dog (24582)	E. P. Morrow
	G-VECD	Robin R.1180T	B. Lee
	G-VECG	Robin R.2160	I. A. Anderson
	G-VECT	Cessna 560XL Citation Excel	Bookajet Aircraft Management Ltd
	G-VEGA	Slingsby T.65A Vega	R. A. Rice (G-BFZN)
	G-VEIL	Airbus A.340-642	Virgin Atlantic Airways Ltd *Queen of the Skies*
	G-VEIT	Robinson R44 II	Field Marshall Helicopters Ltd
	G-VELA	SIAI-Marchetti S.205-22R	D. A. Clarke & N. D. Dixon
	G-VELD	Airbus A.340-313	Virgin Atlantic Airways Ltd *African Queen*
	G-VENC	Schempp-Hirth Ventus 2cT	J. B. Giddins
	G-VENI	DH.112 Venom FB.50 (VV612)	Aviation and Computer Consultancy Ltd
	G-VENM	DH.112 Venom FB.50 (WK436)	Aviation Heritage Ltd (G-BLIE)
	G-VERA	Gardan GY-201 Minicab	D. K. Shipton
	G-VERU	Agusta A109S Grand	MRY Ltd
	G-VETA	Hawker Hunter T.Mk.7	Classic Jet Hritage Ltd (G-BVWN)
	G-VETS	Enstrom 280C-UK Shark	B. G. Rhodes (G-FSDC/G-BKTG)
	G-VEYE	Robinson R22	Manor PC's Ltd (G-BPTP)
	G-VEZE	Rutan Vari-Eze	S. D. Brown & ptnrs
	G-VFAB	Boeing 747-4Q8	Virgin Atlantic Airways Ltd *Lady Penelope*
	G-VFAR	Airbus A.340-313	Virgin Atlantic Airways Ltd *Diana*
	G-VFAS	PA-28R-200 Cherokee Arrow	P. Wood (G-MEAH/G-BSNM)
	G-VFIT	Airbus A.340-642	Virgin Atlantic Airways Ltd *Dancing Queen*
	G-VFIZ	Airbus A.340-642	Virgin Atlantic Airways Ltd *Bubbles*
	G-VFOX	Airbus A.340-642	Virgin Atlantic Airways Ltd *Silver Lady*
	G-VGAG	Cirrus SR20 GTS	Alfred Graham Ltd
	G-VGAL	Boeing 747-443	Virgin Atlantic Airways Ltd *Jersey Girl*
	G-VGAS	Airbus A.340-542	Virgin Atlantic Airways Ltd *Varga Girl*
	G-VGMC	Eurocopter AS.355N Ecureuil II	Eassda Aviation (G-HEMH)
	G-VGOA	Airbus A.340-642	Virgin Atlantic Airways Ltd *Indian Princess*
	G-VGVG	Savannah VG Jabiru(1)	M. A. Jones
	G-VHOL	Airbus A.340-311	Virgin Atlantic Airways Ltd *Jetstreamer*
	G-VHOT	Boeing 747-4Q8	Virgin Atlantic Airways Ltd *Tubular Belle*
	G-VICC	PA-28-161 Warrior II	Freedom Aviation Ltd (G-JFHL)
	G-VICI	DH.112 Venom FB.50 (J-1573)	Aviation and Computer Consultancy Ltd
	G-VICM	Beech F33C Bonanza	Velocity Engineering Ltd
	G-VICS	Commander 114B	Millennium Aviation Ltd
	G-VICT	PA-31-310 Turbo Navajo	Aviation Leasing ACS (G-BBZI)
	G-VIEW	Vinten-Wallis WA-116/100	K. H. Wallis
	G-VIIA	Boeing 777-236	British Airways
	G-VIIB	Boeing 777-236	British Airways
	G-VIIC	Boeing 777-236	British Airways
	G-VIID	Boeing 777-236	British Airways
	G-VIIE	Boeing 777-236	British Airways
	G-VIIF	Boeing 777-236	British Airways

Reg.	Type	Owner or Operator	Notes
G-VIIG	Boeing 777-236	British Airways	
G-VIIH	Boeing 777-236	British Airways	
G-VIIJ	Boeing 777-236	British Airways	
G-VIIK	Boeing 777-236	British Airways	
G-VIIL	Boeing 777-236	British Airways	
G-VIIM	Boeing 777-236	British Airways	
G-VIIN	Boeing 777-236	British Airways	
G-VIIO	Boeing 777-236	British Airways	
G-VIIP	Boeing 777-236	British Airways	
G-VIIR	Boeing 777-236	British Airways	
G-VIIS	Boeing 777-236	British Airways	
G-VIIT	Boeing 777-236	British Airways	
G-VIIU	Boeing 777-236	British Airways	
G-VIIV	Boeing 777-236	British Airways	
G-VIIW	Boeing 777-236	British Airways	
G-VIIX	Boeing 777-236	British Airways	
G-VIIY	Boeing 777-236	British Airways	
G-VIIZ	CZAW Sportcruiser	Skyview Systems Ltd	
G-VIKE	Bellanca 1730A Viking	S. J. Doughty	
G-VILA	Avtech Jabiru UL	G. T. Clipstone (G-BYIF)	
G-VILL	Lazer Z.200 (modified)	The G-VILL Group (G-BOYZ)	
G-VIPA	Cessna 182S	Stallingborough Aviation Ltd	
G-VIPH	Agusta A109C	Cheqair Ltd(G-BVNH/G-LAXO)	
G-VIPI	BAe 125 Srs 800B	Yeates of Leicester Ltd	
G-VIPP	PA-31-350 Navajo Chieftain	Capital Air Charter Ltd	
G-VIPR	Eurocopter EC 120B Colibri	Amey Aviation LLP	
G-VIPU	PA-31-350 Navajo Chieftain	Capital Air Charter Ltd	
G-VIPV	PA-31-350 Navajo Chieftain	Capital Air Charter Ltd	
G-VIPW	PA-31-350 Navajo Chieftain	Capital Air Charter Ltd	
G-VIPX	PA-31-350 Navajo Chieftain	Capital Air Charter Ltd	
G-VIPY	PA-31-350 Navajo Chieftain	Capital Air Charter Ltd	
G-VIRU	Agusta A109E Power	MRY Ltd	
G-VITA	Dassault Falcon 7X	Casanova Air 7X Ltd	
G-VITE	Robin R.1180T	G-VITE Flying Group	
G-VITL	Lindstrand LBL-105A balloon	Vital Resources	
G-VIVA	Thunder Ax7-65 balloon	R. J. Mitchener	
G-VIVI	Taylor JT.2 Titch	D. G. Tucker	
G-VIVM	P.84 Jet Provost T.5	K. Lyndon-Dykes (G-BVWF)	
G-VIVO	Nicollier HN700 Menestrel II	D. G. Tucker	
G-VIVS	PA-28-151 Cherokee Warrior	S. J. Harrison & V. A. Donnelly	
G-VIXN	DH.110 Sea Vixen FAW.2 (XS587) ★	P. G. Vallance Ltd/Charlwood	
G-VIXX	Alpi Pioneer 300	K. P. O'Sullivan (G-CESE/G-CERJ)	
G-VIZA	LBL-260A balloon	A. Nimmo	
G-VIZZ	Sportavia RS.180 Sportsman	Exeter Fournier Group	
G-VJAB	Avtech Jabiru UL	A. Thornton	
G-VJET	Avro 698 Vulcan B.2 (XL426) ★	Vulcan Restoration Trust	
G-VJIM	Colt 77 Jumbo Jim SS balloon	Magical Adventures Ltd/USA	
G-VJMJ	Agusta-Bell 206B JetRanger II	Total Digital Solutions Ltd (G-PEAK/G-BLJE)	
G-VKIT	Shaw Europa	T. H. Crow	
G-VKUP	Cameron Z-90 balloon	Global Brands Ltd	
G-VLCC	Schleicher ASW-27-18E	Viscount Cobham & K. M. H. Wilson	
G-VLCN	Avro 698 Vulcan B.2 (XH558) ★	Vulcan to the Sky Trust/Bruntingthorpe	
G-VLIP	Boeing 747-443	Virgin Atlantic Airways Ltd *Hot Lips*	
G-VMCG	PA-38-112 Tomahawk	W. G. E. James (G-BSVX)	
G-VMEG	Airbus A.340-642	Virgin Atlantic Airways Ltd *Mystic Maiden*	
G-VMJM	SOCATA TB10 Tobago	S. C. Brown (G-BTOK)	
G-VMVM	Cessna Z-77 balloon	Virgin Balloon Flights	
G-VNAP	Airbus A.340-642	Virgin Atlantic Airways Ltd	
G-VNOM	DH.112 Venom FB.50 (J-1632) ★	de Havilland Heritage Museum/London Colney	
G-VNON	Escapade Jabiru (3)	P. A. Vernon	
G-VNTS	Schempp-Hirth Ventus bT	911 Syndicatem	
G-VOAR	PA-28-181 Archer III	Solent Flight Ltd	
G-VOCE	Robinson R22	J. J. Voce (G-BSCL)	
G-VODA	Cameron N-77 balloon	I. Harris	
G-VOGE	Airbus A.340-642	Virgin Atlantic Airways Ltd *Cover Maiden*	
G-VOID	PA-28RT-201 Arrow IV	Doublecube Aviation LLP	

Notes	Reg.	Type	Owner or Operator
	G-VOIP	Westland SA.341G Gazelle	Q. Milne (G-HOBZ/G-CBSJ)
	G-VOLO	Alpi Pioneer 300	J. Buglass
	G-VOLP	Lindstrand LBL-150° balloon	Idea Balloon SAS
	G-VONA	Sikorsky S-76A	Von Essen Aviation Ltd (G-BUXB)
	G-VONB	Sikorsky S-76B	Von Essen Aviation Ltd (G-POAH)
	G-VONC	Sikorsky S-76B	Von Essen Aviation Ltd
	G-VOND	Bell 222	Von Essen Aviation Ltd (G-OWCG/G-VERT/ G-JLBZ/G-BNGB)
	G-VONE	Eurocopter AS355N Twin Squirrel	Von Essen Aviation Ltd (G-LCON)
	G-VONG	AS.355F1 Twin Squirrel	Von Essen Aviation Ltd (G-OILX/G-RMGN/ G-BMCY)
	G-VONH	AS.355F1 Twin Squirrel	Von Essen Aviation Ltd (G-BKUL/G-FFHI/ G-GWHH)
	G-VONJ	Raytheon 390 Premier 1	Von Essen Aviation Ltd
	G-VONK	AS.355F1 Squirrel	Von Essen Aviation Ltd (G-BLRI/G-NUTZ)
	G-VONS	PA-32R-301T Saratoga IITC	W. S. Stanley
	G-VOOM	Pitts S-1S Special	P. G. Roberts
	G-VORN	Aerotechnik EV-97 Eurostar	J. Parker (G-ODAV)
	G-VPAT	Evans VP-1 Srs 2	A. P. Twort
	G-VPER	BAC167 Strikemaster Mk.80A	D. J. Davidson (G-CDHB)
	G-VPPL	SOCATA TB20 Trinidad	P. Murer, L. Printie & P. J. Wood (G-BPAS)
	G-VPSJ	Shaw Europa	J. D. Bean
	G-VRED	Airbus A.340-642	Virgin Atlantic Airways Ltd *Scarlet Lady*
	G-VRMM	Van's RV-9	D. J. Rose
	G-VROC	Boeing 747-41R	Virgin Atlantic Airways Ltd *Mustang Sally*
	G-VROD	Aeroprakt A.22 Foxbat	K. Dickson
	G-VROE	Avro 652A Anson T.21 (WD413)	Air Atlantique Ltd/Coventry (G-BFIR)
	G-VROS	Boeing 747-443	Virgin Atlantic Airways Ltd *English Rose*
	G-VROY	Boeing 747-443	Virgin Atlantic Airways Ltd *Pretty Woman*
	G-VRVB	Van's RV-8	R. J. Verrall (G-CETI)
	G-VSEA	Airbus A.340-311	Virgin Atlantic Airways Ltd *Plane Sailing*
	G-VSGE	Cameron O-105 balloon	G. Sbocchelli
	G-VSHY	Airbus A.340-642	Virgin Atlantic Airways Ltd *Madam Butterfly*
	G-VSIX	Schempp-Hirth Ventus 2cT	V6 Group
	G-VSSH	Airbus A.340-642	Virgin Atlantic Airways Ltd *Sweet Dreamer*
	G-VSUN	Airbus A.340-313	Virgin Atlantic Airways Ltd *Rainbow Lady*
	G-VTAL	Beech V35 Bonanza	R. Chamberlain
	G-VTCT	Schempp-Hirth Ventus-2cT	V26 Syndicate
	G-VTGE	Bell 206L LongRanger	Vantage Helicopters Ltd (G-ELIT)
	G-VTII	DH.115 Vampire T.11 (XX507:74)	Vampire Preservation Group, Bournemouth
	G-VTOL	Hawker Siddeley Harrier T.52 ★	Brooklands Museum of Aviation/Weybridge
	G-VTOP	Boeing 747-4Q8	Virgin Atlantic Airways Ltd *Virginia Plain*
	G-VTUS	Schempp-Hirth Ventus 2cT	Ventus 02 Syndicate
	G-VTWO	Schempp-Hirth Ventus 2c	F. & B. Birlison
	G-VUEA	Cessna 550 Citation II	AD Aviation Ltd (G-BWOM)
	G-VUEM	Cessna 501 Citation I	Frandley Aviation Partnership LLP (G-FLVU)
	G-VUEZ	Cessna 550 Citation II	AD Aviation Ltd
	G-VULC	Avro 698 Vulcan B.2A (XM655) ★	Radarmoor Ltd/Wellesbourne
	G-VVBA	AS.355F2 Ecureuil II	Hinde Holdings Ltd (G-DBOK)
	G-VVBE	Robinson R22 Beta	Hinde Holdings Ltd (G-OTOY/G-BPEW)
	G-VVBF	Colt 315A balloon	Virgin Balloon Flights
	G-VVBK	PA-34-200T Seneca II	Ravenair Aircraft Ltd (G-BSBS/G-BDRI)
	G-VVBL	Robinson R44 II	Hinde Holdings Ltd
	G-VVBO	Bell 206L-3 LongRanger III	Hinde Holdings Ltd
	G-VVIP	Cessna 421C	My Sky Air Charter Ltd (G-BMWB)
	G-VVPA	Bombardier CL600-2B16	TAG Aviation (UK) Ltd
	G-VVTV	Diamond DA42 Twin Star	A. D. R. Northeast
	G-VVVV	Skyranger 912 (2)	J. Thomas
	G-VVWW	Enstrom 280C Shark	P. J. Odendaal
	G-VWEB	Airbus A.340-642	Virgin Atlantic Airways Ltd *Surfer Girl*
	G-VWIN	Airbus A.340-642	Virgin Atlantic Airways Ltd *Lady Luck*
	G-VWKD	Airbus A.340-642	Virgin Atlantic Airways Ltd *Miss Behavin'*
	G-VWOW	Boeing 747-41R	Virgin Atlantic Airways Ltd *Cosmic Girl*
	G-VXLG	Boeing 747-41R	Virgin Atlantic Airways Ltd *Ruby Tuesday*

Reg.	Type	Owner or Operator	Notes
G-VYOU	Airbus A.340-642	Virgin Atlantic Airways Ltd *Emmeline Heaney*	
G-VYPO	DH.115 Sea Vampire T.35 (N6-766)	N. Rose (G-SPDR)	
G-VZON	ATR-72-212A	Aurigny Air Services Ltd	
G-WAAN	MBB Bö.105DB	PLM Dollar Group Ltd (G-AZOR)	
G-WAAS	MBB Bö.105DBS-4	Bond Air Services Ltd (G-ESAM/G-BUIB/ G-BDYZ)	
G-WABB	Dassault Falcon 900EX	TAG Aviation (UK) Ltd	
G-WABH	Cessna 172S Skyhawk	Blackhawk Aviation Ltd	
G-WACB	Cessna F.152 II	Wycombe Air Centre Ltd	
G-WACE	Cessna F.152 II	Wycombe Air Centre Ltd	
G-WACF	Cessna 152 II	Wycombe Air Centre Ltd	
G-WACG	Cessna 152 II	Wycombe Air Centre Ltd	
G-WACH	Cessna FA.152 II	Wycombe Air Centre Ltd	
G-WACI	Beech 76 Duchess	Wycombe Air Centre Ltd	
G-WACJ	Beech 76 Duchess	Wycombe Air Centre Ltd	
G-WACL	Cessna F.172N	A. G. Arthur (G-BHGG)	
G-WACO	Waco UPF-7	R. F. L. Cuypers/Belgium	
G-WACT	Cessna F.152 II	Durham Tees Flight Training Ltd (G-BKFT)	
G-WACU	Cessna FA.152	Wycombe Air Centre Ltd (G-BJZU)	
G-WACW	Cessna 172P	Technical Power & Maintenance Ltd	
G-WACY	Cessna F.172P	Wycombe Air Centre Ltd	
G-WADI	PA-46-350P Malibu Mirage	Air Malibu AG/Liechtenstein	
G-WADS	Robinson R22 Beta	Whizzard Helicopters (G-NICO)	
G-WAGA	Wag-Aero Wagabond	B. Howells (G-BNJA)	
G-WAGG	Robinson R22 Beta II	N. J. Wagstaff Leasing	
G-WAGN	Stinson 108-3 Voyager	S. E. H. Ellcome	
G-WAGS	Robinson R44 II	Wagstaff Homes Ltd	
G-WAHL	QAC Quickie	A. A. A. Wahlberg	
G-WAIN	Cessna 550 Citation Bravo	Williams Aviation Ltd	
G-WAIR	PA-32-301 Saratoga	Finningley Aviation	
G-WAIT	Cameron V-77 balloon	C. P. Brown	
G-WAKE	Mainair Blade 912	J. E. Rourke	
G-WAKY	Cyclone AX2000	R. Knight & R. Hinton	
G-WALI	Robinson R44 II	Casdron Enterprises Ltd	
G-WALY	Maule MX-7-180	J. R. Colthurst	
G-WAMS	PA-28R-201 Arrow	Stapleford Flying Club Ltd	
G-WANT	Robinson R22 Beta	M. Lombardi	
G-WARA	PA-28-161 Warrior III	Aviation Rentals	
G-WARB	PA-28-161 Warrior III	OSF Ltd	
G-WARD	Taylor JT.1 Monoplane	R. P. J. Hunter	
G-WARE	PA-28-161 Warrior II	N. M. G. Pearson	
G-WARH	PA-28-161 Warrior III	KN Singles & Twins Aviation Consultants BV	
G-WARO	PA-28-161 Warrior III	T. G. D. Leasing Ltd	
G-WARP	Cessna 182F Sylane	R. D. Fowden (G-ASHB)	
G-WARR	PA-28-161 Warrior II	B. Huda	
G-WARS	PA-28-161 Warrior III	Blaneby Ltd	
G-WARU	PA-28-161 Warrior III	Smart People Don't Buy Ltd	
G-WARV	PA-28-161 Warrior III	Plane Talking Ltd	
G-WARW	PA-28-161 Warrior III	Lomac Aviators Ltd	
G-WARX	PA-28-161 Warrior III	C. M. A. Clark	
G-WARY	PA-28-161 Warrior III	Transport Command Ltd	
G-WARZ	PA-28-161 Warrior III	Target Aviation Ltd	
G-WASN	Eurocopter EC.135 T2+	Bond Air Services Ltd	
G-WASS	Eurocopter EC.135 T2+	Bond Air Services Ltd	
G-WATJ	Beech B200GT Super King Air	Saxonhenge Ltd	
G-WATR	Christen A1 Husky	S. N. Gregory	
G-WAVA	Robin HR.200/120B	Smart People Don't Buy Ltd	
G-WAVE	Grob G.109B	C. G. Wray	
G-WAVI	Robin HR.200/120B	Plane Talking Ltd (G-BZDG)	
G-WAVN	Robin HR.200/120B	Plane Talking Ltd (G-VECA)	
G-WAVS	PA-28-161 Warrior III	TGD Leasing Ltd (G-WARC)	
G-WAVT	Robin R.2160i	TGD Leasing Ltd (G-CBLG)	
G-WAVV	Robon HR200/120B	TGD Leasing Ltd (G-GORF)	
G-WAVY	Grob G.109B	G-WAVY Group	
G-WAWW	P & M Quik GT450	Oztubs Ltd	
G-WAYS	Lindstrand LBL-105A balloon	Lindstrand Hot Air Balloons Ltd	
G-WAZP	Skyranger 912 (2)	L. V. McClune	
G-WAZZ	Pitts S-1S Special	J. P. Taylor (G-BRRP)	
G-WBEV	Cameron N-77 balloon	T. J. & M. Turner (G-PVCU)	

Notes	Reg.	Type	Owner or Operator
	G-WBLY	Mainair Pegasus Quik	A. J. Lindsey
	G-WBTS	Falconar F-11	W. C. Brown (G-BDPL)
	G-WBVS	Diamond DA.4D Star	G. W. Beavis
	G-WCAO	Eurocopter EC 135T2	Avon & Somerset Constabulary & Gloucestershire Constabulary
	G-WCAT	Colt Flying Mitt SS balloon	Balloon Preservation Flying Group
	G-WCCI	Embraer RJ135BJ Legacy	Altarello Ltd (G-REUB)
	G-WCCP	Beech B200 Super King Air	William Cook Aviation Ltd
	G-WCEI	MS.894E Rallye 220GT	R. A. L. Lucas (G-BAOC)
	G-WCKD	Eurocopter EC130 B4	Eurocopter UK Ltd (G-CFWX)
	G-WCOM	Robinson R44	CDS Aviation Ltd
	G-WCRD	Aérospatiale SA.341G Gazelle	MW Helicopters Ltd
	G-WCUB	PA-18 Super Cub 150	P. A. Walley
	G-WCUP	Cameron Z-77 balloon	A. M. Holly
	G-WDEB	Thunder Ax-7-77 balloon	A. Heginbottom
	G-WDEV	Westland SA.341G Gazelle 1	MW Helicopters Ltd (G-IZEL/G-BBHW)
	G-WDGC	Rolladen-Schneider LS8-18	W. D. G. Chappel (G-CEWJ)
	G-WDKR	AS.355F1 Ecureuil 2	Cheshire Helicopters Ltd (G-NEXT/G-OMAV)
	G-WEAT	Robinson R44 II	C. B. M. Barratt
	G-WEBI	Hughes 369E	M. Webb
	G-WEBY	Ace Magic Cyclone	B. W. Webster
	G-WEBS	American Champion 7ECA Citabria	P. J. Webb
	G-WEED	Ace Magic Laser	R. D. Leigh
	G-WEEK	Skyranger 912(2)	D. J. Prothero
	G-WEFR	Alpi Pioneer 200-M	Cardiff Backpacker Caerdydd Ltd
	G-WEGO	Robinson R44 II	Helimove Ltd
	G-WELY	Agusta A109E Power	Titan Airways Ltd
	G-WENA	AS.355F2 Ecureuil II	Multiflight Ltd (G-CORR/G-MUFF/G-MOBI)
	G-WEND	PA-28RT-201 Arrow IV	Tayside Aviation Ltd
	G-WERY	SOCATA TB20 Trinidad	WERY Flying Group
	G-WESX	CFM Streak Shadow	M. Catania
	G-WETI	Cameron N-31 balloon	C. A. Butter & J. J. T. Cooke
	G-WFFW	PA-28-161 Warrior II	S. Letheren & D. Jelly
	G-WFLY	Mainair Pegasus Quik	D. E. Lord
	G-WFOX	Robinson R22 Beta II	Rotorfun Aviation
	G-WGCS	PA-18 Super Cub 95	S. C. Thompson
	G-WGHB	Canadair T-33AN Silver Star 3	Parkhouse Aviation
	G-WGSC	Pilatus PC-6/B2-H4 Turbo Porter	D. M. Penny
	G-WGSI	Tanarg/Ixess 13 912S(1)	J. A. Ganderton
	G-WHAL	QAC Quickie	A. A. M. Wahiberg
	G-WHAM	AS.350B3 Ecureuil	Horizon Helicopter Hire Ltd
	G-WHAT	Colt 77A balloon	M. A. Scholes
	G-WHEE	Pegasus Quantum 15-912	Airways Airsports Ltd
	G-WHEN	Tecnam P92-EM Echo	N. Harrison
	G-WHIM	Colt 77A balloon	D. L. Morgan
	G-WHOG	CFM Streak Shadow	B. R. Cannell
	G-WHOO	Rotorway Executive 162F	C. A. Saul
	G-WHRL	Schweizer 269C	M. Gardiner
	G-WHST	AS.350B2 Ecureuil	Keltruck Ltd (G-BWYA)
	G-WHYS	Savannah VG Jabiru(3)	D. J. Whysall
	G-WIBB	Jodel D.18	C. J. Bragg
	G-WIBS	CASA 1-131E Jungmann 2000	C. Willoughby
	G-WICH	Clutton FRED Srs II	L. A. Tomlinson
	G-WIEZ	Cameron C-80 balloon	M. B. Young
	G-WIFE	Cessna R.182 RG II	Wife 182 Group (G-BGVT)
	G-WIFI	Cameron Z-90 balloon	Trigger Concepts Ltd
	G-WIGY	Pitts S-1S Special	M. J. Wright (G-ITTI)
	G-WIII	Schempp-Hirth Ventus bT	P. Turner & B. Goodyer
	G-WIIZ	Augusta-Bell 206B JetRanger 2	Tiger Helicopters Ltd (G-DBHH/G-AWVO)
	G-WIKI	Europa XS	J. Greenhaigh
	G-WILB	Ultramagic M-105 balloon	A. S. Davidson, B. N. Trowbridge & W. C. Bailey
	G-WILD	Pitts S-1T Special	N. J. Wakefield
	G-WILG	PZL-104 Wilga 35	M. H. Bletsoe-Brown (G-AZYJ)
	G-WILT	Ikarus C.42 FB 100	A. E. Lacy-Hulbert
	G-WIMP	Colt 56A balloon	T. & B. Chamberlain

Reg.	Type	Owner or Operator	Notes
G-WINA	Cessna 560XL Citation XL	Inclination 1 LLP	
G-WINE	Thunder Ax7-77Z balloon ★	Balloon Preservation Group/Lancing	
G-WINH	EV-97 TeamEurostar UK	H. M. Wooldridge	
G-WINI	SA Bulldog Srs.120/121 (XX546:03)	A. Bole (G-CBCO)	
G-WINK	AA-5B Tiger	B. St. J. Cooke	
G-WINN	Stolp SA.300 Starduster Too	H. Feeney	
G-WINR	Robinson R22	Heli Air Ltd (G-BTHG)	
G-WINS	PA-32 Cherokee Six 300	Cheyenne Ltd	
G-WINT	Pilatus PC-12/47	Air Winton Ltd	
G-WIRL	Robinson R22 Beta	Rivermead Aviation Ltd/Switzerland	
G-WISE	PA-28-181 Archer III	M. Arnold	
G-WISZ	Steen Skybolt	G. S. Reid	
G-WIWI	Sikorsky S-76C	Air Harrods Ltd	
G-WIXI	Avions Mudry CAP-10B	A. R. Harris	
G-WIZA	Robinson R22 Beta	Patriot Aviation Ltd (G-PERL)	
G-WIZI	Enstrom 280FX	A. Gilligan & J. D. Beeson	
G-WIZR	Robinson R22 Beta II	Physio Supplies Ltd	
G-WIZS	Mainair Pegasus Quik	G. R. Barker	
G-WIZY	Robinson R22 Beta	P. P. McCullagh (G-BMWX)	
G-WIZZ	Agusta-Bell 206B JetRanger 2	Rivermead Aviation Ltd	
G-WJAC	Cameron TR-70 balloon	S. J. & J. A. Bellaby	
G-WJAN	Boeing 757-21K	Thomas Cook Airlines Ltd	
G-WJCJ	Eurocopter EC 155B1	Starspeed Ltd	
G-WJCM	CASA 1.131E Jungmann 2000 (S5+B06)	M. L. J. Goff (G-BSFB)	
G-WLAC	PA-18 Super Cub 150	White Waltham Airfield Ltd (G-HAHA/G-BSWE)	
G-WLDN	Robinson R44 Raven	Fly Executive Ltd	
G-WLGC	PA-28-181 Archer III	Sherburn Aero Club Ltd (G-FLUX)	
G-WLKI	Lindstrand LBL-105A balloon	C. Wilkinson	
G-WLLS	Rolladen-Schneider LS8-18	L & A Wells	
G-WLMS	Mainair Blade 912	L. W. Jones	
G-WLSN	Best Off Skyranger 912S (1)	A. Wilson & ptnrs	
G-WLVS	Dassault Falcon 2000EX	Trinity Aviation Ltd	
G-WMAS	Eurocopter EC 135T1	Bond Air Services Ltd	
G-WMLT	Cessna 182Q	P. J. Kloosterman (G-BOPG)	
G-WMTM	AA-5B Tiger	Falcon Flying Group	
G-WNAA	Agusta A109E Power	Sloane Helicopters Ltd (G-TVAC)	
G-WNCH	Beech B200 Super King Air	Winch Air Ltd (G-OMGI)	
G-WNTR	PA-28-161 Warrior II	Fleetlands Flying Group (G-BFNJ)	
G-WOCO	Waco YMF-5C	Classic Aviation Ltd	
G-WOFM	Agusta A109E Power	Quinnasette Ltd (G-NWRR)	
G-WOLF	PA-28 Cherokee 140	K. C. Fitch	
G-WONE	Schempp-Hirth Ventus 2cT	J. P. Wright	
G-WONN	Eurocopter EC135 T2	Bond Air Services Ltd	
G-WOOD	Beech 95-B55A Baron	M. S. Choskey (G-AYID)	
G-WOOF	Enstrom 480	Netcopter.co.uk Ltd & Curvature Ltd	
G-WOOL	Colt 77A balloon	Whacko Balloon Group	
G-WOOO	CZAW Sportcruiser	F. Sayyah & A. Palmer	
G-WORM	Thruster T.600N	Medway Airsports	
G-WOSY	MBB Bö.105DBS/4	Redwood Aviation Ltd (G-PASD/G-BNRS)	
G-WOTW	Ultramagic M-77 balloon	Window on the World Ltd	
G-WOWA	DHC.8-311 Dash Eight	Air Southwest Ltd (G-BRYS)	
G-WOWB	DHC.8-311 Dash Eight	Air Southwest Ltd (G-BRYT)	
G-WOWC	DHC.8-311 Dash Eight	Air Southwest Ltd (G-BRYO)	
G-WOWD	DHC.8-311 Dash Eight	Air Southwest Ltd	
G-WOWE	DHC.8-311 Dash Eight.	Air Southwest Ltd (G-BRYI)	
G-WOWI	Van's RV-7	P. J. Wood	
G-WPAS	MDH MD-900 Explorer	Police Aviation Services Ltd	
G-WRBI	Agusta A.109E Power	Fuel the Jet LLP (G-CRST)	
G-WREN	Pitts S-2A Special	Modi Aviation Ltd	
G-WRFM	Enstrom 280C-UK Shark	A. J. Clark (G-CTSI/G-BKIO)	
G-WRIT	Thunder Ax7-77A balloon	G. Pusey	
G-WRLY	Robinson R22 Beta	Burman Aviation Ltd (G-OFJS/G-BNXJ)	
G-WRSY	Enstrom 480B	Pristheath Ltd	
G-WRWR	Robinson R22 Beta II	MFH Helicopters Ltd	

Notes	Reg.	Type	Owner or Operator
	G-WSKY	Enstrom 280C-UK-2 Shark	B. J. Rutterford (G-BEEK)
	G-WSMW	Robinson R44	M. Wass (G-SGPL)
	G-WSSX	Ikarus C42 FB100	J. M. Crane & D. P. Toulson
	G-WTAV	Robinson R44 II	William Taylor Aviation Ltd
	G-WTEC	Cirrus SR22	B. J. White
	G-WTOR	Dassault Falcon 900EX	Executive Jet Charter Ltd
	G-WTWO	Aquila AT01	J. P. Wright
	G-WUFF	Shaw Europa	M. A. Barker
	G-WULF	WAR Focke-Wulf Fw.190 (8+)	S. Laver
	G-WVBF	Lindstrand LBL-210A balloon	Virgin Balloon Flights Ltd
	G-WVIP	Beech B.200 Super King Air	Capital Air Charter Ltd
	G-WWAL	PA-28R Cherokee Arrow 180	White Waltham Airfield Ltd (G-AZSH)
	G-WWAY	Piper PA-28-181 Archer II	R. A. Witchell
	G-WWBC	Airbus A.330-243	bmi british midland
	G-WWBD	Airbus A.330-243	bmi british midland
	G-WWBM	Airbus A.330-243	bmi british midland
	G-WWOW	Robinson R44 I	Capital Helicopters Ltd
	G-WWZZ	CZAW Sportcruiser	L. Hogan
	G-WYAT	CFM Streak Shadow Srs SA	K. D. MacCuish
	G-WYDE	Schleicher ASW-20BL	461 Syndicate
	G-WYKD	Tanarg/Ixess 15 912S(2)	D. C. Dewey
	G-WYND	Wittman W.8 Tailwind	R. S. Marriott
	G-WYNE	BAe 125 Srs 800B	Club 328 Ltd (G-CJAA/G-HCFR/G-SHEA/ G-BUWC)
	G-WYNT	Cameron N-56 balloon	S. L. G. Williams
	G-WYPA	MBB Bö.105DBS/4	Police Aviation Services Ltd
	G-WYSZ	Robin DR.400/100	R. S. M. Fendt (G-FTIM)
	G-WYVN	DG Flugzeugbau DG-1000S	Army Gliding Association
	G-WZOL	RL.5B LWS Sherwood Ranger	D. Lentell (G-MZOL)
	G-WZOY	Rans S.6-ES Coyote II	S. P. Read
	G-WZRD	Eurocopter EC 120B Colibri	Conductia Enterprises Ltd
	G-XAIM	Ultramagic H-31 balloon	G. Everett
	G-XALT	PA-38-112 Tomahawk	P. J. Crowther
	G-XALZ	Rans S6S-116 Super Six	A. F. & M. Stafford
	G-XARV	ARV Super 2	D. J. Burton (G-OPIG/G-BMSJ)
	G-XAVB	Cessna 510 Citation Mustang	Aviation Beauport Ltd
	G-XAVI	PA-28-161 Warrior II	J. R. Santamaria (G-SACZ)
	G-XAXA	BN-2A-26 Islander	Blue Island Air (G-LOTO/G-BDWG)
	G-XAYR	Raj Hamsa X'Air 582 (6)	P. Jordanou
	G-XBCI	Bell 206B JetRanger 3	BCI Helicopter Charters Ltd
	G-XBEL	Cessna 560XL Citation XLS	Aviation Beauport Ltd
	G-XBGA	Glaser-Dirks DG500/22 Elan	N. Kelly
	G-XBJT	Aerotechnik EV-97 Eurostar	B. J. Tyre (G-WHOA/G-DATH)
	G-XBLU	Cessna 680 Citation Sovereign	Datel Holdings Ltd
	G-XBOX	Bell 206B JetRanger 3	Mainstream Digital Ltd (G-OOHO/G-OCHC/ G-KLEE/G-SIZL/G-BOSW)
	G-XCBI	Schweizer 269C-1	B. Durkan
	G-XCCC	Extra EA.300/L	P. T. Fellows
	G-XCIT	Pioneer 300	A. Thomas
	G-XCRJ	Van's RV-9A	R. Jones
	G-XCUB	PA-18 Super Cub 150	M. C. Barraclough
	G-XDUO	Schempp-Hirth Duo Discus xT	G-XDUO Group
	G-XDWE	P & M Quik GT450	R. J. Harper
	G-XELA	Robinson R44 II	A. Yew
	G-XELL	Schleicher ASW-27-18E	S. R. Ell
	G-XENA	PA-28-161 Warrior II	P. Brewer
	G-XERO	CZAW Sportcruiser	M. R. Mosley
	G-XFLY	Lambert Mission M212-100	Lambert Aircraft Engineering BVBA
	G-XHOT	Cameron Z-105 balloon	S. F. Burden

Reg.	Type	Owner or Operator	Notes
G-XIII	Van's RV-7	Icarus Flying Group	
G-XIIX	Robinson R22 Beta ★	(Static exhibit)/Blackbushe	
G-XINE	PA-28-161 Warrior II	P. Tee (G-BPAC)	
G-XIOO	Raj Hamsa X'Air 133 (1)	M. Ridgway	
G-XIXI	Evektor EV-97 TeamEurostar UK	J. A. C. Cockfield	
G-XIXX	Glaser-Dirks DG-300 Elan	S. D. Black	
G-XJCB	Sikorsky S-76C	J. C. Bamford Excavators Ltd	
G-XJJM	P & M Pegasus Quik	Mainair Microlight Centre Ltd	
G-XJON	Schempp-Hirth Ventus 2b	J. C. Bastin	
G-XKKA	Diamond KH36 Super Dimona	G-XKKA Group	
G-XLAM	Best Off Skyranger 912S	X-LAM Skyranger Syndicate	
G-XLGB	Cessna 560XL Citation Excel	Tosh Air Ltd	
G-XLII	Schleicher ASW-27-18E	N. Hoare & G. Smith	
G-XLLL	AS.355F1 Twin Squirrel	MW Helicopters Ltd (G-PASF/G-SCHU)	
G-XLNT	Zenair CH.601XL	Zenair G-XLNT Group	
G-XLTG	Cessna 182S	D. H. Morgan	
G-XLXL	Robin DR.400/160	L. R. Marchant/Biggin Hill (G-BAUD)	
G-XMGO	Aeromot AMT-200S Super Ximango	G. McLean & R. P. Beck	
G-XMII	Eurocopter EC 135T1	Merseyside Police Authority	
G-XOAR	Schleicher ASW-27-18E	R. A. Browne	
G-XOIL	AS.355N Twin Squirrel	Firstearl Marine and Aviation Ltd (G-LOUN)	
G-XONE	Canadair CL600-2B16	Gama Aviation Ltd	
G-XPBI	Letov LK-2M Sluka	K. H. A. Negal	
G-XPDA	Cameron Z-120 balloon	ABC Flights Ltd	
G-XPII	Cessna R.172K	The Hawk Flying Group (G-DIVA)	
G-XPWW	Cameron TR-77 balloon	Chalmers Ballong Corps/Sweden	
G-XPXP	Aero Designs Pulsar XP	B. J. Edwards	
G-XRAF	X'Air 582(5)	D. J. Rooney	
G-XRAY	Rand-Robinson KR-2	R. S. Smith	
G-XRED	Pitts S-1C Special	J. E. Rands (G-SWUN/G-BSXH)	
G-XRLD	Cameron A-250 balloon	The Cotswold Balloon Co.Ltd	
G-XRVB	Van's RV-8	P. G. Winters	
G-XRVX	Van's RV-10	N. K. Lamping	
G-XRXR	Raj Hamsa X'Air 582 (1)	R. J. Philpotts	
G-XSAM	Van's RV-9A	D. G. Lucas	
G-XSDJ	Shaw Europa XS	D. N. Joyce	
G-XSEA	Van's RV-8	H. M. Darlington	
G-XSEL	Silence Twister	Skyview Systems Ltd	
G-XSFT	PA-23 Aztec 250F	Yager International SA/Spain (G-CPPC/G-BGBH)	
G-XSKY	Cameron N-77 balloon	Phoenix Ballooning	
G-XTEE	Edge XT912-B/Streak III	Airborne Australia UK	
G-XTEK	Robinson R44	Hields viation	
G-XTHT	Edge XT912-B/Streak III-B	H. A. Taylor	
G-XTNI	AirBorne XT912-B/Streak	A. J. Parry	
G-XTOR	BN-2A Mk III-2 Trislander	Aurigny Air Services Ltd (G-BAXD)	
G-XTPG	Edge XT912-B/Streak III-B	P. Greaves (G-XTNR)	
G-XTRA	Extra EA.230	Xtra Aerobatics Ltd	
G-XTUN	Westland-Bell 47G-3B1 (XT223)	P. A. Rogers (G-BGZK)	
G-XVOM	Van's RV-6	A. Baker-Munton	
G-XWEB	Best Off Skyranger 912 (2)	K. B. Woods	
G-XWON	Rolladen-Schneider LS8-18	P. K Carpenter	
G-XXBH	Agusta-Bell 206B JetRanger 3	Coln Aviation Ltd (G-BYBA/G-BHXV/G-OWJM)	
G-XXEB	Sikorsky S-76C	The Queen's Helicopter Flight	
G-XXIV	Agusta-Bell 206B JetRanger 3	Bart Fifty Nine Ltd	
G-XXIX	Schleicher ASW-27-18E	P. R. & A. H. Pentecost	
G-XXRG	Avid Speed Wing Mk.4	R. J. Grainger (G-BWLW)	
G-XXRS	Bombardier BD-700 Global Express	TAG Aviation (UK) Ltd	
G-XXRV	Van's RV-9	D. R. Gilbert & D. Slabbert	
G-XXTR	Extra EA.300/L	Shoreham Extra Group (G-ECCC)	
G-XXVB	Schempp-Hirth Ventus b	R. Johnson	

Notes	Reg.	Type	Owner or Operator
	G-XXVI	Sukhoi Su-26M	A. N. Onn
	G-XXZZ	Learjet 60	Gama Aviation Ltd
	G-XYAK	IDA Bacau Yakovlev Yak-52 (69 blue)	R. Davies
	G-XYJY	Best Off Skyranger 912 (2)	A. V. Francis
	G-XYZT	Aeromot AMT-200S Super Ximango	M. Zacharia & B. Chalabi
	G-XZXZ	Robinson R44 II	Ashley Martin Ltd
	G-YAAK	Yakovlev Yak-50	R. J. Luke (G-BWJT)
	G-YAAZ	Gulfstream 550	Ocean Sky (UK) Ltd
	G-YADA	Ikarus C42 FB100	Ikarus Flying Syndicate (Carlisle)
	G-YAKA	Yakovlev Yak-50	M. Chapman
	G-YAKB	Aerostar Yakovlev Yak-52	Kemble Air Services Ltd
	G-YAKC	Yakovlev Yak-52	T. J. Wilson
	G-YAKF	Aerostar Yakovlev Yak-52	B. Gwynett
	G-YAKH	IDA Bacau Yakovlev Yak-52	Plus 7 minus 5 Ltd
	G-YAKI	IDA Bacau Yakovlev Yak-52 (100 blue)	Yak One Ltd
	G-YAKK	Yakovlev Yak-50	A. P. Wilson
	G-YAKM	IDA Bacau Yakovlev Yak-50 (61 red)	Airborne Services Ltd
	G-YAKN	IDA Bacau Yakovlev Yak-52 (66 red)	Airborne Services Ltd
	G-YAKP	Yakovlev Yak-9	M. V. Rijkse & N. M. R. Richards
	G-YAKR	IDA Bacau Yakovlev Yak-52 (03 white)	G-YAKR Group
	G-YAKT	IDA Bacau Yakovlev Yak-52	G-YAKT Group
	G-YAKU	IDA Bacau Yakovlev Yak-50 (49 red)	D. J. Hopkinson (G-BXND)
	G-YAKV	IDA Bacau Yakovlev Yak-52 (31 grey)	P. D. Scandrett
	G-YAKX	IDA Bacau Yakovlev Yak-52 (27 red)	The X-Flyers Ltd
	G-YAKY	Aerostar Yakovlev Yak-52	W. T. Marriott
	G-YAKZ	IDA Bacau Yakovlev Yak-50 (33 red)	Airborne Services Ltd
	G-YANK	PA-28-181 Archer II	G-YANK Flying Group
	G-YARR	Mainair Rapier	D. Yarr
	G-YARV	ARV Super 2	A. M. Oliver (G-BMDO)
	G-YAWW	PA-28RT-201T Turbo Arrow IV	Barton Aviation Ltd
	G-YBAA	Cessna FR.172J	A. Evans
	G-YCII	LET Yakovlev C-11 (11 yellow)	R. W. Davies
	G-YCUB	PA-18 Super Cub 150	F. W. Rogers
	G-YCUE	Agusta A109A	Oldham Broadway Developments Ltd
	G-YEHA	Schleicher ASW-27	B. L. Cooper
	G-YELL	Murphy Rebel	A. H. Godfrey
	G-YELO	Rotorsport UK MT-03	M. Black
	G-YEOM	PA-31-350 Navajo Chieftain	Foster Yeoman Ltd/Exeter
	G-YEWS	Rotorway Executive 152	R. Turrell & P. Mason
	G-YFLY	VPM M-16 Tandem Trainer	A. J. Unwin (G-BWGI)
	G-YFUT	Yakovlev Yak-52	R. Oliver
	G-YFZT	Cessna 172S	AB Integro
	G-YIII	Cessna F.150L	Merlin Flying Club Ltd
	G-YIPI	Cessan FR.172K	A. J. G. Davis
	G-YIRO	Campbell Cricket Mk.4	R. Boese (G-KGED)
	G-YJET	Montgomerie-Bensen B.8MR	A. Shuttleworth (G-BMUH)
	G-YKCT	Aerostar Yakovlev Yak-52	G-YKCT Group
	G-YKSO	Yakovlev Yak-50	Classic Displays Ltd
	G-YKSS	Yakovlev Yak-55	I. D. Trask
	G-YKSZ	Aerostar Yakovlev Yak-52 (01 yellow)	Tzarina Group
	G-YKYK	Aerostar Yakovlev Yak-52	K. J. Pilling
	G-YLYB	Cameron N-105 balloon	Blackhorse Balloon Club
	G-YMBO	Robinson R22M Mariner	M. Roebuck
	G-YMFC	Waco YMF	S. J. Brenchley
	G-YMMA	Boeing 777-236ER	British Airways
	G-YMMB	Boeing 777-236ER	British Airways
	G-YMMC	Boeing 777-236ER	British Airways
	G-YMMD	Boeing 777-236ER	British Airways
	G-YMME	Boeing 777-236ER	British Airways
	G-YMMF	Boeing 777-236ER	British Airways

Reg.	Type	Owner or Operator	Notes
G-YMMG	Boeing 777-236ER	British Airways	
G-YMMH	Boeing 777-236ER	British Airways	
G-YMMI	Boeing 777-236ER	British Airways	
G-YMMJ	Boeing 777-236ER	British Airways	
G-YMMK	Boeing 777-236ER	British Airways	
G-YMML	Boeing 777-236ER	British Airways	
G-YMMN	Boeing 777-236ER	British Airways	
G-YMMO	Boeing 777-236ER	British Airways	
G-YMMP	Boeing 777-236ER	British Airways	
G-YMMR	Boeing 777-236ER	British Airways	
G-YMMS	Boeing 777-236ER	British Airways	
G-YMMT	Boeing 777-236ER	British Airways	
G-YMMU	Boeing 777-236ER	British Airways	
G-YNOT	D.62B Condor	T. Littlefair (G-AYFH)	
G-YNYS	Cessna 172S Skyhawk	T. V. Hughes	
G-YOBI	Schleicher ASH-25	J. Kangurs	
G-YODA	Schempp-Hirth Ventus 2cT	A. Charlier	
G-YOGI	Robin DR.400/140B	M. M. Pepper (G-BDME)	
G-YOLK	P & M Aviation Quik GT450	M. Austin	
G-YORK	Cessna F.172M	EIMH-Flying Group	
G-YOTS	IDA Bacau Yakovlev Yak-52	YOTS Group	
G-YOYO	Pitts S-1E Special	J. D. L. Richardson (G-OTSW/G-BLHE)	
G-YPDN	Rotorsport UK MT-03	T. M. Jones	
G-YPOL	MDH MD-900 Explorer	West Yorkshire Police Authority	
G-YPRS	Cessna 550 Citation Bravo	Executive Aviation Services Ltd (G-IPAC/G-IPAL)	
G-YPSY	Andreasson BA-4B	D. J. Howell	
G-YRAF	RAF 2000 GTX-SE gyroplane	J. R. Cooper	
G-YRIL	Luscombe 8E Silvaire	C. Potter	
G-YROA	Rotorsport UK MTO Sport	J. P. R. McLaren	
G-YROC	Rotorsport UK MT-03	C. V. Catherall	
G-YROH	Rotorsport UK MTO Sport	J. W. G. Andrews	
G-YROI	Air Command 532 Elite	W. B. Lumb	
G-YROJ	RAF 2000 GTX-SE gyroplane	J. R. Mercer	
G-YROM	Rotorsport UK MT-03	R. T. Reich	
G-YROO	RAF 2000 GTX-SE gyroplane	K. D. Rhodes & C. S. Oakes	
G-YROP	Magni M-16C Tandem Trainer	Magni Guernsey Flying Group	
G-YROR	Magni M.24C	B. D. Denton & R. M. Stanley	
G-YROX	Rotorsport UK MT-03	Surplus Art	
G-YROY	Montgomerie-Bensen B.8MR	S. S. Wilson	
G-YROZ	Rotorsport UK Calidus	P. Chaplin	
G-YRRO	AutoGyro Calidus	W. C. Walters	
G-YRUS	Jodel D.140E	W. E. Massam (G-YRNS)	
G-YSMO	Mainair Pegasus Quik	I. G. Harban	
G-YSTT	PA-32R-301 Saratoga II HP	A. W. Kendrick	
G-YUGE	Schempp-Hirth Ventus cT	E. P. Lambert (G-CFNN)	
G-YUGO	HS.125 Srs 1B/R-522 ★	Fire Section/Dunsfold (G-ATWH)	
G-YULL	PA-28 Cherokee 180E	ASG Leasing Ltd (G-BEAJ)	
G-YUMM	Cameron N-90 balloon	H. Stringer	
G-YUPI	Cameron N-90 balloon	MCVH SA/Belgium	
G-YURO	Shaw Europa ★	Yorkshire Air Museum/Elvington	
G-YVES	Alpi Pioneer 300	M. C. Birchall	
G-YYAK	Aerostar SA Yak-52	A. Bonnet	
G-YYRO	Magni M-16C Tandem Trainer	J. A. McGill	
G-YYYY	MH.1521C-1 Broussard	Aerosuperbatics Ltd	
G-YZYZ	Mainair Blade 912	P. G. Eastlake	
G-ZAAP	CZAW Sportcruiser	L. A. Seers	
G-ZAAZ	Van's RV-8	P. A. Soper	
G-ZABC	Sky 90-24 balloon	P. Donnelly	
G-ZACE	Cessna 172S	Sywell Aerodrome Ltd	
G-ZACH	Robin DR.400/100	A. P. Wellings (G-FTIO)	
G-ZADA	Best Off Skyranger 912S(1)	B. Bisley	
G-ZAIR	Zenair CH 601HD	J. R. Standring	
G-ZANG	PA-28 Cherokee 140	A. M. Khan	
G-ZANY	Diamond DA40D Star	Altair Aviation Ltd	

Notes	Reg.	Type	Owner or Operator
	G-ZAPH	Bell 206B JetRanger 3	WPD Helicopter Unit (G-DBMW)
	G-ZAPK	BAe 146-200QC	Titan Airways Ltd (G-BTIA/G-PRIN)
	G-ZAPN	BAe 146-200QC	Titan Airways Ltd (G-BPBT)
	G-ZAPO	BAe 146-200QC	Titan Airways Ltd (G-BWLG/G-PRCS)
	G-ZAPR	BAe 146-200F	Titan Airways Ltd (G-BOXE)
	G-ZAPV	Boeing 737-3Y0	Titan Airways Ltd (G-IGOC)
	G-ZAPW	Boeing 737-3L9	Titan Airways Ltd (G-BOZB/G-IGOX)
	G-ZAPX	Boeing 757-256	Titan Airways Ltd
	G-ZAPY	Robinson R22 Beta	Heli Air Ltd (G-INGB)
	G-ZAPZ	Boeing 737-33A	Titan Airways Ltd
	G-ZARI	AA-5B Tiger	ZARI Aviation Ltd (G-BHVY)
	G-ZARV	ARV Super 2	P. R. Snowden
	G-ZAVI	Ikarus C42 FB100	M. A. Curtis
	G-ZAZA	PA-18 Super Cub 95	G. J. Harry, The Viscount Goschen
	G-ZAZZ	Lindstrand LBL-120A balloon	Idea Balloon SAS Di Stefano Travaglia and Co./Italy
	G-ZBED	Robinson R22 Beta	P. D. Spinks
	G-ZBLT	Cessna 182S Skylane	Cessna 182S Group/Ireland
	G-ZBOP	PZL-Bielsko SZD-36A Cobra 15	S. Bruce
	G-ZEBO	Thunder Ax8-105 S2 balloon	S. M. Waterton
	G-ZEBY	PA-28 Cherokee 140	G. Gee (G-BFBF)
	G-ZECH	CZAW Sportcruiser	P. J. Reilly
	G-ZEIN	Slingsby T.67M Firefly 260	R. C. P. Brookhouse
	G-ZELE	Westland Gazelle HT.Mk.2	London Helicopter Centres Ltd (G-CBSA)
	G-ZENA	Zenair CH.701UL	A. N. Aston
	G-ZENI	Zenair CH.601HD Zodiac	P. P. Plumley
	G-ZENN	Schempp-Hirth Ventus 2cT	Z. Marczynski
	G-ZENR	Zenair CH.601HD Zodiac	H. Burroughs & A. J. S. Jones (G-BRJB)
	G-ZENY	Zenair CH.601HD Zodiac	T. R. & B. K. Pugh
	G-ZEPI	Colt GA-42 gas airship	P. A. Lindstrand (G-ISPY/G-BPRB)
	G-ZERO	AA-5B Tiger	Emery-Little Insurance Brokers Ltd
	G-ZETA	Lindstrand LBL-105A balloon	S. Travaglia/Italy
	G-ZEXL	Extra EA.300/L	2 Excel Aviation Ltd
	G-ZFOX	Denney Kitfox Mk.2	S. M. Hall
	G-ZGZG	Cessna 182T	J. Noble
	G-ZHKF	Escapade 912(1)	C. D. & C. M. Wills
	G-ZHWH	Rotorway Executive 162F	B. Alexander
	G-ZIGI	Robin DR.400/180	D. C. R. Writer
	G-ZIGY	Europa XS	K. D. Weston
	G-ZIII	Pitts S-2B	Nick Houghton Aerobatics (G-CDBH)
	G-ZINC	Cessna 182S	Zinc Ahead Ltd (G-VALI)
	G-ZING	Learjet 35A	Agrevia Holdings Ltd (G-ZENO/G-GAYL)
	G-ZINT	Cameron Z-77 balloon	D. Ricci
	G-ZIPA	Rockwell Commander 114A	Roissy Technical Services Ltd (G-BHRA)
	G-ZIPI	Robin DR.400/180	A. J. Cooper
	G-ZIPY	Wittman W.8 Tailwind	K. J. Nurcombe
	G-ZIRA	Z-1RA Stummelflitzer	D. H. Pattison
	G-ZITZ	AS.355F2 Twin Squirrel	Heli Aviation Ltd
	G-ZIZI	Cessna 525 CitationJet	Ortac Air Ltd
	G-ZIZZ	Agusta A.109 II	Fortis Property Investment LLP
	G-ZJET	Cessna 510 Citation Mustang	C. J. Reston
	G-ZLLE	Aérospatiale SA.341G Gazelle	MW Helicopters Ltd
	G-ZLOJ	Beech A36 Bonanza	W. D. Gray
	G-ZMAM	PA-28-181 Archer II	Z. Mahmood (G-BNPN)
	G-ZMED	Learjet 35A	Air Medical Fleet Ltd (G-JETL)
	G-ZODY	Zenair CH.601UL Zodiac	Sarum AX2000 Group
	G-ZOGT	Cirrus SR20	M. Banbury
	G-ZONX	Moulai Sonex	A. Carter
	G-ZOOG	Tecnam P2006T	Polarb Air Ltd
	G-ZOOL	Cessna FA.152	W. J. D. Tollett (G-BGXZ)
	G-ZOOS	Balony Kubicek BB20XR balloon	Balony Kubicek Spol Sro
	G-ZORO	Shaw Europa	N. T. Read

Reg.	Type	Owner or Operator	Notes
G-ZOSA	Champion 7GCAA	R. McQueen	
G-ZRZZ	Cirrus SR22	Computerised Training Systems Ltd	
G-ZSDB	PA-28-236 Dakota	Dakota Air Services LLP (G-BPCX)	
G-ZSIX	Schleicher ASW-27-18E	S. J. Riddington	
G-ZSKD	Cameron Z-90 balloon	M. J. Gunston	
G-ZSKY	Best Off Sky Ranger Swift 912S(1)	J. E. Lipinski	
G-ZTED	Shaw Europa	J. J. Kennedy	
G-ZTWO	Staaken Z-2 Flitzer	S. J. Randle	
G-ZUMI	Van's RV-8	S. E. Leach	
G-ZVIP	Beech 200 Super King Air	Capital Air Charter Ltd (G-SAXN/G-OMNH)	
G-ZVKO	Edge 360	P. J. Tomlinson	
G-ZWIP	Silence Twister	Zulu Glasstek Ltd (G-TWST)	
G-ZXCL	Extra EA.300/L	2 Excel Aviation Ltd	
G-ZXEL	Extra EA.300/L	2 Excel Aviation Ltd	
G-ZXZX	Learjet 45	Gama Aviation Ltd	
G-ZYAK	IDA Bacau Yakovlev YAK-52	J. A. H. Van Rossom	
G-ZZAC	Aerotechnik EV-97 Eurostar	S. A. Ivell	
G-ZZAJ	Schleicher ASH-26E	A.T. Johnstone	
G-ZZDG	Cirrus SR20 G2	Little Mouse Productions Ltd	
G-ZZEL	Westland Gazelle AH.1	Tregenna Castle Hotel Ltd	
G-ZZIJ	PA-28-180 Cherokee C	G-ZZIJ Group (G-AVGK)	
G-ZZLE	Westland Gazelle AH.2	Estates (UK) Management Ltd (G-CBSE)	
G-ZZMM	Enstrom 480B	Fly 7 Helicopters LLP (G-TOIL)	
G-ZZOE	Eurocopter EC 120B	J. F. H. James	
G-ZZOW	Medway Eclipse	A. G. Woodward	
G-ZZSA	Eurocopter EC.225LP Super Puma	Bristow Helicopters Ltd	
G-ZZSB	Eurocopter EC.225LP Super Puma	Bristow Helicopters Ltd	
G-ZZSC	Eurocopter EC.225LP Super Puma	Bristow Helicopters Ltd	
G-ZZSD	Eurocopter EC.225LP Super Puma	Bristow Helicopters Ltd	
G-ZZSE	Eurocopter EC.225LP Super Puma	Bristow Helicopters Ltd	
G-ZZSF	Eurocopter EC.225LP Super Puma	Bristow Helicopters Ltd	
G-ZZSG	Eurocopter EC.225LP Super Puma	Bristow Helicopters Ltd	
G-ZZSI	Eurocopter EC.225LP Super Puma	Bristow Helicopters Ltd (G-CGES)	
G-ZZTT	Schweizer 269C	M. V. Chadwick	
G-ZZXX	P & M Quik GT450	R. G. Street	
G-ZZZA	Boeing 777-236	British Airways	
G-ZZZB	Boeing 777-236	British Airways	
G-ZZZC	Boeing 777-236	British Airways	
G-ZZZS	Eurocopter EC.120B Colibri	R. E. S & D. Medway	

ISLE OF MAN REGISTER

Reg.	Type	Owner or Operator	Notes
M-AAAD	Bombardier CL600-2B16 Challenger	Gulf Wings (IOM) Ltd	
M-ABCD	Dassault Falcon 20F-5	Pan Gulf Aviation Ltd	
M-ABCM	Bombardier BD100-1A10 Challenger 300	Cameron Industries Inc	
M-ABCT	Gulfstream IV SP	Pillar Securitisation SARL	
M-ABCU	Bombardier CL600-2B16 Challenger	MeHoria Ltd	
M-ABDF	Boeing 757-23N	Flycraft II Ltd	
M-ABDG	Boeing 757-23N	Flycorp Ltd	
M-ABDH	Boeing 737-790	CIT Group Location (France) SAS	
M-ACPT	BAe. 125 Srs.1000	Remo Investments Ltd	
M-ACRO	Eurocopter AS.350B3 Ecureuil	F. Allani	
M-AFAJ	Dassault Falcon 900EX	Elan Finance Management SA	
M-AGER	Dassault Falcon 50	GEO Aviation Services Ltd	
M-AGGY	Cessna 550 Citation II	Maudib GmbH Deutschland	
M-AGIC	Cessna 680 Citation Sovereign	Trustair Ltd	
M-AIRS	Learjet 60	Maiton Air LLP	
M-AJDM	Cessna 525A Citationjet CJ2	Mazia Investments Ltd	
M-AJOR	Hawker 900XP	INEOS Aviation LLP	
M-AKAK	Embraer 135BJ Legacy	AAK Company	

Notes	Reg.	Type	Owner or Operator
	M-AKAR	Sikorsky S-76C	Starspeed Ltd
	M-AKVI	Bombardier BD100-1A10 Challenger 300	AK VI Ltd
	M-ALCB	Pilatus PC-12/47E	M. S. Bartlett
	M-ALII	Bombardier CL600-2B16 Challenger 604	Western Gulf Assets Ltd
	M-ALMA	Dassault Falcon 7X	Armad Ltd
	M-ALRV	Dassault Falcon 2000EX	Lodgings 2000 LP
	M-ALUN	BAe 125 Srs.700A	Briarwood Products Ltd
	M-AMAN	Pilatus PC-12	Pilatus PC-12 Centre UK Ltd
	M-AMND	Dassault Falcon 2000EX	Doha Capital Ltd
	M-ANGO	Bombardier CL600-2B16 Challenger	Waylawn Ltd
	M-ANSL	Cessna 560 Citation Encore	ITTUR AB
	M-ANTA	Bombardier CL600-2B190 Challenger 85	Tathra International Holdings Inc
	M-APWC	Learjet 60	Trans Aviation Ltd
	M-ARIE	Pilatus PC-12/47E	Guernsey PC-12 Ltd
	M-ARTY	Pilatus PC-12/47E	Creston (UK) Ltd
	M-ASRI	Bombardier BD700-1A10 Global Express	YYA Aviation Ltd
	M-ASRY	Cessna 525B Citationjet CJ3	YYA Aviation Ltd
	M-ATAK	Bombardier BD700-1A10 Global 5000	Greenway Investment Assets Ltd
	M-ATHS	Pilatus PC-12/47E	Altis Partners (Aviation) Ltd
	M-ATOS	Dassault Falcon 900EX	Banton Overseas Ltd
	M-AXIM	CessnaT.206H Turbo Stationair	C. D. B. Cope
	M-AZAG	BAe.125 Srs.800B	Mazag
	M-AZIZ	Boeing 737-505	Azizi Group Ltd
	M-BEST	Cessna 750 Citation X	Lanara Ltd
	M-BFLY	Bombardier BD100-1A10 Challenger 300	Litavio Consulting Ltd
	M-BIGG	Bombardier CL600-2B16 Challenger	Signal Aviation Ltd
	M-BONO	Cessna 172N Skyhawk II	J. McCandless
	M-BWFC	Cessna 560XL Citation XLS	Bakewell Industries Ltd
	M-CEXL	Cessna 560XL Citation Excel	D. Whelan
	M-CHEM	Dassault Falcon 200EX	INEOS Aviation LLP
	M-CHGK	Agusta A109S Grand	Helter Management Ltd
	M-CHLG	Bombardier CL600-1A11 Challenger	Albion Holdings Ltd
	M-CICO	Dassault Falcon 50	BZ Air Ltd
	M-CIRU	Cirrus SR20	Stamp Aviation Ltd
	M-CLAB	Bombardier BD100-1A10 Challenger 300	Shamrock Trading Ltd
	M-COOL	Cessna 510 Citation Mustang	E. Keats
	M-CRVS	Bombardier BD700-1A10 Global Express	Skydream Ltd
	M-DADI	Dassault Falcon 900DX	Rubicon Capital Consulting Co.Ltd
	M-DASO	Dassault Falcon 50	Bramptonia Ltd
	M-DBOY	Agusta A.109C	Herair Ltd
	M-DEJB	Dassault Falcon 200	Baron Aircraft Management SA
	M-DINO	Cessna 525 Citationjet CJ1	J. N. Bentley
	M-DSCL	Embraer 135BJ Legacy	Legacy Aviation Ltd
	M-EAGL	Dassault Falcon 900EX	Faycroft Finance
	M-EANS	Bombardier BD100-1A10 Challenger 300	YH Aviation Ltd
	M-EDOK	Bombardier BD100-1A10 Challenger 300	Jarvirne Ltd
	M-EGGA	Beech B200 Super King Air	Langley Aviation Ltd
	M-EIRE	Bombardier CL600-2B16 Challenger	Mercury Engineering Ltd
	M-ELON	Cessna 525B Citationjet CJ3	Sleepwell Aviation Ltd
	M-EMLI	Bombardier CL600-2B16 Challenger	A. J. Walter Aviation Ltd
	M-ERCI	Bombardier CL600-2B16 Challenger	J & S Holding Ltd
	M-ERIL	Pilatus PC-12/47E	Confidentia Aviation Ltd
	M-ERIT	Agusta-Westland AW139	Merit Engineering Ltd
	M-ERRY	Sikorsky S-76B	Trustair Ltd
	M-ESGR	Embraer ERJ135 Legacy	Hermes Executive Aviation Ltd
	M-ETIS	Boeing 727-2XB	Azer Management Ltd
	M-EXPL	Eurocopter AS.355N Ecureuil 2	Select Plant Hire Co.Ltd
	M-FAHD	Boeing 727-76	Prime Air Corporation
	M-FALC	Falcon 900EX	Noclaf Ltd
	M-FBVZ	Bombardier CL600-2B16 Challenger	Qaltin Enterprises Ltd
	M-FINK	BAe. 125 Srs.1000B	B. T. Fink
	M-FIVE	Beech B300 Super King Air 350	Larvotto LP
	M-FLYI	Beech B300 Super King Air 350	Avtrade Ltd

Reg.	Type	Owner or Operator	Notes
M-FMHG	Gulfstream IV SP	Future Aviation Ltd	
M-FOUR	Beech G36 Bonanza	Quadra Aviation LP	
M-FROG	Beech 390 Premier 1	White and Cope Aviation LLP	
M-FRZN	Hawker 850XP	Iceland Foods Ltd	
M-FUAD	Gulfstream 550	Future Pipe Aviation Ltd	
M-FZMH	Bombardier CL600-2B19 Global Express	AK VI Ltd	
M-GACB	Dassault Falcon 10	Valiant Aviation Ltd	
M-GAPA	Airbus A.320-212	GAIF II Ireland Nine Ltd	
M-GAPB	Airbus A.320-212	GAIF II Ireland Nine Ltd	
M-GBAL	Bombardier BD700-1A10 Global Express	Noclaf Ltd	
M-GENT	Bombardier CL600-2B16 Challenger 605	Genting Singapore Aviation	
M-GFOR	Gulfstream IV	Star Oriental International Ltd	
M-GLAS	Beec C90A King Air	Glasdon Group Ltd	
M-GLOB	Bombardier BD700-1A10 Global Express	Colvic Investment Holdings Ltd	
M-GLRS	Learjet 45	Bombardier Transportation GmbH	
M-GOLF	Cessna FR.182RG	P. R. Piggin & C. J. Harding	
M-GOLX	Dassault Falcon 2000EX	LX Aviation (SPL) Ltd	
M-GPIK	Dassault Falcon 50EX	Dassault Falcon Leasing Ltd	
M-GRAN	Bombardier BD700-1A11 Global 5000	Starflight Investments Ltd	
M-GSKY	Bombardier BD700-1A10 Global Express	Jerand Holdings Ltd	
M-GULF	Gulfsteam IV	Earth One Ltd	
M-GVSP	Gulfstream 550	Business Universe Ltd	
M-GYQM	Bombardier BD700-1A10 Global Express	Head Win Group Ltd	
M-GZOO	Gulfstream 200	Sentrus Overseas Ltd	
M-HAWK	Hawker 800XP	INEOS Aviation LLP	
M-HDAM	BAe 125 Srs.800B	ABG Air Ltd	
M-HELI	Eurocopter EC.155-B1	Flambards Ltd	
M-HNOY	Bombardier CL600-2B16 Challenger 605	Merhav Aviation LP	
M-HOIL	Learjet 60	Begal Air Ltd	
M-HOTB	Gulfstream V SP	Darwin Air Ltd	
M-HSNT	Bombardier BD100-1A10 Challenger 300	Unisky Ltd	
M-IABU	Airbus A.340-313	Klaret Aviation Ltd	
M-ICKY	Pilatus PC12/45	Saxon Logistics Ltd	
M-ICRO	Cessna 525A Citationjet CJ2	Pektron Group Ltd	
M-IDAS	Agusta A109E Power	Trustair Ltd	
M-IFES	Bombardier CL600-1A11 Challenger	Inflite Aviation (IOM) Ltd	
M-IFLY	Pilatus PC-12/47E	N. J. Vetch	
M-IGHT	Learjet 60	High Wing Aviation Ltd	
M-IGOR	Learjet 60	Condamine Enterprises Ltd	
M-IIII	Dassault Falcon 2000	Kredel International Ltd	
M-INOR	Hawker 900XP	INEOS Aviation LLP	
M-INXY	Embraer EMB-500 Phenom 100	Midland Aviation Ltd	
M-IPHS	Gulfstream 550	Islands Aviation Ltd	
M-IRNE	Hawker 850XP	R. N. Edmiston	
M-ISKY	Cessna 550 Citation Bravo	MYSKY LLP	
M-ISLA	Bombardier CL600-2B19 Challenger 850	Knightsdene Ltd	
M-ISLE	Cessna 680 Citation Sovereign	Bakewell Industries Ltd	
M-IVSP	Gulfstream IV SP	Travcorp Air Transportation Ltd	
M-JACK	Beech B200GT King Air	Jetstream Aviation Ltd	
M-JANP	Bombardier BD700-1A10 Global Express	Joannou and Paraskevaides (Aviation) Ltd	
M-JCPO	HS.125 Srs.700A	Saucar Ltd	
M-JETI	BAe 125 Srs 800B	Cassel Invest Ltd	
M-JETT	Dassault Falcon 200	Piraeus Leasing Chrimatodotikes Mishoseis SA	
M-JJTL	Pilatus PC-12/47E	L. Uggia, J. P. Huth & K. Giannamore	
M-JMMM	Dassault Falcon 900B	Executive Aviation (SPV) Ltd	
M-JNJL	Bombardier BD700-1A11 Global Express	Global Thirteen Worldwide Resources Ltd	
M-JOLY	Hawker 900XP	Rooksmead Capital Ltd	
M-JSMN	Bombardier BD700-1A11 Global 5000	Jasmin Aviation Ltd	
M-JSTA	Bombardier CL600-2B16 Challenger	Jetsteff Aviation Ltd	
M-KARN	Bombardier CL600-2B16 Challenger	Joannou and Paraskevaides (Aviation) Ltd	
M-KATE	Airbus A.319-133	Sophar Property Holding	

Notes	Reg.	Type	Owner or Operator
	M-KELY	Embraer EMB-500 Phenom 100	Kelly Air Ltd
	M-KENF	Hawker 4000 Horizon	Avalanche Aviation Ltd
	M-KICK	Embraer EMB-500 Phenom 100	M-KICK LP
	M-KPCO	Embraer EMB-135BJ Legacy	M-KPCO Holding Co.Ltd
	M-KRRR	Learjet 55	R. Rogner
	M-LCJP	Hawker 900XP	Yolenal Ltd
	M-LEKT	Robin DR.400/180	T. D. Allan, P. & J. P. Bromley
	M-LION	Hawker 900XP	Lion Invest and Trade Ltd
	M-LJGI	Dassault Falcon 2000Easy	Ven Air
	M-LNDN	Eurocopter EC155-B1	Larkford Ltd
	M-LRJT	Learjet 40	Chemiplastica Aviation Ltd
	M-LUNA	Eurocopter MBB BK-117C-2	Flambards Ltd
	M-LVIA	Eurocopter AS.365N3 Dauphin 2	Flambards Ltd
	M-MACH	Embraer EMB-500 Phenom 100	Mach Air Ltd
	M-MANX	Cessna 425 Conquest	Mastercraft Ltd
	M-MHDH	Cessna 510 Citation Mustang	Herrenknecht Aviation GmbH
	M-MHMH	Cessna 525B Citationjet CJ3	Herrenknecht Aviation GmbH
	M-MIKE	Cessna 525B Citationjet CJ3	M. F. Jacobson
	M-MMAS	Bombardier BD700-1A10 Global Express	Jana Aviation Ltd
	M-MNAA	Bombardier BD700-1A10 Global Express	JAPAT AG (Isle of Man)
	M-MNBB	Dassault Falcon 7X	JAPAT AG (Isle of Man)
	M-MNDD	Dassault Falcon 900EX	JAPAT AG (Isle of Man)
	M-MOMO	Gulfstream V SP	Fayair (Jersey) Co Ltd
	M-MRBB	Learjet 45	Boultbee Aviation 3 LLP
	M-MSGG	Gulfstream G200	ARTOC Prague
	M-NATH	Embraer EMB-135BJ	Pheebe Ltd
	M-NEWT	Bombardier BD100-1A10 Challenger	Stirling Aviation Properties LLP
	M-NGSN	Pilatus PC-12/47E	N. Stolt-Nielson
	M-NHOI	Bombardier CL600-2B16 Challenger	Hatta Investments Ltd
	M-NICO	Hawker 900XP	Asia Universal Jet Ltd
	M-NINE	Beech G58 Baron	Larvotto LP
	M-NLYY	PA-42-1000 Cheyenne 400LS	Factory Leasing Ltd
	M-NOEL	Bombardier BD100-1A10 Challenger	ABS Service Ltd
	M-NOLA	Bombardier CL600-2B16 Challenger	Nola Aviation Ltd
	M-NYJT	Bombardier BD100-1A10 Challenger	NY Jets Transporter Ltd
	M-ODKZ	Dassault Falcon 900EX	Skylane LP
	M-OGUL	Agusta A109S Grand	Medway Leasing Ltd
	M-OLEG	Embraer 135BJ Legacy	Hermitage Air Ltd
	M-OLLE	Hawker 750	Dunard Engineering Ltd
	M-OLTT	Pilatus PC-12/47E	One Luxury Travel LLP
	M-ONAV	Hawker 900XP	Monavia Ltd
	M-ONDE	Eurocopter MBB BK.117C2	Peyton Ltd
	M-ONEM	Gulfstream 550	G550 Ltd
	M-ONTI	Beech C90A King Air	Air Montgomery (Guernsey) Ltd
	M-ONTY	Sikorsky S-76C	Trustair Ltd
	M-OODY	Cessna 525B Citationjet CJ3	Futures Aviation Services Ltd
	M-OOSE	PA-46-500TP Malibu Meridian	Global Domain Names Ltd
	M-OOUN	Hawker 800XP	United Airgroup Corporation
	M-OPAL	Pilatus PC-12/47E	G-GYC Ltd
	M-OPED	PA-32-301XTC Saratoga	Hock Lai Cham
	M-OSPB	Gulfstream G200	G200 Ltd
	M-OTOR	Beech C90A King Air	Pektron Group Ltd
	M-OUSE	Cessna 510 Citation Mustang	Mouse (IOM) Ltd
	M-OZZA	Bombardier BD100-1A10 Challenger 300	Casam International Ltd
	M-PACF	Eurocopter EC135 P2+	Starspeed Ltd
	M-PARK	Cessna 525 CitationJet	Parkridge (Aviation) Ltd
	M-PBKI	Gulfstream IV SP	GIV-SP Air Service Ltd
	M-PHML	American General AG-5B Tiger	I. J. Ross & J. R. Shannon
	M-PRIT	Pilatus PC-12/47E	J. Pritchard
	M-PRVT	Cessna 750 Citation X	Unifox Holdings Ltd
	M-RACE	Hawker 850XP	First Aircraft Leasing Co.Ltd
	M-RBUS	Airbus A.319-115CJ	Belville Investment Ltd
	M-RCCG	Embraer EMB-135BJ Legacy 650	Russian Copper Co. Holdings Ltd
	M-RLIV	Bombardier CL600-2B16 Challenger	Mobyhold Ltd
	M-ROLL	Dassault Falcon 7X	Pacelli Beteiligungs GmbH and Co KG
	M-ROWL	Dassault Falcon 2000EX	M. Rowley
	M-RUAT	Bombardier BD700-1A10 Global Express	Vipjet Ltd
	M-RURU	Falcon 900B	Opus Nominees Ltd

Reg.	Type	Owner or Operator	Notes
M-SAIL	Pilatus PC-12/47E	G. G. & L. G. Gordon	
M-SAIR	Falcon 900B	W. A. Developments International Ltd	
M-SBAH	Embraer ERJ190ECJ Lineage 1000	National Lineage M-SBAH Holding Co.Ltd	
M-SCMG	Dassault Falcon 7X	BlueSky International Management Ltd	
M-SGCR	Cessna 550 Citation Bravo	Labraid Ltd	
M-SHEP	SOCATA TBM-850	L. W. & J. K. Shephard	
M-SKSM	Bombardier BD700-1A11 Global	Tesker Management Ltd	
M-SKZL	Bombardier CL600-2B16 Challenger	Kerzner Investment Management Ltd	
M-SMJJ	Cessna 414A	Gull Air Ltd	
M-SMKM	Cirrus SR20	K. Mallet	
M-SNAP	Cessna 560XL Citation XLS	AMS Ltd	
M-SPEC	Beech B350 Super King Air	Specsavers Aviation Ltd	
M-SPEX	Beech B350 Super King Air	Specsavers Aviation Ltd	
M-SPOR	Beech B200 King Air	Select Plant Hire Co.Ltd	
M-SRNE	Eurocopter MBB-BK.117C-2	Serena Aviation Ltd	
M-SSSV	Learjet 60XR	Distant Horizon Ltd	
M-STCO	Dassault Falcon F2000EX	STC (Bermuda) Ltd	
M-SUEC	PA-32-301XTC Saratoga	H. L. Chan	
M-SVGN	Cessna 680 Citation Sovereign	Vocalion Ltd	
M-SYGB	Beech B.200GT Super King Air	Rialus Ltd	
M-TAKE	Bombardier CL600-2B19 Challenger 850	Caropan Company SA	
M-TEAM	Cessna 525B Citationjet CJ1+	Mistral Aviation Ltd	
M-TKFR	Gulfstream V SP	Tele-Fonika Kable Sp	
M-TNTJ	Learjet 55	TNT Airways SA	
M-TOMS	Cessna 208B Grand Caravan	CJ Airways	
M-TOPI	Bombardier CL600-2B16 Challenger	Gladiator Flight Ltd	
M-TRIX	Bombardier CL600-2B16 Challenger	Universal Air Services Ltd	
M-TSGP	Cessna 525A Citationjet CJ2	Airjet Ltd	
M-TSRI	Beech C.90GT King Air	Timpson Ltd	
M-UKHA	Hawker 800XP	Nebula III Ltd	
M-UNIS	Bombardier BD700-1A10 Global Express	Lapwing Ltd	
M-UPCO	Cessna 525B CitationJet CJ3	Ulla Popken GmbH	
M-URKA	Sikorsky S-76B	Starspeed Ltd	
M-URUS	Boeing 737-7GC	Ingram Services Ltd	
M-USCA	SOCATA TBM-850	Sterna Aviation Ltd	
M-USHY	Cessna 441 Conquest	Flying Dogs Ltd	
M-USTG	Cessna 510 Citation Mustang	OSM Aviation Ltd	
M-VANG	Bombardier BD700-1A10 Global Express	Elderberry Ltd	
M-VBBQ	Beech 390 Premier 1A	Asia Universal Jet Ltd	
M-VBPO	Beech 390 Premier 1A	Asia Universal Jet Ltd	
M-VQBI	Bombardier BD700-1A10 Global Express	Altitude X3 Ltd	
M-VRNY	Gulfstream 550	Mirtos Ltd	
M-VSSK	Bombardier CL600-2B16 Challenger	Clear Horizon Ltd	
M-WBTA	Airbus A.321-211	M & C Corporate Services Ltd	
M-WHAT	Eurocopter EC.135T2+	Starspeed Ltd	
M-WING	Dassault Falcon 2000	Certico Engineering Ltd	
M-WLLM	Beech C.90GTI King Air	Wilpot Ltd	
M-WMWM	Cessna 525A Citationjet CJ2	Standard Aviation Ltd	
M-WOOD	Cessna 550 Citation Bravo	Horizon Air LLP	
M-XHEC	Eurocopter EC155B	Flambards Ltd	
M-YAAA	Bombardier BD700-1A10 Global Express	Glenn Eagles Research LLP	
M-YAIR	Hawker 390 Premier 1A	RB209 IOM Ltd	
M-YBBJ	Boeing 737-7HE BBJ	Hamilton Jets Ltd	
M-YBST	Bombardier CL600-2B16 Challenger	Kilmarnock Management Ltd	
M-YBUB	Pilatus PC-12/45	H. Nathanson	
M-YEDT	Gulfstream 100	Opal Consulting LLC	
M-YFLY	Bombardier BD100-1A10 Challenger 300	Apollo Traders Ltd	
M-YGIV	Gulfstream IV	Al-Sahab Ltd	
M-YGLK	Gulfstream 450	Overseas Operation Ltd	
M-YHOP	Agusta A109S Grand	Lemsage Ltd	
M-YJET	Dassault Falcon 2000Easy	My Jet Ltd	
M-YNJC	Embraer RJ135BJ Legacy	Newjetco (Europe) Ltd	
M-YNNS	Dassault Falcon 7X	NS Falcon Ltd	
M-YONE	Bombardier CL600-2B16 Challenger	Inflite Aviation (IOM) Ltd	
M-YRGL	Embraer ERJ-170-200LR	Celestial Aviation Trading 71 Ltd	
M-YRGN	Embraer ERJ-170-200LR	Celestial Aviation Trading 71 Ltd	

Notes	Reg.	Type	Owner or Operator
	M-YRGO	Embraer ERJ-170-200LR	ECC Leasing Co.Ltd
	M-YRGP	Embraer ERJ-170-200LR	ECC Leasing Co.Ltd
	M-YSAI	Bombardier BD700-1A10 Global 5000	Capital Investment Worldwide
	M-YSKY	Raytheon 390 Premier 1A	RB209 IOM Ltd
	M-YTOY	Embraer EMB-500 Phenom 100	TD Aviation IOM Ltd
	M-YWAY	Gulfstream IV SP	Blue Sky Leasing Ltd
	M-YUNI	Bombardier CL600-2B16 Challenger	Unitrans Management Ltd
	M-ZUMO	Pilatus PC-12/47	C. C. H. Way Ltd

G-AAOK Curtis Wright Travel Air. *Peter R March*

G-AAYX Southern Martlet. *Peter R March*

G-ADRA Pietenpol Air Camper. *Allan Wright*

G-APIE Tipsy Belfair B. *Peter R March*

G-AZOL Piper PA-34-200 Seneca II. *Allan Wright*

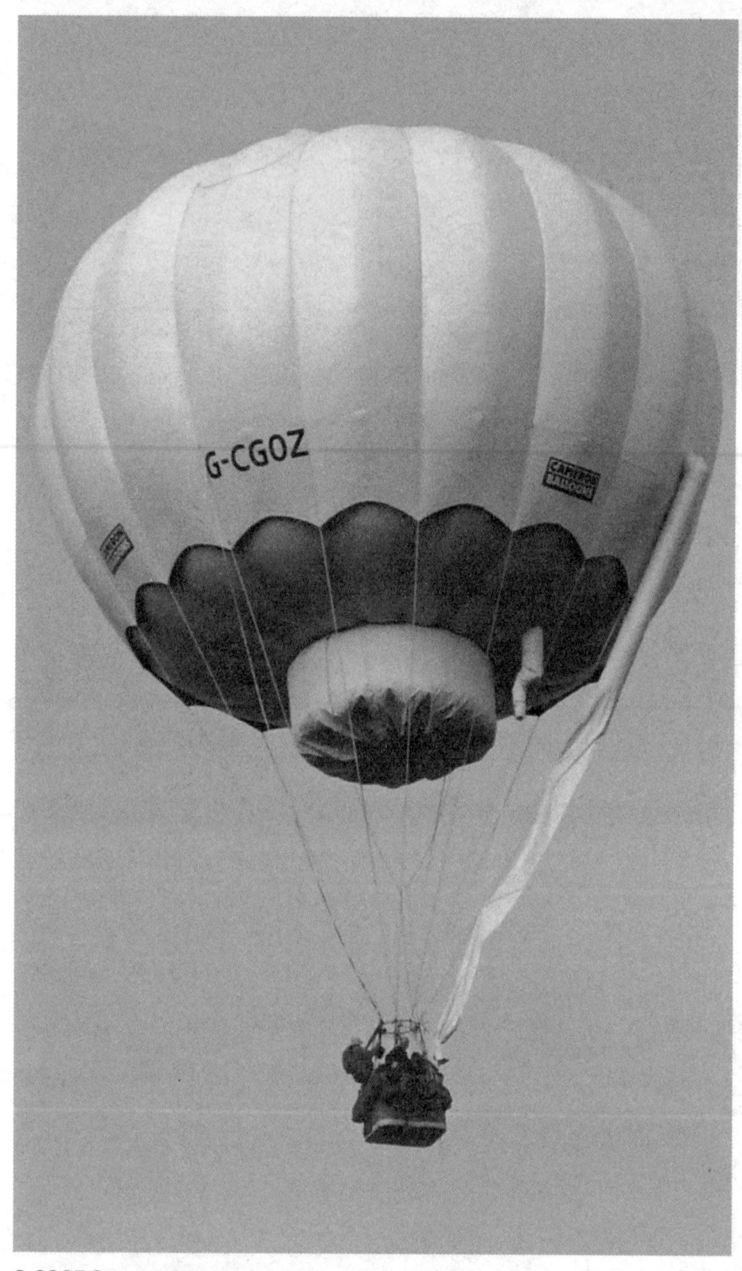

G-CGOZ Cameron GB 1000 Gas Balloon. *Peter R March*

G-BXTS Diamond Katana DA20. *Peter R March*

G-CITJ Cessna 525 Citationjet. *Allan Wright*

G-DIZI Escapade 912 (1). *Allan Wright*

G-EZTH Airbus A.320-214 of Easyjet. *Allan Wright*

G-FEDA Eurocopter EC120B. *Peter R March*

G-FZDG Boeing 737-8K5 of Thomsonfly. *Allan Wright*

G-HORK Pioneer 300 Hawk. *Allan Wright*

G-OPAZ Pazmany PL.2. *Peter R March*

G-RUBE Embraer EMB-135BJ Legacy. *Allan Wright*

G-IIDI Extra EA.300L. *Peter R March*

G-PSST Hunter F58A. *Peter R March*

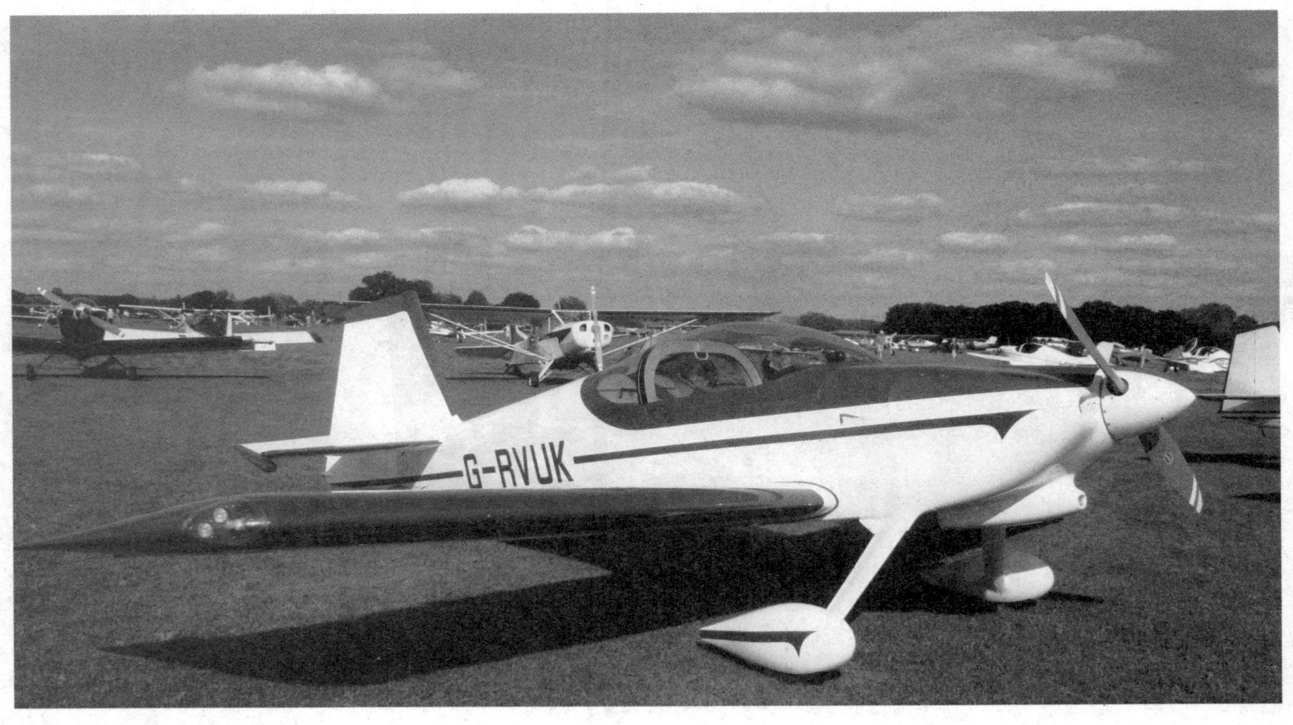

G-RVUK Van's RV-7. *Allan Wright*

G-TLAC Sherwood Ranger ST. *Allan Wright*

G-WOWC Dash 8- 311 of Air Southwest. *Peter R March*

G-ZOOG Tecnam P2006T. *Peter R March*

Military to Civil Cross-Reference

Serial carried	Civil identity
001	G-BYPY
1	G-BPVE
6G-ED (Luftwaffe)	G-BZOB
9 (Soviet AF)	G-OYAK
09 (DOSAAF)	G-BVMU
10 (DOSAAF)	G-BTZB
10 (DOSAAF)	G-CBMD
11 (Soviet AF)	G-YCII
26 (USAAC)	G-BAVO
26 (DOSAAF)	G-BVXK
27 (Soviet AF)	G-YAKX
27 (USN)	G-BRVG
27 (USAAC)	G-AGYY
27 (Soviet AF)	G-YAKX
42 (Soviet AF)	G-CBRU
43:SC (USAF)	G-AZSC
44 (DOSAAF)	G-BXAK
49 (USAAF)	G-KITT
50 (DOSAAF)	G-CBPM
50 (DOSAAF)	G-CBRW
50 (DOSAAF)	G-EYAK
52 (DOSAAF)	G-BWVR
55 (DOSAAF)	G-BVOK
67 (DOSAAF)	G-CBSL
68 (Chinese AF)	G-BVVG
69 (Russian AF)	G-XYAK
78 (French Army)	G-BIZK
82:8 (French AF)	G-CCVH
93 (DOSAAF)	G-JYAK
100 (DOSAAF)	G-YAKI
112 (USAAC)	G-BSWC
113 (Kuwait AF)	G-CFBK
118 (USAAC)	G-BSDS
124 (French Army)	G-BOSJ
143 (French AF)	G-MSAL
156 (French AF)	G-NIFE
157 (French AF)	G-AVEB
161 (Irish Air Corps)	G-CCCA
168 (RFC)	G-BFDE
174 (Royal Netherlands Navy)	G-BEPV
177 (Irish Air Corps)	G-BLIW
311 (Singapore AF)	G-MXPH
379 (USAAC)	G-ILLE
394 (French AF)	G-BIMO
422/15 (Luftwaffe)	G-AVJO
423 / 427 (Royal Norwegian AF)	G-AMRK
425 (Oman AF)	G-SOAF
441 (USN)	G-BTFG
450/17 (Luftwaffe)	G-BVGZ
503 (Hungarian AF)	G-BRAM
540 (USAAF)	G-BCNX
669 (USAAC)	G-CCXA
781-32 (Spanish AF)	G-BPDM
854 (USAAC)	G-BTBH
897:E (USN)	G-BJEV
99+26 (Luftwaffe)	G-BZGL
99+32 (Luftwaffe)	G-BZGK
1018 (Polish AF)	G-ISKA
1102:102 (USN)	G-AZLE
1104 (Royal Saudi AF)	G-SMAS
1125 (Kuwaiti AF)	G-CFBK
1130 (Royal Saudi AF)	G-VPER
1164:64 (USAAC)	G-BKGL
1211(North Korean AF)	G-MIGG
1342 (Soviet AF)	G-BTZD
1363 (Portuguese AF)	G-DHPM
1373 (Portuguese AF)	G-CBJG
1377 (Portuguese AF)	G-BARS
1747 (Portuguese AF)	G-BGPB
2345 (RFC)	G-ATVP
3066	G-AETA
3072:72 (USN)	G-TEXN
3349 (RCAF)	G-BYNF
3397:174 (USN)	G-OBEE
4034 (Luftwaffe)	G-CDTI
4406:12 (USN)	G-ONAF
4513:1 (French AF)	G-BFYO
5964 (RFC)	G-BFVH
6136:205 (USN)	G-BRUJ
7198/18 (Luftwaffe)	G-AANJ
7797 (USAAF)	G-BFAF
8178:FU-178 (USAF)	G-SABR
8449M (RAF)	G-ASWJ
9917	G-EBKY
01420 (Polish AF but in Korean colours)	G-BMZF
14863 (USAAF)	G-BGOR
16693:693 (RCAF)	G-BLPG
18013:013 (RCAF)	G-TRIC
18393:393 (RCAF)	G-BCYK
18671:671 (RCAF)	G-BNZC
20310:310 (RCAF)	G-BSBG
21261:261 (RCAF)	G-TBRD
21509 (US Army)	G-UHIH
24550 (US Army)	G-PDOG
24582 (US Army)	G-VDOG
28521:TA-521 (USAF)	G-TVIJ
30146 (Yugoslav Army)	G-BSXD
30149 (Yugoslav Army)	G-SOKO
31145:G-26 (USAAF)	G-BBLH
3-1923 (USAAF)	G-BRHP
31952 (USAAF)	G-BRPR
39624:D-39 (USAAF)	G-BVMH
40467:19 (USN)	G-BTCC
56321:U-AB (Royal Norwegian AF)	G-BKPY
80105 (US Air Service)	G-CCBN
80425:WT-4 (USN)	G-RUMT
93542:LTA-542 (USAF)	G-BRLV
111836:JZ-6 (USN)	G-TSIX
115042:TA-042 (USAF)	G-BGHU
115227 (USN)	G-BKRA
115302:TP (USMC)	G-BJTP
115373 (USAAF)	G-AYPM
115684 (USAAF)	G-BKVM
121714:201-B (USN)	G-RUMM
124485:DF-A (USAAF)	G-BEDF
126922:402-AK (USN)	G-RADR
150225:123 (USMC)	G-AWOX
18-2001 (USAAF)	G-BIZV
18-5395:CDG (French Army)	G-CUBJ
238410:A-44 (USAAF)	G-BHPK
314887 (USAAF)	G-AJPI
315509:W7-S (USAAF)	G-BHUB
329405:A-23 (USAAF)	G-BCOB
329417 (USAAF)	G-BDHK
329471:F-44 (USAAF)	G-BGXA
329601:D-44 (USAAF)	G-AXHR
329854:R-44 (USAAF)	G-BMKC
329934:B-72 (USAAF)	G-BCPH
330238:A-24 (USAAF)	G-LIVH
330485:C-44 (USAAF)	G-AJES
343251:27 (USAAC)	G-NZSS
413521:5Q-B (USAAF)	G-MRLL

Serial carried	Civil identity
413704: 87-H (USAAF)	G-BTCD
413926: E2-S (USAAF)	G-CGOI
414419:LH-F (USAAF)	G-MSTG
433915 (USAAF)	G-PBYA
436021 (USAAF)	G-BWEZ
454467:J-44 (USAAF)	G-BILI
454537:J-04 (USAAF)	G-BFDL
461748:Y (USAF)	G-BHDK
472035 (USAAF)	G-SIJJ
472216:HO-M (USAAF)	G-BIXL
472218:WZ-I (USAAF)	G-HAEC
474008:VF-R (USAAF)	G-PSIR
479744:M-49 (USAAF)	G-BGPD
479766:D-63 (USAAF)	G-BKHG
480015:M-44 (USAAF)	G-AKIB
480133:B-44 (USAAF)	G-BDCD
480173:57-H (USAAF)	G-RRSR
480321:H-44 (USAAF)	G-FRAN
480480:E-44 (USAAF)	G-BECN
480636:A-58 (USAAF)	G-AXHP
480723:E5-J (USAAF)	G-BFZB
480752:E-39 (USAAF)	G-BCXJ
493209 (US ANG)	G-DDMV
542447 (USAF)	G-SCUB
2632019 (Chinese AF)	G-BXZB
41-33275:CE (USAAF)	G-BICE
42-35870:129 (USN)	G-BWLJ
42-58678:IY (USAAF)	G-BRIY
42-78044 (USAAF)	G-BRXL
42-84555:EP-H (USAAF)	G-ELMH
43-35943 (USN)	G-BKRN
44-79609:44-S (USAAF)	G-BHXY
44-80594 (USAAF)	G-BEDJ
44-83184 (USAAF)	G-RGUS
51-7692 (French AF)	G-TROY
51-11701A:AF258 (USAF)	G-BSZC
51-15319 (USAAF)	G-FUZZ
54-2445 (USAF)	G-OTAN
A-10 (Swiss AF)	G-BECW
A16-199:SF-R (RAAF)	G-BEOX
A17-48 (RAAF)	G-BPHR
A-57 (Swiss AF)	G-BECT
A-806 (Swiss AF)	G-BTLL
A8226	G-BIDW
B595:W	G-BUOD
B1807	G-EAVX
B2458:R	G-BPOB
B6401	G-AWYY
C1904:Z	G-PFAP
C3009	G-BFWD
C3011:S	G-SWOT
C4918	G-BWJM
C4994	G-BLWM
C5430	G-CCXG
C9533:M	G-BUWE
D-692	G-BVAW
D5397/17 (Luftwaffe)	G-BFXL
D7889	G-AANM
D8084	G-ACAA
D8096:D	G-AEPH
E-15 (Royal Netherlands AF)	G-BIYU
E3B-143 (Spanish AF)	G-JUNG
E3B-153:781-75 (Spanish AF)	G-BPTS
E3B-350:05-97 (Spanish AF)	G-BHPL
E449	G-EBJE
E8894	G-CDLI
F141:G	G-SEVA
F235:B	G-BMDB
F904	G-EBIA
F938	G-EBIC
F943	G-BIHF
F943	G-BKDT
F5447:N	G-BKER
F5459:Y	G-INNY
F8010:Z	G-BDWJ
F8614	G-AWAU
G-48-1 (Class B)	G-ALSX
H5199	G-ADEV
J-1573 (Swiss AF)	G-VICI
J-1605 (Swiss AF)	G-BLID
J-1632 (Swiss AF)	G-VNOM
J-1758 (Swiss AF)	G-BLSD
J-4021 (Swiss AF)	G-HHAC
J-4083 (Swiss AF)	G-EGHH
J7326	G-EBQP
J9941:57	G-ABMR
K1786	G-AFTA
K1930	G-BKBB
K2048	G-BZNW
K2050	G-ASCM
K2059	G-PFAR
K2075	G-BEER
K2227	G-ABBB
K2567	G-MOTH
K2572	G-AOZH
K2585	G-ANKT
K2587	G-BJAP
K3241	G-AHSA
K3661	G-BURZ
K3731	G-RODI
K4259:71	G-ANMO
K5054	G-BRDV
K5414:XV	G-AENP
K5600	G-BVVI
K5673	G-BZAS
K5674	G-CBZP
K7985	G-AMRK
K8203	G-BTVE
K8303:D	G-BWWN
L2301	G-AIZG
L6906	G-AKKY
N-294 (RNeth AF)	G-KAXF
N500	G-BWRA
N1854	G-AIBE
N1977:8 (French AF)	G-BWMJ
N3200	G-CFGJ
N3788	G-AKPF
N4877:MK-V	G-AMDA
N5182	G-APUP
N5195	G-ABOX
N5199	G-BZND
N5719	G-CBHO
N5903:H	G-GLAD
N6-766 (Royal Australian Navy)	G-VYPO
N6290	G-BOCK
N6452	G-BIAU
N6466	G-ANKZ
N6537	G-AOHY
N6720:VX	G-BYTN
N6797	G-ANEH
N6847	G-APAL
N6965:FL-J	G-AJTW
N9191	G-ALND
N9192:RCO-N	G-DHZF
P2902:DX-X	G-ROBT
P6382:C	G-AJRS
P9374	G-MKIA
R-151 (RNethAF)	G-BIYR
R-163 (RNethAF)	G-BIRH
R-167 (RNethAF)	G-LION
R1914	G-AHUJ
R3821:UX-N	G-BPIV
R4118:UP-W	G-HUPW
R4922	G-APAO

MILITARY/CIVIL CROSS REFERENCE

Serial carried	Civil identity
R4959:59	G-ARAZ
R5136	G-APAP
R5172:FIJ-E	G-AOIS
R5250	G-AODT
S1287	G-BEYB
S1579:571	G-BBVO
S1581:573	G-BWWK
T5854	G-ANKK
T5879:RUC-W	G-AXBW
T6562	G-ANTE
T6953	G-ANNI
T7230	G-AFVE
T7281	G-ARTL
T7793	G-ANKV
T7794	G-ASPV
T7798	G-ANZT
T7842	G-AMTF
T7909	G-ANON
T8191	G-BWMK
T9707	G-AKKR
T9738	G-AKAT
T9768	G-AIUA
U-0247 (Class B identity)	G-AGOY
U-80 (Swiss AF)	G-BUKK
U-95 (Swiss AF)	G-BVGP
U-99 (Swiss AF)	G-AXMT
U-108 (Swiss AF)	G-BJAX
U-110 (Swiss AF)	G-PTWO
V-54 (Swiss AF)	G-BVSD
V3388	G-AHTW
V7497	G-HRLI
V9312	G-CCOM
V9367:MA-B	G-AZWT
V9673:MA-J	G-LIZY
W2718	G-RNLI
W5856:A2A	G-BMGC
W9385:YG-L	G-ADND
X4276	G-CDGU
Z2033:N/275	G-ASTL
Z5140:HA-C	G-HURI
Z5207	G-BYDL
Z5252:GO-B	G-BWHA
Z7015:7-L	G-BKTH
Z7197	G-AKZN
Z7288	G-AHGD
AB196	G-CCGH
AP506	G-ACWM
AP507:KX-P	G-ACWP
AR213:PR-D	G-AIST
AR501:NN-A	G-AWII
BB697	G-ADGT
BB807	G-ADWO
BE505:XP-L	G-HHII
BI-005 (RNethAF)	G-BUVN
BM597:JH-C	G-MKVB
CW-BG (Luftwaffe)	G-BXBD
DE208	G-AGYU
DE470	G-ANMY
DE623	G-ANFI
DE673	G-ADNZ
DE992	G-AXXV
DF112	G-ANRM
DF128:RCO-U	G-AOJJ
DF155	G-ANFV
DF198	G-BBRB
DG590	G-ADMW
EM720	G-AXAN
EN224	G-FXII
EP120:AE-A	G-LFVB
ES.1-4 (Spanish AF)	G-BUTX
FB226:MT-A	G-BDWM
FE695:94	G-BTXI

Serial carried	Civil identity
FE788	G-CTKL
FH153	G-BBHK
FJ777 (RCAF)	G-BIXN
FR886	G-BDMS
FS628	G-AIZE
FT391	G-AZBN
FX301:FD-NQ	G-TXAN
FZ626:YS-DH	G-AMPO
HB275	G-BKGM
HB751	G-BCBL
HD-75 (R Belgian AF)	G-AFDX
HG691	G-AIYR
HM580	G-ACUU
JF343:JW-P	G-CCZP
JV579:F	G-RUMW
KB889:NA-I	G-LANC
KD345:130-A	G-FGID
KF584:RAI-X	G-RAIX
KF729	G-BJST
KG651	G-AMHJ
KK116	G-AMPY
KN353	G-AMYJ
LB264	G-AIXA
LB294	G-AHWJ
LB312	G-AHXE
LB323	G-AHSD
LB367	G-AHGZ
LB375	G-AHGW
LF858	G-BLUZ
LZ766	G-ALCK
MB293	G-CFGI
MH434:ZD-B	G-ASJV
MJ627:9G-P	G-BMSB
ML407:OU-V	G-LFIX
MP425	G-AITB
MS824 (French AF)	G-AWBU
MT197	G-ANHS
MT438	G-AREI
MT818	G-AIDN
MV268:JE-J	G-SPIT
MW401	G-PEST
MW763:HF-A	G-TEMT
NJ633	G-AKXP
NJ673	G-AOCR
NJ695	G-AJXV
NJ719	G-ANFU
NJ889	G-AHLK
NL750	G-AOBH
NL985	G-BWIK
NM181	G-AZGZ
NX534	G-BUDL
NX611:LE-C/DX-C	G-ASXX
PL965:R	G-MKXI
PL983	G-PRXI
PS853:C	G-RRGN
PT462:SW-A	G-CTIX
PT879	G-BYDE
RG333	G-AIEK
RG333	G-AKEZ
RH377	G-ALAH
RL962	G-AHED
RM221	G-ANXR
RN218:N	G-BBJI
RR232	G-BRSF
RT486:PF-A	G-AJGJ
RT520	G-ALYB
RT610	G-AKWS
RX168	G-BWEM
SM520:KJ-1	G-ILDA
SM969:D-A	G-BRAF
SX336:105-VL	G-KASX
TA634:8K-K	G-AWJV

Serial carried	Civil identity
TA719:6T	G-ASKC
TA805:FX-M	G-PMNF
TD248:CR-S	G-OXVI
TE184:D	G-MXVI
TE517	G-JGCA
TJ534	G-AKSY
TJ569	G-AKOW
TJ652	G-AMVD
TJ672:TS-D	G-ANIJ
TJ704:JA	G-ASCD
TS798	G-AGNV
TW439	G-ANRP
TW467	G-ANIE
TW511	G-APAF
TW536:TS-V	G-BNGE
TW591:N	G-ARIH
TW641	G-ATDN
TX213	G-AWRS
TX310	G-AIDL
VF512:PF-M	G-ARRX
VF516	G-ASMZ
VF526:T	G-ARXU
VF581	G-ARSL
VL348	G-AVVO
VL349	G-AWSA
VM360	G-APHV
VN799	G-CDSX
VP955	G-DVON
VP981	G-DHDV
VR192	G-APIT
VR249:FA-EL	G-APIY
VR259:M	G-APJB
VS356	G-AOLU
VS610:K-L	G-AOKL
VS623	G-AOKZ
VV612	G-VENI
VX113	G-ARNO
VX118	G-ASNB
VX147	G-AVIL
VX281	G-RNHF
VX927	G-ASYG
VZ638:HF	G-JETM
VZ728	G-AGOS
WA576	G-ALSS
WA577	G-ALST
WA591:W	G-BWMF
WB565:X	G-PVET
WB569:R	G-BYSJ
WB571:34	G-AOSF
WB585:M	G-AOSY
WB588:D	G-AOTD
WB615:E	G-BXIA
WB652:V	G-CHPY
WB654:U	G-BXGO
WB671:910	G-BWTG
WB697:95	G-BXCT
WB702	G-AOFE
WB703	G-ARMC
WB711	G-APPM
WB726:E	G-AOSK
WB763:14	G-BBMR
WD286	G-BBND
WD292	G-BCRX
WD305	G-ARGG
WD310:B	G-BWUN
WD327	G-ATVF
WD331:J	G-BXDH
WD363:5	G-BCIH
WD373:12	G-BXDI
WD379:K	G-APLO
WD390:68	G-BWNK
WD413	G-VROE

Serial carried	Civil identity
WE569	G-ASAJ
WE724:062	G-BUCM
WF118	G-DACA
WF877	G-BPOA
WG308:8	G-BYHL
WG316	G-BCAH
WG321:G	G-DHCC
WG348	G-BBMV
WG350	G-BPAL
WG407:67	G-BWMX
WG422:16	G-BFAX
WG465	G-BCEY
WG469:72	G-BWJY
WG472	G-AOTY
WG719	G-BRMA
WJ358	G-ARYD
WJ368	G-ASZX
WJ945:21	G-BEDV
WK163	G-BVWC
WK436	G-VENM
WK512:A	G-BXIM
WK514	G-BBMO
WK517	G-ULAS
WK522	G-BCOU
WK549	G-BTWF
WK577	G-BCYM
WK585	G-BZGA
WK586:V	G-BXGX
WK590:69	G-BWVZ
WK609:93	G-BXDN
WK611	G-ARWB
WK624	G-BWHI
WK628	G-BBMW
WK630	G-BXDG
WK633:A	G-BXEC
WK640:C	G-BWUV
WK642:94	G BXDP
WL626:P	G-BHDD
WM167	G-LOSM
WP308:572CU	G-GACA
WP321	G-BRFC
WP788	G-BCHL
WP790:T	G-BBNC
WP795:901	G-BVZZ
WP800:2	G-BCXN
WP803	G-HAPY
WP805:D	G-MAJR
WP808	G-BDEU
WP809:78 RN	G-BVTX
WP840:9	G-BXDM
WP857:24	G-BDRJ
WP859:E	G-BXCP
WP860:6	G-BXDA
WP896	G-BWVY
WP901:B	G-BWNT
WP903	G-BCGC
WP925:C	G-BXHA
WP928:D	G-BXGM
WP929:F	G-BXCV
WP930:J	G-BXHF
WP970:12	G-BCOI
WP971	G-ATHD
WP983:B	G-BXNN
WP984:H	G-BWTO
WR360:K	G-DHSS
WR410:N	G-BLKA
WR410	G-DHUU
WR421	G-DHTT
WR470	G-DHVM
WT333	G-BVXC
WT722:878/VL	G-BWGN
WT933	G-ALSW

Serial carried	Civil identity
WV198:K	G-BJWY
WV256	G-BZPC
WV318:D	G-FFOX
WV322:Y	G-BZSE
WV372:R	G-BXFI
WV493:29	G-BDYG
WV740	G-BNPH
WV783	G-ALSP
WW453:W-S	G-TMKI
WZ507:74	G-VTII
WZ662	G-BKVK
WZ711	G-AVHT
WZ847:F	G-CPMK
WZ868:H	G-ARMF
WZ872:E	G-BZGB
WZ879	G-BWUT
WZ882:K	G-BXGP
XA880	G-BVXR
XD693:Z-Q	G-AOBU
XE489	G-JETH
XE601	G-ETPS
XE665:876/VL	G-BWGM
XE685:861/VL	G-GAII
XE689:864/VL	G-BWGK
XE856	G-DUSK
XE956	G-OBLN
XF114	G-SWIF
XF300	G-BZPB
XF597:AH	G-BKFW
XF603	G-KAPW
XF690	G-MOOS
XF785	G-ALBN
XF836:J-G	G-AWRY
XG160:U	G-BWAF
XG164:A	G-PRII
XG452	G-BRMB
XH134	G-OMHD
XH558	G-VLCN
XJ389	G-AJJP
XJ398	G-BDBZ
XJ615	G-BWGL
XJ729	G-BVGE
XJ771	G-HELV
XK417	G-AVXY
XK895:19/CU	G-SDEV
XK896	G-RNAS
XK940:911	G-AYXT
XL426	G-VJET
XL500	G-KAEW
XL502	G-BMYP
XL571:V	G-HNTR
XL573	G-BVGH
XL577:V	G-BXKF
XL587	G-HPUX
XL602	G-BWFT
XL621	G-BNCX
XL714	G-AOGR
XL716	G-AOIL
XL809	G-BLIX
XL929	G-BNPU
XL954	G-BXES
XM223:J	G-BWWC
XM370:10	G-BVSP
XM424	G-BWDS
XM479:54	G-BVEZ
XM553	G-AWSV
XM575	G-BLMC
XM655	G-VULC
XM685:513/PO	G-AYZJ
XM819	G-APXW
XN351	G-BKSC
XN437	G-AXWA

Serial carried	Civil identity
XN441	G-BGKT
XN459:N	G-BWOT
XN498	G-BWSH
XN637:03	G-BKOU
XP242	G-BUCI
XP254	G-ASCC
XP279	G-BWKK
XP282	G-BGTC
XP355	G-BEBC
XP907	G-SROE
XP924	G-CVIX
XR240	G-BDFH
XR241	G-AXRR
XR246	G-AZBU
XR486	G-RWWW
XR502:Z	G-CCUP
XR537:T	G-NATY
XR538:01	G-RORI
XR595:M	G-BWHU
XR673:L	G-BXLO
XR724	G-BTSY
XR944	G-ATTB
XR991	G-MOUR
XS111	G-TIMM
XS165:37	G-ASAZ
XS235	G-CPDA
XS587	G-VIXN
XS765	G-BSET
XT223	G-XTUN
XT420:606	G-CBUI
XT435:430	G-RIMM
XT634	G-BYRX
XT671	G-BYRC
XT787	G-KAXT
XT788:316	G-BMIR
XT793:456	G-BZPP
XV130:R	G-BWJW
XV134:P	G-BWLX
XV137	G-CRUM
XV268	G-BVER
XW289:73	G-JPVA
XW293:Z	G-BWCS
XW310	G-BWGS
XW324:K	G-BWSG
XW325:E	G-BWGF
XW333:79	G-BVTC
XW354	G-JPTV
XW422:3	G-BWEB
XW423:14	G-BWUW
XW433	G-JPRO
XW613	G-BXRS
XW635	G-AWSW
XW784:VL	G-BBRN
XW853	G-SWWM
XW854:46/CU	G-TIZZ
XW858:C	G-DMSS
XW866:E	G-BXTH
XX406:P	G-CBSH
XX432	G-CDNO
XX467:86	G-TVII
XX513:10	G-CCMI
XX514	G-BWIB
XX515:4	G-CBBC
XX518:S	G-UDOG
XX521:H	G-CBEH
XX522:06	G-DAWG
XX524:04	G-DDOG
XX525:8	G-CBJJ
XX528:D	G-BZON
XX534:B	G-EDAV
XX537:C	G-CBCB
XX538:O	G-TDOG

Serial carried	Civil identity
XX543:F	G-CBAB
XX546:03	G-WINI
XX549:6	G-CBID
XX550:Z	G-CBBL
XX551:E	G-BZDP
XX554	G-BZMD
XX561:7	G-BZEP
XX611:7	G-CBDK
XX612:A, 03	G-BZXC
XX614:V	G-GGRR
XX619:T	G-CBBW
XX621:H	G-CBEF
XX622:B	G-CBGZ
XX624:E	G-KDOG
XX626:02, W	G-CDVV
XX628:9	G-CBFU
XX629:V	G-BZXZ
XX630:5	G-SIJW
XX631:W	G-BZXS
XX636:Y	G-CBFP
XX638	G-DOGG
XX658:07	G-BZPS
XX667:16	G-BZFN
XX668:1	G-CBAN
XX692:A	G-BZMH
XX693:07	G-BZML
XX694:E	G-CBBS
XX695:3	G-CBBT
XX698:9	G-BZME
XX699:F	G-CBCV
XX700:17	G-CBEK
XX702:P	G-CBCR
XX704	G-BCUV
XX707:4	G-CBDS
XX885	G-HHAA

Serial carried	Civil identity
XZ239	G-BZYD
XZ934:U	G-CBSI
XZ937:Y	G-CBKA
ZA250	G-VTOL
ZA634:C	G-BUHA
ZA652	G-BUDC
ZA730	G-FUKM
ZB500	G-LYNX
ZB627:A	G-CBSK
ZB646:59/CU	G-CBGZ
2+1:7334 Luftwaffe)	G-SYFW
3+ (Luftwaffe)	G-BAYV
4+ (Luftwaffe)	G-BSLX
4-97/MM52801 (Italian)	G-BBII
07 (Russian AF)	G-BMJY
8+ (Luftwaffe)	G-WULF
F+IS (Luftwaffe)	G-BIRW
BU+CC (Luftwaffe)	G-BUCC
BU+CK (Luftwaffe)	G-BUCK
CF+HF (Luftwaffe)	EI-AUY
DM+BK (Luftwaffe)	G-BPHZ
GM+AI (Luftwaffe)	G-SCTH
LG+01 (Luftwaffe)	G-AYSJ
LG+03 (Luftwaffe)	G-AEZX
KG+EM (Luftwaffe)	G-ETME
NJ+C11 (Luftwaffe)	G-ATBG
S4+A07 (Luftwaffe)	G-BWHP
S5+B06 (Luftwaffe)	G-WJCM
6J+PR (Luftwaffe)	G-AWHB
57-H (USAAC)	G-AKAZ
97+04 (Luftwaffe)	G-APVF
+14 (Luftwaffe)	G-BSMD
146-11083 (5)	
G-BNAI	

G-SABR F86A Sabre. *Peter R March*

Republic of Ireland Civil Registrations

Reg.	Type (†False registration)	Owner or Operator	Notes
EI-ABI	DH.84 Dragon	Aer Lingus Iolar (EI-AFK)	
EI-ADV	PA-12 Super Cruiser	R. E. Levis	
EI-AED	Cessna 120	E. McNeill & P. O'Reilly	
EI-AEE	Auster 3/1 Autocrat	B. J. Hogan	
EI-AFE	Piper J3C-65 Cub	4 of Cubs Flying Group	
EI-AFF	B.A. Swallow 2	J. J. Sullivan & ptnrs	
EI-AGD	Taylorcraft Plus D	B. & K. O'Sullivan	
EI-AGJ	Auster J/1 Autocrat	T. G. Rafter	
EI-AHI	DH.82A Tiger Moth	High Fidelity Flyers	
EI-AKM	Piper J-3C-65 Cub	J. A. Kent	
EI-ALH	Taylorcraft Plus D	N. Reilly	
EI-ALP	Avro 643 Cadet	J.C. O'Loughlin (stored)	
EI-AMK	Auster J/1 Autocrat	J. J. Sullivan	
EI-AMY	Auster J/1N Alpha	T. Lennon	
EI-ANT	Champion 7ECA Citabria	T. Croke & ptnrs	
EI-ANY	PA-18 Super Cub 95	Bogavia Group	
EI-AOB	PA-28 Cherokee 140	Knock Flying Group	
EI-AOS	Cessna 310B	Southair	
EI-APS	Schleicher ASK.14	E. Shiel & ptnrs	
EI-ARH	Currie Wot/S.E.5 Replica	L. Garrison	
EI-ARM	Currie Wot/S.E.5 Replica	L. Garrison	
EI-ARW	Jodel D.R.1050	J. Davy	
EI-ASR	McCandless Gyroplane Mk 4	J. J. Fasenfeld	
EI-AST	Cessna F.150H	Ormond Flying Club	
EI-ATJ	B.121 Pup Srs 2	L. O'Leary	
EI-ATK	PA-28 Cherokee 140	Mayo Flying Club	
EI-ATL	Aeronca 7AC Champion	Kildare Flying Club	
EI-ATS	MS.880B Rallye Club	ATS Group	
EI-AUG	MS.894 Rallye Minerva 220	K. O'Leary	
EI-AUM	Auster J/1 Autocrat	T. G. Rafter	
EI-AUO	Cessna FA.150K Aerobat	S. Burke & L. Bagnell	
EI-AUS	Auster J/5F Aiglet Trainer	T. Stevens & ptnrs	
EI-AUT	Forney F-1A Aircoupe	Southair	
EI-AUY	Morane-Saulnier MS.502 (CF+HF)	Historical Aircraft Preservation Group	
EI-AVB	Aeronca 7AC Champion	T. Brett	
EI-AVM	Cessna F.150L	Tojo Air Leasing	
EI-AWD	PA-22 Tri-Pacer 160	J. P. Montcalm	
EI-AWH	Cessna 210J	Rathcoole Flying Club	
EI-AWP	DH.82A Tiger Moth	A. P. Bruton	
EI-AWR	Malmö MFI-9 Junior	A. Szorfy	
EI-AYB	GY-80 Horizon 180	J. B. Smith	
EI-AYD	AA-5 Traveler	V. O'Rourke & ptnrs	
EI-AYF	Cessna FRA.150L	S. Bruton	
EI-AYI	MS.880B Rallye Club	J. McNamara	
EI-AYK	Cessna F.172M	D. Gallagher	
EI-AYN	BN-2A-8 Islander	Aer Arann	
EI-AYR	Schleicher ASK-16	B. O'Broin & ptnrs	
EI-AYT	MS.894A Rallye Minerva	K. A. O'Connor	
EI-AYV	MS.892A Rallye Commodore 150	P. Murtagh	
EI-AYY	Evans VP-1	R. Dowd	
EI-BAJ	Stampe SV.4C	Dublin Tiger Group	
EI-BAR	Thunder Ax8-105 balloon	J. Burke & ptnrs	
EI-BAT	Cessna F.150M	K. Kacprzak	
EI-BAV	PA-22 Colt 108	E. Finnamore & J. Deegan	
EI-BBC	PA-28 Cherokee 180C	Vero Beach	
EI-BBD	Evans VP-1	Volksplane Group	
EI-BBE	Champion 7FC Tri-Traveler (tailwheel)	S. Coughlan	
EI-BBI	MS.892 Rallye Commodore	Ossory Flying & Gliding Club	
EI-BBO	MS.893E Rallye 180GT	G. P. Moorhead	
EI-BBV	Piper J-3C-65 Cub	F. Cronin	
EI-BCE	BN-2A-26 Islander	Aer Arann	
EI-BCF	Bensen B.8M	P. Flanagan	
EI-BCJ	Aeromere F.8L Falco 1 Srs 3	M. P. McLoughlin	
EI-BCK	Cessna F.172N II	K. A. O'Connor	
EI-BCL	Cessna 182P	A. D. Brennan	

Notes	Reg.	Type	Owner or Operator
	EI-BCM	Piper J-3C-65 Cub	Kilmoon Flying Group
	EI-BCN	Piper J-3C-65 Cub	H. Diver
	EI-BCO	Piper J-3C-65 Cub	J. Molloy
	EI-BCP	D.62B Condor	T. Delaney
	EI-BCS	MS.880B Rallye Club	Organic Fruit & Vegetables of Kilmeadan
	EI-BCW	MS.880B Rallye Club	Kilkenny Flying Club
	EI-BDH	MS.880B Rallye Club	Munster Wings
	EI-BDL	Evans VP-2	P. Buggle
	EI-BDM	PA-23 Aztec 250D	G. A. Costello
	EI-BDR	PA-28 Cherokee 180	Cherokee Group
	EI-BEN	Piper J-3C-65 Cub	Capt. J. J. Sullivan
	EI-BEP	MS.892A Rallye 150	H. Lynch & J. O'Leary
	EI-BFE	Cessna F.150G	Southair
	EI-BFF	Beech A.23 Musketeer	J. Lankfer
	EI-BFI	MS.880B Rallye 100ST	J. O'Neill
	EI-BFO	Piper J-3C-90 Cub	D. Gordon
	EI-BGA	SOCATA Rallye 100ST	J. J. Frew
	EI-BGC	MS.880B Rallye Club	P. Moran
	EI-BGD	MS.880B Rallye Club	N. Kavanagh
	EI-BGJ	Cessna F.152 II	Sligo Aero Club
	EI-BGS	MS.893E Rallye	M. Farrelly
	EI-BGT	Colt 77A balloon	M. J. Mills
	EI-BGU	MS.880B Rallye Club	M. F. Neary
	EI-BHF	MS.892A Rallye Commodore 150	B. Mullen
	EI-BHI	Bell 206B JetRanger 2	G. Tracey
	EI-BHM	Cessna F.337E	City of Dublin VE College
	EI-BHN	MS.893A Rallye Commodore 180T	T. Garvan
	EI-BHP	MS.893A Rallye Commodore 180T	Spanish Point Flying Club
	EI-BHT	Beech 77 Skipper	M. Casey
	EI-BHV	Champion 7EC Traveler	P. O'Donnell & ptnrs
	EI-BHW	Cessna F.150F	R. Sharpe
	EI-BIB	Cessna F.152	Sligo Aeronautical Club Ltd
	EI-BID	PA-18 Super Cub 95	S. Coghlan & P. Ryan
	EI-BIG	Zlin 526	P. von Lonkhuyzen
	EI-BIK	PA-18 Super Cub 180	Dublin Gliding Club
	EI-BIM	MS.880B Rallye Club	D. Millar
	EI-BIO	Piper J-3C-65 Cub	H. Duggan
	EI-BIR	Cessna F.172M	Figile Flying Group
	EI-BIS	Robin R.1180TD	Robin Aiglon Group
	EI-BIT	MS.887 Rallye 125	Spanish Point Flying Club
	EI-BIV	Bellanca 8KCAB	Aerocrat Pilots Ltd
	EI-BIW	MS.880B Rallye Club	E. J. Barr
	EI-BJB	Aeronca 7AC Champion	A. W. Kennedy
	EI-BJC	Aeronca 7AC Champion	A. E. Griffin
	EI-BJI	Cessna FR.172E	Irish Parachute Club
	EI-BJJ	Aeronca 15AC Sedan	O. Bruton
	EI-BJK	MS.880B Rallye 110ST	M. Keenen
	EI-BJM	Cessna A.152	K. A. O'Connor
	EI-BJO	Cessna R.172K	The XP Group
	EI-BKC	Aeronca 15AC Sedan	G. Hendrick & M. Farrell
	EI-BKF	Cessna F.172H	D. Darby
	EI-BKK	Taylor JT.1 Monoplane	R. Klimcke
	EI-BLD	Bolkow Bö.105DB	Irish Helicopters
	EI-BLE	Eipper Quicksilver Microlight	R. Smith & P. St. George
	EI-BLN	Eipper Quicksilver MX	O. J. Conway & ptnrs
	EI-BMA	MS.880B Rallye Club	W. Rankin & M. Kelleher
	EI-BMB	MS.880B Rallye 100T	Glyde Court Developments
	EI-BMF	Laverda F.8L Falco srs IV	M. Slazenger
	EI-BMH	MS.880B Rallye Club	N. S. Bracken
	EI-BMI	SOCATA TB9 Tampico	D. Pratt
	EI-BMM	Cessna F.152 II	P. Redmond
	EI-BMN	Cessna F.152 II	K. A. O'Connor
	EI-BMU	Monnet Sonerai IIL	A. Fenton
	EI-BMV	Grumman AA-5 Traveler	E. Tierney & K. A. Harold
	EI-BMW	Vulcan Air Trike	L. Maddock & ptnrs
	EI-BNF	Eurowing Goldwing Canard	T. Morelli
	EI-BNH	Hiway Skytrike	M. Martin
	EI-BNJ	Evans VP-2	G. Cashman
	EI-BNK	Cessna U.206F	Irish Parachute Club
	EI-BNL	Rand-Robinson KR-2	K. Hayes
	EI-BNP	Rotorway 133	R. L. Renfroe

Reg.	Type	Owner or Operator	Notes
EI-BNT	Cvjetkovic CA-65	B. Tobin & ptnrs	
EI-BNU	MS.880B Rallye Club	P. A. Doyle	
EI-BOA	Pterodactyl Ptraveller	A. Murphy	
EI-BOE	SOCATA TB10 Tobago	Tobago Group	
EI-BOH	Eipper Quicksilver	J. Leech	
EI-BOV	Rand-Robinson KR-2	G. O'Hara & G. Callan	
EI-BOX	Jordan Duet	Dr. K. Riccius	
EI-BPE	Viking Dragonfly	G. G. Bracken	
EI-BPL	Cessna F.172K	Phoenix Flying	
EI-BPN	Flexiform Striker	P. H. Collins	
EI-BPO	Southdown Sailwings Lightning DS	A. Channing	
EI-BPP	Quicksilver MX	J. A. Smith	
EI-BPT	Skyhook Sabre	T. McGrath	
EI-BPU	Hiway Demon	A. Channing	
EI-BRK	Flexiform Trike	L. Maddock & ptnrs	
EI-BRS	Cessna P.172D	P. Mathews	
EI-BRU	Evans VP-1	Home Bru Flying Group	
EI-BRV	Hiway Demon	M. Garvey & C. Tully	
EI-BRW	Hovey Deltabird	A & E Aerosport	
EI-BSB	Wassmer Jodel D.112	S. Byrne	
EI-BSC	Cessna F.172N	M. Foreman	
EI-BSG	Bensen B.80	J. Todd	
EI-BSK	SOCATA TB9 Tampico	T. Drury	
EI-BSL	PA-34-220T Seneca III	P. Sreenan	
EI-BSN	Cameron O-65 balloon	C. O'Neill & T. Hooper	
EI-BSO	PA-28 Cherokee 140B	H. N. Hanley	
EI-BSW	Solar Wings Pegasus XL-R	E. Fitzgerald	
EI-BSX	Piper J-3C-65 Cub	J. & T. O'Dwyer	
EI-BUA	Cessna 172M	K. A. O'Connor	
EI-BUC	Jodel D.9 Bébé	B. Lyons & M. Blake	
EI-BUF	Cessna 210N	210 Group	
EI-BUG	SOCATA ST.10 Diplomate	J. Cooke	
EI-BUH	Lake LA.4-200 Buccaneer	P. Redden	
EI-BUJ	MS.892A Rallye Commodore 150	T. Cunniffe	
EI-BUL	Whittaker MW5 Sorcerer	J. Culleton	
EI-BUN	Beech 76 Duchess	K. A. O'Connor	
EI-BUT	MS.893A Commodore 180	T. Keating	
EI-BVB	Whittaker MW6 Merlin	R. England	
EI-BVJ	AMF Chevvron 232	A. Dunn	
EI-BVK	PA-38-112 Tomahawk	M. Martin	
EI-BVT	Evans VP-2	P. Morrison	
EI-BVY	Zenith 200AA-RW	J. Matthews & M. Skelly	
EI-BXL	Polaris F1B-OK350	M. McKeon	
EI-BYA	Thruster TST Mk 1	E. Fagan	
EI-BYF	Cessna 150M	High Kings Flying Group	
EI-BYG	SOCATA TB9 Tampico	M. McGinn	
EI-BYL	Zenith CH.250	M. McLoughlin	
EI-BYO	Aérospatiale ATR-42-310	Aer Arann	
EI-BYX	Champion 7GCAA	P. J. Gallagher	
EI-BYY	Piper J-3C-85 Cub	The Cub Club	
EI-CAC	Grob G.115A	C. Phillips	
EI-CAD	Grob G.115A	C. Phillips	
EI-CAE	Grob G.115A	O. O'Reilly	
EI-CAN	Aerotech MW5 Sorcerer	V. A. Vaughan	
EI-CAP	Cessna R.182RG	M. J. Hanlon	
EI-CAU	AMF Chevvron 232	J. Tarrant	
EI-CAX	Cessna P.210N	K. A. O'Connor	
EI-CAY	Mooney M.20C	Ranger Flights Ltd	
EI-CBK	Aérospatiale ATR-42-310	Aer Arann	
EI-CCD	Grob G.115A	Usher Aviation Flight Academy Ltd	
EI-CCF	Aeronca 11AC Chief	G. McGuinness	
EI-CCJ	Cessna 152 II	P. Cahill	
EI-CCK	Cessna 152 II	P. Cahill	
EI-CCL	Cessna 152 II	P. Cahill	
EI-CCM	Cessna 152 II	E. Hopkins	
EI-CDD	Boeing 737-548	Castle 2003-2 Ireland/Pulkovo Airlines	
EI-CDE	Boeing 737-548	Castle 2003-2 Ireland/Pulkovo Airlines	
EI-CDF	Boeing 737-548	Jetscope Aviation Ireland/Pulkovo Airlines	
EI-CDG	Boeing 737-548	Nordic Aviation Contractor (Ireland) Ltd/Pulkovo Airlines	

Notes	Reg.	Type	Owner or Operator
	EI-CDH	Boeing 737-548	Jetscope Aviation Ireland/Pulkovo Airlines
	EI-CDP	Cessna 182L	Irish Parachute Club
	EI-CDV	Cessna 150G	K. A. O'Connor
	EI-CEG	MS.893A Rallye 180GT	M. Jarrett
	EI-CEN	Thruster T.300	P. A. J. Murphy
	EI-CES	Taylorcraft BC-65	B. J. Douglas
	EI-CFF	PA-12 Super Cruiser	J. & T. O'Dwyer
	EI-CFG	CP.301B Emeraude	F. Doyle
	EI-CFH	PA-12 Super Cruiser	G. Treacy
	EI-CFO	Piper J-3C-65 Cub	J. T. Wilson & ptnrs
	EI-CFP	Cessna 172P (floatplane)	K. A. O'Connor
	EI-CFY	Cessna 172N	K. A. O'Connor
	EI-CGB	TEAM mini-MAX	M. Garvey
	EI-CGC	Stinson 108-3	A. D. Weldon & L. Shoebridge
	EI-CGD	Cessna 172M	G. Cashman
	EI-CGF	Luton LA-5 Major	J. Duggan
	EI-CGG	Erco Ercoupe 415C	Irish Ercoupe Group
	EI-CGH	Cessna 210N	J. Smith
	EI-CGJ	Solar Wings Pegasus XL-R	A. P. Hearty
	EI-CGM	Solar Wings Pegasus XL-R	Microflight Ltd
	EI-CGN	Solar Wings Pegasus XL-R	V. Power
	EI-CGP	PA-28 Cherokee 140C	L. A. Tattan
	EI-CGT	Cessna 152 II	J. Rafter
	EI-CHK	Piper J-3C-65 Cub	N. Higgins
	EI-CHR	CFM Shadow Srs BD	B. Kelly
	EI-CHT	Solar Wings Pegasus XL-R	J. Grattan
	EI-CIA	MS.880B Rallye Club	G. Hackett & C. Mason
	EI-CIF	PA-28 Cherokee 180C	AA Flying Group
	EI-CIG	PA-18 Super Cub 150	K. A. O'Connor
	EI-CIM	Avid Flyer Mk IV	P. Swan
	EI-CIN	Cessna 150K	K. A. O'Connor
	EI-CIV	PA-28 Cherokee 140	L. A. Tatton
	EI-CIW	McD Douglas MD-83	Aergo Leasing 113 Ltd/Meridiana
	EI-CJJ	Slingsby T-31M	J. J. Sullivan
	EI-CJR	SNCAN Stampe SV.4A	P. McKenna
	EI-CJS	Jodel D.120A	A. Flood
	EI-CJT	Slingsby Motor Cadet III	J. Tarrant
	EI-CJV	Moskito 2	M. Peril & ptnrs
	EI-CJZ	Whittaker MW6 Merlin	M. McCarthy
	EI-CKF	Hunt Wing/Avon Trike	M. Leyden
	EI-CKG	Avon Hunt Weightlift	B. Kenny
	EI-CKH	PA-18 Super Cub 95	G. Brady
	EI-CKI	Thruster TST Mk 1	S. Woodgates
	EI-CKJ	Cameron N-77 balloon	A. F. Meldon
	EI-CKM	McD Douglas MD-83	Airplanes Finance/Meridiana
	EI-CKN	Whittaker MW6-S Fatboy Flyer	F. Byrne & M. O.'Carroll
	EI-CKT	Mainair Gemini/Flash	A. C. Burke
	EI-CKU	Solar Wings Pegasus SLR	M. O'Regan
	EI-CKZ	Jodel D.18	J. O'Brien
	EI-CLA	HOAC Katana DV.20	J. Cooke
	EI-CLB	Aerospatiale ATR-72-212	Magellan Aviation Services Ltd
	EI-CLL	Whittaker MW6-S Fat Boy Flyer	F. Stack
	EI-CLQ	Cessna F.172N	E. Finnamore
	EI-CMB	PA-28 Cherokee 140	K. Furnell & Partners
	EI-CMK	Goldwing ST	M. Gavigan
	EI-CML	Cessna 150M	K. A. O'Connor
	EI-CMN	PA-12 Super Cruiser	A. McNamee & ptnrs
	EI-CMR	Rutan LongEz	F. & C. O'Caoimh
	EI-CMT	PA-34-200T Seneca II	Atlantic Flight Training
	EI-CMU	Mainair Mercury	Bill O'Neill
	EI-CMV	Cessna 150L	K. A. O'Connor
	EI-CMW	Rotorway Executive	B. McNamee
	EI-CNA	Letov LK-2M Sluka	G. Doody
	EI-CNC	TEAM mini-MAX	A. M. S. Allen
	EI-CNG	Air & Space 18A gyroplane	P. Joyce
	EI-CNR	McD Douglas MD-83	Aircraft Finance Trust Ireland Ltd
	EI-CNU	Pegasus Quantum 15-912	M. Ffrench
	EI-COE	Shaw Europa	F. Flynn
	EI-COG	Gyroscopic Rotorcraft gyroplane	R. C. Fidler & D. Bracken
	EI-COH	Boeing 737-430	ACS Acft Lsg/Air One
	EI-COK	Boeing 737-430	Constitution Acft Lsg/Air One

Reg.	Type	Owner or Operator	Notes
EI-COM	Whittaker MW6-S Fatboy Flyer	M. Watson	
EI-COO	Carlson Sparrow II	D. Logue	
EI-COT	Cessna F.172N	Tojo Air Leasing	
EI-COY	Piper J-3C-65 Cub	W. Flood	
EI-COZ	PA-28 Cherokee 140C	L. A. Tattan	
EI-CPC	Airbus A.321-211	Aer Lingus St Fergus	
EI-CPD	Airbus A.321-211	Aer Lingus St Davnet	
EI-CPE	Airbus A.321-211	Aer Lingus St Enda	
EI-CPF	Airbus A.321-211	Aer Lingus St Ide	
EI-CPG	Airbus A.321-211	Aer Lingus St Aidan	
EI-CPH	Airbus A.321-211	Aer Lingus St Dervilla	
EI-CPI	Rutan LongEz	D. J. Ryan	
EI-CPN	Auster J/4	E. Fagan	
EI-CPP	Piper J-3C-65 Cub	E. Fitzgerald	
EI-CPT	Aérospatiale ATR-42-320	Aer Arann	
EI-CPX	I.I.I. Sky Arrow 650T	M. McCarthy	
EI-CRB	Lindstrand LBL-90A balloon	J. & C. Concannon	
EI-CRD	Boeing 767-31BER	ILFC Ireland/Alitalia	
EI-CRE	McD Douglas MD-83	AAR Ireland/Meridiana	
EI-CRF	Boeing 767-31BER	ILFC Ireland/Alitalia	
EI-CRG	Robin DR.400/180R	D. & B. Lodge	
EI-CRH	McD Douglas MD-83	Airplanes 111/Meridiana	
EI-CRM	Boeing 767-343ER	GECAS Technical Services/Alitalia	
EI-CRR	Aeronca 11AC Chief	L. Maddock & ptnrs	
EI-CRU	Cessna 152	W. Reilly	
EI-CRV	Hoffman H-36 Dimona	The Dimona Group	
EI-CRW	McD Douglas MD-83	Airplanes IAL/Meridiana	
EI-CRX	SOCATA TB-9 Tampico	Hotel Bravo Flying Club	
EI-CRY	Medway Eclipser	G. A. Murphy	
EI-CSG	Boeing 737-8AS	CIT Aerospace International	
EI-CTC	Medway Eclipser	P. A. McMahon	
EI-CTI	Cessna FRA.150L	J. Logan & T. Bradford	
EI-CTL	Aerotech MW-5B Sorcerer	M. Wade	
EI-CUA	Boeing 737-4K5	Aerco Ireland/Blue Panorama	
EI-CUD	Boeing 737-4Q8	Castle 2003-2 Ireland/Blue Panorama	
EI-CUJ	Cessna 172N	M. Nally	
EI-CUM	Airbus A.320-232	Wilmington Trust SP Services (Dublin) Ltd/Windjet	
EI-CUN	Boeing 737-4K5	Aerco Ireland/Blue Panorama	
EI-CUP	Cessna 335	J. Greany	
EI-CUS	AB-206B JetRanger 3	Doherty Quarries and Waste Management	
EI-CUT	Maule MX-7-180A	Cosair	
EI-CUW	BN-2B-20 Islander	Aer Arann	
EI-CVA	Airbus A.320-214	Aer Lingus St Schira	
EI-CVB	Airbus A.320-214	Aer Lingus St Mobhi	
EI-CVC	Airbus A.320-214	Aer Lingus St Kealin	
EI-CVD	Airbus A.320-214	Aer Lingus St Kevin	
EI-CVL	Ercoupe 415CD	V. O'Rourke	
EI-CVM	Schweizer S.269C	B. Moloney	
EI-CVW	Bensen B.8M	F. Kavanagh	
EI-CVY	Brock KB-2 Gyro	G. Smyth	
EI-CWE	Boeing 737-42C	Rockshaw/Air One	
EI-CWF	Boeing 737-42C	Rockshaw/Air One	
EI-CWR	Robinson R22 Beta	Skywest Aviation Ltd	
EI-CWW	Boeing 737-4Y0	Airplanes Holdings/Air One	
EI-CWX	Boeing 737-4Y0	Airplanes Holdings/Air One	
EI-CXC	Raj Hamsa X'Air 502T	R. Dunleavy	
EI-CXK	Boeing 737-4S3	Bravo Aircraft Management/Transaero	
EI-CXN	Boeing 737-329	VEBL-767-300 Ltd/Transaero	
EI-CXO	Boeing 767-3G5ER	ILFC Aircraft 76B-28111 Ltd/Blue Panorama	
EI-CXR	Boeing 737-329	VEBL-767-300 Ltd/Transaero	
EI-CXS	Sikorsky S-61N	CHC Ireland Ltd	
EI-CXV	Boeing 737-8CX	MASL Ireland(14)Ltd/MIAT Mongolian Airlines	
EI-CXY	Evektor EV-97 Eurostar	G. Doody & ptnrs	
EI-CXZ	Boeing 767-216ER	VEBL-767-300 Ltd/Transaero	
EI-CZA	ATEC Zephyr 2000	P. Whitehouse-Tedd	
EI-CZC	CFM Streak Shadow Srs II	M. Culhane & D. Burrows	
EI-CZD	Boeing 767-216ER	Capablue Ltd/Transaero	
EI-CZH	Boeing 767-3G5ER	ILFC Aircraft 76B-29435 Ltd/Blue Panorama	
EI-CZK	Boeing 737-4Y0	Aergo Leasing 113 Ltd/Transaero	
EI-CZM	Robinson R44	Wellingford Construction	
EI-CZN	Sikorsky S-61N	CHC Ireland	

Notes	Reg.	Type	Owner or Operator
	EI-CZP	Schweizer 269C-1	T. Ng Kam
	EI-DAA	Airbus A.330-202	Aer Lingus St Keeva
	EI-DAC	Boeing 737-8AS	Ryanair
	EI-DAD	Boeing 737-8AS	Ryanair
	EI-DAE	Boeing 737-8AS	Ryanair
	EI-DAF	Boeing 737-8AS	Ryanair
	EI-DAG	Boeing 737-8AS	Ryanair
	EI-DAH	Boeing 737-8AS	Ryanair
	EI-DAI	Boeing 737-8AS	Ryanair
	EI-DAJ	Boeing 737-8AS	Ryanair
	EI-DAK	Boeing 737-8AS	Ryanair
	EI-DAL	Boeing 737-8AS	Ryanair
	EI-DAM	Boeing 737-8AS	Ryanair
	EI-DAN	Boeing 737-8AS	Ryanair
	EI-DAO	Boeing 737-8AS	Ryanair
	EI-DAP	Boeing 737-8AS	Ryanair
	EI-DAR	Boeing 737-8AS	Ryanair
	EI-DAS	Boeing 737-8AS	Ryanair
	EI-DAX	Boeing 737-8AS	Ryanair
	EI-DAY	Boeing 737-8AS	Ryanair
	EI-DAZ	Boeing 737-8AS	Ryanair
	EI-DBF	Boeing 767-3Q8ER	ACG Acquisition Ireland/Transaero
	EI-DBG	Boeing 767-3Q8ER	VEBL-767-300 Ltd/Transaero
	EI-DBH	CFM Streak Shadow SA-11	M. O'Mahony
	EI-DBI	Raj Hamsa X'Air Mk.2 Falcon	E. Hamilton
	EI-DBJ	Huntwing Pegasus XL Classic	P. A. McMahon
	EI-DBK	Boeing 777-243ER	GECAS Technical Services/Alitalia
	EI-DBL	Boeing 777-243ER	GECAS Technical Services/Alitalia
	EI-DBM	Boeing 777-243ER	GECAS Technical Services/Alitalia
	EI-DBO	Air Creation Kiss 400	E. Spain
	EI-DBP	Boeing 767-35H	Centennial Aviation (Ireland) Ltd/Alitalia
	EI-DBU	Boeing 767-37EER	Pegasus Aviation Ireland/Transaero
	EI-DBV	Rand Kar X' Air 602T	S. Scanlon
	EI-DBW	Boeing 767-201	Orix Aircraft Management Ltd/Transaero
	EI-DCA	Raj Hamsa X'Air	S. Cahill
	EI-DCB	Boeing 737-8AS	Ryanair
	EI-DCC	Boeing 737-8AS	Ryanair
	EI-DCD	Boeing 737-8AS	Ryanair
	EI-DCE	Boeing 737-8AS	Ryanair
	EI-DCF	Boeing 737-8AS	Ryanair
	EI-DCG	Boeing 737-8AS	Ryanair
	EI-DCH	Boeing 737-8AS	Ryanair
	EI-DCI	Boeing 737-8AS	Ryanair
	EI-DCJ	Boeing 737-8AS	Ryanair
	EI-DCK	Boeing 737-8AS	Ryanair
	EI-DCL	Boeing 737-8AS	Ryanair
	EI-DCM	Boeing 737-8AS	Ryanair
	EI-DCN	Boeing 737-8AS	Ryanair
	EI-DCO	Boeing 737-8AS	Ryanair
	EI-DCP	Boeing 737-8AS	Ryanair
	EI-DCR	Boeing 737-8AS	Ryanair
	EI-DCS	Boeing 737-8AS	Ryanair
	EI-DCT	Boeing 737-8AS	Ryanair
	EI-DCV	Boeing 737-8AS	Ryanair
	EI-DCW	Boeing 737-8AS	Ryanair
	EI-DCX	Boeing 737-8AS	Ryanair
	EI-DCY	Boeing 737-8AS	Ryanair
	EI-DCZ	Boeing 737-8AS	Ryanair
	EI-DDA	Robinson R44 II	Eirecopter Helicopters Ltd
	EI-DDB	Eurocopter EC 120B	J. Cuddy
	EI-DDC	Cessna F.172M	Trim Flying Club
	EI-DDD	Aeronca 7AC	J. Sullivan & M. Quinn
	EI-DDH	Boeing 777-243ER	GECAS Technical Services/Alitalia
	EI-DDI	Schweizer S.269C-1	B. Hade
	EI-DDJ	Raj Hamsa X'Air 582	J. P. McHugh
	EI-DDK	Boeing 737-4S3	Boeing Capital Leasing/Transaero
	EI-DDO	Montgomerie Merlin	C. Condell
	EI-DDP	Southdown International microlight	M. Mannion
	EI-DDR	Bensen B.8V	P. MacCabe & K. Renolds
	EI-DDW	Boeing 767-3S1ER	Pegasus Aviation Ireland/Alitalia
	EI-DDX	Cessna 172S	Atlantic Flight Training

Reg.	Type	Owner or Operator	Notes
EI-DDY	Boeing 737-4Y0	Aerco Ireland/Transaero	
EI-DEA	Airbus A.320-214	Aer Lingus St Fidelma	
EI-DEB	Airbus A.320-214	Aer Lingus St Nathy	
EI-DEC	Airbus A.320-214	Aer Lingus St Fergal	
EI-DEE	Airbus A.320-214	Aer Lingus St Fintan	
EI-DEF	Airbus A.320-214	Aer Lingus St Declan	
EI-DEG	Airbus A.320-214	Aer Lingus St Fachtna	
EI-DEH	Airbus A.320-214	Aer Lingus St Malachy	
EI-DEI	Airbus A.320-214	Aer Lingus St Kilian	
EI-DEJ	Airbus A.320-214	Aer Lingus St Oliver Plunkett	
EI-DEK	Airbus A.320-214	Aer Lingus St Eunan	
EI-DEL	Airbus A.320-214	Aer Lingus St Ibar	
EI-DEM	Airbus A.320-214	Aer Lingus St Canice	
EI-DEN	Airbus A.320-214	Aer Lingus St Kieran	
EI-DEO	Airbus A.320-214	Aer Lingus St Senan	
EI-DEP	Airbus A.320-214	Aer Lingus St Eugene	
EI-DER	Airbus A.320-214	Aer Lingus St Mel	
EI-DES	Airbus A.320-214	Aer Lingus St Pappin	
EI-DET	Airbus A.320-214	Aer Lingus St Brendan	
EI-DEZ	Airbus A.319-112	VGS Investments One Ltd/Meridiana	
EI-DFA	Airbus A.319-112	VGS Investments One Ltd/Meridiana	
EI-DFG	Embraer ERJ-170-100LR	GECAS Technical Services/Alitalia Express	
EI-DFH	Embraer ERJ-170-100LR	Aldus Portfolio Leasing Ltd/Alitalia Express	
EI-DFI	Embraer ERJ-170-100LR	Aldus Portfolio Leasing Ltd/Alitalia Express	
EI-DFJ	Embraer ERJ-170-100LR	Aldus Portfolio Leasing Ltd/Alitalia Express	
EI-DFK	Embraer ERJ-170-100LR	GECAS Technical Services/Alitalia Express	
EI-DFL	Embraer ERJ-170-100LR	GECAS Technical Services/Alitalia Express	
EI-DFM	Evektor EV-97 Eurostar	G. Doody	
EI-DFN	Airbus A.320-211	Eden Irish Aircraft Leasing MSN 204 Ltd/Windjet	
EI-DFO	Airbus A.320-211	Triton Aviation Ireland/Windjet	
EI-DFP	Airbus A.319-112	Wilmington Trust SP Services (Dublin) Ltd/Meridiana	
EI-DFS	Boeing 767-33AER	Transalpine Leasing Ltd/Transaero	
EI-DFX	Air Creation Kiss 400	L. Daly	
EI-DFY	Raj Hamsa R100 (2)	P. McGirr & R Gillespie	
EI-DGA	Urban Air UFM-11UK Lambada	Dr. P. & D. Durkin	
EI-DGG	Raj Hamsa X'Air 582	P. A. Weldon	
EI-DGH	Raj Hamsa X'Air 582	M. Garvey & T. McGowan	
EI-DGJ	Raj Hamsa X'Air 582	N. Brereton	
EI-DGK	Raj Hamsa X'Air 133	B. Chambers	
EI-DGP	Urban Air UFM-11 Lambada	R. Linehan	
EI-DGR	Urban Air UFM-11UK Lambada	M. Tormey	
EI-DGS	ATEC Zephyr 2000	P. Jones	
EI-DGT	Urban Air UFM-11UK Lambada	P. Walsh & Partners	
EI-DGV	ATEC Zephyr 2000	A. Higgins	
EI-DGW	Cameron Z-90 balloon	J. Leahy	
EI-DGX	Cessna 152 II	K. A. O'Connor	
EI-DGY	Urban Air UFM-11 Lambada	D. McMorrow	
EI-DHA	Boeing 737-8AS	Ryanair	
EI-DHB	Boeing 737-8AS	Ryanair	
EI-DHC	Boeing 737-8AS	Ryanair	
EI-DHD	Boeing 737-8AS	Ryanair	
EI-DHE	Boeing 737-8AS	Ryanair	
EI-DHF	Boeing 737-8AS	Ryanair	
EI-DHG	Boeing 737-8AS	Ryanair	
EI-DHH	Boeing 737-8AS	Ryanair	
EI-DHI	Boeing 737-8AS	Ryanair	
EI-DHJ	Boeing 737-8AS	Ryanair	
EI-DHK	Boeing 737-8AS	Ryanair	
EI-DHL	Airbus A.300B4-203F	European Air Transport/DHL	
EI-DHM	Boeing 737-8AS	Ryanair	
EI-DHN	Boeing 737-8AS	Ryanair	
EI-DHO	Boeing 737-8AS	Ryanair	
EI-DHP	Boeing 737-8AS	Ryanair	
EI-DHR	Boeing 737-8AS	Ryanair	
EI-DHS	Boeing 737-8AS	Ryanair	
EI-DHT	Boeing 737-8AS	Ryanair	
EI-DHV	Boeing 737-8AS	Ryanair	
EI-DHW	Boeing 737-8AS	Ryanair	
EI-DHX	Boeing 737-8AS	Ryanair	
EI-DHY	Boeing 737-8AS	Ryanair	

Notes	Reg.	Type	Owner or Operator
	EI-DHZ	Boeing 737-8AS	Ryanair
	EI-DIA	Solar Wings Pegasus XL-Q	P. Byrne
	EI-DIB	Air Creation Kiss 400	E. Redmond
	EI-DIF	PA-31-350 Navajo Chieftain	Flightwise Aviation Ltd & Partners
	EI-DIP	Airbus A.330-202	Calliope Ltd/Alitalia
	EI-DIR	Airbus A.330-202	ILFC Ireland Ltd/Alitalia
	EI-DIY	Van's RV-4	J. A. Kent
	EI-DJM	PA-28-161 Warrior II	Waterford Aero Club
	EI-DJR	Boeing 737-3YO	Larrett/KLD – KD Avia
	EI-DJS	Boeing 737-3YO	Wodell/KLD – KD Avia
	EI-DJX	Farrington Twinstarr	F. Kavanagh
	EI-DJY	Grob G.115	Atlantic Flight Training
	EI-DJZ	Lindstrand LBL-31A Cloudhopper	M. E. White
	EI-DKC	Solar Wings Quasar	K. Daly
	EI-DKE	Air Creation Kiss 450-582	J. Bennett
	EI-DKI	Robinson R22 Beta	P. Gilboy
	EI-DKJ	Thruster T.600N	C. Brogan
	EI-DKK	Raj Hamsa X'Air Jabiru	M. Tolan
	EI-DKL	Boeing 757-231	Pegasus Palls 99/Blue Panorama
	EI-DKN	ELA Aviacion ELA-07 gyrocopter	S. Brennan
	EI-DKT	Raj Hamsa X'Air 582 (11)	S. O'Reilly
	EI-DKU	Air Creation Kiss 450-582 (1)	P. Kirwan
	EI-DKW	Evektor EV-97 Eurostar	Ormand Flying Club
	EI-DKY	Raj Hamsa X'Air 582	M. Clarke
	EI-DKZ	Reality Aircraft Escapade 912 (1)	J. Deegan
	EI-DLB	Boeing 737-8AS	Ryanair
	EI-DLC	Boeing 737-8AS	Ryanair
	EI-DLD	Boeing 737-8AS	Ryanair
	EI-DLE	Boeing 737-8AS	Ryanair
	EI-DLF	Boeing 737-8AS	Ryanair
	EI-DLG	Boeing 737-8AS	Ryanair
	EI-DLH	Boeing 737-8AS	Ryanair
	EI-DLI	Boeing 737-8AS	Ryanair
	EI-DLJ	Boeing 737-8AS	Ryanair
	EI-DLK	Boeing 737-8AS	Ryanair
	EI-DLL	Boeing 737-8AS	Ryanair
	EI-DLM	Boeing 737-8AS	Ryanair
	EI-DLN	Boeing 737-8AS	Ryanair
	EI-DLO	Boeing 737-8AS	Ryanair
	EI-DLR	Boeing 737-8AS	Ryanair
	EI-DLS	Boeing 737-8AS	Ryanair
	EI-DLT	Boeing 737-8AS	Ryanair
	EI-DLV	Boeing 737-8AS	Ryanair
	EI-DLW	Boeing 737-8AS	Ryanair
	EI-DLX	Boeing 737-8AS	Ryanair
	EI-DLY	Boeing 737-8AS	Ryanair
	EI-DLZ	Boeing 737-8AS	Ryanair
	EI-DMA	MS.892E Rallye 150	J. Lynn & Partners
	EI-DMB	Best Off Skyranger 912S (1)	Fun 2 Fly Ltd
	EI-DMC	Schweizer 269C-1	B. Hade
	EI-DMG	Cessna 441	Dawn Meats Group
	EI-DMM	Boeing 737-33A	GAIF II Ireland Two Ltd/KLD - KD Avia
	EI-DMR	Boeing 737-436	Dillondell Ltd/Air One
	EI-DMU	Whittaker MW6S Merlin	G. W. Maher
	EI-DNA	Boeing 757-231	Rockshaw Ltd/Blue Panorama
	EI-DNH	Boeing 737-3Y5	Boeing Capital Leasing/Kras Air/AiRUnion
	EI-DNL	Bensen B-8M	J. Henry & H. O'Driscoll
	EI-DNM	Boeing 737-4S3	Boeing Capital Leasing/Transaero
	EI-DNN	Bede BD-5G	H. John & E. M. Cox
	EI-DNO	Bede BD-5G	R. A. Gardiner
	EI-DNP	Airbus A.320-212	Aerlift Leasing Ireland MSN 421 Ltd/Wind Jet
	EI-DNR	Raj Hamsa X'Air 582 (5)	N. Furlong & J. Grattan
	EI-DNU	Schweizer 269C-1	Skywest Aviation Ltd
	EI-DNV	Urban Air UFM-11UK Lambada	F. Maughan
	EI-DNW	Skyranger J2.2 (1)	M. Kerrison
	EI-DNZ	Boeing 737-3T0	BCI Aircraft Leasing/Avolar
	EI-DOB	Zenair CH-701	D. O'Brien
	EI-DOD	Airbus A.320-231	Hanover Aircraft Leasing/MyAir
	EI-DOE	Airbus A.320-211	ALS Irish Aircraft Leasing/Wind Jet
	EI-DOH	Boeing 737-31S	Challey Ltd/Air One
	EI-DOP	Airbus A.320-232	ILFC Ireland/Wind Jet

Reg.	Type	Owner or Operator	Notes
EI-DOS	Boeing 737-49R	Celestial Avn Trading/Air One	
EI-DOT	Bombardier CL-600-2D24	Challey Ltd/Air One	
EI-DOU	Bombardier CL-600-2D24	Challey Ltd/Air One	
EI-DOV	Boeing 737-48E	Wilmington Trust SP Services (Dublin) Ltd/Air One	
EI-DOW	Mainair Blade 912	G. D. Fortune	
EI-DOX	Solar Wings XL-R	T. Noonan	
EI-DOY	PZL Koliber 150A	Limerick Flying Club	
EI-DPA	Boeing 737-8AS	Ryanair	
EI-DPB	Boeing 737-8AS	Ryanair	
EI-DPC	Boeing 737-8AS	Ryanair	
EI-DPD	Boeing 737-8AS	Ryanair	
EI-DPE	Boeing 737-8AS	Ryanair	
EI-DPF	Boeing 737-8AS	Ryanair	
EI-DPG	Boeing 737-8AS	Ryanair	
EI-DPH	Boeing 737-8AS	Ryanair	
EI-DPI	Boeing 737-8AS	Ryanair	
EI-DPJ	Boeing 737-8AS	Ryanair	
EI-DPK	Boeing 737-8AS	Ryanair	
EI-DPL	Boeing 737-8AS	Ryanair	
EI-DPM	Boeing 737-8AS	Ryanair	
EI-DPN	Boeing 737-8AS	Ryanair	
EI-DPO	Boeing 737-8AS	Ryanair	
EI-DPP	Boeing 737-8AS	Ryanair	
EI-DPR	Boeing 737-8AS	Ryanair	
EI-DPS	Boeing 737-8AS	Ryanair	
EI-DPT	Boeing 737-8AS	Ryanair	
EI-DPV	Boeing 737-8AS	Ryanair	
EI-DPW	Boeing 737-8AS	Ryanair	
EI-DPX	Boeing 737-8AS	Ryanair	
EI-DPY	Boeing 737-8AS	Ryanair	
EI-DPZ	Boeing 737-8AS	Ryanair	
EI-DRA	Boeing 737-852	Mexican Aircraft Leasing/Aeromexico	
EI-DRB	Boeing 737-852	Mexican Aircraft Leasing/Aeromexico	
EI-DRC	Boeing 737-852	Mexican Aircraft Leasing/Aeromexico	
EI-DRD	Boeing 737-852	Mexican Aircraft Leasing/Aeromexico	
EI-DRE	Boeing 737-752	Mexican Aircraft Leasing/Aeromexico	
EI-DRH	Mainair Blade	J. McErlain	
EI-DRI	Bombardier CL-600-2D24	Challey Ltd/Air One	
EI-DRJ	Bombardier CL-600-2D24	Challey Ltd/Air One	
EI-DRK	Bombardier CL-600-2D24	Challey Ltd/Air One	
EI-DRL	Raj Hamsa X'Air Jabiru	J. O'Connor	
EI-DRM	Urban Air UFM-10 Samba	M. Tormey	
EI-DRO	Tecnam P2002-JF	Ossory Flying & Gliding Club	
EI-DRT	Air Creation Tanarg 912	L. Daly	
EI-DRU	Tecnam P92/EM Echo	P. Gallogly	
EI-DRW	Evektor EV-97R Eurostar	Eurostar Flying Club	
EI-DRX	Raj Hamsa X'Air 582 (5)	M. Sheelan & D. McShane	
EI-DSA	Airbus A.320-216	Aircraft Purchase Company/Alitalia	
EI-DSB	Airbus A.320-216	BF Best Aviation Alpha Ltd/Alitalia	
EI-DSC	Airbus A.320-216	BF Best Aviation Alpha Ltd/Alitalia	
EI-DSD	Airbus A.320-216	BF Best Aviation Alpha Ltd/Alitalia	
EI-DSE	Airbus A.320-216	BF Best Aviation Alpha Ltd/Alitalia	
EI-DSF	Airbus A.320-216	Aircraft Purchase Company/Alitalia	
EI-DSG	Airbus A.320-216	Aircraft Purchase Company/Alitalia	
EI-DSH	Airbus A.320-216	Aircraft Purchase Company/Alitalia	
EI-DSI	Airbus A.320-216	Aircraft Purchase Company/Alitalia	
EI-DSJ	Airbus A.320-216	Aircraft Purchase Company/Alitalia	
EI-DSK	Airbus A.320-216	Aircraft Purchase Company/Alitalia	
EI-DSL	Airbus A.320-216	Aircraft Purchase Company/Alitalia	
EI-DSM	Airbus A.320-216	Aircraft Purchase Company/Alitalia	
EI-DSN	Airbus A.320-216	Aircraft Purchase Company/Alitalia	
EI-DSO	Airbus A.320-216	Aircraft Purchase Company/Alitalia	
EI-DSP	Airbus A.320-216	Aircraft Purchase Company/Alitalia	
EI-DSR	Airbus A.320-216	Aircraft Purchase Company/Alitalia	
EI-DSS	Airbus A.320-216	Aircraft Purchase Company/Alitalia	
EI-DST	Airbus A.320-216	Aircraft Purchase Company/Alitalia	
EI-DSU	Airbus A.320-216	Aircraft Purchase Fleet Ltd/Alitalia	
EI-DSV	Airbus A.320-216	Aircraft Purchase Company/Alitalia	
EI-DSW	Airbus A.320-216	Aircraft Purchase Company/Alitalia	
EI-DSX	Airbus A.320-216	Aircraft Purchase Company/Alitalia	
EI-DSY	Airbus A.320-216	Aircraft Purchase Fleet Ltd/Alitalia	

Notes	Reg.	Type	Owner or Operator
	EI-DSZ	Airbus A.320-216	Aircraft Purchase Fleet Ltd/Alitalia
	EI-DTA	Airbus A.320-216	Aircraft Purchase Fleet Ltd/Alitalia
	EI-DTB	Airbus A.320-216	Aircraft Purchase Fleet Ltd/Alitalia
	EI-DTC	Airbus A.320-216	Aircraft Purchase Fleet Ltd/Alitalia
	EI-DTD	Airbus A.320-216	Aircraft Purchase Fleet Ltd/Alitalia
	EI-DTE	Airbus A.320-216	Aircraft Purchase Fleet Ltd/Alitalia
	EI-DTF	Airbus A.320-216	Aircraft Purchase Fleet Ltd/Alitalia
	EI-DTG	Airbus A.320-216	Herodias Aircraft Leasing Co. No.2 Ltd/Alitalia
	EI-DTH	Airbus A.320-216	Herodias Aircraft Leasing Co. No.2 Ltd/Alitalia
	EI-DTI	Airbus A.320-216	Herodias Aircraft Leasing Co. No.2 Ltd/Alitalia
	EI-DTJ	Airbus A.320-216	Herodias Aircraft Leasing Co. No.2 Ltd/Alitalia
	EI-DTK	Airbus A.320-216	Airbus Financial Services/Alitalia
	EI-DTL	Airbus A.320-216	Airbus Financial Services/Alitalia
	EI-DTM	Airbus A.320-216	Aercap Ireland Asset Investments 2 Ltd/Alitalia
	EI-DTN	Airbus A.320-216	Aercap Ireland Asset Investments 2 Ltd/Alitalia
	EI-DTO	Airbus A.320-216	Aercap Ireland Asset Investments 2 Ltd/Alitalia
	EI-DTR	Robinson R44	R & M Quarries Ltd
	EI-DTS	PA-18 Super Cub	P. Dunne, K. Synnott & M. Murphy
	EI-DTT	ELA-07 R-100 Gyrocopter	N. Steele
	EI-DTU	Boeing 737-5Y0	Celestial Aviation Trading/Transaero
	EI-DTV	Boeing 737-5Y0	Airplanes Holdings/Transaero
	EI-DTW	Boeing 737-5Y0	Airplanes Finance/Transaero
	EI-DTX	Boeing 737-5Q8	Wilmington Trust SP Services (Dublin) Ltd/Transaero
	EI-DUA	Boeing 757-256	ILFC Ireland/Kras Air/AiRUnion
	EI-DUC	Boeing 757-256	ILFC Ireland/Kras Air/AiRUnion
	EI-DUD	Boeing 757-256	ILFC Ireland/Kras Air/AiRUnion
	EI-DUE	Boeing 757-256	ILFC Ireland/Kras Air
	EI-DUF	AS.365N	Dauphin 2 Aviation Ltd
	EI-DUH	Scintex CP.1310C3 Emeraude	W. Kennedy
	EI-DUJ	Evektor EV-97 Eurostar	E. Fitzpatrick
	EI-DUK	Bombardier CL-600-2D24	Challey Ltd/myAir
	EI-DUL	Alpi Aviation Pioneer	J. Hackett
	EI-DUO	Airbus A.330-203	Aer Lingus
	EI-DUS	Boeing 737-32B	Mistral Air
	EI-DUV	Beech 55	J. Given
	EI-DUZ	Airbus A.330-203	Aer Lingus
	EI-DVA	Boeing 737-33A	Mistral Air
	EI-DVC	Boeing 737-33A	Mistral Air
	EI-DVD	Airbus A.319-113	WindJet SpA
	EI-DVE	Airbus A.320-214	Aer Lingus
	EI-DVF	Airbus A.320-214	Aer Lingus
	EI-DVG	Airbus A.320-214	Aer Lingus
	EI-DVH	Airbus A.320-214	Aer Lingus
	EI-DVI	Airbus A.320-214	Aer Lingus
	EI-DVJ	Airbus A.320-214	Aer Lingus
	EI-DVO	Barnett j4b2	T. Brennan
	EI-DVP	CL-600-2D24	Aircraft Purchase Company/Air One
	EI-DVR	CL-600-2D24	Aircraft Purchase Company/Air One
	EI-DVS	CL-600-2D24	Aircraft Purchase Company/Air One
	EI-DVT	CL-600-2D24	Aircraft Purchase Company/Air One
	EI-DVU	Airbus A.319-113	WindJet SpA
	EI-DVZ	Robinson R44 II	D. McAuliffe
	EI-DWA	Boeing 737-8AS	Ryanair
	EI-DWB	Boeing 737-8AS	Ryanair
	EI-DWC	Boeing 737-8AS	Ryanair
	EI-DWD	Boeing 737-8AS	Ryanair
	EI-DWE	Boeing 737-8AS	Ryanair
	EI-DWF	Boeing 737-8AS	Ryanair
	EI-DWG	Boeing 737-8AS	Ryanair
	EI-DWH	Boeing 737-8AS	Ryanair
	EI-DWI	Boeing 737-8AS	Ryanair
	EI-DWJ	Boeing 737-8AS	Ryanair
	EI-DWK	Boeing 737-8AS	Ryanair
	EI-DWL	Boeing 737-8AS	Ryanair
	EI-DWM	Boeing 737-8AS	Ryanair
	EI-DWO	Boeing 737-8AS	Ryanair
	EI-DWP	Boeing 737-8AS	Ryanair
	EI-DWR	Boeing 737-8AS	Ryanair
	EI-DWS	Boeing 737-8AS	Ryanair
	EI-DWT	Boeing 737-8AS	Ryanair

Reg.	Type	Owner or Operator	Notes
EI-DWV	Boeing 737-8AS	Ryanair	
EI-DWW	Boeing 737-8AS	Ryanair	
EI-DWX	Boeing 737-8AS	Ryanair	
EI-DWY	Boeing 737-8AS	Ryanair	
EI-DWZ	Boeing 737-8AS	Ryanair	
EI-DXA	Ikarus C42	M. Kirrane	
EI-DXB	Boeing 737-31S	DSF Aircraft Leasing (Ireland) Ltd/Blu-Express	
EI-DXC	Boeing 737-4Q8	Castle 2003-1 Ireland Ltd/Air One	
EI-DXL	CFM Shadow	F. Lynch	
EI-DXM	Raj Hamsa X'Air 582	B. Nugent	
EI-DXN	Zenair CH.601HD	N. Gallagher	
EI-DXP	Cyclone AX3/503	J. McCann	
EI-DXS	CFM Shadow	R. W. Frost	
EI-DXT	UrbanAir UFM-10 Samba	N. Irwin	
EI-DXU	ELA-07 R115	R. Savage	
EI-DXV	Thruster T.600N	P. Higgins	
EI-DXX	Raj Hamsa X'AIR 582(5)	D. Hanly & C. Wright	
EI-DXY	Airbus A.320-212	ILFC Ireland Ltd/Rossiya	
EI-DXZ	UrbanAir UFM-10 Samba	D. O'Leary	
EI-DYA	Boeing 737-8AS	Ryanair	
EI-DYB	Boeing 737-8AS	Ryanair	
EI-DYC	Boeing 737-8AS	Ryanair	
EI-DYD	Boeing 737-8AS	Ryanair	
EI-DYE	Boeing 737-8AS	Ryanair	
EI-DYF	Boeing 737-8AS	Ryanair	
EI-DYG	Boeing 737-8AS	Ryanair	
EI-DYH	Boeing 737-8AS	Ryanair	
EI-DYI	Boeing 737-8AS	Ryanair	
EI-DYJ	Boeing 737-8AS	Ryanair	
EI-DYK	Boeing 737-8AS	Ryanair	
EI-DYL	Boeing 737-8AS	Ryanair	
EI-DYM	Boeing 737-8AS	Ryanair	
EI-DYN	Boeing 737-8AS	Ryanair	
EI-DYO	Boeing 737-8AS	Ryanair	
EI-DYP	Boeing 737-8AS	Ryanair	
EI-DYR	Boeing 737-8AS	Ryanair	
EI-DYS	Boeing 737-8AS	Ryanair	
EI-DYT	Boeing 737-8AS	Ryanair	
EI-DYV	Boeing 737-8AS	Ryanair	
EI-DYW	Boeing 737-8AS	Ryanair	
EI-DYX	Boeing 737-8AS	Ryanair	
EI-DYY	Boeing 737-8AS	Ryanair	
EI-DYZ	Boeing 737-8AS	Ryanair	
EI-DZA	Colt 21A balloon	P. Baker	
EI-DZB	Colt 21A balloon	P. Baker	
EI-DZE	UrbanAir UFM-10 Samba	P. Keane	
EI-DZF	Pipistrel Sinus 912	Light Sport Aviation Ltd	
EI-DZH	Boeing 767-3Q8ER	ILFC Ireland Ltd/Rossiya	
EI-DZI	Robinson R44	P. Reynolds & T. Kelly	
EI-DZJ	Robinson R44 II	L. Behan & Sons Ltd	
EI-DZK	Robinson R22B2 Beta	Skywest Aviation Ltd	
EI-DZL	Urban Air Samba XXL	M. Tormey	
EI-DZM	Robinson R44 II	A. & G. Thomond Builders Ltd	
EI-DZN	Bell 222	B. McCarty & A. Dalton	
EI-DZO	Dominator Gyroplane Ultrawhite	P. O'Reilly	
EI-DZR	Airbus A.320-212	ILFC Aircraft 32A-427 Ltd/Rossiya	
EI-DZS	BRM Land Africa	M. Whyte	
EI-EAB	Airbus A.300B4-203F	European Air Transport/DHL	
EI-EAC	Airbus A.300B4-203F	European Air Transport/DHL	
EI-EAD	Airbus A.300B4-203F	European Air Transport/DHL	
EI-EAG	Pipistrel Virus 912	R. Armstrong	
EI-EAJ	RAF-2000GTX-SE	J. P. Henry	
EI-EAK	Airborne Windsports Edge XT	M. O'Brien	
EI-EAM	Cessna 172R	Atlantic Flight Training Ltd	
EI-EAP	Mainair Blade	H. D. Lynch	
EI-EAR	Boeing 767-3Q8ER	ILFC Aircraft 76B-27616 Ltd/Rossiya	
EI-EAS	Robinson R22 Beta	Midland Helicopters Ltd	
EI-EAV	Airbus A.330-302	Aer Lingus	
EI-EAW	Airborne Windsports Edge XT582	F. Heary	
EI-EAX	Raj Hamsa X'Air 582 (2)	A. Bray	
EI-EAY	Raj Hamsa X'Air 582 (5)	R. Smith	

Notes	Reg.	Type	Owner or Operator
	EI-EAZ	Cessna 172R	Atlantic Flight Training Ltd
	EI-EBA	Boeing 737-8AS	Ryanair
	EI-EBB	Boeing 737-8AS	Ryanair
	EI-EBC	Boeing 737-8AS	Ryanair
	EI-EBD	Boeing 737-8AS	Ryanair
	EI-EBE	Boeing 737-8AS	Ryanair
	EI-EBF	Boeing 737-8AS	Ryanair
	EI-EBG	Boeing 737-8AS	Ryanair
	EI-EBH	Boeing 737-8AS	Ryanair
	EI-EBI	Boeing 737-8AS	Ryanair
	EI-EBK	Boeing 737-8AS	Ryanair
	EI-EBL	Boeing 737-8AS	Ryanair
	EI-EBM	Boeing 737-8AS	Ryanair
	EI-EBN	Boeing 737-8AS	Ryanair
	EI-EBO	Boeing 737-8AS	Ryanair
	EI-EBP	Boeing 737-8AS	Ryanair
	EI-EBR	Boeing 737-8AS	Ryanair
	EI-EBS	Boeing 737-8AS	Ryanair
	EI-EBT	Boeing 737-8AS	Ryanair
	EI-EBV	Boeing 737-8AS	Ryanair
	EI-EBW	Boeing 737-8AS	Ryanair
	EI-EBX	Boeing 737-8AS	Ryanair
	EI-EBY	Boeing 737-8AS	Ryanair
	EI-EBZ	Boeing 737-8AS	Ryanair
	EI-ECA	Agusta A109A-II	McGarrity & Partners
	EI-ECB	Boeing 767-3Q8ER	ILFC Ireland
	EI-ECC	Cameron Z-90 balloon	J. J. Daly
	EI-ECE	Hawker 800XP	Airlink Airways Ltd
	EI-ECG	BRM Land Africa	J. McGuinness
	EI-ECK	Raj Hamsa X'Air Hawk	N. Geh
	EI-ECO	Raj Hamsa X'Air Hawk	J. McLaughlin
	EI-ECP	Raj Hamsa X'Air Hawk	R. Gillespie & Partners
	EI-ECR	Cessna 525	Aircraft International Renting Ltd
	EI-ECV	Raj Hamsa X'Air Hawk	D. P. Myers
	EI-ECW	BRM Land Africa	D. Bolger & Partners
	EI-ECX	Airbus A.319-132	ILFC Ireland Ltd
	EI-ECY	Airbus A.319-132	ILFC Ireland Ltd
	EI-ECZ	Raj Hamsa X'Air Hawk	M. Tolan
	EI-EDA	Raj Hamsa X'Air Hawk	A. Clarke
	EI-EDB	Cessna 152	K. O'Connor
	EI-EDC	Cessna FA.152	K. O'Connor
	EI-EDI	Ikarus C42	M. Owens
	EI-EDJ	CZAW Sportcruiser	Croftal Ltd
	EI-EDM	Airbus A.319-132	ILFC Ireland Ltd/Windjet
	EI-EDP	Airbus A.320-214	Aer Lingus
	EI-EDR	PA-28R Cherokee Arrow 200	Dublin Flyers
	EI-EDS	Airbus A.320-214	Aer Lingus
	EI-EDV	Cessna 172S	R. Carey
	EI-EDY	Airbus A.330-302	Aer Lingus
	EI-EDZ	Boeing 737-8K5	Transaero
	EI-EEA	Boeing 737-8K5	Transaero
	EI-EEB	Boeing 737-73S	Pembroke 7006 Leasing Ltd/AIRES Colombia
	EI-EED	Boeing 767-31AER	ILFC Aircraft 76B-27619 Ltd/Blue Panorama
	EI-EEF	Raj Jamsa X'Air Jabiru(3)	P. J. Sheehy
	EI-EEG	Raj Hamsa X'Air Hawk	C. Kiernan
	EI-EEH	BRM Land Africa	P. Higgins
	EI-EEI	Airbus A.320-232	ILFC Aircraft 32A-661 Ltd/Avia Nova
	EI-EEL	Airbus A.320-232	ILFC Ireland Ltd
	EI-EES	ELA-07R	D. Doyle & Partners
	EI-EEV	Boeing 737-73S	Pembroke 7006 Leasing Ltd/AIRES Colombia
	EI-EEW	Boeing 737-375	Pindell Ltd/Blue Panorama
	EI-EEZ	Bombardier CL-600-2B19	Airlink Airways Ltd
	EI-EFA	Boeing 737-8AS	Ryanair
	EI-EFB	Boeing 737-8AS	Ryanair
	EI-EFC	Boeing 737-8AS	Ryanair
	EI-EFD	Boeing 737-8AS	Ryanair
	EI-EFE	Boeing 737-8AS	Ryanair
	EI-EFF	Boeing 737-8AS	Ryanair
	EI-EFG	Boeing 737-8AS	Ryanair
	EI-EFH	Boeing 737-8AS	Ryanair
	EI-EFI	Boeing 737-8AS	Ryanair

Reg.	Type	Owner or Operator	Notes
EI-EFJ	Boeing 737-8AS	Ryanair	
EI-EFK	Boeing 737-8AS	Ryanair	
EI-EFL	Boeing 737-8AS	Ryanair	
EI-EFM	Boeing 737-8AS	Ryanair	
EI-EFN	Boeing 737-8AS	Ryanair	
EI-EFO	Boeing 737-8AS	Ryanair	
EI-EFP	Boeing 737-8AS	Ryanair	
EI-EFR	Boeing 737-8AS	Ryanair	
EI-EFS	Boeing 737-8AS	Ryanair	
EI-EFT	Boeing 737-8AS	Ryanair	
EI-EFV	Boeing 737-8AS	Ryanair	
EI-EFW	Boeing 737-8AS	Ryanair	
EI-EFX	Boeing 737-8AS	Ryanair	
EI-EFY	Boeing 737-8AS	Ryanair	
EI-EFZ	Boeing 737-8AS	Ryanair	
EI-EGA	Boeing 737-8AS	Ryanair	
EI-EGB	Boeing 737-8AS	Ryanair	
EI-EGC	Boeing 737-8AS	Ryanair	
EI-EGD	Boeing 737-8AS	Ryanair	
EI-EGG	Robinson R44 Raven	B. Haugh	
EI-EHG	Robinson R22 Beta	G. Jordan	
EI-EHH	Aerospatiale ATR-42-300	Aer Arran	
EI-EHK	Magni Gyro M-22 Voyager	M. Concannon	
EI-EHL	Air Creation Tanarg/Ixess 15 912S	S. Woods	
EI-EHP	Robinson R44	P. Tallis	
EI-EHR	Mainair Blade 912S	B. Liffey	
EI-EHV	CZAW Sportcruiser	G. Doody & Partners	
EI-EHW	Embraer EMB-145MP	ECC Leasing Company Ltd	
EI-EHY	Urban Air Samba XXL	J. K. Woodville	
EI-EIA	Airbus A.320-216	Alitalia	
EI-EIB	Airbus A.320-216	Alitalia	
EI-EIC	Airbus A.320-216	Alitalia	
EI-EID	Airbus A.320-216	Alitalia	
EI-EIE	Airbus A.320-216	Alitalia	
EI-EIG	Airbus A.320-216	Alitalia	
EI-EJG	Airbus A.330-202	Alitalia	
EI-EJH	Airbus A.330-202	Alitalia	
EI-EJR	Robinson R44	Gerair Ltd	
EI-EKA	Boeing 737-8AS	Ryanair	
EI-EKB	Boeing 737-8AS	Ryanair	
EI-EKC	Boeing 737-8AS	Ryanair	
EI-EKD	Boeing 737-8AS	Ryanair	
EI-EKE	Boeing 737-8AS	Ryanair	
EI-EKF	Boeing 737-8AS	Ryanair	
EI-EKG	Boeing 737-8AS	Ryanair	
EI-EKH	Boeing 737-8AS	Ryanair	
EI-EKI	Boeing 737-8AS	Ryanair	
EI-EKJ	Boeing 737-8AS	Ryanair	
EI-EKK	Boeing 737-8AS	Ryanair	
EI-EKL	Boeing 737-8AS	Ryanair	
EI-EKM	Boeing 737-8AS	Ryanair	
EI-EKN	Boeing 737-8AS	Ryanair	
EI-EKO	Boeing 737-8AS	Ryanair	
EI-EKP	Boeing 737-8AS	Ryanair	
EI-EKR	Boeing 737-8AS	Ryanair	
EI-EKS	Boeing 737-8AS	Ryanair	
EI-EKT	Boeing 737-8AS	Ryanair	
EI-EKV	Boeing 737-8AS	Ryanair	
EI-EKW	Boeing 737-8AS	Ryanair	
EI-EKX	Boeing 737-8AS	Ryanair	
EI-EKY	Boeing 737-8AS	Ryanair	
EI-EKZ	Boeing 737-8AS	Ryanair	
EI-ELA	Airbus A.330-302	Aer Lingus	
EI-ELB	Raj Hamsa X'Air 582 (1)	M. Smullen	
EI-ELC	Ikarus C42B	J. Roddy	
EI-ELD	Airbus A.320-232	Avia Nova	
EI-ELE	Airbus A.320-232	ACG Acquisition Ireland II Ltd/Avia Nova	
EI-ELG	Airbus A.340-311	ILFC Ireland Ltd	
EI-ELL	Medway Eclipser	Microflex Ltd	
EI-ELM	PA-18-95 Super Cub	S. Coughlan	
EI-ELN	Airbus A.320-232	ACG Acquisition Ireland II Ltd/Avia Nova	

Notes	Reg.	Type	Owner or Operator
	EI-ELS	Boeing 737-3Q8	Triton Aviation Ireland Ltd
	EI-ELU	Boeing 737-4YO	Dinglewood Ltd
	EI-ELV	Pegasus XL-R	D. Minnock
	EI-ELZ	Boeing 737-4Q8	Ansett Worldwide Aviation Ireland Ltd/Mistral Air
	EI-EMA	Boeing 737-8AS	Ryanair
	EI-EMB	Boeing 737-8AS	Ryanair
	EI-EMC	Boeing 737-8AS	Ryanair
	EI-EMD	Boeing 737-8AS	Ryanair
	EI-EME	Boeing 737-8AS	Ryanair
	EI-EMF	Boeing 737-8AS	Ryanair
	EI-EMH	Boeing 737-8AS	Ryanair
	EI-EMI	Boeing 737-8AS	Ryanair
	EI-EMJ	Boeing 737-8AS	Ryanair
	EI-EMK	Boeing 737-8AS	Ryanair
	EI-EML	Boeing 737-8AS	Ryanair
	EI-EMM	Boeing 737-8AS	Ryanair
	EI-EMN	Boeing 737-8AS	Ryanair
	EI-EMO	Boeing 737-8AS	Ryanair
	EI-EMP	Boeing 737-8AS	Ryanair
	EI-EMR	Boeing 737-8AS	Ryanair
	EI-EMS	McD Douglas MD-11F	Boeing Capital Leasing Ltd/Cagoitalia
	EI-EMT	PA-16 Clipper	J. Dolan
	EI-EMU	Cessna F.152	K. O'Connor
	EI-EMV	CZAW Sportcruiser	A. Grant & partners
	EI-EMW	Boeing 737-45D	Celestial Aviation Trading 40 Ltd
	EI-EMX	Mainair Blade 912S	G. Maher
	EI-ENA	Boeing 737-8AS	Ryanair
	EI-ENB	Boeing 737-8AS	Ryanair
	EI-ENC	Boeing 737-8AS	Ryanair
	EI-ENE	Boeing 737-8AS	Ryanair
	EI-ENF	Boeing 737-8AS	Ryanair
	EI-ENG	Boeing 737-8AS	Ryanair
	EI-ENH	Boeing 737-8AS	Ryanair
	EI-ENI	Boeing 737-8AS	Ryanair
	EI-ENJ	Boeing 737-8AS	Ryanair
	EI-ENK	Boeing 737-8AS	Ryanair
	EI-ENL	Boeing 737-8AS	Ryanair
	EI-ENM	Boeing 737-8AS	Ryanair
	EI-ENN	Boeing 737-8AS	Ryanair
	EI-ENO	Boeing 737-8AS	Ryanair
	EI-ENP	Boeing 737-8AS	Ryanair
	EI-EOA	Raj Hamsa X'Air Jabiru	B. Lynch Jnr
	EI-EOB	Cameron Z-69 balloon	J. Leahy
	EI-EOC	Van's RV-6	D. McCann
	EI-EOD	Boeing 737-45D	Celestial Aviation Trading 40 Ltd
	EI-EOE	Boeing 737-505	Engaly Ltd
	EI-EOH	BRM Land Africa	P. J. Piling
	EI-EOI	Take Off Merlin 1100	N. Fitzmaurice
	EI-EOJ	Boeing 737-8BK	Wilmington Trust SP Services (Dublin) Ltd/Air Italy Polska
	EI-EOL	Airbus A.330-243	Whitney Ireland Leasing Ltd
	EI-EON	Airbus A.330-243	Calliope Ltd
	EI-EOO	Ikarus C42 FB UK	B. Gurnett & Partners
	EI-EOP	Boeing 737-8Q8	Shrewsbury Aircraft Leasing Ltd
	EI-EOT	Airbus A.300B4-622R	GA Telesis Ireland Ltd
	EI-EOV	Boeing 737-7BK	CIT Leasing
	EI-EPA	Boeing 737-8AS	Ryanair
	EI-EPB	Boeing 737-8AS	Ryanair
	EI-EPC	Boeing 737-8AS	Ryanair
	EI-EPD	Boeing 737-8AS	Ryanair
	EI-EPE	Boeing 737-8AS	Ryanair
	EI-EPF	Boeing 737-8AS	Ryanair
	EI-EPG	Boeing 737-8AS	Ryanair
	EI-EPH	Boeing 737-8AS	Ryanair
	EI-EUR	Eurocopter EC 120B	Atlantic Helicopters
	EI-EXC	Robinson R44	S. Geany
	EI-EZL	Airbus A.330-223	CIT Aerospace International Ltd
	EI-EZN	Airbus A.320-232	MCAP Ireland 01 Ltd/Meridiana
	EI-EZO	Airbus A.320-232	MCAP Ireland 01 Ltd/Meridiana
	EI-EZR	Airbus A.320-214	Celestial Aviation Trading 18 Ltd/Meridiana
	EI-EZS	Airbus A.320-214	Gamma Aviation Ltd/Meridiana

Reg.	Type	Owner or Operator	Notes
EI-EZT	Airbus A.320-214	Gamma Aviation Ltd/Meridiana	
EI-FAB	Eurocopter EC.120B	Billy Jet Ltd	
EI-FAC	Aerospatiale AS.350B1	Irish Helicopters Ltd	
EI-FBG	Cessna F.182Q	J. Paxton	
EI-FII	Cessna 172RG	K. O'Connor	
EI-FXA	Aérospatiale ATR-42-300	Air Contractors (Ireland) Ltd	
EI-FXB	Aérospatiale ATR-42-300	Air Contractors (Ireland) Ltd	
EI-FXC	Aérospatiale ATR-42-300	Air Contractors (Ireland) Ltd	
EI-FXD	Aérospatiale ATR-42-300	Air Contractors (Ireland) Ltd	
EI-FXE	Aérospatiale ATR-42-300	Air Contractors (Ireland) Ltd	
EI-FXG	Aérospatiale ATR-72-202	Air Contractors (Ireland) Ltd	
EI-FXH	Aérospatiale ATR-72-202	Air Contractors (Ireland) Ltd	
EI-FXI	Aérospatiale ATR-72-202	Air Contractors (Ireland) Ltd	
EI-FXJ	Aerospatiale ATR-72-202	Air Contractors (Ireland) Ltd	
EI-FXK	Aerospatiale ATR-72-202	Air Contractors (Ireland) Ltd	
EI-GCE	Sikorsky S-61N	CHC Ireland Ltd	
EI-GDL	Gulfstream GV-SP (G550)	Westair Aviation	
EI-GEM	Hawker 850XP	Airlink Airways Ltd	
EI-GER	Maule MX7-180A	R. Lanigan & J.Patrick	
EI-GHT	Bell 206B JetRanger	Duncan High Reach Equipment	
EI-GJL	AS.365N3	AIBP	
EI-GKL	Robinson R22 Beta	Eamonn Duffy (Rosemount) Ltd	
EI-GLA	Schleicher ASK-21	Dublin Gliding Club Ltd	
EI-GLB	Schleicher ASK-21	Dublin Gliding Club Ltd	
EI-GLC	Centrair 101A Pegase	Dublin Gliding Club Ltd	
EI-GLD	Schleicher ASK-13	Dublin Gliding Club Ltd	
EI-GLF	Schleicher K-8B	Dublin Gliding Club Ltd	
EI-GLG	Schleicher Ka 6CR	C. Sinclair	
EI-GLH	AB Sportine LAK-17A	S. Kinnear	
EI-GLL	Glaser-Dirks DG-200	P. Denman & C. Craig	
EI-GLM	Schleicher Ka-6CR	P. Denman, C. Craig & J. Finnan	
EI-GLN	Glasflugel H201 Standard Libelle	D. McMahon	
EI-GLO	Scheibe Zugvogel IIIB	J. Walsh, J. Murphy & N. Short	
EI-GLP	Olympia 2B	J. Cashin	
EI-GLS	Rolladen-Schneider LS-7	M. McHugo	
EI-GLT	Schempp-Hirth Discus b	D. Thomas	
EI-GLU	Schleicher Ka-6CR	K. Cullen & Partners	
EI-GLV	Schleicher ASW-19B	C. Sinclair & B. O'Neill	
EI-GMB	Schleicher ASW-17	ASW-17 Group	
EI-GMC	Schleicher ASK-18	The Eighteen Group	
EI-GMD	Phoebus C	F. McDonnell & Partners	
EI-GMF	Schleicher ASK-13	Ossory Flying and Gliding Club Ltd.	
EI-GML	Grob G.103 Twin Astir	D. McCarthy	
EI-GMN	DG Flugzeugbau DG-808C	K. Houlihan	
EI-GPT	Robinson R22 Beta	Treaty Plant & Tool (Hire & Sales)	
EI-GPZ	Robinson R44 II	G & P Transport	
EI-GSE	Cessna F.172M	K. A. O'Connor	
EI-GSM	Cessna 182S	Westpoint Flying Group	
EI-GTY	Robinson R22 Beta	Executive Helicopter Maintenance Ltd	
EI-GVM	Robinson R22 Beta	G. V. Maloney	
EI-GWY	Cessna 172R	Atlantic Flight Training	
EI-HAM	Light Aero Avid Flyer	J. Duggan & Partners	
EI-HAZ	Robinson R44	Forestbrook Developments Ltd	
EI-HCS	Grob G.109B	H. Sydner	
EI-HER	Bell 206B JetRanger 3	S. Lanigan Ryan	
EI-HOG	Cessna U.206G	Irish Parachute Club Ltd	
EI-HOK	Eurocopter EC.130B4	Heli Leasing Partnership	
EI-HUM	Van's RV-7	G. Humphreys	
EI-IAN	Pilatus PC-6/B2-H4	Irish Parachute Club	
EI-IGC	Boeing 757-230	Constitution Aircraft Leasing (Ireland) 3 Ltd/Air Italy	
EI-IGP	Boeing 737-7GL	AEY Aviation Ltd/Air Italy	
EI-IGR	Boeing 737-36N	Aircraft Finance Trust Ireland Ltd/Air Italy	
EI-IGS	Boeing 737-36N	Aircraft Finance Trust Ireland Ltd/Air Italy	
EI-IKB	Airbus A.320-214	Alitalia	
EI-IKL	Airbus A.320-214	Alitalia	
EI-IKU	Airbus A.320-214	Alitalia	
EI-ILS	Eurocopter EC.135T2+	Irish Helicopters Ltd	
EI-IMB	Airbus A.319-112	Alitalia	
EI-IMC	Airbus A.319-112	Alitalia	
EI-IMD	Airbus A.319-112	Alitalia	
EI-IME	Airbus A.319-112	Alitalia	

Notes	Reg.	Type	Owner or Operator
	EI-IMF	Airbus A.319-112	Alitalia
	EI-IMG	Airbus A.319-112	Alitalia
	EI-IMH	Airbus A.319-112	Alitalia
	EI-IMI	Airbus A.319-112	Alitalia
	EI-IMJ	Airbus A.319-112	Alitalia
	EI-IML	Airbus A.319-112	Alitalia
	EI-IMO	Airbus A.319-112	Alitalia
	EI-ING	Cessna F.172P	21st Century Flyers
	EI-IRE	Canadair CL.600-2B16	Starair (Ireland)
	EI-IRV	AS.350B Ecureuil	S. Harris
	EI-IXB	Airbus A.321-112	Alitalia
	EI-IXC	Airbus A.321-112	Alitalia
	EI-IXD	Airbus A.321-112	Alitalia
	EI-IXF	Airbus A.321-112	Alitalia
	EI-IXG	Airbus A.321-112	Alitalia
	EI-IXH	Airbus A.321-112	Alitalia
	EI-IXI	Airbus A.321-112	Alitalia
	EI-IXJ	Airbus A.321-112	Alitalia
	EI-IXO	Airbus A.321-112	Alitalia
	EI-IXU	Airbus A.321-112	Alitalia
	EI-IXV	Airbus A.321-112	Alitalia
	EI-IXZ	Airbus A.321-112	Alitalia
	EI-JAR	Robinson R44	D. Horan
	EI-JFD	Robinson R44	New World Plant Ltd
	EI-JIM	Urban Air Samba XLA	J. Smith
	EI-JIV	L.382G-44K-30 Hercules	Air Contractors (Ireland)
	EI-JJJ	Hawker 900XP	Airlink Airways Ltd
	EI-JOR	Robinson R44 II	Skywest Aviation Ltd
	EI-JPK	Tecnam P2002-JF	Limerick Flying Club (Coonagh) Ltd
	EI-KDH	PA-28-181 Archer II	K. O'Driscoll & D. Harris
	EI-KEV	Raj Hamsa X'Air Jabiru(3)	P. Kearney
	EI-LAD	Robinson R44 II	J. Harney & Partners
	EI-LAX	Airbus A.330-202	Aer Lingus St Mella
	EI-LCM	TBM-700N	G. Power
	EI-LEM	SOCATA TB9 Tampico	M. Fleing
	EI-LFC	Tecnam P.2002-JF	Limerick Flying Club (Coonagh) Ltd
	EI-LIT	MBB Bö.105CBS	Irish Helicopters
	EI-LMK	Agusta A. 109S	Skyheli Ltd
	EI-LVA	Airbus A.321-231	AWAS Aviation Trading Ltd
	EI-LVD	Airbus A.321-231	GAIF 11 Ireland Four Ltd
	EI-MAX	Learjet 31A	Airlink Airways
	EI-MCF	Cessna 172R	K. O'Connor
	EI-MCG	Cessna 172R	Galway Flying Club
	EI-MCP	Agusta A109C	Quarry & Mining Equipment
	EI-MEJ	Bell 206B JetRanger	Gaelic Helicopters
	EI-MER	Bell 206B JetRanger III	Gaelic Helicopters
	EI-MES	Sikorsky S-61N	CHC Ireland
	EI-MIK	Eurocopter EC 120B	Executive Helicopter Maintenance Ltd
	EI-MIP	SA.365N Dauphin 2	CHC Ireland
	EI-MIR	Roko Aero NG 4HD	H. Goulding
	EI-MIT	Agusta A109E	Fernwave Ireland Ltd
	EI-MJC	Cessna 525B	Munster Jet Partnership Ltd
	EI-MMO	Robinson R44	Tallis Windfield Construction Ltd
	EI-MPW	Robinson R44	Connacht Helicopters
	EI-MSG	Agusta A.109E	Beckdrive Ltd
	EI-MTZ	Urban Air Samba XXL	M. Motz
	EI-MUL	Robinson R44	J. T. Clarke
	EI-NBG	Agusta A.109S	A. Logue
	EI-NFW	Cessna 172S	Galway Flying Club
	EI-NJA	Robinson R44 II	Nojo Aviation Ltd
	EI-NTH	Agusta A.109E	O'Flynn Construction Co.
	EI-NVL	Jora spol S. R. O. Jora	A. McAllister & partners
	EI-ODD	Bell 206B JetRanger	Zero Altitude Ltd
	EI-OFM	Cessna F.172N	C. Phillips
	EI-OOR	Cessna 172S	Sligo Flying Schol Ltd
	EI-ORD	Airbus A.330-301	Aer Lingus St Maeve
	EI-OZA	Airbus A.300B4-203F	European Air Transport/DHL (stored)
	EI-OZB	Airbus A.300B4-103F	European Air Transport/DHL
	EI-OZC	Airbus A.300B4-103F	European Air Transport/DHL
	EI-OZD	Airbus A.300B4-203F	European Air Transport/DHL

Reg.	Type	Owner or Operator	Notes
EI-OZE	Airbus A.300B4-203F	European Air Transport/DHL	
EI-OZF	Airbus A.300B4-203F	European Air Transport/DHL	
EI-OZG	Airbus A.300B4-203F	European Air Transport/DHL	
EI-OZH	Airbus A.300B4-203F	European Air Transport/DHL	
EI-OZI	Airbus A.300B4-203F	European Air Transport/DHL	
EI-PCI	Bell 206B JetRanger	Malcove Ltd	
EI-PII	Robinson R44	P. Barrow & Partners	
EI-PJD	AS.350B2 Twin Squirrel	New World Plant	
EI-PKS	Bell 206B JetRanger	Hawk Springs Ltd	
EI-PMI	Agusta-Bell 206B JetRanger III	Ping Golf Equipment	
EI-POP	Cameron Z-90 balloon	The Travel Department	
EI-RAV	Robinson R44	Glenkill Properties Ltd	
EI-RCG	Sikorsky S-61N	CHC Ireland	
EI-REH	Aérospatiale ATR-72-201	Aer Arann	
EI-REI	Aérospatiale ATR-72-201	Aer Arann	
EI-REJ	Aérospatiale ATR-72-201	Air Contractgors (Ireland) Ltd	
EI-REL	Aerospatiale ATR-72-212	Aer Arann	
EI-REM	Aerospatiale ATR-72-212	Aer Arann	
EI-REO	Aerospatiale ATR-72-212	Aer Arann	
EI-REP	Aerospatiale ATR-72-212	Aer Arann	
EI-REX	Learjet 60	Airlink Airways	
EI-RHM	Bell 407	A. Morrin	
EI-RJA	Avro RJ85	Cityjet	
EI-RJB	Avro RJ85	Cityjet Bere Island	
EI-RJC	Avro RJ85	Cityjet	
EI-RJD	Avro RJ85	Cityjet	
EI-RJE	Avro RJ85	Cityjet	
EI-RJF	Avro RJ85	Cityjet	
EI-RJG	Avro RJ85	Cityjet	
EI-RJH	Avro RJ85	Cityjet	
EI-RJI	Avro RJ85	Cityjet	
EI-RJJ	Avro RJ85	Cityjet	
EI-RJK	Avro RJ85	Cityjet	
EI-RJL	Avro RJ85	Cityjet	
EI-RJM	Avro RJ85	Cityjet	
EI-RJN	Avro RJ85	Cityjet	
EI-RJO	Avro RJ85	Cityjet	
EI-RJP	Avro RJ85	Cityjet Clare Island	
EI-RJR	Avro RJ85	Cityjet	
EI-RJS	Avro RJ85	Cityjet Dursey Island	
EI-RJT	Avro RJ85	Cityjet	
EI-RJU	Avro RJ85	Cityjet	
EI-RJV	Avro RJ85	Cityjet	
EI-RJW	Avro RJ85	Cityjet Garinish Island	
EI-RJX	Avro RJ85	Cityjet	
EI-RJY	Avro RJ85	Cityjet	
EI-RJZ	Avro RJ85	Cityjet	
EI-RMC	Bell 206B JetRanger	Westair Aviation	
EI-ROB	Robin R.1180TD	Extras Ltd	
EI-ROK	Roko Aero NG 4UL	K. Harley	
EI-SAC	Cessna 172P	Sligo Aero Club	
EI-SAF	Airbus A.300B4-203F	European Air Transport/DHL	
EI-SAR	Sikorsky S-61N	CHC Ireland	
EI-SAT	Steen Skybolt	Capt. B. O'Sullivan	
EI-SEA	SeaRey	J. Brennan	
EI-SFA	Cessna 510	Star Fly CJM 1 Ltd	
EI-SFB	Cessna 510	Star Fly CJM 1 Ltd	
EI-SFC	Cessna 510	Star Fly CJM 1 Ltd	
EI-SFD	Cessna 510	Star Fly CJM 1 Ltd	
EI-SFE	Cessna 510	Star Fly CJM 1 Ltd	
EI-SGF	Robinson R44	M. Reilly & S. Filan	
EI-SKB	PA-44-180 Seminole	Shemburn Ltd	
EI-SKC	PA-44-180 Seminole	Shemburn Ltd	
EI-SKD	PA-44-180 Seminole	Shemburn Ltd	
EI-SKE	Robin DR400/140B	Shemburn Ltd	
EI-SKP	Cessna F.172P	Shemburn Ltd	
EI-SKR	PA-44-180 Seminole	Shemburn Ltd	
EI-SKS	Robin R.2160	Shemburn Ltd	
EI-SKT	PA-44-180 Seminole	Shemburn Ltd	
EI-SKU	PA-28RT-201 Arrow IV	Shemburn Ltd	
EI-SKV	Robin R.2160	Shemburn Ltd	

Notes	Reg.	Type	Owner or Operator
	EI-SKW	PA-28-161 Warrior II	Shemburn Ltd
	EI-SLA	Aérospatiale ATR-42-310	Air Contractors (Ireland) Ltd
	EI-SLC	Aérospatiale ATR-42-310	Air Contractors (Ireland) Ltd
	EI-SLF	Aérospatiale ATR-72-201	Air Contractors (Ireland) Ltd
	EI-SLG	Aérospatiale ATR-72-202	Air Contractors (Ireland) Ltd
	EI-SLH	Aerospatiale ATR-72-202	Air Contractors (Ireland) Ltd
	EI-SLI	Aerospatiale ATR-42-310	Air Contractors (Ireland) Ltd
	EI-SLJ	Aerospatiale ATR-72-201	Air Contractors (Ireland) Ltd
	EI-SLK	Aerospatiale ATR-72-212	Air Contractors (Ireland) Ltd
	EI-SLL	Aerospatiale ATR-72-212	Air Contractors (Ireland) Ltd/Aer Arran
	EI-SLM	Aerospatiale ATR-72-212	Air Contractors (Ireland) Ltd/Aer Arran
	EI-SLN	Aerospatiale ATR-72-212	Air Contractors (Ireland) Ltd/Aer Arran
	EI-SMD	Robinson R44	New World Plant Ltd
	EI-SMK	Zenair CH701	S. King
	EI-SPB	Cessna T206H	P. Morrissey
	EI-SQG	Agusta A109E	Quinn Group
	EI-STA	Boeing 737-31S	Air Contractors (Ireland) Ltd/Europe Airpost
	EI-STT	Cessna 172M	Trim Flying Club
	EI-SUB	Robinson R44	EI-SUB Ltd
	EI-TAB	Airbus A.320-233	Wilmington Trust SP Services/TACA
	EI-TAD	Airbus A.320-233	Alvi Leasing/TACA
	EI-TAG	Airbus A.320-233	Wilmington Trust SP ServicesI/TACA
	EI-TDV	Dassault Falcon 2000LX	Herodias Executive Aircraft
	EI-TGF	Robinson R22 Beta	Skyexpress Ltd
	EI-TIM	Piper J-5A	N. & P. Murphy
	EI-TKI	Robinson R22 Beta	J. McDaid
	EI-TON	M. B. Cooke 582 (5)	T. Merrigan
	EI-UFO	PA-22 Tri-Pacer 150 (tailwheel)	W. Treacy
	EI-UNA	Boeing 767-3P6ER	Capablue Ltd/Transaero
	EI-UNB	Boeing 767-3P6ER	Capablue Ltd/Transaero
	EI-UNC	Boeing 767-319ER	ILFC Ireland Ltd/Transaero
	EI-UND	Boeing 767-2P6ER	Capablue Ltd/Transaero
	EI-UNF	Boeing 767-3P6ER	Capablue Ltd/Transaero
	EI-UNI	Robinson R44 II	Unipipe (Irl) Ltd
	EI-UNR	Boeing 777-212ER	VEBL-767-300 Ltd/Transaero
	EI-UNS	Boeing 777-212ER	VEBL-767-300 Ltd/Transaero
	EI-UNT	Boeing 777-212ER	VEBL-767-300 Ltd/Transaero
	EI-UNU	Boeing 777-222ER	VEBL-767-300 Ltd/Transaero
	EI-UNV	Boeing 777-222ER	ALAFCO Iirish Aircraft Leasing One Ltd/Transaero
	EI-UNW	Boeing 777-222	Transaero
	EI-UNX	Boeing 777-222	Transaero
	EI-UNZ	Boeing 777-222	Capablue Ltd/Transaero
	EI-UPE	McD Douglas MD-11F	Pegasus Aviation/Alitalia
	EI-UPI	McD Douglas MD-11F	Pegasus Aviation/Alitalia
	EI-VII	Vans RV-7	B. Sheane
	EI-VLN	PA-18A-150	D. O'Mahony
	EI-WAC	PA-23 Aztec 250E	Westair Aviation
	EI-WAT	Tecnam P.2002-JF	Waterford Aero Club Ltd
	EI-WAV	Bell 430	Westair Aviation
	EI-WFD	Tecnam P.2002-JF	Waterford Aero Club Ltd
	EI-WFI	Bombardier CL600-2B16 Challenger	NMWAA/Westair
	EI-WIG	Sky Ranger 912	M. Brereton
	EI-WJN	HS.125 Srs 700A	Westair Aviation
	EI-WMN	PA-23 Aztec 250F	Westair Aviation
	EI-WWI	Robinson R44 II	J. Murtagh
	EI-WXA	Avro RJ85	Cityjet Ltd
	EI-WXB	Avro RJ85	Cityjet Ltd
	EI-WXP	Hawker 800XP	Westair Aviation Ltd
	EI-XLA	Urban Air Samba XLA	K. Dardis
	EI-XLS	Cessna 560XL	Airlink Airways Ltd
	EI-YBZ	Robinson R44	ILH Enterprises
	EI-YLG	Robin HR.200/120B	Leinster Aero Club
	EI-ZZZ	Bell222	Executive Helicopter Maintenance Ltd

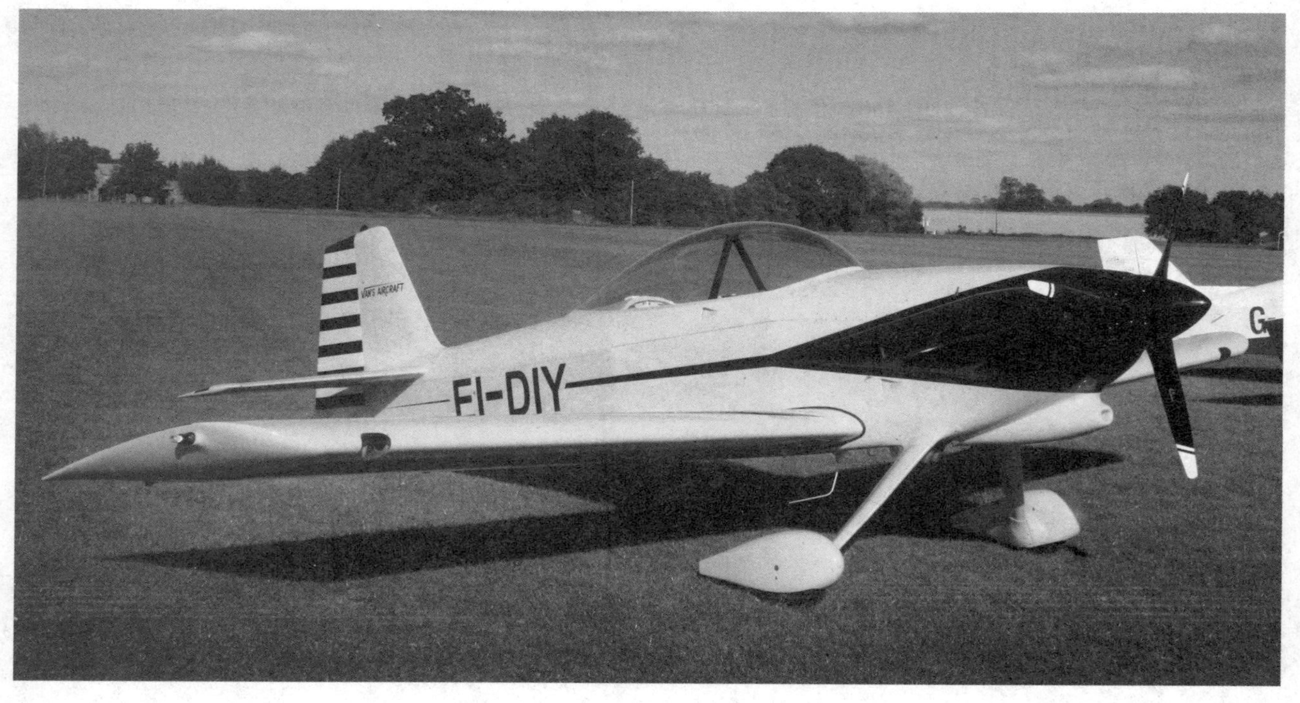

EI-DIY Van's RV-4. *Allan Wright*

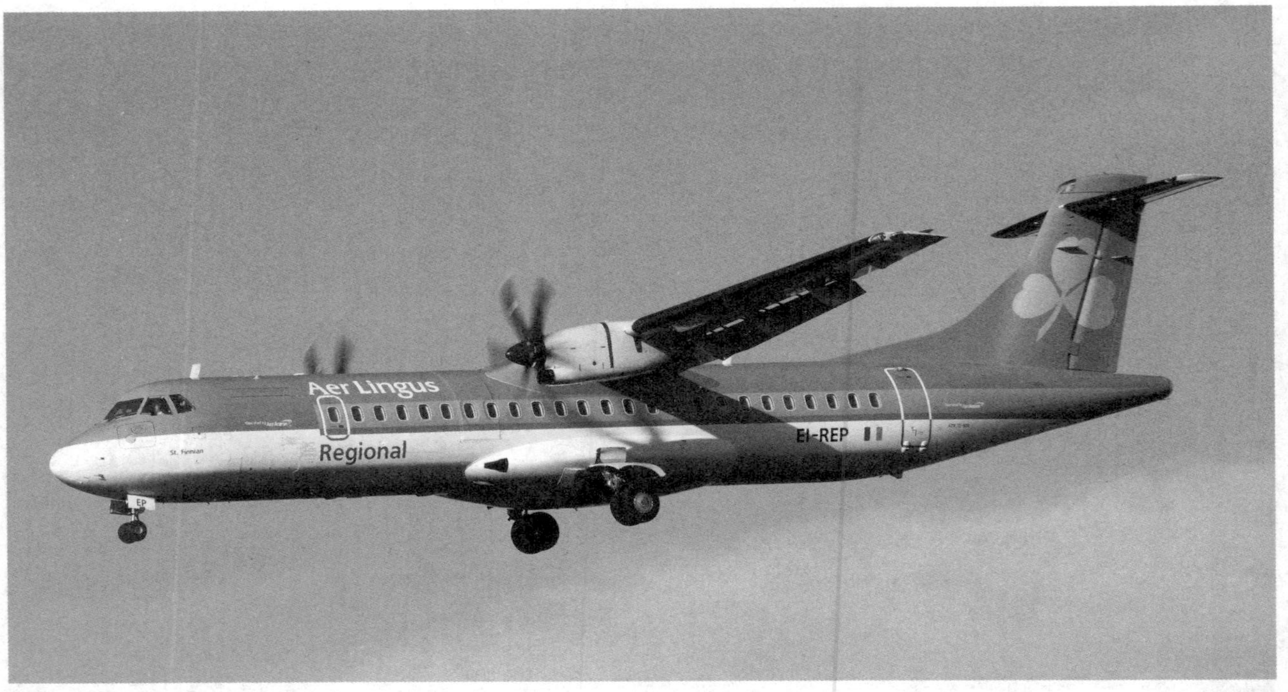

EI-REP ATR72-212 of Aer Lingus Regional. *Peter R March*

Overseas Airliner Registrations

(Aircraft included in this section are those most likely to be seen at UK and nearby European airports or overflying UK airspace.)

A6 (Arab Emirates)

Reg.	*Type*	*Owner or Operator*	*Notes*
A6-AFA	Airbus A.330-343X	Ethiad Airways	
A6-AFB	Airbus A.330-343X	Ethiad Airways	
A6-AFC	Airbus A.330-343X	Ethiad Airways	
A6-AFD	Airbus A.330-343X	Ethiad Airways	
A6-AFE	Airbus A.330-343X	Ethiad Airways	
A6-AFF	Airbus A.330-343X	Ethiad Airways	
A6-EAA	Airbus A.330-243	Emirates Airlines *Spirit of Birmingham*	
A6-EAB	Airbus A.330-243	Emirates Airlines	
A6-EAC	Airbus A.330-243	Emirates Airlines	
A6-EAD	Airbus A.330-243	Emirates Airlines	
A6-EAE	Airbus A.330-243	Emirates Airlines	
A6-EAF	Airbus A.330-243	Emirates Airlines	
A6-EAG	Airbus A.330-243	Emirates Airlines	
A6-EAH	Airbus A.330-243	Emirates Airlines	
A6-EAI	Airbus A.330-243	Emirates Airlines	
A6-EAJ	Airbus A.330-243	Emirates Airlines	
A6-EAK	Airbus A.330-243	Emirates Airlines	
A6-EAL	Airbus A.330-243	Emirates Airlines	
A6-EAM	Airbus A.330-243	Emirates Airlines	
A6-EAN	Airbus A.330-243	Emirates Airlines	
A6-EAO	Airbus A.330-243	Emirates Airlines	
A6-EAP	Airbus A.330-243	Emirates Airlines	
A6-EAQ	Airbus A.330-243	Emirates Airlines	
A6-EAR	Airbus A.330-243	Emirates Airlines	
A6-EAS	Airbus A.330-243	Emirates Airlines	
A6-EBA	Boeing 777-31HER	Emirates Airlines	
A6-EBB	Boeing 777-36NER	Emirates Airlines	
A6-EBC	Boeing 777-36NER	Emirates Airlines	
A6-EBD	Boeing 777-31HER	Emirates Airlines	
A6-EBE	Boeing 777-36NER	Emirates Airlines	
A6-EBF	Boeing 777-31HER	Emirates Airlines	
A6-EBG	Boeing 777-36NER	Emirates Airlines	
A6-EBH	Boeing 777-31HER	Emirates Airlines	
A6-EBI	Boeing 777-36NER	Emirates Airlines	
A6-EBJ	Boeing 777-36NER	Emirates Airlines	
A6-EBK	Boeing 777-31HER	Emirates Airlines	
A6-EBL	Boeing 777-31HER	Emirates Airlines	
A6-EBM	Boeing 777-31HER	Emirates Airlines	
A6-EBN	Boeing 777-36NER	Emirates Airlines	
A6-EBO	Boeing 777-36NER	Emirates Airlines	
A6-EBP	Boeing 777-31HER	Emirates Airlines	
A6-EBQ	Boeing 777-36NER	Emirates Airlines	
A6-EBR	Boeing 777-31HER	Emirates Airlines	
A6-EBS	Boeing 777-31HER	Emirates Airlines	
A6-EBT	Boeing 777-31HER	Emirates Airlines	
A6-EBU	Boeing 777-31HER	Emirates Airlines	
A6-EBV	Boeing 777-31HER	Emirates Airlines	
A6-EBW	Boeing 777-36NER	Emirates Airlines	
A6-EBX	Boeing 777-31HER	Emirates Airlines	
A6-EBY	Boeing 777-36NER	Emirates Airlines	
A6-EBZ	Boeing 777-31HER	Emirates Airlines	
A6-ECA	Boeing 777-36NER	Emirates Airlines	
A6-ECB	Boeing 777-31HER	Emirates Airlines	
A6-ECC	Boeing 777-36NER	Emirates Airlines	
A6-ECD	Boeing 777-36NER	Emirates Airlines	
A6-ECE	Boeing 777-31HER	Emirates Airlines	
A6-ECF	Boeing 777-31HER	Emirates Airlines	
A6-ECG	Boeing 777-31HER	Emirates Airlines	
A6-ECH	Boeing 777-31HER	Emirates Airlines	
A6-ECI	Boeing 777-31HER	Emirates Airlines	
A6-ECJ	Boeing 777-31HER	Emirates Airlines	
A6-ECK	Boeing 777-31HER	Emirates Airlines	
A6-ECL	Boeing 777-31NER	Emirates Airlines	

Notes	Reg.	Type	Owner or Operator
	A6-ECM	Boeing 777-31NER	Emirates Airlines
	A6-ECN	Boeing 777-31NER	Emirates Airlines
	A6-ECO	Boeinb 777-31NER	Emirates Airlines
	A6-ECP	Boeing 777-31NER	Emirates Airlines
	A6-ECQ	Boeing 777-31HER	Emirates Airlines
	A6-ECR	Boeing 777-31HER	Emirates Airlines
	A6-ECS	Boeing 777-31HER	Emirates Airlines
	A6-ECT	Boeing 777-31HER	Emirates Airlines
	A6-ECU	Boeing 777-31HER	Emirates Airlines
	A6-ECV	Boeing 777-31HER	Emirates Airlines
	A6-ECW	Boeing 777-31HER	Emirates Airlines
	A6-ECX	Boeing 777-31HER	Emirates Airlines
	A6-ECY	Boeing 777-31HER	Emirates Airlines
	A6-ECZ	Boeing 777-31HER	Emirates Airlines
	A6-EDA	Airbus A.380-861	Emirates Airlines
	A6-EDB	Airbus A.380-861	Emirates Airlines
	A6-EDC	Airbus A.380-861	Emirates Airlines
	A6-EDD	Airbus A.380-861	Emirates Airlines
	A6-EDE	Airbus A.380-861	Emirates Airlines
	A6-EDF	Airbus A.380-861	Emirates Airlines
	A6-EDG	Airbus A.380-861	Emirates Airlines
	A6-EDH	Airbus A.380-861	Emirates Airlines
	A6-EDI	Airbus A.380-861	Emirates Airlines
	A6-EDJ	Airbus A.380-861	Emirates Airlines
	A6-EDK	Airbus A.380-861	Emirates Airlines
	A6-EDL	Airbus A.380-861	Emirates Airlines
	A6-EDM	Airbus A.380-861	Emirates Airlines
	A6-EDN	Airbus A.380-861	Emirates Airlines
	A6-EDO	Airbus A.380-861	Emirates Airlines
	A6-EDP	Airbus A.380-861	Emirates Airlines
	A6-EDQ	Airbus A.380-861	Emirates Airlines
	A6-EDR	Airbus A.380-861	Emirates Airlines
	A6-EDS	Airbus A.380-861	Emirates Airlines
	A6-EDT	Airbus A.380-861	Emirates Airlines
	A6-EGA	Boeing 777-31HER	Emirates Airlines
	A6-EGB	Boeing 777-31HER	Emirates Airlines
	A6-EGC	Boeing 777-31HER	Emirates Airlines
	A6-EGD	Boeing 777-31HER	Emirates Airlines
	A6-EGE	Boeing 777-31HER	Emirates Airlines
	A6-EHA	Airbus A.340-541	Etihad Airways
	A6-EHB	Airbus A.340-541	Etihad Airways
	A6-EHC	Airbus A.340-541	Etihad Airways
	A6-EHD	Airbus A.340-541	Etihad Airways
	A6-EHE	Airbus A.340-642	Ethiad Airways
	A6-EHF	Airbus A.340-642	Ethiad Airways
	A6-EHH	Airbus A.340-642	Ethiad Airways
	A6-EHI	Airbus A.340-642	Ethiad Airways
	A6-EHJ	Airbus A.340-642	Ethiad Airways
	A6-EHK	Airbus A.340-642	Ethiad Airways
	A6-EHL	Airbus A.340-642	Ethiad Airways
	A6-EKQ	Airbus A.330-243	Emirates Airlines
	A6-EKR	Airbus A.330-243	Emirates Airlines
	A6-EKS	Airbus A.330-243	Emirates Airlines
	A6-EKT	Airbus A.330-243	Emirates Airlines
	A6-EKU	Airbus A.330-243	Emirates Airlines
	A6-EKV	Airbus A.330-243	Emirates Airlines
	A6-EKW	Airbus A.330-243	Emirates Airlines
	A6-EKX	Airbus A.330-243	Emirates Airlines
	A6-EKY	Airbus A.330-243	Emirates Airlines
	A6-EKZ	Airbus A.330-243	Emirates Airlines
	A6-EMD	Boeing 777-21H	Emirates Airlines
	A6-EME	Boeing 777-21H	Emirates Airlines
	A6-EMF	Boeing 777-21H	Emirates Airlines
	A6-EMG	Boeing 777-21HER	Emirates Airlines
	A6-EMH	Boeing 777-21HER	Emirates Airlines
	A6-EMI	Boeing 777-21HER	Emirates Airlines
	A6-EMJ	Boeing 777-21HER	Emirates Airlines
	A6-EMK	Boeing 777-21HER	Emirates Airlines
	A6-EML	Boeing 777-21HER	Emirates Airlines
	A6-EMM	Boeing 777-31H	Emirates Airlines
	A6-EMN	Boeing 777-31H	Emirates Airlines
	A6-EMO	Boeing 777-31H	Emirates Airlines
	A6-EMP	Boeing 777-31H	Emirates Airlines
	A6-EMQ	Boeing 777-31H	Emirates Airlines

Reg.	Type	Owner or Operator	Notes
A6-EMR	Boeing 777-31H	Emirates Airlines	
A6-EMS	Boeing 777-31H	Emirates Airlines	
A6-EMT	Boeing 777-31H	Emirates Airlines	
A6-EMU	Boeing 777-31H	Emirates Airlines	
A6-EMV	Boeing 777-31H	Emirates Airlines	
A6-EMW	Boeing 777-31H	Emirates Airlines	
A6-EMX	Boeing 777-31H	Emirates Airlines	
A6-ERA	Airbus A.340-541	Emirates Airlines	
A6-ERB	Airbus A.340-541	Emirates Airlines	
A6-ERC	Airbus A.340-541	Emirates Airlines	
A6-ERD	Airbus A.340-541	Emirates Airlines	
A6-ERE	Airbus A.340-541	Emirates Airlines	
A6-ERF	Airbus A.340-541	Emirates Airlines	
A6-ERG	Airbus A.340-541	Emirates Airlines	
A6-ERH	Airbus A.340-541	Emirates Airlines	
A6-ERI	Airbus A.340-541	Emirates Airlines	
A6-ERJ	Airbus A.340-541	Emirates Airlines	
A6-ERM	Airbus A.340-313X	Emirates Airlines	
A6-ERN	Airbus A.340-313X	Emirates Airlines	
A6-ERO	Airbus A.340-313X	Emirates Airlines	
A6-ERP	Airbus A.340-313X	Emirates Airlines	
A6-ERQ	Airbus A.340-313X	Emirates Airlines	
A6-ERR	Airbus A.340-313X	Emirates Airlines	
A6-ERS	Airbus A.340-313X	Emirates Airlines	
A6-ERT	Airbus A.340-313X	Emirates Airlines	
A6-ETA	Boeing 777-3FXER	Etihad Airways	
A6-ETB	Boeing 777-3FXER	Etihad Airways	
A6-ETC	Boeing 777-3FXER	Etihad Airways	
A6-ETD	Boeing 777-3FXER	Etihad Airways	
A6-ETE	Boeing 777-3FXER	Etihad Airways	
A6-ETF	Boeing 777-3FXER	Ethiad Airways	
A6-ETG	Boeing 777-3FXER	Ethiad Airways	
A6-EWA	Boeing 777-21HLR	Emirates Airlines	
A6-EWB	Boeing 777-21HLR	Emirates Airlines	
A6-EWC	Boeing 777-21HLR	Emirates Airlines	
A6-EWD	Boeing 777-21HLR	Emirates Airlines	
A6-EWE	Boeing 777-21HLR	Emirates Airlines	
A6-EWF	Boeing 777-21HLR	Emirates Airlines	
A6-EWG	Boeing 777-21HLR	Emirates Airlines	
A6-EWH	Boeing 777-21HER	Emirates Airlines	
A6-EWI	Boeing 777-21HER	Emirates Airlines	
A6-EWJ	Boeing 777-21HLR	Emirates Airlines	
A6-EYD	Airbus A.330-243	Etihad Airways	
A6-EYE	Airbus A.330-243	Etihad Airways	
A6-EYF	Airbus A.330-243	Etihad Airways	
A6-EYG	Airbus A.330-243	Etihad Airways	
A6-EYH	Airbus A.330-243	Etihad Airways	
A6-EYI	Airbus A.330-243	Etihad Airways	
A6-EYJ	Airbus A.330-243	Ethiad Airways	
A6-EYK	Airbus A.330-243	Etihad Airways	
A6-EYL	Airbus A.330-243	Etihad Airways	
A6-EYM	Airbus A.330-243	Etihad Airways	
A6-EYN	Airbus A.330-243	Etihad Airways	
A6-EYO	Airbus A.330-243	Etihad Airways	
A6-EYP	Airbus A.330-243	Etihad Airways	
A6-EYQ	Airbus A.330-243	Etihad Airways	
A6-EYR	Airbus A.330-243	Ethiad Airways	
A6-EYS	Airbus A.330-243	Ethiad Airways	

A7 (Qatar)

Reg.	Type	Owner or Operator	Notes
A7-ACA	Airbus A.330-202	Qatar Airways *Al Wajba*	
A7-ACB	Airbus A.330-202	Qatar Airways *Al Majida*	
A7-ACC	Airbus A.330-202	Qatar Airways *Al Shahaniya*	
A7-ACD	Airbus A.330-202	Qatar Airways *Al Wusell*	
A7-ACE	Airbus A.330-202	Qatar Airways *Al Dhakira*	
A7-ACF	Airbus A.330-202	Qatar Airways *Al Kara'anah*	
A7-ACG	Airbus A.330-202	Qatar Airways *Al Wabra*	
A7-ACH	Airbus A.330-202	Qatar Airways *Al Mafjar*	
A7-ACI	Airbus A.330-202	Qatar Airways *Muathier*	
A7-ACJ	Airbus A.330-202	Qatar Airways *Zikreet*	
A7-ACK	Airbus A.330-202	Qatar Airways	

Notes	Reg.	Type	Owner or Operator
	A7-ACL	Airbus A.330-202	Qatar Airways
	A7-ACM	Airbus A.330-202	Qatar Airways
	A7-AEA	Airbus A.330-302	Qatar Airways *Al Muntazah*
	A7-AEB	Airbus A.330-302	Qatar Airways *Al Sayliyah*
	A7-AEC	Airbus A.330-302	Qatar Airways *Al Markhiya*
	A7-AED	Airbus A.330-302	Qatar Airways *Al Nu'uman*
	A7-AEE	Airbus A.330-302	Qatar Airways *Semaisma*
	A7-AEF	Airbus A.330-302	Qatar Airways *Al Rumellah*
	A7-AEG	Airbus A.330-302	Qatar Airways *Al Duhell*
	A7-AEH	Airbus A.330-302	Qatar Airways
	A7-AEI	Airbus A.330-302	Qatar Airways
	A7-AEJ	Airbus A.330-302	Qatar Airways
	A7-AEM	Airbus A.330-302	Qatar Airways
	A7-AEN	Airbus A.330-302	Qatar Airways
	A7-AEO	Airbus A.330-302	Qatar Airways
	A7-AFL	Airbus A.330-202	Qatar Airways *Al Messilah*
	A7-AFM	Airbus A.330-202	Qatar Airways *Al Udaid*
	A7-AFP	Airbus A-330-202	Qatar Airways *Al Shamal*
	A7-AGA	Airbus A.340-642	Qatar Airways
	A7-AGB	Airbus A.340-642	Qatar Airways
	A7-AGC	Airbus A.340-642	Qatar Airways
	A7-AGD	Airbus A.340-642	Qatar Airways
	A7-AKA	Airbus A.380-861	Qatar Airways
	A7-AKB	Airbus A.380-861	Qatar Airways
	A7-BAA	Boeing 777-3DZ ER	Qatar Airways
	A7-BAB	Boeing 777-3DZ ER	Qatar Airways
	A7-BAC	Boeing 777-3DZ ER	Qatar Airways
	A7-BAE	Boeing 777-3DZ ER	Qatar Airways
	A7-BAF	Boeing 777-3DZ ER	Qatar Airways
	A7-BAG	Boeing 777-3DZ ER	Qatar Airways
	A7-BAH	Boeing 777-3DZ ER	Qatar Airways
	A7-BAI	Boeing 777-3DZ ER	Qatar Airways
	A7-BAJ	Boeing 777-3DZ ER	Qatar Airways
	A7-BAK	Boeing 777-3DZ ER	Qatar Airways
	A7-BAL	Boeing 777-3DZ ER	Qatar Airways
	A7-BAO	Boeing 777-3DZ ER	Qatar Airways
	A7-BAP	Boeing 777-3DZ ER	Qatar Airways
	A7-BAQ	Boeing 777-3DZ ER	Qatar Airways
	A7-BBA	Boeing 777-2DZ LR	Qatar Airways
	A7-BBB	Boeing 777-2DZ LR	Qatar Airways
	A7-BBC	Boeing 777-2DZ LR	Qatar Airways
	A7-BBD	Boeing 777-2DZ LR	Qatar Airways
	A7-BBE	Boeing 777-2DZ LR	Qatar Airways
	A7-BBF	Boeing 777-2DZ LR	Qatar Airways
	A7-BBG	Boeing 777-2DZ LR	Qatar Airways
	A7-BBH	Boeing 777-2DZ LR	Qatar Airways *A.Calail*

A9C (Bahrain)

Notes	Reg.	Type	Owner or Operator
	A9C-KA	Airbus A.330-243 (501)	Gulf Air
	A9C-KB	Airbus A.330-243 (502)	Gulf Air
	A9C-KC	Airbus A.330-243 (503)	Gulf Air
	A9C-KD	Airbus A.330-243 (504)	Gulf Air
	A9C-KE	Airbus A.330-243 (505)	Gulf Air
	A9C-KF	Airbus A.330-243 (506)	Gulf Air *Aldafra*
	A9C-KG	Airbus A.330-243	Gulf Air
	A9C-KH	Airbus A.330-243	Gulf Air
	A9C-KI	Airbus A.330-243	Gulf Air
	A9C-KJ	Airbus A.330-243	Gulf Air
	A9C-LG	Airbus A.340-313X (407)	Gulf Air
	A9C-LH	Airbus A.340-313X (408)	Gulf Air
	A9C-LI	Airbus A.340-313X (409)	Gulf Air
	A9C-LJ	Airbus A.340-313X (410)	Gulf Air

A40 (Oman)

Notes	Reg.	Type	Owner or Operator
	A40-DA	Airbus A.330-243	Oman Air
	A40-DB	Airbus A.330-343	Oman Air
	A40-DC	Airbus A.330-243	Oman Air
	A40-DD	Airbus A.330-343	Oman Air
	A40-DE	Airbus A.330-343	Oman Air

Reg.	Type	Owner or Operator	Notes
A40-DF	Airbus A.330-243	Oman Air	
A40-DG	Airbus A.330-243	Oman Air	

AP (Pakistan)

Reg.	Type	Owner or Operator	Notes
AP-BDZ	Airbus A.310-308	Pakistan International Airlines	
AP-BEB	Airbus A.310-308	Pakistan International Airlines	
AP-BEC	Airbus A.310-308	Pakistan International Airlines	
AP-BEG	Airbus A.310-308	Pakistan International Airlines	
AP-BEQ	Airbus A.310-308	Pakistan International Airlines	
AP-BEU	Airbus A.310-308	Pakistan International Airlines	
AP-BGJ	Boeing 777-240ER	Pakistan International Airlines	
AP-BGK	Boeing 777-240ER	Pakistan International Airlines	
AP-BGL	Boeing 777-240ER	Pakistan International Airlines	
AP-BGY	Boeing 777-240LR	Pakistan International Airlines	
AP-BGZ	Boeing 777-240LR	Pakistan International Airlines	
AP-BHV	Boeing 777-340ER	Pakistan International Airlines	
AP-BHW	Boeing 777-340ER	Pakistan International Airlines	
AP-BHX	Boeing 777-240ER	Pakistan International Airlines	
AP-BID	Boeing 777-240ER	Pakistan International Airlines	
AP-BJA	Airbus A.321-231	AirBlue	
AP-BRJ	Airbus A.321-131	AirBlue	

B (China/Taiwan/Hong Kong)

Reg.	Type	Owner or Operator	Notes
B-HKE	Boeing 747-412	Cathay Pacific Airways	
B-HKF	Boeing 747-412	Cathay Pacific Airways	
B-HKH	Boeing 747-412BCF (SCD)	Cathay Pacific Airways	
B-HKJ	Boeing 747-412BCF	Cathay Pacific Airways	
B-HKS	Boeing 747-412BCF	Cathay Pacific Airways	
B-HKT	Boeing 747-412BCF	Cathay Pacific Airways	
B-HKU	Boeing 747-412	Cathay Pacific Airways	
B-HKV	Boeing 747-412	Cathay Pacific Airways	
B-HKX	Boeing 747-412	Cathay Pacific Airways	
B-HOP	Boeing 747-467	Cathay Pacific Airways	
B-HOR	Boeing 747-467	Cathay Pacific Airways	
B-HOS	Boeing 747-467	Cathay Pacific Airways	
B-HOT	Boeing 747-467	Cathay Pacific Airways	
B-HOV	Boeing 747-467	Cathay Pacific Airways	
B-HOW	Boeing 747-467	Cathay Pacific Airways	
B-HOX	Boeing 747-467	Cathay Pacific Airways	
B-HOY	Boeing 747-467	Cathay Pacific Airways	
B-HOZ	Boeing 747-467F	Cathay Pacific Airways	
B-HUA	Boeing 747-467	Cathay Pacific Airways	
B-HUB	Boeing 747-467	Cathay Pacific Airways	
B-HUD	Boeing 747-467	Cathay Pacific Airways	
B-HUE	Boeing 747-467	Cathay Pacific Airways	
B-HUF	Boeing 747-467	Cathay Pacific Airways	
B-HUG	Boeing 747-467	Cathay Pacific Airways	
B-HUH	Boeing 747-467F (SCD)	Cathay Pacific Airways	
B-HUI	Boeing 747-467	Cathay Pacific Airways	
B-HUJ	Boeing 747-467	Cathay Pacific Airways	
B-HUK	Boeing 747-467F (SCD)	Cathay Pacific Airways	
B-HUL	Boeing 747-467F (SCD)	Cathay Pacific Airways	
B-HUO	Boeing 747-467F (SCD)	Cathay Pacific Airways	
B-HUP	Boeing 747-467F (SCD)	Cathay Pacific Airways	
B-HUQ	Boeing 747-467F (SCD)	Cathay Pacific Airways	
B-HUR	Boeing 747-444BCF	Cathay Pacific Airways	
B-HUS	Boeing 747-444BCF	Cathay Pacific Airways	
B-HXA	Airbus A.340-313X	Cathay Pacific Airways	
B-HXB	Airbus A.340-313X	Cathay Pacific Airways	
B-HXC	Airbus A.340-313X	Cathay Pacific Airways	
B-HXD	Airbus A.340-313X	Cathay Pacific Airways	
B-HXE	Airbus A.340-313X	Cathay Pacific Airways	
B-HXF	Airbus A.340-313X	Cathay Pacific Airways	
B-HXG	Airbus A.340-313X	Cathay Pacific Airways	
B-HXH	Airbus A.340-313X	Cathay Pacific Airways	
B-HXI	Airbus A.340-313X	Cathay Pacific Airways	
B-HXJ	Airbus A.340-313X	Cathay Pacific Airways	
B-HXK	Airbus A.340-313X	Cathay Pacific Airways	
B-HXL	Airbus A.340-313X	Cathay Pacific Airways	
B-KAE	Boeing 747-412BCF	Cathay Pacific Airways	

Notes	Reg.	Type	Owner or Operator
	B-KAF	Boeing 747-412BCF	Cathay Pacific Airways
	B-KAG	Boeing 747-412BCF	Cathay Pacific Airways
	B-KAH	Boeing 747-412SF	Cathay Pacific Airways
	B-KAI	Boeing 747-412BCF	Cathay Pacific Airways
	B-KPA	Boeing 777-367ER	Cathay Pacific Airways
	B-KPB	Boeing 777-367ER	Cathay Pacific Airways
	B-KPC	Boeing 777-367ER	Cathay Pacific Airways
	B-KPD	Boeing 777-367ER	Cathay Pacific Airways
	B-KPE	Boeing 777-367ER	Cathay Pacific Airways
	B-KPF	Boeing 777-367ER	Cathay Pacific Airways
	B-KPG	Boeing 777-367ER	Cathay Pacific Airways
	B-KPH	Boeing 777-367ER	Cathay Pacific Airways
	B-KPI	Boeing 777-367ER	Cathay Pacific Airways
	B-KPJ	Boeing 777-367ER	Cathay Pacific Airways
	B-KPK	Boeing 777-367ER	Cathay Pacific Airways
	B-KPL	Boeing 777-367ER	Cathay Pacific Airways
	B-KPM	Boeing 777-367ER	Cathay Pacific Airways
	B-KPN	Boeing 777-367ER	Cathay Pacific Airways
	B-KPO	Boeing 777-367ER	Cathay Pacific Airways
	B-KPP	Boeing 777-367ER	Cathay Pacific Airways
	B-KPQ	Boeing 777-367ER	Cathay Pacific Airways
	B-KPR	Boeing 777-367ER	Cathay Pacific Airways
	B-KPS	Boeing 777-367ER	Cathay Pacific Airways
	B-KPT	Boeing 777-367ER	Cathay Pacific Airways
	B-KPU	Boeing 777-367ER	Cathay Pacific Airways
	B-KPV	Boeing 777-367ER	Cathay Pacific Airways
	B-KPW	Boeing 777-367ER	Cathay Pacific Airways
	B-KPX	Boeing 777-367ER	Cathay Pacific Airways
	B-LIA	Boeing 747-467ERF	Cathay Pacific Airways
	B-LIB	Boeing 747-467ERF	Cathay Pacific Airways
	B-LIC	Boeing 747-467ERF	Cathay Pacific Airways
	B-LID	Boeing 747-467ERF	Cathay Pacific Airways
	B-LIE	Boeing 747-467ERF	Cathay Pacific Airways
	B-LIF	Boeing 747-467ERF	Cathay Pacific Airways
	B-2385	Airbus A.340-313X	Air China
	B-2386	Airbus A.340-313X	Air China
	B-2387	Airbus A.340-313X	Air China
	B-2388	Airbus A.340-313X	Air China
	B-2389	Airbus A.340-313X	Air China
	B-2390	Airbus A.340-313X	Air China
	B-2409	Boeing 747-412F (SCD)	Air China Cargo
	B-2428	Boeing 747-412F	Great Wall Airlines
	B-2430	Boeing 747-412BCF	Great Wall Airlines
	B-2433	Boeing 747-412F	Great Wall Airlines
	B-2455	Boeing 747-412BCF	Air China Cargo
	B-2456	Boeing 747-4J6BCF	Air China Cargo
	B-2458	Boeing 747-4J6BCF	Air China Cargo
	B-2475	Boeing 747-4FTF (SCD)	Air China Cargo
	B-2476	Boeing 747-4FTF (SCD)	Air China Cargo
	B-2477	Boeing 747-433SF	Air China Cargo
	B-2478	Boeing 747-433SF	Air China Cargo
	B-6070	Airbus A.330-243	Air China
	B-6071	Airbus A.330-243	Air China
	B-6072	Airbus A.330-243	Air China
	B-6073	Airbus A.330-243	Air China
	B-6075	Airbus A.330-243	Air China
	B-6076	Airbus A.330-243	Air China
	B-6079	Airbus A.330-243	Air China
	B-6080	Airbus A.330-243	Air China
	B-6081	Airbus A.330-243	Air China
	B-6082	Airbus A.330-243	China Eastern Airlines
	B-6090	Airbus A.330-243	Air China
	B-6091	Airbus A.330-243	Air China
	B-6092	Airbus A.330-243	Air China
	B-6093	Airbus A.330-243	Air China
	B-6099	Airbus A.330-243	China Eastern Airlines
	B-6113	Airbus A.330-243	Air China
	B-6115	Airbus A.330-243	Air China
	B-6117	Airbus A.330-243	Air China
	B-6121	Airbus A.330-243	China Eastern Airlines
	B-6122	Airbus A.330-243	China Eastern Airlines
	B-6123	Airbus A.330-243	China Eastern Airlines
	B-6130	Airbus A.330-243	Air China
	B-6131	Airbus A.330-243	Air China

B-6132	Airbus A.330-243	Air China	
B-6505	Airbus A.330-243	Air China	
B-16101	McD Douglas MD-11F	EVA Air Cargo	
B-16107	McD Douglas MD-11F	EVA Air Cargo	
B-16108	McD Douglas MD-11F	EVA Air Cargo	
B-16109	McD Douglas MD-11F	EVA Air Cargo	
B-16110	McD Douglas MD-11F	EVA Air Cargo	
B-16111	McD Douglas MD-11F	EVA Air Cargo	
B-16112	McD Douglas MD-11F	EVA Air Cargo	
B-16113	McD Douglas MD-11F	EVA Air Cargo	
B-16402	Boeing 747-45E	EVA Airways	
B-16403	Boeing 747-45E	EVA Airways	
B-16405	Boeing 747-45E	EVA Airways	
B-16408	Boeing 747-45E	EVA Airways	
B-16409	Boeing 747-45E	EVA Airways	
B-16410	Boeing 747-45E	EVA Airways	
B-16411	Boeing 747-45E	EVA Airways	
B-16412	Boeing 747-45E	EVA Airways	
B-16701	Boeing 777-35EER	EVA Airways	
B-16702	Boeing 777-35EER	EVA Airways	
B-16703	Boeing 777-35EER	EVA Airways	
B-16705	Boeing 777-35EER	EVA Airways	
B-16706	Boeing 777-35EER	EVA Airways	
B-16707	Boeing 777-35EER	EVA Airways	
B-16708	Boeing 777-35EER	EVA Airways	
B-16709	Boeing 777-35EER	EVA Airways	
B-16710	Boeing 777-35EER	EVA Airways	
B-16711	Boeing 777-35EER	EVA Airways	
B-16712	Boeing 777-35EER	EVA Airways	
B-16713	Boeing 777-35EER	EVA Airways	
B-16715	Boeing 777-35EER	EVA Airways	
B-16716	Boeing 777-35EER	EVA Airways	
B-16717	Boeing 777-35EER	EVA Airways	
B-18701	Boeing 747-409F (SCD)	China Airlines	
B-18702	Boeing 747-409F (SCD)	China Airlines	
B-18706	Boeing 747-409F (SCD)	China Airlines	
B-18707	Boeing 747-409F (SCD)	China Airlines	
B-18708	Boeing 747-409F (SCD)	China Airlines	
B-18709	Boeing 747-409F (SCD)	China Airlines	
B-18710	Boeing 747-409F (SCD)	China Airlines	
B-18711	Boeing 747-409F (SCD)	China Airlines	
B-18715	Boeing 747-409F (SCD)	China Airlines	
B-18716	Boeing 747-409F (SCD)	China Airlines	
B-18717	Boeing 747-409F (SCD)	China Airlines	
B-18718	Boeing 747-409F (SCD)	China Airlines	
B-18719	Boeing 747-409F (SCD)	China Airlines	
B-18720	Boeing 747-409F (SCD)	China Airlines	
B-18721	Boeing 747-409F (SCD)	China Airlines	
B-18722	Boeing 747-409F (SCD)	China Airlines	
B-18723	Boeing 747-409F (SCD)	China Airlines	
B-18725	Boeing 747-409F (SCD)	China Airlines	
B-18801	Airbus A.340-313X	China Airlines	
B-18802	Airbus A.340-313X	China Airlines	
B-18803	Airbus A.340-313X	China Airlines	
B-18805	Airbus A.340-313X	China Airlines	
B-18806	Airbus A.340-313X	China Airlines	
B-18807	Airbus A.340-313X	China Airlines	

C (Canada)

C-FCAB	Boeing 767-375ER (681)	Air Canada	
C-FCAE	Boeing 767-375ER (682)	Air Canada	
C-FCAF	Boeing 767-375ER (683)	Air Canada	
C-FCAG	Boeing 767-375ER (684)	Air Canada	
C-FDAT	Airbus A.310-308 (305)	Air Transat	
C-FITL	Boeing 777-333ER (731)	Air Canada	
C-FITU	Boeing 777-333ER (732)	Air Canada	
C-FITW	Boeing 777-3Q8ER (733)	Air Canada	
C-FIUA	Boeing 777-233LR (701)	Air Canada	
C-FIUF	Boeing 777-233LR (702)	Air Canada	
C-FIUJ	Boeing 777-233LR (703)	Air Canada	
C-FIUL	Boeing 777-333ER (734)	Air Canada	

Notes	Reg.	Type	Owner or Operator
	C-FIUR	Boeing 777-333ER (735)	Air Canada
	C-FIUV	Boeing 777-333ER	Air Canada
	C-FIUW	Boeing 777-333ER	Air Canada
	C-FIVK	Boeing 777-233LR	Air Canada
	C-FIVM	Boeing 777-333ER	Air Canada
	C-FIVQ	Boeing 777-333ER	Air Canada
	C-FIVR	Boeing 777-333ER	Air Canada
	C-FIVS	Boeing 777-333ER	Air Canada
	C-FMWP	Boeing 767-333ER (631)	Air Canada
	C-FMWQ	Boeing 767-333ER (632)	Air Canada
	C-FMWU	Boeing 767-333ER (633)	Air Canada
	C-FMWV	Boeing 767-333ER (634)	Air Canada
	C-FMWY	Boeing 767-333ER (635)	Air Canada
	C-FMXC	Boeing 767-333ER (636)	Air Canada
	C-FNND	Boeing 777-233LR	Air Canada
	C-FNNH	Boeing 777-233LR	Air Canada
	C-FOCA	Boeing 767-375ER (640)	Air Canada
	C-FPCA	Boeing 767-375ER (637)	Air Canada
	C-FRAM	Boeing 777-333ER	Air Canada
	C-FTCA	Boeing 767-375ER (638)	Air Canada
	C-FXCA	Boeing 767-375ER (639)	Air Canada
	C-GBZR	Boeing 767-38EER (645)	Air Canada
	C-GCTS	Airbus A.330-243	Air Transat
	C-GDUZ	Boeing 767-38EER (646)	Air Canada
	C-GEOQ	Boeing 767-375ER (647)	Air Canada
	C-GEOU	Boeing 767-375ER (648)	Air Canada
	C-GFAF	Airbus A.330-343X (931)	Air Canada
	C-GFAH	Airbus A.330-343X (932)	Air Canada
	C-GFAJ	Airbus A.330-343X (933)	Air Canada
	C-GFAT	Airbus A.310-304 (301)	Air Transat
	C-GFUR	Airbus A.330-343X (934)	Air Canada
	C-GGTS	Airbus A.330-243 (101)	Air Transat
	C-GHKR	Airbus A.330-343X (935)	Air Canada
	C-GHKW	Airbus A.330-343X (936)	Air Canada
	C-GHKX	Airbus A.330-343X (937)	Air Canada
	C-GHLA	Boeing 767-35HER (656)	Air Canada
	C-GHLK	Boeing 767-35HER (657)	Air Canada
	C-GHLM	Airbus A.330-343X (938)	Air Canada
	C-GHLQ	Boeing 767-333ER (658)	Air Canada
	C-GHLT	Boeing 767-333ER (659)	Air Canada
	C-GHLU	Boeing 767-333ER (660)	Air Canada
	C-GHLV	Boeing 767-333ER (661)	Air Canada
	C-GHOZ	Boeing 767-375ER (685)	Air Canada
	C-GHPD	Boeing 767-3Y0ER (687)	Air Canada
	C-GHPF	Boeing 767-3Y0ER (689)	Air Canada
	C-GITS	Airbus A.330-243 (102)	Air Transat
	C-GKTS	Airbus A.330-342 (100)	Air Transat
	C-GLAT	Airbus A.310-308 (302)	Air Transat
	C-GLCA	Boeing 767-375ER (641)	Air Canada
	C-GPAT	Airbus A.310-308 (303)	Air Transat
	C-GPTS	Airbus A.330-243 (103)	Air Transat
	C-GSAT	Airbus A.310-308 (304)	Air Transat
	C-GSCA	Boeing 767-375ER (642)	Air Canada
	C-GTSD	Airbus A.310-304 (341)	Air Transat
	C-GTSF	Airbus A.310-304 (345)	Air Transat
	C-GTSH	Airbus A.310-304 (343)	Air Transat
	C-GTSK	Airbus A.310-304	Air Transat
	C-GTSN	Airbus A.330-243	Air Transat
	C-GTSR	Airbus A.330-243	Air Transat
	C-GTSW	Airbus A.310-304	Air Transat
	C-GTSX	Airbus A.310-304	Air Transat
	C-GTSY	Airbus A.310-304 (344)	Air Transat
	C-GTSZ	Airbus A.330-243	Air Transat
	C-GVAT	Airbus A.310-304 (321)	Air Transat

Note: Airline fleet number when carried on aircraft is shown in parentheses.

CN (Morocco)

Notes	Reg.	Type	Owner or Operator
	CN-RGA	Boeing 747-428	Royal Air Maroc
	CN-RMF	Boeing 737-4B6	Royal Air Maroc
	CN-RMG	Boeing 737-4B6	Royal Air Maroc
	CN-RMV	Boeing 737-5B6	Royal Air Maroc
	CN-RMW	Boeing 737-5B6	Royal Air Maroc

Reg.	Type	Owner or Operator	Notes
CN-RMX	Boeing 737-4B6	Royal Air Maroc	
CN-RMY	Boeing 737-5B6	Royal Air Maroc	
CN-RNB	Boeing 737-5B6	Royal Air Maroc	
CN-RNC	Boeing 737-4B6	Royal Air Maroc	
CN-RND	Boeing 737-4B6	Royal Air Maroc	
CN-RNG	Boeing 737-5B6	Royal Air Maroc	
CN-RNH	Boeing 737-5B6	Royal Air Maroc	
CN-RNJ	Boeing 737-8B6	Royal Air Maroc	
CN-RNK	Boeing 737-8B6	Royal Air Maroc	
CN-RNL	Boeing 737-7B6	Royal Air Maroc	
CN-RNM	Boeing 737-7B6	Royal Air Maroc	
CN-RNP	Boeing 737-8B6	Royal Air Maroc	
CN-RNQ	Boeing 737-7B6	Royal Air Maroc	
CN-RNR	Boeing 737-7B6	Royal Air Maroc	
CN-RNS	Boeing 767-3B6ER	Royal Air Maroc	
CN-RNT	Boeing 767-3B6ER	Royal Air Maroc	
CN-RNU	Boeing 737-8B6	Royal Air Maroc	
CN-RNV	Boeing 737-7B6	Royal Air Maroc	
CN-RNW	Boeing 737-8B6	Royal Air Maroc	
CN-RNX	Airbus A.321-211	Royal Air Maroc	
CN-RNY	Airbus A.321-211	Royal Air Maroc	
CN-RNZ	Boeing 737-8B6	Royal Air Maroc	
CN-ROA	Boeing 737-8B6	Royal Air Maroc	
CN-ROB	Boeing 737-8B6	Royal Air Maroc	
CN-ROC	Boeing 737-8B6	Royal Air Maroc	
CN-ROD	Boeing 737-7B6	Royal Air Maroc	
CN-ROE	Boeing 737-8B6	Royal Air Maroc	
CN-ROF	Airbus A.321-211	Royal Air Maroc	
CN-ROG	Boeing 767-328ER	Royal Air Maroc	
CN-ROH	Boeing 737-8B6	Royal Air Maroc	
CN-ROJ	Boeing 737-8B6	Royal Air Maroc	
CN-ROK	Boeing 737-8B6	Royal Air Maroc	
CN-ROL	Boeing 737-8B6	Royal Air Maroc	
CN-ROM	Airbus A.321-211	Royal Air Maroc	
CN-ROP	Boeing 737-8B6	Royal Air Maroc	
CN-ROR	Boeing 737-8B6	Royal Air Maroc	
CN-ROS	Boeing 737-8B6	Royal Air Maroc	
CN-ROT	Boeing 737-8B6	Royal Air Maroc	
CN-ROU	Boeing 737-8B6	Royal Air Maroc	
CN-ROV	Boeing 767-3Q8ER	Royal Air Maroc	
CN-ROW	Boeing 767-343ER	Royal Air Maroc	
CN-ROY	Boeing 737-8B6	Royal Air Maroc	
CN-ROZ	Boeing 737-8B6	Royal Air Maroc	

CS (Portugal)

Reg.	Type	Owner or Operator	Notes
CS-TDI	Airbus A.310-304	White Airways *Flygreen*	
CS-TEX	Airbus A.310-304	HiFly	
CS-TFM	Boeing 777-212	Euro Atlantic Airways/Bangladesh Biman	
CS-TFS	Boeing 767-3YOER	Euro Atlantic Airways	
CS-TFT	Boeing 767-3YOER	Euro Atlantic Airways	
CS-TFW	Airbus A.340-542	Arik Air	
CS-TFX	Airbus A.340-542	Arik Air *Captain Bob Hayes,OON*	
CS-TGU	Airbus A.310-304	SATA International *Terceira*	
CS-TGV	Airbus A.310-304	SATA International	
CS-TJE	Airbus A.321-211	TAP Portugal *Pero Vaz de Caminha*	
CS-TJF	Airbus A.321-211	TAP Portugal *Luis Vaz de Camoes*	
CS-TJG	Airbus A.321-211	TAP Portugal *Amelia Rodrigues*	
CS-TKI	Airbus A.310-304	White Airways *FlyRed*	
CS-TKJ	Airbus A.320-212	SATA International *Pico*	
CS-TKK	Airbus A.320-214	SATA International *Corvo*	
CS-TKL	Airbus A.320-214	SATA International *Sao Jorge*	
CS-TKM	Airbus A.310-304	SATA International *Autonomia*	
CS-TKN	Airbus A.310-325	SATA International *Macaronesia*	
CS-TKO	Airbus A.320-214	SATA International	
CS-TLO	Boeing 767-383ER	Euro Atlantic Airways/Brussels Airlines	
CS-TLX	Boeing 757-2G5	Euro Atlantic Airways	
CS-TMW	Airbus A.320-214	TAP Portugal *Luisa Todi*	
CS-TNG	Airbus A.320-214	TAP Portugal *Mouzinho da Silveira*	
CS-TNH	Airbus A.320-214	TAP Portugal *Almada Negreiros*	
CS-TNI	Airbus A.320-214	TAP Portugal *Aquilino Ribiera*	
CS-TNJ	Airbus A.320-214	TAP Portugal *Florbela Espanca*	
CS-TNK	Airbus A.320-214	TAP Portugal *Teofilo Braga*	

Notes	Reg.	Type	Owner or Operator
	CS-TNL	Airbus A.320-214	TAP Portugal *Vitorino Nermesio*
	CS-TNM	Airbus A.320-214	TAP Portugal *Natalia Correia*
	CS-TNN	Airbus A.320-214	TAP Portugal *Gil Vicente*
	CS-TNP	Airbus A.320-214	TAP Portugal *Alexandre O'Neill*
	CS-TNQ	Airbus A.320-214	TAP Portugal *Jose Regio*
	CS-TNR	Airbus A.320-214	TAP Portugal
	CS-TNS	Airbus A.320-214	TAP Portugal *D.Alfonso Henriques*
	CS-TNT	Airbus A.320-214	TAP Portugal
	CS-TNU	Airbus A.320-214	TAP Portugal
	CS-TNV	Airbus A.320-214	TAP Portugal
	CS-TOA	Airbus A.340-312	TAP Portugal *Fernao Mendes Pinto*
	CS-TOB	Airbus A.340-312	TAP Portugal *D Joao de Castro*
	CS-TOC	Airbus A.340-312	TAP Portugal *Wenceslau de Moraes*
	CS-TOD	Airbus A.340-312	TAP Portugal *D Francisco de Almeida*
	CS-TOE	Airbus A.330-223	TAP Portugal *Pedro Alvares Cabal*
	CS-TOF	Airbus A.330-223	TAP Portugal *Infante D Henrique*
	CS-TOG	Airbus A.330-223	TAP Portugal *Bartolomeu de Gusmão*
	CS-TOH	Airbus A.330-223	TAP Portugal *Nuno Gongalves*
	CS-TOI	Airbus A.330-223	TAP Portugal *Damiao de Gois*
	CS-TOJ	Airbus A.330-223	TAP Portugal *D.Ja-o II 'O Principe Perfeito*
	CS-TOK	Airbus A.330-223	TAP Portugal *Padre Antonio Vieira*
	CS-TOL	Airbus A.330-202	TAP Portugal *Joao Goncalves Zarco*
	CS-TOM	Airbus A.330-202	TAP Portugal *Vasco da Gama*
	CS-TON	Airbus A.330-202	TAP Portugal *Ja-o XXI*
	CS-TOO	Airbus A.330-202	TAP Portugal *Fernao de Magalhaes*
	CS-TOP	Airbus A.330-202	TAP Portugal *Pedro Nunes*
	CS-TQD	Airbus A.320-214	TAP Portugal
	CS-TQK	Airbus A.320-232	White Airways
	CS-TQO	Airbus A.320-214	White Airways
	CS-TRH	Airbus A.330-343	Orbest
	CS-TTA	Airbus A.319-111	TAP Portugal *Vieira da Silva*
	CS-TTB	Airbus A.319-111	TAP Portugal *Gago Coutinho*
	CS-TTC	Airbus A.319-111	TAP Portugal *Fernando Pessoa*
	CS-TTD	Airbus A.319-111	TAP Portugal *Amadeo de Souza-Cardoso*
	CS-TTE	Airbus A.319-111	TAP Portugal *Francisco d'Ollanda*
	CS-TTF	Airbus A.319-111	TAP Portugal *Calouste Gulbenkian*
	CS-TTG	Airbus A.319-111	TAP Portugal *Humberto Delgado*
	CS-TTH	Airbus A.319-111	TAP Portugal *Antonio Sergio*
	CS-TTI	Airbus A.319-111	TAP Portugal *Eca de Queiros*
	CS-TTJ	Airbus A.319-111	TAP Portugal *Eusebio*
	CS-TTK	Airbus A.319-111	TAP Portugal *Miguel Torga*
	CS-TTL	Airbus A.319-111	TAP Portugal *Almeida Garrett*
	CS-TTM	Airbus A.319-111	TAP Portugal *Alexandre Herculano*
	CS-TTN	Airbus A.319-111	TAP Portugal *Camilo Castelo Branco*
	CS-TTO	Airbus A.319-111	TAP Portugal *Antero de Quental*
	CS-TTP	Airbus A.319-111	TAP Portugal *Josefa d'Obidos*
	CS-TTQ	Airbus A.319-112	TAP Portugal *Agostinho da Silva*
	CS-TTR	Airbus A.319-112	TAP Portugal
	CS-TTS	Airbus A.319-112	TAP Portugal *Guilhermina Suggia*

D (Germany)

Notes	Reg.	Type	Owner or Operator
	D-AALA	Boeing 777-FZN	AeroLogic
	D-AALB	Boeing 777-FZN	AeroLogic
	D-AALC	Boeing 777-FZN	AeroLogic
	D-AALD	Boeing 777-FZN	AeroLogic
	D-AALE	Boeing 777-FZN	AeroLogic
	D-AALF	Boeing 777-FZN	AeroLogic
	D-AALG	Boeing 777-FZN	AeroLogic
	D-AALH	Boeing 777-FZN	AeroLogic
	D-AALI	Boeing 777-FZN	AeroLogic
	D-AALJ	Boeing 777-FZN	AeroLogic
	D-AALK	Boeing 777-FZN	AeroLogic
	D-AALL	Boeing 777-FZN	AeroLogic
	D-AALM	Boeing 777-FZN	AeroLogic
	D-AALN	Boeing 777-FZN	AeroLogic
	D-AALO	Boeing 777-FZN	AeroLogic
	D-ABAA	Boeing 737-76Q	Air Berlin
	D-ABAB	Boeing 737-76Q	Air Berlin
	D-ABAF	Boeing 737-86J	Air Berlin
	D-ABAG	Boeing 737-86J	Air Berlin
	D-ABAP	Boeing 737-86J	Air Berlin
	D-ABAQ	Boeing 737-86J	Air Berlin

Reg.	Type	Owner or Operator	Notes
D-ABAR	Boeing 737-86J	Air Berlin	
D-ABAS	Boeing 737-86J	Air Berlin	
D-ABAV	Boeing 737-86J	Air Berlin	
D-ABBA	Boeing 737-86J	Air Berlin	
D-ABBB	Boeing 737-86J	Air Berlin	
D-ABBC	Boeing 737-86J	Air Berlin	
D-ABBD	Boeing 737-86J	Air Berlin	
D-ABBE	Boeing 737-86J	Air Berlin	
D-ABBF	Boeing 737-86J	Air Berlin	
D-ABBG	Boeing 737-86J	Air Berlin	
D-ABBH	Boeing 737-86J	Air Berlin	
D-ABBI	Boeing 737-86J	Air Berlin	
D-ABBJ	Boeing 737-86Q	Air Berlin	
D-ABBK	Boeing 737-8BK	Air Berlin	
D-ABBS	Boeing 737-76N	Air Berlin	
D-ABBT	Boeing 737-76N	Air Berlin	
D-ABBU	Boeing 737-8Q8	Air Berlin	
D-ABBV	Boeing 737-7Q8	Air Berlin	
D-ABBW	Boeing 737-7Q8	Air Berlin	
D-ABBX	Boeing 737-808	Air Berlin	
D-ABBY	Boeing 737-808	Air Berlin	
D-ABBZ	Boeing 737-85F	Air Berlin	
D-ABCA	Airbus A.321-211	Air Berlin	
D-ABCB	Airbus A.321-211	Air Berlin	
D-ABCC	Airbus A.321-211	Air Berlin	
D-ABCF	Airbus A.321-211	Air Berlin	
D-ABCG	Airbus A.321-211	Air Berlin	
D-ABDA	Airbus A.320-214	Air Berlin	
D-ABDB	Airbus A.320-214	Air Berlin	
D-ABDC	Airbus A.320-214	Air Berlin	
D-ABDD	Airbus A.320-214	Air Berlin	
D-ABDP	Airbus A.320-214	Air Berlin	
D-ABDQ	Airbus A.320-214	Air Berlin	
D-ABDR	Airbus A.320-214	Air Berlin	
D-ABDS	Airbus A.320-214	Air Berlin	
D-ABDU	Airbus A.320-214	Air Berlin	
D-ABDW	Airbus A.320-214	Air Berlin	
D-ABDX	Airbus A.320-214	Air Berlin	
D-ABDY	Airbus A.320-214	Air Berlin	
D-ABEA	Boeing 737-330	Lufthansa *Saarbrücken*	
D-ABEB	Boeing 737-330	Lufthansa *Xanten*	
D-ABEC	Boeing 737-330	Lufthansa *Karlsrühe*	
D-ABED	Boeing 737-330	Lufthansa *Hagen*	
D-ABEE	Boeing 737-330	Lufthansa *Ulm*	
D-ABEF	Boeing 737-330	Lufthansa *Weiden i.d.Obf.*	
D-ABEH	Boeing 737-330	Lufthansa *Bad Kissingen*	
D-ABEI	Boeing 737-330	Lufthansa *Bamberg*	
D-ABEK	Boeing 737-330	Lufthansa *Wuppertal*	
D-ABEL	Boeing 737-330	Lufthansa *Pforzheim*	
D-ABEM	Boeing 737-330	Lufthansa *Eberswalde*	
D-ABEN	Boeing 737-330	Lufthansa *Neubrandenburg*	
D-ABEO	Boeing 737-330	Lufthansa *Plauen*	
D-ABEP	Boeing 737-330	Lufthansa *Naumburg (Saale)*	
D-ABER	Boeing 737-330	Lufthansa *Merseburg*	
D-ABES	Boeing 737-330	Lufthansa *Koethen/Anhalt*	
D-ABET	Boeing 737-330	Lufthansa *Gelsenkirchen*	
D-ABEU	Boeing 737-330	Lufthansa *Goslar*	
D-ABEW	Boeing 737-330	Lufthansa *Detmold*	
D-ABFA	Airbus A.320-214	Air Berlin	
D-ABFB	Airbus A.320-214	Air Berlin	
D-ABFC	Airbus A.320-214	Air Berlin	
D-ABFE	Airbus A.320-214	Air Berlin	
D-ABFF	Airbus A.320-214	Air Berlin	
D-ABFG	Airbus A.320-214	Air Berlin	
D-ABFK	Airbus A.320-214	Air Berlin	
D-ABFL	Airbus A.320-214	Air Berlin	
D-ABFM	Airbus A.320-214	Air Berlin	
D-ABFN	Airbus A.320-214	Air Berlin	
D-ABFO	Airbus A.320-214	Air Berlin	
D-ABGA	Airbus A.319-132	Air Berlin	
D-ABGH	Airbus A.319-112	Air Berlin	
D-ABGI	Airbus A.319-111	Air Berlin	
D-ABGJ	Airbus A.319-112	Air Berlin	
D-ABGK	Airbus A.319-112	Air Berlin	

Notes	Reg.	Type	Owner or Operator
	D-ABGL	Airbus A.319-112	Air Berlin
	D-ABGN	Airbus A.319-112	Air Berlin
	D-ABGO	Airbus A.319-112	Air Berlin
	D-ABGP	Airbus A.319-112	Air Berlin
	D-ABGQ	Airbus A.319-112	Air Berlin
	D-ABGR	Airbus A.319-112	Air Berlin
	D-ABGS	Airbus A.319-112	Air Berlin
	D-ABIA	Boeing 737-530	Lufthansa *Greifswald*
	D-ABIB	Boeing 737-530	Lufthansa *Esslingen*
	D-ABIC	Boeing 737-530	Lufthansa *Krefeld*
	D-ABID	Boeing 737-530	Lufthansa *Aachen*
	D-ABIE	Boeing 737-530	Lufthansa *Hildesheim*
	D-ABIF	Boeing 737-530	Lufthansa *Landau*
	D-ABIH	Boeing 737-530	Lufthansa *Bruchsal*
	D-ABII	Boeing 737-530	Lufthansa *Lörrach*
	D-ABIK	Boeing 737-530	Lufthansa *Rastatt*
	D-ABIL	Boeing 737-530	Lufthansa *Memmingen*
	D-ABIM	Boeing 737-530	Lufthansa *Salzgitter*
	D-ABIN	Boeing 737-530	Lufthansa *Langenhagen*
	D-ABIO	Boeing 737-530	Lufthansa *Wesel*
	D-ABIP	Boeing 737-530	Lufthansa *Oberhausen*
	D-ABIR	Boeing 737-530	Lufthansa *Anklam*
	D-ABIS	Boeing 737-530	Lufthansa *Rendsburg*
	D-ABIT	Boeing 737-530	Lufthansa *Neumünster*
	D-ABIU	Boeing 737-530	Lufthansa *Limburg a.d. Lahn*
	D-ABIW	Boeing 737-530	Lufthansa *Bad Nauheim*
	D-ABIX	Boeing 737-530	Lufthansa *Iserlohn*
	D-ABIY	Boeing 737-530	Lufthansa *Lingen*
	D-ABIZ	Boeing 737-530	Lufthansa *Kirchheim unter Teck*
	D-ABJA	Boeing 737-530	Lufthansa *Bad Segeberg*
	D-ABJB	Boeing 737-530	Lufthansa *Rheine*
	D-ABJC	Boeing 737-530	Lufthansa *Erding*
	D-ABJD	Boeing 737-530	Lufthansa *Freising*
	D-ABJE	Boeing 737-530	Lufthansa *Ingelheim am Rhein*
	D-ABJF	Boeing 737-530	Lufthansa *Aalen*
	D-ABJH	Boeing 737-530	Lufthansa *Heppenheim/Bergstrasse*
	D-ABJI	Boeing 737-530	Lufthansa *Siegburg*
	D-ABKA	Boeing 737-82R	Air Berlin
	D-ABKD	Boeing 737-86J	Air Berlin
	D-ABKE	Boeing 737-86J	Air Berlin
	D-ABKF	Boeing 737-86J	Air Berlin
	D-ABKH	Boeing 737-86J	Air Berlin
	D-ABKI	Boeing 737-86J	Air Berlin
	D-ABKJ	Boeing 737-86J	Air Berlin
	D-ABKK	Boeing 737-86J	Air Berlin
	D-ABKL	Boeing 737-86J	Air Berlin
	D-ABKM	Boeing 737-86J	Air Berlin
	D-ABKN	Boeing 737-86J	Air Berlin
	D-ABKO	Boeing 737-86J	Air Berlin
	D-ABKP	Boeing 737-86J	Air Berlin
	D-ABKQ	Boeing 737-86J	Air Berlin
	D-ABLA	Boeing 737-76J	Air Berlin
	D-ABLB	Boeing 737-76J	Air Berlin
	D-ABLC	Boeing 737-76J	Air Berlin
	D-ABLD	Boeing 737-76J	Air Berlin
	D-ABLE	Boeing 737-76J	Air Berlin
	D-ABLF	Boeing 737-76J	Air Berlin
	D-ABOA	Boeing 757-330	Condor
	D-ABOB	Boeing 757-330	Condor
	D-ABOC	Boeing 757-330	Condor
	D-ABOE	Boeing 757-330	Condor
	D-ABOF	Boeing 757-330	Condor
	D-ABOG	Boeing 757-330	Condor
	D-ABOH	Boeing 757-330	Condor
	D-ABOI	Boeing 757-330	Condor
	D-ABOJ	Boeing 757-330	Condor
	D-ABOK	Boeing 757-330	Condor
	D-ABOL	Boeing 757-330	Condor
	D-ABOM	Boeing 757-330	Condor
	D-ABON	Boeing 757-330	Condor
	D-ABQA	DHC.8Q-402 Dash Eight	Air Berlin
	D-ABQB	DHC.8Q-402 Dash Eight	Air Berlin
	D-ABQC	DHC.8Q-402 Dash Eight	Air Berlin
	D-ABQD	DHC.8Q-402 Dash Eight	Air Berlin

Reg.	Type	Owner or Operator	Notes
D-ABQE	DHC.8Q-402 Dash Eight	Air Berlin	
D-ABQF	DHC.8Q-402 Dash Eight	Air Berlin	
D-ABQG	DHC.8Q-402 Dash Eight	Air Berlin	
D-ABQH	DHC.8Q-402 Dash Eight	Air Berlin	
D-ABQI	DHC.8Q-402 Dash Eight	Air Berlin	
D-ABQJ	DHC.8Q-402 Dash Eight	Air Berlin	
D-ABTB	Boeing 747-430 (SCD)	Lufthansa *Brandenburg*	
D-ABTC	Boeing 747-430 (SCD)	Lufthansa *Mecklenburg-Vorpommern*	
D-ABTD	Boeing 747-430 (SCD)	Lufthansa *Hamburg*	
D-ABTE	Boeing 747-430 (SCD)	Lufthansa *Sachsen-Anhalt*	
D-ABTF	Boeing 747-430 (SCD)	Lufthansa *Thüringen*	
D-ABTH	Boeing 747-430 (SCD)	Lufthansa *Duisburg*	
D-ABTK	Boeing 747-430 (SCD)	Lufthansa *Kiel*	
D-ABTL	Boeing 747-430 (SCD)	Lufthansa *Dresden*	
D-ABUA	Boeing 767-330ER	Condor	
D-ABUB	Boeing 767-330ER	Condor	
D-ABUC	Boeing 767-330ER	Condor	
D-ABUD	Boeing 767-330ER	Condor	
D-ABUE	Boeing 767-330ER	Condor	
D-ABUF	Boeing 767-330ER	Condor	
D-ABUH	Boeing 767-330ER	Condor	
D-ABUI	Boeing 767-330ER	Condor	
D-ABUZ	Boeing 767-330ER	Condor	
D-ABVA	Boeing 747-430	Lufthansa *Berlin*	
D-ABVB	Boeing 747-430	Lufthansa *Bonn*	
D-ABVC	Boeing 747-430	Lufthansa *Baden-Württemberg*	
D-ABVD	Boeing 747-430	Lufthansa *Bochum*	
D-ABVE	Boeing 747-430	Lufthansa *Potsdam*	
D-ABVF	Boeing 747-430	Lufthansa *Frankfurt am Main*	
D-ABVH	Boeing 747-430	Lufthansa *Düsseldorf*	
D-ABVK	Boeing 747-430	Lufthansa *Hannover*	
D-ABVL	Boeing 747-430	Lufthansa *Muenchen*	
D-ABVM	Boeing 747-430	Lufthansa *Hessen*	
D-ABVN	Boeing 747-430	Lufthansa *Dortmund*	
D-ABVO	Boeing 747-430	Lufthansa *Mulheim a.d.Ruhr*	
D-ABVP	Boeing 747-430	Lufthansa *Bremen*	
D-ABVR	Boeing 747-430	Lufthansa *Koln*	
D-ABVS	Boeing 747-430	Lufthansa *Saarland*	
D-ABVT	Boeing 747-430	Lufthansa *Rheinland Pfalz*	
D-ABVU	Boeing 747-430	Lufthansa *Bayern*	
D-ABVW	Boeing 747-430	Lufthansa *Wolfsburg*	
D-ABVX	Boeing 747-430	Lufthansa *Schleswig-Holstein*	
D-ABVY	Boeing 747-430	Lufthansa *Nordrhein Westfalen*	
D-ABVZ	Boeing 747-430	Lufthansa *Niedersachsen*	
D-ABWH	Boeing 737-330	Lufthansa *Rothenburg o. d. Taube*	
D-ABXL	Boeing 737-330	Lufthansa *Neuss*	
D-ABXM	Boeing 737-330	Lufthansa *Herford*	
D-ABXN	Boeing 737-330	Lufthansa *Böblingen*	
D-ABXO	Boeing 737-330	Lufthansa *Schwäbisch-Gmünd*	
D-ABXP	Boeing 737-330	Lufthansa *Fulda*	
D-ABXR	Boeing 737-330	Lufthansa *Celle*	
D-ABXS	Boeing 737-330	Lufthansa *Sindelfingen*	
D-ABXT	Boeing 737-330	Lufthansa *Reutlingen*	
D-ABXU	Boeing 737-330	Lufthansa *Seeheim-Jugenheim*	
D-ABXW	Boeing 737-330	Lufthansa *Hanau*	
D-ABXX	Boeing 737-330	Lufthansa *Bad Homburg v.d. Höhe*	
D-ABXY	Boeing 737-330	Lufthansa *Hof*	
D-ABXZ	Boeing 737-330	Lufthansa *Bad Mergentheim*	
D-ACHE	Canadair CRJ200LR	Lufthansa Regional *Meissen*	
D-ACJC	Canadair CRJ200LR	Lufthansa Regional	
D-ACKA	Canadair CRJ900ER	Lufthansa Regional *Pfaffenhofen a.d.ilm*	
D-ACKB	Canadair CRJ900ER	Lufthansa Regional *Schliersee*	
D-ACKC	Canadair CRJ900ER	Lufthansa Regional *Mettmann*	
D-ACKD	Canadair CRJ900ER	Lufthansa Regional *Wittlich*	
D-ACKE	Canadair CRJ900ER	Lufthansa Regional *Weningerode*	
D-ACKF	Canadair CRJ900ER	Lufthansa Regional *Prenzlau*	
D-ACKG	Canadair CRJ900ER	Lufthansa Regional *Glucksburg*	
D-ACKH	Canadair CRJ900ER	Lufthansa Regional *Radebuel*	
D-ACKI	Canadair CRJ900ER	Lufthansa Regional *Tuttlingen*	
D-ACKJ	Canadair CRJ900ER	Lufthansa Regional *Ilmenau*	
D-ACKK	Canadair CRJ900ER	Lufthansa Regional *Furstenwalde*	
D-ACKL	Canadair CRJ900ER	Lufthansa Regional *Bad Bergzabern*	
D-ACLY	Canadair CRJ200LR	Lufthansa Regional	
D-ACNA	Canadair CRJ900ER	Lufthansa Regional	

Notes	Reg.	Type	Owner or Operator
	D-ACNB	Canadair CRJ900ER	Lufthansa Regional
	D-ACNC	Canadair CRJ900ER	Lufthansa Regional
	D-ACND	Canadair CRJ900ER	Lufthansa Regional
	D-ACNE	Canadair CRJ900ER	Lufthansa Regional
	D-ACNF	Canadair CRJ900ER	Lufthansa Regional
	D-ACNG	Canadair CRJ900ER	Lufthansa Regional
	D-ACNH	Canadair CRJ900ER	Lufthansa Regional
	D-ACNI	Canadair CRJ900ER	Lufthansa Regional
	D-ACNJ	Canadair CRJ900ER	Lufthansa Regional
	D-ACNK	Canadair CRJ900ER	Lufthansa Regional
	D-ACNL	Canadair CRJ900ER	Lufthansa Regional
	D-ACNM	Canadair CRJ900ER	Lufthansa Regional
	D-ACNN	Canadair CRJ900ER	Lufthansa Regional
	D-ACNO	Canadair CRJ900ER	Lufthansa Regional
	D-ACNP	Canadair CRJ900ER	Lufthansa Regional
	D-ACPA	Canadair CRJ700ER	Lufthansa Regional *Westerland/Sylt*
	D-ACPB	Canadair CRJ700ER	Lufthansa Regional *Rudesheim a. Rhein*
	D-ACPC	Canadair CRJ700ER	Lufthansa Regional *Espelkamp*
	D-ACPD	Canadair CRJ700ER	Lufthansa Regional *Vilshofen*
	D-ACPE	Canadair CRJ700ER	Lufthansa Regional *Belzig*
	D-ACPF	Canadair CRJ700ER	Lufthansa Regional *Uhingen*
	D-ACPG	Canadair CRJ700ER	Lufthansa Regional *Leinfelden-Echterdingen*
	D-ACPH	Canadair CRJ700ER	Lufthansa Regional *Eschwege*
	D-ACPI	Canadair CRJ700ER	Lufthansa Regional *Viernheim*
	D-ACPJ	Canadair CRJ700ER	Lufthansa Regional *Neumarkt i. d. Oberfalz*
	D-ACPK	Canadair CRJ700ER	Lufthansa Regional *Besigheim*
	D-ACPL	Canadair CRJ700ER	Lufthansa Regional *Halberstadt*
	D-ACPM	Canadair CRJ700ER	Lufthansa Regional *Heidenheim an der Brenz*
	D-ACPN	Canadair CRJ700ER	Lufthansa Regional *Quedlinburg*
	D-ACPO	Canadair CRJ700ER	Lufthansa Regional *Spaichingen*
	D-ACPP	Canadair CRJ700ER	Lufthansa Regional *Torgau*
	D-ACPQ	Canadair CRJ700ER	Lufthansa Regional *Lübbecke*
	D-ACPR	Canadair CRJ700ER	Lufthansa Regional *Weinheim an der Bergstrasse*
	D-ACPS	Canadair CRJ700ER	Lufthansa Regional *Berchtesgarten*
	D-ACPT	Canadair CRJ700ER	Lufthansa Regional *Altötting*
	D-ACRA	Canadair CRJ200LR	Lufthansa Regional
	D-ACRB	Canadair CRJ200LR	Lufthansa Regional
	D-ACRC	Canadair CRJ200LR	Lufthansa Regional
	D-ACRD	Canadair CRJ200LR	Lufthansa Regional
	D-ACRE	Canadair CRJ200LR	Lufthansa Regional
	D-ACRF	Canadair CRJ200LR	Lufthansa Regional
	D-ACRG	Canadair CRJ200LR	Lufthansa Regional
	D-ACRH	Canadair CRJ200LR	Lufthansa Regional
	D-ACRI	Canadair CRJ200LR	Lufthansa Regional
	D-ACRK	Canadair CRJ200LR	Lufthansa Regional
	D-ACRM	Canadair CRJ200LR	Lufthansa Regional
	D-ACRO	Canadair CRJ200LR	Lufthansa Regional
	D-ACRP	Canadair CRJ200LR	Lufthansa Regional
D-ACSB	D-ACRQ	Canadair CRJ200LR	Lufthansa Regional
	D-ACSC	Canadair CRJ700ER	Lufthansa Regional
	D-ADHA	DHC.8Q-402 Dash Eight	Lufthansa Regional
	D-ADHB	DHC.8Q-402 Dash Eight	Lufthansa Regional
	D-ADHC	DHC.8Q-402 Dash Eight	Lufthansa Regional
	D-ADHD	DHC.8Q-402 Dash Eight	Lufthansa Regional/Brussels Airlines
	D-ADHE	DHC.8Q-402 Dash Eight	Lufthansa Regional
	D-ADHP	DHC.8Q-402 Dash Eight	Lufthansa Regional
	D-ADHQ	DHC.8Q-402 Dash Eight	Lufthansa Regional
	D-ADHR	DHC.8Q-402 Dash Eight	Lufthansa Regional
	D-ADHS	DHC.8Q-402 Dash Eight	Lufthansa Regional
	D-ADHT	DHC.8Q-402 Dash Eight	Lufthansa Regional
	D-ADIH	Boeing 737-3Y0	Germania
	D-AEBA	Embraer ERJ190-200LR	Lufthansa Regional
	D-AEBB	Embraer ERJ190-200LR	Lufthansa Regional
	D-AEBC	Embraer ERJ190-200LR	Lufthansa Regional
	D-AEBD	Embraer ERJ190-200LR	Lufthansa Regional
	D-AEBE	Embraer ERJ190-200LR	Lufthansa Regional
	D-AECA	Embraer ERJ190-100LR	Lufthansa Regional *Deidesheim*
	D-AECB	Embraer ERJ190-100LR	Lufthansa Regional *Meiben*
	D-AECC	Embraer ERJ190-100LR	Lufthansa Regional *Eisleben*
	D-AECD	Embraer ERJ190-100LR	Lufthansa Regional *Schkeuditz*
	D-AECE	Embraer ERJ190-100LR	Lufthansa Regional *Kronach*
	D-AECF	Embraer ERJ190-100LR	Lufthansa Regional
	D-AECG	Embraer ERJ190-100LR	Lufthansa Regional
	D-AECH	Embraer ERJ190-100LR	Lufthansa Regional

Reg.	Type	Owner or Operator	Notes
D-AECI	Embraer ERJ190-100LR	Lufthansa Regional	
D-AEMA	Embraer ERJ190-200LR	Lufthansa Regional	
D-AEMB	Embraer ERJ190-200LR	Lufthansa Regional	
D-AEMC	Embraer ERJ190-200LR	Lufthansa Regional	
D-AEMD	Embraer ERJ190-200LR	Lufthansa Regional	
D-AEME	Embraer ERJ190-200LR	Lufthansa Regional	
D-AEMF	Embraer ERJ190-100LR	Lufthansa Regional	
D-AEMG	Embraer ERJ190-100LR	Lufthansa Regional	
D-AERK	Airbus A.330-322	Air Berlin	
D-AERQ	Airbus A.330-322	Air Berlin	
D-AERS	Airbus A.330-322	Air Berlin	
D-AFKA	Fokker 100	Contact Air/Lufthansa Regional	
D-AFKB	Fokker 100	Contact Air/Lufthansa Regional	
D-AFKC	Fokker 100	Contact Air/Lufthansa Regional	
D-AFKD	Fokker 100	Contact Air/Lufthansa Regional	
D-AFKE	Fokker 100	Contact Air/Lufthansa Regional	
D-AFKF	Fokker 100	Contact Air/Lufthansa Regional	
D-AGEB	Boeing 737-322	Germania	
D-AGEC	Boeing 737-76J	Air Berlin	
D-AGEE	Boeing 737-35B	Germania	
D-AGEG	Boeing 737-35B	Germania	
D-AGEJ	Boeing 737-3L9	Germania	
D-AGEK	Boeing 737-3M8	Germania	
D-AGEL	Boeing 737-75B	Air Berlin	
D-AGEN	Boeing 737-75B	Air Berlin	
D-AGEP	Boeing 737-75B	Air Berlin	
D-AGEQ	Boeing 737-75B	Germania	
D-AGER	Boeing 737-75B	Germania	
D-AGES	Boeing 737-75B	Air Berlin	
D-AGET	Boeing 737-75B	Germania	
D-AGEU	Boeing 737-75B	Air Berlin	
D-AGPH	Fokker 100	Contact Air/Swiss	
D-AGPK	Fokker 100	Contact Air/Swiss	
D-AGWA	Airbus A.319-132	Germanwings	
D-AGWB	Airbus A.319-132	Germanwings	
D-AGWC	Airbus A.319-132	Germanwings	
D-AGWD	Airbus A.319-132	Germanwings	
D-AGWE	Airbus A.319-132	Germanwings	
D-AGWF	Airbus A.319-132	Germanwings	
D-AGWG	Airbus A.319-132	Germanwings	
D-AGWH	Airbus A.319-132	Germanwings	
D-AGWI	Airbus A.319-132	Germanwings	
D-AGWJ	Airbus A.319-132	Germanwings	
D-AGWK	Airbus A.319-132	Germanwings	
D-AGWL	Airbus A.319-132	Germanwings	
D-AGWM	Airbus A.319-132	Germanwings	
D-AGWN	Airbus A.319-132	Germanwings	
D-AGWO	Airbus A.319-132	Germanwings	
D-AGWP	Airbus A.319-132	Germanwings	
D-AGWQ	Airbus A.319-132	Germanwings	
D-AGWR	Airbus A.319-132	Germanwings	
D-AHFA	Boeing 737-8K5	TUIfly	
D-AHFB	Boeing 737-8K5	TUIfly	
D-AHFH	Boeing 737-8K5	TUIfly	
D-AHFI	Boeing 737-8K5	TUIfly	
D-AHFK	Boeing 737-8K5	TUIfly	
D-AHFL	Boeing 737-8K5	TUIfly	
D-AHFM	Boeing 737-8K5	TUIfly	
D-AHFP	Boeing 737-8K5	TUIfly	
D-AHFR	Boeing 737-8K5	TUIfly	
D-AHFS	Boeing 737-86N	Air Berlin	
D-AHFT	Boeing 737-8K5	TUIfly	
D-AHFU	Boeing 737-8K5	TUIfly	
D-AHFV	Boeing 737-8K5	TUIfly	
D-AHFW	Boeing 737-8K5	Air Berlin	
D-AHFX	Boeing 737-8K5	TUIfly	
D-AHFY	Boeing 737-8K5	TUIfly	
D-AHFZ	Boeing 737-8K5	TUIfly	
D-AHIA	Boeing 737-73S	Air Berlin	
D-AHIN	Airbus A.319-112	Air Berlin	
D-AHIO	Airbus A.319-112	Air Berlin	
D-AHXA	Boeing 737-7K5	Air Berlin	
D-AHXB	Boeing 737-7K5	Air Berlin	
D-AHXC	Boeing 737-7K5	Air Berlin	

Notes	Reg.	Type	Owner or Operator
	D-AHXD	Boeing 737-7K5	Air Berlin
	D-AHXE	Boeing 737-7K5	Air Berlin
	D-AHXF	Boeing 737-7K5	Air Berlin
	D-AHXG	Boeing 737-7K5	Air Berlin
	D-AHXH	Boeing 737-7K5	Air Berlin
	D-AHXJ	Boeing 737-7K5	Air Berlin
	D-AIBA	Airbus A.319-114	Lufthansa
	D-AIBB	Airbus A.319-114	Lufthansa
	D-AIBC	Airbus A.319-114	Lufthansa
	D-AIBD	Airbus A.319-114	Lufthansa
	D-AIBE	Airbus A.319-114	Lufthansa
	D-AICA	Airbus A.320-212	Condor
	D-AICC	Airbus A.320-212	Condor
	D-AICD	Airbus A.320-212	Condor
	D-AICE	Airbus A.320-212	Condor
	D-AICF	Airbus A.320-212	Condor
	D-AICG	Airbus A.320-212	Condor
	D-AICH	Airbus A.320-212	Condor
	D-AICI	Airbus A.320-212	Condor
	D-AICJ	Airbus A.320-212	Condor
	D-AICK	Airbus A.320-212	Condor
	D-AICL	Airbus A.320-212	Condor
	D-AICN	Airbus A.320-214	Condor
	D-AIDA	Airbus A.321-231	Lufthansa
	D-AIDB	Airbus A.321-231	Lufthansa
	D-AIDC	Airbus A.321-231	Lufthansa
	D-AIDD	Airbus A.321-231	Lufthansa
	D-AIDE	Airbus A.321-231	Lufthansa
	D-AIDF	Airbus A.321-231	Lufthansa
	D-AIDG	Airbus A.321-231	Lufthansa
	D-AIFA	Airbus A.340-313X	Lufthansa *Dorsten*
	D-AIFB	Airbus A.340-313X	Lufthansa *Gummersbach*
	D-AIFC	Airbus A.340-313X	Lufthansa *Gander/Halifax*
	D-AIFD	Airbus A.340-313X	Lufthansa *Giessen*
	D-AIFE	Airbus A.340-313X	Lufthansa *Passau*
	D-AIFF	Airbus A.340-313X	Lufthansa *Delmenhorst*
	D-AIGA	Airbus A.340-311	Lufthansa *Oldenburg*
	D-AIGB	Airbus A.340-311	Lufthansa *Recklinghausen*
	D-AIGC	Airbus A.340-311	Lufthansa *Wilhelmshaven*
	D-AIGD	Airbus A.340-311	Lufthansa *Remscheid*
	D-AIGF	Airbus A.340-311	Lufthansa *Gottingen*
	D-AIGH	Airbus A.340-311	Lufthansa *Koblenz*
	D-AIGI	Airbus A.340-311	Lufthansa *Worms*
	D-AIGK	Airbus A.340-311	Lufthansa *Bayreuth*
	D-AIGL	Airbus A.340-313X	Lufthansa *Herne*
	D-AIGM	Airbus A.340-313X	Lufthansa *Görlitz*
	D-AIGN	Airbus A.340-313X	Lufthansa *Solingen*
	D-AIGO	Airbus A.340-313X	Lufthansa *Offenbach*
	D-AIGP	Airbus A.340-313X	Lufthansa *Paderborn*
	D-AIGS	Airbus A.340-313X	Lufthansa *Bergisch-Gladbach*
	D-AIGT	Airbus A.340-313X	Lufthansa *Viersen*
	D-AIGU	Airbus A.340-313X	Lufthansa *Castrop-Rauxei*
	D-AIGV	Airbus A.340-313X	Lufthansa *Dinslaken*
	D-AIGW	Airbus A.340-313X	Lufthansa *Gladbeck*
	D-AIGX	Airbus A.340-313X	Lufthansa *Duren*
	D-AIGY	Airbus A.340-313X	Lufthansa *Lünen*
	D-AIGZ	Airbus A.340-313X	Lufthansa *Villingen-Schwenningen*
	D-AIHA	Airbus A.340-642	Lufthansa *Nurnberg*
	D-AIHB	Airbus A.340-642	Lufthansa *Bremerhaven*
	D-AIHC	Airbus A.340-642	Lufthansa *Essen*
	D-AIHD	Airbus A.340-642	Lufthansa *Stuttgart*
	D-AIHE	Airbus A.340-642	Lufthansa *Leverkusen*
	D-AIHF	Airbus A.340-642	Lufthansa *Lübeck*
	D-AIHH	Airbus A.340-642	Lufthansa
	D-AIHI	Airbus A.340-642	Lufthansa
	D-AIHK	Airbus A.340-642	Lufthansa
	D-AIHL	Airbus A.340-642	Lufthansa
	D-AIHM	Airbus A.340-642	Lufthansa
	D-AIHN	Airbus A.340-642	Lufthansa
	D-AIHO	Airbus A.340-642	Lufthansa
	D-AIHP	Airbus A.340-642	Lufthansa
	D-AIHQ	Airbus A.340-642	Lufthansa
	D-AIHR	Airbus A.340-642	Lufthansa
	D-AIHS	Airbus A.340-642	Lufthansa

Reg.	Type	Owner or Operator	Notes
D-AIHT	Airbus A.340-642	Lufthansa	
D-AIHU	Airbus A.340-642	Lufthansa	
D-AIHV	Airbus A.340-642	Lufthansa	
D-AIHW	Airbus A.340-642	Lufthansa	
D-AIHX	Airbus A.340-642	Lufthansa	
D-AIHY	Airbus A.340-642	Lufthansa	
D-AIHZ	Airbus A.340-642	Lufthansa	
D-AIKA	Airbus A.330-343X	Lufthansa *Minden*	
D-AIKB	Airbus A.330-343X	Lufthansa *Cuxhaven*	
D-AIKC	Airbus A.330-343X	Lufthansa *Hamm*	
D-AIKD	Airbus A.330-343X	Lufthansa *Siegen*	
D-AIKE	Airbus A.330-343X	Lufthansa *Landshut*	
D-AIKF	Airbus A.330-343X	Lufthansa *Witten*	
D-AIKG	Airbus A.330-343X	Lufthansa *Ludwigsburg*	
D-AIKH	Airbus A.330-343X	Lufthansa	
D-AIKI	Airbus A.330-343X	Lufthansa	
D-AIKJ	Airbus A.330-343X	Lufthansa	
D-AIKK	Airbus A.330-343X	Lufthansa	
D-AIKL	Airbus A.330-343X	Lufthansa	
D-AIKM	Airbus A.330-343X	Lufthansa	
D-AIKN	Airbus A.330-343X	Lufthansa	
D-AIKO	Airbus A.330-343X	Lufthansa	
D-AIKP	Airbus A.330-343X	Lufthansa	
D-AILA	Airbus A.319-114	Lufthansa *Frankfurt (Oder)*	
D-AILB	Airbus A.319-114	Lufthansa *Lutherstadt Wittenburg*	
D-AILC	Airbus A.319-114	Lufthansa *Russelsheim*	
D-AILD	Airbus A.319-114	Lufthansa *Dinkelsbühl*	
D-AILE	Airbus A.319-114	Lufthansa *Kelsterbach*	
D-AILF	Airbus A.319-114	Lufthansa Italia	
D-AILH	Airbus A.319-114	Lufthansa Italia *Norderstedt*	
D-AILI	Airbus A.319-114	Lufthansa Italia *Roma*	
D-AILK	Airbus A.319-114	Lufthansa *Landshut*	
D-AILL	Airbus A.319-114	Lufthansa *Marburg*	
D-AILM	Airbus A.319-114	Lufthansa *Friedrichshafen*	
D-AILN	Airbus A.319-114	Lufthansa *Idar-Oberstein*	
D-AILP	Airbus A.319-114	Lufthansa *Tubingen*	
D-AILR	Airbus A.319-114	Lufthansa *Tegernsee*	
D-AILS	Airbus A.319-114	Lufthansa *Heide*	
D-AILT	Airbus A.319-114	Lufthansa *Straubing*	
D-AILU	Airbus A.319-114	Lufthansa *Verden*	
D-AILW	Airbus A.319-114	Lufthansa *Donaueschingen*	
D-AILX	Airbus A.319-114	Lufthansa *Feilbach*	
D-AILY	Airbus A.319-114	Lufthansa *Schweinfurt*	
D-AIMA	Airbus A.380-841	Lufthansa *Frankfurt am Main*	
D-AIMB	Airbus A.380-841	Lufthansa	
D-AIMC	Airbus A.380-841	Lufthansa	
D-AIMD	Airbus A.380-841	Lufthansa	
D-AIME	Airbus A.380-841	Lufthansa	
D-AIMF	Airbus A.380-841	Lufthansa	
D-AIMG	Airbus A.380-841	Lufthansa	
D-AIMH	Airbus A.380-841	Lufthansa	
D-AIMI	Airbus A.380-841	Lufthansa	
D-AIMJ	Airbus A.380-841	Lufthansa	
D-AIMK	Airbus A.380-841	Lufthansa	
D-AIPA	Airbus A.320-211	Lufthansa *Buxtehude*	
D-AIPB	Airbus A.320-211	Lufthansa *Heidelberg*	
D-AIPC	Airbus A.320-211	Lufthansa *Braunschweig*	
D-AIPD	Airbus A.320-211	Lufthansa *Freiburg*	
D-AIPE	Airbus A.320-211	Lufthansa *Kassel*	
D-AIPF	Airbus A.320-211	Lufthansa *Deggendorf*	
D-AIPH	Airbus A.320-211	Lufthansa *Munster*	
D-AIPK	Airbus A.320-211	Lufthansa *Wiesbaden*	
D-AIPL	Airbus A.320-211	Lufthansa *Ludwigshafen am Rhein*	
D-AIPM	Airbus A.320-211	Lufthansa *Troisdorf*	
D-AIPP	Airbus A.320-211	Lufthansa *Starnberg*	
D-AIPR	Airbus A.320-211	Lufthansa *Kaufbeuren*	
D-AIPS	Airbus A.320-211	Lufthansa *Augsburg*	
D-AIPT	Airbus A.320-211	Lufthansa *Cottbus*	
D-AIPU	Airbus A.320-211	Lufthansa *Dresden*	
D-AIPW	Airbus A.320-211	Lufthansa *Schwerin*	
D-AIPX	Airbus A.320-211	Lufthansa *Mannheim*	
D-AIPY	Airbus A.320-211	Lufthansa *Magdeburg*	
D-AIPZ	Airbus A.320-211	Lufthansa *Erfurt*	
D-AIQA	Airbus A.320-211	Lufthansa *Mainz*	

Notes	Reg.	Type	Owner or Operator
	D-AIQB	Airbus A.320-211	Lufthansa *Bielefeld*
	D-AIQC	Airbus A.320-211	Lufthansa *Zwickau*
	D-AIQD	Airbus A.320-211	Lufthansa *Jena*
	D-AIQE	Airbus A.320-211	Lufthansa *Gera*
	D-AIQF	Airbus A.320-211	Lufthansa *Halle (Saale)*
	D-AIQH	Airbus A.320-211	Lufthansa *Dessau*
	D-AIQK	Airbus A.320-211	Lufthansa *Rostock*
	D-AIQL	Airbus A.320-211	Lufthansa *Stralsund*
	D-AIQM	Airbus A.320-211	Lufthansa *Nordenham*
	D-AIQN	Airbus A.320-211	Lufthansa *Laupheim*
	D-AIQP	Airbus A.320-211	Lufthansa *Suhl*
	D-AIQR	Airbus A.320-211	Lufthansa *Lahr/Schwarzwald*
	D-AIQS	Airbus A.320-211	Lufthansa *Eisenach*
	D-AIQT	Airbus A.320-211	Lufthansa *Gotha*
	D-AIQU	Airbus A.320-211	Lufthansa *Backnang*
	D-AIQW	Airbus A.320-211	Lufthansa *Kleve*
	D-AIRA	Airbus A.321-131	Lufthansa *Finkenwerder*
	D-AIRB	Airbus A.321-131	Lufthansa *Baden-Baden*
	D-AIRC	Airbus A.321-131	Lufthansa *Erlangen*
	D-AIRD	Airbus A.321-131	Lufthansa *Coburg*
	D-AIRE	Airbus A.321-131	Lufthansa *Osnabrueck*
	D-AIRF	Airbus A.321-131	Lufthansa *Kempten*
	D-AIRH	Airbus A.321-131	Lufthansa *Garmisch-Partenkirchen*
	D-AIRK	Airbus A.321-131	Lufthansa *Freudenstadt/Schwarzwald*
	D-AIRL	Airbus A.321-131	Lufthansa *Kulmbach*
	D-AIRM	Airbus A.321-131	Lufthansa *Darmstadt*
	D-AIRN	Airbus A.321-131	Lufthansa *Kaiserslautern*
	D-AIRO	Airbus A.321-131	Lufthansa *Konstanz*
	D-AIRP	Airbus A.321-131	Lufthansa *Lüneburg*
	D-AIRR	Airbus A.321-131	Lufthansa *Wismar*
	D-AIRS	Airbus A.321-131	Lufthansa *Husum*
	D-AIRT	Airbus A.321-131	Lufthansa *Regensburg*
	D-AIRU	Airbus A.321-131	Lufthansa *Würzburg*
	D-AIRW	Airbus A.321-131	Lufthansa *Heilbronn*
	D-AIRX	Airbus A.321-131	Lufthansa *Weimar*
	D-AIRY	Airbus A.321-131	Lufthansa *Flensburg*
	D-AISB	Airbus A.321-231	Lufthansa *Hamein*
	D-AISC	Airbus A.321-231	Lufthansa *Speyer*
	D-AISD	Airbus A.321-231	Lufthansa *Chemnitz*
	D-AISE	Airbus A.321-231	Lufthansa *Neustadt an der Weinstrasse*
	D-AISF	Airbus A.321-231	Lufthansa *Lippstadt*
	D-AISG	Airbus A.321-231	Lufthansa *Dormagen*
	D-AISH	Airbus A.321-231	Lufthansa
	D-AISI	Airbus A.321-231	Lufthansa
	D-AISJ	Airbus A.321-231	Lufthansa
	D-AISK	Airbus A.321-231	Lufthansa
	D-AISL	Airbus A.321-231	Lufthansa Arnsberg
	D-AISN	Airbus A.321-231	Lufthansa *Goppingen*
	D-AISO	Airbus A.321-231	Lufthansa
	D-AISP	Airbus A.321-231	Lufthansa
	D-AISQ	Airbus A.321-231	Lufthansa
	D-AISR	Airbus A.321-231	Lufthansa
	D-AIST	Airbus A.321-231	Lufthansa
	D-AISU	Airbus A.321-231	Lufthansa *Nordlingen*
	D-AISV	Airbus A.321-231	Lufthansa *Bingen*
	D-AISW	Airbus A.321-231	Lufthansa
	D-AISX	Airbus A.321-231	Lufthansa
	D-AISZ	Airbus A.321-231	Lufthansa
	D-AIZA	Airbus A.320-214	Lufthansa
	D-AIZB	Airbus A.320-214	Lufthansa
	D-AIZC	Airbus A.320-214	Lufthansa
	D-AIZD	Airbus A.320-214	Lufthansa
	D-AIZE	Airbus A.320-214	Lufthansa
	D-AIZF	Airbus A.320-214	Lufthansa
	D-AIZG	Airbus A.320-214	Lufthansa
	D-AIZH	Airbus A.320-214	Lufthansa
	D-AIZI	Airbus A.320-214	Lufthansa
	D-AIZJ	Airbus A.320-214	Lufthansa
	D-AIZK	Airbus A.320-214	Lufthansa
	D-AKNF	Airbus A.319-112	Lufthansa Italia *Torino*
	D-AKNG	Airbus A.319-112	Lufthansa Italia *Varese*
	D-AKNH	Airbus A.319-112	Lufthansa Italia *Bologna*
	D-AKNI	Airbus A.319-112	Lufthansa Italia
	D-AKNJ	Airbus A.319-112	Lufthansa Italia *Milano*

Reg.	Type	Owner or Operator	Notes
D-AKNK	Airbus A.319-112	Germanwings	
D-AKNL	Airbus A.319-112	Germanwings	
D-AKNM	Airbus A.319-112	Germanwings	
D-AKNN	Airbus A.319-112	Germanwings	
D-AKNO	Airbus A.319-112	Germanwings	
D-AKNP	Airbus A.319-112	Germanwings	
D-AKNQ	Airbus A.319-112	Germanwings	
D-AKNR	Airbus A.319-112	Germanwings *Spirit of T-Com*	
D-AKNS	Airbus A.319-112	Germanwings *Spirit of T Mobile*	
D-AKNT	Airbus A.319-112	Germanwings *City of Hamburg*	
D-AKNU	Airbus A.319-112	Germanwings	
D-AKNV	Airbus A.319-112	Germanwings	
D-ALCA	McD Douglas MD-11F	Lufthansa Cargo	
D-ALCB	McD Douglas MD-11F	Lufthansa Cargo	
D-ALCC	McD Douglas MD-11F	Lufthansa Cargo	
D-ALCD	McD Douglas MD-11F	Lufthansa Cargo	
D-ALCE	McD Douglas MD-11F	Lufthansa Cargo	
D-ALCF	McD Douglas MD-11F	Lufthansa Cargo	
D-ALCG	McD Douglas MD-11F	Lufthansa Cargo	
D-ALCH	McD Douglas MD-11F	Lufthansa Cargo	
D-ALCI	McD Douglas MD-11F	Lufthansa Cargo	
D-ALCJ	McD Douglas MD-11F	Lufthansa Cargo	
D-ALCK	McD Douglas MD-11F	Lufthansa Cargo	
D-ALCL	McD Douglas MD-11F	Lufthansa Cargo	
D-ALCM	McD Douglas MD-11F	Lufthansa Cargo	
D-ALCN	McD Douglas MD-11F	Lufthansa Cargo	
D-ALCO	McD Douglas MD-11F	Lufthansa Cargo	
D-ALCP	McD Douglas MD-11F	Lufthansa Cargo	
D-ALCR	McD Douglas MD-11F	Lufthansa Cargo	
D-ALCS	McD Douglas MD-11F	Lufthansa Cargo	
D-ALEA	Boeing 757-236SF	DHL Express	
D-ALEB	Boeing 757-236SF	DHL Express	
D-ALEC	Boeing 757-236SF	DHL Express	
D-ALED	Boeing 757-236SF	DHL Express	
D-ALEE	Boeing 757-236SF	DHL Express	
D-ALEF	Boeing 757-236SF	DHL Express	
D-ALEG	Boeing 757-236SF	DHL Express	
D-ALEH	Boeing 757-236SF	DHL Express	
D-ALEI	Boeing 757-236SF	DHL Express	
D-ALEJ	Boeing 757-23APF	DHL Express	
D-ALEK	Boeing 757-236SF	DHL Express	
D-ALIA	Embraer RJ170-100LR	Cirrus Airlines/Lufthansa Regional	
D-ALIE	Embraer RJ170-100LR	Cirrus Airlines/Lufthansa Regional	
D-ALIN	BAe 146-300	WDL Aviation	
D-ALPA	Airbus A.330-223	Air Berlin	
D-ALPB	Airbus A.330-223	Air Berlin	
D-ALPC	Airbus A.330-223	Air Berlin	
D-ALPD	Airbus A.330-223	Air Berlin	
D-ALPE	Airbus A.330-223	Air Berlin	
D-ALPF	Airbus A.330-223	Air Berlin	
D-ALPG	Airbus A.330-223	Air Berlin	
D-ALPH	Airbus A.330-223	Air Berlin	
D-ALPI	Airbus A.330-223	Air Berlin	
D-ALPJ	Airbus A.330-223	Air Berlin	
D-ALSA	Airbus A.321-211	Air Berlin	
D-ALSB	Airbus A.321-211	Air Berlin	
D-ALSC	Airbus A.321-211	Air Berlin	
D-ALSD	Airbus A.321-211	Air Berlin	
D-ALTB	Airbus A.320-214	Air Berlin	
D-ALTE	Airbus A.320-214	Air Berlin	
D-ALTF	Airbus A.320-214	Air Berlin	
D-ALTH	Airbus A.320-214	Air Berlin	
D-ALTJ	Airbus A.320-214	Air Berlin	
D-ALTK	Airbus A.320-214	Air Berlin	
D-ALTL	Airbus A.320-214	Air Berlin	
D-AMAJ	BAe 146-200	WDL Aviation	
D-AMAX	BAe 146-300	WDL Aviation	
D-AOLB	SAAB 2000	OLT	
D-AOLC	SAAB 2000	OLT	
D-AOLT	SAAB 2000	OLT *Emden*	
D-APBB	Boeing 737-8FH	PrivatAir/Lufthansa	
D-APBC	Boeing 737-8BK	PrivatAir/Lufthansa	
D-APBD	Boeing 737-8BK	PrivatAir/Lufthansa	
D-ATUA	Boeing 737-8K5	TUIfly	

Notes	Reg.	Type	Owner or Operator
	D-ATUB	Boeing 737-8K5	TUIfly
	D-ATUC	Boeing 737-8K5	TUIfly
	D-ATUD	Boeing 737-8K5	TUIfly
	D-ATUE	Boeing 737-8K5	TUIfly
	D-ATUF	Boeing 737-8K5	TUIfly
	D-ATUG	Boeing 737-8K5	TUIfly
	D-ATUH	Boeing 737-8K5	TUIfly
	D-ATUI	Boeing 737-8K5	TUIfly
	D-ATUJ	Boeing 737-8K5	TUIfly
	D-ATUK	Boeing 737-8K5	TUIfly
	D-ATUL	Boeing 737-8K5	TUIfly
	D-AVRA	Avro RJ85	Lufthansa Regional
	D-AVRB	Avro RJ85	Lufthansa Regional
	D-AVRG	Avro RJ85	Lufthansa Regional
	D-AVRH	Avro RJ85	Lufthansa Regional
	D-AVRJ	Avro RJ85	Lufthansa Regional
	D-AVRK	Avro RJ85	Lufthansa Regional
	D-AVRM	Avro RJ85	Lufthansa Regional
	D-AVRN	Avro RJ85	Lufthansa Regional
	D-AVRO	Avro RJ85	Lufthansa Regional
	D-AVRP	Avro RJ85	Lufthansa Regional
	D-AVRQ	Avro RJ85	Lufthansa Regional
	D-AVRR	Avro RJ85	Lufthansa Regional
	D-AWBA	Bae 146-300	WDL Aviation
	D-AWUE	BAe 146-200	WDL Aviation
	D-AXLD	Boeing 737-8FH	XL Airways Germany
	D-AXLE	Boeing 737-8Q8	XL Airways Germany
	D-AXLF	Boeing 737-8Q8	XL Airways Germany
	D-AXLG	Boeing 737-8Q8	XL Airways Germany
	D-BGAE	Dornier 328JET	Cirrus Airlines
	D-BGAL	Dornier 328JET	Cirrus Airlines
	D-BGAQ	Dornier 328JET	Cirrus Airlines
	D-CASB	SAAB SF.340B	OLT *Birdie*
	D-CCIR	Dornier 328-130	Cirrus Airlines
	D-CIRA	Dornier 328-120	Cirrus Airlines
	D-CIRB	Dornier 328-110	Cirrus Airlines
	D-CIRC	Dornier 328-110	Cirrus Airlines
	D-CIRD	Dornier 328-110	Cirrus Airlines
	D-CIRE	Dornier 328-110	Cirrus Airlines
	D-CIRI	Dornier 328-110	Cirrus Airlines
	D-CIRJ	Dornier 328-110	Cirrus Airlines
	D-CIRK	Dornier 328-110	Cirrus Airlines
	D-CIRL	Dornier 328-100	Cirrus Airlines
	D-CIRP	Dornier 328-110	Cirrus Airlines
	D-CMNX	Dornier Do.228	Manx2
	D-COLE	SAAB SF.340A	OLT *Bremen*
	D-COSA	Dornier 328-110	Cirrus Airlines
	D-CPRP	Dornier 328-110	Cirrus Airlines
	D-CPRW	Dornier 328-110	Cirrus Airlines
	D-IFLM	Dornier Do.228	Manx2
	D-ILKA	Dornier Do.228	Manx2

EC (Spain)

Notes	Reg.	Type	Owner or Operator
	EC-ELT	BAe 146-200QT	Pan Air/TNT Airways
	EC-FDB	Airbus A.320-211	Iberia *Lago de Sanabria*
	EC-FNR	Airbus A.320-211	Iberia *Monte el Valle*
	EC-FQY	Airbus A.320-211	Iberia *Joan Miro*
	EC-FVY	BAe 146-200QT	Pan Air/TNT Airways
	EC-FZE	BAe 146-200QT	Pan Air/TNT Airways
	EC-GCV	McD Douglas MD-82	Spanair *Sunburst*
	EC-GGS	Airbus A.340-313	Iberia *Concha Espina*
	EC-GHX	Airbus A.340-313	Iberia *Rosalia de Castro*
	EC-GJT	Airbus A.340-313	Iberia *Rosa Chacel*
	EC-GLE	Airbus A.340-313	Iberia *Concepcion Arenal*
	EC-GOM	McD Douglas MD-83	Spanair *Sunlight*
	EC-GPB	Airbus A.340-313X	Iberia *Teresa de Avila*
	EC-GPS	Swearingen SA227 Metro	Manx 2
	EC-GQG	McD Douglas MD-83	Spanair *Sunrise*
	EC-GQO	BAe 146-200QT	Pan Air/TNT Airways
	EC-GRG	Airbus A.320-211	Vueling Airlines
	EC-GRH	Airbus A.320-211	Vueling Airlines
	EC-GUP	Airbus A.340-313X	Iberia *Agustina De Aragon*

Reg.	Type	Owner or Operator	Notes
EC-GUQ	Airbus A.340-313X	Iberia *Beatriz Galindo*	
EC-GVE	Swearingen SA227AC Metro III	Aeronova	
EC-GVO	McD Douglas MD-83	Spanair *Sunspot*	
EC-GXU	McD Douglas MD-83	Spanair *Sunray*	
EC-HAF	Airbus A.320-214	Iberia *Santiago de Compostela*	
EC-HAG	Airbus A.320-214	Iberia *Senorio de Bertiz*	
EC-HBL	Boeing 737-85P	Air Europa *Travelplan*	
EC-HBM	Boeing 737-85P	Air Europa *La Gaceta*	
EC-HCH	Swearingen SA227AC Metro III	Aeronova	
EC-HDH	BAe 146-200QT	Pan Air/TNT Airways	
EC-HDK	Airbus A.320-214	Iberia *Mar Ortigola*	
EC-HDN	Airbus A.320-214	Iberia *Parque National de Omiedo*	
EC-HDQ	Airbus A.340-313X	Iberia *Sor Juana Ines de la Cruz*	
EC-HDS	Boeing 757-256	Iberia *Paraguay*	
EC-HDT	Airbus A.320-214	Iberia *Museo Guggenheim Bilbao*	
EC-HGO	Boeing 737-85P	Air Europa	
EC-HGP	Boeing 737-85P	Air Europa *Marbella*	
EC-HGQ	Boeing 737-85P	Air Europa *El Mundo-El Dia de Baleares*	
EC-HGR	Airbus A.319-111	Iberia *Ribeira Sacra*	
EC-HGS	Airbus A.319-111	Iberia *Bardenas Reales*	
EC-HGT	Airbus A.319-111	Iberia *Icnitas de Enciso*	
EC-HGU	Airbus A.340-313X	Iberia *Maria de Molina*	
EC-HGV	Airbus A.340-313X	Iberia *Maria Guerrero*	
EC-HGX	Airbus A.340-313X	Iberia *Maria Pita*	
EC-HGZ	Airbus A.320-214	Iberia *Boi Taull*	
EC-HHA	Airbus A.320-214	Vueling Airlines	
EC-HJH	BAe 146-200QT	Pan Air/TNT Airways	
EC-HJP	Boeing 737-85P	Air Europa	
EC-HJQ	Boeing 737-85P	Air Europa	
EC-HKO	Airbus A.319-111	Iberia *Gorbia*	
EC-HKQ	Boeing 737-85P	Air Europa *San Pedro Alcantara*	
EC-HKR	Boeing 737-85P	Air Europa	
EC-HPM	Airbus A.321-231	Spanair *Camillo José Cela*	
EC-HQI	Airbus A.320-214	Vueling Airlines *Merce Sune*	
EC-HQJ	Airbus A.320-214	Vueling Airlines	
EC-HQL	Airbus A.320-214	Vueling Airlines *Click on Vueling*	
EC-HQN	Airbus A.340-313X	Iberia *Luisa Carvajal y Mendoza*	
EC-HQZ	Airbus A.321-231	Spanair	
EC-HRG	Airbus A.321-231	Spanair *Placido Domingo*	
EC-HRP	Airbus A.320-232	Spanair *Juan de Avalos*	
EC-HSF	Airbus A.320-214	Iberia *Mar Menor*	
EC-HTA	Airbus A.320-214	Iberia *Cadaques*	
EC-HTB	Airbus A.320-214	Iberia *Playa de las Americas*	
EC-HTC	Airbus A.320-214	Iberia *Alpujarra*	
EC-HTD	Airbus A.320-214	Vueling Airlines *Unos Vuelan,otros Vueling*	
EC-HUH	Airbus A.321-211	Iberia *Benidorm*	
EC-HUI	Airbus A.321-211	Iberia *Comunidad Autonoma de la Rioja*	
EC-HUJ	Airbus A.320-214	Iberia *Getaria*	
EC-HUK	Airbus A.320-214	Iberia *Laguna Negra*	
EC-HUL	Airbus A.320-214	Iberia *Monasterio de Rueda*	
EC-HXA	Airbus A.320-232	Spanair	
EC-HYC	Airbus A.320-214	Iberia *Cuidad de Ceuta*	
EC-HYD	Airbus A.320-214	Iberia *Maspalomas*	
EC-HZH	Swearingen SA227AC Metro III	Aeronova	
EC-HZS	Boeing 737-86Q	Air Europa	
EC-IAZ	Airbus A.320-232	Spanair	
EC-ICF	Airbus A.340-313X	Iberia *Maria Zambrano*	
EC-ICL	Airbus A.320-232	Spanair	
EC-ICQ	Airbus A.320-211	Vueling Airlines *Iker Ochandorena*	
EC-ICR	Airbus A.320-211	Vueling Airlines	
EC-ICS	Airbus A.320-211	Vueling Airlines	
EC-ICT	Airbus A.320-211	Vueling Airlines	
EC-IDA	Boeing 737-86Q	Air Europa	
EC-IDF	Airbus A.340-313X	Iberia *Mariana Pineda*	
EC-IDT	Boeing 737-86Q	Air Europa	
EC-IEF	Airbus A.320-214	Iberia *Castillo de Loarre*	
EC-IEG	Airbus A.320-214	Iberia *Costa Brava*	
EC-IEI	Airbus A.320-214	Iberia *Monasterio de Valldigna*	
EC-IEJ	Airbus A.320-232	Spanair	
EC-IGK	Airbus A.321-211	Iberia *Costa Calida*	
EC-IIG	Airbus A.321-211	Iberia *Ciudad de Siguenza*	
EC-IIH	Airbus A.340-313X	Iberia *Maria Barbara de Braganza*	
EC-III	Boeing 737-86Q	Air Europa	
EC-IIZ	Airbus A.320-232	Spanair	

Notes	Reg.	Type	Owner or Operator
	EC-IJN	Airbus A.321-211	Iberia *Merida*
	EC-IJU	Airbus A.321-231	Spanair
	EC-ILH	Airbus A.320-232	Spanair
	EC-ILO	Airbus A.321-211	Iberia *Cueva de Nerja*
	EC-ILP	Airbus A.321-211	Iberia *Peniscola*
	EC-ILQ	Airbus A.320-214	Iberia *La Pedrera*
	EC-ILR	Airbus A.320-214	Iberia *San Juan de la Pena*
	EC-ILS	Airbus A.320-214	Iberia *Sierra de Cameros*
	EC-IMB	Airbus A.320-232	Spanair
	EC-INB	Airbus A.321-231	Spanair
	EC-INM	Airbus A.320-232	Spanair
	EC-INO	Airbus A.340-642	Iberia *Gaudi*
	EC-INZ	Airbus A.320-214	Iberworld
	EC-IOB	Airbus A.340-642	Iberia *Julio Romanes de Torres*
	EC-IOH	Airbus A.320-232	Spanair
	EC-IPI	Airbus A.320-232	Spanair
	EC-IQR	Airbus A.340-642	Iberia *Salvador Dali*
	EC-ISE	Boeing 737-86Q	Air Europa
	EC-ISN	Boeing 737-86Q	Air Europa
	EC-ITN	Airbus A.321-211	Iberia *Empuries*
	EC-IVG	Airbus A.320-232	Spanair
	EC-IXD	Airbus A.321-211	Iberia *Vall d'Aran*
	EC-IYG	Airbus A.320-232	Spanair
	EC-IZD	Airbus A.320-214	Vueling Airlines
	EC-IZH	Airbus A.320-214	Iberia *San Pere de Roda*
	EC-IZK	Airbus A.320-232	Spanair
	EC-IZR	Airbus A.320-214	Iberia *Urkiola*
	EC-IZX	Airbus A.340-642	Iberia *Mariano Benlliure*
	EC-IZY	Airbus A.340-642	Iberia *I. Zuloaga*
	EC-JAP	Boeing 737-85P	Air Europa
	EC-JAZ	Airbus A.319-111	Iberia *Las Medulas*
	EC-JBA	Airbus A.340-642	Iberia *Joaquin Rodrigo*
	EC-JBJ	Boeing 737-85P	Air Europa
	EC-JBK	Boeing 737-85P	Air Europa
	EC-JBL	Boeing 737-85P	Air Europa
	EC-JCU	Swearingen SA227AC Metro III	Aeronova
	EC-JCY	Airbus A.340-642	Iberia *Andrés Segovia*
	EC-JCZ	Airbus A.340-642	Iberia *Vicente Aleixandre*
	EC-JDL	Airbus A.319-111	Iberia *Los Llanos de Aridane*
	EC-JDM	Airbus A.321-211	Iberia *Cantabria*
	EC-JDR	Airbus A.321-211	Iberia
	EC-JEI	Airbus A.319-111	Iberia *Xátiva*
	EC-JEJ	Airbus A.321-211	Iberia *Río Frío*
	EC-JFF	Airbus A.320-214	Vueling Airlines *Vueling the world*
	EC-JFG	Airbus A.320-214	Iberia *Valle de Ricote*
	EC-JFH	Airbus A.320-214	Iberia *Trujillo*
	EC-JFN	Airbus A.320-214	Iberia *Sirrea de las Nieves*
	EC-JFX	Airbus A.340-642	Iberia *Jacinto Benavente*
	EC-JGM	Airbus A.320-214	Vueling Airlines *The joy of vueling*
	EC-JGS	Airbus A.321-211	Iberia *Guadelupe*
	EC-JHK	Boeing 737-85P	Air Europa
	EC-JHL	Boeing 737-85P	Air Europa
	EC-JHP	Airbus A.330-343X	Iberworld
	EC-JJD	Airbus A.320-232	Spanair
	EC-JLE	Airbus A.340-642	Iberia *Santiago Ramon y Cajal*
	EC-JLI	Airbus A.321-211	Iberia *Delta del Llobregrat*
	EC-JMR	Airbus A.321-211	Iberia *Aranjuez*
	EC-JNC	Airbus A.320-214	Spanair *Juan Antonio Samaranch*
	EC-JNF	Boeing 737-85P	Air Europa *Mutua Madrileqa*
	EC-JNI	Airbus A.321-211	Iberia *Palmeral de Eiche*
	EC-JNQ	Airbus A.340-642	Iberia *Antonio Machado*
	EC-JPF	Airbus A.330-202	Air Europa
	EC-JPU	Airbus A.340-642	Iberia *Pio Baroja*
	EC-JQG	Airbus A.330-202	Air Europa *Estepona – Costa del Sol*
	EC-JQP	Airbus A.320-214	Iberworld
	EC-JQQ	Airbus A.330-202	Air Europa
	EC-JQV	McD Douglas MD-83	Swiftair
	EC-JQZ	Airbus A.321-211	Iberia *Generalife*
	EC-JRE	Airbus A.321-211	Iberia *Villa de Uncastillo*
	EC-JRU	Airbus A.320-214	Iberworld
	EC-JSB	Airbus A.320-214	Iberia *Benalmadena*
	EC-JSK	Airbus A.320-214	Iberia *Ciudad Encantada*
	EC-JSY	Airbus A.320-214	Vueling Airlines
	EC-JTQ	Airbus A.320-214	Vueling Airlines *Vueling, que es gerundio*

Reg.	Type	Owner or Operator	Notes
EC-JTR	Airbus A.320-214	Vueling Airlines *No Vueling no party*	
EC-JUG	McD Douglas MD-83	Swiftair	
EC-JVE	Airbus A.319-111	Iberia *Puerto de la Cruz*	
EC-JXJ	Airbus A.319-111	Iberia *Ciudad de Baeza*	
EC-JXV	Airbus A.319-111	Iberia *Concejo de Cabrales*	
EC-JYX	Airbus A.320-214	Vueling Airlines *Elisenda Masana*	
EC-JZI	Airbus A.320-214	Vueling Airlines *Vueling in love*	
EC-JZL	Airbus A.330-202	Air Europa	
EC-JZM	Airbus A.321-211	Iberia *Águila Imperial Ibérica*	
EC-JZQ	Airbus A.320-214	Vueling Airlines *I want to Vueling*	
EC-KBJ	Airbus A.319-111	Iberia *Lince Iberico*	
EC-KBU	Airbus A.320-214	Vueling Airlines	
EC-KBV	Boeing 737-85P	Air Europa	
EC-KBX	Airbus A.319-111	Iberia *Oso Pardo*	
EC-KCG	Boeing 737-85P	Air Europa	
EC-KCL	Airbus A.340-311	Iberia	
EC-KCU	Airbus A.320-216	Vueling Airlines	
EC-KCZ	McD Douglas MD-87	Spanair	
EC-KDG	Airbus A.320-214	Vueling Airlines	
EC-KDH	Airbus A.320-214	Vueling Airlines *Ain't no Vueling high enough*	
EC-KDI	Airbus A.319-111	Iberia *Cigu-a Negra*	
EC-KDT	Airbus A.320-216	Vueling Airlines	
EC-KDX	Airbus A.320-216	Vueling Airlines *Francisco Jose Ruiz Cortizo*	
EC-KEC	Airbus A.320-232	Spanair	
EC-KEO	Boeing 737-85P	Air Europa	
EC-KEV	Airbus A.319-111	Iberia *Urogallo*	
EC-KFI	Airbus A.320-216	Vueling Airlines	
EC-KFT	Airbus A.319-111	Iberia *Nutria*	
EC-KHA	McD Douglas MD-87	Spanair	
EC-KHJ	Airbus A.320-214	Iberia	
EC-KHM	Airbus A.319-111	Iberia *Buho Real*	
EC-KHN	Airbus A.320-216	Vueling Airlines	
EC-KHX	Boeing 717-2K9	Spanair	
EC-KJC	Airbus A.319-111	Iberia *Avutarda*	
EC-KJD	Airbus A.320-216	Vueling Airlines	
EC-KJE	McD Douglas MD-87	Spanair	
EC-KKS	Airbus A.319-111	Iberia *Halcon Peregrino*	
EC-KKT	Airbus A.320-214	Vueling Airlines *Vueling Together*	
EC-KLB	Airbus A.320-214	Vueling Airlines *Vuela Punto*	
EC-KLT	Airbus A.320-214	Vueling Airlines	
EC-KMD	Airbus A.319-111	Iberia *Petirrojo*	
EC-KME	Airbus A.319-111	Iberia *Grulla*	
EC-KMI	Airbus A.320-216	Vueling Airlines *How are you? I'm Vueling!*	
EC-KNM	Airbus A.320-214	Iberia *Hoces de Cabriel*	
EC-KOH	Airbus A.320-214	Iberia	
EC-KOM	Airbus A.330-202	Air Europa	
EC-KOU	Airbus A.340-313	Iberia	
EC-KOX	Airbus A.320-232	Spanair	
EC-KOY	Airbus A.319-111	Iberia *Vencejo*	
EC-KPX	Airbus A.320-232	Spanair	
EC-KQC	Boeing 747-412	Pullmantur Air	
EC-KRH	Airbus A.320-214	Vueling Airlines *Vueling me softly*	
EC-KRJ	Embraer RJ190-200SR	Air Europa	
EC-KRO	Boeing 717-23S	Spanair	
EC-KSE	Airbus A.340-313X	Iberia	
EC-KSM	Boeing 747-412	Pullmantur Air	
EC-KTG	Airbus A.330-203	Air Europa	
EC-KUB	Airbus A.319-111	Iberia	
EC-KXD	Embraer RJ190-200SR	Air Europa	
EC-KXN	Boeing 747-4H6	Pullmantur Air	
EC-KYO	Embraer RJ190-200SR	Air Europa	
EC-KYP	Embraer RJ190-200SR	Air Europa	
EC-KYZ	Airbus A.320-214	Iberworld	
EC-KZG	Airbus A.320-214	Iberworld	
EC-KZI	Airbus A.340-642	Iberia *Miguel Hernandez*	
EC-LAA	Airbus A.320-214	Vueling Airlines	
EC-LAB	Airbus A.320-214	Vueling Airlines	
EC-LAJ	Airbus A.320-214	Iberworld	
EC-LAQ	Airbus A.320-214	Iberworld	
EC-LCQ	Embraer ERJ190-20LR	Air Europa	
EC-LCZ	Airbus A.340-642	Iberia	
EC-LEA	Airbus A.320-214	Iberia *Formentera*	
EC-LEI	Airbus A.319-111	Iberia *Vison Europeo*	
EC-LEK	Embraer ERJ190-200LR	Air Europa	

Notes	Reg.	Type	Owner or Operator
	EC-LEQ	Airbus A.330-343E	Iberworld
	EC-LEU	Airbus A.340-642	Iberia
	EC-LEV	Airbus A.340-642	Iberia
	EC-LEY	McD Douglas MD-83	Swiftair/Mint Airways
	EC-LFS	Airbus A.340-642	Iberia
	EC-LFZ	Embraer ERJ190-200LR	Air Europa
	EC-LGL	Boeing 747-412	Pullmantur Air
	EC-LHL	Boeing 757-28A	Mint Airways
	EC-LHM	Airbus A.340-313X	Iberia
	EC-LIN	Embraer ERJ190-200LR	Air Europa
	EC-LKE	Airbus A.330-243	Air Europa
	EC-LKH	Airbus A.320-214	Iberia *Parque de Cabarceno*

EK (Armenia)

Notes	Reg.	Type	Owner or Operator
	EK-32005	Airbus A.320-214	Armavia
	EK-32006	Airbus A.320-214	Armavia
	EK-32007	Airbus A.319-111	Armavia
	EK-32008	Airbus A.320-211	Armavia
	EK-32011	Airbus A.319-132	Armavia
	EK-32012	Airbus A.319-132	Armavia

EP (Iran)

Notes	Reg.	Type	Owner or Operator
	EP-IAA	Boeing 747SP-86	Iran Air
	EP-IAB	Boeing 747SP-86	Iran Air *Khorasan*
	EP-IAC	Boeing 747SP-86	Iran Air
	EP-IAD	Boeing 747SP-86	Iran Air
	EP-IAH	Boeing 747-286B (SCD)	Iran Air *Khuzestan*
	EP-IAI	Boeing 747-230B	Iran Air
	EP-IAM	Boeing 747-186B	Iran Air
	EP-IBA	Airbus A.300B4-605R	Iran Air
	EP-IBB	Airbus A.300B4-605R	Iran Air
	EP-IBC	Airbus A.300B4-605R	Iran Air
	EP-IBD	Airbus A.300B4-605R	Iran Air
	EP-MHO	Airbus A.310-304	Mahan Air
	EP-MNO	Airbus A.310-304	Mahan Air
	EP-MNP	Airbus A.310-308	Mahan Air
	EP-MNV	Airbus A.310-304	Mahan Air
	EP-MNX	Airbus A.310-304ET	Mahan Air

ER (Moldova)

Notes	Reg.	Type	Owner or Operator
	ER-AXP	Airbus A.320-211	Air Moldova
	ER-AXV	Airbus A.320-211	Air Moldova

ES (Estonia)

Notes	Reg.	Type	Owner or Operator
	ES-ABJ	Boeing 737-33R	Estonian Air
	ES-ABK	Boeing 737-36N	Estonian Air *Kalev*
	ES-ABL	Boeing 737-5L9	Estonian Air *Linda*
	ES-ABO	Boeing 737-505	Estonian Air
	ES-ABP	Boeing 737-528	Estonian Air

ET (Ethiopia)

Notes	Reg.	Type	Owner or Operator
	ET-AJS	Boeing 757-260PF	Ethiopian Airlines
	ET-AJX	Boeing 757-260F	Ethiopian Airlines
	ET-AKC	Boeing 757-260	Ethiopian Airlines
	ET-AKE	Boeing 757-260	Ethiopian Airlines
	ET-AKF	Boeing 757-260	Ethiopian Airlines
	ET-ALC	Boeing 767-33AER	Ethiopian Airlines
	ET-ALH	Boeing 767-3BGER	Ethiopian Airlines
	ET-ALJ	Boeing 767-360ER	Ethiopian Airlines
	ET-ALL	Boeing 767-3BGER	Ethiopian Airlines
	ET-ALO	Boeing 767-360ER	Ethiopian Airlines
	ET-ALP	Boeing 767-360ER	Ethiopian Airlines
	ET-ALY	Boeing 757-231	Ethiopian Airlines

Reg.	Type	Owner or Operator	Notes
ET-ALZ	Boeing 757-231	Ethiopian Airlines	
ET-AME	Boeing 767-306ER	Ethiopian Airlines	
ET-AMF	Boeing 767-3BGER	Ethiopian Airlines	
ET-AMG	Boeing 767-3BGER	Ethiopian Airlines	
ET-AMK	Boeing 757-28A	Ethiopian Airlines	
ET-AML	McD Douglas MD-11F	Ethiopian Airlines	
ET-AMQ	Boeing 767-33AER	Ethiopian Airlines	
ET-AMT	Boeing 757-23N	Ethiopian Airlines	
ET-AMU	Boeing 757-23N	Ethiopian Airlines	
ET-AND	McD Douglas MD-11F	Ethiopian Airlines	
ET-ANU	Boeing 767-3Q8ER	Ethiopian Airlines	

EW (Belarus)

Reg.	Type	Owner or Operator	Notes
EW-100PJ	Canadair CRJ200LR	Belavia	
EW-250PA	Boeing 737-524	Belavia	
EW-251PA	Boeing 737-5Q8	Belavia	
EW-252PA	Boeing 737-524	Belavia	
EW-253PA	Boeing 737-524	Belavia	
EW-254PA	Boeing 737-3Q8	Belavia	
EW-276PJ	Canadair CRJ200ER	Belavia	
EW-277PJ	Canadair CRJ200ER	Belavia	
EW-282PA	Boeing 737-3Q8	Belavia	
EW-283PA	Boeing 737-3Q8	Belavia	
EW-290PA	Boeing 737-5Q8	Belavia	
EW-294PA	Boeing 737-505	Belavia	
EW-303PJ	Canadair CRJ200LR	Belavia	

EZ (Turkmenistan)

Reg.	Type	Owner or Operator	Notes
EZ-A010	Boeing 757-23A	Turkmenistan Airlines	
EZ-A011	Boeing 757-22K	Turkmenistan Airlines	
EZ-A012	Boeing 757-22K	Turkmenistan Airlines	
EZ-A014	Boeing 757-22K	Turkmenistan Airlines	

F (France)

Reg.	Type	Owner or Operator	Notes
F-GEXA	Boeing 747-4B3	Air France	
F-GEXB	Boeing 747-4B3	Air France Cargo	
F-GFKH	Airbus A.320-211	Air France *Ville de Bruxelles*	
F-GFKI	Airbus A.320-211	Air France *Ville de Lisbonne*	
F-GFKJ	Airbus A.320-211	Air France *Pays de Roissy*	
F-GFKM	Airbus A.320-211	Air France *Ville de Luxembourg*	
F-GFKR	Airbus A.320-211	Air France *Ville de Barceloune*	
F-GFKS	Airbus A.320-211	Air France *Ville de Marseilles*	
F-GFKV	Airbus A.320-211	Air France *Ville de Bordeaux*	
F-GFKX	Airbus A.320-211	Air France *Ville de Francfort*	
F-GFKY	Airbus A.320-211	Air France *Ville de Toulouse*	
F-GFKZ	Airbus A.320-211	Air France *Ville de Turin*	
F-GHQC	Airbus A.320-211	Air France	
F-GHQG	Airbus A.320-211	Air France	
F-GHQH	Airbus A.320-211	Air France	
F-GHQJ	Airbus A.320-211	Air France	
F-GHQK	Airbus A.320-211	Air France	
F-GHQL	Airbus A.320-211	Air France	
F-GHQM	Airbus A.320-211	Air France	
F-GHQO	Airbus A.320-211	Air France	
F-GHQP	Airbus A.320-211	Air France	
F-GHQQ	Airbus A.320-211	Air France	
F-GHQR	Airbus A.320-211	Air France	
F-GIDK	Douglas DC-3C	Dakota Air Legend	
F-GISC	Boeing 747-428	Air France	
F-GISD	Boeing 747-428	Air France	
F-GITD	Boeing 747-428	Air France	
F-GITE	Boeing 747-428	Air France	
F-GITF	Boeing 747-428	Air France	
F-GITH	Boeing 747-428	Air France	
F-GITI	Boeing 747-428	Air France	
F-GITJ	Boeing 747-428	Air France	
F-GIUA	Boeing 747-428ERF (SCD)	Air France Cargo	
F-GIUC	Boeing 747-428ERF (SCD)	Air France Cargo	

Notes	Reg.	Type	Owner or Operator
	F-GIUD	Boeing 747-428ERF (SCD)	Air France Cargo
	F-GJVB	Airbus A.320-211	Air France
	F-GJVF	Airbus A.320-211	Aigle Azur
	F-GJVG	Airbus A.320-211	Air France
	F-GJVW	Airbus A.320-211	Air France
	F-GKHD	Fokker 100	Brit Air/Air France
	F-GKHE	Fokker 100	Brit Air/Air France
	F-GKHK	Airbus A.320-212	XL Airways France
	F-GKPD	Aerospatiale ATR-72-202	Airlinair/Air France
	F-GKXA	Airbus A.320-211	Air France
	F-GKXD	Airbus A.320-214	Air France
	F-GKXE	Airbus A.320-214	Air France
	F-GKXF	Airbus A.320-214	Air France
	F-GKXG	Airbus A.320-214	Air France
	F-GKXH	Airbus A.320-214	Air France
	F-GKXI	Airbus A.320-214	Air France
	F-GKXJ	Airbus A.320-214	Air France
	F-GKXK	Airbus A.320-214	Air France
	F-GKXL	Airbus A.320-214	Air France
	F-GKXM	Airbus A.320-214	Air France
	F-GKXN	Airbus A.320-214	Air France
	F-GKXO	Airbus A.320-214	Air France
	F-GKXP	Airbus A.320-214	Air France
	F-GKXR	Airbus A.320-214	Air France
	F-GKXS	Airbus A.320-214	Air France
	F-GKXT	Airbus A.320-214	Air France
	F-GKXU	Airbus A.320-214	Air France
	F-GKXV	Airbus A.320-214	Air France
	F-GKXY	Airbus A.320-214	Air France
	F-GKXZ	Airbus A.320-214	Air France
	F-GLZC	Airbus A.340-312	Air France
	F-GLZH	Airbus A.340-312	Air France
	F-GLZI	Airbus A.340-312	Air France
	F-GLZJ	Airbus A.340-313X	Air France
	F-GLZK	Airbus A.340-313X	Air France
	F-GLZL	Airbus A.340-313X	Air France
	F-GLZM	Airbus A.340-313X	Air France
	F-GLZN	Airbus A.340-313X	Air France
	F-GLZO	Airbus A.340-313X	Air France
	F-GLZP	Airbus A.340-313X	Air France
	F-GLZR	Airbus A.340-313X	Air France
	F-GLZS	Airbus A.340-313X	Air France
	F-GLZT	Airbus A.340-313X	Air France
	F-GLZU	Airbus A.340-313X	Air France
	F-GMZA	Airbus A.321-111	Air France
	F-GMZB	Airbus A.321-111	Air France
	F-GMZC	Airbus A.321-111	Air France
	F-GMZD	Airbus A.321-111	Air France
	F-GMZE	Airbus A.321-111	Air France
	F-GNIG	Airbus A.340-313X	Air France
	F-GNIH	Airbus A.340-313X	Air France
	F-GNII	Airbus A.340-313X	Air France
	F-GOHC	Embraer RJ135ER	Regional Airlines/Air France
	F-GOHE	Embraer RJ135ER	Regional Airlines/Air France
	F-GOHF	Embraer RJ135ER	Regional Airlines/Air France
	F-GPEJ	Boeing 757-236	Open Skies
	F-GPEK	Boeing 757-236	Open Skies
	F-GPMA	Airbus A.319-113	Air France
	F-GPMB	Airbus A.319-113	Air France
	F-GPMC	Airbus A.319-113	Air France
	F-GPMD	Airbus A.319-113	Air France
	F-GPME	Airbus A.319-113	Air France
	F-GPMF	Airbus A.319-113	Air France
	F-GPOC	Aerospatiale ATR-72-202	Airlinair/Air France
	F-GPOD	Aerospatiale ATR-72-202	Airlinair/Air France
	F-GPXB	Fokker 100	Brit Air/Air France
	F-GPXC	Fokker 100	Brit Air/Air France
	F-GPXD	Fokker 100	Brit Air/Air France
	F-GPXE	Fokker 100	Brit Air/Air France
	F-GPXF	Fokker 100	Brit Air/Air France
	F-GPYA	Aerospatiale ATR-42-500	Airlinair/Air France
	F-GPYD	Aerospatiale ATR-42-500	Airlinair/Air France
	F-GPYF	Aerospatiale ATR-42-500	Airlinair/Air France
	F-GPYK	Aerospatiale ATR-42-500	Airlinair/Air France

Reg.	Type	Owner or Operator	Notes
F-GPYL	Aerospatiale ATR-42-500	Airlinair/Air France	
F-GPYM	Aerospatiale ATR-42-500	Airlinair/Air France	
F-GPYO	Aerospatiale ATR-42-500	Airlinair/Air France	
F-GRGA	Embraer RJ145EU	Regional Airlines/Air France	
F-GRGB	Embraer RJ145EU	Regional Airlines/Air France	
F-GRGC	Embraer RJ145EU	Regional Airlines/Air France	
F-GRGD	Embraer RJ145EU	Regional Airlines/Air France	
F-GRGE	Embraer RJ145EU	Regional Airlines/Air France	
F-GRGF	Embraer RJ145EU	Regional Airlines/Air France	
F-GRGG	Embraer RJ145EU	Regional Airlines/Air France	
F-GRGH	Embraer RJ145EU	Regional Airlines/Air France	
F-GRGI	Embraer RJ145EU	Regional Airlines/Air France	
F-GRGJ	Embraer RJ145EU	Regional Airlines/Air France	
F-GRGK	Embraer RJ145EU	Regional Airlines/Air France	
F-GRGL	Embraer RJ145EU	Regional Airlines/Air France	
F-GRGM	Embraer RJ145EU	Regional Airlines/Air France	
F-GRGP	Embraer RJ135ER	Regional Airlines/Air France	
F-GRGQ	Embraer RJ135ER	Regional Airlines/Air France	
F-GRGR	Embraer RJ135ER	Regional Airlines/Air France	
F-GRHA	Airbus A.319-111	Air France	
F-GRHB	Airbus A.319-111	Air France	
F-GRHC	Airbus A.319-111	Air France	
F-GRHD	Airbus A.319-111	Air France	
F-GRHE	Airbus A.319-111	Air France	
F-GRHF	Airbus A.319-111	Air France	
F-GRHG	Airbus A.319-111	Air France	
F-GRHH	Airbus A.319-111	Air France	
F-GRHI	Airbus A.319-111	Air France	
F-GRHJ	Airbus A.319-111	Air France	
F-GRHK	Airbus A.319-111	Air France	
F-GRHL	Airbus A.319-111	Air France	
F-GRHM	Airbus A.319-111	Air France	
F-GRHN	Airbus A.319-111	Air France	
F-GRHO	Airbus A.319-111	Air France	
F-GRHP	Airbus A.319-111	Air France	
F-GRHQ	Airbus A.319-111	Air France	
F-GRHR	Airbus A.319-111	Air France	
F-GRHS	Airbus A.319-111	Air France	
F-GRHT	Airbus A.319-111	Air France	
F-GRHU	Airbus A.319-111	Air France	
F-GRHV	Airbus A.319-111	Air France	
F-GRHX	Airbus A.319-111	Air France	
F-GRHY	Airbus A.319-111	Air France	
F-GRHZ	Airbus A.319-111	Air France	
F-GRJE	Canadair CRJ100ER	Brit Air/Air France	
F-GRJF	Canadair CRJ100ER	Brit Air/Air France	
F-GRJG	Canadair CRJ100ER	Brit Air/Air France	
F-GRJI	Canadair CRJ100ER	Brit Air/Air France	
F-GRJJ	Canadair CRJ100ER	Brit Air/Air France	
F-GRJK	Canadair CRJ100ER	Brit Air/Air France	
F-GRJL	Canadair CRJ100ER	Brit Air/Air France	
F-GRJM	Canadair CRJ100ER	Brit Air/Air France	
F-GRJN	Canadair CRJ100ER	Brit Air/Air France	
F-GRJO	Canadair CRJ100ER	Brit Air/Air France	
F-GRJP	Canadair CRJ100ER	Brit Air/Air France	
F-GRJQ	Canadair CRJ100ER	Brit Air/Air France	
F-GRJR	Canadair CRJ100ER	Brit Air/Air France	
F-GRJT	Canadair CRJ100ER	Brit Air/Air France	
F-GRJU	Canadair CRJ100ER	Brit Air/Air France	
F-GRSI	Airbus A.320-214	XL Airways France	
F-GRSQ	Airbus A.330-243	XL Airways France	
F-GRXA	Airbus A.319-111	Air France	
F-GRXB	Airbus A.319-111	Air France	
F-GRXC	Airbus A.319-111	Air France	
F-GRXD	Airbus A.319-111	Air France	
F-GRXE	Airbus A.319-111	Air France	
F-GRXF	Airbus A.319-111	Air France	
F-GRXG	Airbus A.319-115LR	Air France Dedicate	
F-GRXH	Airbus A.319-115LR	Air France Dedicate	
F-GRXI	Airbus A.319-115LR	Air France Dedicate	
F-GRXJ	Airbus A.319-115LR	Air France Dedicate	
F-GRXK	Airbus A.319-115LR	Air France Dedicate	
F-GRXL	Airbus A.319-111	Air France	
F-GRXM	Airbus A.319-111	Air France	

Notes	Reg.	Type	Owner or Operator
	F-GRXN	Airbus A.319-115LR	Air France Dedicate
	F-GRZA	Canadair CRJ700	Brit Air/Air France
	F-GRZB	Canadair CRJ700	Brit Air/Air France
	F-GRZC	Canadair CRJ700	Brit Air/Air France
	F-GRZD	Canadair CRJ700	Brit Air/Air France
	F-GRZE	Canadair CRJ700	Brit Air/Air France
	F-GRZF	Canadair CRJ700	Brit Air/Air France
	F-GRZG	Canadair CRJ700	Brit Air/Air France
	F-GRZH	Canadair CRJ700	Brit Air/Air France
	F-GRZI	Canadair CRJ700	Brit Air/Air France
	F-GRZJ	Canadair CRJ700	Brit Air/Air France
	F-GRZK	Canadair CRJ700	Brit Air/Air France
	F-GRZL	Canadair CRJ700	Brit Air/Air France
	F-GRZM	Canadair CRJ700	Brit Air/Air France
	F-GRZN	Canadair CRJ700	Brit Air/Air France
	F-GRZO	Canadair CRJ700	Brit Air/Air France
	F-GSEU	Airbus A.330-243	XL Airways France
	F-GSPA	Boeing 777-228ER	Air France
	F-GSPB	Boeing 777-228ER	Air France
	F-GSPC	Boeing 777-228ER	Air France
	F-GSPD	Boeing 777-228ER	Air France
	F-GSPE	Boeing 777-228ER	Air France
	F-GSPF	Boeing 777-228ER	Air France
	F-GSPG	Boeing 777-228ER	Air France
	F-GSPH	Boeing 777-228ER	Air France
	F-GSPI	Boeing 777-228ER	Air France
	F-GSPJ	Boeing 777-228ER	Air France
	F-GSPK	Boeing 777-228ER	Air France
	F-GSPL	Boeing 777-228ER	Air France
	F-GSPM	Boeing 777-228ER	Air France
	F-GSPN	Boeing 777-228ER	Air France
	F-GSPO	Boeing 777-228ER	Air France
	F-GSPP	Boeing 777-228ER	Air France
	F-GSPQ	Boeing 777-228ER	Air France
	F-GSPR	Boeing 777-228ER	Air France
	F-GSPS	Boeing 777-228ER	Air France
	F-GSPT	Boeing 777-228ER	Air France
	F-GSPU	Boeing 777-228ER	Air France
	F-GSPV	Boeing 777-228ER	Air France
	F-GSPX	Boeing 777-228ER	Air France
	F-GSPY	Boeing 777-228ER	Air France
	F-GSPZ	Boeing 777-228ER	Air France
	F-GSQA	Boeing 777-328ER	Air France
	F-GSQB	Boeing 777-328ER	Air France
	F-GSQC	Boeing 777-328ER	Air France
	F-GSQD	Boeing 777-328ER	Air France
	F-GSQE	Boeing 777-328ER	Air France
	F-GSQF	Boeing 777-328ER	Air France
	F-GSQG	Boeing 777-328ER	Air France
	F-GSQH	Boeing 777-328ER	Air France
	F-GSQI	Boeing 777-328ER	Air France
	F-GSQJ	Boeing 777-328ER	Air France
	F-GSQK	Boeing 777-328ER	Air France
	F-GSQL	Boeing 777-328ER	Air France
	F-GSQM	Boeing 777-328ER	Air France
	F-GSQN	Boeing 777-328ER	Air France
	F-GSQO	Boeing 777-328ER	Air France
	F-GSQP	Boeing 777-328ER	Air France
	F-GSQR	Boeing 777-328ER	Air France
	F-GSQS	Boeing 777-328ER	Air France
	F-GSQT	Boeing 777-328ER	Air France
	F-GSQU	Boeing 777-328ER	Air France
	F-GSQV	Boeing 777-328ER	Air France
	F-GSQX	Boeing 777-328ER	Air France
	F-GSQY	Boeing 777-328ER	Air France
	F-GSTA	Airbus A.300-608ST Beluga (1)	Airbus Transport International
	F-GSTB	Airbus A.300-608ST Beluga (2)	Airbus Transport International
	F-GSTC	Airbus A.300-608ST Beluga (3)	Airbus Transport International
	F-GSTD	Airbus A.300-608ST Beluga (4)	Airbus Transport International
	F-GSTF	Airbus A.300-608ST Beluga (5)	Airbus Transport International
	F-GTAD	Airbus A.321-211	Air France
	F-GTAE	Airbus A.321-211	Air France
	F-GTAH	Airbus A.321-211	Air France

Reg.	Type	Owner or Operator	Notes
F-GTAI	Airbus A.321-211	Air France	
F-GTAJ	Airbus A.321-211	Air France	
F-GTAK	Airbus A.321-211	Air France	
F-GTAL	Airbus A.321-211	Air France	
F-GTAM	Airbus A.321-211	Air France	
F-GTAN	Airbus A.321-211	Air France	
F-GTAO	Airbus A.321-211	Air France	
F-GTAP	Airbus A.321-212	Air France	
F-GTAQ	Airbus A.321-211	Air France	
F-GTAR	Airbus A.321-211	Air France	
F-GTAS	Airbus A.321-211	Air France	
F-GTAT	Airbus A.321-211	Air France	
F-GTAU	Airbus A.321-211	Air France	
F-GTAV	Airbus A.321-211	Air France	
F-GTAX	Airbus A.321-211	Air France	
F-GTAY	Airbus A.321-211	Air France	
F-GTHL	Airbus A.320-231	XL Airways France	
F-GTUI	Boeing 747-422	Corsair	
F-GUAA	Airbus A.321-211	Aigle Azur	
F-GUAM	Embraer RJ145MP	Regional Airlines/Air France	
F-GUBA	Embraer RJ145MP	Regional Airlines/Air France	
F-GUBB	Embraer RJ145MP	Regional Airlines/Air France	
F-GUBC	Embraer RJ145MP	Regional Airlines/Air France	
F-GUBD	Embraer RJ145MP	Regional Airlines/Air France	
F-GUBE	Embraer RJ145MP	Regional Airlines/Air France	
F-GUBF	Embraer RJ145MP	Regional Airlines/Air France	
F-GUBG	Embraer RJ145MP	Regional Airlines/Air France	
F-GUEA	Embraer RJ145MP	Regional Airlines/Air France	
F-GUFD	Embraer RJ145MP	Regional Airlines/Air France	
F-GUGA	Airbus A.318-111	Air France	
F-GUGB	Airbus A.318-111	Air France	
F-GUGC	Airbus A.318-111	Air France	
F-GUGD	Airbus A.318-111	Air France	
F-GUGE	Airbus A.318-111	Air France	
F-GUGF	Airbus A.318-111	Air France	
F-GUGG	Airbus A.318-111	Air France	
F-GUGH	Airbus A.318-111	Air France	
F-GUGI	Airbus A.318-111	Air France	
F-GUGJ	Airbus A.318-111	Air France	
F-GUGK	Airbus A.318-111	Air France	
F-GUGL	Airbus A.318-111	Air France	
F-GUGM	Airbus A.318-111	Air France	
F-GUGN	Airbus A.318-111	Air France	
F-GUGO	Airbus A.318-111	Air France	
F-GUGP	Airbus A.318-111	Air France	
F-GUGQ	Airbus A.318-111	Air France	
F-GUGR	Airbus A.318-111	Air France	
F-GUMA	Embraer RJ145MP	Regional Airlines/Air France	
F-GUOB	Boeing 777-F28	Air France Cargo	
F-GUOC	Boeing 777-F28	Air France Cargo	
F-GUPT	Embraer RJ145MP	Regional Airlines/Air France	
F-GVGS	Embraer RJ145MP	Regional Airlines/Air France	
F-GVHD	Embraer RJ145MP	Regional Airlines/Air France	
F-GVZL	Aerospatiale ATR-72-500	Airlinair/Air France	
F-GVZM	Aerospatiale ATR-72-212	Airlinair/Air France	
F-GVZN	Aerospatiale ATR-72-500	Airlinair/Air France	
F-GXAH	Airbus A.319-132	Aigle Azur	
F-GYAI	Airbus A.320-211	Air Mediterranée	
F-GYAJ	Airbus A.321-211	Air Mediterranée	
F-GYAN	Airbus A.321-111	Air Mediterranée	
F-GYAO	Airbus A.321-111	Air Mediterranée	
F-GYAP	Airbus A.321-111	Air Mediterranée	
F-GYAQ	Airbus A.321-211	Air Mediterranée	
F-GYAR	Airbus A.321-211	Air Mediterranée	
F-GYAZ	Airbus A.321-111	Air Mediterranée	
F-GZCA	Airbus A.330-203	Air France	
F-GZCB	Airbus A.330-203	Air France	
F-GZCC	Airbus A.330-203	Air France	
F-GZCD	Airbus A.330-203	Air France	
F-GZCE	Airbus A.330-203	Air France	
F-GZCF	Airbus A.330-203	Air France	
F-GZCG	Airbus A.330-203	Air France	
F-GZCH	Airbus A.330-203	Air France	
F-GZCI	Airbus A.330-203	Air France	

Notes	Reg.	Type	Owner or Operator
	F-GZCJ	Airbus A.330-203	Air France
	F-GZCK	Airbus A.330-203	Air France
	F-GZCL	Airbus A.330-203	Air France
	F-GZCM	Airbus A.330-203	Air France
	F-GZCN	Airbus A.330-203	Air France
	F-GZCO	Airbus A.330-203	Air France
	F-GZHA	Boeing 737-8GJ	Transavia France
	F-GZHB	Boeing 737-8GJ	Transavia France
	F-GZHC	Boeing 737-8GJ	Transavia France
	F-GZHD	Boeing 737-8K2	Transavia France
	F-GZHE	Boeing 737-8K2	Transavia France
	F-GZHF	Boeing 737-8HX	Transavia France
	F-GZHN	Boeing 737-8K2	Transavia France
	F-GZHV	Boeing 737-85H	Transavia France
	F-GZNA	Boeing 777-328ER	Air France
	F-GZNB	Boeing 777-328ER	Air France
	F-GZNC	Boeing 777-328ER	Air France
	F-GZND	Boeing 777-328ER	Air France
	F-GZNE	Boeing 777-328ER	Air France
	F-GZNF	Boeing 777-328ER	Air France
	F-GZNG	Boeing 777-328ER	Air France
	F-GZNH	Boeing 777-328ER	Air France
	F-GZNI	Boeing 777-328ER	Air France
	F-GZNJ	Boeing 777-328ER	Air France
	F-GZNK	Boeing 777-328ER	Air France
	F-HAVI	Boeing 757-26D	Open Skies *Violette*
	F-HAVN	Boeing 757-230	Open Skies
	F-HAXL	Boeing 737-8Q8	XL Airways France
	F-HBAB	Airbus A.321-211	Aigle Azur
	F-HBAC	Airbus A.320-214	Aigle Azur
	F-HBAF	Airbus A.321-211	Aigle Azur
	F-HBAL	Airbus A.319-111	Aigle Azur
	F-HBAO	Airbus A.320-214	Aigle Azur
	F-HBII	Airbus A.320-214	Aigle Azur
	F-HBIL	Airbus A.330-243	Corsair
	F-HBLA	Embraer RJ190-100LR	Regional Airlines/Air France
	F-HBLB	Embraer RJ190-100LR	Regional Airlines/Air France
	F-HBLC	Embraer RJ190-100LR	Regional Airlines/Air France
	F-HBLD	Embraer RJ190-100LR	Regional Airlines/Air France
	F-HBLE	Embraer RJ190-100LR	Regional Airlines/Air France
	F-HBLF	Embraer RJ190-100LR	Regional Airlines/Air France
	F-HBLG	Embraer RJ190-100LR	Regional Airlines/Air France
	F-HBLH	Embraer RJ190-100LR	Regional Airlines/Air France
	F-HBLI	Embraer RJ190-100LR	Regional Airlines/Air France
	F-HBLJ	Embraer RJ190-100LR	Regional Airlines/Air France
	F-HBMI	Airbus A.319-114	Aigle Azur
	F-HBNA	Airbus A.320-214	Air France
	F-HBNB	Airbus A.320-214	Air France
	F-HBXA	Embraer RJ170-100LR	Regional Airlines/Air France
	F-HBXB	Embraer RJ170-100LR	Regional Airlines/Air France
	F-HBXC	Embraer RJ170-100LR	Regional Airlines/Air France
	F-HBXD	Embraer RJ170-100LR	Regional Airlines/Air France
	F-HBXE	Embraer RJ170-100LR	Regional Airlines/Air France
	F-HBXF	Embraer RJ170-100LR	Regional Airlines/Air France
	F-HBXG	Embraer RJ170-100LR	Regional Airlines/Air France
	F-HBXH	Embraer RJ170-100LR	Regional Airlines/Air France
	F-HBXI	Embraer RJ170-100LR	Regional Airlines/Air France
	F-HBXJ	Embraer RJ170-100LR	Regional Airlines/Air France
	F-HCAI	Airbus A.321-111	Aigle Azur
	F-HCAT	Airbus A.330-243	Corsair
	F-HCOA	Boeing 737-5LP	Air Mediterranee
	F-HCZI	Airbus A.319-112	Aigle Azur
	F-HDTA	Canadair CRJ900ER	Brit Air/Air France
	F-HDTB	Canadair CRJ900ER	Brit Air/Air France
	F-HEPA	Airbus A.320-214	Air France
	F-HEPB	Airbus A.320-214	Air France
	F-HEPC	Airbus A.320-214	Air France
	F-HEPD	Airbus A.320-214	Air France
	F-HEPE	Airbus A.320-214	Air France
	F-HEPF	Airbus A.320-214	Air France
	F-HEPG	Airbus A.320-214	Air France
	F-HJUL	Boeing 737-8Q8	XL Airways France
	F-HKIS	Boeing 747-422	Corsair

Reg.	Type	Owner or Operator	Notes
F-HLOV	Boeing 747-422	Corsair	
F-HMLA	Canadair CRJ1000	Brit Air/Air France	
F-HMLD	Canadair CRJ1000	Brit Air/Air France	
F-HPJA	Airbus A.380-861	Air France	
F-HPJB	Airbus A.380-861	Air France	
F-HPJC	Airbus A.380-861	Air France	
F-HPJD	Airbus A.380-861	Air France	
F-HPJE	Airbus A.380-861	Air France	
F-HPJF	Airbus A.380-861	Air France	
F-HPJG	Airbus A.380-861	Air France	
F-HPJH	Airbus A.380-861	Air France	
F-HSEA	Boeing 747-422	Corsair	
F-HSEX	Boeing 747-422	Corsair	
F-HSUN	Boeing 747-422	Corsair	
F-OHGV	Airbus A.320-232	Royal Jordanian *Irbid*	
F-OHGX	Airbus A.320-232	Royal Jordanian *Madaba*	
F-OJHH	Airbus A.310-304ET	Mahan Air	
F-OJHI	Airbus A.310-304ET	Mahan Air	
F-OMRN	Airbus A.320-232	Middle East Airlines	
F-OMRO	Airbus A.320-232	Middle East Airlines	
F-ORMA	Airbus A.330-243	Middle East Airlines	
F-ORME	Airbus A.321-231	Middle East Airlines	
F-ORMF	Airbus A.321-231	Middle East Airlines	
F-ORMG	Airbus A.321-231	Middle East Airlines	

HA (Hungary)

Reg.	Type	Owner or Operator	Notes
HA-LKB	Boeing 737-86Q	Travel Service Airlines	
HA-LKE	Boeing 737-86Q	Travel Service Airlines	
HA-LOA	Boeing 737-7Q8	Malev	
HA-LOB	Boeing 737-7Q8	Malev	
HA-LOC	Boeing 737-8Q8	Malev	
HA-LOD	Boeing 737-6Q8	Malev	
HA-LOE	Boeing 737-6Q8	Malev	
HA-LOF	Boeing 737-6Q8	Malev	
HA-LOG	Boeing 737-6Q8	Malev	
HA-LOH	Boeing 737-8Q8	Malev	
HA-LOI	Boeing 737-7Q8	Malev	
HA-LOJ	Boeing 737-6Q8	Malev	
HA-LOK	Boeing 737-8Q8	Malev	
HA-LOL	Boeing 737-7Q8	Malev	
HA-LOM	Boeing 737-8Q8	Malev	
HA-LON	Boeing 737-6Q8	Malev	
HA-LOP	Boeing 737-7Q8	Malev	
HA-LOR	Boeing 737-7Q8	Malev	
HA-LOS	Boeing 737-7Q8	Malev	
HA-LOU	Boeing 737-8Q8	Malev	
HA-LPA	Airbus A.320-233	Wizz Air	
HA-LPB	Airbus A.320-233	Wizz Air	
HA-LPC	Airbus A.320-233	Wizz Air	
HA-LPD	Airbus A.320-233	Wizz Air	
HA-LPE	Airbus A.320-233	Wizz Air	
HA-LPF	Airbus A.320-233	Wizz Air	
HA-LPH	Airbus A.320-233	Wizz Air	
HA-LPI	Airbus A.320-233	Wizz Air	
HA-LPJ	Airbus A.320-232	Wizz Air	
HA-LPK	Airbus A.320-231	Wizz Air	
HA-LPL	Airbus A.320-232	Wizz Air	
HA-LPM	Airbus A.320-232	Wizz Air	
HA-LPN	Airbus A.320-232	Wizz Air	
HA-LPO	Airbus A.320-232	Wizz Air	
HA-LPQ	Airbus A.320-232	Wizz Air	
HA-LPR	Airbus A.320-232	Wizz Air	
HA-LPS	Airbus A.320-232	Wizz Air	
HA-LPT	Airbus A.320-232	Wizz Air	
HA-LPU	Airbus A.320-232	Wizz Air	
HA-LPV	Airbus A.320-232	Wizz Air	
HA-LPW	Airbus A.320-232	Wizz Air	
HA-LPX	Airbus A.320-232	Wizz Air	
HA-LPY	Airbus A.320-232	Wizz Air	
HA-LPZ	Airbus A.320-232	Wizz Air	
HA-LWA	Airbus A.320-232	Wizz Air	
HA-LWB	Airbus A.320-232	Wizz Air	

Notes	Reg.	Type	Owner or Operator
	HA-LWC	Airbus A.320-232	Wizz Air
	HA-LWD	Airbus A.320-232	Wizz Air
	HA-LWE	Airbus A.320-232	Wizz Air
	HA-LWF	Airbus A.320-232	Wizz Air
	HA-LWG	Airbus A.320-232	Wizz Air

HB (Switzerland)

Notes	Reg.	Type	Owner or Operator
	HB-IEE	Boeing 757-23A	PrivatAir
	HB-IHX	Airbus A.320-214	Edelweiss Air *Calvaro*
	HB-IHY	Airbus A.320-214	Edelweiss Air *Upali*
	HB-IHZ	Airbus A.320-214	Edelweiss Air *Viktoria*
	HB-IIR	Boeing 737-86Q	PrivatAir/Swiss International
	HB-IJB	Airbus A.320-214	Swiss International *Embrach*
	HB-IJD	Airbus A.320-214	Swiss International
	HB-IJE	Airbus A.320-214	Swiss International *Arosa*
	HB-IJF	Airbus A.320-214	Swiss International
	HB-IJH	Airbus A.320-214	Swiss International
	HB-IJI	Airbus A.320-214	Swiss International *Basodino*
	HB-IJJ	Airbus A.320-214	Swiss International *Les Diablerets*
	HB-IJK	Airbus A.320-214	Swiss International *Wissigstock*
	HB-IJL	Airbus A.320-214	Swiss International *Pizol*
	HB-IJM	Airbus A.320-214	Swiss International *Schilthorn*
	HB-IJN	Airbus A.320-214	Swiss International *Vanil Noir*
	HB-IJO	Airbus A.320-214	Swiss International *Lissengrat*
	HB-IJP	Airbus A.320-214	Swiss International *Nollen*
	HB-IJQ	Airbus A.320-214	Swiss International *Agassizhorn*
	HB-IJR	Airbus A.320-214	Swiss International *Dammastock*
	HB-IJS	Airbus A.320-214	Swiss International *Creux du Van*
	HB-IJU	Airbus A.320-214	Swiss International *Bietschhorn*
	HB-IJV	Airbus A.320-214	Swiss International *Wildspitz*
	HB-IJW	Airbus A.320-214	Swiss International *Bachtel*
	HB-IJX	Airbus A.320-214	Swiss International *Davos*
	HB-IOC	Airbus A.321-111	Swiss International *Eiger*
	HB-IOD	Airbus A.321-111	Swiss International
	HB-IOF	Airbus A.321-111	Swiss International
	HB-IOH	Airbus A.321-111	Swiss International *Piz Palu*
	HB-IOK	Airbus A.321-111	Swiss International *Biefertenstock*
	HB-IOL	Airbus A.321-111	Swiss International *Kaiseregg*
	HB-IOM	Airbus A.321-212	Swiss International
	HB-IOP	Airbus A.320-214	Air Berlin/Belair
	HB-IOQ	Airbus A.320-214	Air Berlin/Belair
	HB-IOR	Airbus A.320-214	Air Berlin/Belair
	HB-IOS	Airbus A.320-214	Air Berlin/Belair
	HB-IOU	Airbus A.320-214	Air Berlin/Belair
	HB-IOW	Airbus A.320-214	Air Berlin/Belair
	HB-IOX	Airbus A.319-112	Air Berlin/Belair
	HB-IOY	Airbus A.319-112	Air Berlin/Belair
	HB-IOZ	Airbus A.320-214	Air Berlin/Belair
	HB-IPR	Airbus A.319-112	Swiss International *Commune de Champagne*
	HB-IPS	Airbus A.319-112	Swiss International *Weiach*
	HB-IPT	Airbus A.319-112	Swiss International *Stadel*
	HB-IPU	Airbus A.319-112	Swiss International *Hochfelden*
	HB-IPV	Airbus A.319-112	Swiss International *Rumlang*
	HB-IPX	Airbus A.319-112	Swiss International *Steinmaur*
	HB-IPY	Airbus A.319-112	Swiss International *Hori*
	HB-IQA	Airbus A.330-223	Swiss International *Lauteraarhorn*
	HB-IQC	Airbus A.330-223	Swiss International *Breithorn*
	HB-IQH	Airbus A.330-223	Swiss International *Allalinhorn*
	HB-IQI	Airbus A.330-223	Edelweiss Air *Kiburi*
	HB-IQQ	Airbus A.330-223	Swiss International
	HB-IXN	Avro RJ100	Swiss European Airlines *Balmhorn 3699m*
	HB-IXO	Avro RJ100	Swiss European Airlines *Brisen 2404m*
	HB-IXP	Avro RJ100	Swiss European Airlines *Chestenberg 647m*
	HB-IXQ	Avro RJ100	Swiss European Airlines *Corno Gries 2969m*
	HB-IXR	Avro RJ100	Swiss European Airlines *Hoho Winde 1204m*
	HB-IXS	Avro RJ100	Swiss European Airlines *Mont Velan 3731m*
	HB-IXT	Avro RJ100	Swiss European Airlines *Ottenberg 681m*
	HB-IXU	Avro RJ100	Swiss European Airlines *Pfannenstiel 853m*
	HB-IXV	Avro RJ100	Swiss European Airlines *Saxer First 2151m*
	HB-IXW	Avro RJ100	Swiss European Airlines *Shafarnisch 2107m*
	HB-IXX	Avro RJ100	Swiss European Airlines *Silberen 2319m*
	HB-IYQ	Avro RJ100	Swiss European Airlines *Piz Buin 3312m*

Reg.	Type	Owner or Operator	Notes
HB-IYR	Avro RJ100	Swiss European Airlines *Vrenelisgärtli 2904m*	
HB-IYS	Avro RJ100	Swiss European Airlines *Churfirsten 2306m*	
HB-IYT	Avro RJ100	Swiss European Airlines *Bluemlisalp 3663m*	
HB-IYU	Avro RJ100	Swiss European Airlines *Rot Turm 2002m*	
HB-IYV	Avro RJ100	Swiss European Airlines *Pizzo Barone 2864m*	
HB-IYW	Avro RJ100	Swiss European Airlines *Spitzmeilen 2501m*	
HB-IYY	Avro RJ100	Swiss European Airlines *Titlis 3238m*	
HB-IYZ	Avro RJ100	Swiss European Airlines *Tour d'Ai 2331m*	
HB-JHA	Airbus A.330-343	Swiss International	
HB-JHB	Airbus A.330-343	Swiss International *Sion*	
HB-JHC	Airbus A.330-343	Swiss International *Bellinzona*	
HB-JHD	Airbus A.330-343	Swiss International *St.Gallen*	
HB-JHE	Airbus A.330-343	Swiss International *Fribourg*	
HB-JHF	Airbus A.330-343	Swiss International	
HB-JHG	Airbus A.330-343	Swiss International *Glarus*	
HB-JHH	Airbus A.330-343	Swiss International *Neuchatel*	
HB-JHI	Airbus A.330-343	Swiss International	
HB-JHJ	Airbus A.330-343	Swiss International	
HB-JHQ	Airbus A.330-343	Edelweiss Air	
HB-JIE	McD Douglas MD-90-30	Hello	
HB-JIF	McD Douglas MD-90-30	Hello	
HB-JIY	Airbus A.320-214	Hello	
HB-JIZ	Airbus A.320-214	Hello	
HB-JJA	Boeing 737-7AK	PrivatAir/KLM	
HB-JLP	Airbus A.320-214	Swiss International	
HB-JLQ	Airbus A.320-214	Swiss International	
HB-JMA	Airbus A.340-313X	Swiss International *Matterhorn*	
HB-JMB	Airbus A.340-313X	Swiss International *Zurich*	
HB-JMC	Airbus A.340-313X	Swiss International *Basel*	
HB-JMD	Airbus A.340-313X	Swiss International *Liestal*	
HB-JME	Airbus A.340-313X	Swiss International *Dom*	
HB-JMF	Airbus A.340-313X	Swiss International *Liskamm*	
HB-JMG	Airbus A.340-313X	Swiss International *Luzern*	
HB-JMH	Airbus A.340-313X	Swiss International *Chur*	
HB-JMI	Airbus A.340-313X	Swiss International *Schaffhausen*	
HB-JMJ	Airbus A.340-313X	Swiss International *City of Basel*	
HB-JMK	Airbus A.340-313X	Swiss International *Aarau*	
HB-JML	Airbus A.340-313X	Swiss International *Liestal*	
HB-JMM	Airbus A.340-313X	Swiss International	
HB-JMN	Airbus A.340-313X	Swiss International	
HB-JMO	Airbus A.340-313X	Swiss International	
HB-JQA	DHC.8Q-402 Dash Eight	Baboo	
HB-JQB	DHC.8Q-402 Dash Eight	Baboo	
HB-JVC	Fokker 100	Helvetic Airways	
HB-JVE	Fokker 100	Helvetic Airways	
HB-JVF	Fokker 100	Helvetic Airways	
HB-JVG	Fokker 100	Helvetic Airways	
HB-JVH	Fokker 100	Helvetic Airways	
HB-JVI	Fokker 100	Helvetic Airways	
HB-JZF	Airbus A.319-111	easyJet Switzerland	
HB-JZG	Airbus A.319-111	easyJet Switzerland	
HB-JZH	Airbus A.319-111	easyJet Switzerland	
HB-JZI	Airbus A.319-111	easyJet Switzerland	
HB-JZJ	Airbus A.319-111	easyJet Switzerland	
HB-JZK	Airbus A.319-111	easyJet Switzerland	
HB-JZL	Airbus A.319-111	easyJet Switzerland	
HB-JZM	Airbus A.319-111	easyJet Switzerland	
HB-JZN	Airbus A.319-111	easyJet Switzerland	
HB-JZO	Airbus A.319-111	easyJet Switzerland	
HB-JZP	Airbus A.319-111	easyJet Switzerland	
HB-JZQ	Airbus A.319-111	easyJet Switzerland	
HB-JZR	Airbus A.320-214	easyJet Switzerland	
HB-JZS	Airbus A.319-111	easyJet Switzerland	
HB-JZT	Airbus A.319-111	easyJet Switzerland	
HB-JZU	Airbus A.319-111	easyJet Switzerland	
HB-JZV	Airbus A.319-111	easyJet Switzerland	
HB-JZW	Airbus A.319-111	easyJet Switzerland	

HL (Korea)

Reg.	Type	Owner or Operator	Notes
HL7400	Boeing 747-4B5F	Korean Air Cargo	
HL7402	Boeing 747-4B5	Korean Air	
HL7403	Boeing 747-4B5F	Korean Air Cargo	

Notes	Reg.	Type	Owner or Operator
	HL7404	Boeing 747-4B5	Korean Air
	HL7413	Boeing 747-48EBCF	Asiana Airlines Cargo
	HL7414	Boeing 747-48EBCF	Asiana Airlines Cargo
	HL7415	Boeing 747-48EBCF	Asiana Airlines Cargo
	HL7417	Boeing 747-48EBCF	Asiana Airlines Cargo
	HL7419	Boeing 747-48EF (SCD)	Asiana Airlines Cargo
	HL7420	Boeing 747-48EF (SCD)	Asiana Airlines Cargo
	HL7434	Boeing 747-4B5F	Korean Air Cargo
	HL7436	Boeing 747-48EF (SCD)	Asiana Airlines Cargo
	HL7437	Boeing 747-4B5F	Korean Air Cargo
	HL7438	Boeing 747-4B5ERF	Korean Air Cargo
	HL7439	Boeing 747-4B5ERF	Korean Air Cargo
	HL7448	Boeing 747-4B5F (SCD)	Korean Air Cargo
	HL7449	Boeing 747-4B5F (SCD)	Korean Air Cargo
	HL7460	Boeing 747-4B5	Korean Air
	HL7461	Boeing 747-4B5	Korean Air
	HL7462	Boeing 747-4B5F	Korean Air Cargo
	HL7466	Boeing 747-4B5F	Korean Air Cargo
	HL7467	Boeing 747-4B5F	Korean Air Cargo
	HL7472	Boeing 747-4B5	Korean Air
	HL7473	Boeing 747-4B5	Korean Air
	HL7480	Boeing 747-4B5 (SCD)	Korean Air
	HL7482	Boeing 747-4B5BCF	Korean Air Cargo
	HL7483	Boeing 747-4B5BCF	Korean Air Cargo
	HL7484	Boeing 747-4B5BCF	Korean Air Cargo
	HL7485	Boeing 747-4B5BCF	Korean Air Cargo
	HL7486	Boeing 747-4B5BCF	Korean Air Cargo
	HL7487	Boeing 747-4B5	Korean Air
	HL7488	Boeing 747-4B5	Korean Air
	HL7489	Boeing 747-4B5	Korean Air
	HL7490	Boeing 747-4B5	Korean Air
	HL7491	Boeing 747-4B5	Korean Air
	HL7492	Boeing 747-4B5	Korean Air
	HL7493	Boeing 747-4B5	Korean Air
	HL7494	Boeing 747-4B5	Korean Air
	HL7495	Boeing 747-4B5	Korean Air
	HL7498	Boeing 747-4B5	Korean Air
	HL7499	Boeing 747-4B5ERF	Korean Air Cargo
	HL7500	Boeing 777-28EER	Asiana Airlines
	HL7526	Boeing 777-2B5ER	Korean Air
	HL7530	Boeing 777-2B5ER	Korean Air
	HL7531	Boeing 777-2B5ER	Korean Air
	HL7574	Boeing 777-2B5ER	Korean Air
	HL7575	Boeing 777-2B5ER	Korean Air
	HL7596	Boeing 777-28EER	Asiana Airlines
	HL7597	Boeing 777-28EER	Asiana Airlines
	HL7598	Boeing 777-2B5ER	Korean Air
	HL7600	Boeing 747-4B5ERF	Korean Air Cargo
	HL7601	Boeing 747-4B5ERF	Korean Air Cargo
	HL7602	Boeing 747-4B5ERF	Korean Air Cargo
	HL7603	Boeing 747-4B5ERF	Korean Air Cargo
	HL7604	Boeing 747-48EF (SCD)	Asiana Airlines Cargo
	HL7605	Boeing 747-4B5ERF	Korean Air Cargo
	HL7606	Boeing 747-4B5BCF	Korean Air Cargo
	HL7607	Boeing 747-4B5	Korean Air
	HL7608	Boeing 747-4B5BCF	Korean Air Cargo
	HL7616	Boeing 747-446F	Asiana Airlines Cargo
	HL7700	Boeing 777-28EER	Asiana Airlines
	HL7714	Boeing 777-2B5ER	Korean Air
	HL7715	Boeing 777-2B5ER	Korean Air
	HL7721	Boeing 777-2B5ER	Korean Air
	HL7732	Boeing 777-28EER	Asiana Airlines
	HL7733	Boeing 777-2B5ER	Korean Air
	HL7734	Boeing 777-2B5ER	Korean Air
	HL7739	Boeing 777-28EER	Asiana Airlines
	HL7742	Boeing 777-28EER	Asiana Airlines
	HL7743	Boeing 777-2B5ER	Korean Air
	HL7750	Boeing 777-2B5ER	Korean Air
	HL7751	Boeing 777-2B5ER	Korean Air
	HL7752	Boeing 777-2B5ER	Korean Air
	HL7755	Boeing 777-28EER	Asiana Airlines
	HL7756	Boeing 777-28EER	Asiana Airlines
	HL7764	Boeing 777-2B5ER	Korean Air
	HL7765	Boeing 777-2B5ER	Korean Air

Reg.	Type	Owner or Operator	Notes
HL7766	Boeing 777-2B5ER	Korean Air	
HL7775	Boeing 777-28EER	Asiana Airlines	
HL7791	Boeing 777-28EER	Asiana Airlines	

HS (Thailand)

Reg.	Type	Owner or Operator	Notes
HS-TGA	Boeing 747-4D7	Thai Airways International *Srisuriyothai*	
HS-TGB	Boeing 747-4D7	Thai Airways International *Si Satchanulai*	
HS-TGF	Boeing 747-4D7	Thai Airways International *Sri Ubon*	
HS-TGG	Boeing 747-4D7	Thai Airways International *Pathoomawadi*	
HS-TGH	Boeing 747-4D7	Thai Airways International *Chaiprakarn*	
HS-TGJ	Boeing 747-4D7	Thai Airways International *Hariphunchai*	
HS-TGK	Boeing 747-4D7	Thai Airways International *Alongkorn*	
HS-TGL	Boeing 747-4D7	Thai Airways International *Theparat*	
HS-TGM	Boeing 747-4D7	Thai Airways International *Chao Phraya*	
HS-TGN	Boeing 747-4D7	Thai Airways International *Simongkhon*	
HS-TGO	Boeing 747-4D7	Thai Airways International *Bowonrangsi*	
HS-TGP	Boeing 747-4D7	Thai Airways International *Thepprasit*	
HS-TGR	Boeing 747-4D7	Thai Airways International *Siriwatthana*	
HS-TGT	Boeing 747-4D7	Thai Airways International *Watthanothai*	
HS-TGW	Boeing 747-4D7	Thai Airways International *Visuthakasatriya*	
HS-TGX	Boeing 747-4D7	Thai Airways International *Sirisobhakya*	
HS-TGY	Boeing 747-4D7	Thai Airways International *Dararasmi*	
HS-TGZ	Boeing 747-4D7	Thai Airways International *Phimara*	
HS-TNA	Airbus A.340-642	Thai Airways International *Watthana Nakhon*	
HS-TNB	Airbus A.340-642	Thai Airways International *Saraburi*	
HS-TNC	Airbus A.340-642	Thai Airways International *Chon Buri*	
HS-TND	Airbus A.340-642	Thai Airways International *Phetchaburi*	
HS-TNE	Airbus A.340-642	Thai Airways International *Nonthaburi*	
HS-TNF	Airbus A.340-642	Thai Airways International	

HZ (Saudi Arabia)

Reg.	Type	Owner or Operator	Notes
HZ-AIU	Boeing 747-268F	Saudi Arabian Airlines Cargo	
HZ-AKA	Boeing 777-268ER	Saudi Arabian Airlines	
HZ-AKB	Boeing 777-268ER	Saudi Arabian Airlines	
HZ-AKC	Boeing 777-268ER	Saudi Arabian Airlines	
HZ-AKD	Boeing 777-268ER	Saudi Arabian Airlines	
HZ-AKE	Boeing 777-268ER	Saudi Arabian Airlines	
HZ-AKF	Boeing 777-268ER	Saudi Arabian Airlines	
HZ-AKG	Boeing 777-268ER	Saudi Arabian Airlines	
HZ-AKH	Boeing 777-268ER	Saudi Arabian Airlines	
HZ-AKI	Boeing 777-268ER	Saudi Arabian Airlines	
HZ-AKJ	Boeing 777-268ER	Saudi Arabian Airlines	
HZ-AKK	Boeing 777-268ER	Saudi Arabian Airlines	
HZ-AKL	Boeing 777-268ER	Saudi Arabian Airlines	
HZ-AKM	Boeing 777-268ER	Saudi Arabian Airlines	
HZ-AKN	Boeing 777-268ER	Saudi Arabian Airlines	
HZ-AKO	Boeing 777-268ER	Saudi Arabian Airlines	
HZ-AKP	Boeing 777-268ER	Saudi Arabian Airlines	
HZ-AKQ	Boeing 777-268ER	Saudi Arabian Airlines	
HZ-AKR	Boeing 777-268ER	Saudi Arabian Airlines	
HZ-AKS	Boeing 777-268ER	Saudi Arabian Airlines	
HZ-AKT	Boeing 777-268ER	Saudi Arabian Airlines	
HZ-AKU	Boeing 777-268ER	Saudi Arabian Airlines	
HZ-AKV	Boeing 777-268ER	Saudi Arabian Airlines	
HZ-AKW	Boeing 777-268ER	Saudi Arabian Airlines	
HZ-ANA	McD Douglas MD-11F	Saudi Arabian Airlines Cargo	
HZ-ANB	McD Douglas MD-11F	Saudi Arabian Airlines Cargo	
HZ-ANC	McD Douglas MD-11F	Saudi Arabian Airlines Cargo	
HZ-AND	McD Douglas MD-11F	Saudi Arabian Airlines Cargo	

I (Italy)

Reg.	Type	Owner or Operator	Notes
I-AIGG	Boeing 767-304ER	Air Italy	
I-AIGH	Boeing 767-23BER	Air Italy	
I-AIGI	Boeing 767-23BER	Air Italy	
I-AIGJ	Boeing 767-304ER	Air Italy	
I-AIGL	Boeing 737-33A	Air Italy	
I-AIGM	Boeing 737-3Q8	Air Italy	
I-BIKA	Airbus A.320-214	Alitalia *Johann Sebastian Bach*	

Notes	Reg.	Type	Owner or Operator
	I-BIKC	Airbus A.320-214	Alitalia *Zefiro*
	I-BIKD	Airbus A.320-214	Alitalia *Maestrale*
	I-BIKE	Airbus A.320-214	Alitalia *Franz Liszt*
	I-BIKF	Airbus A.320-214	Alitalia *Grecale*
	I-BIKG	Airbus A.320-214	Alitalia *Scirocco*
	I-BIKI	Airbus A.320-214	Alitalia *Girolamo Frescobaldi*
	I-BIKO	Airbus A.320-214	Alitalia *George Bizet*
	I-BIMA	Airbus A.319-112	Alitalia *Isola d'Elba*
	I-BIXA	Airbus A.321-112	Alitalia *Piazza del Duomo Milano*
	I-BIXE	Airbus A.321-112	Alitalia *Piazza di Spagna Roma*
	I-BIXK	Airbus A.321-112	Alitalia *Piazza Ducale Vigevano*
	I-BIXL	Airbus A.321-112	Alitalia *Piazza del Duomo Lecce*
	I-BIXM	Airbus A.321-112	Alitalia *Piazza di San Franceso Assisi*
	I-BIXN	Airbus A.321-112	Alitalia *Piazza del Duomo Catania*
	I-BIXP	Airbus A.321-112	Alitalia *Carlo Morelli*
	I-BIXQ	Airbus A.321-112	Alitalia *Domenico Colapietro*
	I-BIXR	Airbus A.321-112	Alitalia *Piazza dell Campidoglio-Roma*
	I-BIXS	Airbus A.321-112	Alitalia *Piazza San Martino-Lucca*
	I-BIXT	Airbus A.321-112	Alitalia *Piazza dei Miracoli Pisa*
	I-DACR	McD Douglas MD-82	Alitalia *Carrara*
	I-DACS	McD Douglas MD-82	Alitalia *Maratea*
	I-DACT	McD Douglas MD-82	Alitalia *Valtellina*
	I-DACV	McD Douglas MD-82	Alitalia
	I-DACZ	McD Douglas MD-82	Alitalia *Castelfidardo*
	I-DAND	McD Douglas MD-82	Alitalia *Bolzano*
	I-DANF	McD Douglas MD-82	Alitalia *Vicenza*
	I-DANG	McD Douglas MD-82	Alitalia
	I-DANH	McD Douglas MD-82	Alitalia *Messina*
	I-DANQ	McD Douglas MD-82	Alitalia *Lecce*
	I-DANU	McD Douglas MD-82	Alitalia *Trapani*
	I-DANW	McD Douglas MD-82	Alitalia *Siena*
	I-DATC	McD Douglas MD-82	Alitalia *Foggia*
	I-DATE	McD Douglas MD-82	Alitalia *Grosseto*
	I-DATG	McD Douglas MD-82	Alitalia *Arezzo*
	I-DATI	McD Douglas MD-82	Alitalia *Siracusa*
	I-DATQ	McD Douglas MD-82	Alitalia *Modena*
	I-DAVT	McD Douglas MD-82	Alitalia *Como*
	I-DEIG	Boeing 767-33AER	Alitalia *Francesco Agello*
	I-DISA	Boeing 777-243ER	Alitalia *Taromina*
	I-DISB	Boeing 777-243ER	Alitalia *Portor Rotondo*
	I-DISD	Boeing 777-243ER	Alitalia *Cortina d'Ampezzo*
	I-DISE	Boeing 777-243ER	Alitalia *Portofino*
	I-DISO	Boeing 777-243ER	Alitalia *Positano*
	I-DISU	Boeing 777-243ER	Alitalia *Madonna di Campiglio*
	I-EEZE	Airbus A.320-214	Meridiana Fly
	I-EEZF	Airbus A.320-214	Meridiana Fly
	I-EEZG	Airbus A.320-214	Meridiana Fly
	I-EEZH	Airbus A.320-214	Meridiana Fly
	I-EEZI	Airbus A.320-214	Meridiana Fly
	I-EEZJ	Airbus A.330-223	Meridiana Fly
	I-EEZK	Airbus A.320-214	Meridiana Fly
	I-EEZM	Airbus A.330-223	Meridiana Fly
	I-EEZP	Airbus A.320-233	Meridiana Fly
	I-EEZQ	Airbus A.319-112	Meridiana Fly
	I-NEOS	Boeing 737-86N	Neos
	I-NEOT	Boeing 737-86N	Neos
	I-NEOU	Boeing 737-86N	Neos
	I-NEOW	Boeing 737-86N	Neos
	I-NEOX	Boeing 737-86N	Neos
	I-NEOZ	Boeing 737-86N	Neos
	I-NDMJ	Boeing 767-306ER	Neos
	I-NDOF	Boeing 767-306ER	Neos
	I-SMEB	McD Douglas MD-82	Meridiana Fly
	I-SMEC	McD Douglas MD-83	Meridiana Fly
	I-SMEL	McD Douglas MD-82	Meridiana Fly
	I-SMEM	McD Douglas MD-82	Meridiana Fly
	I-SMEN	McD Douglas MD-83	Meridiana Fly
	I-SMEP	McD Douglas MD-82	Meridiana Fly
	I-SMER	McD Douglas MD-82	Meridiana Fly
	I-SMES	McD Douglas MD-82	Meridiana Fly
	I-SMET	McD Douglas MD-82	Meridiana Fly
	I-SMEV	McD Douglas MD-82	Meridiana Fly
	I-SMEZ	McD Douglas MD-83	Meridiana Fly
	I-WEBA	Airbus A.320-214	Volareweb.com

Reg.	Type	Owner or Operator	Notes
I-WEBB	Airbus A.320-214	Volareweb.com	

JA (Japan)

Reg.	Type	Owner or Operator	Notes
JA01KZ	Boeing 747-481F	Nippon Cargo Airlines	
JA02KZ	Boeing 747-481F	Nippon Cargo Airlines	
JA03KZ	Boeing 747-4KZF	Nippon Cargo Airlines	
JA04KZ	Boeing 747-4KZF	Nippon Cargo Airlines	
JA05KZ	Boeing 747-4KZF	Nippon Cargo Airlines *NCA Apollo*	
JA06KZ	Boeing 747-4KZF	Nippon Cargo Airlines	
JA07KZ	Boeing 747-4KZF	Nippon Cargo Airlines *NCA Andromeda*	
JA08KZ	Boeing 747-4KZF	Nippon Cargo Airlines *NCA Aries*	
JA13KZ	Boeing 747-8KZF	Nippon Cargo Airlines	
JA704J	Boeing 777-246ER	Japan Airlines	
JA705J	Boeing 777-246ER	Japan Airlines	
JA706J	Boeing 777-246ER	Japan Airlines	
JA707J	Boeing 777-246ER	Japan Airlines	
JA708J	Boeing 777-246ER	Japan Airlines	
JA709J	Boeing 777-246ER	Japan Airlines	
JA710J	Boeing 777-246ER	Japan Airlines	
JA711J	Boeing 777-246ER	Japan Airlines	
JA731A	Boeing 777-381ER	All Nippon Airways	
JA731J	Boeing 777-346ER	Japan Airlines	
JA732A	Boeing 777-381ER	All Nippon Airways	
JA732J	Boeing 777-346ER	Japan Airlines	
JA733A	Boeing 777-381ER	All Nippon Airways	
JA733J	Boeing 777-346ER	Japan Airlines	
JA734A	Boeing 777-381ER	All Nippon Airways	
JA734J	Boeing 777-346ER	Japan Airlines	
JA735A	Boeing 777-381ER	All Nippon Airways	
JA735J	Boeing 777-346ER	Japan Airlines	
JA736A	Boeing 777-381ER	All Nippon Airways	
JA736J	Boeing 777-346ER	Japan Airlines	
JA737J	Boeing 777-346ER	Japan Airlines	
JA738J	Boeing 777-346ER	Japan Airlines	
JA739J	Boeing 777-346ER	Japan Airlines	
JA740J	Boeing 777-346ER	Japan Airlines	
JA741J	Boeing 777-346ER	Japan Airlines	
JA742J	Boeing 777-346ER	Japan Airlines	
JA743J	Boeing 777-346ER	Japan Airlines	
JA777A	Boeing 777-381ER	All Nippon Airways	
JA778A	Boeing 777-381ER	All Nippon Airways	
JA780A	Boeing 777-381ER	All Nippon Airways	
JA781A	Boeing 777-381ER	All Nippon Airways	
JA782A	Boeing 777-381ER	All Nippon Airways	
JA783A	Boeing 777-381ER	All Nippon Airways	
JA784A	Boeing 777-381ER	All Nippon Airways	
JA785A	Boeing 777-381ER	All Nippon Airways	
JA786A	Boeing 777-381ER	All Nippon Airways	
JA787A	Boeing 777-381ER	All Nippon Airways	
JA788A	Boeing 777-381ER	All Nippon Airways	
JA789A	Boeing 777-381ER	All Nippon Airways	

JY (Jordan)

Reg.	Type	Owner or Operator	Notes
JY-AGM	Airbus A.310-304	Royal Jordanian *Prince Hamzeh*	
JY-AGN	Airbus A.310-304	Royal Jordanian *Princess Haya*	
JY-AGP	Airbus A.310-304	Royal Jordanian	
JY-AGQ	Airbus A.310-304F	Royal Jordanian Cargo	
JY-AGR	Airbus A.310-304F	Royal Jordanian Cargo	
JY-AIA	Airbus A.340-211	Royal Jordanian *Hussein Bin Abdullah*	
JY-AIB	Airbus A.340-211	Royal Jordanian *Princess Iman Bint Abdullah*	
JY-AIC	Airbus A.340-212	Royal Jordanian	
JY-AID	Airbus A.340-212	Royal Jordanian	
JY-AIE	Airbus A.330-223	Royal Jordanian *Jordan River*	
JY-AIF	Airbus A.330-223`	Royal Jordanian *Prince Ali bin Al Hussein*	
JY-AYD	Airbus A.320-232	Royal Jordanian *Amman*	
JY-AYF	Airbus A.320-232	Royal Jordanian *Aqaba*	
JY-AYG	Airbus A.321-231	Royal Jordanian *As-Salt*	
JY-AYH	Airbus A.321-231	Royal Jordanian	
JY-AYJ	Airbus A.321-231	Royal Jordanian *Ramtha*	
JY-AYK	Airbus A.321-231	Royal Jordanian	

Notes	Reg.	Type	Owner or Operator
	JY-AYL	Airbus A.319-132	Royal Jordanian
	JY-AYM	Airbus A.319-132	Royal Jordanian
	JY-AYN	Airbus A.319-132	Royal Jordanian
	JY-AYP	Airbus A.319-132	Royal Jordabian *Ajloun*

LN (Norway)

Notes	Reg.	Type	Owner or Operator
	LN-BRE	Boeing 737-405	SAS *Haakon V Magnusson*
	LN-BRH	Boeing 737-505	SAS *Haakon den Gode*
	LN-BRI	Boeing 737-405	SAS *Harald Haarfagre*
	LN-BRJ	Boeing 737-505	SAS
	LN-BRO	Boeing 737-505	SAS *Magnus Haraldsson*
	LN-BRQ	Boeing 737-405	SAS *Harald Graafell*
	LN-BRV	Boeing 737-505	SAS *Haakon Sverresson*
	LN-BRX	Boeing 737-505	SAS *Sigurd Munn*
	LN-BUC	Boeing 737-505	SAS *Magnus Erlingsson*
	LN-BUD	Boeing 737-505	SAS *Inge Krokrygg*
	LN-BUE	Boeing 737-505	SAS
	LN-BUF	Boeing 737-405	SAS *Magnus den Gode*
	LN-BUG	Boeing 737-505	SAS *Oystein Haraldsson*
	LN-DYA	Boeing 737-8JP	Norwegian Air Shuttle
	LN-DYB	Boeing 737-8JP	Norwegian Air Shuttle
	LN-DYC	Boeing 737-8JP	Norwegian Air Shuttle
	LN-DYD	Boeing 737-8JP	Norwegian Air Shuttle
	LN-DYE	Boeing 737-8JP	Norwegian Air Shuttle
	LN-DYF	Boeing 737-8JP	Norwegian Air Shuttle
	LN-DYG	Boeing 737-8JP	Norwegian Air Shuttle
	LN-DYH	Boeing 737-8JP	Norwegian Air Shuttle
	LN-DYI	Boeing 737-8JP	Norwegian Air Shuttle
	LN-DYJ	Boeing 737-8JP	Norwegian Air Shuttle
	LN-DYK	Boeing 737-8JP	Norwegian Air Shuttle
	LN-DYL	Boeing 737-8JP	Norwegian Air Shuttle
	LN-DYM	Boeing 737-8JP	Norwegian Air Shuttle
	LN-DYN	Boeing 737-8JP	Norwegian Air Shuttle
	LN-DYO	Boeing 737-8JP	Norwegian Air Shuttle
	LN-DYP	Boeing 737-8JP	Norwegian Air Shuttle
	LN-DYQ	Boeing 737-8JP	Norwegian Air Shuttle
	LN-DYS	Boeing 737-8JP	Norwegian Air Shuttle
	LN-KHA	Boeing 737-31S	Norwegian Air Shuttle
	LN-KHB	Boeing 737-31S	Norwegian Air Shuttle
	LN-KHC	Boeing 737-31S	Norwegian Air Shuttle
	LN-KKB	Boeing 737-33A	Norwegian Air Shuttle
	LN-KKC	Boeing 737-3Y5	Norwegian Air Shuttle
	LN-KKD	Boeing 737-33V	Norwegian Air Shuttle
	LN-KKE	Boeing 737-33A	Norwegian Air Shuttle
	LN-KKG	Boeing 737-3K2	Norwegian Air Shuttle *Gidsken Jakobse*
	LN-KKH	Boeing 737-3K2	Norwegian Air Shuttle *Otto Sverdrup*
	LN-KKI	Boeing 737-3K2	Norwegian Air Shuttle *Helge Ingstad*
	LN-KKJ	Boeing 737-36N	Norwegian Air Shuttle *Sonja Henie*
	LN-KKL	Boeing 737-36N	Norwegian Air Shuttle *Roald Amundsen*
	LN-KKM	Boeing 737-3Y0	Norwegian Air Shuttle *Thor Heyerdahl*
	LN-KKN	Boeing 737-3Y0	Norwegian Air Shuttle *Sigrid Undset*
	LN-KKO	Boeing 737-3Y0	Norwegian Air Shuttle *Henrik Ibsen*
	LN-KKP	Boeing 737-3MQ	Norwegian Air Shuttle *Kirsten Flagstad*
	LN-KKQ	Boeing 737-36Q	Norwegian Air Shuttle *Alf Proysen*
	LN-KKR	Boeing 737-3Y0	Norwegian Air Shuttle
	LN-KKS	Boeing 737-33A	Norwegian Air Shuttle *Eduard Munch*
	LN-KKT	Boeing 737-3L9	Norwegian Air Shuttle
	LN-KKU	Boeing 737-3L9	Norwegian Air Shuttle
	LN-KKV	Boeing 737-3Y5	Norwegian Air Shuttle *Niels Henrik Abel*
	LN-KKW	Boeing 737-3K9	Norwegian Air Shuttle
	LN-KKX	Boeing 737-33S	Norwegian Air Shuttle
	LN-KKY	Boeing 737-33S	Norwegian Air Shuttle
	LN-KKZ	Boeing 737-33A	Norwegian Air Shuttle *Silver*
	LN-NOB	Boeing 737-8FZ	Norwegian Air Shuttle *Edward Greig*
	LN-NOC	Boeing 737-81Q	Norwegian Air Shuttle
	LN-NOD	Boeing 737-8Q8	Norwegian Air Shuttle
	LN-NOE	Boeing 737-8Q8	Norwegian Air Shuttle
	LN-NOF	Boeing 737-86N	Norwegian Air Shuttle
	LN-NOG	Boeing 737-86N	Norwegian Air Shuttle
	LN-NOH	Boeing 737-86N	Norwegian Air Shuttle
	LN-NOI	Boeing 737-86N	Norwegian Air Shuttle
	LN-NOJ	Boeing 737-86N	Norwegian Air Shuttle

Reg.	Type	Owner or Operator	Notes
LN-NOL	Boeing 737-8Q8	Norwegian Air Shuttle	
LN-NOM	Boeing 737-86N	Norwegian Air Shuttle	
LN-NON	Boeing 737-86N	Norwegian Air Shuttle	
LN-NOO	Boeing 737-86Q	Norwegian Air Shuttle	
LN-NOP	Boeing 737-86N	Norwegian Air Shuttle	
LN-NOQ	Boeing 737-86N	Norwegian Air Shuttle	
LN-NOR	Boeing 737-86N	Norwegian Air Shuttle	
LN-NOS	Boeing 737-8BK	Norwegian Air Shuttle	
LN-NOT	Boeing 737-8JP	Norwegian Air Shuttle	
LN-NOU	Boeing 737-8FZ	Norwegian Air Shuttle	
LN-NOV	Boeing 737-8FZ	Norwegian Air Shuttle	
LN-NOW	Boeing 737-8JP	Norwegian Air Shuttle	
LN-NOX	Boeing 737-8JP	Norwegian Air Shuttle	
LN-RCN	Boeing 737-883	SAS *Hedrun Viking*	
LN-RCT	Boeing 737-683	SAS *Fridlev Viking*	
LN-RCU	Boeing 737-683	SAS *Sigfrid Viking*	
LN-RCW	Boeing 737-683	SAS *Yngvar Viking*	
LN-RCX	Boeing 737-883	SAS *Hottur Viking*	
LN-RCY	Boeing 737-883	SAS *Eylime Viking*	
LN-RCZ	Boeing 737-883	SAS *Glitne Viking*	
LN-RKF	Airbus A.340-313X	SAS *Godfred Viking*	
LN-RKG	Airbus A.340-313X	SAS *Gudrod Viking*	
LN-RKH	Airbus A.330-343X	SAS *Emund Viking*	
LN-RKI	Airbus A.321-231	SAS *Gunnhild Viking*	
LN-RKK	Airbus A.321-231	SAS *Viger Viking*	
LN-RLE	McD Douglas MD-82	SAS *Ketiil Viking*	
LN-RLF	McD Douglas MD-82	SAS *Finn Viking*	
LN-RMG	McD Douglas MD-87	SAS/Spanair	
LN-RML	McD Douglas MD-82	SAS *Aud Viking*	
LN-RMM	McD Douglas MD-82	SAS *Blenda Viking*	
LN-RMO	McD Douglas MD-82	SAS *Bergljot Viking*	
LN-RMR	McD Douglas MD-82	SAS *Olav Viking*	
LN-RMS	McD Douglas MD-82	SAS *Nial Viking*	
LN-RMT	McD Douglas MD-82	SAS *Jarl Viking*	
LN-RNL	Canadair CRJ900ER	SAS	
LN-RNN	Boeing 737-783	SAS *Borgny Viking*	
LN-RNO	Boeing 737-783	SAS *Gjuke Viking*	
LN-RNU	Boeing 737-783	SAS	
LN-RNW	Boeing 737-783	SAS	
LN-ROP	McD Douglas MD-82	SAS *Bjoern Viking*	
LN-ROT	McD Douglas MD-82	SAS *Ingjaid Viking*	
LN-ROX	McD Douglas MD-82	SAS *Ulvrik Viking*	
LN-RPA	Boeing 737-683	SAS *Arnljot Viking*	
LN-RPB	Boeing 737-683	SAS *Bure Viking*	
LN-RPE	Boeing 737-683	SAS *Edla Viking*	
LN-RPF	Boeing 737-683	SAS *Frede Viking*	
LN-RPG	Boeing 737-683	SAS *Geirmund Viking*	
LN-RPH	Boeing 737-683	SAS *Hamder Viking*	
LN-RPJ	Boeing 737-783	SAS *Grimhild Viking*	
LN-RPK	Boeing 737-783	SAS *Heimer Viking*	
LN-RPL	Boeing 737-883	SAS *Svanevit Viking*	
LN-RPM	Boeing 737-883	SAS *Frigg Viking*	
LN-RPN	Boeing 737-883	SAS *Bergfora Viking*	
LN-RPS	Boeing 737-683	SAS *Gautrek Viking*	
LN-RPT	Boeing 737-683	SAS *Ellida Viking*	
LN-RPU	Boeing 737-683	SAS *Ragna Viking*	
LN-RPW	Boeing 737-683	SAS *Alvid Viking*	
LN-RPX	Boeing 737-683	SAS *Nanna Viking*	
LN-RPY	Boeing 737-683	SAS *Olof Viking*	
LN-RPZ	Boeing 737-683	SAS *Bera Viking*	
LN-RRA	Boeing 737-783	SAS *Steinar Viking*	
LN-RRB	Boeing 737-783	SAS *Cecilia Viking*	
LN-RRC	Boeing 737-683	SAS	
LN-RRD	Boeing 737-683	SAS	
LN-RRE	Boeing 737-883	SAS *Knut Viking*	
LN-RRF	Boeing 737-883	SAS	
LN-RRG	Boeing 737-883	SAS	
LN-RRH	Boeing 737-883	SAS *Freja Viking*	
LN-RRJ	Boeing 737-883	SAS *Frida Viking*	
LN-RRK	Boeing 737-883	SAS *Gerud Viking*	
LN-RRL	Boeing 737-883	SAS *Jarlabanke Viking*	
LN-RRM	Boeing 737-783	SAS *Erland Viking*	
LN-RRN	Boeing 737-783	SAS *Solveig Viking*	
LN-RRO	Boeing 737-683	SAS *Bernt Viking*	

Notes	Reg.	Type	Owner or Operator
	LN-RRP	Boeing 737-683	SAS *Vilborg Viking*
	LN-RRR	Boeing 737-683	SAS *Torbjorn Viking*
	LN-RRS	Boeing 737-883	SAS *Ymir Viking*
	LN-RRT	Boeing 737-883	SAS *Lodyn Viking*
	LN-RRU	Boeing 737-883	SAS *Vingolf Viking*
	LN-RRW	Boeing 737-883	SAS *Saga Viking*
	LN-RRX	Boeing 737-683	SAS *Ragnfast Viking*
	LN-RRY	Boeing 737-683	SAS *Signe Viking*
	LN-RRZ	Boeing 737-683	SAS *Gisla Viking*
	LN-TUA	Boeing 737-705	SAS *Ingeborg Eriksdatter*
	LN-TUD	Boeing 737-705	SAS *Margrete Skulesdatter*
	LN-TUF	Boeing 737-705	SAS*Tyra Haraldsdatter*
	LN-TUH	Boeing 737-705	SAS *Margrete Ingesdatter*
	LN-TUI	Boeing 737-705	SAS *Kristin Knudsdatter*
	LN-TUJ	Boeing 737-705	SAS *Eirik Blodoks*
	LN-TUK	Boeing 737-705	SAS *Inge Bardsson*
	LN-TUL	Boeing 737-705	SAS *Haakon IV Haakonson*
	LN-TUM	Boeing 737-705	SAS *Oystein Magnusson*
	LN-WDE	DHC.8-402 Dash Eight	Wideroe's Flyveselskap
	LN-WDF	DHC.8-402 Dash Eight	Wideroe's Flyveselskap
	LN-WDG	DHC.8-402 Dash Eight	Wideroe's Flyveselskap
	LN-WDH	DHC.8-402 Dash Eight	Wideroe's Flyveselskap
	LN-WDI	DHC.8-402 Dash Eight	Wideroe's Flyveselskap
	LN-WDJ	DHC.8-402 Dash Eight	Wideroe's Flyveselskap
	LN-WDK	DHC.8-402 Dash Eight	Wideroe's Flyveselskap
	LN-WFC	DHC.8-311 Dash Eight	Wideroe's Flyveselskap
	LN-WFD	DHC.8-311 Dash Eight	Wideroe's Flyveselskap
	LN-WFH	DHC.8-311 Dash Eight	Wideroe's Flyveselskap
	LN-WFO	DHC.8Q-311 Dash Eight	Wideroe's Flyveselskap
	LN-WFP	DHC.8Q-311 Dash Eight	Wideroe's Flyveselskap
	LN-WFS	DHC.8Q-311 Dash Eight	Wideroe's Flyveselskap
	LN-WFT	DHC.8Q-311 Dash Eight	Wideroe's Flyveselskap

LX (Luxembourg)

Notes	Reg.	Type	Owner or Operator
	LX-ACV	Boeing 747-4B5BCF	Cargolux
	LX-KCV	Boeing 747-4R7F (SCD)	Cargolux *City of Dudelange*
	LX-LCV	Boeing 747-4R7F (SCD)	Cargolux *City of Grevenmacher*
	LX-LGA	DHC.8Q-402 Dash Eight	Luxair
	LX-LGC	DHC.8Q-402 Dash Eight	Luxair
	LX-LGD	DHC.8Q-402 Dash Eight	Luxair
	LX-LGE	DHC.8Q-402 Dash Eight	Luxair
	LX-LGI	Embraer RJ145LU	Luxair
	LX-LGJ	Embraer RJ145LU	Luxair
	LX-LGK	Embraer RJ135LR	Luxair
	LX-LGL	Embraer RJ135LR	Luxair
	LX-LGQ	Boeing 737-7C9	Luxair *Chateau de Burg*
	LX-LGR	Boeing 737-7C9	Luxair *Chateau de Fischbach*
	LX-LGS	Boeing 737-7C9	Luxair *Chateau de Senningen*
	LX-LGT	Boeing 737-8K5	Luxair
	LX-LGW	Embraer RJ145LU	Luxair
	LX-LGX	Embraer RJ145LU	Luxair
	LX-LGY	Embraer RJ145LU	Luxair
	LX-LGZ	Embraer RJ145LU	Luxair
	LX-NCV	Boeing 747-4R7F (SCD)	Cargolux *City of Vianden*
	LX-OCV	Boeing 747-4R7F (SCD)	Cargolux *City of Differdange*
	LX-PCV	Boeing 747-4R7F (SCD)	Cargolux *City of Diekirch*
	LX-RCV	Boeing 747-4R7F (SCD)	Cargolux *City of Schengen*
	LX-SCV	Boeing 747-4R7F (SCD)	Cargolux *City of Niederanven*
	LX-STA	Airbus A.320-212	Strategic Airlines
	LX-TCV	Boeing 747-4R7F (SCD)	Cargolux *City of Sandweiler*
	LX-UCV	Boeing 747-4R7F (SCD)	Cargolux *City of Bertragne*
	LX-VCA	Boeing 747-8R7F	Cargolux
	LX-VCB	Boeing 747-8R7F	Cargolux
	LX-VCC	Boeing 747-8R7F	Cargolux
	LX-VCD	Boeing 747-8R7F	Cargolux
	LX-VCV	Boeing 747-4R7F (SCD)	Cargolux *City of Walferdange*
	LX-WAO	BAe ATP	West Air Europe
	LX-WAP	BAe ATP	West Air Europe
	LX-WAS	BAe ATP	West Air Europe
	LX-WAT	BAe ATP	West Air Europe
	LX-WAV	BAe ATP	West Air Europe
	LX-WAW	BAe ATP	West Air Europe

Reg.	Type	Owner or Operator	Notes
LX-WCV	Boeing 747-4R7F (SCD)	Cargolux *City of Petange*	
LX-YCV	Boeing 747-4R7F	Cargolux *City of Contern*	
LX-ZCV	Boeing 747-481BCF	Cargolux	

LY (Lithuania)

Reg.	Type	Owner or Operator	Notes
LY-FLC	Boeing 737-31S	Small Planet Airlines	
LY-FLE	Boeing 737-3L9	Small Planet Airlines	
LY-FLH	Boeing 737-382	Small Planet Airlines	
LY-NSC	SAAB 340	Loganair	
LY-SKA	Boeing 737-35B	Aurela	
LY-SKW	Boeing 737-382	Aurela	

LZ (Bulgaria)

Reg.	Type	Owner or Operator	Notes
LZ-BHB	Airbus A.320-212	BH Air	
LZ-BHC	Airbus A.320-212	BH Air	
LZ-BHD	Airbus A.320-212	BH Air	
LZ-BHE	Airbus A.320-211	BH Air	
LZ-BOU	Boeing 737-3L9	Bulgaria Air	
LZ-BOV	Boeing 737-330	Bulgaria Air	
LZ-BOW	Boeing 737-330	Bulgaria Air	
LZ-FBA	Airbus A.319-112	Bulgaria Air	
LZ-FBB	Airbus A.319-112	Bulgaria Air	
LZ-FBC	Airbus A.320-214	Bulgaria Air	
LZ-FBD	Airbus A.320-214	Bulgaria Air	
LZ-FBE	Airbus A.320-214	Bulgaria Air	
LZ-FBF	Airbus A.319-111	Bulgaria Air	
LZ-LDC	McD Douglas MD-82	Bulgarian Air Charter	
LZ-LDF	McD Douglas MD-82	Bulgarian Air Charter	
LZ-LDK	McD Douglas MD-82	Bulgarian Air Charter	
LZ-LDP	McD Douglas MD-82	Bulgarian Air Charter	
LZ-LDR	McD Douglas MD-82	Bulgarian Air Charter	
LZ-LDW	McD Douglas MD-82	Bulgarian Air Charter	
LZ-LDY	McD Douglas MD-82	Bulgarian Air Charter	
LZ-WZA	Airbus A.320-233	Wizz Air Bulgaria	
LZ-WZB	Airbus A.320-232	Wizz Air Bulgaria	
LZ-WZC	Airbus A.320-232	Wizz Air Bulgaria	

N (USA)

Reg.	Type	Owner or Operator	Notes
N108AX	Douglas DC-10-30	Omni Air International	
N152DL	Boeing 767-3P6ER	Delta Air Lines	
N153DL	Boeing 767-3P6ER	Delta Air Lines	
N154DL	Boeing 767-3P6ER	Delta Air Lines	
N155DL	Boeing 767-3P6ER	Delta Air Lines	
N156DL	Boeing 767-3P6ER	Delta Air Lines	
N169DZ	Boeing 767-332ER	Delta Air Lines	
N171DN	Boeing 767-332ER	Delta Air Lines	
N171DZ	Boeing 767-332ER	Delta Air Lines	
N172AJ	Boeing 757-223ET	American Airlines	
N172DZ	Boeing 767-332ER	Delta Air Lines	
N173AN	Boeing 757-223ET	American Airlines	
N173DZ	Boeing 767-332ER	Delta Air Lines	
N174AA	Boeing 757-223ET	American Airlines	
N174DN	Boeing 767-332ER	Delta Air Lines	
N174DZ	Boeing 767-332ER	Delta Air Lines	
N175AN	Boeing 757-223ET	American Airlines	
N175DN	Boeing 767-332ER	Delta Air Lines	
N175DZ	Boeing 767-332ER	Delta Air Lines	
N176AA	Boeing 757-223ET	American Airlines	
N176DN	Boeing 767-332ER	Delta Air Lines	
N176DZ	Boeing 767-332ER	Delta Air Lines	
N177AN	Boeing 757-223ET	American Airlines	
N177DN	Boeing 767-332ER	Delta Air Lines	
N177DZ	Boeing 767-332ER	Delta Air Lines	
N178AA	Boeing 757-223ET	American Airlines	
N178DN	Boeing 767-332ER	Delta Air Lines	
N178DZ	Boeing 767-332ER	Delta Air Lines	
N179AA	Boeing 757-223ET	American Airlines	
N179DN	Boeing 767-332ER	Delta Air Lines	

Notes	Reg.	Type	Owner or Operator
	N180DN	Boeing 767-332ER	Delta Air Lines
	N181AN	Boeing 757-223ET	American Airlines
	N181DN	Boeing 767-332ER	Delta Air Lines
	N182DN	Boeing 767-332ER	Delta Air Lines
	N183AN	Boeing 757-223ET	American Airlines
	N183DN	Boeing 767-332ER	Delta Air Lines
	N184AN	Boeing 757-223ET	American Airlines
	N184DN	Boeing 767-332ER	Delta Air Lines
	N185AN	Boeing 757-223ET	American Airlines
	N185DN	Boeing 767-332ER	Delta Air Lines
	N186AN	Boeing 757-223ET	American Airlines
	N186DN	Boeing 767-332ER	Delta Air Lines
	N187AN	Boeing 757-223ET	American Airlines
	N187DN	Boeing 767-332ER	Delta Air Lines
	N188AN	Boeing 757-223ET	American Airlines
	N188DN	Boeing 767-332ER	Delta Air Lines
	N189AN	Boeing 757-223ET	American Airlines
	N189DN	Boeing 767-332ER	Delta Air Lines
	N190AA	Boeing 757-223ET	American Airlines
	N190DN	Boeing 767-332ER	Delta Air Lines
	N191AN	Boeing 757-223ET	American Airlines
	N191DN	Boeing 767-332ER	Delta Air Lines
	N192AN	Boeing 757-223ET	American Airlines
	N192DN	Boeing 767-332ER	Delta Air Lines
	N193AN	Boeing 757-223ET	American Airlines
	N193DN	Boeing 767-332ER	Delta Air Lines
	N194AA	Boeing 757-223ET	American Airlines
	N194DN	Boeing 767-332ER	Delta Air Lines
	N195DN	Boeing 767-332ER	Delta Air Lines
	N196AA	Boeing 757-223ET	American Airlines
	N196DN	Boeing 767-332ER	Delta Air Lines
	N197AN	Boeing 757-223ET	American Airlines
	N197DN	Boeing 767-332ER	Delta Air Lines
	N198AA	Boeing 757-223ET	American Airlines
	N198DN	Boeing 767-332ER	Delta Air Lines
	N199AN	Boeing 757-223ET	American Airlines
	N199DN	Boeing 767-332ER	Delta Air Lines
	N200UU	Boeing 757-2B7	US Airways
	N201UU	Boeing 757-2B7	US Airways
	N202UW	Boeing 757-2B7	US Airways
	N203UW	Boeing 757-23N	US Airways
	N204UA	Boeing 777-222ER	United Airlines
	N204UW	Boeing 757-23N	US Airways
	N205UW	Boeing 757-23N	US Airways
	N206UA	Boeing 777-222ER	United Airlines
	N206UW	Boeing 757-2B7	US Airways
	N209UA	Boeing 777-222ER	United Airlines
	N216UA	Boeing 777-222ER	United Airlines
	N217UA	Boeing 777-222ER	United Airlines
	N218UA	Boeing 777-222ER	United Airlines
	N219CY	Boeing 767-383ER	ABX Air/DHL
	N219UA	Boeing 777-222ER	United Airlines
	N220UA	Boeing 777-222ER	United Airlines
	N221UA	Boeing 777-222ER	United Airlines
	N222UA	Boeing 777-222ER	United Airlines
	N223UA	Boeing 777-222ER	United Airlines
	N224UA	Boeing 777-222ER	United Airlines
	N225UA	Boeing 777-222ER	United Airlines
	N226UA	Boeing 777-222ER	United Airlines
	N227UA	Boeing 777-222ER	United Airlines
	N228UA	Boeing 777-222ER	United Airlines
	N229UA	Boeing 777-222ER	United Airlines
	N245AY	Boeing 767-201ER	US Airways
	N246AY	Boeing 767-201ER	US Airways
	N248AY	Boeing 767-201ER	US Airways
	N249AU	Boeing 767-201ER	US Airways
	N250AY	Boeing 767-201ER	US Airways
	N250UP	McD Douglas MD-11F	United Parcel Service
	N251AY	Boeing 767-2B7ER	US Airways
	N251UP	McD Douglas MD-11F	United Parcel Service
	N252AU	Boeing 767-2B7ER	US Airways
	N252UP	McD Douglas MD-11F	United Parcel Service
	N253AY	Boeing 767-2B7ER	US Airways
	N253UP	McD Douglas MD-11F	United Parcel Service

Reg.	Type	Owner or Operator	Notes
N254UP	McD Douglas MD-11F	United Parcel Service	
N255AY	Boeing 767-2B7ER	US Airways	
N255UP	McD Douglas MD-11F	United Parcel Service	
N256AY	Boeing 767-2B7ER	US Airways	
N256UP	McD Douglas MD-11F	United Parcel Service	
N257UP	McD Douglas MD-11F	United Parcel Service	
N258UP	McD Douglas MD-11F	United Parcel Service	
N259UP	McD Douglas MD-11F	United Parcel Service	
N260UP	McD Douglas MD-11F	United Parcel Service	
N269WA	McD Douglas MD-11	World Airways	
N270AX	Douglas DC-10-30	Omni Air International	
N270AY	Airbus A.330-323X	US Airways	
N270UP	McD Douglas MD-11F	United Parcel Service	
N270WA	McD Douglas MD-11AH	World Airways	
N271AY	Airbus A.330-323X	US Airways	
N271UP	McD Douglas MD-11F	United Parcel Service	
N271WA	McD Douglas MD-11 (271)	World Airways	
N272AY	Airbus A.330-323X	US Airways	
N272UP	McD Douglas MD-11F	United Parcel Service	
N272WA	McD Douglas MD-11 (272)	World Airways	
N273AY	Airbus A.330-323X	US Airways	
N273UP	McD Douglas MD-11F	United Parcel Service	
N273WA	McD Douglas MD-11 (273)	World Airways	
N274AY	Airbus A.330-323X	US Airways	
N274UP	McD Douglas MD-11F	United Parcel Service	
N274WA	McD Douglas MD-11F (274)	World Airways	
N275AY	Airbus A.330-323X	US Airways	
N275UP	McD Douglas MD-11F	United Parcel Service	
N275WA	McD Douglas MD-11CF (275)	World Airways	
N276AY	Airbus A.330-323X	US Airways	
N276UP	McD Douglas MD-11F	United Parcel Service	
N276WA	McD Douglas MD-11F	World Airways	
N277AY	Airbus A.330-323X	US Airways	
N277UP	McD Douglas MD-11F	United Parcel Service	
N277WA	McD Douglas MD-11 (277)	World Airways	
N278AY	Airbus A.330-323X	US Airways	
N278UP	McD Douglas MD-11F	United Parcel Service	
N278WA	McD Douglas MD-11F (278)	World Airways	
N279UP	McD Douglas MD-11F	United Parcel Service	
N279AY	Airbus A.330-243	US Airways	
N279WA	McD Douglas MD-11 (279)	World Airways/Etihad Airways	
N280AY	Airbus A.330-243	US Airways	
N280UP	McD Douglas MD-11F	United Parcel Service	
N281AY	Airbus A,330-243	US Airways	
N281UP	McD Douglas MD-11F	United Parcel Service	
N282AY	Airbus A.330-243	US Airways	
N282UP	McD Douglas MD-11F	United Parcel Service	
N283AY	Airbus A.330-243	US Airways	
N283UP	McD Douglas MD-11F	United Parcel Service	
N284AY	Airbus A.330-243	US Airways	
N284UP	McD Douglas MD-11F	United Parcel Service	
N285AY	Airbus A.330-243	US Airways	
N285UP	McD Douglas MD-11F	United Parcel Service	
N286AY	Airbus A.330-243	US Airways	
N286UP	McD Douglas MD-11F	United Parcel Service	
N287AY	Airbus A.330-243	US Airways	
N287UP	McD Douglas MD-11F	United Parcel Service	
N288AY	Airbus A.330-243	US Airways	
N288UP	McD Douglas MD-11F	United Parcel Service	
N289AY	Airbus A.330-243	US Airways	
N289UP	McD Douglas MD-11F	United Parcel Service	
N290UP	McD Douglas MD-11F	United Parcel Service	
N291UP	McD Douglas MD-11F	United Parcel Service	
N292UP	McD Douglas MD-11F	United Parcel Service	
N293UP	McD Douglas MD-11F	United Parcel Service	
N294UP	McD Douglas MD-11F	United Parcel Service	
N295UP	McD Douglas MD-11F	United Parcel Service	
N296UP	McD Douglas MD-11F	United Parcel Service	
N301UP	Boeing 767-34AFER	United Parcel Service	
N302UP	Boeing 767-34AFER	United Parcel Service	
N303UP	Boeing 767-34AFER	United Parcel Service	
N304UP	Boeing 767-34AFER	United Parcel Service	
N305UP	Boeing 767-34AFER	United Parcel Service	
N306UP	Boeing 767-34AFER	United Parcel Service	

Notes	Reg.	Type	Owner or Operator
	N307UP	Boeing 767-34AFER	United Parcel Service
	N308UP	Boeing 767-34AFER	United Parcel Service
	N309UP	Boeing 767-34AFER	United Parcel Service
	N310UP	Boeing 767-34AFER	United Parcel Service
	N311UP	Boeing 767-34AFER	United Parcel Service
	N312UP	Boeing 767-34AFER	United Parcel Service
	N313UP	Boeing 767-34AFER	United Parcel Service
	N314UP	Boeing 767-34AFER	United Parcel Service
	N315UP	Boeing 767-34AFER	United Parcel Service
	N316UP	Boeing 767-34AFER	United Parcel Service
	N317UP	Boeing 767-34AFER	United Parcel Service
	N318UP	Boeing 767-34AFER	United Parcel Service
	N319UP	Boeing 767-34AFER	United Parcel Service
	N320UP	Boeing 767-34AFER	United Parcel Service
	N322UP	Boeing 767-34AFER	United Parcel Service
	N323UP	Boeing 767-34AFER	United Parcel Service
	N324UP	Boeing 767-34AFER	United Parcel Service
	N325UP	Boeing 767-34AFER	United Parcel Service
	N326UP	Boeing 767-34AFER	United Parcel Service
	N327UP	Boeing 767-34AFER	United Parcel Service
	N328UP	Boeing 767-34AFER	United Parcel Service
	N329UP	Boeing 767-34AER	United Parcel Service
	N330UP	Boeing 767-34AER	United Parcel Service
	N331UP	Boeing 767-34AER	United Parcel Service
	N332UP	Boeing 767-34AER	United Parcel Service
	N334UP	Boeing 767-34AER	United Parcel Service
	N335UP	Boeing 767-34AF	United Parcel Service
	N336UP	Boeing 767-34AF	United Parcel Service
	N337UP	Boeing 767-34AF	United Parcel Service
	N338UP	Boeing 767-34AF	United Parcel Service
	N339UP	Boeing 767-34AF	United Parcel Service
	N340UP	Boeing 767-34AF	United Parcel Service
	N341UP	Boeing 767-34AF	United Parcel Service
	N342AN	Boeing 767-223ER	American Airlines
	N342UP	Boeing 767-34AF	United Parcel Service
	N343AN	Boeing 767-223ER	American Airlines
	N344AN	Boeing 767-223ER	American Airlines
	N344UP	Boeing 767-34AF	United Parcel Service
	N345AN	Boeing 767-223ER	American Airlines
	N345UP	Boeing 767-34AF	United Parcel Service
	N346AN	Boeing 767-223ER	American Airlines
	N347AN	Boeing 767-223ER	American Airlines
	N348AN	Boeing 767-223ER	American Airlines
	N349AN	Boeing 767-223ER	American Airlines
	N350AN	Boeing 767-223ER	American Airlines
	N351AA	Boeing 767-323ER	American Airlines
	N352AA	Boeing 767-323ER	American Airlines
	N353AA	Boeing 767-323ER	American Airlines
	N354AA	Boeing 767-323ER	American Airlines
	N355AA	Boeing 767-323ER	American Airlines
	N357AA	Boeing 767-323ER	American Airlines
	N358AA	Boeing 767-323ER	American Airlines
	N359AA	Boeing 767-323ER	American Airlines
	N360AA	Boeing 767-323ER	American Airlines
	N361AA	Boeing 767-323ER	American Airlines
	N362AA	Boeing 767-323ER	American Airlines
	N363AA	Boeing 767-323ER	American Airlines
	N366AA	Boeing 767-323ER	American Airlines
	N368AA	Boeing 767-323ER	American Airlines
	N369AA	Boeing 767-323ER	American Airlines
	N369AX	Boeing 757-28A	Omni Air International
	N370AA	Boeing 767-323ER	American Airlines
	N371AA	Boeing 767-323ER	American Airlines
	N372AA	Boeing 767-323ER	American Airlines
	N373AA	Boeing 767-323ER	American Airlines
	N374AA	Boeing 767-323ER	American Airlines
	N376AN	Boeing 767-323ER	American Airlines
	N377AN	Boeing 767-323ER	American Airlines
	N378AN	Boeing 767-323ER	American Airlines
	N379AA	Boeing 767-323ER	American Airlines
	N380AN	Boeing 767-323ER	American Airlines
	N380WA	McD Douglas MD-11F	World Airways
	N381AN	Boeing 767-323ER	American Airlines
	N381WA	McD Douglas MD-11F (381)	World Airways

Reg.	Type	Owner or Operator	Notes
N382AN	Boeing 767-323ER	American Airlines	
N382WA	McD Douglas MD-11F	World Airways	
N383AN	Boeing 767-323ER	American Airlines	
N383WA	McD Douglas MD-11F	World Airways	
N384AA	Boeing 767-323ER	American Airlines	
N384WA	McD Douglas MD-11F	World Airways	
N385AM	Boeing 767-323ER	American Airlines	
N386AA	Boeing 767-323ER	American Airlines	
N387AM	Boeing 767-323ER	American Airlines	
N388AA	Boeing 767-323ER	American Airlines	
N389AA	Boeing 767-323ER	American Airlines	
N390AA	Boeing 767-323ER	American Airlines	
N391AA	Boeing 767-323ER	American Airlines	
N392AN	Boeing 767-323ER	American Airlines	
N393AN	Boeing 767-323ER	American Airlines	
N394AN	Boeing 767-323ER	American Airlines	
N394DL	Boeing 767-324ER	Delta Air Lines	
N395AN	Boeing 767-323ER	American Airlines	
N396AN	Boeing 767-323ER	American Airlines	
N397AN	Boeing 767-323ER	American Airlines	
N398AN	Boeing 767-323ER	American Airlines	
N399AN	Boeing 767-323ER	American Airlines	
N408MC	Boeing 747-47UF	Atlas Air/Emirates SkyCargo	
N412MC	Boeing 747-47UF	Atlas Air	
N415MC	Boeing 747-47UF	Atlas Air/Emirates SkyCargo	
N416MC	Boeing 747-47UF	Atlas Air	
N418MC	Boeing 747-47UF	Atlas Air/TNT Airways	
N419MC	Boeing 747-48EF	Atlas Air	
N429MC	Boeing 747-481	Atlas Air	
N470EV	Boeing 747-273C	Evergreen International Airlines	
N471EV	Boeing 747-273C	Evergreen International Airlines	
N482EV	Boeing 747-212B (SCD)	Evergreen International Airlines	
N485EV	Boeing 747-212B (SCD)	Evergreen International Airlines	
N486EV	Boeing 747-212B (SCD)	Evergreen International Airlines	
N487EV	Boeing 747-230B (SF)	Evergreen International Airlines	
N488EV	Boeing 747-230B (SF)	Evergreen International Airlines	
N489EV	Boeing 747-230B (SF)	Evergreen International Airlines	
N490EV	Boeing 747-230F (SCD)	Evergreen International Airlines	
N491EV	Boeing 747-412F	Evergreen International Airlines	
N493MC	Boeing 747-47UF	Atlas Air/Emirates SkyCargo	
N496MC	Boeing 747-47UF	Atlas Air	
N497MC	Boeing 747-47UF	Atlas Air/Emirates SkyCargo	
N498MC	Boeing 747-47UF	Atlas Air	
N499MC	Boeing 747-47UF	Atlas Air	
N517MC	Boeing 747-243F (SCD)	Atlas Air	
N521FE	McD Douglas MD-11F	Federal Express	
N522AX	Douglas DC-10-30	Omni Air International	
N522FE	McD Douglas MD-11F	Federal Express	
N522MC	Boeing 747-2D7B	Atlas Air	
N523FE	McD Douglas MD-11F	Federal Express	
N523MC	Boeing 747-2D7B (SF)	Atlas Air	
N524FE	McD Douglas MD-11F	Federal Express	
N524MC	Boeing 747-2D7BF	Atlas Air	
N525FE	McD Douglas MD-11F	Federal Express	
N527FE	McD Douglas MD-11F	Federal Express	
N528FE	McD Douglas MD-11F	Federal Express	
N529FE	McD Douglas MD-11F	Federal Express	
N531AX	Douglas DC-10-30	Omni Air International	
N540MC	Boeing 747-243B (SCD)	Atlas Air	
N572FE	McD Douglas MD-11F	Federal Express	
N573FE	McD Douglas MD-11F	Federal Express	
N574FE	McD Douglas MD-11F	Federal Express	
N575FE	McD Douglas MD-11F	Federal Express	
N576FE	McD Douglas MD-11F	Federal Express	
N577FE	McD Douglas MD-11F	Federal Express	
N578FE	McD Douglas MD-11F	Federal Express *Stephen*	
N579FE	McD Douglas MD-11F	Federal Express *Nash*	
N580FE	McD Douglas MD-11F	Federal Express *Ashton*	
N582FE	McD Douglas MD-11F	Federal Express *Jamie*	
N583FE	McD Douglas MD-11F	Federal Express *Nancy*	
N584FE	McD Douglas MD-11F	Federal Express *Jeffrey Wellington*	
N585FE	McD Douglas MD-11F	Federal Express *Katherine*	
N586FE	McD Douglas MD-11F	Federal Express *Dylan*	
N587FE	McD Douglas MD-11F	Federal Express *Jeanna*	

Notes	Reg.	Type	Owner or Operator
	N588FE	McD Douglas MD-11F	Federal Express *Kendra*
	N589FE	McD Douglas MD-11F	Federal Express *Shaun*
	N590FE	McD Douglas MD-11F	Federal Express
	N591FE	McD Douglas MD-11F	Federal Express *Giovanni*
	N592FE	McD Douglas MD-11F	Federal Express *Joshua*
	N593FE	McD Douglas MD-11F	Federal Express *Harrison*
	N594FE	McD Douglas MD-11F	Federal Express
	N595FE	McD Douglas MD-11F	Federal Express *Avery*
	N596FE	McD Douglas MD-11F	Federal Express
	N597FE	McD Douglas MD-11F	Federal Express
	N598FE	McD Douglas MD-11F	Federal Express
	N599FE	McD Douglas MD-11F	Federal Express *Mariana*
	N601FE	McD Douglas MD-11F	Federal Express *Jim Riedmeyer*
	N602FE	McD Douglas MD-11F	Federal Express *Malcolm Baldridge 1990*
	N603AX	Douglas DC-10-30	Omni Air International
	N603FE	McD Douglas MD-11F	Federal Express *Elizabeth*
	N604FE	McD Douglas MD-11F	Federal Express *Hollis*
	N605FE	McD Douglas MD-11F	Federal Express *April Star*
	N606FE	McD Douglas MD-11F	Federal Express *Charles & Theresa*
	N607FE	McD Douglas MD-11F	Federal Express *Christina*
	N608FE	McD Douglas MD-11F	Federal Express *Karen*
	N609FE	McD Douglas MD-11F	Federal Express *Scott*
	N610FE	McD Douglas MD-11F	Federal Express *Marisa*
	N612AX	Douglas DC-10-30	Omni Air International
	N612FE	McD Douglas MD-11F	Federal Express *Alyssa*
	N613FE	McD Douglas MD-11F	Federal Express *Krista*
	N614FE	McD Douglas MD-11F	Federal Express *Christy Allison*
	N615FE	McD Douglas MD-11F	Federal Express *Max*
	N616FE	McD Douglas MD-11F	Federal Express *Shanita*
	N617FE	McD Douglas MD-11F	Federal Express *Travis*
	N618FE	McD Douglas MD-11F	Federal Express *Justin*
	N619FE	McD Douglas MD-11F	Federal Express *Lyndon*
	N620FE	McD Douglas MD-11F	Federal Express
	N621AX	Douglas DC-10-30	Omni Air International
	N621FE	McD Douglas MD-11F	Federal Express *Connor*
	N623FE	McD Douglas MD-11F	Federal Express *Meghan*
	N624FE	McD Douglas MD-11F	Federal Express
	N625FE	McD Douglas MD-11F	Federal Express
	N628FE	McD Douglas MD-11F	Federal Express
	N631FE	McD Douglas MD-11F	Federal Express
	N641UA	Boeing 767-322ER	United Airlines
	N642UA	Boeing 767-322ER	United Airlines
	N643UA	Boeing 767-322ER	United Airlines
	N644UA	Boeing 767-322ER	United Airlines
	N646UA	Boeing 767-322ER	United Airlines
	N647UA	Boeing 767-322ER	United Airlines
	N648UA	Boeing 767-322ER	United Airlines
	N649UA	Boeing 767-322ER	United Airlines
	N651UA	Boeing 767-322ER	United Airlines
	N652UA	Boeing 767-322ER	United Airlines
	N653UA	Boeing 767-322ER	United Airlines
	N654UA	Boeing 767-322ER	United Airlines
	N655UA	Boeing 767-322ER	United Airlines
	N656UA	Boeing 767-322ER	United Airlines
	N657UA	Boeing 767-322ER	United Airlines
	N658UA	Boeing 767-322ER	United Airlines
	N659UA	Boeing 767-322ER	United Airlines
	N660UA	Boeing 767-322ER	United Airlines
	N661UA	Boeing 767-322ER	United Airlines
	N662UA	Boeing 767-322ER	United Airlines
	N663UA	Boeing 767-322ER	United Airlines
	N700CK	Boeing 747-246B	Kalitta Air
	N701CK	Boeing 747-259B (SF)	Kalitta Air
	N702TW	Boeing 757-2Q8	Delta Air Lines
	N703CK	Boeing 747-212B (SF)	Kalitta Air
	N703TW	Boeing 757-2Q8	Delta Air Lines
	N704CK	Boeing 747-246F	Kalitta Air
	N704X	Boeing 757-2Q8	Delta Air Lines
	N705TW	Boeing 757-231	Delta Air Lines
	N705TZ	Douglas DC-10-30	World Airways
	N706TW	Boeing 757-2Q8	Delta Air Lines
	N707CK	Boeing 747-246F (SCD)	Kalitta Air
	N707TW	Boeing 757-2Q8	Delta Air Lines
	N708CK	Boeing 747-212B	Kalitta Air

Reg.	Type	Owner or Operator	Notes
N709TW	Boeing 757-2Q8	Delta Air Lines	
N710TW	Boeing 757-2Q8	Delta Air Lines	
N711ZX	Boeing 757-231	Delta Air Lines	
N712TW	Boeing 757-2Q8	Delta Air Lines	
N712CK	Boeing 747-122F (SF)	Kalitta Air	
N713CK	Boeing 747-2B4B (SF)	Kalitta Air	
N713TW	Boeing 757-2Q8	Delta Air Lines	
N715CK	Boeing 747-209B (SF)	Kalitta Air	
N717TW	Boeing 757-231	Delta Air Lines	
N718TW	Boeing 757-231	Delta Air Lines	
N720AX	Douglas DC-10-30	Omni Air International	
N721TW	Boeing 757-231	Delta Air Lines	
N722TW	Boeing 757-231	Delta Air Lines	
N723TW	Boeing 757-231	Delta Air Lines	
N727TW	Boeing 757-231	Delta Air Lines	
N740CK	Boeing 747-4H6BCF	Kalitta Air	
N740WA	Boeing 747-4H6F	World Airways	
N741CK	Boeing 747-4H6F	Kalitta Air	
N741WA	Boeing 747-4H6F	World Airways	
N742CK	Boeing 747-446BCF	Kalitta Air	
N743CK	Boeing 747-446BCF	Kalitta Air	
N743WA	Boeing 747-412F	World Airways	
N744CK	Boeing 747-446BCF	Kalitta Air	
N745CK	Boeing 747-446BCF	Kalitta Air	
N746CK	Boeing 747-246B	Kalitta Air	
N747CK	Boeing 747-221F	Kalitta Air	
N748CK	Boeing 747-221F	Kalitta Air	
N750AN	Boeing 777-223ER	American Airlines	
N751AN	Boeing 777-223ER	American Airlines	
N752AN	Boeing 777-223ER	American Airlines	
N753AN	Boeing 777-223ER	American Airlines	
N754AN	Boeing 777-223ER	American Airlines	
N755AN	Boeing 777-223ER	American Airlines	
N756AM	Boeing 777-223ER	American Airlines	
N757AN	Boeing 777-223ER	American Airlines	
N758AN	Boeing 777-223ER	American Airlines	
N759AN	Boeing 777-223ER	American Airlines	
N760AN	Boeing 777-223ER	American Airlines	
N761AJ	Boeing 777-223ER	American Airlines	
N762AN	Boeing 777-223ER	American Airlines	
N765AN	Boeing 777-223ER	American Airlines	
N766AN	Boeing 777-223ER	American Airlines	
N767AJ	Boeing 777-223ER	American Airlines	
N768AA	Boeing 777-223ER	American Airlines	
N768UA	Boeing 777-222	United Airlines	
N769UA	Boeing 777-222	United Airlines	
N770AN	Boeing 777-223ER	American Airlines	
N771AN	Boeing 777-223ER	American Airlines	
N771UA	Boeing 777-222	United Airlines	
N772AN	Boeing 777-223ER	American Airlines	
N772UA	Boeing 777-222	United Airlines	
N773AN	Boeing 777-223ER	American Airlines	
N773UA	Boeing 777-222	United Airlines	
N774AN	Boeing 777-223ER	American Airlines	
N774UA	Boeing 777-222	United Airlines	
N775AN	Boeing 777-223ER	American Airlines	
N775UA	Boeing 777-222	United Airlines	
N776AN	Boeing 777-223ER	American Airlines	
N776UA	Boeing 777-222	United Airlines	
N777AN	Boeing 777-223ER	American Airlines	
N777UA	Boeing 777-222	United Airlines	
N778AN	Boeing 777-223ER	American Airlines	
N778UA	Boeing 777-222	United Airlines	
N779AN	Boeing 777-223ER	American Airlines	
N779UA	Boeing 777-222	United Airlines	
N780AN	Boeing 777-223ER	American Airlines	
N780UA	Boeing 777-222	United Airlines	
N781AN	Boeing 777-223ER	American Airlines	
N781UA	Boeing 777-222	United Airlines	
N782AN	Boeing 777-223ER	American Airlines	
N782UA	Boeing 777-222ER	United Airlines	
N783AN	Boeing 777-223ER	American Airlines	
N783UA	Boeing 777-222ER	United Airlines	
N784AN	Boeing 777-223ER	American Airlines	

Notes	Reg.	Type	Owner or Operator
	N784UA	Boeing 777-222ER	United Airlines
	N785AN	Boeing 777-223ER	American Airlines
	N785UA	Boeing 777-222ER	United Airlines
	N786AN	Boeing 777-223ER	American Airlines
	N786UA	Boeing 777-222ER	United Airlines
	N787AL	Boeing 777-223ER	American Airlines
	N787UA	Boeing 777-222ER	United Airlines
	N788AN	Boeing 777-223ER	American Airlines
	N788UA	Boeing 777-222ER	United Airlines
	N789AN	Boeing 777-223ER	American Airlines
	N790AN	Boeing 777-223ER	American Airlines
	N790CK	Boeing 747-251F	Kalitta Air
	N791AN	Boeing 777-223ER	American Airlines
	N791CK	Boeing 747-251F	Kalitta Air
	N791UA	Boeing 777-222ER	United Airlines
	N792CK	Boeing 747-212F	Kalitta Air
	N792AN	Boeing 777-223ER	American Airlines
	N792UA	Boeing 777-222ER	United Airlines
	N793AN	Boeing 777-223ER	American Airlines
	N793UA	Boeing 777-222ER	United Airlines
	N794AN	Boeing 777-223ER	American Airlines
	N794UA	Boeing 777-222ER	United Airlines
	N795AN	Boeing 777-223ER	American Airlines
	N795UA	Boeing 777-222ER	United Airlines
	N796AN	Boeing 777-223ER	American Airlines
	N796UA	Boeing 777-222ER	United Airlines
	N797AN	Boeing 777-223ER	American Airlines
	N797UA	Boeing 777-222ER	United Airlines
	N798AN	Boeing 777-223ER	American Airlines
	N798UA	Boeing 777-222ER	United Airlines
	N799AN	Boeing 777-223ER	American Airlines
	N799UA	Boeing 777-222ER	United Airlines
	N801DE	McD Douglas MD-11 (801)	World Airways
	N801NW	Airbus A.330-323X	Delta Airlines
	N801SY	Boeing 737-8Q8	Sun Country Airlines
	N802NW	Airbus A.330-323X	Delta Airlines
	N803NW	Airbus A.330-323X	Delta Air Lines
	N804DE	McD Douglas MD-11 (804)	World Airways
	N804NW	Airbus A.330-323X	Delta Air Lines
	N804SY	Boeing 737-8Q8	Sun Country Airlines
	N805NW	Airbus A.330-323X	Delta Air Lines
	N805SY	Boeing 737-8Q8	Sun Country Airlines
	N806NW	Airbus A.330-323X	Delta Air Lines
	N806SY	Boeing 737-8Q8	Sun Country Airlines
	N807NW	Airbus A.330-323X	Delta Air Lines
	N808NW	Airbus A.330-323X	Delta Air Lines
	N809NW	Airbus A.330-323E	Delta Air Lines
	N809SY	Boeing 737-8Q8	Sun Country Airlines
	N810AX	Douglas DC-10-30	Omni Air International
	N810NW	Airbus A.330-323E	Delta Air Lines
	N811NW	Airbus A.330-323E	Delta Air Lines
	N812NW	Airbus A.330-323E	Delta Air Lines
	N813NW	Airbus A.330-323E	Delta Air Lines
	N813SY	Boeing 737-8Q8	Sun Country Airlines
	N814NW	Airbus A.330-323E	Delta Air Lines
	N815NW	Airbus A.330-323E	Delta Air Lines
	N816NW	Airbus A.330-323E	Delta Air Lines
	N817NW	Airbus A.330-323E	Delta Air Lines
	N818NW	Airbus A.330-323E	Delta Air Lines
	N819NW	Airbus A.330-323E	Delta Air Lines
	N820NW	Airbus A.330-323E	Delta Air Lines
	N821NW	Airbus A.330-323E	Delta Air Lines
	N825MH	Boeing 767-432ER (1801)	Delta Air Lines
	N826MH	Boeing 767-432ER (1802)	Delta Air Lines
	N827MH	Boeing 767-432ER (1803)	Delta Air Lines
	N828MH	Boeing 767-432ER (1804)	Delta Air Lines
	N829MH	Boeing 767-432ER (1805)	Delta Air Lines
	N830MH	Boeing 767-432ER (1806)	Delta Air Lines
	N831MH	Boeing 767-432ER (1807)	Delta Air Lines
	N832MH	Boeing 767-432ER (1808)	Delta Air Lines
	N833MH	Boeing 767-432ER (1809)	Delta Air Lines
	N834MH	Boeing 767-432ER (1810)	Delta Air Lines
	N835MH	Boeing 767-432ER (1811)	Delta Air Lines
	N836MH	Boeing 767-432ER (1812)	Delta Air Lines

Reg.	Type	Owner or Operator	Notes
N837MH	Boeing 767-432ER (1813)	Delta Air Lines	
N838MH	Boeing 767-432ER (1814)	Delta Air Lines	
N839MH	Boeing 767-432ER (1815)	Delta Air Lines	
N840MH	Boeing 767-432ER (1816)	Delta Air Lines	
N841MH	Boeing 767-432ER (1817)	Delta Air Lines	
N842MH	Boeing 767-432ER (1818	Delta Air Lines	
N843MH	Boeing 767-432ER (1819)	Delta Air Lines	
N844MH	Boeing 767-432ER (1820)	Delta Air Lines	
N845MH	Boeing 767-432ER (1821)	Delta Air Lines	
N851NW	Airbus A.330-223	Delta Air Lines	
N852NW	Airbus A.330-223	Delta Air Lines	
N853NW	Airbus A.330-223	Delta Air Lines	
N854NW	Airbus A.330-223	Delta Air Lines	
N855NW	Airbus A.330-223	Delta Air Lines	
N856NW	Airbus A.330-223	Delta Air Lines	
N857NW	Airbus A.330-223	Delta Air Lines	
N858NW	Airbus A.330-223	Delta Air Lines	
N859NW	Airbus A.330-223	Delta Air Lines	
N860NW	Airbus A.330-223	Delta Air Lines	
N861NW	Airbus A.330-223	Delta Air Lines	
N937UW	Boeing 757-2B7	US Airways	
N938UW	Boeing 757-2B7	US Airways	
N939UW	Boeing 757-2B7	US Airways	
N940UW	Boeing 757-2B7	US Airways	
N941UW	Boeing 757-2B7	US Airways	
N942UW	Boeing 757-2B7	US Airways	
N1200K	Boeing 767-332ER (200)	Delta Air Lines	
N1201P	Boeing 767-332ER (201)	Delta Air Lines	
N1501P	Boeing 767-3P6ER (1501)	Delta Air Lines	
N1602	Boeing 767-332ER (1602)	Delta Air Lines	
N1603	Boeing 767-332ER (1603)	Delta Air Lines	
N1604R	Boeing 767-332ER (1604)	Delta Air Lines	
N1605	Boeing 767-332ER (1605)	Delta Air Lines	
N1607B	Boeing 767-332ER (1607)	Delta Air Lines	
N1608	Boeing 767-332ER (1608)	Delta Air Lines	
N1609	Boeing 767-332ER (1609)	Delta Air Lines	
N1610D	Boeing 767-332ER (1610)	Delta Air Lines	
N1611B	Boeing 767-332ER (1611)	Delta Air Lines	
N1612T	Boeing 767-332ER (1612)	Delta Air Lines	
N1613B	Boeing 767-332ER (1613)	Delta Air Lines	
N7375A	Boeing 767-323ER	American Airlines	
N12109	Boeing 757-224 (109)	Continental Airlines/United Airlines	
N12114	Boeing 757-224 (114)	Continental Airlines/United Airlines	
N12116	Boeing 757-224 (116)	Continental Airlines/United Airlines	
N12125	Boeing 757-224 (125)	Continental Airlines/United Airlines	
N13110	Boeing 757-224 (110)	Continental Airlines/United Airlines	
N13113	Boeing 757-224 (113)	Continental Airlines/United Airlines	
N13138	Boeing 757-224 (118)	Continental Airlines/United Airlines	
N14102	Boeing 757-224 (102)	Continental Airlines/United Airlines	
N14106	Boeing 757-224 (106)	Continental Airlines/United Airlines	
N14107	Boeing 757-224 (107)	Continental Airlines/United Airlines	
N14115	Boeing 757-224 (115)	Continental Airlines/United Airlines	
N14118	Boeing 757-224 (118)	Continental Airlines/United Airlines	
N14120	Boeing 757-224 (120)	Continental Airlines/United Airlines	
N14121	Boeing 757-224 (121)	Continental Airlines/United Airlines	
N16065	Boeing 767-332ER (1606)	Delta Air Lines	
N17085	Douglas DC-10-30	Omni Air International	
N17104	Boeing 757-224 (104)	Continental Airlines/United Airlines	
N17105	Boeing 757-224 (105)	Continental Airlines/United Airlines	
N17122	Boeing 757-224 (122)	Continental Airlines/United Airlines	
N17126	Boeing 757-224 (126)	Continental Airlines/United Airlines	
N17128	Boeing 757-224 (128)	Continental Airlines/United Airlines	
N17133	Boeing 757-224 (133)	Continental Airlines/United Airlines	
N17139	Boeing 757-224 (139)	Continental Airlines/United Airlines	
N18112	Boeing 757-224 (112)	Continental Airlines/United Airlines	
N18119	Boeing 757-224 (119)	Continental Airlines/United Airlines	
N19117	Boeing 757-224 (117)	Continental Airlines/United Airlines	
N19130	Boeing 757-224 (130)	Continental Airlines/United Airlines	
N19136	Boeing 757-224 (136)	Continental Airlines/United Airlines	
N19141	Boeing 757-224 (141)	Continental Airlines/United Airlines	
N21108	Boeing 757-224 (108)	Continental Airlines/United Airlines	
N26123	Boeing 757-224 (123)	Continental Airlines/United Airlines	
N27015	Boeing 777-224ER (015)	Continental Airlines/United Airlines	
N29124	Boeing 757-224 (124)	Continental Airlines/United Airlines	

Notes	Reg.	Type	Owner or Operator
	N29129	Boeing 757-224 (129)	Continental Airlines/United Airlines
	N33103	Boeing 757-224 (103)	Continental Airlines/United Airlines
	N33132	Boeing 757-224 (132)	Continental Airlines/United Airlines
	N34131	Boeing 757-224 (131)	Continental Airlines/United Airlines
	N34137	Boeing 757-224 (13)	Continental Airlines/United Airlines
	N37018	Boeing 777-224ER (018)	Continental Airlines/United Airlines
	N39356	Boeing 767-323ER	American Airlines
	N39364	Boeing 767-323ER	American Airlines
	N39365	Boeing 767-323ER	American Airlines
	N39367	Boeing 767-323ER	American Airlines
	N41135	Boeing 757-224 (135)	Continental Airlines/United Airlines
	N41140	Boeing 757-224 (140)	Continental Airlines/United Airlines
	N48127	Boeing 757-224 (127)	Continental Airlines/United Airlines
	N57016	Boeing 777-224ER (016)	Continental Airlines/United Airlines
	N57111	Boeing 757-224 (111)	Continental Airlines/United Airlines
	N58101	Boeing 757-224 (101)	Continental Airlines/United Airlines
	N59053	Boeing 767-424ER (053)	Continental Airlines/United Airlines
	N59083	Douglas DC-10-30	Omni Air International
	N66051	Boeing 767-424ER (051)	Continental Airlines/United Airlines
	N66056	Boeing 767-424ER (056)	Continental Airlines/United Airlines
	N66057	Boeing 767-424ER (057)	Continental Airlines/United Airlines
	N67052	Boeing 767-424ER (052)	Continental Airlines/United Airlines
	N67058	Boeing 767-424ER (058)	Continental Airlines/United Airlines
	N67134	Boeing 757-224 (134)	Continental Airlines/United Airlines
	N67157	Boeing 767-224ER (157)	Continental Airlines/United Airlines
	N67158	Boeing 767-224ER (158)	Continental Airlines/United Airlines
	N68061	Boeing 767-424ER (061)	Continental Airlines/United Airlines
	N68155	Boeing 767-224ER (155)	Continental Airlines/United Airlines
	N68159	Boeing 767-224ER (159)	Continental Airlines/United Airlines
	N68160	Boeing 767-224ER (160)	Continental Airlines/United Airlines
	N69020	Boeing 777-224ER	Continental Airlines/United Airlines
	N69059	Boeing 767-424ER (059)	Continental Airlines/United Airlines
	N69063	Boeing 767-424ER (063)	Continental Airlines/United Airlines
	N69154	Boeing 767-224ER (154)	Continental Airlines/United Airlines
	N73152	Boeing 767-224ER (152)	Continental Airlines/United Airlines
	N74007	Boeing 777-224ER (007)	Continental Airlines/United Airlines
	N76010	Boeing 777-224ER (010)	Continental Airlines/United Airlines
	N76021	Boeing 777-224ER	Continental Airlines/United Airlines
	N76054	Boeing 767-424ER (054)	Continental Airlines/United Airlines
	N76055	Boeing 767-424ER (055)	Continental Airlines/United Airlines
	N76062	Boeing 767-424ER (062)	Continental Airlines/United Airlines
	N76064	Boeing 767-424ER (064)	Continental Airlines/United Airlines
	N76065	Boeing 767-424ER (065)	Continental Airlines/United Airlines
	N76151	Boeing 767-224ER (151)	Continental Airlines/United Airlines
	N76153	Boeing 767-224ER (153)	Continental Airlines/United Airlines
	N76156	Boeing 767-224ER (156)	Continental Airlines/United Airlines
	N77006	Boeing 777-224ER (006)	Continental Airlines/United Airlines
	N77012	Boeing 777-224ER (012)	Continental Airlines/United Airlines
	N77014	Boeing 777-224ER (014)	Continental Airlines/United Airlines
	N77019	Boeing 777-224ER (019)	Continental Airlines/United Airlines *Larry Kellner*
	N77022	Boeing 777-224ER	Continental Airlines/United Airlines
	N77066	Boeing 767-424ER (066)	Continental Airlines/United Airlines
	N78001	Boeing 777-224ER (001)	Continental Airlines/United Airlines
	N78002	Boeing 777-224ER (002)	Continental Airlines/United Airlines
	N78003	Boeing 777-224ER (003)	Continental Airlines/United Airlines
	N78004	Boeing 777-224ER (004)	Continental Airlines/United Airlines
	N78005	Boeing 777-224ER (005)	Continental Airlines/United Airlines
	N78008	Boeing 777-224ER (008)	Continental Airlines/United Airlines
	N78009	Boeing 777-224ER (009)	Continental Airlines/United Airlines
	N78013	Boeing 777-224ER (013)	Continental Airlines/United Airlines
	N78017	Boeing 777-224ER (017)	Continental Airlines/United Airlines
	N78060	Boeing 767-424ER (060)	Continental Airlines/United Airlines
	N79011	Boeing 777-224ER (011)	Continental Airlines/United Airlines

OD (Lebanon)

Notes	Reg.	Type	Owner or Operator
	OD-MEA	Airbus A.330-243	Middle East Airlines
	OD-MEB	Airbus A.330-243	Middle East Airlines
	OD-MEC	Airbus A.330-243	Middle East Airlines
	OD-MRR	Airbus A.320-232	Middle East Airlines
	OD-MRS	Airbus A.320-232	Middle East Airlines
	OD-MRT	Airbus A.320-232	Middle East Airlines
	OD-RMH	Airbus A.321-231	Middle East Airlines

Reg.	Type	Owner or Operator	Notes
OD-RMI	Airbus A.321-231	Middle East Airlines	
OD-RMJ	Airbus A.321-231	Middle East Airlines	

Middle East Airlines also operate Airbus A.321s, Airbus A.320s and an Airbus A.330 on the French Register

OE (Austria)

Reg.	Type	Owner or Operator	Notes
OE-IHA	Embraer ERJ190-100LR	Niki	
OE-IHB	Embraer ERJ190-100LR	Niki	
OE-IHC	Embraer ERJ190-100LR	Niki	
OE-IHD	Embraer ERJ190-100LR	Niki	
OE-IHE	Embraer ERJ190-100LR	Niki	
OE-LAE	Boeing 767-3Z9ER	Austrian Airlines *Malaysia*	
OE-LAT	Boeing 767-31AER	Austrian Airlines *Enzo Ferrari*	
OE-LAW	Boeing 767-3Z9ER	Austrian Airlines *China*	
OE-LAX	Boeing 767-3Z9ER	Austrian Airlines *Thailand*	
OE-LAY	Boeing 767-3Z9ER	Austrian Airlines *Japan*	
OE-LAZ	Boeing 767-3Z9ER	Austrian Airlines	
OE-LBA	Airbus A.321-111	Austrian Airlines *Salzkammergut*	
OE-LBB	Airbus A.321-111	Austrian Airlines *Pinzgau*	
OE-LBC	Airbus A.321-111	Austrian Airlines *Sudtirol*	
OE-LBD	Airbus A.321-111	Austrian Airlines *Steirisches Weinland*	
OE-LBE	Airbus A.321-111	Austrian Airlines *Wachau*	
OE-LBF	Airbus A.321-111	Austrian Airlines *Wien*	
OE-LBN	Airbus A.320-214	Austrian Airlines *Osttirol*	
OE-LBO	Airbus A.320-214	Austrian Airlines *Pyhrn-Eisenwurzen*	
OE-LBP	Airbus A.320-214	Austrian Airlines *Neusiedler See*	
OE-LBQ	Airbus A.320-214	Austrian Airlines *Wienerwald*	
OE-LBR	Airbus A.320-214	Austrian Airlines *Frida Kahle*	
OE-LBS	Airbus A.320-214	Austrian Airlines *Waldviertel*	
OE-LBT	Airbus A.320-214	Austrian Airlines *Worthersee*	
OE-LBU	Airbus A.320-214	Austrian Airlines *Muhlviertel*	
OE-LCJ	Canadair CRJ200LR	Austrian Arrows *Hannover*	
OE-LCN	Canadair CRJ200LR	Austrian Arrows *Bremen*	
OE-LCR	Canadair CRJ200LR	Austrian Arrows *Baden*	
OE-LDA	Airbus A.319-112	Austrian Airlines *Sofia*	
OE-LDB	Airbus A.319-112	Austrian Airlines *Bucharest*	
OE-LDC	Airbus A.319-112	Austrian Airlines *Kiev*	
OE-LDD	Airbus A.319-112	Austrian Airlines *Moscow*	
OE-LDE	Airbus A.319-112	Austrian Airlines *Baku*	
OE-LDF	Airbus A.319-112	Austrian Airlines *Sarajevo*	
OE-LDG	Airbus A.319-112	Austrian Airlines *Tbilisi*	
OE-LEA	Airbus A.320-214	Niki *Rock 'n Roll*	
OE-LEB	Airbus A.320-214	Niki	
OE-LEC	Airbus A.320-214	Niki *Flamenco*	
OE-LED	Airbus A.319-112	Niki	
OE-LEE	Airbus A.320-214	Niki	
OE-LEF	Airbus A.320-214	Niki	
OE-LEK	Airbus A.319-112	Niki *Tango*	
OE-LEO	Airbus A.320-214	Niki *Soul*	
OE-LES	Airbus A.321-211	Niki	
OE-LET	Airbus A.321-211	Niki	
OE-LEU	Airbus A.320-214	Niki	
OE-LEV	Airbus A.321-211	Niki	
OE-LEX	Airbus A.320-214	Niki *Jazz*	
OE-LFG	Fokker 70	Austrian Arrows *Innsbruck*	
OE-LFH	Fokker 70	Austrian Arrows *Salzburg*	
OE-LFI	Fokker 70	Austrian Arrows *Klagenfurt*	
OE-LFJ	Fokker 70	Austrian Arrows *Graz*	
OE-LFK	Fokker 70	Austrian Arrows *Wien*	
OE-LFL	Fokker 70	Austrian Arrows *Linz*	
OE-LFP	Fokker 70	Austrian Airlines *Wels*	
OE-LFQ	Fokker 70	Austrian Airlines *Dornbirn*	
OE-LFR	Fokker 70	Austrian Airlines *Steyr*	
OE-LGA	DHC.8Q-402 Dash Eight	Austrian Arrows *Karnten*	
OE-LGB	DHC.8Q-402 Dash Eight	Austrian Arrows *Tirol*	
OE-LGC	DHC.8Q-402 Dash Eight	Austrian Arrows *Salzburg*	
OE-LGD	DHC.8Q-402 Dash Eight	Austrian Arrows *Steiermark*	
OE-LGE	DHC.8Q-402 Dash Eight	Austrian Arrows *Oberosterreich*	
OE-LGF	DHC.8Q-402 Dash Eight	Austrian Arrows *Niederosterreich*	
OE-LGG	DHC.8Q-402 Dash Eight	Austrian Arrows *Budapest*	
OE-LGH	DHC.8Q-402 Dash Eight	Austrian Arrows *Vorarlberg*	
OE-LGI	DHC.8Q-402 Dash Eight	Austrian Arrows *Eisenstadt*	

Notes	Reg.	Type	Owner or Operator
	OE-LGJ	DHC.8Q-402 Dash Eight	Austrian Arrows *St Pölten*
	OE-LGK	DHC.8Q-402 Dash Eight	Austrian Arrows *Burgenland*
	OE-LGL	DHC.8Q-402 Dash Eight	Austrian Arrows *Altenrhein*
	OE-LGM	DHC.8Q-402 Dash Eight	Austrian Arrows *Villach*
	OE-LGN	DHC.8Q-402 Dash Eight	Austrian Arrows *Gmunden*
	OE-LNJ	Boeing 737-8Z9	Austrian Airlines *Falco*
	OE-LNK	Boeing 737-8Z9	Austrian Airlines *Freddie Mercury*
	OE-LNL	Boeing 737-6Z9	Austrian Airlines *Kahlenberg*
	OE-LNM	Boeing 737-6Z9	Austrian Airlines *Albert Einstein*
	OE-LNN	Boeing 737-7Z9	Austrian Airlines *Maria Callas*
	OE-LNO	Boeing 737-7Z9	Austrian Airlines *Greta Garbo*
	OE-LNP	Boeing 737-8Z9	Austrian Airlines *George Harrison*
	OE-LNQ	Boeing 737-8Z9	Austrian Airlines *Gregory Peck*
	OE-LNR	Boeing 737-8Z9	Austrian Airlines *Frank Zappa*
	OE-LNS	Boeing 737-8Z9	Austrian Airlines *Miles Davis*
	OE-LNT	Boeing 737-8Z9	Austrian Airlines *Kurt Cobain*
	OE-LPA	Boeing 777-2Z9	Austrian Airlines *Melbourne*
	OE-LPB	Boeing 777-2Z9	Austrian Airlines *Sydney*
	OE-LPC	Boeing 777-2Z9ER	Austrian Airlines *Donald Bradman*
	OE-LPD	Boeing 777-2Z9ER	Austrian Airlines *America*
	OE-LVA	Fokker 100	Austrian Arrows *Riga*
	OE-LVB	Fokker 100	Austrian Arrows *Vilnius*
	OE-LVC	Fokker 100	Austrian Arrows *Tirana*
	OE-LVD	Fokker 100	Austrian Arrows *Belgrade*
	OE-LVE	Fokker 100	Austrian Arrows *Zagreb*
	OE-LVF	Fokker 100	Austrian Arrows *Yerevan*
	OE-LVG	Fokker 100	Austrian Arrows *Krakow*
	OE-LVH	Fokker 100	Austrian Arrows *Minsk*
	OE-LVI	Fokker 100	Austrian Arrows *Prague*
	OE-LVJ	Fokker 100	Austrian Arrows *Bratislava*
	OE-LVK	Fokker 100	Austrian Arrows *Timisoara*
	OE-LVL	Fokker 100	Austrian Arrows
	OE-LVM	Fokker 100	Austrian Arrows *Krasnodar*
	OE-LVN	Fokker 100	Austrian Arrows *Dnepropetrovsk*
	OE-LVO	Fokker 100	Austrian Arrows *Chisinau*

OH (Finland)

Notes	Reg.	Type	Owner or Operator
	OH-AFI	Boeing 757-2K2	Air Finland
	OH-AFJ	Boeing 757-2Q8	Air Finland
	OH-AFK	Boeing 757-28A	Air Finland
	OH-BLG	Boeing 717-2CM	Blue 1
	OH-BLI	Boeing 717-2CM	Blue 1
	OH-BLJ	Boeing 717-23S	Blue 1
	OH-BLM	Boeing 717-23S	Blue 1
	OH-BLP	Boeing 717-23S	Blue 1
	OH-LBO	Boeing 757-2Q8	Finnair
	OH-LBR	Boeing 757-2Q8	Finnair
	OH-LBS	Boeing 757-2Q8	Finnair
	OH-LBT	Boeing 757-2Q8	Finnair
	OH-LEE	Embraer RJ170-100LR	Finnair
	OH-LEF	Embraer RJ170-100LR	Finnair
	OH-LEG	Embraer RJ170-100LR	Finnair
	OH-LEH	Embraer RJ170-100LR	Finnair
	OH-LEL	Embraer RJ170-100LR	Finnair
	OH-LEO	Embraer RJ170-100LR	Finnair
	OH-LGC	McD Douglas MD-11	Finnair Cargo
	OH-LKE	Embraer RJ190-100LR	Finnair
	OH-LKF	Embraer RJ190-100LR	Finnair
	OH-LKG	Embraer RJ190-100LR	Finnair
	OH-LKH	Embraer RJ190-100LR	Finnair
	OH-LKI	Embraer RJ190-100LR	Finnair
	OH-LKK	Embraer RJ190-100LR	Finnair
	OH-LKL	Embraer RJ190-100LR	Finnair
	OH-LKM	Embraer RJ190-100LR	Finnair
	OH-LKN	Embraer RJ190-100LR	Finnair
	OH-LKO	Embraer RJ190-100LR	Finnair
	OH-LQA	Airbus A.340-311	Finnair
	OH-LQB	Airbus A.340-313X	Finnair
	OH-LQC	Airbus A.340-313E	Finnair
	OH-LQD	Airbus A.340-313E	Finnair
	OH-LQE	Airbus A.340-313E	Finnair
	OH-LQF	Airbus A.340-313X	Finnair

Reg.	Type	Owner or Operator	Notes
OH-LQG	Airbus A.340-313X	Finnair	
OH-LTM	Airbus A.330-302	Finnair	
OH-LTN	Airbus A.330-302	Finnair	
OH-LTO	Airbus A.330-302	Finnair	
OH-LTP	Airbus A.330-302	Finnair *St.Munchin*	
OH-LTR	Airbus A.330-302	Finnair	
OH-LTS	Airbus A.330-302	Finnair	
OH-LTT	Airbus A.330-302	Finnair	
OH-LTU	Airbus A.330-302	Finnair	
OH-LVA	Airbus A.319-112	Finnair	
OH-LVB	Airbus A.319-112	Finnair	
OH-LVC	Airbus A.319-112	Finnair	
OH-LVD	Airbus A.319-112	Finnair	
OH-LVE	Airbus A.319-112	Finnair *Silver Bird*	
OH-LVF	Airbus A.319-112	Finnair	
OH-LVG	Airbus A.319-112	Finnair	
OH-LVH	Airbus A.319-112	Finnair	
OH-LVI	Airbus A.319-112	Finnair	
OH-LVK	Airbus A.319-112	Finnair	
OH-LVL	Airbus A.319-112	Finnair	
OH-LXA	Airbus A.320-214	Finnair	
OH-LXB	Airbus A.320-214	Finnair	
OH-LXC	Airbus A.320-214	Finnair	
OH-LXD	Airbus A.320-214	Finnair	
OH-LXE	Airbus A.320-214	Finnair	
OH-LXF	Airbus A.320-214	Finnair	
OH-LXG	Airbus A.320-214	Finnair	
OH-LXH	Airbus A.320-214	Finnair	
OH-LXI	Airbus A.320-214	Finnair	
OH-LXK	Airbus A.320-214	Finnair	
OH-LXL	Airbus A.320-214	Finnair	
OH-LXM	Airbus A.320-214	Finnair	
OH-LZA	Airbus A.321-211	Finnair	
OH-LZB	Airbus A.321-211	Finnair	
OH-LZC	Airbus A.321-211	Finnair	
OH-LZD	Airbus A.321-211	Finnair	
OH-LZE	Airbus A.321-211	Finnair	
OH-LZF	Airbus A.321-211	Finnair	
OH-SAJ	Avro RJ85	Blue1 *Pyhaselka*	
OH-SAK	Avro RJ85	Blue1 *Nasijarvi*	
OH-SAL	Avro RJ85	Blue1 *Orivesi*	
OH-SAO	Avro RJ85	Blue1 *Oulujarvi*	
OH-SAP	Avro RJ85	Blue1 *Pielinen*	

OK (Czech Republic)

Reg.	Type	Owner or Operator	Notes
OK-ASA	Let L410UVP-E	Manx2	
OK-CEC	Airbus A.321-211	CSA Czech Airlines *Nove Mesto nad Metuji*	
OK-CED	Airbus A.321-211	CSA Czech Airlines *Havlikuv Brod*	
OK-CGK	Boeing 737-55S	CSA Czech Airlines *Pardubice*	
OK-DGL	Boeing 737-55S	CSA Czech Airlines *Tabor*	
OK-EGO	Boeing 737-55S	CSA Czech Airlines *Jindrichuv Hradec*	
OK-GEA	Airbus A.320-214	CSA Czech Airlines *Roznovpod Radhostem*	
OK-GEB	Airbus A.320-214	CSA Czech Airlines *Strakonice*	
OK-LEE	Airbus A.320-214	CSA Czech Airlines	
OK-LEF	Airbus A.320-214	CSA Czech Airlines	
OK-LEG	Airbus A.320-214	CSA Czech Airlines	
OK-MEH	Airbus A.320-214	CSA Czech Airlines	
OK-MEI	Airbus A.320-214	CSA Czech Airlines	
OK-MEJ	Airbus A.320-214	CSA Czech Airlines	
OK-MEK	Airbus A.319-112	CSA Czech Airlines	
OK-MEL	Airbus A.319-112	CSA Czech Airlines	
OK-NEM	Airbus A.319-112	CSA Czech Airlines	
OK-NEN	Airbus A.319-112	CSA Czech Airlines	
OK-NEO	Airbus A.319-112	CSA Czech Airlines	
OK-NEP	Airbus A.319-112	CSA Czech Airlines	
OK-OER	Airbus A.319-112	CSA Czech Airlines	
OK-PET	Airbus A.319-112	CSA Czech Airlines	
OK-SWU	Boeing 737-522	Smart Wings	
OK-SWV	Boeing 737-522	Smart Wings	
OK-TCA	Let L410UVP-E	Manx2	
OK-TVB	Boeing 737-8CX	Travel Service Airlines	
OK-TVD	Boeing 737-86N	Travel Service Airlines	

Notes	Reg.	Type	Owner or Operator
	OK-TVF	Boeing 737-8FH	Travel Service Airlines
	OK-TVG	Boeing 737-8Q8	Travel Service Airlines
	OK-TVH	Boeing 737-8Q8	Travel Service Airlines
	OK-TVK	Boeing 737-86N	Travel Service Airlines
	OK-TVL	Boeing 737-8FN	Travel Service Airlines
	OK-TVM	Boeing 737-8FN	Travel Service Airlines
	OK-TVN	Boeing 737-8BK	Travel Service Airlines
	OK-TVO	Boeing 737-8CX	Travel Service Airlines
	OK-TVP	Boeing 737-8K5	Travel Service Airlines
	OK-TVR	Boeing 737-86N	Travel Service Airlines
	OK-TVS	Boeing 737-86N	Travel Service Airlines
	OK-UBA	Let 410UVP-E	Manx2
	OK-WGX	Boeing 737-436	CSA Czech Airlines *Unicov*
	OK-WGY	Boeing 737-436	CSA Czech Airlines
	OK-XGA	Boeing 737-55S	CSA Czech Airlines *Plzen*
	OK-XGB	Boeing 737-55S	CSA Czech Airlines *Olomouc*
	OK-XGC	Boeing 737-55S	CSA Czech Airlines *Ceske Budejovice*
	OK-XGD	Boeing 737-55S	CSA Czech Airlines *Poprad*
	OK-XGE	Boeing 737-55S	CSA Czech Airlines *Kosice*

OM (Slovakia)

Notes	Reg.	Type	Owner or Operator
	OM-AEX	Boeing 737-4YO	AirExplore
	OM-TVA	Boeing 737-86N	Travel Service Airlines

OO (Belgium)

Notes	Reg.	Type	Owner or Operator
	OO-DJK	Avro RJ85	Brussels Airlines
	OO-DJL	Avro RJ85	Brussels Airlines
	OO-DJN	Avro RJ85	Brussels Airlines
	OO-DJO	Avro RJ85	Brussels Airlines
	OO-DJP	Avro RJ85	Brussels Airlines
	OO-DJQ	Avro RJ85	Brussels Airlines
	OO-DJR	Avro RJ85	Brussels Airlines
	OO-DJS	Avro RJ85	Brussels Airlines
	OO-DJT	Avro RJ85	Brussels Airlines
	OO-DJV	Avro RJ85	Brussels Airlines
	OO-DJW	Avro RJ85	Brussels Airlines
	OO-DJX	Avro RJ85	Brussels Airlines
	OO-DJY	Avro RJ85	Brussels Airlines
	OO-DJZ	Avro RJ85	Brussels Airlines
	OO-DWA	Avro RJ100	Brussels Airlines
	OO-DWB	Avro RJ100	Brussels Airlines
	OO-DWC	Avro RJ100	Brussels Airlines
	OO-DWD	Avro RJ100	Brussels Airlines
	OO-DWE	Avro RJ100	Brussels Airlines
	OO-DWF	Avro RJ100	Brussels Airlines
	OO-DWG	Avro RJ100	Brussels Airlines
	OO-DWH	Avro RJ100	Brussels Airlines
	OO-DWI	Avro RJ100	Brussels Airlines
	OO-DWJ	Avro RJ100	Brussels Airlines
	OO-DWK	Avro RJ100	Brussels Airlines
	OO-DWL	Avro RJ100	Brussels Airlines
	OO-JAA	Boeing 737-8BK	Jetairfly/TUI Airlines Belgium
	OO-JAF	Boeing 737-8K5	Jetairfly/TUI Airlines Belgium
	OO-JAN	Boeing 737-76N	Jetairfly/TUI Airlines Belgium
	OO-JAO	Boeing 737-7K5	Jetairfly/TUI Airlines Belgium
	OO-JAP	Boeing 767-38EER	Jetairfly/TUI Airlines Belgium
	OO-JAQ	Boeing 737-8K5	Jetairfly/TUI Airlines Belgium *Vision*
	OO-JAR	Boeing 737-7K5	Jetairfly/TUI Airlines Belgium
	OO-JAS	Boeing 737-7K5	Jetairfly/TUI Airlines Belgium
	OO-JAT	Boeing 737-5K5	Jetairfly/TUI Airlines Belgium
	OO-JAX	Boeing 737-8K5	Jetairfly/TUI Airlines Belgium
	OO-JBG	Boeing 737-8K5	Jetairfly/TUI Airlines Belgium *Gerard Brack*
	OO-LTM	Boeing 737-3M8	Brussels Airlines
	OO-SFM	Airbus A.330-301	Brussels Airlines
	OO-SFN	Airbus A.330-301	Brussels Airlines
	OO-SFO	Airbus A.330-301	Brussels Airlines
	OO-SFV	Airbus A.330-322	Brussels Airlines
	OO-SFW	Airbus A.330-322	Brussels Airlines
	OO-SNA	Airbus A.320-214	Brussels Airlines
	OO-SNB	Airbus A.320-214	Brussels Airlines

Reg.	Type	Owner or Operator	Notes
OO-SSC	Airbus A.319-112	Brussels Airlines	
OO-SSD	Airbus A.319-112	Brussels Airlines	
OO-SSG	Airbus A.319-112	Brussels Airlines	
OO-SSK	Airbus A.319-112	Brussels Airlines	
OO-SSM	Airbus A.319-112	Brussels Airlines	
OO-SSP	Airbus A.319-112	Brussels Airlines	
OO-TAA	BAe 146-300QT	TNT Airways	
OO-TAD	BAe 146-300QT	TNT Airways	
OO-TAE	BAe 146-300QT	TNT Airways	
OO-TAF	BAe 146-300QT	TNT Airways	
OO-TAH	BAe 146-300QT	TNT Airways	
OO-TAJ	BAe 146-300QT	TNT Airways	
OO-TAK	BAe 146-300QT	TNT Airways	
OO-TAQ	BAe 146-200QT	TNT Airways	
OO-TAR	BAe 146-200QT	TNT Airways	
OO-TAS	BAe 146-300QT	TNT Airways	
OO-TAU	BAe 146-200QT	TNT Airways	
OO-TAW	BAe 146-200QT	TNT Airways	
OO-TAY	BAe 146-200QT	TNT Airways	
OO-TAZ	BAe 146-200QC	TNT Airways	
OO-TCH	Airbus A.320-214	Thomas Cook Airlines Belgium *experience*	
OO-TCI	Airbus A.320-214	Thomas Cook Airlines Belgium *relax*	
OO-TCJ	Airbus A.320-214	Thomas Cook Airlines Belgium *inspire*	
OO-TCN	Airbus A.320-212	Thomas Cook Airlines Belgium *dream*	
OO-TCO	Airbus A.320-214	Thomas Cook Airlines Belgium *sensation*	
OO-TCP	Airbus A.320-214	Thomas Cook Airlines Belgium *desire*	
OO-TCR	Airbus A.320-232	Thomas Cook Airlines Belgium	
OO-THA	Boeing 747-4HAERF	TNT Airways	
OO-THB	Boeing 747-4HAERF	TNT Airways	
OO-THC	Boeing 747-4HAERF	TNT Airways/Emirates Airlines	
OO-THD	Boeing 747-4HAERF	TNT Airways/Emirates Airlines	
OO-TNA	Boeing 737-3T0F	TNT Airways	
OO-TNB	Boeing 737-3T0F	TNT Airways	
OO-TNC	Boeing 737-3T0F	TNT Airways	
OO-TNE	Boeing 737-3Q8	TNT Airways	
OO-TNF	Boeing 737-3Q8F	TNT Airways	
OO-TNG	Boeing 737-3Y0QC	TNT Airways	
OO-TNH	Boeing 737-301F	TNT Airways	
OO-TNJ	Boeing 737-301F	TNT Airways	
OO-TNK	Boeing 737-301F	TNT Airways	
OO-TNL	Boeing 737-34SF	TNT Airways	
OO-TNM	Boeing 737-34SF	TNT Airways	
OO-TNN	Boeing 737-45D	TNT Airways	
OO-TUA	Boeing 737-4K5	Jetairfly/TUI Airlines Belgium *Passion*	
OO-TUC	Boeing 767-341ER	Jetairfly/TUI Airlines Belgium *Discover*	
OO-VAC	Boeing 737-8BK	Jetairfly/TUI Airlines Belgium *Rising Sun*	
OO-VEG	Boeing 737-36N	Brussels Airlines	
OO-VEH	Boeing 737-36N	Brussels Airlines	
OO-VEK	Boeing 737-405	Brussels Airlines	
OO-VEN	Boeing 737-36N	Brussels Airlines	
OO-VEP	Boeing 737-43Q	Brussels Airlines	
OO-VES	Boeing 737-43Q	Brussels Airlines	
OO-VET	Boeing 737-4Q8	Brussels Airlines	
OO-VEX	Boeing 737-36N	Brussels Airlines	
OO-VLE	Fokker 50	Cityjet	
OO-VLF	Fokker 50	Cityjet	
OO-VLI	Fokker 50	Cityjet	
OO-VLJ	Fokker 50	Cityjet	
OO-VLL	Fokker 50	Cityjet	
OO-VLM	Fokker 50	Cityjet	
OO-VLN	Fokker 50	Cityjet	
OO-VLO	Fokker 50	Cityjet	
OO-VLP	Fokker 50	Cityjet	
OO-VLQ	Fokker 50	Cityjet	
OO-VLR	Fokker 50	Cityjet	
OO-VLS	Fokker 50	Cityjet	
OO-VLV	Fokker 50	Cityjet	
OO-VLY	Fokker 50	Cityjet	
OO-VLZ	Fokker 50	Cityjet	

OY (Denmark)

Reg.	Type	Owner or Operator	Notes
OY-BJP	Swearingen SA.227AC Metro III	Benair	

Notes	Reg.	Type	Owner or Operator
	OY-JRU	McD Douglas MD-87	Danish Air Transport
	OY-JTA	Boeing 737-33A	Jet Time
	OY-JTB	Boeing 737-3Y0	Jet Time
	OY-JTC	Boeing 737-3L9	Jet Time
	OY-JTD	Boeing 737-3Y0	Jet Time
	OY-JTE	Boeing 737-3L9	Jet Time
	OY-JTF	Boeing 737-382	Jet Time
	OY-KBA	Airbus A.340-313X	SAS *Adalstein Viking*
	OY-KBB	Airbus A.321-231	SAS *Hjorulf Viking*
	OY-KBC	Airbus A.340-313X	SAS *Fredis Viking*
	OY-KBD	Airbus A.340-313X	SAS *Toste Viking*
	OY-KBE	Airbus A.321-231	SAS *Emma Viking*
	OY-KBF	Airbus A.321-231	SAS *Skapti Viking*
	OY-KBH	Airbus A.321-231	SAS *Sulke Viking*
	OY-KBI	Airbus A.340-313X	SAS *Rurik Viking*
	OY-KBK	Airbus A.321-231	SAS *Arne Viking*
	OY-KBL	Airbus A.321-231	SAS *Gynnbjorn Viking*
	OY-KBN	Airbus A.330-343X	SAS *Eystein Viking*
	OY-KBO	Airbus A.319-131	SAS *Christian Valdemar Viking*
	OY-KBP	Airbus A.319-131	SAS *Viger Viking*
	OY-KBR	Airbus A.319-132	SAS *Finnboge Viking*
	OY-KBT	Airbus A.319-131	SAS *Ragnvald Viking*
	OY-KFA	Canadair CRJ900ER	SAS *Johan Viking*
	OY-KFB	Canadair CRJ900ER	SAS *Alfhild Viking*
	OY-KFC	Canadair CRJ900ER	SAS
	OY-KFD	Canadair CRJ900ER	SAS
	OY-KFE	Canadair CRJ900ER	SAS
	OY-KFF	Canadair CRJ900ER	SAS
	OY-KFG	Canadair CRJ900ER	SAS
	OY-KFH	Canadair CRJ900ER	SAS
	OY-KFI	Canadair CRJ900ER	SAS
	OY-KFK	Canadair CRJ900ER	SAS
	OY-KFL	Canadair CRJ900ER	SAS
	OY-KFM	Canadair CRJ900ER	SAS
	OY-KGT	McD Douglas MD-82	SAS *Hake Viking*
	OY-KHE	McD Douglas MD-82	SAS *Saxo Viking*
	OY-KHG	McD Douglas MD-82	SAS *Alle Viking*
	OY-KHM	McD Douglas MD-82	SAS *Mette Viking*
	OY-KHN	McD Douglas MD-82	SAS *Dan Viking*
	OY-KHP	McD Douglas MD-81	SAS *Harild Viking*
	OY-KKS	Boeing 737-683	SAS *Ramveig Viking*
	OY-MBT	Canadair CRJ200LR	Cimber Sterling/SAS
	OY-MRE	Boeing 737-7L9	Cimber Sterling
	OY-MRF	Boeing 737-7L9	Cimber Sterling
	OY-MRG	Boeing 737-7L9	Cimber Sterling
	OY-MRH	Boeing 737-7L9	Cimber Sterling
	OY-MRS	Boeing 737-76N	Cimber Sterling
	OY-MRU	Boeing 737-7L9	Cimber Sterling
	OY-NCA	Dornier 328-100	Sun-Air/British Airways
	OY-NCD	Dornier 328-100	Sun-Air/British Airways
	OY-NCK	Dornier 328-100	Sun-Air/British Airways
	OY-NCL	Dornier 328-300 JET	Sun-Air/British Airways
	OY-NCM	Dornier 328-300 JET	Sun-Air/British Airways
	OY-NCN	Dornier 328-300 JET	Sun-Air/British Airways
	OY-NCP	Dornier 328-300 JET	Sun-Air/British Airways
	OY-NCS	Dornier 328-100	Sun-Air/British Airways
	OY-PBH	Let L410UVP-E20	Benair
	OY-PBI	Let L410UVP-E20	Benair
	OY-PSA	Boeing 737-8Q8	Primera Air Scandinavia
	OY-PSB	Boeing 737-8Q8	Primera Air Scandinavia
	OY-PSC	Boeing 737-86N	Primera Air Scandinavia
	OY-PSD	Boeing 737-86N	Primera Air Scandinavia
	OY-PSE	Boeing 737-809	Primera Air Scandinavia
	OY-PSF	Boeing 737-7Q8	Primera Air Scandinavia
	OY-RCC	Avro RJ100	Atlantic Airways
	OY-RCD	Avro RJ85	Atlantic Airways
	OY-RCE	Avro RJ85	Atlantic Airways
	OY-RJA	Canadair CRJ200LR	Cimber Sterling
	OY-RJB	Canadair CRJ200LR	Cimber Sterling/SAS
	OY-RJC	Canadair CRJ200LR	Cimber Sterling/SAS
	OY-RJD	Canadair CRJ200LR	Cimber Sterling
	OY-RJE	Canadair CRJ200LR	Cimber Sterling/SAS
	OY-RJF	Canadair CRJ200LR	Cimber Sterling
	OY-RJG	Canadair CRJ200LR	Cimber Sterling

Reg.	Type	Owner or Operator	Notes
OY-RJH	Canadair CRJ200LR	Cimber Sterling	
OY-RJI	Canadair CRJ200LR	Cimber Sterling/SAS	
OY-RJJ	Canadair CRJ200LR	Cimber Sterling	
OY-RUE	McD Douglas MD-83	Danish Air Transport	
OY-SRF	Boeing 767-219 (SF)	Star Air	
OY-SRG	Boeing 767-219 (SF)	Star Air	
OY-SRH	Boeing 767-204 (SF)	Star Air	
OY-SRI	Boeing 767-25E (SF)	Star Air	
OY-SRJ	Boeing 767-25E (SF)	Star Air	
OY-SRK	Boeing 767-204 (SF)	Star Air	
OY-SRL	Boeing 767-232 (SF)	Star Air	
OY-SRM	Boeing 767-25E (SF)	Star Air	
OY-SRN	Boeing 767-219 (SF)	Star Air	
OY-SRO	Boeing 767-25E (SF)	Star Air	
OY-SRP	Boeing 767-232 (SF)	Star Air	
OY-TDB	Boeing 737-8K2	Transavia Denmark	
OY-VKA	Airbus A.321-211	Thomas Cook Airlines	
OY-VKB	Airbus A.321-211	Thomas Cook Airlines	
OY-VKC	Airbus A.321-211	Thomas Cook Airlines	
OY-VKD	Airbus A.321-211	Thomas Cook Airlines	
OY-VKE	Airbus A.321-211	Thomas Cook Airlines	
OY-VKF	Airbus A.330-243	Thomas Cook Airlines	
OY-VKG	Airbus A.330-343X	Thomas Cook Airlines	
OY-VKH	Airbus A.330-343X	Thomas Cook Airlines	
OY-VKI	Airbus A.330-343X	Thomas Cook Airlines	
OY-VKM	Airbus A.320-214	Thomas Cook Airlines	
OY-VKS	Airbus A.320-214	Thomas Cook Airlines	
OY-VKT	Airbus A.321-211	Thomas Cook Airlines	

P4 (Aruba)

Reg.	Type	Owner or Operator	Notes
P4-EAS	Boeing 757-2G5	Air Astana	
P4-FAS	Boeing 757-2G5	Air Astana	
P4-GAS	Boeing 757-2G5	Air Astana	
P4-KCA	Boeing 767-306ER	Air Astana	
P4-KCB	Boeing 767-306ER	Air Astana	
P4-MAS	Boeing 757-28A	Air Astana	

PH (Netherlands)

Reg.	Type	Owner or Operator	Notes
PH-AAX	Airbus A.320-231	Amsterdam Airlines	
PH-AAY	Airbus A.320-232	Amsterdam Airlines	
PH-AHQ	Boeing 767-383ER	TUI Airlines Nederland/Arkefly	
PH-AHX	Boeing 767-383ER	TUI Airlines Nederland/Arkefly	
PH-AHY	Boeing 767-383ER	TUI Airlines Nederland/Arkefly	
PH-AOA	Airbus A.330-203	KLM *Dam – Amsterdam*	
PH-AOB	Airbus A.330-203	KLM *Potsdamer Platz – Berlin*	
PH-AOC	Airbus A.330-203	KLM *Place de la Concorde – Paris*	
PH-AOD	Airbus A.330-203	KLM *Plazza del Duomo – Milano*	
PH-AOE	Airbus A.330-203	KLM *Parliament Square – Edinburgh*	
PH-AOF	Airbus A.330-203	KLM *Federation Square – Melbourne*	
PH-AOH	Airbus A.330-203	KLM *Senaatintori/Senate Square-Helsinki*	
PH-AOI	Airbus A.330-203	KLM *Plaza de la Independencia-Madrid*	
PH-AOK	Airbus A.330-203	KLM *Radhuspladsen-Kobenhavn*	
PH-AOL	Airbus A.330-203	KLM *Picadilly Circus – London*	
PH-AOM	Airbus A.330-203	KLM	
PH-AON	Airbus A.330-203	KLM	
PH-BCA	Boeing 737-8K2	KLM	
PH-BDO	Boeing 737-306	KLM *Jacob van Heemskerck*	
PH-BDT	Boeing 737-406	KLM *Gerrit de Veer*	
PH-BDW	Boeing 737-406	KLM *Leifur Eiriksson*	
PH-BFA	Boeing 747-406	KLM *City of Atlanta*	
PH-BFB	Boeing 747-406	KLM *City of Bangkok*	
PH-BFC	Boeing 747-406 (SCD)	KLM *City of Calgary*	
PH-BFD	Boeing 747-406 (SCD)	KLM *City of Dubai*	
PH-BFE	Boeing 747-406 (SCD)	KLM *City of Melbourne*	
PH-BFF	Boeing 747-406 (SCD)	KLM *City of Freetown*	
PH-BFG	Boeing 747-406	KLM *City of Guayaquil*	
PH-BFH	Boeing 747-406 (SCD)	KLM *City of Hong Kong*	
PH-BFI	Boeing 747-406 (SCD)	KLM *City of Jakarta*	
PH-BFK	Boeing 747-406 (SCD)	KLM *City of Karachi*	
PH-BFL	Boeing 747-406	KLM *City of Lima*	

Notes	Reg.	Type	Owner or Operator
	PH-BFM	Boeing 747-406 (SCD)	KLM *City of Mexico*
	PH-BFN	Boeing 747-406	KLM *City of Nairobi*
	PH-BFO	Boeing 747-406 (SCD)	KLM *City of Orlando*
	PH-BFP	Boeing 747-406 (SCD)	KLM *City of Paramaribo*
	PH-BFR	Boeing 747-406 (SCD)	KLM *City of Rio de Janeiro*
	PH-BFS	Boeing 747-406 (SCD)	KLM *City of Seoul*
	PH-BFT	Boeing 747-406 (SCD)	KLM *City of Tokyo*
	PH-BFU	Boeing 747-406 (SCD)	KLM *City of Beijing*
	PH-BFV	Boeing 747-406	KLM *City of Vancouver*
	PH-BFW	Boeing 747-406	KLM *City of Shanghai*
	PH-BFY	Boeing 747-406	KLM *City of Johannesburg*
	PH-BGA	Boeing 737-8K2	KLM
	PH-BGB	Boeing 737-8K2	KLM *Whimbrel/Regenwulg*
	PH-BGC	Boeing 737-8K2	KLM
	PH-BGD	Boeing 737-706	KLM *Goldcrest/Goadhaantje*
	PH-BGE	Boeing 737-706	KLM *Ortolan Bunting/Ortolaan*
	PH-BGF	Boeing 737-7K2	KLM *Great White Heron/Grote Ziverreiger*
	PH-BGG	Boeing 737-706	KLM *King Eider/Koening Seider*
	PH-BGH	Boeing 737-7K2	KLM
	PH-BGI	Boeing 737-7K2	KLM *Vink/Finch*
	PH-BGK	Boeing 737-7K2	KLM
	PH-BGL	Boeing 737-7K2	KLM *Rietzangler/Warbler*
	PH-BGM	Boeing 737-7K2	KLM
	PH-BGN	Boeing 737-7K2	KLM
	PH-BGO	Boeing 737-7K2	KLM
	PH-BGP	Boeing 737-7K2	KLM
	PH-BGR	Boeing 737-7K2	KLM
	PH-BGT	Boeing 737-7K2	KLM
	PH-BPB	Boeing 737-4Y0	KLM *Jan Tinbergen*
	PH-BPC	Boeing 737-4Y0	KLM *Ernest Hemingway*
	PH-BQA	Boeing 777-206ER	KLM *Albert Plesman*
	PH-BQB	Boeing 777-206ER	KLM *Borobudur*
	PH-BQC	Boeing 777-206ER	KLM *Chichen-Itza*
	PH-BQD	Boeing 777-206ER	KLM *Darjeeling Highway*
	PH-BQE	Boeing 777-206ER	KLM *Epidaurus*
	PH-BQF	Boeing 777-206ER	KLM *Ferrara City*
	PH-BQG	Boeing 777-206ER	KLM *Galapagos Islands*
	PH-BQH	Boeing 777-206ER	KLM *Hadrian's Wall*
	PH-BQI	Boeing 777-206ER	KLM *Iguazu Falls*
	PH-BQK	Boeing 777-206ER	KLM *Mount Kilimanjaro*
	PH-BQL	Boeing 777-206ER	KLM *Litomysl Castle*
	PH-BQM	Boeing 777-206ER	KLM *Macchu Picchu*
	PH-BQN	Boeing 777-206ER	KLM *Nahanni National Park*
	PH-BQO	Boeing 777-206ER	KLM *Old Rauma*
	PH-BQP	Boeing 777-206ER	KLM *Pont du Gard*
	PH-BTA	Boeing 737-406	KLM *Fernao Magalhaes*
	PH-BTB	Boeing 737-406	KLM *Henry Hudson*
	PH-BTD	Boeing 737-306	KLM *James Cook*
	PH-BTE	Boeing 737-306	KLM *Roald Amundsen*
	PH-BTF	Boeing 737-406	KLM *Alexander von Humboldt*
	PH-BTG	Boeing 737-406	KLM *Henry Morton Stanley*
	PH-BVA	Boeing 777-306ER	KLM *National Park De Hoge Veluwe*
	PH-BVB	Boeing 777-306ER	KLM *Fulufjallet Ntional Park*
	PH-BVC	Boeing 777-306ER	KLM
	PH-BVD	Boeing 777-306ER	KLM
	PH-BVF	Boeing 777-306ER	KLM
	PH-BVG	Boeing 777-306ER	KLM
	PH-BXA	Boeing 737-8K2	KLM *Zwaan/Swan*
	PH-BXB	Boeing 737-8K2	KLM *Valk/Falcon*
	PH-BXC	Boeing 737-8K2	KLM *Korhoen/Grouse*
	PH-BXD	Boeing 737-8K2	KLM *Arend/Eagle*
	PH-BXE	Boeing 737-8K2	KLM *Harvik/Hawk*
	PH-BXF	Boeing 737-8K2	KLM *Zwallou/Swallow*
	PH-BXG	Boeing 737-8K2	KLM *Kraanvogel/Crane*
	PH-BXH	Boeing 737-8K2	KLM *Gans/Goose*
	PH-BXI	Boeing 737-8K2	KLM *Zilvermeeuw*
	PH-BXK	Boeing 737-8K2	KLM *Gierzwallou/Swift*
	PH-BXL	Boeing 737-8K2	KLM *Sperwer/Sparrow*
	PH-BXM	Boeing 737-8K2	KLM *Kluut/Avocet*
	PH-BXN	Boeing 737-8K2	KLM *Merel/Blackbird*
	PH-BXO	Boeing 737-9K2	KLM *Plevier/Plover*
	PH-BXP	Boeing 737-9K2	KLM *Meerkoet/Crested Coot*
	PH-BXR	Boeing 737-9K2	KLM *Nachtegaal/Nightingale*
	PH-BXS	Boeing 737-9K2	KLM *Buizerd/Buzzard*

Reg.	Type	Owner or Operator	Notes
PH-BXT	Boeing 737-9K2	KLM *Zeestern/Sea Tern*	
PH-BXU	Boeing 737-8BK	Transavia	
PH-BXV	Boeing 737-8K2	KLM *Roodborstje*	
PH-BXW	Boeing 737-8K2	Transavia	
PH-BXY	Boeing 737-8K2	KLM *Fuut/Grebe*	
PH-BXZ	Boeing 737-8K2	KLM	
PH-CKA	Boeing 747-406ERF	KLM Cargo/Martinair *Eendracht*	
PH-CKB	Boeing 747-406ERF	KLM Cargo/Martinair *Leeuwin*	
PH-CKC	Boeing 747-406ERF	KLM Cargo/Martinair *Oranje*	
PH-CKD	Boeing 747-406F	KLM Cargo/Martinair	
PH-DDZ	Douglas DC-3	Dutch Dakota Association	
PH-EZA	Embraer ERJ190-100STD	KLM CityHopper	
PH-EZB	Embraer ERJ190-100STD	KLM CityHopper	
PH-EZC	Embraer ERJ190-100STD	KLM CityHopper	
PH-EZD	Embraer ERJ190-100STD	KLM CityHopper	
PH-EZE	Embraer ERJ190-100STD	KLM CityHopper	
PH-EZF	Embraer ERJ190-100STD	KLM CityHopper	
PH-EZG	Embraer ERJ190-100STD	KLM Cityhopper	
PH-EZH	Embraer ERJ190-100STD	KLM Cityhopper	
PH-EZI	Embraer ERJ190-100STD	KLM CityHopper	
PH-EZK	Embraer ERJ190-100STD	KLM CityHopper	
PH-EZL	Embraer ERJ190-100STD	KLM CityHopper	
PH-EZM	Embraer ERJ190-100STD	KLM CityHopper	
PH-EZN	Embraer ERJ190-100STD	KLM CityHopper	
PH-EZO	Embraer ERJ190-100STD	KLM CityHopper	
PH-EZP	Embraer ERJ190-100STD	KLM CityHopper	
PH-EZR	Embraer ERJ190-100STD	KLM CityHopper	
PH-EZS	Embraer ERJ190-100STD	KLM CityHopper	
PH-HSB	Boeing 737-8K2	Transavia	
PH-HSC	Boeing 737-8K2	Transavia	
PH-HSD	Boeing 737-8K2	Transavia	
PH-HSE	Boeing 737-8K2	Transavia	
PH-HZC	Boeing 737-8K2	Transavia	
PH-HZD	Boeing 737-8K2	Transavia	
PH-HZE	Boeing 737-8K2	Transavia *City of Rhodos*	
PH-HZF	Boeing 737-8K2	Transavia	
PH-HZG	Boeing 737-8K2	Transavia	
PH-HZI	Boeing 737-8K2	Transavia	
PH-HZJ	Boeing 737-8K2	Transavia	
PH-HZK	Boeing 737-8K2	Transavia	
PH-HZL	Boeing 737-8K2	Transavia	
PH-HZM	Boeing 737-8K2	Transavia	
PH-HZN	Boeing 737-8K2	Transavia	
PH-HZO	Boeing 737-8K2	Transavia	
PH-HZW	Boeing 737-8K2	Transavia	
PH-HZX	Boeing 737-8K2	Transavia	
PH-HZY	Boeing 737-8K2	Transavia	
PH-JCH	Fokker 70	KLM CityHopper	
PH-JCT	Fokker 70	KLM CityHopper	
PH-KCA	McD Douglas MD-11	KLM *Amy Johnson*	
PH-KCB	McD Douglas MD-11	KLM *Maria Montessori*	
PH-KCC	McD Douglas MD-11	KLM *Marie Curie*	
PH-KCD	McD Douglas MD-11	KLM *Florence Nightingale*	
PH-KCE	McD Douglas MD-11	KLM *Audrey Hepburn*	
PH-KCF	McD Douglas MD-11	KLM *Annie Romein*	
PH-KCG	McD Douglas MD-11	KLM *Maria Callas*	
PH-KCH	McD Douglas MD-11	KLM *Anna Pavlova*	
PH-KCI	McD Douglas MD-11	KLM *Ingrid Bergman*	
PH-KCK	McD Douglas MD-11	KLM *Marie Servaes*	
PH-KZA	Fokker 70	KLM CityHopper	
PH-KZB	Fokker 70	KLM CityHopper	
PH-KZC	Fokker 70	KLM CityHopper	
PH-KZD	Fokker 70	KLM CityHopper	
PH-KZE	Fokker 70	KLM CityHopper	
PH-KZF	Fokker 70	KLM CityHopper	
PH-KZG	Fokker 70	KLM CityHopper	
PH-KZH	Fokker 70	KLM CityHopper	
PH-KZI	Fokker 70	KLM CityHopper	
PH-KZK	Fokker 70	KLM CityHopper	
PH-KZL	Fokker 70	KLM CityHopper	
PH-KZM	Fokker 70	KLM CityHopper	
PH-KZN	Fokker 70	KLM CityHopper	
PH-KZO	Fokker 70	KLM CityHopper	
PH-KZP	Fokker 70	KLM CityHopper	

Notes	Reg.	Type	Owner or Operator
	PH-KZR	Fokker 70	KLM CityHopper
	PH-KZS	Fokker 70	KLM CityHopper
	PH-KZT	Fokker 70	KLM CityHopper
	PH-KZU	Fokker 70	KLM Cityhopper
	PH-KZV	Fokker 70	KLM Cityhopper
	PH-KZW	Fokker 70	KLM CityHopper
	PH-MCI	Boeing 767-31AER	Martinair *Prins Pieter-Christiaan*
	PH-MCJ	Boeing 767-33AER	Martinair
	PH-MCL	Boeing 767-31AER	Martinair *Koningin Beatrix*
	PH-MCM	Boeing 767-31AER	Martinair *Prins Floris*
	PH-MCP	McD Douglas MD-11CF	Martinair Cargo
	PH-MCR	McD Douglas MD-11CF	Martinair Cargo
	PH-MCS	McD Douglas MD-11CF	Martinair Cargo
	PH-MCT	McD Douglas MD-11CF	Martinair Cargo
	PH-MCU	McD Douglas MD-11F	Martinair Cargo *Prinses Maxima*
	PH-MCW	McD Douglas MD-11CF	Martinair Cargo
	PH-MCY	McD Douglas MD-11F	Martinair Cargo
	PH-MPR	Boeing 747-412BCF	Martinair Cargo
	PH-OFL	Fokker 100	KLM CityHopper
	PH-OFM	Fokker 100	KLM CityHopper
	PH-OFN	Fokker 100	KLM CityHopper
	PH-OFO	Fokker 100	KLM CityHopper
	PH-OFP	Fokker 100	KLM CityHopper
	PH-OYI	Boeing 767-304ER	TUI Airlines Nederland/Arkefly
	PH-PBA	Douglas DC-3C	Dutch Dakota Association
	PH-TFA	Boeing 737-8FH	TUI Airlines Nederland/Arkefly
	PH-TFB	Boeing 737-8K5	TUI Airlines Nederland/Arkefly
	PH-TFC	Boeing 737-8K5	TUI Airlines Nederland/Arkefly
	PH-WXA	Fokker 70	KLM CityHopper
	PH-WXC	Fokker 70	KLM CityHopper
	PH-WXD	Fokker 70	KLM CityHopper
	PH-XRA	Boeing 737-7K2	Transavia *Leontien van Moorsel*
	PH-XRB	Boeing 737-7K2	Transavia
	PH-XRC	Boeing 737-7K2	Transavia
	PH-XRD	Boeing 737-7K2	Transavia
	PH-XRE	Boeing 737-7K2	Transavia
	PH-XRV	Boeing 737-7K2	Transavia
	PH-XRW	Boeing 737-7K2	Transavia
	PH-XRX	Boeing 737-7K2	Transavia
	PH-XRY	Boeing 737-7K2	Transavia
	PH-XRZ	Boeing 737-7K2	Transavia

PP/PR/PT (Brazil)

Notes	Reg.	Type	Owner or Operator
	PT-MUA	Boeing 777-32WER	TAM Linhas aereas
	PT-MUB	Boeing 777-32WER	TAM Linhas aereas
	PT-MUC	Boeing 777-32WER	TAM Linhas aereas
	PT-MUD	Boeing 777-32WER	TAM Linhas aereas

RA (Russia)

Notes	Reg.	Type	Owner or Operator
	RA-82010	An-124	Polet
	RA-82042	An-124	Volga-Dnepr
	RA-82043	An-124	Volga-Dnepr
	RA-82044	An-124	Volga-Dnepr
	RA-82045	An-124	Volga-Dnepr
	RA-82046	An-124	Volga-Dnepr
	RA-82047	An-124	Volga-Dnepr
	RA-82068	An-124	Polet
	RA-82074	An-124	Volga-Dnepr
	RA-82075	An-124	Polet
	RA-82077	An-124	Polet
	RA-82078	An-124	Volga-Dnepr
	RA-82079	An-124	Volga-Dnepr
	RA-82080	An-124	Polet
	RA-82081	An-124	Volga-Dnepr

S2 (Bangladesh)

Notes	Reg.	Type	Owner or Operator
	S2-ACO	Douglas DC-10-30	Bangladesh Biman *City of Shah Makhdum (R.A.)*
	S2-ACP	Douglas DC-10-30	Bangladesh Biman *The City of Dhaka*

Reg.	Type	Owner or Operator	Notes
S2-ACQ	Douglas DC-10-30	Bangladesh Biman *The City of Hazarat-Shah Jalal (R.A.)*	
S2-ACR	Douglas DC-10-30	Bangladesh Biman *The New Era*	
S2-ADF	Airbus A.310-325	Bangladesh Biman *City of Chittagong*	
S2-ADK	Airbus A.310-324	Bangladesh Biman	
S2-AEH	McD Douglas MD-83	United Airways	
S2-AEU	McD Douglas MD-83	United Airways	
S2-AFF	Airbus A.310-325	United Airways	
S2-AFT	Airbus A.310-325	Bangladesh Biman	

S5 (Slovenia)

Reg.	Type	Owner or Operator	Notes
S5-AAD	Canadair CRJ200LR	Adria Airways	
S5-AAE	Canadair CRJ200LR	Adria Airways	
S5-AAF	Canadair CRJ200LR	Adria Airways	
S5-AAG	Canadair CRJ200LR	Adria Airways	
S5-AAH	Canadair CRJ100LR	Adria Airways	
S5-AAI	Canadair CRJ200LR	Adria Airways	
S5-AAJ	Canadair CRJ200LR	Adria Airways	
S5-AAK	Canadair CRJ900LR	Adria Airways	
S5-AAL	Canadair CRJ900LR	Adria Airways	
S5-AAN	Canadair CRJ900LR	Adria Airways	
S5-AAO	Canadair CRJ900LR	Adria Airways	
S5-AAP	Airbus A.319-132	Adria Airways	
S5-AAR	Airbus A.319-132	Adria Airways	
S5-AAS	Airbus A.319-132	Adria Airways	

S7 (Seychelles)

Reg.	Type	Owner or Operator	Notes
S7-AHM	Boeing 767-37DER	Air Seychelles *Vallee de Mai*	
S7-ASY	Boeing 767-3Q8ER	Air Seychelles *Aldabra*	
S7-FCS	Boeing 767-306ER	Air Seychelles	
S7-ILF	Boeing 767-205ER	Air Seychelles	
S7-SEZ	Boeing 767-219ER	Air Seychelles	

SE (Sweden)

Reg.	Type	Owner or Operator	Notes
SE-DIB	McD Douglas MD-87	SAS	
SE-DIK	McD Douglas MD-82	SAS *Stenkil Viking*	
SE-DIL	McD Douglas MD-82	SAS *Tord Viking*	
SE-DIN	McD Douglas MD-82	SAS *Eskil Viking*	
SE-DIP	McD Douglas MD-87	SAS *Margret Viking*	
SE-DIR	McD Douglas MD-82	SAS *Nora Viking*	
SE-DIS	McD Douglas MD-82	SAS *Sigmund Viking*	
SE-DIU	McD Douglas MD-87	City Airline	
SE-DMB	McD Douglas MD-81	SAS *Bjarne Viking*	
SE-DMC	McD Douglas MD-87	City Airline	
SE-DMK	McD Douglas MD-87	City Airline	
SE-DMT	McD Douglas MD-81	Air Sweden	
SE-DNX	Boeing 737-683	SAS	
SE-DOR	Boeing 737-683	SAS	
SE-DTH	Boeing 737-683	SAS *Vile Viking*	
SE-DZB	Embraer RJ145EP	City Airline	
SE-DZK	Boeing 737-804	TUIfly Nordic	
SE-DZN	Boeing 737-804	TUIfly Nordic	
SE-DZV	Boeing 737-804	TUIfly Nordic	
SE-KXP	BAe ATP	West Air Sweden	
SE-LGX	BAe ATP	West Air Sweden	
SE-LGY	BAe ATP	West Air Sweden	
SE-LHX	BAe ATP	West Air Sweden	
SE-LHZ	BAe ATP	West Air Sweden	
SE-LNX	BAe ATP	West Air Sweden	
SE-LNY	BAe ATP	West Air Sweden	
SE-LPU	BAe ATP	West Air Sweden	
SE-LPX	BAe ATP	West Air Sweden	
SE-MAF	BAe ATP	West Air Sweden	
SE-MAH	BAe ATP	West Air Sweden	
SE-MAJ	BAe ATP	West Air Sweden	
SE-MAN	BAe ATP	West Air Sweden	
SE-MAP	BAe ATP	West Air Sweden	
SE-MAR	BAe ATP	West Air Sweden	

Notes	Reg.	Type	Owner or Operator
	SE-MAY	BAe ATP	West Air Sweden
	SE-RAA	Embraer RJ135ER	City Airline *City of Gothenburg*
	SE-RAB	Embraer RJ135LR	City Airline *City of Linkoping*
	SE-RAC	Embraer RJ145LR	City Airline
	SE-RAD	Embraer RJ145EU	City Airline
	SE-RAE	Embraer RJ145EU	City Airline
	SE-RDN	Airbus A.321-231	Novair Airlines
	SE-RDO	Airbus A.321-231	Novair Airlines
	SE-RDP	Airbus A.321-231	Novair Airlines
	SE-REE	Airbus A.330-343X	SAS *Sigrid Viking*
	SE-REF	Airbus A.330-343X	SAS *Erik Viking*
	SE-RFO	Boeing 757-204	TUIfly Nordic
	SE-RFP	Boeing 757-204	TUIfly Nordic
	SE-RFS	Boeing 767-304ER	TUIfly Nordic
	SE-RIA	Embraer RJ145MP	City Airline
	SE-RJM	Airbus A.320-212	Air Sweden
	SE-RJN	Airbus A.320-231	Air Sweden
	SE-RJP	McD Douglas MD-82	Air Sweden

SP (Poland)

Notes	Reg.	Type	Owner or Operator
	SP-LDA	Embraer RJ170 100ST	LOT
	SP-LDB	Embraer RJ170 100ST	LOT
	SP-LDC	Embraer RJ170 100ST	LOT
	SP-LDD	Embraer RJ170 100ST	LOT
	SP-LDE	Embraer RJ170 100LR	LOT
	SP-LDF	Embraer RJ170 100LR	LOT
	SP-LDG	Embraer RJ170 100LR	LOT
	SP-LDH	Embraer RJ170 100LR	LOT
	SP-LDI	Embraer RJ170 100LR	LOT
	SP-LDK	Embraer RJ170 100LR	LOT
	SP-LGE	Embraer RJ145LR	LOT
	SP-LGF	Embraer RJ145MP	LOT
	SP-LGG	Embraer RJ145MP	LOT
	SP-LGH	Embraer RJ145MP	LOT
	SP-LGO	Embraer RJ145MP	LOT
	SP-LIA	Embraer RJ170-200STD	LOT
	SP-LIB	Embraer RJ170-200STD	LOT
	SP-LIC	Embraer RJ170-200STD	LOT
	SP-LID	Embraer RJ170-200STD	LOT
	SP-LIE	Embraer RJ170-200STD	LOT
	SP-LIF	Embraer RJ170-200STD	LOT
	SP-LII	Embraer RJ170-200STD	LOT
	SP-LIK	Embraer RJ170-200STD	LOT
	SP-LIL	Embraer RJ170-200STD	LOT
	SP-LIM	Embraer RJ170-200STD	LOT
	SP-LIN	Embraer RJ170-200STD	LOT
	SP-LIO	Embraer RJ170-200STD	LOT
	SP-LKC	Boeing 737-55D	LOT
	SP-LKD	Boeing 737-55D	LOT
	SP-LKE	Boeing 737-55D	LOT
	SP-LKF	Boeing 737-55D	LOT
	SP-LLB	Boeing 737-45D	LOT
	SP-LLC	Boeing 737-45D	LOT
	SP-LLE	Boeing 737-45D	LOT
	SP-LLF	Boeing 737-45D	LOT
	SP-LLG	Boeing 737-45D	LOT
	SP-LLK	Boeing 737-4Q8	LOT
	SP-LLL	Boeing 737-4Q8	LOT
	SP-LNA	Embraer RJ190-200LR	LOT
	SP-LNB	Embraer RJ190-200LR	LOT
	SP-LNC	Embraer RJ190-200LR	LOT
	SP-LND	Embraer RJ190-200LR	LOT
	SP-LPA	Boeing 767-35DER	LOT *Warszawa*
	SP-LPB	Boeing 767-35DER	LOT *Gdansk*
	SP-LPC	Boeing 767-35DER	LOT *Poznan*
	SP-LPE	Boeing 767-341ER	LOT
	SP-LPF	Boeing 767-319ER	LOT
	SP-LPG	Boeing 767-306ER	LOT

SU (Egypt)

Reg.	Type	Owner or Operator	Notes
SU-BDG	Airbus A.300B4-203F	EgyptAir Cargo *Toshki*	
SU-GAC	Airbus A.300B4-203F	EgyptAir Cargo *New Valley*	
SU-GAS	Airbus A.300F4-622RF	EgyptAir Cargo *Cheops*	
SU-GAY	Airbus A.300B4-622RF	EgyptAir Cargo *Seti I*	
SU-GBM	Airbus A.340-212	EgyptAir *Osirus Express*	
SU-GBN	Airbus A.340-212	EgyptAir *Cleo Express*	
SU-GBO	Airbus A.340-212	EgyptAir *Hathor Express*	
SU-GBP	Boeing 777-266ER	EgyptAir *Nefertiti*	
SU-GBR	Boeing 777-266ER	EgyptAir *Nefertari*	
SU-GBS	Boeing 777-266ER	EgyptAir *Tyie*	
SU-GBT	Airbus A.321-231	EgyptAir *Red Sea*	
SU-GBU	Airbus A.321-231	EgyptAir	
SU-GBV	Airbus A.321-231	EgyptAir	
SU-GBW	Airbus A.321-231	EgyptAir *The Nile*	
SU-GBX	Boeing 777-266ER	EgyptAir *Neit*	
SU-GBY	Boeing 777-266ER	EgyptAir *Titi*	
SU-GCE	Airbus A.330-243	EgyptAir	
SU-GCF	Airbus A.330-243	EgyptAir	
SU-GCG	Airbus A.330-243	EgyptAir	
SU-GCH	Airbus A.330-243	EgyptAir	
SU-GCI	Airbus A.330-243	EgyptAir	
SU-GCJ	Airbus A.330-243	EgyptAir	
SU-GCK	Airbus A.330-243	EgyptAir	
SU-GDL	Boeing 777-36NER	EgyptAir	
SU-GDM	Boeing 777-36NER	EgyptAir	
SU-GDN	Boeing 777-36NER	Egyptair	
SU-GDO	Boeing 777-36NER	Egyptair	
SU-GDP	Boeing 777-36NER	Egyptair	
SU-GDR	Boeing 777-36NER	Egyptair	
SU-KBA	Airbus A.320-212	Koral Blue Airlines	
SU-KBB	Airbus A.319-112	Koral Blue Airlines	
SU-KBD	Airbus A.320-214	Koral Blue Airlines	
SU-KBE	Airbus A.320-214	Koral Blue Airlines	

SX (Greece)

Reg.	Type	Owner or Operator	Notes
SX-DGA	Airbus A.321-231	Aegean Airlines	
SX-DGB	Airbus A.320-232	Aegean Airlines	
SX-DVG	Airbus A.320-232	Aegean Airlines *Ethos*	
SX-DVH	Airbus A.320-232	Aegean Airlines *Nostos*	
SX-DVI	Airbus A.320-232	Aegean Airlines *Kinesis*	
SX-DVJ	Airbus A.320-232	Aegean Airlines *Kinesis*	
SX-DVK	Airbus A.320-232	Aegean Airlines	
SX-DVL	Airbus A.320-232	Aegean Airlines	
SX-DVM	Airbus A.320-232	Aegean Airlines	
SX-DVN	Airbus A.320-232	Aegean Airlines	
SX-DVO	Airbus A.321-232	Aegean Airlines *Philoxenia*	
SX-DVP	Airbus A.321-232	Aegean Airlines	
SX-DVQ	Airbus A.320-232	Aegean Airlines	
SX-DVR	Airbus A.320-232	Aegean Airlines	
SX-DVS	Airbus A.320-232	Aegean Airlines	
SX-DVT	Airbus A.320-232	Aegean Airlines	
SX-DVU	Airbus A.320-232	Aegean Airlines *Pheidias*	
SX-DVV	Airbus A.320-232	Aegean Airlines *Cleisthenes*	
SX-DVW	Airbus A.320-232	Aegean Airlines	
SX-DVX	Airbus A.320-232	Aegean Airlines	
SX-DVY	Airbus A.320-232	Aegean Airlines	
SX-DVZ	Airbus A.321-232	Aegean Airlines	
SX-OAF	Airbus A.319-112	Olympic Air	
SX-OAG	Airbus A.319-112	Olympic Air	
SX-OAH	Airbus A.320-232	Olympic Air	
SX-OAI	Airbus A.320-232	Olympic Air	
SX-OAJ	Airbus A.319-112	Olympic Air	
SX-OAM	Airbus A.320-232	Olympic Air	
SX-OAN	Airbus A.319-132	Olympic Air	
SX-OAO	Airbus A.319-132	Olympic Air	
SX-OAP	Airbus A.320-232	Olympic Air	
SX-OAQ	Airbus A.320-232	Olympic Air	
SX-OAR	Airbus A.320-232	Olympic Air	
SX-OAS	Airbus A.320-232	Olympic Air	

Notes	Reg.	Type	Owner or Operator
	SX-OAT	Airbus A.320-214	Olympic Air
	SX-OAU	Airbus A.320-214	Olympic Air
	SX-SMS	McD Douglas MD-83	Viking Hellas Airlines
	SX-SMT	Airbus A.320-231	Viking Hellas Airlines
	SX-SMU	Airbus A.320-231	Viking Hellas Airlines

TC (Turkey)

Notes	Reg.	Type	Owner or Operator
	TC-AAD	Boeing 737-5Q8	Pegasus Airlines
	TC-AAE	Boeing 737-82R	Pegasus Airlines *Hayirli*
	TC-AAF	Boeing 737-58E	Pegasus Airlines
	TC-AAG	Boeing 737-5L9	Pegasus Airlines
	TC-AAH	Boeing 737-82R	Pegasus Airlines
	TC-AAI	Boeing 737-82R	Pegasus Airlines
	TC-AAJ	Boeing 737-82R	Pegasus Airlines
	TC-AAK	Boeing 737-8FH	Pegasus Airlines
	TC-AAL	Boeing 737-82R	Pegasus Airlines
	TC-AAN	Boeing 737-82R	Pegasus Airlines
	TC-AAO	Boeing 737-86N	Pegasus Airlines
	TC-AAP	Boeing 737-86N	Pegasus Airlines
	TC-AAR	Boeing 737-86N	Pegasus Airlines
	TC-AAS	Boeing 737-82R	Pegasus Airlines
	TC-AAT	Boeing 737-82R	Pegasus Airlines
	TC-AAU	Boeing 737-82R	Pegasus Airlines
	TC-AAV	Boeing 737-82R	Pegasus Airlines
	TC-AAY	Boeing 737-82R	Pegasus Airlines
	TC-AAZ	Boeing 737-82R	Pegasus Airlines
	TC-ABK	Airbus A.300B4-203F	ULS Cargo *Adiyaman*
	TC-ABP	Boeing 737-82R	Pegasus Airlines
	TC-ACD	Airbus A.300B4-203F	ACT Cargo
	TC-ACE	Airbus A.300B4-203F	ACT Cargo
	TC-ACP	Boeing 737-82R	Pegasus Airlines
	TC-ACU	Airbus A.300B4-203F	ACT Cargo
	TC-ACY	Airbus A.300B4-203F	ACT Cargo
	TC-ACZ	Airbus A.300B4-103F	ACT Cargo
	TC-ADP	Boeing 737-82R	Pegasus Airlines
	TC-AGK	Airbus A.300B4-203F	ULS Cargo
	TC-APD	Boeing 737-42R	Pegasus Airlines
	TC-APH	Boeing 737-8S3	Pegasus Airlines
	TC-API	Boeing 737-86N	Pegasus Airlines
	TC-APJ	Boeing 737-86N	Pegasus Airlines
	TC-APR	Boeing 737-4Y0	Pegasus Airlines
	TC-APU	Boeing 737-82R	Pegasus Airlines
	TC-FBE	Airbus A.320-212	Freebird Airlines
	TC-FBF	Airbus A.320-212	Freebird Airlines
	TC-FBG	Airbus A.321-131	Freebird Airlines
	TC-FBH	Airbus A.320-214	Freebird Airlines
	TC-FBJ	Airbus A.320-232	Freebird Airlines
	TC-FBR	Airbus A.320-232	Freebird Airlines
	TC-FBT	Airbus A.321-131	Freebird Airlines
	TC-JCT	Airbus A.310-304F	Turkish Airlines *Samsun*
	TC-JCV	Airbus A.310-304F	Turkish Airlines *Aras*
	TC-JCY	Airbus A.310-304F	Turkish Airlines *Coruh*
	TC-JCZ	Airbus A.310-304F	Turkish Airlines *Ergene*
	TC-JDG	Boeing 737-4Y0	Turkish Airlines *Marmaris*
	TC-JDJ	Airbus A.340-311	Turkish Airlines *Istanbul*
	TC-JDK	Airbus A.340-311	Turkish Airlines *Diyarbakir*
	TC-JDL	Airbus A.340-311	Turkish Airlines *Ankara*
	TC-JDM	Airbus A.340-311	Turkish Airlines *Izmir*
	TC-JDN	Airbus A.340-313X	Turkish Airlines *Adana*
	TC-JFC	Boeing 737-8F2	Turkish Airlines *Diyarbakir*
	TC-JFD	Boeing 737-8F2	Turkish Airlines *Rize*
	TC-JFE	Boeing 737-8F2	Turkish Airlines *Hatay*
	TC-JFF	Boeing 737-8F2	Turkish Airlines *Afyon*
	TC-JFG	Boeing 737-8F2	Turkish Airlines *Mardi*
	TC-JFH	Boeing 737-8F2	Turkish Airlines *Igdir*
	TC-JFI	Boeing 737-8F2	Turkish Airlines *Sivas*
	TC-JFJ	Boeing 737-8F2	Turkish Airlines *Agri*
	TC-JFL	Boeing 737-8F2	Turkish Airlines *Ordu*
	TC-JFM	Boeing 737-8F2	Turkish Airlines *Nigde*
	TC-JFN	Boeing 737-8F2	Turkish Airlines *Bitlis*
	TC-JFO	Boeing 737-8F2	Turkish Airlines *Batman*
	TC-JFT	Boeing 737-8F2	Turkish Airlines *Kastamonu*

Reg.	Type	Owner or Operator	Notes
TC-JFU	Boeing 737-8F2	Turkish Airlines *Elazig*	
TC-JFV	Boeing 737-8F2	Turkish Airlines *Tunceli*	
TC-JFY	Boeing 737-8F2	Turkish Airlines *Manisa*	
TC-JFZ	Boeing 737-8F2	Turkish Airlines *Bolu*	
TC-JGB	Boeing 737-8F2	Turkish Airlines *Eskisehir*	
TC-JGD	Boeing 737-8F2	Turkish Airlines *Nevsehir*	
TC-JGG	Boeing 737-8F2	Turkish Airlines *Erzincan*	
TC-JGH	Boeing 737-8F2	Turkish Airlines *Tokat*	
TC-JGI	Boeing 737-8F2	Turkish Airlines *Siirt*	
TC-JGJ	Boeing 737-8F2	Turkish Airlines *Ayidn*	
TC-JGK	Boeing 737-8F2	Turkish Airlines *Kirsehir*	
TC-JGL	Boeing 737-8F2	Turkish Airlines *Karaman*	
TC-JGM	Boeing 737-8F2	Turkish Airlines *Hakkari*	
TC-JGN	Boeing 737-8F2	Turkish Airlines *Bilecik*	
TC-JGO	Boeing 737-8F2	Turkish Airlines *Kilis*	
TC-JGP	Boeing 737-8F2	Turkish Airlines *Bartin*	
TC-JGR	Boeing 737-8F2	Turkish Airlines *Usak*	
TC-JGS	Boeing 737-8F2	Turkish Airlines	
TC-JGT	Boeing 737-8F2	Turkish Airlines *Avanos*	
TC-JGU	Boeing 737-8F2	Turkish Airlines *Bodrum*	
TC-JGV	Boeing 737-8F2	Turkish Airlines *Cesme*	
TC-JGY	Boeing 737-8F2	Turkish Airlines *Managvat*	
TC-JGZ	Boeing 737-8F2	Turkish Airlines	
TC-JHA	Boeing 737-8F2	Turkish Airlines	
TC-JHB	Boeing 737-8F2	Turkish Airlines	
TC-JHC	Boeing 737-8F2	Turkish Airlines *Iskenderun*	
TC-JHD	Boeing 737-8F2	Turkish Airlines	
TC-JHE	Boeing 737-8F2	Turkish Airlines *Burhaniye*	
TC-JHF	Boeing 737-8F2	Turkish Airlines *Ayvalik*	
TC-JHJ	Boeing 737-86Q	Turkish Airlines	
TC-JIH	Airbus A.340-313X	Turkish Airlines *Kocaeli*	
TC-JII	Airbus A.340-313X	Turkish Airlines *Aydin*	
TC-JIJ	Airbus A.340-313X	Turkish Airlines	
TC-JIK	Airbus A.340-313X	Turkish Airlines	
TC-JJA	Boeing 777-35RER	Turkish Airlines	
TC-JJB	Boeing 777-35RER	Turkish Airlines	
TC-JJC	Boeing 777-35RER	Turkish Airlines	
TC-JJD	Boeing 777-35RER	Turkish Airlines	
TC-JJE	Boeing 777-3F2ER	Turkish Airlines	
TC-JJF	Boeing 777-3F2ER	Turkish Airlines	
TC-JJG	Boeing 777-3F2ER	Turkish Airlines	
TC-JJH	Boeing 777-3F2ER	Turkish Airlines	
TC-JJI	Boeing 777-3F2ER	Turkish Airlines	
TC-JJJ	Boeing 777-3F2ER	Turkish Airlines	
TC-JJK	Boeing 777-3F2ER	Turkish Airlines	
TC-JJL	Boeing 777-3F2ER	Turkish Airlines	
TC-JJM	Boeing 777-3F2ER	Turkish Airlines	
TC-JJN	Boeing 777-3F2ER	Turkish Airlines	
TC-JJO	Boeing 777-3F2ER	Turkish Airlines	
TC-JJP	Boeing 777-3F2ER	Turkish Airlines	
TC-JKJ	Boeing 737-752	Turkish Airlines *Eyup*	
TC-JKK	Boeing 737-752	Turkish Airlines	
TC-JKN	Boeing 737-752	Turkish Airlines	
TC-JKO	Boeing 737-752	Turkish Airlines	
TC-JKR	Boeing 737-7GL	Turkish Airlines	
TC-JKS	Boeing 737-73V	Turkish Airlines	
TC-JKT	Boeing 737-73V	Turkish Airlines	
TC-JLJ	Airbus A.320-232	Turkish Airlines *Sirnak*	
TC-JLK	Airbus A.320-232	Turkish Airlines *Kirklareli*	
TC-JLL	Airbus A.320-232	Turkish Airlines *Duzce*	
TC-JLM	Airbus A.319-132	Turkish Airlines	
TC-JLN	Airbus A.319-132	Turkish Airlines	
TC-JLO	Airbus A.319-132	Turkish Airlines *Ahlat*	
TC-JLP	Airbus A.319-132	Turkish Airlines *Koycegiz*	
TC-JLR	Airbus A.319-132	Turkish Airlines	
TC-JMC	Airbus A.321-231	Turkish Airlines *Aksaray*	
TC-JMD	Airbus A.321-231	Turkish Airlines *Cankiri*	
TC-JME	Airbus A.321-211	Turkish Airlines *Burdur*	
TC-JMF	Airbus A.321-211	Turkish Airlines *Bingol*	
TC-JMH	Airbus A.321-232	Turkish Airlines	
TC-JMI	Airbus A.321-232	Turkish Airlines	
TC-JMJ	Airbus A.321-232	Turkish Airlines	
TC-JMK	Airbus A.321-232	Turkish Airlines	
TC-JML	Airbus A.321-231	Turkish Airlines *Eminonu*	

Notes	Reg.	Type	Owner or Operator
	TC-JMM	Airbus A.321-232	Turkish Airlines
	TC-JMN	Airbus A.321-232	Turkish Airlines
	TC-JMO	Airbus A.321-232	Turkish Airlines
	TC-JMP	Airbus A.321-232	Turkish Airlines
	TC-JMQ	Airbus A.321-232	Turkish Airlines
	TC-JNA	Airbus A.330-203	Turkish Airlines *Gaziantep*
	TC-JNB	Airbus A.330-203	Turkish Airlines *Konya*
	TC-JNC	Airbus A.330-203	Turkish Airlines *Bursa*
	TC-JND	Airbus A.330-203	Turkish Airlines *Antalya*
	TC-JNE	Airbus A.330-203	Turkish Airlines *Kayseri*
	TC-JNF	Airbus A.330-203	Turkish Airlines *Eskisehir*
	TC-JNG	Airbus A.330-203	Turkish Airlines
	TC-JNH	Airbus A.330-343X	Turkish Airlines *Topkapi*
	TC-JNI	Airbus A.330-343X	Turkish Airlines *Konak*
	TC-JNJ	Airbus A.330-343X	Turkish Airlines
	TC-JNK	Airbus A.330-343X	Turkish Airlines
	TC-JPA	Airbus A.320-232	Turkish Airlines *Mus*
	TC-JPB	Airbus A.320-232	Turkish Airlines *Rize*
	TC-JPC	Airbus A.320-232	Turkish Airlines *Erzurum*
	TC-JPD	Airbus A.320-232	Turkish Airlines *Isparta*
	TC-JPE	Airbus A.320-232	Turkish Airlines *Gumushane*
	TC-JPF	Airbus A.320-232	Turkish Airlines *Yozgat*
	TC-JPG	Airbus A.320-232	Turkish Airlines *Osmaniye*
	TC-JPH	Airbus A.320-232	Turkish Airlines *Kars*
	TC-JPI	Airbus A.320-232	Turkish Airlines
	TC-JPJ	Airbus A.320-232	Turkish Airlines *Edremit*
	TC-JPK	Airbus A.320-232	Turkish Airlines *Erdek*
	TC-JPL	Airbus A.320-232	Turkish Airlines *Goreme*
	TC-JPM	Airbus A.320-232	Turkish Airlines *Harput*
	TC-JPN	Airbus A.320-232	Turkish Airlines *Sarikamis*
	TC-JPO	Airbus A.320-232	Turkish Airlines *Kemer*
	TC-JPP	Airbus A.320-232	Turkish Airlines *Harran*
	TC-JPR	Airbus A.320-232	Turkish Airlines *Kusadasi*
	TC-JPS	Airbus A.320-232	Turkish Airlines
	TC-JPT	Airbus A.320-232	Turkish Airlines
	TC-JPU	Airbus A.320-214	Turkish Airlines
	TC-JPV	Airbus A.320-214	Turkish Airlines
	TC-JPY	Airbus A.320-214	Turkish Airlines
	TC-JRA	Airbus A.321-231	Turkish Airlines *Kutayha*
	TC-JRB	Airbus A.321-231	Turkish Airlines *Sanliurfa*
	TC-JRC	Airbus A.321-231	Turkish Airlines *Sakarya*
	TC-JRD	Airbus A.321-231	Turkish Airlines *Balikesir*
	TC-JRE	Airbus A.321-231	Turkish Airlines *Trabzon*
	TC-JRF	Airbus A.321-231	Turkish Airlines
	TC-JRG	Airbus A.321-231	Turkish Airlines
	TC-JRH	Airbus A.321-231	Turkish Airlines *Yalova*
	TC-JRI	Airbus A.321-232	Turkish Airlines *Adiyaman*
	TC-JRJ	Airbus A.321-232	Turkish Airlines *Corum*
	TC-JRK	Airbus A.321-231	Turkish Airlines *Batman*
	TC-JRL	Airbus A.321-231	Turkish Airlines *Tarsus*
	TC-LER	Airbus A.310-308F	ULS Cargo *Aras*
	TC-MCA	Airbus A.300B4-605R	MNG Cargo
	TC-MCB	Airbus A.300B4-203F	MNG Cargo
	TC-MCF	Boeing 737-4K5F	MNG Cargo
	TC-MCI	Boeing 737-4K5F	MNG Cargo
	TC-MNB	Airbus A.300B4-203F	MNG Cargo
	TC-MNC	Airbus A.300B4-203F	MNG Cargo
	TC-MND	Airbus A.300B4-203F	MNG Cargo
	TC-MNJ	Airbus A.300B4-203F	MNG Cargo
	TC-MNU	Airbus A.300B4-203F	MNG Cargo
	TC-MNV	Airbus A.300B4-605R	MNG Cargo
	TC-OAE	Airbus A.321-231	Onur Air
	TC-OAF	Airbus A.321-231	Onur Air
	TC-OAI	Airbus A.321-231	Onur Air
	TC-OAK	Airbus A.321-231	Onur Air
	TC-OAL	Airbus A.321-231	Onur Air
	TC-OAN	Airbus A.321-231	Onur Air
	TC-OBD	Airbus A.320-232	Onur Air
	TC-OBE	Airbus A.320-232	Onur Air
	TC-OBF	Airbus A.321-231	Onur Air
	TC-OBG	Airbus A.320-233	Onur Air
	TC-OBH	Airbus A.320-233	Onur Air
	TC-OBI	Airbus A.320-233	Onur Air
	TC-OGJ	Airbus A.320-232	Onur Air

Reg.	Type	Owner or Operator	Notes
TC-ONJ	Airbus A.321-131	Onur Air	
TC-ONS	Airbus A.321-131	Onur Air	
TC-ONM	McD Douglas MD-88	Onur Air *Yasemin*	
TC-ONN	McD Douglas MD-88	Onur Air *Ece*	
TC-SGF	Boeing 737-83N	Saga Airlines	
TC-SGG	Boeing 737-83N	Saga Airlines	
TC-SGH	Boeing 737-86J	Saga Airlines	
TC-SGI	Boeing 737-86J	Saga Airlines	
TC-SGJ	Airbus A.330-343X	Turkish Airlines *Trabzon*	
TC-SGK	Boeing 737-8S3	Saga Airlines	
TC-SGL	Boeing 737-8S3	Saga Airlines	
TC-SNB	Boeing 757-2Q8	SunExpress	
TC-SNC	Boeing 757-2Q8	SunExpress	
TC-SND	Boeing 757-2Q8	SunExpress	
TC-SNE	Boeing 737-8HX	SunExpress	
TC-SNF	Boeing 737-8HC	SunExpress	
TC-SNG	Boeing 737-8HC	SunExpress	
TC-SNH	Boeing 737-8FH	SunExpress	
TC-SNI	Boeing 737-8FH	SunExpress	
TC-SNJ	Boeing 737-86J	SunExpress	
TC-SNL	Boeing 737-86N	SunExpress	
TC-SNM	Boeing 737-8BK	SunExpress	
TC-SNN	Boeing 737-8HC	SunExpress	
TC-SNO	Boeing 737-8HC	SunExpress	
TC-SNP	Boeing 737-8HC	SunExpress	
TC-SNR	Boeing 737-8HC	SunExpress	
TC-SNT	Boeing 737-8HC	SunExpress	
TC-SNU	Boeing 737-8HC	SunExpress	
TC-SUG	Boeing 737-8CX	SunExpress	
TC-SUH	Boeing 737-8CX	SunExpress	
TC-SUI	Boeing 737-8CX	SunExpress	
TC-SUJ	Boeing 737-8CX	SunExpress	
TC-SUL	Boeing 737-85F	SunExpress	
TC-SUM	Boeing 737-85F	SunExpress	
TC-SUO	Boeing 737-86Q	SunExpress	
TC-SUU	Boeing 737-86Q	SunExpress	
TC-SUV	Boeing 737-86N	SunExpress	
TC-SUY	Boeing 737-86N	SunExpress	
TC-SUZ	Boeing 737-8HX	SunExpress	
TC-TCE	Airbus A.321-211	Turkuaz Airlines	
TC-TCF	Airbus A.321-211	Turkuaz Airlines	
TC-TCG	Airbus A.321-211	Turkuaz Airlines	
TC-TCI	Airbus A.320-214	Turkuaz Airlines	
TC-TCJ	Airbus A.320-232	Turkuaz Airlines	
TC-TJB	Boeing 737-3Q8	Corendon Air	
TC-TJC	Boeing 737-4Q8	Corendon Air	
TC-TJD	Boeing 737-4Q8	Corendon Air	
TC-TJE	Boeing 737-4YO	Corendon Air	
TC-TJF	Boeing 737-4YO	Corendon Air	
TC-TJG	Boeing 737-86J	Corendon Air	
TC-TJH	Boeing 737-86J	Corendon Air	
TC-TLA	Boeing 737-4Q8	Tailwind Airlines	
TC-TLB	Boeing 737-4Q8	Tailwind Airlines	
TC-TLC	Boeing 737-4Q8	Tailwind Airlines	
TC-TLD	Boeing 737-4Q8	Tailwind Airlines	
TC-TLE	Boeing 737-4Q8	Tailwind Airlines	
TC-VEL	Airbus A.310-308F	ULS Cargo	

TF (Iceland)

Reg.	Type	Owner or Operator	Notes
TF-AAA	Boeing 747-236F	Air Atlanta Icelandic/Cargolux	
TF-AAB	Boeing 747-236F	Air Atlanta Icelandic/Saudi Arabian Airlines	
TF-AME	Boeing 747-312	Air Atlanta Icelandic	
TF-AMI	Boeing 747-412BCF	Air Atlanta Icelandic/Saudi Arabian Airlines	
TF-AMJ	Boeing 747-312	Air Atlanta Icelandic/Saudi Arabian Airlines	
TF-AMS	Boeing 747-481	Air Atlanta Icelandic/Saudi Arabian Airlines	
TF-AMT	Boeing 747-481	Air Atlanta Icelandic/Saudi Arabian Airlines	
TF-AMU	Boeing 747-48E	Air Atlanta Icelandic/Saudi Arabian Airlines	
TF-AMV	Boeing 747-412	Air Atlanta Icelandic/Saudi Arabian Airlines	
TF-AMX	Boeing 747-441BCF	Air Atlanta Icelandic/Saudi Arabian Airlines	
TF-ARM	Boeing 747-230BF (SCD)	Air Atlanta Icelandic	
TF-ARU	Boeing 747-344	Air Atlanta Icelandic	
TF-ATX	Boeing 747-236F	Air Atlanta Icelandic	

Notes	Reg.	Type	Owner or Operator
	TF-BBD	Boeing 737-3Y0F	Bluebird Cargo
	TF-BBE	Boeing 737-36EF	Bluebird Cargo
	TF-BBF	Boeing 737-36EF	Bluebird Cargo
	TF-BBG	Boeing 737-36EF	Bluebird Cargo
	TF-BBH	Boeing 737-4YO	Bluebird Cargo
	TF-CIB	Boeing 757-204F	Icelandair Cargo/TNT
	TF-FIA	Boeing 757-256	Icelandair
	TF-FID	Boeing 757-23APF	Icelandair Cargo/TNT
	TF-FIE	Boeing 757-23APF	Icelandair Cargo/TNT
	TF-FIG	Boeing 757-23APF	Icelandair Cargo
	TF-FIH	Boeing 757-208PCF	Icelandair Cargo
	TF-FII	Boeing 757-208	Icelandair
	TF-FIJ	Boeing 757-208	Icelandair *Surtsey*
	TF-FIN	Boeing 757-208	Icelandair *Bryndis*
	TF-FIO	Boeing 757-208	Icelandair *Valdis*
	TF-FIP	Boeing 757-208	Icelandair *Leifur Eiriksson*
	TF-FIR	Boeing 757-256	Icelandair
	TF-FIU	Boeing 757-256	Icelandair
	TF-FIV	Boeing 757-208	Icelandair *Gudridur Porbjarnardottir*
	TF-FIX	Boeing 757-308	Icelandair *Snorri Porfinnsson*
	TF-FIZ	Boeing 757-256	Icelandair

TS (Tunisia)

Notes	Reg.	Type	Owner or Operator
	TS-IMB	Airbus A.320-211	Tunis Air *Fahrat Hached*
	TS-IMC	Airbus A.320-211	Tunis Air *7 Novembre*
	TS-IMD	Airbus A.320-211	Tunis Air *Khereddine*
	TS-IME	Airbus A.320-211	Tunis Air *Tabarka*
	TS-IMF	Airbus A.320-211	Tunis Air *Djerba*
	TS-IMG	Airbus A.320-211	Tunis Air *Abou el Kacem Chebbi*
	TS-IMH	Airbus A.320-211	Tunis Air
	TS-IMI	Airbus A.320-211	Tunis Air *Jughurta*
	TS-IMJ	Airbus A.319-114	Tunis Air *El Kantaoui*
	TS-IMK	Airbus A.319-114	Tunis Air *Kerkenah*
	TS-IML	Airbus A.320-211	Tunis Air *Gafsa el Ksar*
	TS-IMM	Airbus A.320-211	Tunis Air *Le Bardo*
	TS-IMN	Airbus A.320-211	Tunis Air *Ibn Khaldoun*
	TS-IMO	Airbus A.319-114	Tunis Air *Hannibal*
	TS-IMP	Airbus A.320-211	Tunis Air *La Galite*
	TS-IMR	Airbus A.320-211	Tunis Air *Habib Bourguiba*
	TS-IMQ	Airbus A.319-114	Tunis Air
	TS-INA	Airbus A.320-214	Nouvelair
	TS-INB	Airbus A.320-214	Nouvelair
	TS-INC	Airbus A.320-214	Nouvelair
	TS-IND	Airbus A.320-212	Nouvelair/Libyan Airlines
	TS-INE	Airbus A.320-212	Nouvelair/Libyan Airlines
	TS-INF	Airbus A.320-212	Nouvelair
	TS-ING	Airbus A.320-214	Nouvelair
	TS-INI	Airbus A.320-212	Nouvelair
	TS-INL	Airbus A.320-212	Nouvelair
	TS-INN	Airbus A.320-212	Nouvelair
	TS-INO	Airbus A.320-232	Nouvelair
	TS-IOG	Boeing 737-5H3	Tunis Air *Sfax*
	TS-IOH	Boeing 737-5H3	Tunis Air *Hammamet*
	TS-IOI	Boeing 737-5H3	Tunis Air *Mahida*
	TS-IOJ	Boeing 737-5H3	Tunis Air *Monastir*
	TS-IOK	Boeing 737-6H3	Tunis Air *Kairouan*
	TS-IOL	Boeing 737-6H3	Tunis Air *Tozeur-Nefta*
	TS-IOM	Boeing 737-6H3	Tunis Air *Carthage*
	TS-ION	Boeing 737-6H3	Tunis Air *Utique*
	TS-IOP	Boeing 737-6H3	Tunis Air *El Jem*
	TS-IOQ	Boeing 737-6H3	Tunis Air *Bizerte*
	TS-IOR	Boeing 737-6H3	Tunis Air *Tahar Haddad*
	TS-IPA	Airbus A.300B4-605R	Tunis Air *Sidi Bou Said*
	TS-IPB	Airbus A.300B4-605R	Tunis Air *Tunis*
	TS-IPC	Airbus A.300B4-605R	Tunis Air *Amilcar*
	TS-IQA	Airbus A.321-211	Nouvelair
	TS-IQB	Airbus A.321-211	Nouvelair

UK (Uzbekistan)

Notes	Reg.	Type	Owner or Operator
	UK-31001	Airbus A.310-324	Uzbekistan Airways *Tashkent*

Reg.	Type	Owner or Operator	Notes
UK-31002	Airbus A.310-324	Uzbekistan Airways *Fergana*	
UK-31003	Airbus A.310-324	Uzbekistan Airways *Bukhara*	
UK-67001	Boeing 767-33PER	Uzbekistan Airways	
UK-67002	Boeing 767-33PER	Uzbekistan Airways	

UN (Kazakhstan)

Note: Air Astana operates P4- registered Boeing 757s and 767s.

UR (Ukraine)

Reg.	Type	Owner or Operator	Notes
UR-GAH	Boeing 737-32Q	Ukraine International *Mayrni*	
UR-GAK	Boeing 737-5Y0	Ukraine International	
UR-GAM	Boeing 737-4Y0	Ukraine International	
UR-GAN	Boeing 737-36N	Ukraine International	
UR-GAO	Boeing 737-4Z9	Ukraine International	
UR-GAP	Boeing 737-4Z9	Ukraine International	
UR-GAQ	Boeing 737-33R	Ukraine International	
UR-GAS	Boeing 737-528	Ukraine International	
UR-GAT	Boeing 737-528	Ukraine International	
UR-GAU	Boeing 737-5Y0	Ukraine International	
UR-GAV	Boeing 737-4C9	Ukraine International	
UR-GAW	Boeing 737-5Y0	Ukraine International	
UR-GAX	Boeing 737-4Y0	Ukraine International	
UR-PSA	Boeing 737-8HX	Ukraine International	
UR-PSB	Boeing 737-8HX	Ukraine International	
UR-PSC	Boeing 737-8HX	Ukraine International	
UR-PSD	Boeing 737-89P	Ukraine International	
UR-WUA	Airbus A.320-232	Wizz Air Ukraine	
UR-WUB	Airbus A.320-232	Wizz Air Ukraine	
UR-82007	Antonov An-124	Antonov Airlines	
UR-82008	Antonov An-124	Antonov Airlines	
UR-82009	Antonov An-124	Antonov Airlines	
UR-82027	Antonov An-124	Antonov Airlines	
UR-82029	Antonov An-124	Antonov Airlines	
UR-82060	Antonov An-225	Antonov Airlines	
UR-82072	Antonov An-124	Antonov Airlines	
UR-82073	Antonov An-124	Antonov Airlines	

V5 (Namibia)

Reg.	Type	Owner or Operator	Notes
V5-NME	Airbus A.340-311	Air Namibia	
V5-NMF	Airbus A.340-311	Air Namibia	

V8 (Brunei)

Reg.	Type	Owner or Operator	Notes
V8-BLA	Boeing 777-212ER	Royal Brunei Airlines	
V8-BLB	Boeing 777-212ER	Royal Brunei Airlines	
V8-BLC	Boeing 777-212ER	Royal Brunei Airlines	
V8-BLD	Boeing 777-212ER	Royal Brunei Airlines	
V8-BLE	Boeing 777-212ER	Royal Brunei Airlines	
V8-BLF	Boeing 777-212ER	Royal Brunei Airlines	

VH (Australia)

Reg.	Type	Owner or Operator	Notes
VH-OEB	Boeing 747-48E	QANTAS	
VH-OEE	Boeing 747-438ER	QANTAS	
VH-OEF	Boeing 747-438ER	QANTAS	
VH-OEG	Boeing 747-438ER	QANTAS	
VH-OEH	Boeing 747-438ER	QANTAS	
VH-OEI	Boeing 747-438ER	QANTAS	
VH-OEJ	Boeing 747-438ER	QANTAS	
VH-OJA	Boeing 747-438	QANTAS	
VH-OJB	Boeing 747-438	QANTAS	
VH-OJC	Boeing 747-438	QANTAS	
VH-OJD	Boeing 747-438	QANTAS	
VH-OJE	Boeing 747-438	QANTAS	
VH-OJF	Boeing 747-438	QANTAS	
VH-OJG	Boeing 747-438	QANTAS	

Notes	Reg.	Type	Owner or Operator
	VH-OJH	Boeing 747-438	QANTAS
	VH-OJI	Boeing 747-438	QANTAS
	VH-OJJ	Boeing 747-438	QANTAS
	VH-OJL	Boeing 747-438	QANTAS
	VH-OJM	Boeing 747-438	QANTAS
	VH-OJN	Boeing 747-438	QANTAS
	VH-OJO	Boeing 747-438	QANTAS
	VH-OJP	Boeing 747-438	QANTAS
	VH-OJQ	Boeing 747-438	QANTAS
	VH-OJS	Boeing 747-438	QANTAS
	VH-OJT	Boeing 747-438	QANTAS
	VH-OJU	Boeing 747-438	QANTAS
	VH-OQA	Airbus A.380-841	QANTAS
	VH-OQB	Airbus A.380-841	QANTAS
	VH-OQC	Airbus A.380-841	QANTAS
	VH-OQD	Airbus A.380-841	QANTAS
	VH-OQE	Airbus A.380-841	QANTAS
	VH-OQF	Airbus A.380-841	QANTAS
	VH-OQG	Airbus A.380-841	QANTAS
	VH-OQH	Airbus A.380-841	QANTAS
	VH-OQI	Airbus A.380-841	QANTAS
	VH-OQJ	Airbus A.380-841	QANTAS
	VH-OQK	Airbus A.380-841	QANTAS
	VH-OQL	Airbus A.380-841	QANTAS

VP-B/VP-Q (Bermuda)

Notes	Reg.	Type	Owner or Operator
	VP-BAV	Boeing 767-36NER	Aeroflot Russian International *L. Tolstoy*
	VP-BAX	Boeing 767-36NER	Aeroflot Russian International *F. Dostoevsky*
	VP-BAY	Boeing 767-36NER	Aeroflot Russian International *I. Turgenev*
	VP-BAZ	Boeing 767-36NER	Aeroflot Russian International *N. Nekrasov*
	VP-BBR	Boeing 757-22L	Azerbaijan Airlines *Garabagh*
	VP-BBS	Boeing 757-22L	Azerbaijan Airlines
	VP-BDI	Boeing 767-38AER	Aeroflot Russian International *A. Pushkin*
	VP-BDK	Airbus A.320-214	Aeroflot Russian International *G. Sviridov*
	VP-BDM	Airbus A.319-111	Aeroflot Russian International *A. Borodin*
	VP-BDN	Airbus A.319-111	Aeroflot Russian International *A. Dargomyzhsky*
	VP-BDO	Airbus A.319-111	Aeroflot Russian International *I. Stravinsky*
	VP-BDP	McD Douglas MD-11F	Aeroflot Cargo
	VP-BDQ	McD Douglas MD-11F	Aeroflot Cargo
	VP-BDR	McD Douglas MD-11F	Aeroflot Cargo
	VP-BIQ	Airbus A.319-111	Rossiya
	VP-BIT	Airbus A.319-111	Rossiya
	VP-BIU	Airbus A.319-114	Rossiya
	VP-BKC	Airbus A.320-214	Aeroflot Russian International
	VP-BKX	Airbus A.320-214	Aeroflot Russian International *G. Sedov*
	VP-BKY	Airbus A.320-214	Aeroflot Russian International *M. Rostropovich*
	VP-BLX	Airbus A.330-243	Aeroflot Russian International *E. Svetlanov*
	VP-BLY	Airbus A.330-243	Aeroflot Russian International
	VP-BME	Airbus A.320-214	Aeroflot Russian International *N. Mikluho-Maklay*
	VP-BMF	Airbus A.320-232	Aeroflot Russian International *G. Shelihov*
	VP-BPA	Boeing 737-5K5	Transaero
	VP-BPD	Boeing 737-5K5	Transaero
	VP-BQP	Airbus A.320-214	Aeroflot Russian International *A. Rublev*
	VP-BQR	Airbus A.321-211	Aeroflot Russian International *I. Repin*
	VP-BQS	Airbus A.321-211	Aeroflot Russian International *I. Kramskoi*
	VP-BQT	Airbus A.321-211	Aeroflot Russian International *I. Shishkin*
	VP-BQU	Airbus A.320-214	Aeroflot Russian International *A. Nikitin*
	VP-BQV	Airbus A.320-214	Aeroflot Russian International *V. Vasnetsov*
	VP-BQW	Airbus A.320-214	Aeroflot Russian International *V. Vereshchagin*
	VP-BQX	Airbus A.321-211	Aeroflot Russian International *I. Ayvazovsky*
	VP-BRW	Airbus A.321-211	Aeroflot Russian International
	VP-BRX	Airbus A.320-214	Aeroflot Russian International *V. Surikov*
	VP-BRY	Airbus A.320-214	Aeroflot Russian International *K. Brulloff*
	VP-BRZ	Airbus A.320-214	Aeroflot Russian International *V. Serov*
	VP-BUB	Boeing 757-23P	Uzbekistan Airways *Urgench*
	VP-BUD	Boeing 757-23P	Uzbekistan Airways *Shahrisabz*
	VP-BUE	Boeing 767-3CBER	Uzbekistan Airways
	VP-BUF	Boeing 767-33PER	Uzbekistan Airways
	VP-BUH	Boeing 757-231	Uzbekistan Airways
	VP-BUI	Boeing 757-231	Uzbekistan Airways
	VP-BUJ	Boeing 757-231	Uzbekistan Airways
	VP-BUK	Airbus A.319-111	Aeroflot Russian International *Yuri Senkevich*

Reg.	Type	Owner or Operator	Notes
VP-BUM	Airbus A.321-211	Aeroflot Russian International *A.Deineka*	
VP-BUN	Airbus A.319-112	Aeroflot Russian International	
VP-BUO	Airbus A.319-111	Aeroflot Russian International *K. Malevich*	
VP-BUP	Airbus A.321-211	Aeroflot Russian International	
VP-BWA	Airbus A.319-111	Aeroflot Russian International *S. Prokofiev*	
VP-BWD	Airbus A.320-214	Aeroflot Russian International *A. Aliabiev*	
VP-BWE	Airbus A.320-214	Aeroflot Russian International *H. Rimsky-Korsakov*	
VP-BWF	Airbus A.320-214	Aeroflot Russian International *D. Shostakovich*	
VP-BWG	Airbus A.319-111	Aeroflot Russian International *A. Aleksandrov*	
VP-BWH	Airbus A.320-214	Aeroflot Russian International *M. Balakirev*	
VP-BWI	Airbus A.320-214	Aeroflot Russian International *A. Glazunov*	
VP-BWJ	Airbus A.319-111	Aeroflot Russian International *A. Shnitke*	
VP-BWK	Airbus A.319-111	Aeroflot Russian International *S. Taneyev*	
VP-BWL	Airbus A.319-111	Aeroflot Russian International *A. Grechaninov*	
VP-BWM	Airbus A.320-214	Aeroflot Russian International *S. Rakhmaninov*	
VP-BWN	Airbus A.321-211	Aeroflot Russian International *A. Skriabin*	
VP-BWO	Airbus A.321-211	Aeroflot Russian International *P. Chaikovsky*	
VP-BWP	Airbus A.321-211	Aeroflot Russian International *M. Musorgsky*	
VP-BWU	Boeing 767-3T7ER	Aeroflot Russian International *I. Bunin*	
VP-BWV	Boeing 767-3T7ER	Aeroflot Russian International *A. Kuprin*	
VP-BWW	Boeing 767-306ER	Aeroflot Russian International *S. Esenin*	
VP-BWX	Boeing 767-306ER	Aeroflot Russian International *A. Blok*	
VP-BYI	Boeing 737-524	Transaero	
VP-BYJ	Boeing 737-524	Transaero	
VP-BYN	Boeing 737-524	Transaero	
VP-BYO	Boeing 737-524	Transaero	
VP-BYP	Boeing 737-524	Transaero	
VP-BYQ	Boeing 737-524	Transaero	
VP-BYT	Boeing 737-524	Transaero	
VP-BZO	Airbus A.320-214	Aeroflot Russian International *V. Bering*	
VP-BZP	Airbus A.320-214	Aeroflot Russian International *E. Habarov*	
VP-BZQ	Airbus A.320-214	Aeroflot Russian International *Yu. Lisiansky*	
VP-BZR	Airbus A.320-214	Aeroflot Russian International *F. Bellinsgauzen*	
VP-BZS	Airbus A.320-214	Aeroflot Russian International *M. Lazarev*	
VQ-BAQ	Airbus A.319-112	Rossiya	
VQ-BAR	Airbus A.319-112	Rossiya	
VQ-BAS	Airbus A.319-112	Rossiya	
VQ-BAT	Airbus A.319-112	Rossiya	
VQ-BAU	Airbus A.319-112	Rossiya	
VQ-BAV	Airbus A.319-112	Rossiya	
VQ-BAX	Airbus A.320-214	Aeroflot Russian International *G. Nevelskoy*	
VQ-BAY	Airbus A.320-214	Aeroflot Russian International *S. Krasheninnikov*	
VQ-BAZ	Airbus A.320-214	Aeroflot Russian International *V. Obruchev*	
VQ-BBA	Airbus A.319-112	Aeroflot Russian International *S. Cheliuskin*	
VQ-BBB	Airbus A.320-114	Aeroflot Russian International *Yu. Gagarin*	
VQ-BBC	Airbus A.320-214	Aeroflot Russian International	
VQ-BBD	Airbus A.319-112	Aeroflot Russian International *V. Golovnin*	
VQ-BBE	Airbus A.330-243	Aeroflot Russian International *I. Brodsky*	
VQ-BBF	Airbus A.330-243	Aeroflot Russian International *A. Griboedov*	
VQ-BBG	Airbus A.330-243	Aeroflot Russian International *N. Gogol*	
VQ-BBM	Airbus A.320-214	Rossiya	
VQ-BCM	Airbus A.320-214	Aeroflot Russian International	
VQ-BCN	Airbus A.320-214	Aeroflot Russian International	
VQ-BCO	Airbus A.319-111	Aeroflot Russian International	
VQ-BCP	Airbus A.319-112	Aeroflot Russian International *D. Mendeleev*	
VQ-BCQ	Airbus A.330-343	Aeroflot Russian International	
VQ-BCU	Airbus A.330-343	Aeroflot Russian International *W. Majakowski*	
VQ-BCV	Airbus A.330-343	Aeroflot Russian International	
VQ-BDQ	Airbus A.320-214	Rossiya	
VQ-BDR	Airbus A.320-214	Rossiya	
VQ-BDY	Airbus A.320-214	Rossiya	
VQ-BEA	Airbus A.321-211	Aeroflot Russian International *I. Michurin*	
VQ-BED	Airbus A.321-211	Aeroflot Russian International	
VQ-BEE	Airbus A.321-211	Aeroflot Russian International	
VQ-BEF	Airbus A.321-211	Aeroflot Russian International	
VQ-BEG	Airbus A.321-211	Aeroflot Russian International	
VQ-BEH	Airbus A.320-214	Aeroflot Russian International	
VQ-BEI	Airbus A.321-211	Aeroflot Russian International	
VQ-BEJ	Airbus A.320-214	Aeroflot Russian International	
VQ-BEK	Airbus A.330-343	Aeroflot Russian International *A. Tvardovsky*	
VQ-BEL	Airbus A.330-343	Aeroflot Russian International	
VQ-BHK	Airbus A.321-211	Aeroflot Russian International	
VQ-BHL	Airbus A.320-214	Aeroflot Russian International	
VQ-BHM	Airbus A.321-211	Aeroflot Russian International	

Notes	Reg.	Type	Owner or Operator
	VQ-BHN	Airbus A.320-214	Aeroflot Russian International
	VQ-BRD	Airbus A.320-214	Rossiya

VT (India)

Notes	Reg.	Type	Owner or Operator
	VT-ALA	Boeing 777-237LR	Air-India *State of Andhra Pradesh*
	VT-ALB	Boeing 777-237LR	Air-India *Arunachal Pradesh*
	VT-ALC	Boeing 777-237LR	Air-India *State of Assam*
	VT-ALD	Boeing 777-237LR	Air-India *Gujarat*
	VT-ALE	Boeing 777-237LR	Air India *Haryana*
	VT-ALF	Boeing 777-237LR	Air India
	VT-ALG	Boeing 777-237LR	Air India
	VT-ALH	Boeing 777-237LR	Air India
	VT-ALJ	Boeing 777-337ER	Air India *Bihar*
	VT-ALK	Boeing 777-337ER	Air India *Chattisgarh*
	VT-ALL	Boeing 777-337ER	Air-India *State of Assam*
	VT-ALM	Boeing 777-337ER	Air India *Himachel Pradesh*
	VT-ALN	Boeing 777-337ER	Air India *Jammu & Kashmir*
	VT-ALO	Boeing 777-337ER	Air India
	VT-ALP	Boeing 777-337ER	Air India
	VT-ALQ	Boeing 777-337ER	Air India
	VT-ALR	Boeing 777-337ER	Air India *Meghalaya*
	VT-ALS	Boeing 777-337ER	Air India *Mizoram*
	VT-ALT	Boeing 777-337ER	Air India *Nagaland*
	VT-ALU	Boeing 777-337ER	Air India *Orissa*
	VT-ALV	Boeing 777-337ER	Air India
	VT-ALW	Boeing 777-337ER	Air India
	VT-ALX	Boeing 777-337ER	Air India
	VT-ESN	Boeing 747-437	Air-India *Tanjore*
	VT-ESO	Boeing 747-437	Air-India *Khajuraho*
	VT-ESP	Boeing 747-437	Air-India *Ajanta*
	VT-EVA	Boeing 747-437	Air-India *Agra*
	VT-EVB	Boeing 747-437	Air-India *Velha Goa*
	VT-JEG	Boeing 777-35RER	Jet Airways
	VT-JEH	Boeing 777-35RER	Jet Airways
	VT-JEK	Boeing 777-35RER	Jet Airways
	VT-JWD	Airbus A.330-243	Jet Airways
	VT-JWE	Airbus A.330-243	Jet Airways
	VT-JWF	Airbus A.330-243	Jet Airways
	VT-JWG	Airbus A.330-243	Jet Airways
	VT-JWH	Airbus A.330-302	Jet Airways
	VT-JWJ	Airbus A.330-203	Jet Airways
	VT-JWK	Airbus A.330-203	Jet Airways
	VT-JWL	Airbus A.330-203	Jet Airways
	VT-JWM	Airbus A.330-202	Jet Airways
	VT-JWN	Airbus A.330-203	Jet Airways
	VT-JWP	Airbus A.330-203	Jet Airways
	VT-JWQ	Airbus A.330-203	Jet Airways
	VT-VJK	Airbus A.330-223	Kingfisher Airlines
	VT-VJL	Airbus A.330-223	Kingfisher Airlines
	VT-VJN	Airbus A.330-223	Kingfisher Airlines
	VT-VJO	Airbus A.330-223	Kingfisher Airlines
	VT-VJP	Airbus A.330-223	Kingfisher Airlines

YK (Syria)

Notes	Reg.	Type	Owner or Operator
	YK-AKA	Airbus A.320-232	Syrianair *Ugarit*
	YK-AKB	Airbus A.320-232	Syrianair *Ebla*
	YK-AKC	Airbus A.320-232	Syrianair *Afamia*
	YK-AKD	Airbus A.320-232	Syrianair *Mari*
	YK-AKE	Airbus A.320-232	Syrianair *Bosra*
	YK-AKF	Airbus A.320-232	Syrianair *Amrit*

YL (Latvia)

Notes	Reg.	Type	Owner or Operator
	YL-BBD	Boeing 737-53S	Air Baltic
	YL-BBE	Boeing 737-53S	Air Baltic
	YL-BBF	Boeing 737-548	Air Baltic
	YL-BBG	Boeing 737-548	Air Baltic
	YL-BBH	Boeing 737-548	Air Baltic
	YL-BBI	Boeing 737-33A	Air Baltic

Reg.	Type	Owner or Operator	Notes
YL-BBJ	Boeing 737-36Q	Air Baltic	
YL-BBK	Boeing 737-33V	Air Baltic	
YL-BBL	Boeing 737-33V	Air Baltic	
YL-BBM	Boeing 737-522	Air Baltic	
YL-BBN	Boeing 737-522	Air Baltic	
YL-BBP	Boeing 737-522	Air Baltic	
YL-BBR	Boeing 737-315	Air Baltic	
YL-BBQ	Boeing 737-522	Air Baltic	
YL-BBS	Boeing 737-31S	Air Baltic	
YL-BBX	Boeing 737-36Q	Air Baltic	
YL-BBY	Boeing 737-36Q	Air Baltic	
YL-BDB	Boeing 757-256ET	Air Baltic	
YL-BDC	Boeing 757-256ET	Air Baltic	

YR (Romania)

Reg.	Type	Owner or Operator	Notes
YR-ASA	Airbus A.318-111	Tarom	
YR-ASB	Airbus A.318-111	Tarom	
YR-ASC	Airbus A.318-111	Tarom	
YR-ASD	Airbus A.318-111	Tarom	
YR-BAC	Boeing 737-377	Blue Air	
YR-BAE	Boeing 737-46N	Blue Air	
YR-BAF	Boeing 737-322	Blue Air	
YR-BAG	Boeing 737-5L9	Blue Air	
YR-BAH	Boeing 737-505	Blue Air	
YR-BAI	Boeing 737-4Y0	Blue Air	
YR-BAJ	Boeing 737-430	Blue Air	
YR-BAK	Boeing 737-430	Blue Air	
YR-BGA	Boeing 737-38J	Tarom *Alba Iulia*	
YR-BGB	Boeing 737-38J	Tarom *Bucuresti*	
YR-BGD	Boeing 737-38J	Tarom *Deva*	
YR-BGE	Boeing 737-38J	Tarom *Timisoara*	
YR-BGF	Boeing 737-78J	Tarom *Braila*	
YR-BGG	Boeing 737-78J	Tarom *Craiova*	
YR-BGH	Boeing 737-78J	Tarom *Hunedoara*	
YR-BGI	Boeing 737-78J	Tarom *Iasi*	
YR-BGP	Boeing 737-86J	Tarom	
YR-BGR	Boeing 737-86J	Tarom	
YR-BGS	Boeing 737-8GJ	Tarom	
YR-LCA	Airbus A.310-325	Tarom	

YU (Serbia and Montenegro)

Reg.	Type	Owner or Operator	Notes
YU-AND	Boeing 737-3H9	JAT Airways *City of Krusevac*	
YU-ANF	Boeing 737-3H9	JAT Airways	
YU-ANI	Boeing 737-3H9	JAT Airways	
YU-ANJ	Boeing 737-3H9	JAT Airways	
YU-ANK	Boeing 737-3H9	JAT Airways	
YU-ANL	Boeing 737-3H9	JAT Airways	
YU-ANV	Boeing 737-3H9	JAT Airways	
YU-ANW	Boeing 737-3H9	JAT Airways	
YU-AON	Boeing 737-3Q4	JAT Airways	

Z (Zimbabwe)

Reg.	Type	Owner or Operator	Notes
Z-WPE	Boeing 767-2N0ER	Air Zimbabwe *Victoria Falls*	
Z-WPF	Boeing 767-2N0ER	Air Zimbabwe *Chimanimani*	

ZA (Albania)

Reg.	Type	Owner or Operator	Notes
ZA-MAK	BAe 146-100	Albanian Airlines	
ZA-MAL	BAe 146-200	Albanian Airlines	
ZA-MEV	BAe 146-300	Albanian Airlines	

ZK (New Zealand)

Reg.	Type	Owner or Operator	Notes
ZK-NBU	Boeing 747-419	Air New Zealand *Rotorua*	
ZK-NBV	Boeing 747-419	Air New Zealand *Christchurch*	
ZK-NBW	Boeing 747-419	Air New Zealand *Wellington*	

Notes	Reg.	Type	Owner or Operator
	ZK-OKA	Boeing 777-219ER	Air New Zealand
	ZK-OKB	Boeing 777-219ER	Air New Zealand
	ZK-OKC	Boeing 777-219ER	Air New Zealand
	ZK-OKD	Boeing 777-219ER	Air New Zealand
	ZK-OKE	Boeing 777-219ER	Air New Zealand
	ZK-OKF	Boeing 777-219ER	Air New Zealand
	ZK-OKG	Boeing 777-219ER	Air New Zealand
	ZK-OKH	Boeing 777-219ER	Air New Zealand
	ZK-OKM	Boeing 777-319ER	Air New Zealand
	ZK-OKN	Boeing 777-319ER	Air New Zealand
	ZK-OKO	Boeing 777-319ER	Air New Zealand
	ZK-OKP	Boeing 777-319ER	Air New Zealand
	ZK-SUH	Boeing 747-475	Air New Zealand *Dunedin*
	ZK-SUJ	Boeing 747-4F6	Air New Zealand *Auckland*

ZS (South Africa)

Notes	Reg.	Type	Owner or Operator
	ZS-SLA	Airbus A.340-211	South African Airways
	ZS-SLB	Airbus A.340-211	South African Airways
	ZS-SLC	Airbus A.340-211	South African Airways
	ZS-SLD	Airbus A.340-211	South African Airways
	ZS-SLE	Airbus A.340-211	South African Airways
	ZS-SLF	Airbus A.340-211	South African Airways
	ZS-SNA	Airbus A.340-642	South African Airways
	ZS-SNB	Airbus A.340-642	South African Airways
	ZS-SNC	Airbus A.340-642	South African Airways
	ZS-SND	Airbus A.340-642	South African Airways
	ZS-SNE	Airbus A.340-642	South African Airways
	ZS-SNF	Airbus A.340-642	South African Airways
	ZS-SNG	Airbus A.340-642	South African Airways
	ZS-SNH	Airbus A.340-642	South African Airways
	ZS-SNI	Airbus A.340-642	South African Airways
	ZS-SXA	Airbus A.340-313E	South African Airways
	ZS-SXB	Airbus A.340-313E	South African Airways
	ZS-SXC	Airbus A.340-313E	South African Airways
	ZS-SXD	Airbus A.340-313E	South African Airways
	ZS-SXE	Airbus A.340-313E	South African Airways
	ZS-SXF	Airbus A.340-313E	South African Airways
	ZS-SXG	Airbus A.340-313X	South African Airways
	ZS-SXH	Airbus A.340-313X	South African Airways
	ZS-SXU	Airbus A.330-243	South African Airways
	ZS-SXV	Airbus A.330-243	South African Airways
	ZS-SXW	Airbus A.330-243	South African Airways
	ZS-SXX	Airbus A.330-243	South African Airways
	ZS-SXY	Airbus A.330-243	South African Airways
	ZS-SXZ	Airbus A.330-243	South African Airways

3B (Mauritius)

Notes	Reg.	Type	Owner or Operator
	3B-NAU	Airbus A.340-312	Air Mauritius *Pink Pigeon*
	3B-NAY	Airbus A.340-313X	Air Mauritius *Cardinal*
	3B-NBD	Airbus A.340-313X	Air Mauritius *Parakeet*
	3B-NBE	Airbus A.340-313X	Air Mauritius *Paille en Queue*
	3B-NBI	Airbus A.340-313E	Air Mauritius *Le Flamboyant*
	3B-NBJ	Airbus A.340-313E	Air Mauritius *Le Chamarel*

4K (Azerbaijan)

Notes	Reg.	Type	Owner or Operator
	4K-AZ03	Airbus A.319-111	Azerbaijan Airlines
	4K-AZ04	Airbus A.319-111	Azerbaijan Airlines
	4K-AZ05	Airbus A.319-111	Azerbaijan Airlines
	4K-AZ38	Boeing 757-256	Azerbaijan Airlines
	4K-AZ43	Boeing 757-2M6	Azerbaijan Airlines

4O (Montenegro)

Notes	Reg.	Type	Owner or Operator
	4O-AOA	Embraer ERJ190-200LR	Montenegro Airlines
	4O-AOB	Embraer ERJ190-200LR	Montenegro Airlines
	4O-AOC	Embraer ERJ190-200LR	Montenegro Airlines
	4O-AOK	Fokker 100	Montenegro Airlines

Reg.	Type	Owner or Operator	Notes
4O-AOL	Fokker 100	Montenegro Airlines	
4O-AOM	Fokker 100	Montenegro Airlines	
4O-AOP	Fokker 100	Montenegro Airlines	
4O-AOT	Fokker 100	Montenegro Airlines	

4R (Sri Lanka)

Reg.	Type	Owner or Operator	Notes
4R-ADA	Airbus A.340-311	SriLankan Airlines	
4R-ADB	Airbus A.340-311	SriLankan Airlines	
4R-ADC	Airbus A.340-311	SriLankan Airlines	
4R-ADE	Airbus A.340-313X	SriLankan Airlines	
4R-ADF	Airbus A.340-313X	SriLankan Airlines	
4R-ALA	Airbus A.330-243	SriLankan Airlines	
4R-ALB	Airbus A.330-243	SriLankan Airlines	
4R-ALC	Airbus A.330-243	SriLankan Airlines	
4R-ALD	Airbus A.330-243	SriLankan Airlines	
4R-ALG	Airbus A.330-243	SriLankan Airlines	

4X (Israel)

Reg.	Type	Owner or Operator	Notes
4X-ABF	Airbus A.320-232	Israir	
4X-ABG	Airbus A.320-232	Israir	
4X-AXL	Boeing 747-245F (SCD)	El Al Cargo	
4X-EAC	Boeing 767-258ER	El Al	
4X-EAD	Boeing 767-258ER	El Al	
4X-EAE	Boeing 767-27EER	El Al	
4X-EAF	Boeing 767-27EER	El Al	
4X-EAJ	Boeing 767-330ER	El Al	
4X-EAK	Boeing 767-3Q8ER	El Al	
4X-EAP	Boeing 767-3Y0ER	El Al	
4X-EAR	Boeing 767-352ER	El Al	
4X-ECA	Boeing 777-258ER	El Al *Galilee*	
4X-ECB	Boeing 777-258ER	El Al *Negev*	
4X-ECC	Boeing 777-258ER	El Al *Hasharon*	
4X-ECD	Boeing 777-258ER	El Al *Carmel*	
4X-ECE	Boeing 777-258ER	El Al *Sderot*	
4X-ECF	Boeing 777-258ER	El Al *Kiryat Shmona*	
4X-EKA	Boeing 737-858	El Al *Tiberias*	
4X-EKB	Boeing 737-858	El Al *Eilat*	
4X-EKC	Boeing 737-858	El Al *Beit Shean*	
4X-EKD	Boeing 737-758	El Al *Ashkelon*	
4X-EKE	Boeing 737-758	El Al *Nazareth*	
4X-EKF	Boeing 737-858	El Al *Kinneret*	
4X-EKH	Boeing 737-85P	El Al *Yarden*	
4X-EKI	Boeing 737-86N	El Al	
4X-EKJ	Boeing 737-85P	El Al *Degania*	
4X-EKL	Boeing 737-85P	El Al *Nahalal*	
4X-EKO	Boeing 737-86Q	El Al	
4X-EKP	Boeing 737-8Q8	El Al	
4X-EKS	Boeing 737-8Q8	El Al *Caesarea*	
4X-EKT	Boeing 737-8BK	El Al	
4X-ELA	Boeing 747-458	El Al *Tel Aviv-Jaffa*	
4X-ELB	Boeing 747-458	El Al *Haifa*	
4X-ELC	Boeing 747-458	El Al *Beer Sheva*	
4X-ELD	Boeing 747-458	El Al *Jerusalem*	
4X-ELE	Boeing 747-458	El Al	
4X-ELF	Boeing 747-412F	El Al Cargo	

5A (Libya)

Reg.	Type	Owner or Operator	Notes
5A-DLY	Airbus A.300B4-601	Libyan Airlines *Al-Gordabia*	
5A-DLZ	Airbus A.300B4-622R	Libyan Airlines *Derna*	
5A-LAA	Canadair CRJ900ER	Libyan Airlines	
5A-LAB	Canadair CRJ900ER	Libyan Airlines	
5A-LAC	Canadair CRJ900ER	Libyan Airlines	
5A-LAD	Canadair CRJ900ER	Libyan Airlines	
5A-LAE	Canadair CRJ900ER	Libyan Airlines	
5A-LAH	Airbus A.320-214	Libyan Airlines	
5A-LAI	Airbus A.320-214	Libyan Airlines	
5A-LAJ	Airbus A.320-214	Libyan Airlines	
5A-LAK	Airbus A.320-214	Libyan Airlines	

Notes	Reg.	Type	Owner or Operator
	5A-LAM	Canadair CRJ900ER	Libyan Airlines
	5A-LAN	Canadair CRJ900ER	Libyan Airlines
	5A-ONA	Airbus A.320-214	Afriqiyah Airways
	5A-ONB	Airbus A.320-214	Afriqiyah Airways
	5A-ONC	Airbus A.319-111	Afriqiyah Airways
	5A-OND	Airbus A.319-111	Afriqiyah Airways
	5A-ONF	Airbus A.330-202	Afriqiyah Airways
	5A-ONH	Airbus A.330-202	Afriqiyah Airways
	5A-ONI	Airbus A.319-111	Afriqiyah Airways
	5A-ONJ	Airbus A.320-214	Afriqiyah Airways
	5A-ONK	Airbus A.320-214	Afriqiyah Airways
	5A-ONL	Airbus A.320-214	Afriqiyah Airways
	5A-ONM	Airbus A.320-214	Afriqiyah Airways
	5A-ONO	Airbus A.320-214	Afriqiyah Airways
	5A-ONP	Airbus A.320-214	Afriqiyah Airways

5B (Cyprus)

Notes	Reg.	Type	Owner or Operator
	5B-DBA	Airbus A.320-231	Cyprus Airways *Evagoras*
	5B-DBC	Airbus A.320-231	Cyprus Airways *Tefkros*
	5B-DBO	Airbus A.319-132	Cyprus Airways *Nikoklis*
	5B-DBP	Airbus A.319-132	Cyprus Airways *Chalkanor*
	5B-DBS	Airbus A.330-223	Cyprus Airways *Ammochostos*
	5B-DBT	Airbus A.330-223	Cyprus Airways *Keryneia*
	5B-DCF	Airbus A.319-132	Cyprus Airways *Larnaka*
	5B-DCG	Airbus A.320-232	Cyprus Airways *Aphrodite*
	5B-DCH	Airbus A.320-232	Cyprus Airways *Lefkosia*
	5B-DCJ	Airbus A.320-232	Cyprus Airways *Amathus*
	5B-DCK	Airbus A.320-232	Cyprus Airways

5N (Nigeria)

Notes	Reg.	Type	Owner or Operator
	5N-EIA	Airbus A.330-223	Arik Air *Sultan of Sokoto*
	5N-MJN	Boeing 737-86N	Arik Air
	5N-MJO	Boeing 737-86N	Arik Air
	5N-MJP	Boeing 737-8JE	Arik Air
	5N-MJQ	Boeing 737-8JE	Arik Air

5Y (Kenya)

Notes	Reg.	Type	Owner or Operator
	5Y-KQS	Boeing 777-2U8ER	Kenya Airways
	5Y-KQT	Boeing 777-2U8ER	Kenya Airways
	5Y-KQU	Boeing 777-2U8ER	Kenya Airways
	5Y-KQX	Boeing 767-36NER	Kenya Airways
	5Y-KQY	Boeing 767-36NER	Kenya Airways
	5Y-KQZ	Boeing 767-36NER	Kenya Airways
	5Y-KYW	Boeing 767-319ER	Kenya Airways
	5Y-KYX	Boeing 767-3P6ER	Kenya Airways
	5Y-KYY	Boeing 767-3Q8ER	Kenya Airways
	5Y-KYZ	Boeing 777-2U8ER	Kenya Airways

7O (Yemen)

Notes	Reg.	Type	Owner or Operator
	7O-ADP	Airbus A.330-243	Yemenia *Sana'a*
	7O-ADR	Airbus A.310-324	Yemenia
	7O-ADT	Airbus A.330-243	Yemenia *Aden*
	7O-ADV	Airbus A.310-325	Yemenia
	7O-ADW	Airbus A.310-325	Yemenia
	7O-ADX	Airbus A.330-243	Yemenia

7T (Algeria)

Notes	Reg.	Type	Owner or Operator
	7T-VJG	Boeing 767-3D6ER	Air Algerie
	7T-VJH	Boeing 767-3D6ER	Air Algerie
	7T-VJI	Boeing 767-3D6ER	Air Algerie
	7T-VJJ	Boeing 737-8D6	Air Algerie *Jugurtha*
	7T-VJK	Boeing 737-8D6	Air Algerie *Mansourah*
	7T-VJL	Boeing 737-8D6	Air Algerie *Allizi*
	7T-VJM	Boeing 737-8D6	Air Algerie

Reg.	Type	Owner or Operator	Notes
7T-VJN	Boeing 737-8D6	Air Algerie	
7T-VJO	Boeing 737-8D6	Air Algerie	
7T-VJP	Boeing 737-8D6	Air Algerie	
7T-VJQ	Boeing 737-6D6	Air Algerie	
7T-VJR	Boeing 737-6D6	Air Algerie	
7T-VJS	Boeing 737-6D6	Air Algerie	
7T-VJT	Boeing 737-6D6	Air Algerie	
7T-VJU	Boeing 737-6D6	Air Algerie	
7T-VJV	Airbus A.330-202	Air Algerie *Tinhinan*	
7T-VJW	Airbus A.330-202	Air Algerie *Lalla Setti*	
7T-VJX	Airbus A.330-202	Air Algerie *Mers el Kebir*	
7T-VJY	Airbus A.330-202	Air Algerie *Monts des Beni Chougrane*	
7T-VJZ	Airbus A.330-202	Air Algerie	
7T-VKA	Boeing 737-8D6	Air Algerie	
7T-VKB	Boeing 737-8D6	Air Algerie	
7T-VKC	Boeing 737-8D6	Air Algerie	
7T-VKD	Boeing 737-8D6	Air Algerie	
7T-VKE	Boeing 737-8D6	Air Algerie	
7T-VKF	Boeing 737-8D6	Air Algerie	

9A (Croatia)

Reg.	Type	Owner or Operator	Notes
9A-CDA	McD Douglas MD-83	Dubrovnik Airline *Revelin*	
9A-CDB	McD Douglas MD-83	Dubrovnik Airline *Lovrijenac*	
9A-CDC	McD Douglas MD-83	Dubrovnik Airline *Minceta*	
9A-CDD	McD Douglas MD-82	Dubrovnik Airline *Bckar*	
9A-CDE	McD Douglas MD-82	Dubrovnik Airline *Sveti Ivan*	
9A-CTF	Airbus A.320-211	Croatia Airlines *Rijeka*	
9A-CTG	Airbus A.319-112	Croatia Airlines *Zadar*	
9A-CTH	Airbus A.319-112	Croatia Airlines *Zagreb*	
9A-CTI	Airbus A.319-112	Croatia Airlines *Vukovar*	
9A-CTJ	Airbus A.320-214	Croatia Airlines *Dubrovnik*	
9A-CTK	Airbus A.320-214	Croatia Airlines *Split*	
9A-CTL	Airbus A.319-112	Croatia Airlines *Pula*	

9H (Malta)

Reg.	Type	Owner or Operator	Notes
9H-AEF	Airbus A.320-214	Air Malta	
9H-AEG	Airbus A.319-112	Air Malta	
9H-AEH	Airbus A.319-111	Air Malta *Floriana*	
9H-AEJ	Airbus A.319-111	Air Malta *San Pawl il-Bahar*	
9H-AEK	Airbus A.320-214	Air Malta *San Giljan*	
9H-AEL	Airbus A.319-111	Air Malta *Marsaxlokk*	
9H-AEM	Airbus A.319-111	Air Malta *Birgu*	
9H-AEN	Airbus A.320-214	Air Malta	
9H-AEO	Airbus A.320-214	Air Malta	
9H-AEP	Airbus A.320-214	Air Malta	
9H-AEQ	Airbus A.320-214	Air Malta	

9K (Kuwait)

Reg.	Type	Owner or Operator	Notes
9K-ADE	Boeing 747-469 (SCD)	Kuwait Airways *Al-Jabariya*	
9K-ALA	Airbus A.310-308	Kuwait Airways *Al-Jahra*	
9K-ALB	Airbus A.310-308	Kuwait Airways *Gharnada*	
9K-ALC	Airbus A.310-308	Kuwait Airways *Kazma*	
9K-AMA	Airbus A.300B4-605R	Kuwait Airways *Failaka*	
9K-AMB	Airbus A.300B4-605R	Kuwait Airways *Burghan*	
9K-AMC	Airbus A.300B4-605R	Kuwait Airways *Wafra*	
9K-AMD	Airbus A.300B4-605R	Kuwait Airways *Wara*	
9K-AME	Airbus A.300B4-605R	Kuwait Airways *Al-Rawdhatain*	
9K-ANA	Airbus A.340-313	Kuwait Airways *Warba*	
9K-ANB	Airbus A.340-313	Kuwait Airways *Bayan*	
9K-ANC	Airbus A.340-313	Kuwait Airways *Meskan*	
9K-AND	Airbus A.340-313	Kuwait Airways *Al-Riggah*	
9K-AOA	Boeing 777-269ER	Kuwait Airways *Al-Grain*	
9K-AOB	Boeing 777-269ER	Kuwait Airways *Garouh*	

9M (Malaysia)

Reg.	Type	Owner or Operator	Notes
9M-MPB	Boeing 747-4H6	Malaysian Airlines *Shah Alam*	

Notes	Reg.	Type	Owner or Operator
	9M-MPF	Boeing 747-4H6	Malaysian Airlines *Kota Bharu*
	9M-MPK	Boeing 747-4H6	Malaysian Airlines *Johor Bahru*
	9M-MPL	Boeing 747-4H6	Malaysian Airlines *Penang*
	9M-MPM	Boeing 747-4H6	Malaysian Airlines *Melaka*
	9M-MPN	Boeing 747-4H6	Malaysian Airlines *Pangkor*
	9M-MPO	Boeing 747-4H6	Malaysian Airlines *Alor Setar*
	9M-MPP	Boeing 747-4H6	Malaysian Airlines *Putrajaya*
	9M-MPQ	Boeing 747-4H6	Malaysian Airlines *Kuala Lumpur*
	9M-MPR	Boeing 747-4H6F	Malaysian Airlines Cargo
	9M-MPS	Boeing 747-4H6F	Malaysian Airlines Cargo
	9M-MRA	Boeing 777-2H6ER	Malaysian Airlines
	9M-MRB	Boeing 777-2H6ER	Malaysian Airlines
	9M-MRC	Boeing 777-2H6ER	Malaysian Airlines
	9M-MRD	Boeing 777-2H6ER	Malaysian Airlines
	9M-MRE	Boeing 777-2H6ER	Malaysian Airlines
	9M-MRF	Boeing 777-2H6ER	Malaysian Airlines
	9M-MRG	Boeing 777-2H6ER	Malaysian Airlines
	9M-MRH	Boeing 777-2H6ER	Malaysian Airlines
	9M-MRI	Boeing 777-2H6ER	Malaysian Airlines
	9M-MRJ	Boeing 777-2H6ER	Malaysian Airlines
	9M-MRK	Boeing 777-2H6ER	Malaysian Airlines
	9M-MRL	Boeing 777-2H6ER	Malaysian Airlines
	9M-MRM	Boeing 777-2H6ER	Malaysian Airlines
	9M-MRN	Boeing 777-2H6ER	Malaysian Airlines
	9M-MRO	Boeing 777-2H6ER	Malaysian Airlines
	9M-MRP	Boeing 777-2H6ER	Malaysian Airlines
	9M-MRQ	Boeing 777-2H6ER	Malaysian Airlines
	9M-XAB	Airbus A.340-313X	Air Asia X Xcalibur
	9M-XAC	Airbus A.340-313X	Air Asia X *Xcellence*

9V (Singapore)

Notes	Reg.	Type	Owner or Operator
	9V-SFD	Boeing 747-412F	Singapore Airlines Cargo
	9V-SFF	Boeing 747-412F	Singapore Airlines Cargo
	9V-SFG	Boeing 747-412F	Singapore Airlines Cargo
	9V-SFJ	Boeing 747-412F	Singapore Airlines Cargo
	9V-SFK	Boeing 747-412F	Singapore Airlines Cargo
	9V-SFL	Boeing 747-412F	Singapore Airlines Cargo
	9V-SFM	Boeing 747-412F	Singapore Airlines Cargo
	9V-SFN	Boeing 747-412F	Singapore Airlines Cargo
	9V-SFO	Boeing 747-412F	Singapore Airlines Cargo
	9V-SFP	Boeing 747-412F	Singapore Airlines Cargo
	9V-SFQ	Boeing 747-412F	Singapore Airlines Cargo
	9V-SKA	Airbus A.380-841	Singapore Airlines
	9V-SKB	Airbus A.380-841	Singapore Airlines
	9V-SKC	Airbus A.380-841	Singapore Airlines
	9V-SKD	Airbus A.380-841	Singapore Airlines
	9V-SKE	Airbus A.380-841	Singapore Airlines
	9V-SKF	Airbus A.380-841	Singapore Airlines
	9V-SKG	Airbus A.380-841	Singapore Airlines
	9V-SKH	Airbus A.380-841	Singapore Airlines
	9V-SKI	Airbus A.380-841	Singapore Airlines
	9V-SKJ	Airbus A.380-841	Singapore Airlines
	9V-SKK	Airbus A.380-841	Singapore Airlines
	9V-SKL	Airbus A.380-841	Singapore Airlines
	9V-SKM	Airbus A.380-841	Singapore Airlines
	9V-SKN	Airbus A.380-841	Singapore Airlines
	9V-SKO	Airbus A.380-841	Singapore Airlines
	9V-SKP	Airbus A.380-841	Singapore Airlines
	9V-SKQ	Airbus A.380-841	Singapore Airlines
	9V-SKR	Airbus A.380-841	Singapore Airlines
	9V-SKS	Airbus A.380-841	Singapore Airlines
	9V-SVE	Boeing 777-212ER	Singapore Airlines
	9V-SVH	Boeing 777-212ER	Singapore Airlines
	9V-SVI	Boeing 777-212ER	Singapore Airlines
	9V-SVJ	Boeing 777-212ER	Singapore Airlines
	9V-SVK	Boeing 777-212ER	Singapore Airlines
	9V-SVL	Boeing 777-212ER	Singapore Airlines
	9V-SVM	Boeing 777-212ER	Singapore Airlines
	9V-SVN	Boeing 777-212ER	Singapore Airlines
	9V-SVO	Boeing 777-212ER	Singapore Airlines
	9V-SWA	Boeing 777-312ER	Singapore Airlines

Reg.	Type	Owner or Operator	Notes
9V-SWB	Boeing 777-312ER	Singapore Airlines	
9V-SWD	Boeing 777-312ER	Singapore Airlines	
9V-SWE	Boeing 777-312ER	Singapore Airlines	
9V-SWF	Boeing 777-312ER	Singapore Airlines	
9V-SWG	Boeing 777-312ER	Singapore Airlines	
9V-SWH	Boeing 777-312ER	Singapore Airlines	
9V-SWI	Boeing 777-312ER	Singapore Airlines	
9V-SWJ	Boeing 777-312ER	Singapore Airlines	
9V-SWK	Boeing 777-312ER	Singapore Airlines	
9V-SWL	Boeing 777-312ER	Singapore Airlines	
9V-SWM	Boeing 777-312ER	Singapore Airlines	
9V-SWN	Boeing 777-312ER	Singapore Airlines	
9V-SWO	Boeing 777-312ER	Singapore Airlines	
9V-SWP	Boeing 777-312ER	Singapore Airlines	
9V-SWQ	Boeing 777-312ER	Singapore Airlines	
9V-SWR	Boeing 777-312ER	Singapore Airlines	
9V-SWS	Boeing 777-312ER	Singapore Airlines	
9V-SWT	Boeing 777-312ER	Singapore Airlines	

A6-EMM Boeing 777-31H of Emirates Airlines. *Allan Wright*

B-18708 Boeing 747-409F of China Airlines Cargo. *Allan Wright*

CN-ROF Airbus A.321-211 of Royal Air Maroc. *Allan Wright*

D-AECG Embraer ERJ190-200LR of Lufthansa Cityline. *Allan Wright*

D-AIKC Airbus A.330-343X of Lufthansa. *Allan Wright*

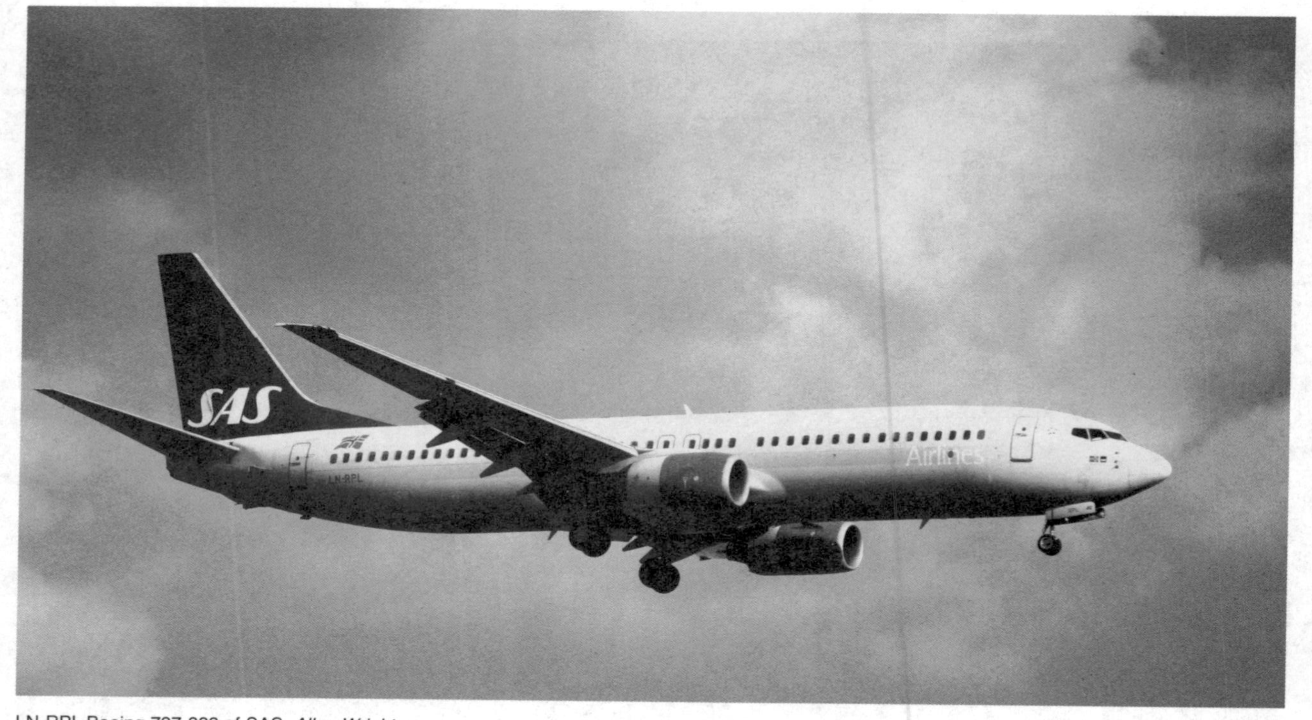

LN-RPL Boeing 737-883 of SAS. *Allan Wright*

N706TW Boeing 757-2Q8 of Delta Air Lines. *Allan Wright*

SP-LGE Embraer RJ145LR of LOT. *Allan Wright*

TS-INM Airbus A.320-211 of Tunis Air. *Allan Wright*

Radio Frequencies

The frequencies used by the larger airfields/airports are listed below. Abbreviations used: TWR – Tower, APP – Approach, A/G – Air-Ground advisory. It is possible that changes will be made from time to time with the frequencies allocated, all of which are quoted in Megahertz (MHz).

Airfield	*TWR*	*APP*	*A/G*
Aberdeen	118.1	119.05	
Alderney	125.35		
Andrewsfield			130.55
Barton			120.25
Barrow			123.2
Beccles			120.375
Belfast International	118.3	128.5	
Belfast City	122.825	130.85	
Bembridge			123.25
Biggin Hill	134.8	129.4	
Birmingham	118.3	118.05	
Blackbushe			122.3
Blackpool	118.4	119.95	
Bodmin		128.725	122.7
Bourn			124.35
Bournemouth	125.6	119.625	
Breighton			129.80
Bristol/Filton	132.35	122.725	
Bristol/Lulsgate	133.85	125.65	
Bruntingthorpe			122.825
Caernarfon			122.25
Cambridge	122.2	123.6	
Cardiff	133.1	125.85	
Carlisle	123.6	123.6	
Clacton			118.15
Compton Abbas			122.7
Conington			129.725
Cosford	128.65	135.875	
Coventry	119.25	119.25	
Cranfield	134.925	122.85	
Denham		126.45	130.725
Doncaster RHA	128.775	126.225	
Dundee	122.9		
Dunkeswell			123.475
Durham Tees Valley	119.8	118.85	
Duxford			122.075
Earls Colne			122.425
Edinburgh	118.7	121.2	
Elstree			122.4
Exeter	119.8	128.15	
Fairoaks			123.425
Farnborough	122.5	134.35	
Fenland			122.925
Fowlmere			135.7
Gamston			130.475
Gatwick	124.225	126.825	
Glasgow	118.8	119.1	
Gloucester/Staverton	128.55	122.9	
Goodwood			122.45
Guernsey	119.95	128.65	
Haverfordwest			122.2
Hawarden	124.95	123.35	
Henstridge			130.25
Headcorn			122.0
Heathrow	118.7 118.5	119.725	
Hethel			122.35
Hucknall			130.8
Humberside	124.9	119.125	
Inverness	118.4	122.6	
Jersey	119.45	120.3	
Kemble			118.9
Land's End	120.25		
Leeds Bradford	120.3	123.75	
Leicester			122.125
Liverpool	126.35	119.85	
London City	118.075	132.7	
Luton	132.55	129.55	
Lydd			120.7
Manchester	118.625	118.575	
Manston	119.925	126.35	
Netherthorpe		126.225	123.275
Newcastle	119.7	124.375	
Newquay	134.375	133.4	
North Denes	123.4		
North Weald			123.525
Norwich	124.25	119.35	
Nottingham EMA	124.0	134.175	
Old Warden			130.7
Oxford	133.425	125.325	
Penzance			118.1
Perth			119.8
Plymouth	118.15	133.55	
Popham			129.8
Prestwick	118.15	120.55	
Redhill	119.6		
Rochester			122.25
Ronaldsway IOM	122.6	120.85	
Sandown			123.5
Sandtoft			130.425
Scilly Isles	123.825	124.875	
Seething			122.6
Sheffield City			128.525
Sherburn			122.6
Shipdham			132.25
Shobdon			123.5
Shoreham	125.4	123.15	
Sibson			122.3
Sleap			122.45
Southampton	118.2	128.85	
Southend	127.725	130.775	
Stansted	123.8	120.625	
Stapleford			122.8
Sumburgh	118.25	131.3	
Swansea			119.7
Sywell			122.7
Tatenhill			124.075
Thruxton			130.45
Tollerton			134.875
Wellesbourne			124.025
Welshpool			128.0
White Waltham			122.6
Wick	119.7		
Wickenby			122.45
Wolverhampton			123.3
Woodford	120.7	130.75	
Woodvale	119.75	121.0	
Wycombe Air Park			126.55
Yeovil	125.4	130.85	

Airline Flight Codes

Those listed below identify the UK and overseas carriers appearing in the book

Code	Airline	Reg
AAF	Aigle Azur	F
AAG	Atlantic Air Transport	G
AAL	American Airlines	N
AAR	Asiana Airlines	HL
AAW	Afriquiyah Airways	5A
ABD	Air Atlanta Icelandic	TF
ABQ	AirBlue	AP
ABR	Air Contractors	EI
ACA	Air Canada	C
ADB	Antonov Airlines	UR
ADH	Air One	I
ADR	Adria Airways	S5
AEA	Air Europa	EC
AEE	Aegean Airlines	SX
AEU	Astraeus	G
AEW	Aerosvit Airlines	UR
AEY	Air Italy	I
AFL	Aeroflot	RA
AFR	Air France	F
AHY	Azerbaijan Airlines	4K
AIC	Air-India	VT
AIZ	Arkia	4X
AJM	Air Jamaica	6Y
AKL	Air Kilroe	G
ALK	SriLankan Airlines	4R
AMC	Air Malta	9H
AMT	ATA Airlines	N
AMV	AMC Airlines	SU
ANA	All Nippon Airways	JA
ANZ	Air New Zealand	ZK
ARA	Arik Air	5N
ATN	Air Transport International	N
AUA	Austrian Airlines	OE
AUI	Ukraine International	UR
AUR	Aurigny A/S	G
AWC	Titan Airways	G
AXM	Air Asia X	9M
AZA	Alitalia	I
AZE	Arcus Air	D
AZW	Air Zimbabwe	Z
BAW	British Airways	G
BBC	Biman Bangladesh	S2
BBD	Bluebird Cargo	TF
BBO	Baboo	HB
BCS	European A/T	OO
BCY	CityJet	EI
BDI	BenAir A/S	OY
BEE	Flybe	G
BEL	Brussels Airlines	OO
BER	Air Berlin	D
BGA	Airbus Tpt International	F
BGH	Balkan Holidays	LZ
BHP	Belair	HB
BID	Binair	D
BIE	Air Mediterranée	F
BIH	CHC Scotia	G
BLC	TAM Linhas Aereas	PT
BLF	Blue 1	OH
BMA	bmi british midland	G
BMI	bmi Baby	G
BMM	Atlas Blue	CN
BOS	Open Skies	F
BOX	AeroLogic	D
BPA	Blue Panorama	I
BRT	BA Citiexpress	G
BRU	Belavia	EW
BTI	Air Baltic	YL
BUC	Bulgarian Air Charter	LZ
BZH	Brit Air	F
CAI	Corendon Airlines	TC
CAJ	Air Caraibes	F-O
CAL	China Airlines	B
CCA	Air China	B
CES	China Eastern	B
CFG	Condor	D
CIM	Cimber Sterling	OY
CKS	Kalitta Air	N
CLH	Lufthansa CityLine	D
CLW	Centralwings	SP
CLX	Cargolux	LX
COA	Continental Airlines	N
CPA	Cathay Pacific	B
CRL	Corsair	F
CSA	CSA Czech Airlines	OK
CTN	Croatia Airlines	9A
CUB	Cubana	CU
CWC	Centurion Air Cargo	N
CYP	Cyprus Airways	5B
DAH	Air Algerie	7T
DAL	Delta Air Lines	N
DBK	Dubrovnik Airline	9A
DHL	DHL Express	D/G/N
DLH	Lufthansa	D
DNM	Denim Air	PH
DTR	Danish Air Transport	OY
EDW	Edelweiss Air	HB
EIA	Evergreen International	N
EIN	Aer Lingus	EI
ELL	Estonian Air	ES
ELY	El Al	4X
ETD	Etihad Airways	A6
ETH	Ethiopian Airlines	ET
EUK	Air Atlanta Europe	TF
EVA	EVA Airways	B
EWG	Eurowings	D
EXS	Jet2	G
EZE	Eastern Airways	G
EZS	easyJet Switzerland	HB
EZY	easyJet	G
FDX	Federal Express	N
FHE	Hello	HB
FHY	Freebird Airlines	TC
FIF	Air Finland	OH
FIN	Finnair	OH
FLI	Atlantic Airways	OY
GEC	Lufthansa Cargo	D
GFA	Gulf Air	A9C
GHA	Ghana Airways	9G
GIA	Garuda	PK
GMI	Germania	D
GTI	Atlas Air	N
GWI	Germanwings	D
GWL	Great Wall Airlines	B
GXL	XL Airways Germany	D
HDA	Dragonair	B
HFY	HiFly	CS
HLF	Hapag-Lloyd	D
HLX	Hapag-Lloyd Express	D
HMS	Hemus Air	LZ
IBE	Iberia	EC
ICB	Islandsflug	TF
ICE	Icelandair	TF
IOS	Isles of Scilly Skybus	G
IRA	Iran Air	EP
IRM	Mahan Air	EP
ISS	Meridianafly	I
IWD	Iberworld	EC
IYE	Yemenia	7O
JAI	Jet Airways	VT
JAL	Japan Airlines	JA
JAT	JAT Airways	YU
JKK	Spanair	EC
JXX	Iceland Express	TF
JOR	Blue Air	YR
JTG	Jet Time	OY
KAC	Kuwait Airways	9K
KAJ	Karthago Airlines	TS
KAL	Korean Air	HL
KBR	Koral Blue	AP
KLC	KLM CityHopper	PH
KLM	KLM	PH
KQA	Kenya Airways	5Y
KZR	Air Astana	UN
KZU	Kuzu Airlines Cargo	TC
LAA	Libyan Airlines	5A
LBC	Albanian Airlines	CC
LBT	Nouvelair	TS
LDA	Lauda Air	OE
LGL	Luxair	LX
LLC	Small Planet Airlines	LY
LOG	Loganair	G
LOT	Polish Airlines (LOT)	SP
LSK	Aurela	LY
LVG	Livingston	I
LZB	Bulgaria Air	LZ
MAH	Malev	HA
MAS	Malaysian Airlines	9M
MAU	Air Mauritius	3B
MEA	Middle East Airlines	OD
MGX	Montenegro Airlines	4O
MLD	Air Moldova	ER
MMZ	Euro Atlantic Airways	CS
MNB	MNG Airlines	TC
MON	Monarch Airlines	G
MPH	Martinair	PH
MSR	EgyptAir	SU
MTL	RAF-Avia	YL
NAX	Norwegian Air Shuttle	LN
NCA	Nippon Cargo Airlines	JA
NEX	Northern Executive	G
NLY	Niki	OE
NMB	Air Namibia	V5
NOA	Olympic Air	SX

NOS	Neos	I
NPT	Atlantic Airlines	G
NVR	Novair Airlines	SE
OAE	Omni Air International	N
OAS	Oman Air	A40
OAW	Helvetic Airways	HB
OBS	Orbest	CS
OGE	Atlasjet	TC
OHY	Onur Air	TC
OLT	OLT	D
PAC	Polar Air Cargo	N
PGT	Pegasus Airlines	TC
PIA	Pakistan International A/L	AP
PLK	Rossiya	RA
POT	Polet	RA
PRI	Primera Airlines	OY
PTG	PrivatAir	D
PTI	PrivatAir	HB
QFA	QANTAS	VH
QTR	Qatar Airways	A7
RCF	Aeroflot Cargo	RA
RAE	Regional Airlines	F
RAM	Royal Air Maroc	CN
RBA	Royal Brunei Airlines	V8
REA	Aer Arann	EI
RJA	Royal Jordanian	JY
RNV	Armavia	EK
ROT	Tarom	YR
RPX	BAC Express Airlines	G
RUS	Cirrus Airlines	D
RYR	Ryanair	EI
RZO	SATA International	CS
SAA	South African Airways	ZS
SAS	SAS	SE/ OY/ LN
SAY	Scot Airways	G
SCW	Malmo Aviation	SE
SCX	Sun Country Airlines	N
SDM	Rossiya	RA
SDR	City Airline	SE
SEU	Star Airlines	F
SEY	Air Seychelles	S7
SVA	Singapore Airlines	9V
SLL	Slovak Airlines	OM
SLM	Surinam Airways	PZ
SQC	Singapore Airlines Cargo	9V
SRR	Starair	OY
STZ	Strategic Airlines	F
SUD	Sudan Airways	ST
SUS	Sun-Air	OY
SVA	Saudi Arabian Airlines	HZ
SVK	Air Slovakia	OM
SWN	West Air Sweden	SE
SWR	Swiss	HB
SXS	SunExpress	TC
SYR	Syrianair	YK
TAP	TAP Portugal	CS
TAR	Tunis Air	TS
TAY	TNT Airways	OO
TCW	Thomas Cook Belgium	OO
TCX	Thomas Cook Airlines	G
TDK	Transavia Denmark	OY
TFL	Arkefly	PH
THA	Thai Airways International	HS
THY	Turkish Airlines	TC
TOM	Thomson Airways	G
TRA	Transavia	PH
TRK	Turkuaz Airlines	TC
TSC	Air Transat	C
TSO	Transaero	RA
TUA	Turkmenistan Airlines	EZ
TUB	TUI Airlines Belgium	OO
TUI	TUIfly	D
TVF	Transavia France	F
TVS	Travel Service/Smart Wings	OK
TWI	Tailwind Airlines	TC
TYR	Tyrolean Airways	OE
UAE	Emirates Airlines	A6
UAL	United Airlines	N
UBD	United Airways	S2
UPS	United Parcel Service	N
USA	US Airways	N
UZB	Uzbekistan Airways	UK
VDA	Volga-Dnepr	RA
VIR	Virgin Atlantic	G
VKH	Viking Hellas	SX
VLG	Vueling	EC
VLM	VLM	OO
VPA	Danube Wings	OM
WDL	WDL Aviation	D
WIF	Wideroe's	LN
WHT	White Airways	CS
WLX	West Air Europe	LX
WOA	World Airways	N
WOW	Air Southwest	G
WZZ	Wizz Air	HA/LZ
XLF	XL Airways France	F

YU-ANI Boeing 737-3H9 of JAT Airways. *Allan Wright*

British Aircraft Preservation Council Register

The British Aircraft Preservation Council was formed in 1967 to co-ordinate the works of all bodies involved in the preservation, restoration and display of historical aircraft. Membership covers the whole spectrum of national, Service, commercial and voluntary groups, and meetings are held regularly at the bases of member organisations. The Council is able to provide a means of communication, helping to resolve any misunderstandings or duplication of effort. Every effort is taken to encourage the raising of standards of both organisation and technical capacity amongst the member groups to the benefit of everyone interested in aviation. To assist historians, the B.A.P.C. register has been set up and provides an identity for those aircraft which do not qualify for a Service serial or inclusion in the UK Civil Register.

Aircraft on the current B.A.P.C. Register are as follows:

Reg.	*Type*	*Owner or Operator*	*Notes*
1	Roe Triplane Type 4 (replica)	Shuttleworth Collection as G-ARSG (not carried)	
2	Bristol Boxkite (replica)	Shuttleworth Collection as G-ASPP (not carried)	
6	Roe Triplane Type IV (replica)	Manchester Museum of Science & Industry	
7	Southampton University MPA	Solent Sky, Southampton	
8	Dixon ornithopter	The Shuttleworth Collection	
9	Humber Monoplane (replica)	Midland Air Museum/Coventry	
10	Hafner R.II Revoplane	Museum of Army Flying/Middle Wallop	
12	Mignet HM.14	Museum of Flight/East Fortune	
13	Mignet HM.14	Brimpex Metal Treatments	
14	Addyman Standard Training Glider	A. Lindsay & N. H. Ponsford	
15	Addyman Standard Training Glider	The Aeroplane Collection	
16	Addyman ultra-light aircraft	N. H. Ponsford	
17	Woodhams Sprite	BB Aviation/Canterbury	
18	Killick MP Gyroplane	A. Lindsay & N. H. Ponsford	
20	Lee-Richards annular biplane (replica)	Visitor Centre Shoreham Airport	
21	Thruxton Jackaroo	M. J. Brett	
22	Mignet HM.14 (G-AEOF)	Aviodome/Netherlands	
23	SE-5A Scale Model	Newark Air Museum	
24	Currie Wot (replica)	Newark Air Museum	
25	Nyborg TGN-III glider	Midland Air Museum	
26	Auster AOP.6 (fuselage frame)	Remains scrapped	
27	Mignet HM.14	M. J. Abbey	
28	Wright Flyer (replica)	Corn Exchange/Leeds	
29	Mignet HM.14 (replica) (G-ADRY)	Brooklands Museum of Aviation/Weybridge	
32	Crossley Tom Thumb	Midland Air Museum	
33	DFS.108-49 Grunau Baby IIb	–	
34	DFS.108-49 Grunau Baby IIb	D. Elsdon	
35	EoN primary glider	–	
36	Fieseler Fi 103 (V-1) (replica)	Kent Battle of Britain Museum/Hawkinge	
37	Blake Bluetit (G-BXIY)	The Shuttleworth Collection/Old Warden	
38	Bristol Scout replica (A1742)	K. Williams & M. Thorn	
39	Addyman Zephyr sailplane	A. Lindsay & N. H. Ponsford	
40	Bristol Boxkite (replica)	Bristol City Museum	
41	B.E.2C (replica) (6232)	Yorkshire Air Museum/Elvington	
42	Avro 504 (replica) (H1968)	Yorkshire Air Museum/Elvington	
43	Mignet HM.14	Newark Air Museum/Winthorpe	
44	Miles Magister (L6906)	Museum of Berkshire Aviation (G-AKKY)/ Woodley	
45	Pilcher Hawk (replica)	Stanford Hall Museum	
46	Mignet HM.14	Stored	
47	Watkins Monoplane	National Museum of Wales	
48	Pilcher Hawk (replica)	Glasgow Museum of Transport	
49	Pilcher Hawk	Royal Scottish Museum/East Fortune	
50	Roe Triplane Type 1	Science Museum/South Kensington	
51	Vickers Vimy IV	Science Museum/South Kensington	
52	Lilienthal glider	Science Museum Store/Hayes	
53	Wright Flyer (replica)	Science Museum/South Kensington	
54	JAP-Harding monoplane	Science Museum/South Kensington	
55	Levavasseur Antoinette VII	Science Museum/South Kensington	
56	Fokker E.III (210/16)	Science Museum/South Kensington	
57	Pilcher Hawk (replica)	Science Museum/South Kensington	

Notes	Reg.	Type	Owner or Operator
	58	Yokosuka MXY7 Ohka II (15-1585)	F.A.A. Museum/Yeovilton
	59	Sopwith Camel (replica) (D3419)	Aerospace Museum/Cosford
	60	Murray M.1 helicopter	The Aeroplane Collection Ltd
	61	Stewart man-powered ornithopter	Lincolnshire Aviation Museum
	62	Cody Biplane (304)	Science Museum/South Kensington
	63	Hurricane (replica) (P3208)	Kent Battle of Britain Museum/Hawkinge
	64	Hurricane (replica) (P3059)	Kent Battle of Britain Museum/Hawkinge
	65	Spitfire (replica) (N3289)	Kent Battle of Britain Museum/Hawkinge
	66	Bf 109 (replica) (1480)	Kent Battle of Britain Museum/Hawkinge
	67	Bf 109 (replica) (14)	Kent Battle of Britain Museum/Hawkinge
	68	Hurricane (replica) (H3426)	Midland Air Museum
	69	Spitfire (replica) (N3313)	Kent Battle of Britain Museum/Hawkinge
	70	Auster AOP.5 (TJ398)	North East Aircraft Museum/Usworth
	71	Spitfire (replica) (P8140)	Norfolk & Suffolk Aviation Museum
	72	Hurricane (model) (V6779)	Gloucestershire Aviation Collection
	73	Hurricane (replica)	–
	74	Bf 109 (replica) (6357)	Kent Battle of Britain Museum/Hawkinge
	75	Mignet HM.14 (G-AEFG)	N. H. Ponsford
	76	Mignet HM.14 (G-AFFI)	Yorkshire Air Museum/Elvington
	77	Mignet HM.14 (replica) (G-ADRG)	Lower Stondon Transport Museum
	78	Hawker Hind (K5414) (G-AENP)	The Shuttleworth Collection/Old Warden
	79	Fiat G.46-4B (MM53211)	British Air Reserve/France
	80	Airspeed Horsa (KJ351)	Museum of Army Flying/Middle Wallop
	81	Hawkridge Dagling	Russavia Collection
	82	Hawker Hind (Afghan)	RAF Museum/Hendon
	83	Kawasaki Ki-100-1b (24)	Aerospace Museum/Cosford
	84	Nakajima Ki-46 (Dinah III)(5439)	Aerospace Museum/Cosford
	85	Weir W-2 autogyro	Museum of Flight/East Fortune
	86	de Havilland Tiger Moth (replica)	Yorkshire Aircraft Preservation Society
	87	Bristol Babe (replica) (G-EASQ)	Bristol Aero Collection/Kemble
	88	Fokker Dr 1 (replica) (102/17)	F.A.A. Museum/Yeovilton
	89	Cayley glider (replica)	Manchester Museum of Science & Industry
	90	Colditz Cock (replica)	Imperial War Museum/Duxford
	91	Fieseler Fi 103 (V-1)	Lashenden Air Warfare Museum
	92	Fieseler Fi 103 (V-1)	RAF Museum/Hendon
	93	Fieseler Fi 103 (V-1)	Imperial War Museum/Duxford
	94	Fieseler Fi 103 (V-1)	Aerospace Museum/Cosford
	95	Gizmer autogyro	F. Fewsdale
	96	Brown helicopter	North East Aircraft Museum
	97	Luton L.A.4A Minor	North East Aircraft Museum
	98	Yokosuka MXY7 Ohka II (997)	Manchester Museum of Science & Industry
	99	Yokosuka MXY7 Ohka II (8486M)	Aerospace Museum/Cosford
	100	Clarke Chanute biplane gliderr	RAF Museum/Hendon
	101	Mignet HM.14	Newark Air Museum/Winthorpe
	102	Mignet HM.14	Not completed
	103	Hulton hang glider (replica)	Personal Plane Services Ltd
	104	Bleriot XI	Sold in France
	105	Blériot XI (replica)	Arango Collection/Los Angeles
	106	Blériot XI (164)	RAF Museum/Hendon
	107	Blériot XXVII	RAF Museum/Hendon
	108	Fairey Swordfish IV (HS503)	RAF Restoration Centre/Wyton
	109	Slingsby Kirby Cadet TX.1	RAF Museum/Henlow store
	110	Fokker D.VII replica (static) (5125)	Stored
	111	Sopwith Triplane replica (static) (N5492)	F.A.A. Museum/Yeovilton
	112	DH.2 replica (static) (5964)	Museum of Army Flying/Middle Wallop
	113	S.E.5A replica (static) (B4863)	Stored
	114	Vickers Type 60 Viking (static) (G-EBED)	Brooklands Museum of Aviation/Weybridge
	115	Mignet HM.14	Norfolk & Suffolk Aviation Museum/Flixton
	116	Santos-Dumont Demoiselle (replica)	Cornwall Aero Park/Helston
	117	B.E.2C (replica)(1701)	Stored Hawkinge
	118	Albatros D.V (replica) (C19/18)	North Weald Aircraft Restoration Flight
	119	Bensen B.7	North East Aircraft Museum
	120	Mignet HM.14 (G-AEJZ)	South Yorkshire Aviation Museum/Doncaster

Reg.	Type	Owner or Operator	Notes
121	Mignet HM.14 (G-AEKR)	South Yorkshire Aviation Society	
122	Avro 504 (replica) (1881)	Stored	
123	Vickers FB.5 Gunbus (replica)	A. Topen (stored)/Cranfield	
124	Lilienthal Glider Type XI (replica)	Science Museum/South Kensington	
125	Clay Cherub	ground trainer/Coventry	
126	D.31 Turbulent (static)	Midland Air Museum/Coventry	
127	Halton Jupiter MPA	The Shuttleworth Collection	
128	Watkinson Cyclogyroplane Mk IV	IHM/Weston-super-Mare	
129	Blackburn 1911 Monoplane (replica)	Cornwall Aero Park/Helston store	
130	Blackburn 1912 Monoplane (replica)	Yorkshire Air Museum	
131	Pilcher Hawk (replica)	C. Paton	
132	Blériot XI (G-BLXI)	Stored	
133	Fokker Dr 1 (replica) (425/17)	Kent Battle of Britain Museum/Hawkinge	
134	Pitts S-2A static (G-CARS)	Toyota Ltd/Sywell	
135	Bristol M.1C (replica) (C4912)	Stored	
136	Deperdussin Seaplane (replica)	National Air Race Museum/USA	
137	Sopwith Baby Floatplane (replica) (8151)	Stored	
138	Hansa Brandenburg W.29 Floatplane (replica) (2292)	Stored	
139	Fokker Dr 1 (replica) 150/17	Stored	
140	Curtiss 42A (replica)	Stored	
141	Macchi M39 (replica)	Switzerland	
142	SE-5A (replica) (F5459)	Stored	
143	Paxton MPA	R. A. Paxton/Gloucestershire	
144	Weybridge Mercury MPA	Cranwell Gliding Club	
145	Oliver MPA	Stored	
146	Pedal Aeronauts Toucan MPA	Stored	
147	Bensen B.7	Norfolk & Suffolk Aviation Museum/Flixton	
148	Hawker Fury II (replica) (K7271)	High Ercall Aviation Museum	
149	Short S.27 (replica)	F.A.A. Museum (stored)/Yeovilton	
150	SEPECAT Jaguar GR.1 (replica) (XX728)	RAF M & R Unit/St. Athan RAF Marketing & Recruitment Unit/St. Athan	
151	SEPECAT Jaguar GR.1 (replica) (XZ363)	RAF M & R Unit/St. Athan	
152	BAe Hawk T.1 (replica) (XX227)	RAF M & R Unit/Bottesford	
153	Westland WG.33	IHM/Weston-super-Mare	
154	D.31 Turbulent	Lincolnshire Aviation Museum/E. Kirkby	
155	Panavia Tornado GR.1 (model) (ZA556)	RAF M & R Unit/St. Athan	
156	Supermarine S-6B (replica)	National Air Race Museum/USA	
157	Waco CG-4A(237123)	Yorkshire Air Museum/Elvington	
158	Fieseler Fi 103 (V-1)	Defence Ordnance Disposal School/Chattenden	
159	Yokosuka MXY7 Ohka II	Defence Ordnance Disposal School/Chattenden	
160	Chargus 18/50 hang glider	Museum of Flight/East Fortune	
161	Stewart Ornithopter Coppelia	Bomber County Museum	
162	Goodhart MPA	Science Museum/Wroughton	
163	AFEE 10/42 Rotabuggy (replica)	Museum of Army Flying/Middle Wallop	
164	Wight Quadruplane Type 1 (replica)	Solent Sky, Southampton	
165	Bristol F.2b (E2466)	RAF Museum/Hendon	
166	Bristol F.2b (D7889)	Stored	
167	Bristol SE-5A	Stored	
168	DH.60G Moth (static replica)	Stored Hawkinge (G-AAAH)	
169	BAC/Sepecat Jaguar GR.1 (XX110)	RAF Training School/Cosford	
170	Pilcher Hawk (replica)	A. Gourlay/Strathallan	
171	BAe Hawk T.1 (model) (XX308)	RAF Marketing & Recruitment Unit/Bottesford	
172	Chargus Midas Super 8 hang glider	Science Museum/Wroughton	
173	Birdman Promotions Grasshopper	Science Museum/Wroughton	
174	Bensen B.7	Science Museum/Wroughton	
175	Volmer VJ-23 Swingwing	Manchester Museum of Science & Industry	
176	SE-5A (replica) (A4850)	South Yorks Aviation Society/Firbeck	
177	Avro 504K (replica) (G-AACA)	Brooklands Museum of Aviation/Weybridge	
178	Avro 504K (replica) (E373)	Bygone Times Antique Warehouse/ Eccleston, Lancs	
179	Sopwith Pup (replica) (A7317)	Midland Air Museum/Coventry	

Notes	Reg.	Type	Owner or Operator
	180	McCurdy Silver Dart (replica)	Reynolds Pioneer Museum/Canada
	181	RAF B.E.2b (replica) (687)	RAF Museum/Hendon
	182	Wood Ornithopter	Manchester Museum of Science & Industry
	183	Zurowski ZP.1 helicopter	Newark Air Museum/Winthorpe
	184	Spitfire IX (replica) (EN398)	Fighter Wing Display Team/North Weald
	185	Waco CG-4A (243809)	Museum of Army Flying/Middle Wallop
	186	DH.82B Queen Bee (LF789)	de Havilland Heritage Museum
	187	Roe Type 1 biplane (replica)	Brooklands Museum of Aviation/Weybridge
	188	McBroom Cobra 88	Science Museum/Wroughton
	189	Bleriot XI (replica)	Stored
	190	Spitfire (replica) (K5054)	P. Smith/Hawkinge
	191	BAe Harrier GR.7 (model) (ZH139)	RAF M & R Unit/St. Athan
	192	Weedhopper JC-24	The Aeroplane Collection
	193	Hovey WD-11 Whing Ding	The Aeroplane Collection
	194	Santos Dumont Demoiselle (replica)	RAF Museum Store/RAF Stafford
	195	Moonraker 77 hang glider	Museum of Flight/East Fortune
	196	Sigma 2M hang glider	Museum of Flight/East Fortune
	197	Scotkites Cirrus III hang glider	Museum of Flight/East Fortune
	198	Fieseler Fi 103 (V-1)	Imperial War Museum/Lambeth
	199	Fieseler Fi 103 (V-1)	Science Museum/South Kensington
	200	Bensen B.7	K. Fern Collection/Stoke
	201	Mignet HM.14	Caernarfon Air Museum
	202	Spitfire V (model) (MAV467)	Maes Artro Craft Centre
	203	Chrislea LC.1 Airguard (G-AFIN)	The Aeroplane Collection
	204	McBroom hang glider	Newark Air Museum
	205	Hurricane (replica) (Z3427)	RAF Museum/Hendon
	206	Spitfire (replica) (MH486)	RAF Museum/Hendon
	207	Austin Whippet (replica) (K.158)	South Yorkshire Aviation Museum/Doncaster
	208	SE-5A (replica) (D276)	Prince's Mead Shopping Precinct/Farnborough
	209	Spitfire IX (replica) (MJ751)	Museum of D-Day Aviation/Shoreham
	210	Avro 504J (replica) (C4451)	Solent Sky, Southampton
	211	Mignet HM.14 (replica) (G-ADVU)	North East Aircraft Museum
	212	Bensen B.8	IHM/Weston-super-Mare
	213	Vertigo MPA	IHM/Weston-super-Mare
	214	Spitfire prototype (replica) (K5054)	Tangmere Military Aviation Museum
	215	Airwave hang-glider prototype	Solent Sky, Southampton
	216	DH.88 Comet (replica) (G-ACSS)	de Havilland Heritage Museum/London Colney
	217	Spitfire (replica) (K9926)	RAF Museum/Bentley Priory
	218	Hurricane (replica) (P3386)	RAF Museum/Bentley Priory
	219	Hurricane (replica) (L1710)	RAF Memorial Chapel/Biggin Hill
	220	Spitfire 1 (replica) (N3194)	RAF Memorial Chapel/Biggin Hill
	221	Spitfire LF.IX (replica) (MH777)	RAF Museum/Northolt
	222	Spitfire IX (replica) (BR600)	RAF Museum/Uxbridge
	223	Hurricane 1 (replica) (V7467)	RAF Museum/Coltishall
	224	Spitfire V (replica) (BR600)	Ambassador Hotel/Norwich
	225	Spitfire IX (replica) (P8448)	RAF Museum/Cranwell
	226	Spitfire XI (replica) (EN343)	RAF Museum/Benson
	227	Spitfire 1A (replica) (L1070)	RAF Museum/Turnhouse
	228	Olympus hang-glider	North East Aircraft Museum/Usworth
	229	Spitfire IX (replica) (MJ832)	RAF Museum/Digby
	230	Spitfire (replica) (AA550)	Eden Camp/Malton
	231	Mignet HM.14 (G-ADRX)	South Copeland Aviation Group
	232	AS.58 Horsa I/II	de Havilland Heritage Museum/London Colney
	233	Broburn Wanderlust sailplane	Museum of Berkshire Aviation/Woodley
	234	Vickers FB.5 Gunbus (replica)	RAF Manston Museum
	235	Fieseler Fi 103 (V-1) (replica)	Eden Camp Wartime Museum
	236	Hurricane (replica) (P2793)	Eden Camp Wartime Museum
	237	Fieseler Fi 103 (V-1)	RAF Museum Store/RAF Stafford
	238	Waxflatter ornithopter	Personal Plane Services Ltd
	239	Fokker D.VIII 5/8 scale replica	Norfolk & Suffolk Aviation Museum/Flixton
	240	Messerschmitt Bf.109G (replica)	Yorkshire Air Museum/Elvington
	241	Hurricane 1 (replica) (L1679)	Tangmere Military Aviation Museum
	242	Spitfire Vb (replica) (BL924)	Tangmere Military Aviation Museum
	243	Mignet HM.14 (replica) (G-ADYV)	P. Ward
	244	Solar Wings Typhoon	Museum of Flight/East Fortune

Reg.	Type	Owner or Operator	Notes
245	Electraflyer Floater hang glider	Museum of Flight/East Fortune	
246	Hiway Cloudbase hang glider	Museum of Flight/East Fortune	
247	Albatross ASG.21 hang glider	Museum of Flight/East Fortune	
248	McBroom hang glider	Museum of Berkshire Aviation/Woodley	
249	Hawker Fury 1 (replica) (K5673)	Brooklands Museum of Aviation/Weybridge	
250	RAF SE-5A (replica) (F5475)	Brooklands Museum of Aviation/Weybridge	
251	Hiway Spectrum hang glider (replica)	Manchester Museum of Science & Industry	
252	Flexiform Wing hang glider	Manchester Museum of Science & Industry	
253	Mignet HM.14 (G-ADZW)	H. Shore/Sandown	
254	Hawker Hurricane (P3873)	Yorkshire Air Museum/Elvington	
255	NA P-51D Mustang (replica) (463209)	American Air Museum/Duxford	
256	Santos Dumont Type 20 (replica)	Brooklands Museum of Aviation/Weybridge	
257	DH.88 Comet (G-ACSS)	The Galleria/Hatfield	
258	Adams balloon	British Balloon Museum	
259	Gloster Gamecock (replica)	Jet Age Museum Gloucestershire	
260	Mignet HM280	–	
261	GAL Hotspur (replica)	Museum of Army Flying/ Middle Wallop	
262	Catto CP-16	Museum of Flight/East Fortune	
263	Chargus Cyclone	Ulster Aviation Heritage/Langford Lodge	
264	Bensen B.8M	IHM/Weston-super-Mare	
265	Spitfire 1 (P3873)	Yorkshire Air Museum/Elvington	
266	Rogallo hang glider	Ulster Aviation Heritage	
267	Hurricane (model)	Duxford	
268	Spifire (model)	–	
269	Spitfire (model) USAF	Lakenheath	
270	DH.60 Moth (model)	Yorkshire Air Museum	
271	Messerschmitt Me 163B	Shuttleworth Collection/Old Warden	
272	Hurricane (model)	Kent Battle of Britain Museum/Hawkinge	
273	Hurricane (model)	Kent Battle of Britain Museum/Hawkinge	
274	Boulton & Paul P.6 (model)	Boulton & Paul Aircraft Heritage Project	
275	Bensen B.7 gyroglider	Doncaster Museum	
276	Hartman Ornithopter	Science Museum/Wroughton	
277	Mignet HM.14	Visitor Centre Shoreham Airport	
278	Hurricane (model)	Kent Battle of Britain Museum/Hawkinge	
279	Airspeed Horsa	Shawbury	
280	DH.89A Dragon Rapide (model)	–	
281	Boulton & Paul Defiant (model)	–	
282	Manx Elder Duck	Isle of Man Airport Terminal	
283	Spitfire (model	Jurby, Isle of Man	
284	Gloster E.28/39 (model)	Lutterworth Leics	
285	Gloster E.28/39 (model)	Farnborough	
286	Mignet HM.14	Caernarfon Air Museum	
287	Blackburn F.2 Lincock (model)	Street Life Museum/Hull	
288	Hurricane (model)	Wonderland Pleasure Park, Mansfield	
289	Gyro Boat	IHM Weston-super-Mare	
290	Fieseler Fi 103 (V1) (model)	Dover Museum	
291	Hurricane (model)	National Battle of Britain Memorial, Capel-le-Ferne, Kent	
292	Eurofighter Typhoon (model)	RAF Museum/Hendon	
293	Spitfire (model)	RAF Museum/Hendon	
294	Fairchild Argus (model)	Visitor Centre, Thorpe Camp, Woodhall Spa	
295	Da Vinci hang glider (replica)	Skysport Engineering	
296	Army Balloon Factory NuIII (replica)	RAF Museum, Hendon	
297	Spitfire (replica)	Kent Battle of Britain Museum/Hawkinge	
298	Spitfire IX (Model)	Kent Battle of Britain Museum/ Hawkinge	
299	Spitfire 1 (model).	National Battle of Britain Memorial, Capel-le-Ferne, Kent	
300	Hummingbird (replica)	Shoreham Airport Historical Association	

Note: Registrations/Serials carried are mostly false identities.
MPA = Man Powered Aircraft, IHM = International Helicopter Museum. The aircraft, listed as 'models' are generally intended for exhibition purposes and are not airworthy although they are full scale replicas. However, in a few cases the machines have the ability to taxi when used for film work

Future Allocations Log

The grid provides the facility to record future registrations as they are issued or seen. To trace a particular code, refer to the left hand column which contains the three letters following the G prefix. The final letter can be found by reading across the columns headed A to Z. For example, the box for G-CGZT is located 6 rows down (CGZ) and then 19 across to the T column.

G-	A	B	C	D	E	F	G	H	I	J	K	L	M	N	O	P	R	S	T	U	V	W	X	Y	Z
CGU																									
CGV																									
CGW																									
CGX																									
CGY																									
CGZ																									
CHA																									
CHB																									
CHC																									
CHD																									
CHE																									
CHF																									
CHG																									
CHH																									
CHI																									
CHJ																									
CHK																									
CHL																									
CHM																									
CHN																									
CHO																									
CHP																									
CHR																									
CHS																									
CHT																									
CHU																									
CHV																									
CHW																									
CHX																									
CHY																									
CHZ																									
CIA																									
CIB																									
CIC																									
	A	B	C	D	E	F	G	H	I	J	K	L	M	N	O	P	R	S	T	U	V	W	X	Y	Z

Credit: *Wal Gandy*

Future Allocation Groups

This grid can be used to record registrations as they are issued or seen. The first column is provided for the ranges prefixed with G-C, ie from G-CYxx to G-CZxx. The remaining columns cover the sequences from G-Dxxx to G-Zxxx and in this case it is necessary to insert the last three letters in the appropriate section.

G-C	G-D	G-F	G-H	G-J	G-L	G-N	G-O	G-P	G-S	G-U
										G-V
	G-E	G-G			G-M	G-O				
				G-K						
										G-W
			G-I							
								G-R		
									G-T	
										G-X
G-D	G-F			G-L	G-N					
										G-Y
										G-Z

Overseas Airliners Registration Log

This grid may be used to record airliner registrations not included in the main section.

Reg.	*Type*	*Operator*